STREET ON TORTS

Twelfth Edition

JOHN MURPHY LLB, LLM

Reader in Law at the University of Manchester

OXFORD
UNIVERSITY PRESS

OXFORD

UNIVERSITY PRESS

Great Clarendon Street, Oxford OX2 6DP

Oxford University Press is a department of the University of Oxford.
It furthers the University's objective of excellence in research, scholarship,
and education by publishing worldwide in

Oxford New York

Auckland Cape Town Dar es Salaam Hong Kong Karachi
Kuala Lumpur Madrid Melbourne Mexico City Nairobi
New Delhi Shanghai Taipei Toronto

With offices in

Argentina Austria Brazil Chile Czech Republic France Greece
Guatemala Hungary Italy Japan Poland Portugal Singapore
South Korea Switzerland Thailand Turkey Ukraine Vietnam

Oxford is a registered trade mark of Oxford University Press
in the UK and in certain other countries

Published in the United States
by Oxford University Press Inc., New York

© Oxford University Press 2007

British Library Cataloguing in Publication Data
Data available

Library of Congress Cataloging in Publication Data
Data available

Typeset by Newgen Imaging Systems (P) Ltd., Chennai, India
Printed in Great Britain
on acid-free paper by
Ashford Colour Press Limited, Gosport, Hampshire

ISBN 978–0–19–929166–3

1 3 5 7 9 10 8 6 4 2

STREET ON TORTS

This book is dedicated to
Lukas Jacobsen-Murphy

PREFACE

In undertaking the task of editing this 12th edition, I have tried to abide by one simple objective: to make this edition the best I have ever known. To this end I have devoted much time and thought to the question of what the ideal textbook on tort should be and contain. Oxford University Press were good enough to consult widely on my behalf in order to obtain the views of fellow teachers of torts in a large number of leading law schools. But I have not ignored the views of my own students. In short, I have tried to produce a book that is comprehensive, readable, up to date, well organised (so as to map neatly on to modern torts courses) and capable of fulfilling the needs of those teaching and studying on undergraduate tort law courses of all shapes and sizes.

In ensuring that the book is up to date, I have of course added a considerable amount of new material. But I have also, through painstaking editing and judicious pruning, made every endeavour to make the book no longer than it was in its previous edition. Partly, this was a response to the fact that many students have told me over the years that their core textbooks are simply too long for their needs. However, while I was sympathetic to their concerns (and conscious, too, that short, semesterized models of teaching now abound), I was also acutely mindful of the history of the book. *Street on Torts* is famous for its comprehensive coverage of tort law. That was a reputation that was simply too precious to sacrifice. Furthermore, while semesterized teaching is very common these days, I wanted the book to remain valuable to those studying traditional year-long courses. Accordingly, my task in editing this edition became a huge challenge: how could I keep the breadth and depth of previous editions without significantly increasing the size of the book? Notwithstanding the magnitude of the task, I think I have succeeded; and any readers familiar with previous editions will still find all the law and most of the detail that sets this book apart. Indeed, there are now more references than ever before to secondary literature, and I have even added, for the more enthusiastic students, a 'Further Reading' section at the end of each chapter.

In the light of the copious information garnered for me by my publishers from a sizeable number of law schools, I was forced to re-order nearly all the chapters (and re-jig the content of some) in order that the book would now map more neatly on to the 'typical' modern tort course. I have also written a brand new chapter on 'Misuse of Private Information'. Taking my lead from Lord Nicholls in *Campbell v MGN*, I have elected to treat this topic as a new (or, at the very least, emerging) tort. The big question was: 'Where should I put it?'. One option was to place it alongside the chapters on defamation since, for now, the tort of Misuse of Private Information looks to be confined to information that is bound up with the claimant's dignity and informational autonomy. However, since the action has evolved from the old equity action for the breach of confidentiality, and since I suspect (notwithstanding what was said in *Douglas v Hello! Ltd (No 6)*) that it will be a mere matter of time before the new tort is extended to commercially exploitable private information, I have elected to place it, in anticipation, alongside the other chapters dealing with the protection of economic interests.

As is always the case with a project of this kind, I find myself indebted to many friends and colleagues, but especially to a former editor, and dear friend, Margot Brazier. While I doubt she would ever have done to this book what I have done to it, I nonetheless consider it a much better book than it would have been had she not greeted my many incursions into her office over the years with cheerful smiles and great insights and wisdom that nearly always left me intellectually enriched and her, I suspect, chasing deadlines. I would also make special mention of Francesca Griffin at OUP who provided great help, encouragement and support from start to finish.

Above all, however, I am thankful for the love and support that I have received from Anne and Lukas. I'm sure there must have been times when they felt my laptop saw more of me than they did. But if they did think that, they never said so.

I have attempted to present the law on the basis of materials available to me as of 10 July 2006.

John Murphy
Manchester
July, 2006

CONTENTS

PART III   INTENTIONAL INVASIONS OF INTERESTS IN THE
PERSON AND PROPERTY

PART IV INTERFERENCE WITH ECONOMIC AND INTELLECTUAL PROPERTY INTERESTS AND RELATED ACTIONS

PART VI INTERESTS IN REPUTATION — DEFAMATION

TABLE OF CASES

TABLE OF STATUTES AND
STATUTORY INSTRUMENTS

PART I

INTRODUCTION

1

OVERVIEW OF THE LAW
OF TORTS

SECTION 1 WHAT IS A TORT?

The very word tort may pose a conundrum for the novice law student. Crime and contract will be terms with which he or she is already familiar, but what does tort mean? What is the law of torts about? Much ink has been spilt in attempts to define tort with only limited success; at least for the student new to the subject. Winfield's classic definition declared:

Tortious liability arises from the breach of a duty primarily fixed by law; such duty is towards persons generally and its breach is redressable by an action for unliquidated damages.[1]

A more recent definition, offered by Peter Birks, suggests that a tort is:

[T]he breach of a legal duty which affects the interests of an individual to a degree which the law regards as sufficient to allow that individual to complain on his or her own account rather than as a representative of society as a whole.[2]

Yet the first of these definitions does little more than point towards one kind of remedy that is available in tort and towards certain distinctions between tort and other branches of the law,[3] while the second may be unhelpfully vague to the newcomer to tort. As we shall see at the end of this chapter, even those distinctions between tort and other branches of law are sometimes blurred.[4] Partly for this reason, a satisfactory definition of tort remains largely elusive. Perhaps the best working explanation that can be offered at this stage is this:

Tort is that branch of the civil law relating to obligations imposed by operation of law on all natural and artificial persons. It concerns the basic duties one person owes to another outside of a contract or the obligations triggered by an unjust enrichment. It enables the person to

---

[1] Winfield, *Province of the Law of Tort* (1931) p 92.

[2] Birks, 'The Concept of a Civil Wrong' in Owen (ed), *Philosophical Foundations of Tort Law* (1995) p 51.

[3] For a fuller account of the distinction between tort and other branches of the civil law, see Fleming, *The Law of Torts* (1998) pp 3–5 and Cane, *The Anatomy of Tort Law* (1997) pp 182–196.

[4] See generally, Waddams, *Dimensions of Private Law: Categories and Concepts in Anglo-American Legal Reasoning* (2003).

whom the duty is owed to pursue a remedy on his own behalf where breach of one of those duties infringes his interests to a degree recognized by the law as such an infringement.

No further attempt at defining tort will be made here. It is the functions and purposes of the law of torts that are of greater importance, and these are matters that can be explained in comparatively simple terms. Tort law defines the obligations imposed on one member of society to his or her fellows and provides a range of remedies for harms caused by breach of those obligations. Tort is often described as centrally concerned with corrective justice – that is, loss-adjustment from the person initially wronged to the wrongdoer.[5] In consequence, the law of torts is often judged by its success or otherwise as a compensation system. In simple terms, since most tort actions have as their objective monetary compensation for a loss inflicted on the claimant by the defendant, the question that most often arises is 'who should bear the relevant cost?' Should it lie where it falls on the unfortunate claimant; or is the conduct of the defendant such that the law should shift the loss to him? In the tort of negligence, as well as many other torts later in this book, loss adjustment is a core issue. Tort's 'success' in these areas must therefore be judged at least in part by its efficacy as a compensation system.

But compensation is not tort's only concern, and monetary damages are not the only available remedy. Torts are also designed to protect fundamental human interests. Here, 'interests' may be defined as the kinds of claims, wants or desires that people seek to satisfy in life, and which a civilized society ought to recognise as theirs as of right. Tort therefore serves to determine which of the many human (and related) interests are so fundamental that the law should impose duties upon us all that are designed primarily to protect those interests and, secondarily, to provide a remedy when those interests are wrongfully violated by others.

In the first edition of this work, Street's emphasis on the claimant's interests as opposed to the defendant's wrongdoing was perceived as radical, even bizarre. While I have elected to abandon the hierarchical interest-based structure that characterized previous editions in favour of one that maps more neatly onto the kinds of tort syllabuses that nowadays exist in most leading law schools in this country, it is nonetheless worth making clear that there is still a great deal to be said for an interest-based approach[6] (albeit that it has its imperfections and some notable inconsistencies[7]). Certainly, no claim in tort can succeed, however morally reprehensible the defendant's conduct, unless the court first recognises some form of harm suffered by the claimant that involves a violation of an interest sufficient to confer on the claimant a legal right to protection of that interest.[8] It is still useful, therefore, to consider the various rights and interests which the law of tort protects.

---

[5] There is now a voluminous literature on tort law and corrective justice, but especially good, if a little difficult, is Weinrib, 'Understanding Tort Law' (1989) 23 *Valparaiso U L Rev* 485. See also Wright, 'Right, Justice and Tort Law' in Owen (ed), *Philosophical Foundations of Tort Law* (1995) p 51.

[6] See Cane, *The Anatomy of Tort Law* (1997).

[7] See Murphy, 'Formularism and Tort Law' [1999] *Adelaide L Rev* 115.

[8] See, eg, *Rogers v Rajendro Dutt* (1860) 25 JP 3; *Bradford Corpn v Pickles* [1895] AC 587; *Pickering v Liverpool Daily Post and Echo Newspapers plc* [1991] 2 AC 370. For academic explanations of this, see Goldberg and Zipursky, 'Unrealized Torts' (2002) 88 *Virginia L Rev* 1625; Perry, 'Risk, Harm and Responsibility' in Owen (ed),

SECTION 2 PROTECTED RIGHTS AND INTERESTS

(A) HUMAN RIGHTS

Tort law has always protected certain human rights, albeit in a somewhat piecemeal and unsystematic way. However, the enactment of the Human Rights Act 1998 significantly enhanced this protection. Indeed, its passing prompted academics and judges almost immediately to rethink the boundaries and substance of tort law,[9] and the full effects of the Act on the law of torts are, no doubt, yet to emerge. To understand the various ways in which the Act was significant for tort law, it is necessary to say a little about the workings of that Act.

Contrary to what is often said, the Human Rights Act did not incorporate the European Convention on Human Rights into English law. Rather, the Act provides (1) that, wherever possible, primary and subordinate legislation must be interpreted in a way that is compatible with 'Convention rights'[10] and (2) that it is unlawful for any public authority (including a court of law,[11] but excluding the legislature[12]) to act in a way that is incompatible with a 'Convention right'.[13] 'Convention rights' are the funda-mental rights and freedoms set out in Articles 2 to 12 and Article 14 of the Convention, as well as Articles 1 to 3 of the First Protocol (concerning rights to property, education and free elections) and Articles 1 and 2 of the Sixth Protocol (abolishing the death penalty).[14] Section 11 of the Human Rights Act 1998 makes it clear that 'Convention rights' exist in addition to, not in substitution for, rights and freedoms already endorsed at common law. Thus, reference to various of these Articles and Protocols will be made from time to time throughout this book.

Philosophical Foundations of Tort Law (1995); Ripstein, *Equality, Responsibility, and the Law* (1999) p 75. For a nuanced argument to the effect that the harm threshold ought sometimes to be lower see Handfield and Pisciotta, 'Is the Risk-Liability Theory Compatible with Negligence Law?' (2006) 12 *Legal Theory* (forthcoming) and McCarthy, 'Liability and Risk' (1996) 25 *Philosophy and Public Affairs* 238. See also the analysis of the decision in *Barker v Corus UK Ltd* [2006] UKHL 20 in ch. 4.

[9] For comprehensive treatment, see Wright, *Tort Law and Human Rights* (2001). And for a useful introduc-tory account see Buxton, 'The Human Rights Act and Private Law' (2000) 116 LQR 48.

[10] Human Rights Act 1998, s 3. For an introductory account of the Act, see Ewing 'The Human Rights Act and Parliamentary Democracy' (1999) 62 MLR 79.   [11] Human Rights Act 1998, s 6(3)(a).

[12] Human Rights Act 1998, s 6(3)(b).

[13] Human Rights Act 1998, s 6(1). For these purposes, 'acts' include 'failures to act' – *eg*, failures to fulfil the several positive obligations that exist under the Convention. See, *eg*, *Z v United Kingdom* (2002) 34 EHRR 97 where local authorities failed to take all reasonable steps to avoid a real and imminent risk of ill-treatment of children of whom they had actual or imputed knowledge. See also *Anufrijeva v Southwark LBC* [2004] QB 1124 and Murphy, 'Children in Need: The Limits of Local Authority Accountability' [2003] *Legal Studies* 102. Note, however, that under s 6(6) a failure to introduce a proposal for legislation does not amount to an unlawful act for these purposes.   [14] Human Rights Act 1998, s 1.

It may at first glance seem odd that no express provision of the Act appears to require that the judges develop the common law in a manner consistent with 'Convention rights'. Two factors explain that apparent omission. First, for some years now, English judges have wherever possible sought to ensure that the common law is consistent with such rights.[15] Secondly, and more importantly, section 6 of the Act makes it unlawful, as we have already seen, for any public authority, including a court, to act in a way that is incompatible with 'Convention rights'. As such, a judge adjudicating on a claim in tort must develop the common law compatibly with 'Convention rights' with a view to ensuring consistency between common law and 'Convention rights'.[16]

Apart from these general points, the most crucial element of the Act for a tort lawyer is the provision that 'Convention rights' are directly enforceable against public authorities, thus permitting an individual who considers his rights to have been violated to sue for damages.[17] However, recourse to such damages under the Act may not be the only option available in response to such violations. This is because the self-same rights conferred by the Convention may already be protected by the law of torts. For example, Article 5 provides for a right to liberty and security and protects the citizen against arbitrary detention. But the ancient tort of false imprisonment does likewise. Equally, a person alleging unlawful arrest by the police will not need to claim a breach of Article 5. He, too, can perfectly well sue in false imprisonment; and, indeed, may well prefer to do so.[18] Even so, in determining whether that arrest was lawful, the court will be mindful of the provisions of Article 5 and the jurisprudence of the European Court of Human Rights.[19]

But what if a 'Convention right' is not so well established in domestic law? Privacy is such a case.[20] The claimant might then elect to bring his claim under the Act alleging breach of Article 8 (which requires respect for private and family life). If he elects for a Convention remedy, the claimant can sue under the Act *so long as* the defendant is a public authority. The question of what constitutes a public authority would then, possibly, arise. If I were to discover that the Home Office is bugging my office, suing a government department as a public authority should be straightforward. But, if a tabloid newspaper invades my home life, splashing my private business all over its front page, what then? It is arguable that the newspaper, too, may be classified as a public authority, for section 6(3)(b) classifies as a public authority 'any person certain of whose functions are functions of a public nature'. State schools and universities thus

---

[15] See, eg, *Rantzen v Mirror Group Newspapers* [1993] 4 All ER 975; *Olotu v Home Office* [1997] 1 WLR 329; *R v Chief Constable of North Wales Police, ex p AB* [1998] 3 WLR 7.

[16] Otherwise the court itself acts unlawfully under the Human Rights Act 1998, s 6. But note that s 6 does not require the courts to create brand new rights that mirror those in the Convention.

[17] Human Rights Act 1998, ss 7–8.

[18] Generally, tort damages are intended to return the claimant to the position he was in prior to the commission of the tort, but in respect of this tort, exemplary damages might be available. Not only would exemplary damages *not* be available under the Act, it is by no means clear that C would even be restored to his or her *ex ante* position since under the Act, 'in considering whether to award compensation and, if so, how much, there is a balance to be drawn between the interests of the victim and those of the public': *Anufrijeva v Southwark LBC* [2004] QB 1124, at [56] *per* Woolf CJ. The Law Commission has suggested a range of factors that would be relevant in this context: *Law Com No 266*, para 4.44; see also *McGregor on Damages* (2003) p 1549 *et seq*.

[19] As is already the case, well illustrated in the judgments of the members of the Court of Appeal in *Olotu v Home Office* [1997] 1 WLR 328.   [20] For the limited extent to which tort law protects privacy, see ch 15.

clearly qualify as public bodies, as do charities such as the NSPCC. But the status of other bodies remains unclear for the present.[21]

Next, let us consider the situation where the wrongdoer is an entirely private individual – let us say, a colleague who invades my privacy by persistently peering through my window and monitoring my private correspondence. Some common law remedy may often be found in such circumstances. The 'snooper' who peers through windows and opens mail could be liable for harassment[22] or trespass to goods.[23] But if the facts of the case do not lend themselves to the invocation of an existing common law action, the position is not entirely clear. This is important because, despite a marked move in the direction of allowing an invasion of privacy to be treated as a full-blown tort (as it is in the USA and New Zealand), English tort law has gone no further than to allow a claimant to sue in respect of the misuse of private personal information.[24] There is full discussion of the protection of privacy in chapter 15 of this book. But for now it suffices to note that the English courts seem generally to be moving towards a convergence of common law and Convention rights in this area. On the other hand, the obligation to develop the common law in a manner consistent with the Convention does not empower the courts to engage in free-and-easy judicial legislation, especially in an area so politically charged as privacy rights.[25] Article 6 (which grants a right to a fair trial) cannot be invoked to chivvy the courts along in this respect, for Article 6 does not carry with it any substantive civil law rights: it merely provides a procedural guarantee.[26]

Finally, in the context of Human Rights, we must note that in relation to primary legislation the courts' role remains limited by the doctrine of Parliamentary sovereignty. As such, section 3 of the Act (which requires the judges to interpret domestic statutes consistently with 'Convention rights' so far as it is possible so to do) does not give the courts the power to strike down legislation that contradicts Convention rights. In such cases, there is merely a power for the higher courts to issue a declaration of incompatibility.[27]

(B) OTHER INTERESTS PROTECTED BY THE LAW OF TORTS[28]

One important issue that must be identified here is that it is not uncommon for the central question in a tort claim to be how the law must reconcile competing interests.

---

[21] But see Sunkin, 'Pushing Forward the Frontiers of Human Rights Protection: The Meaning of Public Authority Under the Human Rights Act' [2004] PL 643 and *Cameron v Network Rail Infrastructure Ltd* [2006] EWHC 1133 (Railtrack was held not to be a public authority for the purposes of maintaining railway safety standards). [22] See ch 8.

[23] See ch 9. [24] See *Campbell v MGN* [2004] 2 AC 457; *Douglas v Hello! Ltd (No 6)* [2006] QB 125.

[25] In *Wainwright v Home Office* [2003] 3 WLR 1137 Lord Hoffmann expressed the view (at [31] – [33]) that that matter was one that would require an Act of Parliament.

[26] See the twin decisions of the European Court of Human Rights, in *Z v United Kingdom* (2002) 34 EHRR 97 and *TP and KM v United Kingdom* (2002) 34 EHRR 42. See also Gearty, 'Osman Unravels' (2002) 65 MLR 87 and *id*, 'Unravelling *Osman*' (2001) 64 MLR 159. [27] Human Rights Act 1998, s 4.

[28] Cane has supplied a simpler list to the one provided here. It covers broadly the same ground, but differs in emphasis. He suggests that tort law protects (i) interests in the person, (ii) property interests, (iii) contractual interests, (iv) non-contractual expectancies, (v) trade values and (vi) wealth: see Cane, *The Anatomy of Tort Law* (1997), pp 66–89.

A classic example concerns the fact that every citizen can assert both a right to free speech as well as a right to freedom from the deliberate publication of words injurious to his or her reputation. Thus, protecting A's compelling interest in the latter may involve restricting B's right to the former. Hence, certain defences that justify what would otherwise constitute defamation may be of crucial importance.

We look now at the kinds of interests that tort law protects.

(1) INTENTIONAL INVASION OF PERSONAL AND PROPRIETARY INTERESTS

The protection of the person from deliberately inflicted physical harm, restrictions on freedom of movement, and the protection of interests in tangible property – especially the right to non-interference with land and goods – were originally the most important concerns of the law of torts. The relevant modern torts include interference with goods and trespass in its various forms. It is these torts which provide the foundation of the protection of 'Convention rights' to life (Article 2), freedom from torture or degrading treatment (Article 3), freedom from slavery (Article 4), liberty (Article 5) and peaceful possession of property (First Protocol, Article 1).

(2) INTERESTS IN ECONOMIC RELATIONS, BUSINESS AND TRADE INTERESTS[29]

The extensive protection afforded to individuals' interests in freedom from physical harm and in their property is not mirrored by similar protection of interests in economic and business activities. The economic torts presently remain somewhat unclear in their scope (even though there are signs that they may well give way to a fairly simplistic, general principle of liability in the none-too-distant future[30]). Furthermore, very real difficulties exist in reconciling protection of one individual's economic interests with another's right to engage in free competition in a market economy. In addition to the classic economic torts of interference with contractual relations, conspiracy and intimidation, other torts of significance in this context are passing off and deceit.

(3) INTERESTS IN INTELLECTUAL PROPERTY

Interests in tangible property, land and goods are, as we shall see, well protected by the common law. By contrast, intellectual property in confidential information, copyright, and patents presents greater problems. Much of the law in this field is statutory; and interests in intellectual property generally overlap with interests in economic relations. But this is not invariably so. For example, the emerging tort based on the misuse of private personal information may soon embrace both a patient's right to confidentiality from his doctor and a multinational company's right to protection of their trade secrets.

---

[29] For thoroughgoing consideration see Carty, *An Analysis of the Economic Torts* (2001). See also chs 12–14.
[30] See further ch 14.

(4) NEGLIGENT INTERFERENCE WITH PERSONAL, PROPRIETARY AND ECONOMIC INTERESTS

If tort law's protection of persons and property were limited only to deliberately inflicted harm, it would be manifestly inadequate in our complex and overcrowded world. Nor would such limited protection reflect the requirements of the Human Rights Act 1998 insofar as it seeks to safeguard and protect life and bodily security. Since the landmark decision in *Donoghue v Stevenson*,[31] however, the courts have developed the tort of negligence to provide further protection to personal safety (including, within limits, mental integrity), property and economic interests. But for a variety of reasons, including the absence of any requirement that harm be inflicted 'directly' in the tort of negligence, the judges have adopted a cautious approach to protecting economic interests from negligently inflicted harm.

(5) FURTHER PROTECTION OF PERSONAL AND PROPRIETARY INTERESTS

Personal and proprietary interests rank so highly within the hierarchy of protected interests in tort law, and within the hierarchy of 'Convention rights', that further torts have emerged offering protection for those interests against conduct which is not necessarily, or cannot be proved to be, either intentional or negligent. There are, for example, torts of ancient origin – such as nuisance – as well as others of more recent vintage – such as the rule in *Rylands v Fletcher* (developed during the height of the industrial revolution when a new range of threats to private property were born almost overnight[32]) – which protect these interests. The former highlights the (arguably perverse[33]) degree of importance vested by the common law in the landowner's interest in his property.

The action for breach of statutory duty represents the common law's response to comparatively recent welfarist legislation, usually designed to improve standards of public health and personal safety. But in addition, albeit at the behest of the European Community, Parliament has also introduced a regime of strict liability for injuries caused by defective products.[34]

(6) REPUTATION

Tort law has long protected an individual's interest in his reputation via the torts of libel and slander. But these torts are of limited scope and fall a long way short of providing comprehensive protection to an individual's privacy interests, as we shall see in chapter 15. In addition, they are also subject to a wide range of partial and complete defences which further circumscribe their import.[35]

---

[31] [1932] AC 562.

[32] For the significance of the industrial revolution in grounding this rule, see Murphy, 'The Merits of *Rylands v Fletcher*' (2004) 24 OJLS 643.

[33] For the argument that, for the purposes of injunctive relief, property is treated more highly than the interest in bodily integrity, see Murphy, 'Rethinking Injunctions in Tort' (forthcoming).   [34] See ch 16.

[35] See, eg, the defences available in defamation discussed in ch 22.

(7) DUE PROCESS

A right to protection from malicious abuse of the judicial process is recognised in the tort of malicious prosecution and its ancillary tort of abuse of process. Now it seems that a tort to prevent abuse of the administrative process is also in its early infancy; and Article 6 of the European Convention on Human Rights may well contribute significantly to its development.[36]

(8) MISCELLANEOUS INTERESTS: 'CONVENTION RIGHTS' AND EUROPEAN COMMUNITY LAW RIGHTS

The antiquity and somewhat piecemeal development of torts means that there are a number of residual torts that defy classification. More importantly, however, a question now arises as to whether the principles developed by the common law offer adequate coverage of 'Convention rights'. Does the European Convention recognise interests unknown to the common law? The most obvious example of a possible lacuna in the law of tort has already been noted: the protection of privacy guaranteed in the ECHR by Article 8. However, privacy is also an excellent example of how dangerous it may be to look at any alleged human right in isolation. Article 10 establishes a right to freedom of expression, to hold opinions and disseminate information. The media and others fear that a right to privacy, if developed without proper safeguards, could undermine that latter right. Unscrupulous individuals whose conduct adversely affects others' interests would seek to use Article 8 to prevent public knowledge of their own activities. But Article 8 would permit the publication and dissemination of such information so long as it could be shown to be necessary within the specific terms mentioned in Article 8(2).[37]

Turning to European Community Law rights, it has for some time been recognised by the English courts that directly applicable European Community Law can create obligations the breach of which entitle affected persons to sue for the harm thereby caused.[38] But as originally understood, these 'Eurotorts'[39] were strictly limited to instances in which the European legislation in question imposed obligations on private individuals. Thus, in one case where the United Kingdom was in breach of its obligations and imposed an unlawful ban on the import of turkeys from France,[40] it was held that no private law right of action arose and that only public law redress by way of judicial review was available. Since then, however, the European Court of Justice has recognised a much wider principle of state liability that undermines the

---

[36] It has already been raised on a number of occasions in connection with the striking out of negligence claims: see, eg, *Z v United Kingdom* (2002) 34 EHRR 97 and *TP and KM v United Kingdom* (2002) 34 EHRR 42. See also Gearty, '*Osman* Unravels' (2002) 65 MLR 87.   [37] See *Campbell v MGN* [2004] 2 AC 457.

[38] *Garden Cottage Foods Ltd v Milk Marketing Board* [1984] AC 130.

[39] It has been confirmed that an action for a breach of Community legislation is of the same order as an action for breach of statutory duty and that therefore the action is one in tort: see *R v Secretary of State for Transport, ex p Factortame (No 7)* [2001] 1 WLR 942.

[40] *Bourgoin SA v Ministry of Agriculture* [1986] QB 716.

reasoning in this case.[41] In *Francovich v Italian Republic*,[42] for example, the European Court held that failure by a member state to implement a directive from the Community designed to create rights on the part of particular individuals would give rise to a claim in damages on the part of those individuals. What was perhaps most significant and remarkable about the decision in *Francovich* was that the Community legislation in question was not directly effective (which meant that, in the absence of an action against the state, there would have been no-one against whom an action could have been brought). But it has now been made clear by the European court that the *Francovich* principle applies equally where the legislation *is* of direct effect,[43] where the breach of Community law entails a legislative act (not merely an omission),[44] and in respect of administrative decisions.[45]

The conditions that must be satisfied in order to sue according to this 'Eurotort' principle were set out by Lord Slynn in *R v Secretary of State for Transport, ex p Factortame Ltd*. He said:

Before a member state can be held liable, a national court must find that

  (i) the relevant rule of Community law is one which is intended to confer rights on individuals;
 (ii) the breach must be sufficiently serious;
(iii) there must be a direct causal link between the breach and the loss complained of.[46]

The similarity between the first requirement and the test adopted in relation to an action for breach of (domestic) statutory duty is immediately striking.[47] Furthermore, it is clear that this requirement can be invoked to restrict the operation of the *Francovich* principle. Thus, in *Three Rivers District Council v Bank of England (No 3)*,[48] the House of Lords held that a failure to comply with a banking directive concerning the regulation of credit institutions was fundamentally concerned with harmonizing banking practice, and not with protecting depositors. As such, the Community legislation in question was not viewed as intended to confer rights on individuals, and the 'Eurotort' action in that case failed at the first stage.

It has since been explained in relation to the second limb, that the pivotal phrase 'sufficiently serious' does not necessarily require negligence or fault (although fault may

---

[41] The House of Lords also doubted its correctness in *Kirklees Metropolitan Borough Council v Wickes Building Supplies Ltd* [1993] AC 227.

[42] [1993] 2 CMLR 66. See Craig, 'Once More unto the Breach: the Community, the State and Damages Liability' (1997) 113 LQR 67.

[43] *Brasserie du Pêcheur SA v Federal Republic of Germany* (Case C-46/93) [1996] ECR 1–1029.

[44] *R v Secretary of State for Transport, ex p Factortame Ltd* (Case C-48/93).

[45] *R v Ministry of Agriculture, Fisheries and Food, ex p Hedley Lomas (Ireland)* (Case C5/94) [1996] ECR 1–2553.

[46] [1999] 4 All ER 906, at 916. These conditions derive directly from the decision of the European Court of Justice in *Brasserie du Pêcheur SA v Federal Republic of Germany* (Case C-46/93) [1996] ECR 1–1029, at [74].

[47] See ch 20.   [48] [2000] 2 WLR 1220.

be a material consideration), and that the seriousness of the breach must be judged in the context of the clarity of the community rule breached and, where appropriate, the legislative discretion afforded to the member state.[49]

SECTION 3 THEORETICAL PERSPECTIVES ON TORT LAW

In recent decades there has been much theorizing about the proper parameters of tort law;[50] about the bases of tortious liability;[51] and about whether tort law should serve individual or collective goals.[52] In this section, some of these perspectives are considered in order to supply readers with a wider theoretical context in which to set the remaining chapters.

(A) A LAW OF TORT OR A LAW OF TORTS?

It is sometimes said that it makes more sense to talk in terms of a law of torts than simply the law of tort, given the various bases of liability that apply to different torts, given the range of interests that these torts protect, and given the peculiar historical genesis of the various nominate torts.[53] There is doubtless something in this, but it is largely an academic point. When considering the vast body of authorities, it is clear that in *practical terms* it counts for little to contend that the infliction of unjustifiable harm is always a tort,[54] or that there is a fixed catalogue of circumstances which alone, and for all time, mark the limit of what are torts.[55] There is no problem peculiar to the law of torts here. Certain situations have been held to involve torts and will continue to do so in the absence of statutory repeal. Similarly, others have been held not to be tortious, and the courts upon which those decisions are binding will likewise continue to follow them.[56] These fundamental points are also often camouflaged behind the Latin maxims

---

[49] *R v Secretary of State for Transport, ex p Factortame Ltd (No 5)* [1999] 4 All ER 960.

[50] See, eg, Weinrib, 'Understanding Tort Law' (1989) 23 *Valparaiso U L Rev* 485; id, *The Idea of Private Law* (1995).

[51] See, eg, Coleman, *Risks and Wrongs* (1992). Cf Abel, 'A Socialist Approach to Risk' (1982) *Maryland L Rev* 695.

[52] See, eg, Weinrib, 'Understanding Tort Law' (1989) 23 *Valparaiso U L Rev* 485. Cf Schwartz, 'Mixed Theories of Tort Law: Affirming Both Deterrence and Corrective Justice' (1997) 75 *Tex L Rev* 1801 and Waldron, 'Moments of Carelessness and Massive Loss' in Owen (ed), *Philosophical Foundations of Tort Law* (1995).

[53] See Ibbetson, *A Historical Introduction to the Law of Obligations* (1999).

[54] An especially good example is the action for breach of confidential information which may be thought of either (as is common) in terms of a breach of an equitable duty or in terms of a tortious breach of duty (see, eg, *Campbell v MGN Ltd* [2004] 2 AC 457, at [14] *per* Lord Nicholls).

[55] See further Murphy, 'Formularism and Tort Law' [1999] *Adelaide L Rev* 115.

[56] This is not to say that the superior courts will not, on occasion, part company with the past: see, eg, *Campbell v MGN* [2004] 2 AC 457 in which Lord Nicholls (at [14]) seemed to want to break free of the shackles

damnum sine injuria and *injuria sine damno*, which (not because of their aid to understanding, but because the student may meet them elsewhere) must be shortly explained. *Damnum sine injuria* – harm without (recognized) injury – merely means that one may have suffered harm and yet have no action for damages in tort; in short, that the damage of which he complains is not an interest protected by the law of tort.[57] *Injuria sine damno* – (recognized) injury without harm – is a shorthand version of the rule that some interests are so important that their violation is an actionable tort without proof of tangible damage. Battery is a classic example of a tort that adopts this principle.

(B) WRONGFULNESS IN TORT LAW

The relationship within tort law between rights and wrongs must very briefly be addressed. It is not enough merely to identify the kinds of interest that tort protects. The kinds of wrongdoing considered sufficient to violate those interests must also be identified.[58] The deliberate invasion of an interest can easily be classified in terms that demand that the law should intervene to require the defendant to compensate for the harm he has caused the claimant. Certain interests, however, may be so crucial to the claimant, and so vulnerable to accidental harm, that negligence on the part of the defendant suffices to engage his liability in tort. Exceptionally, the relationship of the claimant and the defendant, or the nature of the defendant's conduct will give rise to *strict* liability. In such instances, the law requires the defendant to bear a greater (but not absolute) responsibility for protecting the claimant's interests.

It is not, however, necessary to dwell here on the importance of motive or malice. It follows from what has already been said that an act, even though it is malicious, will not incur tortious liability unless the interest that it violates is protected by an extant tort.[59] On the other hand, the interest interfered with is occasionally rated so low in the hierarchy of protected interests that only malicious invasions are forbidden.[60] Which these interests are, the reader will discover as he or she progresses through the remaining chapters of this book.

---

of the action in equity for breach of confidentiality in order to give the protection of tort law to the misuse of private information.

[57] For the argument that *damnum sine injuria* should support a claim for injunctive relief, even though it would not ground an action for damages in certain circumstances, see Murphy, 'Rethinking Injunctions in Tort' (forthcoming). For more general discussion of what amounts to recognized harm see Tettenborn, 'What is a Loss?' in Neyers (ed), *Emerging Issues in Tort Law* (2007).

[58] See Cane, *The Anatomy of Tort Law* (1997).

[59] Fierce competition that damages one's business interests and is prompted by malice, for example, will not by itself usually suffice to invoke the protection afforded by the economic torts. There must normally also be some illegal act on the part of D.

[60] The fact that tort law ranks certain interests higher than others should not be assumed to be either logically coherent or able to withstand detailed scrutiny: see Murphy, 'Formularism and Tort Law' [1999] *Adelaide L Rev* 115.

(C) GHOSTS FROM THE PAST: FORMS OF ACTION[61]

Until the passing of the Common Law Procedure Act 1852 and the Judicature Act 1875, a claimant could only sue in tort if he brought his cause of action within a recognised form of action – that is, one for which some particular writ of summons was available. Although the forms of action have now been abolished, many old cases cannot be understood without some knowledge of what they were.[62] Moreover, classifications of torts derive from the various writs grounding suit, so that rules worked out under them have necessarily been the starting point for any growth in the law of torts which has taken place since. Many seemingly arbitrary divisions today between one tort and another are explained only by reference to the forms of action. Thus, the writ of trespass lay only for direct injuries, while the form of action known as 'action on the case' developed separately for indirect injuries. And it will be seen in due course that, even now, trespass is not committed where the injury is indirect.[63]

A claimant does not have to plead the tort of negligence, trespass or whatever; he merely sets out the relevant facts. Yet torts can overlap so that on any given facts a claimant may succeed by contending at trial that the facts satisfied the requirements of either of two (or more) torts. On the other hand, the claimant may fail where he relies on, say, the rule in *Rylands v Fletcher* rather than private nuisance if he argues only that the facts proved satisfy all the requirements of *Rylands v Fletcher* (but they in fact do not) and he could have advanced further facts (but did not) which would have satisfied the tort of nuisance. The claimant's error will be one of oral argument, not of pleading, except when he fails to plead an allegation of fact which, although not material in one tort, would have been a prerequisite of the other. Strictly speaking, a judge could find for the claimant merely by holding that, on the facts proved, there was a tort. But, given the splitting up into compartments of the law of torts, the judge will ordinarily decide that the claimant wins because the defendant has committed some specific tort. The law does not say that intentionally and carelessly inflicted harm will be tortious in certain circumstances. Instead, it defines the limits of each tort and says to the claimant: 'You win if you establish facts which satisfy the definitions of any one of those torts'. With regard to any particular decided case, the tort student is thus concerned to know, not only that the claimant has succeeded on certain facts, but also which tort has been committed. In short, it is important to know both the ingredients of each particular tort as well as the general principles of tortious liability.[64]

---

[61] See Maitland, *The Forms of Action at Common Law* (1909).

[62] For an accessible account, see Williams and Hepple, *Foundations of the Law of Tort* (1984) ch 2.

[63] See chs 8, 9 and 10.

[64] See Cane, 'General and Special Tort Law: Uses and Abuses of Theory' in Neyers (ed), *Emerging Issues in Tort Law* (2007).

(D) CONFLICT BETWEEN CERTAINTY AND JUSTICE

The conflict between the demands of certainty and justice is a recurrent theme in case law. The claims of certainty are less pressing in the case of the law of torts than in some other branches of the law – for example, the law of property. The purchaser of land must be assured that the law on the faith of which he acquires a good title is not liable to change; it is less important that the law should settle precisely and for all time, say, the limits of liability of doctors for harm caused to their patients. On the other hand, the development of some torts has been seriously affected by the judicial urge for that certainty which is believed by many to result from making rigid categories. The courts, for example, once thought fit to divide entrants on to land into three rigid categories – invitees, licensees and trespassers – in order to determine the duty of occupiers to them in respect of their personal safety, with the result that in 1957 the Occupiers' Liability Act was passed in order to clear up the confusion that this method had brought about.[65]

A significant measure of difficulty in this context stems from the fact that there are profoundly competing accounts of what justice entails. Such disagreement over the appropriate conception of justice – corrective, distributive, or even retributive – bedevils the debate about the appropriate balance between justice and certainty.[66] To some extent, then, the fact that common agreement on the justice of any given case is likely to be elusive perhaps explains why the courts sometimes emphasize certainty,[67] even though the need for certainty within the law of torts is not of paramount importance.

(E) LOSS DISTRIBUTION, DETERRENCE AND ECONOMIC ANALYSIS

The traditional approach of the law of torts has been to ask whether a loss that B has suffered should be shifted to A. If A were at fault, the answer would usually be to shift that loss from innocent victim B to wrongdoer A.[68] There is, however, another view. By spreading the loss from an individual victim to the many that benefit from an activity that has caused it, the loss is more easily and more fairly borne.[69] The employer whose

---

[65] See ch 7.

[66] See, eg, Coleman 'The Practice of Corrective Justice' in Owen (ed), *Philosophical Foundations of Tort Law* (1995).

[67] On the other hand, the judiciary in recent years have made explicit their pursuit of justice within tort law, especially in the twin areas of liability for pure economic loss and for psychiatric harm: see, eg, *White v Jones* [1995] 1 All ER 69 (discussed in Murphy, 'Expectation Losses, Negligent Omissions and the Tortious Duty of Care' [1996] CLJ 43) and *White v Chief Constable of South Yorkshire* [1999] 2 AC 455.

[68] Loosely, this account may be termed corrective justice, and it is based on the conception of torts as being based exclusively on bi-polar relations: see Weinrib, 'Understanding Tort Law' (1989) 23 *Valparaiso U L Rev* 485.

[69] This is what is meant by the term 'distributive justice'. For other arguments against simplistic loss shifting see Cane, *Atiyah's Accidents Compensation and the Law* (2006).

workman is injured can spread the loss through raising the price of his product. The same argument applies where his product injures a consumer. This principle of loss distribution is sometimes, for example, advanced as a justification for the vicarious liability principle which makes an employer answerable for the torts committed by those who work for him.[70] Equally, loss distribution is reinforced by widespread insurance.[71] The vehicle owner can readily insure – and is indeed required by law to do so – against the risk of his negligently inflicting harm on third parties. His premium (and the premium of other drivers) falls short of the amount payable in damages for a typical road accident. Yet in this way the aggregate cost of all car accidents is distributed among all properly insured car drivers. Some judges even acknowledge that they are the readier to find negligence, or to make high compensatory awards, when they know that the damages will be paid by an insurance company (and thus, in turn, premium payers).[72]

But while loss distribution via insurance can better guarantee tort victims that there will be money available to pay them the damages they are awarded in court, it also has the capacity to undermine another of tort law's goals: deterrence. The imposition of tort liability operates not only to transfer the relevant loss from the victim to the tortfeasor, but also (especially where the tort requires intentional wrongdoing or malice) to deter tortious conduct from the outset. Put at its simplest, the more a person commits a tort, the more he will have to pay in damages. Accordingly, he will generally endeavour not to commit such torts in the first place.[73] Good examples include the imposition of strict liability for breaches of statutory duty by employers, and on manufacturers of defective products who are encouraged to maintain high standards of safety in their goods in order to avoid liability.

However, the role of deterrence within tort law should not be overestimated, nor is it without other problems. To begin with, there are many instances in which the tortfeasor's conduct is in no sense deliberately harmful or even what might be termed 'calculated negligence'.[74] In such cases, where his conduct is at worst inadvertent, it is difficult to see how the tortfeasor could have been deterred. Secondly, for the courts to ensure in other areas that 'tort does not pay', recourse to exemplary damages is sometimes thought to be necessary.[75] This is problematic because punishment is not generally taken to be one of tort law's functions; it is, instead, seen as the role of the criminal law. Thirdly, judges are sometimes cautious in general terms about invoking principles of deterrence, fearful that it will lead to over-cautious, defensive conduct. This concern is

---

[70] For critique of this as a complete justification for vicarious liability, see Neyers, 'A Theory of Vicarious Liability' (2005) *Alberta L Rev* 1 and Murphy, 'Juridicial Foundations of Common Law Non-Delegable Duties' in Neyers (ed.), *Emerging Issues in Tort Law* (2007).

[71] See Cane, *The Anatomy of Tort Law* (1997), ch 9; Stapleton 'Tort, Insurance and Ideology' (1995) 58 MLR 520.

[72] See *Murphy v Brentwood District Council* [1990] 2 All ER 908, at 923, *per* Lord Keith. See also *Nettleship v Weston* [1971] 2 QB 691.

[73] This deterrent effect is not entirely absent in contexts where there is compulsory insurance, since repeated car accidents, for example, will lead to the tortfeasor having to pay higher and higher insurance premiums.

[74] The driver who takes the odd chance with amber traffic lights might appropriately be described thus.

[75] See, eg, *Cassell & Co v Broome* [1972] AC 1027 (D published defamatory material concerning C in the expectation that profits would outweigh an award of compensatory damages). See further Law Commission Report, *Exemplary, Aggravated and Restitutionary Damages*, Law Com No 247 (1997).

particularly evident in connection with medical litigation despite the fact that there is scant evidence of defensive medicine.

Finally, we should note in this context that much academic work has been done on the economic analysis of tort law.[76] According to this school of thought, the law is criticised and evaluated according to the criterion of economic efficiency. Thus, in the present context, the crucial issue becomes whether the rule governing a particular tort is cost effective.[77] Perhaps the classic example is the test for negligent conduct propounded by Learned Hand J in *United States v Carroll Towing Co.*[78] It runs as follows: 'if the probability be called P; the injury, L; and the burden, B; liability [in negligence] depends on whether B is less than L multiplied P'. In other words, the test operates by permitting and requiring the defendant to assess the probability and costs of accidents, and then to compare them with the cost of precautions. The defendant is not negligent if his conduct is vindicated according to this test, for the objective is not to eliminate all damage, but rather to deter conduct that results in damage where the cost of preventing the accident is less than the cost (in damages) of the accident occurring. On such criteria, any change from fault-based liability to strict liability would have to depend on proof that the total additional costs to the potential defendants – additional precautions, insurance and so on – did not exceed the total cost to individuals of the risk created by the enterprise. Normal concepts of fairness and justice can be relevant only if susceptible to being assigned economic value.[79]

Economic analysis is a useful tool to attain an understanding of the operation of certain torts, in particular negligence, nuisance and product liability. It offers a measure by which our often confused system of compensation law may be judged and found wanting. However, economic analysis can never be an all-embracing explanation of the objectives of tort law; it fails to account, for example, for broader considerations of justice. As two of the leading lawyer-economists in England have pointed out, '[e]fficiency is, of course, not the only guideline to the right [legal] principles'; thus, efficiency must 'at some points yield before, and at other points compromise with, other guidelines, notably those of justice and fairness'.[80] Not surprisingly, then, English judges are often wary of relying on academic expositions of economic analysis when deciding cases.[81] Quite apart from its limitations, economic analysis has its powerful detractors, foremost among whom is a prominent Canadian private lawyer, Ernest Weinrib.[82]

---

[76] For a general introduction to economic analysis see Burrows and Veljanowski, *Readings in the Economics of Law and Regulation* (1984).

[77] Calabresi, *The Cost of Accidents* (1970); Posner, *The Economic Analysis of Law* (6th ed, 2003).

[78] 159 F 2d 169 (2d Cir 1947) at 173.

[79] Some lawyer-economists, of course, contend that an economic approach to tort law is a fair one precisely because it can be justified in accordance with objective, economic criteria. But this argument presupposes that the objective economic criteria are themselves fair.

[80] Ogus and Richardson, 'Economics and the Environment: A Study of Private Nuisance' [1977] CLJ 284 at 294.

[81] Although they do take economic efficiency into account in determining the limits of liability for negligence on occasion: see, eg, *Stovin v Wise* [1996] AC 923.

[82] See, eg, Weinrib, 'Understanding Tort Law' (1989) 23 *Valparaiso U L Rev* 485. And for a highly accessible account of the various arguments for (and against), and the proponents of, economic analysis, see Cane, 'The Anatomy of Private Law Theory: A 25th Anniversary Essay' (2005) 25 OJLS 203.

(F) THE JUDGES AND *LAISSEZ-FAIRE*

Much of the law relating to economic transactions is only understood if the implied judicial acceptance of *laissez-faire* is considered. This is merely one facet of the individualism of the law of torts, especially prominent during the nineteenth century. It is an influence which still persists, although less pervasively, in the face of the modern tendency towards welfarism.[83]

(G) LIMITS ON THE EFFECTIVENESS OF TORT LAW

Though there is much theorizing about what should and should not be actionable in tort,[84] the law of torts remains essentially practical. Judges have little patience with trivial claims. For example, they may deny a remedy by way of trespass to the person for mere touching.[85] They recognize the limits of the wrongs that the law is capable of redressing, however morally reprehensible they may be. For example, avarice, brutal words and ingratitude cannot form the basis of an action in tort law. Along with this is a judicial dread of a flood of actions. It is often avowedly for this reason that the courts have so far been reluctant to allow claims for negligently inflicted pure economic loss where the range of claimants as a result of one incident might be large.[86] The courts also display a marked caution in the context of awarding damages for non-material harms.

   Another problem is that damages in many torts cannot be fixed with mathematical precision. For example, the calculation of damages in, say, the tort of false imprisonment cannot be conducted in the same way as damages for breach of a contract based on failure to fulfil a sale of goods agreement. For this reason, the courts have rightly been on their guard to restrain 'gold-digging' actions. Nonetheless, it is apparent that they have sometimes been excessively wary; and later courts have had to overrule earlier decisions. The cases on the negligent infliction of psychiatric harm illustrate this point.[87]

SECTION 4 TORT AND OTHER BRANCHES
OF COMMON LAW

For some writers, the juridical divisions between torts and other areas of the common law – principally the law of contract and the law of unjust enrichment – have become so

---

[83] See generally Cane, *Tort Law and Economic Interests* (1996).

[84] And, indeed, what might *properly* be taken to constitute tort law: see, McBride and Bagshaw, *Tort Law* (2005) pp 30–35 and 727–788.   [85] See *Collins v Wilcock* [1984] 1 WLR 1172.

[86] See ch 3. See also Barker, 'Economic Loss and the Duty of Care: A Study in the Exercise of Legal Justification' (forthcoming).

[87] As in *White v Chief Constable of South Yorkshire Police* [1999] 1 All ER 1. For rigorous analysis of the legitimacy of the courts' stance in this context see Murphy, 'Negligently Inflicted Psychiatric Harm – A Re-appraisal' (1995) 15 *Legal Studies* 415.

blurred that they prefer not to talk of three separate branches of the civil law but, instead, of a general law of obligations.[88] Historically, contract law alone was concerned with the obligation to fulfil undertakings voluntarily made (so long as good consideration had been provided). By contrast, as we have seen, the obligations underlying torts require us to refrain from violating another's non-contractual, legally recognised rights and interests. Finally, with its roots in Roman law, the law of unjust enrichment concerns the obligation to reverse unjust and unjustifiable gains.[89] However, while 'obligations lawyers' recognize that it is broadly possible to distinguish these three areas of law in this way, they nonetheless contend that these divisions are imperfect. They believe that there are too many areas of overlap (in terms of the bases of damages awarded and the sources of the obligations) for this tripartite classification to be worthwhile. For example, the burgeoning tort law associated with voluntary assumptions of responsibility stemming from the decision in *Hedley Byrne & Co v Heller & Partners Ltd*,[90] is seen by some to undermine the cardinal principles that only contractual obligations are created by the parties themselves, and that tortious obligations are imposed by rules of law.[91]

Similarly, contract and tort are connected by the fact that they both generally concern awards of damages for harm done (whether broken promises or broken legs).[92] But this is not exclusively the case. For example, contractual remedies may be assessed in the light of benefits acquired by the other party – and herein lies a point of connection with the law of unjust enrichment.[93] While at the same time, both tort and unjust enrichment can be linked in that their obligations derive from rules of law rather than reciprocal undertakings.[94]

In the light of these juridical connections, the argument in favour of reconceptualizing the common law in terms of a law of obligations is not without some force. Certainly, the divisions between tort, contract and unjust enrichment law are far from perfect.[95]

---

[88] For some of the debate see Cane, *The Anatomy of Tort Law* (1997), pp 182–196, and (more thoroughly) Waddams, *Dimensions of Private Law: Categories and Concepts in Anglo-American Legal Reasoning* (2003).

[89] See Giglio, 'A Systematic Approach to "Unjust" and "Unjustified" Enrichment' (2003) 23 OJLS 455.

[90] [1964] AC 465. See also *White v Jones* [1995] 1 All ER 69; *Henderson v Merrett Syndicate* [1994] 3 All ER 506.

[91] For a particularly trenchant attack on the language of assumed responsibility in this context, see Barker, 'Unreliable Assumptions in the Modern Law of Negligence' (1993) 109 LQR 461.

[92] Furthermore, while the measure of damages in contract was once distinctively that of 'expectation loss', this has begun to feature also in the law of tort: see *White v Jones* [1995] 1 All ER 69. See also Murphy, 'Expectation Losses, Negligent Omissions and the Tortious Duty of Care' [1996] CLJ 43.

[93] In contract, if A builds B a fence for which B fails to pay, B is in breach of contract. If the benefit is conferred extra-contractually, however, the action will lie in unjust enrichment (eg, *Greenwood v Bennett* [1973] QB 195: A, believing the car he bought from a thief to be his own, effected several improvements upon it; B, the true owner, to whom the car had to be returned was liable to A in respect of his unjust enrichment in the form of those car improvements).

[94] Occasionally, contractual obligations are imposed by rules of law – eg, the duty to perform a service with reasonable care imposed by the Supply of Goods and Services Act 1982, s 13. But these obligations are imposed only within the pre-existing framework of reciprocal, voluntary obligations.

[95] See Waddams, *Dimensions of Private Law: Categories and Concepts in Anglo-American Legal Reasoning* (2003).

On the other hand, it is submitted that the clearest grasp of the principles, aims and objectives of tort law – together with an appreciation of its distinctiveness in terms of the range of interests protected – may best be derived from its exposition in isolation from the law of contract and the law of unjust enrichment.

Finally, it should be noted that certain types of conduct may simultaneously constitute both a crime and a tort. Thus, it is that the thief who steals your watch commits both the crime of theft and the tort of conversion. This overlap can be explained on the basis that whereas it is the function of criminal law to protect the interest of the public at large (or the state), it is primarily the law of torts that protects the interests of individuals (hence sanctioning compensation and injunctions rather than fines or imprisonment).

FURTHER READING

Birks, 'The Concept of a Civil Wrong' in Owen (ed), *Philosophical Foundations of Tort Law* (1995)

Cane, *The Anatomy of Tort Law* (1997)

Cane, 'General and Special Tort Law: Uses and Abuses of Theory' in Neyers (ed), *Emerging Issues in Tort Law* (2007)

Goldberg and Zipursky, 'Unrealized Torts' (2002) 88 *Virginia L Rev* 1625

Murphy, 'Formularism and Tort Law' [1999] *Adelaide L Rev* 115

Schwartz, 'Mixed Theories of Tort Law: Affirming both Deterrence and Corrective Justice' (1997) 75 *Tex L Rev* 1801

Stapleton, 'Tort, Insurance and Ideology' (1995) 58 MLR 520

Weinrib, 'Understanding Tort Law' (1989) 23 *Valparaiso U L Rev* 485

Wright, 'Right, Justice and Tort Law' in Owen (ed), *Philosophical Foundations of Tort Law* (1995) p 51

PART II

NEGLIGENT INVASIONS OF INTERESTS IN THE PERSON, PROPERTY INTERESTS AND ECONOMIC INTERESTS

2

DUTY OF CARE I: FOUNDATIONAL PRINCIPLES

SECTION 1 INTRODUCTION

Far more people suffer damage from the careless acts of others than from intentional wrongdoing. Accordingly, carelessly inflicted harm occupies a central position in the English law of torts, and it has long been recognized that, in certain circumstances, persons guilty of careless conduct should be liable to their victims. Indeed, the liability of those engaged in certain common callings – such as, smiths and innkeepers – goes back to the fourteenth century. Furthermore, many actions in nuisance and trespass were once based upon negligent conduct. Gradually, however, a large variety of situations in which negligence was the common element got subsumed under the action on the case. But not until maybe 1825 onwards was there any discernible emergence of negligence as a separate tort. There existed merely a list of situations where the victims of careless conduct might recover damages. Thereafter, actions on the case for negligence became common, no doubt spurred on at first by the increase in negligently inflicted injuries through the use of new mechanical inventions such as the railways, and later by the abolition of the forms of action.[1] The concrete emergence of negligence as a separate tort with a distinct set of principles became irresistible, and in practical terms it is now the most common (and most important) tort of all. It must be realised, however, that negligently inflicted harm does not always sound in negligence alone; negligent conduct relating to the use of land may well, for example, give rise to nuisance liability.[2]

It is essential to grasp from the start of any consideration of negligence law that it is not the case that anyone who suffers harm as a result of another's carelessness can sue. The tort of negligence requires more than 'heedless or careless conduct'.[3] The injured party must establish that the defendant owed him a duty to take reasonable care to protect him from the kind of harm suffered,[4] that he was in breach of that duty, and that it was the defendant's breach of duty that caused the claimant's injury. Duty, breach and

---

[1] The main milestones were *Vaughan v Menlove* (1837) 3 Bing NC 468; *Winterbottom v Wright* (1842) 10 M & W 109; *Heaven v Pender* (1883) 11 QBD 503.

[2] But for criticism see Gearty, 'The Place of Nuisance in the Modern Law of Torts' [1989] CLJ 214.

[3] *Lochgelly Iron and Coal Co v M'Mullan* [1934] AC 1, at 25, *per* Lord Wright.

[4] In *Caparo Industries plc v Dickman* [1990] 605, at 627 Lord Bridge said: 'It is never sufficient to ask simply whether A owes B a duty of care. It is always necessary to determine the scope of the duty by reference to the

causation must all be established in every successful claim in negligence.[5] This chapter therefore starts by seeking to identify the fundamental principles underpinning the duty of care.

SECTION 2 THE EMERGENCE OF A GENERAL TEST

The concept of duty of care in negligence[6] emerged towards the end of the eighteenth century, and is now so firmly rooted that there can be no doubt that actions in negligence must fail where a duty is not established.[7] There are many strands to this requirement of duty, as we shall see. But to begin with, it is important to stress that there must be one of those general situations which the law recognises as being capable of giving rise to a duty; for in a number of situations it has been held that there can be no such duty.[8] The first attempt to rationalise the situations in which a duty may be imposed was made in *Heaven v Pender* by Brett MR. He said:

[W]henever one person is by circumstances placed in such a position with regard to another that everyone of ordinary sense who did think would at once recognise that if he did not use ordinary care and skill in his own conduct with regard to those circumstances he would cause danger or injury to the person or property of the other, a duty arises to use ordinary care and skill to avoid such danger.[9]

In 1932 came the famous dictum of Lord Atkin in *Donoghue v Stevenson* in which he enunciated his seminal 'neighbour principle'.

The rule that you are to love your neighbour becomes in law, you must not injure your neighbour; and the lawyer's question, Who is my neighbour? receives a restricted reply. You must take reasonable care to avoid acts or omissions which you can reasonably foresee would be likely to injure your neighbour. Who, then, in law is my neighbour? The answer seems to be persons who are so closely and directly affected by my act that I ought reasonably to have them

---

kind of damage from which A must take care to save B harmless'. Accordingly, where X is instrumental in injuring Y in circumstances where no duty was owed to Y to take care not to injure Y *in that way*, X will not be liable for want of duty: *Sam v Atkins* [2005] EWCA Civ 1452.

[5] However, judges by no means always clearly distinguish between the three. In *Roe v Minister of Health* [1954] 2 QB 66, at 85, Lord Denning LJ opined that the three questions were in many cases simply different ways of looking at one and the same thing: 'Is the consequence fairly to be considered within the risk created by the negligence?'.

[6] Duties similar to those discussed here under common law negligence may also arise under statutes or contracts. See, eg, the 'common duty of care' under the Occupiers' Liability Act 1957, s 2(2).

[7] *Heaven v Pender* (1883) 11 QBD 503, at 507, *per* Brett MR; *Thomas v Quartermaine* (1887) 18 QBD 685, at 694, *per* Bowden LJ; *Le Lievre v Gould* [1893] 1 QB 491, at 497, *per* Lord Esher MR; *Grant v Australian Knitting Mills Ltd* [1936] AC 85, at 101; *Hay (or Bourhill) v Young* [1943] AC 92.

[8] See, eg, *Mulcahy v Ministry of Defence* [1996] QB 732 (no duty owed by one serviceman to another).

[9] (1883) 11 QBD 503, at 509.

in contemplation as being so affected when I am directing my mind to the acts or omissions which are called in question.[10]

This 'neighbour principle' is not the *ratio decidendi* of the case and it is probable that Lord Atkin never intended it to be an exact or comprehensive statement of law.[11] However, the importance of *Donoghue v Stevenson* was two-fold. (1) It firmly established a new category of duty, namely that of a manufacturer of goods to the eventual users of those goods (a category that has since developed far beyond the limits of the facts of that case).[12] (2) It finally set at rest any possible doubts about whether the tort of negligence was capable of further expansion.

Although Lord Atkin's neighbour principle was established as a broad guide to the circumstances in which a duty of care may be imposed, it must not be forgotten that the question of duty is one of law, not fact. As such, the question of whether a duty exists is often straightforward, for there are numerous and extensive categories of situations which are already treated by the courts as imposing a duty of care. Examples include makers or repairers of goods owing a duty to those who use those goods, and those carrying out activities on a highway owing a duty to other highway users. Accordingly, before one falls back on any general test, one must ascertain whether on similar facts the courts have already recognised a duty.

There are, of course, other cases where the law has unequivocally denied the existence of a duty. A landowner, for example, may with impunity abstract percolating water from below the surface of his land even though this results in a settlement of a claimant's adjoining buildings. He is not liable because he owes no duty of care in respect of percolating water.[13] Similarly, there is no duty in respect of economic loss caused by damage to the property of an individual other than a person with a current proprietary interest in the damaged property.[14]

SECTION 3 THE RISE AND FALL OF *ANNS*

Were it to be the case that the courts would hold that no duty exists unless an earlier precedent established such a duty, the law of torts would remain frozen and static for all time. Yet Lord Macmillan stated in *Donoghue v Stevenson* that the 'categories of

[10] [1932] AC 562, at 580.

[11] Cf *Haseldine v CA Daw & Son Ltd* [1941] 2 KB 343, at 362, *per* Scott LJ.

[12] This was an instance of the courts taking account of the new conditions of mass production and complex marketing of goods (wherein there are many intermediaries between manufacturer and consumer), and imposing on manufacturers certain minimum standards of care in favour of the consumer. The clearest exposition of this function of *Donoghue v Stevenson* is located in the speech of Lord Devlin in *Hedley Byrne & Co Ltd v Heller & Partners Ltd* [1964] AC 465.

[13] *Langbrook Properties Ltd v Surrey County Council* [1969] 3 All ER 1424; *Thomas v Gulf Oil Refining Ltd* (1979) 123 Sol Jo 787 (oil company had no duty to avoid fissuring its rock strata so as to deprive neighbour, C, of water in his ponds); *Midland Bank v Bargrove Property Services* (1991) 24 Con LR 98.

[14] *Leigh & Sillivan Ltd v Aliakmon Shipping Co Ltd* [1986] AC 785.

negligence are never closed'.[15] This means at the very least, as Asquith LJ said in *Candler v Crane Christmas & Co*, 'that in accordance with changing social needs and standards new classes of persons legally bound or entitled to the exercise of care may from time to time emerge'.[16] So, over the several decades beginning with Lord Atkin's formulation of the 'neighbour principle', new duty-situations were readily recognised by the courts. Thus, for example, it was held that an education authority owes a duty to the driver of a vehicle to exercise reasonable supervision over children in its nursery adjoining the highway so as to prevent them from endangering his safety on the road, by, for example, running unattended out of the nursery through an unlocked gate onto the roadway and causing him to swerve to avoid injuring them.[17] Equally, an electricity authority that had high-voltage wires near a climbable tree was held liable to the personal representatives of a child who trespassed off a nearby footpath, climbed the tree, and was killed.[18]

What each of the above examples have in common is that the defendant failed his 'neighbour'. He could have foreseen, and should have taken steps to prevent, the injury suffered by the claimant. So was the 'neighbour test' the sole criterion determining whether or not a duty arose? In a series of judgments from 1970 to 1982 the courts came close to accepting as much. First, in *Home Office v Dorset Yacht Co Ltd*, Lord Reid declared:

The time has come when we can and should say that it [*ie*, Lord Atkins's neighbour principle] ought to apply unless there is some justification or valid explanation for its exclusion.[19]

Then in *Anns v Merton LBC*, Lord Wilberforce proposed his now discredited two-stage test:

. . . the position has now been reached that in order to establish that a duty of care arises in a particular situation, it is not necessary to bring the facts of that situation within those of previous situations in which a duty of care has been held to exist. Rather the question has to be approached in two stages. First, one has to ask whether, as between the alleged wrongdoer and the person who suffered damage there is a sufficient relationship of proximity or neighbourhood such that, in the reasonable contemplation of the former, carelessness on his part may be likely to cause damage to the latter, in which case a *prima facie* duty of care arises. Secondly, if the first question is answered affirmatively, it is necessary to consider whether there are any considerations which ought to negative, or to reduce or limit the scope of the duty of the class of person to whom it is owed or the damages to which a breach of it may give rise.[20]

The two-stage test looked deceptively simple. Applied fairly literally, a judge ruling on a novel duty-situation might reason thus. (1) Was the harm to the claimant foreseeable bringing him within the 'neighbour principle'? (2) Was there any valid policy reason to

---

[15] [1932] AC 562, at 619.   [16] [1951] 2 KB 164, at 192.

[17] *Carmarthenshire County Council v Lewis* [1955] AC 549 (in that case the lorry struck a telegraph pole, and the driver was killed); *Barnes v Hampshire County Council* [1969] 3 All ER 746 (a local education authority was liable when a traffic accident ensued after letting children out of a school early before their parents or others came to fetch them).   [18] *Buckland v Guildford Gas Light and Coke Co* [1949] 1 KB 410.

[19] [1970] AC 1004, at 1027.   [20] [1978] AC 728, at 751–2.

deny the existence of a duty to the claimant?[21] In effect, the claimant having established foreseeability raised a presumption of the existence of a duty which the defendant then had to rebut on policy grounds. Lord Wilberforce himself, however, recognized that policy factors had a central role to play in determining the scope of a duty in *McLoughlin v O'Brian*: 'at the margin, the boundaries of a man's responsibilities for acts of negligence have to be fixed as a matter of policy'.[22]

But in the very same case, Lord Scarman who was fearful that judicial conservatism would lead to unjust rigidity in the common law came close to declaring foreseeability to be the *sole* test of the existence of a duty. Rejecting any policy-oriented limitations on liability for psychiatric harm, he argued:

> . . . if principle inexorably requires a decision which entails a degree of policy risk, the court's function is to adjudicate according to principle, leaving policy curtailment to the judgment of Parliament.[23]

Over a period of 14 years from 1970 to 1984 the categories of negligence looked infinitely expandable. The boundaries of liability expanded both in respect of psychiatric harm[24] and, more importantly, pure economic loss.[25] The tort of negligence even looked set to undermine the very boundaries of contract and tort, and, more particularly, the doctrines of consideration and privity of contract.[26] From 1984 onwards, however, judicial caution resurfaced and the House of Lords in particular led a retreat from *Anns*, bringing the tort of negligence back to a much more category-based approach. Their Lordships' determination to restrict the unchecked expansion of the tort and to prevent the emergence of any presumption that all kinds of harm were the responsibility of someone other than the claimant, was summed up neatly by Lord Hoffmann in *Stovin v Wise*.

> The trend of authorities [since 1984] has been to discourage the assumption that anyone who suffers loss is *prima facie* entitled to compensation from a person (preferably insured or a public authority) whose act or omission can be said to have caused it. The default position is that he is not.[27]

The retreat from *Anns* began in *Governors of the Peabody Donation Fund v Sir Lindsay Parkinson & Co Ltd*.[28] There, the House of Lords denied a remedy to a development

---

[21] For example, to refuse a remedy to C, a criminal, who is injured by the negligence of his drunken companion while driving their getaway car. Injury to C was readily foreseeable but as a matter of policy no duty was recognised as owed by one participant in crime to another: *Ashton v Turner* [1981] QB 137. And a claim by a child for 'wrongful life' – ie, a claim that the doctors acted negligently in not aborting her – was rejected on policy grounds. The consequences of failing to diagnose the rubella in her mother were foreseeable, but the Court of Appeal held (*inter alia*) that such claims would, if allowed, undermine the sanctity of human life: *McKay v Essex Area Health Authority* [1982] QB 1166.　　　　　　　　　　　　　　[22] [1983] 1 AC 410, at 421.

[23] *McLoughlin v O'Brian* [1983] 1 AC 410, at 430.

[24] See, eg, *McLoughlin v O'Brian* [1983] 1 AC 410, at 430; *Attia v British Gas plc* [1988] QB 304.

[25] See, eg, *Ross v Caunters* [1980] Ch 297; *Junior Books Ltd v Veitchi Co Ltd* [1983] 1 AC 520 (the high water mark of foreseeability sufficing to impose a duty).

[26] Since then, much of the doctrine of privity has been unpicked by the Contracts (Rights of Third Parties) Act 1999.　　　　　　　　　　　　　　　　　　　　　　　　[27] [1996] AC 923, at 949.

[28] [1985] AC 210.

company suing a local authority for the financial loss occasioned to that company by an inadequate drainage system, the plans for which they alleged the authority had negligently approved. Lord Keith said of the *Anns* test:

There has been a tendency in some recent cases to treat these passages as being themselves of a definitive character. This is a temptation to be resisted in determining whether or not a duty of care of a particular scope was incumbent on the defendant. It is material to take into consideration whether it is just and reasonable that it should be so.[29]

In effect Lord Keith demanded that the *claimant* identify policy grounds why a duty should arise and why the defendant should be made responsible for his welfare. Judicial disapproval for the *Anns* test continued apace.[30] And what is now clear beyond doubt is that foreseeability of harm alone is not enough to create a duty of care.

It has been said almost too frequently to require repetition that foreseeability of likely harm is not in itself a sufficient test of liability in negligence. Some further ingredient is invariably needed to establish the requisite proximity of relationship between the [claimant] and defendant, and all the circumstances of the case must be carefully considered and analysed in order to ascertain whether such an ingredient is present.[31]

Exactly what constitutes the 'necessary proximity' to give rise to a duty-situation is difficult to define precisely in most circumstances.[32] Foreseeability of harm to the claimant remains a necessary precondition of liability; and there can be no proximity without foreseeability. On the other hand, it seems clear that the term 'proximity' is intended to describe the nexus or relationship between the claimant and the defendant. As Lord Atkin insisted, my neighbours are 'persons who are so closely and directly affected by my act that I ought reasonably to have them in contemplation as being so affected'. As we shall see shortly, however, any distinctiveness of the proximity requirement is best gleaned from cases dealing with negligent omissions or negligent failures to control third parties.

In addition to the foreseeability and proximity requirements, it subsequently became clear that the courts would require, also, that there be proper grounds on which to impose on the defendant responsibility for the harm in question; reasons, in other words, why it would be fair to expect the defendant to safeguard the claimant's interests rather than to expect the claimant to look after himself. How difficult a task the claimant faces in this respect will vary depending on the kind of harm he has suffered. The courts are more ready to impose responsibility to safeguard others from physical injury and damage to their property, than from economic losses. Lord Bridge said in *Caparo Industries plc v Dickman*:

One of the most important distinctions always to be observed lies in the law's essentially different approach to the different kinds of damage which one party may have suffered in

---

[29] [1985] AC 210, at 240.

[30] *Yuen Kun-yeu v A-G of Hong Kong* [1988] AC 175, at 190–194; *Rowling v Takaro Properties Ltd* [1988] AC 473, at 501.   [31] *Hill v Chief Constable of West Yorkshire* [1988] 2 All ER 238, at 241, *per* Lord Keith.

[32] See Kidner, 'Resiling from the *Anns* Principle: The Variable Nature of Proximity in Negligence' [1987] *Legal Studies* 319.

consequence of the acts or omissions of another. It is one thing to owe a duty to avoid causing injury to the person or property of others. It is quite another to avoid causing others to suffer purely economic loss.[33]

Where physical harm is caused to a person (or his property) by another's carelessness, establishing that the claimant is proximate and that it is fair that the defendant *ought* to be responsible for the harm thus inflicted is generally unproblematic. As Lord Oliver put it in *Caparo*: 'the nexus between the defendant and the injured claimant can rarely give rise to any difficulty [in such cases]'.[34] And in *Murphy v Brentwood District Council*[35] he further implied the presumption of a duty in such cases stating that '[t]he infliction of physical injury to the person or property of another universally requires to be justified'.

Nonetheless, the House of Lords made it clear in *Marc Rich & Co AG v Bishop Rock Marine Co Ltd*[36] that, even in claims in relation to physical damage, foreseeability alone is insufficient to create a duty of care. Citing Saville LJ in the Court of Appeal, Lord Steyn confirmed[37] that *whatever the nature of the relevant harm* the court must consider, not only the foreseeability of such harm, but address the relationship between the parties and in every case be ' . . . satisfied that in all the circumstances it is fair, just and reasonable to impose a duty of care'. The facts of the case were as follows:

Cs' cargo had been loaded on D1's vessel under contracts incorporating the usual terms and conditions of international shipping contracts. Mid-voyage, the ship put into port with a crack in her hull. A surveyor employed by D3, a classification society responsible for checking the safety of ships at sea, inspected the vessel and certified that after some temporary repairs it should proceed on its voyage. A few days later the ship sank and the cargo worth £6m was lost. Cs recovered some of that sum from D1, but D1's liability was limited by statute. Cs then attempted to recover the balance of the loss from D3. Cs had suffered readily foreseeable physical damage to property as a result of the society's negligent inspection of the ship and the subsequent 'green light' the society's surveyor had given for the ship to carry on with the voyage.

Giving the majority speech in the House of Lords and finding no duty to the cargo owners, Lord Steyn acknowledged that where one person's carelessness *directly* causes physical damage to another, the law will more readily impose a duty. The infliction of loss to the claimants in this case was, however, indirect. There was no contract between the claimant and the society and no direct reliance by the claimants on the expertise of the society. Imposing a duty would undermine the framework established by the Hague-Visby Rules (an international maritime Convention).[38] Equally, it was considered relevant that classification societies are independent, non-profit-making bodies that act in the public interest to promote the collective welfare of people and property on the seas. Faced with litigation of this sort, such societies might act defensively, refusing to

---

[33] [1990] 1 All ER 568, at 574.   [34] [1990] 1 All ER 568, at 585.   [35] [1990] 2 All ER 908, at 935.
[36] [1996] AC 211.   [37] [1996] AC 211, at 235.
[38] For analogous reasoning, see *Raja v Austin Gray* [2002] EWCA Civ 1965.

carry out urgent or problematic inspections carrying a high risk of liability. Furthermore, limited resources would be diverted from the societies' fundamental work to conduct complex litigation. It would thus be unfair and unjust to impose a duty in respect of the claimants' lost cargo. The societies' responsibility was primarily towards the collective welfare of those at sea, and individual cargo owners should be left to their contractual remedies.

Lord Lloyd dissented. He perceived the facts as little more than a straightforward application of *Donoghue v Stevenson*. The surveyor certifying the ship as fit to sail *de facto* controlled its fate. Had he refused a certificate, the shipowners would not have continued the voyage. He argued, therefore, that in instances of physical damage it would require an exceptional case to refuse to impose a duty on the grounds that it would not be fair, just and reasonable. In other words, Lord Lloyd felt that in a case of physical harm to people or property, once foreseeability of harm is proven there should be a strong presumption of liability. He concluded that: '[o]therwise there is a risk that the law of negligence will disintegrate into a series of isolated decisions without any coherent principles at all, and the retreat from *Anns* will turn into a rout'.[39]

But what Lord Lloyd had to say must now be read in the light of *Sutradhar v NERC*[40] where a unanimous House of Lords insisted that proximity must still be shown in cases where physical injury results from careless certification. Crucial to the non-liability of the NERC (who failed to identify the presence of arsenic in a potential Bangladeshi water supply upon testing the water) was the fact that there was 'nothing like the directness and immediacy between the defendant's role in events and the claimant's injuries . . . the essential touchstones of proximity are missing'.[41] In other words, given the testing had been commissioned by a third party, the claimant who suffered arsenical poisoning in consequence of drinking the water was unable to establish a sufficiently close relationship between himself and the NERC, and it was not enough that it was foreseeable that someone would suffer such poisoning if the water was certified to be reasonably pure by the NERC.

One crucial question was left unanswered in *Marc Rich*. Had lives been imperilled when the ship sank, would the classification society have owed a duty to the dead sailors? Counsel for the society appeared to concede a duty in relation to personal injury. Lord Steyn's robust speech, suggesting that it is unreasonable to attach legal consequences to the society's carelessness, makes it difficult to judge whether, if the personal injury issue had arisen, a duty of care would have been held to exist.[42]

Notwithstanding the universal support in *Caparo* for the tripartite test based on foreseeability, proximity and it being just, fair and reasonable to impose a duty, it was simultaneously recognized in that case that the component limbs of the test are inherently vague. Concepts such as proximity and fairness, for instance, were thought by Lord Bridge to be 'not susceptible of any precise definition as would be necessary to

---

[39] [1996] AC 211, at 230.   [40] [2006] UKHL 33.

[41] [2006] UKHL 33, at 47–8, *per* Lord Brown. To like effect see, also, the speech of Lord Hoffmann, at [38].

[42] For some intimation that it might, see *Perrett v Collins* [1998] 2 Lloyd's Rep 255.

give them utility as practical tests.'[43] And the need to introduce some element of predictability into the development of duty-situations perhaps underscores the comment he made immediately after this acknowledgment.

Whilst recognising, of course, the importance of the underlying general principles common to the whole field of negligence, I think the law has now moved in the direction of attaching greater significance to the more traditional categorisation of distinct and recognisable situations as guides to the existence, the scope and the limits of the varied duties of care which the law imposes. We must now, I think, recognise the wisdom of the words of Brennan J in the High Court of Australia in *Sutherland Shire Council v Heyman*,[44] where he said:

It is preferable in my view that the law should develop novel categories of negligence incrementally and by analogy with established categories, rather than by a massive extension of a *prima facie* duty of care restrained only by indefinable 'considerations, which ought to negative, or to reduce or limit the scope of the duty or the class of person to whom it is owed'.[45]

Lord Bridge was not arguing for a return to a pre-*Donoghue v Stevenson* approach. A claimant in an action for negligence will not fail simply because the duty-situation he relies on has never previously been recognised. The House of Lords have not closed the categories of negligence.[46] Rather, a claimant seeking recognition of a novel duty situation *will* now have to argue his case in the context of existing authority and to persuade the court that to extend liability into this new situation accords with previous analyses of policy and justice in analogous cases. Moreover, a finding of no duty in analogous cases will tell against the claimant. So, in *X v Bedfordshire County Council*,[47] it was sought to establish that local authorities owe a duty of care in relation to their powers to protect children from abuse and neglect. There was no precedent in relation to a public authority's administration of a social welfare scheme. However, Lord Browne-Wilkinson[48] looked at analogous powers vested in the police to protect society from crime and in the financial regulatory bodies to protect investors from fraud. Finding no duty in either of those contexts, he suggested that establishing a duty in relation to child protection would be very incongruous.

Similar reasoning has also been applied in relation to economic loss arising out of property damage. In *Leigh & Sillivan Ltd v Aliakmon Shipping Co Ltd*,[49] Lord Brandon[50] denied the existence of a duty of care in respect of economic loss to X arising out damage to Y's property. He noted a line of authority dating back to before 1980[51] insisting that a duty of care would only be owed to those with the requisite proprietary or possessory interest in the property concerned. He was adamant that well-established

---

[43] *Caparo Industries plc v Dickman* [1990] 1 All ER 568, at 574, *per* Lord Bridge. See also the speech of Lord Oliver (at 585): ' . . . to search for any single formula which will serve as a general test of liability is to pursue a will-o-the-wisp'.   [44] (1985) 60 ALR 1, at 43–44.

[45] [1990] 1 All ER 568, at 574. See also *Murphy v Brentwood District Council* [1990] 2 All ER 908, at 915.

[46] See, eg, *Spring v Guardian Assurance plc* [1995] 2 AC 296.   [47] [1995] 2 AC 633.

[48] [1995] 2 AC 633, at 751.   [49] [1986] AC 785.   [50] [1986] AC 785, at 815.

[51] See *Margarine Union v Cambay Prince Steamship Co Ltd* [1969] 1 QB 219; *The Mineral Transporter* [1986] AC 1.

authority had settled the matter,[52] and thus, regardless of how foreseeable consequential loss to others might be, that loss was irrecoverable. There could be no question, he thought, of 'the existence of a duty of care in a factual situation in which the existence of such a duty had been repeatedly held not to exist'.[53]

Judicial refusal to review proposed categories of negligence previously ruled 'out of court' does to some extent fossilise the tort of negligence. But consider some of the reasons justifying such an approach. Principles in tort need to be reasonably predictable otherwise litigation can proliferate fruitlessly; and tort law helps to define those obligations imposed on us by law. Whereas we know what our contractual obligations entail because we chose to enter into them, justice demands that we have some means of knowing what other obligations we must honour. There is also the question of insurance. In many tort cases the dispute is not really between the claimant and defendant but between their insurers.[54] The decision as to when a person should insure against loss to himself and when he should insure against liability to others depends on an understanding of the circumstances in which a duty of care will arise. If you know it is highly likely that a certain kind of loss will be left to lie where it falls, you, as a prudent person, will insure yourself against that loss. Similarly, if you know that a particular sort of careless conduct will probably give rise to liability towards another person, you will prudently insure against that liability.

A final factor to note in the context of the retreat from *Anns* is the parallel growth in the willingness of the judges to address openly the issue of insurance.[55] The fact that one party might be insured was supposed to be irrelevant to liability.[56] However, *who*, given the economic and social realities of the parties' relationship, *ought* sensibly to have insured against the relevant loss is now a factor overtly used to determine whether it is fair, just and reasonable to impose a duty on the defendant.[57] That said, Lord Lloyd in his dissent in *Marc Rich & Co AG v Bishop Rock Marine Co Ltd*[58] sounded a note of caution. He remarked that judicial statements on insurance are not necessarily based on empirical factual evidence and that too often they may be no more than assumptions about common practice unsupported by conclusive evidence.

SECTION 4 MODERN APPROACHES TO THE DUTY OF CARE

Although modern judicial conservatism and the adoption by the House of Lords of Brennan J's dictum in *Sutherland Shire Council v Heyman* have not resulted in a finite

---

[52] See also *Stephens v Anglian Water Authority* [1987] 1 WLR 1381 (refusal to reverse long established rule regarding abstraction of water from land whatever the consequences).

[53] [1986] AC 785, at 815.   [54] See Stapleton, 'Tort, Insurance and Ideology' (1995) 58 MLR 820.

[55] An early example can be seen in the judgment of Lord Denning MR in *Spartan Steel and Alloys Ltd v Martin & Co (Contractors) Ltd* [1973] QB 27, at 38.

[56] *Capital and Counties plc v Hampshire County Council* [1997] 2 All ER 865, at 891.

[57] See *Murphy v Brentwood District Council* [1990] 2 All ER 908, at 923; *Marc Rich & Co AG v Bishop Rock Marine Co Ltd* [1996] AC 211, at 241; *Stovin v Wise* [1996] AC 923, at 954.   [58] [1996] AC 211, at 228.

set of duty categories, they do of course serve to restrain the future growth of the tort. First, by suggesting that new duty-situations ought to develop only incrementally, it is now much harder to establish a new category of negligence that is significantly different from, or wider in scope than, any of its predecessors.[59] Secondly, as we have already seen, where a duty-situation is not entirely novel, but analogous to a category in which courts in earlier decisions refused to recognise a duty, the door indeed seems closed to imposing a new duty.[60] On the other hand, it must not be overlooked that it is the tripartite *Caparo* test that now provides the primary mechanism according to which new duties of care will be ascribed; so the frontiers of negligence are clearly capable of gradual expansion.

(a) THE *CAPARO* TEST

According to their Lordships in *Caparo*, a duty of care may now be imposed if three requirements are satisfied. (1) The claimant must be foreseeable (bearing in mind the kind of harm involved). (2) There must be a relationship of proximity between the claimant and the defendant. (3) It must be fair, just and reasonable in the circumstances for a duty of care to be imposed on the defendant. Each limb of this test requires closer consideration.

(1) THE FORESEEABLE CLAIMANT

Although foreseeability alone is insufficient to create a duty of care, it must not be forgotten that the defendant can only be held subject to a duty of care if he should have foreseen *both* the claimant as an individual (or member of a class) *and* injury of the kind that actually occurred. In other words, there may be important limits to the scope of the defendant's duty of care. In particular, not always will a duty be imposed for the general benefit of the claimant: in some cases it will be imposed in respect of certain types of loss.

The first of these requirements is neatly illustrated by *Haley v London Electricity Board*.[61] There, the defendants dug a trench in the street with statutory authority. They took some measures to help ensure the safety of passers-by, but these precautions were only adequate to the needs of passers-by with decent eyesight. The claimant, who was blind and alone, suffered serious injury when he tripped over a long hammer left lying on the ground by the defendants. The House of Lords held that it was incumbent on the defendants to take reasonable care for the safety of all persons using the highway, including the blind and the infirm. Just because blind

---

[59] Note the reliance placed by Lord Steyn in *Marc Rich & Co AG v Bishop Rock Marine Co Ltd* [1996] AC 211, on the absence of precedent for shipowners suing classification societies.

[60] But see below for the impact of the Human Rights dimension on the negligence liability of public authorities in *D v East Berkshire Community NHS Trust* [2005] 2 AC 373. See also, Murphy, 'Children in Need: The Limits of Local Authority Accountability' [2003] *Legal Studies* 103.   [61] [1965] AC 778.

persons constitute only a small percentage of the population does not make them unforeseeable. As Lord Reid asserted:

We are all accustomed to meeting blind people walking alone with their white sticks on city pavements ... I find it quite impossible to say that it is not reasonably foreseeable that a blind person may pass along a particular pavement on a particular day.[62]

The second requirement – that the duty should extend to the particular kind of harm suffered by the claimant – can be just as important. A simple example of this principle at work occurred where a nurse carelessly jolted ampoules containing fluid for an injection causing tiny cracks in the ampoules. Phenol solution in which the ampoules were later placed seeped into their contents through the almost invisible cracks and this later caused paralysis in the claimant. The nurse escaped liability since she owed no duty to the patient in respect of that particular kind of harm.[63] It was insufficient to show that the defendant owed a general duty of care to the particular claimant. It follows from this that while a defendant may be under a duty to protect the claimant from personal injury, he may not be under a similar duty in respect of, say, economic loss. A general practitioner advising his patient on treatment for her heart condition and high blood pressure owes a duty to safeguard that patient's health, but will not be liable for the financial loss caused to the patient if he also gives her an unsuccessful tip for the Grand National and the horse comes in last!

Furthermore, even where a defendant does owe a duty in respect of economic loss under either the original or extended *Hedley-Byrne* principles considered in the next chapter, there may still be a limit to the scope of the defendant's duty where the so called *SAAMCO* principle applies. This principle, which derives its name from the case in which the principle was introduced – *South Australia Asset Management Corp v York Montague Ltd* [64] – is complicated and multi-faceted making it far from obvious where exposition of the principle is best located.[65] It need only be noted here that the principle operates to set limits on a defendant's liability for certain forms of loss where other factors (extraneous to both parties) play a part in exacerbating the actual loss suffered. Those interested in a full exposition of the principle should skip forward to chapter five.

Even where there is clearly a duty in respect of a certain kind of harm, there may not be liability if the risk which materialises is not of a type envisaged by the law when imposing the duty on the defendant. In the classic American case, *Palsgraf v Long Island Railroad Co*,[66] the facts were as follows.

An employee of D (a railway company), in helping a passenger on to a train, negligently dislodged a parcel which the passenger was carrying. Unbeknown to the employee, it

---

[62] [1965] AC 778, at 791.   [63] *Roe v Minister of Health* [1954] 2 QB 66.   [64] [1997] AC 191.

[65] Apart from the possibility of discussing it here, there are three other possibilities. First, since the principle is in practice chiefly concerned with negligence liability for economic loss, it might well have been dealt with in ch 3 (and it should therefore be borne in mind when reading the relevant section of that chapter). Secondly, since it bears a close relationship with the remoteness of damage principle *in cases of economic loss* it could also be, *and is in fact*, discussed in ch 5. But, thirdly, since the *SAAMCO* principle strictly concerns the quantum of damages to which C is entitled, it might also have appeared in ch 26 (where, once again, it should be borne in mind).   [66] 284 NY 339 (1928).

contained fireworks. These exploded and the shock upset some scales at the other end of the platform. The scales struck C, who was standing on the platform. The majority held that the action failed because, although the conduct was careless, no duty was owed to C to protect him against *this particular hazard*.

The view of the majority, contained in the judgment of Cardozo CJ, that there was no liability to a claimant towards whom harm could not be anticipated, was to have a great influence on English judicial thought. But the decisive moment came in 1943, in *Hay (or Bourhill) v Young*.[67] There, a motor-cyclist carelessly collided with another vehicle. The claimant who was outside the area of foreseeable danger, suffered nervous shock as a result of hearing the noise of the collision. The House of Lords held that the fact that the claimant was outside the area of foreseeable danger was sufficient to prevent her negligence action from succeeding. Their Lordships explicitly rejected the argument that because the defendant violated his duty of care to a third party he was responsible for the damage which he inflicted on the claimant.

But suppose that the claimant is in breach of his duty of care to Z, and that Y has also suffered damage as the result of the same careless act. In the early days, during the genesis of the tort of negligence, there was much support for the view that Y could also recover. In one case, the Court of Exchequer Chamber stated that where the defendant railway company could have foreseen that sparks from their engine would set fire to an adjoining field, they were liable to the owner of a cottage 200 yards away, and across a road, when the fire, fanned by a strong wind, destroyed the cottage. This was despite the fact that they could not have foreseen harm to the claimant's cottage.[68]

(2) PROXIMITY

In many instances proximity and foreseeability may be thought of as coextensive and even, perhaps, interdependent. In the case of road users, for example, the duty of care that is owed is in part founded on the fact that one can readily foresee that careless driving by X may result in adverse consequences for innocent driver Y, who was unfortunate enough to be in X's vicinity. But the thing that makes Y a foreseeable claimant is the fact that he is on the same stretch of road as X at the time of X's careless driving. In other words, Y's proximity (relational and spatial) is a determinant of his foreseeability.[69]

There are instances, however, where the requirement of proximity can be perceived as a distinctive limb of the *Caparo* test. The Court of Appeal's decision in *Goodwill v British Pregnancy Advisory Service*[70] illustrates nicely this potential.

---

[67] [1943] AC 92.   [68] *Smith v London and South Western Rly Co* (1870) LR 6 CP 14.

[69] It might also be thought that the fact that C was both foreseeable and proximate is what makes it fair, just and reasonable to impose a duty of care on D. In other words, it could be argued that the three elements are really only 'three facets of the same thing' and 'not to be treated as wholly separate and distinct requirements': see *Marc Rich & Co AG v Bishop Rock Marine Co Ltd* [1996] AC 211, at 235, *per* Lord Steyn. Cf Witting, 'Duty of Care: An Analytical Approach' (2005) 25 OJLS 33.

[70] [1996] 1 WLR 1397. See also *Roe v Minister of Health* [1954] 2 QB 66.

D performed a vasectomy on a man who three years later became C's lover. Knowing that he had had a vasectomy, the couple did not use contraception. But C became pregnant and gave birth to a child. The vasectomy had, as a tiny number of such procedures do, spontaneously reversed. C claimed that D owed her a duty and was negligent in failing to warn her lover of the possibility that he might regain his fertility. Her claim was struck out.

Peter Gibson LJ suggested, *obiter*, that if the claimant's lover had been her husband or partner, and if the doctor had known that the vasectomy was intended to be as much for her benefit as the patient's, a duty might have been owed to the claimant. But without such a connection between the doctor and the woman – who, after all, was merely one of an indeterminate class of women with whom the man in question might have sexual intercourse during his lifetime – the relationship with the defendant was insufficiently proximate for a duty to be imposed on the doctor in her favour.

Further areas in which the requirement of proximity can quite clearly be distinguished from the first and third limbs of the *Caparo* test are where the gist of the claimant's action is either that the defendant has caused him harm by virtue of a pure omission or by virtue of a failure to control a third party.

(a) Omissions

Where there is no prior relationship between the parties, an omission to act will not constitute actionable negligence, however readily foreseeable the harm to the claimant.[71] A passer-by who stands and watches a child drown in a shallow pool is not liable for failing to intervene to save her, even though he could do so at minimal risk to himself. A 'Bad Samaritan', who neglects even to summon aid to the victims of a road accident and prioritizes getting to work on time, is not liable for his omission. English law imposes no duty to rescue.[72] Lord Nicholls elegantly summed up the distinction between acts and omissions declaring it to be:

. . . one matter to require a person to take care if he embarks on a course of conduct which may harm others. It is another matter to require a person, who is doing nothing to take positive action to protect others from harm for which he is not responsible.[73]

The rule against liability for pure omissions was justified by Lord Hoffmann in *Stovin v Wise* according to an array of political, moral and economic arguments.

In political terms it is less of an invasion of an individual's freedom for the law to require him' to consider the safety of others in his actions than to impose upon him a duty to rescue or protect. A moral version of this point may be called the 'Why pick on me?' argument. A duty to prevent harm to others or to render assistance to a person in danger or distress may apply to a large and indeterminate class of people who happen to be able to do something. Why should one be held liable rather than another? In economic terms, the efficient allocation of resources usually requires an activity should bear its own costs. If it benefits from being able

---

[71] *Sutradhar v NERC* [2006] UKHL 33.
[72] Such a duty is imposed in a number of civil law systems: see *Smith v Littlewoods Organisation Ltd* [1987] 1 All ER 710, at 729, *per* Lord Goff.   [73] *Stovin v Wise* [1996] AC 923, at 930.

to impose some of its costs on other people (what economists call 'externalities') the market is distorted because the activity appears cheaper than it really is. So liability to pay compensation for loss caused by negligent conduct acts as a deterrent against increasing the cost of the activity to the community and reduces externalities. But there is no similar justification for requiring a person who is not doing anything to spend money on behalf of someone else.[74]

This is the rule in cases of pure omissions – that is, where the defendant's omission directly, and without more, causes loss to the claimant. But this presumes a rather difficult issue: that it is easy to classify any given conduct as nonfeasance (an omission) rather than misfeasance (requiring positive conduct). Is, for example, failing to apply the brakes of a car at a red traffic light an omission to act, or is it simply active, careless driving?[75] It is almost certainly the latter. Yet a failure to repair expeditiously a breached sea wall such that subsequent flooding to a claimant occurred was not culpable misfeasance. The threat posed by the breach in the sea wall had arisen naturally, and the defendants' duty did not stretch to the prevention of future damage for which they were not responsible. Nor were they under a duty to shorten the period in which such damage could occur.[76]

One thing that does seem clear is that when the defendant's prior act creates a duty to take care, the fact that an omission is the immediate cause of harm will not prevent the defendant from being liable. Thus, if a hospital admits a patient, a duty to provide care then arises. So, too, does a duty to supervise a drunken soldier arise where the company commander organises the evening's drinking and transportation home.[77] And similarly, as *Kent v Griffiths*[78] illustrates, if an ambulance service once accepts an emergency call, a duty to provide an ambulance in good time then arises in favour of the patient. By contrast, however, if a person injures himself in his (criminal) attempt to escape arrest, no duty is owed, even if the attempted escape was foreseeable.[79]

In other cases there may be an existing relationship from which there flows a positive duty to act. Thus, for example, there may be liability on the part of an education authority in certain circumstances towards a pupil in respect of a negligent omission.[80] Similarly, a general practitioner who has accepted a patient onto his NHS list may be

---

[74] [1996] AC 923, at 943–944. Cf Weinrib, 'The Case for a Duty to Rescue' (1981) 90 Yale LJ and Honoré, 'Are Omissions Less Culpable?' in Cane and Stapleton (eds), *Essays for Patrick Atiyah* (1991).

[75] In *Johnson v Rea Ltd* [1962] 1 QB 373, Ds (who were stevedores), without lack of care, dropped soda ash on a surface over which they subsequently invited C to pass. It was held that D had a duty to take care that the surface was safe, and the failure to remove the ash was actionable. But was this an omission or merely negligence in a chain of positive conduct beginning with the unloading of the bags of soda ash? See also *Kane v New Forest District Council* [2001] 3 All ER 914.

[76] *East Suffolk Rivers Catchment Board v Kent* [1941] AC 74, at 105, *per* Lord Porter.

[77] *Jebson v Ministry of Defence* [2000] 1 WLR 2055. In *Reeves v Metropolitan Police Comr* [2000] 1 AC 360 it was held that the police may owe a duty to even a sane person placed in their cells where it is foreseeable that the prisoner may attempt suicide. But the risk of suicide must certainly be foreseeable: see *Orange v Chief Constable of West Yorkshire* [2002] QB 347.

[78] *Kent v Griffiths* [2001] QB 36. See also *Reeves v Metropolitan Police Comr* [2001] 1 AC 360.

[79] *Vellino v Chief Constable of Greater Manchester* [2002] 1 WLR 218.

[80] See *X v Bedfordshire County Council* [1995] 2 AC 633, at 735, *per* Lord Browne-Wilkinson. Another illustration is where D's conduct lulls C into a false state of dependence on D. A railway company which omitted to lock a crossing on the approach of a train was held liable to a person injured because of its previous regular

liable if he later negligently omits to treat the patient, refusing to visit her, or turning her away from the surgery. Accepting responsibility for the patient's NHS care imposes a positive duty to act. But if a doctor simply 'happened to witness a road accident' there would be no duty since the doctor, in the absence of a previously cemented relationship with the accident victim 'is not under any legal obligation to [provide assistance]'.[81] For exactly the same reason – that is, the absence of proximity – a research body that fails to test for, or detect, arsenic in water is not under a duty to warn of its presence to those that subsequently drink the water.[82]

Despite the fact that these exceptions to the general rule about omissions are not easily explained according to any obvious general principle, it is submitted that they each do have something in common: a sufficient relationship of proximity between the claimant and defendant that is absent in cases that would otherwise be caught by Lord Hoffmann's 'Why me?' principle.[83] In *Kent v Griffiths*, for example, it was the assumption of responsibility upon receipt of the emergency telephone call that forged the proximate link between the claimant and the defendant. For as Stuart-Smith LJ explained in *Capital and Counties plc v Hampshire County Council*:

[a]s a general rule a sufficient relationship of proximity will exist when someone possessed of a special skill undertakes to apply that skill for the assistance of another person who relies upon such skill and there is direct and substantial reliance by the plaintiff on the defendant's skill.[84]

It is notable that assumptions of responsibility other than those associated with persons of special skill seem now also to suffice. Consider *Barrett v Ministry of Defence*.[85]

A sailor drank himself insensible and later asphyxiated on his own vomit after being put in his bunk at a remote base. The Court of Appeal held that the Navy owed no general duty to prevent him abusing alcohol. But when colleagues put him in his bunk the Navy had (vicariously) assumed responsibility for his welfare once he could no longer care for himself.

(b) Failure to control or guard against the acts of third parties[86]

A related problem to the one just considered is that of harm caused to a claimant because of a failure on the part of a defendant to control, or guard against, the acts of one or more third parties. This problem is often dealt with alongside the supposed liability to control dangerous things. But the leading authority for this putative category is *Goldman v Hargrave*,[87] in which nuisance (not negligence) liability was imposed for

practice (on which C reasonably relied) of locking the crossing at the train's approach: *Mercer v South Eastern and Chatham Rly Co's Managing Committee* [1922] 2 KB 549. (This might be viewed as an early case of assumption of responsibility on which see ch 3.)

[81] *Capital and Counties plc v Hampshire County Council* [1997] QB 1004, at 1060, *per* Stuart-Smith LJ (*obiter*).　　　　　　　　　　　　　　　　[82] *Sutradhar v NERC* [2006] UKHL 33.

[83] For fuller accounts of this argument, see Murphy, 'An Accident Waiting to Happen?' [1994] *Tort Law Review* 77 and *id* 'Expectation Losses, Negligent Omissions and the Tortious Duty of Care' [1996] CLJ 43.

[84] *Capital and Counties plc v Hampshire County Council* [1997] QB 1004, at 1060. See also *White v Jones* [1995] 2 AC 207.　　　　　　　　　　　　　　　　　　　　　[85] [1995] 3 All ER 87.

[86] Note that in the human rights context certain positive duties are now imposed on certain public bodies: see, eg, *Keenan v United Kingdom* (2001) 33 EHRR 913. For the general common law position, see Markesinis, 'Negligence, Nuisance and Affirmative Duties of Action' (1989) 105 LQR 104.　　　　[87] [1967] 1 AC 645.

failure to avert the spread of a fire.[88] And even if liability had been imposed in negligence in that case – something Lord Goff perceived to be a distinct possibility in *Smith v Littlewoods Organisation Ltd*[89] – it could certainly be argued that the basis of the duty was an implied assumption of responsibility by one landowner or occupier in favour of his neighbour.[90] As such, the duty would be attributable to the parties pre-existing relationship and not, *per se*, to the dangerous nature of the thing causing harm to the claimant. Furthermore, it is notable that the House of Lords have rejected the notion that mere knowledge of a source of danger created by someone else could give rise to a duty to remove that source of danger.[91]

As a general rule, individuals are not subjected to any general duty to protect their 'neighbours' from others' tortious conduct outside the circumstances in which the principles of vicarious liability operate.[92] And this is so even if the loss or injury in question is readily foreseeable and preventable.[93] An omission to warn a next door neighbour that she has left a door open, or a failure to telephone the police when you see a suspicious person in her garden, results in no liability on your part for the burglary committed by that person. Distilling the various speeches in *Smith v Littlewoods* (but especially that of Lord Goff), it would seem that a positive duty to act to prevent third parties causing harm to another might be grounded if two conditions are satisfied.

1 There must exist either between D and the third party, or between D and C, some special relationship which properly demands of D that he safeguard C from the wrongful conduct of the third party.

2 The damage done by the third party must be closely related to, and a very probable result of, some failure in care by D.

Whether both these issues go to the existence of a duty, or the first to duty, and the second to remoteness of damage, is a nice point. Oliver LJ put the question thus:

I think that the question of the existence of duty and that of whether the damage brought about by the act of a third party is too remote are simply two facets of the same problem: for if there be a duty to take reasonable care to prevent damage being caused by a third party then I find it difficult to see how damage caused by that third party consequent on the failure to take such care can be too remote a consequence of the breach of duty. Essentially the answer to both questions is to be found in answering the question: in what circumstances is a defendant to be held responsible at common law for the independent act of a third person whom he knows or ought to know may injure his neighbour?[94]

---

[88] Other cases such as *Haynes v Harwood* [1935] 1 KB 146 (involving horses that bolted causing injury to a policeman when a boy threw a stone at them) and *Topp v London Country Bus (South West) Ltd* [1993] 1 WLR 976 (involving an unlocked bus with the keys left in it) are both cases in which the actions of a third party were crucial to the final decision. Indeed, in *Smith v Littlewoods Organisation Ltd* [1987] AC 241, Lord Goff explained the former in terms of a danger liable to be 'sparked off' by a third party. [89] [1987] AC 241.

[90] See below. [91] See *Stovin v Wise* [1996] AC 923.

[92] One exception is where D owes his neighbour a non-delegable duty of care in respect of certain operations on D's land: see Murphy, 'The Juridical Foundations of Common Law Non-Delegable Duties' in Neyers (ed), *Emerging Issues in Tort Law* (2007).

[93] *Weld-Blundell v Stephens* [1920] AC 956, at 986, *per* Lord Sumner; *Smith v Leurs* (1945) 70 CLR 256, at 261–262, *per* Lord Dixon CJ. [94] *Perl (P) (Exporters) Ltd v Camden LBC* [1983] 3 All ER 161, at 167.

For convenience, the second condition will be dealt with in this book in the chapter on causation and remoteness. In relation to the first condition, however, there appear to be two factual bases that justify the imposition of a duty of care in respect of a failure to control, or guard against, the injurious actions of third parties: either (i) the existence of a special relationship between the defendant and the third party, *or* (ii) a special relationship between the defendant and the claimant. At first sight, these appear to be alternatives. But in fact – or at least so it is submitted – they are both reducible to, and ought to be viewed as, the proximity requirement central to the operation of the *Caparo* test.

(1) Where D has the right to control the conduct of the third party, a failure of control resulting in the very kind of damage likely to result from lack of control may be actionable by C. Thus, where parents or teachers fail to supervise young children adequately, they may be in breach of a duty not only to the child if she injures herself, but also to any other person injured by intentional or negligent wrongdoing by that child.[95] In *Home Office v Dorset Yacht Co Ltd*,[96] the Home Office's contention that no duty could arise in the case of a wrong committed by a person of full age and capacity who was not the servant of, or acting on behalf of, the defendant, failed. The statutory duty to control the detainees in that case was the source of a duty of care to those who were at immediate risk of loss or damage from any negligent failure to exercise carefully that control. The duty placed the borstal officers in a 'special relationship' with the detainees which, coupled with the existence of an identifiable and determinate class of potential victims (the yacht owners) gave rise to the duty owed to the latter.[97] This was because, in the words of Lord Pearson, 'control imports responsibility'.[98] And in this context, the 'responsibility' was that of the officers towards those members of the public whose property would foreseeably be adversely affected by borstal boys attempting an escape.[99] In other words, 'responsibility' was synonymous with the required relationship of proximity. Lord Diplock was similarly of the view that the critical factor was the relationship of proximity between the officers and the yacht owners. He said:

> To give rise to a duty on the part of the custodian owed to a member of the public to take reasonable care to prevent a borstal trainee from escaping from his custody before

[95] *Eg*, when lack of supervision allows a child to stray onto a road where a driver is injured swerving to avoid him: *Carmarthenshire County Council v Lewis* [1955] AC 549.   [96] [1970] AC 1004.

[97] Note that it was not the statutory duty alone that gave rise to the common law duty. This is because, as Lord Hoffmann explained in general terms in *Commissioners of Customs and Excise v Barclays Bank plc* [2006] UKHL 28, at [39]: '[a] statute either creates a statutory duty or it does not . . . But you cannot derive a common law duty of care directly from a statute'. In similar vein see *Gorringe v Calderdale MBC* [2004] 1 WLR 1057.

[98] [1970] AC 1004, at 1055. See also *LaPlante v LaPlante* (1995) 125 DLR (4th) 569 for a case involving a defendant other than a public body having control over the relevant third party.

[99] Proximity was absent where the mother of a serial killer's last victim sought on behalf of her daughter's estate to sue the police for negligence in failing to apprehend the killer earlier: *Hill v Chief Constable of West Yorkshire* [1989] AC 53. Unlike the Home Office in *Dorset Yacht*, there was, before his arrest, no right vested in the West Yorkshire police to control the killer's conduct; nor was there anything to distinguish Miss Hill from any other member of the public. For similar reasons, a rape victim who was no more foreseeable than any other woman is not owed a duty of care by those negligently releasing the rapist from custody: *K v Secretary of State for the Home Department* [2002] EWCA Civ 775.

completion of the trainee's sentence there should be some special relationship between the custodian and the person to whom the duty is owed which exposes that person to a particular risk of damage in consequence of that escape which is different in its incidence from the general risk of damage from criminal acts of others which he shares with all members of the public.[100]

(2) In the second category of cases – where D has a special relationship with C – the proximity requirement is simply being spelt out. As such, cases within this category are uncontroversial. However, the fact that they are uncontroversial does not necessarily mean it is always easy to identify cases falling within this category: the threshold test of a 'special relationship' is somewhat vague. Consider *Perl (P) (Exporters) Ltd v Camden LBC*.[101]

The local authority owned a block of flats the basement flat of which was unoccupied. Cs were tenants of an adjoining flat. The empty flat was left unsecured and there had been several burglaries in the area. Burglars entered the empty flat, knocked a hole through the 18-inch common wall and burgled Cs' property.

The Court of Appeal found that the authority owed the claimants no duty of care in respect of the loss inflicted by the burglary. The relationship of neighbouring property owners was, of itself, not sufficiently 'special' to justify the imposition of a duty of care to guard the claimants against the foreseeable risk of burglary by way of an unsecured property. Similarly, in *Smith v Littlewoods Organisation Ltd*[102] the House of Lords rejected a claim for damage caused by a fire started by vandals in a disused cinema owned by Ds that spread to the Cs' property. Of crucial importance in both cases was the issue of, if a duty were imposed, how could it be fulfilled? If the only effective precaution was a 24-hour guard on the premises, this was not an obligation that could be viewed as reasonably incidental to the fact that they were neighbours. As Robert Goff LJ put it:

Is every occupier of a terraced house under a duty to his neighbours to shut his windows or lock his door when he goes out, or to keep access to his cellars secure, or even to remove his fire escape, at the risk of being held liable in damages if thieves thereby obtain access to his own house and thence to his neighbour's house? I cannot think that the law imposes any such duty.[103]

If, however, there is something more specific about the relationship between C and D, the courts are more likely to treat that relationship as possessing sufficient proximity to impose a duty of care. In *Stansbie v Troman*,[104] for example, a decorator engaged by C left the door of C's house open while he went to get wallpaper. In his absence, a thief entered the house and stole a diamond bracelet and some clothes. The Court of Appeal held that a duty existed in this case, and that the decorator was liable for C's loss.

---

[100] [1970] AC 1004, at 1070.   [101] [1984] QB 342.   [102] [1987] 1 All ER 710.
[103] *Perl (P) (Exporters) Ltd v Camden LBC* [1983] 3 All ER 161, at 172.
[104] [1948] 2 KB 48.

Two final points ought to be made in this context. First, in relation to the duties of neighbouring property owners, consideration must always also be given to potential duties created by the torts of private nuisance and the rule in *Rylands v Fletcher*. But secondly, Lord Hoffmann's trenchant support in *Stovin v Wise*[105] for rigorously limiting liability for omissions based on political, moral and economic arguments, should not be overlooked, even in the context of these torts.

(3) FAIR, JUST AND REASONABLE

While in *Anns v Merton LBC* the House of Lords made explicit reference to the role of 'policy', it appears that in the wake of *Caparo* the same kinds of concerns as are embraced by the term 'policy' are now to be considered under the banner of what is 'fair, just and reasonable'. Unlike the invocation of policy under *Anns*, however, considerations of fairness, justice and reasonableness can be invoked not just to restrict the imposition of a duty of care (although this is their most common use), but also to supply a reason why a duty of care should be imposed.

Before considering instances of each, however, it is important to appreciate that most of the problematic duty cases that have come before the appellate courts in the past 20 years or so have been dominated by two broad kinds of issue: (1) whether certain areas of activity (for example, the work of public authorities, or certain professionals) warrant the imposition of a duty of care, and (2) whether the risk of certain kinds of harm (for example, economic loss and psychiatric harm) can rightly be ascribed by means of the imposition of a duty. It is in such contexts that arguments about whether it is fair, just and reasonable to impose a duty of care are most likely to surface. And in relation to certain areas of activity, it is economic and political arguments that come to the fore. Thus, for example, it is often thought that the actions of public authorities should be non-justiciable in many respects not only because their limited funding is better spent on discharging their statutory functions but also because they are often involved in the formulation and deployment of matters of public policy with which the courts should not interfere. In relation to certain forms of harm, such as pure economic loss, the concerns tend to centre on ensuring some measure of proportionality between the nature of the defendant's wrongdoing and the extent of his liability. Beyond this guidance, it is difficult to state with any precision what the courts will consider in relation to the question of whether it is fair, just and reasonable. Much will turn on the facts of each case.[106]

In line with the general structure of this book, the level of protection afforded to various interests protected by the law of negligence is dealt with in the next chapter. But it should be borne in mind that the proportionality point just made is, of course, a foundational principle that is equally pertinent to this chapter.

---

[105] [1996] AC 923, at 944.
[106] See, eg, *McLoughlin v Grovers* [2001] EWCA Civ 1743 (very novel case of psychiatric harm).

(a) Fair, just and reasonable: negative usage

In much the same way that policy was invoked under the test formulated in *Anns* to deny the existence of a duty of care, so too, nowadays, are notions of fairness, justice and reasonableness often used to limit the circumstances in which a duty will be imposed. In *Marc Rich & Co AG v Bishop Rock Marine Co Ltd*,[107] the facts of which case we have already seen, the House of Lords held that no duty was owed by the defendant classification society to a cargo owner whose claim in damages had been limited to an amount fixed according to an international maritime Convention. Their Lordships conceded that the requirements of foreseeability and proximity were satisfied in the case, yet held that it was not ultimately fair, just and reasonable to impose a duty of care. In particular, their Lordships noted that a fine balance of risks was established by the Convention in question, and that the recognition of a duty of care in this case would subvert that balance of risks with severe potential consequences for both marine insurance and freight costs. It was also pointed out that the imposition of a duty of care might lead to classification societies refusing to survey high-risk vessels in the future with potentially harmful consequences for public safety at sea.[108]

Other cases decided by the appellate courts also confirm this negative usage of the 'fair, just and reasonable' limb of the *Caparo* test. For example, in *X v Bedfordshire County Council*[109] the risk of defensive practices to which liability *may give rise*,[110] coupled with the fact that it would be improper for the courts to second-guess local authority decisions were cited among the reasons for the non-imposition of a duty of care. Equally, in *Elguzouli-Daf v Metropolitan Police Commissioner*[111] it was felt to be inappropriate, for similar reasons, to impose a duty of care on the Crown Prosecution Service in respect of those suspects they decide to prosecute.

(b) Fair, just and reasonable: positive usage

It was noted at the start of this section that, historically – and certainly in the immediate wake of *Anns* – policy factors have tended to be invoked by the courts in order to justify the *non-imposition* of a duty of care. However, in the post-*Caparo* era, it has since become clear that considerations of fairness, justice and reasonableness can now also be employed to ground the *imposition* of a duty of care; either in circumstances in which no such duty has previously existed, or in circumstances where a duty has previously been denied.

---

[107] [1996] AC 211. See also, *White v Jones* [1995] 2 AC 207.

[108] Cf *Perrett v Collins* [1998] 2 Lloyd's Rep 255 (D, an inspector of private light aircraft, was held to owe a duty of care to a passenger in an aircraft in respect of which a certificate of airworthiness was negligently issued). Arguably, the distinction between the two cases is that a duty of care will more readily be extended in respect of harm to the person than damage to property. See further Witting, 'Negligent Inspectors and Flying Machines' [2000] CLJ 544.   [109] [1995] 2 AC 633.

[110] For doubt about the soundness of this fear see *Phelps v Hillingdon LBC* [2001] 2 AC 619, at 672, *per* Lord Clyde: 'I am not persuaded that the recognition of a liability . . . should inspire some peculiarly defensive attitude in the performance of . . . responsibilities. On the contrary it may have the healthy effect of securing that high standards are sought and secured'. See also *Barrett v Enfield LBC* [2001] 2 AC 550, at 568 and 589, *per* Lords Slynn and Hutton respectively, *Gregg v Scott* [2005] 2 AC 176, at [55]-[56], and the academic criticism of this argument in Markesinis *et al*, *Tortious Liability of Statutory Bodies: A Comparative and Economic Analysis of Five English Cases* (1999) ch 3.   [111] [1995] QB 335.

In *Stovin v Wise*, Lord Hoffmann recognised this judicial about-turn on the *Anns* approach and summarised what he perceived to be its replacement, thus:

[s]ubsequent decisions in this House and the Privy Council have preferred to approach the question the other way round . . . asking whether there are considerations of analogy, policy, fairness and justice for extending [the duty of care] to cover a new situation.[112]

While it is by no means the case that this positive approach has become the norm, as Lord Hoffmann misleadingly intimated,[113] there is certainly ample evidence of policy considerations being used in this way at the highest judicial level. In *White v Jones*,[114] for example, the facts were as follows:

D, a solicitor, was instructed by a testator to draw up a new will to replace an earlier one. Due to D's negligence, the new will had not been drafted by the time the testator died. Under the new will, unlike the old one, the testator's daughters would have been named as beneficiaries. The testator's daughters therefore mounted an action in negligence against D alleging that his negligence had cost them their inheritance. By a majority of three to two, the House of Lords held that the daughters were owed a duty of care.

The foreseeability of the daughters' loss was not in question. Equally, in recognising the solicitor's assumption of a responsibility to draft a replacement will, their Lordships were also satisfied that the requirement of a relationship of proximity between the defendant and the claimants existed.[115] But their Lordships ran up (among other things[116]) against the problem that the case involved an omission to act on the part of the solicitor. As we have already seen, the courts are generally loathe to impose liability in cases of nonfeasance. However, Lord Goff, in a section of his speech headed 'The Impulse to do Practical Justice', noted four reasons why a duty should be imposed; and each of those reasons was clearly rooted in considerations of fairness and justice. He said:

(1) In the forefront stands the extraordinary fact that, if such a duty is not recognised, the only persons who might have a valid claim (ie, the testator and his estate) have suffered no loss, and the only person who has suffered a loss (ie, the disappointed beneficiary) has no claim . . .

(2) The injustice of denying such a remedy is reinforced if one considers the importance of legacies in a society which recognises . . . the right of citizens to leave their assets to whom they please . . .

(3) There is a sense in which the solicitors' profession cannot complain if such a liability may be imposed upon their members. If one of them has been negligent in such a way as to defeat his client's testamentary intentions, he must regard himself as very lucky indeed if the effect of the law is that he is not liable . . .

---

[112] [1996] AC 923, at 949.

[113] Both *Marc Rich* [1996] AC 211, and *Elguzouli-Daf* [1995] QB 335, supply ample evidence of policy factors being invoked in the traditional way to negative the imposition of a duty.   [114] [1995] 2 AC 207.

[115] This is questionable: see Murphy, 'Expectation Losses, Negligent Omissions and the Tortious Duty of Care' [1996] CLJ 43.

[116] See Benson, 'Does *White v Jones* represent Canadian Law?' in Neyers (ed), *Emerging Issues in Tort Law* (2007).

(4) That such a conclusion is required as a matter of justice is reinforced by consideration of the role played by solicitors in society. The point was well made by Cooke J in *Gartside v Sheffield Young and Ellis*:[117]

> To deny an effective remedy in a plain case would seem to imply a refusal to acknowledge the solicitor's professional role in the community. In practice the public relies on solicitors . . . to prepare effective wills. . . .
>
> I respectfully agree with Nicholls V-C [in the Court of Appeal] . . . that the court will have to fashion 'an effective remedy for the solicitor's breach of his professional duty to his client' in such a way as to repair the injustice to the disappointed beneficiary.[118]

While *White v Jones* constitutes an example of the courts invoking the third *Caparo* limb in order to justify the creation of a *new duty situation*,[119] the decision of the House of Lords in *Arthur JS Hall & Co v Simons* arguably goes one step further by employing it to justify the imposition of a duty of care on advocates who had formerly enjoyed a well-established immunity in respect of their conduct of (at least civil) litigation on a client's behalf. In removing that immunity, Lord Hobhouse declared:

> [i]n the civil justice system . . . the legitimate interest of the client, the appropriateness of the tort remedy and the absence of clear or sufficient justification all militate against the recognition of an advocate immunity.[120]

A final cautionary note should be entered here. It is this: just because we can identify clear positive and negative usages of policy considerations does not make the task of predicting the outcome of new cases any easier. Indeed, it is perhaps for the reason that the *Caparo* test (especially the third limb) lends itself so well to individual judicial impressions of where lines should be drawn that a great many of the cases concerning the duty of care have been pursued in recent decades at least to the Court of Appeal, with scores even reaching the House of Lords.

(B) INCREMENTALISM

We have already noted that, in *Caparo*, the House of Lords approved Brennan J's dictum in *Sutherland Shire Council v Heyman* suggesting that '[i]t is preferable . . . that the law should develop novel categories of negligence incrementally and by analogy with established categories'.[121] But we have yet to explore in depth the nature of this incremental approach and its relationship with the tripartite test that also emerged from the *Caparo* decision.

In *Perrett v Collins*, a case in which a certificate of airworthiness was negligently issued in respect of a light aircraft, with the consequence that a passenger in it was subsequently injured, Hobhouse LJ said:

[t]he over-arching formula [in *Caparo*] does not affect the outcome. Established categories, with or without the assistance of 'common sense and justice', provide the answer. The

---

[117] [1983] NZLR 37, at 43.   [118] [1995] 2 AC 207, at 259–260.
[119] To like effect, see also *Spring v Guardian Assurance plc* [1995] 2 AC 296.
[120] [2002] 1 AC 615, at 749–750.   [121] (1985) 60 ALR 1, at 43–44.

certainty provided by the previous authorities is not undermined . . . It is a truism to say that any case must be decided taking into account the circumstances of the case, but where those circumstances comply with established categories of liability, a defendant should not be allowed to seek to escape from liability by appealing to some vaguer concept of justice or fairness; the law cannot be re-made for every case. Indeed, the previous authorities have by necessary implication held that it is fair, just and reasonable that the [claimant] should recover in the situations falling within the principles they have applied. Accordingly, if the present case is covered by the decisions in, or the principles recognised by, previous authorities – and it is . . . we remain bound to follow them.[122]

It is clear from this passage that his Lordship envisaged that the tripartite test could be ousted in circumstances where an incremental step beyond existing authorities could be taken. Certainly, such an approach seeks to guarantee a measure of consistency in the ever-growing body of case law by adherence to the doctrine of precedent. But it is questionable whether, as it may ostensibly appear, this approach is truly a rival to the three-limbed *Caparo* test. For while it is consonant with the technique of analogical reasoning so central to the common law, it does not tell us how far any given incremental step may take us beyond the decided cases. Ultimately, therefore, the courts will have recourse to concepts such as justice and reasonableness in order to set the limits to what amounts to legitimate incrementalism. In doing so, they are effectively applying the very *Caparo* test to which incrementalism is said to be an alternative. This is because if the instant case is closely analogous to a previously decided case in which a duty has been imposed, all the court is doing is assuming that the proximity and foreseeability requirements are probably satisfied in the case before it and simply asking whether it is just, fair and reasonable to extend the duty of care by the marginal amount required in order to cover the particular facts of the case.[123]

(c) ASSUMPTION OF RESPONSIBILITY

In *Hedley Byrne & Co Ltd v Heller & Partners Ltd*[124] the House of Lords recognized the possibility of negligence liability in respect of negligent misstatements where a defendant voluntarily assumes responsibility for the accuracy of a statement made to a claimant in circumstances where a special relationship exists between the two of them and the claimant places reasonable reliance on the accuracy of the statement. At the heart of the decision was the insistence upon the defendant's 'assumption of responsibility'.

Although originally *Hedley Byrne* was only concerned with the question of whether a duty could be imposed in connection with economic loss caused by negligent

---

[122] [1998] 2 Lloyds Rep 255, at 263.

[123] For oblique support see, eg, *Islington LBC v UCL Hospital NHS Trust* [2006] PIQR P29 and *White v Chief Constable of South Yorkshire* [1999] 2 AC 455, at 511, *per* Lord Hoffmann: 'I agree with Jane Stapleton's remark . . . that "once the law has taken a wrong turning . . . incrementalism cannot provide the answer". Consequently, your Lordships are now engaged . . . to preserve the general perception of the law as fair between one citizen and another'. And for an explicit confirmation that the two tests may be used together (with recourse also to the 'assumption of responsibility' test), see *Commissioners of Customs and Excise v Barclays Bank plc* [2006] UKHL 28.

[124] [1964] AC 465.

misstatements, its 'assumption of responsibility' criterion has since been suggested to form a more general test according to which a duty of care may be ascribed, even beyond the confines of economic loss and negligent misstatements. In *White v Jones*, Lord Browne-Wilkinson said that:

> a duty of care will arise if there is a special relationship between the parties. [And] such special relationships can be held to exist . . . where the defendant has voluntarily answered a question or tenders skilled advice or services in circumstances where he knows or ought to know that an identified [claimant] will rely on his answers or advice . . . . [T]he special relationship is created by the defendant voluntarily assuming to act in the matter by involving himself in the [claimant's] affairs or by choosing to speak . . . [And] although the extent of the duty will vary from category to category, some duty of care arises from the special relationship.[125]

In *Bank of Credit and Commerce International (Overseas) Ltd v Price Waterhouse (No 2)* Sir Brian Neill (with whom Brooke and Nourse LJJ agreed) interpreted these words as grounding a separate mechanism for the ascription of duty.[126] However, by its very nature, the assumption of responsibility test most easily lends itself to circumstances involving negligent misstatements or the negligent provision of services by professionals in which case the kind of loss most likely to result is economic loss.[127] As such, it is doubtful whether it is appropriate to view the assumption of responsibility mechanism as a discrete test of general application.[128] It is considered in more depth in the next chapter in the context of economic loss.

SECTION 5 PUBLIC AUTHORITIES AND THE DUTY OF CARE

(A) BACKGROUND

Public authorities, such as the emergency services and local authorities, require special consideration. This is because the foundational principles governing negligence liability in such cases frequently need to be formulated bearing in mind the statutory and public law dimensions (including the Human Rights Act 1998) that are often

---

[125] [1995] 2 AC 207, at 273.

[126] [1998] Lloyd's Rep Bank 85, at [84]-[86]. For criticism of the test see Barker, 'Unreliable Assumptions in the Modern Law of Negligence' (1993) 109 LQR 461, esp at 468–469.

[127] But not always: see *Watson v British Boxing Board of Control* [2001] QB 1134 (provision of inadequate medical services at a professional boxing match in which C suffered severe brain damage); *Phelps v Hillingdon LBC* [2001] 2 AC 619 (negligent failure by an educational psychologist to identify the educational needs of a child); *Vowles v Evans* [2003] 1 WLR 1607 (amateur rugby referee liable for injuries sustained by a player where the referee failed to apply the relevant laws of the game designed to promote the safety of players); *Wattleworth v Goodwood Road Racing Co Ltd* [2004] EWHC 140 (Motor Sports Association provided inaccurate advice on the safety of a racing circuit).

[128] See the doubts about the independence of this test in *Merrett v Babb* [2001] 3 WLR 1, and the suggestion that the test is apt to be invoked in relation to very particular forms of harm: *Parkinson v St James and Seacroft University Hospital NHS Trust* [2001] 3 All ER 97 (costs associated with raising a disabled child born following

present in this arena.[129] These dimensions, as we shall see, impact mainly upon the assessment of whether it is just, fair and reasonable to impose liability on a public authority.[130] But they may also impinge upon the logically prior question of justiciability.

The starting point is to note that there is no general rule granting public authorities immunity from liability in negligence just because they are public, not private, bodies.[131] A pedestrian knocked down by a council truck can perfectly well sue the local council, and a schoolgirl injured by a dilapidated ceiling collapsing on her in the classroom can sue the education authority. On the other hand, difficulties do tend to arise where the alleged negligence of a public body derives from its exercise of, or failure to exercise, statutory powers that are designed to ensure the provision of some public function or other.[132] The essence of a typical claim is that the claimant has suffered damage because the public body has provided an inadequate service. Many such claims are met with considerable obstacles in establishing a duty of care and a number of factors explain the particular complexities inherent in such cases. These include the following:

(1) Many statutory powers enabling public authorities to provide public services confer on the authority a measure of discretion as to how, or even *if*, the relevant power should be exercised.

(2) Very often, what C alleges is not that the authority itself negligently created the danger which befell him, but that it failed to protect him from that danger. This then takes us into the familiar, problematic realm of negligent omissions.

(3) The (presumed) effect of frequent litigation on limited public funds and the manner in which statutory functions would be performed in the face of possible negligence actions.

(4) The fact that it would be inapt for the courts to second-guess certain decisions of public bodies made in accordance with the statutory powers of those bodies.

Just as the decision in *Anns v Merton LBC*[133] appeared to trigger a radical expansion of the tort of negligence generally, so, in its specific consideration of the liability of public authorities, did it appear set to extend the liability of public bodies. In the retreat from *Anns*, there was no better example of the courts' hesitancy to expand the frontiers of

a negligently performed sterilisation operation). Note, too, the insistence in *Commissioners of Customs and Excise v Barclays Bank plc* [2006] UKHL 28 that the courts should take a multi-factoral approach according to which the *Caparo* test, the incrementalism approach and the use of 'assumed responsibilities' should be seen as working in harmony with one another.

[129] Sometimes these public law and statutory features are irrelevant (*eg*, when an action is brought against a public authority *qua* employer – in respect of, say, an unsafe workplace. The duty in such a case would be the ordinary duty of care owed by any employer to an employee). Sometimes, also, the question of negligence liability is irrelevant (eg, if the statute itself creates a civil law action for breach of statutory duty: see ch 20).

[130] For the weight that ought to be attached to these concerns (in the light of certain continental experiences) see Markesinis *et al*, *Tortious Liability of Statutory Bodies: A Comparative and Economic Analysis of Five English Cases* (1999) ch 3.

[131] *Mersey Docks and Harbour Board Trustees v Gibbs* (1866) LR 1 HL 93; *Allen v Gulf Oil Refining Ltd* [1981] AC 1001.

[132] The literature is legion, but especially valuable is Bailey and Bowman 'Public Authority Negligence Revisited' [2000] CLJ 85.   [133] [1978] AC 728.

negligence liability than in relation to public bodies. The decisions of the House of Lords in *X v Bedfordshire County Council*[134] and *Stovin v Wise*[135] sought to place stringent limits on any such actions. And although these limits have since undergone significant refinement – arguably to the point where there is little left of the original *Bedfordshire* decision so far as it allowed for the automatic striking-out of an action against a public body[136] – it may nonetheless remain a considerable task to mount a *successful* negligence action against a public body. Showing a duty of care is, after all, only part of the task: a successful claimant will still need to show a breach of duty (which, it is submitted, future case law will reveal to be far from easy).

(B) JUSTICIABILITY

The point has already been made, but stands reiteration, that in instances in which the public law/statutory dimension is immaterial, the negligence principles governing the liability of public authorities are the same as those applicable in a run-of-the-mill action between two private individuals. But where the statutory powers of a public authority are in issue, the initial question for the courts is whether the alleged negligent act or omission on the part of that public authority is even justiciable.

Ordinarily, public bodies are held to account in respect of their statutory functions by one or more of the following: judicial review, ombudsmen, complaints procedures set out in the enabling legislation,[137] actions based on a breach of the Human Rights Act 1998 and, occasionally, default powers afforded to the relevant secretary of state.[138] In short, public law (in one form or another) ordinarily provides the means of redress in respect of public law wrongs. And allowing private law remedies in such cases might be seen as undermining the public law system. On the other hand, the argument from the corrective justice viewpoint – that damages for negligence ought to be available where a claimant suffers loss or injury – is a powerful one and difficult to resist. As such, the courts have struggled greatly over recent years to identify clearly the touchstones of justiciability in this context.

As regards the fact that certain decisions are taken by reference to a statutory discretion, it was said by Lord Browne-Wilkinson in a case concerning a local authority that:

[i]t is clear both in principle and from the decided cases that the local authority cannot be liable in damages for doing that which Parliament has authorised. Therefore if the decisions complained of fall within the ambit of the statutory discretion they cannot be actionable at common law. However, if the decision complained of is so unreasonable that it falls outside the ambit of the discretion conferred upon the local authority, there is no *a priori* reason for excluding all common law liability.[139]

---

[134] [1995] 2 AC 633.   [135] [1996] AC 923.

[136] See *Barrett v Enfield LBC* [2001] 2 AC 550; *W v Essex County Council* [2001] 2 AC 592; *Phelps v Hillingdon LBC* [2001] 2 AC 619; *B v Attorney General* [2003] 4 All ER 833; *D v East Berkshire Community NHS Trust* [2005] 2 AC 373.   [137] That is, the legislation that confers upon the public body the relevant powers and duties.

[138] For examples of each of these in relation to local authorities' duties towards children in need, see Murphy, 'Children in Need: The Limits of Local Authority Liability' [2003] *Legal Studies* 103. Note, too, that an action based on a 'Eurotort' may also be available in this context: see ch 1.

[139] *X v Bedfordshire County Council*, [1995] 2 AC 633, at 736.

As such, the fact that a public body has exercised a discretionary power conferred by statute does not necessarily preclude the courts from finding that there has been actionable negligence.

(1) GENERAL PRINCIPLES

In *X v Bedfordshire County Council*[140] Lord Browne-Wilkinson sought to rationalise the principles that could be invoked in order to determine the justiciability of public bodies' negligent acts and omissions.[141] The case dealt with two groups of appeals relating to failures in public services. The facts were complex.

The first group of cases, the 'child care' appeals comprised two rather different allegations that local authorities had acted negligently in relation to statutory powers to protect children from abuse. (1) Five children of the same parents, alleged that *Bedfordshire* council acted negligently in failing to take them into care after it had received reports of parental abuse and gross neglect. (2) A mother and daughter alleged that their local council, *Newham*, acted negligently when, on the basis of a mistaken identification of the mother as the child's abuser, the child was removed from its home. Both claimants alleged that their enforced separation had caused them psychiatric harm.

The second group of cases, the 'education' cases, involved three rather different claims that education authorities had acted negligently in the exercise of their powers in relation to the provision of education. (1) In two cases, the actions rested upon the allegation that the children concerned had, because of Ds' negligence, *not* been placed in special schools. (2) In the third case, C alleged that the council had wrongly placed him in a special school, having negligently failed to assess his real needs and potential, and provide appropriate mainstream schooling for him.

Lord Browne-Wilkinson acknowledged the factual diversity of the several claims before him, but nonetheless recognised their common thread: the fact that each case raised the fundamental question of the extent to which public authorities charged with statutory duties can be held liable in negligence in relation to the negligent (non)performance of those duties. Seeking to set out a summary of the relevant principles, his Lordship said:

Where Parliament has conferred a statutory discretion on a public authority, it is for that authority, not for the courts, to exercise the discretion: nothing which the authority does within the ambit of the discretion can be actionable at common law. If the decision complained of falls outside the statutory discretion, it can (but not necessarily will) give rise to common law liability. However, if the factors relevant to the exercise of the discretion include matters of policy, the court cannot adjudicate on such policy matters and therefore cannot reach the conclusion that the decision was outside the ambit of the statutory

---

[140] [1995] 2 AC 633.
[141] See Brodie, 'Public Authorities – Negligence Actions – Control Devices' (1998) 18 *Legal Studies* 1.

discretion. Therefore a common law duty of care in relation to the taking of decisions involving policy matters cannot exist.[142]

In order to understand fully this excerpt – which nowadays provides no more than the starting point in understanding public authority negligence liability – it is necessary to unpick and explain each of its key elements.

(1) To begin with, Lord Browne-Wilkinson sought to forge a distinction between (a) *decision-making* cases, where it is contended that D owes a duty of care in respect of the manner in which D exercises a statutory discretion and (b) *implementation* cases, where what is in issue is the manner in which a previously formulated policy is put into practice.[143] Although this distinction between policy formulation and policy implementation has been shown by academics and judges alike to be an unsustainable and imperfect one,[144] the gist of the supposed distinction is that, for example, decisions about how to ensure pupil safety would fall into the first category while the practical measures actually implemented in order to achieve that policy objective would fall into the second.[145] In relation to the implementation of a policy, his Lordship said that the usual *Caparo* test would apply.

(2) Next, wherever a claim relates purely to the exercise of a statutory discretion, his Lordship stated that 'nothing which an authority does within the ambit of that discretion can be actionable at common law',[146] unless the decision complained of falls outside the statutory discretion in which case 'it *can* (but not necessarily will) give rise to common law liability.'[147] This, expressed in the language of public lawyers, means that any *intra vires* exercise of statutory discretion cannot give rise to a duty of care for the purposes of negligence law, but that a *Wednesbury* unreasonable decision *may* be justiciable.

(3) Thirdly, Lord Browne-Wilkinson sought to place even *Wednesbury* unreasonable decision-making beyond the reach of negligence law where the statutory discretion that is alleged to have been abused relates to matters of policy that are unfit for consideration by the courts. In such cases, he opined, no action would lie because the courts would simply have no jurisdiction to examine (let alone determine) whether there has been an excess of the discretion afforded.

---

[142] [1995] 2 AC 633, at 738.

[143] A decision to close a school clearly falls into the decision-making category and the day-to-day running of a school falls into the implementation category.

[144] The fallacy of this assumption was most succinctly summed up in an American case where it was said that any act can involve some measure of discretion, even the hammering of a nail (*Johnson v State of California* 447 P 2d 352 (1968)). For academic and judicial criticism in this country, see Bailey and Bowman, 'The Policy/Operational Dichotomy: A Cuckoo in the Nest' [1986] CLJ 430, and, *id*, 'Public Authority Negligence Revisited' [2000] CLJ 85 and *Stovin v Wise* [1996] AC 923, at 951, *per* Lord Hoffmann.

[145] The fact that the service is provided pursuant to statute is not necessarily incompatible with a normal relationship of proximity between the school and pupils: [1995] 2 AC 633, at 735.

[146] [1995] 2 AC 633, at 738.   [147] [1995] 2 AC 633, at 738.

These three principles must now be read subject to the reasoning of the House of Lords in *D v East Berkshire Community NHS Trust*.[148]

In that case, there were three conjoined appeals. In the first, C was wrongly accused by health professionals of having harmed her own daughter. She sued in negligence on the basis of the resultant anxiety and stress that she suffered. In the second case, a father and daughter brought an action against social workers who removed the daughter into local authority care on the incorrect basis that the father had sexually abused her. In the third case, Cs were a mother and father who were, again, suing on the ground of false accusations that led to a compulsory separation from their daughter. In all three cases, the social services applied to have the negligence actions struck out on grounds of non-justiciability.

The House of Lords rejected the suggestion that a duty might be owed to any of the parents in these cases because of the *perceived* conflict of interests entailed,[149] but conceded that a duty was arguably owed to the daughter in the second case. Accordingly, their Lordships permitted only the second claim, brought by the daughter, to proceed. It struck out all the remaining actions.

For present purposes, it is also important to note the way in which the Court of Appeal severely circumscribed the principles established in the *Bedfordshire* decision, where it had been held that no duty would be owed in respect of a child wrongfully removed into local authority care. According to the Court of Appeal – and the House of Lords did not disturb this finding – what had materially changed was the enactment of the Human Rights Act 1998. For since its enactment, it had become possible to bring an action directly under that Act in two important circumstances: first, where a child's Article 8 right to respect for privacy and family life would be infringed by taking a child into care where there was no proper basis for so doing, and secondly, for infringement of the child's Article 3 right to be free from inhuman and degrading treatment where he or she should have been removed into care but was left at home with abusive parents.[150] In short, the Human Rights Act 1998 had already undermined the immunity established in the *Bedfordshire* case, so it was supposed that there was no longer any point in trying to preserve one at common law.[151]

---

[148] [2005] 2 AC 373.

[149] It was said to be contrary to public policy to hold, in a case where a child was suspected of being abused, that the relevant public authority investigating the case would owe the parents a duty of care in the conduct of its investigation. The thinking was as follows: while the authority would be statutorily bound to do what it could to ensure the child's welfare – by, for example, removing the child into care in spite of parental opposition – there would necessarily be a conflict of interests if the authority was liable to be sued in negligence by the parents if it should transpire that the child was not in fact in need of protection. Yet as Lord Bingham observed in his dissenting speech (at [37]), this approach is not wholly convincing since it could well be argued that the prospect of liability towards the parents might galvanize the authority into doing its job with particular care and sensitivity, in which case it would then be performing its statutory functions in the way that we would wish it to perform them in an ideal world.

[150] That these actions would lie was made clear by the twin decisions in *TP and KM v United Kingdom* [2001] 2 FLR 549 and *Z v United Kingdom* [2001] 2 FLR 612 which arose directly out of two of the appeals in the *Bedfordshire* case.

[151] Arguably, the Human Rights Act had only partially undermined it, since actions under the 1998 Act are subject to a shorter limitation period of just one year: Human Rights Act 1998, s 7(5) and since damages under

(2) POLICY AND DISCRETION

In the *Bedfordshire* case, although Lord Browne-Wilkinson gave examples of 'social policy, the allocation of finite public resources [and] . . . the balance between pursuing desirable social aims as against the risk to the public inherent in so doing',[152] he failed to provide an exact definition of what he meant by a statutory discretion so imbued with considerations of policy as to render it non-justiciable for the purposes of the law of negligence.[153] This lingering uncertainty simply added to that associated with the some-what illusory policy/implementation dichotomy[154] upon which he also placed great emphasis. So when should a statutory discretion be regarded as so bound up with policy considerations as to be non-justiciable? This is by no means an easy question to answer, but at least Lord Slynn provided some guidance in *Phelps v Hillingdon LBC* when he observed:

The fact that acts which are claimed to be negligent are carried out within a statutory discretion is not in itself a reason why it should be held that no claim in negligence can be brought in respect of them. It is only where what is done has involved the weighing of competing public interests or has been dictated by considerations on which Parliament could not have intended that the courts would substitute their views for the views of ministers or officials that the courts will hold that the issue is not justiciable.[155]

This dictum would appear to explain Lord Browne-Wilkinson's example of competing public interests in the case of decisions concerning the allocation of scarce resources. Take, for example, a local authority that decides to devote certain limited resources to making provision X for children in need rather than provision Y. Its decision so to do (even if negligent) would be non-justiciable because the court is not entitled to substitute its view for that of the public authority on the thorny question of how best to allocate such resources in the furtherance of competing public interests. Applying this approach, it has since been held that the courts are not in a position to second-guess discretionary decisions made by adoption agencies concerning the level of information that is revealed to prospective adopters prior to an adoption.[156] On the one hand, the parents have an interest in knowing a good deal about the child they are proposing to adopt, but on the other, there is the child's interest in keeping certain information confidential (at least so long as the interested parties are merely *prospective* adopters). Parliament has invested adoption agencies with the discretion to decide just how much information to release, and, as the Court of Appeal held, it is not for the courts to second-guess such decisions.

the Act will not be as generous as those under the law of tort, being assessed on quite separate, narrower bases (on which see ch 1).

[152] [1995] 2 AC 633, at 736.

[153] Any such decisions will, of course, remain open to the public law supervision of the courts by way of judi-cial review: see *A v Essex CC* [2004] 1 FLR 749, at [33], *per* Hale LJ.

[154] For details of the problems associated with this dichotomy, see Bailey and Bowman, 'The Policy/Opera-tional Dichotomy: A Cuckoo in the Nest' [1986] CLJ 430.

[155] [2001] 2 AC 619, at 653. To similar effect see *Barrett v Enfield LBC* [2001] 2 AC 550.

[156] *A v Essex CC* [2004] 1 FLR 749.

Apart from these illustrations, however, it is difficult to provide hard-and-fast guidance on when a statutory discretion will be regarded as too intricately bound up with matters of policy as to be non-justiciable. The reality seems to be that the negligent exercise of a statutory discretion must always be addressed on a case-by-case basis in order to decide whether policy (or human rights considerations, bearing in mind the *East Berkshire* decision) will render the negligent exercise of that discretion justiciable or not.

(3) THE AMBIT OF DISCRETION PRINCIPLE?

While it is easy to state that a decision which falls beyond the discretion conferred upon a public authority is justiciable, it is a good deal more difficult to justify this statement (made, as it was, by Lord Browne-Wilkinson in the *Bedfordshire* case). No matter how appealing the proposition may appear, it nonetheless implies the application of a public law test – that of *Wednesbury* unreasonableness – in the sphere of private law.[157] As his Lordship said in that case, a decision purportedly taken according to a statutory discretion should be treated as justiciable within the law of negligence if it was 'so unreasonable that no reasonable authority could have made it'.[158] Just why a public law test should be used to determine the existence of a private law cause of action, however, is difficult to comprehend. Yet despite a notable attempt by one Court of Appeal judge in *Carty v Croydon LBC* to relocate the unreasonableness issue to the court's decision on whether there has been a breach of an already established duty of care,[159] it is difficult to square that approach with Lord Browne-Wilkinson's *dictum* and with the speech of Hale LJ in *A v Essex CC* where she spoke of 'an area of discretion which can only be challenged if it falls outside the realms of reasonableness'.[160] Thus, although the public law principle of *Wednesbury* unreasonableness looks something of a fish out of water in this context, it nonetheless appears fairly well entrenched as a relevant principle of law in this context.

(c) THE APPLICATION OF *CAPARO*

Once it has been decided that a case is at least justiciable, it still remains for the claimant to establish that a duty of care was in fact owed to him. This, according to Lord Browne-Wilkinson in the *Bedfordshire* case, should be decided by applying the usual three-part test established in *Caparo*. And in applying this test, the greatest difficulty that typically arises in relation to establishing a duty of care on the part of public authorities comes at the third stage: showing that it would be fair, just and reasonable to impose such a duty. In the *Bedfordshire* case, Lord Browne-Wilkinson adverted to a number of factors that might impinge on this question. The first was whether Parliament had created specific remedies within the statute conferring the discretion, for it would be inapt for the

---

[157] See *Associated Provincial Picture Houses Ltd v Wednesbury Corp* [1948] 1 KB 223.

[158] [1995] 2 AC 633, at 740, *per* Lord Browne-Wilkinson.

[159] [2005] 1 WLR 2312, at [26] and [32], *per* Dyson LJ.

[160] [2004] 1 FLR 749, at [48]. But cf the remarks made earlier in her judgment (at [33]) where she seemed fleetingly to pre-echo the approach taken in *Carty*.

courts to superimpose a duty of care on the remedies that had been created by Parliament.[161] (At the same time, the *absence* of a specific statutory remedy will also tell against the existence of a common law duty of care: '[i]f the statute does not create a private right of action, it would be . . . unusual if the mere existence of a statutory duty could generate a common law duty of care'.[162]) Secondly, the fact that the statutory framework in the *Bedfordshire* case required the co-operation between many individuals and agencies might mean (a) that it would be unfair to single out any individual or agency for potential liability and (b) that the imposition of a duty of care on the local authority could lead to a disruption in the operation of that partnership. Thirdly, his Lordship was troubled by the fact that no analogous case in relation to a statutory social welfare scheme had been identified where a common law duty had been imposed. This concern, of course, has the capacity – since it was expressed in very general terms – to apply more widely than simply to the facts of the *Bedfordshire* case.

Since then, the appellate courts have stressed a number of other factors relevant to the question of whether it would be fair, just and reasonable to impose a duty of care on a public authority. These include the risk that potential liability might lead to defensive practices on the part of the public authority and the wastefulness of a public authority having to devote sizeable amounts of its limited financial resources to defending negligence actions.[163]

The decided cases have also highlighted problems in establishing a sufficient relationship of proximity between public authorities and claimants; especially where the claimants have been children asserting negligence on the part of social services departments or education authorities. To an extent, such problems might have been predicted since not every single child suffering from some form of familial or educational problem is likely to be known personally to the relevant public authorities. As such, it is not surprising that the courts have more readily found there to be a sufficient relationship of proximity once the authority has undertaken to provide a particular assessment (in the case of children with educational problems) or welfare service (in the case of children who have been formally admitted to local authority care). In *Barrett v Enfield LBC*, where a child in care complained of a series of negligent acts and omissions on the part of the local authority during his time in local authority care, Lord Hutton made the following point:

[I]n the present case the [claimant] was not a member of a wide class of society which the defendant was obliged to seek to protect, but was an individual person who had been placed in the care of the defendant by statute, and I consider that it would not constitute a novel category of negligence to hold that the defendant owed him a common law duty of care.[164]

---

[161] [1995] 2 AC 633, at 748–751. The point was endorsed in *Gorringe v Calderdale MBC* [2004] 1 WLR 1057, at [70], *per* Lord Scott.

[162] *Gorringe v Calderdale MBC* [2004] 1 WLR 1057, at [23] and [90], *per* Lords Hoffmann and Rodger respectively.

[163] *Stovin v Wise* [1996] AC 923; *Gorringe v Calderdale MBC* [2004] 1 WLR 1057; *A v Essex CC* [2004] 1 FLR 749. For a growing judicial scepticism, see *Gregg v Scott* [2005] 2 AC 176 (contrast the speeches of Lords Hoffmann and Lord Nicholls); and for academic critique of this thinking, see Markesinis *et al*, *Tortious Liability of Statutory Bodies: A Comparative and Economic Analysis of Five English Cases* (1999).

[164] *Barrett v Enfield LBC* [2001] 2 AC 550, at 589. Note that this reasoning was followed by Lord Woolf in the later Court of Appeal case of *Kent v Griffiths* [2000] 2 WLR 1158 where it was held (at 1170) that the statutory

In similar vein, recognising the actual connection that existed between the claimant and the defendant, Lord Slynn said in *Phelps v Hillingdon LBC* (where an educational psychologist engaged by the local education authority failed to diagnose the claimant's dyslexia and thence organise special educational provision):

I see no reason why in this situation [the educational psychologist who failed to diagnose the claimant's dyslexia] did not have a duty of care . . . Her relationship with the child and what she was doing created the necessary nexus and duty.[165]

A second difficulty associated with the proximity requirement has arisen in particularly sharp relief where the allegation made is that the public authority has *failed to perform* a statutory function; in other words, where there has been a negligent omission.

Stovin v Wise[166] is illustrative, and the facts were refreshingly simple.

C suffered serious injuries when his motor cycle collided with a car driven by D1 who came out of a junction. The junction was dangerous because a bank on adjoining land obscured road users' views. Accidents had occurred at the junction on at least three earlier occasions. The local council, which was the authority responsible for the highway, was joined as a second defendant. It was alleged that the council owed a common law duty of care to road users. The council was aware of the danger posed by the junction. At a meeting prior to the accident in which C was injured, the council had acknowledged the visibility problems and recommended removal of at least part of the bank so long as the owners of the land, British Rail, agreed. The owners simply did not respond to the council's proposal. They did, however, possess statutory powers to issue a notice compelling British Rail to act to eliminate the danger to the highway.

One question that arose was whether the council could be liable for their failure to exercise their statutory power to issue a notice to British Rail. Public law demands that councils exercise their power responsibly, but it does not follow that an authority 'necessarily owes a duty of care which may require that the power should actually be exercised'.[167] Thus, while a public authority exercising its statutory powers so as to cause independent or additional damage can sometimes be liable in negligence, it would be rare indeed if the courts were to subvert a discretionary statutory 'power' by imposing a common law 'duty' that effectively removed that discretion, and forced the authority to act.[168]

Notwithstanding the rejection of a common law action in that case, it should be observed that *Stovin v Wise* did not completely rule out negligence actions in respect of failures to exercise statutory powers. The minimum preconditions for any such duty

power granted to the ambulance service to answer an emergency call crystallised into a specific duty to respond to a particular 999 call which was owed to C as a particular individual.

[165] [2001] 2 AC 619, at 656.

[166] [1996] AC 923.

[167] [1996] AC 923, at 950, *per* Lord Hoffmann. He reiterated this view in *Gorringe v Calderdale* MBC [2004] 1 WLR 1057, at [39]-[40] (and (at [73]), Lord Scott made the same point).

[168] Cf *Kane v New Forest DC (No 1)* [2001] 3 All ER 914 where the authority had entered into a formal undertaking to improve (but had failed to improve by the time of the accident) visibility where a footpath met the inside of a bend on a main road. It was held that there was a strong possibility of the action succeeding.

were said to be (1) that it would be irrational not to have exercised the power so that there would be a public law duty to act and (2) that there were 'exceptional grounds for holding that the policy of the statute requires compensation to be paid to persons who suffer loss because the power was not exercised'. Since then, Lord Hoffmann has clarified this rather hazy proposition, explaining that an assumption of responsibility of the extended *Hedley Byrne* variety is what is required to transform a statutory *power* into a common law *duty*, and that it was just such assumptions of responsibility that underpinned the decisions in *Barrett v Enfield LBC* and *Phelps v Hillingdon LBC*.[169] In such cases, then, claimants will be required to show evidence of *general reliance* within the community on the provision of the service in question. At the very least, it is difficult to see any clear evidence of *especial reliance* by the children in the *Barrett* and *Phelps* cases. In the context of general reliance, then, it should be established that patterns of behaviour depend on a near universal and reasonable expectation that the public authority will deliver protection from particular kinds of harm almost as a matter of routine and that the service would be one which was much the same whoever it was provided for. Indeed, Lord Hoffmann suggested that routine building inspections by local authorities might fall within the test as being something upon which there would be universal reliance. By contrast, not all motorists are foolish enough to treat the occasional absence of warning signs along the road as a licence to disregard the obvious risks associated with driving too fast at the crest of a hill. As such, there will be no liability on the part of a highway authority in respect of a failure to signpost each and every potential hazard on the road.[170]

(D) VICARIOUS LIABILITY

One further issue that arose in *X v Bedfordshire County Council* concerned the possibility of vicarious liability on the part of public bodies in respect of the acts of their employees.[171] The House of Lords said of such vicarious liability for public service employees generally[172] that the employee would only owe a duty of care to the individual member of the public where (1) the existence of such a duty is 'consistent with the proper performance of his duties to the . . . authority' and (2) it is appropriate to impose such a duty on the employee. In both *X v Bedfordshire County Council*[173] and *Phelps v Hillingdon LBC*[174] it was recognised that a duty of care was incumbent on the individual professionals for which the council could be vicariously liable.[175] The perceived advantage of

---

[169] *Gorringe v Calderdale MBC* [2004] 1 WLR 1057 15, at [39]–[40].

[170] *Gorringe v Calderdale MBC* [2004] 1 WLR 1057.

[171] As to the distinction between direct and vicarious liability in this context see *X v Bedfordshire County Council* [1995] 2 AC 633, at 739–740, *per* Lord Browne-Wilkinson.   [172] [1995] 2 AC 633, at 739–740.

[173] [1995] 2 AC 633, at 763, 766 and 770.

[174] [2000] 3 WLR 776 (negligence of an educational psychologist in failing to diagnose C's dyslexia causing C's future education to suffer could result in the employer-council being held vicariously liable).

[175] See also *Carty v Croydon LBC* [2005] 2 All ER 51 (local education authorities could be liable in respect of professional education officers' discharge of statutory functions).

pursuing an action on the basis of vicarious liability is, of course, that it becomes much easier to demonstrate the requisite elements of foreseeability and proximity.

(E) THE FUTURE?

The decisions of the House of Lords in *X v Bedfordshire County Council* and *Stovin v Wise* illustrate well the former reluctance of the judiciary to impose a duty in tort in respect of the exercise of, or failure to exercise, statutory powers by public authorities. An earlier case, in which there was an equally if not more pronounced reluctance to impose such duties was *Hill v Chief Constable of West Yorkshire*[176] where their Lordships refused to impose a duty of care on the police in favour of the estate of a young woman murdered by a serial killer. But this trilogy of cases granting public authorities something fairly close to immunity from negligence liability has been greatly circumscribed by the effect of the Human Rights Act 1998,[177] three important decisions of the Strasbourg court,[178] and the various subsequent decisions of the House of Lords considered above. In the light of these developments, it will now be a good deal more difficult for a public authority to have a negligence action against it struck out.[179] But this does not mean that public authorities are nowadays more likely to be held liable in negligence. Instead, future decisions are likely to be characterised by three particular difficulties that may just as well present insurmountable hurdles for claimants. These are: (1) showing that in all the circumstances of the case it will be fair, just and reasonable to impose a duty of care; (2) showing that the claimant was in a sufficient relationship of proximity with the public authority;[180] (3) showing that, even if a duty of care existed, the local authority was in breach of that duty of care (given the ongoing resource limitations under which all such authorities continue to operate).

SECTION 6 DUTIES IN TORT AND CONTRACT

There are many circumstances when liability for negligence could arise concurrently in tort and contract. In such cases, the implied duty of care derives from the contract between the parties,[181] the relevant proximity stemming from their contractual nexus.

---

[176] [1989] AC 53.   [177] See *D v East Berkshire Community NHS Trust* [2005] 2 AC 373.

[178] *Osman v UK* (1998) 29 EHRR 245 (on the effects of this see Gearty, '*Osman* Unravels' (2002) 65 MLR 87; Murphy, 'Children in Need – The Limits of Local Authority Liability' [2003] *Legal Studies* 103, and the 11th edition of this work at pp 209–210), *TP and KM v United Kingdom* [2001] 2 FLR 549 and *Z v United Kingdom* [2001] 2 FLR 612.

[179] But not impossible: see *Brooks v Commissioner of Police of the Metropolis* [2005] 1 WLR 1495 (C was the victim of a racist gang attack but treated most insensitively by the police in their investigation of that attack in which C's friend was actually killed. The police were entitled to an immunity on the basis that their primary duty was to ensure the full and proper investigation of crime, not to treat witnesses with especial kindness.)

[180] See, eg, *Cowan v Chief Constable of Avon and Somerset* [2002] HLR 44.

[181] For an example of a duty of care implied by statute into a contract for services see the Supply of Goods and Services Act 1982, s 13.

Concurrent liability was always recognised where the defendant exercised a 'common calling', for example a blacksmith, innkeeper or common carrier. In such cases, the 'calling' in question imposed a duty to show the degree of skill normally expected of a person exercising that particular 'calling', irrespective of any contract. But in the case of many professionals, such as solicitors and architects, it was traditionally held that, where there was a contract between the parties, the claimant was confined to a remedy in contract alone.[182] A number of Court of Appeal decisions sought to put an end to any such restrictive rule.[183] But subsequent to those decisions, Lord Scarman sought to resurrect the traditional rule and exclude concurrent liability in contract and tort in *Tai Hing Cotton Mill Ltd v Liu Chong Hing Bank Ltd*. He said:

[t]hough it is possible as a matter of legal semantics to conduct an analysis of the rights and duties inherent in some contractual relationships either as a matter of contract law when the question will be what, if any, terms are to be implied, or as a matter of tort law when the task will be to identify a duty arising from the proximity and character of the relationship between the parties, their Lordships believe it to be correct on principle and necessary for the avoidance of confusion in the law to adhere to the contractual analysis, on principle because it is a relationship in which the parties have, subject to a few exceptions, the right to determine their obligations to each other, and for avoidance of confusion because different consequences do follow according to whether liability arises from contract or tort, eg, in the limitation of action.[184]

A series of conflicting decisions from the Court of Appeal followed *Tai Hing*.[185] At the heart of these cases was an essentially practical question: 'When a person enters into a contract, in circumstances where, were there no contract, there would nonetheless be a duty in tort, should he forfeit the potential advantages that suing in tort may have over contract?'.[186] The House of Lords in *Henderson v Merrett Syndicates Ltd*[187] finally resolved the issue holding that concurrent liability in contract and tort is generally applicable. Providing that a duty in tort is not contrary to the terms of the contract, a duty in tort arising out of the special relationship between the parties lies concurrently with the obligations imposed by the contract. Lord Goff declared:

. . . the common law is not antipathetic to concurrent liability, and there is no sound basis for a rule which automatically restricts the [claimant] to either a tortious or contractual remedy. The result may be untidy; but given that the tortious duty is imposed by the general law, and

---

[182] *Bagot v Stevens, Scanlan & Co Ltd* [1966] 1 QB 197.

[183] *Esso Petroleum Co Ltd v Mardon* [1976] QB 801; *Midland Bank Trust Co Ltd v Hett, Stubbs & Kemp* [1979] Ch 384; *Batty v Metropolitan Property Realisations Ltd* [1978] QB 554.   [184] [1986] AC 80, at 107.

[185] Contrast, *eg, Forsikringsaktieselskapet Vesta v Butcher* [1988] 2 All ER 43 with *Lee v Thompson* (1989) 6 PN 91. See also the disagreement within the Court of Appeal in *Johnstone v Bloomsbury Health Authority* [1992] QB 333.

[186] Such advantages most regularly relate to the rules of limitation of actions. That is, C will normally have longer in which to bring his action if he sues in tort. In contract the limitation period begins to run from the date of the breach of contract. In tort the start may be delayed until the date when C could reasonably have become aware of the breach of the duty. Furthermore, extensions under the Latent Damage Act 1986 apply only to tort actions: *Iron Trades Mutual Insurance Ltd v Buckingham (JK) Ltd* [1990] 1 All ER 808.

[187] [1995] 2 AC 145. See Whittaker, 'The Application of the 'Broad Principle' in *Hedley-Byrne* as between Parties to a Contract' [1997] *Legal Studies* 169.

the contractual duty is attributable to the will of the parties, I do not find it objectionable that the [claimant] may be entitled to take advantage of the remedy which is most advantageous to him, subject only to ascertaining whether the tortious duty is so inconsistent with the applicable contract that, in accordance with ordinary principle the parties must be taken to have agreed that the tortious remedy is to be limited or excluded.[188]

A claimant who has either expressly or implicitly agreed to give up any remedy in tort cannot go back on his word. He cannot assert a duty in tort quite contrary to the framework of agreed contractual terms. However, where a contract deals with only part of the relationship between the parties, a duty of care wider than the contractual duty may arise from the circumstances of the case. Such duties may be concurrent but not co-extensive.[189] Thus, if we entrust our portfolio of shares in US companies to a paid financial adviser, our contract will govern his professional liability to us. If that contract excludes a duty in tort, we cannot elect to sue in tort in respect of those dealings between us. If, however, that same defendant also gives us general advice on how to reinvest our US profits elsewhere, no bar exists to a duty of care in respect of those aspects of our relationship not governed by the contract.

It must not be assumed that tort always offers advantages over contract. The disadvantage of a tort action in comparison with contract must also be noted in this context. A surgeon treating an NHS patient can owe him no obligation higher or stricter than that of reasonable care. He does not contract with his patient to 'guarantee' success. In *Thake v Maurice*[190] the claimant paid for a private vasectomy. The operation was carefully and competently performed. Some time later, the minute risk of natural reversal of the surgery materialised. The claimant's wife conceived again. In his action for breach of contract the claimant's counsel argued thus. (1) The surgeon never mentioned the possibility of the vasectomy 'failing' therefore, (2) he should be taken to have contracted to render Mr Thake sterile in which case (3) when he failed to do so, he was in breach of contract. The Court of Appeal ultimately dismissed that claim holding that in such a contract a term 'guaranteeing' success could not reasonably be implied.[191] But the argument could never even have been attempted in tort.

Consider also the famous American case of *Hawkins v McGee*.[192] The claimant in that case severely burnt his hand. The defendant, a plastic surgeon, undertook to treat the hand and restore it to perfect condition. After treatment the hand was in fact much worse than before. The measure of damages awarded in contract was the difference between the hand after treatment and a perfect hand. In tort it would have been the difference between the burned hand and the hand after surgery. In contract the claimant is awarded damages for his expectation loss; that is, damages for not obtaining

---

[188] [1995] 2 AC 145, at 193–194.
[189] *Holt v Payne Skillington* [1996] PNLR 179.   [190] [1986] QB 644.
[191] C lost 2–1 in the Court of Appeal. See, however, the judgment at first instance [1984] 2 All ER 513. Peter Pain J held for C in contract and his judgment is instructive on the relationship between tort and contract.
[192] 84 NH 114, 146 .A 641 (1929).

the result he contracted for. In tort he is generally[193] only awarded compensation to return him to the position he enjoyed prior to the tort.

The relationship between tort and contract continues to be relevant not only to questions of concurrent liability, but also to cases where a third party seeks to establish that A who owes a duty in contract to B also owes a duty in tort to him.[194] *Donoghue v Stevenson*[195] dismissed the fallacy that privity of contract *per se* prevents such a duty to the third party ever arising. If there is the necessary proximity between the parties then a duty in tort may arise independently of any contract between A and B. Nonetheless, the courts will be wary of extending liability in tort to third parties where the defendant's primary duty rests on a contractual obligation to someone else. They will seek to ensure that a duty in tort to the third party does not conflict with the primary contractual duty. The decision of the House of Lords in *White v Jones*[196] (discussed fully in the next chapter) confirms, however, that liability in tort for breach of an obligation owed in contract to another party can arise in appropriate circumstances. Furthermore, in *Williams v Natural Life Health Foods Ltd*[197] the House of Lords acknowledged that tort may play an interstitial role where contract law fails to deliver justice. Privity of contract, then, is not a bar to liability; it is simply a consideration which should not be overlooked.

FURTHER READING

Bailey and Bowman, 'The Policy/Operational Dichotomy: A Cuckoo in the Nest' [1986] CLJ 430

Bailey and Bowman, 'Public Authority Negligence Revisited' [2000] CLJ 85

Honoré, 'Are Omissions Less Culpable?' in Cane and Stapleton (eds), *Essays for Patrick Atiyah* (1991)

Kidner, 'Resiling from the *Anns* Principle: The Variable Nature of Proximity in Negligence' [1987] *Legal Studies* 319

Markesinis *et al*, *Tortious Liability of Statutory Bodies: A Comparative and Economic Analysis of Five English Cases* (1999)

Murphy, 'An Accident Waiting to Happen?' [1994] *Tort Law Review* 77

Murphy, 'Children in Need: The Limits of Local Authority Accountability' [2003] *Legal Studies* 103

---

[193] For a rare example of expectation losses recovered in tort see *White v Jones* [1995] 2 AC 207, discussed in Murphy, 'Expectation Losses, Negligent Omissions and the Tortious Duty of Care' [1996] CLJ 43.

[194] For a third party statutorily to acquire the benefit of terms included in a contract between two others, three conditions must be satisfied. First, it must be clear that the contract purports to confer a benefit on that third party; secondly, there must be no contrary agreement in the contract; thirdly, the third party must be expressly identified in the contract: Contracts (Rights of Third Parties) Act 1999: ss 1(1)(b), 1(2) and 1(3).

[195] [1932] AC 562.   [196] [1995] 1 All ER 691.   [197] [1998] 2 All ER 577.

Stapleton, 'Duty of Care Factors: A Selection from the Judicial Menus' in Cane and Stapleton (eds), *The Law of Obligations: Essays in Honour of John Fleming* (1998)

Weir, 'The Staggering March of Negligence' in Cane and Stapleton (eds), *The Law of Obligations: Essays in Honour of John Fleming* (1998)

Whittaker, 'The Application of the "Broad Principle" in *Hedley-Byrne* as between Parties to a Contract' [1997] *Legal Studies* 169

Witting, 'Duty of Care – An Analytical Approach' (2005) 25 OJLS 33

3

DUTY OF CARE II:
RECOGNIZED HARM

SECTION 1 INTRODUCTION

Lord Atkin's famous phrase – '[t]he rule that you are to love your neighbour becomes in law, you must not injure your neighbour' – begs one vital question. What kinds of injury must one take reasonable care to avoid inflicting on one's neighbour? Failing to return his affection may offend him, but no-one would suggest that he could sue on this basis. Accordingly, whereas the previous chapter considered the broad framework within which a duty of care will be imposed, this chapter focuses on the kinds of harm that are protected by any such duty.

In the modern era, duties may be imposed to protect against injury to the person (including psychiatric harm), damage to property, and economic losses. But such a simple statement provides no hint as to the many intricacies in the law. As we shall see, not always are the distinctions between these categories obvious, nor is each of these interests afforded the same level of protection. As such, the following principles must be borne in mind throughout the chapter.

(1) There are kinds of harm which are currently irremediable in English law even if intentionally and maliciously inflicted: privacy, *per se*, continues for the present to be just such an interest.[1] Furthermore, when the harm of which C complains does not give rise to a tort if committed intentionally, the courts are naturally reluctant to say that such harm gives rise to a cause of action if inflicted carelessly.

(2) Liability for careless acts and omissions has to be confined within manageable proportions. The courts will strive to avoid liability that is wholly disproportionate to the mere carelessness of which D is guilty. As Lord Steyn put it in *White v Chief Constable of South Yorkshire Police*:

[W]e do not live in Utopia: we live in a practical world where the tort system imposes limits to the classes of claims that rank for consideration as well as to the heads of recoverable

---

[1] Over the years, via *ad hoc* applications of several existing torts and the Human Rights Act 1998, many privacy-related interests have received increased protection. But no common law tort based solely on the invasion of privacy has yet emerged. *Campbell v MGN* [2005] 2 AC 457 seems to create an action for the misuse of private information but *Douglas v Hello! Ltd (No 6)* [2006] QB 125 makes clear that no tort based on an invasion of privacy more generally has yet emerged.

damages. This results, of course, in imperfect justice but it is by and large the best that the common law can do.[2]

(3) The proper functions of tort and contract and the borderline between them may be in issue. Where the substance of C's action is that D failed to provide value for money in terms of services rendered, and where no contract existed between the parties, would imposing a duty of care in such circumstances trespass too greatly on the privity of contract principle (or such of it as remains in the wake of the Contract (Rights of Third Parties) Act 1999[3])?

(4) Since the Human Rights Act 1998 came into force, the courts have been forced to re-think some of tort law's foundational principles. In the previous chapter we observed that the (potential) negligence liability of public authorities has had to be reappraised quite significantly in the light of the decisions of the European Court of Human Rights in *Z v United Kingdom*[4] and *TP and KM v United Kingdom*.[5] We also noted that since it became independently possible to hold public authorities liable in respect of breaches of the Human Rights Convention[6] it was necessary for the courts to show a new-found generosity towards claimants seeking to sue public authorities on the basis of common law negligence.[7]

SECTION 2 HARM TO PERSONS

(A) DUTY TO THE UNBORN

Whether a duty of care was owed to a child damaged by another's negligence before its birth remained unresolved at common law until 1992. In *Burton v Islington Health Authority*[8] the Court of Appeal finally held that a duty is owed to the unborn child, but that the duty does not crystallise until the live birth of the child. Prior to that decision, however, Parliament had intervened in the form of the Congenital Disabilities (Civil Liability) Act 1976. There it is provided that a child who is born alive but disabled as a result of an occurrence before its birth may in certain circumstances have a cause of action against the person responsible for that occurrence.[9] Section 4(5) provides that the 1976 Act supersedes the common law in respect of births occurring after its passing. As such, the common law rule in *Burton*, *so far as it is superseded* by the 1976 Act, applies only in relation to children born before 1976.

---

[2] [1999] 1 All ER 1.   [3] See *White v Jones* [1995] 2 AC 207, at 262–265, *per* Lord Goff.
[4] (2002) 34 EHRR 97.   [5] (2002) 34 EHRR 42.   [6] Human Rights Act 1998, s 7.
[7] *D v East Berkshire Community NHS Trust* [2005] 2 AC 373.
[8] [1993] QB 204; and see *De Martell v Merton and Sutton Health Authority* [1992] 3 All ER 820.
[9] Congenital Disabilities (Civil Liability) Act 1976, s 1(1). Note that s 44 of the Human Fertilisation and Embryology Act 1990 extends the 1976 Act to cover negligently inflicted disability in the course of licensed fertility treatment.

On the other hand, the Act only applies in respect of children born with a 'disability', and 'disability' is defined in terms of 'any deformity, disease or abnormality including predisposition (whether or not susceptible of immediate prognosis) to physical or mental defect in the future'.[10] It is therefore arguable that any injury which falls short of a disability remains governed by the common law rule established in *Burton*.[11] There are also other limits to the scope of the Act that thus leave untouched a still wider residual role for the common law. It is therefore necessary to provide some account of the Act.

The duty imposed under the Act relates to any occurrence, whether it is one affecting the reproductive capacity of either parent before conception, or one affecting the mother during pregnancy. The peculiarity of the duty to the child is that it is derivative only. The relevant occurrence must have been capable of giving rise to liability in tort to the affected parent. But it is no answer that the parent suffered no actionable injury so long as 'there was a breach of legal duty which, [had it been] accompanied by injury, would have given rise to ... liability.'[12]

Not surprisingly, mothers are made immune from general liability under the Act.[13] How could a mother damaging her baby by smoking or drinking too much be in breach of a duty to herself? Would she be in breach of a duty to the father in damaging his child? Section 2 does expressly provide for the only direct duty owed to her unborn child under the 1976 Act. A woman may be liable for damage to her child inflicted by her negligent driving of a motor vehicle when she knows or ought to know herself to be pregnant. The justification for this exceptional instance of maternal liability is probably that, in such circumstances, her insurers will meet the cost of the child's claim.

One crucial question in the context of pre-natal injuries is the extent to which negligence law recognizes 'wrongful life' claims. In *McKay v Essex Area Health Authority*,[14] it was held that English common law recognizes no such claims.

C was born before the 1976 Act with terrible disabilities resulting from her mother having contracted rubella during pregnancy. The mother had undergone pregnancy tests when she realized that she had been in contact with the disease and had been negligently told that the tests were negative. She would have opted for an abortion had tests proved positive. Subsequently, the child sued in respect of the harm caused to her by being born disabled. The Court of Appeal held that it was impossible to measure the harm resulting from entry into a life afflicted by disability where the only alternative was no life at all. They were therefore unprepared to impose on doctors a duty of care that was in essence a duty to abort.

In relation to births subsequent to the 1976 Act, Ackner LJ said in *McKay*[15] that the Act gave a cause of action only in respect of occurrences causing disabilities which would otherwise not have afflicted the child. It did not afford a remedy to a child whose birth

---

[10] Congenital Disabilities (Civil Liability) Act 1976, s 4(1).

[11] See Murphy, 'The Civil Liability of Obstetricians for Injuries Sustained During Childbirth' (1994) 10 *Professional Negligence* 94. [12] Congenital Disabilities (Civil Liability) Act 1976, s 1(3).

[13] See Congenital Disabilities (Civil Liability) Act 1976, s 1. Fathers are not immune. But what sorts of circumstance could create paternal liability – infecting the mother and baby with AIDS?

[14] [1982] QB 1166. [15] [1982] QB 1166, at 1187.

was caused by the defendant's alleged negligence (even though the child born was afflicted by a disability). His Lordship also emphasized the fact that the Act was equally unsupportive of a claim for 'wrongful life'. And it is eminently sensible that English law and the English courts should set their faces against actions which suggest that it would be better to have never been born at all.[16]

(B) A DUTY TO RESCUERS?

Recognition of a duty in respect of physical and emotional injury to rescuers raises two important questions about the ambit of the duty to avoid harm to persons since the rescuer is only indirectly at risk from the negligent conduct. First, is he a foreseeable claimant? Secondly, if he is, and given that he 'elects' to undertake the rescue, can he properly claim that the originator of the danger owes him any obligation in respect of his safety since he has 'chosen' to imperil himself?

In 1935 the Court of Appeal held for the first time that a defendant who owed a duty to another also owed a duty to those who might foreseeably attempt to rescue him from the acute peril in which the defendant's negligence had placed him.[17] Subsequent case law has consistently confirmed the notion that rescuers are foreseeable claimants since it is well understood that '[d]anger invites rescue . . . [and] [t]he cry of distress is a summons to relief'.[18] Whether the rescuer is a member of the emergency services, whose public duty it is to embark on the rescue mission, or a well-meaning member of the public,[19] the courts will now hold that a duty is owed to him personally.[20] On the other hand, there is no especially favourable duty owed to such persons. It suffices to note here that the usual rules apply[21] and that the controversial question of whether it is generally appropriate to compensate professional servicemen in circumstances where ordinary citizens would recover nothing for psychiatric harm in respect of witnessing is considered fully in the following section.

The duty to a rescuer is imposed not only on those who endanger other people or their property so as to invite rescue, but also on anyone endangering himself or his own property so as to make rescue likely. Thus, a householder who negligently set his own roof alight was held liable to the fireman who was later burnt when fighting the blaze.[22]

---

[16] See Symmons, 'Policy Factors in Actions for Wrongful Birth' (1987) 50 MLR 269.

[17] *Haynes v Harwood* [1935] 1 KB 146.   [18] *Wagner v International Rly Co* 232 NY Rep 176 (1921).

[19] *Baker v T E Hopkins & Son Ltd* [1959] 3 All ER 225 (damages awarded to the widow of a doctor rescuer); *Chadwick v British Transport Commission* [1967] 2 All ER 945 (nearby resident coming to the aid of victims of a rail disaster and suffering nervous shock).

[20] In *Videan v British Transport Commission* [1963] 2 QB 650 it was held that a duty was owed to a station-master rescuing his small son who had been trespassing on the lines. At that time, no duty was owed to the child trespasser. But the duty owed to the stationmaster was not derived from, or dependant upon, any duty owed to the son. An emergency requiring a rescue was foreseeable thus creating a direct, personal duty towards the stationmaster.   [21] *White v Chief Constable of South Yorkshire Police* [1999] 1 All ER 1.

[22] *Ogwo v Taylor* [1988] AC 431.

(C) LIABILITY FOR PSYCHIATRIC HARM

Damages cannot be awarded at common law for ordinary grief and sorrow experienced when a relative or friend is killed or injured,[23] or when a person is distressed by the sight of some dreadful incident or disaster. The courts have traditionally been cautious about awarding damages for non-physical harm to the person, even if that harm goes well beyond normal distress resulting in some obvious physical symptoms. The reasons for caution are easy to catalogue. They include the difficulties of putting a monetary value on such harm, the risk of fictitious claims and excessive litigation, and the problems of proving the link between the defendant's negligence and the injury to the claimant. Gradual, if belated, judicial recognition of the genuine nature of psychiatric harm led to the abandonment of the nineteenth century attitude that non-physical harm to the person was totally irrecoverable.[24] The courts began to award damages for what was for many years called 'nervous shock'.[25] A claimant who became mentally ill because of the shock to his nervous system caused by an incident that either threatened his own safety[26] or involved witnessing exceptionally distressing injuries to others[27] could in certain circumstances[28] recover compensation for psychiatric harm.[29]

It will become apparent that what the law labels psychiatric harm, often but not invariably, describes the condition known to psychiatrists and the media as post-traumatic stress disorder (PTSD).[30] Such psychiatric harm can follow from an incident in a number of ways. First, and most obviously, a claimant who suffers severe physical injury, for example in a road accident, may well also succumb to mental illness triggered by the terror of the accident and his or her consequent pain and suffering. Secondly, a person may be so badly treated following a traumatic event that psychiatric harm ensues.[31] Thirdly, an accident may occur in which the claimant is involved but in which he or she suffers no bodily injury, only shock and fear that cause psychiatric illness.

[23] But note that statute allows for the limited provision of bereavement damages for spouses and parents of children under 18 in the Fatal Accidents Act 1976, s 1A.
[24] For the nineteenth century view see *Victorian Railways Comrs v Coultas* (1888) 13 App Cas 222. For an analysis of how the law has always 'limped behind medicine' see Sprince, 'Negligently Inflicted Psychiatric Damage: A Medical Diagnosis and Prognosis' [1998] *Legal Studies* 55.
[25] The phrase can be misleading and should be regarded as no more than a customary means of grouping together cases where C becomes mentally ill as a consequence of an assault upon his nervous system: see *Alcock v Chief Constable of South Yorkshire* [1991] 4 All ER 907, at 923, *per* Lord Oliver. See also *McLoughlin v O'Brian* [1982] 2 All ER 298, at 301, *per* Lord Wilberforce.
[26] *Dulieu v White & Sons* [1901] 2 KB 669 (C had a miscarriage after just missing being run over).
[27] *Hambrook v Stokes Bros* [1925] 1 KB 141 (C saw a driverless lorry career down the road in the direction of her children).
[28] Note the refusal of damages in *Hay (Bourhill) v Young* [1943] AC 92 (C heard but did not see the accident involving a cyclist unrelated to her).
[29] The term now preferred to nervous shock: *Attia v British Gas plc* [1987] 3 All ER 455, at 462, *per* Bingham LJ.
[30] See *Vernon v Bosley (No 1)* [1997] 1 All ER 577; *White v Chief Constable of South Yorkshire Police* [1999] 1 All ER 1, at 30–31, *per* Lord Steyn.
[31] See, eg, *Brooks v Commissioner of Police of the Metropolis* [2005] 1 WLR 1495 (although on the facts, there was no duty owed by the police to C, a murder witness). Consider, too, *McLoughlin v Grovers* [2002] QB 1312 where the traumatic occurrence was C's wrongful conviction due to the negligence of his solicitors; and in

Fourthly, the claimant may not be directly involved in the original accident, and be at no personal risk of physical injury, but nonetheless witness injury to others and suffer psychiatric harm in consequence. (A good example would be a mother who witnesses an horrific injury to her children.[32]) In such cases, the claimant is classified as a *secondary* victim of the defendant's negligence. A series of decisions have set limits, often referred to as 'control mechanisms', on who may claim as a secondary victim of psychiatric harm.[33] These limits will be discussed fully later. But here it suffices to note that they are primarily intended to keep litigation in this area within manageable limits. In essence, and very briefly, to recover damages, a *secondary* victim must generally establish (1) a close tie of love or affection with the primary victim (such a tie being presumed to exist between certain persons such as spouses, or parents and their children) and (2) proximity in time and place to the accident.

Victims of psychiatric illness in the first three categories are *regarded as primary* victims of the defendant's negligence. A person who suffers psychiatric illness as well as physical injury causes us no problems. Such psychiatric harm is part and parcel of his claim for injury. There is no decided case in which liability has been imposed for a claimant in the second category which leaves only the third category. Here *Page v Smith*[34] is the leading case.

C was involved in a collision with a car negligently driven by D. He suffered no physical injury. However, almost immediately, he succumbed to a revival in an acute form of the chronic fatigue syndrome (ME) from which he had periodically suffered in the past. He became so ill that he was unable to work. D argued that, as C suffered no physical injury, he was not liable for injury through shock. A normal person with no previous history of psychiatric illness would not be expected to become ill as a result of a minor collision.

The House of Lords found for the claimant. In cases involving 'nervous shock', they said, a clear distinction must be made between primary and secondary victims. In claims by the latter, certain 'control mechanisms' limit the potential liability for psychiatric harm. Shock in a person of normal fortitude must be foreseeable. But Mr Page, the claimant, was a primary victim of the defendant's negligence. It was readily foreseeable that he would be exposed to personal injury, and physical and psychiatric harm were not to be regarded as different kinds of damage.[35] Once *physical* injury to a primary victim is foreseeable, he can recover both for any actual physical harm that he suffers and for any recognised psychiatric illness ensuing from the defendant's breach of duty. Indeed, even if only distress to the claimant is foreseeable, he or she may nonetheless sue in respect of any recognised form of psychiatric harm that goes beyond *mere distress* even though that specific illness was not foreseeable.[36] Even so, in the case

which case it was held that C had an arguable case that he may be entitled to recover in negligence for the psychiatric illness he developed as a consequence of that wrongful conviction.

[32] Eg, *Hambrook v Stokes Bros* [1925] 1 KB 141.

[33] *Bourhill v Young* [1943] AC 92; *McLoughlin v O'Brian* [1983] 1 AC 410. The leading case is now in *Alcock v Chief Constable of South Yorkshire Police* [1992] 1 AC 310.   [34] [1996] AC 155.

[35] For the argument that we should follow our intuition and treat them separately, see Jones, 'Liability for Psychiatric Damage: Walking a Path Between Pragmatism and Principle' in Neyers (ed), *Emerging Issues in Tort Law* (2007).

[36] *Essa v Laing* [2004] ICR 746. See also *Corr v IBC Vehicles Ltd* [2006] EWCA Civ 331 (ensuring suicide covered, too).

of primary (just like secondary) victims, damages are available only in relation to a recognised psychiatric illness.[37] And until the decision in *Vernon v Bosley*[38] the courts had insisted that a secondary victim of psychiatric harm must show post-traumatic stress disorder (PTSD). In that case the facts were as follows:

C's two young children were passengers in a car driven by D, their nanny, when it veered off the road and crashed into a river. C did not witness the original accident, but was called to the scene immediately afterwards and watched unsuccessful attempts to salvage the car and rescue his children. These efforts failed and the children drowned. C became mentally ill and his business and marriage both failed. D accepted that C's illness resulted from the tragic deaths of his children but argued that his illness was caused not by the shock of what he experienced at the riverside, but by pathological grief at his loss in an illness distinct from PTSD called pathological grief disorder.

The Court of Appeal held that although damages for ordinary grief and bereavement remain irrecoverable,[39] a secondary victim can recover damages for psychiatric illness where he establishes the general pre-conditions for such a claim (set out above), and that the negligence of the defendant caused or contributed to his mental illness. The claimant in this case was able to do so and could recover compensation regardless of the fact that his illness consisted partly of an *abnormal* grief reaction.[40] On the other hand, the decision in *Vernon v Bosley* does not imply that every person who loses a loved one and becomes ill through grief can sue the negligent individual responsible for the death of the primary victim. For example, the grandmother in Newcastle who is told of the death in a car crash of her grandson in Norwich has no claim in negligence. She cannot establish the requisite conditions limiting any claim by secondary victims.

The conditions for liability to a secondary victim established by analysis of the case law up to 1982 generally required that the claimant should be present at the scene of the accident, or very close by, so that he perceived what happened with his unaided senses. But then *McLoughlin v O'Brian*[41] was decided, the facts of which case were as follows:

C's husband and three children were involved in a car accident caused by D's negligence. All four of her family were injured, one so seriously that she died almost immediately. An hour later, a friend told her of the accident at her home two miles away. They went to the hospital

---

[37] But where the primary victim suffers physically and psychologically, the psychological harm need not be a recognised psychiatric condition. Thus, in *Gregg v Scott* [2005] 2 AC 176, it was held that C could claim for the anxiety caused by a physical condition for which D was answerable in negligence: the anxiety merely falls within the recognized head of 'pain and suffering' that have long been recognized as recoverable in conjunction with physical injuries. If however the anxiety is freestanding, there is no liability. Thus, in *Grieves v FT Everard & Sons* [2006] EWCA Civ 27, C developed pleural thickening caused by exposure to asbestos; yet because this pleural thickening was held by the majority of the Court of Appeal to be a condition falling within the *de minimis non curat lex* principle, C's anxiety about the prospects of some future onset of a long-term, perhaps even fatal, disease was held to be freestanding and therefore non-remediable. [38] [1997] 1 All ER 577.

[39] See also *Alcock v Chief Constable of South Yorkshire Police* [1991] 4 All ER 907, at 917.

[40] Note that the courts are prepared to make a discount in the award of damages where C's grief merges with a recognizable psychiatric disorder: see, eg, *Rahman v Arearose Ltd* [2001] QB 351. Furthermore, D will only be liable for that part of C's psychiatric harm that he actually caused: *Hatton v Sutherland* [2002] 2 All ER 1.

[41] [1983] 1 AC 410. For more recent insistence on first-hand experience of traumatic sights, see *Palmer v Tees Health Authority* [1999] Lloyd's Rep Med 351.

where C was told of the death and then saw the three remaining family members before they had been properly cleaned up. Though a woman of reasonable fortitude, C suffered severe shock, organic depression and a change of personality.

The House of Lords insisted that the claimant should demonstrate her proximity in time and space to the traumatic events. But they held also that in coming upon the 'immediate aftermath' of the accident in which her family had been so grievously injured, she was well within the scope of the duty to avoid nervous shock. Witnessing the aftermath, they said, was equivalent to witnessing the incident itself since nothing in the horror of the sight that met her had changed.

Beyond that, there were distinct differences of approach among their Lordships. But since the decision was made within the now discredited test for the imposition of a duty laid down by Lord Wilberforce in *Anns v Merton London Borough Council*, these divergent views need not concern us here.[42] The leading case on liability for psychiatric harm is now *Alcock v Chief Constable of South Yorkshire Police*.[43]

In April 1989, 95 people died and over 400 were injured when South Yorkshire police allowed an excessive number of spectators to crowd into Hillsborough football ground. People were quite literally crushed to death. Cs' actions were for psychiatric illness ensuing from the horror of what had happened to their relatives (or in one case, a fiancé). In the House of Lords two issues were pre-eminent. First, could relatives other than parents or spouses bring an action for psychiatric harm? Secondly, could those who witnessed coverage of the disaster on television recover?

(1) Their Lordships refused to prescribe rigid categories of potential secondary claimants in nervous shock claims. They held that there must generally be a close tie of love and affection between the claimant and the primary victim of the sort normally enjoyed by spouses and by parents and children.[44] Siblings and other more remote relatives, it was held, would generally fall outside such a relationship in the absence of special factors. Consequently claims by brothers, sisters and brothers-in-law failed in *Alcock*, while the claim on the part of a fiancée was allowed. However, claims by more distant relatives were not totally debarred. So, for instance, a grandmother who had brought up a grandchild since infancy might qualify upon proof of the required bond of love and affection.

(2) Lord Ackner suggested that in cases of exceptional horror, where a reasonably strong-nerved individual would suffer shock-induced psychiatric injury, even a bystander unrelated to the victim should be able to recover.[45]

(3) A degree of proximity in time and space between the claimant and the accident is required. The claimant must normally either witness the accident himself or come upon the aftermath within a very short period of time.[46] Identifying a relative

---

[42] Details can be found in the 10th edition of this work.   [43] [1992] 1 AC 310.
[44] [1991] 4 All ER 907, at 914, 919–920, 930 and 935, *per* Lords Keith, Ackner, Oliver and Jauncey.
[45] [1991] 4 All ER 907, at 919. See also, at 930, *per* Lord Oliver.
[46] [1991] 4 All ER 907, at 914–915, 920–921, 930–932 and 936, *per* Lords Keith, Ackner, Oliver and Jauncey. See also *Hunter v British Coal* [1998] 2 All ER 97.

several hours after death will not usually suffice. Nor will witnessing the accident via the medium of television generally be sufficient.[47] Parents who watched the Hillsborough disaster unfold on television had their claims rejected. Television pictures cannot normally be equated with actual sight or hearing of the event or its aftermath since the broadcasting code of ethics prohibits graphic coverage of individual suffering.[48] Once again there might be exceptional cases where simultaneous broadcasts of a disaster that cannot be edited will equate to personal presence at the accident.[49] Indeed, in the Court of Appeal, Nolan LJ gave the example of a balloon carrying children at some live broadcast event suddenly bursting into flames.[50]

(4) The relevant psychiatric illness must be shown to result from the trauma of the event or its immediate aftermath.[51] Psychiatric illness resulting from being informed of a loved one's death, however gruesome the circumstances, is not recoverable in English law.[52] So if a young child is crushed by falling masonry at school and, within an hour, her mother comes to her deathbed at the hospital, the mother may recover for the trauma of coming upon the immediate aftermath of the accident. But if the child's father has a heart attack when told over the phone of the girl's fate, his loss remains irrecoverable.[53]

Their Lordships in *Alcock* adopted an avowedly pragmatic approach to psychiatric harm. They rejected a simplistic approach based on fixed categories of who can recover, and in what circumstances. They also refused to extend liability for psychiatric harm indefinitely. Lord Oliver expressly conceded that he could not 'regard the present state of the law as either satisfactory or logically defensible'.[54] He suggested further that Parliamentary intervention may be timely.[55] One nice point was left open. Could a primary victim be liable for harm to another person caused by shock where he was the author of his own injury? As we saw in *Ogwo v Taylor*,[56] a negligent householder was liable to a fire-fighter injured in a fire caused by his carelessness. But in *Greatorex v Greatorex*[57] it was held that a drunk driver who caused an accident did not owe a duty of care to his father (who happened to be the fireman called to the scene of the accident) in respect of his father's psychiatric harm. To impose such a duty would, the court said, amount to too much of an imposition on the drunken man's right to conduct himself broadly as he pleased. Our self-determination, the court reasoned, involves the right to injure ourselves without owing others a duty in respect of them witnessing our injury.

---

[47] [1991] 4 All ER 907, at 937, *per* Lord Jauncey.   [48] [1991] 4 All ER 907, at 921, *per* Lord Ackner.

[49] [1991] 4 All ER 907, at 921 and 931, *per* Lords Keith and Oliver.   [50] [1991] 3 All ER 88, at 122.

[51] After *Vernon v Bosley* [1997] 1 All ER 577 it is no longer necessary that it be exclusively shock that triggers C's illness.

[52] [1991] 4 All ER 907, at 914–15, *per* Lord Keith. Cf the position taken by the High Court of Australia in *Tame v New South Wales* [2002] HCA 35 and *Gifford v Strang Patrick Stevedoring Pty Ltd* [2003] HCA 33. Now that the rule in *Wilkinson v Downton* [1897] 2 QB 57 has been viewed as anomalous (see ch 8), and preferably seen as a case involving negligence, it is a moot point whether in future this rather arbitrary obstacle to recovery for shock-induced psychiatric illness will be upheld in any pertinent future litigation.

[53] As it would be if his illness were precipitated by identifying his daughter at the mortuary next day.

[54] [1991] 4 All ER 907, at 932, *per* Lord Oliver.   [55] [1991] 4 All ER 907, at 931, *per* Lord Oliver.

[56] [1988] AC 431.   [57] [2000] 1 WLR 1970.

Perhaps one distinction between the two cases is that in *Ogwo* the claimant suffered physical harm (burns) whereas the fireman in *Greatorex* suffered only psychiatric harm. But as the House of Lords, relying on the formulations contained in the Limitation Acts pointed out in *Page v Smith*,[58] psychiatric harm is merely part of the broader species, 'personal injury'. A second possible distinction is that in *Ogwo* the fireman would have satisfied the test of primary victim set out in *White v Chief Constable of South Yorkshire Police*,[59] whereas the claimant in *Greatorex* was in no personal danger (nor in a position to claim reasonably that that he thought he was in personal danger). But this, too, is unconvincing for the primary/secondary victim distinction operates to differentiate between two types of claimant, both of whom are suing for *psychiatric harm*. A third explanation might be that a person rescuing property (as in *Ogwo*) will be owed a duty more readily than a person rescuing fellow human beings (as in *Greatorex*). But such a distinction – if we accept that the law seeks to treat rescuers kindly – runs counter to the usual hierarchy of protected interests in tort law. Perhaps the simplest explanation of the decision in *Greatorex* is the one implicit in the fact that not a single mention of *Ogwo* was made in that case.

Alcock might at first sight appear to have settled some firm principles delimiting liability for psychiatric harm. But the decision provoked as many questions as it answered. Let us look first at liability to bystanders. Lord Ackner, as we have noted, suggested that a truly horrific disaster might entitle even unrelated bystanders to recover damages for psychiatric illness. Yet consider *McFarlane v E E Caledonia Ltd*.[60]

C witnessed the destruction of an oil rig from aboard a support vessel involved in attempts to rescue survivors of the explosion which tore apart the rig. He was not himself involved in the rescue effort and was far enough away from the burning rig to be in no personal danger. However, a more horrifying spectacle is difficult to imagine.

The Court of Appeal refused his claim. A rescuer personally at risk in such circumstances would have been entitled to compensation as a participant in the terrifying event. But crucially the claimant was neither a rescuer nor otherwise a participant (that is, at no objective risk nor in a position reasonably to believe himself to be risk).[61] As a bystander only, it was not foreseeable that he would suffer such shock. Stuart-Smith LJ effectively sought to close the door, left ajar in *Alcock*, on liability to bystanders. Practical and policy reasons, he said, militated against such liability: reactions to horrific events were 'entirely subjective'.[62]

White v Chief Constable of South Yorkshire Police[63] further explored the boundaries of *Alcock*.

Cs were police officers who claimed damages for psychiatric illness resulting from their professional involvement in events at the Hillsborough disaster in which many died or were

---

[58] [1996] AC 155.   [59] [1999] 1 All ER 1.

[60] [1994] 2 All ER 1. For critique, see Murphy, 'Negligently Inflicted Psychiatric Harm: A Re-Appraisal' [1995] *Legal Studies* 415. See also *Hegarty v E E Caledonia Ltd* [1996] 1 Lloyd's Rep 413.

[61] [1994] 2 All ER 1, at 13.   [62] [1994] 2 All ER 1, at 14.

[63] [1999] 1 All ER 1, overturning the decision of the Court of Appeal.

seriously injured in the crush at the football ground. Five of the six claimants assisted the injured and sought to ensure that, subsequent to the full height of the disaster, no further danger faced those leaving the ground. The sixth claimant was on duty at the mortuary. None of the officers were exposed to any personal risk of physical injury. The Court of Appeal held by 2–1 that a duty of care was owed to the officers actually present at the ground (but not the one at the mortuary).[64] The decision provoked outrage from the many relatives of those killed and injured at Hillsborough who had been refused compensation in the *Alcock* case. The House of Lords therefore reversed the findings of the Court of Appeal openly acknowledging the argument that it would be perceived as unacceptable to compensate police officers at the ground in the course of their job and yet deny any remedy to brothers and sisters who saw their relatives die horrifically.[65]

First, by a majority of 4–1, their Lordships ruled that the claimants were not to be classified as primary victims of the defendants' negligence. The first point they made was that an employer's duty to safeguard his employees from personal injury is simply part of the ordinary law of negligence. As such, the claimants' first argument (resting upon the assertion that their relationship with the chief constable was to akin to a contract of employment) failed: they were in no better position than normal bystanders to sue in respect of psychiatric harm simply by virtue of this relationship. Employers undoubtedly owe a duty where an employee is subjected to such a burdensome workload that stress-related illness is readily foreseeable.[66] But where it is a form of psychiatric harm (as opposed to mere distress) that results, not from anything directly done to the employee by the employer but, rather, from his traumatic experience of what is done to others, he is to be treated in exactly the same way as any other secondary victim.[67] The Hillsborough police officers witnessed the disaster at close quarters, but lacked the requisite close ties of love or affection with the victims in order to be able to sue.

The claimants' alternative argument was that they were owed a duty of care in their capacity as rescuers. Yet here, too, the House of Lords insisted that *in relation to psychiatric harm* rescuers must meet the same conditions as any other witnesses of injury to third parties. They must either objectively have exposed themselves to danger or reasonably believed themselves to have done so.[68] They must also meet the other conditions limiting recovery by secondary victims outlined above.

It appears, then, that *White* has to some extent closed the door on further expansion of liability for psychiatric harm. On the other hand, the courts' repeated insistence

---

[64] *White v Chief Constable of South Yorkshire Police* [1997] 1 All ER 540.

[65] [1999] 1 All ER 1, at 48, *per* Lord Hoffmann.

[66] See, eg, *Walker v Northumberland County Council* [1995] 1 All ER 737; *Hatton v Sutherland* [2002] 2 All ER 1. (Analogous principles apply in relation to the duty owed by a school to a bullied pupil: *Bradford-Smart v West Sussex County Council* [2002] 1 FCR 425.) It may be material to the question of negligence whether, in a job that is known to be stressful, the employer failed to provide counselling services: *Hartman v South Essex Mental Health and Community Care NHS Trust* [2005] ICR 782.

[67] In *Farley v Skinner* [2002] AC 732 it was held that C would have a contractual claim in respect of distress arising out a breach *where the contract was specifically designed to protect C from distress*. Extrapolating from this, there seems no reason in principle why a tort claim could not be brought in respect of distress if a *tortious duty* to protect C from distress could be found.

[68] See also *Cullin v London Fire and Civil Defence Authority* [1999] PIQR P314.

upon shock-induced injury now enjoys a lenient enough interpretation so as to embrace a reaction to a protracted event that lasted some 36 hours.[69] Equally, a further important issue that has never much troubled the judiciary is that of the application of the 'egg-shell skull' rule in this context. It may be invoked equally with respect to psychiatric harm as it may in relation to physical injury.[70] Thus, if psychiatric harm would have been foreseeable in respect of a reasonably mentally tough individual, the extenuated degree to which the claimant actually suffers psychiatric harm is irrelevant.[71] And even if psychiatric harm *per se* is not foreseeable, so long as the physical injury which triggers or otherwise leads to psychiatric harm is foreseeable, the claimant may nonetheless recover for the psychiatric illness.[72]

As Lord Steyn admitted in *White v Chief Constable of South Yorkshire* 'the law on the recovery of compensation for pure psychiatric harm is a patchwork quilt of distinctions which are difficult to justify'.[73] Even after judicial attempts to clarify the principles governing liability for psychiatric harm and package claims neatly according to a scheme of primary and secondary victims, loose ends remain. Reflect on the following examples:

(1) A final year student arrives home to witness her hall of residence burning to the ground. In her room are all her revision notes and the only copy of her dissertation. Unsurprisingly she succumbs to clinical depression. Can she recover damages? If the fire was caused by faulty wiring and the university can be shown to have been negligent in its maintenance of the residence, could she argue that she is a primary victim because her psychiatric illness is consequent on the damage to her property? Might she assert, if a secondary victim, 'a close tie of love and affection to her work'. In *Attia v British Gas plc*,[74] decided before *Alcock*, a woman did win damages after suffering a nervous breakdown caused by witnessing her home burn down.

(2) A second, equally unlucky, student is working in a university laboratory when an explosion rocks the building. He feels the shockwaves and hears the blast, but only minimal damage ensues in the laboratory where he is at the time. Even so, it is immediately clear that the neighbouring laboratory has been completely destroyed and his four closest friends were working there. His fears are justified.[75] All four were killed in the blast. The surviving student succumbs to psychiatric

---

[69] In *North Glamorgan NHS Trust v Walters* [2003] PIQR P232, the Court of Appeal allowed a claim in respect of a woman who 'reeled under successive blows [to her psyche]' as the condition of her child visibly worsened before her eyes when medics failed to diagnose that the child was suffering from acute hepatitis.

[70] *Brice v Brown* [1984] 1 All ER 997; *Vernon v Bosley* [1997] 1 All ER 577.

[71] *Brice v Brown* [1984] 1 All ER 997.

[72] *Simmons v British Steel Plc* [2004] ICR 565 at [55], *per* Lord Rodger (with whose speech the remaining members of the House of Lords agreed). For the argument that the egg-shell skull principle is inappropriately applied in the context of psychiatric harm, see Jones, 'Liability for Psychiatric Damage: Walking a Path Between Pragmatism and Principle' in Neyers (ed), *Emerging Issues in Tort Law* (2007).

[73] [1999] 1 All ER 1, at 38.   [74] [1988] QB 304.

[75] For a case on broadly analogous facts, where C succeeded, see *Dooley v Cammell Laird & Co Ltd* [1951] 1 Lloyd's Rep 271. In *White*, Lord Hoffmann suggested that this case might have to be treated as falling outside the general rules and control mechanisms for secondary victims.

illness. If he shows that his illness resulted from reasonable fear to himself, does he recover as a primary victim? If he admits that it was the shock of his friends' fate which triggered his illness, does he fail because of the absence of the requisite 'close tie of love and affection'?

This area of the law is unquestionably very complex, and without any obviously coherent background principles.[76] Reform is often called for. Three very different solutions have been advanced. Stapleton advocates the abolition of recovery in tort for pure psychiatric harm.[77] She argues the case for a return to the harsh, but clear rules of the Victorian judges contending that 'no reasonable boundaries for the cause of action [can] be found and this [is] an embarrassment to the law'. Mullany and Handford contend that no special rules should limit claims for psychiatric illness.[78] Foreseeability of psychiatric injury should be the only condition of recovery of compensation. Finally, the Law Commission recommends a 'middle way'.[79] The condition that secondary victims enjoy a close tie of love or affection with the individual who suffers physical harm would stay. All other 'control mechanisms' would go.[80]

SECTION 3 POLICY ISSUES AND HARM TO THE PERSON

The ebb and flow of judicial readiness to limit liability for foreseeable harm by invoking 'public policy' was dealt with in the previous chapter. But in relation to cases involving harm to the person, some particular policy concerns arise that warrant especial consideration here.

As is clear from two cases raising genuinely moral questions, the existence of a duty may be refused on the bases that (1) one participant in crime should not be able to sue his co-criminal in tort,[81] and (2) it would be morally improper to impose a duty to

---

[76] For an attempt to fit the seemingly *ad hoc* requirements relating to secondary victims into a framework that is consistent with the bulk of the remainder of negligence law, see Murphy, 'Negligently Inflicted Psychiatric Harm: A Re-Appraisal' [1995] *Legal Studies* 415. But even if such rationalization is possible, it has to be said that it seems beyond the courts at present. They talk of primary and secondary victims as though the categories were watertight, when they are not, and as all encompassing which they are not (as the two previous hypothetical examples illustrate) and in circumstances where the language seems inapt (because of the absence of a traumatic event and the absence of even the possibility of a secondary victim): see, eg, *Barber v Somerset CC* [2002] ICR 613 (revsd on other grounds [2004] 1 WLR 1089) and *Grieves v FT Everard & Sons* [2006] EWCA Civ 27).

[77] 'In Restraint of Tort' in Birks (ed), *Frontiers of Liability* (1994).

[78] *Tort Liability for Psychiatric Damage: The Law of Nervous Shock* (1993). See also Mullany, 'Hillsborough Replayed' (1998) 113 LQR 410 and Teff, 'Liability for Negligently Inflicted Psychiatric Harm: Justifications and Boundaries' [1998] CLJ 91. [79] *Liability for Psychiatric Illness*, Law Com No 249 (1998).

[80] For the argument that most of the extant control mechanisms can be rationalized in terms of the general test for the imposition of a duty of care see Murphy, 'Negligently Inflicted Psychiatric Harm: A Re-Appraisal' [1995] *Legal Studies* 415.

[81] *Clunis v Camden and Islington Health Authority* [1998] QB 978 (the Court of Appeal went as far as to say that a remedy in tort can never arise from C's own criminal act).

terminate a child's existence before its birth.[82] But in a number of other decisions the courts have shown themselves unwilling to mount the unruly horse of public policy in claims where the policy factors raised were essentially matters of public morality and society's values. The applicability of this sort of public interest limitation on the scope of the tort of negligence has been tested in a series of cases concerning the question of whether damages are recoverable in respect of the birth of an unplanned baby subsequent to a negligently performed sterilization. In *Udale v Bloomsbury Area Health Authority*,[83] Jupp J refused the mother compensation towards the upkeep of the child despite the defendant's admission of negligence. Limiting her damages to compensation for the discomfort of her pregnancy, he said that the child's birth was a 'blessing' and that the financial cost associated with such a 'blessing'[84] was irrecoverable. It offended both society's notion of what is right and the value afforded to human life. He also thought that the knowledge that his parents had claimed damages in respect of his birth might later distress and damage the child emotionally as he grew to maturity.

A year later, the Court of Appeal in *Emeh v Kensington Area Health Authority*[85] overruled Jupp J on the policy issue. They were unconvinced that the policy objections should prevent recovery of damages. Then, subsequently, in *McFarlane v Tayside Health Board*[86] – another case involving an unplanned child – the House of Lords suggested that damages could be made payable in respect of the pain and suffering associated with an unwanted pregnancy and confinement, but that the costs of bringing up the child were irrecoverable. Largely attempting to side-step the policy issues, their Lordships took the view that child-rearing costs were a form of pure economic loss and thus irrecoverable.[87] Furthermore, it would seem to make no difference if the woman who undergoes a negligently performed sterilization operation and gives birth is herself disabled: the costs of rearing a healthy child remain irrecoverable.[88] On the other hand, the woman will now be able to recover a fixed sum of £15,000 for the loss of autonomy associated with having the child;[89] and if the child is born with a disability, the *special costs* associated with bringing up that disabled child following a negligently performed sterilization will be recoverable.[90] Even so, the courts continue to take the view that the

---

[82] *McKay v Essex Area Health Authority* [1982] QB 1166.   [83] [1983] 2 All ER 522.

[84] 'I would have to regard the financial disadvantages as offset by her gratitude for the gift of a boy after four girls': [1983] 2 All ER 522, at 531, *per* Jupp J.   [85] [1985] QB 1012.

[86] [2000] 2 AC 59.

[87] On the other hand, Lord Steyn ([2000] AC 59, at 82) did recognise the cogency of the policy arguments against the imposition of liability based on the sanctity and value of human life, and Lord Hope (at 97) acknowledged the benefits associated with having a child that (were they calculable) would have to be set off against the costs of bringing up a child (were they recoverable, which they were not).

[88] *Rees v Darlington Memorial Hospital NHS Trust* [2004] 1 AC 309, at [9] and [18], *per* Lords Bingham and Nicholls respectively.

[89] *Rees v Darlington Memorial Hospital NHS Trust* [2004] 1 AC 309, at [123], *per* Lord Millett. A subsequent endorsement of compensation for loss of autonomy can be found in the speech of Lord Steyn in *Chester v Afshar* [2005] 1 AC 134, at [18].

[90] *Parkinson v St James and Seacroft University Hospital NHS Trust* [2002] QB 266. This is so regardless of whether it is a matter of pure bad luck that the child comes to be born with a disability, or whether it manifests within a few weeks of birth: *Groom v Selby* (2001) 64 BMLR 47.

birth of *any* child is an unquantifiable benefit at least equivalent to the costs associated with raising a healthy child.[91]

Goodwill v British Pregnancy Advisory Service[92] is also worthy of mention in this context.

C sued the clinic which she alleged had failed to warn her lover of the potential failure rate of vasectomy. Their relationship had begun some time after his surgery. But C nonetheless argued that, had her partner been adequately advised by D, he would have communicated the relevant information to her so that she would then have taken appropriate contraceptive precautions. She argued that the birth of her child was a consequence of the defendants' negligence.

It was held that the defendants owed no duty of care to the claimant because the claimant was not a person whom they could be expected to identify as immediately affected by the services they rendered to her lover. The man's future sexual partners were not persons for whose benefit the vasectomy was performed.

Classifying failed sterilization as economic loss to the parent(s) – whether or not that claim succeeds – has a certain logic to it. The main purpose of compensation will be to meet the costs of raising the child. Yet classifying the loss in this way does not simplify the question of recoverability. The special costs of raising a disabled child, or the special costs of a disabled woman raising *any* child are equally forms of pure economic loss, yet recoverable according to the Court of Appeal. It is submitted that these decisions were reached only by clever judicial manipulation of 'convenient aspects' of the tripartite *Caparo* test and the extended *Hedley Byrne* assumption of responsibility test. We considered each of these tests in general terms in the previous chapter and will return to their respective applications in the context of pure economic loss in due course. But it is worth setting out in full the compound reasoning of Brooke LJ in *Parkinson v St James and Seacroft University Hospital NHS Trust*.

I would apply the battery of tests which the House of Lords has taught us to use . . . My route would be as follows: (i) for the reasons given by Waller LJ in *Emeh v Kensington and Chelsea and Westminster Area Health Authority* the birth of a child with congenital abnormalities was a foreseeable consequence of the surgeon's careless failure to clip a fallopian tube effectively; (ii) there was a very limited group of people who might be affected by this negligence, *viz* Mrs Parkinson and her husband (and, in theory, any other man with whom she had sexual intercourse before she realised that she had not been effectively sterilized); (iii) there is no difficulty in principle in accepting the proposition that the surgeon should be deemed to have assumed responsibility for the foreseeable and disastrous economic consequences of performing his services negligently; (iv) the purpose of the operation was to prevent Mrs Parkinson from conceiving any more children, including children with congenital abnormalities, and the surgeon's duty of care is strictly related to the proper fulfilment of that purpose; (v) parents in Mrs Parkinson's position were entitled to recover damages in these circumstances for 15 years between the decisions in *Emeh's* case and *McFarlane's* case, so that

---

[91] *Rees v Darlington Memorial Hospital NHS Trust* [2004] 1 AC 309.   [92] [1996] 2 All ER 161.

this is not a radical step forward into the unknown; (vi) for the reasons set out in (i) and (ii) above, Lord Bridge of Harwich's tests of foreseeability and proximity are satisfied, and for the reasons given by the Supreme Court of Florida in *Fassoulas v Ramey*[93] an award of compensation which is limited to the special upbringing costs associated with rearing a child with a serious disability would be fair, just and reasonable; (vii) if principles of distributive justice are called in aid, I believe that ordinary people would consider that it would be fair for the law to make an award in such a case, provided that it is limited to the extra expenses associated with the child's disability.[94]

SECTION 4 DAMAGE TO PROPERTY

Recognition of a duty to avoid physical damage to another's property, as much as to his person, raises no unique problem of principle.[95] Should a negligent driver manage by the narrowest of margins to prevent his vehicle actually injuring me, but the impact does ruin my new designer suit, I may recover the cost of the suit without problems. Should the careless driver, swerving to avoid me, crash into my colleague's front wall, he may recover the cost of repairing the wall. Whether the damaged property is a chattel or real property, a duty to take reasonable care not to inflict that kind of harm arises.[96] Where, however, the parties are neighbours, the action may lie in nuisance rather than negligence.

The class of persons to whom a duty in respect of damage to property is owed and the manner in which harm is classified as physical damage to property as opposed to 'pure' economic loss do however call for careful consideration.[97] The House of Lords in *Leigh & Sillivan Ltd v Aliakmon Shipping Co Ltd* confirmed the rule that a duty in respect of loss or damage to property is owed only to a person having 'legal ownership of, or a possessory title to, the property concerned at the time when the loss or damage occurred'.[98] Should an old house in the process of conversion to flats be destroyed by a fire caused by negligence, only the owner of the house, or a tenant, may recover compensation. The builders, the plumbers, the decorators all of whom lose out on valuable contracts to convert the property are left remediless. Contractual rights in relation to property may well be adversely affected by loss or damage to that property, but they are insufficient to give rise to a duty of care.

---

[93] 450 So 2d 822 (1984).   [94] [2002] QB 266, at [50].

[95] But note that foreseeability alone is not enough: *Marc Rich & Co AG v Bishop Rock Marine Co Ltd* [1996] AC 211.

[96] [1986] AC 785. See also *The Mineral Transporter* [1986] AC 1; *Tate & Lyle Industries Ltd v Greater London Council* [1983] 2 AC 509.

[97] See Witting, 'Distinguishing Between Property Damage and Pure Economic Loss: a Personality Thesis' [2001] *Legal Studies* 481.

[98] [1986] 2 All ER 145, at 149. See also *Simaan General Contracting Co v Pilkington Glass Ltd (No 2)* [1988] QB 758.

Where the claimant has the necessary title to the damaged property the further question arises of how harm is classified. All harm, be it personal injuries or physical damage to property, is quantified in economic terms. What loss of earnings did the claimant's injuries occasion him? How much will it cost to repair or replace a damaged wall? As we shall see, although the courts have attempted to draw lines of demarcation, they are not wholly satisfactory in terms of providing a general account of distinguishing physical harm from economic loss.[99]

It has always been clear that physical damage to, or defects in, property which simply render it less than value for money, but *not* dangerous, will be classified as economic loss. So if one buys a central heating boiler which heats the house inefficiently and at vast expense, the loss one suffers is economic loss alone, readily recoverable in contract, but not normally in tort. Where the defective property is dangerous, however, a line of authority relating to buildings suggests that if there is an imminent danger of damage to person or other property, the cost of rectifying the defect and avoiding the danger could be categorized as physical damage, albeit that no tangible physical damage has yet materialized.[100] The decision of the House of Lords in *Murphy v Brentwood District Council*[101] rejected that line of authority as being close to heresy. Physical damage means just what it says: actual physical harm to persons or other property. Where no such damage has materialized, the loss caused by the need to repair defective property, to obviate the danger, constitutes merely an economic loss.

C had purchased a house built on an in-filled site over a concrete raft foundation. In 1981 he discovered cracks in the house threatening the whole fabric of the property. Had he done nothing, the house might have collapsed on top of him. He sued the local council for negligently approving the plans for the foundations. The House of Lords held (*inter alia*) that the council could not be liable unless the builder would have been so liable.[102] The first question to address was what was the nature of C's loss. Their Lordships conceded that a builder of premises is subject to the same duty of care in tort as the manufacturers of chattels to 'avoid injury through defects in the premises to the person or property of those whom he should have in contemplation as likely to suffer such injury if care is not taken'.[103] So, to illustrate the points made, if the ceiling had actually collapsed on Mr Murphy, injuring him or destroying his piano, he might have had a claim for personal injuries or property damage against the builder. However, unless and until such actual physical damage occurs, the loss associated with the cost of making the house safe (or any diminution in its value) is purely economic.

---

[99] For an erudite suggestion as to why we should want to distinguish between the two types of harm, see Witting, 'Distinguishing Between Property Damage and Pure Economic Loss: A Personality Thesis' [2001] *Legal Studies* 481.

[100] *Batty v Metropolitan Property Realisations Ltd* [1978] QB 554; *Anns v Merton London Borough Council* [1978] AC 728.   [101] [1991] 1 AC 398.

[102] For direct authority on the liability of builders see *Department of the Environment v Thomas Bates & Son Ltd* [1991] 1 AC 499.

[103] [1991] 1 AC 398, at 461, *per* Lord Keith. Note that the question of the liability of the council even for physical injury was left open.

One matter must be made clear. Mr Murphy's house at the time of his action was already suffering from serious cracks in the internal walls. Physical damage, you might have thought. Not so; for that damage was damage to, and a defect in, the very property in question. There was no question of the defective property causing damage to quite separate property. In an earlier decision of the House of Lords it had been suggested that where there was a 'complex structure', defects in one part of the structure causing damage to some other part might be regarded as having damaged 'other property'.[104] In *Murphy* this doctrine was questioned, yet not in terms rejected.[105] It has since received further tacit judicial approval.[106] There are, however, limits to this so called complex structure exception. It can only apply if some distinct and separate item, which is combined with, but distinct from the product in question, causes damage to the latter. For example, it might apply where C buys a house built by X with a central heating system made and installed by Y, and some months after the purchase an explosion damages the house (but injures no-one). In such a circumstance, an action would lie against Y for his negligently manufactured item that has damaged separate property, the house itself.[107]

Another limit to the complex structure approach applies where distinct product X is combined with distinct product Y to make product Z – for example, where two products (one a gas, one a liquid) are combined to make a carbonated drink. In such circumstances it has been held to be inappropriate to speak in terms of the first product damaging the second because there is merely the production of a defective third product (product Z in our example).[108]

Where defective design causes another form of harm to occur – for example, fire damage that would have been avoided if a fire wall had been properly designed and constructed – a duty of care *may* be imposed on the architects responsible. But the scope of their duty to a subsequent occupier of the premises is determined by reference to the extent of their original contractual duty. Thus, if they were only contracted to provide the plans for such a wall, but not to supervise its actual construction, no duty would be imposed in respect of the negligent erection of the wall.[109]

Finally in this context it is worth noting that there can be some strange consequences to applying the *Murphy* doctrine. Assume an impecunious house-owner becomes aware of the worsening condition of her property, but she does nothing about it because she cannot afford to pay for the necessary repairs. Several months later the house collapses injuring her and damaging her priceless furniture. It seems she may

---

[104] In *D & F Estates Ltd v Church Comrs for England* [1988] 2 All ER 992, at 1006–7, *per* Lord Bridge.

[105] [1990] 2 All ER 908, at 926–8, 932–933 and 942, *per* Lords Bridge, Oliver and Jauncey.

[106] *Bacardi-Martini Beveridges Ltd v Thomas-Hardy Packaging Ltd* [2002] 1 Lloyd's Rep 62.

[107] *Murphy v Brentwood District Council* [1990] 2 All ER 908, at 928, *per* Lord Bridge.

[108] *Bacardi-Martini Beveridges Ltd v Thomas-Hardy Packaging Ltd* [2002] 1 Lloyd's Rep 62. See further, Tettenborn, 'Components and Product Liability' [2000] LMCLQ 338.

[109] *Bellefield Computer Services v E Turner & Sons Ltd* [2002] All ER (D) 272 (Dec).

then sue to recover compensation for that physical damage.[110] It should be noted that for the most part Commonwealth jurisdictions have declined to follow the *Murphy* 'doctrine' and preferred to allow claimants in circumstances analogous to Mr Murphy's to succeed.[111]

There are also some rather difficult borderline cases on what constitutes economic loss. For example, the need to decontaminate a ship after it has been doused in acid which causes no tangible damage to the ship has been characterized as physical damage.[112] A similar interpretation has been placed on the ingress of water into a gas supply line such that householders become deprived of a gas supply for several days.[113]

SECTION 5 'PURE' ECONOMIC LOSS

Classifying the claimant's loss as purely economic does not preclude recovery of that loss altogether. But it does require the claimant to convince the court that the defendant owed him a duty to safeguard him against just that sort of loss. As noted earlier,[114] the courts are generally much less willing to find the existence of such a duty than a duty to protect others from physical injury or damage. According to Lord Fraser in *The Mineral Transporter* 'some limit or control mechanism has to be imposed on the liability of a wrongdoer towards those who have suffered economic damage as a consequence of his negligence'.[115] This restrictive approach to economic loss means that, in practice, economic loss is generally only recoverable when the claimant can establish a 'special relationship' between himself and the defendant (the latter having undertaken an assumption of responsibility of one form or another[116]), or where the loss is consequential upon physical damage also suffered by the claimant. It is as well to note at the outset that 'special relationships' characterized by assumptions of responsibility exist not just where the defendant has made a statement or proffered advice upon which the claimant relies, but also where he has undertaken to perform various forms of service. However, historical development of the law in this area makes it simpler to begin by examining economic loss resulting from inaccurate statements and advice.

---

[110] See *Nitrigin Eireann Teoranta v Inco Alloys Ltd* [1992] 1 All ER 854. Would D be able to plead contributory negligence? See ch 6.

[111] See, eg, *Invercargill City Council v Hamlin* [1996] 1 All ER 756.

[112] *The Orjula* [1995] 2 Lloyd's Rep 395.

[113] *Anglian Water Services Ltd v Crawshaw Robbins Ltd* [2001] BLR 173.

[114] [2001] BLR 173, at 177–178. And see generally Stapleton, 'Duty of Care and Economic Loss: A Wider Agenda' (1991) 107 LQR 249; *id*, 'Duty of Care: Peripheral Parties and Alternative Opportunities for Deterrence' (1995) 111 LQR 301.

[115] [1985] 2 All ER 935, at 945. See also *White v Chief Constable of South Yorkshire Police* [1999] 1 All ER 1, at 31, *per* Lord Steyn.

[116] *Williams v Natural Life Health Foods Ltd* [1998] 2 All ER 577; *Henderson v Merrett Syndicates Ltd* [1995] 2 AC 145.

(A) STATEMENTS AND 'SPECIAL RELATIONSHIPS'

Two difficulties beset the imposition of any duty to avoid making careless statements. First, there is generally a difference in the potential effects of careless words and careless acts. For while negligent acts will generally have a limited range of impact, negligent words may be widely broadcast without the consent or foresight of the speaker. Secondly, careless statements are, in general, likely to inflict only economic loss. But it should not be overlooked that careless words, whether written or spoken, do have the potential to cause harm to the person.[117] Thus, a doctor whose negligent certification of one claimant as a person of unsound mind leading to his detention in a mental hospital was held liable,[118] while a similar result was reached in a more recent case involving the negligent certification of a light aircraft as suitable to fly.[119]

The development of the duty to avoid statements causing pecuniary loss is inextricably linked to the troubled history of liability for economic loss in general. The original difficulty relating to economic loss resulting from careless statements was this. A person suffering economic loss through relying on a fraudulent statement could sue in the tort of deceit. In *Derry v Peek*[120] the House of Lords held that to establish deceit the claimant must prove fraud – that is, broadly, that the defendant knew that his statement was untrue, or was reckless as to its untruth. Mere negligence was considered insufficient.[121] The fallacy in this early case law was exposed by the House of Lords in the landmark decision in *Hedley Byrne & Co Ltd v Heller & Partners Ltd*.[122]

Cs asked their bankers to inquire into the financial stability of a company with which they were having business dealings. Their bankers made inquiries of Ds, the company's bankers, who carelessly gave favourable references about the company. Reliance on these references caused Cs to lose £17,000. Cs sued Ds for the careless statements. The action failed only because Ds had expressly disclaimed any responsibility.

All five Law Lords re-examined the authorities on liability for careless statements. They rightly limited the rule in *Derry v Peek* to its proper function of defining the limits of the tort of deceit and thus held it to be irrelevant to the issue of whether a duty of care arose in negligence. The absence of a contract was also irrelevant. As Lord Devlin said:

[a] promise given without consideration to perform a service cannot be enforced as a contract by the promisee, but if the service is in fact performed and done negligently the promisee can recover in an action in tort.[123]

Their Lordships were not however prepared to recognize a duty of care in respect of negligent statements on the basis of the *Donoghue v Stevenson* neighbour principle alone. For liability for statements resulting in economic loss to be imposed, some

---

[117] See, eg, *Perrett v Collins* [1998] 2 Lloyd's Rep 255; *Sharp v Avery and Kerwood* [1938] 4 All ER 85; *Bird v Pearce* (1979) 77 LGR 753; *Clayton v Woodman & Son (Builders) Ltd* [1961] 3 All ER 249 (revsd on other grounds [1962] 2 All ER 33).   [118] *De Freville v Dill* (1927) 96 LJKB 1056.
[119] *Perrett v Collins* [1998] 2 Lloyd's Rep 255.   [120] (1889) 14 App Cas 337.
[121] *Candler v Crane, Christmas & Co* [1951] 2 KB 164.   [122] [1964] AC 465.
[123] [1964] AC 465, at 526.

narrower test than that of foreseeability of the loss had to be satisfied.[124] The House was cautious not to formulate rules that might expose a maker of careless statements to liability to a large indeterminate class of claimants. For instance, newspapers were not to be accountable to everybody who read their advice columns and suffered loss through relying on their negligent advice.[125] Instead, their Lordships said that the claimant seeking to recover for negligent misstatements must establish that the statement was made within a relationship where the claimant could reasonably rely on the skill and care of the defendant in making the statement. He must show some 'special relationship' with the defendant which properly resulted in the defendant undertaking responsibility for the accuracy of the statements made. These concerns were captured succinctly by Lord Reid:

[q]uite careful people often express definite opinions on social or informal occasions, even when they see that others are likely to be influenced by them; and they often do that without taking that care which they would take if asked for their opinion professionally, or in a business.[126]

Subsequent case law to some extent elucidated the crepuscular phrase 'special relationship'. In *Mutual Life and Citizens' Assurance Co Ltd v Evatt*[127] Lord Diplock suggested that liability for misstatements should arise only in the context of certain professional relationships where giving advice was the primary purpose of the relationship. So, solicitors would be responsible for legal advice offered to clients, and stockbrokers for financial guidance, but an insurance company volunteering financial advice to a policy holder should not be liable. The Court of Appeal, however, largely ignored *Evatt*. In *Chaudhry v Prabhakar*[128] the defendant who considered himself something of an expert on motor cars was held liable to his friend whom he agreed to assist with the purchase of a car when his advice proved to be negligent. Indeed, the trend up until 1989 appeared to be to allow a liberal interpretation of what constituted a special relationship. But two subsequent decisions of the House of Lords – *Caparo Industries plc v Dickman*[129] and *Smith v Bush*[130] – outlined more authoritatively the parameters of liability for economic loss arising from negligent advice. Although *Caparo* was decided subsequently to *Smith v Bush*, it helps to consider *Caparo* first.

Ds were auditors who acted for Fidelity plc. They had prepared annual accounts on the strength of which Cs bought shares in Fidelity and then mounted a successful takeover bid. Cs alleged that the accounts were inaccurate and misleading showing a large pre-tax profit when they should have recorded a sizeable loss. Had Cs been aware of this, they would never have bid for Fidelity.

The House of Lords found against the claimants on a preliminary point of law. The auditors owed no duty of care in respect of the accuracy of the accounts either to members of the public who relied on the accounts to invest in the company or to any

---

[124] [1964] AC 465, at 483 and 537, *per* Lords Reid and Pearce.   [125] [1971] AC 793.

[126] [1964] AC 465, at 487.   [127] [1971] AC 793.

[128] [1988] 3 All ER 718. See also *Esso Petroleum Co Ltd v Mardon* [1976] QB 801.

[129] [1990] 2 AC 605.   [130] [1990] 1 AC 831.

individual existing shareholder who similarly relied on those accounts to increase his shareholding.[131] Auditors prepare accounts, not to promote the interests of potential investors, but to assist the shareholders collectively to exercise their right of control over the company.[132] Their Lordships held that four conditions must be met for a defendant to be liable for economic loss resulting from negligent advice or information. (1) The defendant must be *fully* aware of the nature of the transaction which the claimant had in contemplation as a result of receipt of the information. (2) He must either have communicated that information to the claimant directly, or know that it would be communicated to him (or a restricted class of persons of which the claimant is an identifiable member). (3) He must specifically anticipate that the claimant would *properly* and *reasonably* rely on that information when deciding whether or not to engage in the transaction in question. (4) The purpose for which the claimant does rely on that information must be a purpose connected with interests that it is reasonable to require the defendants to protect.

No duty is owed to all potential investors for such a duty would in truth result in unlimited liability. If auditors were liable to *any* investor who relied on the published accounts to deal with the company simply because such conduct is foreseeable, they would equally be liable to anyone else who dealt with the company to his detriment, for example, banks lending the company money, or tradesmen extending credit terms.[133] Caparo sought to argue that the vulnerability of Fidelity to takeover should have alerted the auditors to the likelihood of a company, such as Caparo, mounting a takeover bid, and that they were not just *any* potential investor, but existing shareholders. Their Lordships held that the defendants were under no duty to safeguard the economic interests of predators,[134] and that the statutory duty imposed on them by Parliament was to protect the interests, and existing holdings, of the shareholders in the client company,[135] not to facilitate investment decisions whether by existing shareholders or others.

A positive avalanche of cases on the limits of *Hedley Byrne* liability followed. Just a few examples are given here to illustrate the application of the *Caparo* principles.

In one case it was held that directors of a company who issued a prospectus to invite shareholders to take up a rights issue were not under a duty to those shareholders who relied on the prospectus to make further investments.[136] Nor were accountants advising a creditor company on the appointment of a receiver liable to that company's debtors.[137] In both cases, the relationship between the parties lacked the necessary proximity. The defendants had done nothing to make themselves responsible for the

---

[131] The Court of Appeal had held that existing shareholders were owed such a duty distinguishing the shareholder investors from other members of the public: [1989] 1 All ER 798.

[132] [1990] 1 All ER 568, at 580–1 and 600–601, *per* Lords Bridge and Oliver respectively.

[133] See *Al Saudi Banque v Clark Pixley* [1990] Ch 313.

[134] Why should auditors be responsible for the success of those actively seeking to destroy their client?

[135] As to whether an existing shareholder might sue if his existing proprietary interest was damaged by negligence on the part of the auditors (*ie*, sold at an undervalue) see Lord Bridge [1990] 1 All ER 568, at 580–1 (probably yes) and Lord Oliver, at 601 (leaving the question open).

[136] *Al-Nakib Investments (Jersey) Ltd v Longcroft* [1990] 3 All ER 321.

[137] *Huxford v Stoy Hayward & Co* (1989) 5 BCC 421.

financial welfare of the claimants. But what if some express representation has been made directly to the claimant on the basis of which he argues that he then decided to go ahead with a particular transaction? Much may turn on the facts of the case. In *James McNaughton Paper Groups v Hicks Anderson*[138] the defendant accountants became aware that the claimants were considering a takeover of their clients. At a meeting between the two companies, the defendants were asked to confirm the accuracy of draft accounts, and they did this in very general terms. The Court of Appeal found that no duty was owed to the claimants. The draft accounts were not prepared for their benefit, and the defendants would reasonably expect a party to a takeover bid to take independent advice and not rely exclusively on draft accounts. However, in another case where it was pleaded that the defendants had prepared profit forecasts expressly in order to induce the claimants to increase their bid for a company at risk of takeover, the Court of Appeal refused to strike out the claim and ordered a full trial on the facts.[139]

Perhaps the key question in this sort of case is whether advice given by the defendant has been given in a context in which the assumption that claimants should generally look after their own financial interests can be displaced.[140] Have the defendants in effect induced the claimants to place faith in their judgment?

In *Henderson v Merrett Syndicates Ltd*[141] managing agents at Lloyds who placed monies entrusted to them by Names at Lloyds in underwriting contracts owed a duty of care to 'their' Names. The agents undertook responsibility for advising the claimants and finding appropriate investments for their money. They effectively 'took over' the claimants' financial affairs. *Williams v Natural Life Health Food Ltd*[142] is also instructive. The second defendant set up a company to franchise out health food businesses. The claimants approached the company to obtain a franchise. Having received from the company, Natural Life, a glowing brochure and prospectus which included testimonies to the second defendant's experience and success, the claimants went ahead and obtained a franchise. At no stage in the pre-contractual negotiations did they have any contact with the second defendant personally. The enterprise was a disaster and the claimants' shop failed to make money, resulting in severe financial loss to the claimants. The claimants sued both the company, Natural Life, and the second defendant personally. The company went into liquidation so the action proceeded against the second defendant alone. The House of Lords found that there was no special relationship between the second defendant and the claimants because there were no personal dealings between them and neither directly nor indirectly did the second defendant convey to the claimants that he assumed personal responsibility for their affairs. Nor was there evidence that the claimants relied on his personal undertakings to

---

[138] [1991] 2 QB 113.   [139] *Morgan Crucible v Hill Samuel Bank Ltd* [1991] 1 All ER 148.

[140] For closer analysis see Witting, 'Justifying Liability to Third Parties for Negligent Misstatements' (2000) 20 OJLS 615.

[141] [1995] 2 AC 145. As to concurrent liability in tort and contract see ch 2. See also Whittaker, 'The Application of the "Broad Principle of *Hedley Byrne*" as Between Parties to a Contract' [1997] *Legal Studies* 169.

[142] [1998] 2 All ER 577.

safeguard their economic well-being as franchisers. The dealings were all with the company. Unlike the Lloyds' agents, the second defendant took on no role as an individual in 'managing' the claimants' business interests.

We move now to look at *Smith v Bush*; but we do so noting that in *Caparo*[143] Lord Oliver described *Smith v Bush*[144] as the outer limit of *Hedley Byrne* liability.

Ds were surveyors acting for the mortgagees. They gave favourable reports on properties to be purchased by C, the mortgagor. An express disclaimer denied any liability to C.[145] Nonetheless the evidence was that 90% of house purchasers do in fact rely on the mortgagees' report[146] and do not engage their own surveyor. C paid the surveyor's fee and Ds were well aware that C (whose identity they knew) would rely on the report and would suffer loss if that report were negligently prepared.

The House of Lords unanimously found that in such circumstances a duty of care is owed to the mortgagor. Unlike in *Caparo*, the defendants were well aware of the identity of the claimant, knew that their advice would be transmitted to the claimant and appreciated exactly how the claimant would act in reliance on that advice. There was no element of uncertainty relating to the transaction consequent on that advice. There was no question of liability other than to one identifiable claimant.[147] There was no conflict between the interests of the surveyors' client and the mortgagors. If the surveyors had done the job properly and produced a proper valuation, they would have discharged their duty to both mortgagee and mortgagor. The claimants who paid their fees were properly entitled to rely on their professional skill and advice.[148]

It is important, of course, to remember that proof of a duty to act carefully in giving advice or information is only the first stage in the claim. Claims may, of course, fail for other reasons. If, for example, it can be shown that the duty extended merely in respect of the provision of information (for example, the value of property suggested as security for a loan) upon which the claimant could (but need not) base his financial decisions, the defendant will not be liable for he has not advised upon the wisdom of

---

[143] [1998] 2 All ER 577, at 598.   [144] [1990] 1 AC 831.

[145] The disclaimer was invalid under the Unfair Contract Terms Act 1977.

[146] *Smith v Bush* was a consolidated appeal concerning two separate claimants. In one case the mortgagee showed the actual report to C1. In the other, the report itself was not disclosed to C2.

[147] The likelihood that *a* purchaser may emerge in the future who will suffer loss if a survey is carelessly conducted is insufficient. A particular individual who will almost inevitably place faith in the report and act to his detriment must be within D's contemplation: *The Morning Watch* [1990] 1 Lloyd's Rep 547. Contrast *Smith v Bush* with *Goodwill v British Pregnancy Advisory Service* [1996] 2 All ER 161 (no liability to a subsequent partner of a man whose vasectomy failed. C argued that had her lover been properly advised of the risk of failure she would have been told and taken suitable precautions. Gibson LJ doubted that she could be considered an identifiable C: 'The defendants could know nothing about the likely course of action of future sexual partners').

[148] Lord Griffiths and Lord Jauncey both made references to the reasonableness of purchasers at the lower end of the market relying on the building society survey rather than facing the additional expense of an independent report. Yet the *Smith v Bush* approach was applied to a property worth £100,000 in *Beaumont v Humberts* [1990] 49 EG 46. Is the value of the property perhaps more relevant to the validity and reasonableness of any disclaimer than whether a duty is owed at all?

the financial decision finally taken (because, for instance, the market value of property is susceptible to rapid drops in price).[149] Equally, as with other actions in negligence, want of care may not be proved.[150] Or, alternatively, the claimant may fail to show that his loss resulted from the defendant's carelessness,[151] or, more problematically, that all his loss resulted from the defendant's carelessness.[152] Thus, if the claimant, albeit he believed the information, would have acted as he did regardless of the defendant's negligence, his loss is not caused by that negligence.[153]

(B) THE EXTENDED *HEDLEY BYRNE* PRINCIPLE

What then is the basis of *Hedley Byrne* liability? Lord Griffiths, in *Smith v Bush*, dismissed as unhelpful the notion that liability rests on an assumption of responsibility by the defendant.[154] Indeed, the defendants in *Smith v Bush* manifested every intention to the contrary, attempting expressly to disclaim liability. A duty, Lord Griffiths argued, can arise, not only where the defendant either expressly or implicitly undertakes responsibility to the claimant for advice or information, but also where the particular relationship between the two is such that it is just that the defendant be subject to such responsibility.[155] Lord Griffiths' criticism of any principle of assumption of responsibility was strongly supported by a number of academic commentators.[156] However, subsequent decisions of the House of Lords have forcefully endorsed the 'assumption of responsibility' test as the basis of an extended *Hedley Byrne* principle which embraces negligent performance of services as much as negligent statements and

---

[149] *South Australia Asset Management Corp v York Montague Ltd* [1997] AC 191; *Aneco Reinsurance Underwriting Ltd v Johnson & Higgins Ltd* [2002] 1 Lloyd's Rep. 157.

[150] *Stafford v Conti Commodity Services Ltd* [1981] 1 All ER 691; *Argy Trading Developments Co Ltd v Lapid Developments Ltd* [1977] 3 All ER 785.

[151] *Banque Financière de la Cité v Westgate Insurance Ltd* [1991] 2 AC 249 (note that their Lordships also found no duty in that case).

[152] The most problematic issues arise where C's financial losses are attributable partly to D's negligent advice and partly to fluctuations in market prices; only those properly attributable to the former being recoverable: *South Australia Asset Management Corp v York Montague Ltd* [1997] AC 191; *Aneco Reinsurance Underwriting Ltd v Johnson & Higgins Ltd* [2002] 1 Lloyd's Rep 157.

[153] *J E B Fasteners Ltd v Marks, Bloom & Co* [1983] 1 All ER 583 (C failed to prove that he relied on negligently prepared accounts when making his investment). See also *Williams v Natural Life Health Foods Ltd* [1998] 2 All ER 577, at 836.

[154] [1998] 2 All ER 577, at 865, confirming the decision of the Court of Appeal in *Ministry of Housing and Local Government v Sharp* [1970] 2 QB 223.

[155] See *Al Saudi Banque v Clark Pixley* [1989] 3 All ER 361, at 367, *per* Millet J (there should either be an assumption of responsibility or a relationship 'equivalent to contract').

[156] See, eg, Barker 'Unreliable Assumptions in the Modern Law of Negligence' (1993) 109 LQR 461; Hepple 'Negligence: The Search for Coherence' (1997) 50 CLP 69. For a limited defence see Murphy, 'The Juridical Foundations of Common Law Non-Delegable Duties' in Neyers (ed), *Emerging Issues in Tort Law* (2007).

advice;[157] and which – if the courts have not erred in applying the principle – now extends to cases characterized by *both* dependency *and* reliance on the part of the claimant.[158] In *Henderson v Merrett Syndicates Ltd*,[159] for example, Lord Goff rested his finding of liability on the part of the managing agents on their assumption of responsibility towards those who relied on their special expertise in underwriting. In *White v Jones*, Lord Browne-Wilkinson affirmed the centrality within *Hedley Byrne* liability of discovering whether the defendant had assumed responsibility for the advice or task undertaken. Notably, however, he stressed that what is crucial is 'a conscious assumption of responsibility for the *task* rather than a conscious assumption of legal responsibility to the claimant for its careful performance'.[160] (This approach, however, is difficult to square with the notion that an assumption of responsibility is really only a way of characterizing the relationship of proximity necessary for the imposition of a duty of care.[161])

More generally, the three decisions of the House of Lords in *Henderson v Merrett Syndicates Ltd*, *White v Jones* and *Williams v Natural Life Ltd*, have confirmed that *Hedley Byrne* opened the doors to much wider liability in respect of economic loss in tort than had previously been available.[162] In *Hedley Byrne* itself, Lord Devlin stated:

[c]ases may arise in the future in which a new and wider proposition, quite independent of contract, will be needed. There may, for example, be cases in which a statement is not supplied for the use of any particular individual.[163]

Seeking to extend yet further the boundaries of a duty to avoid inflicting financial loss on others, a robust approach was taken by Megarry V-C in *Ross v Caunters*.

D, a solicitor, negligently drew up a will and thereby failed to fulfil his client-testator's instruction to benefit C. C then sued D in negligence.[164]

The claimant could in no sense be said to have relied on the solicitor, yet his action succeeded. The judge held that the law had by 1979 so developed that he should apply

---

[157] *Williams v Natural Life Health Foods Ltd* [1998] 2 All ER 577.

[158] Even with this description of the extended *Hedley-Byrne* principle problems can arise in explaining the decided cases. In some, the courts have had to alight upon tenuous notions of 'an assumption of responsibility' (see, eg, *White v Jones* [1995] 2 AC 207). Equally, there are some rather fictitious instances of reliance to be found in the cases. For some judicial recognition of this, see *Customs and Excise Commissioners v Barclays Bank plc* [2005] 1 WLR 2082 (revsd on other issues [2006] UKHL 28). See also *Clerk and Lindsell* (2006) pp 448–450 and fn 194, below.   [159] [1995] 2 AC 145, at 182.

[160] [1995] 2 AC 207, at 274.

[161] See Murphy, 'Expectation Losses, Negligent Omissions and the Tortious Duty of Care' [1996] CLJ 43. Note, however, that *White* has been followed in this respect in an analogous case: *Gorham v British Telecommunications plc* [2000] 1 WLR 2129 (an insurance company owes a duty to those it advises on insurance matters and, in the event of their death, to their dependants).

[162] But note that 'extended *Hedley-Byrne*' liability is not necessarily confined to economic loss. It has been accepted, for example, that it could in principle be invoked in relation to psychiatric illness caused by being wrongfully convicted due to the negligence of C's solicitors: *McLoughlin v Grovers* [2002] QB 1312.

[163] [1964] AC 465, at 530.   [164] [1980] Ch 297. And see *Al-Kandari v JR Brown & Co* [1988] QB 665.

the neighbour principle in *Donoghue v Stevenson* in the absence of any policy factors negativing or limiting the scope of such a duty. There was close proximity between the claimant and the defendant. His contemplation of her was 'actual, nominate and direct', so proximity arose out of the duty he undoubtedly owed to the testator. It was in no way 'casual, accidental or unforeseen'. The liability arising from the duty was to one person alone.[165] Accordingly, the spectre of indeterminate liability did not arise.

In *White v Jones*,[166] the House of Lords found for the claimant on facts reminiscent of (but different to) those in *Ross v Caunters*.

After a family quarrel, the testator (aged 78) disinherited Cs (his two daughters). A few months later the family was reconciled and on 17 July the testator instructed Ds (his solicitors), to draw up a new will including legacies of £9,000 to each daughter. Ds failed to act on those instructions before the testator died some months later. As a result of Ds' negligent delay in acting on the testator's instructions, Cs failed to be awarded their legacies.

The House of Lords held that the claimants' could recover. Lord Goff made it clear that their Lordships did not endorse Megarry V-C's simplistic approach basing liability on the neighbour principle alone.[167] The claim by the claimants in *White v Jones*, as in *Ross v Caunters*, posed a number of conceptual difficulties,[168] but principally the following.

(1) D's contractual duty was owed only to his client, the now dead testator. Privity of contract rules excluded the extension of *this* duty to the disappointed beneficiaries.

(2) Cs' actions, being founded on pure economic loss, could succeed only on the basis of some form of application of *Hedley Byrne*; yet there was no obvious assumption of responsibility towards Cs and, still less obviously, any corresponding reliance on their part. For this reason, it was straining logic to suggest that Cs had actually lost anything at all.[169]

(3) If liability were to be imposed, establishing clear and manageable limits to such liability would be near to impossible to achieve.

The majority in the House of Lords thought these difficulties could be surmounted;[170] but the conceptual grounds on which their Lordships did in fact establish liability must be read with some caution.[171] Lord Goff was entirely frank in admitting that he was strongly motivated by an impulse to do practical justice. He pointed out the 'extraordinary fact' that if no duty in tort were owed to the claimants, the only persons who might have a valid claim (the testator and his estate) had suffered no loss, and the only persons

---

[165] See *Caltex Oil (Australia) Pty Ltd v Dredge Wellemstad* (1976) 136 CLR 529 (note the importance in relation to economic loss of there being a single identifiable C rather than a diffuse class of potential Cs).

[166] [1995] 2 AC 207.   [167] [1995] 2 AC 207, at 268.

[168] Detailed in full in [1995] 2 AC 207, at 260–262.

[169] See Benson, 'Does *White v Jones* Represent Canadian Law?' in Neyers (ed), *Emerging Issues in Tort Law* (2007).   [170] Note the powerful dissent of Lord Mustill.

[171] See Murphy, 'Expectation Losses, Negligent Omissions and the Tortious Duty of Care' [1996] CLJ 43.

who suffered any kind of loss (the disappointed beneficiaries) would have no claim.[172] Lord Browne-Wilkinson warned that his analysis was only what was necessary for the purposes of this case. He made clear that he was 'not purporting to give any comprehensive statement of this aspect of the law'.[173]

So what did *White v Jones* decide? (1) The existence of a contract between the defendants and a third party (the testator) did not by virtue of the rules on privity of contract exclude a duty in tort to the claimant. (2) Such a duty could arise if, quite apart from the contract, the circumstances of the case gave rise to a special relationship between the parties. (3) On the facts of *Hedley Byrne* itself, proof that the claimant relied on the advice given, or statements made, by the defendants, and that the defendants should have foreseen such reliance, was an 'inevitable' condition of liability. However reliance is *not* a necessary condition for the creation of a special relationship in every case giving rise to a duty to safeguard another from economic loss. (4) A special relationship will arise when the defendant assumes responsibility for providing services knowing and accepting that 'the future economic welfare of the intended beneficiary is dependent on his careful execution of the task'.[174] (5) On the facts of *White v Jones*, there were no reasons of policy why such a duty should not be imposed on the defendants, and indeed very good reasons why it should be so imposed. The actual outcome of the decision in *Ross v Caunters* imposing liability on solicitors for negligently executed wills had worked well and had not given rise to unlimited claims. In such cases there was no conflict of interest[175] between the duty owed to the testator in contract, and the duty owed to the claimants in tort. Fulfilling the contractual obligation to the defendant at one and the same time would have discharged the duty of care owed to the claimants.

White v Jones does, therefore, make clear at least three crucial principles. (1) A duty to avoid causing economic loss is confined to special relationships within which the defendant has assumed responsibility for protecting the claimant's economic welfare.[176] (2) Such a relationship will arise only where the claimant is readily identifiable as an individual or a member of a class of persons for whom the defendant undertakes responsibility (in the loosest sense[177]) in the performance of a particular task. (3) 'Extended *Hedley Byrne*' relationships are not confined to negligent misstatements and careless advice. Provision of services, including services provided at the behest of a third party, may create a special relationship in appropriate

---

[172] [1995] 2 AC 207, at 259–60.

[173] [1995] 2 AC 207, at 274. But see the application of *White v Jones* in *Gorham v British Telecommunications plc* [2000] 1 WLR 2129.   [174] [1995] 2 AC 207, at 275, *per* Lord Browne-Wilkinson.

[175] Compare *White v Jones* with *Clarke v Bruce Lance & Co* [1988] 1 All ER 364 (no duty to C in advising the testator in another transaction which ultimately reduced the value of C's legacy under the will).

[176] Whether all the cases supposedly decided according to this principle actually meet this requirement upon close scrutiny of their particular facts is, however, questionable. See, *eg*, *Merrett v Babb* [2001] QB 1174 (surveyor had no personal knowledge of a purchaser of property upon which he had negligently prepared a survey and valuation at the time of that survey).

[177] See Murphy, 'Expectation Losses, Negligent Omissions and the Tortious Duty of Care' [1996] CLJ 43.

conditions.[178] Reliance is not an essential ingredient of a special relationship,[179] though in its absence there must be dependency on the part of the claimant (in the sense that the claimant's well-being depends upon the care and skill of the defendant). Thus, a passenger in a light aircraft who has not personally relied on the negligent certification of its airworthiness is entitled to sue in respect of physical injury consequent upon that negligent certification.[180] In short, *White v Jones* confirms the wider interpretation of *Hedley Byrne* prophesied by Lord Devlin, albeit equally clearly rejecting any suggestion that liability for economic loss can simply be equated with liability for physical harm.

A willingness to give a liberal, extended interpretation to *Hedley Byrne* liability married to an apparent impetus to do justice to a hard-done-by claimant is once again apparent in *Spring v Guardian Assurance plc*.[181]

C sued his former employers for negligence (among other things). The reference D provided for him when he sought to be appointed as an agent for another insurance company was so unfavourable that the company refused to appoint him. The reference suggested that C was dishonest. The trial judge found that the reference had been carelessly (but not maliciously) prepared and found for C in negligence. In the House of Lords, the majority held that there had been an implied term in the contract of employment that any subsequent reference be supplied with due care. The Law Lords also ruled in C's favour in tort. In supplying a reference – at least in circumstances such as those in the instant case where references were required as a matter of regulation[182] – D assumed the responsibility to prepare the reference with care.

That the defendants owed such a duty to the recipient of the reference was established by *Hedley Byrne*. But in the instant case, the duty claimed was one owed to the person about whom it was written, not the person to whom it was sent. It therefore represented an extension of the *Hedley Byrne* principle that could be justified on the basis that an employee relies on his employer to carry out this service with appropriate care. His interests are 'entrusted' to the skill of the referee. His financial prospects are significantly in the hands of that person.

But we must not lose sight of the fact that in *Spring* there was a significant policy issue present that arguably militated against the imposition of liability. Allegations of dishonesty are clearly defamatory. Yet had the claimant sued in defamation, his claim

---

[178] In *West Bromwich Albion FC v El-Safty* [2005] EWHC 2866, it was held that, *if* the three limbs of the *Caparo* test were met, a surgeon whose treatment of a professional player that had been arranged through the club's physiotherapist *would* owe a duty of care to the club in respect of the economic loss it would suffer if the player were to receive negligent treatment ending his career. On the facts, however, the *Caparo* test was not satisfied (affd [2006] EWCA Civ 1299). See also *Williams v Natural Life Health Foods Ltd* [1998] 2 All ER 577; *Carr-Glynn v Frearsons* [1998] 4 All ER 225.

[179] C's reliance is often the means by which causation can be established, but it has no normative significance of its own; it tells us nothing about the nature of D's conduct such that it is appropriate for D to be made liable to C. [180] *Perrett v Collins* [1998] 2 Lloyd's Rep 255.

[181] [1995] 2 AC 296. Note also the growing impetus in negligence law simply to do justice in *Parkinson v St James and Seacroft University Hospital NHS Trust* [2002] QB 266, *Rees v Darlington Memorial Hospital NHS Trust* [2004] 1 AC 309 and *Chester v Afshar* [2005] 1 AC 134.

[182] The regulatory authority (LAUTRO) which governs the conduct of insurance companies required both that the company seeking to appoint C must seek a reference and that Ds must supply such a reference.

would have been met by a defence of qualified privilege (given the absence of malice). Indeed, the giving of references prepared without malice is a classic example of qualified privilege. It was at least arguable, therefore, that to allow the claimant's action in negligence would be to undermine the principles of defamation law. This, conceivably, might cause employers and others supplying references to be inhibited in what they were prepared to say, and possibly even lead to them being unprepared to supply references at all. Their Lordships nonetheless were dismissive of this line of argument. Lord Woolf acknowledged that public policy required that references be full and frank but countered that public policy also required that references 'should not be based upon careless investigations'. If a negligently written favourable reference could give rise to liability, thought his Lordship, there should be no objection in principle to imposing liability for a negligently written adverse reference. The law should encourage referees to act carefully with proper regard for the interests of both the recipient and the subject of the reference.

A strong desire to offer the claimant redress for a perceived injustice can be seen in the opinions of the Law Lords.[183] Addressing the need to prove malice to succeed in defamation, Lord Woolf declared that:

[t]he result of this requirement is that an action for defamation is a wholly inadequate remedy for an employee who is caused damage by a reference which due to negligence is inaccurate. This is because it places a wholly disproportionate burden on the employee. Malice is extremely difficult to establish . . . Without an action for negligence, the employee may, therefore, be left with no practical prospect of redress even though the reference may have permanently prevented him from obtaining employment in his chosen vocation.[184]

The decision in *Williams v Natural Life Health Foods Ltd*[185] attempted to consolidate and confirm the present state of extended *Hedley Byrne* liability via the relatively brief speech delivered by Lord Steyn. He made three crucial points. (1) Once it is established that a case falls within the extended *Hedley Byrne* principle – that is, where there is a special relationship between the parties[186] – 'there is no need to embark on any further inquiry whether it is fair, just and reasonable to impose liability for economic loss'.[187] (2) He acknowledged, and commended, the 'essential gap-filling role' of the law of tort so that, while contractual privity rules might prevent substantial justice being done in that branch of law, this should not prevent torts from filling that gap. *Spring*, indeed, illustrates that this interstitial role may operate between different torts as well. For, there, negligence was utilized to correct what their Lordships regarded as a deficiency in defamation law. (3) Outside any special relationships blessed by the extended *Hedley*

---

[183] Cf *Kapfunde v Abbey National plc* [1999] ICR 1.   [184] [1994] 3 All ER 129, at 172.

[185] [1998] 2 All ER 577.   [186] [1998] 2 All ER 577, at 581.

[187] How this is to be reconciled with the clear emphasis on the endeavour to do practical justice in both *Spring* and *White v Jones* is by no means clear. See also the approach of Brooke LJ in *Parkinson v St James and Seacroft University Hospital NHS Trust* [2002] QB 266, at [17].

Byrne principle, claimants suffering pure economic loss will not, it seems, recover that loss in tort. Lord Steyn declared:

The extended *Hedley Byrne* principle is the rationalization or technique adopted by English law for the recovery of damages in respect of economic loss caused by the negligent perform-ance of services.[188]

It is to the claims by claimants unable to bring themselves within that principle that we now turn.

(c) BEYOND *HEDLEY BYRNE*

Self-evidently, there are several other ways in which one person's negligence can cause another economic loss very different from the situations giving rise to extended *Hedley Byrne* liability. In 1966, the difficult but instructive case of *Weller & Co v Foot and Mouth Disease Research Institute*[189] was decided. The defendants had carelessly allowed cattle to become infected by foot and mouth disease. The claimants were auctioneers whose business suffered badly when quarantine restrictions prevented them holding auction sales of cattle. Widgery J said that no duty of care was owed to the claimants for their loss of profits. The scope of any duty owed was limited to cattle owners who suffered physical damage to their property when cattle had to be destroyed. The loss occasioned to the auctioneer was readily foreseeable but so was economic loss to countless other enterprises: the pubs, the cafes, the car parks, the shops who would benefit from the influx into the town of crowds on market day. Policy required that a cut-off point be set. Widgery J set it at those suffering physical harm and, on the facts of *Weller*, it is easy to understand why.

A series of decisions on the damages recoverable when services such as water, gas or electricity were negligently interrupted confirmed Widgery J's finding that economic loss unrelated to physical damage was irrecoverable. In *British Celanese Ltd v Hunt*[190] and *S C M (UK) Ltd v W J Whittall & Son Ltd*[191] the cutting off of electricity supplies damaged the claimant's machines and materials resulting in a loss of production. The claimants recovered both their additional expenditure in replacing and repairing machinery and their loss of profits on the lost production run. The Court of Appeal in the latter case held that the economic loss (that is, loss of profits) was recoverable, as it was immediately consequent on physical damage to the claimant's property. In 1973 the Court of Appeal again considered economic loss in *Spartan Steel and Alloys Ltd v Martin & Co (Contractors) Ltd*.[192] The defendants' negligence caused the cable carrying

---

[188] *Williams v Natural Life Health Foods Ltd* [1998] 2 All ER 577, at 581.

[189] [1966] 1 QB 569. And see *Cattle v Stockton Waterworks Co* (1875) LR 10 QB 453 (C could not recover for loss on a contract to tunnel under land belonging to another after that land had been flooded by D's negligence).

[190] [1969] 2 All ER 1252.   [191] [1971] 1 QB 337.

[192] [1973] QB 27 and see *Electrochrome Ltd v Welsh Plastics Ltd* [1968] 2 All ER 205; *The Kapetan Georgis* [1988] 1 Lloyd's Rep 352.

electricity to the claimant's factory to be cut through interrupting the supply for $14\frac{1}{2}$ hours. To avoid molten metal solidifying in the furnaces, the claimants used oxygen to melt it and pour it out of the furnaces. This reduced the value of the metal and lost the claimants the £400 profit they would have expected to make on that melt. The claimants also lost a further £1,767 on the other four melts which they would normally have completed in the time that the electricity was cut off. The majority of the Court of Appeal held that they could recover only the loss in value of the metal actually in the furnaces and the loss of profit on that melt. The remaining loss was pecuniary loss unrelated to any physical damage and thus irrecoverable. Edmund-Davies LJ, dissenting, considered that such foreseeable and direct economic loss should be recoverable. For him, the occurrence or non-occurrence of physical damage was a fortuitous event with no relevance in legal principle. In language similar to that later employed by Megarry V-C in *Ross v Caunters*, he argued that if that very kind of economic loss to that claimant was a reasonably foreseeable and direct consequence of want of care, a duty to avoid that kind of loss arose. Firm endorsement of the majority opinion in *Spartan Steel* was nonetheless supplied by the Court of Appeal in *Muirhead v Industrial Tank Specialties Ltd.*[193]

C, a fish merchant, devised a plan to buy lobsters in the summer when prices were low and store them to sell at profit on the Christmas market. The lobsters had to be stored in tanks through which seawater was constantly pumped, filtered and recirculated. The pumps proved to be defective because the electric motors were not suitable for use in the UK. C sued the manufacturers of the electric motors for (1) the loss of several lobsters that died in the tanks, (2) expenditure on attempts to correct the fault, and (3) loss of profits on the enterprise.

The Court of Appeal affirmed *Spartan Steel*. The claimant could recover only for the loss of his property (dead lobsters) and any loss of profit consequent on those dead lobsters. Only that economic loss directly consequent on physical damage could be recovered in tort. In the absence of any evidence of express reliance on, or close proximity to, the defendants, the defendants owed no duty to protect the claimant against financial loss whether that loss be wasted expenditure or loss of profit. Manufacturers owe no duty in tort to ensure products are value for money.

Outside the extended *Hedley Byrne* principle, it seems that the courts take the view that no duty to protect others from pure economic loss will arise however predictable that loss may be,[194] and however just and reasonable it might appear that the defendant should bear the loss. There is no obvious reason for this stance;[195] yet the judicial

---

[193] [1985] 3 All ER 705.

[194] See, eg, *Simaan General Contracting Co v Pilkington Glass Ltd (No 2)* [1988] 1 All ER 791.

[195] For one explanation of the case law based on what the authors (but not the courts) call 'the dependency principle' – which can be distinguished from some (but not all) judicial conceptions of the extended *Hedley-Byrne* principle – see McBride and Bagshaw, *Tort Law* (2005) pp 140–148. Their principle itself is neat, self-contained and coherent. But in saying, as they do, that certain cases do not fit the extended *Hedley-Byrne* principle, the authors conveniently overlook the fact that the judges in many instances believed themselves to be applying the extended *Hedley-Byrne* principle. For this reason, it seems equally possible to argue that the extended *Hedley-Byrne* principle has undergone further extension than the courts have consciously acknowledged,

sympathy for the claimant abundantly evidenced in *White v Jones* was notably absent in *Murphy v Brentwood District Council.*[196]

First, in *Murphy v Brentwood District Council*, as we have seen, their Lordships classified the loss suffered by the claimant (a subsequent purchaser of a defective dwelling) as pure economic loss. This was notwithstanding the fact that his home, if not repaired, would ultimately have collapsed. Such pecuniary loss is irrecoverable in tort whether the defendant is the builder or the local council approving the original building plans. In the absence of a special relationship of proximity, neither manufacturers of chattels nor builders of property are subject to a duty of care in relation to the quality of their work. To impose any such general duty would introduce into the law of tort transmissible warranties of quality.[197] Such guarantees are provided only by contract. Thus, there was generally perceived to be no need for tort to fulfil an interstitial role.[198] However, the simplicity of this statement is marred somewhat by a *dictum* of Lord Bridge suggesting that, even in the absence of a special relationship with the builder:

if a building stands so close to the boundary of the building owner's land that after discovery of the dangerous defect it remains a potential source of injury to persons or property on neighbouring land or the highway, the building owner ought, in principle, to be entitled to recover in tort . . . the cost of obviating the danger . . . *to protect himself from potential liability to third parties.*[199]

The Lord Bridge exception, doubted by Lord Oliver,[200] could theoretically drive a coach and horses through the *Murphy* rule. Assume Mr Murphy had children. The cracks in the walls of his house, if left unrepaired with the family remaining in the house, posed a potential source of injury to them. Could Mr Murphy argue he should recover the cost of protecting himself against liability to the children or his visitors? On the one hand, beyond *Hedley Byrne*, the courts strive to provide predictability and restrict claims for economic loss; yet on the other hand they want to retain the ability to meet the really 'hard case'.

A second category of cases where the House of Lords have declared that economic loss is *never* recoverable is more straightforward. A claimant who suffers economic loss consequent on physical damage to another person, or consequent on damage to property in which, at the time damage occurred, he had no proprietary or possessory interest, cannot recover that loss in tort.[201]

---

so that it now embraces cases not just of reliance, but also those of dependency. The latest edition of *Clerk and Lindsell* (2006) seems implicitly (at p 443) to share this view.

[196] [1991] 1 AC 398. See also *Department of the Environment v Bates* [1991] 1 AC 499; *D & F Estates Ltd v Church Comrs for England* [1988] 2 All ER 992.

[197] *D & F Estates Ltd v Church Comrs for England* [1988] 2 All ER 992, at 1010, *per* Lord Oliver.

[198] See *Williams v Natural Life Health Foods Ltd* [1998] 2 All ER 577.

[199] [1990] 2 All ER 908, at 926 (emphasis added).   [200] [1990] 2 All ER 908, at 936.

[201] For a statutory exception in relation to C's economic loss arising from harm to another, see the Fatal Accidents Act 1976. Note also the Latent Damage Act 1986, s 3.

In *Leigh & Sillivan Ltd v Aliakmon Shipping Ltd*[202] C had contracted to buy a cargo of steel coils to be shipped from Korea. The cargo was damaged at sea. The contractual and credit arrangements between C and the sellers of the steel coils were such that, although the risk in the cargo had passed to C, C did not own the coils. (Such arrangements where the party likely to suffer loss is not the owner of a cargo is not uncommon.) Loss to C was readily foreseeable. Nonetheless, the loss was held to be irrecoverable at common law.

Three reasons may explain the refusal to countenance recovery of economic loss in such circumstances.

(1) The indeterminate liability which would otherwise arise requires a fixed cut-off point in the interests of clarity: recall *Weller v Foot & Mouth Institute* where the list of potential claimants – café owners, local shop owners, etc – was virtually endless.

(2) The claimants in *Leigh & Sillivan* suffered damage to their *business* interests. True, the defendants 'caused' that damage, but on what grounds should they have undertaken responsibility for protecting the claimants' business? The risk was as foreseeable to the claimants as it was to the defendants, so they could have protected themselves against that risk via insurance. The defendants had done nothing to indicate their willingness to shoulder the responsibility themselves.[203]

(3) An individual's personality is to some extent constituted by the property he owns. As such, that property can be seen as integral to that person's self-defini-tion. Accordingly, damage to his property can be seen as a form of personality damage. It follows, so the argument runs, that such a form of 'consequential' economic loss (as distinct from pure economic loss) 'can be viewed as little more than extra compensation for those who have suffered property damage'.[204] Any loss not thus associated with the claimant's property (and hence his personality) can be viewed as less deserving of compensation in accordance with the general hierarchy of protected interests described in this chapter.

Leaving theory to one side, however, it seems that, for the present, extended *Hedley Byrne* liability marks the limits of recovery for economic loss. Yet a final note of caution must be entered. In *White v Jones* the notion of assumption of responsibility was broadened beyond predictable limits, and the previous insistence on claimant reliance was abandoned. The cynic may therefore conclude that if one looks hard enough, and wants to find one, a *Hedley Byrne* relationship may nearly always be discovered. And if

---

[202] [1986] AC 785. Note that in this case as in others, an essential difficulty in imposing a duty in tort derives from the relationship between D's contractual duty to a third party and the purported tortious duty to C. If D (the shippers) had excluded or limited their duty in contract to the sellers, how would that exclusion or limita-tion affect their duty in tort? See the judgment of Robert Goff LJ in the Court of Appeal: [1985] QB 350, at 399.

[203] But what happens where there is dislocation in time between the time at which D is negligent (C having no proprietary interest at that stage) and the time at which the negligence causes harm (by which time C does have a proprietary interest)? For the suggestion that an interest at the time of harm occurring is enough see *The Starsin* [2001] 1 Lloyd's Rep 437.

[204] Witting, 'Distinguishing Between Property Damage and Pure Economic Loss in Negligence: A Personal-ity Thesis' [2001] *Legal Studies* 481, 489.

this argument is accepted, the assumption of responsibility test tends to collapse into little more than a means of illustrating the requisite degree of proximity between the claimant and the defendant for the purposes of the more orthodox tripartite *Caparo* test.[205]

FURTHER READING

Hepple, 'Negligence: The Search for Coherence' (1997) 50 *Current Legal Problems* 69

Jones, 'Liability for Psychiatric Damage: Walking a Path Between Pragmatism and Principle' in Neyers (ed), *Emerging Issues in Tort Law* (2007)

Mullany, 'Hillsborough Replayed' (1998) 113 LQR 410

Mullany and Handford, *Tort Liability for Psychiatric Damage: The Law of Nervous Shock* (1993)

Murphy, 'The Civil Liability of Obstetricians for Injuries Sustained During Childbirth' (1994) 10 *Professional Negligence* 94

Stapleton, 'Duty of Care and Economic Loss: A Wider Agenda' (1991) 107 LQR 249

Stapleton, 'Duty of Care: Peripheral Parties and Alternative Opportunities for Deterrence' (1995) 111 LQR 301

Teff, 'Liability for Negligently Inflicted Psychiatric Harm: Justifications and Boundaries' [1998] CLJ 91

Witting, 'Distinguishing Between Property Damage and Pure Economic Loss: A Personality Thesis' [2001] *Legal Studies* 481

Witting, 'Duty of Care – An Analytical Approach' (2005) 25 OJLS 33

---

[205] For oblique support for this suggested synergy between the 'assumption test' and the '*Caparo* test', see the recent decision of the House of Lords in *Customs and Excise Commissioners v Barclays Bank* [2006] UKHL 28.

4

BREACH OF DUTY

SECTION 1 THE STANDARD OF CARE

So far, only the range of persons to whom the defendant owes a duty of care and the types of harm to which the duty of care extends have been considered. Although it is not uncommon for the standard of care to be treated as part of the 'duty', it seems preferable to confine 'duty' to the question of whether the defendant is under an obligation to the claimant and to treat separately the question of the extent of the duty owed. The conduct of the defendant, and especially the nature of the duty of care imposed on him or her, must therefore now be considered. The question, as a whole, of whether the defendant has broken a duty of care is a mixed one of law and fact;[1] but the standard of care required of the defendant is an exclusively legal construct and based on the standard of a hypothetical reasonable person. If the defendant causes loss or injury to the claimant, but is able to show that he acted in a way that a reasonable person would have acted, no liability will attach.[2]

In *Glasgow Corpn v Muir*, Lord Thankerton explained (after deciding that the appellants owed a duty to take reasonable care for the safety of children on the premises), that a further question had to be settled, namely, 'the test by which ... the standard of care is to be judged'.[3] Similarly, in *Bolton v Stone*, Lord Normand commenced his speech as follows:

My Lords, it is not questioned that the occupier of a cricket ground owes a duty of care to persons on an adjacent highway or on neighbouring property who may be in the way of balls driven out of the ground by the batsman. But it is necessary to consider the measure of the duty owed.[4]

In relation to the question of the 'measure of the duty owed', *Paris v Stepney Borough Council*[5] is also instructive. For in that case – where a claim in negligence was brought by a workman, blind in one eye, who had been injured in his one good eye while working without the use of goggles – Lord Oaksey stated that 'the duty of an employer towards his servant is to take reasonable care for the servant's safety in all the circumstances of the case'.[6] Taking a lead from this guidance, subsequent cases have

---

[1] See, eg, *Barber v Somerset CC* [2004] 1 WLR 1089: the appeal to the House of Lords turned on the question of whether the Court of Appeal had been entitled to disturb the trial judge's finding of fact that D had failed to meet the standard of reasonable care.   [2] See, eg, *Al-Sam v Atkins* [2005] EWCA Civ 1452.

[3] [1943] AC 448, at 454.   [4] [1951] AC 850, at 860.   [5] [1951] AC 367.

[6] [1951] AC 367, at 384(emphasis added).

now made clear that, as a matter of law, if A owes B a duty of care, A must attain the standard of a 'reasonable person' in order to discharge that duty. In short, the duty is one to take *reasonable care*.

The courts have recourse to a range of considerations in deciding whether this standard has been met. Some of these concern matters extraneous to the defendant – such as whether he acted in an emergency situation created by no fault of his own – while others refer to attributes of the defendant, not as an individual, but as a member of a class, such as his standing as a professional person possessing (or at least professing to possess) certain skills. The factors considered here reflect those commonly referred to by the courts, but they are not presented on the basis that they constitute an absolutely comprehensive list.

SECTION 2 FACTORS RELEVANT TO ESTABLISHING THE REQUIRED STANDARD[7]

(A) FACTORS EXTRANEOUS TO THE DEFENDANT

(1) THE LIKELIHOOD OF HARM

Lord Wright in *Northwestern Utilities Ltd v London Guarantee and Accident Co Ltd* said:

The degree of care which that duty involves must be proportioned to the degree of risk involved if the duty of care should not be fulfilled.[8]

The amount of caution required tends to increase with the likelihood that the defendant's conduct will cause harm, and *vice versa*. *Bolton v Stone*[9] provides a good illustration:

Miss Stone was hit by a cricket ball struck from a cricket ground surrounded by a fence 17 feet above the level of the square. The batsman was 80 yards away. The ball was only the 6th in about 30 years to be hit out of the ground. The House of Lords held that there had been no breach of duty by the club in allowing cricket to be played without taking further precautions.

Lord Radcliffe stressed two points: first, the fact that the ball had to clear the fence which itself was a remote possibility and, secondly, that, having cleared the fence the ball would then have to strike a passer-by (an even more remote possibility). Lord Oaksey said:

an ordinarily careful man does not take precautions against every foreseeable risk . . . life would be almost impossible if he were to attempt to take precautions against every risk.[10]

---

[7] See Kidner, 'The Variable Standard of Care, Contributory Negligence and *Volenti*' [1991] *Legal Studies* 1.

[8] [1936] AC 108, at 126(approved by Lord Normand in *Paris v Stepney Borough Council* [1951] AC 367, at 381). Cf Cardozo CJ, in *Palsgraf v Long Island Railroad Co* 284 NY 339(1928): 'The risk reasonably to be perceived defines the duty to be obeyed', and Lord Macmillan in *Glasgow Corpn v Muir* [1943] AC 448, at 456: 'the degree of care required varies directly with the risk involved'. [9] [1951] AC 850.

[10] [1951] AC 850, at 863.

In *Bolton v Stone*, the chance of harm occurring was so small that a reasonable person in the position of the cricket club could not be expected to take additional precautions against such a remote possibility. By contrast, where the risk of injury to a road user from a football being kicked from a patch of open land was much greater, the defendant responsible for the land was held to be in breach of a duty of care.[11]

Furthermore, it is important to appreciate that the test is not one, merely, of whether the risk in question was foreseeable. Instead, the standard of care is set at a level which is commensurate with the degree of risk. That said, the fact that contemplation of possible risks does not reveal them to be present – in other words, the fact that they remain unforeseen – does provide good evidence that the risk involved was sufficiently slight so as not to require the taking of precautions.[12]

Finally, particular vulnerability on the part of the claimant will be taken to increase the likelihood of harm if the defendant knew, or ought to have known, of that vulnerability. This should not be seen as subjectivizing the standard of care: it is just that the standard of care is judged according to the standard of what the reasonable, prudent defendant would do given actual or constructive knowledge of the claimants vulnerability. Thus, in *Barber v Somerset CC*,[13] for example, it was held by the Court of Appeal that an overworked teacher known to his employers to be suffering from stress was entitled to be treated according to the standard of a reasonable and prudent employer taking positive steps for the safety of his workers in the light of what he knew or ought to have known about their susceptibilities.

(2) THE MAGNITUDE OF HARM

Just as the likelihood of harm affects the standard of care demanded, so too does the magnitude of that harm. In *Paris v Stepney Borough Council*[14] the House of Lords held that the gravity of the consequences of an accident befalling an already disabled man had to be taken into account in fixing the level of care required of the defendant.[15] Thus, the risk to the only good eye of the claimant in that case was a material consideration in fixing the standard of care. For a normally sighted individual, there would have been 'merely' the risk of being struck and blinded in one eye. For the claimant, however, the risk of being struck in his one good eye meant a risk of total blindness.

---

[11] *Hilder v Associated Portland Cement Manufacturers Ltd* [1961] 1 WLR 1434. See also *Miller v Jackson* [1977] QB 966 (breach of duty where cricket balls were struck out of a ground about eight or nine times every season).

[12] *Orange v Chief Constable of West Yorkshire* [2002] QB 347(drunken prisoner committed suicide in a police cell; there was no evidence to suggest he was a suicide risk: no breach of duty to prevent suicide by placing him in a cell without the kind of horizontal bar from which he hanged himself).

[13] [2004] 1 WLR 1089. See also *Haley v LEB* [1965] AC 778: D's standard of care was set according to the fact that D ought to have foreseen the possibility of blind persons coming into the vicinity of the hole dug by D in the pavement.   [14] [1950] 1 KB 320.

[15] [1951] AC 367. Cf *Withers v Perry Chain Co Ltd* [1961] 3 All ER 676 (the health risk to C had to be balanced against her interest in keeping her job).

(3) THE SOCIAL UTILITY OF THE DEFENDANT'S ACT

In setting the standard of care, the courts will also take into account any relevant social utility associated with the defendant's conduct. This involves determinations of the general public interest so that matters other than merely those in dispute between the claimant and defendant may be taken into account in assessing the standard of care required of the defendant. A good illustration of such an approach can be found in the case law concerning the standard of care demanded of doctors counselling patients on the risks of proposed medical treatment. In *Sidaway v Bethlem Royal Hospital*[16] the House of Lords held by a majority of 4–1 that the test should be whether the doctor conformed to a practice of disclosure sanctioned by responsible medical opinion. In rejecting the contention that the standard of care ought to be what the reasonable patient would want to know,[17] rather than what the reasonable doctor was prepared to tell, their Lordships made several references to what they saw as undesirable social consequences of adopting a patient-centred standard. These included the fact that patients might irrationally reject necessary treatment, that, in general,[18] lay people would not understand further information if they were given it, and their Lordships' view that most people were in any case content to leave the decision on the risk/benefit analysis to their doctors.

Daborn v Bath Tramways Motor Co Ltd[19] provides another useful illustration of this factor. The relevant issue was whether, during wartime, the driver of a left-hand-drive ambulance had been negligent in turning into a lane on the off-side of the road without giving a signal. Holding that she had not broken her duty of care, Asquith LJ said:

In determining whether a party is negligent, the standard of reasonable care is that which is reasonably to be demanded in the circumstances. A relevant circumstance to take into account may be the importance of the end to be served by behaving in this way or that. As has often been pointed out, if all the trains in this country were restricted to a speed of five miles an hour, there would be fewer accidents, but our national life would be intolerably slowed down. The purpose to be served, if sufficiently important, justified the assumption of abnormal risk. The relevance of this applied to the present case is this: during the war which was, at the material time, in progress, it was necessary for many highly important operations to be carried out by means of motor vehicles with left-hand drives, no others being available. So far as this was the case, it was impossible for the drivers of such cars to give the warning signals which could otherwise be properly demanded of them. Meanwhile, it was essential that the ambulance service should be maintained. It seems to me, in those circumstances, it would be demanding too high and an unreasonable standard of care from the drivers of such cars to say to them: 'Either you must give signals which the structure of your vehicle renders impossible or you must not drive at all'.[20]

---

[16] [1985] AC 871.

[17] The 'prudent patient' test is the standard adopted in a number of American states: see, eg, *Canterbury v Spence* 464 F 2d 772(1972), at 780. This was the approach endorsed by Lord Scarman in his dissenting opinion in *Sidaway*. Note also the very different analysis of public interest by the High Court of Australia in *Rogers v Whittaker* [1993] 4 Med LR 79.

[18] But not where the lay-person happened to be a highly educated Law Lord: see *Sidaway v Bethlem Royal Hospital* [1985] AC 871, at 659, *per* Lord Diplock.`   [19] [1946] 2 All ER 333.

[20] [1946] 2 All ER 333, at 336. Cf *Quinn v Scott* [1965] 2 All ER 588, at 593, *per* Glyn Jones J: 'the safety of the public must take precedence over the preservation of the amenities and [I] cannot hold that the [National]

Similarly, what might be want of care towards an employee in a commercial enterprise will not necessarily be want of care towards a fireman, for 'one must balance the risk against the end to be achieved', and 'the commercial end to make profit is very different from the human end to save life or limb'.[21] As such, the extent of the duty owed by a police officer to a suspect whom he is pursuing must similarly be judged in the light of the end to be attained – that is the lawful arrest of the suspect.[22]

This taking into account of the social utility of the defendant's (would-be) activities has now been given statutory force. By section 1 of the Compensation Act 2006, it is now provided that where a court is considering a claim in negligence, it shall, in setting the required standard of care, 'have regard to whether a requirement to take those steps [necessary to meet that standard] might (a) prevent a desirable activity from being undertaken at all, to a particular extent or in a particular way, or (b) discourage persons from undertaking functions in connection with a desirable activity'. Since it reflects the existing law, it is suggested that this provision is unlikely to have any material impact on the way in which the courts approach the question of breach of duty. And while this suggestion is of course borne of speculation, it is at least a case of informed speculation since a rather similar provision contained in a piece of New South Wales legislation has caused no appreciable change to the common law in that jurisdiction.[23] Perhaps the most useful observation that can be made in relation to section 1 is that it provides an example of distributive justice concerns featuring in the English law of tort.

Whether the utility of what the defendant has done was already implicit within other legislation is a moot point. Take first *Budden v BP Oil Ltd.*[24]

An action was brought on behalf of a child alleging that the child had suffered brain damage caused by excessive lead in his blood. The high level of lead was assumed to result from lead particles emitted from vehicles using petrol supplied by D. The lead had been deliberately added to the petrol. Parliament was progressively phasing down the permitted lead content in petrol. At the time of the child's injury the level of lead in petrol complied with the permitted limits but would not have done so later. The relevant legislation did not provide that it was a defence to any action that the limit was not exceeded – it merely made it a crime to exceed the limit.

The Court of Appeal held that, in setting the limit, Parliament must be regarded as having conclusively determined what lay in the public interest and that it must also be

---

Trust's duty to care for the countryside diminishes to any degree the duty not to subject users of this highway to unnecessary danger'.

[21] *Watt v Hertfordshire County Council* [1954] 2 All ER 368, at 371, *per* Denning LJ. On the other hand, where D can reasonably expect that others will take care for their own safety, and where the cost of eliminating a danger would involve the removal of a social amenity, the social amenity's benefit may well outweigh the obvious risks that exist: see *Tomlinson v Congleton BC* [2004] 1 AC 46 (but note that this is technically a case of whether there was breach of the duty owed under the Occupiers' Liability Act 1984).

[22] *Marshall v Osmond* [1983] QB 1034. See also *Rigby v Chief Constable of Northamptonshire* [1985] 2 All ER 985 (police using CS gas in a shop to flush out a dangerous psychopath).

[23] See Civil Liability Act 2002(NSW), s 5B(2)(d).   [24] (1980) 124 Sol Jo 376.

regarded as having taken into account all the relevant factors, of which health risk was only one. As such, at the relevant time, it could be concluded that it was reasonable to add that amount of lead to petrol. But should the courts have felt themselves precluded by Parliament in that instance from making an independent judgment on the standard of care in a negligence action? The legislation was silent on civil liability for lead-induced injury. By contrast, in *Froom v Butcher*,[25] the key issue was whether the claimant was contributorily negligent in not wearing a seatbelt. At the time of the accident, legislation to make the wearing of seatbelts compulsory (and the non-use of them a crime) had not yet been passed. The Court of Appeal nonetheless felt able to conclude that not wearing a seatbelt constituted contributory negligence.

(4) EMERGENCIES

Closely related to the previous factor is that of acts undertaken in an emergency. Frequently, a defendant may act in an emergency, with little time for reflective decision-making, in a manner that falls below the standard of care normally expected of him.[26] It is equally the case that he may act somewhat incautiously in an emergency with a view to assisting another. In either case, the courts will fix the appropriate standard of care mindful of the circumstances. *Watt v Hertfordshire County Council*[27] provides a good illustration.

The fire service in this case was called upon to save a woman trapped under an over-turned lorry. In order to do so, they needed to use a heavy jack that stood on wheels. They could not transport the jack in the usual vehicle because that vehicle was otherwise engaged. They instead tried to get the jack to the required destination in a surrogate vehicle. While en route, the driver of the vehicle made an emergency stop causing the jack to shoot forwards whereupon it injured C, one of the firemen.

It was held that there was no breach of duty given the short amount of time that the fire service had to act, and in view of the endeavour they were making to save the woman trapped underneath a lorry. On the other hand, it is important to appreciate that an emergency does not exonerate the defendant from displaying any level of care at all; it merely reduces the standard demanded. Thus, if a fire engine goes recklessly through a red light on the way to a fire, there may still be liability.[28]

(5) THE RELATIVE COST OF AVOIDING THE HARM

It is relevant to consider how extensive and costly would be the measures necessary to eliminate the risk. In essence there is a balancing of costs: the cost of averting a danger

---

[25] [1976] QB 286.
[26] Many of the cases on the standard of care in emergencies deal with contributory negligence: see, eg, *Jones v Boyce* (1816) 1 Stark 493. On primary liability and emergency, see *Parkinson v Liverpool Corpn* [1950] 1 All ER 367; *Ng Chun Pui v Lee Chuen Tat* [1988] RTR 298; *Marshall v Osmond* [1983] QB 1034.
[27] [1954] 2 All ER 368. See also *S (A Child) v Keyse* [2001] All ER (D) 236.
[28] *Ward v London County Council* [1938] 2 All ER 341.

measured against the cost of the danger transpiring.[29] In *Latimer v AEC Ltd*[30] an exceptional storm had caused a factory floor to become flooded. When the water receded, the floor was found to be covered with a slimy mixture of oil and water so that its surface was slippery. The issue was whether the factory owners were in breach of their duty towards a workman who, some hours later, was injured through slipping on the floor. In holding there to have been no breach, Lord Tucker said:

The only question was: Has it been proved the floor was so slippery that, remedial steps not being possible, a reasonably prudent employer would have closed down the factory rather than allow his employees to run the risks involved in continuing work?[31]

In *The Wagon Mound (No 2)* the Judicial Committee stated, in similar vein:

A reasonable man would only neglect . . . a risk [of small magnitude] if he had some valid reason for doing so, eg, that it would involve considerable expense to eliminate the risk.[32]

But just how far can this principle be stretched? In the case of a private individual or enterprise there comes a point where, if the defendant lacks the resources to minimize a significant risk of injury to others, he must cease to engage in the relevant activity. Put otherwise, if the defendant does not possess sufficient resources to undertake an activity with reasonable care, then he should not engage in it at all. Thus, if a sports club cannot afford to replace a wooden spectator stand constituting a fire risk, for example, it should not allow spectators to use that stand.[33] By contrast, where the defendant is a public authority, the position may well be different. In *Knight v Home Office*[34] the claimant's husband committed suicide while detained in a prison hospital wing. The judge accepted that the standard of care and supervision for suicidal prisoners may well have fallen below that to be expected in an NHS psychiatric facility. Yet he dismissed her claim saying:

In making the decision as to the standard demanded the court must . . . bear in mind as one factor that resources available for the public service are limited and that the allocation of resources is a matter for Parliament.[35]

What arguably justifies such a finding is the fact that public authorities are notoriously short of resources, in which case a lack of resources is something that would characterise even the reasonable public authority in the position of the defendant.

---

[29] The idea is that if great expense is required to reduce only slightly an existing risk, then it will be acceptable to do nothing. The American judge, Learned Hand, in *United States v Carroll Towing Co* 159 F 2d 169 (1947), at 173 expressed the matter in terms of a formula: 'if the probability be called P; the injury, L; and the burden, B; liability depends upon whether B is less than L multiplied by P; ie, whether $B < PL$'.

[30] [1952] 2 QB 701, at 711. Cf *Watt v Hertfordshire County Council* [1954] 2 All ER 368 (duty of fire authority to firemen in respect of equipment) where the *dictum* of Asquith LJ, in *Daborn v Bath Tramways Motor Co Ltd* [1946] 2 All ER 333 was also approved.   [31] [1953] AC 643, at 659.

[32] [1967] 1 AC 617, at 642. For the relevance of D's financial resources, see *Goldman v Hargrave* [1967] 1 AC 645, at 663.   [33] See *Latimer v AEC* [1953] AC 643, at 659.

[34] [1990] 3 All ER 237.

[35] [1990] 3 All ER 237, at 243. See the similar reasoning in *Walker v Northumberland County Council* [1995] 1 All ER 737: 'The practicability of remedial measures must clearly take into account the resources and facilities

(6) THE 'HURLY BURLY' OF LIFE

The tort of negligence does not demand perfection.[36] It does not require that those to whom a duty of care is owed should be safeguarded against every conceivable risk. The reasonable person test rests largely upon matters of common sense and the exigencies of everyday life. A good example of the allowance made by the law for the 'hurly burly of life' can be seen in cases relating to parental and quasi-parental duties. In *Carmarthenshire County Council v Lewis*[37] the defendant council were held liable when a small boy wandered out of his nursery school and onto a nearby road causing an accident in which the claimant's husband died. The council were negligent because premises where there are small children should be designed to ensure that children cannot wander off endangering themselves or others. But Lord Reid said that the teacher who had not noticed the boy leave her classroom while she attended to a child with a cut knee was not negligent.[38] The gist of his reasoning was that those in charge of small children cannot have eyes in the back of their heads.

In *Surtees v Kingston-upon-Thames Borough Council*[39] a child was scalded when her foster mother left her for a moment or two by a wash-basin and she somehow managed to turn on the hot tap and ran scalding water over her foot. The majority of the Court of Appeal held that the foster mother's apparent oversight was not negligence. Courts should be slow to characterize incidents in family life as negligence 'given the rough and tumble of home life'. Beldam LJ dissented. He argued that it would have required only momentary thought to remove the child from the vicinity of the tap. Was the majority decision fair to the injured child or does it go further than simply acknowledging the realities of life and its conflicting demands? Was the court in effect saying reasonable mothers make mistakes and should not be penalized for them? In other contexts, such as professional liability, no such allowance is made. Perhaps the concept of children suing their parents is seen as unedifying? Or was the Court of Appeal simply acknowledging that a risk-free existence is not feasible, nor in all circumstances desirable. In *Porter v Barking and Dagenham London Borough Council*[40] a 14-year-old boy, injured when he and a friend were allowed to practice the shot-put unsupervized, failed in his action for negligence against the school authorities. The standard of care in relation to children should not be framed so as to stifle initiative.

---

at the disposal of the person or body owing the duty of care and the purpose of the activity giving rise to the risk of injury'.

[36] See *Banque Bruxelles Lambert SA v Eagle Star Insurance Co Ltd* [1997] AC 191, where, in considering whether there had been a negligent valuation, the court recognised as reasonable a range of different valuations. See also *Caldwell v Maguire and Fitzgerald* [2002] PIQR P45.　　　　[37] [1955] AC 549.

[38] [1955] AC 549, at 564. See also *Kearn-Price v Kent County Council* [2003] PIQR P11(no liability in respect of injury to a pupil sustained in a school yard before school started).　　　　[39] [1991] 2 FLR 559.

[40] (1990) *Times*, 9 April.

(7) GENERAL PRACTICE OF THE COMMUNITY

Commonly, a defendant will support his claim to have exercised due care by showing that he conformed to the common practice of those engaged in the activity in question. Such evidence is obviously relevant. Indeed, conforming to the practice of a trade or profession will often (but not always) be conclusive in claims against tradesmen[41] or professionals. So a specialist who failed to diagnose the complaint of the claimant was held not to have been negligent when he used the normal methods of British medical specialists, although the use of an instrument usually employed in the United States might have resulted in a correct diagnosis.[42] By contrast, consider *Cavanagh v Ulster Weaving Co Ltd*.

C slipped coming down a roof ladder. Despite unchallenged evidence that the 'set-up' was in perfect accord with established practice, the House of Lords restored the jury's verdict that D was negligent.[43]

Commercial enterprises must take steps to keep abreast of scientific developments. Growing understanding of the effects of industrial noise and its role as a causative factor in deafness was not matched by action by employers. In *Thompson v Smith's Shiprepairers (North Shields) Ltd*[44] it was held that once there was general awareness of the dangers of noise, and after protective equipment became available from about 1963 onwards, the defendants could be made liable for hearing impairment caused after that date.

Failure to conform to a standard imposed by a statute, although of course it may constitute a breach of statutory duty, is not in itself conclusive evidence of negligence.[45] It may, however, constitute *prima facie* evidence.[46]

(B) FACTORS PERTAINING TO THE DEFENDANT

Before considering various attributes associated with the defendant that have the capacity to affect the standard of care demanded, it is useful to consider a fundamental background principle concerning negligence.

---

[41] *Gray v Stead* [1999] 2 Lloyd's Rep 559 (non-provision of buoyancy aids to trawlermen was not the norm, and thus D, who had failed to provide such aids, was not held liable).

[42] *Whiteford v Hunter* (1950) 94 Sol Jo 758. Cf *Vancouver General Hospital v McDaniel* (1934) 152 LT 56; *Wright v Cheshire County Council* [1952] 2 All ER 789.   [43] [1960] AC 145.

[44] [1984] QB 405.

[45] In *Powell v Phillips* [1972] 3 All ER 864, it was held that breach of the *Highway Code*, despite s 37(5) of the Road Traffic Act 1972, creates no presumption of negligence calling for an explanation. It is just one relevant circumstance. In *Trotman v British Railways Board* [1975] ICR 95, it was held that breach of a regulation in the British Railways' Rule Book created a rebuttable inference of negligence. A breach of a navigational bye-law is particularly cogent evidence of negligence: *Cayzer, Irvine & Co v Cannon Co* (1884) 9 App Cas 873, at 880–1, *per* Lord Blackburn.

[46] *Blamires v Lancashire and Yorkshire Rly Co* (1873) LR 8 Exch 283; *Phillips v Britannia Hygienic Laundry Co* [1923] 1 KB 539, at 548, *per* McCardie J (affd [1923] 2 KB 832); *Anglo-Newfoundland Development Co Ltd v Pacific Steam Navigation Co* [1924] AC 406, at 413, *per* Lord Dunedin. See also *Harrison v National Coal Board*

Negligence is the omission to do something that a reasonable man, guided upon those considerations which ordinarily regulate the conduct of human affairs, would do, or doing something which a prudent and reasonable man would not do.[47]

It follows from this definition that the standard of care is not the standard of the defendant himself, but of 'a man of ordinary prudence',[48] a man using 'ordinary care and skill',[49] a 'hypothetical' man.[50] Lord Macmillan said:

The standard of foresight of the reasonable man ... eliminates the personal equation and is independent of the idiosyncrasies of the particular person whose conduct is in question.[51]

In short, it is important to appreciate that the standard of care is objectively set. But even so, it is inaccurate to state that no reference may be made to the attributes of the particular defendant. The definition of the reasonable person is not complete unless the words 'in the circumstances' are appended. And, plainly, these words import the need to take account of the particular defendant. But the overwhelming majority of the cases that explicitly recognize the relevance of who the defendant is, do so in terms that eliminate considerations pertaining to the defendant's idiosyncrasies. Instead, they consider those of his attributes that are characteristic of a class to which the defendant belongs.

(1) CHILD DEFENDANTS

In *Mullin v Richards*[52] the Court of Appeal confirmed that, in relation to a child, the test is what degree of care and foresight can reasonably be expected of a child of the defendant's age. In that case, two 15-year-old girls were fooling about during a mathematics lesson, fencing with plastic rulers. One of the rulers snapped and a fragment of plastic entered the claimant's eye ultimately causing her to lose any effective sight in that eye. Adopting the approach of the High Court of Australia in *McHale v Watson*,[53] the Court of Appeal held that the claimant had failed to establish that her school-friend was negligent. A 15-year-old, unlike an adult, might well not foresee the risk of her behaviour, particularly as this kind of tomfoolery had never been banned at school, nor had any similar accident occurred previously. Some degree of irresponsibility may be expected of children playing together.[54]

[1951] AC 639; *National Coal Board v England* [1954] AC 403. And compliance with a statutory requirement does not exclude liability in negligence: *Bux v Slough Metals Ltd* [1974] 1 All ER 262. See also *Budden v BP Oil Ltd* (1980) 124 Sol Jo 376.

[47] *Blyth v Birmingham Waterworks Co* (1856) 11 Exch 781, at 784, *per* Alderson B.

[48] *Vaughan v Menlove* (1837) 3 Bing NC 468, at 475, *per* Tindal CJ.

[49] *Heaven v Pender* (1883) 11 QBD 503, at 507, *per* Brett MR.

[50] *King v Phillips* [1953] 1 QB 429, at 441, *per* Denning LJ.

[51] *Glasgow Corpn v Muir* [1943] AC 448, at 457. Cf the earlier *dictum* of Holmes J in *The Germanic* 196 US 589 (1904): 'The standard of conduct ... is an external standard, and takes no account of the personal equation of the man concerned'.

[52] [1998] 1 All ER 920. See also, in relation to contributory negligence, *Yachuk v Oliver Blais Co Ltd* [1949] AC 386; *Gough v Thorne* [1966] 3 All ER 398; *Morales v Eccleston* [1991] RTR 151.

[53] (1964) 111 CLR 384.   [54] *Mullin v Richards* [1998] 1 All ER 920, at 928, *per* Butler-Sloss LJ.

An unresolved question, in relation to the standard of care demanded of children, is whether the test is entirely objective or whether it will it take into account the child's *actual* mental ability, maturity and experience.[55]

(2) INTELLIGENCE AND KNOWLEDGE

The defendant's actions must conform to certain criteria expected of a person of normal intelligence in a given situation. It is no defence that someone acted 'to the best of his own judgment' if his 'best' is below that of the reasonable man.[56] A man whose intellect is lower than average is not thereby excused. And likewise, a woman whose intelligence is superior is not liable for failing to use those above-average qualities, unless she has professed to have some special skill or expertise in which case the law demands that she must manifest that skill or expertise to a reasonable degree.[57]

Two branches of knowledge must be considered separately. The first is that of memory and experience. If X had been on a certain highway several times, and a reasonable man who had been there as often would know that it was busy, then X also is expected to know it to be busy, even though his memory is so poor that he does not actually remember it. Similarly, people are deemed to know those things which adults from their experience are expected to know: that some things easily explode, that others burn, that gravity exists etc.[58] There is one refinement of this rule. Where, in the circumstances, the status of the defendant is relevant, the standard is set according to that status. Thus, in *Caminer v Northern and London Investment Trust* the knowledge required of a landowner with regard to elm trees on his estate, their proneness to disease, lack of wind resistance and the like, was of a standard between that of an urban observer and a scientific arboriculturist.[59] Taking a similar approach, the Privy Council in *The Wagon Mound (No 2)*[60] said that the shipowner was liable for a fire caused by discharging oil into Sydney harbour because the chief engineer should have known that the discharge created a real risk of the oil on the water catching fire. Finally, if someone elects to take on a particular task, albeit he is not an expert or professional in the field, he will be expected to have the necessary degree of knowledge to complete the task competently.[61]

Secondly, what knowledge of the facts and circumstances surrounding him must the defendant have? He will not be excused for failing to observe what a reasonable man

---

[55] Compare *Yachuk v Oliver Blais Co Ltd* [1949] AC 386, at 396 with *McHale v Watson* (1964) 111 CLR 384 where Owen J's yardstick was a 'child of the same age, intelligence and experience'.

[56] *Vaughan v Menlove* (1837) 3 Bing NC 468, at 474, *per* Tindal CJ.

[57] See *Wooldridge v Sumner* [1963] 2 QB 43.

[58] *Caminer v Northern and London Investment Trust* [1951] AC 88. Cf *Haynes v Harwood* [1935] 1 KB 146, at 153, *per* Greer LJ.

[59] [1951] AC 88, at 100, *per* Lord Normand. See also *Clarke v Holmes*(1862) 7 H & N 937 (employer required to know more about the dangers of unfenced machinery than workman); *Quinn v Scott* [1965] 2 All ER 588.

[60] [1967] 1 AC 617.

[61] See *Chaudhry v Prabhakar* [1989] 1 WLR 29 (friend agreeing to act as gratuitous agent in connection with the purchase of a car).

would have observed. Thus, a dock authority that does not know, but ought to know, that the dock is unsafe may be held negligent.[62] Furthermore, even if a reasonable person could not be expected to know something, he or she may be required to get and follow expert advice. Thus, the landlord of flats must consult a specialist engineer about the safety of his lift if he lacks the relevant expertise himself.[63] In addition, actual knowledge of the circumstances on the part of the defendant will increase the standard of care imposed,[64] although it is less clear that the greater one's memory or experience, the greater the standard of care imposed.

Knowledge – in particular expert knowledge – does not remain static over the years. Scientific and technological advances lead to constant revision of, and improvements in, safety standards. In a negligence action, therefore, the defendant must always be judged in the light of the state of scientific, technological or other expert knowledge which should have been available to him at the time of the alleged breach. Concrete evidence that a drug damaged a foetus is not conclusive evidence that either the doctor prescribing the drug, or the pharmaceutical company marketing the drug, were negligent.[65] The test in negligence must be: 'At the time when the drug was prescribed or marketed, should the risk of injury to the foetus have been foreseen?'. As Lord Denning put it, when a claimant sought damages in respect of a medical accident which had never occurred before: 'We must not look at the 1947 accident with 1954 spectacles'.[66]

(3) SKILL

It has been seen that a person's conduct must conform to the standard of a person of normal intelligence. When a person holds himself out as being capable of attaining standards of skill in relation to the public generally – for example, by driving a car – he is required to display the skill normally possessed by persons doing that thing.[67] A doctor failing to diagnose a disease cannot excuse himself by showing that he acted to the best of his skill if a reasonable doctor would have diagnosed it.[68] Nor can a young hospital doctor escape liability simply by pleading that he is inexperienced or overworked. He must still attain the level of competence expected from a person

---

[62] *Mersey Docks and Harbour Board Trustees v Gibbs* (1866) LR 1 HL 93.

[63] *Haseldine v Daw & Son Ltd* [1941] 2 KB 343, at 356, *per* Scott LJ.

[64] *Brooks v London and North Western Rly Co* (1884) 33 WR 167.

[65] The drug thalidomide undoubtedly caused serious deformities in babies whose mothers took the drug in early pregnancy. One of the major obstacles confronting claims for compensation by the damaged children was doubt whether, at the time the drug was first available, as opposed to after the births of several deformed babies, doctors and embryologists appreciated that drugs could cross the placental barrier and injure the foetus.

[66] *Roe v Minister of Health* [1954] 2 QB 66, at 84.

[67] It is immaterial if D does not in fact have that skill; if he engages in conduct usually associated with persons having that skill, the standard demanded is that of those who actually do possess that skill: *Adams v Rhymney Valley District Council* [2000] Lloyd's Rep PN 777. In *Nettleship v Weston* [1971] 2 QB 691, although the standard of a qualified driver was expected of a learner driver, the point was made that if a uniform standard were not applied, the courts would face insuperable difficulties in assessing the skills and competencies of every individual defendant.   [68] *Bolam v Friern Hospital Management Committee* [1957] 2 All ER 118.

holding his 'post' and entrusted with his responsibilities.[69] The same principle presumably applies to newly qualified solicitors.[70] But in such cases, one must be careful to ascertain exactly what skill the defendant did hold himself out to possess.

It is also important to realize that where a skilled person conforms to practices accepted as proper by *some* responsible members of his profession, he will not be held liable in negligence merely because other members of his trade or profession would take a different view. This principle is most frequently applied in the context of medical negligence where there are often differences in opinion as to the best way to address any given medical problem. In such circumstances, the courts will not choose between rival schools of professional thought.[71] Nor, in other circumstances where two non-negligent courses of action were possible, will the courts hold a defendant liable for failing to take that course which has been revealed, with the benefit of hindsight, to have been the preferable course.[72]

In one case in which the claimant had her ears pierced by a jeweller and subsequently contracted a disease that might have been avoided had the work been done with normal medical skill, the jeweller was required only to show the skill of a jeweller doing such work, not that of a doctor.[73] A similar approach was taken in *Wells v Cooper* where a householder fitted a new door handle insecurely. When the claimant pulled on it, he lost his balance and was injured. The defendant householder was only required to show the standard of care of a normal DIY enthusiast, not that of a qualified carpenter.[74] On the other hand, while someone who practises alternative medicine is only liable if he fails to meet the standard applicable to his art, it will nonetheless be relevant to take into account findings within conventional medicine which reveal dangers associated with aspects of his art.[75]

Where someone has not held himself out as having special skill, he is not liable when he shows merely average skill in the circumstances although he does in fact have special skill.[76] Skill, just like every other aspect of the standard of care, has to be assessed in the light of all the circumstances surrounding the alleged breach of duty, and the degree to which the defendant represents that he holds a particular skill is merely one among several considerations.

Where negligence is alleged in the course of playing a sport, the fact that the object of competitive sport is to win and the fact that spectators attend sporting occasions to see

---

[69] *Wilsher v Essex Area Health Authority* [1987] QB 730 (revsd on a different point [1988] AC 1074).

[70] *Nettleship v Weston* [1971] 2 QB 691, at 709, *per* Megaw LJ.

[71] *Bolam v Friern Hospital Management Committee* [1957] 2 All ER 118.

[72] *Adams v Rhymney Valley District Council* [2000] Lloyd's Rep PN 777. An example given in the case is of a driver who on approaching an amber light notices a car very close behind: should that driver pull up sharply and hope the car behind can avoid a collision, or should the driver risk a collision with another vehicle by proceeding through the junction?   [73] *Philips v William Whiteley Ltd* [1938] 1 All ER 566.

[74] [1958] 2 QB 265 If the householder employed a professional carpenter no doubt the latter would be under a contractual duty to him to use the skill of a professional, but what standard would the professional owe to members of the public?   [75] *Shakoor v Situ* [2001] 1 WLR 410.

[76] *Wooldridge v Sumner* [1962] 2 All ER 978, at 989, *per* Diplock J.

competitors exhibit their skill at the game will be relevant. So, in *Wooldridge v Sumner*[77] Diplock LJ held that where a show-jumper was concentrating his attention and exerting his skill to complete his round of the show-jumping circuit, this must be taken into account in determining whether a momentary misjudgement constituted negligence.[78] By contrast, in *Condon v Basi*[79] a footballer successfully managed to sue in negligence when he suffered a broken leg as a result of a tackle by the defendant which was found by the referee to be serious foul play. The Court of Appeal held that a clear breach of the rules of the game would be a relevant (though not conclusive consideration) in deciding whether there had been actionable negligence. The overall test – which has since been confirmed by the Court of Appeal[80] – is whether the defendant's disregard for the claimant's safety can be characterized as deliberate or reckless (bearing in mind the level of competency to be expected from players of the defendant's class) in which case the defendant will be held to be in breach.

(4) DISABILITY AND INFIRMITY?

It is unclear to what extent the standard of the reasonable person will be adjusted to allow for the incapacities and infirmities of individual adults. In *Daly v Liverpool Corpn*[81] it was held that in deciding whether a 67-year-old woman was guilty of contributory negligence in crossing a road, one had to consider a woman of her age, not a hypothetical pedestrian. But this is only a case on contributory negligence and it is, in any event, by no means easy to square with the objective approach advocated on many occasions since it was decided.

In practice, the matter of the defendant's disability or infirmity will seldom arise in respect of the standard of care demanded for the following reason. If X causes an injury to another because X suffers from some disability or infirmity, he will usually be held negligent, not because of want of care at the time of the accident, but because, being aware of his disability, he allowed himself to be in the situation in the first place. Thus, a motorist with seriously impaired eyesight who collides with another car because she fails to see it approaching is not negligent because she is partially sighted, but because, given her defective vision, she was careless enough to drive at the outset.

On the other hand, not all defendants will know of their problem. In *Roberts v Ramsbottom*,[82] for example, the defendant suffered a slight stroke just before getting into his car. He was completely unaware that he had had a stroke although he admitted that he felt somewhat dizzy. A few minutes after starting his journey he was involved in a collision injuring the claimant. It was held that even though his carelessness resulted from impaired consciousness of which he was, at the time of the collision, unaware, he was nonetheless liable in negligence. Neill J suggested two grounds to support the

---

[77] [1963] 2 QB 43.
[78] See, in similar vein, *Caldwell v Maguire and Fitzgerald* [2002] PIQR P45 (skill required of a jockey in a fast-moving sport).   [79] [1985] 2 All ER 453.
[80] *Caldwell v Maguire* [2002] PIQR P6; *Blake v Galloway* [2004] 1 WLR 2844.
[81] [1939] 2 All ER 142.   [82] [1980] 1 All ER 7.

finding of negligence. He said that the defendant was liable first, because he 'continued to drive when he was unfit to do so and when he should have been aware of his unfitness' and, secondly, because any disability affecting a defendant's ability to drive could only exempt him from the normal, objective standard of care where the disability placed his actions 'wholly beyond his control'. In *Mansfield v Weetabix Ltd*,[83] however, the Court of Appeal rejected the second of these reasons on the basis that it came close to equating liability in negligence with strict liability.[84] There, a lorry driver was involved in a collision when he partially lost consciousness as a result of a hypoglycaemic state induced by a malignancy of which he was completely unaware. Overruling the trial judge's finding of negligence, the Court of Appeal held that where a disability or infirmity prevented the defendant from meeting the objective standard of care, and the defendant was not, and could not reasonably have been, aware of his condition, that condition must be taken into account in determining whether or not the defendant was negligent.

It is submitted that *Mansfield* appears out of kilter with the general approach which overlooks the idiosyncrasies of the defendant *unless* it is interpreted as focusing on the standard of care of *all* defendants who suddenly become unconscious, instead of merely *this defendant* who suddenly became unconscious.

(5) SPECIAL KNOWLEDGE CONCERNING THE CLAIMANT

The defendant's actual knowledge of the claimant's frailties and susceptibilities will affect the required standard of care. Thus, the level of care owed to a woman known to be pregnant,[85] to a workman with one eye,[86] or to employees especially susceptible to stress[87] will take account of these conditions *so long as* the defendant knows of them. If the defendant neither knows, nor ought to know of these circumstances, however, the standard of care will be unaffected by the claimant's susceptibility. As Lord Sumner explained:

. . . a measure of care appropriate to the inability or disability of those who are immature or feeble in mind or body is due from others, who know of or ought to anticipate the presence of such persons within the scope and hazard of their own operations.[88]

In *Haley v London Electricity Board*[89] the House of Lords applied Lord Sumner's *dictum* when they held that a body conducting operations on a city highway should foresee that blind persons would walk along the pavement, and that it owes a duty to take those precautions reasonably necessary to protect them from harm. On the facts, it was held

---

[83] [1998] 1 WLR 1263.

[84] But the decision in *Nettleship v Weston* [1971] 2 QB 691 is hard to distinguish from strict liability!

[85] *Hay (or Bourhill) v Young* [1943] AC 92, at 109, *per* Lord Wright.

[86] *Paris v Stepney Borough Council* [1951] AC 367, at 385 and 386, *per* Lords Oaksey and Morton.

[87] *Sutherland v Hatton* [2002] PIQR P241.

[88] *Glasgow Corpn v Taylor* [1922] 1 AC 44, at 67. Of course, there are numerous cases where Ds have not been held in breach of a duty to infants (eg, *Donovan v Union Cartage Co Ltd* [1933] 2 KB 71) or to blind persons (eg, *Pritchard v Post Office*(1950) 114 JP 370).   [89] [1965] AC 778.

liable although a person with normal vision would not have been injured in consequence of its operations. Similarly, in *Johnstone v Bloomsbury Health Authority*[90] in which the level of care owed by an employer to junior doctors who were required to work excessive hours was in issue, Stuart Smith LJ said:

[I]t must be remembered that the duty of care is owed to an individual employee and different employees may have a different stamina. If the authority in this case knew or ought to have known that by requiring him to work the hours they did, they exposed him to risk of injury to his health, then they should not have required him to work in excess of the hours that he safely could have done.

It is no answer to a claim in negligence to respond that you did not appreciate the risk that your conduct would injure the claimant, if the reasonable defendant with your knowledge of the claimant and the circumstances would have perceived that risk. Human frailty must be taken into account and defendants cannot shift their duty to such claimants by arguing that all claimants must always look out for themselves. So, in *Pape v Cumbria County Council*[91] it was found to be insufficient for employers to supply their workers with rubber gloves. They had also to warn them of the risk of dermatitis unless the gloves were worn since the prudent employer would take all reasonable steps to ensure that safety equipment is properly understood and used by employees. By contrast, in *Eastman v South West Thames Regional Health Authority*[92] the defendants were held not liable when the claimant was thrown out of her seat in an ambulance and injured when the driver braked hard. She claimed that the driver had been negligent in not expressly instructing her to wear her seat-belt. But a notice in the ambulance carried just that instruction. The claimant was not herself a patient. She was accompanying her mother-in-law to hospital. The court held that the ambulance staff had done all that was reasonably required in the circumstances. Had the claimant been herself a sick and confused elderly lady, the outcome might well have been different.

(6) DEFENDANT'S ABILITY TO FORESEE ACTS OF THIRD PARTIES

Even where the courts are prepared to find a duty in respect of the act of third parties, it will often be difficult to decide, when there has been an intervening act of a third party, whether the defendant's act has caused the damage suffered by the claimant. It is important to note that the issue of causation becomes material only after the failure of the defendant to take due care has been proved. Whether the defendant has shown that standard of care will frequently depend on what acts or omissions of another he could reasonably have anticipated. If the claimant is injured because a third party has done something that the defendant could not reasonably foresee he would do, the defendant is not liable.[93] Yet, in *London Passenger Transport Board v Upson*,[94] Lord Uthwatt said:

It is common experience that many do not [assume a fellow road user will act with reasonable care]. A driver is not, of course, bound to anticipate folly in all its forms, but he is not, in my

---

[90] [1992] QB 333.   [91] [1992] 3 All ER 211.   [92] [1991] 2 Med LR 297.
[93] *Donaldson v McNiven* [1952] 2 All ER 691.   [94] [1949] AC 155.

opinion, entitled to put out of consideration the teachings of experience as to the form those follies commonly take.[95]

Nor can one excuse oneself by relying on another to do an act unless that reliance was reasonable. *Manchester Corpn v Markland*[96] illustrates the point.

The appellants were the statutory authority for the supply of water to the borough of Eccles. One of the appellants' service pipes in a road in Eccles burst. Three days later, the resulting pool of water froze, and a car skidded on the ice knocking down and killing a man. In a negligence action brought by the dependants of the deceased against the appellants, it was held to be no defence that the appellants chose to rely on Eccles Corporation to notify them of bursts: they should themselves have taken proper precautions.

SECTION 3 THE CONNECTION BETWEEN THE STANDARD AND DUTY OF CARE

Accepting, then, that the standard of care is fixed as a matter of law in the light of the *factual* considerations just outlined, one must ask the further question of whether the standard of care has to be particularized in detail in terms of 'duty'. A motorist fails to sound his horn at a crossing and is held liable in negligence to another motorist with whom he collides. The court holds that he should have sounded his horn. Would such a decision thenceforth be authority for the proposition that a motorist has a duty at law to sound his horn when approaching an intersection? Although such a suggestion is superficially attractive, we must be cautious of adopting this approach. In running down cases, for example, it will usually be relevant to consider the speed of the vehicles, the degree of visibility, the state of the road, the distance within which the vehicles could have pulled up etc. Also, how often will the facts of any particular case be exactly replicated in a subsequent case? Are not the circumstances of each case sufficiently different in at least one material respect to make it inapt to formulate a catalogue of duties based on each individual decision?

Given this backdrop, it is perhaps unsurprising that, in terms of judicial practice, the higher courts have generally[97] rejected forcefully attempts to particularise duties. In *Baker v E Longhurst & Sons Ltd*,[98] for example, Scrutton LJ appeared to lay down a principle that a person driving in the dark must be able to pull up within the limits of his vision. Shortly afterwards, in another road traffic case, Lord Wright said that:

no one case is exactly like another, and no principle of law can in my opinion be extracted from those cases. It is unfortunate that questions which are questions of fact alone should be

---

[95] [1949] AC 155, at 173. Cf *Grant v Sun Shipping Co Ltd* [1948] AC 549, at 567, *per* Lord Du Parcq.
[96] [1936] AC 360.
[97] Though, for the contrary approach see, eg, *Caminer v Northern and London Investment Trust Ltd* [1951] AC 88.   [98] [1933] 2 KB 461, at 468.

confused by importing into them as principles of law a course of reasoning which has no doubt properly been applied in deciding other cases on other sets of facts.[99]

When counsel again relied on the *dictum* of Scrutton LJ in *Morris v Luton Corpn*, Lord Greene adopted the *dictum* of Lord Wright 'in the hope that this suggested principle [of Scrutton LJ] may rest peacefully in the grave in future'.[100] Most important of all is the 1959 decision of the House of Lords in *Qualcast (Wolverhampton) Ltd v Haynes*.[101] There, the House of Lords went out of its way to stress that a judge's reasons for finding want of reasonable care are matters of fact, not law, for otherwise 'the precedent system will die from a surfeit of authorities'.[102] That judges now give reasons for conclusions formerly arrived at by juries without reasons must not be allowed to elevate these decisions of fact into propositions of law.

Naturally, in certain common kinds of claim – notably those arising out of road traffic accidents – factual situations do repeat themselves. Judges may properly refer to earlier decisions for guidance as to what constitutes reasonableness in the circumstances. The infinite variability of human conduct, however, makes it undesirable to express such a standard in terms of an inflexible legal duty. *Worsfold v Howe*[103] illustrates the point.

D, a car driver, edged blind from a side road across stationary tankers and collided with a motorcyclist approaching on the main road past the tankers. Because the Court of Appeal had held in a previous case that a driver so edging out was not negligent, the trial judge felt bound to absolve D from liability.

The Court of Appeal held that the previous decision laid down no legal principle, that such decisions were to be treated as ones of fact, and, in the instant circumstances, held the defendant negligent. In *Foskett v Mistry*,[104] the Court of Appeal reinforced that approach. They ruled that, in running down claims, the question of whether reasonable care had been taken must be judged in the light of all the facts of the particular incident.

SECTION 4 PROFESSIONAL NEGLIGENCE[105]

(A) THE BACKGROUND

There is, in terms of fundamental principle, no distinction between the guidelines ascertaining the standard of care of professionals from those applicable to any other person. Whether the defendant is a plumber or an architect or a consultant surgeon, the primary question is whether in all the circumstances the defendant acted with the skill

---

[99] *Tidy v Battman* [1934] 1 KB 319, at 322. Cf *SS Heranger (Owners) v SS Diamond (Owners)* [1939] AC 94, at 101.　　[100] [1946] KB 114, at 116. See also *Easson v London and North Eastern Rly Co* [1944] KB 421.

[101] [1959] AC 743.　　[102] [1959] 2 All ER 38, at 43–4, *per* Lord Somervell.

[103] [1980] 1 All ER 1028.　　[104] [1984] RTR 1.

[105] For full treatment of this important topic, see Powell, *Jackson and Powell on Professional Negligence* (2005).

and competence to be expected from a person undertaking his particular activity and professing his specific skill. But problems do arise in actions against professionals, and include the following:

(1) There may be disputes within the profession as to what constitutes proper practice.

(2) The implications of professional negligence are likely to be more far reaching. When a carpenter makes an error fixing a new door, the householder may suffer personal injury if the door falls off, but the range of potential harm is limited. Should an architect make a design error in his plans for a tower block of flats, however, hundreds of people are at risk, and the financial cost of correcting the error in several blocks of flats may be astronomic.

(3) The potentially high cost of professional negligence has resulted in massive increases in insurance premiums for architects, solicitors, accountants etc. Many professions are now calling for statutory limits on damages awards made against the relevant professionals even though limited liability partnerships can help.

(4) Particularly acute difficulties affect doctors. Limited funding of the NHS can mean that doctors may often be overworked and hospitals under-resourced, and patients increasingly wish to play a greater part in decision-making these days.

(5) Finally, and rather obviously, a professional defendant will normally be worth suing. The rules of the profession are likely to oblige him to take out professional indemnity cover. On the other hand, professional negligence actions are thus apt to be defended vigorously by the professional backed by his insurers.

Some further guidelines are therefore given here on the current state of the law in England and Wales relating to professional negligence.

(B) DUTY AND BREACH

Very often, the duty of care will arise concurrently in tort and within the contract between the professional and his client. Save where an NHS professional is treating a patient, most professional/client relationships are founded on a contract for services. The client, for example, pays the solicitor or the accountant for her advice. A duty of care will be implied into that contract,[106] but will a duty in tort arise concurrently allowing the client to opt whether to sue in contract or tort? After years of conflicting decisions, the House of Lords in *Henderson v Merrett Syndicates Ltd*[107] ruled in favour of concurrent liability providing that imposing a duty in tort does not conflict with the contractual terms agreed between the parties.[108] When duties of care do arise concurrently, the question of whether there has been a breach of duty will generally be

---

[106] See s 13 of the Supply of Goods and Services Act 1982.   [107] [1995] 2 AC 145.

[108] Note, also, *Bellefield Computer Services Ltd v E Turner & Sons Ltd* [2002] EWCA Civ 1823 in which the limit of the contractual duty was relevant to construing the limit of the tortious duty.

determined on exactly the same principles, whether the action is framed in tort or contract. However, contract may impose duties beyond those covered by the tortious duty of care.

In *Thake v Maurice*[109] a surgeon failed to warn a private patient of the risk that a vasectomy may be reversed by nature restoring the patient's fertility. The patient argued that the surgeon contracted to render him sterile and that he was therefore liable for that breach of contract regardless of whether or not he was negligent when the patient's wife conceived again. The Court of Appeal eventually held, by a majority, that no reasonable man would infer from his contract with a doctor that the doctor guaranteed success.[110]

The case graphically illustrates the separate roles of tort and contract where the claimant seeks to establish a liability independent of classic negligence. The argument pursued by the claimant – that sterility would be guaranteed – could not even have been attempted had he been an NHS patient.

In a number of professional relationships, the core of the professional's duty is to offer advice. Liability in negligence will depend largely on the principles governing liability for negligent misstatements. In *Caparo Industries plc v Dickman*,[111] auditors prepared a report on a company on the basis of which the claimant mounted a successful takeover bid of that company. The claimants alleged that the report negligently suggested pre-tax profits of £1.2m when in fact there had been losses of £400,000. The House of Lords held that no duty was owed to the claimants. Mere foreseeability of financial loss to a third party was insufficient to create a duty on the part of the professional. For a duty to arise to a third party: (1) the professional must be aware that his advice will be transmitted to the claimant, or to an identifiable class of persons of which the claimant is a member; (2) that advice must be transmitted in order to forward a specific purpose or transaction of the claimants; (3) it must be reasonable in all the circumstances for the claimant to rely on that advice, rather than to seek independent advice of his own, and the professional must be well aware that the claimant will so rely on his advice.[112] But note that no duty will be owed if the professional's contract with his or her client conflicts with the alleged duty owed to a third party.[113]

(C) THE REASONABLE PROFESSIONAL

The basic test of whether the defendant conformed to the standard of the 'reasonable professional', must be elaborated a little. The defendant must exhibit the degree of skill which a member of the public would expect from a person in his or her position.

---

[109] [1986] QB 644. See also *Eyre v Measday* [1986] 1 All ER 488.

[110] But the Court of Appeal unanimously held the surgeon liable in negligence. The failure to warn was held to be negligent, and as a result the wife failed to recognize the symptoms of pregnancy soon enough to be able to opt for an abortion.   [111] [1990] 2 AC 605.

[112] For examples of these criteria being fulfilled, see *Smith v Bush* [1990] 1 AC 831 and *White v Jones* [1995] 2 AC 207.   [113] See, eg, *Clarke v Bruce Lance & Co* [1988] 1 All ER 364.

Pressures on him – even pressures for which he is in no way responsible – will not excuse an error on his part. Negligence is not to be equated with moral culpability or general incompetence. In *Wilsher v Essex Area Health Authority*,[114] for example, a premature baby was admitted to a specialist neo-natal unit. An error was made in that the medical staff failed to notice that the baby was receiving too much oxygen and the baby became blind. The Court of Appeal held that the doctors were negligent and, by a majority, that they must be judged by reference to their 'posts' in the unit. It would be irrelevant that they were inexperienced, or doing a job which should have been done by a consultant, or just grossly overworked. The dissenting judge argued that the doctors should be assessed individually. If a particular doctor was too junior for his 'post', then it should be the health authority that was directly liable to the claimant for providing inadequate staffing and resources.[115]

In determining the standard demanded in a particular 'post', expert evidence of proper practice must be called. Where practice is disputed, however, conformity with a responsible body of opinion within the profession will generally suffice.[116] Nonetheless, the court remains the ultimate arbiter of what constitutes reasonable and responsible professional practice. In *Edward Wong Finance Co Ltd v Johnson*,[117] the defendant solicitors followed a uniform practice among the profession in Hong Kong. They paid the purchase price to the vendors in return for the promise to ensure that the property was free of encumbrances. The vendors fraudulently failed to do so, and the claimant thus failed to obtain an unencumbered title to the property. The Privy Council held that, while evidence of the practice of the profession went a long way towards showing that the defendant was not negligent, it was not conclusive. The risk of fraud should have been foreseen and precautions taken to avoid that risk.

Until recently, judges in claims against doctors seemed more than usually unwilling to challenge expert professional opinion. Lord Scarman castigated a trial judge for presuming to prefer one body of distinguished professional opinion to another.[118] However, in *Bolitho v City and Hackney Health Authority*,[119] Lord Browne-Wilkinson stressed that to constitute evidence of proper, non-negligent practice, expert opinion must be shown to be reasonable and responsible: 'the court has to be satisfied that the exponents of the body of opinion relied on can demonstrate that such opinion has a logical basis'.[120] If 'in a rare case' it can be shown that professional opinion cannot withstand logical analysis, then in a claim against a doctor, as much as in a claim against any other professional, a judge is entitled to find that expert opinion is not reasonable or responsible.

Errors of judgment are often the essence of professional negligence. An error of itself is not negligence. The issue in all cases is whether the error in question evidenced

---

[114] [1987] QB 730 (reversed on the issue of causation [1988] AC 1074).

[115] On the direct liability of health authorities to patients see Murphy, 'The Juridical Foundations of Common Law Non-Delegable Duties' in Neyers (ed), *Emerging Issues in Tort Law* (2007).

[116] *Bolam v Friern Hospital Management Committee* [1957] 2 All ER 118.   [117] [1984] AC 296.

[118] *Maynard v West Midlands Regional Health Authority* [1984] 1 WLR 634, at 639.

[119] [1998] AC 232. See also *Hucks v Cole* [1993] 4 Med LR 393.   [120] [1997] 3 WLR 1151, at 1159.

a failure of professional competence. The virtual immunity offered to doctors for errors of clinical judgment was firmly condemned by the House of Lords in *Whitehouse v Jordan*. As Lord Edmund Davies put it:

The test [of negligence] is the standard of the ordinary skilled man exercising or professing to have that special skill. If a surgeon fails to measure up to that standard in any respect ('clinical judgment or otherwise) he has been negligent.[121]

In assessing that standard, care must be taken to relate what is expected of the professional to the expertise he claims to hold, and not to demand unrealistic standards of skill and knowledge. In *Luxmoore-May v Messenger May-Baverstock*[122] the claimant took a painting to a local auctioneer for valuation and sale. The defendants were held not liable for failing to discover that it was a painting by a well-known artist of the eighteenth century. Similarly, if a general practitioner were to be consulted by a patient complaining of stomach trouble, she would not be expected to have the same level of knowledge as a consultant gastro-enterologist. She must, however, recognize her own limitations and know when the patient needs to be referred to a specialist.

SECTION 5 BREACH OF AN EMPLOYER'S DUTY TO HIS EMPLOYEES

The risk of personal injury either suffered in an accident at work, or by contracting an industrial disease, is particularly acute in certain types of employment. The general liability of employers[123] remains liability in negligence alone but it is one of the most highly developed and thoroughly litigated areas of the law of negligence.[124] The circumstances in which an employer will be held to have been in breach of the duty he owes his employees thus warrants separate consideration.

As will be seen, some of the language deployed to analyse employers' responsibilities, is the language of duty. But despite this language, at the core of the majority of cases on employers' liability is the issue of the standard of care. The central question discussed here, therefore, is just what kinds of safeguards must employers put in place to discharge their duty in tort for the health and safety of their workers?

---

[121] [1981] 1 WLR 246, at 258.   [122] [1990] 1 All ER 1067.

[123] Of course in certain cases specific statutory duties in respect of safety are imposed on employers and in such cases an action for breach of statutory duty may lie: see ch 20. Breach of the general statutory code on safety provided for by the Health and Safety at Work Act 1974 is not actionable as a breach of statutory duty. Section 17(1) expressly provides that breach of the code of practice under the Act is not of itself tortious. But it may be that, in assessing negligence, judges may tend to treat conformity with the code as evidence that reasonable care has been taken (and vice versa).

[124] Compensation for industrial injuries is provided for by way of the state scheme relating to industrial injuries. Nonetheless, the higher level of common-law damages ensures that many employees continue to elect for the common-law remedy in negligence. In order to ensure that an employee awarded compensation for negligence against his employer receives the money due to him, the Employers' Liability (Compulsory Insurance)

(A) A PERSONAL, NON-DELEGABLE DUTY

The employer's duty is a personal one of a general nature. As will be seen later,[125] there is another form of tortious liability, known as vicarious liability, whereby an employer is held liable not for a breach of his own personal duty, but for the tort of his employee. Until the Law Reform (Personal Injuries) Act 1948, an employer sued by a workman on account of the employer's vicarious liability for the tort of a fellow-workman could successfully raise the defence of common employment. As such, the personal duties of employers have been kept strictly separate from those for which their responsibility is vicarious. It is true that, since that Act abolishes the defence of common employment, this strict marking off of personal duty has become less important in circumstances where the claimant can in any event prove fault by a fellow-employee. But it would be misleading to state that the distinction can now be ignored.[126] There will still be many cases where the employer is in breach of his personal duty without any employee being at fault.[127] Furthermore, the distinction remains the basis of judicial thinking on the subject, and the development and implications of the cases cannot be understood if this is not grasped.

Employers' responsibilities fall naturally into three divisions: (1) personnel (that is, the provision of competent staff); (2) those concerned with the place of work, machinery, tools and raw materials (that is, the provision of a safe place of work with proper plant and equipment); (3) the general management or system of work (including supervision).

An important feature of the employer's duty is the fact that it is non-delegable.

In *McDermid v Nash Dredging and Reclamation Co Ltd*[128] C was employed by Ds as a deckhand. He was sent to work on a rig owned by a Dutch company under the control of a Dutch captain employed by that Dutch company. C had no idea that he was not continuing to work on one of Ds' boats under one of Ds' captains. C suffered serious injuries as a result of the Dutch captain's carelessness. Ds denied responsibility on the basis that they were not vicariously liable for the conduct of someone else's employee. The House of Lords held Ds liable on very simple grounds. The evidence showed that C was injured because no safe system of work was in operation. The duty incumbent on his employers to devise and ensure the operation of such a system had not been fulfilled.

Act 1969 requires employers to insure against liability for injury sustained by employees in the course of their employment.

[125] Ch 24.

[126] See Murphy, 'The Juridical Foundations of Common Law Non-Delegable Duties' in Neyers (ed), *Emerging Issues in Tort Law* (2007).

[127] It may be that there is simply an inadequate system of working (see, eg, *General Cleaning Contractors Ltd v Christmas* [1953] AC 180); or it may be that the individual at fault is not an employee of the employer sued as in *McDermid v Nash Dredging and Reclamation Co Ltd* [1987] 3 WLR 212.

[128] [1987] AC 906. See also *Kondis v State Transport Authority* (1984) 154 CLR 672.

The essential characteristic of the employer's non-delegable duty:

is that, if it is not performed, it is no defence for the employer to show that he delegated its performance to a person, whether his servant or not his servant, whom he reasonably believed to be competent to perform it. Despite such delegation the employer is liable for the non-performance of the duty.[129]

Although the duty is personal, and cannot be discharged by entrusting it to a competent delegate, fault must still be proved for negligence liability to be imposed.[130] Thus, Lord Tucker has stressed the importance of not enlarging the employer's duty until it is barely distinguishable from his absolute statutory obligations.[131] On the other hand, an employer may be liable for a mere omission:[132] actual knowledge of a danger on his part is not insisted on; it suffices if he ought to have known of it.[133] It is a question of fact whether there has been a breach of the duty;[134] precedents relating to industrial practice form guidance as to an employer's breach of duty, but no more than that.[135] Compliance with common practice will constitute strong, but not conclusive, evidence that the employer has discharged his duty. Nevertheless, once a substantial risk of industrial disease, for example, is well known, failure to protect employees against that disease will be actionable even if it is the 'customary practice' of the trade to go on ignoring the risk.[136]

The same defences are available here as in the general law of negligence. But it is worth stressing that the courts are generally reluctant to find that a workman has voluntarily encountered a danger with obvious consequences for the *volenti* defence.[137] On the other hand, where employment necessarily involves particular risks – for example, working as a stuntman – the employer is under no duty to remove these risks, and an employee injured in consequence of undertaking them will not recover in negligence. There is, however, a duty to warn prospective new employees of such risks before they accept the job.[138]

In one respect a distinction has to be made between defective equipment and failure to provide competent staff or a proper system of working. The Employers' Liability (Defective Equipment) Act 1969 applies only to defective equipment (including plant

---

[129] *McDermid v Nash Dredging and Reclamation Co Ltd* [1987] 3 WLR 212, at 223, *per* Lord Brandon. For discussion of the case see McKendrick, 'Vicarious Liability and Independent Contractors – A Re-examination' (1990) 53 MLR 770.

[130] Cf Stevens, 'Non-Delegable Duties and Vicarious Liability' in Neyers (ed), *Emerging Issues in Tort Law* (2007).

[131] *Latimer v AEC Ltd* [1953] AC 643, at 658. See also *Cook v Square D* [1992] ICR 262 (sub nom *Square D v Cook* [1992] IRLR 34). In *Richardson v Stephenson Clarke Ltd* [1969] 3 All ER 705, the employers left it to C, an employee, to choose his equipment. He chose carelessly and was hurt. It was held that the employers had discharged their duty by providing safe equipment and leaving the selection of the equipment to C; C's negligence alone caused the accident.

[132] *Williams v Birmingham Battery and Metal Co* [1899] 2 QB 338; *Barber v Somerset CC* [2004] 1 WLR 1089.

[133] *Baker v James* [1921] 2 KB 674, at 681, *per* McCardie J.

[134] *Latimer v AEC Ltd* [1953] AC 643, at 655, *per* Lord Oaksey. Furthermore, the *res ipsa loquitur* doctrine applies: *Ballard v North British Rly Co* 1923 SC (HL) 43, at 53, *per* Lord Dunedin.

[135] *King v Smith* [1995] ICR 339.

[136] *Thompson v Smiths Shiprepairers(North Shields) Ltd* [1984] QB 405.

[137] *Smith v Baker & Sons* [1891] AC 325.   [138] See *White v Holbrook Precision Castings* [1985] IRLR 215.

and machinery, vehicles, aircraft and clothing provided by the employer for the purpose of his business[139]). Here, even though the defect is attributable to the negligence of a third party, the employer remains liable to his employee for those personal injuries suffered in consequence of using substandard equipment in the course of his employment. The proclamation in *McDermid v Nash Dredging & Reclamation Co Ltd* that the employer's duty is 'non-delegable' means just what it says. And the principle would seem to apply in respect of any of the components of the duty owed by the employer.

Remembering always that the basic question is whether the employer has failed to take reasonable care for the safety of his employee,[140] and that the tripartite division – based loosely on competent staff, safe places of work and safe systems of work – is not necessarily an exhaustive list of all possible aspects of an employer's duty towards his employees, it is nonetheless convenient to examine each of those three categories.

(B) THE PROVISION OF COMPETENT STAFF

Prior to 1948, an employee injured by the incompetence of his fellow employee could recover damages in negligence from his employer only by establishing that the employer was himself negligent in employing the fellow employee in the circumstances. Although the negligent engagement of incompetent staff will still today give rise to potential liability, this aspect of an employer's duty towards his employees is no longer of great practical significance: the defence of common employment has ceased to absolve the employer from vicarious liability. Indeed, modern-day cases in this category will now only be relevant where the claimant cannot prove any fault on the part of the other employee and yet can show that his injury results from negligent staffing provision. The most common case will be where the employer appoints an insufficiently qualified or experienced person for a particular task.[141]

(C) ADEQUATE PREMISES AND PLANT

The employer must take reasonable care to provide safe premises[142] and plant for his workers. Both the failure to provide some necessary equipment and the provision of defective appliances will constitute breaches of this duty. So, for example, the failure

---

[139] The Act will not apply, eg, where a domestic cleaner is injured because an electrician has carelessly installed a plug in her employer's home. Nor is the employer liable at common law if he has carefully chosen the electrician: *Cook v Broderip* (1968) 206 *Estates Gazette* 128.

[140] Emphasized again by the House of Lords in *General Cleaning Contractors Ltd v Christmas* [1953] AC 180. Cf *Drummond v British Building Cleaners Ltd* [1954] 3 All ER 507.

[141] *Black v Fife Coal Co Ltd* [1912] AC 149 (employment of a colliery manager without experience of carbon monoxide in a pit where its presence was a possible danger); especially, *per* Lord Shaw, at 170. In *Hudson v Ridge Manufacturing Co Ltd* [1957] 2 QB 348, knowingly to employ a workman continually indulging in horseplay was held to violate this duty.

[142] 'Whether the servant is working on the premises of the master or on those of a stranger, that duty is still the same; but . . . its performance and discharge will probably be vastly different in the two cases. The master's

of ship-owners to provide essential spare ropes for a voyage was actionable negligence.[143] There is probably also a duty not merely to provide the material, but also to maintain it.[144]

(D) A PROPER SYSTEM OF WORKING

The scope of this requirement was considerably increased by the decision of the Court of Appeal in *Speed v Thomas Swift & Co Ltd*.[145]

C was engaged in loading a ship from a barge. Normally, the particular part of this loading operation (requiring the port and starboard winches to be used together), was carried out while the ship's rails were left in position. Only when one winch was being used was it ordinarily necessary to remove a section of the rails in order to prevent their being caught by the hook. The following special circumstances, however, made it dangerous on that occasion to load with two winches without removing the section of the rail. Other sections of the rail had been damaged by accident and had been removed out of necessity; timber was lying against the rails so that it was likely easily to be dislodged; the port winch was not in perfect order. A hook caught in the rail, and the rail and timber fell into the barge injuring C. It was held that he could recover in negligence because D had not, in these particular circumstances, provided a safe system of work.

Lord Greene MR, approved the following description of 'system of work':

What is system and what falls short of system may be difficult to define . . . but, broadly stated, the distinction is between the general and the particular, between the practice and method adopted in carrying on the master's business of which the master is presumed to be aware and the insufficiency of which he can guard against, and isolated or day to day acts of the servant of which the master is not presumed to be aware and which he cannot guard against; in short, it is the distinction between what is permanent or continuous on the one hand, and what is merely casual and emerges in the day's work on the other hand.[146]

He added:

It . . . may include . . . the physical lay-out of the job – the setting of the stage, so to speak – the sequence in which the work is to be carried out, the provision in proper cases of warnings and notices, and the issue of special instructions. A system may be adequate for the whole course

own premises are under his control: if they are dangerously in need of repair he can and must rectify the fault at once if he is to escape the censure of negligence. If, however, a master sends his plumber to mend a leak in a respectable private house, no one could hold him negligent for not visiting the house himself to see if the carpet in the hall creates a trap': *Wilson v Tyneside Window Cleaning Co* [1958] 2 QB 110, at 121, *per* Pearce LJ.

[143] *Vaughan v Roper & Co Ltd* (1947) 80 Ll LR 119.

[144] Dicta in *Wilsons & Clyde Coal Co Ltd v English* [1938] AC 57, and the much cited judgment of Sir Arthur Channel in *Toronto Power Co Ltd v Paskwan* [1915] AC 734, at 738.

[145] [1943] KB 557 (approved by the House of Lords in *Colfar v Coggins and Griffith(Liverpool) Ltd* [1945] AC 197, where (at 202), however, Viscount Simon LC suggested that the principles laid down there marked the limit of the duty).

[146] [1943] KB 557, at 562, citing *English v Wilsons and Clyde Coal Co Ltd* in the Court of Session 1936 SC 883, at 904.

of the job or it may have to be modified or improved to meet circumstances which arise. Such modifications or improvements appear to me equally to fall under the head of system.[147]

On the other hand, in *Winter v Cardiff RDC*,[148] the House of Lords held that a workman, who was injured because a rope provided by the employer for that purpose had not in fact been used to lash a regulator being carried on a lorry in which he was travelling, could not complain of the system of work. Lord Porter said:

The difference . . . is between a case where sufficient and adequate provisions have been made, which will, if carried out, protect the workman unless one of his fellows does not use proper care in carrying out the system, and a case where the system itself makes no such provision.[149]

Does this suggest that, provided a safe system is devised, any failure in operation of the system will not be actionable as a breach of the employer's personal duty? This proposition must be treated with caution after *McDermid v Nash Dredging and Reclamation Co Ltd*. For there, Lord Brandon asserted unequivocally that the duty extended to the operation of the system,[150] the crucial factor in that case being perhaps that the relevant carelessness in operating the system was that of the man in control of the operation and not just a fellow employee of the claimant.

The House of Lords has also emphasized that in considering whether the employers are negligent, regard must be had to their knowledge of physical defects of particular workmen, so that it was relevant, in deciding whether the employers had taken reasonable care to protect a workman from flying metal by providing him with goggles, that the employers knew him to be one-eyed.[151]

Many of the decided cases on employers' liability focus on responsibility for physically dangerous work environments. The risk to the employee is usually of crude injury whether by a mechanical device or via industrial disease. Yet other sorts of risk, for example, also come within the employers' duty. Claims for stress-related illness are rapidly becoming commonplace. In *Johnstone v Bloomsbury Area Health Authority*[152] the Court of Appeal refused to strike out a claim by a junior doctor that the excessive hours which he was required to work had damaged his health. And in *Walker v Northumberland County Council*[153] a social worker recovered damages after his employers failed to reduce his workload on his return from sick leave after suffering a nervous breakdown.[154] The continued stress triggered a second bout of illness. The court held that, given the obvious risk of further mental injury to the claimant, the

---

[147] [1943] KB 557, at 563.   [148] [1950] 1 All ER 819.   [149] [1950] 1 All ER 819, at 822.

[150] [1987] 3 WLR 212, at 223.

[151] *Paris v Stepney Borough Council* [1951] AC 367. On the other hand, in *Charlton v Forrest Printing Ink Co Ltd* [1980] IRLR 331, it was held that an employee attacked by robbers after collecting wages from the bank could not sue his employers on the ground that they neglected his safety by not employing a security firm instead.   [152] [1992] QB 333.

[153] [1995] 1 All ER 737.

[154] See also *Sutherland v Hatton* [2002] PIQR P241 (stress at work: D must take into account C's susceptibility, not the susceptibilities of those of ordinary fortitude).

employer should have taken steps to reduce the level of stress to which the claimant was exposed by his work.

Notwithstanding, the foregoing, it must not be forgotten that employers' liability is not unlimited and that an employer does not have to 'insure' his personnel against all work-related risk. In *Reid v Rush & Tompkins Group plc*,[155] for example, an employer was held not liable for failing to provide his employee posted abroad with insurance against risks encountered in that posting.

Consider, too, the rights of workmen on premises. If the workman is merely employed by an independent contractor of the occupier, he will of course, have the rights of a visitor against the occupier. He will only have the greater rights of an employee against an employer in respect of the defect on the premises if he shows that the defect was tantamount to a failure on the employer's part to take reasonable care to protect his safety as, for instance, in *General Cleaning Contractors Ltd v Christmas*,[156] where the employee of a firm of window cleaners was held to be entitled to recover from the firm for failure to lay out a safe system on the premises of a customer whose windows he was cleaning. Subject to that, he will normally be limited to the rights of a visitor contained in the Occupiers' Liability Act 1957 or any right of action for breach of statutory duty that there may be. However, even beyond these actions, an employer will be liable for defective equipment negligently provided by a third party in circumstances where, under the Occupiers' Liability Act 1957, an occupier would not be liable for that independent contractor's fault. Furthermore, the employer must insure against this risk.[157]

Particular difficulty may arise where the employee is, at the time of the accident, actually working on a site abroad. In *Cook v Square D*,[158] the claimant suffered injury while working in Saudi Arabia. The Court of Appeal held that the employers did not have a duty to guarantee the safety of premises occupied by third parties. The question must be whether in the light of all the circumstances the employer had done enough to take reasonable steps to protect his staff.

Finally it should be noted that an employer's negligence can incur liability to the employee's family as well as the employee himself. If the employee is exposed to toxic substances at work, or to a transmissible disease,[159] so that unwittingly he endangers his wife who washes his work-clothes, or his family who contract the disease, the employer may owe a duty of care to the family as well. But there must be adequate proof that the level of toxicity, or the risk of infection, did endanger the employee so as to create a real risk to the family.[160]

---

[155] [1989] 3 All ER 228.

[156] [1953] AC 180; *Drummond v British Building Cleaners* [1954] 3 All ER 507; *Smith v Austin Lifts Ltd* [1959] 1 All ER 81.   [157] The Employers' Liability (Compulsory Insurance) Act 1969.

[158] [1992] IRLR 34 (compare the outcome of this decision with *McDermid v Nash Dredging and Reclamation Ltd* [1987] 3 WLR 212).

[159] Consider the potential liability if a health worker becomes infected with hepatitis B and passes on the disease to her husband or any other sexual partner.

[160] *Hewett v Alf Brown's Transport* [1992] ICR 530 (no evidence that the levels of lead waste to which the husband was exposed were sufficient to cause the wife's lead poisoning).

SECTION 6 PROVING NEGLIGENCE

(A) LAW AND FACT

Historically, negligence actions were tried by judge and jury; the judge deciding matters of law and the jury matters of fact. Nowadays, however, they are heard by a judge sitting without a jury: the judge trying issues of both law and fact. It should not, therefore, be surprising that many modern judgments do not meticulously separate matters of law from questions of fact. This then begs the question of where the boundary lies between law and fact.

The following are matters of law:

(1) All questions of duty – was the duty owed to the claimant? What was the scope of the duty? etc.

(2) The standard of care – what was the standard required?

(3) The principles to be applied in determining whether the damage was too remote, and whether there was any evidence of such damage, and whether any recognized heads of damage have not been taken into account.

By contrast, matters of fact include:

(1) Resolving conflicts in the evidence and determining what the circumstances were and what the parties did.

(2) Evaluating the conduct of the parties in the light of the facts found and deciding whether there was a failure to take care, having regard to the standard of care required of the defendant.

(3) Deciding, in the light of the facts found, whether the damage was caused by the defendant, the extent of the damage[161] and the appropriate level of damages.[162]

When appellate courts largely heard appeals from judges sitting with a jury, they were concerned solely with those matters defined as matters of law. Today the appellate jurisdiction from the judge sitting alone is much broader. '[The court] has ... jurisdiction to review the record of the evidence in order to determine whether the conclusion originally reached upon that evidence should stand; but this jurisdiction has to be exercised with caution.'[163] The court should be 'satisfied that any advantage enjoyed by the trial judge by reason of having seen and heard the witnesses, could not be sufficient to explain or justify the trial judge's conclusion',[164] before it disturbs his findings of fact. On the other hand, where, as often happens, the facts are not in dispute,

---

[161] These and (2) are matters of inference from (1).   [162] See chs 26 and 27.
[163] *Watt v Thomas* [1947] AC 484, at 486, *per* Viscount Simon.
[164] *Watt v Thomas* [1947] AC 484, at 488, *per* Lord Thankerton.

but the case rests on the inference to be drawn from them, an appellate court is in as good a position as the trial judge to decide the case.[165]

(B) ONUS OF PROOF

Whether what is in issue is the veracity of primary facts alleged or the validity of the inferences to be drawn from those facts, the claimant shoulders the burden of establishing (1) that the defendant was negligent, and (2) that his negligence resulted in the claimant's loss or injury. Should the evidence be evenly balanced so that the accident might have been the result of lack of care or competence, but might just as easily have occurred without carelessness, the claimant fails for he will not have established negligence to the required standard of proof.[166] In *Ashcroft v Mersey Regional Health Authority*,[167] for example, the claimant suffered a partial paralysis in her face when in the course of surgery on her left ear the surgeon cut into a facial nerve. Some expert evidence showed this to be an inherent risk of such surgery even when performed with the greatest skill, while other experts acknowledged that it also sometimes occurred because of a failure in skill. The claimant's action failed.

At least Mrs Ashcroft knew what had happened even though her counsel failed, ultimately, to establish negligence on the defendant's part. In many cases of alleged negligence, the claimant knows only that he has been injured. How he came to be hit on the head by a falling object or a collapsing wall, or why a swab remained in his abdomen after surgery, is a closed book to him. In a number of such cases, however, the claimant may be able to invoke the principle of *res ipsa loquitur*. In others, section 11 of the Civil Evidence Act 1968 may be of use to him.

(1) *RES IPSA LOQUITUR*

In *Scott v London and St Katherine's Docks Co*[168] the facts were as follows.

While near the door of D's warehouse, C was injured by some sugar bags falling on him. The judge directed the jury to find a verdict for D on the ground of lack of evidence of negligence by D, who called no evidence. On appeal a new trial was directed.

The court justified this direction of a new trial in the following terms, which have since become known as the *res ipsa loquitur* principle.[169]

There must be reasonable evidence of negligence. But where the thing is shown to be under the management of the defendant or his servants, and the accident is such as in the ordinary

---

[165] *Powell v Streatham Manor Nursing Home* [1935] AC 243, at 267, *per* Lord Wright. See also *Benmax v Austin Motor Co Ltd* [1955] AC 370. Appellate courts are these days exercising this power so freely that many decisions now turn solely on matters of inference from facts. *Morris v West Hartlepool Steam Navigation Co Ltd* [1956] AC 552, is a typical example of the House of Lords substituting its own evaluation of the facts for that of the trial judge: nothing else is in issue, yet the case appears in the Law Reports. See also *Whitehouse v Jordan* [1981] 1 All ER 267.   [166] As to why, see Porat and Stein, *Tort Liability Under Uncertainty* (2001) ch 1.
[167] [1983] 2 All ER 245 (affd [1985] 2 All ER 96n).   [168] (1865) 3 H & C 596.
[169] (1865) 3 H & C 596, at 601, *per* Erle CJ. It is not necessary to plead the doctrine; it is enough to prove facts which make it applicable: *Bennett v Chemical Construction (GB) Ltd* [1971] 3 All ER 822.

course of things does not happen if those who have the management use proper care, it affords reasonable evidence, in the absence of explanation by the defendant, that the accident arose from want of care.

In the past there has been a tendency to elevate *res ipsa loquitur* to the status of a principle of substantive law or at least a doctrine. In the 1970s, however, the Court of Appeal decisively swung away from that approach. In *Lloyde v West Midlands Gas Board*, Megaw LJ said:

I doubt whether it is right to describe *res ipsa loquitur* as a 'doctrine'. I think that it is no more than an exotic, although convenient, phrase to describe what is in essence no more than a common-sense approach, not limited by technical rules, to the assessment of the effect of evidence in certain circumstances. It means that a [claimant] *prima facie* establishes negligence where (i) it is not possible for him to prove precisely what was the relevant act or omission which set in train the events leading to the accident, but (ii) on the evidence as it stands at the relevant time it is more likely than not that the effective cause of the accident was *some* act or omission of the defendant or of someone for whom the defendant is responsible, which act or omission constitutes a failure to take proper care for the [claimant's] safety.[170]

It is still necessary to examine the content of the *res ipsa loquitur* principle, but always with that warning in mind. Three separate requirements must be satisfied.

(a) The absence of explanation [171]

This limb merely means that if the court finds on the evidence adduced how and why the occurrence took place, then there is no room for inference. So, in *Barkway v South Wales Transport Co Ltd*[172] – where the tyre of a bus burst and the bus mounted the pavement and fell down an embankment – *res ipsa loquitur* did not apply because the court had evidence of the circumstances of the accident and was satisfied that the system of tyre inspection in the defendants' garage was negligent.

The word 'explanation' must be qualified in this context by the adjective 'exact'.[173] This is to make it clear that a claimant who is able to present a partial account of how an accident happened is still not precluded from relying on *res ipsa loquitur* for further inferences essential to winning his case. The partial explanation may make it more obvious that an inference of negligence can be drawn. But of course, as in the *Barkway*

---

[170] [1971] 2 All ER 1240, at 1246. The Court of Appeal in *Turner v Mansfield Corpn* (1975) 119 Sol Jo 629 unanimously affirmed that decision. See also *Ng Chun Pui v Lee Chuen Tat* [1988] RTR 298.

[171] *Barkway v South Wales Transport Co Ltd* [1950] 1 All ER 392, at 394, *per* Lord Porter.

[172] [1950] 1 All ER 392. And see *Swan v Salisbury Construction Co Ltd* [1966] 2 All ER 138. In *Richley v Faull* [1965] 3 All ER 109, D's car hit C's car when D's car was on the wrong side of the road. D proved that he skidded. Without mentioning *res ipsa loquitur*, the court reached the solution supported by common sense that D was liable unless he showed that the skid occurred through no fault on his part. Similarly in *Henderson v Henry E Jenkins & Sons* [1970] AC 282, the sudden failure of brakes on a lorry owing to a corroded pipe in the hydraulic braking system was held to impute negligence to the owners.

[173] *Ballard v North British Rly Co* 1923 SC (HL) 43, at 54, *per* Lord Dunedin.

case, even if *res ipsa loquitur* is inapplicable because all the material facts are proved, those facts may still be found to constitute negligence.[174]

(b) The harm must be of such a kind that it does not ordinarily happen if proper care is being taken

The courts have applied *res ipsa loquitur* to things falling from buildings,[175] and to accidents resulting from defective machines, apparatus or vehicles.[176] It applies also where motor cars mount the pavement,[177] or where aircraft crash on taking off.[178] On the other hand, it was held inapplicable when neighbouring rooms were damaged by fire spreading from a lodger's room in which a fire had been left alight in the grate.[179]

It will be recalled that the classic definition of Erle CJ referred to accidents happening 'in the ordinary course of things'. *Mahon v Osborne*[180] raised the question of whether this means that it must be a matter of common experience, so that the experience of the expert is irrelevant. Goddard LJ held that the principle applied where swabs had been left in the body of a patient after an abdominal operation.[181] But Scott LJ thought that the principle did not apply where the judge could not, as he could with surgical operations, have enough knowledge of the circumstances to draw an inference of negligence.[182] Since then, the Court of Appeal has held it to be *prima facie* evidence of negligence that a man leaving hospital after a course of radiography treatment on his hand and arm should suffer four stiff fingers and a useless hand.[183] Equally, a court of first instance was influenced by expert evidence in rejecting the application of *res ipsa loquitur* to a case where a patient sustained a fractured jaw as a result of a dental extraction.[184] Yet where an unexplained accident occurs from a thing under the control of the defendant, and medical or other expert evidence shows that such accidents would not happen if proper care were used, there is strong evidence of negligence.[185]

---

[174] Conversely, D is not liable for an unexplained accident, to which *res ipsa loquitur* might otherwise apply, if he establishes that he himself was not negligent: *Barkway v South Wales Transport Co Ltd* [1948] 2 All ER 460, at 463, *per* Bucknill LJ.

[175] *Byrne v Boadle* (1863) 2 H & C 722 (flour barrel falling from upper window onto C walking on the street below); *Kearney v London and Brighton Rly Co* (1870) LR 5 QB 411.

[176] *Ballard v North British Rly Co* 1923 SC (HL) 43 (defective coupling on train); *Kealey v Heard* [1983] 1 All ER 973 (collapsing scaffolding).

[177] *McGowan v Stott* (1930) 143 LT 219n; *Ellor v Selfridge & Co Ltd* (1930) 46 TLR 236; *Laurie v Raglan Building Co Ltd* [1942] 1 KB 152.

[178] *Fosbroke-Hobbes v Airwork Ltd and British-American Air Services Ltd* [1937] 1 All ER 108.

[179] *Sochacki v Sas* [1947] 1 All ER 344.   [180] [1939] 2 KB 14.   [181] [1939] 2 KB 14, at 50.

[182] [1939] 2 KB 14, at 23. It is impossible to be certain of the view of MacKinnon LJ, in view of the conflicting reports perhaps the fullest of which is at (1939) 108 LJKB 567.

[183] *Cassidy v Ministry of Health* [1951] 2 KB 343. *Saunders v Leeds Western Health Authority* [1993] 4 Med LR 355 (child suffering cardiac stoppage under anaesthetic).

[184] *Fish v Kapur* [1948] 2 All ER 176. Cf the patient who swallows a throat pack: *Garner v Morrell* (1953) *Times*, 31 October.

[185] *Lillywhite v University College London Hospitals NHS Trust* [2005] EWCA Civ 1466.

(c) The instrumentality causing the accident must be within the exclusive control of the defendant

(i) The meaning of 'control'

If the defendant is not in control, *res ipsa loquitur* does not apply. *Turner v Mansfield Corpn*[186] is illustrative.

C, a driver of D's dust-cart was injured when its back raised itself up as C drove it under a bridge. It was held that, since C was in control, it was for him to explain the accident. As he was unable to furnish any evidence from which negligence could be inferred, he failed.

McGowan v Stott[187] is an important case also in that it called a halt to previous attempts to insist on complete control of all the circumstances before the rule could apply. Previously, Fletcher Moulton LJ had indicated[188] that the scope of *res ipsa loquitur* was severely limited in highway accidents because all the essential surrounding circumstances were seldom under the defendant's control. Yet, the court in *McGowan v Stott* refused to follow this approach declaring the doctrine to be applicable to accidents on the highway where the defendant was in control of the vehicle causing the damage. Two actions brought against railway companies by claimants who had fallen out of trains illustrate the degree of control essential for the doctrine to apply:

In *Gee v Metropolitan Rly Co*,[189] a few minutes after a local train had started its journey, C leaned against the offside door, which flew open. This was held to be evidence of negligence on the part of the railway company.

In *Easson v London and North Eastern Rly Co*,[190] C's claim failed, Goddard LJ holding that 'it is impossible to say that the doors of an express corridor train travelling from Edinburgh to London are continuously under the sole control of the railway company'.

(ii) Where one of two or more persons is in control

If the instrumentality is in the control of one of several employees of the same employer, and the claimant cannot point to the particular employee who is in control, the rule may still be invoked so as to make the employer vicariously liable. Thus, a hospital authority has been held answerable for negligent treatment where the claimant could not show which of several members of the staff was responsible.[191] Furthermore, if a surgeon is shown to be in general control of an operation, and the patient cannot establish whether it was the malpractice of the surgeon or one of the theatre staff which inflicted damage on him in the course of

---

[186] The case is briefly reported at (1975) 119 Sol Jo 629, but the text here is based on a full Court of Appeal transcript.

[187] (1930) 143 LT 219n. Where the apparatus is in C's house – eg, gas apparatus – the onus is on C to show that it was improbable that persons other than D could have interfered with it. Only then can he invoke *res ipsa loquitur*: *Lloyde v West Midlands Gas Board* [1971] 2 All ER 1240. In *Ward v Tesco Stores Ltd* [1976] 1 All ER 219, C slipped on yoghurt that had been spilt onto the floor of D's supermarket. Even though there was no evidence as to how long the yoghurt had been on the floor it was held to be a case of *prima facie* negligence.

[188] *Wing v London General Omnibus Co* [1909] 2 KB 652, at 663–4.   [189] (1873) LR 8 QB 161.

[190] [1944] KB 421, at 424.   [191] *Cassidy v Ministry of Health* [1951] 2 KB 343.

that operation, it seems that *res ipsa loquitur* applies in an action for negligence against the surgeon.[192] If, on the other hand, the surgeon is not in control of all the relevant stages of the treatment, and if the claimant cannot prove that the act complained of took place at a time when the defendant surgeon was in control, *res ipsa loquitur* cannot be invoked.[193]

Walsh v Holst & Co Ltd[194] extends the principle further. When the defendant's duty is so extensive that he is answerable for the negligence of his independent contractor, and an accident occurs while the independent contractor is performing the work delegated to him, the claimant can invoke *res ipsa loquitur* against both the defendant and his independent contractor.[195]

A related, though distinct, problem is the position of a claimant who establishes, without invoking the rule of *res ipsa loquitur*, that the damage to him was caused either by the negligence of A or the negligence of B. If he is merely able to show that only A or B but not both must have been negligent then he is not entitled to a judgment against both unless the defendants have refused to give evidence, in which case adverse inferences against them may be drawn.[196] It is, however, the duty of the trial court to come to a definite conclusion on the evidence. It must not dismiss the action because of uncertainty as to which party was free from blame.[197] If the inference is that one or other or both have been negligent, the claimant has made out a *prima facie* case against either A or B, or both.[198] Of course, if the circumstances do not warrant the inference that one or other has been negligent, the claimant fails.[199]

Beyond setting out the above guidance, it is submitted that one cannot define the circumstances where the *res ipsa loquitur* principle applies. As usual in negligence, some writers list all the circumstances where *res ipsa loquitur* has been applied as if they were precedents on points of law. But the Court of Appeal has held that such cases do not lay down any principles of law; they are merely guides to the kinds of circumstances in which the *res ipsa loquitur* principle may successfully be invoked.[200]

---

[192] *Mahon v Osborne* [1939] 2 KB 14, *per* Goddard and Mackinnon LJJ (Scott LJ dissenting).

[193] *Morris v Winsbury-White* [1937] 4 All ER 494. Perhaps Somervell LJ disagreed with this statement of law in *Roe v Minister of Health* [1954] 2 QB 66, at 80.

[194] [1958] 3 All ER 33; *Kealey v Heard* [1983] 1 All ER 973.

[195] Apparently, the employer conceded that he was liable even though C had not established that the act did not occur within that area of the independent contractor's operations for which the employer is not answerable: *viz*, acts of collateral negligence.

[196] *Baker v Market Harborough Industrial Co-operative Society Ltd* [1953] 1 WLR 1472; *Cook v Lewis* [1952] 1 DLR 1 decided that where either X or Y has committed a tort against C and it is the careless act of both of them which prevents C from knowing which caused the harm, both are liable (X and Y were hunters, one or other of whom fired the shot which hit C). [197] *Bray v Palmer* [1953] 2 All ER 1449.

[198] *Roe v Minister of Health* [1954] 2 QB 66, *per* Denning LJ; *France v Parkinson* [1954] 1 All ER 739. Where vehicles collide either at cross-roads or on the brow of a hill, and both drivers are dead, a passenger has a *prima facie* case, in the absence of other evidence, against both drivers or either of them: *Davison v Leggett* (1969) 133 JP 552 (head-on collision in the centre lane, negligence by both drivers inferred and more fully reported in *Knight v Fellick* [1977] RTR 316). [199] *Knight v Fellick* [1977] RTR 316.

[200] *Easson v London and North Eastern Rly Co* [1944] KB 421, at 423, *per* Goddard LJ.

(d) The effect of *res ipsa loquitur*[201]

In some cases the inference to be drawn by resorting to the principle is twofold: that the defendant caused the accident, and that he was negligent. In others, the cause is known, and only the inference of negligence arises.[202]

As we have seen, on any given facts it may be just as likely that the event happened without negligence as that it happened in consequence of negligence, in which case there is no hint of negligence. If, however, in such circumstances, *res ipsa loquitur* applies, its effect is to make it 'relevant to infer negligence'[203] from the fact of the accident. This simply means that there is in law evidence on which the judge may properly find for the claimant.[204] The distinctive function of the rule is to permit an inference of negligence from proof of the injury and the physical instrumentality causing it, even though there is no proof of the facts identifying the human agency responsible. Looked at in this way, its affinity to the ordinary rule of evidence that circumstantial evidence is admissible to prove negligence is clear. As Atkin LJ put it:

all that one wants to know is whether the facts of the occurrence do as a matter of fact make it more probable that a jury may reasonably infer that the damage was caused by want of care on the part of the defendants than the contrary.[205]

It is clear, then, that the effect of *res ipsa loquitur* is to afford *prima facie* evidence of negligence. It does not shift the burden of proof to the defendant[206] in the sense that, in the absence of the defendant rebutting the inference on the balance of probabilities, the courts must find for the claimant. But once *res ipsa loquitur* has been successfully invoked to raise an inference of negligence against the defendant, if the defendant fails to adduce any countervailing evidence, the judge will be entitled to find for the claimant. Historically, the judge could not have withdrawn the case from the jury. But it may now be that certain facts are so clear that the inference of negligence is sufficiently cogent that the judge must rule in favour of the claimant. On the other hand, this will by no means always be the case. As Du Parcq LJ said:

The words *res ipsa loquitur* . . . are a figure of speech, by which sometimes is meant that certain facts are so inconsistent with any view except that the defendant has been negligent that any jury [or judge] which, on proof of these facts, found that negligence was not proved would be giving a perverse verdict. Sometimes, the proposition does not go as far as that, but is merely that on proof of certain facts an inference of negligence may be drawn by a reasonable jury [or judge].[207]

---

[201] For the clearest judicial statement, see the eight rules laid down by Evatt J in *Davis v Bunn* (1936) 56 CLR 246, at 267–8.

[202] *Barkway v South Wales Transport Co Ltd* [1950] 1 All ER 392, at 399–400, *per* Lord Normand.

[203] *Ballard v North British Rly Co* 1923 SC (HL) 43, at 54.

[204] *Cole v De Trafford (No 2)* [1918] 2 KB 523, at 528, *per* Pickford LJ.

[205] *McGowan v Stott* (1923), in (1930) 143 LT 219n. Cf *Langham v Governors of Wellingborough School and Fryer* (1932) 101 LJKB 513, at 518, *per* Greer LJ.

[206] On burden of proof generally see *Wilsher v Essex Area Health Authority* [1988] AC 1074.

[207] *Easson v London and North Eastern Rly Co* [1944] KB 421, at 425.

To sum up, the effect of *res ipsa loquitur* depends on the cogency of the inference to be drawn, and will vary from case to case. If, for instance, a vehicle mounts the pavement, this *may be* evidence of negligence, but reasonable people may differ about the inference to be drawn from these facts, so that a verdict of no negligence may not be upset. Yet something may fall from the defendant's window in such circumstances that only an inference of negligence can be drawn, in which case a verdict of no negligence should be set aside.

The effect of *res ipsa loquitur* where the defendant gives evidence must also be considered. Plainly, the effect of the doctrine is to shift the onus to the defendant in the sense that the principle continues to operate unless the defendant calls credible evidence which explains how the accident may have occurred without negligence; and it seems that the operation of the rule is not displaced merely by expert evidence showing theoretically possible ways in which the accident might have happened without the defendant's negligence. But beyond this, the courts describe its effect in two different ways. Sometimes they state that once the defendant has furnished evidence of the cause of the accident consistent with his having exercised due care it becomes a question of whether, upon the whole of the evidence, the defendant was negligent or not; and the defendant will succeed unless the court is satisfied that he was negligent.[208] On other occasions they state that the defendant loses unless he proves that the accident resulted from a specific cause which does not connote negligence on his part but, on the contrary, points to its absence as more probable.[209] There is possibly no inconsistency in these judicial utterances; all may depend on the context of the cases and the cogency of the rebutting evidence in the particular case.[210]

A useful example of how a defendant can rebut an inference of *res ipsa loquitur* can be seen in *Ng Chun Pui v Lee Chuen Tat*.[211]

A coach veered across the road colliding with a bus coming in the opposite direction. C called no evidence and the Privy Council held that the facts *per se* raised an inference of negligence. But Ds testified that an unidentified car cut across their coach causing the driver to brake suddenly and skid across the road. Ds were found to have rebutted any inference of negligence since the driver's reaction to an emergency beyond his control did not constitute any breach of duty.

(2) CIVIL EVIDENCE ACT 1968, S 11

Whereas *res ipsa loquitur* can be a seen as a partial exception to the general rule that the claimant must prove the defendant's negligence in that it raises a rebuttable presumption of that negligence, section 11 of the Civil Evidence Act 1968 goes slightly further. It in fact reverses the burden of proof in certain circumstances. Where a defendant has

---

[208] Eg, *Ballard v North British Rly Co* 1923 SC (HL) 43, at 54, *per* Lord Dunedin; *The Kite* [1933] P 154; *Colvilles Ltd v Devine* [1969] 2 All ER 53. [209] Eg, *Moore v R Fox & Sons Ltd* [1956] 1 QB 596.

[210] See, eg, *Lillywhite v University College London Hospitals NHS Trust* [2005] EWCA Civ 1466.

[211] [1988] RTR 298.

previously been convicted of a criminal offence against the claimant, and the claimant subsequently brings civil proceedings on the basis of the same facts that led to the defendant's conviction, section 11 makes that conviction *prima facie* evidence of the defendant's civil liability. It then falls to the defendant to demonstrate to the judge (on the balance of probabilities) in civil proceedings that he should not be held liable in damages.[212] This, he is entitled to attempt to do,[213] although the court must be mindful of a potential abuse of process whereby the defendant is effectively attempting to re-litigate his criminal conviction.[214] Thus, in *Grealis v Opuni*[215] the fact that the defendant had been in breach of Road Traffic legislation (by driving at 38mph in a 30mph zone) did not detract from his ability to show that the claimant was contributorily negligent (80% to blame, in fact).

FURTHER READING

Kidner, 'The Variable Standard of Care, Contributory Negligence and *Volenti*' [1991] *Legal Studies* 1

McKendrick, 'Vicarious Liability and Independent Contractors – A Re-examination' (1990) 53 MLR 770

---

[212] See *Wauchope v Mordecai* [1970] 1 WLR 317.   [213] *J v Oyston* [1999] 1 WLR 694.
[214] *McCauley v Hope* [1999] PIQR P185.   [215] [2003] 12 LS Gaz R 32.

5

CAUSATION AND REMOTENESS[1]

Causation is relevant in all torts since problems arise generally in relation to the twin questions of whether the defendant's wrongful conduct did in fact cause the claimant's damage and whether the defendant ought to be held responsible for the full extent of the claimant's damage.

Causation will be dealt with in this chapter in two stages. First, we will consider causation in fact – the matter of how (and to what standard of proof) the claimant can establish that the harm of which he complains resulted from the defendant's negligent conduct. Next, we will consider cases in which a subsequent intervening cause – a *novus actus interveniens* – may be said to sever the chain of causation such that the subsequent cause is treated in law as the only relevant cause of the claimant's injury. Finally, we shall consider the principles governing the related question of remoteness of damage in negligence.

A further introductory point that should be made, however, is this. While causation is relevant throughout tort law, it is dealt with in this early part of the book for two reasons. First, very many, though not all, of the more complex cases in causation arise in negligence. Secondly, in negligence, unlike those torts actionable *per se*, causation of actual damage must be proved before any liability will be imposed. Causation in relation to a tort actionable *per se* (such as trespass) relates only to the extent of the defendant's liability. Beyond this, the only other matter that might usefully be mentioned at this stage is that the principles governing remoteness of damage can vary from one tort to another. Where the remoteness rules in certain torts differ from those explained here, exposition of the applicable principles will be supplied in the relevant chapters. They are therefore dealt with in the relevant analysis of each tort in the various chapters of this book.

---

[1] There is an excellent analysis of the general principles of causation in Hart and Honoré, *Causation in the Law* (2nd ed, 1985) and Honoré, *Responsibility and Fault* (1999). See also Wright, 'Causation in Tort Law' (1985) 75 *Cal L Rev* 1735 and Perry, 'Risk, Harm and Responsibility' in Owen (ed), *Philosophical Foundations of Tort Law* (1995). For an account of the hard cases centring on evidential uncertainty, and a novel thesis of how of they should be dealt with, see Porat and Stein, *Tort Liability Under Uncertainty* (2001).

SECTION 1 CAUSATION IN FACT

(A) THE 'BUT-FOR' TEST

Establishing cause and effect in law can be far from easy. Every occurrence is the result of a combination of several different events. Thus, an incident resulting in injury to a claimant is the product not simply of the negligent acts and omissions of the defendant, but also of the conditions in which those events took place. This series of events includes incidents both prior and subsequent to the allegedly tortious conduct of the defendant. Consider the facts of *Wright v Lodge*.[2]

D2 was driving her car at night along a dual carriageway in the fog. The road was unlit. Her engine failed and the car came to a stop in the near-side lane. A few minutes later, as D2 was trying to restart her car, an articulated lorry being driven at 60 mph by D1 crashed into her car virtually destroying it and seriously injuring a passenger in the back seat. After hitting the car, the lorry careered across the central reservation. The lorry fell onto its side blocking the road. Four vehicles collided with it. One driver died of his injuries and another was seriously injured.

What or who caused those additional injuries? Had the second defendant not chosen to go out that evening, or had it not been foggy, or had the road been lit, the accident might never have happened. In one sense each of those factors is a cause without which the accident would not have occurred. But the law, of course, first looks to the human actors. The unlit road and the fog are part of the complex of conditions which produced the accident, but they are not causes in law. On the other hand, not all human acts constitute the cause in law of an event. No-one would suggest that by driving out that night, the driver of the car (or lorry) was responsible for the three claimants' injuries. What must be identified is the operative legal cause or causes. And this, it must be recognized, involves considerations of policy as much as it does any strict notion of factual cause and effect.[3] Lord Wright captured the point when he said, '[t]he choice of the real or efficient cause from out of the whole complex of facts must be made by applying common sense standards'.

'Causation,' he continued, 'is to be understood as the man in the street, and not as either the scientist or the metaphysician would understand it.'[4] In similar vein, Laws

---

[2] [1993] 4 All ER 299.

[3] In *Gregg v Scott* [2005] 2 AC 176, Lord Hoffmann admitted openly that 'an apparently arbitrary distinction [in the law] obviously rests on grounds of policy'. See also the open use of policy in *Fairchild v Glenhaven Funeral Services Ltd* [2002] 3 All ER 305 and *Barker v Corus UK Ltd* [2005] UKHL 20.

[4] *Yorkshire Dale Steamship Co Ltd v Minister of War Transport* [1942] AC 691, at 706. In similar vein, see *Kuwait Airways Corp v Iraq Airways Co* [2002] 2 AC 883, at [74], *per* Lord Nicholls. See also Stapleton, 'Law, Causation and Common Sense' (1988) 8 OJLS 431 and Robertson, ' The Common Sense of Cause in Fact' (1996–7) 75 *Tex L Rev* 1765.

LJ has said that '[t]he law has dug no deeper in the philosophical thickets of causation than to distinguish between a *causa sine qua non* and a *causa causans*'.[5]

It is thus partly as a matter of convenience that the law settles upon a basic 'but-for' test of causation whereby the question that the court generally addresses is whether, but for the defendant's negligence, the accident would have occurred. If the question receives a negative answer, and there is no evidential complication in the case, the court will hold the defendant liable (subject to the harm in question being too remote to permit recovery). Thus, where a man who later died of poisoning was sent home from a casualty department without treatment after complaining of acute stomach pains, his widow's claim against the hospital failed even though the hospital admitted negligence.[6] The court found that even if he had been given prompt and competent medical treatment, he would still have died as a result of the arsenic that had poisoned him. And in *Wright v Lodge* the question for the court was whether 'but for' the car driver's initial negligence the subsequent pile-up would have occurred. The Court of Appeal held that while she could be held jointly liable with the lorry driver for the injury that was caused to her passenger by failing to move her car out of the way, she was not responsible for the injuries caused to the drivers of the other cars involved in the second collision. Her initial negligence was not a legally operative cause of those injuries. They were solely the responsibility of the lorry driver who had driven in such a grossly careless fashion that night. Not every cause 'without which' an accident would not have occurred is therefore a relevant cause in law. We shall consider this issue in more detail later in the chapter.

(B) EVIDENCE OF CAUSATION

In *Wright v Lodge* there was at least no doubting what had been done (or not done), by the two defendants. Other cases, however, are less straightforward. It is in those cases that the standard of proof becomes a relevant consideration. In this connection, it is well-established that it must be shown that it is more likely than not that the alleged cause – that is, the wrongful conduct of the defendant – caused the claimant's loss or injury.[7]

Where there is some evidence that the defendant's conduct *may* have contributed to the claimant's injury, the burden remains with the claimant. It does not fall to the defendant to rebut the possibility that his conduct *may* have caused the claimant's loss. It thus follows that when the harm in question is a disease, the claimant's task may be a very formidable one.[8] Consider the example of a man claiming that he developed

---

[5] *Rahman v Arearose Ltd* [2001] QB 351, at [32].

[6] *Barnett v Chelsea and Kensington Hospital Management Committee* [1969] 1 QB 428.

[7] *Hotson v East Berkshire Area Health Authority* [1987] AC 750. For a range of reasons as to why this is the appropriate standard, see Porat and Stein, *Tort Liability Under Uncertainty* (2001) ch 1.

[8] Though it is not only cases relating to disease which can be complex: see, eg, *Allied Maples Group Ltd v Simmons and Simmons* [1995] 4 All ER 907.

dermatitis because of contact with substances at work caused by his employer's failure to supply proper protective clothing. The medical evidence may well reveal that contact with the substances at work was just one possible cause. But it may also indicate that several other possible causes can be identified. The issue of whether the claimant has produced sufficient evidence of causation – that is, sufficient evidence that 'but for' the defendant's conduct he would not have suffered injury – is a question of law, not fact. And the essence of the exercise in which the courts are engaged is once again that of identifying the legally operative cause, that of selecting from among the menu of possible causes the 'responsible cause'.

(c) CASES OF EVIDENTIAL UNCERTAINTY

(1) CASES INVOLVING THE 'LOSS OF A CHANCE'

A number of cases involving 'the loss of a chance' have come before the English courts, and they have served to illustrate the importance of the standard of proof in this context.

In *Hotson v East Berkshire Area Health Authority*[9] C fell several feet from a tree injuring his hip. He was rushed to hospital but his injury was not diagnosed until five days later. The hospital admitted negligence and responsibility for the pain C suffered during the five days that treatment was negligently delayed. D denied liability for the avascular necrosis C developed as a result of a failure in the blood supply to his injured hip. The trial judge found[10] that there was a 75% chance that avascular necrosis would have developed as a result of the injury even if promptly treated, and a 25% chance that the delay contributed to the development of the condition. He held that the hospital was liable for loss of that chance and awarded damages assessed at 25% of the compensation which would have been payable had D been 100% liable for C's condition. In the House of Lords, it was held fatal to C's case that the accident was more likely than not to have caused the avascular necrosis.[11]

According to the House of Lords, there was no basis for the judge's decision to award the claimant 25% damages to represent the lost 'chance' of complete recovery. If the alleged cause could be proved or inferred to be more likely than not the actual cause of the damage, the claimant would be entitled to full compensation. If it could not, the claimant was entitled to nothing.[12] Though a highly contentious decision,[13] it has since

---

[9] [1987] AC 750. See also, Stapleton, 'The Gist of Negligence: Part II' (1988) 104 LQR 389. Cf Reece, 'Losses of Chances in the Law' (1996) 59 MLR 188 and Lunney, 'What Price a Chance?' [1995] *Legal Studies* 1.

[10] [1985] 3 All ER 167.   [11] [1985] 3 All ER 167, at 240 and 248, *per* Lords Mackay and Ackner.

[12] See also *Kay v Ayrshire and Arran Health Board* [1987] 2 All ER 417 (C unable to prove on the balance of probabilities that D who supplied C with an overdose of penicillin had caused C's deafness). *Pickford v Imperial Chemical Industries plc* [1998] 3 All ER 462 (C was unable to prove, on the balance of probabilities, that her injury was due to an organic, not psychogenic, cause).

[13] See Stapleton, 'The Gist of Negligence: Part II' (1988) 104 LQR 389. Cf Reece, 'Losses of Chances in the Law' (1996) 59 MLR 188 and Lunney, 'What Price a Chance?' [1995] *Legal Studies* 1.

been followed by a majority of the House of Lords in *Gregg v Scott*[14], where the claimant sought to claim on the basis of a reduced prospect of surviving cancer based on a doctor's misdiagnosis of his condition and consequent failure to refer him to a specialist for confirmation (or otherwise) of that diagnosis. In fact, the claimant had a malignant lymphoma, but this was not discovered until over one year later. Medical evidence showed that even had there been an immediate referral, the claimant would not, on the balance of probabilities, have secured any greater life expectancy.

It was by only a bare majority that the House of Lords confirmed the decision of the Court of Appeal to dismiss the claimant's case. Yet in the Court of Appeal, too, there was a difference of opinion. What this tells us is that this is a highly controversial area of law on which our most senior judges are themselves divided. On the one hand, allowing generally for claims for lost chances in the shape of proportionate damages would radically change the shape of tort law. It would open the way for many more claimants to litigate their cases and might even have serious repercussions for the National Health Service given that the deleterious effects of medical mishaps are often uncertain. It would also mean (presumably) a reduction in the damages available to those who were only able to show a greater-than-even chance that the defendant's negligence caused them to lose the prospect of a total cure from, or avoidance of, a particular condition. Weighing up the pros and cons of each approach is by no means easy since a good deal of speculation is required either way. Fully recognizing these difficulties, Lord Phillips (in the majority) confined himself to deciding no more than he had to in *Gregg v Scott*. He thus left open the question of whether he would have been prepared to develop the law along the lines of loss of chance in misfeasance cases in which the question of causation is one of historical fact (that is, following the defendant's negligence, whether the claimant did or did not have a certain prospect of recovering from a given condition). That being the case, it may well be that notwithstanding the decisions in *Hotson* and in *Gregg*, the House of Lords may at some future time be required again to address this difficult issue.[15]

Leaving these misfeasance cases to one side, it is at least clear that the loss of a chance is recoverable in circumstances where the claimant's loss depends on a negligent omission and the question of causation is not one of historical fact but rather turns on the hypothetical action of a third party. In *Allied Maples Group Ltd v Simmons and Simmons*[16] the facts were as follows.

Cs had been advised by Ds (solicitors) in negotiations to purchase certain businesses from another company. At one stage, the proposed contract included an undertaking by the vendor company that there were no outstanding liabilities in respect of their properties. In the course of negotiations, that undertaking was deleted. After purchasing the business, Cs found themselves liable for substantial sums arising from leases previously held by the vendor.

---

[14] [2005] 2 AC 176.

[15] At the very least, *Gregg v Scott* leaves unanswered the question of why loss of a chance is recoverable in professional negligence cases resulting in economic loss (see, eg, *Allied Maples Group Ltd v Simmons & Simmons* [1995] 1 WLR 1602) but not where the professional negligence is that of a doctor.

[16] [1995] 1 WLR 1602. See further Lunney, 'What Price a Chance?' [1995] *Legal Studies* 1.

The original undertaking would have protected them from such liabilities. Cs argued that Ds were negligent in not advising them to approach the vendors and to seek to retain the original clause in the contract. The issue was whether the vendors would have agreed to do so.

The Court of Appeal held that the claimants must prove that it was more likely than not that, properly advised, they would have approached the vendors. They held further that the claimant need not prove that it was more probable than not that the latter would have agreed. The claimants had only to establish that there was a 'substantial chance' that the vendors would have provided them with the protection requested.[17] Evaluating the value of that lost chance was viewed as a matter of quantification of damage. Another case, however, in which a claim for a lost chance succeeded was *Spring v Guardian Assurance plc*.[18] There, an employer was found liable for negligently giving the claimant a bad reference to a new prospective employer. The claimant recovered for his loss of a chance of employment with the new employer. He could not prove that he definitely would have been given the job, but he could at least prove that with a properly written reference he would have had a decent chance of getting the job.

These cases, as well as others in which *Allied Maples* has been applied,[19] can be distinguished from *Hotson*. In that case, it was argued that the boy had lost a 25% chance of recovering had he been treated. But the probability in that case was calculated according to expert evidence; evidence which was grounded on statistical analysis of outcomes in previous cases. Yet the truth is that, when the boy came to hospital, either he had enough blood vessels to save the hip, or he did not. He could not have 'possibly avoided the condition' in the same way that, for example, the claimant might 'possibly have got the job' in *Spring*. Rather, after the necrosis had set in, it was impossible to say whether he had ever had a chance of recovery (assuming the provision of proper treatment). There was far greater uncertainty in that case.[20]

In the cases just considered, the courts did not perceive the need to depart from the usual 'but for' test that must be proved on the balance of probabilities. It is true that they possessed a certain amount of evidential uncertainty, but there was enough that was known for sure to stick to the usual rules. In *Allied Maples*, it was certain that the claimant lost the chance to renegotiate the terms of the purchase agreement; in *Spring*, it was certain that the claimant had lost the chance of employment. Furthermore, in both cases there was only one possible cause of the loss of the respective chances: the negligence of the defendant.

By contrast, other cases present far greater problems of evidential uncertainty that go far beyond whether a chance has been lost. In such cases, as we shall see shortly, the

---

[17] In a subsequent case involving a lost chance of litigation, it was held that C need not prove that his or her action would, on the balance of probabilities, have succeeded; it was enough to show that he had some prospect of succeeding (ie, that it was not an entirely groundless claim): *Dixon v Clement Jones Solicitors* [2005] PNLR 6.

[18] [1995] 2 AC 296.

[19] See, eg, *Dixon v Clement Jones Solicitors* [2005] PNLR 6 and *Batty v Danaher* [2005] EWHC 2763.

[20] See also *Gregg v Scott* [2005] 2 AC 176, where an earlier diagnosis of C's cancer may or may not have given C better long-term survival prospects. For detailed analysis of these 'indeterministic' and 'quasi-indeterministic' cases, see Reece, 'Losses of Chances in the Law' (1996) 59 MLR 188. See also Perry, 'Risk, Harm and Responsibility' in Owen (ed), *Philosophical Foundations of Tort Law* (1995).

courts have rather unsystematically dealt with problems of evidential uncertainty. These largely *ad hoc* decisions of the English courts seem to create as many problems as they solve, for they are of uncertain scope, and they fail to supply any principle of universal application to deal with the various kinds of evidential uncertainty that have arisen (or may arise in the future[21]). It is submitted that the absence of any such principle means that future cases are likely to be dealt with by a combination of recourse to 'best-fit' analogies and incremental extensions to the several principles that might arguably be gleaned from the various decisions to date. With this in mind, let us consider the responses so far developed in the English courts.[22]

(2) CASES INVOLVING HYPOTHETICAL CONDUCT BY THE CLAIMANT

Where it is certain or virtually certain what the claimant would have done had the defendant not acted negligently, there are especial problems for the law of causation. Take, for example, *Cummings (or McWilliams) v Sir William Arrol & Co Ltd*.[23] In that case, an employer failed to comply with a statutory duty to provide a safety harness to an employee who ended up falling from a great height to his death. It was established that even when harnesses had been supplied in the past the employee in question had seldom if ever worn one. As such, it was virtually certain that even if the employer had supplied one on the occasion in question, the employee would not have worn it and accordingly the defendant's negligent non-provision of the harness could not be regarded as the 'but for' cause of the employee's death. (Importantly, the employer's duty was limited merely to providing, but not ensuring or supervising the wearing of, the harness.[24])

Where, by contrast, there is enduring uncertainty about what the claimant would have done had the defendant not acted negligently, matters become much more difficult. The kinds of problem that arise were considered in depth by the House of Lords in *Chester v Afshar*.[25]

C had a long history of back pain and was advised by D, her surgeon, that she required spinal surgery. What the surgeon failed to tell her was that the operation, which she underwent some

---

[21] Porat and Stein have identified five (sometimes overlapping) kinds of evidential uncertainty: (i) cases of wrongful damage where the wrongdoer is unidentifiable, (ii) cases of wrongful damage where the precise injured party is unidentifiable (eg, cases in which, say, D has emitted radiation affecting many citizens but it is not certain whether C was among their number), (iii) cases of wrongful conduct that may or may not have resulted in damage, (iv) cases of damage wrongfully inflicted by separate wrongdoers, and (v) cases of damage arising from both a wrongful and a non-wrongful cause: *Tort Liability Under Uncertainty* (2001) ch 2.

[22] For solutions in a range of other jurisdictions see Porat and Stein, *Tort Liability Under Uncertainty* (2001). And for a lawyer-economist's account of the market-share liability solution that is often recommended in relation to harm caused by (defective) generic pharmaceutical products, see Rose-Ackerman, 'Market-Share Allocations in Tort Law: Strengths and Weaknesses' [1990] *Journal of Legal Studies* 739.

[23] [1962] 1 All ER 623.

[24] On the relationship between scope of duty and causation see Stapleton, 'Cause-in-Fact and the Scope of Liability for Consequences' (2003) 119 LQR 388.

[25] [2005] 1 AC 134. For critical commentary on this case see Stevens, 'An Opportunity to Reflect' (2005) 121 LQR 189.

three days later, carried with it a risk of neurological damage reckoned at 1–2%. In the event, the injury materialized (even though the surgery was not performed negligently) and C brought an action based on the surgeon's negligent failure to disclose the risk of injury.

The difficulty of the case turned on the fact that, had she been advised of the risk, she would have sought further medical advice before deciding what to do, and, following that advice, may or may not have had the operation at a later date. Now, if she had merely delayed treatment until after she had received further advice, the overwhelming probability is that the injury would not have materialized. The operation at that later date would still only have carried a 1–2% chance of the neurological damage occurring. Alternatively, had she ultimately decided not to have the surgery, it would have been impossible to succumb to the neurological damage. So either way, it would have been highly unlikely that she would have suffered the injury that she ultimately suffered. As such, on usual 'but for' principles, the defendant could be held to have caused the claimant's injury. But only by a bare majority did the House of Lords hold that the defendant had caused the claimant's injury; and then on grounds of policy rather than upon conventional 'but for' principles.[26]

What then, was the complicating factor that the House of Lords perceived in the case that caused two members to dissent and the others to reach a policy (as opposed to principled) decision? Put briefly, the complication that their Lordships perceived there to be in this case was that all that the defendant's failure to warn had caused was the patient to undergo the operation on the day that she did. The failure to warn did not, they thought, increase the risk inherent in the surgery: a constant 1–2%.[27] On this analysis, their Lordships seemed to be hinting (but not saying explicitly) that the surgery, rather than the failure to warn, was the overwhelming cause of the claimant's injury. However, if one accepted that the failure to warn was legally eclipsed by the subsequent surgery, then this would lead to the conclusion that the duty to warn counted for nothing. As Lord Hope put it, the duty would be 'a hollow one, stripped of all practical force and devoid of all content'.[28] As such, he went on, '[the claimants' loss]

---

[26] The majority *did* accept that the 'but for' test was satisfied: [2005] 1 AC 134, at [19], [61] and [94] *per* Lords Steyn, Hope and Walker respectively); but their analysis did not stop there.

[27] See, eg, [2005] 1 AC 134, at [7], [31] and [61], *per* Lords Bingham, Hoffman and Hope respectively. This assumption is questionable, however, since there may have been something about the patient *or* the surgeon on the particular day that made the risk of injury more likely to occur. All that the 1–2% statistic represents is the fact that either one or two persons out of one hundred undergoing such surgery would succumb to the syndrome that afflicted the claimant. We therefore assert (quite reasonably) in the case of any individual patient, that there is a 1–2% risk of injury. This can be described as 'epistemic probability'. But it does not reflect the actual, subjective probability (which might well vary for any given patient), but which is unknown due to an information deficit (about, for instance, the particular susceptibilities of the claimant, or the relative skills of different surgeons). In short, we simply do not know the precise risk on any given occasion, we merely alight upon an epistemic risk derived from knowledge of generalities. For further explanation of the difference between epistemic and subjective probability and of their application to causation problems, see Perry, 'Risk, Harm and Responsibility' in Owen (ed), *Philosophical Foundations of Tort Law* (1995); *id*, 'Protected Interests and Undertakings in the Law of Negligence' (1992) 42 *U Toronto LJ* 247 at 252–262.

[28] This is questionable. If the patient would have not have delayed the operation while she sought further advice, but would declined the operation outright, then the duty to warn would clearly have counted for

can be regarded as having been caused, in the legal sense, by the breach of that duty'.[29] In order to make the decision more palatable still, their Lordships identified the loss to the claimant as a loss of autonomy (that is, the loss of her right to choose whether to have or delay until after further advice, her operation).[30] For all we know, following further consultation, she may have found a way to reduce the inherent risk!

Notably, this approach makes the gist of the action patient autonomy rather than neurological damage; yet it seems that it was for the neurological damage that compensation was awarded. This is by no means explicable in logical terms.[31] In the light of its controversial nature, the Court of Appeal has since been keen to emphasize that the result in *Chester v Afshar* was an extraordinary one reached on policy grounds, and to confine it to its own limited context: that is, cases involving a negligent failure to warn a patient of the dangers associated with a particular medical treatment or procedure.[32] Whether, if the opportunity arises, the House of Lords will be as keen to confine *Chester v Afshar* in this way remains to be seen. But for the present, it would appear wise to treat the decision as exceptional, and one that does not lay down any general rule capable of universal application.

(3) THE MATERIAL CONTRIBUTION TO HARM PRINCIPLE

English law allows negligence claims to be brought by a claimant able to show (1) that the defendant was in breach of a duty of care, and (2) that the breach of duty materially contributed to his injury. The fact that the claimant cannot identify precisely the degree to which the defendant's wrongdoing caused his injury is not regarded as a sufficient basis on which to refuse the claimant a remedy.

In *Bonnington Castings Ltd v Wardlaw*[33] C, who was D's employee, contracted pneumoconiosis after inhaling silicon dust at work. The dust came from two sources – swing grinders and pneumatic hammers. Only the dust thrown out by the swing grinders was avoidable by use of a proper extraction mechanism. In the absence of such a mechanism, the exposure of C to this dust was regarded as tortious. The dust generated by the hammers was not, however, tortiously produced. The question that arose, then, was whether it was the 'innocent' or the 'tortious' dust that had caused C's condition. There was no evidence at all as to the proportions of innocent and tortious dust that C had inhaled. It was therefore impossible to apply the usual 'but-for' test since C could not show on the balance of

---

something. Perhaps this is why Lord Walker did not entirely agree, but preferred to state that the duty would be empty in many [but not all] cases': [2005] 1 AC 134, at [101].

[29] [2005] 1 AC 134, at [87] (emphasis added).

[30] Lord Bingham noted that the rationale of the duty to warn was 'to enable adult patients of sound mind to make for themselves decisions intimately affecting their own lives and bodies' [2005] 1 AC 134, at [5]. See in similar vein the speeches of Lords Hoffmann and Hope at [33] and [56] respectively.

[31] Recognizing this, Lord Hoffmann expressly suggested that in respect of the infringement of the patient's right to choose 'there might be a case for a modest solatium': [2005] 1 AC 134, at [34].

[32] See, eg, *White v Paul Davidson & Taylor* [2005] PNLR 15 (*Chester* inapplicable to solicitor's negligent advice); *Beary v Pall Mall Investments* [2005] PNLR 35 (*Chester* inapplicable to negligent advice regarding financial matters). There were clear hints that this should be done in *Chester v Afshar* itself.

[33] [1956] AC 613.

probabilities that had a proper extraction mechanism been used, he would not have contracted the disease. The House of Lords nonetheless found for C.

Lord Reid captured the essence of their Lordships' approach when he said that 'the source of [the claimant's] disease was the dust from both sources, and the real question is whether the dust from the swing grinders materially contributed to the disease'.[34] Notably, the claimant recovered damages in full despite the fact that the tortious dust only contributed to his illness. By contrast, where successive employers expose the claimant to the same harmful agent in cases of cumulative disease, each defendant will only be held liable for that part of the claimant's harm for which he is responsible.[35]

(4) THE MATERIAL CONTRIBUTION TO THE RISK OF HARM PRINCIPLE

The principle in *Bonnington Castings v Wardlaw* was later extended in *McGhee v National Coal Board*.[36]

D failed to provide adequate after-work washing facilities so that employees could not remove from themselves, at the end of the working day, the brick dust to which they were innocently exposed during the working day. The brick dust to which C's skin was exposed caused him to contract dermatitis. But it was unclear whether C would have contracted dermatitis if he had not been exposed to the dust for the prolonged period attributable to D's failure to provide proper washing facilities. C, in other words, could not invoke the usual but-for test. The House of Lords nonetheless found for C.

Crucial to the decision in *McGhee* was the tortious quality of the prolonged exposure to the brick dust. The increased danger that the claimant would develop dermatitis could be treated, according to their Lordships, *as though* it had made a material contribution to the claimant's injury. The claimant recovered full damages from the defendant.

Because the claimant in *Bonnington* suffered the onset of pneumoconiosis – a cumulative disease, the severity of which increases in proportion to the level of exposure to the harmful agent – the House of Lords were at least able to say that the tortious dust had made his illness worse, even if they could not specify the precise extent to which this was the case. Furthermore, there was no doubt that it was silicon dust that had caused the condition in the claimant. In *McGhee*, by contrast, there was no evidence to the effect that the claimant's disease had been caused by occupational

---

[34] [1956] AC 613, at 621. A similar approach was taken in *Nicholson v Atlas Steel Foundry and Engineering Co Ltd* [1957] 1 All ER 776 where it was held on very similar facts that liability could be imposed although it was impossible even to estimate in very general terms the proportions of innocent and tortious dust. See also *Hutchinson v Epsom & St Helier NHS Trust* [2002] EWHC 2362.

[35] *Holtby v Brigham & Cowan (Hull) Ltd* [2000] PIQR Q293 (C was exposed to asbestos over 40 years of employment. He suffered a cumulative disease in respect of which it was possible to identify the contribution made by D. A reduced damages award was made to reflect this fact. Stuart-Smith LJ (at Q298) was content that there had been no reduction of damages in *Bonnington* simply because this had not been argued). See also *Allen v British Rail Engineering* [2001] EWCA Civ 242.   [36] [1972] 3 All ER 1008.

exposure to brick dust (whether negligent or not). The experts providing evidence in that case would go no further than to say that unnecessary exposure to brick dust after work, caused by the non-provision of showering facilities, materially increased *the risk* of the claimant contracting dermatitis. There was, therefore, greater evidential uncertainty in *McGhee* than in *Bonnington*. But the House of Lords, while acknowledging the difference, was prepared to treat the two types of evidential uncertainty as if they were the same. Lord Salmon said:

In the circumstances of the present case, the possibility of a distinction existing between (a) having materially increased the risk of contracting the disease, and (b) having materially contributed to causing the disease may no doubt be a fruitful source of interesting academic discussions between students of philosophy. Such a distinction is, however, far too unreal to be recognized by the common law.[37]

(5) THE MATERIAL CONTRIBUTION TO THE RISK OF HARM AMONG SEVERAL WRONGDOERS PRINCIPLE

In *McGhee*, the medical evidence confirmed that the claimant's dermatitis could have begun with a single abrasion, either non-tortiously (while he was working), or tortiously (after work, while he was cycling home with brick dust still on his body because of the defendant's failure to provide showering facilities). It was conceivable, too, that the disease may have had a non-occupational origin. What at least was clear, however, was that there was only one wrongdoer. In the case of *Fairchild v Glenhaven Funeral Services Ltd*,[38] by contrast, there was even greater evidential uncertainty.[39]

C contracted mesothelioma – an invariably fatal form of cancer – by exposure to asbestos during his earlier working life. One complication in the case was the fact that C had worked for several employers, all of whom had negligently exposed him to asbestos. A second complication arose from the fact that medical science does not fully understand the aetiology of mesothelioma so that it was impossible to say when he had first contracted the condition, or at least its origins. This meant that the responsible employer could not be identified. Thirdly, because mesothelioma is not a cumulative disease, it was not a case in which the material contribution to harm principle could be applied. Finally, some of C's former employers had ceased to trade so C was limited in the number of former employers he could attempt to sue.

The House of Lords reasserted the principle espoused in *McGhee* and found for the claimant.[40] But the case, it is suggested here, can be distinguished from *McGhee* in that, if the condition had already been triggered by a period of prior employment, it is entirely feasible that the defendants did not in any meaningful way contribute even to

---

[37] [1972] 3 All ER 1008, at 1018.   [38] [2002] 3 All ER 305.

[39] For analysis, see Stapleton, 'Lords a-Leaping Evidentiary Gaps' (2002) 10 *Torts LJ* 276; Morgan, 'Lost Causes in the House of Lords: *Fairchild v Glenhaven Funeral Services*' (2003) 66 MLR 277.

[40] Lords Hoffmann, Hutton and Rodger saw the case as an application of the principle in *McGhee* notwithstanding the additional evidential uncertainty associated with the fact that there were multiple wrongdoers in *Fairchild*: [2002] 3 All ER 305, at [74], [116] and [153].

the risk of harm.[41] Further exposure to asbestos would have been more like stabbing a corpse than stabbing the merely wounded.[42] Similarly, if some of the relevant employers had not been in breach of a duty in exposing the claimant to asbestos, but the condition had been triggered while in the employment of one such employer, the defendant would again find himself liable despite the entirely innocent way in which the disease was contracted. He would have contributed to neither the harm itself, nor even the risk of the harm.

Somewhat radically, and picking up on the point that was never argued in *McGhee*, the House of Lords later held in *Barker v Corus UK Ltd*[43] that, so long as the claimant had contracted mesothelioma, (1) each defendant could be held liable for exposing the claimant to asbestos dust and (2) that each defendant should be held liable *only* for his or her relative contribution to the chance of the claimant contracting mesothelioma. In other words, the House of Lords took the view that employers who expose employees to asbestos should be treated as several, not joint, tortfeasors.[44] The effect of the *Barker* decision *in relation to several tortfeasance* was nullified by section 3 of the Compensation Act 2006. That section now makes it clear that the claimant should be entitled to claim in full from a single defendant (whether or not he was the only one exposing the claimant to asbestos in breach of duty).

There was certainly a case for some statutory intervention following *Barker* since it was by no means clear from their Lordships' decision in that case just how the relative shares of responsibility between various employers was to be computed.[45] However, the unsatisfactory state of the law was hardly resolved satisfactorily by the enactment of the 2006 Act. This is because the statute expressly recognizes the right of the defendant[46] to claim a contribution from fellow wrongdoers who also unjustifiably exposed the claimant to asbestos.[47] And in so doing, the Act puts in place a presumptive apportionment between those wrongdoers based on 'the relative lengths of the periods of exposure for which each [tortfeasor] was responsible'.[48] As such, the statute imports part of what was inadequate in their Lordships decision, albeit that it is now applied to contribution issues rather than to the extent of an individual wrongdoer's several liability.

---

[41] For the view that each employer can be treated as having, in law, contributed to the risk of harm and that he can be liable for that risk creation (assuming mesothelioma has transpired in the claimant), see *Barker v Corus UK Ltd* [2006] UKHL 20.

[42] Lord Bingham recognized the point given that he remarked: 'In *McGhee*'s case . . . unlike the present appeals, the case was not complicated by the existence of additional or alternative wrongdoers' [2002] 3 All ER 305, at [21]. Cf *Barker v Corus UK Ltd* [2006] UKHL 20.   [43] [2006] UKHL 20.

[44] On the distinction between these two categories of tortfeasor, see ch 25.

[45] Two of their Lordships did suggest, somewhat vaguely, that the respective shares should be determined by reference to the length and intensity of exposure to asbestos dust: [2006] 2 WLR 1027, at [48] and [109], *per* Lords Hoffmann and Rodger respectively.

[46] The Act does not refer to a defendant, *per se*, but instead uses the term 'responsible person' defined to be someone who has 'negligently or in breach of statutory duty caused or permitted another person ('the victim') to be exposed to asbestos': Compensation Act 2006, s 3(1)(a). As such, no liability may attach under the Act to anyone other than a common law or statutory wrongdoer.

[47] Compensation Act 2006, s 3(2). The subsection simultaneously recognizes the right to apply the principle of contributory negligence in order to reduce the extent of a wrongdoer's liability.

[48] Compensation Act 2006, s 4.

More particularly, the presumption is of dubious merit since one wrongdoer's share of responsibility will never be a simple linear function of the proportionate amount of time spent working for him. This is because, even if the Act factored in the relative intensity of the different periods of exposure, there would still be the problem that a person who had inhaled the fatal asbestos fibres while working for employer X could never have been further jeopardized or harmed by working for later employers Y and Z.

Perhaps in recognition of the rough and ready nature of this presumption, the Act does go on, in the very same section, to state that the presumption *can* be ousted either (a) where some contrary agreement as to respective responsibility among the various wrongdoers is reached or (b) the situation is one in which 'the court thinks that another basis for determining contributions is more appropriate in the circumstances of a particular case'.[49] What these two bases for ousting the application of the presumption perhaps have in common is the *suggestion* that a decent amount of available evidence will generally be needed in order to compute an equitable division of responsibility for supposed risk.[50] However, if we reflect upon the actual wording of these two exceptions, we might reasonably conclude that the Act is a good deal less helpful than it attempts to be. In relation to the first – quite apart from the fact that it does no more than inscribe into the statute the kind of practice that dominates the settlement of tort claims outside the courts in any event – it is difficult to envisage just when it will be the case that a commercially orientated employer will agree to pay more than he would be required to pay by an apportionment based purely on temporal considerations.[51] And in relation to the second exception, it is next to impossible to predict just when a court will consider that 'another basis for determining contributions is more appropriate',[52] or what that other basis for determining contributions will be. At the very least, it might have been more sensible to entitle a court to depart from the presumption in section 3(4)on the basis of the familiar considerations in contribution cases: namely, what it considers to be just and equitable.[53] Without any such constraints, there would appear to be the danger that the statute could give rise to a fairly unprincipled and *ad hoc* body of case law.

In summary then, *Fairchild*, the now-reversed decision in *Barker* and the 2006 Act (insofar as it deals with liability to contribute) all fail to display or suggest any logically defensible approach to causation. Certainly, both the cases are characterized by speeches of a rather *ad hoc* and balance-of-justice nature which, in any event, are intended to be of very limited scope. Taking *Fairchild* first, Lord Nicholls readily

---

[49] Compensation Act 2006, s 4(a), (b).

[50] Indeed, the presumption itself may well have been introduced in recognition of the evidentiary problems that typically surround mesothelioma cases (given that the disease is widely thought to occur by means of a series of medical processes that take decades to unfold).

[51] Perhaps employer X for whom C worked for five years, may agree to pay, say, 60% of the damages even though C also spent five years working for the actual defendant, Y, if he knows that his workplace was twice as dusty as X's workplace. But even here, why would Y agree to pay 40% of the damages (except perhaps to avoid the hidden costs associated with litigation)?   [52] Compensation Act 2006, s 3(4)(b).

[53] Cf Civil Liability (Contribution) Act 1978, s 2(1). This is equally fluid, but at least imports consistency into the law of contribution.

admitted that the decision was ultimately rooted in policy rather than established legal principle. He said:

The unattractive consequence, that one of the [potential wrongdoers] will be held liable for an injury he did not in fact inflict, is outweighed by the even less attractive alternative, that the innocent [claimant] should receive no recompense even though one of the [potential defendants] injured him. It is this balance ('outweighed by') which justifies a relaxation in the standard of causation required. Insistence on the normal standard of causation would work an injustice.[54]

Yet while his Lordship was prepared to concede that, in cases such as *Fairchild*, 'the court is applying a different and less stringent test', he did not explain precisely what that test was. In fact, the only judges to offer any kind of rule-based explanation of the decision were Lords Bingham, Hoffmann and Rodger. But their three explanations differed significantly from each other.

For Lord Bingham, the claimant's case succeeded because it satisfied the following six-part test:

(1) C was employed at different times and for differing periods by both A and B, and (2) A and B were both subject to a duty to take reasonable care or to take all practicable measures to prevent C inhaling asbestos dust because of the known risk that asbestos dust (if inhaled) might cause a mesothelioma, and (3) both A and B were in breach of that duty to C during the periods of C's employment by each of them with the result that during both periods C inhaled excessive quantities of asbestos dust, and (4) C is found to be suffering from a mesothelioma, and (5) any cause of C's mesothelioma other than the inhalation of asbestos dust at work can be effectively discounted, but (6) C cannot (because of the current limits of human science) prove, on the balance of probabilities, that his mesothelioma was the result of his inhaling asbestos dust during his employment by A or during his employment by B or during his employment by A and B taken together.[55]

Lord Rodger offered a far more general test, albeit implicitly, in his somewhat lengthy explanation of the principle applied in *McGhee* (as *he* understood it). He said:

First, the principle is designed to resolve the difficulty that arises where it is inherently impossible for the claimant to prove exactly how his injury was caused . . . Secondly, part of the underlying rationale of the principle is that the defendant's wrongdoing has materially increased the risk that the claimant will suffer injury. *It is therefore essential not just that the defendant's conduct created a material risk of injury to a class of persons but that it actually created a material risk of injury to the claimant himself.* Thirdly, it follows that the defendant's conduct must have been capable of causing the claimant's injury. Fourthly, the claimant must prove that his injury was caused by the eventuation of the kind of risk created by the defendant's wrongdoing . . . [As such] the principle does not apply where the claimant has merely proved that his injury could have been caused by a number of different events, only one of which is the eventuation of the risk created by the defendant's wrongful act. *Wilsher's* case[56] is an example. Fifthly, this will usually mean that the claimant must prove that his injury was caused, if not by exactly the same agency as was involved in the defendant's wrongdoing,

---

[54] [2002] 3 All ER 305, at [39].   [55] [2002] 3 All ER 305, at [2].   [56] See below.

at least by an agency that operated in substantially the same way . . . Sixthly, the principle applies where the other possible source of the claimant's injury is a similar wrongful act or omission of another person, but it can also apply where, as in *McGhee*'s case, the other possible source of the injury is a similar, but lawful act or omission of the same defendant.[57]

Different again was Lord Hoffmann's reasoning. In his view, the critical factors justifying the imposition of liability were as follows:

First, [there must be] . . . a duty specifically intended to protect employees against being unnecessarily exposed to the risk of (among other things) a particular disease. Secondly, the duty is one intended to create a civil right to compensation for injury relevantly connected with its breach. Thirdly, it is established that the greater the exposure to asbestos, the greater the risk of contracting that disease. Fourthly, except in the case in which there has been only one significant exposure to asbestos, medical science cannot prove whose asbestos is more likely than not to have produced the cell mutation which caused the disease. Fifthly, the employee has contracted the disease against which he should have been protected.[58]

There are notable differences between each of these approaches.[59] On the one hand, Lord Bingham's speech is couched in very narrow terms. It emphasizes both the necessity of the claimant having been employed by successive employers both of whom exposed him to asbestos dust, and the requirement that the relevant form of harm should be mesothelioma. In effect, his reasoning was designed to resolve the dispute in *Fairchild*, but did not support any general principle of law. Lord Hoffmann's approach was almost as narrow, being applicable only to employees exposed to asbestos dust. Thus, elsewhere in his speech, he remarked upon the fact that 'a rule requiring proof of a link between the defendant's asbestos and the claimant's disease would . . . empty the duty of content'.[60] Only Lord Rodger seemed prepared to propound a relatively broad test. But, if one adopts the usual *ex post facto* approach to causation in interpreting the italicized sentence in the passage extracted above,[61] it appears that there is a logical flaw in his reasoning. If the defendant must have 'created a material risk of injury to the claimant himself', how can this ever be shown definitively in a case involving anyone other than the first employer in the chain? If we suppose that the claimant's condition was triggered at the first place of employment – which is entirely feasible – how can any subsequent employer have exposed him to, or contributed to, a material risk of mesothelioma. So far as the condition is presently understood, all that would have been necessary to occur for him to have contracted the disease, would have already occurred.

---

[57] [2002] 3 All ER 305, at [170] (emphasis added).   [58] [2002] 3 All ER 305, at [61].

[59] Curiously, Lord Nicholls agreed with all his brethren: [2002] 3 All ER 305, at [36].

[60] [2002] 3 All ER 305, at [62]. This is, of course, untrue. For as Stapleton has pointed out, the employer would still owe a meaningful duty in relation to other conditions, such as asbestosis: see Stapleton, 'Lords a-leaping Evidentiary Gaps' (2002) 10 *Torts LJ* 276, at 296.

[61] An *ex post facto* interpretation would also appear warranted given the past tense in which his *dictum* is couched: ie, since the language is framed in terms of what D has done, rather than what D may do, it is appropriate to question what may have taken place in fact, rather than what might occur in theory.

Notwithstanding these differences in approach, the Court of Appeal in *Gregg v Scott* wasted no time in trying to clarify the gist of the *Fairchild* decision. Favouring the more limited approaches of Lords Bingham and Hoffmann, Simon Brown LJ said:

As *Fairchild* makes plain, however, this more relaxed approach to the proof of causation – 'treat[ing] a material increase in risk as sufficient to satisfy the causal requirements for liability' (*per* Lord Hoffmann at paragraph 67) – will apply only in the most narrowly defined circumstances (see Lord Bingham at paragraph 2 and Lord Hoffmann at paragraph 61). There is nothing in the speeches to suggest a more relaxed approach generally to proof of causation nor, to my mind, to invite any fresh attempt to advance the *Hotson* argument.[62]

But such narrowing of the *Fairchild* exception did not answer all the questions to which the case gave rise. And here we must turn to the *Barker* case, albeit that it has since been nullified by statute *in so far* as it propounded the idea that negligent employers in mesothelioma cases should be treated as several (not joint) tortfeasors.

The best starting point for considering *Barker* is not in fact *Barker* itself, but rather the decision in *Holtby v Brigham & Cowan (Hull) Ltd*[63], for it was held there that the damages should be reduced in circumstances where a defendant was only partly responsible for the claimant's *cumulative* disease. This naturally caused some lawyers to wonder whether liability should also be allocated severally in cases involving an indivisible disease (a matter not pleaded or considered in *Fairchild*). The question, then, following *Fairchild*, was whether a single employer should be held liable for the full amount of a claimant's suffering where multiple previous employers had equally acted in breach of their duties of care towards employees. Certainly, in the immediate wake of *Fairchild*, it seemed possible to recover in full from a single employer. Yet if such recovery were possible, it would mean, counter-intuitively, that the less the claimant could show in cases of industrial exposure to asbestos (as is the case with mesothelioma where knowledge about the aetiology and triggers of the diseases are shrouded in mystery), the better off he would be in terms of damages. Thus, if the employee suffered a cumulative disease – such as asbestosis – only a proportion of the damages would be recoverable if several former employers had ceased to exist; whereas if he suffered an indivisible disease – like mesothelioma – he could recover in full. As things turned out, it was just this conundrum that fell to be considered in *Barker*,[64] the second House of Lords mesothelioma case.

There, in a spirited attempt to set the limits to the *Fairchild* exception, a majority of the House of Lords held that full recovery from one among several tortfeasors should not be permitted. Liability, they said, 'must be apportioned to the defendants according to their contributions to the risk [of mesothelioma being contracted]'.[65] But in answering one question, their Lordships undoubtedly raised several others. One of

---

[62] *Gregg v Scott* [2002] EWCA Civ 1471, at [100]. But is this simply an endeavour to protect the NHS given that cases of evidential uncertainty abound in the context of medical negligence?

[63] [2000] PIQR Q293.   [64] [2006] UKHL 20.

[65] [2006] UKHL 20, at [48], *per* Lord Hoffmann. Lord Scott, Lord Walker and Baroness Hale all expressly agreed with Lord Hoffmann who also clarified (at [24]) that the *Fairchild* exception was only applicable to cases in which only one agent (or causatively similar/identical agent) caused the disease. Their Lordships unanimously held that it did not matter if not all the exposures were tortious.

these – namely, the way in which we should calculate contributions to the risk of contracting mesothelioma – we have already met. But equally, in characterizing risk creation as a recoverable head of damage in this way, the majority would seem to have taken English tort law into territory that may well offer some rewards,[66] but which is nonetheless fraught with dangers where the remedy sought is damages rather than an injunction.[67] Furthermore, there is nothing in the 2006 Act (which merely reinstates joint liability in such cases) that addresses this problem. Indeed, the contribution provisions of section 3 of the Act leave intact the idea that risk creation alone (albeit only in relation to the risk of mesothelioma) is a wrong that warrants the payment of damages.

(6) THE ONE AMONG SEVERAL CAUSATIVE AGENTS PRINCIPLE

Whether *Fairchild* will be interpreted in the future as having given rise to any clear principle of law remains to be seen.[68] What also remains to be resolved is where the principle in *McGhee* stops, and the rule in *Wilsher v Essex Area Health Authority*[69] begins.

In *Wilsher*, junior doctors negligently administered excess oxygen to C, a premature infant. C later developed retrolental fibroplasia (RLF) a condition that ultimately left him completely blind. Medical practice required careful monitoring of infants receiving oxygen because of evidence that excess oxygen might cause RLF in premature babies. But there were said to be five other possible causes of RLF in very sick, very premature babies. The trial judge ruled that C, having proved a breach of duty arising from a failure to protect him from the risk of the very sort of damage which in fact materialized, was able to shift the onus of proof to the defendants to prove that some other cause actually resulted in that damage.

The trial judge was severely rebuked by the House of Lords for his endeavour to shift the onus of proof. Nor could their Lordships accept the argument of the majority in the Court of Appeal[70] that the principle in *McGhee* could extend to the facts of *Wilsher*. The claimants had not established that it was more probable than not that excess oxygen rather than any of the other possible causes had caused the claimant to succumb to RLF.[71] Indeed, although the trial judge largely overlooked it, there was a good deal of conflicting scientific evidence in the case. Their Lordships made it clear that in no circumstances did the burden of proof shift to the defendant and ordered a retrial on

---

[66] See Murphy, 'Rethinking Injunctions in Tort Law' (forthcoming).

[67] See the dissenting speech of Lord Rodger in *Barker*: [2006] UKHL 20, at [85]: 'The new analysis which the House is adopting will tend to maximise the inconsistencies in the law by turning the *Fairchild* exception into an enclave where a number of rules apply which have been rejected for use elsewhere in the law of personal injuries. Inside the enclave victims recover damages for suffering the increased risk of developing mesothelioma (or suffering the loss of a chance of not developing mesothelioma) while, just outside, patients cannot recover damages for suffering the increased risk of an unfavourable outcome to medical treatment (or suffering the loss of a chance of a favourable outcome to medical treatment)'. For other difficulties and dangers with treating risk as a form of harm see, S Perry, 'Risk, Harm and Responsibility' in Owen (ed), *Philosophical Foundations of Tort Law* (1995); Goldberg and Zipursky, 'Unrealized Torts' (2002) 88 *Virginia Law Review* 1625.

[68] In *Barker*, there was a noted – indeed, highly charged – difference of views as to just what had been decided in *Fairchild*.   [69] [1988] AC 1074.

[70] [1987] QB 730. But see, too, the dissenting view of Sir Nicholas Browne-Wilkinson V-C.

[71] Confirming the decision in *Bonnington Castings Ltd v Wardlaw* [1956] AC 613.

the issue of causation. Lord Bridge warned against the dangers of allowing sympathy for the claimant to overrule the established principles of proof:

[W]hether we like it or not, the law, which only Parliament can change, requires proof of fault causing damage as the basis of liability in tort. We should do society nothing but disservice if we made the forensic process still more unpredictable and hazardous by distorting the law to accommodate the exigencies of what may seem hard cases.[72]

The question that naturally arises, and in respect of which there remains no convincing answer, is why a case like *Fairchild* and *Barker* (in which there is a single agent, but several wrongdoers that may have caused the claimant's harm) should be treated differently from a case like *Wilsher* (in which there is a single wrongdoer, but several agents that may have caused the claimant's harm). In both types of case, it is entirely conceivable that there is a lower than 50% chance that an isolated defendant/agent caused harm to the claimant.[73]

(D) CONCURRENT TORTIOUS CAUSES

Various types of acts which may be described as 'concurrent causes' must be looked at separately. If two tortious acts result in damage, and either one would have produced the same damage – as, for example, when two fires are started and merge to burn out a building – then the perpetrator of each act is responsible for the whole damage, because each act is a substantial factor in producing the result. Similarly, if two independent acts simultaneously bring about the same damage – as where two ships negligently collide, injuring a third party[74] – those responsible for the respective negligent acts are each fully liable.

By contrast, if the defendant commits a tort (or an act which will become a tort if non-remote damage ensues) and, before his act spends its force, some later tortious act combines with it to produce a particular result which would not have been produced without the operation of the second act, then the defendant will be liable if, and only if, it is found by applying the rules already stated, that his act caused the damage.[75] In *Hale v Hants and Dorset Motor Services Ltd*, the facts were as follows.[76]

A corporation negligently allowed tree branches to overhang a highway. C was a passenger in a bus negligently driven by a servant of D (a bus company) in such a way that a branch struck the window of the bus with the result that he was blinded by broken glass.

---

[72] [1988] AC 1074, at 1092.

[73] This assumes roughly equal exposures at employers A, B and C in the multiple wrongdoer scenario, and a roughly equal chance of causing the harm in the multiple agents scenario.

[74] *The Koursk* [1924] P 140. Should D remain liable if the other 'cause' is the non-tortious act of another person, or a natural cause, or the act of C himself? Cf *Cummings (or McWilliams) v Sir William Arrol & Co Ltd* [1962] 1 All ER 623.

[75] *Rouse v Squires* [1973] QB 889, at 898, *per* Cairns LJ: 'If a driver so negligently manages his vehicle as to cause it to obstruct the highway and constitute a danger to other road users, including those who are driving too fast or not keeping a proper lookout, but not those who deliberately or recklessly drive into the obstruction, then the first driver's negligence may be held to have contributed to the causation of an accident of which the immediate cause was the negligent driving of the vehicle which because of the presence of the obstruction collides with it or with some other vehicle or some other person'.

[76] [1947] 2 All ER 628; *Robinson v Post Office* [1974] 2 All ER 737.

It was held that the corporation and the bus company were each liable in full to the claimant. Each was negligent in not foreseeing that this harm was likely to result in combination with the negligence of the other.

Where an act takes place almost contemporaneously with the first negligent act, it seems that the rules on concurrent causes rather than the rules on intervening subsequent causes applies. In *Fitzgerald v Lane*,[77] the claimant was crossing a pelican crossing when he was hit by a car driven by D1. The collision threw him onto the bonnet of the car and back onto the road where he was immediately struck by a car driven by D2. He suffered severe injuries including damage to his neck resulting in partial tetraplegia. Whether it was contact with the car driven by D1 or D2 which caused the injury to the neck could not be established. Both were held jointly liable, and the claimant was held contributorily negligent.

SECTION 2 RELATIONSHIP BETWEEN CAUSATION AND BREACH OF DUTY

In the overwhelming majority of cases, the evidential difficulties in causation cases centre solely on the question 'what would have happened if?'. But occasionally, the question that needs to be addressed is 'what *should* have happened?'. *Bolitho v City and Hackney Health Authority*[78] offers an example.

A doctor negligently failed to respond to a nurse's request to attend a sick child. A little later the child stopped breathing and suffered a cardiac arrest. It was, however, disputed among the expert witnesses at the trial whether, had the doctor attended, good medical practice would have suggested that she intubate the child (to assist him to breathe).

The House of Lords held that to establish that the negligent failure to attend the child caused his cardiac arrest, C needed to prove, not just that the doctor did not intubate the child, but that in not doing so she was negligent. They needed to establish, in other words, that the negligent failure to attend the child resulted in his being deprived of a treatment that he should have received and which would have prevented his cardiac arrest.

SECTION 3 NEW INTERVENING CAUSES: CAUSATION IN LAW

In many instances, a contingency may arise subsequent to the defendant's negligent conduct, which results in further injury to the claimant. For example, the claimant may initially suffer minor injuries at the hands of the defendant, but later die as a result of

---

[77] [1989] AC 328.   [78] [1998] AC 232.

bungled medical treatment. In such a case, the defendant is not liable for all the ulterior harm. In marking off the limits of his liability it will not ordinarily matter whether we use the language of risk or cause. The man run down by the defendant's negligence cannot recover for the extra damage sustained when a tile falls off a roof onto his head while he is on his way to hospital. This is because the defendant's conduct did not create a special risk of harm from that kind of contingency, or because the falling tile was a coincidence. The original negligent driving and the subsequent falling of the tile were independent acts; the conjunction of the two events was abnormal and not contrived by human agency. The falling of the tile broke the chain of *legal* causation. It constituted what is called a *novus actus interveniens* – that is, a new intervening act sufficient to relieve the defendant of further liability for the consequences of his own conduct.

A *novus actus interveniens* may take one of three settled forms.

(1) The intervening event may be an act of nature[79] (or act of God, as it is sometimes described[80]). For example, imagine a child is injured while playing football at school, and, as she is wheeled across the playground to the waiting ambulance she is struck by lightning. The injury inflicted by the lightning is not in any sense a consequence of her sports injury. It is important to note, however, that for an act of nature to constitute a *novus actus*, it must be something overwhelming and unpredictable and in no sense linked to D's negligence.

(2) C's own conduct may constitute a *novus actus*.

(3) The act of a third party may break the chain of causation.[81]

Before considering examples of each type of *novus actus interveniens*, two general points may be made. First, it should be noted that the more foreseeable the intervening cause, the more likely that the court will *not* treat it as breaking the chain of causation. *Reeves v Metropolitan Police Comr*[82] illustrates the point.

C's husband hanged himself in his prison cell. There was no evidence that he had been diagnosed as suffering from any mental disorder but he had been identified as a 'suicide risk'. The Court of Appeal held that his suicide did not constitute a *novus actus interveniens*. The evidence available to Ds of his emotionally disturbed state and suicidal tendencies imposed on them a duty to protect the deceased, effectively from himself. Suicide was a kind of harm which they should have contemplated and guarded against, and they were thus liable when it occurred.

Similarly, damage incurred in rescuing a person imperilled by the act of the defendant does not break the chain of causation where such rescue could have been

---

[79] *Carslogie Steamship Co Ltd v Royal Norwegian Government* [1952] AC 292.

[80] *Nichols v Marsland* (1876) 2 Ex D 1.

[81] There is an argument that a natural event should not be treated as a *novus actus*. Acts of C and acts of third parties have in common the fact that they tend to involve reactions to (or conduct conditioned by) tortious events. Often they involve acts which are designed in some way to 'deal with' D's initial tortious act. Such acts are therefore intimately related to that initial tortuous conduct so that no question of factual causation arises. The only question is one of whether the law is prepared to recognise the fact that D's initial tort was also a cause of the subsequent event. Natural intervening events cannot, of course, be characterized in this way.

[82] [2000] 1 AC 360.

anticipated.[83] And where the injuries negligently inflicted by the defendant on a claimant's husband induced a state of acute anxiety neurosis which persisted for 18 months and caused him ultimately to take his own life, the defendant was held liable to the claimant.[84] In each of these cases, the ulterior harm was within the foreseeable risk.

Secondly, in respect of intervening causes in the second and third categories, it is generally the case that the smaller the degree to which the conduct in question is a voluntary act of folly, the less likely will be the courts to treat that conduct as a *novus actus*. In *Scott v Shepherd*[85] it was held to be no defence to the man who first threw a firework into the crowd that the claimant would have suffered no loss had a third party not picked it up and thrown it again after the defendant had thrown it, because the third party, in throwing it, was acting for his self-preservation. In another case, the claimant's ship lost her compass and charts when the defendant's ship negligently collided with it. The claimant's ship consequently ran aground while trying to make port. The defendant was held liable for this further harm.[86] In both cases, the subsequent events were not sufficiently abnormal responses to the situation created by the defendant's negligence.

With these two general points in mind, let us now consider examples of each type of *novus actus interveniens*.

(A) INTERVENING NATURAL CAUSES

In *Carslogie Steamship Co v Royal Norwegian Government*[87] D negligently caused C's ship to be damaged and require repairs. The ship was out of commission for some time, but she later set sail again for the USA. *En route*, she suffered storm damage that required further repairs. C argued that the storm repairs would not have been necessary had the ship left for the USA on time and that, since the delay was due to D's initial negligence, D must be held liable in respect of the cost of the further repairs.

It was held that the chain of causation was broken by the storm since the severity of the storm was so unforeseeable that it would be improper to regard it as is any way connected to D's negligence.

In *Jobling v Associated Dairies Ltd*[88] C was partially incapacitated by an accident at work. Later, but before the trial, he suffered the onset of a supervening illness of a kind causing the same type of incapacitation. The House of Lords held that D was only responsible for C's loss of earnings up until the time he succumbed to the illness.

The House of Lords stressed the fact that the object of damages in tort is to put the claimant as far as possible in the position he would have been in 'but for' the tort.

---

[83] *Baker v TE Hopkins & Sons Ltd* [1959] 3 All ER 225.

[84] *Pigney v Pointers Transport Services Ltd* [1957] 2 All ER 807. See also *Kirkham v Chief Constable of Greater Manchester Police* [1990] 2 QB 283; *Corr v IBC Vehicles Ltd* [2006] 2 All ER 929.

[85] (1773) 2 Wm Bl 892.   [86] *The City of Lincoln* (1889) 15 PD 15.   [87] [1952] AC 292.

[88] [1982] AC 794.

Claimants are not, they said, supposed to profit (hence the erstwhile principle of common law that a widow's damages for loss of her husband would be calculated taking into account her prospects of remarriage). The claimant in *Jobling* would eventually have been unable to work even if the tort had never been committed. Disease, according to the House of Lords, is a vicissitude of life and one in respect of which, on policy grounds, their Lordships were unprepared to make the defendants responsible.

(B) CLAIMANT'S OWN CONDUCT

There is no doubt that the claimant's own conduct can constitute a *novus actus* in appropriate circumstances.

In *McKew v Holland & Hannens & Cubitts (Scotland) Ltd*[89] D's negligence caused injury to C's leg. C later broke his ankle attempting, while still suffering from the effects of the first injury, to descend a steep staircase unaided. C's imprudent and unreasonable conduct constituted a fresh and separate cause of the second injury. D was only liable for the initial injury.[90]

Compare this with the case of *Wieland v Cyril Lord Carpets Ltd*[91] where the claimant suffered neck injuries and had to wear a collar in consequence of the defendants' negligence. She later fell downstairs because, as a result of the initial injury and the neck collar, she could not use her bifocal lenses with her usual skill. Her further injury was found to be attributable to the defendants' original negligence. Unlike the rash Mr McKew, Mrs Wieland suffered a further injury triggered by her original disability. There was no unreasonable conduct on her part that could be taken to constitute a *novus actus interveniens* breaking the chain of causation.

Defining unreasonable conduct will not always be easy or uncontentious as *Emeh v Kensington, Chelsea and Westminster Area Health Authority*[92] amply illustrates.

C conceived a child after an operation to sterilize her carried out by D. D admitted negligence but denied liability for the cost of the upkeep of the child. That loss to C, he contended, resulted from her 'unreasonable' decision not to seek an abortion, and the judge at first instance agreed with him. The Court of Appeal, however, held that, since by the time C realized she was pregnant she was well into the second trimester of pregnancy, it was not unreasonable for her to refuse the trauma and risk of a late abortion.

Slade LJ made it clear that, save in exceptional circumstances, he would never regard it as unreasonable to refuse an abortion, even early on in pregnancy when the procedure is relatively simple and free of risk.[93] Waller LJ, however, was far less clear about this.[94] The divergence of views simply serves to exemplify the fact that it will frequently be difficult to classify acts or omissions on the part of the claimant as unreasonable where

---

[89] [1969] 3 All ER 1621.   [90] In similar vein, see *Wilson v Coulson* [2002] PIQR P300.
[91] [1969] 3 All ER 1006.   [92] [1985] QB 1012.
[93] [1985] QB 1012, at 1053. See also *McFarlane v Tayside Health Board* [1999] 3 WLR 1301.
[94] [1985] QB 1012, at 1048.

a moral dimension is present.[95] And an additional complication is this: even if the claimant's act may be viewed as immoral or unreasonable, it will not constitute a *novus actus interveniens* where the defendant could foresee such an act and was under a duty to take care to prevent it occurring. Thus, in *Reeves v Metropolitan Police Comr*,[96] the fact that a prisoner was a known suicide risk combined with the fact that the defendants were under a duty to take care to prevent that suicide meant that the defendants were causally responsible when the prisoner did in fact commit suicide. As Lord Hoffmann explained: 'it would make nonsense of the existence of such a duty if the law were to hold that the occurrence of the very act that ought to have been prevented negatived causal connection between the breach of duty and the loss'.[97]

A final point worth noting is that, in just the same we saw[98] that professional status will cause the standard of care to be raised in relation to professional persons who cause harm to others, so too will higher expectations be placed upon them in respect of the protection of their own interests in this context. Thus, a former solicitor's failure to take heed of limitation periods of which he was fully aware constituted a *novus actus* in an action he was attempting to bring against a firm of solicitors acting on his behalf.[99]

(c) ACTS OF THIRD PARTIES

The relevant principles in this category are comparatively flexible and their application is sometimes difficult. The central issue in any case is whether the defendant's negligence was responsible in law for the damage that occurred, even though that damage required the combination of the defendant's negligent act with a subsequent act by a third party. The difficulties in this context stem from the different ways in which the two general principles outlined earlier can be combined. Thus, while it can be asserted with some confidence that an unforeseeable and unreasonable premeditated act by a third party will almost certainly sever the chain of causation (and vice versa), it is more difficult to classify unforeseeable reasonable acts, and foreseeable unreasonable acts, as new intervening causes. Furthermore, it is not necessarily a straightforward matter to determine the reasonableness (or otherwise) of the third party's behaviour.

In *The Oropesa*,[100] a collision at sea was caused by D's negligence. In the ensuing circumstances, the captain of the damaged vessel ordered a life-boat to be put to sea so that salvage arrangements could be made with D. In traversing the waters between the two ships, the lifeboat capsized and several crew members were lost, including C's son.

While the death of C's son was caused by a combination of the defendant's initial negligence with the captain's subsequent decision to board the life-boat in rough seas, it

---

[95] On the related issue of the duty to minimize damages by accepting medical treatment, see *Selvanayagam v University of the West Indies* [1983] 1 All ER 824.   [96] [2000] 1 AC 360.

[97] [2000] 1 AC 360, at 367–368. Cf *Grieves v FT Everard & Sons* [2006] EWCA 27 where C's anxiety about the onset of a long-term asbestos-related disease was foreseeable, but there was no duty to take reasonable care to prevent C suffering such anxiety.   [98] See ch 4.

[99] *Kaberry v Freethcartwright (A Firm)* [2002] EWCA Civ 1966.   [100] [1943] P 32.

was nonetheless held that his decision was reasonable in the circumstances.[101] But even where conduct of the third party is necessitated by the initial negligence of the defendant, it is still possible that the subsequent act will constitute a *novus actus*. In *Rahman v Arearose Ltd* the facts were as follows.

C had been assaulted by two youths. The assault left C needing surgery. The surgery that followed was undertaken negligently by D, and as a result C was left blind in one eye. Partly in response to the blindness and partly in consequence of the assault, C also suffered a psychiatric response that fell within the definition of PTSD.

It was held that the blindness was exclusively attributable to the negligent surgery even though that surgery had been necessitated by the original torts of the two youths.[102] On the other hand, the careless surgery was only part of the cause of the psychiatric harm and the youths remained partly responsible for that.[103]

Issues of remoteness and policy may also complicate matters in this context. In *Lamb v Camden London Borough Council*,[104] for example, the defendants carelessly broke a water main outside the claimant's Hampstead house. The escaping water undermined the foundations and the house subsided so that, until repaired, it was uninhabitable. Squatters moved into the unoccupied house, and by the time they were evicted they had done damage totalling £30,000. The only issue was whether that damage was too remote. Lord Denning MR held that it was a question of policy whether the damage was too remote. Considering that the claimant could readily have insured against the risk and could have taken more steps to guard against squatting, and that the defendants had no right to enter the premises, policy dictated that the damage should be held too remote even though it was foreseeable.[105] Oliver LJ wrestled with the contention that the ratio of Lord Reid's speech in *Home Office v Dorset Yacht Co Ltd*[106] was that the subsequent act was too remote unless that act was likely to happen. He found Lord Reid's statement to be *obiter* and that the subsequent act was neither likely, nor even reasonably foreseeable. He added that he did not dissent from the view of Lord Denning that, on grounds of policy, foreseeable acts could still be too remote. Watkins LJ held that words such as 'possibility' or 'unlikely' did not assist him. Even though the act was reasonably foreseeable it was too remote.[107] He reached this conclusion by taking 'a robust and sensible approach'. His conclusion was:

I have the instinctive feeling that squatters' damage is too remote. I could not possibly come to any other conclusions, although on the primary facts I, too, would regard the damage or something like it as reasonably foreseeable in these times.[108]

---

[101] See also *Knightley v Johns* [1982] 1 All ER 851, where D negligently overturned his car in a road tunnel and C, a police cyclist, riding the wrong way in the tunnel was then injured in a collision with another car, a police inspector having carelessly failed to order the closure of the tunnel. C's injuries were held to be too remote because they were not reasonably foreseeable.   [102] [2001] QB 351.

[103] [2001] QB 351, at [34]. See also *Webb v Barclays Bank plc and Portsmouth Hospitals NHS Trust* [2001] EWCA Civ 1141.   [104] [1981] QB 625.

[105] [1981] QB 625, at 637.   [106] [1970] AC 1004, at 1030.

[107] [1981] QB 625, at 644. See *Rahman v Arearose Ltd* [2001] QB 351.

[108] [1981] QB 625, at 647.

A final complication arises where the third party's act is said to aggravate a form of harm or loss occasioned by the defendant in circumstances where, but for that initial harm or loss, the subsequent damage associated with the third party would never have occurred. In *Baker v Willoughby*[109] the defendants admitted negligently injuring the claimant in the leg. After that injury, the claimant was forced to take a new job. While working at the new job, but before the action came to trial, burglars shot the claimant in the same leg and it had to be amputated. The House of Lords held that the defendants remained liable for the loss of amenity occasioned by the injury inflicted by them. The fortuitous event of the second tort did not relieve them of liability. Lord Reid explained that a claimant:

> is not compensated for the physical injury: he is compensated for the loss which he suffers as a result of the injury. His loss is not in having a stiff leg: it is his inability to lead a full life, his inability to enjoy those amenities which depend on freedom of movement . . . In this case the second injury did not diminish any of these. So why should it be regarded as having obliterated or superseded them?[110]

Though the logic in this reasoning is easy to appreciate, what is less clear is how the *approach* to the occurrence of subsequent harm in this case can be reconciled with the approach taken in *Jobling* (considered earlier). Why the onset of a natural disease should be regarded as having 'obliterated or superseded' the effects of the defendant's negligence in *Jobling* while the gun-shot in *Baker v Willoughby* should be treated as having had no such effect is difficult to understand. The only explanation hinted at in *Jobling* – the later of the two cases – is that the onset of a natural disease can be regarded as a 'vicissitude of life' severing the chain of causation, whereas a subsequent tortious act is not such a vicissitude. But the Court of Appeal has since added to the confusion by stating that subsequent tortious acts are immediately to be disregarded in assessing the damage for which the first tortfeasor will be held responsible.[111]

(d) DEFENDANT'S SUPERVENING ACT

It seems well settled that a defendant may not invoke his or her own supervening tortious conduct in order to evidence a break in the chain of causation stemming from the first tortious act.[112] But in the wake of *Chester v Afshar* it can legitimately be asked whether, in certain circumstances, a subsequent non-tortious act on the part of the defendant may be taken to be a *novus actus interveniens*. In that case, it will be recalled, there was unquestionably a breach of duty on the part of the doctor who failed to disclose the risk attending the suggested surgery. But their Lordships stressed the fact that the negligent failure to warn the claimant did not increase the risk associated with

---

[109] [1970] AC 467.   [110] [1970] AC 467, at 492.   [111] *Heil v Rankin* [2001] PIQR Q16.
[112] *Coudert Bros v Normans Bay Ltd* [2004] EWCA Civ 215; *Bolitho v City and Hackney HA* [1998] AC 232, at 240, *per* Lord Browne-Wilkinson: 'A defendant cannot escape liability by saying that the damage would have occurred in any event because he would have committed some other breach of duty thereafter'.

the surgery.[113] In so doing, they were all but saying that the non-negligent surgery was unconnected to, and in no way flowed from, the tortious failure to warn. In other words, that, on conventional analysis, it might be seen as a supervening proximate cause. Furthermore, given that their Lordships imposed liability *in that particular case* on the basis of *policy reasons*, and given that they fully recognized that on conventional causation principles there would have been no liability, one wonders whether a different result might arise in a case not carrying with it sensitive questions of patient autonomy. If, for example, there were to be a case in which the supervening, non-negligent, proximate cause were to be something else than surgery, and in which the initial negligence were to take the form of something other than negligent medical advice, might the second, non-negligent act be taken to constitute a *novus actus*?

SECTION 4 REMOTENESS OF DAMAGE

Rules which make the wrongdoer liable for all the consequences of his wrongful conduct are exceptional and need to be justified by some special policy. Normally the law limits liability to those consequences which are attributable to that which made the act wrongful.[114] There are however torts – deceit is one example – where imposing liability for all the damage factually related to the relevant wrongdoing is considered justifiable. Such extensive liability is exceptional.[115] In negligence,[116] by contrast, certain consequences of the defendant's tortious conduct will be considered too remote from his wrongdoing to impose on him responsibility for those consequences. It is simply considered to be unjust to make the defendant answerable for events thought to be too far removed from his original breach of duty. As such, we must now consider the content of such rules on remoteness of damage.

(A) *THE WAGON MOUND*

The decision in *The Wagon Mound (No 1)*[117] is the leading modern authority on the rules governing the remoteness of damage in negligence.

Ds carelessly discharged oil from their ship into Sydney Harbour. About six hours later the ship set sail and left the harbour. The oil was carried by wind and tide beneath Cs' wharf, 200

---

[113] [2005] 1 AC 134, at [22], [81] and [94] *per* Lords Steyn, Hope and Walker respectively.

[114] *Banque Bruxelles Lambert SA v Eagle Star Insurance Co Ltd* [1997] AC 191, at 213, *per* Lord Hoffmann.

[115] In respect of wrongful interference with goods, the test for remoteness may, depending on whether D's conduct was intentional or negligent (since both may suffice), be the one relating to the directness of the consequence (as in deceit), or the one (as in negligence) based on the foreseeability of the kind of harm: *Kuwait Airways Corp v Iraq Airways Co* [2002] 2 AC 883.

[116] As is also the case in (*inter alia*) nuisance, the rule in *Rylands v Fletcher*, and breach of statutory duty.

[117] *Overseas Tankship (UK) Ltd v Morts and Dock & Engineering Co Ltd* [1961] AC 388.

yards away. After being advised that they could safely do so, Cs continued welding operations on their wharf. Some 55 to 60 hours after the original discharge of the oil, molten metal from the welding operations on the wharf, when fanned by the wind, set fire to some cotton waste or rag floating in the oil beneath the wharf. The burning cloth set fire to the oil whereupon the flames quickly developed into a conflagration which severely damaged the wharf. The oil also congealed upon the slipways adjoining the wharf and interfered with Cs' use of the slips. Ds neither knew nor ought to have known that the oil was capable of being set alight when spread on water.[118]

The Judicial Committee of the Privy Council held that the defendants were not liable in negligence because they could not reasonably have foreseen that the claimants' wharf would be damaged by fire when they carelessly discharged the oil into the harbour. It was, in short, harm of an unforeseeable kind.

(B) FORESEEABLE TYPE OF HARM

The Wagon Mound established that if the damage which materializes is damage by fire, then, for the defendant to be liable, he must have been able reasonably to anticipate damage by fire. It was insufficient that he could anticipate damage by fouling the wharf's slipways. An unbroken succession of subsequent cases at all levels – House of Lords,[119] Privy Council,[120] Court of Appeal[121] and first instance[122] – has followed the principle that the harm suffered must be of a kind, type or class that was reasonably foreseeable as a result of the defendant's negligence.

  Bradford v Robinson Rentals Ltd[123] is a typical illustration of the working of this principle.

Ds carelessly exposed their employee, C, a van driver, to extreme cold in the course of his duties. In consequence, C suffered frost-bite. The court held that Ds had exposed C to severe cold and fatigue likely to cause a common cold, pneumonia or chilblains. It held further that since frost-bite was of the same type and kind as these forms of harm, Ds could be held liable.

Where a wife sustained foreseeable psychological damage, the fact that some of it resulted from the effect of her husband's changed behaviour (he was also injured in the

---

[118] Some of these facts can only be gleaned from the reports in the courts below: [1958] 1 Lloyd's Rep 575, [1959] 2 Lloyd's Rep 697. In subsequent proceedings arising out of the same discharge of oil, the owners of other damaged ships recovered damages in negligence on the ground that the damage was foreseeable: *Overseas Tankship (UK) Ltd v Miller Steamship Co Pty, The Wagon Mound (No 2)* [1967] 1 AC 617. Cs in *The Wagon Mound* did not dare advance the evidence suggesting it was foreseeable that the oil would ignite on water for fear they would be held contributorily negligent in continuing welding operations. At that time, contributory negligence was a complete defence in New South Wales.

[119] *Hughes v Lord Advocate* [1963] AC 837; *Donaghey v Boulton and Paul Ltd* [1968] AC 1, at 26, *per* Lord Reid; *Banque Financière de la Cité SA v Westgate Insurance Co Ltd* [1991] 2 AC 249.

[120] *The Wagon Mound (No 2)* [1967] 1 AC 617.

[121] *Stewart v West African Terminals Ltd* [1964] 2 Lloyd's Rep 371, at 375, *per* Lord Denning MR; *Doughty v Turner Manufacturing Co Ltd* [1964] 1 QB 518, at 529.

[122] *Wieland v Cyril Lord Carpets Ltd* [1969] 3 All ER 1006, at 1009, *per* Eveleigh J; *Tremain v Pike* [1969] 3 All ER 1303, at 1308, *per* Payne J.   [123] [1967] 1 All ER 267.

accident) did not prevent her from claiming: the damage was of a foreseeable type and 'the fact that it arises or is continued by reason of an unusual complex of events does not avail the defendant'.[124]

Notwithstanding the apparent simplicity of the test for the remoteness of damage, there remain areas of uncertainty in defining 'kind of damage', as *Tremain v Pike* illustrates.[125]

C, a herdsman, while working for Ds contracted a rare condition called Weil's disease. The disease was caused by coming into contact with rats' urine. Weil's disease, *per se*, was not foreseeable, even though other diseases associated with rats were foreseeable. Ds were held not liable.

Payne J stated:

[Weil's disease] was entirely different in kind from the effect of a rat bite, or food poisoning by the consumption of food or drink contaminated by rats. I do not accept that all illness or infection arising from an infestation of rats should be regarded as of the same kind.[126]

It is also worth noting the difference between the approaches of the Court of Appeal and House of Lords in *Jolley v Sutton LBC*.[127] There, a 14-year-old boy was injured while playing with a disused boat. In the Court of Appeal, his injury (sustained while crawling underneath the boat which had been propped up) was held to be of an unforeseeable kind. In their Lordships' view, the foreseeable kinds of injury associated with fooling around with such a boat were those that would occur while climbing upon it, by virtue of rotten planking giving way while being walked upon. In the House of Lords, however, the foreseeable type of harm was cast much more broadly so as to include any injury occurring in consequence of messing about with a disused boat. As a result, the harm that the Court of Appeal had treated as too unforeseeable became suddenly – because of the broad conception applied – foreseeable.

(C) MEANS BY WHICH THE HARM WAS CAUSED

Since *The Wagon Mound*, the courts have frequently reiterated that the defendant may be liable even though he could not envisage that precise set of circumstances which caused harm of the foreseeable kind.

In *Hughes v Lord Advocate*,[128] C, aged 8, and another boy aged 10, were playing on an Edinburgh highway. Near the edge of the roadway was a manhole some nine feet deep, over which a shelter tent had been erected. Post Office workmen working on underground cables left the area after dark, placed red paraffin warning lamps there and took the ladder from the

---

[124] *Malcolm v Broadhurst* [1970] 3 All ER 508, at 511, *per* Geoffrey Lane J. See also *Brice v Brown* [1984] 1 All ER 997 (shock foreseeable: therefore D liable for C's acute mental illness. No need to foresee exact mental process leading to the ultimate result); cf *French v Chief Constable of Sussex* [2006] EWCA Civ 312.

[125] [1969] 3 All ER 1303.   [126] [1969] 3 All ER 1303, at 1308.

[127] [1998] 1 WLR 1546 (CA); [2000] 1 WLR 1082 (HL). For analysis, see Stauch, 'Risk and Remoteness of Damage in Negligence' (2001) 64 MLR 191.   [128] [1963] AC 837.

manhole and laid it on the ground. The boys came up and started meddling with this equipment and C, while swinging one of the lamps by a rope over the hole, stumbled over the lamp, and knocked it into the hole. An explosion followed. C was thrown into the manhole and was severely burned. The explosion occurred because paraffin from the lamp escaped, vaporized and was ignited by the flame. This particular development of events was not foreseeable, but D was held liable for the negligence of the workmen.

The defendant was liable because the claimant was injured as a result of the type or kind of accident or occurrence that could reasonably have been foreseen, even though the workmen could not have foreseen (1) the exact way in which he would play with the alluring objects that had been left lying around, or (2) the exact way in which, in so doing, he might get hurt. The workmen's conduct created a risk of the relevant kind of harm – personal injury by burning – and this in fact materialized.

If harm of a foreseeable kind occurs, it will normally be no defence that the precise mechanics of the way in which the negligent act results in that harm could not be foreseen.[129] Thus, since it was foreseeable that a defendant's pack of terrier dogs would knock over and scratch children, he was liable when one of them bit the claimant child without knocking him over.[130] Equally, the fact that an explosion much greater in magnitude than was foreseeable resulted in damage to the claimant will be no defence.[131] In general, it is only when the accident is caused by the intrusion of some new and unforeseen factor that the way in which the damage was caused is relevant. Lord Reid in *Hughes v Lord Advocate* discussed *Glasgow Corpn v Muir*,[132] where the facts were as follows.

Two picnickers were allowed to carry a tea urn through a passage of D's tea house. For a reason never made explicit, one of the picnickers slipped, and children buying sweets at a counter in the passage were scalded. An action by the children in negligence against D failed.

Lord Reid said of this case that a person carelessly carrying a hot tea urn near children would not be liable if it were upset and caused damage because the ceiling collapsed; the fall of the ceiling would be an extraneous cause. Yet one case is particularly difficult to reconcile with the principles set out in this section: *Doughty v Turner Manufacturing Co Ltd*.[133]

Ds placed an asbestos cement cover over a heat treatment bath containing sodium cyanide as a very hot molten liquid. Ds' employees carelessly dislodged this cover so that it slid into the bath. The molten liquid exploded. It erupted from the bath and injured C, a nearby workman. Although it was reasonably foreseeable that damage by splashing would result from dislodging the cover, it was not reasonably foreseeable that an explosion would ensue.

The defendants were held not liable, even though the relevant kind of harm – damage by burning – was foreseeable. They would have been liable for damage by splashing. But since the risk of damage by explosion was not foreseeable, and since this risk differed so

---

[129] *Draper v Hodder* [1972] 2 QB 556.
[130] *Wieland v Cyril Lord Carpets Ltd* [1969] 3 All ER 1006, *per* Eveleigh J.
[131] *Vacwell Engineering Co Ltd v BDH Chemicals Ltd* [1971] 1 QB 88 (on appeal [1971] 1 QB 111n).
[132] [1943] AC 448.   [133] [1964] 1 QB 518.

substantially from the one that was foreseeable, *Hughes v Lord Advocate* was distinguished. Even so, the distinction drawn between a burn caused by a splash and a burn caused by an explosion is a fine one. This point was noted by the Privy Council in *Att-Gen v Hartwell* where Lord Nicholls specifically questioned whether the decision in *Doughty* was correct[134] (though of course he was in no position *qua* Privy Council judge to attempt to overturn the decision in that case).

(D) EXTENT OF THE DAMAGE

Where the very kind of harm that was foreseeable has occurred, it has always been the case that the defendant cannot plead that the claimant was earning more than the average victim, or that goods were exceptionally valuable in order to reduce his liability in damages. This is because damages are not restricted to the average loss of earnings or average value of goods in the circumstances, even supposing that such a sum is calculable. Similarly, if the facts can be proven, the shop assistant who usually earns £200 per week will recover her full loss if she is knocked down on her way to fulfil a highly lucrative, once-in-a-lifetime television contract.

At one time, it was thought that the claimant's impecuniosity could be relevant in this context. Thus, in *Liesbosch (Dredger) v Edison*[135] where the claimants' dredger was sunk owing to the negligence of the defendants, it was held that the (exorbitant) cost of hiring a replacement dredger to fulfil an existing contract was too remote a loss to recover. The claimants had only hired the replacement because they were too impecunious to purchase immediately a replacement vessel for the one that had been sunk. According to the House of Lords, while the market price of a comparable dredger would, ultimately, be covered by the award of damages, the hire costs of the interim replacement were seen to result from an 'extraneous' cause,[136] the claimant's poverty. It was this supposedly extraneous cause that made the exorbitant cost of hire too remote. Since then, however, the House of Lords has overruled *The Liesbosch*. In *Lagden v O'Connor*, their Lordships decided that a claimant's impecuniosity should in fact be treated no differently from any physical weakness with which the claimant may be afflicted.[137] Thus, a claimant with feeble finances is to be treated according to the same 'egg-shell skull rule' that governs the claimant with a feeble body.

(E) THE 'EGG-SHELL SKULL' RULE

Before *The Wagon Mound* was decided, it was well established at common law that, in relation to personal injury, the defendant had to 'take the claimant as he found him'.

---

[134] [2004] PIQR P27, at [29].   [135] [1933] AC 449. Cf *The Daressa* [1971] 1 Lloyd's Rep 60.
[136] [1933] AC 449, at 460, *per* Lord Wright.
[137] [2004] 1 AC 1067 (after C's own car had been damaged by D's negligence, C was forced to hire a replacement car through a very costly credit hire company rather than through a regular hire company because C lacked the funds to pay the cost of car hire up front).

This meant that the victim could claim damages for the entire harm to his person, even though, owing to some special bodily sensitivity, it was greater than would have been suffered by the ordinary individual. Thus, a haemophiliac,[138] or an extreme neurotic,[139] who sustains greater damage than the ordinary person, may nonetheless recover the full extent of their damage, even though the defendant could not have foreseen such extensive harm.[140] The courts have held that *The Wagon Mound* has not affected this principle, commonly described as the 'egg-shell skull' rule. *Smith v Leech Brain & Co Ltd*[141] is illustrative.

A negligently inflicted burn on C's lip resulted in him dying of cancer. The tissues in his lip in which the cancer developed were in a pre-malignant condition at the time when the burn occurred. Ds were held liable for the damage resulting from the death.

In similar vein, in *Robinson v Post Office*,[142] the defendants carelessly lacerated the claimant's leg. A doctor's subsequent anti-tetanus injection caused encephalitis because the claimant was allergic to the injected serum. The defendants were held liable.

There is no authoritative ruling whether the same principle applies to property damage in tort. In *Parsons v Uttley Ingham*,[143] the defendants negligently failed to install proper ventilation in a hopper used to feed the claimant's pigs. The ground nuts fed to the pigs went mouldy and the pigs died of a rare disease. Some mild 'food poisoning' might have been foreseen as a consequence of feeding pigs mouldy nuts, but death was a highly unusual consequence. The Court of Appeal held, in effect, that the defendants had to 'take the pigs as they found them', and awarded full compensation for the loss of the claimant's pigs. The decision resulted from a claim for breach of contract but the Court of Appeal acted on the interesting, and rather novel, basis that the rules of remoteness in contract and tort were the same.[144]

Presumably, the defendant takes as he finds them, not only the physical state of the damaged person or property, but also the surrounding external physical circumstances. This is the crux of *Great Lakes Steamship Co v Maple Leaf Milling Co*.[145]

Ds negligently failed to lighten Cs' ship at the time stipulated. When the water level fell, the ship grounded and was damaged. This damage was more extensive because the ship settled on a large submerged anchor which Ds neither knew nor could have expected to be there. Ds were liable for all the damage to the ship.

---

[138] *Bidwell v Briant* (1956) *Times*, 9 May.

[139] *Love v Port of London Authority* [1959] 2 Lloyd's Rep 541; *Malcolm v Broadhurst* [1970] 3 All ER 508 (exacerbation of pre-existing nervous disturbance); *Brice v Brown* [1984] 1 All ER 997.

[140] Whether this principle can be justified is considered in depth in Waldron, 'Moments of Carelessness and Massive Loss' in Owen (ed), *Philosophical Foundations of Tort Law* (1995) and (in respect of psychiatric harm) in Jones, 'Liability for Psychiatric Damage: Searching for a Path Between Pragmatism and Principle' in Neyers (ed), *Emerging Issues in Tort Law* (2007).   [141] [1962] 2 QB 405.

[142] [1974] 2 All ER 737.   [143] [1978] QB 791.

[144] This view has since been discredited in that, in contract, the remoteness test turns on what was foreseeable to *both the contracting parties*, as opposed to what was foreseeable to the reasonable man: *Jackson v Royal Bank of Scotland* [2005] UKHL 3. But in relation to the foreseeability of illness caused to pigs by mouldy nuts, this later decision is of no import. Illness would be equally foreseeable to both the contracting parties and the hypothetical reasonable man.   [145] (1924) 41 TLR 21.

The decision is assuredly correct: the damage was of a foreseeable type; it was of a greater extent than foreseeable, not because of internal characteristics of the property, but because of special external circumstances. No doubt the same rule applies to personal injuries. Accordingly, the defendant who negligently causes the claimant to stumble, so that he slides off the edge of a precipice concealed from view, would be liable for those consequences of the risk of stumbling, either before or after *The Wagon Mound*. Once the 'stage is set', the defendant's liability is adjudged accordingly.

(F) SCOPE OF DUTY AND REMOTENESS

In *Caparo Industries v Dickman* Lord Bridge outlined in general terms the important connection between the scope of a duty of care in negligence and the kind of harm for which a claimant will be entitled to sue. He said: 'It is never sufficient to ask simply whether A owes B a duty of care. It is always necessary to determine the scope of the duty by reference to the kind of damage from which A must take care to save B harmless'.[146] In other words, although the defendant's negligence may be *causa sine qua non* of a wide range of foreseeable losses, he should only be held liable in relation to those that are specifically within the specific remit of the duty of care actually owed.[147]

This important interrelation between scope of duty and remoteness has particular significance in cases where a defendant owes a claimant a duty of care either in the performance of a task or in the furnishing of advice, where the duty is specifically owed so as to enable the claimant to avoid a loss or obtain a benefit. In such circumstances, the defendant will only be able to sue the defendant in respect of those losses which are properly attributable to a breach of that particular duty.[148] This principle is generally referred to as the *SAAMCO* principle and it has its origins in the case of *South Australia Asset Management Corp v York Montague Ltd* (hence the abbreviated name). The way in which the principle works can usefully be illustrated by recourse to the case itself.

There were three joined appeals in which Ds were asked by Cs to supply open market valuations of various properties on which Cs were considering lending money by way of mortgages. In the light of the advice given, Cs lent the money, but in respect of each property, the borrowers defaulted. It turned out that the properties had been negligently over-valued. But a further complication was the fact that the market for the properties had also fallen. In one case, C1 had advanced £11 million on a property valued at £15 million, but the true value (at the time of the valuation) was really only £5 million. In the end, the property was sold for only £2.5 million. In a second case, C2 lent £1.75 million on a property valued at £2.5 million. The true value at the time of valuation was £1.8 million, yet after the fall in market value, the property was eventually sold for only £950,000.

---

[146] [1990] 2 AC 605, 627.

[147] Thus, a car driver does not owe a duty of care to protect pedestrians from their own folly when they inappropriately step into the path of an oncoming vehicle: *Al-Sam v Atkins* [2005] EWCA Civ 1452.

[148] Note that since the duty could be of two kinds – to help C avoid a loss or to help C gain a benefit – the losses in question may, correspondingly, be of two kinds: either (i) losses *simpliciter*, or (ii) losses in the form

It fell to the House of Lords to assess the extent to which the claimants could recover their losses from the negligent defendants. It was held that the valuer's duty of care to a lender was to supply a careful estimate of the market value of the property at the date of valuation. As such, the extent of a valuer's liability will be limited to the foreseeable consequences of the information being wrong. This does not take into account losses associated with the unforeseeable drop in market value since a loss of that kind is not a consequence of the valuer's negligence. When applied to the highlighted cases, then, the effects were as follows. In the first case, due to the defendant's negligence, the claimant had £10 million less security than it thought. So as things turned out, the whole of C1's loss (£8.5 million) could be attributed fairly to the defendant. In the second case, by contrast, only part of C2's total loss (£800,000) could be attributed to the defendant, because the claimant had £700,000 less security than it thought. The remaining £100,000 of C2's loss was attributable purely to the unforeseeable drop in market price.

The crucial point in the *SAAMCO* case was that the claimants had requested from the defendant a valuation *for the specific purpose of avoiding a loss when lending money*. As such, recoverable losses were confined to those amounts that were attributable to the defendants overvaluation.

For the sake of completeness, it should be noted that the *SAAMCO* principle can be applied in other kinds of case than merely those involving money lending. Indeed, Lord Hoffmann, in the course of his speech in *SAAMCO*, provided an example of how the principle might apply in a case of personal injury. He gave the following example:

A mountaineer about to undertake a difficult climb is concerned about the fitness of his knee. He goes to a doctor who negligently makes a superficial examination and pronounces the knee fit. The climber goes on the expedition, which he would not have undertaken if the doctor had told him the true state of his knee. He suffers an injury which is an entirely foreseeable consequence of mountaineering but has nothing to do with his knee.[149]

According to simplistic analysis, it could be argued that the doctor should be held liable because the mountaineer would not have undertaken the expedition in question had he received accurate advice about his knee. But applying the *SAAMCO* principle, we take a more sophisticated approach that restricts the doctor's liability not *generally* by reference to loss or injury that is reasonably foreseeable (the usual remoteness test), but *more specifically* by reference to those losses that are reasonably foreseeable *and* within the scope of the duty owed. As Lord Hoffmann put it:

The doctor was asked for information on only one of the considerations which might affect the safety of the mountaineer on the expedition. There seems no reason of policy which requires that the negligence of the doctor should require the transfer to him *of all the foreseeable risks of the expedition*.[150]

---

of C's failure to obtain the benefit that would have been obtained (where the purpose of the duty was to confer a benefit).

[149] [1997] AC 191, 213.   [150] [1997] AC 191, 213 (emphasis added).

FURTHER READING

Lunney, 'What Price a Chance?' [1995] *Legal Studies* 1

Mullany, 'Common Sense Causation – An Australian View' (1992) 12 OJLS 431

Porat and Stein, *Tort Liability Under Uncertainty* (2001)

Reece, 'Losses of Chances in the Law' (1996) 59 MLR 188

Stapleton, 'Law, Causation and Common Sense' (1988) 8 OJLS 431

Stapleton, 'Lords a-Leaping Evidentiary Gaps' (2002) 10 *Torts LJ* 276

Stapleton, 'Cause-in-Fact and the Scope of Liability for Consequences' (2003) 119 LQR 388

Stauch, 'Risk and Remoteness of Damage in Negligence' (2001) 64 MLR 191

Weir, 'Making it Happen versus Making it More Likely' [2003] CLJ 219

Wright, 'Causation in Tort Law' (1985) 75 *Cal L Rev* 1735

6

DEFENCES TO NEGLIGENCE

SECTION 1 CONTRIBUTORY NEGLIGENCE

At common law, it was a complete defence if the defendant proved that the claimant was guilty of contributory negligence. The Law Reform (Contributory Negligence) Act 1945 now provides that contributory negligence no longer affords a complete defence, but merely reduces the damages to the extent to which the claimant has been contributorily negligent. Nonetheless, the early case of *Butterfield v Forrester*[1] can still be invoked to supply a useful example of what contributory negligence involves.

D partially obstructed the highway by putting a pole across part of it. C, riding very rapidly at dusk, did not observe the pole and ran into it, suffering injury. Had he been using ordinary care, he would have seen and avoided the pole.

On the basis that at that time it constituted a complete defence, Lord Ellenborough provided the following, still useful, guide:

One person being in fault will not dispense with another's using ordinary care for himself. Two things must concur to support this action, an obstruction in the road by the fault of the defendant, and no want of ordinary care to avoid it on the part of the [claimant].[2]

According to more recent authority, any defendant seeking to establish contributory negligence must specifically plead and then prove that:

(1) the injury of which the claimant complains resulted from the particular risk to which the claimant exposed himself by virtue of his own negligence;

(2) the negligence of the claimant contributed to his injury;

(3) there was fault or negligence on the part of the claimant.[3]

But in addition to these three elements, we must of course consider the scope of the Law Reform (Contributory Negligence) Act 1945 and the principles it enshrines governing the apportionment of damages.

---

[1] (1809) 11 East 60.   [2] (1809) 11 East 60, at 61.   [3] *Fookes v Slaytor* [1979] 1 All ER 137.

(A) RISK

The rule relating to risk in the context of contributory negligence may be compared with the rule that, in a negligence action, the claimant must prove that the risk that in fact materialized was the one against which the defendant was under a duty to guard. In other words, the defendant must show that the harm sustained by the claimant belongs to that general class of perils to which the claimant was exposed by his own negligent conduct. *Jones v Livox Quarries Ltd* illustrates the point.[4]

C was riding down a slope leading to the bottom of a quarry on the back of Ds' vehicle, contrary to their orders, when another vehicle belonging to Ds was negligently driven into the back of the first vehicle. As a result, C was injured. By so riding, C exposed himself not only to the risk of falling off the vehicle but also to the risk of being injured in the particular way in which he was injured. The court found that he was contributorily negligent.

It is plain from the judgments delivered in the case that the defence would have failed if the damage sustained by the claimant had been totally foreign to the risk to which he exposed himself by virtue of his negligent conduct.[5] So, for example, had the driver of the vehicle negligently set fire to it thus causing the claimant injury by burns, the claimant would have suffered just the same injury regardless of his own lack of care. On the other hand, the risk to which the claimant subjects himself may still be important even if the self-endangerment occurs prior to any negligence on the part of the defendant, so long as the defendant's duty is to take reasonable care of the claimant after the risk to which he exposed himself has materialized. Take, for example, *Barrett v Ministry of Defence*.[6] In that case, a naval airman drank himself unconscious and subsequently died by choking on his own vomit. His widow sued the defendants in negligence. The Court of Appeal held that once the deceased had collapsed and the defendants had taken steps to care for him, the defendants had thereby undertaken a duty of care in respect of the claimant. And since the steps they took were clearly inadequate, the defendants were held liable in negligence subject to a reduction of damages attributable to the claimant's contributory negligence in subjecting himself to harm through excessive drunkenness.

(B) CLAIMANT'S 'NEGLIGENCE' WAS A CONTRIBUTORY FACTOR

The claimant's 'negligence' is undoubtedly the aspect of the defence of contributory negligence that calls for the most careful examination. The key to understanding the development of the case law on this subject is a full appreciation of the absolute rule

---

[4] [1952] 2 QB 608.

[5] [1952] 2 QB 608. Singleton LJ took the view (at 612) that there would be no defence where C negligently sat upon an unsafe wall, and a driver negligently ran into the wall and injured C. By contrast, Denning LJ thought (at 616) that C would succeed, if, while riding on the vehicle, he had been hit in the eye by a shot from a gun fired by a negligent sportsman. [6] [1995] 3 All ER 87.

of common law which deprived the claimant of a remedy if he himself was guilty of *any fault*, however slight, contributing to the damage suffered.

The essence of the matter is causation. Lord Atkin put it thus:

if the [claimant] were negligent but his negligence was not a cause operating to produce the damage there would be no defence. I find it impossible to divorce any theory of contributory negligence from the concept of causation.[7]

Not unnaturally, the courts sought to mitigate the harshness of this doctrine of contributory negligence.[8] In so doing, they evolved various exceptions to the rule, the best known of which is the so-called 'last opportunity rule' on which *Davies v Mann*[9] is the leading case.

C negligently left his ass, fettered by its forefeet, in a highway. D drove his wagon and horses into it at a rapid pace, thereby killing it. Had he used proper care, D could have avoided colliding with the ass, but he was driving too fast. It is uncertain when he saw the ass, if indeed he saw it at all.

It was held that, notwithstanding his own negligence, the claimant could recover full damages because the defendant, had he been driving properly, could still have avoided the consequences of that negligence.[10] Subsequent attempts were made to apply this rule to analogous cases. In each case, two things were crucial: first, the time of both the claimant's and the defendant's acts and, secondly, the respective knowledge of the parties.[11]

In the maritime context, the Maritime Conventions Act 1911 had authorized the court, in cases of collisions at sea, to apportion the loss according to the degree to which each party was at fault; and this principle was made generally applicable by the Law Reform (Contributory Negligence) Act 1945.[12] Since the passing of these Acts, the need for the courts to select some particular cause as the predominant cause has disappeared. A claimant whose own acts contributed to his injury or damage is no longer completely defeated. He simply has his damages proportionately reduced to the extent to which he was at fault. The courts are free to look for all the relevant causes and apportion responsibility accordingly. As Lord Porter said of the 1945 Act:

It enables the court (be it judge or jury) to seek less strenuously to find some ground for holding the [claimant] free from blame, or for reaching the conclusion that his negligence played no part in the ensuing accident, in as much as, owing to the change in the law, the blame can now be apportioned equitably between the two parties.[13]

Plainly, the courts are no longer concerned with the subtleties of the 'last opportunity rule' and other such devices. In order to decide whether the claimant's negligent

---

[7] *Caswell v Powell Duffryn Associated Collieries Ltd* [1940] AC 152, at 165.

[8] *Stapley v Gypsum Mines Ltd* [1953] AC 663, at 677, *per* Lord Porter.   [9] (1842) 10 M & W 546.

[10] See, eg, *Radley v London and North Western Rly Co* (1876) 1 App Cas 754.

[11] Especially *British Columbia Electric Rly Co Ltd v Loach* [1916] 1 AC 719; *The Eurymedon* [1938] P 41, at 49–50, *per* Greer LJ.

[12] Maritime Conventions Act 1911, s 1; Law Reform (Contributory Negligence) Act 1945, s 1.

[13] *Stapley v Gypsum Mines Ltd* [1953] AC 663, at 677.

conduct is contributory, one simply applies the relevant rules of causation discussed in chapter 5. The earliest important case – and one on which the courts still rely – was *Admiralty Comrs v SS Volute*.[14] It was actually decided under the Maritime Conventions Act, but the key principles are the same as those in the 1945 Act.

The Volute, a convoy leader, changed her course without signalling. *The Radstock*, on discovering that she was thereby endangered, negligently put on full steam ahead. Although this negligence was subsequent to that of *The Volute*, both vessels were held to blame for their ensuing collision, and apportionment under the Act was directed.

In a speech warmly supported by the other Law Lords, Viscount Birkenhead pointed out that, despite the fact that cases of 'strictly synchronous negligence' were rare, the courts could, nevertheless, still find that the negligence of both parties contributed to the resulting injury even though their acts were not 'synchronous'. He added:

Upon the whole I think that the question of contributory negligence must be dealt with some-what broadly and upon common sense principles as a jury would probably deal with it. And while, no doubt, where a clear line can be drawn, the subsequent negligence is the only one to look at, there are cases in which the two acts come so closely together, and the second act of negligence is so much mixed up with the state of things brought about by the first act, that the party secondly negligent, while not held free from blame under the *Bywell Castle* rule, might, on the other hand, invoke the prior negligence as being part of the cause of the collision so as to make it a case of contribution. And the Maritime Conventions Act with its provisions for nice qualifications as to the quantum of blame and the proportions in which contribution is to be made may be taken as to some extent declaratory of the Admiralty rule in this respect.[15]

The test, he said, is whether the claimant 'in the ordinary plain common sense of this business . . . contributed to the accident'. This does not mean, of course, that whenever the negligence of the defendant is preceded by negligence on the part of the claimant, there is always contributory negligence. The acts may be so severable that only the defendant's act can be said to have caused the damage; but there is no need to retain a separate rule of 'last opportunity' in order to reach this conclusion. Evershed LJ explained this clearly in *Davies v Swan Motor Co (Swansea) Ltd*.[16]

As I understand the *Davies v Mann* principle . . . it is this: in that case the [claimant's] negli-gence or fault consisted in placing the donkey upon the highway; but it having been observed in due time by the defendant . . . the negligence of the [claimant] had really ceased to be an operating factor in the collision . . . the [claimant] . . . as a negligent actor, was at the material time, *functus officio*, one might say *functus culpa*.[17]

The difficulties encountered in determining whether the claimant's negligence is con-tributory are usually not of law but of fact. Accordingly, there is often scope for a difference of opinion on whether, in any particular case, the negligence of the claimant has ceased

---

[14] [1922] 1 AC 129.   [15] [1922] 1 AC 129, at 144.   [16] [1949] 2 KB 291, at 317.
[17] Cf *Boy Andrew (Owners) v St Rognvald (Owners)* [1948] AC 140, at 149, where Viscount Simon opined: 'The negligence of the donkey-owner was therefore a fault not contributing to the collision: it was merely a *causa sine qua non*'.

to be an operating factor. Yet if it can be inferred that it has so ceased, the claimant's conduct will not be treated as contributory negligence.

Since *The Volute*, the House of Lords has frequently stressed this test of causation in contributory negligence. Thus, in *Swadling v Cooper*[18] (where the Court of Appeal had attempted to frame elaborate classifications[19]), the House of Lords reversed the decision and upheld the direction of the trial judge to the jury, which in substance was this. 'Whose negligence was it that substantially caused the injury?'[20] The Privy Council has also followed *The Volute* and issued a forceful warning against the dangers of 'attempts to classify acts in relation to one another with reference to time or with regard to the knowledge of one party at a particular moment of the negligence of the other party'.[21]

These various principles may be clarified by an examination of some of the more important cases decided since the enactment of the 1945 Act. In *Henley v Cameron*,[22] the defendant chose to leave his car unlighted on the highway at night, and C's husband, riding a motorcycle, carelessly collided with it and was killed. An apportionment under the 1945 Act was made. Applying the rule laid down in *The Volute*, Tucker LJ pointed out that 'it must always remain a question of fact whether the negligence of B is "so mixed up" with the state of things brought about by A's negligence as to make the negligence of both contributory causes to the accident'.[23] He also pointed out the illogicality of asserting that the rules of contributory negligence differ from those of causation, saying:

I cannot understand how, when considering whether the negligence of A or B or of both has been the effective cause of an accident, the answer can depend on whether A or B happens to be the [claimant] in the action or whether they are both defendants.[24]

In *Boy Andrew (Owners) v St Rognvald (Owners)*,[25] as one vessel negligently overtook another, the latter negligently changed course, collided with the first vessel, and sank. The House of Lords followed *The Volute* and found both parties blameworthy. Viscount Simon said:

The suggested test of 'last opportunity' seems to me inaptly phrased and likely in some cases to lead to error, as the Law Revision Committee said in their report (Cmd 6032 of 1939, p 16): 'In truth, there is no such rule – the question, as in all questions of liability for a tortious act, is not who had the last opportunity of avoiding the mischief, but whose act caused the wrong?'.[26]

In *Davies v Swan Motor Co (Swansea) Ltd*,[27] the following occurred:

Contrary to orders, C was standing on the steps on the off-side of a dust lorry. The driver of the lorry turned to the right without warning just as a following vehicle was overtaking

---

[18] [1931] AC 1 (collision at crossroads between D's car and the motorcycle of C's husband, who was killed).
[19] [1930] 1 KB 403.
[20] See *Stapley v Gypsum Mines Ltd* [1953] AC 663 (especially the speech of Lord Reid).
[21] *Marvin Sigurdson v British Columbia Electric Rly Co Ltd* [1953] AC 291, at 299.
[22] [1949] LJR 989. Cf *Harvey v Road Haulage Executive* [1952] 1 KB 120; *Rouse v Squires* [1973] QB 889.
[23] [1949] LJR 989, at 992–3.   [24] [1949] LJR 989, at 993.   [25] [1948] AC 140.
[26] [1948] AC 140, at 149.   [27] [1949] 2 KB 291.

him, and C was injured in the ensuing collision. Both drivers were negligent, but it was also held that C was contributorily negligent.

Evershed LJ began by considering the *Davies v Mann* type of case. He saw this case as distinct in that, in his opinion, the negligence of the defendant alone caused the accident. He then turned to the 'last opportunity' rule and said:

Now that as a doctrine I venture to think has suffered a demise independently altogether of the Act of 1945 . . . No doubt, in practice, such a rule was found useful by judges who were anxious in the interests of justice to avoid coming to a conclusion wholly adverse to a [claimant] merely because, at the material time, the [claimant] was still a negligent actor to some perhaps quite trivial extent. Now the Law Reform (Contributory Negligence) Act 1945 has rendered it no longer necessary to resort to devices of that kind.[28]

Denning LJ stressed that the matter is purely one of causation. Of the *Davies v Mann* type of case – where the claimant negligently leaves an obstruction in the highway and the defendant negligently runs into it – he said that the fact that the defendant sees the obstruction 'may mean in some cases that the obstruction is not the cause of the accident'. In short, one does not apply a mechanical rule of 'last opportunity', but one asks whether 'his conduct would be so powerful a factor in producing the damage that the presence of the parked vehicle would not be itself a cause of the damage'.[29] Similarly, in *Jones v Livox Quarries Ltd*, Denning LJ said:

There is no clear guidance to be found in the books about causation. All that can be said is that causes are different from the circumstances in which, or on which, they operate. The line between the two depends on the facts of each case. It is a matter of common sense more than anything else . . . The man's negligence here was so much mixed up with his injury that it cannot be dismissed as mere history. His dangerous position on the vehicle was one of the causes of his damage.[30]

(c) THE 'NEGLIGENCE' OF THE CLAIMANT

There is an important difference between the defence of contributory negligence and the tort of negligence. To establish the defence, the defendant need not prove that the claimant owed the defendant a duty of care. As was said in *Nance v British Columbia Electric Rly Co Ltd*:

all that is necessary to establish such a defence is to prove to the satisfaction of the jury that the injured party did not in his own interest take reasonable care of himself and contributed, by this want of care, to his own injury.[31]

So far as proving this is concerned, it is well established that the lack of care on the part of the claimant must be proved by the defendant according to the usual civil standard of proof, the balance of probabilities.[32]

---

[28] [1949] 2 KB 291, at 318.   [29] [1949] 2 KB 291, at 323.   [30] [1952] 2 QB 608, at 616.
[31] [1951] AC 601, at 611, *per* Viscount Simon. Cf *Jones v Livox Quarries Ltd* [1952] 2 QB 608, at 615, *per* Denning LJ.   [32] *Owens v Brimmell* [1977] QB 859; *Limbrick v French* [1993] PIQR P 121.

It may also be assumed that decisions on the standard of care demanded of *defendants* in negligence cases apply equally to determine whether the *claimant* has taken reasonable care for his own safety in the context of contributory negligence.[33] As such, many of the problems concerning 'reasonableness' discussed in connection with the tort of negligence also arise here. This is especially the case in relation to children (where, it will be recalled, the age of the child is considered material[34]), and in relation to the rule that 'a prudent man will guard against the possible negligence of others when experience shows such negligence to be common'.[35] The warning issued earlier in the context of the discussion of breach of duty in negligence must be repeated here: *viz*, that decisions on particular facts ought not readily to be regarded as establishing legal principles.[36] The Court of Appeal is as free to infer contributory negligence – and thereby reverse the trial judge – as it is to infer negligence.[37]

Examples of contributory negligence include the following: a moped driver who does not wear a crash helmet,[38] or simply fails to fasten it securely;[39] an employee who has wrongfully been exposed to asbestos fibres who continues to smoke in full knowledge of the risk to his lungs;[40] a car passenger who does not wear a seatbelt,[41] or who knows that the car's foot-brake does not work;[42] a passenger injured by negligent drunken driving (so long as he either travelled knowing that his driver was so drunk that his capacity to drive carefully was impaired, or that he was later going to be a passenger with a driver he accompanied on a drinking bout which affected both the driver's capacity to drive safely and his own capacity to appreciate the danger);[43] a pedestrian who crosses a pelican crossing with the lights on green.[44]

By contrast, a coach passenger was held not to be contributorily negligent in 2002 where her injuries were exacerbated by the fact that she failed to wear one of the fitted lap belts.[45] Importantly, there was at the time no legal requirement that adults should wear such belts; there was no recommendation in the Highway Code that they should be worn and she had never been warned – either by way of public information or specifically by the coach driver – of the need to wear a lap belt. Similarly, a house

---

[33] Whereas a workman suing for breach of statutory duty is not necessarily 'contributorily negligent' because his conduct would have been sufficiently careless to make his employer vicariously liable, the standard of care required of a workman who sues in negligence is apparently the same as that required of him if he were the defendant in a negligence action: *Staveley Iron and Chemical Co Ltd v Jones* [1956] AC 627.

[34] See *Gough v Thorne* [1966] 3 All ER 398; *Mullin v Richards* [1998] 1 All ER 920; *Morales v Eccleston* [1991] RTR 151. Note, too, *Baxter v Woolcombers Ltd* (1963) 107 Sol Jo 553, where C's contributory negligence lay in not complying with instructions. The court refused, with respect to contributory negligence, to take account of his known low intelligence but agreed that it was relevant in measuring the standard of care required of D (the employer).   [35] *Grant v Sun Shipping Co Ltd* [1948] AC 549, at 567, *per* Lord Du Parcq.

[36] *SS Heranger (Owners) v SS Diamond (Owners)* [1939] AC 94, at 101.

[37] *Hicks v British Transport Commission* [1958] 2 All ER 39.

[38] *O'Connell v Jackson* [1972] 1 QB 270.   [39] *Capps v Miller* [1989] 2 All ER 333.

[40] *Badger v Ministry of Defence* [2005] EWHC 2941.

[41] *Froom v Butcher* [1976] QB 286. Cf *Mackay v Borthwick* 1982 SLT 265 where it was held that a woman with a hiatus hernia who did not wear a seatbelt on a short journey was not contributorily negligent. Failure to wear a seatbelt is now a criminal offence: Motor Vehicles (Wearing of Seat Belts) Regulations 1982 (SI 1982 No 176).

[42] *Gregory v Kelly* [1978] RTR 426.   [43] *Owens v Brimmell* [1977] QB 859.

[44] *Fitzgerald v Lane* [1989] AC 328. Cf *Tremayne v Hill* [1987] RTR 131.

[45] *Welsh v Messenger* [2006] 3 CL 238.

buyer who relies on the valuation of his building society's surveyor is not contributorily negligent in not having his house independently surveyed.[46] But if the survey undervalues the premises and a loan to purchase is made on the strength of that valuation, the lender will be contributorily negligent if the borrower defaults in repayment and the lender incurs losses by virtue of the negligent undervaluation. In such circumstances the lender is expected independently to take reasonable measures to verify the borrower's ability to repay the loan.[47]

Importantly, if the negligence of the defendant puts the claimant in a position of imminent personal danger, conduct by the claimant which in fact operates to produce harm to him (but which is nevertheless reasonable in the agony of the moment) does not amount to contributory negligence according to the decision in *Jones v Boyce*.[48]

C, a passenger in a coach, reasonably believed that the coach was about to overturn through the negligent driving of D, the coach proprietor. C therefore jumped off, breaking his leg. As things transpired, the coach did not overturn, but C was adjudged not to be contributorily negligent and he successfully recovered in full from D.

The critical question in such cases is whether the claimant behaved reasonably in the dilemma in which the defendant had placed him, due account being taken of the alarm which such a situation would engender in the reasonably prudent person. The rule was subsequently extended in *Brandon v Osborne, Garrett & Co*.[49]

C and her husband were in Ds' shop as customers. Owing to Ds' negligence, broken glass falling from the roof imperilled C's husband. C instinctively clutched her husband to try to pull him to a place of safety and was herself injured. Had she remained in her original position she would not have been injured. Her injury was held not to be the result of her own contributory negligence.

These cases mark the limits to which the courts have thus far taken the doctrine. But whether it extends to instinctive acts to protect strangers, or interests other than personal safety, is as yet undecided. However, so far as such acts may avail one of a defence in respect of what would otherwise be a trespass to the person, it is submitted that it would be appropriate to consider such acts reasonable conduct unsuited to being dealt with as contributory negligence.

Where the claimant is exercising some right – such as passage along a highway, or some common approach to his premises which the landlord has retained – his deliberately encountering a risk of danger created by the defendant is not necessarily contributory negligence. It will only amount to contributory negligence if, after making due allowance for his right to be there, the claimant is showing an unreasonable neglect for his own safety.[50]

---

[46] *Yianni v Edwin Evans & Sons* [1982] QB 438.

[47] *Legal & General Mortgage Services Ltd v HPC Professional Services* [1997] PNLR 567; *Platform Home Loans Ltd v Oyston Shipways Ltd* [1998] Ch 466; *UCB Bank plc v David J Pinder plc* [1998] PNLR 398.

[48] (1816) 1 Stark 493.   [49] [1924] 1 KB 548.

[50] *Clayards v Dethick and Davis* (1848) 12 QB 439 (C, a cabman, was prevented from taking his horse out of a mews by the only access to the highway because Ds had dug and negligently fenced a trench at the junction of the mews and highway. In trying to get his horse out, he injured it. His action for damages succeeded despite Ds' plea of contributory negligence). See also *Behrens v Bertram Mills Circus Ltd* [1957] 2 QB 1.

Just as the defendant employer may be answerable for the negligence of his employee, so too does the contributory negligence of an employee of the claimant afford the defendant a good defence where that employee was acting in the course of his employment. Thus, in one case, where A, driving B's van for B was struck by C, but A's careless driving contributed to the damage to the van, B's damages were reduced accordingly.[51] On the other hand, the contributory negligence of an independent contractor is not imputed to the principal, and that of a driver is not imputed to a passenger,[52] nor is that of a spouse imputed to his or her wife or husband.[53] And when a child is accompanied by an adult, the contributory negligence of the adult is not imputed to the child.[54] Consider *Oliver v Birmingham and Midland Motor Omnibus Co Ltd*.[55]

C, an infant in the care of his grandfather, was crossing a road when he was injured by the negligent driving of Ds' bus by their servant. Although his grandfather was also negligent, the infant was entitled to recover in full.

A final point that requires mention in this context is that contributory negligence is not merely confined to cases in which the contributory element supplied by the claimant can be characterised in terms of 'negligence' in the sense of carelessness or folly. It also embraces circumstances in which the claimant has *deliberately* harmed himself. Thus, in *Reeves v Metropolitan Police Comr*,[56] where a sane police prisoner committed suicide, it was held that, notwithstanding the duty owed by the police to protect the deceased from taking his own life, the act of suicide constituted contributory negligence such that the damages could be reduced by 50%.

(D) THE SCOPE OF THE LAW REFORM (CONTRIBUTORY NEGLIGENCE) ACT 1945

The primary object of the Law Reform (Contributory Negligence) Act 1945 is to provide that, where the defence of contributory negligence was previously available, the courts may now, instead of exonerating the defendant from liability, reduce the damages awarded against him to the extent to which the claimant was contributorily negligent. But

---

[51] *Kenfield Motors v Hayles and Rees* [1998] CLY 3919.

[52] *Mills v Armstrong, The Bernina* (1888) 13 App Cas 1 (the same principle was held to apply in the case of ships).

[53] *Mallett v Dunn* [1949] 2 KB 180; *Berrill v Road Haulage Executive* [1952] 2 Lloyd's Rep 490 (wife driving husband's car not as his servant or agent; her contributory negligence did not prevent the husband recovering in full for damage to the car). Both the case last cited and *France v Parkinson* [1954] 1 All ER 739 held that the contributory negligence of a bailee is not to be imputed to a bailor. *Lampert v Eastern National Omnibus Co Ltd* [1954] 2 All ER 719 decided that where a wife is injured in a collision between her car (driven by her husband) and another car, in which the two drivers are equally to blame, the wife's damages are to be reduced to one half.

[54] Where a disabled child's action rests on the Congenital Disabilities (Civil Liability) Act 1976 his damages are reduced if it is shown that the parent affected shared the responsibility for his being born disabled: s 1(7).

[55] [1933] 1 KB 35. Cf *Murray v Harringay Arena Ltd* [1951] 2 KB 529. Note, however, that if the parent is in breach of his duty to safeguard the child's safety, D may seek a contribution from the negligent parent under the Civil Liability (Contribution) Act 1978.   [56] [2000] 1 AC 360.

the actual wording of the Act is rather complex and requires closer consideration. Section 1(1) reads as follows.

Where any person suffers damage as the result partly of the fault of any other person or persons, a claim in respect of that damage shall not be defeated by reason of the fault of the person suffering the damage, but the damages recoverable in respect thereof shall be reduced to such extent as the court thinks just and equitable having regard to the [claimant's] share in the responsibility for the damage.

Section 4 defines 'damage' as including loss of life and personal injury, and thus probably embraces any loss for which damages at common law can be awarded.[57] The use of the word 'result' is a neutral term regarded by the courts as leaving them free to continue to treat contributory negligence as a matter of causation.[58] What is clear, then, is that, under the Act, contributory negligence which contributes to the injuries suffered by the claimant is as relevant as contributory negligence contributing to the incident in which the injuries are suffered. Thus, a passenger failing to wear a seatbelt cannot be said to be in any way responsible for *the collision* in which he is thrown against the windscreen. But he is nonetheless responsible for those injuries that would have been avoided had he worn the belt. The correct question is not 'what was the cause of the accident?' but rather, 'what was the cause of the damage?'.[59] In *Capps v Miller*[60] a young man suffered devastating brain injury when he was knocked off his moped by a drunken driver. He had not fastened the chin-strap of his helmet and the helmet came off before he hit the road. The Court of Appeal held that the failure to wear a securely fastened helmet exacerbated the claimant's injuries and thus constituted contributory negligence.

The definition of 'fault' in the 1945 Act has proved to be very problematic. 'Fault' is defined in section 4 as 'negligence, breach of statutory duty or other act or omission which gives rise to liability in tort or would, apart from this Act, give rise to the defence of contributory negligence'.[61] The first limb of the definition of 'fault' appears to make the defence of contributory negligence applicable to all torts. Yet section 11 of the Torts (Interferences with Goods) Act 1977 expressly excludes contributory negligence as a defence to conversion or intentional trespass to goods. Equally, it is now established, though not uncontroversially, that the Act does not apply to deceit[62] or to other torts based on dishonesty.[63] In the context

---

[57] In *Drinkwater v Kimber* [1951] 2 All ER 713, the trial judge held that it excluded pecuniary loss, but the Court of Appeal, although affirming the decision, did so on other grounds and disagreed with this narrow interpretation of 'damage': [1952] 2 QB 281, at 290, *per* Singleton LJ.

[58] Thus, where C's own negligence prior to his act of rescue contributed to his injuries, his damages were reduced. C (a train guard) went to the rescue of D, who was negligently trying to board a moving train without first applying the emergency brake: *Harrison v British Railways Board* [1981] 3 All ER 679.

[59] *Froom v Butcher* [1976] QB 286; *O'Connell v Jackson* [1972] 1 QB 270 (injured motorcyclist not wearing helmet).   [60] [1989] 2 All ER 333.

[61] In *Reeves v Metropolitan Police Comr* [2000] 1 AC 360, at 369, Lord Hoffmann said that the opening words – 'negligence, breach of statutory duty or other act or omission which would give rise to liability in tort' – apply to D's initial, liability-creating act, whereas the closing words of the provision refer to C's fault.

[62] *Alliance and Leicester Building Society v Edgestop Ltd* [1994] 2 All ER 38; *Nationwide Building Society v Thimbleby & Co* [1999] Lloyd's Rep PN 359.

[63] *Corporacion Nacional de Cobre de Chile v Sogemin Metals Ltd* [1997] 1 WLR 1396.

of product liability, contributory negligence is expressly included as a defence under the Consumer Protection Act 1987. It is not, however, a defence that is conceptually easy to apply in the context of negligent misstatements (where the law presupposes that the claimant's contribution to his loss – his reliance – be reasonable, and therefore not negligent[64]).

A still more problematic question is whether the defence of contributory negligence can be invoked in an action for breach of contract.[65] Despite earlier *dicta* to the effect that where the parties have defined their mutual obligations in a contract, a concurrent duty in tort should not arise,[66] it is now clear that where a duty of care arises within a contractual relationship, or where one party assumes responsibility to perform carefully a professional service (and the other party relies upon that assumption of responsibility) the claimant may opt to sue in contract or tort.[67] It has even been held by the Court of Appeal that the tortious duty can be wider than the contractual one.[68] From this, it follows that a private patient suing in respect of the negligent delivery of her baby has a choice of contractual or tortious damages.[69] Furthermore, it has been held at first instance that the client of a negligent solicitor may make a similar choice whether to sue in contract or in tort.[70] On the other hand, an NHS patient has no such choice; nor did a disappointed legatee suing a solicitor for negligence in respect of the preparation of a will.[71] In relation to the hospital patient, it would scarcely accord with common sense to say that the NHS patient who was contributorily negligent should suffer a reduction in damages but that her wealthier sister, who paid for treatment, should not.[72]

Since there may be concurrent duties in tort and contract, is it any more sensible to assert that the defence of contributory negligence should, on a single set of facts, be available only so long as the claimant frames his action in tort? Although it has no place where the action may *only* be framed in contract,[73] the Court of Appeal has nonetheless held that where the defendant's liability in contract is concurrent with a breach of duty

---

[64] *JEB Fasteners Ltd v Marks, Bloom & Co* [1981] 3 All ER 289.

[65] See, eg, *De Meza and Stuart v Apple, Van Straten, Shena and Stone* [1975] 1 Lloyd's Rep 498. See also Spowart-Taylor, 'Contributory Negligence – A Defence to Breach of Contract' (1986) 49 MLR 102.

[66] *Tai Hing Cotton Mill Ltd v Liu Chong Hing Bank Ltd* [1986] AC 80, at 107; *National Bank of Greece SA v Pinios Shipping Co* [1989] 1 All ER 213; *Lee v Thompson* (1989) 2 PN 91; *Johnstone v Bloomsbury Health Authority* [1992] QB 333.

[67] *Henderson v Merrett Syndicates Ltd* [1994] 3 All ER 506. Note also that if a concurrent tortious duty is held not to exist, the Latent Damage Act 1986 cannot be applied to contractual negligence for that Act has been held not to be relevant in respect of breach of contract: *Iron Trade Mutual Insurance Co Ltd v J K Buckenham Ltd* [1990] 1 All ER 808. [68] *Holt v Payne Skillington (a firm)* [1995] PNLR 179.

[69] See *Kralj v McGrath* [1986] 1 All ER 54.

[70] *Midland Bank Trust Co Ltd v Hett, Stubbs & Kemp* [1979] Ch 384 (doubted by Lloyd LJ in *Lee v Thompson* (1989) 2 PN 91).

[71] See *Ross v Caunters* [1980] Ch 297; *White v Jones* [1995] 2 AC 207. But consider now the possibility of such an action if the terms of the Contracts (Rights of Third Parties) Act 1999 Act are met.

[72] Unless one contends that by providing consideration for the duty undertaken by D, C 'buys' protection from her own, as well as his, lack of care.

[73] *AB Marintrans v Comet Shipping Ltd (No 5)* [1985] 3 All ER 442. See also *Barclays Bank plc v Fairclough Building Ltd* [1995] 1 All ER 289: C's fault is an irrelevancy where D is 'guilty' of a breach of a strict contractual duty *unless* C's conduct, rather than D's breach, was the true cause of C's loss.

in tort – that is, where the defendant is *negligently in breach* of contract – the 1945 Act *can* be invoked.[74] On the other hand, where the defendant is in breach of a contractual term that is framed in terms of exercising reasonable care,[75] the Act cannot be applied to reduce the award of damages, if the defendant does not owe a concurrent duty of care in tort.[76] In these cases, of course, the difficulty lies in answering the far from obvious questions of where and why no concurrent common law duty exists.

Another complication concerns the operation of the Act in cases involving careless third parties. Suppose a child is injured partly because his parents fail to be sufficiently careful as to his well-being and partly because of the negligence of the defendant. What, then, occurs in relation to the child's action against the defendant? In fact, the child may sue the defendant in respect of the whole amount;[77] and the defendant cannot invoke the 1945 Act for the child himself was not contributorily negligent. On the other hand, the defendant will have the option of joining the negligent parents in the action so that they, too, will ultimately be held liable for their proportion of the damages.[78]

A final problem in this context arises where the defendant is a professional who performs a service for a third party, where the service is designed to benefit the claimant, but both the professional and the third party are negligent. Just this problem arose in *Gorham v British Telecommunications plc*.[79] There, the claimants were the wife and children of a deceased gentleman who had been the customer of an insurance company that had given him negligent advice concerning pensions and life assurance. Prior to his death, the deceased had also been negligent in failing to take steps to rectify the situation created by the defendant's negligence. A majority of the Court of Appeal held that the deceased's negligence constituted a *novus actus interveniens*. Interestingly, however, Sir Murray Stuart-Smith suggested that broad considerations of justice dictated (1) that the claimants should be able to claim, but (2) that the damages should be reduced to take account of the deceased's negligence.

(E) APPORTIONMENT OF DAMAGES

The 1945 Act directs courts to reduce the award of damages as they think 'just and equitable having regard to the claimant's share in responsibility for the damage'. If the claimant's lack of care is found to have contributed to his damage, some reduction must be made. His carelessness cannot be totally disregarded on the ground that that course of action would be 'just and equitable',[80] nor may a judge evade apportionment by pleading the difficulty of ascertaining the precise degree to which the claimant's own carelessness exacerbated his injury.[81] Decisions on apportionment will generally be reached on a common sense

---

[74] *Forsikringsaktieselskapet Vesta v Butcher* [1989] AC 852. See also *Gran Gelato Ltd v Richcliff (Group) Ltd* [1992] Ch 560, stating that contributory negligence can apply to a claim under s 2(1) of the Misrepresentation Act 1967 where the claim lies concurrently with a claim in negligence.

[75] For example, Supply of Goods and Services Act 1982, s 13.

[76] *Forsikringsaktieselskapet Vesta v Butcher* [1989] AC 852.

[77] *Jones v Wilkins* (2001) *Times*, 6 February. [78] See ch 25. [79] [2000] 1 WLR 2129.

[80] *Boothman v British Northrop Ltd* (1972) 13 KIR 112. [81] *Capps v Miller* [1989] 2 All ER 333.

basis; and the Court of Appeal will only interfere with the trial judge's conclusions on apportionment if he or she can be shown plainly to be wrong.[82] Lord Reid summed up the basic guidelines for apportionment in *Stapley v Gypsum Mines Ltd*:

A court must deal broadly with the problem of apportionment, and, in considering what is just and equitable, must have regard to the blameworthiness of each party, but the [claimant's] share in the responsibility for the damage cannot, I think, be assessed without considering the relative importance of the acts in causing the damage apart from his blameworthiness.[83]

Two factors, therefore, have to be considered: the causative potency of the act,[84] and the blameworthiness of the claimant's conduct (evidenced generally by the extent to which he deviates from the standard of the reasonable man who cares for his own safety[85]). Where there are two or more defendants, the extent of the claimant's contributory negligence must be assessed before addressing the respective responsibilities of the defendants.[86] So, for example, where a claimant walked across a pelican crossing when the lights were on green and was hit first by D1 and then by D2, the House of Lords ruled that the first stage of the apportionment exercise should be to determine the extent to which his own folly contributed to his injuries, so as to assess the totality of the damages due to him. Only after completion of this exercise should the respective contributions to the damages by the two tortfeasors be settled. But it is worth stressing that this exercise does not involve a precise arithmetical calculation of the respective contributions: the Act, it must be remembered, speaks only of apportionment in terms of what 'the court thinks just and equitable'.[87]

One common example of contributory negligence – failing to wear a seatbelt – provides a useful illustration of how apportionment ought to work in practice. Lord Denning, in *Froom v Butcher*,[88] suggested the norm of a 25% reduction if wearing the seatbelt would have prevented the injury, and a 15% reduction where it would simply have reduced the severity of the injuries. In *Gregory v Kelly*,[89] however, where the

---

[82] *Hannam v Mann* [1984] RTR 252.

[83] [1953] AC 663, at 682. Note that, on one reading, *Quintas v National Smelting Co Ltd* [1961] 1 All ER 630, could be read as suggesting that if the trial judge finds D liable for breach of statutory duty, and the Court of Appeal reverses that finding, but holds D liable for negligence, this is a ground for reducing the amount deducted from C's damages for his contributory negligence.

[84] *Davies v Swan Motor Co (Swansea) Ltd* [1949] 2 KB 291, at 326; *Pride Valley Foods Ltd v Hall & Partners* [2001] EWCA Civ 1001.

[85] *Sahib Foods Ltd, Co-operative Insurance Society Ltd v Paskin Kyriakides Sands (a firm)* [2003] EWHC 142. It is clear, however, that blameworthiness is a relative concept. So, if D's wrongful conduct takes the form of a breach of statutory duty, D will be regarded as relatively more blameworthy than if he or she had simply been negligent and, as such, C's damages will not be reduced as much as they otherwise would be on account of his contributory negligence: *Badger v Ministry of Defence* [2005] EWHC 2941.

[86] *Fitzgerald v Lane* [1989] AC 328.

[87] See the overt rejection of any attempt to be precise in *Reeves v Metropolitan Police Comr* [2000] 1 AC 360, at 372, *per* Lord Hoffmann.

[88] [1976] QB 286. See also *O'Connell v Jackson* [1972] 1 QB 270 (motorcyclist; 15% reduction for not wearing a crash helmet); *Capps v Miller* [1989] 2 All ER 333 (10% where C was wearing his helmet but had not fastened it securely). Cf *Owens v Brimmell* [1977] QB 859 (where the passenger accepted a lift knowing the driver was drunk). See Symmons, 'Contributory Negligence Defences for the Drunken Driver' (1977) 40 MLR 350.

[89] [1978] RTR 426.

claimant was not wearing his seatbelt and knew also that the car had a faulty foot-brake, a reduction of 40% was made. Of course, if it can be shown that the claimant would have suffered injuries of equal severity (albeit of a different type) even if he had worn his seatbelt, no reduction at all would be ordered.[90] In each case, the judge must exercise his discretion to determine just what share of responsibility for the accident the claimant should, in fairness, bear. But it is not an unlimited discretion. In *Pitts v Hunt*, Beldam LJ commented, *obiter*, that it was not possible for a court to order a 100% contribution from the claimant under the 1945 Act.[91] The terms in which the Act is framed presuppose at least *some* element of fault on the part of the defendant, and thus any notion of 100% contributory negligence, necessarily falls outside its purview.

SECTION 2 VOLUNTARY ASSUMPTION OF RISK

(A) IS ASSUMPTION OF RISK PROPERLY REGARDED AS A DEFENCE?

Consent of the claimant may take two forms: (1) consent to the actual invasion of his interest – for example, where he invited someone to walk onto his land – or (2) consent to the risk of a tort being committed. Only the latter is discussed here, since, although the defence is not confined to cases of negligence, the usual argument in any case that is founded on negligence will be that the claimant assumed the risk of defendant's negligent (but not his deliberate) conduct.[92]

The Latin maxim *volenti non fit injuria* is commonly used instead of the phrase 'assumption of risk' and the two terms will be used interchangeably in this chapter for its meaning has been described thus:[93]

If the defendants desire to succeed on the ground that the maxim *volenti non fit injuria* is applicable, they must obtain a finding of fact that the [claimant] freely and voluntarily, with full knowledge of the nature and extent of the risk he ran, impliedly agreed to incur it.

The courts have looked at the assumption of risk in two different ways. On one view, it suggests that the defendant has not in the circumstances broken a duty of care. On the other, it is conceded that there has been a breach of duty, but a successful plea of *volenti* removes the effect of that negligence.[94] Whichever of these two judicial approaches is taken, the consequences are likely to be the same even though a conceptual

---

[90] *Condon v Condon* [1978] RTR 483.   [91] [1990] 3 WLR 542, at 547.

[92] This does not mean that a negligence action can never be founded on deliberate wrongdoing: see J. Murphy, 'Rethinking Injunctions in Tort Law' (forthcoming).

[93] *Letang v Ottawa Electric Rly Co* [1926] AC 725, at 731 (citing *Osborne v London and North Western Rly Co* (1888) 21 QBD 220).   [94] See the discussion in *Reeves v Metropolitan Police Comr* [2000] 1 AC 360.

grasp of the application of the *volenti* principle is somewhat easier under the first approach.

Examples illustrate the two different stances. Suppose that X is walking along a busy highway when he is hit by a golf ball struck from a tee placed dangerously near to that highway. If X is an ordinary pedestrian, he may be able to sue the golf club in negligence, but if, on the other hand, he is a golfer who is crossing the highway in order to reach the next tee, he would fail. One could say that the claimant fails if the defendant shows that the claimant assumed the risk of the defendant's negligence. On the other hand, the fact that the claimant is a golfer is merely one of the circumstances pertinent to the question of whether the defendant took reasonable care in respect of *this* claimant. Sometimes, it will not emerge from the claimant's evidence that the claimant comprehended the risk and then, of course, the defendant will himself have to prove that fact (if it is not obvious[95]), if he seeks to rebut the claimant's claim. For example, a claimant who has been injured while being driven in the defendant's speed boat may make out a *prima facie* case without revealing that the defendant was, to the claimant's knowledge, drunk. If the defendant wishes to rely on that further factor, he must prove it. On one view he is merely adducing evidence of matters which are material in deciding whether, in all the circumstances of the case, there has been a breach of the duty to take care.[96] Alternatively, one could say that the claimant consented to the risk of negligent driving.

By contrast, a case such as *Blake v Galloway*[97] is more easily understood by treating it as one where there was no breach of duty. The facts were as follows:

Two youngsters engaged in a game involving throwing bark at one another. Although there were no formal rules to their horseplay, there were nonetheless certain, objectively identifiable understandings or conventions to which the defendant had adhered when, in a slight error of judgement, he threw some bark that struck the claimant in the eye.

The same 'no breach of duty' approach was taken in *Murray v Harringay Arena Ltd*[98] where a six-year-old boy was injured when the puck at an ice hockey match was hit out of the rink in the course of play and landed among the spectators. The Court of Appeal held that his claim in negligence failed. It would be straining logic to say that the child concerned had in fact assumed the risk. Indeed, it may be regarded as a policy decision that organizers of sporting events owe no duty to any spectators to guard against

---

[95] *Darby v National Trust* [2001] PIQR P372 (risks involved in swimming in D's murky ornamental pond were 'perfectly obvious', thus C could not claim ignorance of the danger in this case decided under the ('statutory negligence') provisions of the Occupiers' Liability Act 1957. Cf *Tomlinson v Congleton Borough Council* [2003] 2 WLR 1120 (a case decided under the Occupiers' Liability Act 1984, but involving analogous principles).

[96] *Insurance Comr v Joyce* (1948) 77 CLR 39. *Nettleship v Weston* [1971] 2 QB 691, shows both techniques in use: Salmon LJ applied the breach of duty approach to the question of whether a learner driver was liable for injuring his car passenger whereas Lord Denning MR adopted the standard *volenti* approach. See also *Morris v Murray* [1990] 3 All ER 801, at 806–7, *per* Fox LJ and *Watt v Hertfordshire County Council* [1954] 2 All ER 368. (C was a fireman injured because a jack on the back of the lorry on which he was travelling in the course of his duties slewed forward when the driver had to apply his brakes suddenly. It was held that *volenti non fit injuria* was irrelevant; the issue was whether, in the circumstances, the employers were negligent in requiring C to travel on the back of a lorry together with an untethered heavy jack and found that there was no failure to take reasonable care.)   [97] [2004] 1 WLR 2844.

[98] [1951] 2 KB 529.

certain dangers incidental to the ordinary conduct of the game. As such, some judges clearly favour the 'no duty' approach. Thus, as Asquith J once said:

As a matter of strict pleading it seems that the plea of *volenti* is a denial of any duty at all, and, therefore, of any breach of duty, and an admission of negligence cannot strictly be combined with the plea.[99]

The Court of Appeal decision in *Wooldridge v Sumner*[100] is also important. There, a non-paying spectator, who was also a photographer, was injured by a horse competing at a jumping show. It was held that the rider was not liable in negligence even though he was guilty of an error of judgment.[101]

The court explained that *volenti non fit injuria* in English law 'presupposes a tortious act by the defendant'.[102] This does not mean, however, that there can never be actionable negligence within a sporting context. Where, as in *Smolden v Whitworth*,[103] for example, the referee neglects to officiate a rugby game so as to keep it within the rules (which are designed, in part, to ensure the players' safety), it is quite possible for an injured competitor to sue the referee for his negligence without being met by the defence of *volenti*.[104]

In an employment context, the courts appear to favour the assumption of risk approach. Thus, in *ICI Ltd v Shatwell*,[105] the House of Lords eschewed the *Wooldridge* interpretation and held that an injured shot-firer could not sue his employer for the conduct of a fellow shot-firer because he had, in the special circumstances of the case,[106] assumed the risk of his fellow shot-firer's negligence. It is suggested here that the House of Lords found it more convenient to exempt the employer by finding a defence of consent to negligence than it might have done had it asked whether there was, in the circumstances, a breach of duty. That is why the survival of both approaches to the assumption of risk defence can be expected. And this perhaps explains why, in *Morris v Murray*[107] the Court of Appeal declined to enter into the niceties of which theoretical argument was correct preferring simply to judge the merits of the case before them.

(B) ILLUSTRATIONS OF WHEN A CLAIMANT IS DEEMED TO HAVE ASSUMED THE RISK

(1) ACTIONS BY EMPLOYEES AGAINST EMPLOYERS

The defendant is not liable whenever the claimant is deemed to have absolved him from liability for the consequences. The rule used to be especially important in actions by

---

[99] *Dann v Hamilton* [1939] 1 KB 509, at 512.

[100] [1963] 2 QB 43. In *Baker v T E Hopkins & Son Ltd* [1959] 3 All ER 225, at 243, Willmer LJ provided another sound exposition of the principle, saying of a claim by an injured rescuer that, 'once it is determined that the act of the rescuer was the natural and probable consequence of the defendant's wrongdoing, there is no longer any room for the application of the maxim *volenti non fit injuria*'.

[101] He would be liable if he failed to take the care expected of a reasonable competitor in a sporting event: *Wilks v Cheltenham Home Guard Motor Cycle and Light Car Club* [1971] 2 All ER 369.

[102] [1962] 2 All ER 978, at 990, *per* Diplock LJ.   [103] [1997] PIQR P133.

[104] *Smolden v Whitworth* [1997] PIQR P133; *Watson v British Boxing Board of Control Ltd* [2001] QB 1134. See also Yeo, 'Accepted Inherent Risks Among Sporting Participants' (2001) 9 *Tort L Rev* 114.

[105] [1965] AC 656.   [106] See below.   [107] [1990] 3 All ER 801, at 806.

workmen alleging negligence by their employers. Thus, in nineteenth century cases in which workmen sued employers for injuries sustained at work it was generally held that if the employee knew of the danger, this would be enough, regardless of whether in reality he had any choice but to obey his 'boss'. The House of Lords (no doubt reflecting shifting social and economic attitudes) changed this approach by disapproving one of these early cases,[108] in *Smith v Baker & Sons*[109] where the facts were as follows.

C, who was D's employee, was employed in drilling holes in a rock cutting, and was aware of the danger caused by a crane continually swinging crates of stones above his head. A stone fell out of a crate and injured him. He brought an action in negligence against D, who pleaded *Volenti*.

The House of Lords held that, notwithstanding the claimant's knowledge of the risk, the evidence justified a finding by the jury that he had not voluntarily undertaken it. Although the House of Lords accepted that 'a particular consent may be inferred from a general course of conduct',[110] it was held that knowledge alone is not enough: the jury must affirm 'that he consented to the particular thing being done which would involve the risk, and consented to take the risk upon himself'. Lord Watson said:

The question which has most frequently to be considered is not whether he voluntarily and rashly exposed himself to injury, but whether he agreed that, if injury should befall him, the risk was to be his and not his master's. [Whether continuing at work knowing of the danger is an assumption of the risk] depends ... upon the nature of the risk, and the workman's connection with it, as well as upon other considerations which must vary according to the circumstances of each case.[111]

Since then, there has been a series of employer-employee cases in which this defence has been pleaded unsuccessfully on the ground of the employee's want of consent. *Bowater v Rowley Regis Corpn* is typical.[112]

C, a carter, was ordered by his employers, Ds to take out a horse known by them to be unsafe. C protested but eventually took out the horse. Later, C was thrown off the cart when the horse bolted. C sued in negligence in respect of his injuries.

The Court of Appeal rejected the defence of *volenti non fit injuria*. Goddard LJ said:

it can hardly ever be applicable where the act to which the servant is said to be '*volens*' arises out of his ordinary duty, unless the work for which he is engaged is one in which danger is necessarily involved.[113]

Thus, in one case where the claimant was susceptible to dermatitis, and both she and her employer knew this, and her employer found her work that entailed a slight risk of

---

[108] *Thomas v Quartermaine* (1887) 18 QBD 685.
[109] [1891] AC 325. Cf *Yarmouth v France* (1887) 19 QBD 647.
[110] [1891] AC 325, at 338, *per* Lord Halsbury LC.   [111] [1891] AC 325, at 355.
[112] [1944] KB 476.   [113] [1944] KB 476, at 480–1.

the disease, the employer was held not liable for her then contracting it. He was not obliged either to dismiss her or to make the work safe for her with her particular susceptibility. She took the risk and could not then complain.[114] In *ICI Ltd v Shatwell*,[115] the House of Lords expressly supported the general principle that assumption of risk will not ordinarily defeat a claim by an employee against his employer. At the same time, their Lordships recognized that where the claim rested on vicarious liability for joint and flagrant disobedience of a safety rule by the claimant and his wrongdoing fellow-servant, and where the latter was not the claimant's superior (or one whose orders he bound to obey), the employer could exceptionally invoke the defence against the employee.

(2) DRUNKEN PILOTS/DRUNKEN DRIVERS[116]

In invoking the defence of *volenti*, it is important to show that the claimant was well aware that he ran a risk of injury. In *Nettleship v Weston*[117] the friend teaching the claimant how to drive naturally knew that as a very inexperienced learner she was more likely to cause an accident endangering him than an experienced driver. But he had expressly asked for reassurance that she was properly insured. He did not, in other words, accept full responsibility for whatever befell him. He neither undertook not to sue her, nor to absolve her from any duty otherwise owed to him.

Where no pre-existing relationship exists between the parties, *volenti* can rarely apply. In such cases, the defence will only be relevant in strictly defined and fairly exceptional circumstances. Cases relating to drunken drivers/pilots and their passengers are instructive. Consider first *Dann v Hamilton*.[118]

C voluntarily accompanied D as a passenger in a car driven by D, knowing that D was under the influence of drink to such an extent that the chances of a collision from negligent driving were substantially increased. She was injured by his negligent driving and her action was held not to be barred by the defence of *volenti non fit injuria*.

Asquith J held that the maxim applied 'where a dangerous physical condition has been brought about by the negligence of the defendant, and, after it has arisen, the [claimant], fully appreciating its dangerous character, elects to assume the risk thereof'.[119] Although he doubted whether the defence could lie where the consent of the claimant preceded the act of negligence complained of, the *ratio* of his judgment is probably no more than a finding of fact that the claimant:

---

[114] *Withers v Perry Chain Co Ltd* [1961] 3 All ER 676. (But might this decision be better explained in terms of no breach of duty in the circumstances?). Cf *Paris v Stepney Borough Council* [1951] AC 367.

[115] [1965] AC 656.

[116] Cases of drunken drivers are useful to illustrate the underlying principles but must now be dealt with subject to the Road Traffic Act 1988. See below.   [117] [1971] 2 QB 691.

[118] [1939] 1 KB 509.   [119] [1939] 1 KB 509, at 517.

by embarking in the car . . . with knowledge that through drink the driver had materially reduced his capacity for driving safely, did not impliedly consent to, or absolve the driver from, liability for any subsequent negligence on his part whereby she might suffer harm.[120]

Indeed, it is suggested here that the preferable view is that *volenti* is crucially concerned with consent to *future* risks. Certainly, this understanding of the defence is supported by a considerable body of case law[121] as well as academic writing.[122] But are the two notions mutually exclusive? Only if they are is it necessary to select between the alternative interpretations just outlined. According to Diplock LJ, they would indeed appear to be mutually exclusive on the basis that *volenti* only applies where the claimant consents to future risks. He stated forthrightly that it would make a nonsense to say that the claimant 'agreed to run the risk that the defendant might be negligent . . . [where] the claimant would only play his part after the defendant had already been negligent'.[123]

For several years in England, though not in other Commonwealth jurisdictions,[124] *Dann v Hamilton* was accepted as authority for the proposition that accepting a lift from an obviously inebriated driver would almost certainly constitute contributory negligence[125] but would not give rise to a successful plea of *volenti*. Indeed, it might almost be said that *volenti* went out of fashion. But half a century later *Pitts v Hunt*[126] was decided.

C was a pillion passenger on a motorcycle ridden by D. He knew that D was uninsured and had no licence. After four hours of drinking together, C 'egged-on' D in 'reckless, irresponsible and idiotic' riding of the motorcycle culminating in a disastrous accident. Section 148(3) of the Road Traffic Act 1972 [now section 149 of the Road Traffic Act 1988] prevented the defence of *volenti* from applying in road traffic cases, but apart from that provision, the Court of Appeal judged that, notwithstanding *Dann v Hamilton*, a plea of *volenti* would have defeated C's claim.

In the event, the court held that the claimant's grossly irresponsible conduct and participation in several road traffic offences gave rise to a successful defence of *ex turpi causa non oritur actio*.[127] But then came *Morris v Murray*.[128]

C and the deceased spent the afternoon drinking together. The latter, C agreed, had consumed about 17 whiskies. C then agreed to the deceased's proposal that he take him up for a flight in

---

[120] [1939] 1 KB 509, at 518 (approved in *Slater v Clay Cross Co Ltd* [1956] 2 QB 264). But note that the partial defence of contributory negligence may be available to the drunken driver: *Owens v Brimmell* [1977] QB 859.

[121] See, eg, *Wooldridge v Sumner* [1962] 2 All ER 978, at 990, *per* Diplock LJ; *Baker v T E Hopkins & Son Ltd* [1959] 1 WLR 966, at 983, *per* Willmer LJ and *Morris v Murray* [1991] 2 QB 6, at 17, 28 and 32, *per* Fox, Stocker and Waller LJJ.

[122] See, eg, Jaffey, '*Volenti Non Fit Injuria*' [1985] CLJ 87; Kidner, 'The Variable Standard of Care, Contributory Negligence and *Volenti*' [1991] *Legal Studies* 1 and Murphy, 'Negligently Inflicted Psychiatric Harm – A Re-appraisal' [1995] *Legal Studies* 415.

[123] *Wooldridge v Sumner* [1962] 2 All ER 978, at 990, *per* Diplock LJ. See also *Nettleship v Weston* [1971] 3 All ER 581, at 587, *per* Lord Denning MR and *ICI v Shatwell* [1965] AC 656.

[124] See in particular *Insurance Comr v Joyce* (1948) 77 CLR 39.   [125] *Owens v Brimmell* [1977] QB 859.

[126] [1991] 1 QB 24.   [127] For a full account of this defence see ch 11.   [128] [1991] 2 QB 6.

a light aircraft. At the aerodrome, C helped to prepare the aeroplane. Soon after take-off, the plane crashed killing the pilot and severely injuring C who brought an action against the deceased's estate.

The Court of Appeal upheld the plea of *volenti*. They said that accepting a flight with an obviously drunken pilot was akin to confronting deliberately some dangerous physical condition brought about by the defendant. Whether one says that the claimant could not have supposed that the defendant was capable of discharging any normal duty of care, or that the claimant, impliedly by his conduct, waived any duty towards him, the result is the same. A person voluntarily co-operating in a flight with an intoxicated pilot takes the risk upon himself. Flying is of a different order of danger to driving on the roads.

Morris v Murray raises two wider questions about *volenti*. The first is whether the test for *volenti* is an objective or a subjective one. Earlier (slight) authority suggested an objective test,[129] but Stocker LJ[130] later cast doubt on this approach in *Morris v Murray*. On the facts, he said, such an answer would require that a drunken claimant be excused from the consequences of his own actions, for no sober person would have done as the claimant did. Accordingly, the question must be answered on the facts of the case: 'did the claimant appreciate the danger he faced, and was he capable of accepting responsibility for what happened to him?'. The second question is one of policy. Might one argue that, in some circumstances, to allow a defence of *volenti* runs counter to the public interest because the defendant is allowed to escape the consequences of his own *gross irresponsibility*. Fox LJ answered the point in this way:

It seems to me . . . that the wild irresponsibility of the venture is such that the law should not intervene to award damages and should leave the loss where it falls.[131]

(3) DANGEROUS ACTIVITIES

A final context in which *volenti* may be applicable concerns participation in dangerous activities, including sport. Before the defence can arise, of course, the defendant must show that the claimant consented not only to some risk of harm intrinsic to the game, but also to the particular risk which culminated in injury to him. *Gillmore v LCC*[132] illustrates the point.

C was a member of Ds' physical training class. During an exercise in which the members of the class were lunging at each other, C was injured through losing his balance on a floor which was slippery due to Ds' negligence.

Du Parcq LJ held[133] that the claimant had not consented to the risk incidental to doing physical training on a slippery floor (although, of course, he had consented to the physical contacts which might occur in the course of the lunging exercise) and therefore the defence of assumption of risk failed.[134]

---

[129] *Bennett v Tugwell* [1971] 2 QB 267.   [130] [1990] 3 All ER 801, at 817.
[131] [1990] 3 All ER 801, at 807.   [132] [1938] 4 All ER 331.   [133] [1938] 4 All ER 331, at 336.
[134] *Cleghorn v Oldham* (1927) 43 TLR 465 is also explicable on this ground. It involved C recovering damages against her golf companion who had injured her with a golf club on the course.

(c) VOLUNTARY ACT

Not only must the claimant consent to the risk, he must also assume the risk freely and voluntarily. The decisions on claims by employees constitute, in effect, judicial recognition that economic pressures negative voluntary conduct in the sense indicated by Scott LJ in *Bowater v Rowley Regis Corpn*.[135] In that case, his Lordship said:

For the purposes of the rule . . . a man cannot be said to be truly 'willing' unless he is in a position to choose freely, and freedom of choice predicates, not only full knowledge of the circumstances on which the exercise of choice is conditioned, so that he may be able to choose wisely, but the absence from his mind of any feeling of constraint so that nothing shall interfere with the freedom of his will.[136]

Accordingly, the courts have, with one early exception,[137] consistently refused to allow the *volenti* defence to lie against rescuers.[138] They are not genuine volunteers. Nor do they, in responding to the call for rescue (even if their job requires them to go to a citizen's aid[139]), take upon themselves the risk of injury and impliedly waive any duty owed to them.[140]

An analogous case applies with respect to suicides who are owed a protective duty by either hospital or prison authorities. The question that arises is whether such authorities may raise the defence of *volenti non fit injuria* when a patient/inmate attempts or commits suicide. And the House of Lords in *Reeves v Metropolitan Police Comr*,[141] had to grapple with this very question. Their Lordships held that once it has been established[142] that the defendant was under a duty to prevent the inmate attempting suicide, the defendant could not later invoke the *volenti* defence to escape liability in respect of the inmate's suicide. Allowing the defence to be raised in this way, they said, would effectively empty the initial duty of any real content. The state of the inmate's mind (and the related question of whether his act was truly voluntary) could be disregarded as irrelevant. The same approach would therefore apply to a mental patient.[143]

---

[135] [1944] KB 476.

[136] Cf *Christmas v General Cleaning Contractors Ltd* [1952] 1 KB 141, at 151, *per* Hodson LJ (affd sub nom, *General Cleaning Contractors Ltd v Christmas* [1953] AC 180).

[137] *Cutler v United Dairies (London) Ltd* [1933] 2 KB 297.   [138] *Haynes v Harwood* [1935] 1 KB 146.

[139] *Ogwo v Taylor* [1988] AC 431 (a fireman).

[140] *D'Urso v Sanson* [1939] 4 All ER 26 (night-watchman extinguishing fire on employers' premises). Cf *Merrington v Ironbridge Metal Works Ltd* [1952] 2 All ER 1101; *Baker v T E Hopkins & Son Ltd* [1959] 3 All ER 225 (doctor-rescuer); *Sylvester v Chapman Ltd* (1935) 79 Sol Jo 777: C mauled by leopard at an animal show of D's when he crossed the barrier to extinguish a cigarette smouldering in the straw between the barrier and the cage 'was not rescuing anyone from imminent danger of death, nor even preventing damage to property, since there were people who could easily have done with precautions what he did' (*per* Lord Wright MR); therefore he had no cause of action against D.   [141] [2000] 1 AC 360.

[142] See *Orange v Chief Constable of West Yorkshire Police* [2002] QB 347.

[143] The same approach was taken with respect to the argument that the inmate's suicide constituted a *novus actus interveniens*, and the argument (in the Court of Appeal) that the *ex turpi causa* defence could be raised.

In rare instances, mere knowledge of a risk will bar the claimant: for example, if he is the gratuitous bailee of a defective chattel. The defendant can say to the claimant: 'Take it or leave it'. Conversely, since it is clear that one cannot speak of some constant defence of assumption of risk, reasons of policy will sometimes dictate that a claimant will not fail even though he has freely encountered a known risk (for example, where the claimant has a right to face the risk, such as where he walks along a highway or exercises a right of access[144]). This last class of case illuminates the relationship between assumption of risk and the defence of contributory negligence.[145] Where the defendant cannot show that the claimant has assumed the risk, he may nonetheless demonstrate that the claimant's conduct was sufficiently unreasonable in the light of the risk involved to constitute contributory negligence. Because the effect of establishing the defence of contributory negligence used to be the same as *volenti*, the courts were sometimes, in the past, not especially careful to heed the distinctions between them. But, since the passing of the Law Reform (Contributory Negligence) Act 1945 the distinction has become critical. This is because whereas *volenti* is a complete defence (the claimant recovering nothing),[146] contributory negligence is, necessarily, only a partial defence (damages simply being reduced in proportion to the claimant's responsibility for the loss or injury).

Section 149 of the Road Traffic Act 1988 applies where vehicles are being used in circumstances where third party insurance is compulsory. It rules out the defence of *volenti non fit injuria* in any action brought by a passenger against the driver of a vehicle on a public road.[147] It provides:

if any other person is carried in or upon the vehicle while the user is so using it, any antecedent agreement or understanding between them (whether intended to be legally binding or not) shall be of no effect so far as it purports or might be held to negative or restrict any such liability of the user . . . [to passengers] . . . and the fact that a person so carried has willingly accepted as his the risk of negligence on the part of the user shall not be treated as negativing any such liability of the user.

The theoretical basis for the defence of *volenti non fit injuria* has attracted considerable academic interest and debate.[148] Yet, current judicial attitudes are perhaps most clearly expressed by Lord Herschell in *Smith v Baker & Sons*. He said:

The maxim is founded on good sense and justice. One who has invited or assented to an act being done towards him cannot, when he suffers from it, complain of it as a wrong.[149]

---

[144] *Clayards v Dethick and Davis* (1848) 12 QB 439. In *Burnett v British Waterways* [1973] 2 All ER 631 C, a lighterman, was injured in D's dock having read a notice that he entered at his own risk. *Volenti* did not apply: C had not agreed to be bound by its terms and had no choice in the matter.

[145] See further Kidner, 'The Variable Standard of Care, Contributory Negligence and *Volenti*' [1991] 11 *Legal Studies* 1.   [146] As in *Morris v Murray* [1991] 2 QB 6.

[147] *Pitts v Hunt* [1990] 3 All ER 344, at 356–7, 359 and 366 (but note the applicability of the defence of *ex turpi causa*).

[148] See Jaffey, '*Volenti Non Fit Injuria*' [1985] CLJ 87; Kidner, 'The Variable Standard of Care, Contributory Negligence and *Volenti*' [1991] *Legal Studies* 1.

[149] [1891] AC 325, at 360. Cited with approval by Fox LJ in *Morris v Murray* [1990] 3 All ER 801, at 807.

SECTION 3 EXCLUDING LIABILITY

The already limited application of the defence of *volenti* is further restricted by the operation of the Unfair Contract Terms Act 1977. That Act misrepresents itself by its title. In certain circumstances, it in fact applies to tort as well as contract where there is a purported unilateral exclusion of liability by the defendant. To complicate matters further, the Act must sometimes be read in conjunction with the Unfair Terms in Consumer Contracts Regulations 1994[150] which impose even greater restrictions on the ability to exclude liability than those discussed below where (i) the tortious duty co-exists beside a contractual obligation in a *consumer contract* and (ii) the terms of that contract have not been individually negotiated.

The 1977 Act applies[151] to 'business liability' only. That term refers to liability arising from 'things done or to be done by a person in the course of a business' and the occupation of premises used for 'business purposes'. Section 2 prohibits altogether exclusion or limitation of liability for death or personal injury resulting from negligence.[152] Any contract term or notice purporting so to do is invalid. In the case of loss other than death or personal injury, or in the case of a death or personal injury resulting from a tort other than negligence, an exclusion or limitation of liability is invalid 'except in so far as the term or notice satisfies the requirement of reasonableness'.[153] Finally, section 2(3) provides:

Where a contract term or notice purports to exclude or restrict liability for negligence a person's agreement to or awareness of it is not of itself to be taken as indicating his voluntary acceptance of any risk.

Several questions must be addressed in relation to the operation of the 1977 Act. Business liability is nowhere comprehensively defined. Professions[154] and central and local government are expressly included within the term. But what of the work of a charity? It is suggested here that such work probably is included. The test does not appear to be whether the defendant is a profit-making commercial enterprise. The distinction is one between the domestic and the business sector of life. In view of section 2(3), can *volenti* ever now operate against a business? There is as yet no conclusive authority on the point. Clearly, knowledge of the unilateral exclusion of liability by notice will be insufficient, but it would also be so at common law. An agreement *per se* will not be binding.

In *Johnstone v Bloomsbury Area Health Authority*[155] a junior hospital doctor brought an action against his employers alleging damage to his health caused by the unreasonable hours he was

---

[150] SI 1994 No 3159.   [151] Unfair Contract Terms Act 1977, s 1.
[152] Unfair Contract Terms Act 1977, s 2(1).
[153] Unfair Contract Terms Act 1977, s 2(2). And for a definition of reasonableness see s 11 and *Governor and Company of the Bank of Scotland v Fuller Peiser* [2002] PNLR 289.
[154] See *Smith v Eric S Bush* [1990] 1 AC 831.   [155] [1992] QB 333.

required to work. Refusing to strike out the claim, the Court of Appeal took the view that a clause in his contract imposing those hours of work could only constitute *volenti* or an attempt to limit the employer's duty of care. If it was the latter, it might well fall foul of the 1977 Act. It remains to be seen whether there are residual circumstances – perhaps when the claimant takes the initiative – where *volenti* might still operate.

The crux of the question in many cases where the operation of the 1977 Act is in issue will often be bifurcated. (1) Has a breach of duty been proved yet purportedly excluded? (2) In the case of loss other than death or personal injury, was the exclusion of liability reasonable? The first question may be difficult to answer. Consider a lecturer asked by a student to advise him on a lease for a flat saying to the student 'This is only general advice . . . I am not a practising solicitor . . . I cannot accept liability for what I say'. Is the lecturer excluding liability, or simply attempting to limit the duty he owes (if any) to the student. Or is it simply a statement that flags up the standard of care to be expected from him?

What is now clear is that the effect of sections 11(3)[156] and 13(1)[157] of the Act ensure that where, 'but for' a purported disclaimer, a common law duty of care would have arisen, the Act operates to strike down or limit the extent of that disclaimer. In *Smith v Eric S Bush*,[158] surveyors were instructed by the building society to inspect and report on a house the claimant wished to buy. The surveyors expressly excluded any liability to the claimant herself. The House of Lords found: first, in the absence of the purported disclaimer, a duty of care was owed to the claimant;[159] and, secondly, in the circumstances, the disclaimer was unreasonable. In the vast majority of cases, house purchasers, as surveyors well know, rely on the report commissioned by the building society (a report for which the purchaser will in fact pay).

Lord Griffiths[160] suggested four factors by which to gauge reasonableness under the Act: (1) whether the parties were of equal bargaining power; (2) whether it was practicable to expect the claimant to obtain independent advice; (3) the complexity of the task which formed the subject of the disclaimer; (4) the practical consequences of striking down the disclaimer.[161]

---

[156] Section 11(3) provides: ' . . . the requirement of reasonableness under the Act is that it should be fair and reasonable to allow reliance [on the disclaimer], having regard to all the circumstances obtaining when the liability arose or (but for this notice) would have arisen'.

[157] Section 13(1) provides: 'To the extent that this Part of this Act prevents the exclusion or restriction of any liability it also prevents – (a) making liability or its enforcement subject to restrictive or onerous conditions; (b) excluding or restricting any right or remedy in respect of the liability, or in subjecting a person to any prejudice in consequence of his pursuing any such right or remedy; (c) excluding or restricting rules of evidence or procedure; and (to that extent) sections 2 and 5 to 7 also prevent excluding or restricting liability by reference to terms and notices which exclude or restrict the relevant obligation or duty'.   [158] [1990] 1 AC 831.

[159] [1990] 1 AC 831, at 839–841.

[160] Had the Unfair Contract Terms Act 1977 been in force at that time, would the disclaimer in *Hedley Byrne & Co v Heller & Partners* [1964] AC 465 have survived judicial scrutiny?

[161] Would such action increase the cost/availability of the service?

The practical operation of the 1977 Act and the 1994 Regulations both still require further elaboration. What is clear, however, is that there can no longer be any foolproof exclusion notice or agreement.

FURTHER READING

Jaffey, 'Volenti Non Fit Injuria' [1985] CLJ 87.

Kidner, 'The Variable Standard of Care, Contributory Negligence and Volenti' [1991] Legal Studies 1

Spowart-Taylor, 'Contributory Negligence – A Defence to Breach of Contract' (1986) 49 MLR 102

Symmons, 'Contributory Negligence Defences for the Drunken Driver' (1977) 40 MLR 350

Yeo, 'Accepted Inherent Risks Among Sporting Participants' (2001) 9 Tort L Rev 114

7

LIABILITY FOR DEFECTIVE PREMISES AND STRUCTURES

Liability for defective premises[1] to those who suffer loss or damage on those premises[2] may in general rest with two main types of defendant. First, the person actually occupying the premises may be held responsible. Here, responsibility is generally for personal injuries such as a broken ankle sustained when a rotten floorboard gives way. Secondly, someone other than the occupier may be liable for defects in the premises. This latter category of potential defendants is broad in scope and includes landlords, builders and professionals such as architects and consulting engineers. While in some cases the relevant defect may cause personal injury – for example, an employee may sustain a broken ankle caused by a landlord's failure to repair the premises rented by his employer – in many cases the claimant may suffer only economic loss (such as the discovery that the house one bought from a development company is falling apart after the development company has gone into liquidation). An action against the original builder or architect in such circumstances is designed to recover the financial loss represented by the property's diminished value and/or the cost of repair. In line with the general trend in negligence cases, the liability of non-occupiers for economic loss associated with defective premises is significantly restricted in scope.

SECTION 1 OCCUPIERS' LIABILITY

Occupiers' liability is predominantly defined by statute, but there remains (at least according to case law) a small, residual role for the common law in relation to certain negligently performed activities taking place on the defendant's premises.[3] For this reason, it is necessary to consider the liability of occupiers under three headings: first, the Occupiers' Liability Act 1957 (governing liability to visitors to the defendant's

---

[1] For the purposes of this chapter, the term 'premises' shall be used for convenience to connote not just any building owned by D, but also any land owned by him, regardless of whether there are any buildings on it. An action is equally viable, under the Occupiers' Liability Acts, in either case.

[2] If C was elsewhere than on the D's premises when he was injured, he must frame his action in terms of negligence, nuisance (whether private or public) or the rule in *Rylands v Fletcher*.

[3] See, eg, *Ferguson v Welsh* [1987] 3 All ER 777; *Ogwo v Taylor* [1988] AC 431; *Fowles v Bedfordshire County Council* [1995] PIQR P389.

premises); secondly, the Occupiers' Liability Act 1984 (governing liability to non-visitors); and finally the residual common law rules applicable to both visitors and non-visitors injured by particular activities on the defendant's premises.

(A) THE OCCUPIERS' LIABILITY ACT 1957

(1) WHO IS AN OCCUPIER?

The first precondition of a defendant's liability under the Occupiers' Liability Act 1957 is that he must be the occupier of the premises on which the claimant's loss occurs. The Occupiers' Liability Act 1957 provides no statutory definition of occupier. Instead, it states that those who would be treated as occupiers at common law should be treated likewise for the purposes of the Act;[4] and the leading definition of 'occupier' derives from *Wheat v E Lacon & Co Ltd*.[5]

Ds owned a public house of which Mr R was their manager. Mr R and his wife were allowed by agreement to live in the upper floor, access to which was by a door separate from the licensed premises. Mrs R was allowed to take paying guests on the upper floor. An accident was sustained by a paying guest on the staircase leading to the upper floor. It was held that although C was injured in the private area of the premises, Ds (along with Mr and Mrs R) were still liable. They had enough residual control over that part of the premises to be treated as occupiers.

The case thus clarifies that there may be two or more occupiers simultaneously and that exclusive occupation is not required. The test of occupation, then, is whether a person has some degree of control associated with, and arising from, his presence in and use of, or his activity in, the premises. A good example of the scope for multiple occupancy can be seen in the case of *AMF International Ltd v Magnet Bowling Ltd*[6] where both a contractor and the owner were held to have sufficient control to be joint occupiers of the premises in which the claimant's equipment was damaged by rainwater entering the building via a leaking doorway.[7]

On the question of who may qualify as a sole occupier for the purposes of the Act, it is clear that the following earlier decisions remain sound. A concessionaire without a lease in a fairground is an occupier.[8] So, too, is a local authority that has requisitioned a

---

[4] Occupiers' Liability Act 1957, s 1(2). [5] [1966] AC 552.

[6] [1968] 2 All ER 789. See also *Fisher v CHT Ltd (No 2)* [1966] 2 QB 475 (both D, who ran a restaurant in a club, and the owners of the club were held to be occupiers). Note, however, that a highway authority that has a statutory obligation to maintain a footpath which lies on land owned by another is not the occupier of that footpath: *Whiting v Hillingdon London Borough Council* (1970) 68 LGR 437. Nor is it the occupier of a highway that has not been adopted, even if the occupier owns the relevant land: *Holmes v Norfolk County Council* (1981) 131 NLJ 401. On the other hand, where the occupier has adopted the highway, there will be liability for both negligent misfeasance and negligent nonfeasance under the Highways Act 1980, s 58 (save where the loss is pure economic loss: *Wentworth v Wiltshire County Council* [1993] 2 All ER 256).

[7] In such cases, the degree of care that C may expect from each occupier is determined by the degree of control held by each: *Wheat v Lacon* [1966] AC 552, at 581 and 601, per Lords Denning and Pearson respectively.

[8] *Humphreys v Dreamland (Margate) Ltd* [1930] All ER Rep 327.

house[9] (even in respect of those parts of the house in which it allows homeless persons to live),[10] and a contractor converting a ship into a troopship in dry dock.[11] By contrast, a decorator undertaking to do no more than paint a house does not have sufficient control to be regarded as its occupier.[12]

(2) SCOPE OF THE ACT

Prior to the Occupiers' Liability Act 1957, the duty owed by an occupier to entrants upon his land varied according to their common law status. The highest standard of care was owed to those, such as hotel guests, who were on his land by virtue of contract. A lesser duty was owed to his invitees,[13] and a lower duty still was owed to mere licensees (who were permitted, but not requested, to be there). In relation to trespassers, the occupier was obliged to do no more than refrain from deliberately or recklessly causing them injury.[14]

A further complexity in the common law lay in the fact that the content of the duty varied according to the manner in which the claimant's injury was sustained. A distinction was drawn between injuries sustained by virtue of something done on the defendant's premises and injuries caused merely by the dangerous state of the premises.[15] The Occupiers' Liability Act 1957 was enacted to give effect to the recommendations contained in the Law Reform Committee's Third Report[16] which were designed to eliminate the confusion surrounding the common law rules on liability to entrants. Thus, sections 2 and 3 of the Occupiers' Liability Act 1957 'have effect, in place of the rules of the common law, to regulate the duty which an occupier of premises owes to his visitors in respect of dangers due to the state of the premises or to things done or omitted to be done on them'.[17]

(a) Visitors

The Occupiers' Liability Act 1957 imposes a duty in respect of 'visitors'.[18] And 'visitors' for the purposes of the Act are those persons who were invitees or licensees at common law:[19] that is, anyone to whom an occupier gave any invitation or permission to enter or use his premises. Accordingly, in terms of the level of duty owed, the common law distinction between invitees and licensees is no longer of any real importance.[20] It does,

---

[9] *Hawkins v Coulsdon and Purley UDC* [1954] 1 QB 319.

[10] *Greene v Chelsea Borough Council* [1954] 2 QB 127; *Harris v Birkenhead Corpn* [1976] 1 All ER 341 (a local authority, having acquired a house by compulsory purchase, occupies it even before its staff enter it).

[11] *Hartwell v Grayson Rollo and Clover Docks Ltd* [1947] KB 901.   [12] *Page v Read* (1984) 134 NLJ 723.

[13] That is, those who had a mutual business interest with the occupier, such as customers in a shop.

[14] *Robert Addie & Sons (Collieries) Ltd v Dumbreck* [1929] AC 358.

[15] These were termed, respectively, the 'activity duty' and the 'occupancy duty'.   [16] Cmd 9305.

[17] Occupiers' Liability Act 1957, s 1.

[18] In doing so, it envisages not only personal injury suffered by a visitor, but also any property damage he may suffer: Occupiers' Liability Act 1957, s 1(3)(b).

[19] Occupiers' Liability Act 1957, s 1(2). It is also provided that contractual entrants, in so far as they have not legitimately provided otherwise in their contract, shall also be afforded the common duty of care.

[20] *Campbell v Northern Ireland Housing Executive* [1996] 1 BNIL 99. For an argument that it ought, in a limited set of circumstances, to have importance see Murphy, 'Public Rights of Way and Private Law Wrongs' (1997) Conv 362.

however, remain important to distinguish between visitors and other types of entrant since the duties of an occupier to those other entrants who fall within the definition 'non-visitors' are exclusively governed by the later Occupiers' Liability Act of 1984.[21] This raises the question of whether, in the case of multiple occupiers, a person may be a visitor in relation to Occupier A but a trespasser in relation to Occupier B. Lord Goff answered this question in *Ferguson v Welsh*.

If it is the case that only one such occupier authorizes a third person to come onto the land, then plainly the third person is *vis-à-vis* that occupier, a lawful visitor. But he may not be a lawful visitor *vis-à-vis* the other occupier. Whether he is so or not must, in my opinion, depend on the question whether the occupier who authorized him to enter had authority, actual (express or implied) or ostensible, from the other occupier to allow the third party onto the land . . . if he had not, then the third party will be, *vis-à-vis* that other occupier, a trespasser.[22]

Those entrants covered by the Occupiers' Liability Act 1984 are often called trespassers, but the class, 'non-visitors', is not confined only to persons whose presence constitutes a trespass. If they are on the premises of the defendant without his permission, then even though they have not gone there voluntarily[23] – for example, if they have been thrown or chased there – they fall within this group, just as much as if they have committed the tort of trespass. Similarly, although he is not a trespasser:

[a] person entering any premises in exercise of rights conferred by virtue of (a) section 2(1) of the Countryside and Rights of Way Act 2000,[24] or (b) an access agreement or order under the National Parks and Access to the Countryside Act 1949, is not, for the purposes of this Act, a visitor of the occupier of the premises.[25]

It has also been held that the same non-visitor status extends to those using a private right of way.[26] But a more complex situation exists with respect to persons who sustain injury on a public right of way. At one time it was thought that no-one using a public right of way could be classed as a visitor for the purposes of the Occupiers' Liability Act 1957.[27] However, the matter was shown possibly to be less straightforward in *McGeown v Northern Ireland Housing Executive*.[28]

C's husband was the tenant of a house on Ds' housing estate. The house was accessed by a path over which the public had acquired a right of way. It was upon this path that C tripped and

---

[21] *Stone v Taffe* [1974] 3 All ER 1016 is one of the few cases since the Occupiers' Liability Act 1957 to turn on this distinction. (Pub manager in breach of contract allowed C and others to have a party after hours. C, who was unaware of that restriction in the contract, was held to be a visitor, not a trespasser, *vis-à-vis* the brewery as occupier.)   [22] [1987] 3 All ER 777, at 785.

[23] If D's negligence causes a licensee involuntarily and unpremeditatedly to encroach slightly on land where he has no permission to go, he retains the rights of a licensee: *Braithwaite v Durham Steel Co Ltd* [1958] 3 All ER 161.

[24] This subsection refers to those exercising a right of access to open land for recreational purposes.

[25] Occupiers' Liability Act 1957, s 1(4).   [26] *Vodden v Gayton* [2001] PIQR P52.

[27] *Greenhalgh v British Railways Board* [1969] 2 QB 286, at 292–3, *per* Lord Denning MR. On the other hand, although no action will lie for nonfeasance according to *McGeown v Northern Ireland Housing Executive* [1995] 1 AC 233, contrast *Thomas v British Railways Board* [1976] QB 912 where it was said that an action can be brought in respect of any injury caused by D's misfeasance – eg, digging and leaving uncovered a hole in the right of way into which C later falls).   [28] [1995] 1 AC 233.

sustained a broken leg. She argued that Ds were liable to her as a visitor under the Occupiers' Liability Act (Northern Ireland) 1957.[29] The House of Lords held that she was not a visitor and therefore could not sue under the statute.

The complexity in this case stems from the fact that their Lordships confined their decision to persons using a public right of way *qua* member of the general public (for example, a hill-walker who neither knows, nor is interested in, who owns the *solum* of the right of way[30]). As Lord Keith put it: '[o]nce a public right of way has been established, there is no question of permission being granted by the owner of the *solum* by [sic] those who choose to use it'.[31] The idea of using a right of way by virtue of 'permission' is similar to that of using it *qua* licensee. But what, wondered Lord Browne-Wilkinson, of those who are expressly invited onto the land?

In the case of an invitee there is no logical inconsistency between the claimant's right to be on the premises in exercise of the right of way and his actual presence there in response to the express or implied invitation of the occupier. It is the invitation which gives rise to the occupier's duty of care to an invitee.[32]

This *obiter* proposition has since been dismissed by the Court of Appeal in *Campbell v Northern Ireland Housing Executive*[33] where a claimant who was injured on a public right of way, on the way to the shops, was held to be outside the scope of the Occupiers' Liability Act 1957. Despite this rejection of Lord Browne-Wilkinson's distinction, there is much to be said for the logic underscoring his view, even though it would mean giving new life, in the limited context of persons using public rights of way, to the significance of an invitee/licensee dichotomy.[34]

Whether one accepts or rejects Lord Browne-Wilkinson's reasoning, the pre-Act cases on *implied* permissions and invitations to be on the occupier's premises do remain in full force. This is because the Act defines visitors in terms of those who were formerly regarded as invitees and licensees at common law. In *Edwards v Railway Executive* it was held that permission should not be implied merely because the occupier knew of the claimant's presence or because he failed to take the necessary steps to prevent his entry. Rather, '[t]here must be evidence either of express permission or that the land-owner has so conducted himself that he cannot be heard to say that he did not give it'.[35]

In each case, it is a question of fact whether permission to enter can be implied and the burden of proving it rests with the claimant seeking to rely on it.[36] The rules seem particularly pertinent in relation to children who are sometimes able to show an implied permission on the basis of an 'allurement' that would present no temptation to an adult. In *Glasgow Corpn v Taylor*,[37] for example, shiny red berries growing in the

---

[29] This Act is the same, in all material respects, as the English Act of that name and year.

[30] But note that those exercising access rights under the Countryside and Rights of Way Act 2000 are now specifically denied the status of visitor under the amended Occupiers' Liability Act 1957, s 1(4)(a).

[31] [1995] 1 AC 233, at 246. Presumably, his Lordship meant to say granted '*to* those who choose to use it'.

[32] [1995] 1 AC 233, at 248.   [33] [1996] 1 BNIL 99.

[34] See further, Murphy, 'Public Rights of Way and Private Law Wrongs' (1997) 61 Conv 362.

[35] [1952] AC 737, at 747, *per* Lord Goddard.   [36] [1952] AC 737.   [37] [1922] 1 AC 44.

open on the defendant's land were held to be an allurement to a child aged seven, to whom the berries looked like cherries or blackcurrants. Similarly, and more recently, the House of Lords held that a rotting boat was a sufficiently alluring plaything to constitute an implied permission.[38] The presence of an allurement in a location that is accessible to children will tend to aid the inference of permission to enter.[39] But the mere fact that the occupier has on his premises a dangerous and alluring object will not, *ipso facto*, make him liable to every child who comes onto his land. For example, the child may be old enough to read a notice to the effect that the owner did not want him to be present there in which case the child will be a trespasser, and thus forced to rely on the lower level of protection afforded by the Occupiers' Liability Act 1984. Furthermore, in some circumstances occupiers are deemed only to permit young children onto their land subject to the condition that they are accompanied by a responsible adult.[40]

Of course, in cases concerning adults, it is clearly inapposite to talk of implied permission based on allurements. But even in such cases, a permission may still be implied. As Lord Porter pointed out in the *Edwards* case:

an open pathway, as in *Cooke v Midland Great Western Rly of Ireland*,[41] or a knowledge that a track is and has long been constantly used, coupled with a failure to take any steps to indicate that ingress is not permitted, as in *Lowery v Walker*,[42] may well amount to a tacit licence.[43]

Persons entering as of right – such as police with search warrants and a host of other officials statutorily empowered to enter premises – are specifically deemed by the Occupiers' Liability Act 1957 to be present with the occupier's permission,[44] and as such they are afforded the same duty of care as visitors. So, too, potentially, are contractual entrants; for under section 5(1) there is an implied term in the contract whereby, subject to effective contrary provision, the claimant is afforded the very same duty of care.[45]

---

[38] *Jolley v Sutton London Borough Council* [2000] 1 WLR 1082.

[39] *Hardy v Central London Rly Co* [1920] 3 KB 459; *Latham v R Johnson and Nephew Ltd* [1913] 1 KB 398.

[40] *Latham v R Johnson and Nephew Ltd* [1913] 1 KB 398; *Bates v Stone Parish Council* [1954] 3 All ER 38 (no circumstances to qualify the permissions given by Ds to infant children to enter their playground; three-year-old child held to be a licensee). In *Phipps v Rochester Corpn* [1955] 1 QB 450, Devlin J criticised this rule on the ground that it was lacking in precision: eg, what degree of incapacity on the part of the child and what qualifications on the part of his companion are called for? But the rule still stands on the authority of the Court of Appeal.

[41] [1909] AC 229 (D, a railway company, kept an unlocked turntable close to a public road; children were in the habit of playing with it, having gained access through a gap in D's fence – D was held liable to such a child, a licensee, for injuries sustained while playing on the turntable). [42] [1911] AC 10.

[43] [1952] AC 737, at 744, *per* Lord Porter. See also *Robert Addie & Sons (Collieries) Ltd v Dumbreck* [1929] AC 358, at 372–3, *per* Viscount Dunedin and *Darby v National Trust* [2001] PIQR P 372. Cf *Gough v National Coal Board* [1954] 1 QB 191.

[44] Occupiers' Liability Act 1957, s 2(6). Police officers pursuing inquiries without a warrant may take advantage of the generally implied licence to approach a front door via the garden path: *Robson v Hallett* [1967] 2 QB 939. But like other visitors they will cease to have visitor status if they fail to leave immediately the licence is expressly withdrawn: *Snook v Mannion* [1982] RTR 321. [45] See further below.

(b) Against what risks does the Occupiers' Liability Act 1957 afford protection?

The Occupiers' Liability Act 1957 plainly governs the duty of the occupier in relation to structural defects or other dangers due to the state of the premises themselves, or indeed 'things' on the premises such as vicious dogs roaming free in the garden.[46] That this is not the limit of its scope is made clear by the fact that, in addition to dangers arising from the state of the premises, the Act refers also to dangers due to 'things done or omitted to be done on them'. At the very least, then, the Act covers acts or omissions which have created a dangerous condition of a continuing nature which later causes harm. But a more difficult question is whether the Act also extends to acts (whether of the occupier or others) which themselves directly cause harm to the visitor. Section 1(2) provides that the Act 'shall regulate the nature of the duty imposed by law in consequence of a person's occupation or control of premises'. At common law an occupier had a duty not to permit others to use his premises in such a way that would foreseeably harm other persons on those premises.[47] Regardless of whether such cases previously fell within that branch of the law of negligence imposing special duties on occupiers towards invitees or licensees, it is submitted that the joint effect of subsections (1) and (2) is to bring those situations within the Act – the duty of care arises in consequence of the fact that the defendant is an occupier.[48] On the other hand, activities not directly associated with occupation that caused harm to visitors – such as firing arrows – were governed by ordinary principles of negligence, and not by the special rules relating to occupiers.[49] It has been stated judicially that the Act does not apply to such activities (regardless of whether the act in question was the occupier's, a contractor's or a visitor's), since the duty of care is imposed on the actor by virtue of him performing an act foreseeably likely to cause harm to others present on the premises, and not because the actor occupies the land.[50]

Before the Occupiers' Liability Act 1957, it had been held in some cases that a claimant might sometimes have the choice of suing either under the general law of negligence or by virtue of the special duty owed by occupiers.[51] Since the Act seemingly only displaces the common law rules imposed in consequence of occupation, it follows

---

[46] *Hill v Lovett (OH)* 1992 SLT 994. At common law, if the danger confronted the visitor while on the premises, although he actually suffered the harm off the premises – eg, falling off an unfenced cliff into the sea – the rules regulating the duties of occupiers towards visitors applied: *Perkowski v Wellington Corpn* [1959] AC 53. The wording of s 1(1) of the Act is also wide enough to cover this situation.

[47] *Glasgow Corpn v Muir* [1943] AC 448.

[48] All three judges in *Videan v British Transport Commission* [1963] 2 QB 650 were of the same opinion (*obiter*).

[49] See *Ferguson v Welsh* [1987] 3 All ER 777; *Fairchild v Glenhaven Funeral Services Ltd* [2002] 1 WLR 1052.

[50] *Revill v Newbery* [1996] 1 All ER 291. The rationale here is that the restrictive wording of the Occupiers' Liability Act 1957, s 1(2) – 'The rules so enacted shall regulate the nature of the duty imposed by law *in consequence of a person's occupation or control* of premises' – excludes this class of acts. Thus, when premises were set alight by their occupier, this was clearly a negligent act performed otherwise than *in consequence of occupation or control*, and one for which damages in under the general law of negligence (rather than the Occupiers' Liability Act 1957) were available: *Ogwo v Taylor* [1988] AC 431.

[51] See, eg, *Slade v Battersea and Putney Group Hospital Management Committee* [1955] 1 All ER 429 (A visitor of a patient in a state hospital was injured because polish had recently been spread on the floor and the visitor had not been warned of it. She could invoke negligence *simpliciter*.)

that if some other duty is imposed by the common law or statute (for some reason independent of occupation) the claimant may rely on either the Occupiers' Liability Act 1957 *or* the other cause of action (or both). Thus, a workman injured on his employer's premises may rely either on the common duty of care set out in the Act, the duty of the employer to provide a safe system of work, or even some statutory duty of the employer to provide safe access or the like.[52]

(3) THE COMMON DUTY OF CARE

(a) General principles

The common duty of care is a duty to take such care as in all the circumstances of the case is reasonable to see that the visitor will be reasonably safe in using the premises for the purposes for which he is invited or permitted by the occupier to be there.[53] Thus, a hotelier was not liable in respect of a guest who sustained head injuries from falling out of a window when, in all probability, the guest (who could not recall the incident) had been leaning out too far.[54] There had been no breach of duty because the hotelier had taken reasonable care on the facts thus illustrating the fact that the duty under the Act is virtually identical to the duty imposed under the common law of negligence (hence the inclusion of occupiers' liability in this part of the book). Another example is *Laverton v Kiapasha*[55] where a takeaway food outlet could not prevent the floor of their premises becoming wet because customers were constantly coming in with wet feet on a rainy evening. There was no liability under the 1957 Act when a customer slipped and injured her ankle since, on the facts, the takeaway restaurant had done what was reasonable on a very rainy night to keep the floor as dry as possible. Had the case been brought under the common law, the owners would presumably have escaped liability in negligence for precisely the same reason.

Even though the Act stipulates particular considerations that impinge on the standard of care required in relation to child visitors and those who have a particular trade, profession or skill, the Act still amounts to little more than an echo of well-established common-law principles in these respects. Section 2(3) of the Occupiers' Liability Act 1957 states:

The circumstances relevant for the present purpose include the degree of care, and of want of care, which would ordinarily be looked for in such a visitor, so that (for example) in proper cases:

(a) an occupier must be prepared for children to be less careful than adults; and

(b) an occupier may expect that a person, in the exercise of his calling, will appreciate and guard against any special risks ordinarily incident to it, so far as the occupier leaves him free to do so.

---

[52] Eg, *Ward v Hertfordshire County Council* [1970] 1 All ER 535 (duties of local authority both as education authority and occupier considered when child hurt by playground flint wall, though D held not liable under either head because the wall was not dangerous).   [53] Occupiers' Liability Act 1957, s 2(2).
[54] *Lewis v Six Continents plc* [2005] EWCA Civ 1805.   [55] [2002] NPC 145.

Bearing in mind the similarity between the gist of this provision and the ordinary law of negligence, it would seem appropriate to invoke parallel common-law decisions as guides to the way in which this subsection should be applied. In particular, the following common-law principles would appear to be important. First, in deciding whether there was a danger, regard must be had to the limited physical and mental powers of a child visitor: for, what is not a danger to an adult may well be a danger to a child.[56] As such, in determining the standard of care owed to a child who is not accompanied by a guardian, it will be material to enquire whether, in the circumstances, the occupier could reasonably have expected the presence of the unaccompanied infant.[57] (If the unaccompanied child cannot be expected by the occupier, that child will inevitably be a trespasser. But since the passage of the Occupiers' Liability Act 1984, it is of much less significance that he cannot sue for his injuries *qua* visitor.[58])

The significance of section 2(3)(b) in so far as it deals with the care to be shown to visitors possessed of a particular profession may also be illuminated by decisions at common law. A window cleaner injured through the insecurity of some part of the exterior of the premises which he uses as a foothold or handhold for the purpose of cleaning the outside of the windows can be expected by the occupier to have guarded against this special risk which is ordinarily incidental to the job of a window cleaner.[59] But there is no reason why the occupier should not be liable if the window cleaner is injured through some defect in the staircase which leads to his injury when he is going upstairs, in the ordinary way, to reach the windows on an upper floor.[60] Similarly, an occupier can expect a chimney sweep to guard against dangers from flues.[61] But a self-employed plasterer injured when scaffolding collapses beneath him may recover damages from an occupier since the risk was inherent in the defective state of the premises, and was not an expected risk of his employment as a plasterer.[62] In short, the special skills of the entrant are *relevant* to the determination of whether the occupier is in breach of the common duty of care, but they will not

---

[56] *Cooke v Midland Great Western Rly of Ireland* [1909] AC 229, at 238, *per* Lord Atkinson. Cf *Gough v National Coal Board* [1954] 1 QB 191. The cases are legion but they all turn on their particular facts – eg, *Williams v Cardiff Corpn* [1950] 1 KB 514 (a grassy slope with broken glass at the foot is a trap for a four-year-old child). The principle stated in the text also applied at common law in the case of adults suffering from mental or physical handicap, and, it is submitted, will continue to apply to them under the Act.

[57] See *Phipps v Rochester Corpn* [1955] 1 QB 450, containing a thoroughgoing review by Devlin J of the rights of child visitors. Applied in *Simkiss v Rhondda Borough Council* (1982) 81 LGR 460.

[58] The Occupiers' Liability Act 1984 replaced the harsh rules of common law that had traditionally been applied to trespassers. The difference in the child's protection is therefore equal to the discrepancy between the duties imposed by the 1957 and 1984 Acts.

[59] *Christmas v General Cleaning Contractors Ltd* [1953] AC 180. Similarly, a deliveryman injured when making deliveries cannot sue for the inherent dangers in handling heavy goods; he may reasonably be expected by the occupier to use his expertise in making those deliveries: *Phillips v Perry* (1997) unreported.   [60] See *Bates v Parker* [1953] 2 QB 231.

[61] *Roles v Nathan* [1963] 2 All ER 908. A factory occupier owes a lesser standard of care to a fireman trying to put out a fire than to his employees and has no duty to provide alternative escape facilities: *Bermingham v Sher Bros* 1980 SLT 122.   [62] *Kealey v Heard* [1983] 1 All ER 973.

automatically absolve the occupier from responsibility (especially where the risk is not one ordinarily encountered by a person possessed of the particular entrant's skills[63]).

Another similarity between the duty of care owed under the ordinary law of negligence and the duty owed under the 1957 Act inheres in the fact that no duty is owed under the Act to those who use the premises in excess of their permission to be there. So, someone who was a lawful visitor to the shores of a lake on a hot day became a trespasser once he entered the water in order to swim, when swimming was prohibited.[64] Scrutton LJ neatly encapsulated the principle when he said: '[w]hen you invite a person into your house to use the stairs, you do not invite him to slide down the banisters'.[65] Thus, there is 'no difference between a person who comes upon land without permission and one who, having come with permission, does something which he has not been given permission to do'.[66] This approach, of course, bears a close resemblance to the 'scope of duty' principle in the ordinary law of negligence whereby one asks whether 'the consequence [is] fairly to be considered within the risk created by the negligence'.[67]

A final similarity inheres in the fact that – as was held in *Jolley v Sutton London Borough Council*[68] – the same test for the remoteness of damage applies under the 1957 Act as applies in the ordinary law of negligence.[69] In other words, in order to recover damages, the claimant must be able to show that he suffered loss or injury of a kind that was reasonably foreseeable.

One apparent, if questionable, difference between the two regimes is that the defendant's failure to discharge the common duty of care need not, according to authority, amount to negligent misfeasance. Thus, a football club that can anticipate crowd trouble from visiting supporters, yet fails to make the game all-ticket or ban those visiting supporters, may still be liable in respect of injuries sustained by a policeman when those supporters use loose pieces of concrete as projectiles.[70] But it is difficult to see why the failure of the football club to take preventive steps would not be actionable as common-law negligence. Similar events had occurred at earlier games (making the injury to the policeman foreseeable) and the contractual nexus between the parties would presumably satisfy the proximity requirement.

---

[63] *Eden v West & Co* [2002] EWCA Civ 991; *Simpson v A I Dairies Farms Ltd* [2001] NPC 14.

[64] *Tomlinson v Congleton Borough Council* [2004] 1 AC 46.   [65] *The Carlgarth* [1927] P 93, at 110.

[66] *Tomlinson v Congleton Borough Council* [2004] 1 AC 46, at [13], *per* Lord Hoffmann. Applied in *Maloney v Torfaen CBC* [2005] EWCA Civ 1762.

[67] *Roe v Minister of Health* [1954] 2 QB 66, at 85, *per* Lord Denning MR. See also *South Australia Asset Management Corp v York Montague Ltd* [1997] AC 191.   [68] [1998] 3 All ER 559.

[69] The decision on the facts (but not the *ratio*) in this case is highly questionable. A boy had jacked up an old and rotten boat on D's land with a view to repairing it. It later collapsed on him. The Court of Appeal categorised the harm – injury caused by an 'alluring', dangerous old boat – as too remote on the basis that the injury was caused in an unforeseeable fashion. This reasoning is difficult to square with the *Wagon Mound* principle that it is the *type* of harm (not the manner in which it is occasioned) that determines remoteness.

[70] *Cunningham v Reading Football Club* [1992] PIQR P141.

A second difference between the common law and the duty owed under the 1957 Act – and one mentioned briefly in passing – inheres in the fact that, under section 2(6) of the Act, those entering the occupier's premises by virtue of a right conferred by law will also be afforded the common duty of care. Importantly, this subsection *does not* extend the notion of 'visitor' to such persons; it merely broadens the circumstances in which an entrant will be owed the common duty of care by providing that such persons are to be treated as if they were permitted by the occupier to be there for the particular purpose of exercising the specific right conferred by law.[71] By contrast, the common law of negligence does not afford special duties to those exercising rights conferred by law.[72]

(b) Warning

At common law, an occupier discharged his duty to a visitor by a warning sufficient to convey to the visitor full knowledge of the nature and extent of the danger. That rule was changed by section 2(4)(a) of the 1957 Act which now provides that:

where damage is caused to a visitor by a danger of which he had been warned by the occupier, the warning is not to be treated without more as absolving the occupier from liability, unless in all the circumstances it was enough to enable the visitor to be reasonably safe.

For example, then, the farmer who warns the veterinary surgeon whom he has summoned to the farm at night to attend a sick cow: 'Be careful how you go down the yard or you may fall into a tank', or the railway company which warns of the dangerous roof over what is the sole approach to the ticket office, no longer absolve themselves from liability by such warnings alone. In *Roles v Nathan*[73] Lord Denning provided a helpful example of where the mere provision of a warning would not discharge the duty under the 1957 Act. He suggested that simply warning visitors of the danger of a footbridge over a stream would be insufficient to ensure a visitor's safety if there was only one footbridge and it was essential to use that bridge to enter the defendant's land. But he added that if there were two bridges and one of them was safe, a warning about the unsafe bridge would then fulfil his duty.[74]

In line with the requirement that the warning must be enough to enable the visitor to be safe, a warning has also been held to be ineffective where it was very small in size and posted in an insufficiently prominent position.[75] On the other hand, if a warning is given, but ignored by the visitor – for example, where a customer fails to observe a shopkeeper's warning not to go to the far end of the shop because of a slippery floor – a court would probably hold that, in all the circumstances, the common duty of care had been discharged. If the defendant does not know of the danger, it is obvious that he cannot rely on section 2(4)(a) of the 1957 Act although he may still have a defence based on exclusion of liability (discussed below).[76]

---

[71] *Greenhalgh v British Railways Board* [1969] 2 QB 286, at 292–3, *per* Lord Denning MR.
[72] See, eg, *White v Chief Constable of South Yorkshire Police* [1999] 1 All ER 1.
[73] [1963] 2 All ER 908.   [74] [1963] 2 All ER 908, at 913.   [75] *D v AMF Bowling* [2002] 12 CL 476.
[76] *White v Blackmore* [1972] 2 QB 651.

(c) Assumption of risk

The common duty of care does not impose on an occupier any obligation to a visitor in respect of risks willingly accepted as his by the visitor (where the question of whether a risk is so accepted is to be decided on the same principles as in other cases in which one person owes a duty of care to another).[77] Section 2(5) of the Occupiers' Liability Act 1957 makes clear that an occupier is not in breach of his duty of care where the claimant voluntarily assumed the risk.

At common law no duty of care was owed to a visitor who had full knowledge of the nature and extent of the danger.[78] But case law confirms that knowledge of self-evident dangers relieves the occupier of his duty under section 2(2) of the Occupiers' Liability Act 1957. In *Cotton v Derbyshire Dales District Council*,[79] for example, the Court of Appeal held that the owner of a path which lay adjacent to cliffs and presented an obvious danger was under no duty to visitors who were injured by falling from those cliffs. Similarly, in *Staples v West Dorset District Council*,[80] damages were refused where the claimant slipped and was injured on the defendant council's algae-covered rocks. He had full knowledge of the danger and it was proven that even if there had been a warning, he would have ignored it. Finally, actions will also fail where they are based on mishaps caused either by swimming in deep and murky ornamental ponds that are obviously perilous *for swimmers*, or diving into shallow water.[81]

(d) Contributory negligence

Section 2(3) of the Occupiers' Liability Act 1957 states that in deciding whether the occupier has discharged his common duty of care, the want of care which would ordinarily be looked for in such a visitor is a relevant circumstance. In other words, the claimant cannot by his own carelessness enlarge the duty of care owed to him by the defendant. It is therefore implicit in section 2(3) that the apportionment provisions of the Law Reform (Contributory Negligence) Act 1945 apply to an action for breach of the common duty of care in exactly the same way that they do to any action for negligence *simpliciter*. And a number of cases decided under the Occupiers' Liability Act 1957 have applied these very provisions.[82]

---

[77] Occupiers' Liability Act 1957, s 2(5). But where the occupier occupies the premises for business purposes, note the application of the Unfair Contract Terms Act 1977, s 2(3).

[78] *London Graving Dock Co Ltd v Horton* [1951] AC 737.   [79] (1994) *Times*, 20 June.

[80] (1995) 93 LGR 536.

[81] See, respectively, *Darby v National Trust* [2001] PIQR P372 and *Tomlinson v Congleton Borough Council* [2004] 1 AC 46. Note, however, that it has been held on the highest authority that there is nothing *per se* dangerous about lakes *for those on land*: *Tomlinson v Congleton Borough Council* [2004] 1 AC 46. But a refinement to this point is required: namely, that for a very young child trespasser, unsteady on his feet and unable to swim, a lake may well constitute a danger. Certainly, in *Donoghue v Folkestone Properties Ltd* [2003] QB 1008 the Court of Appeal held that s 1 of the 1984 Act permits the court to take account of differences between adults and children who are non-visitors in deciding whether a duty is owed under the Act.

[82] Eg, *Bunker v Charles Brand & Son Ltd* [1969] 2 QB 480. See also *McMillan v Lord Advocate* 1991 SLT 150.

(e) Liability for independent contractors

Section 2(4)(b) of the Occupiers' Liability Act 1957 provides that where damage is caused to a visitor by virtue of a danger attributable to the faulty execution of any work of construction, maintenance or repair[83] by an independent contractor employed by the occupier, the occupier is not to be treated, without more,[84] as answerable for the danger if in all the circumstances he had acted reasonably in entrusting the work to an independent contractor and had taken such steps (if any) as he reasonably ought in order to satisfy himself that the contractor was competent and that the work had been properly done. Notably, the instances of defective construction, maintenance and repair mentioned in section 2(4)(b) are specifically stated to be no more than examples of the kinds of dangers that can be attributed to independent contractors. Thus, where independent contractors run an amusement facility on the occupier's land, and that facility causes injury to a visitor, the occupier may still be liable if he does not check the contractor's competence in just the same way as he would be liable if he failed to check, say, construction work although only the latter is referred to in section 2(4)(b).[85]

Given that section 2(4)(b) is important both *per se* and by extension, its terms warrant further analysis. First, in applying this subsection, the courts must consider whether, initially, it was reasonable for the occupier to engage an independent contractor to undertake the construction, maintenance or repair work. It is not obvious what this entails for it is difficult to envisage a situation in which the court would expect the occupier to have performed construction work himself in preference to an independent contractor.[86] As such, we might be tempted to say that it is presumptively reasonable for an occupier to engage a contractor wherever, as in *Haseldine v C A Daw & Son Ltd*,[87] the work to be done requires special skill or equipment not possessed by the occupier.[88] On the other hand, it has been suggested that enquiring as to whether

---

[83] This expression covers work incidental to construction: *AMF International Ltd v Magnet Bowling Ltd* [1968] 2 All ER 789. It also extends, curiously, to demolition work: *Ferguson v Welsh* [1987] 3 All ER 777, at 783.

[84] In *Coupland v Eagle Bros Ltd* (1969) 210 *Estates Gazette* 581, C was electrocuted by a live wire which the electrical contractor had not switched off while carrying out electrical work. D knew that the wire was dangerous and had not warned anyone. The 'without more' provision did not absolve him from liability, for he was concurrently careless with the contractor. Even though the cause of harm falls outside these words – eg, the stowing of cargo by a stevedore – D may still discharge his common duty of care by relying on the stevedore as his independent contractor: *Mullis v United States Lines Co* [1969] 1 Lloyd's Rep 109. This is because the Occupiers' Liability Act 1957, s 2(4)(b) is only an 'example' of the common duty of care.

[85] *Gwilliam v West Hertfordshire Hospitals NHS Trust* [2002] 3 WLR 1425. Cf *Bottomley v Todmorden Cricket Club* [2003] EWCA Civ 1575.

[86] On the other hand, where the contractor is permitted to run a fairground concession which necessarily carries a risk of injury, the occupier will be required to check whether the contractor is properly insured: *Gwilliam v West Hertfordshire Hospitals NHS Trust* [2002] 3 WLR 1425.   [87] [1941] 2 KB 343.

[88] In *Maguire v Sefton MBC* [2006] EWCA Civ 316 it was held that the owner of a gym was entitled presumptively to rely on an expert's extra-contractual inspection of machines in a gymnasium prior to their use. Extrapolating from this case – where the machines had been bought from the expert in question and were subsequently to be maintained by the self-same expert – it seems inconceivable that the courts would not apply a similar presumption where an inspection had been *contractually* performed.

a contractor carries proper insurance is a sensible question that might provide some indication as to his general competence.[89] Delegation should, at the very least, be reasonable where it is normal commercial practice to engage contractors for such work. A good example might be office cleaning.

Secondly, the Occupiers' Liability Act 1957 stipulates that the occupier *may* have to check the competence of the contractor. Here, again, it would seem that if the work is of a fairly standard nature the contractor may be trusted.[90] Where, however, the work entrusted to a contractor is of a kind that, after its completion, necessarily involves a risk to future visitors if it has been carelessly executed,[91] the occupier *will* be under a duty to check the competence of the contractor. Thirdly, the occupier will need 'to take such steps as he reasonably ought (if any) in order to satisfy himself that . . . the work had been properly done'.[92] It is unclear from the statute whether this involves a subjective test or an objective one. If a subjective test were adopted, limited financial resources might provide a sufficient reason for not engaging, say, an architect to assess the quality of the work. If an objective test were used, the only relevant factor would be the degree of risk inherent in the kind of work done.

Since the Occupiers' Liability Act 1957 uses the past tense in relation to work done, it is clear that section 2(4)(b) does not envisage the occupier employing a suitable professional to supervise the ongoing work of an independent contractor. Instead, section 2(4)(b) provides only an example of how the common duty of care might be discharged in such cases. Thus, in some circumstances, it may be expected of the occupier that he will have the contractor's work supervised. In *AMF International Ltd v Magnet Bowling Ltd*,[93] for instance, it was said that if the occupier was going to invite the claimant to bring valuable timber onto the site while construction work was ongoing, then to escape liability he may have to employ a supervising architect to ensure that the contractors had made the premises sufficiently safe for that timber safely to be brought there. On the other hand, it was said in *Ferguson v Welsh*[94] (and reiterated by the Court of Appeal in *Fairchild v Glenhaven Funeral Services Ltd*[95]) that an occupier will not normally be liable to the contractor's employee for injuries sustained because the premises were unsafe by virtue of the dangerous system of work adopted by the independent contractors. But if, according to Lord Keith, the occupier knows or has reason to know that the contractor is using an unsafe system of work, he may be liable for not ensuring that a safe system was employed.[96]

---

[89] *Gwilliam v West Hertfordshire Hospitals NHS Trust* [2002] 3 WLR 1425, at [15], *per* Lord Woolf; *Naylor v Paling* [2004] EWCA Civ 560, at [19]-[25], *per* Latham LJ.

[90] In *Cook v Broderip* (1968) 206 *Estates Gazette* 128, D was not liable to his domestic help injured by a new switch fuse negligently installed by a contractor; D was entitled to trust the contractor.

[91] Eg, the repair of a lift which, if carelessly done, clearly poses a risk to subsequent visitors. In one such case, it was central to the court's decision that D was under a duty 'to obtain and follow good technical advice': *Haseldine v Daw & Son Ltd* [1941] 2 KB 343, at 356.   [92] Occupiers' Liability Act 1957, s 2(4)(b).

[93] [1968] 2 All ER 789.   [94] [1987] 3 All ER 777, at 783.   [95] [2002] 1 WLR 1052.

[96] [1987] 3 All ER 777. Note, however, that any such liability would not arise *qua* occupier but rather *qua* joint tortfeasor with the contractor: see [1987] 3 All ER 777, at 786, *per* Lord Goff.

(4) SOME SPECIAL CASES FALLING WITHIN THE OCCUPIERS' LIABILITY ACT 1957

(a) Fixed or movable structures

Section 1(3) of the Occupiers' Liability Act 1957 provides that:

The rules so enacted in relation to an occupier of premises and his visitors shall also apply, in like manner and to the like extent as the principles applicable at common law to an occupier of premises and his invitees or licensees would apply, to regulate:

> (a) the obligations of a person occupying or having control[97] over any fixed or movable structure, including any vessel, vehicle or aircraft.

The term 'movable structures' covers such things as gangways and ladders, as well as vessels, vehicles and aircraft. The test is probably whether one might go into or upon the structure. It is, however, much more difficult to interpret the expression 'fixed structure', for this term, mentioned in section 1(3), and 'premises', mentioned in section 1(1), must presumably be mutually exclusive under the Act. It is clear that the term 'premises' is not confined simply to land: it also includes permanent buildings erected on the land. Thus, 'fixed structures' must be taken to connote some non-movable chattels constructed on land. No doubt the draftsmen doubted whether docks or erections on part of the land such as garden sheds, or swings in a playground, or even scaffolding or lifts were 'premises' and yet realised that the term 'movable structure' did not cover them either. In the end, all of the aforementioned structures are probably within the Occupiers' Liability Act 1957. Yet it remains important whether a structure falls within section 1(1) or section 1(3) because different approaches may need to be taken under these respective subsections. If Mr X provides a defective ladder for an independent contractor to repair Mr X's premises, the Act does not apply for the benefit of the injured contractor, for Mr X has ceased to have enough control of the ladder to be an occupier of it.[98] On the other hand, he may still be liable either as the bailor of goods or as an occupier of premises who intends that the claimant should use his appliances on his land.[99]

(b) Damage to property[100]

Section 1(3) of the Occupiers' Liability Act 1957 also covers:

> (b) the obligations of a person occupying or having control over any premises or structure in respect of damage to property, including the property of persons who are not themselves his visitors.

This subsection will impose a duty on the occupier to prevent damage to goods on the premises arising from the defective physical condition of the premises. The injured

---

[97] Note that an engineering firm did not abandon control of a machine roller when they called in a specialist contractor to modify it, so they retained the obligations of occupiers within the Occupiers' Liability Act 1957, s 1(3)(a): *Bunker v Charles Brand & Son Ltd* [1969] 2 QB 480. [98] *Wheeler v Copas* [1981] 3 All ER 405.
[99] [1981] 3 All ER 405.
[100] See North, 'Damage to Property and the Occupiers' Liability Act 1957' (1966) 30 Conv 264.

visitor would, for example, be able to recover damages for her torn clothes and presumably for damage to her property, even if she is herself uninjured.[101] Where the entrant is carrying the goods of a third party, it is doubtful whether the Act gives the third party an action.[102] Furthermore, the expression 'damage to property' is not apt to cover loss of property so that the section will not cover the duty of boarding-house keepers to keep safe custody of visitors' goods. Still less will it reverse the common-law decision that a publican owes no duty of care to prevent a customer's motorcycle from being stolen from the yard of the public house.[103] On the other hand, it seems consistent with what was said in the preceding section that, whenever the occupier would have owed a duty at common law to prevent damage to goods on his land (whether due to the state of the premises or due to acts or omissions thereon), the common duty of care will now apply.[104]

(c) Liability in contract

At common law, contracts for the use of premises were deemed to contain various implied terms relating to the safety of the premises.[105] *In lieu* of those implied terms,[106] section 5 of the Occupiers' Liability Act 1957 provides that:

(1) Where persons enter or use, or bring or send goods to, any premises in exercise of a right conferred by contract with a person occupying or having control of the premises, the duty he owes them in respect of dangers due to the state of the premises or to things done or omitted to be done on them, in so far as the duty depends on a term to be implied in the contract by reason of its conferring that right, shall be the common duty of care.

(2) The foregoing subsection shall apply to fixed and movable structures as it applies to premises.

The effect of this section is as follows. Where a person enters the occupier's premises under a contract between himself and the occupier, the occupier is obliged to extend the common duty of care to that entrant, subject to any effective contrary term in their contract.[107] It is, of course, open to the occupier specifically to increase the level of care by express provision in the contract. And any such protection bargained for in the main contract may extend to certain third parties so long as the terms of the Contracts

---

[101] *AMF International Ltd v Magnet Bowling Ltd* [1968] 2 All ER 789. It would also seem that loss consequential on damage to property is recoverable. Thus, C, a car-hire firm, could recover loss of earnings when C's car was damaged after having been driven onto D's land by the car *owner*.

[102] Thus, if the visitor's car is damaged he has a remedy, but the finance company, from whom he has it on a credit agreement, does not.

[103] *Tinsley v Dudley* [1951] 2 KB 18. It would seem that, whatever the common-law position, the combined effect of s 1(3)(b) and s 1(1) is to deny the visitor a remedy for loss of property if she is injured and, eg, her valuable necklace falls off her person to be carried away in an adjoining stream.

[104] Supported by *AMF International Ltd v Magnet Bowling Ltd* [1968] 2 All ER 789.

[105] See especially *Francis v Cockrell* (1870) LR 5 QB 501; *Gilmore v LCC* [1938] 4 All ER 331.

[106] The expression 'the duty . . . shall be the common duty of care' shows that the duty replaces, and is not merely alternative to, the terms implied at common law.

[107] See, eg, *Maguire v Sefton* [2006] EWCA Civ 316.

(Rights of Third Parties) Act 1999 are met.[108] On the other hand, the extent to which he is free to exclude or limit his responsibilities towards contractual entrants is governed by the operation of the rules discussed in the next section.

Section 5 of the Occupiers' Liability Act 1957 is not limited in its operation to personal injury caused by the defective state of the occupier's premises; it also covers damage to goods. What is less clear on the face of the Act is whether an action by a contractual entrant must be based solely on contract – on the basis of the term implied into the agreement by virtue of section 5 – or whether he has the alternative of suing in tort. However, the matter was resolved in *Sole v W J Hallt Ltd*.[109] There, a tradesman who had come onto the occupier's premises to perform some plastering work was injured when he fell down an unprotected stair-well. It was held by Swanick J that contractual entrants had the option of suing in either contract (under section 5(1)), or in tort (under section 2(1)).[110]

Another question not resolved by the Act is whether section 5(1) operates where the contract is silent on the issue of the occupier's liability, but it is of a kind that, at common law, traditionally attracted a different implied term. An example would be a passenger on a railway platform who, at common law, was historically protected by a duty owed by the railway company to make the platform reasonably safe.[111] Others present on the platform, such as relatives saying farewell, were afforded the usual duty extended to licensees. But are fare-paying passengers now protected by the traditional common-law implied term which, apart from the statute, would form part of the contract of carriage, or can they invoke only the common duty of care by virtue of section 5(1)? It is submitted that the implied term under the Act applies since the statutory implied term is to be included in the contract *wherever* 'the duty depends upon *a term* to be implied in the contract'.

(5) EXCLUSION OF LIABILITY

Section 2(1) of the Occupiers' Liability Act 1957 provides:

An occupier of premises owes the same duty, the 'common duty of care', to all his visitors, except in so far as he is free to and does extend, restrict, modify or exclude his duty to any visitor or visitors by agreement or otherwise.

The occupier thus has two options if he wishes to modify the common duty of care owed to his visitors. First, where the visitor enters by virtue of a contract – for example,

---

[108]   Under this legislation, there are three such conditions. First, it must be clear that the contract purports to confer a benefit on a third party (eg, the employee or contractor who has agreed to do work for the occupier); secondly, there must be no contrary agreement in the contract; thirdly, the third party must be expressly identified in the contract: Contracts (Rights of Third Parties) Act 1999: s 1(1)(b), (2) and (3).

[109]   [1973] 1 All ER 1032. *Quaere* the effect of any contributory negligence.

[110]   This decision is almost certainly wrong since the Act specifically limits visitors (to whom the Occupiers' Liability Act 1957, s 2(1) refers) to those who were either invitees or licensees at common law. The whole purpose of s 5 is to ensure some protection to contractual entrants where no such protection is mentioned in the contract. It is a decision at first instance and there is no obligation for any future court to follow it.

[111]   *Protheroe v Railway Executive* [1951] 1 KB 376.

a contractor who enters to carry out work on premises – an express term of the contract may be drafted to govern the situation. Secondly, in respect of non-contractual entrants, a clear and unequivocal notice,[112] either affixed at the point of entry to the land,[113] or included in a programme or ticket giving access to the land,[114] will suffice. These two broad options must, however, be read subject to section 3 of the 1957 Act which sets out some important limits on the occupier's freedom to limit or exclude his liability.

Section 3(1) of the Occupiers' Liability Act 1957 provides that the duty of care owed by an occupier to those visitors he is bound to admit onto his premises by virtue of a contract, who are nonetheless 'strangers to the contract',[115] cannot be excluded or restricted.[116] On the other hand, the subsection also provides that any term of the contract which obliges him to increase the level of care shown to such entrants will be effective in determining the standard of care to be shown. Section 3(1) is designed to ensure the protection of employees of the person with whom the occupier has a contract. Thus, if the occupier contracts with Mr A for Mr A's employees to do work on his premises, he may not restrict or exclude any liability to them.

Section 3(2) of the Occupiers' Liability Act 1957 further provides:

A contract shall not by virtue of this section have the effect, unless it expressly so provides, of making an occupier who has taken all reasonable care answerable to strangers to the contract for dangers due to the faulty execution of any work of construction, maintenance or repair or other like operation by persons other than himself, his servants and persons acting under his direction and control.

On reflection, it is apparent that the burden on the defendant under section 3 appears to be greater than that imposed by the common duty of care because he is unable to delegate to independent contractors any part of his duty to take care.[117] Furthermore, while section 3 places some restrictions on the ability of an occupier to limit or exclude his liability, further restrictions upon his freedom to do so are also imposed under the Unfair Contract Terms Act 1977. This later Act drastically reduces the scope for a person who occupies premises for 'business purposes' to exclude or restrict his liability.[118]

---

[112] Note the difference between a notice (excluding or restricting liability) and a warning (alerting entrants to a danger present on the premises).   [113] *Ashdown v Samuel Williams & Sons Ltd* [1957] 1 QB 409.

[114] *White v Blackmore* [1972] 2 QB 651.

[115] Defined as 'a person not for the time being entitled to the benefit of the contract as a party to it or as the successor by assignment or otherwise of a party to it, and accordingly includes a party to the contract who has ceased to be so entitled': s 3(3).

[116] A similar effect is achieved in relation to contractors who enter premises under a contract with the landlord, where the tenant has agreed with the landlord (extra-contractually) to allow such contractors to enter the premises.

[117] The duty in respect of independent contractors now imposed by s 3(1) and (2) is not exactly the same as the common duty of care imposed by s 2(4)(b). First, s 3(2) limits the liability not only in respect of, as in s 2(4)(b), 'the faulty execution of any work of construction, maintenance or repair' but also in respect of any 'other like operation'. Secondly, whereas s 2(4)(b) specifies in detail what would be reasonable care by the occupier in relation to the conduct of the independent contractor, s 3(2) states that he shall take 'all reasonable care' without further particularizing this standard – it cannot simply be assumed that the two standards are identical.

[118] Note that the Unfair Contract Terms Act 1977 and Occupiers' Liability Act 1957, s 3 will often work in tandem since most, if not all, s 3 cases are likely to involve an occupier for 'business purposes'.

The Unfair Contract Terms Act 1977 renders invalid any contract term or notice purporting to exclude or restrict liability for death or personal injury[119] resulting from breach of the common duty of care under the Occupiers' Liability Act 1957 where the premises are occupied for the business purposes of the occupier.[120] In the case of other loss or damage, any contract term or notice designed to restrict or exclude liability is subject to the requirement of reasonableness.[121] If the exclusion is in the form of a contract term, its reasonableness is to be gauged by reference to 'the circumstances which were, or ought reasonably to have been, known to or in the contemplation of the parties when the contract was made'.[122] If the exclusion of liability is in the form of a notice, then its reasonableness is to be judged in the light of 'all the circumstances obtaining when the liability arose'.[123] Of the two tests, the one relating to notices is the more claimant-friendly, for 'all the circumstances' presumably include those both within and beyond the actual or imputed contemplation of the parties. The less claimant-friendly test applied to contract terms can be justified on the basis that the claimant had a chance, at the time of contracting, to bargain against the inclusion of any such term.

Agreement to, or knowledge of, the term or notice will not necessarily be evidence that the visitor has assumed the risk of injury giving rise to the defence of *volenti non fit injuria*.[124] Equally, oral stipulation of any such term or notice, made at the time of the entrant's visit will similarly fail to render the entrant necessarily *volens*; for under the Unfair Contract Terms Act 1977, any such announcement itself constitutes a notice.[125]

The Unfair Contract Terms Act 1977 clearly leaves an occupier free (via a notice on a front gate) to exclude liability to some of his visitors since its operation is limited to those entering in connection with business purposes;[126] and the Act makes clear that it is the business purposes of the occupier alone which are relevant.[127] In some cases it will be clear that the occupier's business purposes are in issue. Consider, for example, *Ashdown v Samuel Williams & Sons Ltd.*[128]

By a licence granted by D, C crossed D's land. A notice board purported to curtail the liabilities of D to licensees. The Court of Appeal held that because D had taken reasonable steps to bring the conditions of the notice to the attention of C, these conditions (designed to exclude liability for damage sustained in the way in which C's injuries were caused) were effective in excluding D's liability. But if the case had arisen after 1977, D would not have been able to exclude his liability under the Occupiers' Liability Act 1957.

---

[119] Unfair Contract Terms Act 1977, s 2(1).
[120] Unfair Contract Terms Act 1977, s 1(1)(c).
[121] Unfair Contract Terms Act 1977, s 2(2).
[122] Unfair Contract Terms Act 1977, s 11(1).
[123] Unfair Contract Terms Act 1977, s 11(3).
[124] Unfair Contract Terms Act 1977, s 2(3).
[125] Unfair Contract Terms Act 1977, s 14.

[126] Ibid, s 14 defines 'business' so as to include 'a profession and the activities of any government department or public or local authority'. So if I invite a research student to my home for supervision, do I then occupy my home for 'business purposes'?

[127] What happens, however, if I let a room of my house to a postgraduate student? Should the premises as a whole be treated as business premises? Equally, what if the premises are under dual control, and only one of the occupiers is a business occupier? On both these matters see Mesher, 'Occupiers, Trespassers and the Unfair Contract Terms Act 1977' (1979) 43 Conv 58.
[128] [1957] 1 QB 409.

But what would happen if the facts of *White v Blackmore*[129] were to recur? There, notices at the entrance to the racetrack and in the programme handed to spectators and competitors excluded liability for injuries occurring in jalopy races. The races were being run to raise money for charity. In 1972 the notices sufficed to exclude the organisers' and occupiers' liability. Today, a preliminary question would be whether the track was occupied for business purposes. Similarly, is a Sunday school within the Unfair Contract Terms Act 1977 when a jumble sale is being held there, but not on a Sunday morning? And what of the housewife who does some part-time hairdressing at home, and whose customer is hurt coming downstairs from the bathroom?

The only further attempt at clarification of the definition of 'business purposes' is to be found in section 2 of the Occupiers' Liability Act 1984. That section amends the Unfair Contract Terms Act 1977 to provide:

but liability of an occupier of premises for breach of an obligation or duty toward a person obtaining access to the premises for recreational or educational purposes, being liability for loss or damage suffered by reason of the dangerous state of premises is not a business liability of the occupier unless granting that person such access for the purposes concerned falls within the business purposes of the occupier.[130]

The purpose of this tortuously worded provision appears to be to allow farmers and owners of countryside areas to exclude liability to day-trippers. The land is occupied for 'business purposes': namely, farming or forestry. But any duty owed to entrants coming to the land to picnic and so on can nonetheless be excluded by agreement or notice.[131]

(B) THE OCCUPIERS' LIABILITY ACT 1984

Liability to trespassers and all other uninvited entrants (such as those using a private right of way[132]) is now governed by section 1 of the Occupiers' Liability Act 1984[133] which provides that the Act:

shall have effect in place of the rules of common law[134] to determine –

    (a) whether any duty is owed by a person as occupier of premises to persons other than his visitors in respect of any risk of their suffering injury on the premises by reason of any danger due to the state of the premises or to things done or omitted to be done on them;

    (b) if so, what that duty is.

Although the Occupiers' Liability Act 1984 avowedly replaces the rules of common law in relation to an occupier's liability towards uninvited entrants, three exceptional

---

[129] [1972] 2 QB 651.

[130] Unfair Contract Terms Act 1977, s 1(3)(b).

[131] See Bragg and Brazier, 'Occupiers and Exclusion of Liability' (1986) 130 Sol Jo 251 & 274.

[132] See, eg, *Vodden v Gayton* [2001] PIQR P52.

[133] The Act is based on proposals from the Law Commission Report No 75, *Liability for Damage or Injury to Trespassers and Related Questions of Occupiers' Liability* (Cmnd 6428).

[134] As to which see *British Railways Board v Herrington* [1972] AC 877.

instances fall outside the Act because of the terms in which it is drafted. First, section 1(8) expressly confines liability to personal injuries. It therefore follows that the common law rules in respect of damage to a trespasser's[135] (or other uninvited entrant's) personal property have survived the enactment of the Occupiers' Liability Act 1984. Secondly, the Act's remit is further limited in that no duty is owed by the occupier of the *solum* of a public right of way to persons using that right of way.[136] (It is arguable, however, that since the Act specifically provides that nothing in its provisions affects any duty otherwise owed to such persons, that users of public rights of way are owed the duty of common humanity formulated in *British Railways Board v Herrington*.[137]) Finally, it was held in *Revill v Newbery*[138] that acts of the occupier that are not done in connection with its occupation fall outside the purview of the Act. Put otherwise, liability for acts which do not in themselves affect the safety of the premises is to be determined according to the common law.[139]

A duty to uninvited entrants in respect of any danger due to the state of the premises arises only when three conditions are met.[140]

(1) The occupier must be aware of the danger or have reasonable grounds to believe it exists.

(2) He must have known, or had reasonable grounds to know, that the uninvited entrant either was in, or might come into, the vicinity of the danger. (So, where occupiers had no reason to expect that trespassers were taking shortcuts across their land, no duty arose.[141] And where a trespasser decides to go swimming in a harbour at midnight in mid-winter, the occupier has no reason to suppose that he will be there.[142])

(3) The risk of injury to an uninvited entrant resulting from that danger was one against which, in all the circumstances of the case, the occupier might reasonably be expected to offer the uninvited entrant some protection.

The test for the existence (as opposed to substance) of the duty of care imposed by the 1984 Act appears, at first sight, to comprise a curious admixture of objective and subjective elements. The first and second limbs seem ostensibly to contain both in referring not only to the *individual occupier's* actual knowledge, but also to that knowledge which he ought reasonably to have. However, it has been held that even the

---

[135] That such common-law liability did arise on the principle in *British Railways Board v Herrington* [1972] AC 877 is clear from *Tutton v A D Walter Ltd* [1986] QB 61 where there was liability for negligently spraying crops so as to kill a neighbour's bees. The bees were probably not trespassers but liability to their keeper would still arise even if the bees were trespassing.   [136] Occupiers' Liability Act 1984, s 1(7).

[137] [1972] AC 877. See further Buckley, 'The Occupiers' Liability Act 1984 – Has *Herrington* Survived?' (1984) 48 Conv 413; Murphy, 'Public Rights of Way and Private Law Wrongs' (1997) 61 Conv 362.

[138] [1996] 1 All ER 291.

[139] However, in *Revill v Newbury* it was said that, in applying the common law, the same principles as those contained in the Occupiers' Liability Act 1984 should be applied: [1996] 1 All ER 291, at 298, *per* Neill LJ.

[140] Occupiers' Liability Act 1984, s 1(3).

[141] *White v St Albans City and District Council* (1990) *Times*, 12 March.

[142] *Donoghue v Folkestone Properties Ltd* [2003] QB 1008.

second part of the test contains a subjective element. That is, the occupier must have either actual knowledge of the danger or presence of a non-visitor *or* he must have actual knowledge of the relevant facts from which a reasonable man would draw the relevant inference (even if he does not himself draw that inference).[143] If he neither knows of the danger, nor of the state of affairs, then he will not be liable just because a reasonable occupier would have known of that state of affairs. As such, a landowner who very seldom looks round his grounds, and fails to notice the emergence of a danger, could not be held liable whereas a landowner who regularly surveys his premises and turns a blind eye to an obvious source of danger would be caught by the subsection.[144] The third limb is mainly objective in nature, emphasizing, as it does, all the circumstances of the case. However it is clear that it does not constitute an entirely objective test since it demands only that level of protection which can reasonably be expected of the particular occupier.[145] For these purposes, the personal characteristics of the occupier and the limits on his financial resources may be taken as relevant.

As already noted, section 1(4) of the 1984 Act states that the duty is one 'to take such care as is reasonable in all the circumstances of the case'. Such circumstances will certainly include the age and capabilities of the entrant[146] so that greater protection needs to be shown to a child than an adult trespasser where the danger concerned would be more apparent to the latter than the former.[147] Similarly, the entrant's purpose may be relevant, so that a burglar can expect far less by way of protection than, say, an 'innocent' child trespasser.[148] On the other hand, where a burglar is injured because of a negligent act on the part of the occupier, the common law will still afford him a remedy. *Revill v Newbery* illustrates this point. There, a burglar whom the defendant negligently shot was able to sue the occupier in negligence even though the case fell outside the Occupiers' Liability Act 1984.[149]

A significant difference between the Occupiers' Liability Act 1984 and Occupiers' Liability Act 1957 exists in section 1(5) of the later Act. There it is stipulated that any duty arising under the Occupiers' Liability Act 1984 can:

in an appropriate case, be discharged by taking such steps as are reasonable in all the circumstances of the case to give warning of the danger concerned or to discourage a person from incurring the risk.

Unlike under the 1957 Act, the warning need not enable the uninvited entrant to be or remain safe on the land. If the occupier of a building site with dangerous concealed

---

[143] *Swain v Natui Ram Puri* [1996] PIQR P442.

[144] In *Swain v Natui Puri* [1996] PIQR P442, the court added the gloss that an occupier cannot be heard to say that he had deliberately shut his eyes to dangers on his land in order to escape liability: knowledge of glaringly obvious dangers will be imputed to him.

[145] This interpretation seems to be borne out by the decision in *Ratcliff v McConnell* [1999] 1 WLR 670, at 680, *per* Stuart-Smith LJ.   [146] See *Ratcliff v McConnell* [1999] 1 WLR 670.

[147] *Ratcliffe v McConnell* [1999] 1 WLR 670, at 683, *per* Stuart-Smith LJ; and see Jones, 'The Occupiers' Liability Act 1984 – The Wheels of Law Reform Turn Slowly' (1984) 47 MLR 713, 721.

[148] See also *Murphy v Culhane* [1977] QB 94, at 98, where Lord Denning MR suggested *obiter* that the defence of *ex turpi causa non oritur actio* might be available in this context.

[149] The court also refused to entertain D's claim that the defence of *ex turpi causa* should apply.

trenches puts up notices[150] around the perimeter of the site saying 'Danger: Concealed Trench', such warnings would be insufficient to discharge the occupier's duty towards his visitors. But since they make specific mention, as the Act demands, of 'the danger concerned', it would almost certainly suffice *vis-à-vis* an uninvited adult entrant.[151] The fact that a warning notice has been read by an uninvited entrant will not, of itself, render that person *volens*,[152] but the Act does provide for the operation of a very similar defence in this context. It states:

No duty is owed by virtue of this section to any person in respect of risks willingly accepted as his by that person (the question of whether a risk was so accepted to be decided on the same principles as in other cases in which one person owes a duty of care to another).[153]

In this context it has been held that there need be no warning of obvious dangers, such as those associated with diving head first into the shallow end of a swimming pool with hardly any water in it.[154] Whether a danger is obvious or not may vary according to whether the non-visitor is an adult or a child. But just because a non-visitor is a child does not mean that – even allowing for his lesser appreciation of danger – it will never be appropriate in respect of children to treat a given risk as obvious. Obviousness is a question of fact and degree and it is wrong simply to treat all dangers as non-obvious on the basis of a claimant's immaturity.[155]

As already noted, by virtue of section 1(8) of the 1984 Act, non-visitors are not entitled to sue in respect of property damage occasioned by breach of the section 1 duty. Accordingly, a trespasser who, due to the perilous state of the premises, trips and falls on the occupier's land while snooping there may sue under the Act in respect of his personal injuries but not for the damage caused to his camera.[156]

Finally in this context, we must consider the new provisions that were added to the Occupiers' Liability Act 1984 by the Countryside and Rights of Way Act 2000. As we noted when considering the 1957 Act, those exercising a right of access to open land for recreational purposes under section 2(1) of the 2000 Act are specifically excluded from

---

[150] NB. The Unfair Contract Terms Act 1977 does not apply to the duty created by the 1984 Act and therefore has no impact on the efficacy of such notices so far as they seek to exclude liability.

[151] In relation to an illiterate young child who is allured onto the premises, it is less likely that such a notice would suffice. In any event, he might be classified as a visitor by implied licence.

[152] *Titchener v British Railways Board* [1983] 3 All ER 770.

[153] Occupiers' Liability Act 1984, s 1(6). The difference between this statutory version of *volenti* and its common law cousin lies in the fact that at common law, C, to be *volens*, must accept both the risk of injury *and* the fact that any resulting loss should be his own. Under the 1984 Act, D can raise the defence in s 1(6) on proof of the former alone. Furthermore, properly understood, *volenti* is to be confined to the assumption of risk in relation to future rather than extant dangers: *Morris v Murray* [1991] 2 QB 6, at 17, 28 and 32, *per* Fox, Stocker and Waller LJJ respectively.

[154] *Ratcliff v McConnell* [1999] 1 WLR 670. On the other hand, the fact that someone takes such foolhardy action does not negate the existence of a duty to take reasonable steps to prevent such persons from doing those things: see *Tomlinson v Congleton Borough Council* [2004] 1 AC 46.

[155] *Keown v Coventry Healthcare NHS Trust* [2006] 1 WLR 953 (11-year held *volens* in respect of dangers associated with climbing the exterior of a fire escape).

[156] He may, however, have an action based on the common law which remains untouched by the Act in respect of property damage.

the category, 'visitors'.[157] As such, they are non-visitors and are owed only a more limited duty under the Occupiers' Liability Act 1984. More specifically, it is now provided that in determining the duty owed to those entering the occupier's land on this basis, regard must be had to 'the fact that the existence of that right ought not to place an undue burden (whether financial or otherwise) on the occupier [and to] ... the importance of maintaining the character of the countryside'.[158] Furthermore, the occupier's duty will generally be excluded in the circumstances governed by the new section 1(6A) of the Occupiers' Liability Act 1984;[159] that is, where there is:

(a) a risk resulting from the existence of any natural feature of the landscape, or any river, stream, ditch or pond whether or not a natural feature, or

(b) a risk of [the claimant] suffering injury when passing over, under or through any wall, fence or gate, except by proper use of the gate or of a stile.

It could be argued that these provisions could be interpreted as conferring greater protection on a trespasser than on someone exercising their right to roam since claims by those exercising the right to roam are unquestionably barred where their injury results from a natural feature of the landscape etc. But in practice, this may do no more than reflect the law as it stands under the 1984 Act. Take, for example, *Tomlinson v Congleton Borough Council*.[160] In that case, a trespasser was injured in a lake under the control of the defendant council. But it was held that the council did not owe a duty by virtue of section 1 of the 1984 Act as there was no especial danger on the occupier's land, lakes not being inherently dangerous. As Lord Hoffmann put it: '[T]here were no hidden dangers. It was shallow in some places and deep in others, but that is the nature of lakes'.[161]

Suppose the facts were substantially to recur in connection with a lake in the countryside that constituted a natural feature of the land. Any claim based on injury associated with that lake would now fail on the basis of section 1(6A). All that the new provision will have achieved then, is the same result via a different route (albeit a more certain route that provides occupiers with some degree of reassurance that they need not be especially careful in respect of those exercising the right to roam). It eliminates the need for the occupier to argue that, taking account of 'all the circumstances of the case' – one of which would presumably be that if the lake happened to be located in an area of natural beauty (which typically attract those exercising the right to roam) – it would have been unreasonable to expect him to undermine or diminish the beauty of the land by erecting artificial fences, warning signs and the like.[162]

---

[157] Occupiers' Liability Act 1957, s 1(4)(a).   [158] Occupiers' Liability Act 1984, s 1A(a), (b).

[159] Inserted by the Countryside and Rights of Way Act 2000, s 13(2).   [160] [2004] 1 AC 46.

[161] [2004] 1 AC 46, at [26].

[162] In *Tomlinson v Congleton Borough Council* [2004] 1 AC 46, the House of Lords held that it would have been unreasonable to turn the sandy beaches by the side of the lake that featured in that case into marshland at the cost of the enjoyment of thousands of people who used the beaches for sunbathing. As Lord Hobhouse observed (at [81]): '[it] should never be the policy of the law to require the protection of the foolhardy or reckless few to deprive, or interfere with, the enjoyment by the remainder of society'.

The only exceptions to the general exclusion of liability under section 1(6A) of the Occupiers' Liability Act 1984 are those set out in section 1(6C). These relate to dangers either intentionally or recklessly created by the occupier. It is submitted that these exceptions are likely to be of little practical significance on the footing that there are likely to be few deliberately or recklessly created perils in the countryside in locations that tend to attract walkers. On the other hand, it is not clear why liability remains excluded in relation to reckless omissions to eliminate dangers that occur otherwise than by occupier's own creation. If, for example, on a known crumbling cliff-top a favourite viewing point reaches the point of imminent collapse, there is no liability for a failure to address that danger.

(C) COMMON – LAW LIABILITY AND ACTIVITIES ON LAND

Naturally, an occupier who intentionally harms a person whom he has permitted to be on his premises is answerable for so doing under the law of battery considered in Chapter 8. But in addition, the occupier may also be under a duty according to the ordinary law of negligence to take reasonable care when conducting certain activities on his land that are foreseeably likely to harm visitors of whose presence he is, or ought to be, aware.[163]

The scope for the residual role of the common law stems from the wording of section 1 of the 1957 Act. It states, first, that the Act 'shall have effect, in place of the rules of common law, to regulate the duty which an occupier of premises owes to visitors in respect of dangers due to the state of the premises *or to things done* or omitted to be done on them'.[164] If it went no further, it would seem that activities – such as driving one's car on the land – would fall within the Act. But it does not stop there: it goes on to provide that the statutory rules shall also 'regulate the nature of the duty imposed by law *in consequence of a person's occupation or control* of premises'.[165] As such, it is arguable that activities on the land that are performed otherwise than as a *consequence* of occupation fall beyond the statute. Thus, driving a tractor on a farm may fall within the Act on the basis that tractor driving will be a normal (and, thus, consequential) act performed by the occupier of a modern arable farm. By contrast, riding a bicycle on the farm could well be seen as an act that is anything but naturally ancillary or incidental to farm occupation.

The fact that there is probably a small residual role for the common law in relation to visitors[166] is doubtless a largely academic point, in both the literal and pejorative senses,

---

[163] In *Chettle v Denton* (1951) 95 Sol Jo 802 (D, while shooting game on private land, hit C who was a licensee on the land. D was held liable in negligence in that he would have seen C if he had taken reasonable care).

[164] Occupiers' Liability Act 1957, s 1(1) (emphasis added).

[165] Occupiers' Liability Act 1957, s 1(2) (emphasis added).

[166] For examples of the kinds of activities that could fall within the small remaining pocket of common law liability, see the equivalent section of the corresponding chapter in the 11th edition of this book.

since, as we noted at length earlier, there is very little difference between the common duty of care imposed under the Act and the standard of care demanded by the ordinary law of negligence.

So far as the Occupiers' Liability Act 1984 is concerned, however, there are no words equivalent to those located in the 1957 legislation, which might be construed to exclude statutory liability in respect of activities performed on the land. As such, as regards the physical injury of non-visitors, the pre-existing common law has definitely not survived the passage of the 1984 Act.[167]

(D) LIABILITY TO THOSE OUTSIDE ONE'S PREMISES

The dangers caused by the defective state of premises is not confined to entrants to those premises. Slates falling from roofs, crumbling walls and dangerous activities carried out on premises are further examples of risks just as likely to endanger passers by and those on adjoining premises. The circumstances in which the occupier of premises owes a duty to such persons therefore require brief consideration. As will be seen in due course,[168] an action in public nuisance sometimes lies in respect of injuries or loss caused on a highway as a result of harmful conditions on adjoining land. But a claimant may just as well sue for personal injuries in negligence in such cases.[169] Furthermore, occupiers are under a general duty to take reasonable care to prevent dangers on their premises damaging persons or property on adjoining premises.[170] This is so whether the danger arises from the disrepair of the premises, or some man-made or natural hazard such as fire caused by lightning striking a tree.[171] Also, where adjoining properties have mutual rights of support, negligently allowing one property to fall into dereliction so as to damage the adjoining premises is actionable in negligence as well as in private nuisance.[172]

There are two issues of particular difficulty affecting the duties of care owed by the occupiers of adjoining premises. First, where a claimant tenant sues his landlord for

---

[167] See, eg, *Scott v Associated British Ports* 2000 WL 1741511 (youths injured when 'surfing' a ride on a slow-moving goods train). [168] Ch 17.

[169] Eg, *Hilder v Associated Portland Cement Manufacturers Ltd* [1961] 3 All ER 709 (D, who occupied a field and allowed children to play football there was liable to a motor-cyclist who, when driving along the adjacent highway, was knocked off by a ball kicked by the children from the field).

[170] *Hughes v Percival* (1883) 8 App Cas 443 (the premises benefited by the present rule are those in respect of which someone other than D has a vested interest in possession). Note also, *Murphy v Brentwood District Council* [1990] 2 All ER 908, at 926, *per* Lord Bridge, and the fact that damage to C's land/property may well sound in private nuisance.

[171] *Goldman v Hargrave* [1967] 1 AC 645. If water normally percolates from D's land to C's land, and D pumps out the water from his land, and by so stopping the subterranean flow causes settlement damage to C's land, C has no remedy because D has no duty to adjoining occupiers in respect of percolating water: *Langbrook Properties Ltd v Surrey County Council* [1969] 3 All ER 1424.

[172] *Bradburn v Lindsay* [1983] 2 All ER 408.

damage resulting from the defective state of repair of premises retained by the landlord, the case law is confused. Take first *Cunard v Antifyre Ltd*.[173]

Some defective roofing and guttering, which formed part of the premises retained by D, a landlord, fell into a part of the premises let by him to C. As a result, C's wife was injured and C's goods were damaged. Damages in negligence were awarded both to C and his wife.

By contrast, in *Cheater v Cater*[174] the Court of Appeal held that a landlord, who had let a field to a tenant at a time when there was a yew tree on the adjoining premises retained by the landlord, was not liable in negligence when the tenant's horse died through eating leaves from the tree which was then in just the same state as at the date of the lease. Then, in *Shirvell v Hackwood Estates Co Ltd*,[175] the court doubted *Cunard v Antifyre Ltd* holding that the workman of a tenant could not recover in negligence from the landlord whose tree on adjoining land fell on him. Finally, came *Taylor v Liverpool Corpn*.[176]

C, the daughter of a tenant of one of D's flats, was injured by the fall of a chimney stack belonging to these flats into the yard adjoining the premises. D had negligently maintained this chimney, which formed part of the building retained by D.

Stable J found for the claimant in negligence, and did so following *Cunard v Antifyre Ltd* while distinguishing *Cheater v Cater* on the ground that the tenant there had impliedly agreed to take the risk in respect of danger existing on the premises at that time. The observations in *Shirvell's* case were treated as *obiter* on the basis that no negligence had in any event occurred. In any case, the principle in *Cunard v Antifyre Ltd* would appear to be preferable to the one which affords landlords blanket immunity in respect of retained premises in a state of disrepair.[177]

The second area of difficulty in delimiting the duty owed by an occupier to those on adjoining premises relates to damage inflicted on those adjoining premises by third parties. No duty will generally be found to lie where damage is inflicted on a neighbour's property by vandals or burglars[178] even though the wrongdoers' conduct may have been facilitated by a state of disrepair or lax security on the defendant occupier's premises.[179] This approach is in line with the general reluctance on the part of the courts to impose liability on a person who has no special relationship with the relevant third party, for the conduct of that third party.

---

[173] [1933] 1 KB 551. The principle on which this case was based was approved, *obiter*, in *Bishop v Consolidated London Properties Ltd* (1933) 102 LJKB 257, at 262, *per* du Parcq J.

[174] [1918] 1 KB 247 (not cited in *Cunard v Antifyre Ltd*).   [175] [1938] 2 KB 577, at 594–5, *per* Green LJ.

[176] [1939] 3 All ER 329.

[177] It is submitted that the Court of Appeal thought wrongly in *Shirvell's* case that the decisions where landlords with no control of defective premises had been held not liable applied in the case before them.

[178] In *P Perl (Exporters) Ltd v Camden London Borough Council* [1984] QB 342 the court did not entirely rule out special circumstances which might give rise to such a duty to adjoining occupiers.

[179] *Smith v Littlewoods Organisation Ltd* [1987] AC 241.

SECTION 2 LIABILITY OF NON-OCCUPIERS

An occupier of premises may have immediate control over the state of those premises and the capacity to repair defects in them, but in a number of instances – particularly in relation to structural defects – nothing he has done will have caused the relevant defect. Cracks in a house resulting from inadequate foundations will often be the result of the negligence of the builder and they may endanger the occupier as much as any visitor to the property. Parliament passed the Defective Premises Act in 1972 to impose on persons providing dwellings some limited responsibility to subsequent purchasers and their families, and to clarify the responsibilities of landlords. As will be seen, the Act is a far from perfect example of legislation.

(A) THE DEFECTIVE PREMISES ACT 1972

One key feature of the decision in *Murphy v Brentwood District Council*[180] is the repeated insistence of their Lordships that the courts should not seek to impose common-law rules of liability where Parliament, via the Defective Premises Act 1972, had already done so. Since *Murphy*, therefore, the primacy of the 1972 Act cannot be doubted, especially since, under section 6(3) of the 1972 Act its provisions are made non-derogable.

Section 1 of the Defective Premises Act 1972 imposes on any 'person taking on work for or in connection with the provision of a dwelling' a strict liability to ensure that the work he takes on is 'done in a workmanlike, or, as the case may be professional manner, with proper materials and so that as regards that work the dwelling will be fit for habitation when completed'.[181] Thus, a builder who, reasonably believing that his materials were suitable, used asbestos in roofing materials at a time before the dangers of asbestos were appreciated, would still be in breach of his duty under section 1. The provision covers all those involved in building new homes: from builders and contractors, to architects and developers.[182] However, while fine in theory, section 1 is in practice more or less a dead letter.[183] First, houses built under the National House

---

[180] [1990] 2 All ER 908. See also *Department of the Environment v Thomas Bates & Son Ltd* [1991] 1 AC 499.

[181] The section applies to omissions as much as to acts: *Andrews v Schooling* [1991] 3 All ER 723; but it is confined to defects rendering the dwelling (but, importantly, not commercial properties) uninhabitable: *Thompson v Clive Alexander and Partners* (1992) 59 BLR 81.

[182] See the Defective Premises Act 1972, s 1(3) (including local authorities). The fact that all such persons may be liable creates the potential for difficulties in establishing causation. The test to be applied is whether D's breach of the section is a 'significant cause' of the unfitness of the dwelling: *Bayoumi v Protim Services Ltd* [1996] EGCS 187.

[183] See Spencer, 'The Defective Premises Act 1972 – Defective Law and Defective Law Reform' [1974] CLJ 307 and [1975] CLJ 48.

Building Council scheme, and covered by a National House Building Registration Council Certificate, are exempted from the strict liability regime created by section 1.[184] Secondly, and much more importantly, the limitation period under the 1972 Act begins to run as soon as the dwelling is completed, which may be a very considerable time prior to a structural defect manifesting itself (defects in foundations, for example, usually taking a long time to appear).[185] By contrast, the limitation period in a negligence action begins to run only when the claimant should reasonably have known of the relevant damage (subject to a long-stop of 15 years after which any action in respect of property damage is barred completely).[186]

Other provisions of the Defective Premises Act – in particular sections 3 and 4 concerning the survival of a duty of care after disposal of the premises, and landlords' duties of care where there is an obligation to repair – are rather more useful, as we shall see below.

(B) BUILDERS AND CONTRACTORS: PHYSICAL DAMAGE

A builder or contractor actually engaged in construction or repair work on land and premises affixed to that land owes a duty of care[187] to the occupier of the premises, his visitors, and, where their presence is foreseeable, probably to trespassers as well.[188] Any universal exemption from a duty of care in respect of real property did not survive the decision in *AC Billings & Sons Ltd v Riden*[189] where building contractors were employed to make an alteration to the front of part of a house. In the course of this work, the contractors failed to take reasonable care to make access to the house safe and Riden, a visitor, was injured when leaving the house in the hours of darkness. The contractors were held liable in negligence.

Subsequent decisions held the original builders of a property liable for personal injury (or physical damage to other property) resulting from the negligent construction or repair of buildings both to subsequent occupiers and to their visitors.[190] Thus, if the defendant contractor negligently erects an unsafe roof which some time later collapses injuring the occupier and her dinner party guests, the victims have a claim against the contractor for those injuries. And if the collapse of the roof also smashes the windows in the adjoining house, the neighbours may also sue the contractor.

The fact that the contractor at the time of the erection of the property was also the landowner no longer affords him immunity from liability in negligence. Most of the

---

[184] Defective Premises Act 1972, s 2. For a time most new houses built were erected within the NHBC scheme, but no longer so: see Wallace, '*Anns* Beyond Repair' (1991) 107 LQR 228.

[185] For an example of the theoretical scope of s 1 made futile by the limitation provisions, see *Rimmer v Liverpool City Council* [1985] QB 1.   [186] Under the Latent Damage Act 1986.

[187] *Miller v South of Scotland Electricity Board* 1958 SC (HL) 20.

[188] The contractor may of course also be the occupier, in which case his liability to trespassers will be governed by the Occupiers' Liability Act 1984. In other circumstances ordinary principles of negligence apply: *Railway Comr v Quinlan* [1964] AC 1054; *Miller v South of Scotland Electricity Board* 1958 SC(HL) 20 (D liable to a child trespasser after carelessly disconnecting electricity in a condemned building so that C suffered a shock from a live cable).   [189] [1958] AC 240.

[190] *Gallagher v N McDowell Ltd* [1961] NI 26; *Sharpe v ET Sweeting & Sons Ltd* [1963] 2 All ER 455.

content of the maxim *caveat emptor* in relation to the sale of land in this context has now been eroded: '[a] landowner who designs or builds a house or flat is no more immune from personal responsibility for faults of construction than a building contractor, or from personal responsibility than an architect, simply because he has disposed of his house or flat by selling or letting'.[191]

But this principle covers only negligence in the original construction of the building, not inadequate repairs or maintenance conducted by the original owner and vendor. However, section 3 of the Defective Premises Act provides that where:

work of construction, repair, maintenance or demolition or any other work is done on or in relation to premises, any duty of care owed because of the doing of the work to persons who might reasonably be expected to be affected by defects in the state of the premises by the doing of the work shall not be abated by the subsequent disposal of the premises by the person who owed the duty.

Thus, a botched job in repairing floorboards will create liability to visitors while the owner remains the occupier; and that liability will survive for the benefit of subsequent occupiers and their visitors when the owner sells or lets the house. But section 3 of the 1972 Act is not comprehensive because it does not cover all possible sources of danger on premises; particularly those caused by omissions. Leaving dangerous refuse on premises and failing to remedy or warn the subsequent occupier about a ruinous defect existing before the vendor came into occupation are probably not covered by the words used in section 3: namely, 'work of construction, repair, maintenance[192] or demolition or any other work'. Thus, the common law principle that there is no duty not to sell or let a ruinous house probably survives albeit in attenuated form. Only the House of Lords can finally take up Lord Denning's invitation in *Dutton v Bognor Regis UDC*[193] to overrule the old cases.[194]

It is suggested that today the crucial point is not whether the defendant contractor is or was the landowner but, rather, what kind of damage resulted from his negligence. If actual physical injury to some person, or separate property, is inflicted as a consequence of his incompetence, that injury is likely to be recoverable just as it would be if the 'guilty' cause of the injury were a negligently manufactured chattel.[195]

(c) BUILDERS AND CONTRACTORS: OTHER LOSS

No duty of care will be imposed on a builder or contractor in respect of economic loss occasioned by negligent work of construction or repair, save where some special relationship is found to exist between him and the claimant. Thus, contractors and development companies owe no duty in tort in respect of financial losses occasioned to

---

[191] *Rimmer v Liverpool City Council* [1984] 1 All ER 930, at 938, *per* Stephenson LJ.
[192] Could omissions to remove or repair pre-existing defects be caught by the word 'maintenance'?
[193] [1972] 1 QB 373, at 394.   [194] Eg, *Otto v Bolton and Norris* [1936] 1 All ER 960.
[195] See *Murphy v Brentwood District Council* [1990] 2 All ER 908, at 917 and 925–6, *per* Lords Keith and Bridge respectively.

subsequent occupiers of property with whom they have no contractual relationship. *D & F Estates Ltd v Church Comrs for England*[196] is illustrative.

D built a block of flats later occupied by C. Crumbling plasterwork caused by D's negligence forced C to expend considerable sums of money on repairs. The House of Lords found that D was not liable for C's loss. By analogy with liability for chattels, D owed a duty to safeguard C against physical damage to person or property caused by negligent construction of the property, but not against loss caused by a defect in the quality of the property itself. Damage to the property itself was a mere defect in quality – the property was simply not value for money.

Recoverable physical damage must be occasioned to separate property.[197] On the other hand, the House of Lords left open the question of 'complex structure' buildings. If a defect in the foundations threatens the structure of a particular flat in a block of flats, or a dwelling house threatens damage to the garden wall, is there damage to separate property?[198]

Some of the questions left open in *D & F Estates* were at least partially answered by the House of Lords in *Murphy v Brentwood District Council*.[199] *Murphy*, strictly speaking, relates to the liability of local authorities, but its applicability to builders and contractors was expressly confirmed in the short judgment in *Department of the Environment v Thomas Bates & Son Ltd*.[200] The facts of *Murphy* were as follows.

C had purchased from a construction company a semi-detached dwelling constructed on a concrete raft foundation over an in-filled site. Eleven years later C noticed cracks in the house which proved to be caused by serious defects in the concrete raft. Repairs which were essential to make the house safe and habitable would have cost £45,000. C could not afford that sum and had to sell the house for £35,000 less than he would have received but for the damage caused by the defective foundations. C sued the local council whom he alleged had negligently approved the plans for the foundations.

The House of Lords rejected his claim, classifying the damage he suffered as irrecoverable economic loss. When the claimant argued that the nature of the damage to his home posed an immediate and imminent danger to his and his family's health, the Law Lords unanimously dismissed that contention as irrelevant since the loss was purely economic.[201] Lord Bridge described the distinction between physical damage and financial loss in this way:[202]

If a builder erects a structure containing a latent defect which renders it dangerous to persons or property, he will be liable in tort for injury to persons or property resulting from that

---

[196] [1989] AC 177.

[197] See *Bellefield Computer Services Ltd v E Turner & Sons Ltd* [2000] BLR 97 (damage caused by a fire spreading across a poorly constructed wall from one part of a dairy to another part of the dairy. This was merely 'damage to the same property') and *Payne v Setchell Ltd* [2002] PNLR 146. Cf *Baxall Securities Ltd v Sheard Walshaw Partnership* [2001] PNLR 257.

[198] See the analysis in *Murphy v Brentwood District Council* [1990] 2 All ER 908, at 1006–7, *per* Lord Bridge.

[199] [1990] 2 All ER 908.   [200] [1990] 2 All ER 908.

[201] In the Commonwealth courts the slavish adherence to the irrecoverability of economic loss caused by defective building work has been, to varying degrees, rejected. In Australia and New Zealand, the negligent builder enjoys no such immunity: *Bryan v Moloney* (1995) 128 ALR 163; *Invercargill City Council v Hamlin* [1994] 3 NZLR 513. In Canada, an intermediate position, depending on a threat to health and safety, has been adopted: *Winnipeg Condominium No 36 v Bird Construction Co* (1995) 121 DLR (4th) 193. See also *Fairgrove Pty Ltd v Todd Group Holding Pty Ltd* [1999] 2 Qd R 236.   [202] [1990] 2 All ER 908, at 926.

dangerous defect. But, if the defect becomes apparent before any injury or damage has been caused, the loss sustained by the building owner is purely economic.

The effect of *Murphy* would seem to be this. Outside a contractual relationship, negligent construction (and presumably also repair and extension) of a building only results in liability if actual physical damage is caused to a person or property that is not part and parcel of the building. Thus, if defective foundations cause cracks in the walls or threaten damage to any fixture in the building installed by the defendant, the cost of remedying the damage is irrecoverable economic loss. By contrast, if A negligently installs a defective central heating boiler in a building erected by B but which is later bought and occupied by C, and then later still that boiler explodes damaging the building, that loss is recoverable by C against A. A's negligence has caused actual damage to property quite separate from the inherently defective component he installed. Lord Bridge, in *Murphy*, also suggested a new exception to the general refusal of recovery for economic loss. He said that where the defect in the building requiring repair threatens damage to adjoining land or the highway:

the building owner ought, in principle, to be entitled to recover in tort from the negligent builder the cost of demolition, so far as that cost is necessarily incurred in order to protect himself from potential liability to third parties.[203]

Consideration of the decision in *Murphy* prompts a number of questions.[204]

(1) Is it just to leave the occupier to bear the loss? Lord Keith maintained that in reality it was not ordinary home-owners who suffered. Disputes such as the one in *Murphy* were essentially quarrels between insurers.[205]

(2) Just how far can Lord Bridge's *caveat* concerning third party liability be stretched? If one may recover that economic loss occasioned by the need to ensure one's crumbling house does not damage a neighbour's house or crash onto a passer-by on the highway, why is one not able to recover the loss occasioned by the need to ensure that one does not incur similar liability to one's visitors?[206]

(3) Finally, is the following the logical result of *Murphy*? Imagine that X discovers that his house has a latent defect which he has no funds to repair. Three months later the ceiling falls in injuring X and his spouse, and it also smashes the grand piano. Does X then recover for that loss and all its consequences or can he be said to be contributorily negligent for not minimising the loss he suffers, or for not rectifying the defect at his own expense?[207]

---

[203] [1990] 2 All ER 908.

[204] See Howarth, 'Negligence after *Murphy* – Time to Re-think' [1991] CLJ 58.

[205] [1990] 2 All ER 908, at 923. No evidence is advanced to support the proposition.

[206] One difference is that I could of course 'obviate' that danger by having no visitors. Another is that I could reasonably warn my visitors; but I could not, for example, practicably warn all passers-by who walk beneath a dangerous overhanging gable.

[207] For a partial answer see *Nitrigin Eireann Teoranta v Inco Alloys Ltd* [1992] 1 All ER 854. See also *Targett v Torfaen Borough Council* [1992] 3 All ER 27: where D lets property, it may in some circumstances be unreasonable to expect a tenant to do repairs that D is obliged to perform.

Leaving aside economic loss, it has also been held, in *Smith v Drumm*,[208] that builders are liable under section 1 of the Defective Premises Act if their work leaves the premises in a state that is not fit for habitation. In this case, the converted flat was left without either electricity or gas, and on that basis deemed to be unfit for habitation. Had the work simply been rectification work (instead of 'construction, conversion or enlargement', as *per* the Act), no duty under section 1 would have been owed.[209]

(D) PROFESSIONAL ADVISERS

The strict liability imposed by section 1 of the Defective Premises Act in respect of the construction of buildings is equally incumbent on architects and other professionals involved in the design of the building. Additionally, those professionals owe a duty of care to any person who may be injured on the site in the course of the building work,[210] and to subsequent occupiers of the premises in respect of both their personal safety and damage to property separate from the original property itself. The reasoning in *Murphy* relating to builders applies equally to architects and engineers. Thus these professionals will not be liable in tort for economic loss arising from the defective nature of the building whether that loss takes the form of the cost of repairs or the diminution in the value of the property.

On subsequent disposal of the premises, surveyors engaged to inspect the property will be liable for any failure to value the property competently or to discover and report on relevant defects in the property. Where the surveyor has been engaged by the building society which is contemplating financing the claimant's house purchase, he will generally be liable, not only to his client (that is, the building society), but also to the purchasers where they have relied on his survey rather than commissioned an independent surveyor.[211] Where, however, a surveyor is expressly commissioned only to value property, he is not under a duty to report on defects generally or to advise on possible difficulties with resale of the property.[212]

---

[208] [1996] EGCS 192.

[209] *Jacobs v Morton & Partners* (1994) 72 BLR 92.

[210] In *Clay v A J Crump & Sons Ltd* [1964] 1 QB 533 (D, an architect, was liable for directing a wall to be left standing during demolition whereupon it collapsed on C who was working on the site. The court rejected the argument that D's only duty was his contractual one to his employer). This decision was followed in *Driver v William Willett (Contractors) Ltd* [1969] 1 All ER 665 (a consulting engineer was liable to a workman for failing to advise a builder about an unsafe hoist which caused C's injuries). See also *Baxall Securities Ltd v Sheard Walshaw Partnership* [2001] PNLR 257 (architect liable for sub-standard roof design causing subsequent water damage). But note, also, that the limited scope of an architect's original instructions will define the extent of his or her liability in tort by confining the extent of the duty of care: *Bellefield Computer Services Ltd v E Turner & Sons Ltd (No 2)* [2002] EWCA Civ 1823.

[211] *Smith v Eric S Bush* [1990] 1 AC 831.   [212] *Sutcliffe v Sayer* [1987] 1 EGLR 155.

(E) LOCAL AUTHORITIES

Local authorities owe duties to tenants and subsequent purchasers of local authority dwellings as builders and contractors. In *Rimmer v Liverpool City Council*[213] the defendants were held liable to a council tenant injuring himself when he fell against a negligently used, thin, glass panel and the glass shattered.

The decision in *Murphy* removes from local authorities the greatest potential area of liability for defective premises since it is local authorities that are entrusted with the function of inspecting and approving all building work. Negligent exercise of these powers may result in local people purchasing and living in defective, even dangerous, property. *Murphy* makes clear, however, that the local authority will not be liable in tort for any economic loss occasioned by the defects in the property. But would the authority be liable if actual injury was caused to a resident or any of his property that was not an integral part of the premises? The House of Lords suggested that the builder would be so liable. But what if the builder has gone into liquidation? That question was left open by their Lordships.[214] In the current climate, where restrictions on the duty of care owed by public authorities are being increasingly relaxed, it is very difficult to say. Nonetheless, while it is true that local authorities are granted inspection powers for the purpose of protecting the health and welfare of local people,[215] it is difficult to characterize this as a duty owed to individuals as opposed to the public more generally (hence an absence of proximity). And why, in any event, should the council be liable for what is, at bottom, the negligence of a third party, the builder?

(F) LANDLORDS

Historically, the liability of landlords for defects arising from disrepair on premises let by them was largely limited to contractual liability. A person other than the tenant had no remedy even if the landlord was in breach of a contractual duty to carry out maintenance and repairs.[216] And like vendors, the landlord owed no duty in respect of defects arising before the tenancy was granted. As we have seen, landlords are now liable to tenants, their families and others injured on the premises just like anyone else in respect of *their* negligent installations or repairs in the premises let by them.[217]

---

[213] [1985] QB 1.

[214] [1990] 2 All ER 908, at 912 and 917, *per* Lords Mackay and Keith respectively.

[215] See the powerful arguments to this effect in the speech of Lord Wilberforce in *Anns v Merton London Borough Council* [1978] AC 728. Note *Anns* was only overruled as far as recovery for economic loss was concerned.

[216] But in some circumstances, the Contracts (Rights of Third Parties) Act 1999 may now apply.

[217] *Rimmer v Liverpool City Council* [1984] 1 All ER 930; *Boldack v East Lindsey District Council* (1998) 31 HLR 41 (where a third party did the defective work, however, the landlord remained immune at common law).

Section 4 of the Defective Premises Act established important duties in respect of landlords under an obligation[218] to carry out repairs or maintenance on the premises, or who are empowered to carry out repairs.[219] A landlord owes to all persons who might reasonably be expected to be affected by defects in the state of the premises a duty to take such care as is reasonable in all the circumstances to see that they are reasonably safe from personal injury or from damage to their property caused by the relevant defects.[220] The landlord is still liable although he did not know of the defect so long as he ought to have known of it.[221] A defect is relevant if it is one in the state of the premises arising from, or continuing because of, an act or omission by the landlord which constitutes or would, if he had had notice of the defect, have constituted a failure by him to carry out his obligation to the tenant for the maintenance or repair of the premises.[222] The duty is wide: it extends to trespassers and those outside the premises. It also applies where the landlord merely has a right to enter to carry out maintenance or repairs.

The liability of non-occupiers for actual physical damage is now fairly extensive, but by no means comprehensive. If an owner knows of a defect in his premises (not created by him) before he sells or lets, but neither repairs it, nor gives warning of the defect, the 1972 Act imposes no liability on him for harm which results after he has disposed of the premises by sale or lease, and there is no liability at common law.[223] A landlord who fails to repair where he has no obligation or power to do so has no liability under either the Act or the common law.

FURTHER READING

Bragg and Brazier, 'Occupiers and Exclusion of Liability' (1986) 130 *Sol Jo* 251 & 274

Buckley, 'The Occupiers' Liability Act 1984 – Has *Herrington* Survived?' (1984) 48 *Conveyancer* 413

Howarth, 'Negligence after *Murphy* – Time to Re-think' [1991] CLJ 58

Jones, 'The Occupiers' Liability Act 1984 – The Wheels of Law Reform Turn Slowly' (1984) 47 MLR 713

Cf the position in Australia in respect of defects caused by another that were capable of reasonable discovery by the landlord: *Northern Sandblasting Pty Ltd v Harris* (1997) 71 ALJR 1428.

[218] This includes statutory obligations.

[219] Defective Premises Act 1972, s 4(4). This extension to the case – where the tenant cannot legally insist on a repair; but where the landlord has a power to repair – is important in view of cases like *Mint v Good* [1951] 1 KB 517, deciding that landlords of small houses let on periodic tenancies, have such a power. For application of this principle resulting in liability under the Act see *McAuley v Bristol City Council* [1992] QB 134; *Sykes v Harry* [2001] 3 WLR 62.

[220] In the case of children who are injured, however, the landlord is entitled to expect that the parents of the child will take proper precautions to ensure the child's safety: see *B (a child) v Camden London Borough Council* [2001] PIQR P143 (landlord not liable to four-year old burnt by hot pipes).

[221] Defective Premises Act 1972, s 4(2).

[222] Defective Premises Act 1972, s 4(3). Failures to remedy such defects are actionable, alternatively, on the basis of common law negligence: see *Targett v Torfaen Borough Council* [1992] 3 All ER 27.

[223] *Cavalier v Pope* [1906] AC 428; *Bromley v Mercer* [1922] 2 KB 126; *Davis v Foots* [1940] 1 KB 116 (although this case would now be decided differently because of housing legislation; the principle is unaffected).

Law Commission Report No 75, *Liability for Damage or Injury to Trespassers and Related Questions of Occupiers' Liability* (Cmnd 6428)

Mesher, 'Occupiers, Trespassers and the Unfair Contract Terms Act 1977' (1979) 43 *Conveyancer* 58

Murphy, 'Public Rights of Way and Private Law Wrongs' (1997) *Conveyancer* 362

Spencer, 'The Defective Premises Act 1972: Defective Law and Defective Law Reform' [1974] CLJ 307 & [1975] CLJ 48

Wallace, '*Anns* Beyond Repair' (1991) 107 LQR 228

PART III

INTENTIONAL INVASIONS OF INTERESTS IN THE PERSON AND PROPERTY

8

TRESPASS TO THE PERSON AND RELATED TORTS

SECTION 1 INTRODUCTION

The torts of battery, assault and false imprisonment are among the most ancient and the law relating to them is fairly well settled which accounts, in part, for the fact that there are relatively few reported cases on these torts in the modern era. But there are other reasons, too, why cases turning on these torts seldom find their way into the law reports these days. These reasons need not be discussed here; it simply suffices to note that it would be a mistake to deduce from the fact that cases involving these torts are seldom reported, that they are nowadays unimportant in practical terms.[1]

Any detailed analysis of the intentional torts to the person (as we might collectively describe the torts considered in this chapter) demonstrates that in protecting bodily integrity and liberty, tort law may be limited in its scope by its historical antecedents. The language associated with these torts is also, on occasion, rather archaic. Yet these torts continue to safeguard the most basic of human rights, and the judges have shown a willingness to innovate in order to ensure that tort law keeps pace with modern society. Even prior to the enactment of the Human Rights Act 1998, the judiciary sought to test how far the conditions of a particular tort matched the relevant provisions of the European Convention on Human Rights.[2] Articles 2 and 3 respectively guarantee the right to life, and freedom from torture or degrading treatment. Article 5 asserts the right to liberty and security of person and seeks to ensure that the state cannot detain persons without substantial grounds justifying that deprivation of liberty.[3] As we shall see in this chapter, the very same fundamental interests are protected by the existing common law, albeit to a slightly lesser degree and without such clarity of articulation as is found in the Convention.

In time, of course, the protection offered by the Convention and the common law will probably converge now that the Human Rights Act is in force. On the one hand, the courts will have to develop the common law in a manner that is compatible with the Convention rights,[4] while, on the other, claims for battery and false imprisonment against public authorities, such as the police, may well be litigated in the alternative under the Act.[5]

---

[1] For a full discussion of the continuing significance of these torts, see the 11th edition of this work pp 27–29 and Trindale, 'Intentional Torts: Some Thoughts on Assault and Battery' (1982) 2 OJLS 211.
[2] See, eg, *Olotu v Home Office* [1997] 1 All ER 385.   [3] See Art 5(2)–(5) and Art 6.
[4] Human Rights Act 1998, s 6.   [5] Human Rights Act 1998, s 7.

SECTION 2 BATTERY

There are several key elements in the tort of battery that are evident from the following working definition of the tort:

Battery is any act of the defendant that directly and intentionally or negligently causes some physical contact with the person of the claimant without the claimant's consent.

(A) DEFENDANT'S STATE OF MIND

Compensation for injuries to the person and to property was first given by the courts from at least the thirteenth century onwards.[6] A suit in trespass could succeed only where the interference was 'direct' and this remains the case today.[7] But if the injury is caused directly, and is attributable to careless conduct on the part of the defendant, must the claimant frame his or her action in negligence, or might battery be an option?

(1) NEGLIGENTLY INFLICTED BATTERY?

Until the middle of the twentieth century and the decision in *Letang v Cooper*,[8] one would have said with confidence that the torts of battery and negligence were both available in cases of direct injuries sustained as a result of careless conduct. This conclusion would have arisen from the fact that, historically, trespass actions would succeed unless the defendant could show inevitable accident.[9] In other words, mere carelessness on the defendant's part would not allow him to escape liability in trespass.

The largely academic confusion that still surrounds the relationship between negligence and trespass began, however, not in *Letang v Cooper*, but some six years earlier in *Fowler v Lanning*.[10] This latter case concerned a technical point of law concerning the burden of proof, but in the course of his judgment Diplock J sought to ensure that the claimant could not gain an unfair advantage by relying on trespass rather than negligence on the basis that, according to the former tort, the burden of proof would lie with the defendant to disprove any *negligence* on his part. In so holding, Diplock J aligned trespass to the person with the hitherto anomalous principle applied only in the context of trespass on the highway: namely, that the burden of proof lay on the claimant to show the defendant's negligence.[11]

---

[6] See Maitland, The Forms of Action at Common Law (1909).
[7] *Sterman v E W & W J Moore Ltd* [1970] 1 QB 596.   [8] [1965] 1 QB 232.
[9] *Weaver v Ward* (1616) Hob 134.   [10] [1959] 1 QB 426.
[11] *Holmes v Mather* (1875) LR 10 Ex 261.

Although *Fowler v Lanning* did not *per se* abolish the principle that trespass to the person can be committed negligently, it did leave the claimant with the burden of proving negligence where his injury was caused by negligent conduct. But then came *Letang v Cooper*, the facts of which were as follows.[12]

D negligently drove his car over C's legs while C was sunbathing on the grass car park of a hotel. More than three years later, C sued D. The rules on limitation of actions provided that actions for 'negligence, nuisance or breach of duty' were barred after three years while other tort actions were barred after six years. C relied on trespass in an effort to prevent her action from being time-barred.

Naturally, the Court of Appeal did not wish to reach the absurd conclusion that an action for negligent trespass would lie while an action for negligence *simpliciter* would not. For their part, Lord Denning MR and Danckwerts LJ insisted that there was no overlap between trespass and negligence. They thought that if an act was intentional it would result in trespass (not negligence) liability, and that if an act was negligent it would lead to negligence (not trespass) liability.[13] By contrast, Diplock LJ thought that trespass could still be committed negligently, but that in such cases the claimant must prove *both* the negligence alleged *and* that there was resulting harm.[14] In other words, the claimant would gain no practical advantage from framing his action in trespass rather than negligence.

In the wake of *Letang v Cooper*, therefore, it would appear that actions for negligent trespass have effectively disappeared: either in juridical terms (for Lord Denning MR and Danckwerts LJ), or in practical terms (for Diplock LJ). But in academic terms we still cannot conclusively assert that trespass has no relevance when negligent conduct is relied on.[15] There may still be particular cases where a claimant perceives there to be an advantage to be gained from framing a claim in trespass rather than in negligence. It is within the divergent principles governing remoteness of damage that this rare advantage may lie. For in negligence law, the defendant is only responsible for injuries or harm of a kind that were reasonably foreseeable,[16] whereas in trespass all the damage actually ensuing from the defendant's unlawful act is generally recoverable.[17]

This minor technical point aside, most modern trespass actions are likely to be based on an intentional act on the part of the defendant. But this merely raises the second, more fundamental question in this context , namely, 'What is meant by an "intentional act" for these purposes?'

---

[12] [1965] 1 QB 232.   [13] [1965] 1 QB 232, at 240.

[14] Compare intentional trespass which is actionable *per se*.

[15] See Trindale, 'Intentional Torts: Some Thoughts on Assault and Battery' (1982) 2 OJLS 211.

[16] *The Wagon Mound* [1961] AC 388.

[17] *Williams v Humphrey* (1975) *Times*, 20 February. C recovered in trespass when he suffered an unforeseeable, serious ankle injury after D pushed him into a swimming pool. See also *Allan v New Mount Sinai Hospital* (1980) 109 DLR (3d) 634.

(2) MEANING OF 'INTENTIONAL ACT'

In determining the meaning of 'intentional act' in this context, there are two broad possibilities.

(1) D intended only to act in the way that he did.

(2) D intended *both* to act in the way that he did *and* he intended the resulting contact with C.

In most cases, the distinction is of little consequence. If A aims a punch at B and succeeds in striking B, there is nothing to separate A's act (the thrown punch) from the outcome of that act (for example, B's broken nose). But in some circumstances, A may do a thing without intending a particular outcome. If D aims his rifle at C, then pulls the trigger, there is no doubt that he intended to shoot C. But if D aims his rifle at a partridge on a hunting trip but accidentally shoots C, it is clear that D intended the act (firing the gun) but not necessarily the outcome (C's injury). In such circumstances it may be stretching the tort too far to hold D liable in battery. But if D aimed his gun at a third party, T, then pulled the trigger missing T and shooting C, standing next to T, we might well wish to hold D liable.

In terms of D's mental state in the first example, there is a genuine accident (possibly even without carelessness on D's part). In the second example, D's act was reckless. This may be the basis upon which the English courts might, like the Americans, borrow the criminal law notion of 'transferred intent' and apply it in tort law.[18] Yet, thus far, there is but limited support for adopting this approach in English law. In addition to a technically non-binding but supportive first instance decision,[19] there is the argument of principle arising from the fact that battery is both a tort and a crime. Thus, as De Grey CJ observed in *Scott v Shepherd*, 'though criminal cases are no rule for civil ones . . . yet in trespass I think there is an analogy'.[20] In that case there was held to be a battery where D threw a lighted squib into a crowded market place that was tossed from one trader to another before it eventually exploded in the face of C. Nonetheless, the case is inconclusive since the main issue there was whether there was sufficient directness to satisfy the requirements of the tort. Further oblique authority can be gleaned from the case of *Haystead v Chief Constable of Derbyshire*.[21] There the defendant punched a woman in the face with the result that she dropped the baby she was holding. He was charged with criminal assault in relation to the baby. Clearly the tortious counterpart of this crime is a battery. The Divisional Court did not even consider the

---

[18] American Restatement, Torts (2d) & 32. See also Prosser, 'Transferred Intent' (1967) 45 *Tex L Rev* 650. In the Northern Ireland case of *Livingstone v Ministry of Defence* [1984] NI 356, it was held that where D fired a baton round injuring C it mattered not whether he fired at C or another person – D was liable in battery unless he could prove lawful justification for his act. But that case is not, technically, an authority for the purposes of the law in England and Wales.

[19] *Bici v Ministry of Defence* [2004] EWHC 786, at 71, *per* Elias J.

[20] (1773) 2 Wm Bl 892, at 899. Cf *Coward v Baddeley* (1859) 4 H & N 478, at 480, *per* Pollock CB.

[21] [2000] 3 All ER 890.

application of the transferred intent doctrine but did say (implying that at a battery action may lie) that:

There is no difference in logic or good sense between the facts of this case and one where the defendant might have used a weapon to fell the child to the floor, save only that this is a case of reckless and not intentional battery.

Here, although the court emphasized the requirement of a sufficiently direct act to ground liability, and although it neglected to address head-on the question of whether the defendant's intention must apply only to his actions, or whether it must also extend to the outcome of those actions, the case does signal a clear unwillingness on the part of the courts to allow defendants in such cases to escape liability.[22] On balance, then, it seems that there is broad, if still not binding, judicial support for the application of the transferred intent principle in English battery cases. On the other hand, there is a plausible counter-argument that can be made. This is that although certain forms of conduct should be branded morally wrong, and thus deserving of criminal punishment, they may not warrant a remedy in tort to which branch of the law both motive and malice are normally irrelevant in determining liability (if not the amount of damages).[23]

In cases where contact with the claimant is unproblematic, it is well established that the defendant need not have intended the claimant any harm. Battery is actionable *per se* – that is, without proof of any injury or damage to the claimant. He must merely have understood that his conduct was beyond the bounds of physical contact 'generally acceptable in the ordinary conduct of everyday life'.[24] The Court of Appeal said in *Wilson v Pringle*[25] that the claimant must show that the defendant's touching of the claimant was a 'hostile' touching. Yet the term 'hostility' is not to be equated with ill-will or malevolence. It means merely that the defendant is doing something to which the claimant may object, something that the claimant may regard as an unlawful intrusion on his rights to physical integrity. Thus, the bare allegation that one 13-year-old boy jumped on another in the course of horseplay was insufficient of itself to establish a battery in that case. Further evidence of intent to injure or distress the claimant had to be shown if liability for battery was to be imposed, yet no such evidence was presented (another hearing would be required to establish that). Had a grown man engaged in similar conduct, the result would almost certainly have been different. Away from the rugby field, mature adults do not generally regard it as acceptable conduct for their colleagues to leap on them or wrestle them to the ground.

In *F v West Berkshire Health Authority*[26] Lord Goff doubted that the use of the word 'hostile', however defined, was appropriate to describe the necessary state of mind in battery. A surgeon operating on a patient to preserve her life and health may be motivated by his judgment as to her best interests, not hostility towards her. Yet if she is

---

[22] In similar vein see *Livingstone v Ministry of Defence* [1984] NI 356.

[23] NB *Haystead* was a criminal (not tort) law case!   [24] *Collins v Wilcock* [1984] 3 All ER 374, at 378.

[25] [1987] QB 237. Cf *Williams v Humphrey* (1975) *Times*, 20 February (15-year-old schoolboy liable for the prank of pushing another boy into a swimming pool).   [26] [1989] 2 All ER 545, at 564.

competent to do so, and has refused to consent to a particular course of treatment, the surgeon commits a battery. Lord Goff preferred the following approach. Any deliberate touching of another's body, beyond the bounds of acceptable everyday conduct, is, in the absence of lawful excuse, capable of constituting a battery. Where a person by reason of some permanent or temporary mental incapacity cannot himself consent to medical or other necessary procedures,[27] the requisite lawful excuse may have to be found in the principle of necessity.

(B) NO CONSENT BY THE CLAIMANT

The absence of consent is so inherent in the notion of a tortious invasion of interests in the person that the absence of consent must be established by the claimant. This might at first sight seem rather odd, but any lingering doubt that the onus of proving absence of consent lies on the claimant was laid to rest in *Freeman v Home Office (No 2)*.[28] There, a prisoner alleged that he had been injected with powerful mood-changing drugs against his will. The judge held that since the essence of battery is a specific and unpermitted intrusion on the claimant's body, it was for the claimant to establish that the intrusion was unpermitted. This he failed to do.

Part of the rationale for this approach is that a contrary result would potentially have posed severe problems for all doctors, not just prison medical officers. Any contact with a patient – for example, vaccinations or even examining sore throats with a spatula – would *prima facie* constitute battery. To escape liability, the doctor would have to prove consent which would be extremely difficult in cases involving minor procedures where no written consent had been obtained, or if records had been lost, or if the doctor had died.[29]

On the other hand, in the context of actions by suspects against the police, or prisoners against prison authorities, casting the burden of proof on the claimant might vitiate the effectiveness of a battery action as a mechanism for vindicating their civil liberties.[30] In such circumstances, cases would turn on the contest between the word of the prisoner and the word of 'respectable' members of society in a position of responsibility.

That which constitutes a valid consent is often a fundamental issue, especially in cases of trespass in the medical context. There may be a question of exactly what the patient consented to, or indeed whether he was competent to give consent in the first place.[31] Logically, as it is for the claimant to prove absence of consent, it might be

[27] There is a statutory definition of incapacity in the Mental Capacity Act 2005, ss 2 and 3. The gist of this definition is that the defendant was unable to make a decision for himself because of impaired brain function, where the inability to make a decision is to be understood in terms of an inability to understand, retain or evaluate the information.   [28] [1983] 3 All ER 589, at 594–5, *per* McCowan J; affd [1984] QB 524.

[29] As had the prison doctor in *Freeman v Home Office (No 2)* [1984] QB 524.

[30] But see *R (on the application of Wilkinson) v Broadmoor Hospital* [2002] 1 WLR 419.

[31] Where medical treatment is administered to a mental patient without his consent, that treatment may nonetheless be justified so long as it does not amount to inhuman or degrading treatment contrary to Art 3 of

expected that we should deal with consent here. But in practice, once the claimant has raised sufficient evidence to cast doubt on the reality of a purported consent, consent is still treated as a defence.[32]

(c) THE CHARACTER OF THE DEFENDANT'S ACT

There can be no battery unless there is an act by the defendant. Merely to obstruct the entrance to a room by standing in someone's way is not of itself enough[33] (although there may be an assault if it is clear that if A tries to pass B, B will forcibly attempt to prevent that happening[34]). Also, no battery is committed if an incident involving contact over which the defendant has no control occurs.[35]

Equally, there can be no battery unless there is contact with the claimant. But is any contact, however slight, enough? Lord Goff has suggested that battery protects a person 'not only against physical injury but against any form of physical molestation'.[36] And this formulation explains why spitting in someone's face is battery while touching another accidentally in a crowd is not. It also explains the view of Holt CJ, 'that the least touching of another in anger is battery' but that 'if two or more meet in a narrow passage, and without any violence or design of harm, the one touches the other gently, it is no battery'.[37] The courts cannot, and should not be expected to, give protection against these unavoidable contacts in everyday life, and thus the second statement just quoted can be classed as an example of a permitted contact.[38] Battery, then, protects a person against all unpermitted contacts, irrespective of whether there is any physical harm. So, taking fingerprints,[39] spitting in another's face (as we have already noted[40]), cutting another's hair against his or her will[41] are all batteries.

As with all trespasses to the person, the requirement of directness applies in battery. It is not enough that the act 'causes' the contact. Contact must follow immediately from

the European Convention on Human Rights: *R (on the application of Wilkinson) v Broadmoor Hospital* [2002] 1 WLR 419.

[32] The ingredients of a genuine consent are discussed in ch 11.

[33] *Innes v Wylie* (1844) 1 Car & Kir 257, at 263, *per* Lord Denman CJ. A motorist who accidentally drives his car onto a police constable's foot while he is parking commits no battery, but does commit a battery if he then ignores the constable's plea to 'Get off my foot'. See the criminal law case of *Fagan v Metropolitan Police Commissioner* [1969] 1 QB 439 (D convicted).

[34] *Hepburn v Chief Constable of Thames Valley Police* [2002] EWCA Civ 1841.

[35] D was not liable when a frightened horse ran away with him and collided with C: see *Gibbons v Pepper* (1695) 2 Salk 637. See also *Holmes v Mather* (1875) LR 10 Exch 261.

[36] See *F v West Berkshire Health Authority* [1989] 2 All ER 545, at 563.

[37] *Cole v Turner* (1704) 6 Mod Rep 149.

[38] This explains, too, the *dictum* in *Tuberville v Savage* (1669) 1 Mod Rep 3 to the effect that striking another on the breast in discourse is not actionable. But what if a police constable who knows that a passing pedestrian does not wish to answer his questions continues to tap him on the shoulder so that he will stop to be interrogated? See *Donnelly v Jackman* [1970] 1 All ER 987.

[39] *Dumbell v Roberts* [1944] 1 All ER 326, at 330, *per* Scott LJ; *Callis v Gunn* [1964] 1 QB 495.

[40] *R v Cotesworth* (1704) 6 Mod Rep 172.

[41] *Forde v Skinner* (1830) 4 C & P 239. Cf *Nash v Sheen* (1953) *Times*, 13 March (actionable to apply to C's hair a 'tone-rinse' which caused a rash).

the act of the defendant;[42] or at least be a continuation of his act.[43] Thus, for a ship to ram another may be a trespass despite the effect of the current.[44] Similarly, it is battery where A strikes B's horse so that the horse bolts throwing B to the ground,[45] or where D punches a third party so that injury results to C.[46] It is also a trespass to the person to overturn a carriage or chair in which the claimant is sitting.[47]

If battery protected against insult generally, and not merely against bodily harm, then any intentional contact with anything closely attached to, or associated with, the person of the claimant could conceivably be treated as battery. This very matter was investigated in *Pursell v Horn*[48] where it was decided that throwing water onto the clothes being worn by the claimant was not necessarily battery. This case suggests that contact with things attached to the claimant can only constitute battery if there is also a transmission of force to the body of the claimant.[49] The protection from insult or indignity afforded by the tort of battery is limited to insult or indignity arising from the touching, however trivial that touching may be.[50]

(D) DAMAGES

As we have already noted, battery, like all suits in trespass, is actionable *per se*. As such, damages can be awarded even if the claimant suffers no tangible harm. Furthermore, it seems also that, once the tort is proved, consequential loss in respect of goods, as well as the personal damage sustained, can be recovered.[51] And the courts can also award additional damages on account of insult or injury to feelings in respect of a battery that has caused harm.[52]

SECTION 3 ASSAULT

Though the commission of an assault will often occur just before the commission of a battery, it makes sense to deal with assault second because the tort's definition refers to battery.

---

[42] *Leame v Bray* (1803) 3 East 593, at 603, *per* Le Blanc J.

[43] *Scott v Shepherd* (1773) 2 Wm Bl 892, at 899, *per* De Grey CJ.   [44] *Covell v Laming* (1808) 1 Camp 497.

[45] *Dodwell v Burford* (1669) 1 Mod Rep 24.

[46] *Haystead v Chief Constable of Derbyshire* [2000] 3 All ER 890 (*obiter*): D punched a woman causing her to drop a child she was holding.   [47] *Hopper v Reeve* (1817) 7 Taunt 698.

[48] (1838) 8 Ad & El 602.

[49] 'It must imply personal violence' (1838) 8 Ad & El 602, at 604, *per* Lord Denman CJ. In *R v Day* (1845) 1 Cox 207 Parke B held that it was the crime of battery to slit with a knife a victim's clothes, and although the victim was cut, this did not seem material.   [50] Thus, an unwanted kiss is actionable.

[51] *Glover v London and South Western Rly Co* (1867) LR 3 QB 25 (C may have been able to claim for the loss of his race glasses had he not carelessly left them behind when he was wrongfully removed from a railway carriage).

[52] *Loudon v Ryder* [1953] 2 QB 202. There is doubt as to whether such damages are available in cases where the battery does not occasion any physical harm.

An assault is any act of the defendant that directly and intentionally or negligently[53] causes the claimant reasonably to apprehend the imminent infliction of a battery.

The law of assault is substantially similar to the law of battery except that, in assault, an apprehension of contact (rather than contact itself) must be established. Usually when there is a battery, there will also be an assault, but not, for instance, when a person is hit from behind. To point a loaded gun at the claimant, to shake a fist under his nose, to curse him in a threatening manner, to aim a blow at him which is intercepted, or to surround him with a display of force,[54] is to assault him. Clearly, if the defendant by his act intends to commit a battery and the claimant apprehends it, it is an assault. Within the tort of assault[55] what must be apprehended, however, is actual physical contact. Photographing a person against his will is not an actionable assault.[56]

The effect of the origins of this tort on the present law is seen when one asks whether to brandish an unloaded pistol is an assault. In 1840 it was still being said that this was not assault because the defendant could not have intended a battery.[57] Tindal CJ had said 10 years previously that 'it is not every threat, when there is no actual physical violence, that constitutes an assault, there must, in all cases, be the means of carrying the threat into effect'.[58] These cases have not been overruled, but in criminal law it is firmly established that pointing an unloaded gun at someone is an assault.[59] Reasoning by analogy, it is submitted that a modern-day court would reach the equivalent conclusion in tort. The gist of the tort of assault is an act which would cause a reasonable person to apprehend an imminent battery.[60] The test for what constitutes reasonable apprehension of an imminent battery is objective not subjective, and a reasonable person could not be expected to know that the gun was not loaded. Conversely, if the claimant is paranoid and perceives the defendant's innocuous waving of his hand in the air during conversation as a threat, there is no assault.

Where interventions of the police, or other protective intrusions, ensure that defendants cannot carry out threats of violence and abuse, there is no assault committed. Thus, where working miners were driven on buses into their collieries with

---

[53] By analogy with battery, it would seem to be in accordance with principle to include foreseeable though unintended harm (although actual decisions are lacking). Thus, if D unintentionally brandishes a stick close to a woman, but without intending to hit or alarm her, it is submitted that D's conduct ought to be regarded as a tortious assault if D could reasonably foresee that his act would have the requisite effect.

[54] *Read v Coker* (1853) 13 CB 850.

[55] In criminal law it has been held that threatening telephone calls amount to a criminal assault: *R v Ireland* [1998] AC 147.

[56] *Murray v Minister of Defence* [1985] 12 NIJB 12. On the other hand, publishing such photographs might give rise to an action based on the misuse of private personal information. See *Campbell v MGN* [2004] 2 AC 457 and ch 15.   [57] *Blake v Barnard* (1840) 9 C & P 626.

[58] *Stephens v Myers* (1830) 4 C & P 349, at 349–50. In *Osborn v Veitch* (1858) 1 F & F 317 it was held that to point a loaded gun at half-cock at C was an assault but this was because there was 'a present ability of doing the act threatened', the cocking of the gun taking just a split second.   [59] *R v St George* (1840) 9 C & P 483.

[60] *Mbasogo v Logo Ltd (No 1)* [2005] EWHC 2034 (a threatened *coup d'état* was not a sufficiently imminent threat to the President of Equitorial Guinea).

police guards, the threats yelled at them by striking miners were not assaults.[61] The claimants could not reasonably have apprehended that those threats would be carried out there and then and thus fell outside the scope of this tort. It is therefore clear that the tort of assault provides only limited protection from the infliction of mental anxiety.

At one time it was thought that mere words could not constitute an assault.[62] But the House of Lords in *R v Ireland*[63] quashed that fallacy in criminal law. By analogy, words that instil a reasonable fear of an imminent battery should equally amount to a tortious assault for '[the] means by which persons of evil disposition may intentionally or carelessly cause another to fear immediate and unlawful violence vary according to circumstances'.[64] On the other hand, words accompanying an act may explain away what might otherwise be an assault. Thus, there was no assault in one ancient case where the defendant with his hand on his sword said: '[i]f it were not assize-time, I would not take such language from you'.[65]

SECTION 4 'INTENTIONAL' PHYSICAL HARM OTHER THAN TRESPASS TO THE PERSON?

This somewhat uncertain tort arose from the case of *Wilkinson v Downton*.[66]

C was told by D, who knew it to be untrue, that her husband had been seriously injured in an accident. Believing this, she suffered nervous shock resulting in serious physical illness, and was held to have a cause of action.

In the case itself, Wright J held the practical joker in the case itself liable on the basis that he had 'wilfully done an act calculated to cause physical harm to the plaintiff . . . which in fact caused physical harm to her'.[67] But, it was by no means clear that the joker had actually intended the harm caused. For this reason, Wright J explained a little later in his judgment that this intention may sometimes need to be imputed, and duly went on to impute such intention to the defendant. But this seems a rash step given that the defendant intended only a joke. The defendant's act is rather more redolent of

---

[61] *Thomas v NUM* [1985] 2 All ER 1, at 24, *per* Scott J.

[62] The case usually relied on is *R v Meade and Belt* (1823) 1 Lew CC 184, where it was said *obiter* (at 185, *per* Holroyd J), that 'no words or singing are equivalent to an assault'.   [63] [1998] AC 147.

[64] [1997] 3 WLR 534, at 550, *per* Lord Hoffmann. *R v Ireland* centred on a telephone call, but unless the call is made from a mobile phone just outside C's house, it seems contrary to principle to embrace such a case within the tort of assault for want of the prospect of an imminent battery.

[65] *Tuberville v Savage* (1669) 1 Mod Rep 3.

[66] [1897] 2 QB 57, 66 LJQB 493 (the fuller report). The Court of Appeal later upheld and applied the decision in this case in *Janvier v Sweeney* [1919] 2 KB 316.   [67] [1897] 2 QB 57, at 58.

negligence even though the joke was intentionally played. And as McPherson J observed in the Australian case of *Carrier v Bonham*.[68]

Most everyday acts of what we call actionable negligence are in fact wholly or partly a product of intentional conduct. Driving a motor vehicle at high speed through a residential area is an intentional act even if injuring people or property on the way is not a result actually intended. *Wilkinson v Downton* is an example of that kind.[69]

He then went on to note that 'the expression calculated . . . is one of those weasel words that is capable of meaning either *subjectively contemplated and intended* or, *objectively likely to happen*', before concluding that in *Wilkinson v Downton* those words were 'being used in the latter, not the former sense'.[70] In short, he effectively recast the decision in *Wilkinson v Downton* as a negligence case. And this, it is submitted, is the better way in which *that case* should nowadays be understood given that it was highly improbable that the practical joker had *subjectively intended* anything more than fleeting or, at most, short term, distress. What was crucial to Wright J's *particular decision* was the likelihood of harm occurring from the joke (which should be instantly recognised a central question posed in negligence cases[71]).

There is an historical explanation as to why *Wilkinson v Downton* has traditionally been presented as a kind of intentional tort *sui generis*. The fleeting and insubstantial nature of the 'harm' that was actually intended by the defendant (as opposed that which actually occurred) would not, at the time, have sufficed to found an action on the case. The Privy Council decision in *Victorian Railways Commissioners v Coultas*[72] prohibited recovery – at least at that point in history – for nervous shock induced by negligence. It is thus probably partly for this reason that Wright J preferred to impute to the defendant an intention to 'produce some effect *of the kind* that was [actually] produced',[73] even though *that kind of harm* was almost certainly never in the defendant's mind. In the light of the more generous, modern approach to cases of psychiatric harm,[74] it seems high time that we abandoned Wright J's historically rooted legal fiction, and reclassified *Wilkinson v Downton* as a negligence case in which the defendant failed to take appropriate care to avoid causing psychiatric harm to the claimant. Strong support for this reclassification of *the actual decision* in *Wilkinson v Downton* can be gleaned from the recent decision of the House of Lords in *Wainwright v Home Office*.[75]

A mother and her son with learning difficulties were subjected to a strip search before they could enter a prison to visit a second son who was imprisoned there. Although no physical contact was made with the mother, she nonetheless complained of the humiliating and procedurally improper way in which the search was conducted. Her complaint was that the prison staff, in forcing her to undergo the search, had wilfully caused her to do something that infringed her legal right to privacy and exacerbated her existing depression.

---

[68] [2001] QCA 234.   [69] [2001] QCA 234, at [27].   [70] [2001] QCA 234, at [25].

[71] See, eg, *Bolton v Stone* [1951] AC 850.   [72] (1888) 13 App Cas 222.   [73] [1897] 2 QB 57, at 59.

[74] See, eg, *Alcock v Chief Constable of South Yorkshire* [1992] 1 A.C. 310.   [75] [2004] 2 AC 406.

In relation to whether liability could be imposed on the basis of the rule in *Wilkinson v Downton*, Lord Hoffmann (with whom the other Law Lords agreed) said:

[t]he claimants can build nothing on *Wilkinson v Downton*. It does not provide a remedy for distress which does not amount to recognised psychiatric injury and so far as there may be a tort of intention under which such damage is recoverable, the necessary intention was not established. I am also in complete agreement with Buxton LJ [in the Court of Appeal in this case] that *Wilkinson v Downton* has nothing to do with trespass to the person.[76]

Notwithstanding these comments, however, it would be a mistake to discard *Wilkinson v Downton* wholesale.[77] This is because the rule in that case was promulgated in terms wide enough to range well beyond distress falling short of recognized psychiatric harm. There are, quite simply, many intentional (or reckless) acts besides the spoken word that can *indirectly* cause harm and thus defy classification as forms of trespass. And without the rule in *Wilkinson v Downton*, it is debatable whether there would be a cause of action available in such cases.[78] Thus, putting poison in another's tea or digging a pit into which it is intended that another shall fall are not trespasses, but might comfortably be brought within the *stated* rule in *Wilkinson v Downton*. Furthermore, there are some rather ancient cases declaring that it is a tortious act deliberately to set spring guns or other mechanical devices with the intention of injuring trespassers which might still be explained according to Wright J's principle.[79] The only other way of dealing with such cases would be to allow negligence suits based on intentional and reckless conduct. And while this is not *per se* objectionable,[80] it does run up against the objection that, in *Letang v Cooper*,[81] Lord Denning MR and Danckwerts LJ made a strenuous effort to keep apart negligence and the intentional torts against the person. At the very least, it is to be noted that there has been a marked reluctance to abandon the rule in *Wilkinson v Downton* in the inferior courts.[82]

Even if, notwithstanding what was said in *Wainwright*, we are able to salvage the rule in *Wilkinson v Downton*, it is nonetheless true that it has been a little used tort. For a time, during the mid-1990s, it looked as though the principle would be extended beyond the protection of physical and mental health, to the protection from harassment.[83] Yet *dicta* in the Court of Appeal decision in *Wong v Parkside Health NHS*

---

[76] [2004] 2 AC 406, at [47].   [77] Cf McBride and Bagsahw, *Tort Law* (2005) pp 68–69.

[78] Another point is that actions that might fail in negligence because the loss is regarded as too remote, yet may nonetheless succeed on the basis of the rule in *Wilkinson v Downton* (assuming that the trespass rules on remoteness of damage apply to that tort).

[79] *Deane v Clayton* (1817) 7 Taunt 489 (court equally divided whether it was actionable on the case to set iron spikes for dogs); *Bird v Holbrook* (1828) 4 Bing 628 (setter of spring gun liable in case to pursuer of stray fowl). Cf *Townsend v Wathen* (1808) 9 East 277.

[80] For the suggestion that the tort of negligence logically embraces *intentional* wrongs, see Murphy, 'Rethinking Injunctions in Tort Law' (forthcoming).

[81] [1965] 1 QB 232.

[82] See, eg, *C v D* [2006] EWHC 166 and *Bici v Ministry of Defence* [2004] EWHC 786. See also the view in the Hong Kong decision in *Wong Kai Wai v Hong Kong Special Administrative Region* (2005) CACV 19/2003 where the Hong Kong Court of Appeal expressly declined to abandon the rule in *Wilkinson v Downton*.

[83] The decision in *Khorasandjian v Bush* [1993] QB 727 looked for a time as though it might be taking the rule in *Wilkinson v Downton* into new territory: the protection of privacy with no requirement of mental or physical harm. See also *Burris v Azadani* [1995] 1 WLR 1372 (some recognition of protection from mere harassment on the part of the then Master of the Rolls).

Trust[84] halted this expansion of the tort in its tracks. In cases of distress falling short of negligently inflicted psychiatric harm or assault, the preferred route to redress will now ordinarily be the Protection from Harassment Act 1997.[85]

SECTION 5 PROTECTION FROM HARASSMENT ACT 1997

This Act creates two criminal offences. The first, created by Section 1(1) of this Act, is the general offence of harassing *one* other person. Under this subsection, conduct amounting to harassment of another person[86] is a criminal offence unless justifiable for the purpose of detecting or preventing crime,[87] or authorized by law, or, in the particular circumstances, the conduct was reasonable.[88] The victim of such harassment, be it actual or apprehended, is granted a right to sue in tort – either for damages or for an injunction[89] – by virtue of section 2 of the Act. But, simple as this sounds, the subsection is not entirely straightforward. For a start, although the Act provides no concrete definition of harassment, it is at least clear that the defendant's conduct can only constitute harassment if he knows or ought to know that his acts amount to harassment.[90] Equally, the precise degree of distress or harm required to

---

[84] [2001] EWCA Civ 1721.

[85] There are three factors which may serve to make the remnants of the rule in *Wilkinson v Downton* preferable to an action under the 1997 Act. First, where C's complaint turns on a one-off incident rather than a 'course of conduct', as is required by the Act (see below), C may need to invoke the rule. Secondly, although there is no specific time-frame under the Act within which the relevant 'course of conduct' must take place, 'the fewer the occasions and the wider they are spread, the less likely it would be that a finding of harassment can reasonably be made [under the Act]': *Lau v DPP* [2000] 1 FLR 799, at [15] *per* Schiemann J (cited with approval in the Court of Appeal in *Pratt v DPP* [2001] EWHC Admin 483, at [9]–[10] *per* Latham LJ; but cf *Jones v Hipgrave* [2005] 2 FLR 174). Thirdly, in cases involving persons who formerly shared an affectionate bond, it seems that pestering conduct that falls short of stalking may prove inadequate for the purposes of invoking the Act: see *R v Hills* [2001] 1 FCR 569, at [31], *per* Otton LJ.

[86] A corporate entity cannot claim under the Act (although individual employees targetted by the harassment will be able to do so): *Daiichi Pharmaceuticals UK Ltd v Stop Huntingdon Animal Cruelty* [2004] 1 WLR 1503.

[87] The test for what is necessary in the prevention of crime is to be interpreted objectively and, so far as investigations involve the repeated questioning of certain people, any resulting invasion of their Art 8 right to respect for privacy must satisfy the twin tests of necessity and proportionality: *KD v Chief Constable of Hampshire* [2005] EWHC 2550.

[88] In one case, Lord Phillips MR stated, less than transparently, that a newspaper running a campaign against a specific individual would only be acting unreasonably for these purposes if the campaign was 'an abuse of the freedom of press which the pressing social needs of a democratic society require should be curbed': *Thomas v News Group Newspapers Ltd* [2002] EMLR 78, at [50]. No doubt, his Lordship was mindful of the right to freedom of expression afforded to the press under Art 10 of the European Convention on Human Rights.

[89] Protection from Harassment Act 1997, s 3(1). Where an injunction is sought, the civil standard of proof applies: *Jones v Hipgrave* [2005] 2 FLR 174.

[90] For these purposes D ought to know that which a reasonable person in possession of the same information would know: Protection from Harassment Act 1997, s 1(2). The test is a purely objective one: *Banks v Ablex Ltd* [2005] ICR 819, at [20] *per* Kennedy LJ. As such, no account is to be taken of any mental deficiency on D's part.

invoke the Act remains to be determined. And the courts may choose to be lenient in this respect preferring not to characterise many forms of undesirable conduct as criminal harassment. Certainly, it has been said that it will be more difficult to rely on pestering that occurs following a relationship breakdown than stalking.[91] In any event, because the 1997 Act offence requires there to have been a course of conduct – that is, conduct on at least two occasions[92] – it is clear that one-off incidents of harassing conduct do not fall within the statute.

The second offence contained in the Act was created by an amendment wrought by section 125 of the Organised Crime and Police Act 2005. According to this amendment, there is now also an offence, under section 1(1A), where the defendant pursues a course of conduct that involves harassment of two or more persons, and this harassment is intended to persuade any person *either* not to do something he or she is entitled or obliged to do, *or* to do something that he or she is not obliged to do. In respect of this offence, there is no right to sue for damages, but an injunction may be sought.[93] The test of what the defendant knows or ought to know will be the effect of his conduct applies equally to this offence.[94]

SECTION 6 FALSE IMPRISONMENT

This somewhat inadequately named tort[95] may be defined in the following terms.

An act of the defendant which directly and intentionally (or possibly negligently) causes the confinement of the claimant within an area delimited by the defendant.

Usually when there is a false imprisonment there will also be an assault or battery, but not, for example, where A voluntarily enters a room and B then locks the door trapping A inside. The tort protects the interest in freedom from confinement and against the loss of liberty more generally.

(A) DEFENDANT'S STATE OF MIND

Normally this tort must be intentional in the sense that the defendant must intend to do an act which is at least substantially certain to effect the confinement. There is no need

---

Thus, a schizophrenic who sends threatening letters to a local MP is not exempt: *R v Colohan* [2001] 2 FLR 757, at [21], *per* Hughes J.

[91]   *R v Hills* [2001] 1 FCR 569, at [31] *per* Otton LJ.

[92]   Protection from Harassment Act 1997, s 7(3). Interestingly, this may include a series of newspaper articles, or a series of threatening letters from someone unknown to C, or a series of threatening emails: see, respectively, *Thomas v News Group Newspapers* [2002] EMLR 78, *R v Colohan* [2001] 2 FLR 757 and *Potter v Price* [2004] EWHC 781.   [93]   Protection from Harassment Act 1997, s 3A.

[94]   Protection from Harassment Act 1997, s 1(1A).

[95]   The term 'false' conveys little to nothing of what this tort concerns.

to show malice. Indeed, even where there is good faith on the part of the defendant, he may still be liable for his intentional confinement of the claimant. Thus, in *R v Governor of Brockhill Prison, ex p Evans (No 2)*[96] a prison governor who calculated the claimant's day of release in accordance with the law as understood at the time of her conviction was held liable when a subsequent change in the law meant that the prisoner should have been released 59 days earlier. On the other hand, since the governor was actually *obliged* to detain the claimant until the law applicable to the calculation of the prisoner's release date was changed – on which date she was duly released – it is difficult to see why the governor could not rely on the defence of necessity, it being required of him that he should detain her until that change in the law occurred.[97] If the law were to have changed before the actual date of release, it would be quite proper that the detainee should be able to sue. This is because an honest mistake – whether negligently made or not – as to the right to continue detention 'does not excuse a trespass to the person':[98] the requisite intention to detain will be present; and that is all that counts in the absence of a recognised justification (such as necessity). But why she could sue on the actual facts of the case is something of a mystery.

Happily, *R v Governor of Brockhill Prison, ex p Evans (No 2)* has at least been confined to errors on the part of the prison governor by the Court of Appeal's decision in *Quinland v Governor of Swalesdale Prison*.[99] In this case, it was judicial error in stating the sentence to be three months longer than it ought to have been that caused the claimant to be detained longer than should have been the case. The Court of Appeal stated that since the prisoner was unduly detained by virtue of a court order, there would be no remedy apart from the correction of the arithmetical error that had occurred in adding together the various periods of confinement attributable to the various offences of which the claimant had been convicted.

On principle, negligence ought to be enough to engage liability for false imprisonment. Accordingly, if a person locks a door, being negligently unaware of the presence of somebody in the room, this should suffice. On the other hand, a remedy was made available in one case under the auspices of the tort of negligence, but not false imprisonment, when a prisoner was negligently detained for a period that exceeded that authorized by the court.[100] This suggests that the courts might take a dim view of any claim based on 'negligent false imprisonment'.

---

[96] [2001] 2 AC 19. Cf *Olotu v Home Office* [1997] 1 WLR 328 (prisoner held beyond proper term of confinement but no liability for false imprisonment because the prisoner could not lawfully be released in the absence of court order authorizing such release).

[97] Their Lordships noted that this involved a hardship to the governor, but felt that it was outweighed by the hardship that would otherwise be done to C were she unable to sue. What perhaps ought to happen, then, is to extend the legislation that currently allows compensation for miscarriages of justice – namely, the Criminal Justice Act 1988, s 133 – to cases like Evans' case (for it currently only applies to cases where an innocent prisoner was wrongly convicted). At any rate, the decision in *Evans* now casts doubt on the decision in *Percy v Hall* [1997] QB 924 where C was held to be unable to sue in respect of arrests made under byelaws that were later declared void for uncertainty.

[98] *Hepburn v Chief Constable of Thames Valley Police* [2002] EWCA Civ 1841.   [99] [2003] QB 306.

[100] *Clarke v Crew* [1999] NLJR 899.

(B) CHARACTER OF THE DEFENDANT'S ACT

Like other forms of trespass to the person, this tort is actionable *per se*. However, the courts do insist upon total (as opposed to partial) restraint of the person.[101] Thus, to prevent a man from crossing a bridge except by making a detour around part of the area of the bridge which has been closed off is not false imprisonment. Nor is it false imprisonment if A is able to escape from his confinement by a nominal trespass on the land of a third party.[102] However, there is a breach of Art 5(1) of the Human Rights Convention (the right to liberty) if a mental patient is 'technically' free to leave a mental hospital, but in reality is constantly monitored and subject to immediate compulsory detention should he try to leave.[103]

It is well established that although confinement must be total, it need not be in a prison as the name of the tort perhaps suggests. One may be confined in a house,[104] in a prison,[105] in a mine,[106] or even in a vehicle.[107] How large the area of confinement can be obviously depends on the circumstances of each particular case. It could be tortious to restrict a man to a large country estate, or perhaps even to restrain him from leaving, say, the Isle of Man. Yet if A prevented B from landing in England from mainland Europe, that act could not be a false imprisonment.[108] The important point is that the boundaries of the area of confinement must be fixed by the defendant. As Coleridge J said in *Bird v Jones*:[109]

Some confusion seems . . . to arise from confounding imprisonment of the body with mere loss of freedom . . . Imprisonment . . . includes the notion of restraint within some limits defined by a will or power exterior to our own.

Lord Denman, in his dissenting judgment in the same case, said:[110]

As long as I am prevented from doing what I have a right to do, of what importance is it that I am permitted to do something else? . . . If I am locked in a room, am I not imprisoned because I might effect my escape through a window, or because I might find an exit dangerous or inconvenient to myself, as by wading through water . . . ?

Although this contention was rejected so far as the adequacy of a partial restraint is concerned, it is suggested that, if someone can only escape at the risk of personal injury,

---

[101] Partial restraint was the subject of an action on the case, on proof of damage: *Wright v Wilson* (1699) 1 Ld Raym 739; *Bird v Jones* (1845) 7 QB 742, at 752, *per* Patterson J.

[102] *Wright v Wilson* (1699) 1 Ld Raym 739; the court thought that a special action on the case would lie.

[103] *HL v United Kingdom* (2005) EHRR 32, at para 91.   [104] *Warner v Riddiford* (1858) 4 CBNS 180.

[105] *Cobbett v Grey* (1849) 4 Exch 729.   [106] *Herd v Weardale Steel, Coal and Coke Co Ltd* [1915] AC 67.

[107] *Burton v Davies* [1953] QSR 26 (Queensland), driving a car at such a speed as to prevent a passenger from alighting is false imprisonment.

[108] But in *Kuchenmeister v Home Office* [1958] 1 QB 496, it was held to be imprisonment for immigration officers to prevent an alien from proceeding from an airport to an aircraft and from embarking on it, even though the Aliens Order 1953 authorised them to prescribe limits within which he must remain.

[109] (1845) 7 QB 742, at 744.   [110] (1845) 7 QB 742, at 754–5.

or if it is otherwise unreasonable[111] for him to escape, it constitutes the tort of false imprisonment. On the other hand, the barriers need not be physical. Thus, when a Commissioner in Lunacy wrongfully used his authority to dissuade the claimant from leaving his office, he was liable in false imprisonment.[112] By contrast, where a voluntary mental patient is only restrained in the sense that he would be compulsorily detained under mental health legislation *if he attempted to leave*, there is, according to the present House of Lords authority, no false imprisonment for the purposes of English tort law.[113] This is because the tort turns on actual, not merely potential or conditional, imprisonment.[114] When the case was taken to Strasbourg, however, it was held by the European Court of Human Rights that there was, in these circumstances, an abrogation of Art 5(1) of the Convention.[115] In the light of this later decision, it is likely that the House of Lords will seek to come into line with the Strasbourg ruling at the first opportunity.

Restraint on movement in the street even by a mere threat of force that intimidates a person into compliance without laying hands on him is false imprisonment.[116] A restraint effected by an assertion of authority is enough – so those who seek compensation because they have been wrongfully arrested by policemen claim for false imprisonment, and need not establish that the policeman touched them.[117] The claimant need not risk violence by resisting his arrester even though he or she is entitled to use reasonable force to resist unlawful restraint.[118]

Once a person is lawfully detained, changes in the conditions of his detention will not render that detention unlawful. In a series of cases, certain prisoners sought to assert that detention in intolerable or unsanitary cells constituted false imprisonment. The House of Lords finally rejected such claims.[119] Once a prisoner is lawfully imprisoned by virtue of the Prison Act 1952, he no longer enjoys any 'residual liberty', and the prison authorities are entitled to restrain and define his movements. This does not mean, however, that a prisoner subjected to intolerable hardship is remediless. In appropriate circumstances he may have an action for assault and battery, for misfeasance in public office,[120] or, if the conditions of confinement affect his health, under the tort of negligence. It is suggested that similar analysis may be applied to

---

[111] If A removes B's bathing costume in a swimming pool and B does not leave the pool until she has found someone to lend her another costume, is he falsely imprisoned?   [112] *Harnett v Bond* [1925] AC 669.

[113] *R v Bournewood Community and Mental Health NHS Trust, ex p L* [1999] 1 AC 458.

[114] But note the dissent of Lord Steyn in that case ([1999] 1 AC 458, at 495) that it was a 'fairy tale' to suggest that the patient was free to leave.   [115] *HL v United Kingdom* (2005) 40 EHRR 32.

[116] But can one be imprisoned by telephone, and would a threat of force to a family member suffice?

[117] *Warner v Riddiford* (1858) 4 CBNS 180, especially at 204, *per* Willes J; *Chinn v Morris* (1826) 2 C & P 361; *Grainger v Hill* (1838) 4 Bing NC 212. What if C is accused of shoplifting, but in order to avoid the embarrassment of a conversation in a crowded store he accompanies the store detective to the office? See *Conn v David Spencer Ltd* [1930] 1 DLR 805.   [118] *R v McKoy* [2002] EWCA Crim 1628.

[119] *R v Deputy Governor of Parkhurst Prison, ex p Hague* [1992] 1 AC 58. But note the *obiter* suggestion in *Toumia v Evans* (1999) *Times*, 1 April that it is arguable that a gaoler who locks a prisoner in his cell in violation of the governor's orders may be liable under this tort.

[120] This, however, would require proof of malice: *Three Rivers District Council v Bank of England (No 3)* [2000] 2 WLR 1220.

detention by police officers who retain the right to detain (albeit not in the unlawful manner). For, if a remedy in false imprisonment lay, once an arrested person could establish that the conditions of his detention render his further detention unlawful, the logical consequence would be that from that moment on he could go free, using reasonable force, if necessary, to effect his escape.

Similarly, it has been held that a person held on remand beyond the 112-day limit set by regulations could not sue the prison authorities for false imprisonment.[121] The claimant was lawfully in the custody of the prison governor and only an order of the Crown Court could secure her release. The failure of the Crown Prosecution Service to bring her to trial or arrange her release on bail, and her own surprising failure to apply for bail, did not affect the validity of her detention. The claimant's right was not to be released from prison *per se*, but to an order of the court releasing her on bail.

False imprisonment must result from a direct act of the defendant which deprives the claimant of his liberty. So, it is not false imprisonment to cause a person to be temporarily detained in an asylum by making false statements to the authorities about his behaviour.[122] However short the period of detention, an action for false imprisonment will lie, provided that the other requirements of the tort are satisfied.

A false imprisonment will normally result from some positive act; but in *Herd v Weardale Steel, Coal and Coke Co*[123] the question arose as to whether there might be liability in respect of a mere omission.[124]

C, a miner employed by Ds, descended into the mine in pursuance of his contract of employment. During his shift C requested that Ds carry him to the surface in their cage. In refusing this request Ds committed no breach of contract: their contractual obligation was to transport C to the surface at the end of his shift. The action in false imprisonment also failed.[125]

This case is authority for the proposition that failure to provide a means of egress from premises is not a tort where there is no duty to provide one. Thus, if A falls down B's mine while trespassing on B's land, it is not false imprisonment should B refuse to bring him to the surface in his lift. What the *Herd* case left undecided, however, is whether the failure to carry out a duty – contractual or otherwise – may constitute false imprisonment even though there has been no positive act on the part of the defendant. But the House of Lords in *R v Governor of Brockhill Prison, ex p Evans (No 2)*[126] has now made

---

[121] *Olotu v Home Office* [1997] 1 WLR 328 (the Court of Appeal expressly addressed how far their findings were compatible with Art 5 of the Human Rights Convention); *Quinland v Governor of Swaleside Prison* [2002] 3 WLR 807.

[122] But an action on the case lay against a medical practitioner, who negligently certified that C was insane, whereupon she was detained in a mental hospital: *De Freville v Dill* (1927) 96 LJKB 1056. *Quaere*: is it false imprisonment to deflate the tyres of the invalid chair in which a cripple is travelling, or to take away the ladder of a tiler who is on the roof?   [123] [1913] 3 KB 771; affd [1915] AC 67.

[124] Because both are acts of commission, not of omission, consider the example of a student forbidden to leave the lecture room until the end of the lecture, and a conductor who will not allow one who has boarded the wrong bus to alight without paying his fare.

[125] Cf *Robinson v Balmain New Ferry Co Ltd* [1910] AC 295, at 299, *per* Lord Loreburn: 'There is no law requiring the defendants to make the exit from their premises gratuitous to people who come there upon a definite contract which involves their leaving the wharf by another way'.

[126] [2001] 2 AC 19. Cf *Olotu v Home Office* [1997] 1 WLR 328.

it clear that the tort is committed where an obligation to release a prisoner who has served his full term is not fulfilled on time.

(C) KNOWLEDGE OF THE CLAIMANT

Surprisingly, perhaps, there is no requirement that the claimant alleging false imprisonment was aware of the relevant restraint on his freedom at the time of his confinement. Prior to 1988 the authorities on this issue were in conflict. In *Herring v Boyle*[127] an action brought on behalf of a schoolboy detained at school by his headmaster during the holidays because his parents had not paid the fees failed. The judge was influenced by the fact that the boy was unaware of his detention. By contrast, in *Meering v Grahame-White Aviation Co*[128] a man persuaded by works police to remain in an office, but unaware that had he tried to leave he would have been prevented from doing so, successfully recovered damages for his imprisonment. The House of Lords in *Murray v Ministry of Defence*[129] endorsed that latter judgment stating that actual knowledge of detention is not a necessary element of false imprisonment. According to Lord Griffiths, proof of a total restraint should suffice. He said:

The law attaches supreme importance to the liberty of the individual and if he suffers a wrongful interference with that liberty it should remain actionable even without proof of special damage.[130]

It would also seem to follow from this that, if a 'prisoner' has a reasonable means of escape at his disposal, but does not know of it, there will also be a false imprisonment. The 'prisoner' may, however, need to show that a reasonable man would not have known of the escape route, either.

(D) WHO IS LIABLE FOR A FALSE IMPRISONMENT?

The usual question to be asked when deciding who can be sued for false imprisonment is: who was 'active in promoting and causing' the confinement?[131] It is often necessary to determine who can be sued when a person is detained and charged for an offence where the arrest is unjustified by law.[132] (The separate question of lawful arrest as a defence is examined in chapter 11.)

Giving information to the police, on the basis of which a police officer exercises his own judgement and arrests the claimant, does not impose on the informer responsibility for that arrest, however likely it is that an arrest will ensue from the information proffered. Thus, a store detective was not liable when the claimant was arrested on the

---

[127] (1834) 1 Cr M & R 377.   [128] (1919) 122 LT 44.   [129] [1988] 2 All ER 521.
[130] [1988] 1 WLR 692, at 704.   [131] *Aitken v Bedwell* (1827) Mood & M 68.
[132] See *Pike v Waldrum and P & O Navigation Co* [1952] 1 Lloyd's Rep 431 on the liability of naval authorities and a ship's captain for the arrest of a seaman.

basis of information which she gave to police officers, even though her information proved to be erroneous.[133] Even signing the charge sheet at the police station will not necessarily render the private citizen liable for the detention of the claimant.[134] It must be shown that the claimant's detention was truly the act of the defendant rather than of the police officers concerned. So where a police officer refused to take the claimant into custody unless the defendant charged him and signed the charge sheet, the defendant, not the police officer, was held responsible for that detention.[135]

If the defendant wrongfully delivers the claimant into custody and then the magistrate remands the claimant, the defendant is answerable in false imprisonment for damages only up to the time of the judicial remand. Once a judicial act interposes, liability for false imprisonment ceases.[136] It is important to distinguish false imprisonment from malicious prosecution. The latter is a tort concerned with the abuse of the judicial process, and which, unlike false imprisonment, calls for proof of malice and of absence of reasonable cause.[137] Therefore, if A wrongfully places a complaint against B before a magistrate who then issues a warrant or tries him forthwith or remands him, A has not committed the tort of false imprisonment,[138] even if the magistrate has no jurisdiction.[139]

(E) DAMAGES

Like the other intentional torts considered in this chapter, false imprisonment is actionable without proof of damage. In addition to damages for loss of liberty, the court may also compensate for injury to feelings and loss of reputation.[140] In claims for false imprisonment, awards of damages are currently made by juries. The amounts of such awards against the police escalated in recent years with an award of £200,000 in exemplary damages being made in one such action brought by Mr Hsu in *Thompson v Metropolitan Police Commissioner*.[141] There, the police appealed against the award to Mr Hsu, and the Court of Appeal issued guidelines on the criteria which should now determine awards of compensation for false imprisonment and malicious prosecution. Judges directing the jury on the issue of damages must address the following matters.

Save in exceptional cases, damages are to be awarded only to compensate the claimant for the injury suffered, not to punish the defendant. Basic damages to

---

[133] *Davidson v Chief Constable of North Wales* [1994] 2 All ER 597. See also *Gosden v Elphick* (1849) 4 Exch 445.

[134] *Sewell v National Telephone Co* [1907] 1 KB 557; *Grinham v Willey* (1859) 4 H & N 496.

[135] *Austin v Dowling* (1870) LR 5 CP 534. See also *Ansell v Thomas* [1974] Crim LR 31 where it was recognised that a person may be liable in false imprisonment either because he himself effected the arrest or – in line with the general principle that he who instigates another to commit a tort is a joint tortfeasor – because he actively promoted the arrest of another.   [136] *Lock v Ashton* (1848) 12 QB 871.

[137] See ch 23.   [138] *Brown v Chapman* (1848) 6 CB 365.

[139] *West v Smallwood* (1838) 3 M & W 418.   [140] *Hook v Cunard Steamship Co Ltd* [1953] 1 All ER 1021.

[141] [1998] QB 498.

compensate the claimant for loss of liberty would generally start at about £500 for the first hour of detention, but thereafter be calculated on a reducing scale to allow around £3,000 for 24 hours unlawful imprisonment and a 'progressively reducing scale' for subsequent days. An additional compensatory amount by way of aggravated damages was at one time available in respect of the humiliation, distress and indignation that are likely to arise upon the commission of an intentional tort against the person. And certainly there is good authority that such an award may be made where the claimant has been humiliated during his or her false imprisonment by the police.[142] But in relation to assault and battery where distress, anger, indignation and hurt feelings are likely to be present in most cases, it is now thought that the appellation 'aggravated damages' is inappropriate. These forms of injury are, in the context of these torts, merely part and parcel of what a defendant is expected to compensate under the head of general damages. As such, aggravated damages should now only be awarded in a 'wholly exceptional case' of assault and battery.[143]

Exemplary damages are always exceptional. They are only granted where the sum of basic and aggravated damages is inadequate to punish the defendant for oppressive and arbitrary behaviour. Juries must note that an award of exemplary damages constitutes a windfall for the claimant and that where damages come out of police funds, the burden of payment falls on the police budget affecting perhaps the operational efficiency of the police service. The amount of exemplary damages must be no more than is sufficient to mark the jury's disapproval of police behaviour. A particularly disgraceful instance of misbehaviour might merit an award of £25,000; and £50,000 should be regarded as an absolute maximum. As such, the Court of Appeal in *Thompson* reduced the award of £200,000 to £15,000.

Given the facts in both Mr Hsu's case, and the second case with which the police's appeal against his award was joined, it might be asked why, in the light of the gross brutality involved in those cases, the Court of Appeal was so anxious to reduce levels of damages for false imprisonment. Was it solely to protect police funds, and if so, can this be justified in terms of justice?[144] Ironically, it may actually be easier to argue that there should never be exemplary damages by way of vicarious liability in respect of the intentional torts of a police officer (or any other employee), since the employer who would be required to pay will not have been *personally* 'guilty' of outrageous or arbitrary behaviour.[145] As the law currently stands, exemplary damages might be awarded against an employer, but where they are so awarded, there should be no necessary implication that aggravated damages should also be awarded.[146] Another

---

[142] See *Wainwright v Home Office* [2002] 3 WLR 405; affd [2004] 2 AC 406.

[143] *Richardson v Howie* [2005] PIQR Q3, at [23], *per* Thomas LJ.

[144] In relation to the question of whether retributive justice ought to play any part in tort law, see generally Law Com No 247, *Aggravated, Exemplary and Restitutionary Damages* (1997).

[145] For the view that, on this basis, exemplary damages should never be imposed on an employer under the vicarious liability principle, see *Kuddus v Chief Constable of Leicestershire* [2002] 2 AC 122, at 128, *per* Lord Scott (*obiter*).   [146] *Isaac v Chief Constable of West Midlands* [2001] EWCA Civ 1405.

crucial factor might well inhere in the fact that awards for pain and suffering in personal injury claims remain relatively low. A claimant suffering two broken legs, enduring weeks of hospitalization and some continuing incapacity, might be awarded only about £50,000. Accordingly, how should compensation for loss of liberty and transient humiliation compare to compensation for injury?

Quite apart from the common law, it must not be forgotten that an action may lie under the Human Rights Act in respect of a breach of the Article 5 right to liberty. In such cases, the court is required to grant damages that provide 'just satisfaction' to the claimant.[147] This is a vindicatory award and therefore need not, on principle, be limited to the same compensatory figure that would be awarded under the nominate tort of false imprisonment. For even though there will be some degree of overlap between an action premised on Convention rights and one based on the common law, the two are not coextensive and there is no reason to treat the two causes of action as mutually exclusive.[148] If, however, a claimant does pursue a remedy under the 1998 Act, he or she must demonstrate a causal link between the breach of Article 5 and his or her detention.[149]

SECTION 7 OTHER FORMS OF COMPENSATION

Many of the torts discussed in this chapter will also be crimes. And any court which has convicted a person of an offence (other than a road traffic offence) may require him to pay compensation to the victim for any personal injury, loss or damage resulting.[150] The amount of compensation payable is to be determined by the court on the basis of what it considers to be appropriate, having regard to any evidence and to any representations made by or on behalf of the accused or prosecutor.[151] In addition, the Criminal Injuries Compensation Scheme also provides for awards of compensation to victims of crime who have sustained personal injuries.[152] However, detailed discussion of that scheme falls outside the scope of this book.[153]

---

[147] Human Rights Act 1998, s 8(3). For further details see *R (on the application of KB) v Mental Health Review Tribunal* [2004] QB 936.

[148] See the Human Rights Act 1998, s 8(3) which specifically requires the court to take into account 'any other relief or remedy granted' and the analagous Privy Council decision in *Merson v Cartwright* [2005] UKPC 38 (the Trinidadian constitutional right to liberty was infringed in this case).

[149] *R (on the application of Richards) v Secretary of State for the Home Department* [2004] EWHC 93.

[150] Powers of Criminal Courts (Sentencing) Act 2000, s 130.

[151] Powers of Criminal Courts (Sentencing) Act 2000, s 130(4).

[152] See Criminal Injuries Compensation Act 1995.

[153] For details, see the Criminal Injuries Compensation Authority website at www.cica.gov.uk.

FURTHER READING

Cane, 'Mens Rea in Tort Law' (2000) 20 OJLS 533

Finnis, 'Intention in Tort Law' in D.G. Owen (ed), *Philosophical Foundations of Tort Law* (1995)

Prosser, 'Transferred Intent' (1967) 45 *Texas Law Review* 650

Trindale, 'Intentional Torts: Some Thoughts on Assault and Battery' (1982) 2 OJLS 211

9

WRONGFUL INTERFERENCE
WITH GOODS

SECTION 1 INTRODUCTION

The law might be expected to protect persons whose title to, or possession of, goods is interfered with, or whose goods are damaged by intentional conduct. Broadly speaking, English law does this, but not in any systematic way; and this is so despite a comprehensive review of these chattel torts by the Law Reform Committee[1] that led to a recommendation that the various torts relating to intentional interferences with goods should be replaced by a single tort of 'wrongful interference with chattels'. In fact, this recommendation was only implemented to a very limited extent in the form of the Torts (Interference with Goods) Act 1977.[2] As such, it is still important to attempt to understand the various chattel torts.

The action for *trespass to goods* affords a remedy where there has been an intentional or careless direct interference with goods in the claimant's possession at the time of the trespass, whether that be by taking the goods from him, or by damaging the goods without removing them. But it is of no help where the relevant interference with the goods was indirect. Nor is a trespass action generally available where the goods were not in the possession of the claimant. Thus if student A lends his book overnight to student B, who gives it or sells it to C, an action in trespass will not lie against C.

The oldest of the chattel torts – the writ of *detinue* – developed to provide a remedy for wrongful detention of goods. A person with a right to immediate possession of goods could, by way of an action in detinue, recover the goods themselves or payment of their value and consequential damages for their detention upon evidence that the defendant had wrongfully refused to surrender the goods on demand. In many instances, the facts that gave rise to a remedy in detinue simultaneously created a cause of action in conversion, the latest of the major chattel torts to evolve. Detinue was abolished by the Torts (Interference with Goods) Act 1977. But the one clear instance of detinue that did not constitute conversion at common law – the loss or destruction of

---

[1] See the 18th Report of the Law Reform Committee (Conversion and Detinue) (1971) Cmnd 4774.
[2] See Palmer, 'The Application of the Torts (Interference with Goods) Act 1977 to Actions in Bailment' (1978) 41 MLR 629.

goods in breach of duty by a bailee[3] – was 'transformed' into a *statutory conversion* by section 2(2) of that Act.

The action for *conversion* (originally called trover) developed upon a legal fiction.[4] The original form of the pleadings alleged that the defendant had found the claimant's chattels and had wrongfully converted them to his own use. The allegation of finding could not be contested and the essence of the tort became the wrongful conversion of the goods to the use of the defendant. As seizing goods and carrying them away is quite clearly a wrongful conversion of goods, conversion is also often available concurrently with trespass. But merely moving or damaging goods without converting them to the defendant's own use remains remediable in trespass alone.[5] The action for conversion lies not only where the claimant has actual possession of the relevant goods but also where he has a right to immediate possession of the goods. Consider again the earlier example of the aggrieved student, A. Should B refuse to return the book to him, he commits conversion. Should B have sold the book to C who also refuses to deliver the book back to A, both B and C may be sued for conversion.

The major chattel torts of trespass and conversion protect interests in possession. But there are also several residual torts derived from the action on the case that protect the rights of owners not in possession in certain cases. Also, where goods are lost or damaged as a result of the defendant's breach of a duty of care, an action may lie in negligence.

The rich history associated with the chattel torts adds to the intrinsic difficulty of the topic of wrongful interference with goods. That difficulty is unavoidable in that, as the essence of trespass or conversion is very often whether the defendant wrongfully and unlawfully dealt with the claimant's goods, the basic question of law in issue may be one of contract or personal property,[6] or even one of mercantile law.[7] For example, if A enters into a conditional sale agreement with B to purchase a car, and before A has completed all the payments on the car he sells it to C, when B seeks to recover the car or its value from C via an action for conversion, the court will have to consider the authority (if any) of A to sell the car to B. That authority will depend on (1) the terms of the contract between A and B; and (2) the relevant personal property rules on title to goods.

The Torts (Interference with Goods) Act 1977 introduces a collective description 'wrongful interference with goods'[8] to cover conversion, trespass to goods, negligence resulting in damage to goods or an interest in goods, and any other tort in so far as it results in damage to goods or an interest in goods. This is done to facilitate common treatment of all chattel torts in respect of remedies and procedure. But the Act neither

---

[3] When goods are entrusted by one person (the bailor) to another (the bailee) a bailment is created which imposes on the bailee duties towards the bailor in respect of those goods. The nature of the bailment – whether gratuitous or for reward, voluntary or involuntary – will determine the scope of the duty owed by the bailee.

[4] For details of the history of detinue and conversion and the interplay between the historic chattel torts, see Milsom, 'Not Doing is No Trespass' [1954] CLJ 105; Simpson, 'The Introduction of the Action on the Case for Conversion' (1959) 75 LQR 364.

[5] *Bushel v Miller* (1718) 1 Stra 128; *Fouldes v Willoughby* (1841) 8 M & W 540.

[6] See Bell, *Modern Law of Personal Property* (1989).   [7] See *The Future Express* [1993] 2 Lloyd's Rep 542.

[8] Torts (Interference with Goods) Act 1977, s 1.

redefines nor replaces the existing substantive rules on trespass, conversion or any of the residual chattel torts. The substantive impact of the Act is thus limited. One novel provision, however, does allow bailees to dispose of uncollected goods.[9] But apart from this, the main impact of the 1977 Act is to simplify and rationalize the remedies and procedures relating to chattel torts. This leaves the intricacies of conversion and trespass actions still to be explored.

SECTION 2 CONVERSION

Conversion involves an intentional[10] dealing with 'goods'[11] that is seriously inconsistent with the possession or right to immediate possession of another person. The tort protects the claimant's interest in the dominion and control of his goods (so long as the interference occurs in this country[12]). It does not protect his interest in their physical condition. This is why the tort is so much concerned with problems of title to personal property, and so often involves complex rules of commercial law.[13]

(A) INTEREST OF THE CLAIMANT

The claimant must have *either* possession *or* the right to immediate possession in order to sue.[14] Equitable rights do not suffice for these purposes,[15] and in any event the law on conversion favours possession at the expense of ownership. Thus, if a landlord has rented out furnished accommodation for a fixed term and a third party commits an act of conversion in respect of some of the furniture, the landlord has no right to sue in conversion; but the tenant may do so.[16]

---

[9] Without statutory authority to do so bailees (*eg*, drycleaners) disposing of uncollected goods would be liable for conversion for so doing. Sections 12,13 and Sch 1 repeal and replace the earlier and unsatisfactory Disposal of Uncollected Goods Act 1952.

[10] At common law an act of conversion had to be a voluntary act; hence the need to make the wrongful loss or destruction of goods by a bailee in breach of duty a statutory conversion once detinue was abolished.

[11] The term 'goods' is used as a matter of convenience. Technically, conversion is based on property and possession, but it is limited to tangible, movable property. It does not apply to real property (such as land) or intellectual property (such as copyright). It was said in *OBG Ltd v Allan* [2005] QB 76, at [56], *per* Peter Gibson LJ, that an invalidly appointed receiver cannot be liable for conversion of contractual rights since conversion cannot be invoked in relation to a *chose in action*. But thus stated, this rule is too wide, for the conversion of a cheque – a form of *chose in action* – is relatively uncontroversial: see, eg, *Hounslow LBC v Jenkins* [2004] EWHC 315.

[12] *Mazur Media Ltd v Mazur Media GmbH* [2005] 1 Lloyd's Rep 41.

[13] As in *The Future Express* [1993] 2 Lloyd's Rep 542. The tort appears to be actionable without proof of special damage: *Hiort v London and North Western Rly Co* (1879) 4 Ex D 188.

[14] *The Future Express* [1993] 2 Lloyd's Rep 542; *Gordon v Harper* (1796) 7 Term Rep 9. See also Curwen, 'Title to Sue in Conversion' [2004] *Conv* 308. [15] *Hounslow LBC v Jenkins* [2004] EWHC 315.

[16] *Gordon v Harper* (1796) 7 Term Rep 9 and see *Roberts v Wyatt* (1810) 2 Taunt 268; *City Motors (1933) Pty Ltd v Southern Aerial Super Service Pty Ltd* (1961) 106 CLR 477.

(1) BAILMENT

Where goods have been entrusted to another so as to create a bailment, the bailee can sue third parties in conversion.[17] If the bailment is determinable at will, the bailor may also sue because he is then deemed to have an immediate right to possession.[18] A bailment which originally gave to the bailor no immediate right to possess may become a bailment at will. *Manders v Williams*[19] is illustrative.

C supplied porter in casks to a publican on condition that he was to return the empty casks within six months. It was held that C could sue a sheriff who seized some empty casks (within six months of their being supplied) in connection with a debt owed by the publican. Under the contract, once the casks were empty, the publican became a bailee at will, whereupon C was entitled to immediate possession.

Where a bailor and bailee enjoy concurrent rights to sue in conversion, they cannot both exercise those rights and so effect double recovery against the defendant.[20] The successful claimant who sues first must then account to the other for the proportion of the damages representing his interest in the property. So, where the owner of a car had lent the vehicle to his girlfriend, and the car was damaged while in her possession, his successful claim for damages based on his right to recover the car at will precluded a second action by the girlfriend albeit she had possession of the car at the time the damage was done.[21] In very many cases, however, the crucial issue for the bailor who owns the goods is whether he enjoys a right to immediate possession: is the bailment, or has it become, a bailment at will? Or has some wrongful act of the bailee ended the bailment? For if a bailee does a wrongful act which may be deemed to terminate the bailment, the bailor may sue. Sale of the goods by the bailee will ordinarily terminate the bailment and the bailor can then sue either the bailee or the third party.[22] Destruction of the goods[23] or dealing with them in a manner wholly inconsistent with the terms of the bailment,[24] will have the same result. Thus, it will often be a matter of interpreting the contract to decide whether a particular act of the bailee determines the bailment, or, at least, makes it determinable at will. This is especially true in the case of hire-purchase agreements which normally prohibit the hirer from selling or otherwise

---

[17] The bailment gives him the right to possession of the goods for the period of the bailment. In *The Winkfield* [1902] P 42, the Postmaster-General, as bailee, could recover the full value of mail lost through D's wrongdoing.

[18] As the bailment can be terminated at will, the owner retains the right to demand the goods back instantly: *Nicolls v Bastard* (1835) 2 Cr M & R 659; *Kahler v Midland Bank Ltd* [1950] AC 24, at 56, *per* Lord Radcliffe.

[19] (1849) 4 Exch 339.

[20] *Nicolls v Bastard* (1835) 2 Cr M & R 659 (once one has sued, the case is closed).

[21] *O'Sullivan v Williams* [1992] 3 All ER 385.

[22] *Cooper v Willomatt* (1845) 1 CB 672; *Scotland v Solomon* [2002] EWHC 1886. Of course, at the conclusion of the purported act of sale, the bailee's interest is forfeited and the bailor is entitled to immediate possession. But if the sale is one which passes a good title, when can the bailor be said to have an immediate right to possess (ie, a right to sue the bailee in conversion)? [23] *Bryant v Wardell* (1848) 2 Exch 479, at 482.

[24] *Plasycoed Collieries Co Ltd v Partridge, Jones & Co Ltd* [1912] 2 KB 345, at 351, *per* Hamilton J. Presumably, this does not extend to excess of permitted user.

disposing of the goods,[25] and empower the owner to terminate the agreement if the prohibition is disregarded. If, for example, the agreement dispenses with notice of termination to the hirer, the owner can sue a party who purchases from the hirer in unwitting contravention of such a prohibition.[26] Consider *Whiteley Ltd v Hilt*.[27]

The hire-purchase agreement allowed the hirer to purchase a piano after payment of the final instalment. It did not prohibit her from transferring the piano during the hiring period. It was held that the owners had no cause of action against the transferee who had paid all the instalments that remained owing.

This may be compared with *Belsize Motor Supply Co v Cox*.[28]

The owners were authorized to determine the agreement if the hirers parted with possession of the hired goods. It was held that (i) the owners could recover from a pledgee of the hirer only the instalments that were still owing, and (ii) that the agreement continued in force despite the transfer of the goods.

In effect, the courts treat hire-purchase agreements as *sui generis* in that they are regarded as creating a proprietary interest separate from the contractual interest under the bailment agreement.[29]

(2) LIEN AND PLEDGE

In certain cases where goods are entrusted to another to carry out particular services (for example, repairs or storage), the person in possession of those goods acquires a lien over the goods. As such, he will ordinarily be entitled to retain the goods until he is paid for the services.[30] But if title to the goods has passed to some third party (now the claimant), and the defendant who is holding the goods knows this, the defendant loses his right to retain the goods and must deliver them up to claimant.[31] The holder of a lien has a sufficient possessory interest to sue in conversion.[32] But if a lien holder once wrongfully parts with possession of the goods, he loses his lien, and his act is itself a conversion which ends the bailment and entitles the owner to sue him.[33] A pledge (that is, the deposit of goods as security for a debt), however, confers something more than a lien. It confers a power to sell in default of payment on the agreed date. So, in *Donald v*

---

[25] It is standard practice in hire-purchase agreements, by express terms, to make the benefits of the hirer's option to purchase unassignable: *Helstan Securities Ltd v Hertfordshire County Council* [1978] 3 All ER 262.

[26] *North Central Wagon and Finance Co Ltd v Graham* [1950] 2 KB 7 (sale by bailee made hiring determinable at will of bailor: as explained in *Reliance Car Facilities Ltd v Roding Motors* [1952] 2 QB 844); *Union Transport Finance Ltd v British Car Auctions Ltd* [1978] 2 All ER 385 (damages recovered from auctioneer who sold car on instructions of a hire-purchaser).   [27] [1918] 2 KB 808.

[28] [1914] 1 KB 244; *Wickham Holdings Ltd v Brooke House Motors Ltd* [1967] 1 All ER 117.

[29] Cf *Karflex Ltd v Poole* [1933] 2 KB 251, at 263–4, *per* Goddard J; *On Demand Information plc v Michael Gerson (Finance) plc* [2001] 1 WLR 155, at 171, *per* Robert Walker LJ.

[30] See Bell, *Modern Law of Personal Property* (1989) ch 6.

[31] *Pendragon plc v Walon Ltd* [2005] EWHC 1082.

[32] In *Lord v Price* (1873) LR 9 Exch 54, the buyer of goods in possession of the seller, who had a lien for the price, could not sue a third party. Is it desirable to prevent the owner from suing a third party if a carrier has a lien?   [33] *Mulliner v Florence* (1878) 3 QBD 484.

Suckling[34] it was held that a re-pledge by the pledgee did not end the pledge and the original pledgor could not sue the second pledgee without tendering the sum owing. Similarly, the assignee of a pledgor cannot sue the pledgee who sells the goods because, until the sum owing is paid, there is no immediate right to possession.[35]

(3) SALE

It is often difficult to discover which of the parties to a contract for the sale of goods has an interest sufficient to support an action in conversion. The crucial question is whether at the date of the alleged conversion the buyer has a sufficient right to immediate possession of the goods.[36] In *Empresa Exportadora de Azucar v IANSA*,[37] the claimants had contracted to buy, and had paid for, two cargoes of sugar to be shipped to them in Chile by the defendants from Cuba. On the orders of the Cuban government, after a military take-over in Chile, the ship discharging the first cargo sailed away with the cargo only partially unloaded and the second ship was diverted back to Cuba part way through its voyage. The buyers were held to have an immediate right to possession of both the partially unloaded cargo and the diverted cargo and succeeded in their action for conversion against the sellers.

Sales on credit terms pose rather more difficulties. In *Bloxam v Sanders*[38] it was held that, where goods were sold on credit, the buyer could ordinarily sue the seller in conversion if he wrongfully sold them to a third party, but that, if the seller exercised his right of stoppage *in transitu* upon the buyer becoming insolvent, the buyer could no longer sue. In the absence of credit terms, the buyer, although he may have property in the goods, has no right to immediate possession until he tenders or pays the price.[39]

(4) LICENSEE

Sometimes a licensee may be able to sue in conversion. In *Northam v Bowden*[40] the claimant had a licence to prospect certain land for tin, and the defendant, without permission, carted away some of the soil on this land. It was held that 'if the claimant had a right to the gravel and soil for the purpose of getting any mineral that could be found in it, he had such a possession of the whole as entitled him to maintain an action for its conversion against a wrongdoer'.[41] Apart from such cases of *profits à prendre*, licensees of goods are bailees and call for no separate treatment.

---

[34] (1866) LR 1 QB 585.

[35] *Halliday v Holgate* (1868) LR 3 Exch 299. Cf *Bradley v Copley* (1845) 1 CB 685. The assignee of a bill of sale which authorizes the borrower to remain in possession of the goods cannot sue in conversion for a wrongful seizure of the goods by a sheriff, because, until the assignee has demanded payment and been refused, or the borrower has otherwise defaulted in payment, he has no immediate right to possession.

[36] See, eg, *Wood v Bell* (1856) 5 E & B 772 (the punching of a name on the keel of ship evinced intention to pass property from the ship to C who had commissioned it).

[37] [1983] 2 Lloyd's Rep 171 (a defence of 'act of state' was rejected).   [38] (1825) 4 B & C 941.

[39] Cf *Chinery v Viall* (1860) 5 H & N 288 where the court decided the case without regard to the fact that the contract was a sale on credit.   [40] (1855) 11 Exch 70.

[41] (1855) 11 Exch 70, at 73, *per* Martin B.

(5) FINDER

The rule that possession is sufficient to ground a claim in conversion means that in certain circumstances someone who finds a chattel can keep it and protect his right to do so against third parties. The rules regarding finding were authoritatively settled in *Parker v British Airways Board* although, as Donaldson LJ pointed out in that case, their application to particular cases is often difficult.

The finder of a chattel acquires rights over it if the true owner is unknown and the chattel appears to have been abandoned or lost and he takes it into his care and control. He acquires a right to keep it against all but the true owner or one who can assert a prior right to keep the chattel which was subsisting at the time when the finder took the chattel into his care and control.[42]

In the classic case of *Armory v Delamirie*[43] a chimney sweep's boy who found a jewel was able to sue when the goldsmith's apprentice to whom he had handed the jewel for valuation refused to return it to him. On the other hand, any employee or agent who finds goods in the course of his employment does so on behalf of his employer who acquires a finder's rights. Anyone with finder's rights has an obligation to take reasonable steps to trace the true owner.

Finally, an occupier of land or a building has rights superior to those of a finder over goods in, under, or attached to that land or building. Thus, a medieval gold brooch buried eight inches under the soil in a public park found by the use of a metal detector,[44] and a prehistoric boat embedded in the soil six feet below the surface,[45] belonged to the respective landowners. Similar rules apply to ships, vehicles and aircraft. Yet an occupier of premises has rights superior to those of a finder over goods upon or in, but not attached to, the premises only if, before the finding, he has manifested an intention to exercise control over the building and the things which may be upon it or in it.[46]

(6) JUS TERTII (THIRD PARTY RIGHTS)

By virtue of the Torts (Interference with Goods) Act 1977[47] the defendant in an action for conversion or other wrongful interference is entitled to prove that a third party has a better right than the claimant with respect to all or any part of the interest claimed by the claimant. The aims of this provision are to avoid a multiplicity of actions by allowing interested third parties to apply to be joined in actions, to protect defendants against the risk of being liable to two different claimants in respect of the same

---

[42] [1982] QB 1004, at 1017.   [43] (1722) 1 Stra 505.

[44] *Waverley Borough Council v Fletcher* [1996] QB 334. See also *South Staffordshire Water Co v Sharman* [1896] 2 QB 44.   [45] *Elwes v Brigg Gas Co* (1886) 33 Ch D 562.

[46] *Parker v British Airways Board* [1982] QB 1004. (C found a gold bracelet on the floor at an airport and handed it in with his name and address and a request that it be returned if unclaimed. D failed to return it and sold it but the court held the proceeds were rightly C's. D, on the facts, had shown no intention beforehand to exercise such control over the lounge as to displace C's rights as a finder.) In similar vein see *Bridges v Hawkesworth* (1851) 21 LJQB 75 and *Hannah v Peel* [1945] KB 509. Cf *London Corpn v Appelyard* [1963] 2 All ER 834 (goods attached to premises).   [47] Torts (Interference with Goods) Act 1977, s 8(1).

interference, and to limit the claimant's damages to his actual loss. The relevant date for ascertaining the interest of the third party is the date of the alleged conversion.[48]

Although the Act abolished the former principle that a possessor of goods could recover for the full amount of their value although he was not the owner, and even though he was not personally liable to the owner to that extent, it is unclear whether the Act has this effect where the relevant third party cannot be found or joined in the proceedings.[49] That said, the rules do abolish the principle that a bailee is estopped from denying the bailor's title: when sued by his bailor, he can now have a named third party joined in.

(B) THE SUBJECT MATTER

Any goods can be converted. Although cheques are of value only as *choses in action*, the courts have allowed the full value represented by them to be recovered in conversion, except where the cheque has been altered, so as to become a worthless piece of paper.[50] So, where bankers do not handle actual cash, but merely make the appropriate entries by credit or debit balances, the courts treat the conversion as being of the cheque under which the money was transferred, and the value as the sum represented by the cheque.[51] This doctrine, applicable to all negotiable instruments, shows that conversion may occasionally lie in respect of rights in intangible property. But this is not the limit. In *Bavins Jnr and Sims v London and South Western Bank*[52] the Court of Appeal thought that the full value of a non-negotiable document evidencing a debt could be recovered in an action for conversion. Equally, any intangible right that is represented in the ordinary course of business by a special written instrument, even though not negotiable, seems to be recoverable. Thus, a life insurance policy[53] or a guarantee[54] may also be converted.

Advances in medical science pose some fascinating problems concerning property rights in human body products. For example, if a husband about to undergo chemotherapy stores sperm to enable his wife to conceive via artificial insemination at some later date, is the sperm bank liable for conversion if it takes that sperm and uses it, without the donor's consent, to inseminate a patient other than his wife? In relation to such a case, the clearest judicial guidance is to be gleaned from the decision in *Dobson v North Tyneside Health Authority*.[55] There, the claimants' daughter's brain was removed after she had died in hospital. The brain was initially stored at the second defendant's hospital, but then subsequently disposed of. The claimants sued in conversion alleging that the defendants' failure to keep and preserve the brain deprived them of the opportunity to discover whether the deceased's tumours were benign or malignant.

---

[48] *De Franco v Metropolitan Police Comr* (1987) *Times*, 8 May.

[49] See, eg, *The Winkfield* [1902] P 42, for the pre-Act principle. Notwithstanding the literal wording of the Act, it seems that the rule in *The Winkfield* may have survived in such circumstances: see *Costello v Chief Constable of Derbyshire Constabulary* [2001] 1 WLR 1437.

[50] *Smith v Lloyd's TSB Group plc* [2001] QB 541.

[51] *Lloyds Bank v Chartered Bank of India, Australia and China* [1929] 1 KB 40, at 55–6, *per* Scrutton LJ.

[52] [1900] 1 QB 270.   [53] *Wills v Wells* (1818) 2 Moore CP 247; *Watson v MacLean* (1858) EB & E 75.

[54] *M'Leod v M'Ghie* (1841) 2 Man & G 326.   [55] [1996] 4 All ER 474.

The Court of Appeal dismissed the claim for conversion re-affirming the principle that generally there is no property right in a corpse, or its parts. Only where some significant process has been undertaken to alter that body, or preserve it for scientific or exhibition purposes, can any title to the body be claimed.[56] So, a museum possessing a valuable Egyptian mummy can assert a claim to that mummy, and, apparently, doctors who deliberately preserved a two-headed foetus could maintain a similar claim.[57]

Dobson expressly addressed property in tissues and organs taken from the dead. But *obiter dicta* in the case suggest that a similar approach should be taken in relation to products taken from living human bodies. In England, as in the US,[58] unless and until some special process alters the very nature of the body product a claim in conversion for misuse of such products looks likely to fail.[59] Equally, the fact that section 32 of the Human Tissue Act 2004 prohibits commercial dealings in organs for transplant has been argued to be indicative of 'a legislative intent to preclude actions for damages reckoned by their value'.[60]

(C) DEFENDANT'S STATE OF MIND

Save for the statutory conversion created by section 2(2) of the Torts (Interference with Goods Act 1977), there can only be a conversion if there is intentional *positive conduct* that interferes with the claimant's goods. *Ashby v Tolhurst*[61] is illustrative.

A third party had driven away C's car which he had left in D's car park. At the trial C gave evidence that the attendant told him that he had 'given' the car to the third party. His case in conversion rested upon the assertion that this word 'imports that the attendant took some active step to place this thief in possession of the motor car' but it was found 'impossible to collect that meaning out of the words'. There was therefore no conversion, quite apart from the fact that the conditions on the ticket were also deemed to exclude liability.

If the defendant deals intentionally with the goods in a manner which interferes with the claimant's proprietary control, his act will constitute conversion, even if he does not 'intend to challenge the property or possession of the true owner'.[62] In other words, liability is strict and it matters not that the defendant commits a conversion by mistake or in good faith.[63] So, *vis-à-vis* the true owner, it is no defence for an auctioneer, after selling goods on behalf of a client, honestly delivering them to the buyer, and paying the proceeds of sale to his client, to say that he was unaware that his client did not own

---

[56] *AB v Leeds Teaching Hospital* (2004) 77 BMLR 145.

[57] *Doodeward v Spence* (1908) 6 CLR 406. And see now *R v Kelly* [1998] 3 All ER 741.

[58] See the famous case of *Moore v Regents of the University of California* 793 P 2d 479 (Cal 1990) where C failed to assert property rights in a cell-line developed from his excised spleen.

[59] See generally Matthews, 'Whose Body? People as Property' [1983] CLP 193.

[60] *Clerk and Lindsell on Torts* (2006) p 1024.   [61] [1937] 2 KB 242.

[62] *Caxton Publishing Co Ltd v Sutherland Publishing Co* [1939] AC 178, at 202, *per* Lord Porter; *Douglas Valley Finance Co Ltd v S Hughes (Hirers) Ltd* [1969] 1 QB 738.

[63] *Fowler v Hollins* (1872) LR 7 QB 616, at 639, *per* Cleasby B; affd sub nom *Hollins v Fowler* (1875) LR 7 HL 757 (followed in *Union Transport Finance Ltd v British Car Auctions Ltd* [1978] 2 All ER 385, and *R H Willis & Son v British Car Auctions Ltd* [1978] 2 All ER 392).

the goods.[64] On the other hand, if the auctioneer simply redelivers the goods to the apparent owner, there is no conversion since redelivery (as opposed to sale) changes only the position of the goods, not the property in them.[65]

(D) ACTS OF CONVERSION

In some instances, especially those involving a sale of the goods, it is eminently clear that the act is sufficiently inconsistent with the true owner's rights to be conversion. In many other instances, however, the courts have a discretion as to whether they will treat the act as sufficiently inconsistent with the true owner's rights to be conversion. This is particularly true in the case of physical damage to the goods and breach of bailment. Regrettably, the courts have not spelt out fully the factors which go to the exercise of their discretion. But the most important are probably the extent and duration of the control or dominion exercised over the goods, the intention and motive of the defendant, the amount of damage to the goods, and the cost and inconvenience to the true owner.

(1) TAKING GOODS OR DISPOSSESSING

To take goods out of the possession of another may be to convert them. To steal, or to seize under legal process without justification,[66] is certainly conversion. If, after lopping off the branches of his neighbour's apple tree when they overhang his land, a householder appropriates the fruit, he also commits conversion.[67] Merely to move goods from one place to another, however, is not conversion.[68] Thus, where a porter moved another's goods in order to reach his own, and negligently failed to replace them, he was not liable in conversion for their subsequent loss.[69] It may be conversion, however, if they are moved to an unreasonable place with an intrinsic risk of loss. In *Forsdick v Collins*,[70] for instance, the defendant came into possession of land on which the claimant had a block of Portland stone and the removal of the Portland stone by the defendant 'to a distance' was held to be a conversion. A deprivation of goods that is more than a mere moving (that is, deprives the claimant of their use for however long), will be conversion,[71] as will forcing the claimant to hand over goods under duress.[72]

---

[64] *Consolidated Co v Curtis & Son* [1892] 1 QB 495. In *Moorgate Mercantile Co Ltd v Finch and Read* [1962] 1 QB 701, the borrower of a car had it confiscated upon conviction for carrying in it uncustomed watches. This was rightly held to be a conversion, for the confiscation was the result of his intentional act of carrying the watches in the car. See also *Chubb Cash Ltd v John Crilley & Son* [1983] 2 All ER 294.

[65] *Marcq v Christie Manson and Wood Ltd* [2004] QB 286.

[66] *Tinkler v Poole* (1770) 5 Burr 2657; *Burton v Hughes* (1824) 2 Bing 173; *Chubb Cash Ltd v John Crilley & Son* [1983] 2 All ER 294. [67] *Mills v Brooker* [1919] 1 KB 555.

[68] *Fouldes v Willoughby* (1841) 8 M & W 540, where D removed C's horses from a ferry boat on to the shore because he did not wish C to travel in the boat. [69] *Bushel v Miller* (1718) 1 Stra 128.

[70] (1816) 1 Stark 173. Cf *Sanderson v Marsden and Jones* (1922) 10 Ll L Rep 467 (D removing timber from a quay to his premises was not a conversion).

[71] *Empresa Exportadora de Azucar v IANSA* [1983] 2 Lloyd's Rep 171. But see to the contrary 384238 *Ontario Ltd v The Queen in Right of Canada* (1983) 8 DLR (4th) 676. [72] *Grainger v Hill* (1838) 4 Bing NC 212.

(2) DESTROYING OR ALTERING

To destroy goods is to convert them, if the destruction is intentional.[73] The quantum of harm constituting a destruction for this purpose is clearly a question of degree, but mere damage is not a conversion.[74] A change of identity not amounting to destruction is also enough. For example, to draw out part of a vessel of liquor and fill it up with water is conversion;[75] but perhaps merely to cut a log in two is not.[76] If goods are used for a purpose which eliminates their utility as goods in their original form – for example, making a fur coat from animal skins – this is conversion.[77] But it is not conversion to bottle another's wine in order to preserve it.[78]

(3) USING

To use goods as one's own is ordinarily to convert them. It was thus conversion for a person, to whom carbolic acid drums were delivered by mistake, to deal with them as his own by pouring the contents into his tank.[79] Equally, a claim 'would not be defeated by the fact that the defendant whom he sues for the misuse of his temporary dominion of the property claims to be an agent for someone else'.[80] However, a mere misuse by a bailee, unaccompanied by any denial of title, is not a conversion, although it may constitute some other tort.[81]

(4) RECEIPT, DISPOSITION AND DELIVERY

Voluntarily[82] to receive goods in consummation of a transaction which is intended by the parties to give to the recipient some proprietary rights in the goods may be a conversion actionable by the owner.[83] It has been held to be a conversion for a purchaser

---

[73] Purely accidental destruction is not conversion: *Simmons v Lillystone* (1853) 8 Exch 431.

[74] *Fouldes v Willoughby* (1841) 8 M & W 540, at 549, *per* Alderson B.

[75] *Richardson v Atkinson* (1723) 1 Stra 576.

[76] *Simmons v Lillystone* (1853) 8 Exch 431, at 442, *per* Parke B.

[77] *Jones v de Marchant* (1916) 28 DLR 561 (approved in *Foskett v McKeown* [2001] 1 AC 102). In such cases, the owner of the materials becomes the owner of the product if the material can be wholly or substantially identified in the product: *Glencore International AG v Metro Trading International Inc* [2001] 1 Lloyd's Rep 284.

[78] *Philpott v Kelley* (1835) 3 Ad & El 106.

[79] *Lancashire and Yorkshire Rly Co v MacNicoll* (1918) 88 LJKB 601. It has also been said that '[t]he wearing of a peal is conversion': *Lord Petre v Heneage* (1701) 12 Mod Rep 519, at 520, *per* Holt CJ. See also the many examples given in *Mulgrave v Ogden* (1591) Cro Eliz 219.

[80] *Morison v London County and Westminster Bank Ltd* [1914] 3 KB 356, at 386, *per* Phillimore LJ (*obiter*).

[81] *Lee v Atkinson and Brooks* (1609) Yelv 172 (when the hirer of a horse deviates, an action on case lies); approved in *Donald v Suckling* (1866) LR 1 QB 585, at 615, *per* Blackburn J, who said that if the act is repugnant to the bailment, it is conversion, but 'where the act, though unauthorized, is not repugnant to the contract as to show a disclaimer' it is not. See also *Penfolds Wines Pty Ltd v Elliott* (1946) 74 CLR 204.

[82] Receipt by an involuntary bailee is not conversion.

[83] Cf *M'Combie v Davies* (1805) 6 East 538, at 540, *per* Lord Ellenborough CJ: 'Certainly a man is guilty of a conversion who takes my property by assignment from another who has no authority to dispose of it; for what is that but assisting that other in carrying his wrongful act into effect?'

so to receive goods from someone who has no title.[84] If, however, the defendant receives the goods in good faith for the purposes of storage or transport,[85] he does not commit conversion because there is no assertion of a proprietary interest in the goods. Receipt of goods by way of pledge is conversion if the delivery is conversion.[86]

In relation to disposition and delivery, there is generally no conversion where a person agrees to sell goods to which he has no title, but does not transfer possession of them. This is because bargain and sale are void if the seller has no rights in the goods.[87] On the other hand, a person who without lawful authority disposes of goods with the intention of transferring the title to another, and does deliver the goods, thereby commits a conversion. A sale and a pledge[88] may each constitute such a disposition. In *Syeds v Hay*[89] a sea-captain was liable for delivering goods to another in the wrongful belief that he had a lien on them. In certain circumstances, however, the courts and Parliament have developed exceptions to the *nemo dat* rule (whereby a person who does not have good title, may not pass a good title to another). The nature of, and reasons for, these exceptions are not dealt with here, however, for they are properly to be seen as matters of commercial (not tort) law.[90]

(5) MISDELIVERY BY CARRIER

A carrier[91] or warehouseman[92] who by mistake delivers goods to the wrong person, commits a conversion whether or not his mistake is innocent.[93] But failure to deliver because the goods have been lost or destroyed by accident or carelessness is not conversion.[94] Nor is it conversion for a bailee[95] or pledgee[96] without notice of the claim of the true owner to return goods to the person from whom he received them.

---

[84] *Farrant v Thompson* (1822) 5 B & Ald 826.

[85] *Hollins v Fowler* (1875) LR 7 HL 757, at 767, *per* Blackburn J. Cf *Sheridan v New Quay Co* (1858) 4 CBNS 618 (carrier).   [86] Sale of Goods Act 1979, s 11(2).

[87] *Lancashire Waggon Co v Fitzhugh* (1861) 6 H & N 502; he may, however, be liable for malicious falsehood: see ch 13.   [88] *Parker v Godin* (1728) 2 Stra 813.

[89] (1791) 4 Term Rep 260. But if someone entrusts another with a chattel to be used by him, the bailor impliedly authorizes the bailee to allow a lien for the cost of necessary repairs to be created over it: *Green v All Motors Ltd* [1917] 1 KB 625; *Tappenden v Artus* [1964] 2 QB 185.

[90] Some illustrative cases were discussed in the 10th edition of this book.

[91] *Youl v Harbottle* (1791) Peake 68, NP.   [92] *Devereux v Barclay* (1819) 2 B & Ald 702.

[93] If the carrier delivers in accordance with the seller's instructions (or even as a carrier would interpret his instructions according to the usual course of business although he in fact delivered them to a person to whom the seller did not intend delivery to be made) this is not a misdelivery: *McKean v McIvor* (1870) LR 6 Exch 36. It is conversion by a carrier to deliver goods to another carrier by whom they are misappropriated, unless the defendant carrier is authorized to make a sub-contract: *Garnham, Harris and Elton Ltd v Alfred W Ellis (Transport) Ltd* [1967] 2 All ER 940.

[94] *Owen v Lewyn* (1672) 1 Vent 223; *The Arpad* [1934] P 189, at 232, *per* Maugham LJ.

[95] *Hollins v Fowler* (1875) LR 7 HL 757, at 767, *per* Blackburn J. Otherwise the bailee would be in an impossible position, for if he retained the goods he could not plead a title paramount of which he was unaware.

[96] *Union Credit Bank Ltd v Mersey Docks and Harbour Board* [1899] 2 QB 205.

(6) REFUSAL TO SURRENDER ON DEMAND

A refusal to surrender goods upon lawful and reasonable demand is a conversion.[97] In particular, this covers the situation where the possession of the defendant was originally lawful. It may be invoked, for example, where the receiving is not itself actionable. The most important case since the abolition of detinue by the Torts (Interference with Goods) Act 1977 is *Howard E Perry & Co Ltd v British Railways Board*.[98] The defendants, fearing industrial action by their employees during a national steelworkers strike, refused to surrender to the claimants steel belonging to the claimants that was being held in the defendants' depots. The defendants admitted that the claimants were entitled to immediate possession and it was held that their refusal to allow the claimants to enter the depots and collect the steel was wrongful.

There is a large amount of case law on this topic, but the principles are quite simple. Even if the defendant no longer has possession at the time of the demand and refusal, it is no defence for him to prove that, prior to the accrual of the claimant's title, he wrongfully parted with them.[99] On the other hand, the defendant may postpone surrender until after he has had a reasonable time in which to confirm the title of the claimant,[100] or, if he is an employee, to consult his employer.[101] This reasonableness is a question of fact. Many factors may be relevant – the time of the demand, the expense and inconvenience of immediate compliance, the knowledge on the part of the defendant of the claimant's title, and of his identity, and whether the defendant has adequately conveyed to the claimant the grounds for his temporary refusal. An estoppel may sometimes operate to prevent the defendant from setting up facts which would otherwise have justified a refusal.[102]

If an auctioneer redelivers goods to their apparent owner after he has failed to sell those goods, he cannot be held liable in conversion upon the suit of the true owner so long as his redelivery was made in good faith and without knowledge of the true owner's title.[103]

(7) GOODS LOST OR DESTROYED

At common law there could be no conversion where there was no voluntary act. Section 2(2) of the Torts (Interference with Goods) Act 1977 therefore provides as follows:

An action lies in conversion for loss or destruction of goods which a bailee has allowed to happen in breach of his duty to his bailor (that is to say it lies in a case which is not otherwise conversion, but would have been detinue before detinue was abolished).

---

[97] *Marcq v Christie Manson and Wood Ltd* [2004] QB 286; *Isaack v Clark* (1615) 2 Bulst 306, at 310, *per* Dodderidge J.   [98] [1980] 2 All ER 579.

[99] *Bristol and West of England Bank v Midland Rly Co* [1891] 2 QB 653.

[100] *Clayton v Le Roy* [1911] 2 KB 1031. Cf *Gough v Chief Constable of the West Midlands* [2004] EWCA Civ 206 (goods detained by the police past the point where the police were seeking to establish the goods' true owners was a conversion. They are permitted only a reasonable time for such purposes under the Police (Property) Act 1997).   [101] *Alexander v Southey* (1821) 5 B & Ald 247.

[102] *Seton, Laing & Co v Lafone* (1887) 19 QBD 68; *Henderson & Co v Williams* [1895] 1 QB 521.

[103] *Marcq v Christie Manson and Wood Ltd* [2004] QB 286.

Bailees are required to take reasonable care of goods in their keeping and are liable for the loss or destruction of such goods unless they can disprove fault;[104] but they are not insurers of the goods. In *Sutcliffe v Chief Constable of West Yorkshire*[105] an arson attack destroyed the claimant's car which had been lawfully seized by the police and which was being held in a police station yard. The Court of Appeal dismissed the claimant's claim for conversion. The attack was unprecedented, and in respect of the claimant's property the defendant had done all that was reasonable to take care of the vehicle.

Denial of title is not of itself conversion.[106] There may, however, be conversion of goods although the defendant has not physically dealt with them,[107] or been in physical possession of them,[108] if his acts deprive the claimant of his right to possession or amount to a substantial interference with that right.[109] But a mere threat to prevent an owner in possession from removing his goods will not of itself amount to conversion.[110]

Where goods are left on land and occupier B acquires the land on which the goods lie from occupier A, then if occupier B refuses to allow the true owner to enter the land and retrieve them, the refusal is not necessarily conversion.[111] It may become conversion, however, if occupier B himself asserts any right in respect of the goods,[112] or denies the claimant most of the rights of ownership, including the right to possession, for a period which is plainly indefinite.[113] But this needs to be established as a question of fact.

(8) RESIDUAL ACTS AMOUNTING TO CONVERSION

The foregoing categories of conversion are not exhaustive. There are other acts, not capable of being readily classified, which may yet fall within the definition of conversion.[114] In these residual cases, judicial discretion to treat the act as sufficiently inconsistent with the true owner's rights for a conversion is especially important.

---

[104] A bailee will ordinarily be liable unless he disproves fault: *Houghland v R R Low (Luxury Coaches) Ltd* [1962] 1 QB 694. An involuntary bailee is not liable for failure to return merely because he has lost the goods: *Howard v Harris* (1884) 1 Cab & El 253. However, he is liable if he destroys or damages the goods. If the bailee is unaware that the goods on his premises are not his property (*ie*, he is an 'unconscious bailee'), he is under a duty to exercise reasonable care to ascertain that they were his own before he destroys them: *AVX Ltd v EGM Solders Ltd* (1982) *Times*, 7 July. [105] [1996] RTR 86.

[106] Torts (Interference with Goods) Act 1977, s 11(3).

[107] *Van Oppen & Co Ltd v Tredegars Ltd* (1921) 37 TLR 504. [108] Eg, *Oakley v Lyster* [1931] 1 KB 148.

[109] *Oakley v Lyster* [1931] 1 KB 148; *Lancashire and Yorkshire Rly Co, London and North Western Rly Co and Graeser Ltd v MacNicoll* (1918) 88 LJKB 601. [110] *England v Cowley* (1873) LR 8 Exch 126.

[111] *Wilde v Waters* (1855) 24 LJCP 193, at 195, *per* Maule J; *British Economical Lamp Co Ltd v Empire Mile End Lane Ltd* (1913) 29 TLR 386.

[112] *Walker v Clyde* (1861) 10 CBNS 381; *H E Dibble Ltd v Moore* [1970] 2 QB 181.

[113] *Howard E Perry & Co Ltd v British Railways Board* [1980] 2 All ER 579, at 583, *per* Sir Robert Megarry VC; *Bryanston Leasings Ltd v Principality Finance Ltd* [1977] RTR 45.

[114] See the *dictum* of Bramwell B in *England v Cowley* (1873) LR 8 Exch 126.

(E) CONVERSION AS BETWEEN CO-OWNERS[115]

Section 10(1)(a) of the Torts (Interference with Goods) Act 1977 provides that co-ownership is no defence to an action founded on conversion where the defendant, without the authority of the other co-owner, destroys the goods, or disposes of them in a way giving a good title to the entire property in the goods, or otherwise does anything equivalent to the destruction of the other interest in the goods. Thus, a partner who paid cheques into a third person's bank account was, by excluding his co-owner's right to enjoy the proceeds, liable for conversion.[116] A co-owner cannot, however, be sued for conversion if he merely makes use of the common property in a reasonable way.[117] Nor was there necessarily a conversion where the co-owner took and kept the goods.[118] The law requires a destruction of the goods or something equivalent to it.[119] The Torts (Interference with Goods) Act 1977 further provides in section 10(1)(b) that it is also no defence to an action founded on conversion where the defendant, without the authority of the other co-owner, purports to dispose of the goods in such a way as would give a good title to the entire property in the goods if he were acting with the authority of all the co-owners of the goods.

These rules do not affect the law concerning execution or enforcement of judgments, or the law concerning any form of distress.[120]

(F) DAMAGES[121]

As was noted at the start of this chapter, the major impact of the Torts (Interference with Goods) Act 1977 was to rationalize the remedies available to claimants suing in conversion, both in relation to the damages which may be awarded and in making provision for specific return of the goods by way of orders for delivery. On the other hand, the related issue of remoteness of damage is still governed by the common law, and the test is one of reasonable foreseeability.[122]

---

[115] Note the Sale of Goods Act 1979, ss 20A and 20B whereby a buyer of a quantity of goods forming part of a larger bulk becomes a proportionate co-owner of those goods.

[116] *Baker v Barclays Bank Ltd* [1955] 2 All ER 571.

[117] As, for instance, by cutting grass and making hay in the common field (*Jacobs v Seward* (1872) LR 5 HL 464) or extracting the oil and the other valuable parts of a dead whale which is owned in common: *Fennings v Lord Grenville* (1808) 1 Taunt 241.

[118] The bailee of common property from one co-owner is not guilty of conversion if he refuses to deliver the property on the demand of another co-owner (*Atwood v Ernest* (1853) 13 CB 881; *Harper v Godsell* (1870) LR 5 QB 422) unless the latter has a special property in the entire chattel (*Nyberg v Handelaar* [1892] 2 QB 202).

[119] *Morgan v Marquis* (1853) 9 Exch 145; *Baker v Barclays Bank Ltd* [1955] 2 All ER 571.

[120] Torts (Interference with Goods) Act 1977, s 11(2). The rules apply equally to intentional trespass to goods as they apply to conversion.

[121] See Tettenborn, 'Damages in Conversion: The Exception or the Anomaly?' [1993] CLJ 128; *id*, 'Conversion, Tort and Restitution' in Palmer and McKendrick (eds), *Interests in Goods* (1998).

[122] *Saleslease Ltd v Davis* [1999] 1 WLR 1664; *Kuwait Airways Corpn v Iraqi Airways Co (Nos 4 and 5)* [2001] 3 WLR 1117.

(1) At common law, the claimant with a limited interest in the goods could normally recover their full value from a third party. Under section 8 of the Torts (Interference with Goods) Act 1977 and rules of court, however, the claimant now has to identify any other person whom he knows to have an interest in the goods and any such interested party may be joined, whereupon the damages may be apportioned among the interested parties in proportion to their respective interests.[123] Where the other interested party is not traced – as in cases of finding, or a missing bailor – the claimant in possession can recover the full value of the goods, but is liable to account to the true owner.[124]

Where the defendant has an interest in the goods, the claimant's damages in respect of the interference with his interest are limited to the value of that interest.[125] An unpaid seller who sold to a third party was held liable to the original buyer, to whom he had not delivered the goods,[126] who was not in default, for only the value of the goods less the contract price owing to him.

(2) The claimant, in conversion, is entitled to be compensated to the extent of the value to him of the goods of which he has been deprived. This will often appropriately be the market value of the goods. Where goods are of a kind which can be readily bought in the market, the actual market value will be the appropriate measure; otherwise the replacement value in a comparable state,[127] or the original cost minus depreciation will be the standard. Where the actual value of the claimant's interest in the goods is less than the market value, he may be awarded the value of that interest and not the higher market value.[128] In *Wickham Holdings Ltd v Brooke House Motors*,[129] the hirer of a car sold the car in breach of his hire-purchase agreement. The finance company that owned the car was held able to recover from the ultimate purchaser of the vehicle only the value of the outstanding hire-purchase instalments due, and not the higher value of the car itself. In *Chubb Cash Ltd v John Crilley & Son (a firm)*[130] the claimant sold a cash register on hire-purchase terms. He then assigned the instalments due under the agreement to a credit company in return for a loan agreeing to pay all instalments due should the purchaser of the register default on the hire purchase. In his action for conversion against bailiffs who had seized the cash register, the claimant was awarded only the market value of the goods and not the higher amount due under his agreement with the credit company. That consequential loss was held to be irrecoverable.

---

[123] Torts (Interference with Goods) Act 1977, s 7(2).

[124] *Wilson v Lombank Ltd* [1963] 1 All ER 740; *O' Sullivan v Williams* [1992] 3 All ER 385.

[125] *Johnson v Stear* (1863) 15 CBNS 330 (owner suing pledgee); *Belsize Motor Supply Co v Cox* [1914] 1 KB 244 (owner suing assignee of hirer).

[126] If an unpaid seller takes goods out of the buyer's possession he is liable in conversion for the full value of the goods without deduction for the unpaid price: *Healing (Sales) Pty Ltd v Inglis Electrix Pty Ltd* (1968) 42 ALJR 280, following *Gillard v Britton* (1841) 8 M & W 575.

[127] *J & E Hall Ltd v Barclay* [1937] 3 All ER 620.

[128] But see *Edmondson v Nuttall* (1864) 17 CBNS 280 and *Wilson v Lombank Ltd* [1963] 1 All ER 740 (a case in trespass).   [129] [1967] 1 All ER 117.

[130] [1983] 2 All ER 294.

Where a negotiable instrument or other document ordinarily representing a *chose in action* is converted, the value which the document represents, and not merely its value as a piece of paper, is the basis of the quantum of damages. On the other hand, a purely intangible *chose in action* cannot be converted.[131]

(3) 'The general rule is that a [claimant] whose property is irreversibly converted has vested in him a right to damages for conversion measured by the value of the property at the date of conversion.'[132] Once a claim for conversion has accrued to the claimant, it is not open to him to delay the issue of his writ and thereby base his action on a subsequent demand and refusal – the duty to mitigate damages operates.[133]

A rule basing damages on the value at the date of conversion can be seen to work to the claimant's benefit in certain circumstances. If the goods decrease in value between the date of the conversion and the date of judgment, the claimant may still recover the value at the date of conversion.[134]

However, the general rule is not immutable. In conversion, as in other torts, the normal purpose of an award of damages is to compensate the claimant for the loss he actually sustains.[135] Thus, the market value (even where ascertainable) at the date of conversion will not necessarily mark the top limit of damages recoverable in the following instances.

(1) Evidence later turns up to show what was the value at the date of conversion.[136]

(2) The market value of the goods rises between the date of the cause of action and trial. If the act of conversion relied on by the claimant is a sale, and by the time when the claimant knows or ought to know of the sale the value has increased, the claimant can recover that higher value.[137] There is some authority also for the view that, from a broker who has sold his stock, the claimant may recover its increased value within a reasonable time for buying replacement stock;[138] that is, the court estimates the value of the chance of a profit.[139] *Greening v Wilkinson*[140] is illustrative.

D refused to hand over to C warrants for cotton belonging to C. At the time of the demand and refusal, the warrants were worth 6d *per* lb, but at the time of the trial they were worth $10\frac{1}{2}$ d *per* lb. The jury awarded damages on the basis of $10\frac{1}{2}$ d *per* lb in accordance with Abbott CJ's ruling that they 'may give the value at the time of the conversion, or at any subsequent time, at their discretion, because the [claimant] might have had a good opportunity of selling the goods if they had not been detained'.[141]

---

[131] *OBG Ltd v Allan* [2005] QB 76, at [56], *per* Peter Gibson LJ.
[132] *BBMB Finance (Hong Kong) Ltd v Eda Holdings Ltd* [1991] 2 All ER 129.
[133] *Empresa Exportadora de Azucar v IANSA* [1983] 2 Lloyd's Rep 171.
[134] *Rhodes v Moules* [1895] 1 Ch 236 (D converted C's shares, the market price of which dropped before judgment. D was not permitted simply to purchase the same number of shares for C). See also the similar results in *Solloway v McLaughlin* [1938] AC 247 and *BBMB Finance v Eda Holdings Ltd* [1991] 2 All ER 129.
[135] *Brandeis Goldschmidt & Co v Western Transport Ltd* [1981] QB 864; *IBL Ltd v Coussens* [1991] 2 All ER 133.   [136] *Caxton Publishing Co Ltd v Sutherland Publishing Co* [1939] AC 178, at 203, *per* Lord Porter.
[137] *Sachs v Miklos* [1948] 2 KB 23.   [138] *Samuel and Escombe v Rowe* (1892) 8 TLR 488.
[139] *Aitken v Gardiner* (1956) 4 DLR (2d) 119.   [140] (1825) 1 C & P 625.
[141] Lord Porter left open the soundness of this judgment in *Caxton Publishing Co Ltd v Sutherland Publishing Co* [1939] AC 178, at 203.

(3) If the defendant converts the claimant's goods and then increases their value, the claimant cannot ordinarily recover that increased value.[142] Thus, where the defendant converted a partially built ship which he then completed at his own expense, the court's view was that the claimant was entitled to recover the market value of the completed ship less the expense incurred by the defendant in completing it.[143] Where the act of conversion relied on takes place after the improvement made to the goods, section 6(1) of the 1977 Act now applies. If the defendant has improved the goods in the mistaken but honest belief that he had a good title to them, an allowance is made for the extent to which (at the time at which the goods fall to be valued in assessing damages) the value of the goods is attributable to the improvement. If, for example, the improver is sued for later selling the goods, the statutory allowance applies.[144] A similar allowance is enjoyed by purported purchasers of goods improved by another, provided again that the purchaser acted in good faith.[145] Subsequent purchasers enjoy the same protection.[146] Thus an eventual buyer in good faith of a stolen car when sued by the true owner will have the damages reduced to reflect any improvements made to it since the theft. The Act leaves it uncertain whether the common law rule that an improver who did not act in good faith was entitled to a deduction still survives, or whether the statutory requirement of good faith must be taken to supersede the common law. At common law special rules applied to goods severed from the land such as coal, other minerals,[147] and timber.[148] If, for instance, the defendant innocently severed the claimant's coal he was liable only for the value of the coal in the seam, but if his act was wilful, he was liable for its value immediately after severance.[149] These rules may be unaffected by the Act.[150]

(4) Whether or not the claimant incurs pecuniary loss (or a potential pecuniary loss) as a direct consequence of the conversion he may still recover special damages in addition to the market value of the goods. Thus, for example, a workman deprived of his tools recovered loss of wages,[151] and the owner of a converted pony could claim the cost of hiring another.[152] In *Strand Electric and Engineering Co Ltd v Brisford Entertainments Ltd*[153] (a detinue case), it was held to be irrelevant that the

---

[142] *Caxton Publishing Co Ltd v Sutherland Publishing Co* [1939] AC 178; *Greenwood v Bennett* [1973] QB 195.

[143] *Reid v Fairbanks* (1853) 13 CB 692 (the parties settled the size of the damages awarded).

[144] And see *Munro v Willmott* [1949] 1 KB 295 at common law (where C relied on a demand and refusal rather than an earlier conversion, C could not recover the value as increased by D's improvement).

[145] Torts (Interference with Goods) Act 1977, s 6(2).

[146] Torts (Interference with Goods) Act 1977, s 6(3).

[147] The English cases have concerned coal. But see the New Zealand case of *Blenheim Borough and Wairau River Board v British Pavements (Canterbury) Ltd* [1940] NZLR 564 concerning shale.

[148] *Burmah Trading Corpn v Mirza Mahomed Allay Sherazee and Burmah Co Ltd* (1878) LR 5 Ind App 130; *Union Bank of Canada v Rideau Lumber Co* (1902) 4 OLR 721; *Greer v Faulkner* (1908) 40 SCR 399 (Canada).

[149] *Wood v Morewood* (1841) 3 QB 440.

[150] The Act applies only where D improves goods; it seems doubtful whether severing minerals to make them saleable amounts to improving them. [151] *Bodley v Reynolds* (1846) 8 QB 779.

[152] *Davis v Oswell* (1837) 7 C & P 804.

[153] [1952] 2 QB 246; confirmed in *Inverugie Investments v Hackett* [1995] 3 All ER 841. Where D converted a Rolls Royce on hire from Cs and then put it out of his power to return it, he remained liable for the hiring

claimants would not have been able to hire out for the whole period of that wrongful detention those goods that the defendants wrongfully failed to return. This is because the usual 'but for' test of causation does not apply in conversion.[154] Similarly, in *Kuwait Airways Corp v Iraqi Airways Co (Damages)*,[155] it was held that the claimant was not bound to show any actual or probable loss associated with the wrongful retention of aircraft parts. The claimant was entitled to damages representing a reasonable sum by way of hire or rent. On the other hand, there will be a time limit to the period for which he can claim a loss of hire because there will come a time when he will be expected to obtain an alternative chattel to hire out.[156]

(5) Although detinue was abolished by section 2(1) of the Torts (Interference with Goods) Act 1977, section 3 of that Act preserved the remedies for what would previously have been detinue by making them available in conversion.[157] Where the defendant has possession of the goods at the time that proceedings are begun, he cannot, by disposing of the goods, reduce to its market value his liability for loss caused by detention of a profit-earning chattel. However, where the remedy lies in damages, while the general rule in conversion is that the value of the converted goods is ascertained at the date of conversion, in detinue it was the date of judgment. The approach under the Act was set out in *IBL Ltd v Coussens*.[158] There, the Court of Appeal held that in cases of temporary deprivation of property (in this case, two cars), where no irreversible act of conversion is committed, evidence must be adduced as to the true loss suffered by the owner. The measure of damages was not to be fixed arbitrarily at either the date of conversion or the date of judgment. Their Lordships remitted the case back to the master for evidence of (a) the value of the cars, and (b) what the claimants would have done with the cars had they been returned when requested. If, for example, the claimants would have sold the cars between the dates of conversion and judgment, the value of the cars at that time, plus interest, would represent a proper measure of damages.

(6) Since the effect of a judgment for damages is to transfer the title to the defendant,[159] it follows that the court will not award damages both for loss of use and the value of the goods where the effect would be doubly to compensate the claimant. The capacity for profitable use is part of the value of the goods. Thus where the defendant converted manufacturing plant belonging to the claimant, he was liable for the value of the plant when converted but not for loss of use between that date and trial.[160] On the other hand, if the defendant wrongfully detains goods and later sells them, it seems that the claimant can recover, in addition to their value, for the loss of use from the date of the unlawful detention

charges, which came to over £13,000, until it was returned, although its value when converted was only £7,500: *Hillesden Securities Ltd v Ryjak Ltd* [1983] 2 All ER 184.

[154] *Kuwait Airways Corpn v Iraqi Airways Co (Nos 4 and 5)* [2001] 3 WLR 1117 (aircraft seized by the Iraqi government were converted, and Cs were entitled to their full value even though they would probably have been destroyed had they not been requisitioned). [155] [2004] EWHC 2603.

[156] *Greer v Alstons Engineering Sales and Services Ltd* [2003] UKPC 46.

[157] *Hillesden Securities Ltd v Ryjak Ltd* [1983] 2 All ER 184. [158] [1991] 2 All ER 133.

[159] *Ellis v John Stenning & Son* [1932] 2 Ch 81. [160] *Re Simms, ex p Trustee* [1934] Ch 1.

until sale,[161] and indeed until the claimant had a reasonable opportunity to buy a replacement after learning of that sale,[162] but not for loss of use until trial.

(7) It is doubtful in what circumstances a buyer who does not recover his goods can claim a loss of re-sale profit.[163] Where a conversion action based on non-delivery is an alternative to an action in contract and the seller is unaware of the re-sale contract, the loss of profit is not recoverable as such in conversion. However, where there is no market in the goods, the re-sale price may be evidence of value.[164]

If the defendant returns the goods before trial, the courts will reduce the damages in conversion by the amount of its value at that time.[165] In short, the court will not enforce a sale on the defendant, and 'subject to the payment of costs and special damages (if there are any) an action for damages for conversion can always be stayed if the defendant offers to hand over the property in dispute'.[166] The value of the goods when returned is set off against the damages calculated *per* the preceding paragraphs. Where goods acquired by the claimant for use in a manufacturing process have been wrongfully detained but later returned, the claimant must show that a loss of profit or other pecuniary loss has resulted from the detention.[167] If he fails to prove that he would have used the goods at any time before their return, he cannot recover the fall in their market value over the period of their detention and may receive only nominal damages.[168] It will, of course, be otherwise where he purchased the goods for re-sale during the period of detention.[169]

(8) If the general preconditions necessary for an award of exemplary damages (discussed in Chapter 26 below) are satisfied, such damages may now be claimed in conversion.[170]

(G) OTHER REMEDIES

The Torts (Interference with Goods) Act 1977 introduced common remedies for all forms of 'wrongful interferences with goods'. Section 3 provides that in proceedings for conversion, or any other chattel tort, against a person in possession or control of the

---

[161] *Strand Electric and Engineering Co Ltd v Brisford Entertainments Ltd* [1952] 2 QB 246, at 255, *per* Denning LJ.

[162] *Re Simms, ex p Trustee* [1934] Ch 1, at 30, *per* Romer LJ.

[163] This loss was recovered in *France v Gaudet* (1871) LR 6 QB 199.

[164] *The Arpad* [1934] P 189. Conversely, a buyer still recovered the market value from a seller not delivering to him, although the loss of the buyer on his contract of re-sale was less than this sum: *D Joseph Ltd v Ralph Wood & Co Ltd* [1951] WN 224.

[165] *Fisher v Prince* (1762) 3 Burr 1363; *Solloway v McLaughlin* [1938] AC 247.

[166] *USA and Republic of France v Dollfus Mieg et Compagnie SA and Bank of England* [1952] AC 582, at 619, *per* Lord Radcliffe.

[167] *Brandeis Goldschmidt & Co Ltd v Western Transport Ltd* [1981] QB 864, at 870, *per* Brandon LJ; *Williams v Peel River Land and Mineral Co Ltd* (1886) 55 LT 689, at 692–693, *per* Bowen LJ. See also *Williams v Archer* (1847) 5 CB 318; *Barrow v Arnaud* (1846) 8 QB 595.

[168] *Williams v Peel River Land and Mineral Co Ltd* (1886) 55 LT 689, at 692–693, *per* Bowen LJ; *Bryanston Leasings Ltd v Principality Finance Ltd* [1977] RTR 45; *Brandeis Goldschmidt & Co Ltd v Western Transport Ltd* [1981] QB 864, at 871, *per* Brandon LJ.

[169] *Brandeis Goldschmidt & Co Ltd v Western Transport Ltd* [1981] QB 864, at 873, *per* Brandon LJ.

[170] *Borders (UK) Ltd v Metropolitan Police Commissioner* [2005] EWCA Civ 197.

goods, the following relief may be given, as far as is appropriate:[171] (1) an order for delivery and for payment of any consequential damages;[172] (2) an order for delivery of the goods, but giving the defendant the alternative of paying damages by reference to the value of the goods, together in either alternative with payment of any consequential damages;[173] or (3) damages.[174]

If it is shown to the court's satisfaction that an order for delivery and payment of any consequential damages has not been complied with, the court may revoke the order (or the relevant part of it)[175] and make an order for payment of damages by reference to the value of the goods.[176] Where an order is made for delivery but giving the defendant the alternative of paying damages,[177] the defendant may satisfy the order by returning the goods at any time before execution of judgment, but without prejudice to liability to pay any consequential damages.[178] Where goods are not detained – for example, where they have been destroyed – the normal form of judgment is for damages.

SECTION 3   TRESPASS TO GOODS

This tort protects several interests. First, like conversion (which is more commonly invoked), this tort also protects the claimant's interest in the possession of his goods. Secondly, trespass protects his interest in the physical condition of the goods and, thirdly, it protects the inviolability of the goods, so that meddling with the goods, such as wrongful wheel clamping, for example, will constitute trespass to goods.[179]

---

[171] Torts (Interference with Goods) Act 1977, s 3(1). See *Secretary of State for Defence v Guardian Newspapers Ltd* [1985] AC 339.

[172] Torts (Interference with Goods) Act 1977, s 3(2)(a). Cf *Howard E Perry & Co Ltd v British Railways Board* [1980] 2 All ER 579.

[173] Torts (Interference with Goods) Act 1977, s 3(2)(b). For principles governing the application of s 3(2)(b) orders see *IBL Ltd v Coussens* [1991] 2 All ER 133. Cf *Howard E Perry & Co Ltd v British Railways Board* [1980] 2 All ER 579.   [174] Torts (Interference with Goods) Act 1977, s 3(2)(c).

[175] Torts (Interference with Goods) Act 1977, s 3(4)(a).

[176] Torts (Interference with Goods) Act 1977, s 3(4)(b).

[177] That is, under the Torts (Interference with Goods) Act 1977, s 3(2)(b). An order for delivery of the goods under s 3(2)(a) or 3(2)(b) of the Act may impose such conditions as may be determined by the court, or pursuant to rules of court and, in particular, where damages by reference to the value of the goods would not be the whole of the value of the goods, C may be required to make an allowance to reflect the difference: s 3(2)(b). For example, a bailor's action against the bailee may be one in which the measure of damages is not the full value of the goods. Then, the court may order delivery of the goods, but require the bailor to pay the bailee a sum reflecting the difference. Where an allowance is to be made under s 6(1) or 6(2) of the Act in respect of an improvement of the goods, and an order is made under s 3(2)(a) or 3(2)(b), the court may assess the allowance to be made in respect of the improvement and by the order require, as a condition for delivery of the goods, that allowance be made by C.   [178] Torts (Interference with Goods) Act 1977, s 3(5).

[179] *Vine v Waltham Forest LBC* [2000] 1 WLR 2383 (absence of consent to the *risk* of wheel clamping made the clamping in this case wrongful and thus a trespass). Cf *Arthur v Anker* [1997] QB 564 (C knew of risk of clamping when the car was parked in a private car park with clear signs warning of this prospect: no conversion).

(A) FORMS OF TRESPASS

Trespass takes various forms. Taking goods out of the possession of another,[180] moving them from one place to another,[181] or even bringing one's person into contact with them,[182] or directing a missile at them[183] have all been held to be trespasses.

(B) CHARACTER OF THE DEFENDANT'S ACT

There cannot be a trespass if the interference is indirect.[184] Thus, to lock the room in which the claimant has his goods is not a trespass to them.[185] Although he who mixes a drug with the feed of a racehorse commits a trespass to the feed, he does not commit a trespass to the racehorse when it is later given the feed.[186] Nor is it clear whether it is trespass to cause the goods of a claimant to come into harmful contact with some other object; for example, to drive sheep over the edge of a cliff into the sea.[187] It is, however, trespass to goods to wheel-clamp unlawfully,[188] cut and take away trees,[189] beat a dog[190] or shoot racing pigeons[191] (whether the goods were capable of being stolen is irrelevant[192]).

A *dictum* of Lord Blanesburgh in *Leitch & Co Ltd v Leydon*[193] is often cited to support the view that trespass to goods is always actionable *per se*. But technically the matter was left undecided in that case. Some, on the other hand, state that there is clear authority for the proposition that trespass is actionable *per se*, but only where there is a dispossession of the claimant. Yet in *Kirk v Gregory*[194] a woman who moved rings belonging to a man who had just died from one room in his house to another was held liable in nominal damages for this. This case has been treated as consistent with this latter view, but an asportation (that is, a moving of the goods) is not necessarily a dispossession.[195] If in gently reversing my car I touch the bumper of another car, the brake of which has not been applied, and, without damaging it, cause it to move a few inches, I have not dispossessed the owner, though I have asported it. On the other hand, there are good reasons for making all trespasses to goods actionable *per se*, and this

---

[180] *Brewer v Dew* (1843) 11 M & W 625.

[181] *Kirk v Gregory* (1876) 1 Ex D 55; *Fouldes v Willoughby* (1841) 8 M & W 540, at 544–5, *per* Lord Abinger.

[182] *Fouldes v Willoughby* (1841) 8 M & W 540, at 549, *per* Alderson B (*obiter*): 'Scratching the panel of a carriage would be a trespass'. [183] *Hamps v Darby* [1948] 2 KB 311.

[184] *Covell v Laming* (1808) 1 Camp 497. [185] *Hartley v Moxham* (1842) 3 QB 701.

[186] *Hutchins v Maughan* [1947] VLR 131.

[187] It is not trespass merely because one's animal inflicts direct injury on goods: see *Manton v Brocklebank* [1923] 2 KB 212 (especially at 229, *per* Atkin LJ).

[188] *Vine v Waltham Forest London Borough Council* [2000] 1 WLR 2383. It is unlawful to clamp without a licence: see the Private Security Industry Act 2001, s 3(2)(j).

[189] *Heydon v Smith* (1610) 2 Brownl 328. [190] *Wright v Ramscot* (1667) 1 Saund 84.

[191] *Hamps v Darby* [1948] 2 KB 311. [192] [1948] 2 KB 311, at 322, *per* Evershed LJ.

[193] [1931] AC 90, at 106. [194] (1876) 1 Ex D 55.

[195] Cf *Burroughes v Bayne* (1860) 5 H & N 296, at 305–6, *per* Channell B.

approach is consistent with the authorities as well as the general principle in the trespass torts. Otherwise the law would leave remediless the perhaps not oversensitive person who declined to wear her Armani blouse again after her flatmate had 'borrowed' it to wear to a party. Perhaps the correct question, in concert with other trespasses, is whether the relevant touching was beyond what is acceptable in everyday life.[196] Picking up and admiring a friend's Armani blouse (worth £300) may not be so objectionable as wearing it without her permission.

(c) DEFENDANT'S STATE OF MIND

The problem of whether there is liability for trespasses which are neither intentional nor negligent has been examined in chapter 8. The same approach is taken in this context so that there is no liability in respect of an act that is neither intentional nor negligent.[197] There is, then, no liability for an accidental trespass to goods.[198] But, if the defendant intended to interfere, his trespass is intentional even though he did not know that his act amounted to a trespass (for example, if he believed the goods to be his own).

(d) THE INTEREST OF THE CLAIMANT

The claimant must be in possession of the goods at the time of the interference. Possession connotes both the power (*factum*) of exercising physical control and the intention (*animus*) to exercise such control on his own behalf. Whether the claimant is the owner is immaterial. So, if A intends to catch a butterfly, which is in his garden, and before he can do so it flies over to the highway where B catches it, A has no possession – there is *animus* but not *factum*. Lord Esher has said that '[t]he [claimant] in an action of trespass must at the time of the trespass have the present possession of the goods, either actual or constructive, or a legal right to the immediate possession'.[199] Thus, a cyclist leaving his cycle outside a shop remains in possession of it but, if a thief rides away on it, the thief then has possession although he obtained it wrongfully.[200]

Therefore, if A took B's gun and handed it to C, B could not sue the claimant in trespass (unless he showed that the claimant authorized or ratified A's act), because B would have had no possession at the time when the claimant received possession

---

[196] Cf trespass to the person: *F v West Berkshire Health Authority* [1989] 2 All ER 545.

[197] *National Coal Board v J E Evans & Co (Cardiff) Ltd* [1951] 2 KB 861. Although the *ratio* is probably that the injury was caused by C's conduct (see especially *per* Cohen LJ, at 875), all three judges gave considered judgments to the effect that there was no liability for accidental trespass to goods.

[198] In *Manton v Brocklebank* [1923] 2 KB 212, at 229, Atkin LJ held that 'whether a horse directly injures goods, or a dog accomplishes an "asportavit" of a golf ball, he does not involve his owner in liability for trespass to goods, at any rate unless the owner has intentionally caused the act complained of'.

[199] *Johnson v Diprose* [1893] 1 QB 512, at 515.

[200] *Costello v Chief Constable of Derbyshire Constabulary* [2001] 1 WLR 1437 (confirms that a thief may sue; thus the police who detain a stolen car are liable to C (not actually the thief) when they are unable to identify the real owner).

from A.[201] If a lodger holds goods on sale or return from a shopkeeper, and those goods are seized in pursuance of a lawful execution on the landlord's goods, this is trespass to the lodger.[202] And if X and Y both claim the right to goods which neither has previously possessed, and in a scuffle for them X snatches them from Y's hand, Y has no possession upon which to found a suit in trespass.[203] Any bailee, even a gratuitous one,[204] can sue in trespass. The Crown could therefore sue in respect of the loss of Post Office mail.[205] Where a landlord demised land to the claimant for 21 years, with liberty to dig a half acre of brick-earth annually, and to dig in excess of that at an agreed price, the claimant could sue a third party who took away brick-earth from the land.[206] A bailor does not have possession and therefore cannot ordinarily sue in trespass for an act done to the goods bailed.[207] If, however, the bailor has an immediate right to possession as in the case of a bailment at will – for example, where a young man had lent his car to his girl-friend while he was on holiday[208] – he may then sue.[209]

Want of possession precluded success in an action brought by the assignees of a bankrupt against a sheriff who seized goods when unaware of a secret act of bankruptcy by the bankrupt.[210] For the same reason a telephone subscriber would have no action if the police tapped his telephone line. But there are three apparent exceptions to the rule that possession is essential.

(1) In *White v Morris*[211] it was held that, where goods were assigned as security for a loan upon trust to permit the assignor to remain in possession until default in repayment, the assignee could sue in trespass while the goods were still in the assignor's possession. It may be assumed, despite lack of authority for such a general proposition, that all trustees may sue for trespass to goods in the hands of the beneficiary on the basis that they share possession with him.[212]

(2) The title of executors or administrators relates back to the death of the deceased, and this entitles them to sue for a trespass between the date of the death and the date of the grant.[213]

(3) The owner of a franchise in wrecks has been deemed to have constructive possession of a wreck so as to enable him to sue in trespass a person who seized a cask of whisky before he could do so.[214]

---

[201] *Wilson v Barker* (1833) 4 B & Ad 614. Cf *Badkin v Powell* (1776) 2 Cowp 476. See also *Wilson v Lombank Ltd* [1963] 1 All ER 740.

[202] *Colwill v Reeves* (1811) 2 Camp 575. Cf Lord Ellenborough (at 576, *obiter*): 'If a man puts corn into my bag ... because it is impossible to distinguish what was mine from what was his'.

[203] *Peachey v Wing* (1826) 5 LJOSKB 55. [204] *Rooth v Wilson* (1817) 1 B & Ald 59.

[205] *The Winkfield* [1902] P 42. [206] *Attersoll v Stevens* (1808) 1 Taunt 183.

[207] *Gordon v Harper* (1796) 7 Term Rep 9; *Ward v Macauley* (1791) 4 Term Rep 489 Cf *United States of America and Republic of France v Dollfus Mieg et Cie SA* [1952] AC 582, at 611, *per* Lord Porter.

[208] *O' Sullivan v Williams* [1992] 3 All ER 385.

[209] *Lotan v Cross* (1810) 2 Camp 464; *Penfolds Wines Pty Ltd v Elliott* (1946) 74 CLR 204, at 226–8, *per* Dixon J.

[210] *Balme v Hutton* (1833) 9 Bing 471. See also *Taylor v Rowan* (1835) 7 C & P 70. Cf *Wennhak v Morgan* (1888) 20 QBD 635. [211] (1852) 11 CB 1015.

[212] See *Barker v Furlong* [1891] 2 Ch 172 (conversion). [213] *Tharpe v Stallwood* (1843) 5 Man & G 760.

[214] *Dunwich Corpn v Sterry* (1831) 1 B & Ad 831.

'Trespass to goods' is expressly included in the definition of a 'wrongful interference with goods' within the Torts (Interference with Goods) Act 1977.[215] Thus, by virtue of the Act's application, the defence of *jus tertii* is no longer available,[216] and the statutory rules regarding co-ownership apply, as do all forms of relief provided by that Act in appropriate cases.[217]

(E) DAMAGES

(1) MEASURE

Where the claimant has been deprived of the goods, he is entitled to their value by way of damages. This rule applies to suits by bailees against third parties, but when the assignee under a bill of sale wrongfully seized from the assignor goods comprised in the bill, the damages awarded to the assignor were limited to the value of his interest in them.[218] A claimant may recover general damages for loss of use of goods (as distinct from special damages for loss of profits from the goods) although he would not have been using them during the period within which he has been deprived of their use.[219] The provisions of the Torts (Interference with Goods) Act 1977, considered earlier, apply equally in this context.

(2) TRESPASS *AB INITIO*

Where any person having by authority of law[220] entered on land or seized goods, or arrested a person, subsequently commits a trespass, his original act will in certain circumstances be deemed itself to be a trespass.[221] The doctrine has little practical relevance today. Its importance is mainly limited to the fact that, presumably, damages may be assessed on the basis that the entire conduct of the defendant, and not merely his subsequent wrongful act, is tortious.[222]

SECTION 4 RESIDUAL TORTS

There are many circumstances where the violation of interests in goods is not protected by trespass, conversion or even the tort of negligence. The action analogous to the old action on the case has generally proved fruitful in filling these gaps. What follows,

---

[215] Torts (Interference with Goods) Act 1977, s 1(b).

[216] Torts (Interference with Goods) Act 1977, s 8(1). Section 11(1) excludes contributory negligence as a defence in proceedings based on intentional trespass.

[217] Torts (Interference with Goods) Act 1977, s 10(1).   [218] *Brierly v Kendall* (1852) 17 QB 937.

[219] *The Mediana* [1900] AC 113, at 117–8, *per* Earl of Halsbury LC.

[220] Authority of law is distinct from permission of another – eg, it covers one who enters an inn, but not the buyer of a ticket for a seat at a theatre.

[221] The Distress for Rent Act 1737, s 19, abolished this rule in the case of distress for rent.

[222] *Shorland v Govett* (1826) 5 B & C 485.

therefore, is to be treated as merely illustrative of this wider right of action, and not as an exhaustive account of the circumstances in which it may be held available in the future. These torts, too, are forms of 'wrongful interference with goods' so that, where relevant, the provisions of the Torts (Interference with Goods) Act 1977 apply.

Trespass and conversion are especially restrictive in that they are not available to a claimant who neither possesses nor has an immediate right to possess the goods. Yet the case of *Mears v London and South Western Rly Co*[223] has firmly established that if goods are destroyed or damaged, the owner may sue without having possession or an immediate right to possess. The rule benefits, for example, a bailor, a purchaser where the vendor has a lien for unpaid purchase money, and a mortgagee. He must prove damage to his interest; taking the goods from the possessor without affecting title is insufficient. Presumably, the act complained of must be wrongful in the sense that it is one which, had the claimant had possession of the chattel (or the immediate right to it), it would have grounded a suit in trespass, or conversion. So, where the employer of the claimant, a conductor on a public transport vehicle, endorsed on the claimant's licence (which was in the employer's possession) the words 'discharged for being 1s 4d short' he was liable in case for defacing it.[224]

Credit agreements also present interesting problems in this respect. If a car which is the subject of a credit agreement is seriously damaged, can the owner sue in case? If the hirer exercises his option to buy, what does the owner lose? And, yet, if (as is likely in such an event) the hirer does not exercise his option, the owner would be left without an effective remedy other than in case. It seems, therefore, that, until the hirer opts, the owner is to be regarded as the reversioner and entitled to sue.

It will be recalled, too, that a bailee disregarding the terms of his bailment may sometimes be liable in case, though not in conversion, and that to deny the claimant access to his goods or to interfere with his freedom of using them is also actionable on the case. Further, to place baited traps on one's land near the highway so as to attract dogs into the traps, and in consequence of which dogs are so trapped, is a tort in this category.[225]

FURTHER READING

Curwen, 'Title to Sue in Conversion' [2004] *Conveyancer* 308

Milsom, 'Not Doing is No Trespass' [1954] CLJ 105

Palmer, 'The Application of the Torts (Interference with Goods) Act 1977 to Actions in Bailment' (1978) 41 MLR 629

Simpson, 'The Introduction of the Action on the Case for Conversion' (1959) 75 LQR 364

Tettenborn, 'Conversion, Tort and Restitution' in Palmer and McKendrick (eds), *Interests in Goods* (1998)

Tettenborn, 'Damages in Conversion: The Exception or the Anomaly?' [1993] CLJ 128

---

[223] (1862) 11 CBNS 850.
[224] *Rogers v Macnamara* (1853) 14 CB 27. Cf *Hurrell v Ellis* (1845) 2 CB 295 (C recovered damages for loss of employment where an action for libel did not lie).　　　[225] *Townsend v Wathen* (1808) 9 East 277.

10

TRESPASS TO LAND

SECTION 1 TRESPASS

This tort protects the interest of the claimant in having his land free from the unjustified physical intrusion of another. Because of this emphasis on physical interference with possession, it follows that it is not the function of the tort to protect ownership as such. Nonetheless, the purpose of many lawsuits in trespass is not the recovery of damages but rather the settlement of disputed rights over land, and a judgment may be backed by the sanction of an injunction if the action succeeds. Furthermore, the use of this action in tort as a means of resolving disputes over title has been facilitated by the rule that trespass is actionable *per se*.[1]

(A) TYPES OF ACT THAT CONSTITUTE TRESPASS

As with all forms of trespass, there must be directness. As such, a claimant landowner who complains that the defendant has erected a spout to drain away water from the eaves of the house of the defendant, as a result of which water has dripped on to the claimant's adjoining land, can sue only in nuisance, not in trespass because of the indirectness of the invasion.[2] The difficulty with drawing the line between 'direct' and 'indirect' invasions is illustrated by two cases. In *Gregory v Piper*[3] it was held to be trespass where rubbish that was placed near the claimant's land, on drying, rolled on to it because of natural forces. By contrast, in *British Waterways Board v Severn Trent Water Ltd*[4] it was made clear that an action may only be brought by the riparian right owner in respect of the direct fouling of a river or other watercourse, but that an action would not lie in respect of the fouling of adjoining land.

---

[1] *Bush v Smith* (1953) 162 *Estates Gazette* 430. The growing awareness of the scope of the declaratory judgment could lead to a declining use of trespass for this purpose: see *Loudon v Ryder (No 2)* [1953] Ch 423; *Acton Corpn v Morris* [1953] 2 All ER 932 (D locked the door of his house, thereby denying C access to his upper flat. Though the court doubted whether this was trespass, it held that C could have a declaration of his right of access.) The action for recovery of land is also important in this connection: see Section 2(C) below. Where C does not mention trespass to land in his pleadings, he is not restricted to the alternative claim for breach of contract; he may still claim exemplary damages for the trespass: *Drane v Evangelou* [1978] 2 All ER 437.

[2] *Reynolds v Clark* (1725) 2 Ld Raym 1399. Cf *Lemmon v Webb* [1894] 3 Ch 1, at 24, *per* Kay LJ: the encroachment of boughs and roots of trees is not trespass, but a nuisance. [3] (1829) 9 B & C 591.

[4] [2002] Ch 25. This decision is more in line with existing authority such as the decision of Denning LJ in *Southport Corpn v Esso Petroleum Co Ltd* [1954] 2 QB 182, at 195–6 (supported by Lords Radcliffe and

Directly causing some foreign matter[5] to enter or come into physical contact with the land of the claimant is a trespass. Thus, firing a gun into the claimant's soil,[6] or placing a ladder against his wall,[7] or driving nails into it,[8] or encouraging a dog to run onto his land,[9] or removing his doors and windows,[10] or throwing a person onto his land,[11] are all trespasses. But in all cases the intrusion onto the claimant's land must result from some act or omission on the part of the defendant, or persons for whom he is responsible.

Simply to enter another's land is a trespass.[12] But such an entry may be an assertion of title, in which case an action in trespass will, in effect, determine who has title.[13] To remain on the land after a trespassory entry thereon is in itself also a trespass: a 'continuing trespass', as it is commonly called. Similarly, if A places goods on B's land and is successfully sued by B in trespass for this act, he is also liable to further actions in trespass for the continued presence of the goods on the land if he fails thereafter to remove them.[14] If, on the other hand, he merely commits an act such as digging a hole, or removing goods – that is, if he does not wrongfully allow anything to remain on the land – the fact that the harm thus occasioned continues is not enough to make it a continuing trespass; damages can be recovered only once for such a trespass.[15] In short, there is a continuing trespass only when that which continued after the first action is itself a trespass.

Tucker: see [1956] AC 218, at 242 and 244 respectively) where discharge of oil from a ship, which, when carried by tide on to C's foreshore, was held not to constitute a trespass, because it involved consequential, not direct, damage.

[5] Perhaps anything having size or mass, including gases, flames, beams from searchlights and mirrors, but not vibrations.   [6] *Pickering v Rudd* (1815) 4 Camp 219, at 220, *per* Lord Ellenborough.

[7] *Westripp v Baldock* [1938] 2 All ER 779; affd [1939] 1 All ER 279.

[8] *Simpson v Weber* (1925) 133 LT 46.

[9] *Beckwith v Shordike* (1767) 4 Burr 2092. But note *League Against Cruel Sports Ltd v Scott* [1986] QB 240 where it was held that the intrusion of D's hounds onto C's land does not necessarily constitute a trespass by D: C must prove that D either intended the hounds to enter C's land, or that D negligently failed to exercise suitable control over the hounds.

[10] *Lavender v Betts* [1942] 2 All ER 72. But this does not apply to D turning off the gas and electricity at the meter in his cellar, for the purpose of evicting the tenant of rooms on an upper floor, because the consequence is indirect: *Perera v Vandiyar* [1953] 1 All ER 1109. This is now a criminal offence under s 1 of the Protection from Eviction Act 1977; but no action for breach of statutory duty lies: *McCall v Abelesz* [1976] QB 585.

[11] *Smith v Stone* (1647) Sty 65.

[12] A squatter – ie, 'one who, without any colour of right, enters on an unoccupied house or land, intending to stay there as long as he can' – is a trespasser: *McPhail v Persons (Names Unknown)* [1973] Ch 447, at 456, *per* Lord Denning MR. But as to a squatter's ability to dispossess the true paper title owner of his right of possession by acting inconsistently with it for a fixed period of time, without ever himself having any intention of acquiring legal title, see *J A Pye (Oxford) Ltd v Graham* [2003] 1 AC 419; Limitation Act 1980, s 17 (*re.* unregistered land) and Land Registration Act 2002, s 98 (*re.* registered land).

[13] If D has not entered, it will normally be impossible to use an action in trespass as a means of settling a dispute in title.

[14] *Holmes v Wilson* (1839) 10 Ad & El 503. If C seeks an injunction, the court has a discretion to award damages *in lieu* of such injunction which also take into account the likely future damage. This, in effect, settles the price which D must pay for the right to commit the trespass in the future, and no subsequent action will lie in respect thereof: *Leeds Industrial Co-operative Society v Slack* [1924] AC 851. Nevertheless, the landowner is *prima facie* entitled to his injunction even where the acts complained of cause no harm: see *Patel v WH Smith (Eziot) Ltd* [1987] 1 WLR 853; *Harrow London Borough Council v Donohue* [1993] NPC 49.

[15] *Clegg v Dearden* (1848) 12 QB 576.

A person who is on land with the permission of the possessor has been held a trespasser if he remains there for an unreasonable time after the termination of that permission.[16] Also:

[w]hen a householder lives in a dwelling-house to which there is a garden in front and does not lock the gate of the garden, it gives an implied licence to any member of the public who has lawful reason for doing so to proceed from the gate to the front door or back door, and to inquire whether he may be admitted and to conduct his lawful business.[17]

If the licence is withdrawn, he is also not a trespasser during the reasonable time which he takes to leave the premises.[18] There is also the additional reasoning here that trespass is a wrong against possession. Thus, since the termination of the tenancy does not coincide exactly with the claimant assuming possession, it follows that a time lag will almost always exist before an action can be brought. But where the claimant has acquired possession and the trespass continues, a lawsuit may be brought. *Konskier v B Goodman Ltd*[19] is illustrative.

D, a builder had permission from the possessor of a building to leave rubbish there while demolishing part of it. During the currency of this licence, C became tenant of the building and was held entitled to recover in trespass from the builder when the latter did not remove the rubbish after the expiry of the licence.

If a tenant, with the consent of the landlord, stays on at the expiration of his term, so that he thereby becomes a tenant, either from year to year or at will, his remaining there is not an act of trespass so long as the tenancy has not been properly determined.[20] If however, he is a mere tenant at sufferance (thus remaining without the permission of the landlord) the landlord may enter and demand possession and sue in trespass.[21]

Finally, *Watson v Murray & Co* provides an illustration (if not an extension[22]) of the types of acts that may constitute trespass to land.[23]

Ds, who were sheriff's officers, seized goods in C's shop under writs of execution. It was held that each of the following acts amounted to trespass: locking C's premises so as to exclude her therefrom when they had lotted the goods for the purpose of a sale; opening her premises for a public viewing of the goods; affixing posters on her premises.

---

[16] *Minister of Health v Bellotti* [1944] KB 298. Cf the conflicting *obiter dicta* of Lord Ellenborough and Bayley J in *Winterbourne v Morgan* (1809) 11 East 395, at 402 and 405 respectively.

[17] *Robson v Hallett* [1967] 2 QB 939 at 953–4, *per* Diplock LJ. In *Brunner v Williams* (1975) 73 LGR 266, a weights and measures inspector was held to have no implied licence to enter C's garden to see whether a coal dealer was infringing the Weights and Measures Act 1963; all he may do is go to C's door and ask permission.

[18] *Robson v Hallett* [1967] 2 QB 939, at 953–4, *per* Diplock LJ.

[19] [1928] 1 KB 421. Presumably, D's successor in title to the chattels would also be liable in trespass for knowingly allowing them to remain on C's land.

[20] *Dougal v McCarthy* [1893] 1 QB 736, at 739–40, *per* Lord Esher; *Meye v Electric Transmission Ltd* [1942] Ch 290.

[21] If the deceased tenant's widow remains there after his death she, too, can be sued in trespass: *Thompson v Earthy* [1951] 2 KB 596.

[22] Were all the acts here held to be trespasses sufficiently direct? See *Acton Corpn v Morris* [1953] 2 All ER 932 (not cited in the present case).   [23] [1955] 2 QB 1.

(B) WHAT MAY CONSTITUTE THE SUBJECT MATTER OF AN ACTION?

The tort is trespass to land. Obviously, then, merely walking on the surface of the claimant's land is enough to constitute the tort of trespass. Anything attached to the soil, and capable of being separately possessed, may also be the subject matter of trespass such as grass[24] or crops,[25] or a *profit à prendre* (for example, a fishery).[26]

Possession of land may be separated horizontally, as it were, so that, for instance, A may possess the pasturage, B the surface and subsoil, and C the minerals underneath. Each of them may sue if the subject matter of his possession is invaded. Highway authorities, for example, often have the surface of streets vested in them by statute. As such, it is those authorities (and not the owners of the subjacent or adjoining land[27]) that may sue for surface trespasses, such as breaking up the street,[28] or erecting structures on the highway.[29] Yet a highway is subject to a public right of way. Thus, if a person uses a highway for purposes other than those 'reasonably incident to its user'[30] as a highway (which may include a peaceful demonstration[31]), his act is a trespass. The purpose need not be unlawful in itself. Interrupting a shoot[32] and obtaining information on the speed and performance of racehorses on the adjoining land of the owner of the highway soil,[33] have both been held to be trespasses.

It may be trespass to tunnel beneath the surface of land, to mine there, to use a cave beneath it or to drive building foundations through the soil. In the absence of specific provision to the contrary, the owner of the surface is presumed to own that which is underground. It is also trespass to invade that portion of the airspace which is necessary for the ordinary use of the land and the structures upon it.[34] However, an aircraft does not infringe any of the claimant's rights to airspace by being flown over his land for the purpose of photographing it.[35]

---

[24] *Richards v Davies* [1921] 1 Ch 90, at 94–5, *per* Lawrence J.

[25] *Wellaway v Courtier* [1918] 1 KB 200; *Monsanto v Tilly* [2000] Env LR 313.

[26] Cf *Hill v Tupper* (1863) 2 H & C 121, at 127, *per* Pollock CB; *Mason v Clarke* [1955] AC 778 (right to take rabbits). The principle does not, however, extend to an easement: see *Paine & Co v St Neots Gas and Coke Co* [1939] 3 All ER 812.

[27] In *Hubbard v Pitt* [1976] QB 142 Lord Denning held that where the surface of a pavement was vested in the local highway authority the adjoining owner could not sue for trespass to the pavement.

[28] *Hyde Corpn v Oldham, Ashton and Hyde Electric Tramway Ltd* (1900) 64 JP 596.

[29] *Sewai Jaipur v Arjun Lal* [1937] 4 All ER 5. See also *Tunbridge Wells Corpn v Baird* [1896] AC 434; *Cox v Glue* (1848) 5 CB 533.

[30] *Liddle v Yorkshire (North Riding) County Council* [1934] 2 KB 101, at 127, *per* Slesser LJ.

[31] *DPP v Jones* [1999] 2 AC 240, at 256, *per* Lord Irvine LC: 'the law should not make unlawful what is commonplace and well accepted'.   [32] *Harrison v Duke of Rutland* [1893] 1 QB 142.

[33] *Hickman v Maisey* [1900] 1 QB 752. Cf *Randall v Tarrant* [1955] 1 All ER 600 (a motorist who parked his car on the highway and then trespassed on the adjoining field was held not to be a trespasser on the highway).

[34] *Kelsen v Imperial Tobacco Co of Great Britain and Ireland Ltd* [1957] 2 QB 334 (D's advertising sign projecting into airspace above C's shop was held to be a trespass); *Anchor Brewhouse Developments v Berkley House Docklands Developments Ltd* (1987) 284 *Estates Gazette* 625 (a crane passing over land without permission was a trespass).   [35] *Baron Bernstein of Leigh v Skyviews and General Ltd* [1978] QB 479.

Apart from the position at common law, the Civil Aviation Act 1982 provides that, with the exception of aircraft belonging to, or exclusively employed in, the service of Her Majesty,[36] no action shall lie in respect of trespass or nuisance by reason only of the flight of an aircraft over any property at a height above the ground, which, having regard to weather and other circumstances of the case, is reasonable.[37] Subject to the same exception, the owner of an aircraft is liable for all material loss or damage to persons or property caused by that aircraft, whether in flight, taking off[38] or landing, or by a person in it or articles falling from it, without proof of negligence or intention or other cause of action.[39]

(C) DEFENDANT'S STATE OF MIND

The leading case on what is required by way of the trespasser's intention is the decision of the House of Lords in *JA Pye (Oxford) Ltd v Graham*.[40]

Cs had once had an agreement with Ds whereby Ds acquired grazing rights over a portion of Cs' land. Although the agreement came to an end in 1993, Ds continued to use the land exactly as they had done under the agreement for about the next 15 years. Despite Ds' repeated requests, Cs refused to renew the agreement. In 1999, Cs brought possession proceedings against Ds arguing that so long as Ds expressed the hope that the agreement would be renewed, Ds could not have formed the requisite intention to dispossess Cs.

Lord Browne-Wilkinson indicated that possession requires two elements: factual possession *plus* the intention to possess. In relation to the critical second element he approved[41] the *dictum* of Slade J in *Powell v McFarlane* that there must be an intention 'to exclude the world at large, including the owner with the paper title if he be not himself the possessor, so far as is reasonably practicable and so far as the processes of the law will allow'.[42]

Mistake, as such, is no defence in trespass. It will not avail the defendant that he innocently thought that he was on his own land.[43] On the other hand, there is no liability if the entry was totally involuntary. Thus, for example, a person who is carried onto the land of the claimant by a third party is not liable in trespass.[44] Also, notwithstanding the decision in *Letang v Cooper*,[45] it must be assumed for the time

---

[36] Civil Aviation Act 1982, ss 49(3) & 76(1).

[37] Civil Aviation Act 1982, s 76(1). The section applies to all flights which are at a reasonable height and comply with statutory requirements. But the ordinary liabilities in trespass or nuisance would arise for any other wrongful activity carried on by or from the aircraft, such as deliberate emission of vast quantities of smoke that polluted C's land: *Baron Bernstein of Leigh v Skyviews and General Ltd* [1978] QB 479, at 489, *per* Griffiths J.

[38] The ordinary common law applies to accidents caused by the aircraft, while taxiing to the take-off point: *Blankley v Godley* [1952] 1 All ER 436.   [39] Civil Aviation Act 1982, s 76(2).

[40] [2003] 1 AC 419.   [41] [2003] 1 AC 419, at [42].

[42] (1979) 38 P & CR 452.

[43] *Basely v Clarkson* (1681) 3 Lev 37; *Nelson v Nicholson* (2001) *Independent*, 22 January.

[44] *Smith v Stone* (1647) Sty 65. But note that entering the land of others pursuant to threats is no defence for such an entry will be regarded as having been voluntary: *Gilbert v Stone* (1647) Style 72.

[45] [1965] 1 QB 232. For discussion see ch 8.

being that a negligent unintentional act of trespass is enough.[46] Thus, if A intentionally throws a stone on to C's land and, as he should have foreseen, it ricochets on to B's land, this is probably trespass to B's land as well as C's.

(D) WHO MAY SUE?

It is generally said that it is possession of the land that entitles a claimant to sue in trespass. Thus, if the claimant has a legal estate and exclusive possession he may sue in trespass. But at the same time, the tenant (not the landlord) can sue if a third party trespasses on the land demised;[47] the owner of an equitable interest with possession can sue;[48] and a statutory possession will also found a trespass action.[49]

The Court of Appeal has held that 'a person may have such a right of exclusive possession of property as will entitle him to bring an action for trespass against the owner of that property but which confers no interest whatever in the land'.[50] Those whose interests fall short of those of a lessee may also be able to sue in trespass if in fact they have exclusive occupation. Thus, whether a lodger can sue in trespass would depend on whether, on the facts, he had exclusive occupation – in other words, it would be relevant whether he had an outdoor key and whether he could bar access to the rooms.[51]

In *National Provincial Bank Ltd v Ainsworth*[52] the House of Lords unanimously held that a deserted wife at that time had only a personal, but no proprietary, interest in the matrimonial home. Nonetheless, Lord Upjohn held that as she had exclusive

---

[46] Certainly in *League Against Cruel Sports Ltd v Scott* [1986] QB 240 Park J expressed the view that liability in trespass could ensue from the negligent failure of D to control hounds properly so that they enter C's land.

[47] *Cooper v Crabtree* (1882) 20 Ch D 589. C with an *Interesse termini* could not sue if he never took possession: *Wallis v Hands* [1893] 2 Ch 75.

[48] *Mason v Clarke* [1955] AC 778. Another example is *Loudon v Ryder* [1953] 2 QB 202, where C was entitled to the premises under a declaration of trust merely and yet recovered damages for trespass to the land. A beneficiary under a trust for sale may also sue: *Bull v Bull* [1955] 1 All ER 253, at 255, *per* Denning LJ (*obiter*).

[49] *Cruise v Terrell* [1922] 1 KB 664; *Lewisham Borough Council v Maloney* [1948] 1 KB 50. Whether the landlord of a tenant at will can sue third parties in trespass is undecided: *Attersoll v Stevens* (1808) 1 Taunt 183, cf *Shrewsbury's (Countess) Case* (1600) 5 Co Rep 13b.

[50] *Marcroft Wagons Ltd v Smith* [1951] 2 KB 496, at 501, *per* Evershed MR. *Brown v Brash and Ambrose* [1948] 2 KB 247 and *Thompson v Ward* [1953] 2 QB 153 show that a statutory tenant who leaves his premises even for a period of five to ten years with the intention of eventually returning there has the right to sue in trespass. It is sufficient, eg, if he installs someone as licensee yet signals his intention to return by, say, leaving furniture there.

[51] *Lane v Dixon* (1847) 3 CB 776; *Monks v Dykes* (1839) 4 M & W 567; *Helman v Horsham and Worthing Assessment Committee* [1949] 2 KB 335, at 347, *per* Evershed LJ; *R v St George's Union* (1871) LR 7 QB 90. Similarly, a claimant who could not rely on possession under his lease from the Crown because it was void for non-compliance with a statute was held to have 'actual possession . . . sufficient to entitle the party possessing it to maintain trespass against persons who have no title at all, and are mere wrongdoers': *Harper v Charlesworth* (1825) 4 B & C 574, at 591, *per* Bayley J. The House of Lords in *Street v Mountford* [1985] AC 809 held that where the intention evidenced by the agreement between the parties was to grant exclusive possession for a period of time and at a rent, there will normally be found to be a tenancy in any case.   [52] [1965] AC 1175.

occupation she could therefore bring proceedings against trespassers. In *Hill v Tupper*[53] the facts were as follows.

X Co leased to C certain land, which adjoined X Co's canal. C was also given 'the sole and exclusive rights' to rent out pleasure boats for use on the canal. Subsequently, D set up a rival concern, whereupon he was sued in trespass by C. C conceded that X Co could sue D in trespass, but at the same time C argued that he could also sue.

Since the claimant's concession was tantamount to an admission that he did not have exclusive occupation, the court dismissed the action. It did however add that if a claimant could show that his interest amounted to a new species of property right he would be able to succeed, subject to the caveat that it was not the policy of the law to allow the courts to create new rights in land. However, in *Manchester Airport plc v Dutton* a licensee who had not yet entered into occupation was entitled to eject trespassers who had set up a protest camp. As Laws LJ explained in that case: 'a licensee not in occupation may claim possession against a trespasser if that is a necessary remedy to vindicate and give effect to such rights of occupation as by contract with his licensor he enjoys'.[54] On the other hand, it was made clear that an action for damages would not have been available on those facts. The action was limited to exercising a superior right in the land in order to gain possession.

It is generally no defence to a trespasser that the claimant's possession of the land is unlawful. The simple fact of possession is normally enough.[55] But as against the true owner, the rule is different. In *Delaney v TP Smith Ltd*[56] the claimant entered property held under a lease that was unenforceable because it did not comply with the requirements of section 40 of the Law of Property Act 1925 relating to a memorandum in writing. As such, he was unable to sue his landlord in trespass for ejecting him. Two extracts from earlier cases that were cited in that case are important here:

A mere trespasser cannot, by the very act of trespass, immediately and without acquiescence, give himself what the law understands by possession against the person whom he ejects, and drive him to produce his title, if he can, without delay, reinstate himself in his former possession.[57]

If there are two persons in a field, each asserting that the field is his, and each doing some act in the assertion of the right of possession, and if the question is, which of those two is in actual possession, I answer, the person who has the title is in actual possession, and the other is a trespasser.[58]

---

[53] (1863) 2 H & C 121.

[54] [2000] 1 QB 133, at 150. See also *Hounslow London Borough Council v Twickenham Garden Developments Ltd* [1971] Ch 233, at 257, *per* Megarry J. But cf *Street v Mountford* [1985] AC 809 on the distinction between tenancies and occupational licences.

[55] *Graham v Peat* (1801) 1 East 244. In *Mason v Clarke* [1955] AC 778, Viscount Simonds and Lord Oaksey held that the bare possession of a *profit à prendre* was enough to found an action in trespass.

[56] [1946] KB 393.

[57] *Browne v Dawson* (1840) 12 Ad & El 624, at 629. (In *Portland Managements Ltd v Harte* [1977] QB 306, it was held that if C proves ownership and his intention to resume possession, the onus is on D to prove that he is not a trespasser.)

[58] *Jones v Chapman* (1847) 2 Exch 803, at 821, *per* Maule J (approved *Lows v Telford* (1876) 1 App Cas 414, at 426, *per* Lord Selborne).

If a claimant has a right to immediate possession of the land, he can seek a summary remedy to obtain possession[59] or, if he has already entered upon the land, sue for trespasses committed by third parties between the date of accrual of his right of possession and the actual date of his entry.[60] This is often called trespass by relation.[61] It operates according to the legal fiction whereby, upon his entry onto the land, the party entitled to possession is deemed to have been in possession from the date of his right to such possession accruing.

Although damages in trespass are not available to those without possession whose interests in land are violated, such persons are not entirely without a remedy. A landlord will ordinarily have contractual rights against tenants who damage his interest – for example, by allowing the premises to fall into disrepair – and the law of property will also afford a remedy of a tortious nature to a landlord who establishes that his tenant has damaged the reversionary interest.[62]

If a non-possessory interest in land is violated by a third party, an action derived from the old action on the case may lie. The claimant must prove 'such permanent injury as would be necessarily prejudicial to the reversioner'.[63] Thus, in one case, it was not enough to prove that the defendant's cart-wheels had made an impression on the surface of the land;[64] the impressions lacked permanency.

SECTION 2 REMEDIES

(A) DAMAGES

The claimant is entitled to full reparation for his loss. Generally, the depreciation in selling value will be an adequate measure for destruction of, or damage to, land and buildings. On occasion, though, the claimant can also recover special damages such as business profits,[65] or the cost of replacement premises.[66] Equally, where the cost of reinstatement or repair exceeds the diminution in value of the property, those costs may be awarded as damages provided expenditure on such reinstatement and repair is reasonable.[67] And for these purposes, reasonableness is to be gauged by applying

---

[59] Civil Procedure Rules, r 55.21.   [60] *Barnett v Earl of Guildford* (1855) 11 Exch 19.

[61] Suppose that the effect of a proviso for forfeiture in a lease is that the lease subsists until proceedings for forfeiture are brought; this doctrine of trespass by relation would not then allow a lessor, who is entitled by the terms of the lease to forfeit it, to claim damages for the period between the act giving ground for forfeiture and the issue of the writ: *Elliott v Boynton* [1924] 1 Ch 236.

[62] Landlord-tenant relationships of this kind are customarily, and appropriately, dealt with in textbooks on real property, not in those on torts.   [63] *Baxter v Taylor* (1832) 5 B & Ad 72, at 75, *per* Taunton J.

[64] *Baxter v Taylor* (1832) 5 B & Ad 72.

[65] *Watson v Murray & Co* [1955] 2 QB 1. Cf *Dunn v Large* (1783) 3 Doug KB 335 (when D ejected C from an inn, closed it down and sent custom elsewhere, C refused loss of sale value, but only because he did not specially plead it).   [66] *Dominion Mosaics and Tile Co v Trafalgar Trucking Co* [1990] 2 All ER 246.

[67] *Heath v Keys* [1984] CLY 3568. Damages based on the cost of repair are only available when C does in fact intend to carry out repairs: *Perry v Sidney Phillips & Son* [1982] 3 All ER 705.

cost-benefit analysis not only to the reinstatement sought, but also to other options that might be available (including halfway-house solutions and the simple payment of damages).[68] Whatever the court's conclusion, the cost of repair will provide important evidence of the claimant's loss, especially where there is no market in which the value of the property may be ascertained, or where the claimant can prove that it was reasonable to have the property restored.[69] All measures of damages – whether based on market value or replacement cost – are subordinate to the general and overriding tort principle of restoring the claimant to the same position he was in before the tort was committed.[70]

The measure of damages for wrongful occupancy of land (*mesne profits*) is generally assessed in terms of the reasonable rental value of the land during the time of the defendant's occupancy. So in *Inverugie Investments Ltd v Hackett*,[71] the claimants were awarded the equivalent of the letting value of the whole of the holiday apartment block wrongfully occupied by the defendant trespassers, even though in practice only about 35–40% of the apartments were actually rented out by the defendants, or could have been by the claimants. The claimants were entitled to compensation for the wrongful use of their property, regardless of whether they had suffered any actual loss from being deprived of the use of that property or whether the defendants had in fact benefited from their wrongdoing. However, the decision in *Davies v Ilieff*[72] provides an important rider to this approach in that, if the premises concerned are also the claimant's home (rather than merely commercial residential premises), the court should add to the ordinary letting value a sum in general damages to reflect the insult of the trespass.

Where goods such as coal, minerals or trees are severed from the land, the measure of damages depends on whether the act is wilful or innocent.[73] If the defendant's severance is innocent, the claimant's damages amount to the value of the goods in their raw state (for example, coal still in a seam) minus the cost of severance and removal.[74] If the act is wilful, however, the claimant's damages will reflect the market value of the goods when they first became a chattel minus only the cost of removal – for example, hauling coal to the surface – but not the cost of severance.[75] Whether in either case the defendant can also deduct an additional sum by way of profit for his work, or whether the claimant is entitled to the value of the severed goods less only the defendant's actual

---

[68] *Bryant v Macklin* [2005] EWCA Civ 762.

[69] For a lucid statement, see *Hutchinson v Davidson* 1945 SC 395.

[70] *Farmer Giles Ltd v Wessex Water Authority* [1990] 18 EG 102. In *Bisney v Swanston* (1972) 225 *Estates Gazette* 2299, D put a trailer on C's transport café ground so as to interfere with C's business as much as possible. As well as damages for loss of business, £250 aggravated damages were awarded against D for intending to interfere with malice and spite.

[71] [1995] 1 WLR 713. See also *Whitwham v Westminster Brymbo Coal and Coke Co* [1896] 1 Ch 894; affd [1896] 2 Ch 538.   [72] 2000 WL 33201551.

[73] 'Wilful' includes 'fraudulent'; whether it includes 'negligent' is doubtful: *Wood v Morewood* (1841) 3 QB 440; *Re United Merthyr Collieries Co* (1872) LR 15 Eq 46. In *Trotter v Maclean* (1879) 13 Ch D 574, at 587 Fry J said (*obiter*) that the burden of proving wilfulness is on C.

[74] *Jegon v Vivian* (1871) 6 Ch App 742.

[75] *Martin v Porter* (1839) 5 M & W 351; *Morgan v Powell* (1842) 3 QB 278. If C could not himself reach the seam in order to extract the mineral, his damages are based on what a third party would pay him by way of royalty for permission to extract: *Livingstone v Rawyards Coal Co* (1880) 5 App Cas 25.

expenses, is not settled.[76] But in the future, it may be that the courts will approach these cases on the basis of the steadily developing law of unjust enrichment rather than the law of trespass (though a sum for the actual trespass will, of course, remain available).

Finally, a tenant who is unlawfully evicted by his landlord may recover exemplary damages in trespass.[77]

(B) INJUNCTIONS

Injunctions, even of the interim variety, are available in the case of continuing trespasses to restrain the trespasser.[78] And mandatory injunctions can be obtained in order to require a trespasser to restore the land to its former state. In *Nelson v Nicholson*,[79] for example, the facts were these.

Cs had recently resolved a boundary dispute with their neighbours. In resolving the dispute, it became apparent that Ds had planted a leylandii hedge on Cs' land. They conceded that this constituted a trespass. Cs then sought a mandatory injunction to require Ds to remove the hedge since they could not do so themselves under the terms of a restrictive covenant that prevented them from removing any fence, hedge, tree or shrubs within 30 feet of the boundary between the two plots of land.

Despite the defendants proposing an undertaking whereby they, the defendants, would keep the hedge trimmed to a height no greater than seven feet, the court granted the injunction sought, making the point that the proposed undertaking would not bind the defendants' successors in title.

Finally, a *quia timet* injunction may be granted to restrain the prospective trespasser; that is, where a trespass is merely threatened. Thus, in one case where the owners of certain incinerators anticipated a trespass by environmental protestors, an injunction was granted to prevent the trespass from occurring. Interestingly, the injunction was granted without the precise identity of the trespassers being ascertained: it was merely aimed at the generic class 'intending trespassers'.[80]

(C) RECOVERY OF LAND

It is an established rule of common law that the person entitled to possession may use reasonably necessary force to remove a trespasser.[81] But in many instances, the rightful

---

[76] *Jegon v Vivian* (1871) 6 Ch App 742 and *A-G v Tomline* (1880) 14 Ch D 58 would allow the innocent D his profit. Cf *Re United Merthyr Collieries Co* (1872) LR 15 Eq 46. In *Tai Te Wheta v Scandlyn* [1952] NZLR 30 it was held that even an innocent trespasser could not set off the value of improvements done by him to the land. See also *Lord Cawdor v Lewis* (1835) 1 Y & C Ex 427.

[77] *Drane v Evangelou* [1978] 2 All ER 437. Surprisingly, however, in *Devonshire v Jenkins* (1979) 129 NLJ 849 it was held that exemplary damages were not recoverable if in fact the evicting landlord did not obtain that profit which he sought by his attempted unlawful eviction.

[78] *Patel v WH Smith (Eziot) Ltd* [1987] 1 WLR 853.   [79] (2001) *Independent*, 22 January.

[80] *Hampshire Waste Services Ltd v Intending Trespassers upon Chineham Incinerator* [2004] Env LR 9.

[81] *Hemmings v Stoke Poges Golf Club* [1920] 1 KB 720.

occupant may prefer to pursue an action for recovery of land. In order to succeed, the claimant must demonstrate the relative weakness of the defendant's possessory rights. In other words, the claimant need not show that he has perfect title, merely a better title than the defendant. The clearest modern authority on this remedy is *Manchester Airport plc v Dutton*.[82] Manchester Airport needed to remove certain trees in neighbouring woods and they were granted a licence by the owner to 'enter and occupy the woods' in this connection. Prior to this, however, protestors had occupied the woods. In order to carry out the work, the airport sought an order for possession against the protestors. Noting that although Manchester Airport was not the owner of the woods, the Court of Appeal nonetheless granted the order on the basis that the airport had a superior right to occupation than the protestors. What was significant was the fact that the owner had included in the licence a right of occupation. Accordingly, in the ostensibly similar case of *Countryside Residential (North Thames) Ltd v Tugwell*[83] the court refused such an order on the grounds that the licence in question merely conferred permission to carry out work on the land, but not a right to occupy it.

SECTION 3 DEFENCES

(A) JUSTIFICATION

Occasionally it will be possible to show legal justification for one's presence on another's land. In such circumstances, there is no actionable trespass. Thus, for example, under the Countryside and Rights of Way Act 2000 rights are conferred to enter land to make arrangements for the general public to have access to open countryside. In such circumstances no tort is committed so long as the entrant complies with the specified statutory restrictions within which he must act.[84] Equally, in certain circumstances police officers are permitted to enter land to make an arrest and to search the premises following such an arrest[85] and private individuals have certain similar common law rights to enter another's land to abate a nuisance or reclaim wrongfully taken personal property.[86]

In fact, there are many forms of justification – whether originating in statute or ancient rules of common law – that are simply too numerous to list here.[87] For present purposes, it suffices to note two general principles: (1) that a recognized legal authority to enter another's land will defeat any prospective trespass action; and (2) that a

---

[82] [2000] 1 QB 133.　　[83] [2000] 34 EG 87.

[84] See the Countryside and Rights of Way Act 2000, s 2.

[85] Police and Criminal Evidence Act 1984, ss 17–18.

[86] See also the statutory procedure set out in the Access to Neighbouring Land Act 1992 which permits an applicant to seek an access order from the court in order to enter a neighbour's land to carry out reasonably necessary works for the preservation of his own land.

[87] For full details, see *Clerk and Lindsell* (2006) paras 19–35 *et seq*.

distinction must be drawn between an absolute right to do an act and a mere power to do an act which the defendant elected to do in a fashion that involved an avoidable trespass.[88]

(B) LICENCE

The defendant may raise the defence of licence where the claimant landowner has granted him a permission, whether express or implied, to enter the land. Such licences do not require that the entrant be granted any proprietary rights in respect of the land; a permission simply to be there suffices. On the other hand, if the entrant exceeds the permission conferred by the licence he becomes a trespasser. Thus, for example, if A is granted permission to enter B's land for the purposes of photographing wildlife, he may not fish in his lake without becoming a trespasser. Similarly, if the landowner revokes the licence, the entrant may not remain on his land. And this is so regardless of whether the licence was conferred gratuitously or by virtue of a contract.[89]

(C) SEARCH WARRANTS

Under section 8 of the Police and Criminal Evidence Act 1984, magistrates have, in certain circumstances, the power to grant search warrants. The details of this jurisdiction, and the case law associated with the extent of the powers contained in a warrant are beyond the scope of this book.[90]

FURTHER READING

Birts, *Remedies for Trespass* (1990)

Pollock and Wright, *Possession in the Common Law* (1888)

---

[88] In *British Waterways Board v Severn Trent Water Ltd* [2002] Ch 25 it was stressed that while a statute authorized certain waterworks, it did not impliedly also confer upon D a right to discharge surplus water into another's watercourse. The court adverted to the crucial difference between mere *convenient* ways of carrying out statutory operations and methods that are *necessary*. A similarly restrictive approach is applied to rights conferred by way of conveyance: see *Martin v Childs* [2002] EWCA Civ 283.

[89] Revocation of a contractual licence, it seems, does not require mutually agreed contractual variation. Any complaint about such revocation – effectively a breach of contract – must be pursued under the law of contract: see *Wood v Leadbitter* (1845) 13 M & W 838 (contractual entrant to a racecourse ejected in breach of contract: only remedy lay in contract).   [90] For full details, see *Clerk and Lindsell* (2006) para 19–60.

11

DEFENCES TO INTENTIONAL TORTS AGAINST THE PERSON OR PROPERTY

This chapter considers all the important defences which may be available in respect of the torts so far described. It must not, however, be thought that these defences apply only to these torts. Many of them – for example, consent, statutory authority, *ex turpi causa* – are general defences, and are capable of being defences to almost any tort. Nevertheless, these defences have a particular importance in the present context because the key question in claims for trespass and the like is often likely to centre on whether, in the actual circumstances of the case, there is any lawful excuse or justification for the conduct complained of. Thus, taking false imprisonment as an example, most common law claims tend to turn on whether the detention of an alleged criminal was justifiable. Articles 5 and 6 of the European Human Rights Convention which protect the rights to liberty and security of the person do so in just ten brief words. By contrast, over a page is devoted to possible justifications for the deprivation of such rights. In short, defences to intentional torts are crucial in defining individual rights.

SECTION 1 MISTAKE[1] AND INEVITABLE ACCIDENT

Previous chapters have revealed that mistake is no defence to the intentional torts. If the defendant intended to drive his tractor onto the claimant's land, then his reasonable mistake that the land was his own will be no defence.[2] Mistake must, however, be distinguished from inevitable accident. If the defendant shows that the tractor went onto the claimant's land solely because of a defect in the steering which no amount of care could have prevented, he will not be liable. In such a case he neither intended to end up on the claimant's land, nor could he have avoided doing so by taking every care.

---

[1] See Trindale, 'Intentional Torts: Some Thoughts on Assault and Battery' (1982) 2 OJLS 211.

[2] Similarly where there is liability for negligent acts, if, though his act is not intentional, he foresees the consequences, mistake about the surrounding circumstances will not afford him a defence.

Although mistake *per se* is no defence, it may be relevant to know in the context of some other defence whether the defendant was mistaken as to some matter of fact. If, for example, a policeman arrests someone without a warrant who in fact is not committing or about to commit an offence, false imprisonment will generally occur. However, if the officer mistakenly believes on reasonable grounds that the claimant was either committing or about to commit an offence at the time of arrest, he will have open to him the defence of lawful arrest.[3]

In *Fowler v Lanning*,[4] the claimant's pleadings in a claim for trespass asserted baldly that 'the defendant shot the claimant'. Diplock J held that the pleadings disclosed no valid cause of action. For trespass to lie, he said, the claimant must aver and prove that the defendant acted either intentionally or negligently. And since the onus of proving such conduct now rests on the claimant, there is no longer any practical need for the ancient defence of 'inevitable accident': if the facts of the case rest on a brief assertion of this kind, no cause of action will exist.

SECTION 2 CONSENT

(A) GENERAL

The common law will not permit someone who has freely consented to conduct by another to sue that other for damages resulting from that conduct. Consent may take two related forms.[5] The first occurs where the claimant expressly consents to an invasion of his interest in a manner that would otherwise constitute a tort, and this form may properly be labelled consent. The second occurs where there is a willingness on the part of the claimant to run the risk of injury from a particular source of danger where the claimant was fully aware of the nature and extent of the risk.[6] This form is often referred to as 'assumption of risk' or by the Latin maxim, *volenti non fit injuria* ('no wrong is done to one who consents'). The difference between the two forms can be captured as follows. Where the tort in question turns upon intentional acts, it is more appropriate to speak of consent. But where the tort in question requires only inadvertent conduct – like, for example, negligence – it is more accurate to speak of *volenti non fit injuria*. Thus, while a hospital patient may well consent to invasive surgery; he may do so without assuming the risk that the surgeon will operate negligently.

It is convenient to treat consent as a defence even though it is now clear that, in trespass to the person (but not in trespass to land), the burden of proving want of

---

[3] Police and Criminal Evidence Act 1984, s 24(1).   [4] [1959] 1 QB 426.

[5] The two forms were set out *Morris v Murray* [1991] 2 QB 6.

[6] *Letang v Ottawa Electric Rly Co* [1926] AC 725, at 731, *per* Lord Shaw.

consent lies with the claimant.[7] Consent may be given expressly or it may be inferred from conduct. A boxer cannot complain if his opponent hits him with a straight left to the nose; and a teenager engaged in horseplay with a friend cannot complain when injured by that friend so long as the latter stays within the accepted rules of that horseplay.[8] Similarly, a footballer consents not only to those tackles which the rules permit, but also, probably, to those tackles which result only in a minor, technical breach of the rules of the game. Where, however, an opponent commits a 'professional foul', the conduct involved is entirely beyond what the player agreed to risk when embarking on the game.[9]

Establishing just what can reasonably be inferred from conduct can be problematic. If a claimant has habitually allowed children to play on his field, the consent defence may arise in respect of a frolicking child. But it is unlikely that it could be invoked in relation to adults using the field for a firework display. *Arthur v Anker*[10] explored the boundaries of consent in a modern context. It was held that where a person had unlawfully parked his car on another's land, knowing that the owners asserted a right to wheel-clamp trespassing vehicles and charge for their release, he had impliedly consented not only to the otherwise unlawful detention of his car (so that there was no trespass to goods), but also to being required to pay a reasonable fee to ensure the un-clamping of the vehicle.[11]

One limit upon the consent principle is that it must relate to the class of act complained of, but it need not relate to the exact act that causes harm. Thus, as already noted, in the context of a contact sport, consenting generally to the prospect of blows being struck will suffice to furnish a good defence.[12] On the other hand, a tenant may consent to her landlord entering the premises in order to undertake repairs of various kinds, but she must not be taken to have consented to his physically assaulting her.

Fraud *may* invalidate an apparent consent if the fraud relates to the very nature of the act consented to, but the law is complex and needs to be dealt with in various stages. To begin with, two nineteenth century decisions holding that a woman's consent to sexual intercourse was not vitiated by her ignorance that her lover was infected with syphilis[13] now require some qualification. In such a case there are two issues at stake: (1) does she consent to intercourse? and (2) does she consent to being infected? In *R v Dica*,[14] it was

---

[7] *Freeman v Home Office (No 2)* [1984] QB 524; affd [1984] 1 All ER 1036. On one interpretation, Lord Blanesburgh in *William Leitch & Co Ltd v Leydon* [1931] AC 90, at 109, could have been applying the rule relating to assault to trespass to goods. In *Jolliffe v Willmett & Co* [1971] 1 All ER 478, a wife living apart from her husband authorized an inquiry agent to enter her husband's flat; the inquiry agent's defence of leave and licence failed when the husband sued him for trespass to land.   [8] *Blake v Galloway* [2004] 3 All ER 315.

[9] See *Condon v Basi* [1985] 2 All ER 453.

[10] [1997] QB 564. Contrast the position in Canada in *Non-Marine Underwriters, Lloyd's of London v Scalera* [2000] 1 SCR 551.

[11] Cf *Vine v Waltham Forest London Borough Council* [2000] 1 WLR 2383 where it was held that if the release fee is exorbitant, consent to its payment cannot be implied where the person parking the car does not actually see the sign (albeit that such a sign would normally be described as both prominently posted and clear in its terms). The difference would seem to lie purely in the fee charged for un-clamping.

[12] *Blake v Galloway* [2004] 1 WLR 2844, at [20].

[13] *R v Clarence* (1888) 22 QBD 23, at 44; *Hegarty v Shine* (1878) 14 Cox CC 124.   [14] [2004] QB 1257.

held that consensual sexual intercourse does not preclude the possibility of a man being convicted of grievous bodily harm if he knowingly or recklessly transmits HIV infection to a woman. *Dica*, of course, was a criminal law case, but the separation of 'consent to sexual intercourse' and 'consent to being infected' would appear to be a perfectly sensible step to take in the context of the tort of battery as well. What is more difficult is the case in which the defendant's motive is in question. For instance, the defendant may do something that could constitute *either* a mildly sexual act or, alternatively, one of a purely comforting nature. An example would be a male police officer 'cuddling' a distressed woman whom he is questioning. If he puts his arms around her purely to eliminate some of the stress caused by the occasion, and she welcomes such comforting, there will be no tort. But what if he does it for prurient reasons that only transpire later? Here, the criminal law would render the police officer guilty of an offence on the basis that the defendant deceived the complainant as to the nature or purpose of the act,[15] but it is undecided whether a claimant's consent is thus vitiated in tort[16] (although on principle it is submitted that it should be treated as vitiated).

If consent is obtained under duress, then it is treated in law as being no consent.[17] Nor is consent procured by a show of authority valid. So, for example, where a policeman, without formally arresting or charging a suspect, asks him with an authoritative air to accompany him to the police station,[18] the claimant is not to be treated as having granted a valid consent. Likewise, if the claimant is drunk or otherwise incapable of giving consent, any putative consent is treated as invalid, and no defence lies.[19]

The overriding interest of the state in maintaining order and punishing wrongdoers is such that it is not necessarily a defence in criminal law that the victim has consented to the criminal act.[20] But no considerations of policy prevent the courts from holding that consent to a crime is a valid defence in tort, and it may be assumed that the courts will hold that consent will be a valid defence in tort in such circumstances.[21]

---

[15] Sexual Offences Act 2003, s 76(2).   [16] *KD v Chief Constable of Hampshire* [2005] EWHC 2550.

[17] Yet in *Latter v Braddell* (1881) 50 LJQB 448, a servant who complied, reluctantly, crying and under protest, with an order of her mistress that she be medically examined to check whether she was pregnant, was held to have consented. In modern parlance, this would be regarded as a case of undue influence; and mere undue influence does not suffice to vitiate consent: *Mrs U v Centre for Reproductive Medicine* [2002] Lloyd's Rep Med 259 (pressure short of duress applied by a nurse to a patient).

[18] *Warner v Riddiford* (1858) 4 CBNS 180. Submissions in *Freeman v Home Office (No 2)* [1984] QB 524; affd [1984] 1 All ER 1036 that the relationship between prisoner and prison doctor was such that the former could never freely consent to treatment by the latter failed. But the judge at first instance made it clear that in looking at the reality of a prisoner's consent to medical treatment the doctor's power to affect the prisoner's situation must be borne in mind.

[19] Must C's consent be manifested to D? Is it enough if D reasonably believes that C has consented?

[20] *R v Brown* [1994] 1 AC 212. The European Court of Human Rights subsequently ruled that the decision in *Brown* did not constitute a violation of Article 8 of the Convention: *Laskey, Jaggard and Brown v United Kingdom* (1997) 24 EHRR 39.

[21] *Barnes v Nayer* (1986) *Times*, 19 December; *Murphy v Culhane* [1977] QB 94 (it was held that the defence of consent might be available in respect of a crime, and at the same time it was also held that a plea of *ex turpi causa* might also be open to D).

(B) CONSENT TO MEDICAL TREATMENT

The law concerning consent to medical treatment could almost form the basis for a book in itself. What follows, then, is very much an abbreviated account of the main principles of the law; and interested readers concerned to know the detail would ordinarily be advised to consult a specialist text on medical law. However, at the time of writing, there are none that are sufficiently current to take account of the Mental Capacity Act 2005.[22]

In order to sketch the law on consent to medical treatment we need to distinguish four classes of patient: adults with capacity to consent; children; adults suffering from mental incapacity and receiving treatment under the Mental Health Act 1983; adults lacking capacity but falling outside the Mental Health Act 1983. As we shall see, however, even these categories are not watertight, and there is some degree of overlap between them.

(1) ADULTS WITH CAPACITY TO CONSENT

As a starting point, any physical contact with a competent adult patient without his or her consent to that contact is *prima facie* a battery.[23] This requirement of consent to treatment reflects a basic right to self-determination. Thus, as Lord Goff put it in *F v West Berkshire Health Authority*[24] '[e]very human being of adult years and sound mind has a right to determine what shall be done with his own body'.[25] For these purposes, consent need not be written and may well be implied from conduct such as holding out one's arm to receive an injection. Where surgery or more serious invasive treatment is contemplated, patients will usually be asked to sign a standard consent form agreeing to the operation or other treatment. Such consent is ineffective unless an adequate explanation of the broad nature of what is to be done to the patient is provided.[26] It follows that a failure to warn the patient of the risks or side-effects of the treatment proposed will not vitiate the patient's consent.[27] At most it will constitute a breach of the doctor's duty to give the patient proper and skilled advice and be actionable as negligence.[28] Only when the defendant actively misleads the patient will a claim in battery normally be appropriate.[29] And even where it is unclear whether a patient freely,

---

[22] A good account of its provisions can, however, be found in *Clerk and Lindsell on Torts* (2006) ch 15.

[23] *F v West Berkshire Health Authority* [1989] 2 All ER 545. See also Brazier, *Medicine, Patients and the Law* (2003) ch 4.   [24] [1989] 2 All ER 545, at 564.

[25] *Schloendorff v Society of New York Hospital* 211 NY 125 (1914), *per* Cardozo J.

[26] *Chatterton v Gerson* [1981] QB 432, at 443, *per* Bristow J.

[27] *Chatterton v Gerson*, [1981] QB 432, at 444, *per* Bristow J; *Freeman v Home Office (No 2)* [1984] QB 524; affd [1984] 1 All ER 1036. The bringing of actions in battery where the essence of the claim is inadequate advice was deplored by their Lordships in *Sidaway v Board of Governors of Bethlem Royal Hospital and the Maudsley Hospital* [1985] 2 WLR 480.

[28] See *Sidaway v Board of Governors of Bethlem Royal Hospital and the Maudsley Hospital* [1985] 2 WLR 480.

[29] See *Appleton v Garrett* [1996] PIQR P 1. See also the criminal conviction in *R v Tabassum* [2000] 2 Cr App Rep 328 where D had no qualifications whatever. Cf *R v Richardson* [1999] QB 444 where D, a dentist, had merely been suspended from practice.

and with full understanding, rejected life-saving treatment, it has been held that doctors act lawfully in erring on the side of preserving life.[30] If however the patient makes clear in advance that he or she would not wish to receive treatment of a particular kind, such advance directives – like the refusal of a blood transfusion by a Jehovah's Witness – must be respected.[31] Equally, where a competent patient requests that a ventilator be disconnected, those providing care must oblige, for continuing the ventilator is to continue to apply force; and for this consent must be forthcoming.[32]

One difficulty concerning competent adults that may arise relates to the situation in which the patient is unconscious – say, because he or she has been involved in a road accident, or because a complication during surgery arises while the patient is under anaesthesia. In such a case, a doctor will act lawfully in providing treatment. In *F v West Berkshire Health Authority* the House of Lords made it clear that the basis for such treatment was necessity.[33] And what is 'necessary' is to be judged according to the best interests of the patient (usually taken to mean preservation of life or the prevention of any permanent damage to health). Lord Goff also made clear that a doctor may only do that which is reasonably required before the patient recovers consciousness, and in any event, he may only provide treatment that would be endorsed by a reasonable body of medical opinion.[34]

(2) CHILDREN

The Family Law Reform Act 1969 provides that a minor over 16 may provide an effective consent to surgical, medical or dental treatment. As such, although such children are not technically adults, their consent to treatment is placed on a par with that of a competent adult. In the case of children under 16, the 1969 Act preserves the common law rule that, providing the individual child is mature enough to make his or her own decision on the treatment proposed, the child herself can give an effective consent.[35] Thus, Mrs Gillick's attempt to ensure that no girl under 16 could lawfully be prescribed the contraceptive pill without parental agreement failed. The House of Lords held that, if such a girl seeking contraception or abortion should refuse adamantly to consult with her parents, the doctor may lawfully treat her provided he is satisfied that she has sufficient understanding of what is involved in the treatment and its implications for her.[36] Yet while a '*Gillick* competent' child can provide a valid consent to treatment, it is apparently necessary to take a more complicated approach to the question of such a child's capacity to *refuse* treatment. This is because the Court of Appeal has held that the parental power to consent on the minor's behalf continues even after the minor acquires an independent capacity to consent for herself.[37] So if

---

[30] *Re T (adult: refusal of medical treatment)* [1992] 4 All ER 649.
[31] Mental Capacity Act 2005, s 26(1).   [32] *B v an NHS Hospital Trust* [2002] 2 All ER 449.
[33] [1989] 2 All ER 545, at 565–6, *per* Lord Goff.
[34] See *Bolam v Friern Hospital Management Committee* [1957] 1 WLR 582.
[35] Family Law Reform Act 1969, s 8(3).   [36] *Gillick v West Norfolk and Wisbech AHA* [1986] AC 112.
[37] *Re W (a minor) (medical treatment)* [1993] Fam 64.

a child seeks to refuse treatment but her parent gives consent, the child may nonetheless be treated lawfully.

In the case of very young children, parental consent to treatment is effective to authorize treatment that is beneficial to the child.[38] No battery is therefore committed when a doctor vaccinates a protesting four-year-old if her parent has given consent. Where the procedure proposed is not clearly and unequivocally beneficial to the child, however, parental consent alone may not be sufficient. In such cases – including, for example, sterilization – the authorization of the court must be sought before any such serious and generally irreversible surgery is performed.[39] When the patient is under 18, authorization is best sought by invoking the inherent jurisdiction of the High Court.[40]

(3) PATIENTS LACKING CAPACITY AND FALLING WITHIN THE MENTAL HEALTH ACT 1983

Where patients are mentally disordered and detained in a mental hospital, the terms under which they may be treated for their mental disorder are governed by the Mental Health Act 1983. The details of this statute cannot be given here. It suffices to note that the Act provides for such treatment according to a complex system of procedural and (in relation to certain kinds of treatment) substantive safeguards.[41]

(4) PATIENTS LACKING CAPACITY BUT FALLING OUTSIDE THE MENTAL HEALTH ACT 1983

The position in relation to patients who lack capacity (as opposed to patients who are competent but unconscious), yet fall outside the Mental Health Act 1983,[42] is now governed by the Mental Capacity Act 2005. Again, a detailed account of this legislation is beyond the scope of this book. Nonetheless, it can be noted here that the Act puts in place a presumption of capacity[43] that is only ousted if the patient is shown to lack capacity (judged according to a test based on the ability to understand, retain and evaluate information relevant to a treatment decision *coupled with* an ability to communicate his or her decision). Where the person lacks capacity, he or she may be treated, subject to a number of safeguards (concerning matters such as known previous wishes and religious beliefs[44]), if the person providing treatment reasonably believes it to be in the patient's best interests.

---

[38] *Re D* [1976] Fam 185. See also *Re B* [1981] 1 WLR 1421. But note that in *Re T* [1997] 1 WLR 242 the Court of Appeal, endorsing parental refusal of a liver transplant for their son, regarded parental objections to treatment as crucial in defining the child's interests.

[39] *Re B (a minor) (wardship: sterilisation)* [1987] 2 All ER 206, at 214, *per* Lord Templeman.

[40] *Practice Note (Sterilisation: minors and mental health patients)* [1993] 3 All ER 222.

[41] For details, see *Clerk and Lindsell on Torts* (2006) ch 15.

[42] Generally, these will be patients who are not liable to be detained in a mental hospital.

[43] Mental Capacity Act 2005, s 1(2).   [44] Mental Capacity Act 2005, ss 4–6.

SECTION 3 CONTRIBUTORY NEGLIGENCE

This frequently invoked defence is fully examined in chapter 6. Nonetheless, it can usefully be noted here that while contributory negligence *is* available in respect of battery actions, it is not available in proceedings founded on conversion or an intentional trespass to goods.[45]

SECTION 4 SELF-DEFENCE

An act which might otherwise constitute trespass to the person may be justified if the defendant is able to establish that he acted in self-defence:[46] that is, that he was merely repelling an attack (or threatened attack[47]) on the part of the claimant. The defendant must prove that in the circumstances it was reasonable that he should defend himself and that the force used by him was reasonable. Consider *Cockcroft v Smith*.[48]

The clerk of a court sued an attorney for biting off his forefinger in a scuffle in court. Holt CJ held that, in itself, it was no defence that C had first run his fingers towards D's eyes, for a man must not 'in case of a small assault, give a violent or an unreasonable return'.[49]

The right to use reasonable force to protect oneself against injury or threat of injury applies equally to resisting unlawful arrest.[50] However, what constitutes reasonable force is a question of fact to be determined in each case.[51] It will be material to consider whether the claimant could have escaped, whether he resisted with the most reasonable means available, whether the act of the defendant went beyond the limits of defence to pure revenge, whether the defendant continued to use violence after the danger had passed, and whether the claimant's attack was, or was reasonably expected to be, violent.[52] Thus, it is not simply a question of comparing the evil of the response to the evil of the attack.[53] So suppose that A pins B against a wall and repeatedly kisses her against her will, and suppose also that the only means whereby B can compel A to desist is by lacerating his hands with scissors, having failed to push him away because of his

---

[45] Torts (Interference with Goods) Act 1977, s 11(1), except that the defence is open to a collecting banker sued for conversion of a cheque: Banking Act 1979, s 47.

[46] Even though the provocation by C may not on the facts justify the battery, it may be a ground for reducing damages: *Fraser v Berkeley* (1836) 7 C & P 621, at 624, *per* Lord Abinger; *Lane v Holloway* [1968] 1 QB 379.

[47] *Dale v Wood* (1822) 7 Moore CP 33 (though on the fact D's response was greater than was warranted).

[48] (1705) 2 Salk 642.   [49] In fact C failed on a finding that his act did endanger D's eye.

[50] *R v McKoy* (2002) *Times*, 17 June; *Codd v Cabe* (1876) 1 Ex D 352.

[51] The notion of any duty to retreat was expressly condemned by the Court of Appeal in *R v Bird* [1985] 2 All ER 513. As to force exerted where the danger is miscalculated but the intervention was based on a reasonable mistake, see *Albert v Lavin* [1982] AC 546.   [52] *Revill v Newbery* [1996] QB 567.

[53] *Turner v Metro-Goldwyn-Meyer Pictures Ltd* [1950] 1 All ER 449, at 471, *per* Lord Oaksey (*obiter*): 'If you are attacked by a prize-fighter you are not bound to adhere to the Queensbury rules in your defence'.

superior strength. It is not certain that her defence will fail simply because the wounding is more severe than the unwanted kisses! Furthermore, there need not be *exact* proportionality between the attack and the response as *Cross v Kirkby*[54] makes clear. There, A struck B with the self-same baseball bat that B had used to attack A (once A had grappled it from him). The blow fractured B's skull and A's blow involved much greater than average force. Nonetheless, it was held to be a reasonably proportionate blow struck instinctively in the heat of the moment.

SECTION 5 DEFENCE OF ANOTHER PERSON

The cases clearly establish that an employee may justify a battery in defence of his employer, and an employer[55] may lawfully strike someone in defence of his employee.[56] Equally, a wife may defend her husband, and a man may defend any member of his household.[57] It may be that this form of defence extends to the protection of other persons, although authority is lacking. For instance, a guard may be permitted to defend railway passengers. It is submitted that the key in each case is whether it is reasonable for the defendant to protect the other person. And as with self-defence, the conduct of the defendant must be reasonable in all the circumstances, and it is conceivable that one relevant factor may be the relationship between the defendant and the person whom he defended (that is, one may use greater force in defence of a close relative than of a stranger). At the very least, the facts must normally be such as to have justified the third person in defending himself.[58]

Historically, if the defendant acted in order to prevent the claimant from perpetrating a felony jeopardizing the life of a third party, that was a defence in itself.[59] Felonies were abolished by the Criminal Law Act 1967, but it is submitted that any general right to intervene to prevent a criminal attack on another is now provided for almost exclusively by section 3 of that Act (there being one further provision to like effect within the context of schools[60]). But if the attack is not criminal – for example, if it comes from someone with a mental disability unable to form the requisite *mens rea* for the purposes of a crime – then the common law should still apply.[61]

---

[54] (2000) *Times*, 5 April.   [55] *Barfoot v Reynolds* (1734) 2 Stra 953.

[56] *Seaman v Cuppledick* (1615) Owen 150; *Tickell v Read* (1773) Lofft 215. Cf *Leward v Basely* (1695) 1 Ld Raym 62.

[57] *A-G's Reference (No 2 of 1983)* [1984] QB 456; *Leward v Basely* (1695) 1 Ld Raym 62. Today, we may assume that both propositions apply equally to men and women.

[58] For an exception see *Re A* [2001] Fam 147 where the Court of Appeal allowed doctors to separate conjoined twins even though the separation would result in the near immediate death of one of the twins (as opposed to the slower, inevitable death of both of them were the separation not to be carried out).

[59] *Handcock v Baker* (1800) 2 Bos & P 260, at 265, *per* Chambre J. See also *Coupey v Henley* (1797) 2 Esp 539.

[60] Education Act 1996, s 550A (teachers may act to prevent the commission of an offence or the causing of personal injury or property damage).

[61] The Criminal Law Act, s 3(2) provides only that the statutory defence created by s 3(1) replaces the common law in relation to acts done in order to prevent a crime. Therefore, the common law rules that apply outside the commission of crime should remain intact.

SECTION 6 DEFENCE OF ONE'S PROPERTY

One may use reasonable force to defend land or chattels in one's possession against any person threatening to commit or actually committing a trespass to the property; but the defendant must have such possession as would enable him to sue the claimant in trespass. Thus the captain of a cricket club who removed the claimant from the field could not plead that he had ejected a trespasser, because the captain did not have possession of the field.[62] A lack of possession was also crucial in *Scott v Matthew Brown & Co Ltd*.[63]

D was on the land merely as a result of ejecting C by an act of trespass whereupon C, the true owner, at once re-entered. D forcibly removed him, and was held not to have sufficient possession to sue in trespass, and therefore had no defence against C's battery action.

If the defendant has a mere right to possess, but no actual possession, he may have some other defence – re-entry in the case of land, or recaption in the case of chattels[64] – but he cannot successfully plead that he was defending his property.[65]

To remain on land after permission has expired is a trespass: therefore the defence of protecting property may be invoked by those who eject such persons.[66] A threatened intrusion is also sufficient to trigger the defence; so if the claimant has taken the key of the defendant's car and is about to enter the car, the defendant may resist this potential trespass to his chattel. As with defence of the person, if the defendant has a reasonable belief that force is essential to end the trespass, he may use it although he is mistaken in thinking it to be necessary. But if he mistakenly believes that the claimant is a trespasser when she is not, he has no defence. What is reasonable force in this context also depends on the facts, though guidance may be sought from the decided cases.

If a person enters another's house with force and violence, the owner of the house may justify turning him out (using no more force than is necessary), without a previous request to depart; but if the person enters quietly, the other party cannot justify turning him out, without a previous request to depart.[67]

As the law does not generally value interests in property as highly as those in the person,[68] the use of force in defence of the former is harder to justify than in the case of self-defence. Firing a shotgun at a burglar breaking into a garden shed, but who shows no overt sign of violence towards the owner, was held in *Revill v Newbery*[69] to be disproportionate force in

---

[62] *Holmes v Bagge* (1853) 1 E & B 782; *Dean v Hogg* (1834) 10 Bing 345.   [63] (1884) 51 LT 746.

[64] Recaption of chattels amounts to the right to commit a battery in order to recover chattels.

[65] *Roberts v Tayler* (1845) 1 CB 117, at 126–7, *per* Tindal CJ.

[66] *Green v Bartram* (1830) 4 C & P 308; *Moriarty v Brooks* (1834) 6 C & P 684, Ex Ch.

[67] *Tullay v Reed* (1823) 1 C & P 6, *per* Park J. Cf *Green v Goddard* (1702) 2 Salk 641; *Polkinhorn v Wright* (1845) 8 QB 197.

[68] But note that in relation to the availability of injunctive relief the opposite appears to be true: see Murphy, 'Rethinking Injunctions in Tort Law' (forthcoming).

[69] [1996] QB 567. See also *Collins v Renison* (1754) Say 138; *Moriarty v Brooks* (1834) 6 C & P 684 Ex Ch. Cf *Stroud v Bradbury* [1952] 2 All ER 76.

defence of property; but the claimant's damages were reduced by two thirds in the light of his contributory negligence. May it be, then, that unless the claimant resists his expulsion so as to bring the rules of self-defence into play, the courts will treat force likely to cause death or serious bodily harm as unjustifiable in the defence of property?[70]

The courts have often had to consider the extent to which a defendant could use mechanical devices or other methods to protect his property. The test appears, once again, to be one of reasonableness. Thus, attempting to deter trespassers or burglars by placing barbed wire or spiked railings on the confines of one's land is reasonable, and there is no liability if another is subsequently injured by them.[71] On the other hand, if one deliberately and without notice sets spring guns or any other such device that is calculated to kill or cause grievous bodily harm, the courts will not consider it to be reasonable.[72]

Where dogs (or, theoretically, other animals) are used to protect one's property, the relevant rules concerning defence of one's property are contained in the Animals Act 1971. Under the legislation, a person is not liable 'for any damage caused by an animal kept on any premises or structure to a person trespassing there, if it is proved either (a) that the animal was not kept there for the protection of persons or property; or (b) (if the animal was kept there for the protection of persons or property) that keeping it there for that purpose was not unreasonable'.[73]

SECTION 7 DEFENCE OF ANOTHER'S PROPERTY

According to Blackstone, it is a defence to act in protection of the property of other members of one's household;[74] and although one might expect the courts to permit this defence only within narrow limits, by analogy with defence of another, it may nonetheless be assumed to exist.

SECTION 8 PREVENTING CRIME

Section 3 of the Criminal Law Act 1967 confers a general right to use 'such force as is reasonable in the prevention of crime'. Clearly there is some overlap with the common law. But the two can be distinguished in at least two instances. First, it is unclear whether

---

[70] As to when killing intruding animals may be justified, see *Hamps v Darby* [1948] 2 KB 311.

[71] See *Deane v Clayton* (1817) 7 Taunt 489. Presumably the danger would need to be obvious in order to escape liability under the Occupiers' Liability Act 1984 (on which see ch 7).

[72] *Bird v Holbrook* (1828) 4 Bing 628; distinguished in *Jordin v Crump* (1841) 8 M & W 782. But see now the Offences Against the Person Act 1861, s 31. In *A-G's Reference (No 2 of 1983)* [1984] QB 456. (D had armed himself with petrol bombs to repel rioters who had earlier smashed into his shop. The court held that D was entitled to acquittal if his object was to protect his family or his property from imminent attack and the force employed was reasonable.) [73] Animals Act 1971, s 5(3). See further ch 19.

[74] Book III, 3; no modern cases can be found.

a common law right exists to use force to repel an attack on a stranger whereas this is plainly within section 3. Secondly, the right to use force under section 3 is clearly inferior to the common law right of self-defence in that if an attacker is insane, or a child is under 10 years old, no crime can be committed, hence section 3 cannot be invoked.

SECTION 9 NECESSITY

(A) DISTINGUISHED FROM DEFENCE OF PROPERTY

The difference between the defence of necessity and that of defence of property is that while the latter presupposes that the claimant is *prima facie* a wrongdoer, the former contemplates the infliction of harm on an innocent claimant. When, for instance, the defendant barricades his land against flood-water and, in consequence, the claimant's land is flooded, the defence of necessity may lie against the claimant who is in no way respon-sible for creating the threat of danger.[75] Here, the law may be expected to give greater weight to the claimant's interest, and, accordingly, to restrict the scope of the defence.

(B) SCOPE

The necessity defence has two forms: private necessity and public necessity. In relation to the former, one may lawfully protect one's person and property[76] (and that of another[77]) against the threat of harm even though the consequence is that an innocent person suffers a loss. Thus, as we have just noted, one may do what is necessary to protect one's property against a threatened flood, even though flooding of a neighbour's land ensues. Similarly, it is justifiable to divert pests away from one's land although they then damage a neighbour's crops instead.[78] But homeless persons who enter empty housing awaiting development cannot invoke the defence: there must be an urgent situation of imminent peril in order to invoke this defence.[79]

As we have already seen, necessity has been extended to the context of medical treatment. A doctor may, for example, invoke this defence after operating to save the life

---

[75] *Nield v London and North Western Rly Co* (1874) LR 10 Exch 4, at 7, *per* Bramwell B; *Maxey Drainage Board v Great Northern Rly Co* (1912) 106 LT 429, at 430, *per* Lush J; *Gerrard v Crowe* [1921] 1 AC 395. If D's land is already flooded he may not divert that flood water onto C's land: *Whalley v Lancashire and Yorkshire Rly Co* (1884) 13 QBD 131.

[76] *Cope v Sharpe (No 2)* [1912] 1 KB 496 (D justified in burning heather on C's land in order to prevent fire on C's land spreading to land on which D's master had shooting rights).

[77] *Proudman v Allen* [1954] SASR 336 (D, believing that C's unoccupied car was about to run into another vehicle, jumped into the driving seat so that the car ran into the sea and sank – no trespass). See also *Kirk v Gregory* (1876) 1 Ex D 55 (moving a dead person's valuables to a safer place is only justified if necessary for the safety of those goods).

[78] *Greyvensteyn v Hattingh* [1911] AC 355 (D entered land of a 3rd party while diverting the pests).

[79] *Southwark London Borough Council v Williams* [1971] Ch 734.

of an unconscious patient.[80] But there is no defence if the doctor knows that the competent patient freely, and with full understanding of the seriousness of a decision to refuse treatment, refuses life-saving treatment.[81] Equally, advance directives made while the patient was still competent, must also be followed.[82] And in the latter stages of pregnancy where the interests of a viable foetus are at stake, the maternal right to bodily integrity now prevails.[83] Finally, prisoners on hunger strike cannot lawfully be force-fed.[84]

Turning to public necessity, several ancient cases establish that a citizen might lawfully enter another's land to erect fortifications for the defence of the realm[85] or to fight fires,[86] or to justify throwing cargo overboard in order to save the lives of the ship's passengers[87] (although whether compensation is payable to the victims of such acts is uncertain[88]). More recently, the public interest in preserving life has been used to invoke this defence where genuine doubt existed as to whether the patient had freely refused life-saving treatment.[89] And necessity may also be invoked to justify restraining a section of a crowd of protestors in a fashion that would otherwise be a false imprisonment if the police reasonably believe it to be necessary to protect public safety.[90]

In order to raise a defence of either public or private necessity there must be both an actual (or what seems to a reasonable man to be actual) danger, and the steps taken must be reasonable in the light of all the facts.[91] One important further point can be gleaned from the case of *Rigby v Chief Constable of Northamptonshire*.[92] There, the police were held liable for firing a CS gas canister into the claimant's shop in order to flush out a dangerous psychopath without having adequate fire-fighting equipment available. The shop was burned out. The judge held that while necessity was a good defence to trespass in such an emergency, the police were nonetheless liable in negligence for their failure to ensure that they had sufficient fire-fighting back-up when the canister was fired.

---

[80] *F v West Berkshire Health Authority* [1989] 2 All ER 545.   [81] Mental Capacity Act 2005, s 26(1).

[82] *Re AK* [2001] 1 FLR 129 (and nothing in the European Human Rights Convention alters this position).

[83] *Re MB* [1997] 8 Med LR 217; *St George's Healthcare NHS Trust v S* [1998] 3 All ER 673.

[84] *Secretary of State for the Home Department v Robb* [1995] Fam 127.

[85] YB 21 H 7 – the point was taken on demurrer but no judgment given on it; *The Case of the King's Prerogative in Saltpetre* (1606) 12 Co Rep 12 (*obiter*).

[86] *Dewey v White* (1827) Mood & M 56 (D justified in throwing down C's chimney because of the risk that it would otherwise fall onto highway below); *Case of Saltpetre* (1606) 12 Co Rep 12 (justified in destroying buildings). Fire brigades now have statutory authority dating from the Metropolitan Fire Brigade Act 1865, s 12 to do such things.

[87] *Mouse's case* (1608) 12 Co Rep 63. Cf *Southport Corpn v Esso Petroleum Co Ltd* [1954] 2 QB 182; revsd [1956] AC 218. Cf also the restricted common law right to deviate from a foundrous highway at least where it is public, and the land entered belongs to a person responsible for the highway's foundrous state: *Stacy v Sherrin* (1913) 29 TLR 555.

[88] 'No': *Bohlen* 39 HLR 370; 'yes': *British Cast Plate Manufacturers (Governor & Co) v Meredith* (1792) 4 Term Rep 794, at 797, per Buller J (*obiter*); Inconclusive *dicta* in *Burmah Oil Co (Burma Trading) Ltd v Lord Advocate* [1965] AC 75.   [89] *Re T (adult: refusal of medical treatment)* [1997] 1 WLR 242.

[90] *Austin v Metropolitan Police Commissioner* [2005] HRLR 20. This application of the necessity defence was held to be consistent with the derogation provision in Art 5(1)(c) of the European Human Rights Convention.

[91] *Cope v Sharpe (No 2)* [1912] 1 KB 496, illustrates both these requirements.   [92] [1985] 2 All ER 985.

SECTION 10 THE MENTAL HEALTH ACTS

Persons who suffer from such a degree of mental disorder as to pose a risk of harm to themselves or to others may be subject both to detention and compulsory treatment against their will under the Mental Health Act 1983 and the Mental Health (Patients in the Community) Act 1995. These Acts permit what would otherwise constitute false imprisonment and battery; but the detailed provisions of the legislation are beyond the scope of this book.[93]

SECTION 11 DISCIPLINE

Where force is used neither in self-defence nor in the prevention of crime, but rather to punish another, that punishment – which would otherwise constitute battery or false imprisonment – must now generally be justified by statutory authority (for example, the Prison Act 1952). The sanction given by the common law to those in authority disciplining those subject to their authority is today virtually a matter of legal history. Exercise of disciplinary powers remains a defence in tort only in relation to children and in the odd case of passengers on ships and aircraft.

(A) CHILDREN

(1) BY PARENTS

Save in the case of injuries inflicted before birth where children are expressly excluded from suing their mothers, children are not prevented from suing their parents even while they remain minors.[94] On the other hand, those with parental responsibility of a child have the right to administer forcible chastisement provided only reasonable corrective force is used, [95] and so long as it does not transgress the threshold of 'actual bodily harm'.[96] Parents are also justified in detaining their children by way of punishment so long as such detention – otherwise a false imprisonment – is reasonable

---

[93] For details see *Clerk and Lindsell on Torts* (2006) ch 15.

[94] Eg, *Ash v Lady Ash* (1696) Comb 357 (a daughter was able to sue her mother in trespass to the person); *Roberts v Roberts* (1657) Hard 96 (an infant obtained an injunction against her father).

[95] In *R v H (Reasonable Chastisement)* [2001] 2 FLR 431, it was held that reasonableness will be judged by reference to (i) the nature and context of D's behaviour, (ii) the duration of D's behaviour, (iii) the physical and mental consequences to the child, (iv) the age and personal characteristics of the child, and (v) the reasons given by D for administering the punishment.

[96] Under s 58(3) of the Children Act 2004, any tortious battery of a child that causes 'actual bodily harm' cannot be justified under the reasonable chastisement principle; and by s 58(4) 'actual bodily harm' bears the same meaning in this context as it does under s 47 of the Offences Against the Person Act 1861.

in all the circumstances,[97] and so long as it does not amount to inhuman or degrading treatment which is prohibited under Article 3 of the European Convention on Human Rights (into line with which English common law must come). In assessing whether there has been an abrogation of Article 3, it will be necessary for the courts to take account of the parent's Article 7 right not to be held guilty of any criminal offence that did not constitute a criminal offence under national or international law at the time it was committed.[98] In other words, in cases where the parent's act does not constitute a criminal offence – for example cruelty as *per* section 1 of the Children and Young Persons Act 1933 – this factor will be a *prima facie* (but by no means conclusive) indication of the reasonableness of the chastisement.

(2) BY SCHOOLTEACHERS AND OTHERS RESPONSIBLE FOR CHILDREN OR FOR THEIR TRAINING AND EDUCATION

At one time schoolteachers, both at boarding and day schools, and in the maintained and the independent sectors, had the right to use reasonable force to correct the children under their tutelage.[99] Nowadays, however, and not least against the background of the European Human Rights Convention, the rights of persons other than parents to punish children in a manner that would otherwise be tortious are extremely limited. Section 548 of the Education Act 1996, for example, prohibits corporal punishment in both state and independent schools.[100] Furthermore, in relation to detention after school, or confiscating a child's property, it seems that a serious breach of discipline must be shown.[101] Similar rules apply to children in community homes[102] or in local authority foster placements.[103]

(B) PASSENGERS ON SHIPS AND AIRCRAFT

The captain of a ship may use reasonable force against anyone on his ship who commits 'some act calculated in the apprehension of a reasonable man to interfere with the safety of the ship or the due prosecution of the voyage',[104] provided also, it seems, that he believes it necessary for the purpose.[105] A captain was not, therefore, justified in detaining a passenger in his cabin for a week because the passenger thumbed his nose to the captain and did not apologise.[106] A similar power exists in favour of the captain

---

[97] *R v Rahman* (1985) 81 Cr App Rep 349.   [98] *R v H (Reasonable Chastisement)* [2001] 2 FLR 431.

[99] *Fitzgerald v Northcote* (1865) 4 F & F 656 (headmaster, boarding school); *Ryan v Fildes* [1938] 3 All ER 517 (assistant mistress, day school).

[100] The Act's extension to independent schools, not merely in respect of state-funded pupils, was made clear in *R (on the application of Williamson) v Secretary of State for Education and Employment* [2002] 1 FLR 493.

[101] *Fitzgerald v Northcote* (1865) 4 F & F 656.

[102] Children's Homes Regulations 1991 (SI 1991/1506), reg 8(2)(a).

[103] Foster Placement (Children) Regulations 1991 (SI 1991/910), Sch 2, para 5.

[104] *Aldworth v Stewart* (1866) 4 F & F 957, at 961, *per* Channell B.

[105] *Hook v Cunard Steamship Co Ltd* [1953] 1 All ER 1021.   [106] *Aldworth v Stewart* (1866) 4 F & F 957.

of an aircraft in flight where a person is jeopardizing or likely to jeopardize the safety of the flight or persons on board.[107]

SECTION 12 ARREST, SEARCH AND SEIZURE

The powers of arrest, search and seizure conferred on police officers, and to a limited extent on private citizens, by the Police and Criminal Evidence Act 1984 are in practice the most important of all the defences discussed in this chapter. Lawful arrest, search or seizure may constitute a defence to false imprisonment, battery, trespass to land or an interference with goods. In the case of unlawful arrest, the victim may use force that would otherwise be a battery in order to resist that unlawful arrest. The Police and Criminal Evidence Act 1984 to some extent codified earlier case law and legislation on police powers. But it also conferred new powers on the police. Nevertheless, a fair amount of pre-1984 Act case law remains relevant to the definition of police powers.[108] The Human Rights Act 1998 also requires that provision for lawful arrest meets the principles set out in Article 5 of the Convention.

(A) ARREST

(1) BY A POLICEMAN WITH A WARRANT

A policeman who arrests a person under a warrant acts lawfully and commits no trespass. Even if there is a 'defect of jurisdiction' in the magistrate who issued the warrant, a constable is statutorily exempt from liability if he acts in obedience to the warrant.[109] Thus, a constable commits no tort if he obeys even an 'invalid or unlawful warrant'.[110] Obedience to the warrant is always central: thus he is liable if he arrests the wrong person, or acts outside his jurisdiction.[111] Furthermore, he must produce the warrant on demand,[112] and will be liable if he fails so to do.

(2) BY A POLICEMAN WITHOUT WARRANT[113]

The power of arrest without warrant is governed by a new section 24 of the Police and Criminal Evidence Act 1984.[114] To begin with, the section provides that a constable may arrest without warrant anyone who is committing or about to commit an offence, or

---

[107] Civil Aviation Act 1982, s 94.

[108] *Lewis v Chief Constable of South Wales Constabulary* [1991] 1 All ER 206, at 208, *per* Balcombe LJ.

[109] Constables Protection Act 1750, s 6.

[110] *McGrath v Chief Constable of the Royal Ulster Constabulary* [2001] 3 WLR 312; *Horsfield v Brown* [1932] 1 KB 355, at 369.   [111] As to constables' jurisdiction see now the Magistrates' Courts Act 1980, s 125(2).

[112] Magistrates' Courts Act 1980, s 125(3).

[113] At the time of writing this chapter, the powers under the Police and Criminal Evidence Act 1984 that are described in the following paragraphs were not in force. The powers derive from sections of the 1984 Act that were inserted or amended by the Serious Organised Crime and Police Act 2005 (which was not fully in force at that time). I anticipated, however, that the various provisions would be in force at the time of publication or shortly thereafter.   [114] This was substituted by the Serious Organised Crime and Police Act 2005, s 110.

anyone whom he believes on reasonable grounds to be doing either of these two things.[115] In addition, if a constable reasonably believes that an offence has been committed, he may also arrest without warrant anyone whom he has reasonable grounds to suspect is guilty of it.[116] It is noteworthy that in relation to this second power there need not in fact have been any offence committed; but where an offence has actually been committed, the constable is of course entitled to arrest anyone guilty of that offence, or anyone he reasonably suspects to be guilty of that offence.[117]

An overarching condition that is applicable to each of these summary powers of arrest is that the constable must have reasonable grounds to believe that an arrest is necessary for any one or more of a list of prescribed reasons.[118] These statutory reasons relate, loosely, to matters such as ascertaining the name and address of the person in question, preventing the infliction of physical injury (either to the person in question or to some third party), protecting a child and facilitating the swift investigation of the offence or conduct of the person in question.[119]

(3) ARREST BY A PRIVATE CITIZEN

A person other than a constable may also arrest anyone in the act of committing (or reasonably suspected to be committing) an indictable offence.[120] Here, private citizens act at their peril; for if, despite appearances, no offence has actually been committed, they may well be liable for false imprisonment in respect of the unlawful arrest.[121] Just as with constables, private citizens may only arrest another where they believe on reasonable grounds that an arrest is necessary according to a list of statutory reasons; but in addition, it must also appear to the person making the arrest that it is not reasonably practicable for a constable to make that arrest instead.[122]

The final point to note in this context is that the common law powers to intervene to prevent breaches of the peace are unaffected by the 1984 Act.[123] Both constables and private citizens may arrest without warrant a person committing a breach of the peace or a person who, having committed one, is reasonably believed to be about to renew that breach.[124] Equally, there is a common law power to intervene where an imminent breach of the peace is reasonably apprehended.[125] Exceptionally a

---

[115] Police and Criminal Evidence Act 1984, s 24(1).   [116] Police and Criminal Evidence Act 1984, s 24(2).
[117] Police and Criminal Evidence Act 1984, s 24(3).   [118] Police and Criminal Evidence Act 1984, s 24(4).
[119] Police and Criminal Evidence Act 1984, s 24(5).
[120] Police and Criminal Evidence Act 1984, s 24A(1).
[121] *R v Self* [1992] 3 All ER 476 (a store detective arrested a customer whom she saw putting a bar of chocolate in his pocket; he was acquitted of theft and the arrest was found to be unlawful).
[122] Police and Criminal Evidence Act 1984, s 24A(3). The list of reasons appears at s 24A(4). It contains some concerns similar to those applicable in relation to a constable's summary arrest – *eg*, fear that a person will otherwise suffer physical injury or property damage – but adds the particular reason that there is a danger of the (suspected) offender making off before a constable can assume responsibility for him.
[123] *Bibby v Chief Constable of Essex* (2000) 164 JP 297.
[124] *Timothy v Simpson* (1835) 1 Cr M & R 757. Police are not entitled to arrest for obstruction of an officer in the execution of his duty unless the disturbance caused, or was likely to cause, a breach of the peace: *Wershof v Metropolitan Police Commissioner* [1978] 3 All ER 540.
[125] *Foulkes v Chief Constable of Merseyside Police* [1998] 3 All ER 705.

person may be detained without a formal arrest in order to prevent or stop a breach of the peace.[126]

(4) REASONABLE GROUNDS FOR SUSPICION

The powers of arrest considered in this section make frequent reference to reasonable grounds for suspicion about the actual or imminent commission of an offence. The terminology is not new, and there is a rich body of case law on the meaning of reasonable suspicion. Detailed consideration of that case law falls beyond the scope of this book,[127] and it suffices to note just two things here. First, that reasonable grounds for suspicion are to be judged as a question of fact in each case, and secondly, that the basic test is one of whether, in all the circumstances, the information available to the person making the arrest, at the time of the arrest, was sufficient to give rise *objectively* to reasonable grounds for suspicion.

(B) ENTRY, SEARCH AND SEIZURE

The Police and Criminal Evidence Act 1984 confers on constables powers far greater in extent than those ill-defined powers enjoyed by the police at common law to enter premises, search persons and property and to seize evidence.[128] Exercise of powers of entry, search and seizure will in an appropriate case provide a good defence to actions for trespass whether to land, person, or goods, and to actions for conversion. But detailed exposition of the relevant powers contained in the Police and Criminal Evidence Act 1984 is again beyond a book on torts.[129] It is enough to note here that these police powers include a power to stop and search persons in public places for stolen or prohibited articles and a power of entry to effect a lawful arrest or to save life or prevent serious damage to property. All these powers are additional to the power to seek a search warrant from magistrates.

SECTION 13 JUDICIAL ACTS

Judges and magistrates have generally enjoyed immunity from tort actions. The law is complex,[130] but the basic position is that it may be a defence to false imprisonment, trespass or conversion if the defendant's act was done in execution of the judicial

---

[126] *Albert v Lavin* [1982] AC 546.
[127] Interested readers should consult *Clerk and Lindsell on Torts* (2006) ch 19.
[128] See also the additional powers of seizure conferred by the Criminal Justice and Police Act 2001, ss 50–51.
[129] For details of the various provisions, see *Clerk & Lindsell on Torts* (2006) ch 15.
[130] For details, see *Clerk and Lindsell on Torts* (2006) ch 5.

process. Where, however, a judicial act done in good faith results in an arrest or detention in contravention of the principles embodied in Article 5 of the Human Rights Convention, an action for damages will lie under section 9 of the Human Rights Act 1998.

SECTION 14 STATUTORY AUTHORITY

Public bodies and officials – such as prison officers and those empowered to act under the Mental Health legislation – may sometimes perform acts that would otherwise be unlawful if they are specifically authorized by statute to do them. In tort cases of this kind, the central question before the courts is whether the Act in question authorized the official to perform the act complained of.[131] Certain guiding principles have been developed by the courts in order to answer this question. Either a duty or a power to do the act will afford a defence.[132] The defendant must prove that the tort would be an inevitable result of performing the act authorized. If, for instance, a local authority built an efficient electricity generating station, the fumes from which damaged crops of the claimant, the authority would only have a defence if it proved not merely that an efficient station had been built, but also that it had used all reasonable care in the light of current technical and scientific skill to prevent the commission of a tort.[133] On the other hand, the authority will have an absolute defence, regardless of proving these precautions, if it can discharge the very heavy burden of proving that the Act authorized it to disregard these matters.[134]

In determining whether Parliament intended to deprive the claimant of a right to sue, the presence of some alternative special provision in the Act for compensating those injured by the statutory activity may be material, and sometimes even decisive. It is also important to look at the nature of the power. Powers to execute some particular work, or carry on some particular undertaking (such as building a reservoir or a gasworks), 'are, in the absence of clear provision to the contrary in the Act, limited to the doing of the particular things authorized without infringement of the rights of others, except in so far as any such infringement may be a demonstrably necessary consequence of doing what is authorized to be done'.[135] If, however, a public body is required to execute a variety of works at its discretion (many of which are likely to affect private rights), the body will rarely be prevented from infringing those rights, *so long as*

---

[131] *IRC v Rossminster Ltd* [1980] AC 952 is an example of the difficult problems of statutory construction which may arise.   [132] *Hammersmith and City Rly Co v Brand* (1868) LR 4 HL 171.

[133] *Tate & Lyle Industries Ltd v Greater London Council* [1983] 2 AC 509.

[134] *Manchester Corpn v Farnworth* [1930] AC 171; *Geddis v Bann Reservoir Proprietors* (1878) 3 App Cas 430.

[135] *Marriage v East Norfolk Rivers Catchment Board* [1950] 1 KB 284, at 307, *per* Jenkins LJ; *British Waterways Board v Severn Trent Water Ltd* [2002] ch 25.

ensuring non-infringement would prevent it from doing the very task it was set up to perform.[136]

SECTION 15 *EX TURPI CAUSA*

(A) JURIDICAL UNCERTAINTY

There is probably no more juridically confusing defence in the whole of the law of tort than that of *ex turpi causa non oritur actio*. Loosely translated, this means that no cause of action should arise from illegal acts. Accordingly, the defence is sometimes referred to as illegality.[137] It is submitted, however, that illegality is an inapposite label in the context of tort actions. It is one thing to assert a claim squarely on the basis of injury sustained by virtue of one's own illegal act (and thus have one's claim rejected on the ground of illegality), but it is quite another to have committed crime X, yet base one's claim on another person's quite independent tort (which is often the case when the defence is raised in tort). Two examples help illustrate the difference.

Imagine that A makes an illegal contract with B and B fails to honour his side of the agreement.[138] In such circumstances, A is barred by the defence of illegality from seeking a remedy in contract because, to assert his claim, A must found his cause of action on what was an illegal agreement in the first place.

Contrast this with the case of X, who, while driving a stolen getaway car, is injured in a collision caused entirely by the negligent driving of Y. Here, X is certainly a wrong-doer, but his claim against Y is based firmly upon Y's tort, not his own, coincidental, illegal act. Even so, there may be great reluctance to allow X's claim to succeed in such circumstances.

But arguing that 'illegality' *per se* is an inapt label for this defence only takes us so far. If *ex turpi causa* is to be viewed as preferable we must immediately adapt our understanding of the maxim to say that tort law may offer a defence where a claimant's action either arises from, or in connection with, the claimant's illegal act. But even this, judged against the backdrop of the existing cases, proves, as we shall see in due course, to be an inadequate description of the defence.[139] As the case law reveals, the defence may sometimes be raised without the claimant's act being strictly a criminal offence;[140]

---

[136] [1950] 1 KB 284, at 307–8, *per* Jenkins LJ. The cases on this defence of statutory authority are numerous, yet it is needless to discuss them all here (since they each turn on particular words in specific statutes). For one example, however, in which D was held liable for not having done something authorized by statute in a manner that *did not* infringe C's rights, see *British Waterways Board v Severn Trent Water Ltd* [2002] Ch 25.

[137] See, eg, Glofcheski, 'Plaintiff's Illegality as a bar to Recovery of Personal Injury Damages' [1999] *Legal Studies* 372.   [138] See, eg, *Taylor v Chester* (1869) LR 4 QB 309.

[139] See doubts as to this Latin maxim in *Pitts v Hunt* [1990] 3 WLR 542, at 565, *per* Dillon LJ.

[140] That the defence has never historically been confined to criminal acts on C's part is clear from *Holman v Johnson* (1775) 1 Cowp 341 in which case Lord Mansfield CJ declared: '[n]o court will lend its aid to a man

and even where the claimant is guilty of an offence, his claim in tort need not always be barred. One important case – *Revill v Newbery*[141] – bears out this second point.

C, a burglar, who did not threaten any personal violence, was allowed to sue D, a householder, who fired a shotgun at him without warning after C attempted to break into D's garden shed. D's response was said to be 'disproportionate' to C's criminal conduct.

In the light of these various qualifications, it might be said that the gist of this defence is caught no more accurately by the Latin maxim '*ex turpi causa non oritur actio*' than it is by the term, 'illegality'. As such, perhaps the best that can be offered by way of a description of this defence is the following:

Where C seeks to assert a claim in tort against D, D may have a defence against C if either (i) C's claim arises out of, or is closely connected with a criminal or flagrantly immoral act on C's part, or (ii) D's tort arises out of the self-same wrongdoing on C's part.

The problem in defining the defence is in large part attributable to the fact that there is no single rationale that explains what this defence is attempting to do. There are at least three partly plausible rationales that can be advanced.[142] But each can be subjected to varying degrees of principled objection. To start with, it has sometimes been said that the *ex turpi causa* defence is based on the idea that it would be 'an affront to the public conscience' to afford the claimant a remedy.[143] But this can be opposed on the basis that it affords a trial judge too much discretion in deciding whether there was adequate moral turpitude on the part of the claimant to ground the defence in any particular case.[144] Furthermore, the Court of Appeal has since resoundingly rejected it.[145]

    A second test, based on the assertion that the claimant's wrongdoing makes it impossible for the court to fix a standard of care owed to him by the defendant,[146] is flawed on at least two grounds, despite any possible ostensible appeal. First, questions concerning 'the appropriate standard of care' only really apply where the claimant's action is based on negligence (but not the intentional torts). As such, this test is unable to be of universal application. Secondly, however, even where the action *is* grounded on

who founds his cause of action upon an immoral or illegal act'. But note the comparable *negligence* cases of *E v Souls Garages Ltd* (2001) *Times*, January 23 and *Vellino v Chief Constable of Greater Manchester* [2002] 3 All ER 78 (in both of which C contended, effectively, that D owed C a duty to deny C the opportunity to injure himself). In the first of these cases, C's conduct was morally reprehensible but not illegal and the *ex turpi* defence failed; while in the latter case, C's conduct was both morally reprehensible and illegal and the *ex turpi* defence succeeded.

[141] [1996] QB 567.

[142] A fourth that is sometimes mentioned – ie, not allowing C to profit by his own wrongdoing – has no obvious application in tort where, if C receives damages he is merely compensated for loss, but not put into any position of what would ordinarily be understood by the word 'profit'.

[143] See, eg, *Kirkham v Chief Constable of the Greater Manchester Police* [1990] 2 QB 283; *Euro-Diam v Bathurst* [1990] 1 QB 1, at 35, *per* Kerr LJ.   [144] See *Tinsley v Milligan* [1994] 1 AC 340.

[145] In *Hewison v Meridian Shipping Services Pte Ltd* [2003] ICR 766 Tuckey said (at [49]) that, 'we all agree that the "affront to public conscience test" is not helpful', while Ward LJ spelt out (at [60]) the reason: namely, that 'it is a false guide'.   [146] See, eg, *Pitts v Hunt* [1990] 3 WLR 542.

negligence, the standard required of the defendant may well be clear and easy to ascertain. If we return to the earlier example of the getaway driver, it would be fanciful in the extreme to suggest that a judge would be unable to determine the appropriate standard of care required of the defendant who negligently drove into him. The standard would, of course, be the usual standard applicable in such cases since the claimant is merely one among many road users and it would be entirely fortuitous that it was the claimant who was injured on account of the defendant's negligent driving.

The third putative explanation of *ex turpi causa* is based on the desire to uphold the integrity of the legal system.[147] But this account is no more compelling than the previous two, for there will typically be equal and opposite arguments concerning the purpose of the law in any given *ex turpi causa* case. Thus, while on the one hand allowing the defence enables the defendant to escape liability for what was unquestionably wrong on his part; denying the defendant the right to invoke this defence may be viewed as allowing a claimant who does not abide by the law herself to insist that the defendant must do so.

(B) THE LEADING CASE LAW

In *Clunis v Camden and Islington Health Authority*, [148] Christopher Clunis had a history of mental illness. After his release from detention in a mental hospital, and having missed four appointments with his doctors, he made an unprovoked attack on a man at a tube station, stabbing and killing him. Clunis was convicted of manslaughter. He sought to sue the health authority responsible for his care in negligence alleging that their failure to provide him with adequate treatment resulted in his deranged killing of his unfortunate victim and thus his subsequent conviction for manslaughter. The Court of Appeal upheld a plea of *ex turpi causa*. In this case, Clunis' claim was doomed because the very basis of his claim – his conviction – was the result of his own criminal act. Thus, while his criminal conduct was not *per se* the basis of his claim, it was sufficiently closely bound up with it for the *ex turpi* defence to be allowed. The public conscience, thought the Court of Appeal, would be appalled if he had succeeded in his negligence action. Similar thinking also featured in *Cross v Kirkby*.[149] There Beldam LJ focused on the way that the claimant's action though not strictly based *upon* his own wrongdoing, was nonetheless closely bound up with his criminal conduct saying:

I have no doubt that in this case the court ought not to have turned a blind eye to the criminal conduct of the claimant. He was guilty of several serious criminal offences. He had committed an offence of having an offensive weapon in a public place contrary to the Prevention of Crime Act 1953, an offence carrying a maximum term of imprisonment of two years. He had

---

[147] See, eg, *Hall v Hebert* (1993) 101 DLR (4th) 129.   [148] [1998] 3 All ER 180.

[149] (2000) *Times*, 5 April.

committed the offence of affray under the Public Order Act 1986 with a maximum sentence of three years. He had assaulted the defendant causing him actual bodily harm and he had made a threat to kill which, even on the assumption that he did not intend the defendant to believe he would carry it out, nevertheless amounted to a further offence under the Public Order Act.[150]

The approach taken in *Clunis* and *Cross* confirms and explains a series of decisions denying a remedy in tort to, among others, a burglar seeking to sue the driver of his getaway car,[151] and the widow of a burglar claiming loss of dependency against the driver responsible for her husband's death in a road accident[152] (her dependency being the loss of his income from crime). But other decisions are now difficult to explain. In *Revill v Newbery*,[153] the claimant's very presence on the defendant's property was intimately bound up with his criminal conduct (that is, trying to break into the defendant's shed): but for his attempting to break into the shed, he would not have been injured. In *Cross v Kirkby* the Court of Appeal attempted to explain the decision in *Revill* on the basis that the injury suffered was not 'sufficiently interwoven or linked with the claimant's criminal activity'. But it is submitted that the case is very close to the borderline and that another judge on another day may well have ruled differently.

Consider, too, *Lane v Holloway*.[154]

An elderly man provoked an argument with D by striking him on the shoulder (a minor criminal assault). D retaliated by way of a violent assault on C. A plea of *ex turpi causa* raised by D failed. D's response was out of all proportion to C's wrongful conduct.

In both cases the claimant's criminal wrongdoing triggered the harm of which they subsequently complained and for this reason they are both far from easy to square with the sensible approach propounded in *Clunis*. That said, one plausible explanation is that the very injury of which Clunis complained was the inevitable consequence of his crime, whereas in *Revill* and *Lane* the claims related to injuries that were not, arguably, the inevitable consequence of their wrongdoing. In other words, in the latter cases, the claimants' wrongdoing was a mere *causa sine qua non* of their injuries, but not the *causa causans*.

Alternatively, one might seek to reconcile the various cases by stating that while criminal conduct on the claimant's part will *normally* entitle the defendant to invoke the defence,[155] it will not do so where the defendant's tortious conduct is a direct response to the claimant's illegal conduct, but it is wholly disproportionate to the claimant's initial criminal act. On this footing, *Lane* and *Revill* could be said to be correctly decided by virtue of the fact that the defendant's response to the claimant's relatively trivial crime was out of all proportion to the claimant's criminality,

---

[150] Quotation taken from *Lexis* transcript.   [151] *Ashton v Turner* [1981] QB 137.

[152] *Burns v Edman* [1970] 2 QB 541.   [153] [1996] QB 567.   [154] [1968] 1 QB 379.

[155] In all cases in which D's tort precedes C's criminal act, the defence will be available if D's tort only caused C harm *because* C subsequently committed the crime in question.

whereas in *Clunis* and *Cross* the defendant's wrongdoing could not be described thus.[156]

There is also a third kind of case in which the defendant's tort comes second in time; and this is where the critical tort occurs after the claimant's crime, but is not a response to that crime (even though the tort could not have been committed without the crime having been committed first). In such circumstances, there is no sufficiently close link between the crime and the tort and, as such, the defence will not be available.[157]

Beyond reiterating that the case law is somewhat confused on this defence, there is little that can be said further in relation to it. Indeed, the only additional point that might be made is that section 329 of the Criminal Justice Act 2003 effectively replicates the common law position on when a defendant will be entitled to invoke the claimant's own criminal conduct as a bar to recovery in cases where the defendant's tort takes the shape of an assault, battery or false imprisonment.[158]

SECTION 16 OTHER SELF-HELP REMEDIES

In addition to the defences so far discussed, the law sanctions a number of 'self-help' remedies enabling a person against whom some prior tort has been committed to take action to remedy the damage done in a manner that would otherwise itself be tortious. These include retaking chattels wrongly withheld from the claimant,[159] abatement of nuisance,[160] distress damage feasant[161] and replevin.[162] Such defences need not be discussed here in depth. It suffices to note that the courts are generally reluctant to allow ancient remedies to be revived in order to expand the freedom of the citizen to resort to self-help. Nonetheless, such remedies refuse to fade away entirely, as is witnessed by a comparatively recent attempt to defend wheel clamping by invoking distress damage feasant.[163]

---

[156] Disproportionality may be of factual (as opposed to technical, legal) relevance here. As the Lexis transcript of *Cross v Kirkby* reveals, 'In many if not most cases, if the defendant's behaviour is truly disproportionate overall then, as a matter of fact rather than law, this may well provide powerful evidence that the claimant's criminal conduct is not sufficiently linked to the injuries he has sustained for the purposes of *ex turpi causa*'.

[157] *Hewison v Meridian Shipping Service Pte Ltd* [2003] ICR 766 (C lied his way into a job and subsequently suffered injury while at work due to D's breach of the Employers' Liability (Defective Equipment) Act 1969).

[158] For closer analysis of this provision, see McBride and Bagshaw, *Tort Law* (2005) pp 517–8.

[159] This defence known as recaption of chattels can therefore be used where a trespass to, or conversion of, C's goods has taken place. See *Blades v Higgs* (1865) 11 HL Cas 621; *Patrick v Colerick* (1838) 3 M & W 483; *Anthony v Haney* (1832) 8 Bing 186.

[160] Eg, chopping off branches of overhanging trees: see *Lemmon v Webb* [1895] AC 1.

[161] Seizing a chattel unlawfully on your land as security until compensation is paid (eg, until the bus company pays for the damage done to your rose bed by a bus which has veered off the road and into your garden). Distress damage feasant may no longer be utilised to seize animals: Animals Act 1971, s 7(1).

[162] An action to reclaim goods taken under some wrongful judicial process.

[163] *Arthur v Anker* [1997] QB 564.

FURTHER READING

Fridman, 'The Wrongdoing Plaintiff' (1972) 18 *McGill Law Journal* 275

Glofcheski, 'Plaintiff's Illegality as a Bar to Recovery of Personal Injury Damages' [1999] *Legal Studies* 372

Law Commission Consultation Paper No 139, *Consent in the Criminal Law* (1995)

Law Commission Consultation Paper No 160, *The Illegality Defence in Tort Law* (2001)

Trindale, 'Intentional Torts: Some Thoughts on Assault and Battery' (1982) 2 OJLS 211

PART IV

INTERFERENCE WITH ECONOMIC AND INTELLECTUAL PROPERTY INTERESTS AND RELATED ACTIONS

12

INTERFERENCE WITH ECONOMIC AND INTELLECTUAL PROPERTY INTERESTS: BACKGROUND ISSUES

SECTION 1 GENERAL ECONOMIC INTERESTS

(A) RIGHTS AND ECONOMIC INTERESTS[1]

The law of torts affords every member of society comprehensive protection from deliberately inflicted harm to his person, his goods and his land by means of the torts discussed in the previous part of this book. Protection of legitimate interests in a person's livelihood, business and trading interests, however, is significantly less comprehensive. Should my economic prosperity be diminished because I have been physically attacked and can no longer work, my attacker must compensate me for my loss of income. Where the defendant claims some justification or authority for what he did to me, the onus lies on him to establish lawful grounds for interfering with my right to bodily security. If one workman takes the tools of another, he does so at his peril. A misguided belief that the tools were his own will not avail him. Yet if a businessman is motivated by pure spite and mounts a campaign to destroy another man's business, to seduce away from him his customers or to dissuade other traders from dealing with him, the injured party *may* have no remedy in tort for his loss of livelihood.

In *Allen v Flood*[2] the House of Lords, by a majority, stifled the growth of any general principle of liability in tort for intentional and malicious interference with economic and business interests.[3]

Flood and Taylor were shipwrights taken on for the day by the Glengall Iron Company to work on the woodwork of a ship. During the day, other employees of the company, who were boilermakers, discovered that Flood and Taylor had previously been employed by another

---

[1] See generally Carty, *An Analysis of the Economic Torts* (2001); Weir, *Economic Torts* (1997).
[2] [1898] AC 1, at 14.
[3] In *Keeble v Hickeringall* (1706) 11 East 574n Holt CJ enunciated a broad principle to this effect.

firm working on ironwork. The boilermakers belonged to a union that strongly opposed shipwrights being employed to do ironwork. Allen, an official of the union, sought an interview with an officer of the Glengall Iron Company and told him that unless the respondents were dismissed, all the boilermakers would 'knock off work'. At the end of the day, Flood and Taylor were told that their services would no longer be required. They brought an action against Allen for maliciously inducing the company not to employ them on subsequent occasions: that is, for intentionally interfering with their livelihood.

The claimants' case depended largely on establishing a right to the protection of their economic interests. Although Hawkins J, in the minority, conceived there to be a right 'to pursue freely and without hindrance, interruption or molestation that profession, trade or calling which he has adopted for his livelihood',[4] the majority refused to recognize such a *right*. They recognized only a *freedom* to pursue one's livelihood or business. But Allen was equally free to seek to arrange affairs in what he thought were the interests of the members of his union by persuading the company not to re-engage the respondents. Furthermore, having found nothing intentionally unlawful in what Allen had done, the House of Lords also rejected the contention that Allen's motive, to 'punish' the respondents for their earlier breach of the boilermakers' desired 'monopoly' of ironwork, transformed an otherwise lawful act into an actionable tort.

The absence of any general *right* to protection of economic interests in English law has had several consequences. First, it has restricted the scope of tort law in guarding claimants against unfair practices by others. An English claimant in the equivalent circumstances of the American claimant in *Tuttle v Buck*[5] – where the wealthy defendant set up a rival barber's shop with much lower prices purely to drive the claimant out of business – would be left remediless. In Minnesota, the claimant recovered for his losses.[6]

Secondly, the development of the economic torts – as will become clear in the following two chapters – has been rather haphazard.[7] The prior existence of specific torts of inducing breach of contract and conspiracy was confirmed in *Allen v Flood*. But the next 80 years or so saw the extension of that first tort[8] as well as the development of the tort of intimidation and other innominate torts of unlawful interference. Much later, Lord Diplock suggested a common thread linking these economic torts. He referred to it as a 'genus tort' of unlawful interference with the trade or business of another; and the traditional economic torts were viewed as mere 'species' of this 'genus tort'.[9]

---

[4] [1898] AC 1, at 14.   [5] 107 Min 145 (1909).

[6] On the development of rights in economic interests in the US generally, see Heydon, *Economic Torts* (1978).

[7] See the comment of Lord Wedderburn that the economic torts have been at best 'a ramshackle construction for decades' (cited in Carty, *An Analysis of the Economic Torts* (2001) n 1, p15). See also Carty, 'Intentional Violation of Economic Interests: the Limits of Common Law Liability' (1988) 104 LQR 250.

[8] This tort in later years embraced the more general wrongdoing of *interference* with existing contracts.

[9] *Merkur Island Shipping Corpn v Laughton* [1983] 2 AC 570. The boundaries of any such tort remain hazy. It is at best still a developing tort: see *Lonrho plc v Fayed* [1989] 2 All ER 65, at 71, *per* Dillon LJ. For an analysis of the implication of such a 'genus' tort and consideration of the role of tort in this area see Carty, 'Intentional Violation of Economic Interests: the Limits of Common Law Liability' (1988) 104 LQR 250.

Thirdly, the restricted development of liability for deliberately inflicted harm to economic interests has necessarily had an effect on the development of negligence in relation to damage to economic interests. Can a rational system of law refuse a remedy to a businessman who suffers financial losses because of the deliberate and spiteful conduct of a rival, and grant a remedy where identical losses result from mere negligence?[10] If a firm of cattle auctioneers lose business because a rival firm undercut their fees and offer farmers inducements to send cattle only to them, the firm's loss is irrecoverable. But what if that same firm suffers an identical loss of business because a neighbouring research institute negligently allows foot and mouth disease to spread to local cattle, and government restrictions on the movement of cattle stop all cattle auctions for a period of months?[11] It will be seen later that it is not necessarily inconsistent to make the latter liable in negligence while the former remains free of liability for his deliberate actions.

(B) FREE COMPETITION, UNFAIR COMPETITION[12]

What must next be considered is why the English courts reject a general right to the protection of economic interests. The clearest explanation is to be found in the following *dictum* of Atkin LJ in *Ware and de Freville Ltd v Motor Trade Association*.

[T]he right of the individual to carry on his trade or profession or execute his own activities, whatever they may be, without interruption, so long as he refrains from tort or crime, affords an unsatisfactory basis for determining what is actionable, in as much as the right is conditioned by a precisely similar right in the rest of his fellow men. Such co-existing rights do in a world of competition necessarily impinge upon one another . . . The true question is, was the power of the [claimant] to carry on his trade etc, interrupted by an act which the law deems wrongful.[13]

Historically, English law has favoured free competition. Such a stance is manifestly inconsistent with any assumption that the interest in pursuing a livelihood or a trade is entitled to absolute legal protection.[14] Acts of competitors, or others, damaging a person in his business are to be regarded as tortious only if the act causing the damage was in itself 'unlawful'. Importantly, there appear to be three discernible categories of 'unlawful act'. The first comprises those specific torts concerned with false

---

[10] For the suggestion that it cannot, see Sales and Stilitz, 'Intentional Infliction of Harm by Unlawful Means'(1999) 115 LQR 411.

[11] See *Weller & Co v Foot and Mouth Disease Research Institute* [1966] 1 QB 569.

[12] See generally, Rodger and MacCulloch (eds), *The UK Competition Act: A New Era for UK Competition Law* (2000).

[13] [1921] 3 KB 40, at 79. For the origins of the doctrine of free competition within the common law, see the *Case of Gloucester Grammar School* (1410) YB 11 Hen 4 fo 47 pl 21.

[14] Modern competition law is governed by Arts 81 and 82 of the EC Treaty (which treaty is directly applicable in England) and the Competition Act 1998. Discussion of these instruments is beyond the scope of this book; but see MacCulloch, 'Private Enforcement of the Competition Act Prohibitions' in Rodger and MacCulloch (eds), *The UK Competition Act: A New Era for UK Competition Law* (2000).

representations.[15] Free competition does not validate the use of lies and fraud to do down one's competitors. Thus, the tort of deceit imposes liability for false representations in reliance on which the claimant suffers damage. Passing off prevents the defendant falsely cashing in on the reputation of the claimant by misrepresenting to customers either the provenance or quality of his goods. And injurious falsehood 'punishes' the trader who falsely disparages his competitors. All these torts are in a very real sense 'unfair competition' torts, and are fully discussed in the next chapter.

Secondly, there are the classic economic torts of inducing breach of contract, conspiracy and intimidation. These are the torts which Lord Diplock has now suggested belong to one 'genus' of unlawful acts interfering with trade or business. Historically, these torts were seen (and taught) as almost exclusively labour law torts of little interest to mainstream tort students. However, the bitter and long-running litigation over the takeover of Harrods did a great deal to 'liberate'them from their labour law straight-jacket.[16]

Thirdly, and finally, there is a growing group of torts concerned with the protection of intellectual property. Many are largely statutory – for example, actions for breach of copyright and infringement of patents – but the residual action for breach of confidence remains subject to development by the common law, especially in the light of the Human Rights Act 1998.[17]

The categories of torts concerned with economic interests will be dealt with in the order outlined above. No attempt will be made to adumbrate or consider in any detail the immunities of trade unions in respect of torts in the second category. The emphasis will be placed on the broad function of these torts in the context of fair competition, and the civil rights of employers and workers. Detailed examination of statutory provisions for breach of copyright etc, also fall beyond the scope of this book; but section 2 of this chapter does provide a short account of these torts simply to complete the picture of liability in respect of interferences with economic interests.

(c) ECONOMIC LOSS AND NEGLIGENCE

An attempt must now be made to answer the question posed earlier of whether the common law can rationally impose liability for negligent violation of economic interests while intentional violations remain non-actionable. Two primary issues need to be considered. Do the reasons for not imposing liability in respect of intentional violations apply with equal force to negligence? If it is correct to explain the basic principle of liability for intentional interference with economic interests in terms of a 'genus' tort of liability for any unlawful act violating economic interests, can negligence be regarded as a further 'species'of unlawful act?

---

[15] But note deceit may also be relevant in other 'classic'economic torts: *Lonrho plc v Fayed* [1990] 2 QB 479.

[16] See *Lonrho plc v Fayed* [1992] 1 AC 448.

[17] See Phillipson and Fenwick, 'Breach of Confidence as a Privacy Remedy in the Human Rights Act' (2000) 63 MLR 660. See also *Campbell v MGN* [2004] 2 AC 457; *Douglas v Hello! Ltd (No 6)* [2006] QB 125.

The rationale for regarding the 'right' to pursue a trade or livelihood as a *freedom* to carry on that trade or livelihood (as opposed to a *right* as such), derives from the judicial perception of the demands of free competition. Just as I am free to set up in business as a greengrocer and to choose to whom I will sell, and from whom I will buy, so is my neighbour generally free[18] to do the same regardless of whether it drives me out of business. The market economy encourages success, and it favours the survival of the fittest. But if my business suffers because of another's negligence – for example, if a careless contractor fractures a gas main and the road leading to my shop is blocked off for several days while repairs are carried out – there is no harm done to the doctrine of free competition in imposing liability upon the negligent actor. Indeed, the opposite is true: a competitive economy requires that each enterprise should maximize its skill, enhance its own profitability and offer the optimum service.

So let us turn to the second question of whether negligence can properly be regarded as a species of 'unlawful act'. The first point to note is that mere carelessness can no more constitute a tort in relation to economic interests than malicious or spiteful motives on their own. A negligently caused explosion in South Manchester which, because of the vagaries of the city's ancient sewage system, results in part of the city centre being blocked to traffic for several hours will not, and should not, result in liability for all the consequent business losses. However, where the relationship of the claimant and the defendant is sufficiently close that the claimant relies and depends upon the care and skill of the defendant to safeguard his economic interests, a failure to exercise that skill – a breach of duty, in other words – can be regarded as an unlawful act creating liability for the ensuing loss subject to two possible caveats.

The first concerns the respective roles of contract and tort. At one time, it might have been thought that no liability should be imposed by the law of tort in favour of the claimant where he had no contract with the defendant in respect of the provision of goods or services upon which the claimant relies.[19] However, in the light of the broadening of liability ushered in by the Contracts (Rights of Third Parties) Act 1999, and the House of Lords decision in *White v Jones*,[20] it may well be that the courts would now be more receptive to negligence claims in this context than in the past.[21]

The second caveat relates to the implications of liability for negligently inflicted economic loss. Where would the limits of liability be drawn to avoid the spectre of liability 'in an indeterminate amount for an indeterminate time to an indeterminate class'?[22] Part of the answer to this question will, of course, be supplied by the rules on remoteness of damage; but part also is to be gleaned by reference to the scope of the defendant's duty. A combination of the two restrictions will help to keep liability for pure economic loss within acceptable limits.

---

[18] His rights are, of course, subject to legal restrictions such as the prohibition on the abuse of a dominant market position contained in Art 82 of the EC Treaty.

[19] See Cane, 'Contract, Tort and Economic Loss' in Furmston (ed), *The Law of Tort* (1986).

[20] [1995] 2 AC 207.   [21] See *Murphy v Brentwood District Council* [1991] 1 AC 398.

[22] *Ultramares Corpn v Touche* 174 NE 441, at 444 (1931), *per* Cardozo J; *Caparo Industries plc v Dickman* [1990] 2 AC 605.

While both caveats illustrate the very real problems associated with the imposition of liability in negligence for pure economic loss, neither constitutes an unanswerable case that such loss should never be recoverable. They do, however, support the general stance that recovery for pure economic loss should be the exception rather than the rule. To put it crudely: the law will always be readier to require others to take care to protect you and your property from physical harm than to demand that they look after your financial and other economic interests for no reward.[23]

(D) ECONOMIC TORTS AND ECONOMIC REGULATION[24]

The discussion so far in this chapter has largely ignored the important fact that the principle of free competition has been reshaped considerably by legislation in order to eliminate unfair trade practices[25] and by the judiciary's insistence that free competition be fair competition.[26] These developments must be borne in mind when reading the next two chapters.

SECTION 2 INTELLECTUAL PROPERTY INTERESTS

The nature of intellectual property and the way in which it is afforded protection under English law is now a well-established, discrete area of study. What follows, therefore, cannot pretend to be more than the very briefest of outlines. Nonetheless, such an account is justified in a book of this kind in order to provide a more complete picture of tort's protection of economic and related interests than would be afforded by an analysis of the economic torts alone.

(A) COPYRIGHT, PATENTS AND SIMILAR INTERESTS

Intellectual property can be defined broadly as the intangible products of a person's mind and skill. Tangible property, be it land or goods, is protected from intentional interference by trespass and conversion, and from carelessly inflicted harm by the tort

---

[23] See further Witting, 'Distinguishing Between Property Damage and Pure Economic Loss: a Personality Thesis' [2001] *Legal Studies* 481.

[24] See Carty, *An Analysis of the Economic Torts* (2001).

[25] Competition Act 1998. For analysis see Rodger and MacCulloch, *The UK Competition Act: A New Era for UK Competition Law* (2000).

[26] See, eg, *Erven Warnink BV v J Townend & Sons (Hull) Ltd* [1979] 2 All ER 927, at 933, where Lord Diplock noted that the 'increasing recognition by Parliament of the need for more rigorous standards of commercial honesty is a factor which should not be overlooked by a judge confronted by the choice whether or not to extend

of negligence. By contrast, contractual rights are, as we have seen, safeguarded to a limited extent by the general economic torts, while goodwill (built up in the course of a business) is protected by the tort of passing off. But what of a person's interest in the results of his intellectual efforts? To what extent are works of literature or art, or scientific inventions afforded protection by the law of torts? The truth is that such intellectual property interests are generally protected by statute. The Copyright, Designs and Patents Act 1988 protects authors, artists and musicians from those who would 'pirate' their efforts; the Patents Act 1977 safeguards new scientific and technological inventions; the Trade Marks Act 1994 supplements the tort of passing off by enabling traders to register their trade mark, rendering any infringement of that mark actionable;[27] and designs, both registered and unregistered, are protected by the Registered Designs Act 1949 and the Copyright, Designs and Patents Act 1988 respectively.

While the protection afforded by these various statutes is potentially fairly wide ranging, it does not typically apply automatically. The would-be 'intellectual property owner' must generally register his or her claim in order to acquire protection. Thus, for example, the inventor of a product must register a patent in order to protect his intellectual property interest. On the other hand, certain rights are protected by the criminal law, while the equitable remedy of account of profits can also occasionally be invoked in this context.

While the details of this regulatory web are beyond the scope of this work, it should nonetheless be noted that actions based on infringements of copyright, patents or trade marks are essentially tort actions. The remedies generally sought include damages, injunctions and search orders. But given the potential for intellectual property to be the source of huge economic wealth, a number of judges have averred that, in respect of infringement of patents at least, exemplary damages may be available.[28] And in the wake of the decision in *Kuddus v Chief Constable of Leicestershire*,[29] this view would seem more plausible than ever.

(B) BREACH OF CONFIDENCE[30]

(1) THE OBLIGATION OF CONFIDENTIALITY

The grant of a patent protects research processes only once they have concluded in a novel invention. At that stage, anyone who produces of a cheaper, 'copycat' version may infringe the patent. But where details are leaked to a competitor while the idea is still in

---

by analogy to circumstances in which it has not previously been applied in a previous case whether the circumstances although different had some features in common with those of the case which he has to decide'.

[27] In two difficult cases for the orthodox view of passing off – those involving claimants who have no trading base in the jurisdiction but either (a) an international trading reputation or (b) a pre-trading publicity campaign in their favour – the Trade Marks Act 1994, s 56(2) protects reputation alone: see Carty, 'Passing Off and the Concept of Goodwill' [1995] JBL 139.

[28] See *Morton-Norwich Products Inc v Intercen Ltd (No 2)* [1981] FSR 337 doubted in *Catnic Components Ltd v Hill & Smith Ltd* [1983] FSR 512.   [29] [2002] 2 AC 122.

[30] See also the related material in ch 15.

the process of refinement and has yet to be expressed in written or other form, there can be no such infringement. How, then, does the law protect such secrets? One partial answer is that, when a competitor seeks to induce an employee to divulge trade secrets, an action for inducing breach of contract may lie.[31] But what of other confidential information, such as lists of clients, special manufacturing processes and so on? Certainly, the law of equity extends a degree of protection to all victims of breaches of confidential information. The detailed principles need not be reproduced here.[32] They are discussed in full in chapter 15, and it suffices to note that an obligation of confidentiality will arise where information is entrusted by X to Y in circumstances where Y is relied upon to keep the confidence.[33]

Although not true of all confidential information,[34] some confidential information may well be valuable as part of a claimant's business and economic interests. Yet even here there may be no need to have recourse to tort law or equity as, sometimes, protection will be available within the law of contract.[35] For example, the duty of fidelity owed by an employee not to disclose his employer's trade secrets derives from his contract of employment. However, an action in contract will not always be available. Consider *Seager v Copydex Ltd*.[36]

C had told D about a new type of carpet grip. Without conscious plagiarism, D developed this idea which had been divulged in confidence. C was awarded damages to compensate him for the use of his idea without paying for it. It was held that, for damages to be available, the information in question must not have been in the public domain; it must not have been public knowledge.

Notwithstanding the availability of damages outside of a breach of contract, and in the absence of any harm to tangible or intangible property, the precise nature of the action for breach of confidence remains unclear. Criteria used to determine the measure of damages indicate a judicial perception of the action as one analogous to tort.[37] Equally, the recognition of a *duty* of confidentiality is reminiscent of the law of negligence, while the development of a public interest defence – somewhat akin to qualified privilege in defamation – again suggests a nascent tort.[38] But as will be explained fully in chapter 15,

---

[31]   *Hivac Ltd v Park Royal Scientific Instruments Ltd* [1946] Ch 169.

[32]   This is mainly because the equitable action looks set to be overtaken by the nascent tort of misuse of private information: see ch 15.

[33]   See *Coco v AN Clark (Engineers) Ltd* [1969] RPC 41; *Dunford and Elliott Ltd v Johnston* [1978] FSR 143; *WB v H Bauer Publishing Ltd* [2002] EMLR 145.

[34]   See, eg, *Duchess of Argyll v Duke of Argyll* [1967] Ch 302 where C was granted an injunction to prohibit her former husband disclosing certain marital confidences. Equally, the relationship between a doctor and her patients gives rise to an obligation on the doctor to keep her patient's confidences: *X v Y* [1988] 2 All ER 648; *W v Egdell* [1990] Ch 359.

[35]   See, eg, *Peter Pan Manufacturing Corpn v Corsets Silhouette Ltd* [1964] 1 WLR 96. The duty may even survive a repudiation of the contract: *Campbell v Frisbee* [2002] EMLR 656. But note that it is highly questionable whether such a term can ever be implied into a contract: see Murphy, 'Contractual Liability for Breach of Medical Confidentiality?'(1996) 2 *Law and Medicine* 1.

[36]   [1967] 2 All ER 415. See also *WB v H Bauer Publishing Ltd* [2002] EMLR 145.

[37]   See *Seager v Copydex Ltd* [1967] 2 All ER 415.

[38]   *Initial Services Ltd v Putterill* [1968] 1 QB 396, at 405, *per* Lord Denning MR; *Fraser v Evans* [1969] 1 QB 349, at 362, *per* Lord Denning MR; *Khashoggi v Smith* (1980) 124 Sol Jo 149.

the action for breach of confidence remains an equitable action (albeit one that, because of the developments it has undergone in the last few decades, has prompted the emergence of a new tort based on the misuse of private information). Recognizing the juridical confusion in this area, the Law Commission proposed some years ago clarification in the form of a statutory tort of breach of confidence,[39] but such a step has yet to be taken.

(2) REMEDIES

The most common remedy for a breach of confidence is the injunction. It is clearly preferable to anticipate and prevent the disclosure to the public at large of the relevant information than to wait for such disclosure, then sue for damages. On the other hand, where a breach of confidence has already occurred, damages may of course be awarded. And where the confidential information is of commercial value, an account of profits is also often sought.

FURTHER READING

Carty, 'Intentional Violation of Economic Interests: The Limits of Common Law Liability' (1988) 104 LQR 250

Carty, *An Analysis of the Economic Torts* (2001) ch 1

Phillipson and Fenwick, 'Breach of Confidence as a Privacy Remedy in the Human Rights Act' (2000) 63 MLR 660

Sales and Stilitz, 'Intentional Infliction of Harm by Unlawful Means' (1999) 115 LQR 411

Witting, 'Distinguishing Between Property Damage and Pure Economic Loss: A Personality Thesis' [2001] *Legal Studies* 481

---

[39] Law Com No 110 *Breach of Confidence* (Cmnd 8388). To some extent, it could be argued that one already exists in that the Data Protection Act 1998 makes damages available in respect of unauthorized disclosures of personal data held in electronic form.

13

FALSE REPRESENTATIONS

SECTION 1 DECEIT

Deliberately false representations on which the claimant is induced to, and does, rely to his detriment have for more than 200 years been actionable under the tort of deceit.[1] Judicial recognition that fraud never constituted fair competition has a much longer history;[2] but whether early authorities were founded on contract, equity or tort is not entirely clear. Whatever their basis, it remains true that the law relating to false representations cannot be understood fully by considering tort alone. A misrepresentation may concurrently create rights of action in tort and contract. A misrepresentation not actionable in tort may give rise to a right to rescind a contract, and misrepresentations unconcerned with contract may create an estoppel. The relationship between common law and equitable remedies for misrepresentation further complicate the picture.

Nonetheless, the development of the separate tort of deceit – with which tort we are centrally concerned in this chapter – can be traced fairly precisely to the decision in *Pasley v Freeman*[3] where the defendant falsely misrepresented to the claimant that X was a person to whom the claimant might safely sell goods on credit. The claimant suffered loss by relying on this representation and was held to have an action on the case for deceit. Subsequently, the tort has been defined in terms of several key elements: namely: a false representation made '(1) knowingly, or (2) without belief in its truth, or (3) recklessly, careless whether it be true or false',[4] with the intention that C should act in reliance upon the representation, which causes damage to C in consequence of his reliance upon it.

(A) FALSE REPRESENTATIONS

Usually the representation will consist of written or spoken words. But it may be assumed that any conduct calculated to mislead will suffice[5] – for example, turning back the mileage indicator on the odometer of a car prior to negotiating its sale. Furthermore, '[w]here the defendant has manifestly approved and adopted a representation

---

[1] *Pasley v Freeman* (1789) 3 Term Rep 51.   [2] There has been a writ of deceit since 1201.
[3] (1789) 3 Term Rep 51.   [4] *Derry v Peek* (1889) 14 App Cas 337, at 374, *per* Lord Herschell.
[5] Cf *R v Barnard* (1837) 7 C & P 784.

made by some third person' he may himself be held to commit the tort.[6] And where a statement is simultaneously capable of bearing a true and a false interpretation, and the defendant knows of the false one, there is a false representation for present purposes.[7]

Active concealment of the truth whereby the claimant is prevented from getting information which he otherwise would have got is a sufficient misrepresentation although no positive misstatement is made.[8] Equally, although mere non-disclosure is not enough for this tort,[9] a statement which is misleading because it is incomplete may be actionable. Thus, Lord Cairns held in *Peek v Gurney*:[10] 'there must . . . be some active misstatement of fact, or, at all events, such a partial and fragmentary statement of fact, as that the withholding of that which is not stated makes that which is stated absolutely false'.

Where a statement by the defendant was accurate when made but, owing to a change of circumstances of which the defendant has become aware, it ceases to be true, there is an actionable misrepresentation if the defendant, by remaining silent, induces the claimant to act to his detriment on the basis of the original statement. Consider *Incledon v Watson*.[11]

In an advertisement for the sale of his school, D stated the number of scholars at that time. That statement was not proved to be inaccurate. During the course of negotiations, the number decreased. C, who bought on the faith of the representation, and who was not informed of the reduction in numbers, was held to have an action in deceit for damages.

What the case illustrates is that what counts is that the statement must be false when the claimant acts upon it.[12] There is some,[13] albeit inconclusive, support for the view that an action lies if the defendant, though believing the statement to be true when he made it, later learns of its falsity but does not disclose this to the claimant who subsequently relies on the statement. There are some contracts – for example, contracts of insurance – in which, because only one party can know the material facts, there is a legal duty on that party to disclose all the material information. Breach of this duty renders the contract voidable. Yet whether such failures to disclose amount to the tort of deceit is undecided.

---

[6] *Bradford Third Equitable Benefit Building Society v Borders* [1941] 2 All ER 205, at 211, *per* Lord Maugham.

[7] *Smith v Chadwick* (1884) 9 App Cas 187, at 201, *per* Lord Blackburn. If the court construes documents as false, but is not satisfied that D intended to give them that false meaning, he is not liable in deceit: *Gross v Lewis Hillman Ltd* [1970] Ch 445.

[8] Cf *Schneider v Heath* (1813) 3 Camp 506 (buyer of ship obtained rescission of a contract induced by seller taking ship from slipway into water, thereby concealing its rotten timbers).

[9] There is generally no duty of candour. Even in the exceptional case of insurance contracts, avoidance of the contract (rather than an action in deceit) is the appropriate remedy: *Banque Keyser Ullmann SA v Skandia (UK) Insurance Co Ltd* [1990] 1 QB 665; *HIH Casualty and General Insurance Ltd v Chase Manhattan Bank* [2001] 2 Lloyd's Rep 483.

[10] (1873) LR 6 HL 377, at 403. See also *Banque Financière de la Cité v Westgate Insurance Co Ltd* [1990] 2 All ER 947.   [11] (1862) 2 F & F 841; *Jones v Dumbrell* [1981] VR 199.

[12] Cf *Briess v Woolley* [1954] AC 333.

[13] *Brownlie v Campbell* (1880) 5 App Cas 925, at 950, *per* Lord Blackburn (*obiter*).

(B) KNOWLEDGE OF FALSITY

As already noted, in order for the defendant to be liable, he must have made the statement knowingly, or without belief in its truth, or recklessly, careless whether it be true or false. In short, the claimant must prove that the defendant did not honestly believe the statement to be true.[14] Importantly, there is no tort of deceit merely because the claimant does not have reasonable grounds for believing the truth of his statement.[15] The facts of *Derry v Peek* illustrate how onerous a burden of proof will therefore be.

A company was empowered by private Act to run trams by animal power, or, if the consent of the Board of Trade was obtained, by steam power. The directors, believing that the Board of Trade would give this consent as a matter of course (since the Board of Trade raised no objection when the plans were laid before it) issued a prospectus saying that the company had the power to run trams by steam power. Relying on this prospectus, the respondent bought shares in the company. The Board of Trade eventually refused its consent, and later the company was wound up.

The House of Lords held that an action in deceit against the directors failed because no want of honest belief on the part of any director was established by the respondent, and it has since been stated that the absence of any injurious intent – though motive is technically immaterial in deceit – may nonetheless constitute good evidence of an honest belief in the truth of a statement.[16] In the light of this, their Lordships have since held a special rule for barristers: namely, that before a barrister could put his signature to an allegation of fraud, he must have received instructions to do so and have evidence before him to make good the allegation.[17] The receipt of instructions is not itself enough; and however negligent a defendant may have been, that is not sufficient to make him liable in deceit.

(C) INTENTION TO DECEIVE

In deceit cases, the claimant must prove that the statement was 'made with the intention that it should be acted upon by the claimant, or by a class of persons which will include the claimant'.[18] Thus, a deceit action may be based on an advertisement in a newspaper if the claimant shows that he was one of a class of persons at whom the advertisement was directed.[19] Lord Cairns in *Peek v Gurney*[20] might be taken as saying that the

---

[14] Although C need not shoulder a criminal standard of proof, his burden of proving fraud is stricter than that of the ordinary civil standard: see *Hornal v Neuberger Products Ltd* [1957] 1 QB 247.

[15] See, eg, *Niru Battery Manufacturing Co v Milestone Trading Ltd* [2004] QB 985.

[16] *Barings plc v Coopers & Lybrand (No 5)* [2002] PNLR 823. But see now the Companies Act 1985, ss 67–69 (statutory liability for false prospectuses).   [17] *Medcalf v Mardell* [2002] 3 All ER 721.

[18] *Bradford Third Equitable Benefit Building Society v Borders* [1941] 2 All ER 205, at 211, *per* Lord Maugham.

[19] *Richardson v Silvester* (1873) LR 9 QB 34 (C misled by a false advertisement in the press that a farm was for sale).   [20] (1873) LR 6 HL 377.

claimant must prove that the defendant 'intended' – in the sense that he desired or had the purpose – that the claimant should act on the statement. Intention is, however, best interpreted in the way in which it is normally interpreted in torts: that is, if the misrepresentation is calculated, or if its necessary consequence is to induce the claimant.[21]

A misrepresentation need not be communicated to the claimant by the defendant, provided that the defendant intended that it should be communicated to him and that he should rely on it. Furthermore, *Pilmore v Hood*[22] seems to support the imputation of such intention.

A, who was negotiating the sale of a public house to B, made certain false statements to B concerning the takings of the public house. The transaction fell through. To A's knowledge, B passed on to C these false statements. A then sold to C without correcting these statements and was held to be liable in deceit.

The claimant must also have been influenced in the manner intended. If, therefore, company promoters issue a prospectus to the claimant, who buys shares (not by subscribing to this issue, but by purchasing subsequently on the market), and the prospectus was not calculated to influence market dealings, no action will lie.[23] The motive of the defendant is irrelevant. As such, it was no excuse that the defendant who made a false statement about some company shares genuinely believed that investment in that company would be advantageous to the claimant,[24] or that the defendant did not intend the claimant to suffer any loss in consequence of the misrepresentation.[25] On the other hand, promoters will be liable where they issue false information about a company in order to inflate the market value of shares in that company for their personal gain.[26]

(d) RELIANCE OF THE CLAIMANT

The claimant must prove that the misrepresentation of the defendant both influenced him[27] and caused him to act to his own prejudice as he did.[28] The action lies even if the

---

[21] *Polhill v Walter* (1832) 3 B & Ad 114; *Richardson v Silvester* (1873) LR 9 QB 34 and see support for this view in *Peek v Gurney* (1873) LR 6 HL 377, at 399 and 401, *per* Lords Chelmsford and Colonsay respectively.

[22] (1838) 5 Bing NC 97. See also *Langridge v Levy* (1837) 2 M & W 519.

[23] *Peek v Gurney* (1873) LR 6 HL 377 had similar facts. Cf *Andrews v Mockford* [1896] 1 QB 372. The Stock Exchange now makes a public advertisement of an issue a condition precedent to the grant of a market quotation, and intention to induce marketing dealings will presumably now be imputed.

[24] *Smith v Chadwick* (1884) 9 App Cas 187, at 201, *per* Lord Blackburn.

[25] *Brown, Jenkinson & Co Ltd v Percy Dalton (London) Ltd* [1957] 2 QB 621.

[26] *Possfund Custodian Trustee Ltd v Diamond* [1996] 2 All ER 774.

[27] *Downs v Chappell* [1996] 3 All ER 344.

[28] *Smith v Chadwick* (1884) 9 App Cas 187; *MacLeay v Tait* [1906] AC 24. There must be some conduct of C's in reliance on the representation. Harmful effects produced directly on C (eg, if the false statement causes him to be ill) are not the subject of a claim for this tort, even though C does not recover in the same action for loss suffered through acts performed in reliance: *Wilkinson v Downton* [1897] 2 QB 57.

misrepresentation was only one of several factors impinging on the mind of the claimant. And if the court is satisfied that the false statement was 'actively present to his mind' when the claimant acted, it will not readily hold that he might have acted as he did in any event, even if the false statement had not been made.[29] Relatedly, the courts sometimes say that the misrepresentation must be material. When they do so, they mean that if the claimant acted in a way that a person was likely to act in reliance on the statement of the defendant, this would be *prima facie* evidence that he did so rely on it.[30] Furthermore, the fact that the claimant acted foolishly is of no moment, because, first, there is no scope for invoking the defence of contributory negligence in the tort of deceit,[31] and secondly, the claimant's act of reliance need not be of the precise kind intended by the defendant.[32]

It is sometimes doubted whether a misrepresentation of an opinion is actionable. An example is the seller who inflatedly describes his house as highly desirable and commodious and whose sales talk – which is really an expression of opinion – does not incur liability in deceit. Furthermore, if both parties have equal access to information about goods, and one falsely describes them as first class, no action will lie. But when the opinion purports to impart information to another who is not on an equal footing – for example, if a dealer states to a customer that a new machine of the type sold by him can lift 5,000lb – an action will lie.[33]

The same general principles govern statements of law.[34] If the representations refer to legal principles as distinct from the facts on which these principles operate, and the parties are on an equal footing, those representations are only expressions of belief and of the same effect as expressions of opinion between parties on an equal footing. In other cases where the defendant professes legal knowledge beyond that of the claimant, the ordinary rules of liability for deceit apply.

Misrepresentations of intention supply further problems. Certainly, if a defendant promises to do something and fails to carry out his promise, the claimant will ordinarily look to the law of contract for his remedy. If, however, the defendant at the time of his statement lacks either the will or the power to carry out the promise, there is a misrepresentation capable of giving rise to liability for deceit. Thus, it was actionable to state in a company's invitation to the public to subscribe to an issue of debentures that the loan was being floated in order to improve buildings, when the real purpose was to discharge existing liabilities.[35]

---

[29] *Edgington v Fitzmaurice* (1885) 29 Ch D 459.

[30] *Arnison v Smith* (1889) 41 Ch D 348, at 369, *per* Lord Halsbury LC.

[31] *Standard Chartered Bank v Pakistan National Shipping Corpn (Nos 2 and 4)* [2003] 1 AC 959. On the other hand, a claimant who is aware of the falsity and, perhaps also one who is misled by any patent defect, cannot recover damages. Cf *Horsfall v Thomas* (1862) 1 H & C 90.

[32] *Goose v Wilson Sandford & Co (No 2)* [2001] Lloyd's Rep PN 189.

[33] Cf *Brown v Raphael* [1958] Ch 636.

[34] *West London Commercial Bank Ltd v Kitson* (1884) 13 QBD 360.

[35] *Edgington v Fitzmaurice* (1885) 29 Ch D 459.

(E) LOSS

There is no cause of action unless the claimant proves that he sustained loss or damage.[36] And while, ordinarily, the damages will be for pecuniary loss, damages for personal injuries[37] and for loss of property[38] are sometimes also recoverable. Furthermore, the claimant is entitled to recover all the actual damage directly flowing from the fraud, even if not all of the damage was foreseeable.[39] If, for example, he is induced by fraud to buy business property, he can claim not only the difference between the price paid and the market value, but also for expenses reasonably incurred in trying to run the business fraudulently sold to him,[40] interest on loans entered into to facilitate the purchase of the property,[41] and the loss of the profit which he might reasonably have earned but for the defendant's deceit.[42]

It is technically unclear whether exemplary damages can be awarded in deceit;[43] but in the light of the decision in *Kuddus v Chief Constable of Leicestershire*,[44] such damages certainly ought to be available in such cases. By contrast, aggravated damages can definitely be obtained in deceit.[45]

(F) AGENCY

Agency is generally of little relevance in the law of torts, but deceit provides an exception to this rule. As well as being vicariously liable for false statements made by agents who are employees, a principal may also be liable for representations made on his behalf by independent persons acting for him in relation to a particular transaction – for example, an estate agent or broker. A principal who expressly authorizes a statement which he and the agent know to be untrue is liable with the agent as a joint tortfeasor.

---

[36] Damage need not be proved in order to obtain rescission: *Goldrei Foucard & Son v Sinclair and Russian Chamber of Commerce in London* [1918] 1 KB 180, at 192, *per* Sargant LJ; *Lemprière v Lange* (1879) 12 Ch D 675 (a minor, on becoming a tenant, made a false representation – the landlord could rescind although he could not recover damages for value of use and occupation).

[37] *Langridge v Levy* (1837) 2 M & W 519; *Graham v Saville* [1945] 2 DLR 489 (C was induced to 'marry' D by D's fraudulent claim that he was a bachelor. C became pregnant by D and later recovered damages in deceit for physical injuries consequent on the pregnancy and for reduced matrimonial prospects.)

[38] *Mullett v Mason* (1866) LR 1 CP 559 (there was a fraudulent misrepresentation that a cow was free from disease; the loss of five other infected cows was also held recoverable in deceit).

[39] See, eg, *AIC Ltd v ITS Testing Services (UK) Ltd* [2005] EWHC 2122.

[40] *Doyle v Olby (Ironmongers) Ltd* [1969] 2 QB 158; *Banque Bruxelles Lambert SA v Eagle Star Insurance Co Ltd* [1997] AC 191.

[41] *Archer v Brown* [1985] QB 401 (loss resulting from C's impecuniosity did not prevent its recovery).

[42] *East v Maurer* [1991] 2 All ER 733; *Clef Aquitaine Sarl v Laporte Materials (Barrow) Ltd* [2001] QB 488.

[43] *Mafo v Adams* [1970] 1 QB 548; *Archer v Brown* [1985] QB 401; *Metall und Rohstoff AG v ACLI Metals (London) Ltd* [1984] 1 Lloyd's Rep 598. See more generally, Law Com No 247, *Exemplary, Aggravated and Restitutionary Damages* (1997).   [44] [2002] 2 AC 122.

[45] *Archer v Brown* [1985] QB 401; *Saunders v Edwards* [1987] 2 All ER 651; *Shaw v Sequence (UK) Ltd* [2004] EWHC 3249.

He is vicariously liable for statements known to be untrue by the agent, and will further be liable where one agent passes on to another information which he knows to be false in order that the second 'innocent' agent may pass it on to the claimant who then acts on it to his detriment.[46] It is unclear whether, if an agent makes a statement without knowing it to be untrue, and without authority to make that statement, the principal is liable in deceit if he would have known of the falsity of the statement.[47]

The key question in relation to liability for deceit by agents is generally whether the false representation was made within the scope of the agent's actual or ostensible authority. Was it a representation which the agent was actually authorized to make, or which the principal's conduct of affairs allowed him to appear to be authorized to make?[48] At any rate, where the agent is also an employee,[49] the fact that he sets out to deceive his employer as well as the claimant, and intends to benefit himself alone, will not relieve the principal from liability for the agent's deceit.[50] The principal will not be liable simply because the agent is his employee. Rather, the false representation must be one which the agent had ostensible authority to make or, presumably nowadays, one that was made opportunistically by the agent in a context that was closely connected to his position as the principal's agent.[51] For the purposes of the tort of deceit, then, the employee's course of employment is delimited by the scope of his authority.[52] Lord Keith explained the rationale of the rule governing a principal's vicarious liability for deceit thus:

In the end of the day the question is whether the circumstances under which a servant has made a fraudulent representation which has caused loss to an innocent party contracting with him are such as to make it just for the employer to bear the loss. Such circumstances exist where the employer by words or conduct has induced the injured party to believe that the servant was acting in the lawful course of the employer's business. They do not exist where such belief, although it is present, has been brought about through misguided reliance on the servant himself, when the servant is not authorized to do what he was purporting to do, when what he is purporting to do is not within the class of acts that an employee in his position is usually authorized to do and when the employer has done nothing to represent that he is authorized to do it.[53]

---

[46] *London County Freehold and Leasehold Properties Ltd v Berkeley Property and Investment Co Ltd* [1936] 2 All ER 1039 (as explained in *Anglo-Scottish Beet Sugar Corpn Ltd v Spalding UDC* [1937] 2 KB 607).

[47] *Armstrong v Strain* [1952] 1 KB 232 (held not to be tortious); but was this decision *per incuriam*? See *Woyka & Co v London and Northern Trading Co* (1922) 10 HL Rep 110.

[48] In *Kooragang Investments Pty Ltd v Richardson & Wrench Ltd* [1982] AC 462; *Petrotrade Inc v Smith* [2000] 1 Lloyd's Rep 486.

[49] When the agent is not a servant and the fraud is initially aimed at the principal there will be no vicarious liability to other victims of the fraud: *Kwei Tek Chao v British Traders and Shippers Ltd* [1954] 2 QB 459.

[50] *Lloyd v Grace Smith & Co Ltd* [1912] AC 716.

[51] The liability of a principal for an agent so far as it has historically been delineated by reference to the agent's actual or ostensibly authority is a form of vicarious liability. But now that vicarious liability is no longer confined to torts capable of being viewed as 'authorized acts' – see *Lister v Hesley Hall Ltd* [2002] 1 AC 215 – it seems that someone who takes advantage of his position as D's agent to commit an unauthorized deceit should also be subjected to the same 'close connection' test promulgated in *Lister*: *Man Nutzfahrzeuge AG v Ernst & Young* [2005] EWHC 2347. For details of the 'close connection' test, see ch 24.

[52] *Armagas Ltd v Mundogas SA, The Ocean Frost* [1986] AC 717.

[53] *Armagas Ltd v Mundogas SA, The Ocean Frost* [1986] AC 717, at 781.

A principal whose agent has been bribed to induce him to enter into a transaction on the principal's behalf has a claim in tort against the briber for damages.[54] He cannot, however, receive double compensation by pursuing both his equitable remedy to recover the bribe from the agent and his tort action against the briber. He must elect between these two remedies. Where an agent offers a bribe and is acting within the scope of his actual or ostensible authority, the principal will be vicariously liable for that fraud as much as for any other act of deceit.[55]

(g) STATUTE OF FRAUDS AMENDMENT ACT 1828

By section 6 of the Statute of Frauds Amendment Act 1828:

No action shall be brought whereby to charge any person upon or by reason of any representation or assurance made or given concerning or relating to the character, conduct, credit, ability, trade, or dealings of any other person, to the intent or purpose that such other person may obtain credit, money, or goods . . . unless such representation or assurance be made in writing signed by the party to be charged therewith.

The section prevents evasion of the Statute of Frauds (which requires guarantees to be in writing) by suing in tort instead of contract, and, in interpreting it, the courts have consistently taken heed of this legislative purpose.[56] The Act does not apply to actions for breach of contract, and in all probability is confined to 'actions upon representations as such'.[57] The signature of an agent does not satisfy the requirements of the section.[58] Even though the defendant has induced the claimant to give credit to secure a pecuniary gain for himself, it seems the Act applies.[59]

(h) MISREPRESENTATION ACT 1967

The Misrepresentation Act 1967, s 2(1) provides:

Where a person has entered into a contract after a misrepresentation has been made to him by another party thereto and as a result thereof he has suffered loss, then, if the person making the misrepresentation would be liable to damages in respect thereof had the misrepresentation been made fraudulently, that person shall be so liable notwithstanding that the misrepresentation was not made fraudulently, unless he proves that he had reasonable ground

---

[54] *Mahesan S/O Thambiah v Malaysian Government Officers' Co-operative Housing Society Ltd* [1979] AC 374.

[55] *Armagas Ltd v Mundogas SA, The Ocean Frost* [1986] AC 717.

[56] *Lyde v Barnard* (1836) 1 M & W 101; *Banbury v Bank of Montreal* [1918] AC 626.

[57] *Banbury v Bank of Montreal* [1918] AC 626.

[58] *Swift v Jewsbury and Goddard* (1874) LR 9 QB 301. A signature on behalf of a company by its duly authorized agent is, for the purposes of s 6, the signature of the company: *UBAF Ltd v European American Banking Corpn* [1984] QB 713.

[59] So held the House of Lords when interpreting the equivalent provisions of a Scottish statute in *Clydesdale Bank Ltd v Paton* [1896] AC 381.

to believe and did believe up to the time the contract was made that the facts represented were true.

The important effect of this provision is that where the misrepresentation by a party induces the claimant to enter into a contract with him, the claimant can recover damages for resulting loss without proving fraud. A claimant may succeed under this Act although he fails in negligence (for want of a duty of care), and the usual burden of proof is reversed: the onus is on the representor to show his belief in the truth of the representation.[60] The Act does not extend the scope of the tort of negligence. Rather, it supplements the tort of deceit,[61] and the rules of deceit, not negligence, govern the measure of damages.[62] On the other hand, contributory negligence is an available defence when liability under the Act is concurrent with liability in common law negligence.[63]

Where the representation falls outside the scope of the Act – for example, where it is made by a person who is not a party to the contract – the victim of negligence will still have to rely on the tort of negligence. The 1967 Act does not impose liability on an agent personally if he makes false representations to induce the making of a contract. His liability, too, remains to be established at common law, in either deceit or negligence.[64]

Prior to the 1967 Act, there were circumstances in which the victim of an innocent misrepresentation could seek rescission of a contract although he could not have sued for deceit. To meet such circumstances, section 2(2) provides the court with a discretion to require the victim of an innocent misrepresentation to accept damages *in lieu* of rescission. And since rescission can be obtained even though damage is not proven, presumably the court might award damages *in lieu* of rescission to a person who has not proved damage.

SECTION 2 PASSING OFF[65]

The action for deceit affords a remedy to businessmen who are the direct target of fraudulent misrepresentation. By contrast, the tort of passing off protects traders against misrepresentations aimed at their customers that are calculated to damage the trader's business or goodwill. The classic tort of passing off was limited to the use by A of the trade name or trade mark of a rival, B, with a view to inducing B's customers to

---

[60] *Howard Marine and Dredging Co Ltd v A Ogden & Sons (Excavations) Ltd* [1978] QB 574.
[61] The Act does not apply where the representation was made by a third party, including the defendant's agent: *Resolute Maritime Inc v Nippon Kaiji Kyokai* [1983] 2 All ER 1.
[62] *Royscott Trust Ltd v Rogerson* [1991] 2 QB 297.
[63] *Gran Gelato Ltd v Richcliff (Group) Ltd* [1992] Ch 560.
[64] *Resolute Maritime Inc v Nippon Kaiji Kyokai* [1983] 2 All ER 1.
[65] See Carty, *An Analysis of the Economic Torts* (2001) ch 8.

believe that the goods were produced by B thus cashing in on B's goodwill. But the scope of the tort gradually expanded during the twentieth century so that in 1979, Lord Parker described the right protected by this tort as the 'property in the business or goodwill likely to be injured by the misrepresentation'.[66]

This broader tort was tested in *Erven Warnink BV v J Townend & Sons (Hull) Ltd*.[67]

C manufactured an alcoholic drink known as Advocaat. Its principal ingredients were eggs, spirits and wine. Ds had for several years manufactured another alcoholic egg drink composed of egg and fortified wine known as Egg Flip and up to 1974 marketed it under that name. Because of the vagaries of the excise laws which impose higher duties on spirits than fortified wine, Egg Flip sold at a lower price than Advocaat. In 1974, D began selling their product as Keeling's Old English Advocaat and gained a large share of the English Advocaat market.

The House of Lords held that no-one was likely to be deceived into believing that the defendants' drink was Dutch Advocaat (that is, that they were buying the claimants' product), and so no cause of action for passing off in its classic form arose. Nevertheless, the name Advocaat was generally understood to denote a distinct species of drink by virtue of which the claimants had built up their goodwill, and the defendants' misrepresentation had induced the public to believe they were buying a form of Advocaat with resulting damage to the claimants' business and goodwill. On these findings, a cause of action arose in tort.

Lord Diplock identified five characteristics necessary to found an action for passing off in its wider form, namely:

(1) a misrepresentation;

(2) made by a trader in the course of trade;

(3) to his prospective customers, or to ultimate consumers of his goods;

(4) calculated to injure the business or goodwill of another trader; and

(5) which causes actual damage to the business or goodwill of the trader by whom the action is brought, or will probably do so.[68]

This broad approach arguably unhinges the tort from its origins, purportedly protecting 'business' (a broad class of interests), rather than goodwill (as originally intended).[69] Thus, analysis of the tort will be undertaken here in accordance with the tripartite framework of the tort that has regained popularity, and which Lord Oliver has described as the 'classic trinity'[70] of misrepresentation, goodwill and damage.

---

[66] *A G Spalding & Bros v A W Gamage Ltd* (1915) 84 LJ Ch 449, at 452.

[67] [1979] AC 731. And see *Associated Newspapers plc v Insert Media Ltd* [1991] 3 All ER 535; *Mirage Studios v Counter-Feat Clothing Co Ltd* [1991] FSR 145; *Kimberley-Clark Ltd v Fort Sterling Ltd* [1997] FSR 877.

[68] [1979] 2 All ER 927, at 932. See also the slightly more restrictive definition given (at 943) by Lord Fraser. Both opinions are considered in *Anheuser-Busch Inc v Budejovicky Budvar NP* [1984] FSR 413.

[69] Dworkin, 'Unfair Competition: Is the Common Law Developing a New Tort?' [1979] EIPR 241.

[70] *Reckitt & Colman Products Ltd v Borden Inc* [1990] RPC 340, at 341.

(A) MISREPRESENTATION

The first requirement in any passing off action is that the defendant must have made a misrepresentation.[71] As Lloyd J has stated, it is insufficient if there has been no misrepresentation, for 'people make assumptions, jump to unjustified conclusions . . . [and] these are cases of non-actionable confusion'.[72]

(1) KINDS OF MISREPRESENTATION

Misrepresentations may take many forms, and various titles may be applied to the different kinds.[73] Here, we simply note that they may take the following forms.[74]

(a) Marketing a product as that of the claimant

One must not market one's product claiming falsely that it is the claimant's product.[75]

(b) Using the claimant's name

To engage in the same line of business as the claimant and to use a similar name may be passing off.[76] If the defendant carries on business in his own name (or one which he has assumed for some time[77]) then he does not commit this tort unless there are further special circumstances showing dishonesty.[78] This is so because he is entitled knowingly to take advantage of the benefits which may accrue to him from the trade use of his own name.[79] On the other hand, if confusion arises from describing his goods by his own name, it is no defence that his use is *bona fide*.[80] A company does not, however, acquire and incorporate the individual rights of its promoters to carry on business under their names.[81]

---

[71] For emphatic endorsement of the point see *Boehringer Ingleheim KG v Swingward Ltd* [2004] EWCA Civ 129, at [2], *per* Jacob LJ.   [72] *HFC Bank plc v Midland Bank plc* [2000] FSR 176, at 201.

[73] See, eg, Carty, *An Analysis of the Economic Torts* (2001) pp 187–202.

[74] The list in the text is not necessarily exhaustive. For example, in *Francis Day and Hunter Ltd v Twentieth Century Fox Corpn Ltd* [1939] 4 All ER 192, at 199, Lord Wright thought the tort would be made out where people went to a performance of D's work under the impression that they were going to witness C's work.

[75] *Lord Byron v Johnston* (1816) 2 Mer 29 (D advertised poems as Byron's when they were written by another person with a different name); *C G Vokes Ltd v F J Evans and Marble Arch Motor Supplies Ltd* (1931) 49 RPC 140.

[76] *Tussaud v Tussaud* (1890) 44 Ch D 678; *Boswell-Wilkie Circus (Pty) Ltd v Brian Boswell Circus (Pty) Ltd* [1985] FSR 434.   [77] *Jay's Ltd v Jacobi* [1933] Ch 411.

[78] *Sykes v Sykes* (1824) 3 B & C 541. Cf *Croft v Day* (1843) 7 Beav 84. In *Wright, Layman and Umney Ltd v Wright* (1949) 66 RPC 149 (D could use his own name, but committed passing off once he traded as 'Wright's Chemical Co').

[79] *John Brinsmead Ltd v Brinsmead and Waddington & Sons Ltd* (1913) 29 TLR 237; on appeal (1913) 29 TLR 706; *Burgess v Burgess* (1853) 3 De GM & G 896. There is no similar protection for a nickname: *Biba Group Ltd v Biba Boutique* [1980] RPC 413.

[80] *Parker-Knoll Ltd v Knoll International Ltd* [1962] RPC 265; *W H Allen & Co v Brown Watson Ltd* [1965] RPC 191 (C published a very successful, unexpurgated edition of Frank Harris' *My Life and Loves*; D committed passing off when he bought the rights then published an expurgated, abridged version under the same title).

[81] *Tussaud v Tussaud* (1890) 44 Ch D 678. Nor has a foreign company a right to set up in England in competitive business with C, a company of the same name: *Sturtevant Engineering Co Ltd v Sturtevant Mill Co of USA Ltd* [1936] 3 All ER 137.

(c) Using the claimant's trade name

To use the claimant's trade name – that is, the designation adopted by the claimant to identify goods or services he markets or supplies – may constitute misrepresentation for the purposes of this tort. The following are examples.

To describe and sell sauce as 'Yorkshire Relish' was to commit a tort against the original manufacturer of sauce under that name.[82]

At the request of D, C used the name, 'Dr Crock and his Crackpots' when broadcasting with his band on D's programme. When C left this programme, he was entitled to restrain D from putting another band on the programme with the title 'Dr Crock and his Crackpots'.[83]

Using internet domain names that closely resemble (or incorporate parts of) those used by C.[84]

If the trade name merely describes the goods or their characteristics, then ordinarily the claimant cannot prevent others from using it. For example the terms vacuum cleaner,[85] gripe water,[86] cellular textiles,[87] nourishing stout[88] and shredded wheat[89] may all be used with impunity. A very heavy burden of proof is cast on the claimant who seeks to establish that a name which is merely descriptive of the product has acquired a technical secondary meaning, so exclusively associated with the claimant's own product, that its use by others is calculated to deceive purchasers. This burden was nonetheless discharged by the makers of 'Camel Hair Belting' in the leading case of *Reddaway v Banham*.[90] The task is a little easier where the descriptive words connect the product with the place of its manufacture. Thus, the manufacturers of 'Glenfield Starch',[91] 'Stone Ales'[92] and 'Chartreuse liqueurs',[93] have all succeeded in passing off actions.

The courts are much more willing to protect the use of a fanciful name, and one that does not describe the quality of the goods – for example, 'Apollinaris'.[94] It has been suggested, however, that a person originally entitled to protection for a fanciful name may lose that right if the name later becomes a mere description of the type of product rather than a word associated with goods of the claimant.[95] Yet no case

---

[82] *Powell v Birmingham Vinegar Brewery Co* [1896] 2 Ch 54.

[83] *Hines v Winnick* [1947] Ch 708. Cf *Forbes v Kemsley Newspapers Ltd* [1951] 2 TLR 656 (*The Sunday Times* could not publish articles under the name of Mary Delane, unless they were written by C, its former correspondent of that name).

[84] *Tesco Stores Ltd v Elogicom Ltd* [2006] EWHC 403; *Global Projects Management Ltd v Citigroup Inc* [2005] EWHC 2663.   [85] *British Vacuum Cleaner Co Ltd v New Vacuum Cleaner Co Ltd* [1907] 2 Ch 312.

[86] *Re Woodward's Trade Mark, Woodward Ltd v Boulton Macro Ltd* (1915) 85 LJ Ch 27.

[87] *Cellular Clothing Co v Maxton and Murray* [1899] AC 326.

[88] *Raggett v Findlater* (1873) LR 17 Eq 29.

[89] *Canadian Shredded Wheat Co Ltd v Kellogg Co of Canada Ltd* [1938] 1 All ER 618.

[90] [1896] AC 199.   [91] *Wotherspoon v Currie* (1872) LR 5 HL 508.

[92] *Montgomery v Thompson* [1891] AC 217.

[93] *Rey v Lecouturier* [1908] 2 Ch 715; affd sub nom *Lecouturier v Rey* [1910] AC 262.

[94] *Apollinaris Co Ltd v Norrish* (1875) 33 LT 242.   [95] Eg, *Ford v Foster* (1872) 7 Ch App 611 (*obiter*).

confirms this,[96] and the attempt failed in *Havana Cigar and Tobacco Factories Ltd v Oddenino*.[97]

C was the original manufacturer of Corona cigars. D supplied other cigars described as Corona cigars. C successfully sued in passing off, the court rejecting D's argument that the word no longer described a brand of cigar, but only a particular size of cigar.

(d) Using the claimant's trade mark[98]

Historically it was tortious to use the claimant's trade mark – that is, a design, picture or other arrangement affixed by him to goods which he markets so as to identify them with him.[99] And although the Trade Marks Act 1994 creates separate rights of action in respect of trade mark infringements, section 2(2) of that Act also expressly preserves the common-law action of passing off in respect of trade marks. That it does so may prove valuable where the claimant fails to prove registration, or where the registration does not extend to the goods in question, or where it is invalid. For in such cases, the statutory action for infringement of the claimant's trade mark will fail and it will be necessary to have recourse to the common-law action.

(e) Imitating the appearance of the claimant's goods

To imitate the appearance of the claimant's goods may be passing off (especially where this is accompanied by other sources of confusion, such as a similar name[100]). So, where claimants had for over 30 years marketed lemon juice in a distinctive yellow plastic squeeze-pack shaped like a natural lemon, they could sue for passing off the defendants who marketed their juice in a similar container. They were entitled to protect the distinctive 'get-up' of their product.[101]

If the appearance complained of is dictated by functional considerations – for example, the purpose or performance of the goods, or simplicity in handling or processing them – the courts will be reluctant to interfere. An action to prevent the use by the defendant of the normal shape of shaving stick container accordingly failed.[102] Yet the manufacturer of laundry blue which had a knobbed stick through the middle of the container was able to prevent the defendant from marketing a product similar in

---

[96]   The cases usually cited here are *Liebig's Extract of Meat Co Ltd v Hanbury* (1867) 17 LT 298 and *Lazenby v White* (1871) 41 LJ Ch 354n. A further case, much more in point is *G H Gledhill & Sons Ltd v British Perforated Toilet Paper Co* (1911) 28 RPC 429. In *Norman Kark Publications v Odhams Press Ltd* [1962] 1 All ER 636, C lost the protection of a trade name in a magazine seven years after its amalgamation with another magazine.

[97]   [1924] 1 Ch 179. The same outcome was reached in *Antec International Ltd v South Western Chicks (Warren) Ltd* [1998] 18 LS Gaz R 32 ('farm fluid' was held to be a trade name – derived from Antec Farm Fluid S – and not merely a generic term).

[98]   Compare the related wrong of infringement of a trade mark under the Trade Marks Act 1994. But note that under that Act, there is no need to prove goodwill in a trade mark: *Fisons plc v Norton Healthcare Ltd* [1994] FSR 745.

[99]   *Millington v Fox* (1838) 3 My & Cr 338; *Singer Machine Manufacturers v Wilson* (1877) 3 App Cas 376, at 391–2, *per* Lord Cairns LC.   [100]   *Massam v Thorley's Cattle Food Co* (1880) 14 Ch D 748.

[101]   *Reckitt & Colman Products Ltd v Borden Inc* [1990] 1 All ER 873.

[102]   *J B Williams Co v H Bronnley & Co Ltd* (1909) 26 RPC 765.

appearance, since he satisfied the court that this appearance was more than merely functional. The defendant was at liberty to have a stick in his product, but not one of the same 'get-up' as the claimant's.[103] Protection will not be afforded where the defendant's product is merely similar to that of the claimant in particulars which are common to all types of that product.[104]

(f) Selling goods inferior to claimant's goods, thereby misleading the purchaser

A defendant must not sell goods which are in fact, and which are described as, the goods of the claimant, but which are of a quality inferior to that of the normal new and current product of the claimant, in such a way as to cause prospective purchasers to believe that the goods are the normal, new and current product of the claimant.

Thus, the manufacturers of Gillette razor blades obtained an injunction restraining the defendant from selling used Gillette blades as 'genuine' ones.[105] On the other hand, a general dealer in a working-class area who advertised in his shop: 'All types of electric lamps and fittings at cut prices' was held not liable in passing off to the manufacturers of Osram lamps for selling old Osram lamps, because it was not established that his acts were calculated to deceive the public into thinking that new lamps were being offered for sale.[106] Judicial reluctance to decide the respective merits of various products[107] led to a denial of a remedy in *Harris v Warren and Phillips*.[108]

The publishers of a songwriter, who had recently attained fame, were unable to restrain D from passing off as new work the writer's early work (in which D had the copyright, and which, it was contended, was of greatly inferior quality to her latest work) as new work. The court held that it could draw no sharp dividing line between the quality of her early and more recent songs.

(g) False advertising

False advertising is largely governed by regulations which provide for complaint to the Director of Fair Trading.[109] However, three cases illustrate when false advertising may also amount to passing off. The first is *Cadbury Schweppes Pty Ltd v Pub Squash Co Pty Ltd*.[110]

---

[103] *William Edge & Sons Ltd v William Niccolls & Sons Ltd* [1911] AC 693.

[104] *Jamieson & Co v Jamieson* (1898) 14 TLR 160.

[105] *Gillette Safety Razor Co and Gillette Safety Razor Ltd v Franks* (1924) 40 TLR 606. Cf *AG Spalding & Bros v AW Gamage Ltd* (1915) 84 LJ Ch 449 (D restrained from selling C's footballs with the false inference that they were of the type currently marketed by C); *Wilts United Dairies Ltd v Thomas Robinson Sons & Co Ltd* [1958] RPC 94 (D sold canned milk under C's trade name without revealing that the contents were appreciably older than those habitually marketed by C); *Morris Motors Ltd v Lilley* [1959] 3 All ER 737 (D sold a car as a 'new Morris' when he bought it from a retail customer who had taken delivery of it as a new car immediately before. D was representing himself as authorized by C, the car manufacturers, and such passing off therefore injured the goodwill of C).

[106] *General Electric Co and British Thomson-Houston Co v Pryce's Stores* (1933) 50 RPC 232.

[107] Cf *White v Mellin* [1895] AC 154.   [108] (1918) 87 LJ Ch 491.

[109] Control of Misleading Advertisement Regulations (SI 1988 No 915) as amended by the Control of Misleading Advertisements (Amendment) Regulations (SI 2000 No 914).

[110] [1981] 1 All ER 213. Cf *United Biscuits (UK) Ltd v Asda Stores Ltd* [1997] RPC 513 (launching and advertising a biscuit called 'Puffin', which was presented in a similar manner to C's market leader, called 'Penguin', was passing off).

C successfully launched a new canned lemon drink with a big media advertising campaign. The following year, D launched a similar drink with a media campaign in which D imitated the slogans and visual images of C's advertising. It was held that such advertising could be passing off, but the action failed: C failed to prove that there had been a confusing misrepresentation.

In *Masson Seeley & Co Ltd v Embosotype Manufacturing Co*,[111] D deliberately created a market for their goods by copying C's catalogue so as to induce the public to believe that goods offered by D were those of C. Customers of C normally ordered goods by reference to certain key words in the catalogue, and D used the same artificial words in their catalogue. Although D's goods were inferior to those sold by C, this was held to be passing off.

In *Associated Newspapers plc v Insert Media Ltd*,[112] D arranged to insert advertising material into C's newspapers without their authority. Readers would assume that the newspaper had sanctioned the inserts, with consequent potential damage to C's reputation and goodwill. D's conduct was found to constitute a misrepresentation amounting to passing-off.

On the other hand, if the defendant merely makes inflated claims about his own product, a rival may not sue for passing off even though he thereby suffered loss.[113]

(h) Character merchandising

The developing trade of character merchandising allows great profits to be made from exploiting the popularity of famous television characters, both real and fictional. In particular, children's cartoons have spawned industries of their own. Having seen the Teenage Mutant Ninja Turtles on television, child viewers pestered their parents for Turtle paraphernalia such as Turtle mugs. Recognizing that unlicensed distributors would try to cash in on the craze, an injunction was granted to prevent unauthorized use of the 'Turtle' connection in *Mirage Studios v Counter-Feat Clothing*.[114]

(2) REPRESENTATION MUST BE LIKELY TO DECEIVE THE CLAIMANT'S CUSTOMERS

The misrepresentation must be made either to prospective customers of the claimant or to ultimate consumers of goods or services supplied by him.[115] It must also be likely to deceive them. Likelihood of deceit is a question of law. The judge must decide on the

---

[111] (1924) 41 RPC 160. Cf *Purefoy Engineering Co Ltd v Sykes Boxall & Co Ltd* (1955) 72 RPC 89.

[112] [1991] 3 All ER 535.

[113] *BBC v Talksport Ltd* [2001] FSR 53 (the BBC lost audience when Talksport misrepresented that their commentators were broadcasting live from a football stadium: no remedy was available because there was no injury to goodwill).

[114] [1991] FSR 145. See also *BBC Worldwide Ltd v Pally Screen Printing Ltd* [1998] FSR 665 (D made T-shirts bearing prints of the Teletubbies). But do the public care who makes such T-shirts, and, if not, in what sense have the public been deceived?

[115] *Erven Warnink BV v J Townend & Sons (Hull) Ltd* [1979] AC 731, at 742, *per* Lord Diplock. As regards foreign-based companies, the law is uncertain. According to one account, the foreign-based company must establish that it has customers in England: see the *Warnink* case [1979] AC 731, *per* Lord Fraser and *Athletes Foot Marketing Associates Inc v Cobra Sports Co* [1980] RPC 343. On the other hand, Maxim's, the famous Paris restaurant, succeeded in preventing a Norfolk restaurant from trading under that name despite having no

balance of probabilities whether a substantial number of the members of the public would be misled by the representation.[116] In assessing this, the court will take account of who the likely customers for the product or service are.[117] Thus, although the ordinary standard to be applied is that of the unwary member of the public,[118] if the particular trade is exclusively with experts, the test must be whether such an expert is likely to be deceived.[119] To an extent, then, each case must be decided on its own facts, in the light of the particular product or service in question. One case that illustrates this point involved a defendant who put a design of two elephants on yarn tickets of material to be sold in rural districts of India. The fact that his design was different from that of the two elephants pictured on the claimant's yarn tickets did not prevent the House of Lords from finding for the claimant.[120]

Even if the parties have no common field of activity, an action may still lie provided that injury to goodwill from confusion is established. Thus, a moneylender who sets up in trade under the same name as an established bank can be restrained on the ground that it would endanger the bank's reputation if it were thought also to be a money-lender.[121] *The Times* newspaper obtained an injunction against the defendant who represented it to be his principal or business associate in his cycle dealer business.[122] On the other hand, Granada TV could not prevent Ford from calling a new model, Granada, for there was neither a connection or association between the two activities, nor any proved confusion of the public.[123] A well-known children's broadcaster who used the pseudonym Uncle Mac could not prevent the defendants from marketing 'Uncle Mac's Puffed Wheat' for the same reason: no damage to his goodwill.[124] Nor could the creator of 'The Wombles' prevent the marketing of 'Wombles Skips'.[125] But in the light of the developments of a trade in 'character' itself, might these cases be decided differently today? The defendants in the latter case might not be harming the reputation of the originator of the Wombles *per se*, but what about limiting the profit to be exploited from the character?[126]

Where the misrepresentation relates to a product produced by a group of traders, rather than one single claimant, the group must establish that they constitute a distinctive class of traders who have built up goodwill by the use of a particular name or description

---

trading base in England: *Maxim's Ltd v Dye* [1978] 2 All ER 55. Note also the perhaps surprising decision in *Burge v Haycock* [2002] RPC 553 where C (a political party) successfully restrained D from dishonestly standing in their name.

[116] *Neutrogena Corpn v Golden Ltd* [1996] RPC 473; *Arsenal Football Club plc v Reed* [2001] RPC 922.

[117] *Bollinger v Costa Brava Wine Co Ltd* [1961] 1 All ER 561.

[118] *Reckitt & Colman Products Ltd v Borden Inc* [1990] 1 All ER 873, at 888, *per* Lord Oliver.

[119] *Singer Manufacturing Co v Loog* (1882) 8 App Cas 15.

[120] *Johnston & Co v Orr-Ewing* (1882) 7 App Cas 219. Cf *William Edge & Sons Ltd v William Niccolls & Sons Ltd* [1911] AC 693; *Lee Kar Choo v Lee Lian Choon* [1967] 1 AC 602.

[121] *Harrods Ltd v R Harrod Ltd* (1923) 40 TLR 195.   [122] *Walter v Ashton* [1902] 2 Ch 282.

[123] *Granada Group Ltd v Ford Motor Co Ltd* [1973] RPC 49.

[124] *McCulloch v Lewis A May (Produce Distributors) Ltd* [1947] 2 All ER 845.

[125] *Wombles Ltd v Wombles Skips Ltd* [1977] RPC 99. Cf *Annabel's (Berkeley Square) Ltd v G Schock* [1972] RPC 838 (Annabel's Club and Annabel's Escort Agency).

[126] See *Mirage Studios v Counter-Feat Clothing* [1991] FSR 145.

of goods. Thus, the French producers of champagne succeeded by establishing they all operated from the Champagne region in France.[127]

(3) REPRESENTATION IN THE COURSE OF A TRADE

The representation must be made in the course of a trade. Trade is liberally defined and includes pursuit of a profession[128] and a person's interest in his literary and perform-ance rights.[129] The tort is even available to protect the name of a political party where the party in question can demonstrate that it has valuable property in the form of the goodwill in its name.[130]

(B) GOODWILL[131]

Nearly all the examples so far given constitute passing off in the form of inducing con-sumers to believe that they are purchasing the claimant's products. But passing off extends beyond such cases. In *A G Spalding & Bros v A W Gamage Ltd*[132] Lord Parker stated that the tort protected goodwill – that is, 'the attractive force that brings in custom'.[133] This theme was picked up in *J Bollinger v Costa Brava Wine Co Ltd*.[134]

D marketed 'Spanish Champagne', a sparkling Spanish wine. C was one of several manufac-turers of champagne in the Champagne region of France. The court found that members of the public bought D's wine in the mistaken belief that they were buying champagne from the vineyards of Champagne. It was held D had committed the tort of passing off.

Crucially, Danckwerts J held that the description 'champagne' was part of the claimants' goodwill and a *right of property*. A group of persons producing goods in a certain local-ity and naming those goods by reference to that locality were entitled to protection against competitors who sought to cash in on their goodwill and reputation by attach-ing that name to a product originating from a different locality and with which the

---

[127] *J Bollinger v Costa Brava Wine Co* [1960] Ch 262.
[128] *Society of Incorporated Accountants v Vincent* (1954) 71 RPC 325. But note the curious decision in *Pontiac Marina Pte Ltd v CDL Hotels International Ltd* [1997] FSR 725 where Chao Hick Tin J held that trading need not have actually commenced for goodwill to have arisen (and therefore be vulnerable).
[129] See *Lord Byron v Johnston* (1816) 2 Mer 29; *Hines v Winnick* [1947] Ch 708; *Illustrated Newspapers Ltd v Publicity Services (London) Ltd* [1938] Ch 414.
[130] *Burge v Haycock* [2002] RPC 553. The earlier, seemingly contrary decision in *Kean v McGivan* [1982] FSR 119 was distinguished as an extempore decision confined to its own particular facts.
[131] Carty, 'Passing off and the Concept of Goodwill' [1995] JBL 139.   [132] (1915) 84 LJ Ch 449.
[133] *IRC v Muller & Co's Margarine Ltd* [1901] AC 217, at 223–4.
[134] [1960] Ch 262. Followed in *Vine Products Ltd v Mackenzie & Co Ltd* [1969] RPC 1 ('sherry' to be confined to products from Jerez in Spain). See also *Consejo Regulador de las Denominaciones v Matthew Clark & Sons* [1992] FSR 525 and *John Walker & Sons Ltd v Henry Ost & Co Ltd* [1970] 2 All ER 106 (injunction granted to one whisky blender to restrain D from passing off as 'Scotch Whisky', whisky mixed with cane spirit). But note also *Taittinger SA v Allbev Ltd* [1993] FSR 641.

competing product has no rational association.[135] The limitation to goods produced in a certain locality was considered immaterial in *Erven Warnink BV v J Townend & Sons (Hull) Ltd*.[136] The Dutch traders in that case recovered for the loss in their business resulting from the defendants' misleading appropriation of the name Advocaat for their different and cheaper alcoholic egg drink. The crucial issues were:

(1) that there was a 'distinctive class of goods'; and

(2) that those goods were marketed in England by a class of persons whose product was genuinely indicated by the use of the name Advocaat.

An earlier decision, *Illustrated Newspapers Ltd v Publicity Services (London) Ltd*,[137] that was not confined to goods or services *per se*, further exemplifies the protection afforded to goodwill.

C owned certain illustrated periodicals. D, on C's behalf, supplied hotels with folders into which the periodical in question was clipped in such a way that it could not be removed. D also inserted into the periodical a four-page advertisement that was printed with the same typeface etc used by C. The advert was headed, 'Supplement'. D argued that no-one would be induced to deal with D in the mistaken belief that they were actually dealing with C. The court rejected this argument and held, further, that C could also sue for the harm caused to C's goodwill among the advertising media by D's misrepresentation.

(c) DAMAGE

A passing-off action can be brought even where no damage can be proved.[138] The probability of damage suffices;[139] and the misuse of a famous person for the purposes of a false endorsement will generate damages that reflect a reasonable royalty.[140] The crucial test is whether a false representation has in fact been made, fraudulently or otherwise,[141] and whether this will foreseeably result in consumers being misled.[142]

---

[135] See also *Chocosuisse Union des Fabricants Suisses de Chocolat v Cadbury Ltd* [1998] RPC 117 (chocolate manufacturers in Switzerland granted an injunction to protect their 'Swiss chocolate').

[136] [1979] AC 731.

[137] [1938] Ch 414. And see *Associated Newspapers plc v Insert Media Ltd* [1991] 3 All ER 535; *Bristol Conservatories Ltd v Conservatories Custom Built Ltd* [1989] RPC 455.

[138] *Draper v Trist* [1939] 3 All ER 513; *Procea Products Ltd v Evans & Sons Ltd* (1951) 68 RPC 210.

[139] *HP Bulmer Ltd and Showerings Ltd v J Bollinger SA* [1978] RPC 79. Only want of damage prevented an action for this tort from being available in *McCulloch v Lewis A May (Produce Distributors) Ltd* [1947] 2 All ER 845. Other cases where the action failed for this reason are *A-G and General Council of Medical Education of United Kingdom Registration v Barrett Proprietaries Ltd* (1932) 50 RPC 45 (publishers of *British Pharmacopoea* could not recover against defendants who used letters 'BP' on cartons of drugs made by them) and *Taittinger SA v Allbev Ltd* [1993] FSR 641.   [140] *Irvine v Talksport Ltd (Damages)* [2003] 2 All ER 881.

[141] Indeed, in *Gillette UK Ltd v Edenwest Ltd* [1994] RPC 279 it was held that innocence on the part of D was no defence to an action for damages against him.

[142] *AG Spalding & Bros v AW Gamage Ltd* (1915) 84 LJ Ch 449, at 452, *per* Lord Parker. For cases where there was held to be no confusion, see *Grand Hotel Co of Caledonia Springs v Wilson* [1904] AC 103 (C's product was 'Caledonian Waters' – D found a new spring in Caledonia and marketed its product as 'from our spring at

Proof of intention to deceive is also not essential (by contrast with the tort of deceit).[143] It is unnecessary (though desirable, where possible) to prove that any members of the public were actually deceived. Thus, where the defendant had done no more than sell to middlemen who were not themselves deceived, the action still lay where it was to be expected that in due course the act of the defendant would be calculated to cause confusion in the minds of the purchasing public.[144]

It is not essential that the person deceived should know the name of the claimant: it is enough 'if a person minded to obtain goods which are identified in his mind with a certain definite commercial source is led by false statements to accept goods coming from a different commercial source'.[145] If the public would not in any sense be confused, there is no tort.[146] But when a cordial was marketed as 'elderflower champagne' it was held that some consumers might link the drink with real champagne, thus damaging the reputation of the genuine article.[147]

(D) DEFENCES[148]

None of the general defences to torts that might apply calls for special attention here. But it is perhaps worth noting that consent is probably the most important in this context.[149]

(E) REMEDIES

(1) INJUNCTION

This remedy is often the most important to the claimant. As always, it is awarded at the discretion of the court, and the actual form of the injunction is often one of the most contested points in this class of litigation.[150] If the defendant's conduct is calculated to

---

Caledonia'); *Office Cleaning Services Ltd v Westminster Office Cleaning Association* (1944) 61 RPC 133; affd (1946) 63 RPC 39 (rival firms of office cleaners trading under the above names, respectively).

[143] *Baume & Co Ltd v A H Moore Ltd* [1958] Ch 907.   [144] *Draper v Trist* [1939] 3 All ER 513.

[145] *Plomien Fuel Economiser Co Ltd v National School of Salesmanship Ltd* (1943) 60 RPC 209, at 214, *per* Lord Green MR. The same applies even though the drug passed off by imitating get-up was sold on prescription only so that the public had no choice of supplier: *F Hoffman-La Roche & Co AG v DDSA Pharmaceuticals Ltd* [1969] FSR 410.

[146] Examples of failure for this reason include *Cadbury Schweppes Pty Ltd v Pub Squash Co Pty Ltd* [1981] 1 All ER 213 and *Newsweek Inc v BBC* [1979] RPC 441 (the owners of the magazine *Newsweek* could not prevent the BBC from using the same name for a new current affairs programme for nobody would confuse a programme with a magazine).   [147] *Taittinger SA v Allbev Ltd* [1993] FSR 641.

[148] For full treatment of defences to passing off, see *Clerk and Lindsell on Torts* (2006), pp1768–1770.

[149] *Ex turpi causa* is a defence: *Lee v Haley* (1869) 5 Ch App 155; *Ford v Foster* (1872) 7 Ch App 611, at 630–1, *per* Mellish LJ.

[150] In the absence of a threat to continue the acts complained of, the courts may grant a declaration but not an injunction (though giving liberty to apply for an injunction, eg, if D does continue): *Treasure Cot Co Ltd v Hamley Bros* (1950) 67 RPC 89.

divert customers, even though no sale has occurred, then in accordance with general principles, an injunction will lie to prevent the apprehended wrong.[151]

(2) DAMAGES

In the archetypal case, claimants recover damages for the loss of profits sustained in consequence of customers being diverted from them to the defendant. But it is not *per se* in respect of such loss that they may claim. Rather, all loss must be referable to goodwill, which lies at the heart of the classic trinity. But goodwill has been recognised as capable of being harmed in several ways beyond mere diversion of customers. Loss of business reputation,[152] restriction of the claimant's expansion potential (within limits),[153] and dilution (of the effectiveness of distinctive symbols)[154] are some examples.

The alternative to the common-law inquiry into damages is the equitable remedy of an account of the profits made by the defendant by virtue of the passing off.[155] There are *dicta* to the effect that an account of profits will not be directed for such period as the defendant's action was innocent.[156] It is uncertain whether more than nominal damages may be awarded when the defendant neither knew nor ought to have known[157] that he was committing the tort of passing off.[158]

(F) UNFAIR TRADING AND PASSING OFF

The House of Lords, in *Erven Warnink BV v J Townend & Sons (Hull) Ltd*, extended the classic tort of passing off to a wider class of misrepresentations resulting in damage to a rival's goodwill. It also paved the way towards the tort becoming a means of controlling unfair trading practices.[159] Lord Diplock recognised that Parliament has progressively intervened to impose on traders higher standards of commercial candour.[160] He clearly indicated that the steady trend in legislation reflecting the legislative view of what is today acceptable conduct in the marketplace should be matched by the development of

---

[151] *Reddaway v Bentham Hemp-Spinning Co* [1892] 2 QB 639, at 648, *per* Smith LJ.

[152] *AG Spalding and Bros v AW Gamage Ltd* (1918) 35 RPC 101; *Treasure Cot Co Ltd v Hamley Bros* (1950) 67 RPC 89.

[153] *Alfred Dunhill Ltd v Sunoptic SA* [1979] FSR 337; *LRC International v Lilla Edets Sales Company* [1973] RPC 560.   [154] *Taittinger SA v Allbev Ltd* [1993] FSR 641.

[155] In computing this profit, sales by D to middlemen can be considered, although the middlemen were not deceived, and had not passed the goods on to the public: *Lever v Goodwin* (1887) 36 Ch D 1.

[156] *Edelsten v Edelsten* (1863) 1 De GJ & Sm 185, at 199, *per* Lord Westbury.

[157] This is what 'innocent' means: *Edward Young & Co Ltd v Holt* (1947) 65 RPC 25.

[158] *Draper v Trist* [1939] 3 All ER 513; *Marengo v Daily Sketch and Sunday Graphic Ltd* (1948) 65 RPC 242, at 251, *per* Lord Simonds.

[159] Cf *Hodgkinson and Corby Ltd v Wards Mobility Ltd* [1995] FSR 169. See also Carty, *An Analysis of the Economic Torts* (2001) pp 235–237 and note the protection afforded to a political party to restrain a person standing for election in that party's name in *Burge v Haycock* [2002] RPC 553 (D was a member of the British National Party attempting to stand as a member of the 'Countryside Alliance').

[160] [1979] 2 All ER 927, at 933.

the common law. Consequently, earlier decisions that misleading trade practices did not amount, on their facts, to the tort of passing off may now need to be regarded with some caution.[161] However, there may come a point when the extension of passing off becomes a means of protecting a monopoly and of excluding all competition? Lord Bridge in *Reckitt & Colman Products Ltd v Borden Inc* warned of this danger.[162]

SECTION 3 MALICIOUS FALSEHOOD

The tort of malicious falsehood also operates to protect interests in goodwill and economic reputation.[163] Passing off generally prevents competitors from using false representations to cash in on the claimant's goodwill. Malicious falsehood, by contrast, affords a remedy where business reputations are maliciously disparaged even though no aspersion is cast upon the character of an individual sufficient to give rise to a cause of action in defamation. The Court of Appeal set out the parameters of this tort as follows:

[A]n action will lie for written or oral falsehoods . . . where they are maliciously published, where they are calculated in the ordinary course of things to produce, and where they do produce, actual damage.[164]

(A) INTERESTS PROTECTED[165]

Originally, this tort protected persons against unwarranted attacks on their title to land, by virtue of which they might be hampered in the disposal of that land. Hence, it was called 'slander of title'.[166] Later, it was held equally applicable to goods, in which case the tort was usually called 'slander of goods'.[167] By 1874 it was established that disparagements of the quality of property, as well as aspersions on title to it, were tortious.[168] Before the end of the century, *Ratcliffe v Evans*[169] made it clear that the tort could be committed whenever damaging lies about a business were uttered (hence, another

---

[161] See, eg, *Cambridge University Press v University Tutorial Press* (1928) 45 RPC 335 where D's conduct in deceiving the public that their book was of a particular class was not actionable by C whose book fell within that class. Would that case now be treated as 'reverse passing off' as in *Bristol Conservatories Ltd v Conservatories Custom Built Ltd* [1989] RPC 455 (D using C's catalogues to sell their own goods)?

[162] [1990] 1 All ER 873, at 877.   [163] *CHC Software Care Ltd v Hopkins & Wood* [1993] FSR 241.

[164] *Ratcliffe v Evans* [1892] 2 QB 524, at 527.

[165] See Newark, 'Malice in Actions on the Case for Words' (1944) 60 LQR 366.

[166] Eg, *Gerard v Dickenson* (1590) Cro Eliz 196.

[167] *Malachy v Soper* (1836) 3 Bing NC 371. Cf *Green v Button* (1835) 2 Cr M & R 707 (D told the person who had contracted with C to sell him timber that he, D, had a lien on it, and thereby prevented C from obtaining delivery).   [168] *Western Counties Manure Co v Lawes Chemical Manure Co* (1874) LR 9 Exch 218.

[169] [1892] 2 QB 524.

name given to this tort – 'trade libel'). Since then, the tort has been referred to by many names;[170] but the term malicious falsehood is preferred here because it is the generic term used in the Defamation Act 1952.[171] The potential ambit and utility of this tort was considerably expanded by two decisions of the Court of Appeal which (1) endorsed its applicability wherever one's economic interests are threatened,[172] and (2) rejected the idea that only truly *commercial* interests are protected. In so saying, the demarcation between malicious falsehood and defamation became partly blurred.[173]

Any type of interest in land, whether vested in possession or not,[174] is protected. Trade marks,[175] patents,[176] trade names,[177] copyright[178] and company shares,[179] may all be the subject of actionable disparagements. The following random illustrations of circumstances treated by the courts as being within the scope of the tort demonstrate its extent. An untrue statement by the defendant to a customer that the claimant – a commercial traveller with whom the customer had formerly dealt – was now in the employment of the defendant's firm;[180] failure to delete the name of the claimant (a musical accompanist), from the programme of a concert series in which she was no longer to appear (because, as a result of this, others might not offer her engagements);[181] a false statement in the defendant's newspaper that the claimant had ceased to carry on business;[182] an erroneous statement that the claimant's wife (who helped the claimant in his drapery business) had committed adultery in the shop with the parson newly appointed to the parish.[183] Finally, *Joyce v Motor Surveys Ltd*[184] is a particularly useful example of a successful action in malicious falsehood.

C became the tenant of one of D's lock-up garages in order to have premises at which he could be registered as a tyre dealer. D subsequently wished to evict C in order to sell the entire property with vacant possession. D therefore told the Post Office not to forward any more mail to him at that address, and told the tyre manufacturers' association that he was no longer trading there. D's conduct was held to constitute malicious falsehood.

The essence of the tort is that the defendant's lies cause economic damage to the claimant, and *Kaye v Robertson*[185] provides a good example of the point. There, an actor was photographed without his genuine consent as he lay in a hospital bed recovering from near-fatal injuries. A newspaper printed a story concerning him as though it had been obtained with his full authority and thereby deprived Mr Kaye of the opportunity to market his own account. So doing was enough to constitute malicious

---

[170] See Carty, *An Analysis of the Economic Torts* (2001) p 151.   [171] Defamation Act 1952, s 3.
[172] *Kaye v Robertson* [1991] FSR 62; *Joyce v Sengupta* [1993] 1 All ER 897.
[173] See also Gibbons, 'Defamation Reconsidered' (1996) 16 OJLS 587.
[174] *Vaughan v Ellis* (1608) Cro Jac 213.   [175] *Greers Ltd v Pearman and Corder Ltd* (1922) 39 RPC 406.
[176] *Wren v Weild* (1869) LR 4 QB 730.
[177] *Royal Baking Powder Co v Wright, Crossley & Co* (1900) 18 RPC 95.
[178] *Dicks v Brooks* (1880) 15 Ch D 22.   [179] *Malachy v Soper* (1836) 3 Bing NC 371.
[180] *Balden v Shorter* [1933] Ch 427. The action failed for a different reason.
[181] *Shapiro v La Morta* (1923) 130 LT 622. The action failed for other reasons.
[182] *Ratcliffe v Evans* [1892] 2 QB 524; *Danish Mercantile Co v Beaumont* (1950) 67 RPC 111 (D's bare statement that he was the only authorized importer of certain machines).
[183] *Riding v Smith* (1876) 1 Ex D 91.   [184] [1948] Ch 252.   [185] [1991] FSR 62.

falsehood because the story would misrepresent the fact that Mr Kaye had given the newspaper an exclusive interview, when the truth was that he was not fully conscious and in fact had no recollection of speaking to the newspaper in question.[186] In *Joyce v Sengupta*[187] the defendant newspaper published an article insinuating that the claimant had abused her position as lady's maid to the Princess Royal in order to steal from her employer personal letters. The claimant argued that the article might well prejudice her future employment prospects and her malicious falsehood claim was allowed to proceed.

(B) DISPARAGEMENT

It is a disparagement if there is some misstatement as to the extent of the claimant's interest in his property or as to the quality of his goods. Thus, a false statement by a newspaper owner that the circulation of his newspaper greatly exceeded that of the claimant's rival newspaper was held to be capable of being tortious.[188]

A threat of proceedings for infringement of a patent[189] or a trade mark[190] may be enough. Section 70 of the Patents Act 1977,[191] section 21 of the Trade Marks Act 1994, section 26 of the Registered Designs Act 1949 and section 253 of the Copyright, Designs and Patents Act 1988 all make it a statutory tort for a person by circulars, advertisements or otherwise to threaten proceedings for infringement wherever the defendant is unable to prove that the claimant's act constitutes an infringement of the defendant's patent, trade mark, registered design or design rights.[192] On the other hand, an assertion by way of mere 'puffery' that the defendant's goods are better than the claimant's, is not actionable[193] (unless the defendant's claims are couched in terms of verifiable facts, and those facts can be shown to be untrue, in which case an action will lie[194]). And the courts will not, in such cases, decide the relative merits of competing products.[195] The test in such cases is whether a reasonable man would take the claim that denigrates the claimant's goods as one made seriously.[196]

---

[186] It is also worthy of mention that the Court of Appeal was keen to offer protection against the gross invasion of the actor's privacy.   [187] [1993] 1 All ER 897.

[188] *Lyne v Nicholls* (1906) 23 TLR 86. Cf *Evans v Harlow* (1844) 5 QB 624.

[189] *Mentmore Manufacturing Co Ltd v Fomento (Sterling Area) Ltd* (1955) 72 RPC 157.

[190] *Colley v Hart* (1890) 44 Ch D 179, at 183, *per* North J.

[191] See *Johnson Electric Industrial Manufacturing Ltd v Mabuchi-Motor KK* [1986] FSR 280.

[192] For full details of the statutory actions see *Clerk and Lindsell on Torts* (2006) ch 26.

[193] *Young v Macrae* (1862) 3 B & S 264; *Hubbuck & Sons v Wilkinson, Heywood and Clark* [1899] 1 QB 86.

[194] *De Beers Abrasive Products Ltd v International General Electric Co of New York Ltd* [1975] 2 All ER 599; *DSG Retail Ltd v Comet Group plc* [2002] FSR 58.

[195] *White v Mellin* [1895] AC 154. D claimed D's product was better in particular respects than any other; but the claim by a competitor failed on the basis that the claim was a mere puff.

[196] *De Beers Abrasive Products Ltd v International General Electric Co of New York Ltd* [1975] 2 All ER 599; test subsequently applied in *Vodaphone Group plc v Orange Personal Communications Services Ltd* [1997] FSR 34.

(C) FALSE STATEMENT

The claimant has the burden of establishing that the statement was untrue.[197] The statement must be a false one *about the claimant or his property*; it is not enough that just any false statement resulted in harm to the claimant.

(D) PUBLICATION

Because the essence of the tort is the effect produced by the false statement on persons entering into relations with the claimant, the falsehood must be published to persons other than the claimant.[198] Whether a negligent or accidental publication is sufficient is undecided. However, it is clear that the defendant is liable for a re-publication that is the natural and probable result of his original publication.[199]

(E) MALICE

Since malice is always required to ground liability for this tort, it naturally follows that good faith on the part of the defendant will always be a good defence.[200] But whether the mere absence of good faith should be taken necessarily to imply the presence of malice is unclear due to the different tests for malice that have been put forward from time to time. Malice has been variously defined as 'improper motive',[201] 'intention to injure',[202] or 'want of honest belief in the truth of the statement'.[203] Significantly, the courts have not indicated a preference for any one of these definitions above the others.[204] Thus, while the House of Lords in *White v Mellin*[205] held that either an intention to injure or knowledge of the falsity of the statement would suffice, Lord Coleridge LCJ was of the view in *Halsey v Brotherhood* that mere 'want of *bona fides* or the presence of *mala fides*' would suffice.[206]

---

[197] *Royal Baking Powder Co v Wright, Crossley & Co* (1900) 18 RPC 95, at 99, *per* Lord Davey. And see also *Joyce v Sengupta* [1993] 1 All ER 897, at 901, *per* Sir Donald Nicholls VC. Note that where the statement is 'not obviously untrue', no action will lie: *MacMillan Magazines Ltd v RCN Publishing Co Ltd* [1998] FSR 9.

[198] Cf *Malachy v Soper* (1836) 3 Bing NC 371.

[199] *Cellactite and British Uralite Ltd v H H Robertson & Co* (1957) *Times*, 23 July.

[200] *Spring v Guardian Assurance plc* [1994] 3 All ER 129.

[201] *Balden v Shorter* [1933] Ch 427, at 430, *per* Maugham J.

[202] *Steward v Young* (1870) LR 5 CP 122, at 127, *per* Montague Smith J.

[203] *Greers Ltd v Pearman and Corder Ltd* (1922) 39 RPC 406, at 417, *per* Scrutton LJ.

[204] Indeed, *British Railway Traffic and Electric Co v CRC Co and LCC* [1922] 2 KB 260, is one of the few cases where the court has held that some particular type of these variants of malice has to be proved. Equally, on only the non-binding authority of a first instance judge, it has been suggested that malice in this context bears the same meaning as in the context of defamation law: *Dorset Flint & Stone Blocks Ltd v Moir* [2004] EWHC 2173.

[205] [1895] AC 154 (the *ratio* is to be found most clearly in the opinion of Lord Herschell LC, at 160). Cf *Shapiro v La Morta* (1923) 130 LT 622, at 628, *per* Atkin LJ and *Greers Ltd v Pearman and Corder Ltd* (1922) 39 RPC 406, at 417–8, *per* Scrutton LJ. [206] (1881) 19 Ch D 386, at 388. Cf *Wren v Weild* (1869) LR 4 QB 730.

The claimant may discharge his burden of proving this element of bad faith in any one of several ways. He may do so by proving that the defendant made the statement knowing it to be false, or that he made it recklessly, careless whether it was true or false.[207] A defendant shown to have been actuated by ill-will, shall also be held to have acted with 'malice'.[208] He will be liable if his purpose was to damage the claimant's business, even, it seems, although he was secondarily acting for the benefit of his own interests.[209] It also seems to suffice that the defendant knew his statement to be untrue: the claimant does not also have to prove that he intended (or even knew) that the statement was disparaging.[210]

(f) DAMAGE

The claimant must prove that the false statement caused him pecuniary loss.[211] A debatable point has been whether the requirement that special damage has to be proved can be discharged by showing general loss of custom without adducing evidence that particular customers have withdrawn their business in consequence of the falsehood.[212] Whether evidence of general loss of business will be sufficient depends on 'the nature and circumstances of the falsehood'.[213] For example, a claimant cannot be expected to identify individuals affected by a statement in a newspaper. Evidence of general business loss will be acceptable in such a case. The same rule has been extended to a circular to customers, where, in the circumstances, the circular was reasonably likely to cause a decline in business.[214] On the other hand, a claimant who complained that the defendants had stated in their newspaper that his house was haunted, but who neither produced witnesses giving evidence that the statement had influenced them to the detriment of the claimant, nor showed that the house had depreciated in value as a result of it, failed.[215] The expenses of bringing litigation in order to remove a cloud hanging over the title caused by the defendant's statement are to be treated as special damages.[216]

---

[207] *Kaye v Robertson* [1991] FSR 62, at 67, *per* Glidewell LJ.

[208] *Dunlop v Maison Talbot* (1904) 20 TLR 579.

[209] The *ratio* of *Joyce v Motor Surveys Ltd* [1948] Ch 252 (where D wanted to make his property saleable with vacant possession) is supported by the judgment of Collins MR in *Alcott v Millar's Karri and Jarrah Forests Ltd* (1904) 91 LT 722, at 723. Cf *Mentmore Manufacturing Co Ltd v Fomento (Sterling Area) Ltd* (1955) 72 RPC 157.

[210] *Wilts United Dairies Ltd v Thomas Robinson Sons & Co Ltd* [1957] RPC 220; affd (but this point was not considered) [1958] RPC 94; *London Ferro-Concrete Co Ltd v Justicz* (1951) 68 RPC 261.

[211] *Ajello v Worsley* [1898] 1 Ch 274; *Shapiro v La Morta* (1923) 130 LT 622; *Allason v Campbell* (1996) *Times*, 8 May. When the damage complained of is physical injury, this tort is presumably not applicable and *Wilkinson v Downton* [1897] 2 QB 57 must be relied on. Cf *Guay v Sun Publishing Co Ltd* [1952] 2 DLR 479; affd [1953] 4 DLR 577.   [212] *Malachy v Soper* (1836) Bing NC 371 decided that the tort is not actionable *per se*.

[213] *Ratcliffe v Evans* [1892] 2 QB 524, at 533, *per* Bowen LJ.

[214] *E Worsley & Co Ltd v Cooper* [1939] 1 All ER 290. Cf *Lyne v Nicholls* (1906) 23 TLR 86.

[215] *Barrett v Associated Newspapers Ltd* (1907) 23 TLR 666.   [216] *Elborow v Allen* (1622) Cro Jac 642.

The difficulties inherent in proving actual loss caused actions for malicious falsehood to become extremely rare.[217] In consequence, the common law rules on damage have been modified by the Defamation Act 1952, section 3 of which provides:

In an action for slander of title, slander of goods or other malicious falsehood, it shall not be necessary to allege or prove special damage – (a) if the words upon which the action is founded are calculated to cause pecuniary damage to the [claimant] and are published in writing or other permanent form;[218] or (b) if the said words are calculated to cause pecuniary damage to the [claimant] in respect of any office, profession, calling, trade or business[219] held or carried on by him at the time of the publication.[220]

For the purpose of this section, 'calculated to cause pecuniary damage' means harm that is objectively likely or probable.[221] And as a result of the section, in the vast majority of cases concerning this tort, it will now no longer be necessary to prove special damage.[222] This is especially important in view of the doubt as to whether an injunction could be obtained before the Act where damage was merely likely to accrue.[223] The economic damage inflicted on the claimant by the falsehood may be accompanied by considerable mental distress and injury to feelings.[224] The Court of Appeal in *Joyce v Sengupta*[225] suggested that injury to feelings was not *per se* recoverable. But Sir Michael Kerr suggested that within general damages, an award of aggravated damages might partly reflect the injury to the claimant's feelings and dignity.

(G) DEFENCES

In those circumstances where a defendant in defamation could plead legislative immunity or absolute privilege – for example, in relation to statements in judicial proceedings – the same defence will be available here. Formerly, it might have been apt to say that the defences of qualified privilege in defamation were similarly applicable, but the requirement of malice in this tort defeats any such claim.

---

[217] This was the view expressed in *Joyce v Sengupta* [1993] 1 All ER 897.

[218] This includes broadcasting.

[219] These words probably have the same meaning here as in the context of defamation.

[220] Note, too, in *Joyce v Sengupta* [1993] 1 All ER 897 the court said that the Defamation Act 1952, s 3 is not confined to nominal damages.   [221] *IBM v Web-Sphere Ltd* [2004] EWHC 529.

[222] A claimant who relies on s 3 of the Defamation Act 1952 is not allowed to prove special damage unless he has specifically pleaded it: *Calvet v Tomkies* [1963] 3 All ER 610.

[223] *Dunlop Pneumatic Tyre Co Ltd v Maison Talbot* (1904) 20 TLR 579. Cf *White v Mellin* [1895] AC 154, at 163–4 and 167, *per* Lords Herschell LC and Lord Watson respectively. Note that *Easycare Inc v Bryan Lawrence & Co* [1995] FSR 597 establishes that the normal rules applicable to the granting of interlocutory injunctions do not apply in cases of malicious falsehood.

[224] In *Fielding v Variety Inc* [1967] 2 QB 841 Lord Denning stated that damages for injured feelings were not recoverable for the tort of malicious falsehood.   [225] [1993] 1 All ER 897.

(H) MALICIOUS FALSEHOOD AND DEFAMATION

There are clear similarities between malicious falsehood and the related tort of defamation.[226] It is apparent, for example, that there are occasions when the claimant has a choice between the two. In *Joyce v Sengupta*, where the claimant argued that allegations that she had stolen from the Princess Royal constituted a malicious falsehood threatening her employment prospects, the defendants contended that her proper remedy lay in defamation. By electing to sue in malicious falsehood, the claimant was able to obtain legal aid (which was unavailable in defamation[227]) and the defendant lost the right to trial by jury. The Court of Appeal refused to strike out the claimant's claim.

There is no principle of law that a claimant must pursue the most appropriate remedy. She is entitled to elect the action that best suits her following *Joyce v Sengupta*. As long as one has an arguable case that defamatory allegations may damage one's financial prospects as well as one's reputation, one may choose whether to sue in defamation or malicious falsehood. That said, three key differences between malicious falsehood on the one hand, and libel and slander on the other, can be identified. First, while malice is a prerequisite to suing in malicious falsehood, it is not in defamation. Secondly, X cannot defame Y unless the statement casts aspersions on Y's character, whereas other classes of untruth – such as false statements about Y's business – will suffice in malicious falsehood. This, it has been judicially intimated, may have repercussions in terms of the inter-relation of the tort with Article 10 of the European Convention on Human Rights.[228] Finally, in defamation, the burden of proof lies with the defendant to establish the truth of a defamatory statement, whereas in malicious falsehood it rests with the claimant to show that the defendant's statement was untrue.

FURTHER READING

Carty, *An Analysis of the Economic Torts* (2001) ch 8

Carty, 'Passing Off and the Concept of Goodwill' [1995] *Journal of Business Law* 139

Dworkin, 'Unfair Competition: Is the Common Law Developing a New Tort?' [1979] *European Intellectual Property Review* 241

Newark, 'Malice in Actions on the Case for Words' (1944) 60 LQR 366

---

[226] See Gibbons, 'Defamation Reconsidered' (1996) 16 OJLS 587.
[227] And is nowadays also unavailable in malicious falsehood.
[228] *Charterhouse Clinical Research Unit Ltd v Richmond Pharmacology Ltd* [2003] EWHC 1099, at [14], *per* Morland J.

14

THE ECONOMIC TORTS AND ASSOCIATED CAUSES OF ACTION

In this chapter we consider not only the well-established economic torts of conspiracy, inducing breach of contract and intimidation, but also two torts of more recent vintage: namely, inducing breach of non-contractual obligations and harming another's trade (or other economic interests) by unlawful means. As we shall see, there is not merely a considerable degree of overlap between the various torts discussed in this chapter, but there is also a good deal of debate associated with the best way in which to describe them. In the hope that it promotes a clear exposition of what is undoubtedly a complex area of law, and in an attempt to remain reasonably faithful to the judicial language preponderantly attached to each of these torts, the various sections of this chapter are given headings that are in some places perhaps a little dated but which nonetheless best enable the newcomer to tort to appreciate their juridical contours and the law's development.

SECTION 1 INTRODUCTION TO THE ECONOMIC TORTS[1]

Allen v Flood[2] established the ground rules for liability in tort for interference with economic interests otherwise than by way of false representations. A person has no absolute right to pursue his trade or livelihood. He merely enjoys a freedom to promote his business and financial interests which the law must reconcile with the equivalent freedoms enjoyed by all his fellows. It was thus held in *Allen v Flood* that where the conduct of X damages the business interests of Y, or interferes with Y's freedom to advance his trade or livelihood, the 'existence of a bad motive, in the case of an act which is not otherwise illegal, will not convert that act into a civil wrong'.[3]

For nearly a century after *Allen v Flood*, the development of tort liability for interference with trade was sporadic. There appeared a somewhat haphazard list of

---

[1] For thoroughgoing treatment of this topic, see Carty, *An Analysis of the Economic Torts* (2001) ch 2.
[2] [1898] AC 1. [3] [1898] AC 1, at 92, *per* Lord Herschell.

nominate torts, prime among which were conspiracy, inducing breach of contract and intimidation. Much later, in an attempt to rationalize these torts, Lord Diplock suggested that there was a genus tort of 'interfering with the trade or business of another person by doing unlawful acts'[4] of which the various nominate economic torts, were merely 'species'. Though it would perhaps make life easier for the tort student if this were the case, the truth is that this proposition amounts to an inadequate and inexact explanatory account of the various economic torts since not all the economic torts (in all their guises, at least) can be said to fit Lord Diplock's description of the genus tort.[5] In particular, conspiracy actions based on the decision in *Crofter Hand Woven Harris Tweed Co Ltd v Veitch*[6] and direct inducement of breach of contract do not fit this account because they do not demand (unlike the genus tort) the proof of unlawful means on the part of the defendant.[7] Even so, Lord Diplock's proposition does help to explain the link between the 'false representation' torts considered in the previous chapter and the 'general' economic torts discussed in this chapter.[8] But that said, there seems considerable potential for the genus tort to give rise to a general form of tortious liability based on using unlawful means to harm another; and thus viewed, there is no particular reason to confine actionable loss to interferences with trade or business.[9]

SECTION 2 CONSPIRACY[10]

The tort of conspiracy takes two forms, the principal distinction between which is the requirement of unlawful means for the first of these. They are:

(1) 'unlawful means conspiracy' – where two or more persons cause loss to a claimant by combining to do an unlawful act, or a lawful act by unlawful means; and

(2) 'simple conspiracy' – where (a) two or more persons combine wilfully, and without justification, to injure another in his trade, and (b) damage to his trade results.[11]

---

[4] *Merkur Island Shipping Corpn v Laughton* [1983] 2 AC 570, at 608.

[5] See further Bagshaw, 'Can the Economic Torts be Unified?' (1998) 18 OJLS 729. Cf Weir, *Economic Torts* (1997).

[6] [1942] AC 435.   [7] For a contrary view, see Weir, *Economic Torts* (1997).

[8] See Carty, 'Intentional Violation of Economic Interests: the Limits of Common Law Liability' (1988) 104 LQR 250.

[9] A number of writers would subscribe (albeit not uncritically) to this potential: see, eg, Sales and Stilitz, 'Intentional Infliction of Harm by Unlawful Means' (1999) 115 LQR 411; McBride & Bagshaw, *Tort Law* (2005) ch 20.   [10] See Carty, *An Analysis of the Economic Torts* (2001) ch 2.

[11] *Quinn v Leathem* [1901] AC 495. For the argument that the tort is far from simple and thus better described as the 'the tort in *Quinn v Leathem*', see McBride & Bagshaw, *Tort Law* (2005) ch 21. But contrast, for example, the language of 'conspiracy' used by the House of Lords in *Crofter Hand Woven Harris Tweed Co Ltd v Veitch* [1942] AC 435.

The first form of conspiracy is now largely superfluous in that, if unlawful means are used to interfere with trade, the genus tort adumbrated above will necessarily be committed.[12] The second kind of conspiracy is anomalous in that it contradicts the fundamental proposition in *Allen v Flood* that motive alone cannot render illegal that which would otherwise be legal conduct. It can be justified only as 'a crude (and arbitrary) method of attacking an abuse of market power'.[13] In *Lonrho Ltd v Shell Petroleum Co Ltd (No 2)* the House of Lords recognised simple conspiracy as a 'highly anomalous cause of action' but considered it too well established to be discarded.[14]

(A) COMBINATION

The requirement of combination is generally straightforward. The ancient fiction that a husband and wife were one person in the eyes of the common law no longer prevents spouses being liable together for the tort of conspiracy.[15] Directors and their company may conspire together since the company is a separate legal entity.[16] However, to establish such a conspiracy, it is essential to identify the relevant 'mind and will' of the company (normally found in the director who had management or control over the particular act in question).[17] From this, it follows that the relevant alter ego of the company will be located in different people for different purposes (usually discoverable from the company's articles of association).[18]

Combinations with which the tort of conspiracy is concerned may take many forms. Examples include traders combining to ward off the competition of a rival trader;[19] trade union officials combining to compel an employer to dismiss a non-union employee;[20] an employers' federation and a trade union combining to deprive a worker belonging to another union of his job so as to promote collective bargaining in the industry concerned;[21] employees collectively threatening a strike unless the employer dismissed a worker belonging to another union.[22] But this list is not exhaustive.

---

[12] See *Lonrho plc v Fayed* [1991] 3 All ER 303, at 312, *per* Lord Bridge. On the other hand, the fact that there has been a combination may help to persuade the court more readily to grant an injunction or a higher award of damages: *Kuwait Oil Co SAK v Al Bader* [2000] 2 All ER (Comm) 271. Equally, the tort of conspiracy may also be a useful mechanism to make *both* conspirators joint-tortfeasors and thus expand the remit of liability: see Sales, 'The Tort of Conspiracy and Civil Secondary Liability' [1990] CLJ 491.

[13] See Carty, *An Analysis of the Economic Torts* (2001) ch 2. See also *Clerk and Lindsell* (2006) where it is pertinently suggested that a combination of two street corner grocers is unlikely to be more oppressive to competitors than the actions of a supermarket chain in single ownership.

[14] [1982] AC 173, at 188, *per* Lord Diplock. See also *Lonrho plc v Fayed* [1991] 3 All ER 303, at 307, *per* Lord Bridge.   [15] *Midland Bank Trust Co Ltd v Green (No 3)* [1982] Ch 529.

[16] *Belmont Finance Corpn Ltd v Williams Furniture Ltd* [1979] Ch 250. And see *Taylor v Smyth* [1991] 1 IR 142 (conspiring with companies under the accused's control).

[17] *El Ajou v Dollar Land Holdings plc* [1994] 2 All ER 685.

[18] *Meridian Global Funds Management Asia Ltd v Securities Commission* [1995] 3 All ER 918, at 923, *per* Lord Hoffmann.   [19] *Mogul Steamship Co v McGregor, Gow & Co* [1892] AC 25 (action failed).

[20] *Quinn v Leathem* [1901] AC 495 (action succeeded).

[21] *Reynolds v Shipping Federation Ltd* [1924] 1 Ch 28 (action failed).

[22] *White v Riley* [1921] 1 Ch 1 (action failed).

(B) UNLAWFUL MEANS

In the context of unlawful means conspiracy, it is essential to establish the sense in which the relevant act is 'unlawful'. *Marrinan v Vibart*[23] illustrates the point.

C pleaded that D1 and D2, who were both policemen, had conspired to make defamatory statements about him to the DPP, and to give false evidence at the Old Bailey and at a later enquiry by the Masters of his Inn. None of these three statements could ever form the subject of a civil action because of the absolute privilege afforded judicial proceedings. But neither was there an actionable conspiracy because the acts allegedly causing the damage were incapable of supporting any form of civil action.[24]

The decision illustrates not only that unlawful means conspiracy is not confined to interference with economic interests, but more importantly that it has little practical significance as an independent tort. Had the statements in *Marrinan* not been privileged, the defendants would have been liable in defamation as joint tortfeasors. There would have been no need to resort to an action framed in terms of conspiracy.

(C) THE PURPOSE OF THE DEFENDANTS

The principles underpinning simple conspiracy can be stated quite simply; and the decision in *Crofter Hand Woven Harris Tweed Co Ltd v Veitch*[25] assists in this exposition.

Cs produced tweed cloth on an island in the Outer Hebrides. Only the weaving of their cloth took place on the island; they imported yarn from the mainland. Other firms had their cloth spun as well as woven on the island. Ds were trade union officials of the union to which most of the spinners employed in the island mills belonged. Employers of these men informed Ds that the competition of Cs prevented them from raising wages. Ds (assumed by some of their Lordships to be acting in combination with the mill-owners) instructed dockers at the island's port to refuse to handle yarn imported from the mainland and consigned to Cs. Without breaking their contracts of employment, the dockers (who were members of the same union as Ds) consented. Cs sought to stop this embargo on the ground that it was an actionable conspiracy. They failed. The House of Lords held that the predominant purpose of the combination was the legitimate promotion of Ds' interests.

The tort of simple conspiracy is thus committed only when the predominant purpose of the defendants' combination is deliberately to inflict damage on the claimant.[26] It is not enough to demonstrate that the defendants were well aware that damage to the claimants was an inevitable consequence of their collective action as the House of Lords made clear in *Lonrho Ltd v Shell Petroleum Co Ltd (No 2)*.[27]

---

[23] [1963] 1 QB 528.

[24] The requirement that the unlawful means must be actionable in their own right was emphatically underlined in *Michaels v Taylor Woodrow Developments Ltd* [2001] Ch 493, at 511, *per* Laddie J. See also *Rookes v Barnard* [1964] AC 1129, at 1204, *per* Lord Devlin.   [25] [1942] AC 435.

[26] [1942] AC 435.   [27] [1982] AC 173.

Ds breached sanctions orders against the illegal regime in Rhodesia, substantially increasing their profits at C's expense. Rejecting the claim in conspiracy, the House of Lords found that even if unlawful means were used to further the conspiracy, no liability arose unless Ds acted 'for the purpose not of protecting their own interests but of injuring the interests of [C]'.[28]

How, then, does unlawful means conspiracy differ from simple conspiracy? According to the House of Lords in *Lonrho plc v Fayed*,[29] there is a critical distinction to be drawn based on the difference between intention and motive.

C, who had sought to take over the House of Fraser (including Harrods), alleged that D had unlawfully made false and fraudulent representations to the Secretary of State for Trade and Industry,[30] thus procuring a successful takeover of the disputed company. There could be no doubt that D's predominant intention was to advance D's own interests. So the Court of Appeal struck out C's claim in conspiracy.[31] However, in the House of Lords, Lord Bridge affirmed that (1) in *any* action for conspiracy, proof of intent to injure C is required, and (2) in unlawful means conspiracy that intention need not be D's primary design.

Thus we may make the following propositions:

(1) If, in simple conspiracy, the defendants' predominant purpose is the protection of their own interests, there will be no actionable conspiracy *even though* a subsidiary purpose is to damage the claimant.

(2) In unlawful means cases, the leading direct authorities suggest that defendants probably cannot excuse the use of such means by proving that their main purpose was to protect or advance their own interests,[32] even though some doubt has been cast on this proposition by the Court of Appeal decision in a genus tort case.[33]

(3) If, in simple conspiracy, the defendants' predominant purpose is to harm the claimant, there will be no legal justification of their action even if it was a subsidiary purpose of their conspiracy to further their own interests.

In cases of simple conspiracy, the defendants' legitimate interests extend beyond merely material interests. Thus, if trade union officers further a purpose which is not calculated to improve the financial state of their members, but which is honestly believed by them to be desirable, and has in fact the support of their members – for example, officers of a musicians' union opposing racial discrimination among dance-hall patrons[34] – this is a legitimate interest. Beyond that, the meaning of 'legitimate interest' is not clear. Perhaps a combination for the purpose of making the claimant pay a debt owed by him to the defendant union (on pain of otherwise being deprived of work), is an example of an

---

[28] [1982] AC 173, at 189, *per* Lord Diplock.   [29] [1992] 1 AC 448.

[30] But will it be necessary at the full trial to prove that the misrepresentation on the part of D constituted actionable deceit? See *Michaels v Taylor Woodrow Developments Ltd* [2001] Ch 493; *Lonrho plc v Fayed* [1989] 2 All ER 65, at 69.   [31] [1989] 2 All ER 65.

[32] *Lonrho v Fayed* [1991] 3 All ER 303, at 309–10, *per* Lord Bridge.

[33] *Douglas v Hello! Ltd (No 6)* [2006] QB 125, at [214].

[34] *Scala Ballroom (Wolverhampton) Ltd v Ratcliffe* [1958] 3 All ER 220. After *Rookes v Barnard*, this decision might be different unless no breach of contract was threatened.

illegitimate interest.[35] But once the *bona fides* of the defendants is established, it is irrelevant that the damage inflicted to secure the purpose is disproportionately severe.[36] Nor does it matter that, secondarily, the defendants are glad to see the claimant suffer a loss.[37] Furthermore, there is no need for the conspirators to share a common, justificatory, predominant purpose: 'it is sufficient if all the various combining parties have their own legitimate trade or business interests to gain, even though these interests may be of differing kinds'.[38]

It is uncertain whether the burden of proving the predominant purpose of damaging the claimant lies with the claimant. In the *Veitch* case, Lords Wright[39] and Porter[40] thought it was; Viscount Maugham held that it lay with the defendant, while the other two Law Lords were silent on the matter. However, the first view seems preferable[41] since it accords with earlier decisions of the House of Lords and with the expressed intention of the Law Lords in *Lonrho Ltd v Shell Petroleum Co Ltd* to confine the ambit of the anomalous tort of simple conspiracy.[42]

(D) JUSTIFICATION

Wherever the burden of proof lies, it is clear that the scope of justification in simple conspiracy is wider than in the 'general' economic torts. The defendant who proves that his primary object was to further his legitimate trade interests escapes liability. As we shall see, however, that does not *per se* justify procuring a breach of contract. In practice, conspirators will almost always be able to show that they were actuated by self-interest. The chances of a successful action, where no alternative cause of action would lie, are thus remote. This is the inevitable result of the judicial reluctance to look beyond the purposes of the parties to the economic consequences of their conduct:

we live in a competitive or acquisitive society, and the English common law may have felt that it was beyond its power to fix by any but the crudest distinctions the metes and bounds which divide the rightful from the wrongful use of the actor's own freedom, leaving the precise application in any particular case to the jury or judge of fact. If further principles of regulation or control are to be introduced, that is a matter for the legislature.[43]

---

[35] *Giblan v National Amalgamated Labourers' Union of Great Britain and Ireland* [1903] 2 KB 600.

[36] *Crofter Hand Woven Harris Tweed Co Ltd Veitch* [1942] AC 435, at 447, *per* Viscount Simon. Cf *Trollope & Sons v London Building Trades Federation* (1895) 72 LT 342.

[37] In *Crofter Hand Woven Harris Tweed Co Ltd v Veitch* [1942] AC 435, Lord Wright said (at 471): 'I cannot see how the pursuit of a legitimate practical object can be vitiated by glee at the adversary's expected discomfiture'. Cf Viscount Simon, at 444–5 and Viscount Maugham, at 450. Yet the court must inquire into the state of knowledge of Ds whenever it is relevant for the ascertainment of their purpose: *Huntley v Thornton* [1957] 1 All ER 234; *Bird v O'Neal* [1960] AC 907.

[38] *Crofter Hand Woven Harris Tweed Co Ltd v Veitch* [1942] AC 435, at 453, *per* Viscount Maugham. Cf the judgment of Evatt J in *McKerman v Fraser* (1931) 46 CLR 343.   [39] [1942] AC 435, at 471.

[40] [1942] AC 435, at 495.   [41] Certainly, it was applied in *Huntley v Thornton* [1957] 1 All ER 234.

[42] And see *Sorrell v Smith* [1925] AC 700.

[43] *Crofter Hand Woven Harris Tweed Co Ltd v Veitch* [1942] AC 435, at 472, *per* Lord Wright.

As for unlawful means conspiracy, its future practical utility would seem to be inextricably bound up with the genus tort[44] which itself would seem to have given way to a more general principle of tortious liability based on using unlawful means to inflict harm.[45]

SECTION 3 INDUCING BREACH OF AN EXISTING CONTRACT[46]

(A) CONTOURS OF THE TORT

For well over a century a distinct tort of inducing breach of contract has been recognised.[47] The tort is committed when the defendant knowingly induces a third party to break his contract with the claimant with the result that the claimant suffers loss. In direct inducement cases, it is not necessary to prove that the defendant used unlawful means.[48] As such, directly inducing breach of contract does not fit within Lord Diplock's genus tort of unlawful interference with trade. Furthermore, although the original tort of inducing breach of contract has evolved in three main ways, only two of these developments obviously fit within Lord Diplock's genus tort. First, inducing breach of non-contractual obligations may now be actionable. Secondly, indirect inducement of a breach of contract may be actionable so long as unlawful means are used. Thirdly, interference with a contract short of procuring an actual breach may also now be actionable upon proof of unlawful means. Only the last two extensions of the tort can convincingly be argued to be species of the genus tort.[49]

(B) DIRECTLY INDUCING A BREACH OF CONTRACT

The tort of directly inducing breach of contract without lawful justification or excuse dates from *Lumley v Gye*.[50] There, the court held that the following facts could constitute a tort.

---

[44] See *Michaels v Taylor Woodrow Developments Ltd* [2001] Ch 493, at 516, *per* Laddie J; *Lonrho plc v Fayed* [1992] 1 AC 448, *per* Lord Templeman; *Douglas v Hello! Ltd (No 6)* [2006] QB 125.

[45] *Douglas v Hello! Ltd (No 6)* [2006] QB 125, at [174]. Just what kinds of harm are covered, however, remains a matter of debate: see Tettenborn, 'Liability for Interfering with Intangibles: Invalidly Appointed Receivers, Conversion, and the Economic Torts' (2006) 122 LQR 31.

[46] See Bagshaw, 'Inducing Breach of Contract' in Horder (ed), *Oxford Essays in Jurisprudence, 4th Series* (2000); Carty, *An Analysis of the Economic Torts* (2001) ch 3.   [47] *Lumley v Gye* (1853) 2 E & B 216.

[48] *Thomson & Co Ltd v Deakin* [1952] Ch 646.

[49] See Carty, *An Analysis of the Economic Torts* (2001).

[50] (1853) 2 E & B 216. For an analysis of the case see Waddams, 'Johanna Wagner and the Rival Opera Houses' (1998) 117 LQR 431.

A famous opera singer was under a contract to sing at C's theatre *and nowhere else*, but she was not C's servant. C claimed that the singer had been induced by D, who knew of this contract,[51] to break it so that she would sing at D's theatre instead.

The claim succeeded on demurrer with the majority of the court indicating that that it would be tortious not merely to induce breach of contracts of service, but also, more broadly, to induce breach of contractual rights generally. Thus, although the claimant's action ultimately failed in that case, the tort of directly inducing breach of contract had been conceived, and its genesis was completed in *Bowen v Hall*[52] where, on similar facts, the Court of Appeal accepted the broad principle enunciated in *Lumley v Gye*. Later, in various *dicta*, certain judges contemplated the application of the principle to advantageous business relations not embodied in contracts.[53] But the decision of the House of Lords in *Allen v Flood*[54] – albeit a case more closely associated with the genus tort than the narrow tort of inducing breach of contract – restricted the scope of the latter to interferences with existing contracts (or, at most, other enforceable civil obligations).

(1) KINDS OF CONTRACT

Any valid and enforceable contract can found an action upon subsequent interference.[55] Meagre evidence of its terms will suffice;[56] but interference with a void contract is, of course, not actionable.[57]

(2) KINDS OF BREACH

The Court of Appeal decision in *Law Debenture Trust Corpn v Ural Caspian Oil Corpn*[58] made it clear that inducing a breach of any contractual obligation – including the secondary contractual duty to pay damages when a primary contractual obligation has been broken – can give rise to tortious liability.[59] Furthermore, on the authority of *Torquay Hotel Co Ltd v Cousins*,[60] the breach need not itself be actionable.

An injunction was granted against Ds who, in the course of industrial action, were attempting to stop a supplier fulfilling his contract with C. The contract expressly exempted either party from liability for events beyond their control – such as labour disputes – if those events led to a failure to perform. The Court of Appeal interpreted the clause as 'an exception from liability

---

[51] C failed at the subsequent trial, the jury finding that D did not believe the contract between C and Wagner to be binding: see Waddams, 'Johanna Wagner and the Rival Opera Houses' (2001) 117 LQR 431.

[52] (1881) 6 QBD 333.

[53] *Temperton v Russell* [1893] 1 QB 715 (preventing C from making a contract); *Bowen v Hall* (1881) 6 QBD 333.

[54] [1898] AC 1; *Sorrell v Smith* [1925] AC 700.

[55] Cf *Thomson & Co Ltd v Deakin* [1952] Ch 646, at 677, *per* Evershed MR; *Findlay v Blaylock* 1937 SC 21.

[56] *Daily Mirror Newspapers Ltd v Gardner* [1968] 2 QB 762.

[57] *Shears v Mendeloff* (1914) 30 TLR 342 (infant's contract); *Said v Butt* [1920] 3 KB 497 (mistake); *Joe Lee Ltd v Lord Dalmery* [1927] 1 Ch 300 (gaming); *British Motor Trade Association v Gray* 1951 SC 586 (contract void in restraint of trade – *obiter dictum* of Lord Keith).   [58] [1995] Ch 152.

[59] [1994] 3 WLR 1221, at 1235, *per* Beldam LJ.   [60] [1969] 2 Ch 106.

for non-performance rather than an exception from the obligation to perform'.[61] Accordingly, the defendant's conduct still constituted inducing a breach of that latter obligation.

Many actions turn on such interpretations of the contract in order to decide whether there has been a breach, and may even require consideration of implied terms. *Hivac Ltd v Park Royal Scientific Instruments Ltd*[62] is a good example.

C had been the only English maker of midget valves for hearing aids. Setting up in competition, D employed some of C's staff in their spare time. It was held that an implied term must be read into the engagement of this staff that the latter should not break their fidelity to C by doing things which would injure C's business. In view of the fact that C had a monopoly on this type of work, and the staff held a monopoly over the relevant skill, an injunction restraining the inducement of breach of contract could be granted.

On the other hand, if a contract is determinable by either party at will, it is not actionable if the defendant induces a party to determine that contract.[63] This is because there has been no breach, but merely a lawful termination of the contract. Similarly, inducing someone to give proper notice in order to terminate a contract lawfully cannot give rise to a tort action.[64] On the other hand, giving notice of a forthcoming strike is not notice to terminate, but notice of a forthcoming breach of contract. It thus follows that where there is a no-strike clause in the contract, inducing a strike will amount to inducing breach of contract.[65] Union officials inducing strike action are thus *prima facie* open to tort liability. In reality, however, they enjoy certain statutory immunities (which fall outside the scope of a book on torts[66]).

Even if the defendant is not responsible for the initial breach of a contract, he will still be liable in tort if he is responsible for procuring the continuing breach of a subsisting contract.[67] Thus, where the defendant engaged a servant in ignorance of an existing contract of service between the servant and the claimant, he could not escape liability where he continued to employ the servant after learning the facts.[68]

But is it still necessary to prove a breach of an obligation under the contract? On principle, it is not necessary because interference with a contract that does not technically procure a breach is often as capable of causing the claimant harm as an actual breach of the primary terms of the contract. Thus it was in *Torquay Hotel Co Ltd v Cousins* that Lord Denning sensibly argued that even if an exclusion clause meant that

---

[61] [1969] 2 Ch 106, at 143, *per* Russell LJ.   [62] [1946] Ch 169.

[63] *McManus v Bowes* [1938] 1 KB 98.

[64] See, eg, *Boxfoldia Ltd v National Graphic Association (1982)* [1988] ICR 752; *Thomson & Co Ltd v Deakin* [1952] Ch 646.   [65] *Rookes v Barnard* [1964] AC 1129.

[66] Those interested should consult a specialist work on labour law, such as Deakin and Morris, *Labour Law* (2005).

[67] *Smithies v National Association of Operative Plasterers* [1909] 1 KB 310. Cf *Denaby and Cadeby Main Collieries Ltd v Yorkshire Miners' Association* [1906] AC 384. There must be a continuing obligation at the time of the breach – where, then, is the tort committed if A agrees to sell his house to B, and C (knowing A has broken this agreement) buys it from A?

[68] *Blake v Lanyon* (1795) 6 Term Rep 221; *Fred Wilkins & Bros Ltd v Weaver* [1915] 2 Ch 322. Cf *Read v Friendly Society of Operative Stonemasons* [1902] 2 KB 88, at 95, *per* Darling J; on appeal [1902] 2 KB 732. See also *Jones Bros (Hunstanton) Ltd v Stevens* [1955] 1 QB 275.

there was technically no breach of contract, the defendant should remain liable for 'interfering' with the contract. The trouble, however, is that there is little support elsewhere for such a tort.[69] On the other hand, if unlawful means are used, the interference may well be actionable as *Dimbleby & Sons Ltd v NUJ*[70] illustrates.

Journalists employed by C refused, in breach of their contracts of employment, to prepare copy. As a result, C faced severe difficulties in fulfilling his contract with the publishing company. Nevertheless, C managed to procure alternative copy. Sir John Donaldson MR held the NUJ liable for unlawful interference with C's contractual obligations. Hindrance, *where unlawful means were employed*, was sufficient.

Dimbleby & Sons Ltd v NUJ is probably best seen, then, as an example of the genus tort rather than an extension of the distinct tort of directly inducing breach of contract.[71]

(3) KNOWLEDGE OF THE CONTRACT

The defendant must be shown to have had actual or constructive knowledge[72] of the existence[73] of the contract which has been broken.[74] Furthermore, the courts have shown themselves willing to impute to the defendant the knowledge that he was inducing a breach.[75]

(c) THE WIDER TORT: INTERFERENCE WITH AN EXISTING CONTRACT

The tort of directly inducing a breach of contract – established in *Lumley v Gye*[76] – has developed considerably since its emergence into English law well over a hundred years ago. In consequence of this development, tort law's protection of *contractual rights* is by no means confined to occasions on which a defendant directly induces a breach of

---

[69] See *Associated British Ports v Transport and General Workers' Union* [1989] 3 All ER 796.

[70] [1984] 1 All ER 117. See also *Shipping Co Uniform Inc v ITWF* [1985] ICR 245.

[71] For the argument that it may constitute a sort of 'half-way' tort of unlawful interference with contract: see Carty, *An Analysis of the Economic Torts* (2001).

[72] *British Industrial Plastics Ltd v Ferguson* [1940] 1 All ER 479; *Middlebrook Mushrooms Ltd v TGWU* [1993] ICR 612. But in *Lumley v Gye* (1853) 2 E & B 216 Lord Campbell directed the jury that 'if the defendant *bona fide* believed that the agreement with the [claimant] had ceased to be binding upon Miss Wagner the *scienter* was not proved and the defendant would be entitled to the verdict': the jury then found for D.

[73] The contract must be in existence at the time of the inducement; it is insufficient if the contract is merely one that is certain to come into being at some defined point in the future: *Allen v Flood* [1898] AC 1. Furthermore, D need not know details of its terms: *J T Stratford & Son Ltd v Lindley* [1965] AC 269; *Greig v Insole* [1978] 3 All ER 449.

[74] *Long v Smithson* (1918) 118 LT 678; *British Homophone Ltd v Kunz and Crystallate Gramophone Record Manufacturing Co Ltd* [1935] All ER Rep 627. In *Thomson & Co Ltd v Deakin* [1952] ch 646 it is suggested (at 687, *per* Evershed MR) that 'common knowledge about the way business is conducted' would be sufficient constructive knowledge; *Cunard Steamship Co Ltd v Stacey* [1955] 2 Lloyd's Rep 247 (official of seaman's union deemed to know seaman's contract would conform with Merchant Shipping Act 1894). It is enough if D deliberately disregards means of knowledge: *Emerald Construction Co v Lowthian* [1966] 1 All ER 1013.

[75] *J T Stratford & Son Ltd v Lindley* [1965] AC 269, at 307.   [76] (1853) 2 E & B 216.

contract. In *Thomson & Co Ltd v Deakin*,[77] Jenkins LJ enumerated what he considered to be the various forms of the tort as he saw it in 1952.[78] These were:

(1) direct inducement of a breach of a contract;

(2) direct intervention in the contract (for example, disabling a contracting party);

(3) indirect procurement or intervention (for example, secondary industrial action preventing performance of the contract); and

(4) inconsistent dealings.

Authority establishes that interference with a claimant's *contractual rights* in any of these four circumstances may be tortious. But we shall see that forms 2 and 3 – that is, direct intervention in the contract, and indirect procurement or intervention – both require proof of unlawful means in order for a tort action to be grounded. They might, therefore, be better regarded as species of the genus tort, as originally conceived:[79] namely, unlawful interference with trade.[80]

(1) DIRECT PERSUASION OR INDUCEMENT

Direct persuasion or procurement or inducement applied by the defendant to the contract-breaker is, as we have already seen, sufficient.[81] If the contract-breaker is a limited company, an approach to some person in the company with actual or ostensible authority to make contracts on behalf of the company is required.[82] There has been much discussion of how to distinguish advice from persuasion, but this seems to miss the point since a rigid distinction between advice and persuasion is not strictly necessary.[83] The appropriate test is simply whether the breach of contract is 'fairly attributable to any . . . pressure, persuasion or procuration'.[84] In other words, the issue is one of causation; and it has just the same capacity to present difficulties as other problems of causation in tort law. For example, where a trade union official sent to managers of the claimants' public houses a circular questionnaire asking for details of

---

[77] [1952] Ch 646.

[78] Whether all these ought properly be regarded as the progeny of the original tort is highly doubtful: see, eg, Bagshaw, 'Inducing Breach of Contract' in Horder (ed) *Oxford Essays in Jurisprudence 4th Series* (2000). Nonetheless, it is convenient to deal with the following cases in one place since they all turn on loss arising from the non-fulfilment of contractual obligations.

[79] As noted at the outset, the original notion of the genus tort was confined to the protection of trade and business interests, but as we shall see below, this has now given way, on the authority of the Court of Appeal in *Douglas v Hello! Ltd (No 6)* [2006] QB 125 to a broader principle of harming another through unlawful means.

[80] See Carty, *An Analysis of the Economic Torts* (2001); Elias and Ewing, 'Economic Torts and Labour Laws: Old Principles and New Feasibilities' [1982] CLJ 321.

[81] *Thomson v Deakin* [1952] Ch 646, at 681 and 694, *per* Evershed MR and Jenkins LJ, respectively.

[82] *Thomson v Deakin* [1952] Ch 646, at 681, *per* Evershed MR.

[83] *Torquay Hotel Co Ltd v Cousins* [1969] 2 Ch 106, at 147, *per* Winn LJ.

[84] *Thomson v Deakin* [1952] Ch 646, at 686, *per* Evershed MR (*ratio*). On the difficulty of deciding whether there is merely a transmission of information, and no inducement, see *Camellia Tanker Ltd v International Transport Workers' Federation* [1976] ICR 274, and Bagshaw, 'Inducing Breach of Contract' in Horder (ed), *Oxford Essays in Jurisprudence, 4th Series* (2000).

the receipts and profits of their houses. The various managers disclosed the information believing that the defendant's union might ultimately secure them better wages and conditions. It was held that the official's distribution of the questionnaires had, on balance, caused the managers to break their contractual obligation not to disclose confidential information.[85]

It is important to decide whether the inducement is direct or indirect because if indirect procurement is pleaded, (1) the breach must be a necessary consequence of the defendant's act, and (2) unlawful means must be used. An inducement may be direct even though a federation transmits it through its members to a contracting party.[86] And where the inducement is direct, it is only the other contracting party (and not the one induced) who may sue for this tort.[87] But liability has its limits. If the 'inducement' is couched in terms that could equally provoke *either* a lawful *or* an unlawful response on the part of the contract breaker, there will be no liability if the contract breaker elects to respond unlawfully.[88]

(2) DIRECT INTERVENTION

An action will lie if the defendant intervenes (otherwise than by inducement) so as to prevent a contracting party from performing his contract, for example by kidnapping or otherwise restraining him,[89] or by removing essential tools from him.[90] The wrongful act against the one contractor creates a cause of action for interference with the contract in the hands of the other. *GWK Ltd v Dunlop Rubber Co Ltd*[91] exemplifies the point:

A car manufacturer had contracted with C that, when he exhibited his car at a motor show, it would have tyres made by C fitted to it. D unlawfully removed C's tyres and substituted them with tyres made by D. That trespass to the car owner's goods created liability to C.

In *D C Thomson & Co Ltd v Deakin*, Evershed MR[92] limited liability for direct intervention resulting in a breach of contract to tortious acts (as in *GWK Ltd v Dunlop Rubber Co Ltd*). But there are conflicting *dicta* suggesting that a wrongful act by the defendant which, had it been done by the contractor so as to constitute a breach of contract, will also ground an action in this tort.[93] By contrast, it is at least clear that not every breach of a penal statute will suffice,[94] for the unlawful means must be *directed*

---

[85] *Bent's Brewery Co Ltd v Hogan* [1945] 2 All ER 570. See also, *Jasperson v Dominion Tobacco Co* [1923] AC 709.

[86] *Daily Mirror Newspapers Ltd v Gardner* [1968] 2 QB 762. In *J T Stratford Ltd v Lindley* [1965] AC 269, at 307, Lord Pearce alone thought the inducement direct.

[87] *Williams v Hursey* (1959) 103 CLR 30. And see *Brekkes Ltd v Cattel* [1972] Ch 105. The party induced has *locus standi* to obtain a declaration: *Greig v Insole* [1978] 3 All ER 449.

[88] *Sanders v Snell* (1998) 157 ALR 491.

[89] *Thomson & Co Ltd v Deakin* [1952] Ch 646, at 678 and 694–5, *per* Evershed MR and Jenkins LJ.

[90] *Thomson v Deakin* [1952] Ch 646, at 702, *per* Morris LJ.

[91] (1926) 42 TLR 376; on appeal (1926) 42 TLR 593.   [92] *Thomson v Deakin* [1952] Ch 646, at 678.

[93] *Thomson v Deakin* [1952] Ch 646, at 694, *per* Jenkins LJ; *Statnigros v Storhaug & Partners* [1953] CLY 3556 (a landlord covenanted with C, a tenant, to leave open a particular door on Saturday mornings; the landlord's agent locked it and was held liable in damages on the principle of *Lumley v Gye* (1853) 2 E & B 216).

[94] *Lonrho Ltd v Shell Petroleum Co Ltd (No 2)* [1982] AC 173.

against the claimant in order to ground the action. Of course, this tends to square 'direct intervention' cases with the genus tort of unlawful interference with trade. But to treat them in this way may conceal the fact that the bulk of the decided cases reveal a lingering judicial commitment to dealing with them as cases of interfering with existing contracts.

(3) INDIRECT INDUCEMENT OR PROCUREMENT

This version of the classic economic tort has typically been invoked to stop secondary industrial action. It is committed when the defendant induces a third party to do a wrongful act – normally, breach his contract of employment – in order to prevent performance of some other contract. For example, it covers the situation where union officials persuade men working for a supplier of parts to a car manufacturer to strike, thus preventing their employer from performing his contract with the manufacturers. This conduct, involving an unlawful act on the part of the strikers, may enable the manufacturer to sue.

For liability to be established, there needs to be more than general exhortations issued in the course of a trade dispute such as 'stop supplies to A'. Rather, it must be clear that the defendant intends a specific contract to be broken.[95] This will normally require either (a) that the defendant specifically intended the contract to be broken as an end in itself, or (b) that the defendant intended the contract to be broken as a means to achieving some ulterior aim. However, in two recent cases,[96] the Court of Appeal has suggested that either of these forms of intention may sometimes be inferred from the defendant's knowledge that harm to the other contracting party will be an inevitable (as opposed to a mere likely, or possible) consequence of his actions.[97] Consider now *J T Stratford & Sons Ltd v Lindley*.[98]

C let out barges on hire to customers. These customers were under a contractual obligation to return the barges to C's moorings. Ds, who were union officials, instructed their members to break their contracts of employment with C's customers by not returning the barges. The members obeyed those instructions and did not work the barges back to C's moorings. The House of Lords held that this amounted to the tort of indirectly procuring a breach of the contract between C and C's customers: the breach of contract being a necessary consequence of D's conduct.

Equally, in *Falconer v ASLEF*[99] the defendants were held liable to the claimant for the hotel expenses he incurred when they called railwaymen out on strike, thus preventing the claimant from travelling on the ticket he had purchased for a planned journey. The interference with the performance of the contract between British Rail and the

---

[95] *Mainstream Properties v Young* [2005] EWCA Civ 125.

[96] *Douglas v Hello! Ltd (No 6)* [2006] QB 125; *Mainstream Properties v Young* [2005] EWCA Civ 861.

[97] But is such an inference reconcilable with the firmly stated requirement that there must be specific intention? It is submitted that it is not, for inherent in any such inference is the admission that (a) something else was specifically intended by D, and that (b) harm to C was a mere by-product of that ulterior goal.

[98] [1965] AC 269.   [99] [1986] IRLR 331 (county court).

claimant was found to be a necessary consequence of the defendants' actions and thus indicative of the requisite intention.

Indirect inducement (or procurement as it is sometimes – perhaps more accurately – referred to) is actionable only upon proof of unlawful means. While this will often consist of breaches of contract by a third party, other unlawful acts – such as the commission of an independent tort – will also suffice.[100] Thus, for example, the tort of public nuisance committed by demonstrators hindering distribution of the claimants' newspapers was held to constitute the necessary unlawful means in *News Group Newspapers Ltd v SOGAT '82 (No 2)*.[101] It is yet to be finally resolved whether the requirement of 'unlawful means' is synonymous with the commission of any actionable civil wrong as it is in the case of unlawful means conspiracy. But the argument that the term does bear this meaning – especially if both are to be viewed as sibling, sub-species of the genus tort – would seem a compelling one.[102]

(4) INCONSISTENT DEALINGS[103]

In *Thomson & Co Ltd v Deakin*, Jenkins LJ harboured no doubt that if a third party, with knowledge of a contract between the contract breaker and another, had dealings with the contract breaker which the third party knows to be inconsistent with the contract, he has committed an actionable interference'.[104] This is doubtless correct if harm to the claimant is an inevitable consequence of those inconsistent dealings.[105] But it is not always easy to decide whether the defendant, in making the inconsistent dealings, has merely taken advantage of a voluntary decision already made by the contract breaker to discontinue his contract, or whether he has been primarily responsible for that discontinuation. Only if he has induced that discontinuance will he be liable. *British Motor Trade Association v Salvadori* illustrates the point.[106]

Third parties had entered into covenants with C not to resell cars except under certain conditions. D had bought some cars from these third parties with a view to reselling at a profit. Roxburgh J noted that D had offered a price high enough to cause a man (who would not otherwise have broken his covenant) to sell in breach of covenant. Accordingly, he found D liable. He added, however, that 'any active step taken by a defendant having knowledge of the covenant by which he facilitates a breach of that covenant is enough', and that 'a defendant by agreeing to buy, paying for and taking delivery of a motor car known by him to be on offer in breach of covenant' commits the tort.[107]

---

[100] *Merkur Island Shipping Corpn v Laughton* [1983] 2 AC 570.   [101] [1987] ICR 181.

[102] See *Michaels v Taylor Woodrow Developments Ltd* [2001] Ch 493.

[103] For critical analysis of this version of the tort see Bagshaw, 'Inducing Breach of Contract' in Horder (ed), *Oxford Essays in Jurisprudence, 4th Series* (2000) 144–145.

[104] [1952] Ch 646, at 694; not considered by the other judges.

[105] At least if the word 'dealings' is limited to 'the making of a contract'. Jenkins LJ may have intended to include other dealings – eg, accepting benefits under a contract already made. In *De Francesco v Barnum* (1890) 63 LT 438, an action succeeded against a theatrical manager who continued to employ show girls after receiving notice of a prior inconsistent contract which they had with C.   [106] [1949] Ch 556.

[107] *British Industrial Plastics Ltd v Ferguson* [1940] 1 All ER 479.

The case can be contrasted with *Batts Combe Quarry Ltd v Ford.*[108]

On selling his quarry to C, a father contracted not to assist in setting up any rival quarry in the neighbourhood. His sons, Ds, decided to set up such a quarry and the father financed them in this enterprise. It was held that the acceptance of this gift by the sons was not an actionable interference with C's contract. They had already decided to set up the rival quarry independently of their father's promise of financial help and as such had procured no breach.

(5) DEFENDANT'S STATE OF MIND

A defendant is liable if he intends to bring about a breach of the contract, and it is irrelevant that he did not act with malice in the sense of spite or ill-will.[109] The decision of the Court of Appeal in *Exchange Telegraph Co Ltd v Gregory & Co*[110] is illustrative.

C had a monopoly of information about Stock Exchange prices and circulated this information to subscribers who had contracted not to communicate it to others. They also published it in a newspaper, issued six times daily. D, a stockbroker, induced a subscriber to give him information contained in C's circular, and posted it in his own office for the benefit of his clients. He was held liable for interference with a contract.

If the defendant does an act, the substantially certain consequence of which is to bring about a breach of a contract of which he is aware, then an intention to bring about the breach will be imputed to him, and he will be liable unless the presumption is rebutted.[111] A negligent interference with a contract does not however constitute this tort,[112] as the current tendency of the courts in such cases is to insist upon a deliberate and intentional act aimed at the claimant.[113] That said, it remains to be established clearly whether the defendant must merely intend the act that causes a breach, or whether he must intend not simply the act, but also that it will cause a breach. The leading case, *Millar v Bassey*,[114] is hopelessly confused on the matter. Two Court of

---

[108] [1943] Ch 51.
[109] There are *dicta* in *Lumley v Gye* (1853) 2 E & B 216 and *Bowen v Hall* (1881) 6 QBD 333 that malice is essential, but later cases such as *Quinn v Leathem* [1901] AC 495, at 510, *per* Lord Macnaughton, *South Wales Miners' Federation v Glamorgan Coal Co Ltd* [1905] AC 239, *The Kaliningrad and The Nadezhda Krupskaya* [1997] 2 Lloyd's Rep 35 and *Thomson & Co Ltd v Deakin* [1952] Ch 646, at 676, *per* Evershed MR have made it abundantly clear that spite or ill-will is not required. Good faith is no defence: *Greig v Insole* [1978] 3 All ER 449.
[110] [1896] 1 QB 147; *British Motor Trade Association v Salvadori* [1949] Ch 556; *Emerald Construction Co v Lowthian* [1966] 1 All ER 1013.
[111] *White v Riley* [1921] 1 Ch 1; *Inshore Services (International) Ltd v NFFO Services Ltd* [2001] EWCA Civ 1722, at [21], *per* Brooke LJ; *Emerald Construction Co v Lowthian* [1966] 1 All ER 1013, at 1019, *per* Diplock LJ. Dealing with a plea that the tort is not committed when D has an honest doubt whether he was interfering with the contract, Browne-Wilkinson J held in *Swiss Bank Corpn v Lloyds Bank Ltd* [1979] Ch 548, at 580, that, if D chooses to adopt a course which to his knowledge will undoubtedly interfere with C's contract, on one view of the law, he must at least show that he was advised and honestly believed he was legally entitled to take that course.
[112] *Cattle v Stockton Waterworks Co* (1875) LR 10 QB 453; *Société Anonyme de Remorquage à Hélice v Bennetts* [1911] 1 KB 243.
[113] *Bennett v Metropolitan Police Comr* [1995] 2 All ER 1; *Northern Territory v Mengel* (1995) 69 ALJR 527.
[114] [1994] EMLR 44.

Appeal judges adopted diametrically opposed views, while the third was unfathomably equivocal.[115]

(6) DAMAGE

It must be proved that the breach of the contract has caused damage (or, at least, that damage can be inferred from the circumstances[116]). An illustration of this need to prove damage is furnished by *Jones Bros (Hunstanton) Ltd v Stevens*.[117]

D continued to employ a servant after learning that the servant, in entering into his employment, was breaking his contract with C. It was shown, however, that the servant would not in any event have returned to C's employment. It was held, therefore, that C's action based on this tort failed: no damage had been occasioned.

(7) JUSTIFICATION

It is established law that, exceptionally, certain circumstances may justify interference with contracts. As yet the courts have not laid down any detailed rules for this defence, but the *dictum* of Romer LJ is widely cited.[118]

[R]egard might be had to the nature of the contract broken; the position of the parties to the contract; the grounds for the breach; the means employed to procure the breach; the relation of the person procuring the breach to the person who breaks the contract; and to the object of the person in procuring the breach.

In that case it was held that the defendants were not justified in calling the miners out on strike in order to keep up the price of coal by which the miners' pay was regulated.[119] The breach by a claimant of his contract with the defendant will not justify the defendant in inducing a third party to break his contract with the claimant.[120] On the other hand, *Brimelow v Casson* is one of the rare cases in which the defence has succeeded.[121]

---

[115] But see *The Kalingrad and The Nadezhda Krupskaya* [1997] 2 Lloyd's Rep 35 where Rix J emphasized (at 39) the need to intend a breach of contract. And see also the suggestion of Laddie J in *Michaels v Taylor Woodrow Developments Ltd* [2001] Ch 493 that intention in this context (and equally among the other economic torts) should embrace recklessness.

[116] *Exchange Telegraph Co Ltd v Gregory & Co* [1896] 1 QB 147; *Goldsoll v Goldman* [1914] 2 Ch 603 (on appeal [1915] 1 Ch 292); *Bents Brewery Co Ltd v Hogan* [1945] 2 All ER 570.

[117] [1955] 1 QB 275.

[118] *Glamorgan Coal Co Ltd v South Wales Miners' Federation* [1903] 2 KB 545, at 574–5 (approved by Lord Lindley in *South Wales Miners' Federation v Glamorgan Coal Co Ltd* [1905] AC 239, at 252).

[119] Cf *Temperton v Russell* [1893] 1 QB 715 where trade union officials were not justified in interfering in order to enforce certain conditions of labour in a particular trade; *Read v Friendly Society of Operative Stonemasons of England, Ireland and Wales* [1902] 2 KB 88.

[120] *Smithies v National Association of Operative Plasterers* [1909] 1 KB 310. Of course if a contract which X has made with Y is so inconsistent with an earlier contract between X and Z that the later contract interfered with the performance of the earlier one, the very act of X in making the contract with Y constitutes a tort. See the analysis of this defence by Goff J in *Pritchard v Briggs* [1980] 1 All ER 294, at 326 *et seq*.

[121] [1924] 1 Ch 302. Yet Simonds J in *Camden Nominees Ltd v Forcey* [1940] Ch 352 treated that decision (at 366) as being based on the separate ground of *ex turpi causa*.

D represented various theatrical unions, and C owned a touring theatrical company. D induced a theatre manager to break his contract with C because C was paying such low wages to his company that some chorus girls were compelled to resort to prostitution. The interest that D had in maintaining professional theatrical standards was held to justify D procuring the breach.

This was a case of direct inducement; and it may well be that in cases of indirect inducement – where unlawful means are required – the unlawful means used will negate any possibility of the justification defence succeeding.[122] At the very least, it seems clear that the defence is not very wide. For instance, it cannot be invoked on the basis of facts which would absolve the defendants in the tort of conspiracy: namely, that those acts were done for the purpose of protecting the trade interests of the defendant. In addition, it has been judicially stated that the role for justification is highly exceptional in relation to procuring a breach of contract.[123] There is a simple reason for this restrictive approach: the interest in maintaining the security of contracts almost always outweighs that of protecting free trade. On the other hand, lawfully exercising one's own contractual rights (as against A) with the consequence that it will inevitably cause A to break his contract with B is probably justified. As Rix J explained in *The Kaliningrad and The Nadezhda Krupskaya*:

[If] a shipowner enters into a time-charter on terms (which are standard) which entitles him to withdraw his vessel for late payment of hire, it seems to me that he remains entitled and is justified in validly exercising that right even if he thereby interferes knowingly and intentionally with another contract.[124]

(D) REMEDIES

(1) DAMAGES

Higher damages will often be recoverable in this tort than could be obtained in an action for breach of contract against the contract-breaker.[125]

(a) The damages will be assessed in the light of the facts as at the date of the breach, not when the contract was made.

(b) Any damage which the defendant intended to cause is recoverable in tort, for example, if the defendant intended to make the claimant bankrupt.[126]

(c) The damages may be more extensive than those awarded in contract.[127] For example, damages for injured feelings *may* be recoverable.[128]

---

[122] *Camden Nominees Ltd v Forcey* [1940] Ch 352. Cf *Green v Button* (1835) 2 Cr M & R 707.

[123] *SOS Kinderdorf International v Bittaye* [1996] 1 WLR 987, at 994, *per* Lord Keith.

[124] [1997] 2 Lloyd's Rep 35, at 39.   [125] *Lumley v Gye* (1853) 2 E & B 216, at 233–4, *per* Erle CJ.

[126] *Lumley v Gye* (1853) 2 E & B 216.

[127] See, eg, *Gunter v Astor* (1819) 4 Moore CP 12 (enticement of servants by a rival piano manufacturer; although only in breach for one half-day, the court rejected a claim that the damages in tort be so restricted, and awarded two years' loss of profits).

[128] See *Pratt v BMA* [1919] 1 KB 244. Cf the doubt arising from the conspiracy case of *Lonrho v Fayed (No 5)* [1993] 1 WLR 1489.

(d) Damages are at large in this tort. Thus in *GWK Co Ltd v Dunlop Rubber Co Ltd*,[129] the court included compensation for loss of prestige in its award of general damages. Furthermore, in *British Motor Trade Association v Salvadori*, Roxburgh J held that the expenses incurred in unravelling and detecting the devices of the defendants for evading the covenant system were recoverable. He acknowledged that 'the maintenance of fixed prices, and the covenant system as an integral feature of that policy, is a trade interest which the [claimants] are entitled to protect against unlawful interference'.[130]

Sometimes the action in tort will succeed where one in contract would fail – for example, where, if physical restraint were used, frustration might be pleaded in contract. Equally, the complications that arise from the claimant's election to sue for breach of contract can be avoided in this action; and the duty of the claimant to mitigate his damage may be less strict when he is the victim of an intentional tort.[131]

(2) INJUNCTION

The remedy often sought in this context is an injunction. As with other torts, an injunction is not granted as of right and may be refused even though the tort is established.[132] That said, an injunction may be awarded even if an action for damages fails.[133] Thus, Lumley failed to recover damages from Gye (because Gye did not believe Lumley's contract with Wagner was binding), but he did obtain an injunction. Equally, an injunction may be granted to prevent conduct which would lead to a breach of contract although there is insufficient 'interference' for damages to be awarded. The basis for such an injunction is that there is a 'proprietary' or 'property-like' interest at stake.[134] By contrast, an injunction will be refused against a defendant who persuades an employee of the claimant to leave his employment and work for the defendant, where the effect of the injunction would be to tie a reluctant employee to the claimant.[135]

---

[129] (1926) 42 TLR 376.   [130] [1949] Ch 556, at 568–9.

[131] See *Carmen v Fox Film Corpn* 204 App Div 776 (1923) (NY). Interesting problems about the effect of satisfaction of a judgment in contract on the claim in tort remain unsolved: see, eg, *Bird v Randall* (1762) 3 Burr 1345.

[132] See, eg, *Rely-a-Bell Burglar and Fire Alarm Co Ltd v Eisler* [1926] Ch 609, where the effect of granting an injunction would have been to prevent the servant from working at all. An injunction against the new employer who enticed him was refused.

[133] In *Esso Petroleum Co Ltd v Kingswood Motors (Addlestone) Ltd* [1974] QB 142, a mandatory injunction was ordered requiring the reconveyance of a garage sold in breach of a solus-tie agreement.

[134] For academic analysis explaining this contention, see Waddams, 'Johanna Wagner and the Rival Opera Houses' (1998) 117 LQR 431; Murphy, 'Rethinking Injunctions in Tort Law' (forthcoming). For cases supporting it, see *Manchester Ship Canal Co v Manchester Racecourse Co* [1901] 2 Ch 37 (applying *Lumley v Wagner* (1852) 1 De G M & G 604); *Earl Sefton v Tophams Ltd and Capital and Counties Property Co Ltd* [1965] Ch 1140 (revsd on other grounds [1967] 1 AC 50); *A-G for New South Wales v Perpetual Trustee Co Ltd* (1951) 85 CLR 237, at 297, *per* Kitto J. Note also that injunctions are freely given under this head when disclosure of trade secrets is involved: *Printers and Finishers Ltd v Holloway* [1964] 3 All ER 731; *Swiss Bank Corpn v Lloyds Bank Ltd* [1979] Ch 548; *Pritchard v Briggs* [1980] Ch 338.

[135] *Lotus Cars Ltd v Jaguar Cars Ltd* [1982] LS Gaz R 1214.

In practice, claimants often apply for an injunction *ex parte* and the courts will generally grant an interlocutory injunction based on the claimant's affidavit. This happened in *JT Stratford & Son Ltd v Lindley*[136] and *Torquay Hotel Co Ltd v Cousins*.[137] But in any such case, the court must be satisfied that the balance of convenience favours granting the injunction.[138]

SECTION 4 INDUCING BREACHES OF OTHER OBLIGATIONS

It now seems to be fairly well established that it is tortious deliberately to procure the violation of any enforceable obligation providing a violation of that obligation is itself actionable.[139] So, by analogy with inducing breach of contract, it would seem to be tortious to induce a breach of statutory duty if performance of that duty would confer a benefit on the claimant to which he had a right.[140] It is also tortious to induce the breach of an equitable obligation;[141] except a breach of trust.[142] And it has been held that in principle the tort may extend to inducing breach of copyright.[143] Like directly inducing breach of contract, proof that unlawful means were used to induce the breach would seem to be unnecessary.[144] The tortious nature of the act inheres in the procurement itself: the 'unjustifiable interference with legal rights'.[145]

---

[136] [1965] AC 269.   [137] [1969] 2 Ch 106.

[138] *NWL Ltd v Woods* [1979] 3 All ER 614. On the factors to be considered in deciding whether a court in its discretion grants an interlocutory injunction, see *Hadmor Productions Ltd v Hamilton* [1983] 1 AC 191 and *American Cyanamid Co v Ethicon Ltd* [1975] AC 396; *Dimbleby & Sons Ltd v NUJ* [1984] 1 All ER 751; *Associated British Ports v Transport and General Workers' Union* [1989] 3 All ER 796.

[139] Cf Bagshaw, 'Inducing Breach of Contract' in Horder (ed), *Oxford Essays in Jurisprudence, 4th Series* (2000) who argues (at 149) that the critical test is 'whether such obligations should be recognized as having a dimension which should be protected against *the rest of the world*'.

[140] *Meade v Haringey London Borough Council* [1979] 2 All ER 1016; *Associated British Ports v Transport and General Workers' Union* [1989] 3 All ER 796 (revsd on other grounds [1989] 3 All ER 822). The suggestion that the breach of statute would not need to be itself actionable seems doubtful notwithstanding what was suggested in *Wilson v Housing Corpn* [1997] IRLR 346. Otherwise, it is difficult to identify any infringement of a *right* sufficient to ground an action by C.

[141] *Prudential Assurance Co Ltd v Lorenz* (1971) 11 KIR 78; *Lonrho plc v Fayed (No 2)* [1991] 4 All ER 961.

[142] Where D procures such a breach of trust, he himself (by operation of the rules of equity) becomes liable as trustee, thus affording C adequate protection. See *Metall und Rohstoff AG v Donaldson Lufkin and Jenrette Inc* [1990] 1 QB 391.

[143] *CBS Songs v Amstrad Consumer Electronics plc* [1988] AC 1013 (no liability on the facts where D had only provided X with tape machines that were capable of being used to infringe C's copyright). By contrast, no independent tort lies in respect of inducing breach of tortious obligations; but a separate tort is unnecessary here since such an act would engage the principles of joint tortfeasance

[144] *Associated British Ports v Transport and General Workers' Union* [1989] 3 All ER 796.

[145] *F v Wirral Metropolitan Borough Council* [1991] Fam 69. Quaere: does this approach withstand the arguments made by Laddie J in *Michaels v Taylor Woodrow Developments Ltd* [2001] Ch 493 in favour of harmonizing the notion of 'unlawful means' throughout the economic torts?

SECTION 5 INTIMIDATION[146]

(A) INTRODUCTION

Although parts of the law associated with inducing breach of contract and conspiracy do not fit squarely with Lord Diplock's description of them as mere 'species' of his genus tort of unlawful interference with trade, the same cannot be said of intimidation. It involves the defendant using an unlawful threat successfully to compel another to act (or refrain from acting) in a particular manner that will cause harm to the claimant.[147] Sometimes the tort will be committed where the coercive threat is issued directly to the claimant, but more often the person threatened will be a third party. It follows, then, that there are two forms of intimidation: two-party intimidation and three-party intimidation.

Both versions of the tort may be of less practical importance than formerly due not only to the fact that a claimant will now be free to invoke the wider principle of intentionally harming another by unlawful means, but also because an alternative cause of action may lie under the Protection from Harassment Act 1997. Under section 3(2) of that Act, damages are available not only for any anxiety caused by harassment of the victim, but also in respect of any financial loss resulting from that harassment. That said, if the courts take the probable view that *indirect* financial losses are not covered by the statute,[148] recourse to the common law will still remain important (although there can be no guarantee that it will be the law of intimidation that is used in preference to the genus tort).

(B) UNLAWFUL THREATS

Intimidation is committed whenever an unlawful threat is successfully used deliberately[149] in order to cause another to do something they would not otherwise do, or to cause them to refrain from doing something that they would otherwise do with the result (in either case) that harm is caused either to the subject of the threat or to a third party. The requirement that the threat must be coercive in one of these ways is well established.[150]

---

[146] See Carty, *An Analysis of the Economic Torts* (2001) ch 4.

[147] *News Group Newspapers Ltd v SOGAT '82 (No 2)* [1987] ICR 181.

[148] See *Waters v Metropolitan Police Comr* [2000] 1 WLR 1607. But note that the action in this case against an employer, D, that was brought by C in respect of the harassment of C by fellow employees was founded on negligence and not indirect harassment of the employer.

[149] *Cheticamp Fisheries Co-operative Ltd v Canada* (1995) 123 DLR (4th) 121, at 127, *per* Chipman JA.

[150] See *Hodges v Webb* [1920] 2 Ch 70; *J T Stratford & Sons Ltd v Lindley* [1965] AC 269.

In terms of the unlawfulness of the conduct threatened, the early authorities on intimidation involved threats of violence.[151] However, the modern tort of intimidation is by no means confined to threats of this kind, and indeed it was defined in considerably broader terms in *Rookes v Barnard*.[152]

C was an employee of the airline BOAC who had resigned from his trade union. Ds were union officials. They threatened BOAC that all union members employed at BOAC would strike unless C was dismissed. BOAC consequently gave C notice and (lawfully) dismissed him.

The House of Lords held that the breach of contract threatened by the union members in that case was a sufficiently unlawful form of conduct to substantiate the tort. On the other hand, if the act threatened by the defendant is something that the defendant is entitled to do, there can be no tort. As Lord Reid said: 'so long as the defendant only threatens what he has a legal right to do he is on safe ground'.[153]

Importantly, while threats of breach of contract will suffice to supply the requisite unlawfulness in cases of three-party intimidation (where X threatens to break his contract with Y thereby causing loss to Z in respect of which Z can sue),[154] such threats will give rise only to contractual remedies in the context of two-party intimidation (where the threatened breach is of the defendant's contract with the claimant).[155] Such remedies may take the form of an injunction, or avoidance of the 'new' contract in cases of economic duress.[156]

A threat to commit a criminal act of violence will always suffice for the purposes of the law of intimidation, but mere breach of a penal statute is not *per se* sufficient: the statute must also be intended to create private rights.[157] Following the logic of this, breach of an equitable obligation may be sufficient.[158]

(C) DEFENDANT'S STATE OF MIND

It seems beyond doubt that the defendant must intend his threat to cause harm to the claimant. So, for example, in *News Group Newspapers Ltd v SOGAT '82 (No 2)*, Stuart-Smith J insisted that the claimant 'must be a person whom [the defendant] intended to injure'.[159]

---

[151] For a modern example see *Godwin v Uzoigwe* [1993] *Fam Law* 65.

[152] [1964] AC 1129.

[153] *Rookes v Barnard* [1964] AC 1129, at 1168–9. See also *Hardie and Lane Ltd v Chilton* [1928] 2 KB 306 and *Ware and De Freville Ltd v Motor Trade Association* [1921] 3 KB 40.   [154] *Rookes v Barnard* [1964] AC 1129.

[155] *Pao On v Lau Yiu Long* [1980] AC 614.

[156] In such cases, the courts insist upon coercion of the will of the threatened party (see, eg, *Pao On v Lau Yiu Long* [1980] AC 614, at 635, *per* Lord Scarman), but whether coercion is the true basis has been subjected to very powerful criticism: see Atiyah, 'Economic Duress and the Overborne Will' (1982) 98 LQR 197 and Birks, 'The Travails of Duress' [1990] LMCLQ 342. See also Bigwood, 'Economic Duress by (Threatened) Breach of Contract' (2001) 117 LQR 376.   [157] *Lonrho Ltd v Shell Petroleum Co Ltd (No 2)* [1982] AC 173.

[158] *Dixon v Dixon* [1904] 1 Ch 161.   [159] [1987] ICR 181, at 204.

SECTION 6 INTENTIONALLY HARMING ANOTHER'S TRADE OR OTHER ECONOMIC INTERESTS BY UNLAWFUL MEANS

The precise boundaries of Lord Diplock's genus tort – originally conceived to cover 'interfering with the trade or business of another person by doing unlawful acts'[160] – still need to be established. What is clear, though, is that the genus tort now has a freestanding existence.[161] But whatever those boundaries may turn out to be, there seems no good reason to confine the genus tort to the protection of trade or business interests at the expense of broader economic interests. To do so appears rather arbitrary when one bears in mind that the defendant has not only specifically employed unlawful means, but done so with the intention of causing loss to the claimant.

The argument that the genus tort provides 'scope for development of general principles of liability in respect of harm suffered intentionally'[162] arises chiefly from the fact that at its heart lie two main considerations: namely, (1) the infliction of intentional harm[163] and (2) the requirement that unlawful means be used. So much is clear from *Barretts & Baird (Wholesale) Ltd v IPCS*.[164]

Cs were members of the Association of British Abattoir Owners and companies in the meat trade. The defendant union (D) represented fat-stock officers employed by the Meat and Livestock Commission (MLC) in connection with the certification of slaughtered meat. D was engaged in a dispute with the MLC over pay and conditions. The officers voted to take strike action and a one-day strike had already created considerable difficulties for Cs' business. They alleged that D was liable for interfering in their business by unlawful means either by inducing breach of the officers' contracts of employment or by breach of statutory duty by the MLC.

Henry J, attempting to define the genus tort, according to its original conception, held that four ingredients must be established, namely:

(1) interference with the claimant's trade or business;

(2) unlawful means;

(3) intent to injure the claimant; and

(4) actual injury.

On the facts, he refused the claimants' application for an interlocutory injunction on two grounds. The alleged breach of statutory duty by the MLC was not made out.

---

[160] *Merkur Island Shipping Corpn v Laughton* [1983] 2 AC 570, at 608.

[161] See *Douglas v Hello! Ltd (No 6)* [2006] QB 125.

[162] Sales and Stilitz, 'Intentional Infliction of Harm by Unlawful Means' (1999) 115 LQR 411, 436.

[163] *Associated British Ports v TGWU* [1989] ICR 557. In this case Stuart-Smith LJ made it clear (at 586) that 'deliberate and intended damage' is required. That view also appears in *Douglas v Hello! Ltd (No 6)* [2006] QB 125 and *Mainstream Properties v Young* [2005] EWCA Civ 861. Cf the academic view that recklessness in the sense of foresight of inevitable or highly probable harm should be insufficient: Carty, *An Analysis of the Economic Torts* (2001) pp105–108.   [164] [1987] IRLR 3.

Statute required them to provide a system of inspection, not a strike-free system. Secondly, even if the breach of their contracts of employment by the fat-stock officers constituted unlawful means, no intention to injure the claimants was proved.

The two main outstanding problems that arise in connection with the genus tort are, first, whether it protects any interests not otherwise (or adequately) protected by the three classic economic torts of conspiracy, inducing breach of contract and intimidation, and, second, what constitutes unlawful means in this context? There is, however, a third and lesser concern; and this turns on the specific mental element required.

(A) THE INTERESTS PROTECTED

As already noted, the notion that the genus tort *must* be confined to interferences with economic interests apt to be described as the claimant's business or trade interests seems wrong on principle. Confining the genus tort in this way leads to the counter-intuitive result that it is narrower in scope than the so-called species torts. Even so – perhaps partly because of this – it now looks set to develop into a more expansive, general principle of liability based on the intentional infliction of harm by unlawful means[165] as something of a counterpart to the way in which the tort of negligence has developed largely on the basis of the non-intentional infliction of harm.[166] In *Dimbleby & Sons Ltd v NUJ*,[167] for example, the claimant, though able to produce his newspaper, found it a greater hardship (and thus less profitable) to do so in the face of the defendant's interference. He was thus able to invoke the tort. Similarly, in the (admittedly only county court) case of *Falconer v ASLEF*,[168] an award was made to a disappointed rail traveller where a strike caused him to incur hotel expenses.

(B) UNLAWFUL MEANS

The proper understanding of unlawful means for the purposes of this tort was for some years a topic of debate.[169] And it is still worth considering the various strands to this debate, even though the Court of Appeal has recently suggested that the doing of anything that one is not entitled to do under either the civil or criminal law will now suffice. This is because, although the unanimous Court of Appeal in *Douglas v Hello! Ltd (No 6)*[170] felt that, on balance, '[i]t would be more consistent and more likely to lead to just results if any

---

[165] Sales and Stilitz, 'Intentional Infliction of Harm by Unlawful Means' (1999) 115 LQR 411. The authors see the usual emphasis on unlawful means as misplaced and consider D's intention to harm C as the critical link between D and C in the paradigm case where D's act against X is done with a view (ultimately) to causing harm to C. The article received unequivocal endorsement in *Douglas v Hello! Ltd (No 6)* [2006] QB 125, at [174].

[166] While negligence law has developed in this way does not necessarily mean that negligence liability must be confined to cases of harm that have been inflicted non-intentionally.

[167] [1984] 1 WLR 67.   [168] [1986] IRLR 331.

[169] For a useful account of the conflicting case law, see the review supplied by Laddie J in *Michaels v Taylor Woodrow Developments Ltd* [2001] Ch 493.   [170] [2006] QB 125.

unlawful act could be' "unlawful means",[171] they nonetheless conceded that '[t]here is scope for argument as to what can and cannot amount to unlawful means for the purposes of the tort of interference with business by unlawful means'.[172] In other words, the guarded way in which the Court of Appeal reached its conclusion provides some lingering doubt as to what constitutes unlawful means in this tort. But in another sense, too, there is doubt. This second form of doubt inheres in the fact that the case, at the time of writing, is on appeal to the House of Lords where the normal chaos of the economic torts may well be restored. Without attempting to anticipate the outcome of that appeal, it seems nonetheless premature to discard the previous complex array of authorities.

What was certainly clear before, and remains clear after, the *Douglas* case is that unlawful acts capable of giving rise to tortious liability to B definitely constitute unlawful means for the purposes of any claim brought by C on the basis of the present tort.[173] Thus, if A commits a battery against B, and he does so with the intention of harming C (say, by depriving C of an employee), the tort against B will constitute the unlawful means for the purposes of the tort of using unlawful means to harm C. It is even the case that a tort against B that results in no actionable loss for B may nonetheless constitute unlawful means for the purposes of the tort against C.[174] Threats to breach a contract also amount to unlawful means; and actual breaches of contract would also seem to suffice, at least in three-party cases, since it would be a veritable oddity if a mere threat would suffice (as it does, for example, in intimidation), but an actual breach would not. The doubts relating to whether a breach of contract will suffice in two-party cases are considered separately, below.

Other civil wrongs – such as a breach of an equitable obligation – may also be enough in this context.[175] But much less clear is the status of the defendant's use of means that constitute the use of an arrangement that is unlawful only in the sense that it is in restraint of trade. In one House of Lords case[176] it was held that an agreement made in restraint of trade is void and therefore unenforceable without being unlawful as such. Yet in two subsequent Court of Appeal cases it was suggested that such unenforceable agreements are sufficiently 'unlawful means' to ground this tort.[177]

Another contentious issue centres on criminal acts. In certain cases, policy considerations may militate against implementation of civil liability. *Chapman v Honig*[178] furnishes an example where, even though the landlord who maliciously evicted a tenant

---

[171] *Douglas v Hello! Ltd (No 6)* [2006] QB 125, at [228].

[172] *Douglas v Hello! Ltd (No 6)* [2006] QB 125, at [227].

[173] See, eg, *Plessey Co plc v Wilson* [1982] IRLR 198.

[174] See *National Phonographic Co Ltd v Edison-Bell* [1908] 1 Ch 335 (D lied to a third party in order to gain an economic advantage over C and could be sued by C although the lies to the third party did not constitute actionable deceit, there being no loss to the third party); *Lonrho plc v Fayed* [1990] 2 QB 479, at 489, *per* Dillon LJ (substantially endorsing the approach in *Edison-Bell*).

[175] *Jarman & Platt Ltd v I Barget Ltd* [1977] FSR 260; *Indata Equipment Supplies Ltd v ACL Ltd* [1998] FSR 248, at 264, *per* Otton LJ.

[176] *Mogul Steamship Co v McGregor Gow & Co* [1892] AC 25. See also *Newport Association Football Club Ltd v Football Association of Wales Ltd* [1995] 2 All ER 87.

[177] *Daily Mirror Newspapers Ltd v Gardner* [1968] 2 QB 762; *Associated British Ports v TGWU* [1989] ICR 557.

[178] [1963] 2 QB 502. See also *Hargreaves v Bretherton* [1959] 1 QB 45 (no cause of action arising in respect of harm resulting from D's perjury); but in *Acrow (Automation) Ltd v Rex Chainbelt Inc* [1971] 3 All ER 1175, Ds

subpoenaed to give evidence against him acted in contempt of court, no action was found to lie in tort. Similarly, simple commission of a statutory crime – for example, where a lone driver speeds on behalf of his employer X in order to assist X in taking business from Y – cannot sensibly be thought to give rise to tortuous liability towards Y.[179] Such a case, in any event, might be argued to be covered by the protective decision in *Douglas v Hello! Ltd (No 6)* where it was suggested that acts primarily intended to advance the business interests of X (as opposed to being primarily designed to harm Y) will bring into play (the limited) defence of justification.[180]

The decision of the House of Lords in *Lonrho Ltd v Shell Petroleum Co Ltd (No 2)*[181] poses difficulties of a far more general nature.

C complied with sanctions orders prohibiting the supply of oil to the illegal regime in Southern Rhodesia. D, in breach of the orders, continued to supply oil to that regime. C alleged that those unlawful acts resulted in losses to them caused by the prolongation of the illegal regime increasing D's business at C's expense.

The claimants sought to establish liability for their business losses on three grounds: conspiracy, breach of statutory duty and interference with trade by unlawful means. The conspiracy argument failed because no intent to injure the claimants was proved; there was merely an endeavour to promote the interests of the defendants. The breach of statutory duty argument also failed because the statutory prohibition on supplying oil was not shown to be a duty imposed for the benefit or protection of a class of which the claimants were members. The claimants were thus forced, in pursuit of their third claim, to rely heavily on the broad principle enunciated by Lord Denning in *Ex p Island Records*[182] that, 'whenever a lawful business carried on by one individual in fact suffers damage as the consequence of a contravention by another individual of any statutory prohibition, the former has a civil right of action against the latter for such damage'. Dillon LJ expressed the view, *obiter*, that only where breach of a statute supports a civil cause of action will it amount to unlawful means for the purposes of the commission of the genus tort. The decision in *Lonrho* received further support from the Court of Appeal in *RCA Corpn v Pollard*.[183] But Dillon LJ's approach cannot be reconciled with the later Court of Appeal judgment of Stuart-Smith LJ in *Associated British Ports v Transport and General Workers' Union*[184] to the effect that any breach of a statute will suffice to constitute the requisite unlawful means.

Technically, the matter is an open one that needs to be settled by the Court of Appeal (or, preferably, House of Lords). But it is submitted that the simple commission of any breach of statute should not be regarded as sufficient unlawful means. What ought to be

---

were held liable for business losses resulting from Ds' aiding and abetting breach of an injunction not to impede C's manufacture of certain equipment.

[179] Example and point drawn from *Michaels v Taylor Woodrow Developments Ltd* [2001] Ch 493, at 502, *per* Laddie J.

[180] [2006] QB 125. For detailed discussion, see part C of this section.   [181] [1982] AC 173.

[182] [1978] Ch 122.

[183] [1983] Ch 135. The court was careful to state that it was not pronouncing on the soundness of earlier cases such as *Springhead Spinning Co v Riley* (1868) LR 6 Eq 551 where property rights were protected by injunction.   [184] [1989] 1 WLR 939, at 966.

required is an unlawful act that is integral to the harm caused by A to B, for, as was said in *Barretts & Baird v IPCS*, intent to injure is an essential ingredient of the tort.[185]

(C) DEFENDANT'S STATE OF MIND

In *Douglas v Hello! Ltd (No 6)*[186] the Court of Appeal made clear that the required intention to injure the claimant must take the form of a specific intention to occasion harm.

The editor of *Hello!* magazine published unauthorized photographs taken covertly at a celebrity wedding between Michael Douglas and Catherine Zeta-Jones. A rival magazine, *OK!*, had commercially negotiated an exclusive right to publish photos of the wedding and *OK!* brought an action based, *inter alia*, on the assertion that *Hello!* had committed the genus tort of interfering with the business interests of *OK!* (those business interests taking the form of the enhanced market position to which the exclusive photos would naturally contribute). While the editor of *Hello!* admitted that he had been motivated by a desire to maintain the market share of his own magazine, he denied any specific intention to damage the commercial gains that *OK!* expected to make from the publication of their photos, *even though* such damage would inevitably follow from any success in maintaining the market share of *Hello!*. One question for the Court of Appeal, then, was what was meant by 'intent to injure' in this context. Did it mean a specific intention to cause harm, or would subjective recklessness suffice? In the result, the Court of Appeal held that 'it must be shown that the object or purpose of the defendant is to inflict harm on the claimant, either as an end in itself, or as a means to another end'.[187] Thus, on the facts, there was an insufficient basis on which to make *Hello!* liable for the commission of the genus tort: harm to *OK!* was merely an inevitable (but not specifically sought) result of pursuing a legitimate business interest.

As a result of this decision (taken in tandem with another decision of a differently constituted Court of Appeal not long afterwards[188]), there has been a net reduction in the degree of uncertainty enshrouding the role of justification in relation to the genus tort. But the case falls short of constituting an authority for the broad proposition that 'justification' constitutes a *general* defence to this tort. On the question of whether it should constitute a general defence, there are arguments both ways. On the one hand, it can be argued that, so long as the commission of a legal wrong constitutes a threshold requirement for the commission of the tort, it is difficult to see how any resulting harm to the claimant can be justified. As Webster J put it in *Shearson Lehman Hutton Inc v Maclaine*

---

[185] On the centrality of intent, see Sales and Stilitz, 'Intentional Infliction of Harm by Unlawful Means' (1999) 115 LQR 411.   [186] [2006] QB 125.

[187] [2006] QB 125, at [223]. Adding a layer of confusion, however, his Lordship had earlier in his speech suggested that an inference as to either of these forms of intention *may* arise where harm to C is an inevitable consequence of what D alleges was his primary motive in acting as he did. In other words, D may be deemed to have intended harm – either as a means in itself, or as a means to some other end – where harm is an inevitable consequence of D's course of action, even if D alleges that that course of action is primarily designed to achieve some other end: [2006] QB 125, at 159. Whether such an inference is actually reconcilable with the requirement emphatically stated that there must be specific intention is questionable. Inherent in it is the admission that (a) something else was specifically intended by D, and that (b) harm to C was a mere by-product of that ulterior goal.   [188] *Mainstream Properties v Young* [2005] EWCA Civ 861.

Watson & Co Ltd: 'there can be no justification for a civil wrong'.[189] On the other hand, however, it can be argued that the simple fact that an independent civil wrong has been committed is by no means an obvious or inevitably suitable yardstick by which to gauge the tortious nature of the interference with another's business interests that arises from the commission of that civil wrong.[190] For now, then, we can only really say with any degree of confidence that a primary endeavour to advance one's own legitimate commercial interests (albeit that the means employed to pursue those legitimate interests constitute illegitimate means) may constitute an effective justification.

(D) TWO-PARTY CASES

There seems to be slender support for the notion that the genus tort can be committed in a two-party scenario.[191] If A breaks his contract with B intending not merely to cause B's disappointment on the contract, but also intending to bring about B's complete commercial ruin, there would be an undesirable multiplication of liability; one, indeed, that would conceivably lead to exemplary damages.[192] This, objectionably, would potentially circumvent the remoteness rules in contract.[193] There may also be a more general argument against the application of the genus tort – in either in its original or extended guise – in two party-cases. This objection would turn on the tort's redundancy where the unlawful means constituted some other actionable tort committed by A against B; for here, B could simply invoke the other tort to pursue a claim for damages. Thus, if A were to defame B with a view to causing B economic harm, there would be no need of the genus tort: B could simply sue in defamation, and may even obtain exemplary damages. As such, it is questionable whether the availability of the tort in two-party scenarios will be confirmed judicially.

SECTION 7 ECONOMIC TORTS AND TRADE UNIONS[194]

It is virtually impossible for a trade union to take effective action in the traditional manner (that is, by striking or threatening a strike) without risking liability arising from one of the economic torts discussed in this chapter. Calling members out on strike

---

[189] [1989] 2 Lloyd's Rep 570, at 633.

[190] Weir, for example, believes there to be some scope for the defence where the unlawful means constitute 'white lies' told to a third party, or a 'trivial breach of contract with a third party': see Weir, *Economic Torts* (1997), p 230. See also, Bagshaw, 'Unauthorised Wedding Photographs' (2005) 121 LQR 550.

[191] See *Cornwall Gardens Pte Ltd v R O Garrard & Co Ltd* [2001] EWCA Civ 699.

[192] *Kuddus v Chief Constable of Leicestershire Constabulary* [2001] 2 WLR 1789.

[193] See further Carty, *An Analysis of the Economic Torts* (2001) p 111.

[194] For fuller treatment see Carty, *An Analysis of the Economic Torts* (2001) pp 11–14.

may constitute inducing breach of contract. Threatening a strike to preserve a closed shop or to protect a demarcation agreement risks liability for intimidation. Thus, since 1906,[195] the common law has been modified by statutory immunities afforded to trades unions and their officials for acts done in contemplation or furtherance of a trade dispute. The details of such immunities fall beyond the scope of this book.

FURTHER READING

Bagshaw, 'Can the Economic Torts be Unified?' (1998) 18 OJLS 729

Bagshaw, 'Inducing Breach of Contract', in Horder (ed), *Oxford Essays in Jurisprudence, 4th Series* (2000)

Bigwood, 'Economic Duress by (Threatened) Breach of Contract' (2001) 117 LQR 376

Carty, *An Analysis of the Economic Torts* (2001)

Sales, 'The Tort of Conspiracy and Civil Secondary Liability' [1990] CLJ 491

Sales and Stilitz, 'Intentional Infliction of Harm by Unlawful Means' (1999) 115 LQR 411

Tettenborn, 'Liability for Interfering with Intangibles: Invalidly Appointed Receivers, Conversion, and the Economic Torts' (2006) 122 LQR 31

Waddams, 'Johanna Wagner and the Rival Opera Houses' (1998) 117 LQR 431

Weir, *Economic Torts* (1997)

---

[195] Trade Disputes Act 1906.

15

MISUSE OF PRIVATE INFORMATION

SECTION 1 INTRODUCTION

Whereas the wrongful invasion of privacy has for some time been recognized as the basis for an action in tort in the United States[1] and New Zealand,[2] there is as yet no comparable tort under English common law. Indeed, in *Wainwright v Home Office*, Lord Hoffmann saw great danger in the courts attempting to fashion a tort based on the unjustified invasion of privacy. He much preferred the idea that this should be a job for Parliament rather than the courts, not least because of the patent need for any such tort to carry with it a carefully thought-through menu of exceptions and defences.[3]

On the other hand, this does not mean that English common law more generally fails to recognize the interest we all have in our privacy being protected from wrongful invasions. For a start, Article 8 of the European Convention on Human Rights – now imported into English law by virtue of the Human Rights Act 1998 – imposes the obligation on all public authorities to grant positive respect to our private lives. And because the courts are public authorities for these purposes, coupled with the fact that they are required to develop the common law consistently with the rights embodied in the Convention,[4] it is apparent that the Convention is likely to enjoy a measure of horizontal effect in this context: that is, it will indirectly influence litigation between two private bodies.[5]

But even beyond the application of the Human Rights Act 1998, there are several extant torts that provide some, albeit specious, protection to our interest in privacy. For example, the law of private nuisance is helpful inasmuch as it confers a cause of action in relation to substantial and unreasonable interferences with the use or enjoyment of land. Equally, the tort of trespass to land offers protection against physical intrusions; while the laws of defamation and malicious falsehood seek to guard reputation and goodwill against the publication of untruths that cause them to suffer. Most significantly, however – at least in common law terms – has been the rapid evolution of the

---

[1] *Second Restatement of Torts* at §§ 652A-652I (1977). [2] *Hosking v Runting* [2004] NZCA 34.
[3] [2003] 3 WLR 1137, at [31]-[33]. [4] Human Rights Act 1998, ss 2 and 6.
[5] See Bamforth, 'The Application of the Human Rights Act 1998 to Public Authorities and Private Bodies' [1999] CLJ 159.

protection of privacy out of the longstanding equitable obligation to respect confidences. Indeed, as one judge explained quite recently:

[i]n the great majority of situations where the protection of privacy was justified, an action for breach of confidence would provide the necessary protection . . . A duty of confidence would arise whenever the party subject to the duty was in a situation where he either knew or ought to know that the other party could reasonably expect his privacy to be protected. The range of situations in which protection can be provided is therefore extensive.[6]

At the turn of the Millennium, however, the prevailing view was still that any general protection of privacy was 'grounded . . . in the *equitable doctrine* of breach of confidence'.[7] It took another half a decade before a senior member of the English judiciary was prepared to offer a firm indication that a new *tort* based on misuse of private information had emerged (or was emerging). In the leading case of *Campbell v MGN*,[8] and cognisant of Commonwealth authority,[9] Lord Nicholls noted that the relevant cause of action had 'shaken off the limiting constraint of the need for an initial confidential relationship' before suggesting that '*the tort* is better encapsulated now as a misuse of private information'.[10] Although his Lordship was the only member of the House of Lords to describe the action in terms of a tort in that case, there are now (as will be noted at various points in this chapter) so many differences between the action for misuse of private information and the action for breach of confidence that it seems right that he should have seen the action in this way. We shall take it, then, that a new tort – albeit one falling short of the general protection of privacy – was created in *Campbell v MGN*, the facts of which case were as follows.

C, a famous model, claimed damages from D, a newspaper group, in respect of an alleged breach of confidence and an infringement of her privacy rights under the Human Rights Act 1998. D had published (1) stories about C attending Narcotics Anonymous (NA), (2) details of her treatment for drug addiction and (3) a photograph of her at a place where NA held meetings. C was prepared to concede that the *Daily Mirror* was entitled to publish the fact that she was a drug addict and that she was in need of treatment, but she alleged that publication of the details of her treatment together with the photograph were a step too far and that this amounted to a wrongful publication by the newspaper of private information.

Recognizing fully the need to balance the newspaper group's right to freedom of expression (under Article 10) against Ms Campbell's right to respect for privacy (under Article 8), the House of Lords held by a bare majority that publication of Ms Campbell's treatment details along with the photograph suggesting her attendance of an NA meeting was a step too far. These details were more than was necessary to put the record straight (bearing in mind that Ms Campbell had previously lied in public, denying her

---

[6] *A v B plc (a company)* [2002] EMLR 371, at 382, *per* Lord Woolf CJ.

[7] *Douglas v Hello! Ltd (No 1)* [2001] QB 967, at 1001, *per* Sedley LJ (emphasis added). For details of the equitable doctrine see *Clerk and Lindsell on Torts* (2006) pp 1779–1786 and Cornish, *Intellectual Property* (2003) ch 8.

[8] [2004] 2 AC 457.

[9] *Hosking v Runting* [2004] NZCA 34. In that case, the New Zealand Court of Appeal identified two heads of liability: one, in equity, protecting confidentiality; the other, in tort, protecting wrongful publicity about private lives.   [10] [2004] 2 AC 457, at [14] (emphasis added).

drug addiction). As such, her Article 8 right to privacy outweighed the newspaper's Article 10 right to freedom of expression and her action succeeded. However, as has already been observed, the most remarkable feature of the case was the way in which the action was viewed: namely, as an action based on a *common law* right of privacy;[11] or more particularly, as an action derived from the misuse of private information.

SECTION 2 CONTENT OF THE TORT

In the immediate wake of *Campbell*, it was highly probable that the misuse of private information of a *personal* kind would ground an action in tort. But shortly after that case was decided, the opportunity arose in *Douglas v Hello! Ltd (No 6)*[12] to consider whether the tort action could be extended to protect *commercially exploitable* private information. However, instead of dealing with such information in the same way that Lord Nicholls dealt with private personal information in *Campbell*, the Court of Appeal preferred to treat the misuse of commercially exploitable information along the traditional lines of breach of confidence.[13] While acutely aware of the way in which the protection of privacy had developed over recent years, and while indicating that further development was both inevitable and necessary along human rights lines, Lord Phillips MR, delivering the judgment of the court, said:

the Human Rights Act 1998 . . . [requires that] [t]he court should, in so far as it can, develop the action for breach of confidence in such a manner as will give effect to both article 8 and article 10 rights.[14]

On the one hand, this decision would appear to be a step backwards in that it represents a return to the less-than-ideal manipulation of the action in equity for breach of confidence. On the other hand, however, there was some indication elsewhere in his speech that the action may have broken free of its traditional equitable constraints, since, after highlighting Lord Nicholls' reference to a tort action, Lord Phillips MR also referred to the 'action *formerly described* as breach of confidence'.[15] Thus we are left with a sense of ambivalence about this decision. Taken as a whole, Lord Phillips' speech suggests clearly only the following limited proposition: namely, that for the present, it is preferable if the courts continue to deal with cases capable of falling within established breach of confidence categories – such as misuse of artistic and literary confidences[16] – along the lines of the traditional equity action.

---

[11] Lord Nicholls took especial note of an academic article canvassing this possibility: namely, Phillipson, 'Transforming Breach of Confidence? Towards a Common Law Right of Privacy under the Human Rights Act' (2003) 66 MLR 726.

[12] [2006] QB 125. For detailed analysis of the case see Bagshaw, 'Unauthorized Wedding Photographs' (2005) 121 LQR 550.

[13] [2006] QB 125, at [120], *per* Lord Phillips MR. In similar vein see *Fraser v Thames Television* [1984] QB 44; *Lansing Linde Ltd v Kerr* [1991] 1 WLR 251.   [14] [2006] QB 125, at [53].

[15] [2006] QB 125, at [51]–[53].   [16] See, eg, *Shelley Films Ltd v Rex Features Ltd* [1994] EMLR 134.

A second limit of the tort, and one recognized by Lord Nicholls, centres on the fact that only *unjustified* disclosures of private personal information will trigger liability. This, of course, begs the question of what amounts to an 'unjustified disclosure'; and it necessarily involves the balancing of two competing human rights – *viz*, the right to respect for our private lives and the right to freedom of expression – neither of which is absolute. But before considering the way in which this balancing exercise is to be undertaken, it is necessary to point out the crucial distinction between, on the one hand, failing to respect privacy rights by *unjustifiably disclosing* private personal information, and, on the other, simply invading our privacy (for example, by use of a powerful zoom lens on a camera[17]). Only the former is capable of generating tortious liability on the basis of what Lord Nicholls said in *Campbell*.[18]

As regards the human rights dimension, it has been recognized for some time that there are important limits to both the Article 8 and Article 10 rights. As regards the latter, the then President of the Family Division in *Venables v News Group Newspapers Ltd*[19] held that the right to freedom of expression in Article 10(1) was a strong one that could only be overridden in accordance with the exceptions in Article 10(2). Furthermore, her Ladyship insisted that these exceptions – that is, that any restriction on free expression must be in accordance with the law, necessary in a democratic society and, in every case, proportionate to the legitimate aim pursued – were to be construed narrowly and that the burden of showing an Article 10(2) exception lies firmly with the party seeking to restrain publication of potentially injurious information. On the other hand, in *Campbell*, Baroness Hale identified that there were different classes of speech each of which warranted different levels of protection. Thus, while she clearly saw political free speech as central to a democratic society, she also indicated that mere gossip serving no political, educational or artistic purpose would be more difficult to justify (even though it may help to sell certain publications) if it were to impact negatively on another's privacy interest.[20]

In precisely the same passage, however, her Ladyship also pointed out that the right to privacy was similarly to be understood in relative terms. Thus, for example, she envisaged a much greater general freedom to discuss the private lives of 'public figures, especially those in elective office' since this otherwise private information might well be 'relevant to their participation in public life'.[21] In essence, what she was describing was a 'public interest' justification for the disclosure of otherwise private information.[22]

---

[17] In the case itself, two Law Lords drew a similar distinction between the simple spying through such a lens with the (probably tortious) publication of a photograph taken in such a fashion: see *Campbell v MGN* [2004] 2 AC 457, at [76] and [121]-[123], *per* Lords Hoffmann and Hope respectively.

[18] But note that if the invasion is deliberately undertaken by a public authority – say, in the form of unjustified state surveillance of an individual – then there can nonetheless be direct liability under section 7 of the Human Rights Act 1998 for breach of Article 8: see, eg, *Halford v UK* (1997) 24 EHRR 523; *Wainwright v Home Office* [2003] 3 WLR 1137.   [19] [2001] 2 WLR 1038.

[20] *Campbell v MGN* [2004] 2 AC 457, at [148].   [21] *Campbell v MGN* [2004] 2 AC 457, at [148].

[22] See further Section 5, below.

And here it is noteworthy that the legitimacy of breaking confidences on the basis of the public interest is a well-established justification for disclosures of private information within the context of the equity action for breach of confidence.[23] Indeed, it is hard to imagine that, even if the courts henceforth deal with misuses of private personal information on the basis of *tort law*, they will ignore the substantial body of law on public interest disclosure built up within the context of the action in equity. And this is so even though the balancing exercise for the purposes of compliance with the European Human Rights Convention may require a slightly different approach to the one developed in relation to the action for breach of confidentiality. As such, it is worth considering some of the existing equity cases.

According to the established equitable principles, the competing public interests in maintaining the bond of confidence[24] and access to particular information must be weighed against each other.[25] An example of competing interests is the patient's right to confidentiality versus the potential risk to third parties. Here it seems that a doctor is almost certainly entitled to break his duty of confidentiality if maintaining it would entail a serious risk of physical harm to a third party. But it is important to stress that a small or insignificant risk will not suffice. In *X v Y*,[26] for example, publication of the names of two doctors found to be HIV positive was banned by Rose J. There was found to be no significant risk to their patients which outweighed the doctors' right to confidentiality. By contrast, the defendant psychiatrist in *W v Egdell*[27] had been engaged to prepare a report on W who was seeking to be transferred from a special hospital to a lower security unit in preparation for his ultimate discharge from hospital. W had been detained under the Mental Health Act 1983 after being convicted of multiple manslaughter. Dr Egdell concluded that far from being 'cured', W remained dangerously ill with a morbid interest in explosives. The Court of Appeal held that Dr Egdell was justified in breaching W's confidence and sending a copy of his report to the hospital where W was detained, and to the Home Secretary.[28]

So far as cases based on the equity action for breach of confidence are concerned, a legitimate public interest in the subject matter of the information has to be proved. Curiosity alone is insufficient. So, too, is prurient interest. There is, after all, a critical distinction between that which is in the public interest and that which merely interests the public.[29] In order to justify a disclosure, then, the information must of its very nature be of a kind that ought to be disclosed.[30] So, for example, the expression of

[23] Decisions on confidentiality and the state suggesting that the public interest in information is accorded a low priority compared with 'state secrets' should be treated with caution and confined to their special facts: see *A-G v Jonathan Cape Ltd* [1976] QB 752 (Crossman diaries) and *A-G v Guardian Newspapers* [1987] 3 All ER 316 (*Spycatcher* affair).

[24] Note that there is a public as well as a private interest in confidentiality in many contexts: *X v Y* [1988] 2 All ER 648; *W v Egdell* [1990] Ch 359.

[25] *Church of Scientology of California v Miller* (1987) *Times*, 23 October.   [26] [1988] 2 All ER 648.

[27] [1990] Ch 359.

[28] For further confirmation of the legitimacy of disclosures made with a view to preventing the commission of a crime, see *Hellewell v Chief Constable of Derbyshire* [1995] 1 WLR 804.

[29] *Stephens v Avery* [1988] Ch 449.   [30] *Cambridge Nutrition Ltd v BBC* [1990] 3 All ER 523.

legitimate doubt about the safety of criminal convictions may well be taken to be a matter of public interest. Take, for example, *Lion Laboratories Ltd v Evans*.[31]

Cs sought to prevent publication of internal memoranda leaked by employees to the press. The memoranda cast doubt on the reliability of the intoximeter manufactured by Cs and used by the police to test alcohol levels in drivers. The Court of Appeal refused to grant an injunction. The public interest in the reliability of the product which could, if unreliable, result in unfair prosecutions outweighed any private rights of Cs. Disclosure of this information to the proper authorities was therefore justified.

It remains to be seen just how differently from these equity cases the courts will undertake the balancing exercise involving the weighing of the Article 8 right to respect for privacy against the Article 10 right to freedom of expression. But in so far as Article 10(2) is substantially synonymous with the notion of public interest disclosures, we may with some degree of confidence predict that the courts will draw a good deal of guidance from the above cases as regards what is and is not a legitimate aim in a democratic society. Equally, there are clear indications from the speeches of Lord Hope and Baroness Hale in *Campbell* that the courts ought to adopt a 'relative merits' approach whereby the respective benefits of protecting one right rather than the other are compared and contrasted (given that one or other right must give way where the two come into conflict).[32] In making this assessment, it seems that the following factors will be pertinent considerations: the extent of the harm or distress that is likely to be caused by the disclosure, the manner in which the information was obtained, the kind of information involved and the degree of intrusion.[33]

SECTION 3 THE 'REASONABLE EXPECTATION' TEST

Not all information that can be described as private personal information attracts the protection of the emerging tort. This is because, as the *Campbell* case insists, the claimant must also be able to show that he held a reasonable expectation that the information in question would be kept private.[34] This of course begs the question of what factors will be taken to generate the requisite 'reasonable expectation' of privacy. And while there is currently no clear-cut answer to this, it is at least apparent that a claimant will not be able to rely upon his peculiar susceptibility to embarrassment to transform an ordinarily innocuous disclosure into an actionable one. As Lord Hope explained in the *Campbell* case, '[t]he law of privacy is not intended for the unduly sensitive'.[35] But this only takes us so far. It does not resolve the way in which the phrase 'reasonable

---

[31] [1985] QB 526.   [32] *Campbell v MGN* [2004] 2 AC 457, at [105] and [141] respectively.

[33] See *Clerk and Lindsell on Torts* (2006) pp 1793–1994.

[34] *Campbell v MGN* [2004] 2 AC 457, at [21] and [85], *per* Lords Nicholls and Hope respectively, and at [134], *per* Baroness Hale.   [35] [2004] 2 AC 457, at 94.

expectation' should be understood. It could, for example, be taken to mean the equivalent of a rational, actual expectation; or it could be taken to connote a legitimate (but not necessarily actual) expectation. So if, for example, certain salacious facts concerning X, a famous pop star, were to come to the attention of a well-known, sensationalist tabloid newspaper, X could hardly be thinking rationally he if genuinely expected that the newspaper would withhold those facts from the public when their publication would undoubtedly generate higher sales. Yet at the same time, he may well have a legitimate expectation that those facts be kept secret.

According to the various speeches in the *Campbell* case, it would seem that the second interpretation is nearer the mark. What concerned Baroness Hale was that misuse of private information could amount to an infringement of 'the individual's informational autonomy', while Lord Hoffmann stressed the 'protection of human autonomy and dignity'.[36] The lowest common denominator here would seem to be the right to control the dissemination of private information (since this would seem to be an aspect of both human autonomy and informational autonomy). But this does not mean that the two categories are co-extensive. Indeed, only information that has the capacity to embarrass or cause a decline in one's public standing would seem to fit the thinking of Lord Hoffmann. So, while details of a pop star's drug addiction would fit both tests, publication of his or her mobile telephone number would have no obvious impact on his or her human dignity or social standing. Even so, a publication of the latter kind would almost certainly fall within the category of information the publication of which the pop star would reasonably expect to be able to control.

Since their Lordships were wary of creating a general tort centring on the protection of privacy, it would seem more sensible to adopt the narrower test based on 'human autonomy and dignity' in order to explain the case. Such a test commands broader support from the various speeches in the *Campbell* case which, taken together, in general viewed the action as being centred upon personal information bearing the capacity to cause embarrassment or offence.[37] It also reconciles *Campbell* with the *Douglas* case where the Court of Appeal failed to extend the *Campbell* principle to commercially exploitable information (which, of course, would fall within the 'informational autonomy' test).

So, to summarize, what appears to lie at the heart of the new tort is a reasonable expectation (judged objectively from the perspective of the claimant) that certain private personal information should not be misused, where that expectation arises out of the fact that misuse (in the form of *unjustified disclosure* to the public) will have a direct negative impact on the claimant's autonomy and dignitary interests. Thus, recalling the facts of *Campbell*, we can see that while certain disclosures – themselves capable of causing embarrassment – were justified in order to set the record straight, other disclosures, that were not so justified, gave rise to a successful action in tort. Similarly, in

---

[36] *Campbell v MGN* [2004] 2 AC 457, at [51].

[37] Lord Hope favoured the adoption of a 'substantial offence' test like the one propounded by Gleeson CJ in the High Court of Australia in *Australian Broadcasting Corporation v Lenah Game Meats Pty Ltd* (2001) 208 CLR 199. Cf the doubts of Lord Nicholls in the *Campbell* case about this being 'suggestive of a stricter test of private information than a reasonable expectation of privacy' [2004] 2 AC 457, at [22].

Theakston v MGN,[38] it was thought to be acceptable to publish written details of a celebrity's visit to a brothel, but that it was also necessary to draw the line at publication of photographic evidence of the event.

For the present, then, it would seem that a wrongful disclosure of a good deal of private information will not fall within the *Campbell* principle. An individual's private financial information provides a good example. For while there may well be a desire to keep something such as the details of one's earnings or expenditure a secret, it is difficult to see how disclosures about these matters would have any impact on the claimant's autonomy or dignitary interests. On the other hand, a good case can be made for extending the new tort in this direction.

SECTION 4 INFORMATION COVERED BY THE TORT

As the tort is limited to the misuse of private information, it follows that misuse of public information will never suffice to ground an action. Drawing on the existing case-law relating to breaches of confidentiality we might begin by asserting that no protection will be afforded to information that is already public knowledge. But in so saying we should also bear in mind the principle according to which something should *not* be construed as being common knowledge just because all the relevant component parts of a particular piece of information are already in the public domain. Thus, just because the public could find something out by putting A and B together in order to get C (when A and B are common knowledge), does not mean that C cannot be regarded as protected information. If a member of the public has to go through the process of putting A and B together in order to possess the precise information constituting C, then C may well be regarded as confidential information even though A and B were already clearly in the public domain.[39]

(A) COMPROMISING AND EMBARRASSING PHOTOGRAPHS

Notwithstanding what has just been said about information already in the public domain, it is apparent that special rules apply to compromising or embarrassing photographs. This is because, as Baroness Hale put it in the *Campbell* case, '[a] picture is "worth a thousand words" because it adds to the impact of what the words convey'.[40] In other words, while it is one thing to report in words that X is a drug addict, it is quite another to publish a photograph of X in all his drug-addicted misery. Thus it was that

---

[38] [2002] EMLR 137.   [39] *Saltman Engineering Co v Campbell Engineering Co* (1948) 65 RPC 203.
[40] [2004] 2 AC 457, at [155].

the Court of Appeal held in the *Douglas* case that repeated publications of photographs already in the public domain may on each occasion amount to a misuse of private information. The reasoning ran thus: '[i]n so far as a photograph does more than convey information and intrudes on privacy by enabling the viewer to focus on intimate personal detail, there will be a fresh intrusion of privacy when each additional viewer sees the photograph'.[41] As such, '[t]he agreement [with *OK! Magazine*] that certain authorized photographs can be published will not, however, provide a defence to a claim . . . [based on] the publication of unauthorized photographs'.[42] Furthermore, the fact that pictures are taken in a public place does not necessarily undermine their intrusiveness if published. If their taking and publication was unauthorized, and particularly if the photographs were taken covertly, an action will lie if 'the person publishing the information knows or ought to know that there is a reasonable expectation that the information in question will be kept confidential'.[43]

(B) INFORMATION ABOUT HEALTH AND MEDICAL CONDITIONS

In just the same way that disclosures of medical information have generally been taken to be capable of grounding an action in equity based on breach of confidentiality, so too – as is apparent from the decision in *Campbell*[44] – may we take it that such information can also form the basis for an action under the new tort of misuse of private information. On the other hand, there would appear to be an important distinction between the two actions in this context. The tort only permits claims by those to whom the information relates personally. By contrast, it would appear possible for, say, a hospital that compiles and holds patients' medical records, to sue on the basis of the action in equity since it, too, has a sufficient interest in their confidentiality being maintained.[45]

(C) SEXUAL INFORMATION

Unauthorized disclosure of private details concerning one's sexual relationships (or even sexuality[46]) should also generally ground the tort. However, as a caveat to this point, it might well be the case that such information will not always give rise to a reasonable expectation of privacy. If, for example, the claimant were a public figure

---

[41] *Douglas v Hello! Ltd (No 6)* [2006] QB 125, at [105].

[42] *Douglas v Hello! Ltd (No 6)* [2006] QB 125, at [107].

[43] *Campbell v MGN* [2004] 2 AC 457, at [134], *per* Hale B. See also *Peck v UK* [2003] EMLR 15 where an attempted suicide was captured on CCTV and the European Court of Human Rights held that it was a breach of Article 8 of the European Convention to disclose that footage to newspapers and broadcasters.

[44] See also *Z v Finland* (1997) 25 EHRR 371.

[45] See *Ashworth Security Hospital v MGN* [2001] FSR 559.

[46] See, eg, *Dudgeon v UK* (1981) 4 EHRR 149.

whose honesty could be seen to turn on the disclosure of such factual information, then there may be a case for disclosing so much of the otherwise private information as is necessary in the public interest to confirm or refute the allegations about that person's honesty. So, as Lord Woolf CJ put it in one case: 'where a public figure chooses to make untrue pronouncements about his or her life, the press will normally be entitled to put the record straight'.[47]

SECTION 5 DEFENCES AND REMEDIES

It has already been mentioned in passing that a disclosure of private information in the public interest provides a justification for that disclosure. But there are four further points worthy of note. First, so far as the action for breach of confidence is concerned, it is well established that the matter disclosed must have been of genuine public concern,[48] and one in respect of which the recipient has a genuine interest.[49] Yet, while there were echoes of this principle in the *Campbell* case, it is difficult to see what general interest the public has in learning of a model's drug addiction and treatment for that addiction (even though on the facts of the case the principle of putting the record straight applied[50]). Secondly, so far as the tort action is not constrained by the traditional maxims of equity, it seems unnecessary for the courts to continue to invoke the oft-quoted *dictum* that 'there is no equity in the disclosure of an iniquity'[51] in order to show justification for any given disclosure. Thirdly, as regards additional defences, one rather more obvious one will be that of prior consent/authorization; while another, based on the fact that the information is already in the public domain, may also apply to information other than that contained in photographs (to which, as we have seen, special rules apply).

Finally, as regards remedies, both injunctions (prior to disclosure) and compensatory damages (after disclosure) will be available. It may also be possible to obtain damages based on an account of profits where disclosure of private information has netted the defendant profits that exceed the amount payable by way of compensatory damages.[52] And where X has obtained possession of certain private personal information concerning Y, it seems on principle, by extrapolation from the breach of confidence case law, that Y may be able to obtain an order for the return of the confidential documents.[53]

---

[47] *A v B* [2003] QB 195, at [43].

[48] See, eg, *Hubbard v Vosper* [1972] 2 QB 84 where a disclosure which was clearly in the public interest was justified notwithstanding a specific undertaking not to make that disclosure.

[49] See, eg, *Initial Services v Putterill* [1968] 1 QB 396.

[50] For earlier cases in which this principle was enunciated see *Woodward v Hutchins* [1977] 2 All ER 75; *Campbell v Frisbee* [2002] EMLR 656.   [51] *Gartside v Outram* (1857) 26 LJ Ch 113.

[52] See Jones, 'Restitution of Benefits Obtained in Breach of Another's Confidence' (1970) 80 LQR 463.

[53] See, eg, *Saltman Engineering Co v Campbell Engineering Co* (1948) 65 RPC 203.

FURTHER READING

Bagshaw, 'Unauthorized Wedding Photographs' (2005) 121 LQR 550

Jones, 'Restitution of Benefits Obtained in Breach of Another's Confidence' (1970) 80 LQR 463

Phillipson, 'Transforming Breach of Confidence? Towards a Common Law Right of Privacy under the Human Rights Act' (2003) 66 MLR 726

PART V

TORTS INVOLVING STRICT OR STRICTER LIABILITY

The common element in the torts discussed in this Part is that a defendant who is not merely being held accountable for the acts of an employee need not have committed the act complained of either intentionally or negligently. They are often referred to as torts of strict liability; yet as the following chapters reveal, the liability threshold in some of these torts is less strict than that in others of them. As such, it is better to see only some of these torts as involving pure strict liability, while the others impose merely stricter liability than that which characterizes the archetypal, fault-based tort of negligence.

16

PRODUCT LIABILITY[1]

SECTION 1 INTRODUCTION

The complex history of liability for loss or injury caused by defective products illustrates well the gradual development and changing perceptions of the role of tort law and its inter-relationship with the law of contract. The classical common law stance towards faulty or useless goods was that of *caveat emptor* (that is, let the buyer beware). The person buying goods was expected either to take steps to ensure that the goods were safe for use and value for money, or to make contractual arrangements which would provide him with a remedy should the goods prove to be defective. If he failed to protect himself, he would bear any resulting loss. In 1893 Parliament gave some protection to purchasers of goods via the first Sale of Goods Act. Then, in 1932, in *Donoghue v Stevenson*,[2] the House of Lords held that the ultimate user of a product might also, in certain circumstances, sue in negligence the manufacturers of a product causing injury to his person or his property. The extent of manufacturers' negligence liability has since been further developed and refined by the courts.

In the meantime, Parliament strengthened the contractual rights of purchasers of goods[3] and services[4] with increasingly interventionist consumer protection laws.[5] And in respect of certain types of goods, the criminal law was used to protect safety standards, and an action for breach of statutory duty[6] was expressly created to allow individuals injured by goods in the specified categories to recover compensation from the manufacturers. Thus, by 1987 little survived of the *caveat emptor* principle. The social and legal climate had changed, but there was a confusing multiplicity of potential remedies available under a range of limited causes of action. Furthermore, the difficulty of proving negligence had become especially problematic in relation to products. As such, several official bodies[7] advocated that manufacturers should be made strictly liable for defective products.[8] The final victory for proponents of strict liability was won

---

[1] See generally Howells, *Product Liability* (2000).   [2] [1932] AC 562.

[3] See the Sale of Goods Act 1979.

[4] See the Supply of Goods and Services Act 1982. Note also the Unfair Contract Terms Act 1977.

[5] Domestic consumer protection legislation has been strengthened further by the European Directive on Unfair Terms in Consumer Contracts 1993.   [6] Consumer Protection Act 1987, s 41.

[7] See *Law Commission Report on Liability for Defective Products* (1977); *Royal Commission on Civil Liability and Compensation for Personal Injury* (1978) (Cmnd 7054–1).

[8] For the reasons and relevant history, see the 10th edition of this book.

in Europe when on 25 July 1985 the Council of the European Communities issued a Directive[9] requiring all member states to implement a regime of strict liability for defective products. The UK Government responded by enacting the Consumer Protection Act 1987. The Act leaves untouched contractual claims against the retailer, the action in negligence and, where appropriate, actions for breach of statutory duty. The Act is further limited in its effect in that it provides only for claims in relation to personal injury and damage to private property. Damage to business property and economic loss resulting from defective products are outside its remit.

SECTION 2 CONSUMER PROTECTION AND THE CHANGING COMMON LAW

(A) THE LIMITATIONS OF CONTRACT LAW

The primary means invoked to protect consumers against faulty goods has traditionally been the law of contract. The original Sale of Goods Act 1893 has now been replaced by the Sale of Goods Act 1979 (itself amended by the Sale and Supply of Goods Act 1994). It is that 1979 Act which, among other things, incorporates into every contract of sale terms of satisfactory quality[10] and fitness for purpose.[11] Identical terms are implied by the Supply of Goods and Services Act 1982 into any contract for services in the course of which goods are supplied.[12] Thus, if in the course of private dental treatment a dentist provides her patient with dentures which crumble within the week, it matters not whether any contract of sale for the dentures exists. The patient clearly had a contract for services under which unsuitable dentures were supplied. Terms implied by virtue of the 1979 and 1982 Acts cannot be excluded against the consumer,[13] liability is strict, and it is not limited to protection against injury to the person or property.

There are, however, limitations to the effectiveness of contract as a means of general consumer protection against defective goods. These arise from the rules of privity of contract.[14] A person who is not a party to a contract cannot generally benefit from that contract. So if one receives as a gift an electric blanket bought by a friend, one has no contractual right to sue the retailer if it proves to be faulty; and where one purchases the faulty blanket oneself, and the retailer goes out of business, one has no contractual claim against the wholesaler.[15] The Contracts (Rights of Third Parties) Act 1999 is

---

[9] 1985/374/EEC.   [10] Consumer Protection Act 1987, s 14(2).

[11] Consumer Protection Act 1987, s 14(3). Satisfactory quality means 'the standard that a reasonable person would regard as satisfactory taking into account any description of the goods, the price (if relevant) and all the other relevant circumstances'. So, an electric blanket that fails to heat a bed as expected would incur liability as easily as one that causes an electric shock or fire.   [12] Consumer Protection Act 1987, s 4.

[13] Unfair Contract Terms Act 1977, s 6; Supply of Goods and Services Act 1982, s 13.

[14] See Furmston, *Cheshire, Fifoot and Furmston's Law of Contract* (2001) ch 14.

[15] There may, however, be a collateral contract with the manufacturer to the effect that any guarantee given is effective in the hands of the ultimate purchaser. But even if there is no such collateral contract, Art 6 of Directive 1999/44/EC now requires that manufacturers' guarantees should be legally enforceable.

unlikely to be of much use in this context, for that Act only confers rights on third parties in respect of whom it is clear that the contract was designed to confer a benefit and who are identified by name, class or description in the contract.[16]

A number of devices have occasionally been used to evade the consequences of rules of privity. In *Lockett v Charles*,[17] for instance, a wife whose husband bought her a restaurant meal was able to claim for her food poisoning on the basis that her husband had acted as her agent. But the circumstances allowing for an inference of agency are strictly limited. The same is true of the other devices that have been employed to avoid the privity rule.[18] It is thus to tort that a claimant must generally look if she did not purchase the product herself.

(B) THE ACTION FOR NEGLIGENCE

The early development of liability in negligence for defective goods began with *Dixon v Bell*[19] where a master who entrusted a loaded gun to his young servant was found liable to a third party injured by the servant firing the gun on the ground that the goods 'were in a state capable of doing mischief'. However, the court in *Langridge v Levy*[20] declined an invitation to deduce from *Dixon v Bell* a general principle of liability for putting into circulation things 'of a dangerous nature'. In *Winterbottom v Wright*,[21] the driver of a coach was seriously injured as a result of a defect in the coach. His action against the defendant (who supplied his employers with coaches and horses) failed because of privity of contract: the claimant could not take advantage of express terms in the contract as to the repair and maintenance of the coach. But what the court in *Winterbottom v Wright* failed to analyse was the possibility of a separate and independent obligation arising within the tort of negligence.

Case law between 1851 and 1932 continued to deny any general duty to take care in the manufacture and distribution of goods although some exceptional cases did hold that a duty existed. Liability was eventually recognized in relation to goods 'dangerous in themselves',[22] in respect of known defects of which no warning was given by the supplier.[23] In addition, occupiers were held liable to their invitees in respect of appliances on their premises which proved to be defective.[24] The boundaries of these instances of liability for defects were unclear, and the need to prove knowledge of the defect in the second category was often fatal to the success of a claim. The decision of the House of Lords in *Donoghue v Stevenson*[25] heralded a new age.

---

[16] Contracts (Rights of Third Parties) Act 1999, ss 1(1)(b) and (3).
[17] *Lockett v A & M Charles Ltd* [1938] 4 All ER 170.
[18] Furmston, *Cheshire, Fifoot and Furmston's Law of Contract* (2001) pp 502–507.
[19] (1816) 5 M & S 198.
[20] (1837) 2 M & W 519. The court nevertheless found for C on the ground of fraud.
[21] (1842) 10 M & W 109.   [22] See *Longmeid v Holliday* (1851) 6 Exch 761.
[23] *Heaven v Pender* (1883) 11 QBD 503, at 517; *Clarke v Army and Navy Co-operative Society* [1903] 1 KB 155.
[24] *Heaven v Pender* (1883) 11 QBD 503.   [25] [1932] AC 562.

C drank a bottle of ginger beer, manufactured by D, which a friend bought from a retailer and gave to C. The bottle allegedly contained the decomposed remains of a snail which were not, and could not be, detected (as the bottle was opaque) until most of the bottle had been consumed. C alleged that she was ill as a result, and sued D. The House of Lords had to decide whether the facts disclosed a cause of action. They found for C by a majority of 3 to 2.

Lord Atkin held that:

a manufacturer of products, which he sells in such form as to show that he intends them to reach the ultimate consumer in the form in which they left him with no reasonable possibility of intermediate examination, and with the knowledge that the absence of reasonable care in the preparation or putting up of the products will result in an injury to the consumer's life or property, owes a duty to the consumer to take that reasonable care.[26]

Others among their Lordships had other reasons for reaching the same result, but since then, negligence liability for defective products has extended its scope and remains important notwithstanding the passage of the Consumer Protection Act 1987. Throughout the remainder of this chapter, therefore, readers ought to bear in mind the following questions:

(1) Are there any persons who may be liable in negligence in respect of defective goods who would not be classified as 'producers' for the purposes of the Consumer Protection Act 1987 (and thus not liable within the terms of the Act)?

(2) Are there any kinds of loss remediable in negligence but not under the Act?

(3) What is the nature of the special limitation rules under the Consumer Protection Act 1987?

(4) How radical a departure from common law negligence is the strict liability regime introduced by the Consumer Protection Act 1987?

With these in mind, let us turn to the modern approach of negligence law.

(1) RANGE OF DEFENDANTS

Although Lord Atkin imposed liability only on manufacturers, later case law extended liability to, among others, assemblers,[27] repairers[28] and suppliers of drinking water.[29] Mere suppliers of goods have also been held liable where their function went beyond simple distribution. For example, a car dealer selling vehicles reconditioned by him,[30] and a retail chemist[31] failing to observe the manufacturers' instructions to test the product before labelling it, were both found liable to injured users. Indeed, wherever the circumstances are such that a supplier would normally be expected to check a product, a duty to do so has often been imposed. Second-hand car dealers will be

---

[26] [1932] AC 562, at 599. This proposition will be called the 'narrow rule' in the case; and the 'neighbour principle', the broad rule.   [27] *Malfroot v Noxal Ltd* (1935) 51 TLR 551 (fitting a sidecar).

[28] *Haseldine v C A Daw & Son Ltd* [1941] 2 KB 343 (lift repairer).

[29] *Read v Croydon Corpn* [1938] 4 All ER 631; *Barnes v Irwell Valley Water Board* [1939] 1 KB 21.

[30] *Herschtal v Stewart and Ardern Ltd* [1940] 1 KB 155.   [31] *Kubach v Hollands* [1937] 3 All ER 907.

expected to check the steering on used cars.[32] Wholesalers who fail to test a hair dye of dubious provenance will also be held negligent.[33]

A number of categories of persons owing a common law duty of care will also shoulder responsibility for compensating victims of defective products under the Consumer Protection Act 1987. But this is not so of all those owing a common law duty of care. For example, suppliers failing to carry out tests may avoid liability under the statute by simply naming the person who supplied the goods to them. Repairers are also beyond the scope of the statute.

(2) PRODUCTS

The term 'products' today includes not only food and drink[34] but quite clearly any product in normal domestic use. Underwear,[35] hair dye,[36] motor cars,[37] computer software,[38] installations in houses,[39] exterior staircases,[40] have all been treated as proper subjects of a duty of care. Pre-*Donoghue v Stevenson* distinctions[41] between products 'dangerous in themselves' and other goods can now be largely disregarded.[42] The distinction remains relevant only in that the greater the potential danger inherent in a product, the more stringent must be the precautions needed to protect the user against injury or loss.[43]

(3) ULTIMATE 'CONSUMER'

It follows from what has been said about the courts' willingness to expand negligence liability since *Donoghue v Stevenson* that a wide range of claimants may now sue for injuries caused by defective products. Thus, in *Barnett v H and J Packer & Co*,[44] the proprietor of a sweet shop who was injured by a piece of metal protruding from a sweet recovered damages from the sweet's manufacturers. And in *Stennett v Hancock and Peters*[45] a bystander was able to sue after a defendant garage owner negligently

---

[32] *Andrews v Hopkinson* [1957] 1 QB 229. See also *Fisher v Harrods Ltd* [1966] 1 Lloyd's Rep 500 (D, a retailer, was liable to the donee of a customer for an eye injury caused by a jewellery cleaning fluid).

[33] *Watson v Buckley, Osborne Garrett & Co Ltd* [1940] 1 All ER 174.

[34] *Barnes v Irwell Water Board* [1939] 1 KB 21(water).

[35] *Grant v Australian Knitting Mills Ltd* [1936] AC 85.

[36] *Watson v Buckley, Osborne, Garrett & Co Ltd* [1940] 1 All ER 174.

[37] *Herschtal v Stewart and Ardern Ltd* [1940] 1 KB 155.

[38] *St Albans City and District Council v International Computers Ltd* [1996] 4 All ER 481.

[39] *Haseldine v C A Daw & Son Ltd* [1941] 2 KB 343.

[40] *Targett v Torfaen Borough Council* [1992] 3 All ER 27.

[41] See *Dominion Natural Gas Co Ltd v Collins and Perkins* [1909] AC 640.

[42] See *Billings (AC) & Sons Ltd v Riden* [1958] AC 240.

[43] But that must not be construed as a rule distinct from negligence that there is a separate class of dangerous things which D must keep safe at his peril. See *Read v J Lyons & Co Ltd* [1947] AC 156, at 172–3, *per* Lord Macmillan.

[44] [1940] 3 All ER 575. Cf *Mason v Williams and Williams Ltd and Thomas Turton & Sons Ltd* [1955] 1 All ER 808 (manufacturers of chisel liable to C when a splinter flew off the negligently made chisel supplied to C's employers and injured C's eye).   [45] [1939] 2 All ER 578.

reassembled the flange on the wheel of X's lorry so that the flange came off, mounted the pavement and injured the claimant, a pedestrian. The defendant was held liable for his negligent repair. In neither case was the claimant strictly a 'consumer'.

(4) SALE

There seems no reason why the rule should not apply even where there is no sale of goods distributed in the course of a business, for example, where manufacturers supply free samples.[46] The liability for goods supplied in a domestic or social context is more disputable. Would a housewife who baked a fish pie for a charity fair be liable to the person who bought it, ate it and succumbed to food poisoning? Would she be liable to her own children who ate a second pie made for their dinner?[47]

(5) INTERMEDIATE EXAMINATION

Lord Atkin envisaged that a manufacturer should be liable where:

he sells in such a form as to show that he intends [his products] . . . to reach the ultimate consumer in the form in which they left him with no reasonable possibility of intermediate examination.

If the rule is to apply, 'the customer must use the article exactly as it left the maker, that is in all material features, and use it as it was intended to be used'.[48] The effect of intermediate examination seems, therefore, to be this: if someone in the place of the manufacturer would reasonably contemplate that the defect in the goods would remain there at the time of their use by the claimant despite their passing through the hands of intermediaries, he is still liable.[49] The test is not whether intermediate examination is possible.[50] However, where an intermediary does specifically test and certify a product as safe, he may himself incur negligence liability.[51]

This test with respect to defective goods is stricter than it might be for other forms of negligence. *Clay v A J Crump & Sons Ltd*[52] illustrates the point.

Under the supervision of an architect, D, demolition contractors were demolishing a building, and builders were to construct a new one. On D's advice a wall was left standing on the site.

---

[46] See *Hawkins v Coulsdon and Purley UDC* [1954] 1 QB 319, at 333, *per* Denning LJ.

[47] The narrow rule in *Donoghue v Stevenson* is probably inapplicable to gratuitous transfers. There are cases where liability has been established in respect of dangers known to the transferor: see, eg, *Hodge & Sons v Anglo-American Oil Co* (1922) 12 Ll L Rep 183; *Hurley v Dyke* [1979] RTR 265. Where the defect is not known to the transferor, however, there seems no reason in principle why the *broad rule* should not apply to gratuitous transfers. What would be the standard of care demanded of the housewife in the example in the text?

[48] *Grant v Australian Knitting Mills Ltd* [1936] AC 85, at 104.

[49] [1936] AC 85 at 105, *per* Lord Wright; *Haseldine v C A Daw & Son Ltd* [1941] 2 KB 343, at 376, *per* Goddard LJ. And see *Nitrigin Eireann Teoranta v Inco Alloys* [1992] 1 All ER 854 (fractured pipe would not have been discovered even by the use of reasonable care).

[50] *Dransfield v British Insulated Cables Ltd* [1937] 4 All ER 382, holding the opposite, is probably best regarded as wrongly decided.

[51] *Perrett v Collins* [1998] 2 Lloyd's Rep 255 (negligent certification of safety of an aircraft).

[52] [1964] 1 QB 533.

It subsequently collapsed onto C, an employee of the builders. D pleaded that the demolition contractors and their employees had had the opportunity of intermediate examination.

This was held to be a case not of the narrow products rule but of the broad principle, so that the intermediate examination principle did not apply to defeat the claimant's claim against the architect.

(6) PREPARATION OR PUTTING UP

There may be liability for a defect in the design of a product,[53] in the container and, probably also, in the labelling of the package.[54]

(7) CONTINUING DUTY OF CARE

What if the product when first put on the market was not manufactured with any lack of care? Imagine at that time, on all the reasonably available evidence, the manufacturers could have discovered no defect in their product. Suppose, however, that evidence later transpires of risks to person or property posed by a latent defect. Do the manufacturers then owe any duty (1) to attempt to recall the goods, and/or (2) to warn consumers of the danger? It is clear beyond doubt that, even though originally the design of a product may have been made with all due care, once a design defect becomes patent, the manufacturer is liable in negligence if he continues to produce and market the unsafe product.[55] In respect of unsafe products already in circulation, a continuing duty of care is owed to do whatever is reasonable to recall the defective product and warn users of the risk the defect may pose to their health and/or property.[56] As regards the duty to warn, it may be sufficient, according to Canadian authority,[57] if the manufacturer passes the warning on to the intermediary (in that case, a doctor) who supplied the consumer (a patient) with the product rather than warning the consumer directly. So far as the duty to recall goes, it is clear that the recall procedure must also be conducted non-negligently if further liability is to be avoided.[58]

(8) RECOVERABLE LOSS

The duty of care in respect of defective products remains, in general, limited to a duty to avoid inflicting injury to the ultimate consumer's life or property.[59] But in relation to damage to property, no liability is imposed in respect of damage to the defective

---

[53] *Hindustan Steam Shipping Co Ltd v Siemens Bros & Co Ltd* [1955] 1 Lloyd's Rep 167.

[54] *Kubach v Hollands* [1937] 3 All ER 907.   [55] *Wright v Dunlop Rubber Co Ltd* (1972) 13 KIR 255.

[56] *Hobbs (Farms) v Baxenden Chemicals* [1992] 1 Lloyd's Rep 54; *Walton v British Leyland UK Ltd* (1978) *Times*, 13 July; *Rivtow Marine Ltd v Washington Ironworks* (1974) 40 DLR (3rd) 530.

[57] *Hollis v Dow Corning Corpn* (1995) 129 DLR (4th) 609.

[58] *McCain Foods Ltd v Grand Falls Industries Ltd* (1991) 80 DLR (4th) 252.

[59] The property damage must arise from a use to which D might reasonably have expected the property to be put. There was no liability where a waterproofing compound was lost when pails manufactured by D melted in the intense heat of Kuwait: *Aswan Engineering Establishment Co v Lupdine Ltd* [1987] 1 All ER 135.

product itself. Thus, if pistons in a car's engine fail causing further damage to the engine, there is no liability imposed in respect of the further engine damage.[60] This is pure economic loss and it is not generally recoverable in negligence.[61] It is only where non-integral parts of a car malfunction and cause further damage – such as a CD player that overheats and causes a fire – that an action *may* lie.[62] It would be inapt to conceive of a car without tyres; therefore the tyres are merely parts of an overall defective product. But where an accessory such as a CD player is added, it is possible to talk of product A (the CD player) damaging product B (the car). This example should not be confused, however, with a case in which defective product A is combined with product B to make product C – for example, where two products (a gas and a liquid) are combined to make a carbonated drink. In such a case it is inappropriate to talk of product A damaging product B. Instead, there is merely the production of a defective product, product C, in respect of which the defects are to be treated as irrecoverable, pure economic loss.[63]

(9) PROVING NEGLIGENCE

The scope of liability for negligent manufacture, distribution and repair that has evolved from the rule in *Donoghue v Stevenson* is now very considerable. Yet it is in the formidable task of proving negligence in the narrow sense that claimants confront the greatest difficulty. In the classic application of the narrow rule in *Donoghue v Stevenson* – where the ultimate consumer is suing the manufacturer – it is often verging on impossible to prove absence of reasonable care, at least by direct evidence. The consumer's difficulties may be further compounded by problems of causation; especially, for example, in claims relating to drug induced injury. Yet the burden of proof remains with the claimant. Lord Macmillan said in *Donoghue v Stevenson* that the burden of proof:

must always be upon the injured party to establish that the defect which caused the injury was present in the article when it left the hands of the party whom he sues, that the defect was occasioned by the carelessness of that party . . . There is no presumption of negligence in such a case at present, nor is there any justification for applying the maxim *res ipsa loquitur*.[64]

However, the Privy Council modified this rigid approach in *Grant v Australian Knitting Mills Ltd*.[65] There, the claimant was concerned to prove that the dermatitis he

---

[60] Analogy drawn from *Hamble Fisheries Ltd v Gardner & Sons Ltd, The Rebecca Elaine* [1999] 2 Lloyd's Rep 1.

[61] *Murphy v Brentwood District Council* [1991] 1 AC 398; *Simaan General Contracting Co v Pilkington Glass Ltd (No 2)* [1988] QB 758; *Muirhead v Industrial Tank Specialities Ltd* [1986] QB 507; *Aswan Engineering Establishment Co v Lupdine Ltd* [1987] 1 All ER 135.

[62] For an analogous application of this so-called 'complex structure' approach, see *Jacobs v Moreton & Partner* (1994) 72 BLR 92. (D constructed faulty foundations to remedy the existing defects in the foundations of C's property. There had always been problems with the foundations but the further damage to C's property was caused by the defects in D's 'remedial' foundations.)

[63] *Bacardi-Martini Beverridges Ltd v Thomas-Hardy Packaging Ltd* [2002] 1 Lloyd's Rep 62. See also, Tettenborn, 'Components and Product Liability' [2000] LMCLQ 338.   [64] [1932] AC 562, at 622.

[65] [1936] AC 85.

contracted was caused by the presence of invisible excess sulphites in the underwear he purchased and which was made by the defendants. It was explained that the test was whether, on the balance of probabilities, it was a reasonable inference to be drawn from the evidence that the harm was so caused.[66] On the issue of negligence, it was said:

if excess sulphites were left in the garment, that could only be because someone was at fault. The appellant is not required to lay his finger on the exact person in all the chain[67] who was responsible, or to specify what he did wrong. Negligence is found as a matter of inference from the existence of the defects taken in connection with all the known circumstances.[68]

This approach is eminently practical and good law,[69] and it is certainly to be preferred to the *obiter dicta* of Lord Macmillan in so far as the two are in conflict.[70] Where the presence of the defect (in combination with the known circumstances) gives rise to an inference of negligence against the manufacturers, the burden shifts to the defendant to rebut that inference. This may be done either by pinpointing the exact cause giving rise to the defect and establishing that it does not arise from any want of care, or by the manufacturer producing evidence as to his system and establishing that the system was consistent with all due care. In *Daniels and Daniels v R White & Sons Ltd and Tabbard*,[71] the claimant was seriously injured when he drank lemonade containing a large quantity of carbolic acid. The acid presumably came from the washing process used by the defendant manufacturer. The judge accepted evidence of the precautions taken by the defendants to avoid such a contingency and found that the claimants had failed to prove negligence.

The problems faced by the claimant are compounded where the relevant defect is not a construction defect but a design defect.[72] Design defects occur where the basic design of the product proves to be inherently dangerous. Although a construction defect – where something goes wrong that does not normally go wrong – allows the possibility of the court inferring negligence, a similar inference cannot be made with respect to a design defect. In design cases, the claimant must prove (1) that the manufacturer should have been aware of the risk of the defect, and (2) that he could reasonably have avoided the defect. The issue all too often becomes one of whether, at the time the

---

[66] [1936] AC 85, at 96–7, *per* Lord Wright.

[67] What if C does not know whether the negligence is that of the manufacturer, the bottler, the wholesaler, the carrier or the retailer?

[68] [1936] AC 85, at 101, *per* Lord Wright. Thus, where there is no evidence of a defect at the time of manufacture, and there exist several alternative explanations of why a malfunction may have occurred, liability will not be imposed on a manufacturer: see *Evans v Triplex Safety Glass Co Ltd* [1936] 1 All ER 283. Cf *Carroll v Fearon* [1998] PIQR P416 (evidence of fault in tyre manufacture sufficient to incur liability even when tyre was seven years old).

[69] For a lucid and similar explanation of the burden of proof see *Mason v Williams and Williams Ltd and Thomas Turton & Sons Ltd* [1955] 1 All ER 808, at 810, *per* Finnemore LJ.

[70] This was exactly the approach of the House of Lords in the Scottish case of *Lockhart v Barr* 1943 SC 1 where the purchaser of aerated water contaminated with phenol recovered from the manufacturer although he could not prove how the phenol came to be in the aerated water. [71] [1938] 4 All ER 258.

[72] The construction/design dichotomy was rejected as an analytical device in *A v National Blood Authority* [2001] 3 All ER 289. But why? In terms of both conceptual distinctiveness and practical repercussions, the two are readily distinguishable.

product was put on the market, scientific and technical knowledge available to the manufacturer should have enabled him to identify the danger.

The classic example of the difficulties posed in this connection arise in the medical context where a drug is first marketed without foresight of its possible repercussions, but in the firm belief (based on the best available scientific knowledge), that the drug is safe. In such cases, an action in negligence requires a claimant to prove that according to the state of scientific knowledge at the time of marketing, the manufacturer should recognize the risk.[73]

(10) PROVING CAUSATION

The next problem faced by the claimant is that of proving causation. Normally, this is done in accordance with the usual 'but for' test.[74] But in relation to certain types of product – especially pharmaceutical products – great difficulties can arise.[75] In the case of such products the claimant will frequently already be suffering from some form of illness. Where the claimant's condition deteriorates, or she suffers the onset of a related illness, the question is whether the drug caused the additional illness. Similarly, it is one thing to allege that a drug has caused injurious side-effects, but quite another to prove that it has done so. Thus, in *Loveday v Renton*[76] the action failed because it could not be proved, on the balance of probabilities, that the claimant's brain damage had been caused by the administration of the pertussis vaccine. This was despite the fact that it was known that the pertussis vaccine *could* cause brain damage in children. On the other hand, the courts need not abandon common sense. So in *Best v Wellcome Foundation Ltd*,[77] for example, the Irish Supreme Court held that causation could be inferred from the fact that the first sign of the claimant's brain damage followed closely on the heels of the administration of the pertussis vaccine. There was no other plausible explanation of its cause and it thus satisfied the balance of probabilities threshold.

(c) ACTION FOR BREACH OF STATUTORY DUTY

Before considering the strict liability regime contained in the Consumer Protection Act 1987, a brief mention must be made of the possibility of an action for breach of statutory duty in respect of certain limited categories of goods. The Secretary of State has the power to make safety regulations prescribing detailed rules as to, among other things, the design, manufacture and packaging of specified classes of goods.[78] Breach of such regulations is a criminal offence.[79] But section 4 of the Consumer Protection Act 1987 also provides that an individual injured by a breach of the regulations will have an

---

[73] While it is very difficult to establish negligence in design defects, it is not absolutely impossible: see *Independent Broadcasting Authority v EMI Electronics and BICC Construction Ltd* (1980) 14 BLR 1.

[74] See ch 5.   [75] See, eg, Porat and Stein, *Tort Liability Under Uncertainty* (2000) *passim*.

[76] [1990] 1 Med LR 117.   [77] [1994] 5 Med LR 81.   [78] Consumer Protection Act 1987, s 41.

[79] See General Product Safety Regulations SI 2005/1803.

action for breach of statutory duty.[80] The regulations cover only a limited class of goods and the action for damages lies only where the defect in the goods derives from breach of the regulations. The action is also subject to the due diligence defence in section 39.

SECTION 3 THE STRICT LIABILITY REGIME

(A) THE CONSUMER PROTECTION ACT 1987

Three prefatory points must be borne in mind when considering the 1987 Act. First, the regime it contains derives from the European Community Directive of 12 July 1985.[81] And although the Directive allows for some variation in the rules throughout member states, the basic regime throughout the Community is the same. British industry is subjected to the same strict liability rules as its European competitors.[82] Secondly, industry in the UK – particularly the pharmaceutical industry – persuaded the government to adopt the controversial 'development risks' defence despite every official report on product liability advising against such a course of action. (The defence, as we shall see, does much to undermine the strictness of liability under the Act.) Thirdly, although it was possible to give direct statutory effect to the Directive, that was not done. Thus, where the interpretation of the 1987 Act is in doubt, it should be construed in the light of the Directive. And should there be any serious conflict between the provisions of the Act and the Directive, the dispute may ultimately have to be decided by the European Court of Justice.[83] That said, there is clear domestic judicial support for the view that the wording of the Directive should prevail in such cases.[84]

(B) WHO CAN SUE UNDER THE ACT?

Wherever a defect in a product wholly or partly causes personal injury or death, the victim or his dependants may sue under the Act.[85] The injured individual need not be a purchaser or even a direct user of the faulty goods. If defective brakes in a new car

---

[80] Note that it is only breach of specific safety regulations that gives rise to an action for breach of statutory duty and not infringement of the general safety duty provided for by Consumer Protection Act 1987, s 10.

[81] 1985/374/EEC.

[82] Notably, the European Court of Justice has held that member states may not implement rules more stringent than those contained in the Directive (*European Commission v France*, Case C-52/00, 25 April 2002), nor may they retain pre-existing rules that are more stringent than those in the Directive (*Sanchez v Medicina Asturiana SA*, Case C-183/00, 25 April 2002).

[83] Interestingly, in *EC Commission v United Kingdom*, C-300/95 [1997], the Commission refused to accept that the UK's adoption of the development risk defence is, despite plausible arguments to the contrary, compatible with Art 7 of the Directive.

[84] See *A v National Blood Authority* [2001] 3 All ER 289, at 297, *per* Burton J.

[85] Consumer Protection Act 1987, s 2(1).

bought by A suddenly fail causing a road accident in which A, his passenger B, and C, a pedestrian, are seriously injured, all three can sue the car's manufacturer. Where a defective product causes damage to a baby before birth, the baby may later sue in respect of its disabilities.[86] Moreover, although the Act is primarily aimed at protection against personal injuries and death, consumers can also invoke its provisions where a product causes damage to private property (including land) providing the amount to be awarded to compensate for that damage exceeds £275.[87] Damage to the product itself is expressly excluded;[88] and other forms of pure economic loss are also clearly irrecoverable.[89]

(c) ON WHOM IS STRICT LIABILITY IMPOSED?

Liability is not limited to manufacturers alone. Essentially, all those involved in the primary production and marketing of goods are made liable. Repairers and distributors who may owe consumers a duty of care at common law are generally outside the scope of the new strict liability regime.

The Act imposes liability on the following categories of persons.

(1) Liability is imposed on 'producers';[90] and producers are defined as:

(a) manufacturers;[91]

(b) in the case of products which are not made, but won or abstracted (for example coal and minerals) the person who won or abstracted the product;[92] and

(c) in respect of products which are neither made, nor won or abstracted (for example crops), but where essential characteristics of the product are attributable to an industrial or other process, the person carrying out that process.[93]

(2) Liability is imposed on any person who brand names a product or by other means holds himself out as a producer.[94] This does not necessarily mean, however, that if you buy a food processor at Marks & Spencer which bears the brand name 'St Michael', and a part of the machine flies off and injures you, that you may sue Marks & Spencer on this basis. Simply placing the 'St Michael' stamp on

---

[86] Consumer Protection Act 1987, s 6(3).

[87] See the Consumer Protection Act 1987, s 5(4). By s 5(3) property used for business purposes is excluded. See Bell, 'Product Liability Damages in England and Wales' (1992) 20 *Anglo-American Law Review* 371.

[88] Consumer Protection Act 1987, s 5(2).

[89] Economic loss consequent upon physical injury or damage to private property should in principle, however, be recoverable.   [90] Consumer Protection Act 1987, s 2(2)(a).

[91] Consumer Protection Act 1987, s 1(2)(a).   [92] Consumer Protection Act 1987, s 1(2)(b).

[93] Consumer Protection Act 1987, s 1(2)(c). The cumbersome definition of this category of producer is explained by reference to the former exemption of primary agricultural produce from the regime instituted by the 1987 Act. This exemption was removed by the Consumer Protection Act 1987 (Product Liability) (Modification) Order 2000 (SI 2000, 2771) giving effect to Directive 1999/34/EC.

[94] Consumer Protection Act 1987, s 2(2)(b).

the processor is probably insufficient, since, in addition, the company must thereby hold itself out as having actually produced the product.

(3) Liability is imposed on any person importing a product into Europe from outside Europe.[95] Had you bought a Japanese food processor you need not concern yourself with the intricacies of suing in Japan; you can proceed against whichever European imported it into Europe.

(4) Liability is also potentially imposed on distributors. Section 2(3) provides that any supplier of a product will be liable to the injured person *unless* he complies with a request to name, within a reasonable time, the person supplying him with the product. (Recall that a consumer may not know the identity of a manufacturer in a long chain of supply.)

(5) The Directive expressly defines manufacturers of component parts as 'producers' so they, too, are subject to strict liability.[96] The Act achieves the same end by more tortuous means: namely, defining 'product' so as to embrace component parts.[97] The effect is simply illustrated. Should defective brakes in a new car fail causing personal injuries, the injured person may sue both the 'producer' of the finished product (that is, the car manufacturer) as well as the 'producer' of the defective component (the manufacturer of the brakes). Section 1(3), however, provides that a supplier of the finished product shall not be deemed to be liable for defects in all component parts simply because he cannot name the actual manufacturer of each and every component.

(D) PRODUCTS

'Products' are defined in the Act[98] as 'any goods or electricity' and include component parts, certain substances[99] and agricultural crops.

In earlier drafts of the Directive, blood and human tissues were expressly excluded from the Directive, but it has since been held that blood and blood products do fall within its compass, even though the Directive and the Act were ultimately silent on the matter.[100] By contrast, the Act does not cover immovable property – that is, land and fixtures on land.[101] But products which become fixtures within immovable property – for example, central heating boilers – are probably within the scope of the Act.[102]

---

[95] Consumer Protection Act 1987, s 2(2)(c). Note that a person importing a product into the UK from another member state is not made strictly liable under the Act. He may, however, be liable in negligence.

[96] Article 3(1).   [97] See the Consumer Protection Act 1987, s 1(2).

[98] Consumer Protection Act 1987, s 1(2).

[99] Eg, blood and blood products: see *A v National Blood Authority* [2001] 3 All ER 289.

[100] *A v National Blood Authority* [2001] 3 All ER 289.

[101] Liability for defectively constructed buildings remains subject to the general rules of negligence and the Defective Premises Act 1972.

[102] See the Consumer Protection Act 1987, s 45(1) and Art 2 of the Directive.

(E) DEFINING 'DEFECT'

Proof that a product resulted in injury is not sufficient to establish liability. The claimant, must show also that *a defect in the product* caused the injury. If a defect can be proved, carelessness *per se* is irrelevant. Thus, if a chef is badly cut when the blade from his new food processor flies off the machine, he will succeed in his claim simply on proof of the obvious: that the processor is unsafe and defective.

Defect is defined in section 3 of the Act in terms that there is a defect in a product if the safety of that product is not such as persons generally are entitled to expect.[103] It is important to note that the standard that a person may be entitled to expect – perfection in some circumstances – may in fact transcend the standard they do *in fact* expect.[104] In assessing what persons generally are entitled to expect, section 3(2) states that all the circumstances are to be taken into account including:

(a) the manner in which, and purposes for which, the product has been marketed, its get-up, the use of any mark in relation to the product and any instructions for, or warnings with respect to, doing or refraining from doing anything with or in relation to the product;

(b) what might reasonably be expected to be done with or in relation to the product; and

(c) the time when the product was supplied by its producer to another;

and nothing in this section shall require a defect to be inferred from the fact alone that the safety of a product which is supplied after that time is greater than the safety of the product in question.

It remains for the claimant to prove that, taking into account the criteria outlined in section 3, the product is defective. Hardly any product is entirely safe and free of risk. The test is whether the risk to person and property posed by the product in the context of its common use or uses exceeds what is generally acceptable. Take the example of a sharp knife marketed as a kitchen knife for chopping vegetables and packaged so as to be reasonably child-proof on display. If the knife cuts off the tip of one's finger, one cannot claim that the injury resulted from a defect. A sharp cutting edge is a risk one accepts as the price for a knife which does its job. But if the same knife were marketed as a 'Marvellous Magic Dagger' and a child should cut himself, then the defect would be easier to prove: a risk to children in such a product (clearly aimed at children) would be generally unacceptable. Ultimately, the question is one of whether the manufacturer ought to issue a warning as to dangers one would not expect the product to present. If the danger is both obvious and inherent, and if it is part and parcel of what the consumer would expect, then there is no defect. Thus, hot coffee which inevitably carries the potential to scald is not a defective product.[105]

---

[103] See generally Stoppa, 'The Concept of Defectiveness in the Consumer Protection Act 1987' [1992] *Legal Studies* 210.   [104] See *A v National Blood Authority* [2001] 3 All ER 289.

[105] *B v McDonald's Restaurants Ltd* [2002] EWHC 409.

The test for a defect set out in section 3(2)(a) and (b) is likely to involve the courts in risk/benefit analysis. This can best be illustrated by examples of liability for drugs.[106] Imagine a new and effective antibiotic is introduced. In 99.5% of cases it works well with fewer side-effects than other antibiotics. But 0.5% of consumers develop serious kidney damage caused by the drug. If an identifiable group of persons should or could have been foreseen as susceptible to damage, the failure to warn doctors of the potential allergic reaction may conclude the issue of defect.[107] But in cases where no such reaction is foreseeable, much may turn on the nature of the drug and the condition it is designed to combat. Thus, while a new minor tranquilliser posing a risk of liver damage to however small a group would probably be found defective, an AIDS drug designed to prolong sufferers' lives would probably justify a much higher degree of risk to life and health. Where the consumer of the drug faces a prospect of almost certain and painful death, any product offering a realistic hope of cure or palliation may generally be thought acceptable, even if it is inherently dangerous to some of its users. Existing chemotherapy treatments, for example, fit this analysis.

Section 3(2)(c) of the Act warrants separate consideration. It has two main implications. First, the time when the product was put into circulation is obviously relevant to determine whether the defect was inherent in the product or merely the result of 'fair wear and tear'. Thus, when a child-seat is eight years old and has been used by three different children, can it be expected to be as safe as when new?[108] Secondly, section 3(2)(c) also provides that safety standards must be judged by the generally acceptable standards at the time at which the product was put on the market, and not with hindsight, according to standards prevailing when the claim reaches court. Thus, a 15-year-old car without rear seatbelts ought not to be regarded as defective *purely because* of that absence.

In relation to construction and presentation defects, strict liability will probably be easy to establish. Where the manufacturing process breaks down – for example, where snails get into ginger beer bottles – the product will be patently defective. Equally, where instructions on use are inadequate, or warnings as to use fail to make the consumer safe, a defect will also be easy to establish.[109] The need to engage in a rigorous examination of risks and benefits of a product will generally be reserved for design defects[110] where the implications for industry of design defects are potentially much more profound.[111]

---

[106] See Newdick, 'Liability for Defective Drugs' (1985) 101 LQR 405.

[107] By analogy with *A v National Blood Authority* [2001] 3 All ER 289, and the emphasis placed on strict liability in that case, it is conceivable that even a 0.05% risk would not excuse the manufacturer in the case of this hypothetical.

[108] Consider the juridical underpinnings of product liability regimes in Clark, 'The Conceptual Basis of Product Liability' (1985) 48 MLR 325.

[109] If, however, a warning leaflet is lost, or a consumer chooses not to replace a lost leaflet, the manufacturer cannot be held responsible: *Worsley v Tambrands Ltd* [2000] PIQR P95.

[110] See, eg, *Abouzaid v Mothercare (UK) Ltd* 2000 WL 1918530, where Pill LJ thought the question for the court was one of whether the public could legitimately expect a higher degree of safety from the product than that which was actually present.

[111] Compensating 10 victims of a freak construction defect is a less daunting prospect than compensating the thousands who may have suffered injury before a design defect became patent.

The question of what the defendant could (reasonably or otherwise) have done to eliminate or reduce the risks will be irrelevant under the 1987 Act.

(F) GENERAL DEFENCES

Section 4 of the Consumer Protection Act 1987 provides several defences to strict liability. They include the following incidents:

(1) The defect is attributable to compliance with any requirement imposed by legislation (whether domestic or European).[112] On the other hand, the defence is not available where there are no statutory rules on how the product is to be made, but there are rules requiring licensing of the product by a public body before it can be marketed.

(2) If the defendant proves he never supplied the product to another[113] – for example, if experimental drugs are stolen from a drug company's laboratory and sold by the thieves.

(3) If the defendant did not supply the goods in the course of business.[114] Thus, the defendant is not strictly liable for defects in the food he serves to colleagues at a dinner party.

(4) If the defendant proves that the defect did not exist in the product when it was supplied by the defendant to another.[115] Thus, a chocolate manufacturer would not be liable for chocolates injected with poison on the supermarket shelves by some third party.

(5) Where the defendant makes components, he will not be liable where the defect arose in the finished product and was caused by the faulty design of the finished product or inadequate installation of D's component into the finished product by the manufacturers of that product.[116]

In addition to the defences provided for by section 4 of the Act, section 6(4) provides that the contributory negligence of the consumer is a defence under the Act. Two difficult questions arise, however. The Law Reform (Contributory Negligence) Act 1945 provides that when a finding of contributory negligence is made, apportionment of responsibility between the claimant and defendant (and hence the level of damages) is based on relative fault. But where the defendant is strictly liable, and the claimant has been careless of his own safety, does this mean that the claimant will generally have to bear the lion's share of responsibility, or will the courts at this stage have to revert to considering any evidence of want of care on the part of the defendant?

More problematic still is the matter of defining the circumstances in which a product that is put to improper use is evidence of contributory negligence. Imagine a stepladder

---

[112] Consumer Protection Act 1987, s 4(1)(a). For example drugs which must be licensed under the Medicines Act 1968.   [113] Consumer Protection Act 1987, s 4(1)(b).
[114] Consumer Protection Act 1987, s 4(1)(c).   [115] Consumer Protection Act 1987, s 4(1)(d).
[116] Consumer Protection Act 1987, s 4(1)(f).

is bought for cleaning windows. The 17-year-old son of the purchaser uses it to build an assault course. After a 14-stone friend of his has thundered across it, the wood cracks as the son himself is on the ladder. He falls and breaks a leg. Is he guilty of a degree of contributory negligence, or was the ladder put to a use that it would not generally be expected to withstand (in which case it may not even have been defective)?

(G) THE 'DEVELOPMENT RISKS' DEFENCE[117]

The incorporation of the development risks defence into the Act via section 4(1)(e) is the most controversial part of the legislation. Permitting member states to incorporate such a defence was a compromise by the European Community in order to end the long-drawn-out process of agreeing to implement strict liability at all. Section 4(1)(e) provides that a defendant shall not be liable where he can show:

that the state of scientific and technical knowledge at the relevant time was not such that a producer of products of the same description as the product in question might be expected to have discovered the defect if it had existed in his products while they were under his control.

The effect of the defence can be explained as follows. Consider a drug-induced injury. A claimant establishes that the product fails to comply with society's legitimate expectations for the safety of that type of product. This means he proves that the risks created by the drug outweigh its potential benefits. The defendant may still escape liability by virtue of the 'development risks' defence if he can prove that the nature of the defect was such that, at the time he marketed the drug,[118] the very best available scientific and technical knowledge[119] would not have revealed the defect.[120] Imagine, for example, that a drug has been developed to alleviate sickness during pregnancy. Imagine further that it leads to unforeseen disabilities in the children born subsequently. In such circumstances, the development risks defence would confer one significant advantage on the parents of the damaged babies. In negligence they would have to prove that the defendants should have foreseen the risk. But under the statute,

---

[117] See generally Newdick, 'The Development Risks Defence of the Consumer Protection Act 1987' [1988] CLJ 455 and *id*, 'Risk, Uncertainty and "Knowledge" in the Development Risk Defence' (1992) 20 *Anglo-American Law Review* 309.

[118] It will not, once and for always, be enough simply to establish that at the time the design was first put on the market the defect was not discoverable. Once the defect becomes apparent, any further marketing of batches of the drug will engage liability both under the Act and in negligence: see *Wright v Dunlop Rubber Co Ltd* (1972) 13 KIR 255.

[119] The development risks defence in Art 7(e) of the Directive is defined in terms of, 'the state of scientific and technical knowledge at the time when he put the product into circulation was not such as to enable the existence of the defect to be discovered'. There is no reference to whether a 'producer of products of the same description might have been expected to have discovered the defect' as *per* the Consumer Protection Act 1987, s 4(1)(e). But notwithstanding the seemingly more generous test under the Act, relevant case law points to what is unknown to the world of science rather than merely what is unknown to the defendant: see *Richardson v LRC Products Ltd* [2000] Lloyd's Rep Med 280; *A v National Blood Authority* [2001] 3 All ER 289.

[120] It follows that if a risk is known, or ought to be known, in the light of accessible information, the defence is not available: *A v National Blood Authority* [2001] 3 All ER 289.

the onus is on the defendants to prove that they could not have anticipated the danger. As such, self-interest impels manufacturers to disclose all reports of tests on a product as well as the expert opinion made available to them.

In summary, the Consumer Protection Act 1987 purports to benefit claimants by implementing a regime of strict liability, and despite academic doubts about just how strict liability would prove to be under the Act,[121] the decision of Burton J in *A v National Blood Authority*[122] displays a firm commitment to its strictness. There, the claimants who had received blood transfusions, were infected with the Hepatitis C virus. The risk of infection had been known, but there was nothing that the defendants could have done to identify which blood products were thus infected. The defendants were not at fault in causing the claimants' infection. They were nonetheless held liable. Since the overwhelming majority of the blood was free from the virus, it was held that the claimants were entitled to expect a transfusion that was free from the virus (notwithstanding the known, and unavoidable risk). Of course, *A v National Blood Authority* is only a first instance decision, and may well not be the final word on the matter.[123]

(H) CAUSATION

The burden of proof rests with the claimant to show that there was a 'defect' in the product, and that the relevant injury or damage was wholly or partly caused by that defect.[124] This often presents a problem in establishing causation where an improper or unexpected use of the product leads to the claimant's injury: is it the improper use or the defect which caused the injury? Consider the following difficult scenarios.

(1) A new antibiotic is marketed. Information to doctors includes a warning not to prescribe the drug to pregnant women. The drug is only available on prescription. Dr X prescribes the drug for Y. Y feels better the next day. Y discontinues the tablets and gives the remainder to his colleague Z who is 10-weeks pregnant. Z takes the tablets and her baby is born seriously damaged.[125]

(2) A trendy student buys a lurid pink dye in a dressmaking shop. She uses it to dye her hair and suffers acute dermatitis as a result.[126]

(3) A wealthy businessman buys domestic heaters and installs them in his swimming pool. One heater explodes destroying the pool.

---

[121] See, eg, Stapleton, 'Products Liability Reform – Real or Illusory?' (1986) 6 OJLS 392. See also Newdick, 'The Future of Negligence in Product Liability' (1987) 104 LQR 288.

[122] [2001] 3 All ER 289, esp at [69].

[123] For academic discussion of the case, see Howells and Mildred, 'Infected Blood: Defect and Discoverability' (2002) 65 MLR 95; Hodges, 'Compensating Patients' (2001) 117 LQR 528.

[124] See the Consumer Protection Act 1987, s 2(1) and Art 4 of the Directive.

[125] Questions of causation can be seen from this example to be inextricably bound up with the definition of a 'defect'. D could argue that the manner in which the product was marketed as a 'prescription only' drug, with appropriate information supplied to GPs, rendered it acceptably safe.

[126] Should dye intended for use on materials be marked 'Not to be used on the hair'?

One causation issue is, however, somewhat clearer. Intermediate examination of the product will no longer exculpate the manufacturer from liability for defects in the product existing at the time that he put the product into circulation. That some third party may share liability for the injury to the claimant is relevant only to the issue of contribution between the tortfeasors.[127] Equally, certain factual difficulties associated with causation for the consumer seeking to identify and sue the manufacturer will largely be alleviated by the obligation on each supplier to name his supplier or be deemed strictly liable himself.[128] Only where the last party identified is bankrupt will problems arise.

In the US, claims have been litigated where the actual manufacturer of the product – a generic drug – injuring the claimant cannot be traced. The American courts have held that liability should be apportioned between all companies manufacturing the drug in proportion to their share in the market for that drug.[129]

(i) LIMITATION

Actions under Part I of the Consumer Protection Act 1987 are subject to the usual limitation periods with the exception of two special periods of limitation:

(1) The action must be brought within three years of the date on which injury or damage was suffered by the claimant, or, if later, the date on which the claimant becomes aware of the injury or damage.[130] Only in the case of personal injuries does the court have a discretion to override that three-year period.

(2) No action may be brought in any circumstances more than 10 years from the date on which the defendant supplied the relevant product to another.[131]

Claims such as those brought before the courts in the US by several young women who had developed cervical cancer as a result of a drug (DES) taken by their mothers in pregnancy could not, therefore, have been brought under the 1987 Act. In this country, the young women would have had to fall back on the common law action for negligence.

---

[127] See Art 8(1) of the Directive. Contribution is not limited to tortfeasors but is available between all persons liable for the same damage: see the Civil Liability (Contribution) Act 1978 discussed in ch 25. Retailers liable to purchasers for breach of the implied conditions of the contract of sale may also seek a contribution from the manufacturers.   [128] See the Consumer Protection Act 1987, s 2(3).

[129] See *Sindell v Abbott Laboratories* 26 Cal 3d 588 (1980). See also Porat and Stein, *Tort Liability Under Uncertainty* (2001); Newdick, 'Liability for Defective Drugs' (1985) 101 LQR 405.

[130] For example, a person who took a particular drug in 2006 but only became aware of the kidney damage caused by that drug in 2011.

[131] The time of supply is not necessarily straightforward. In *O'Byrne v Sanofi Pasteur MSD Ltd* (Case C-127/04), company X sent the product in question to company Y (which was a wholly owned subsidiary of company X). It was held that the product was supplied within the Directive from the moment when it left the production process and entered a marketing process in which it would ultimately be offered to the public (which included the despatch from X to Y).

FURTHER READING

Bell, 'Product Liability Damages in England and Wales' (1992) 20 *Anglo-American Law Review* 371

Clark, 'The Conceptual Basis of Product Liability' (1985) 48 MLR 325

Howells and Mildred, 'Infected Blood: Defect and Discoverability' (2002) 65 MLR 95

Newdick, 'Liability for Defective Drugs' (1985) 101 LQR 405

Newdick, 'The Future of Negligence in Product Liability' (1987) 104 LQR 288

Newdick, 'The Development Risks Defence of the Consumer Protection Act 1987' [1988] CLJ 455

Stoppa, 'The Concept of Defectiveness in the Consumer Protection Act 1987' [1992] *Legal Studies* 210

Stapleton, 'Products Liability Reform – Real or Illusory?' (1986) 6 OJLS 392

Tettenborn, 'Components and Product Liability' [2000] LMCLQ 338

17

NUISANCE

SECTION 1 NUISANCE AS A SEPARATE TORT

(A) SCOPE OF THE LAW OF NUISANCE

This chapter deals with two torts: public nuisance and private nuisance. Though both may be actionable under the civil law, the commission of a public nuisance, such as obstructing a public highway, is primarily a criminal offence.[1] We therefore consider public nuisance separately. To begin with, however, and for the greater part of this chapter, we are concerned only with the more prevalent tort of private nuisance.

A private nuisance may be defined as any activity or state of affairs causing a substantial and unreasonable interference with a claimant's land or his use or enjoyment of that land. From this definition we can discern three kinds of interests to which nuisance law affords protection:[2] the protection of land *per se*; the protection of the use of land; the protection of the enjoyment of land.[3] In each case, the damage must always be referable to the land, and not merely chattels which happen to be on the land.[4]

---

[1] Whether there is, in truth, anything left of the common law offence of public nuisance is a moot point. On the one hand, many of the established forms of public nuisance are now proscribed as *statutory nuisances*. On the other hand, the flexibility of the common law offence – which has historically outlawed a miscellany of public 'mischiefs' – may be the only available means of punishing activities not yet prohibited by Parliament (albeit at the cost of transgressing the *nulla poena sine lege* principle): see further Spencer, 'Public Nuisance – a Critical Examination' [1989] CLJ 55.

[2] Though the enjoyment of land and the use of land may, at one level, be seen as distinct interests, it is important to recognise that they are inter-related and that it is not uncommon for both to be violated at any one time. See, eg, *Dodds Properties v Canterbury City Council (Kent) Ltd* [1980] 1 All ER 928 (interruption to *use of*, and *damage to*, a garage used for business purposes, caused by D's pile-driving operations). Furthermore, in the important decision in *Hunter v Canary Wharf Ltd* [1997] 2 All ER 426, it was said, *obiter*, by Lord Lloyd (at 442) and Lord Hoffmann (at 451–2) that the enjoyment of land was only a protected interest in so far as the destruction of that enjoyment represents a diminution in the value of the property affected. Cf Lord Cooke (at 463) and Gearty, 'The Place of Nuisance in the Modern Law of Torts' [1989] CLJ 214.

[3] In *Hunter v Canary Wharf Ltd* [1997] 2 All ER 426, at 452, Lord Hoffmann sought to equate 'sensible discomfort' with an injury to the land rather than to the person. However, it should be noted that (a) he was only speaking *obiter* and (b) the distinction, apart from being inherently vague, is difficult to sustain: see Oliphant, 'Unblurring the Boundaries of Nuisance' (1998) 6 *Tort Law Review* 21 and O'Sullivan, 'Nuisance in the House of Lords – Normal Service Resumed' [1997] CLJ 483, 485.

[4] In *Anglian Water Services Ltd v Crawshaw Robbins & Co Ltd* 2002 WL 31523191, at [142], Stanley Burnton J opined (in relation to a disrupted gas supply) that 'it is possible to regard the interruption to the supply of gas

It follows from this that not every interference caused by A to B will amount to an actionable nuisance. Instead, the law calls for reasonable tolerance between neighbours *vis-à-vis* the respective uses to which each puts his land.[5] Indeed, from time to time, it is almost inevitable that each neighbour will put his land to a use that causes some irritation to the other.[6] It would be absurd for the law to allow an action in nuisance for every minor irritation so caused, for it would unjustifiably circumscribe the freedom to enjoy one's own land. It is for this reason that the law of nuisance insists not simply that there be an interference with the claimant's land (or any right or interest in that land), but also that that interference be both *substantial and unreasonable*.[7]

The range of activities that may give rise to an action in nuisance are manifold. They commonly include the emission of noxious fumes, smoke, noise and heat, or the generation of violent vibrations. But not every instance of smoke or noise emission will sustain a nuisance action: it is impossible to characterize any of the activities just listed as inevitably and incontrovertibly a nuisance. At most, all that can be said about them is that they each have the *potential* to constitute a nuisance. Imagine, for example, that a neighbour's very young child manages momentarily to turn a CD player up to full volume. Naturally, the noise will create a disturbance until the neighbour turns it back down again. In such an instance it would be a very unjust law that characterized such a fleeting disturbance as an actionable nuisance, and in the example given here, it would be difficult to say that the disturbance caused by a momentary increase in the volume of a CD was either substantial or unreasonable.

While the rigours of the law of nuisance are tempered in this way, it is important to appreciate that there are no precise thresholds beyond which any given disturbance becomes either substantial or unreasonable. The concepts of magnitude and unreasonableness are context-dependent;[8] and gauging each depends upon a series of factors explored in depth later in this chapter. One cautionary note that should be entered here, however, is that, unlike the law of negligence, reasonableness in nuisance refers not to the defendant's conduct, as such, but to the outcome of his conduct. We are not strictly concerned with whether the defendant passes the 'reasonable man test' (in the sense of taking reasonable care to avoid causing harm) that is central to the tort of negligence. Rather, we are concerned to assess the reasonableness of the harm occasioned to the claimant.[9] Thus, as Lindley LJ observed in *Rapier v London Tramways Co* – where the nuisance emanated from too many horses crammed into the defendant's stable – 'If I am sued for nuisance, and nuisance is proved, it is no defence to say and to

as an interference with the use of gas appliances rather than with a use of land [since replacement electrical appliances can be obtained]'. But this seems a rather tenuous distinction.

[5] In *Bamford v Turnley* (1862) 3 B & S 66, for example, Bramwell B described nuisance as 'A rule of give and take, live and let live'; and the give and take principle was echoed by Lord Goff in *Cambridge Water Co Ltd v Eastern Counties Leather plc* [1994] 2 AC 264.

[6] Eg, a 21st birthday celebration that goes on until late at night.

[7] The *magnitude* and *unreasonableness* of an interference should not be assumed to be mutually exclusive: the existence of the former is often a precondition to the existence of the latter: see below.

[8] *Sturges v Bridgman* (1879) 11 Ch D 852.

[9] *Walter v Selfe* (1851) 4 De G & Sm 315. See also, Gearty, 'The Place of Nuisance in the Modern Law of Torts' [1989] CLJ 214, 231–3 and Lee, 'What is Private Nuisance?' (2003) 119 LQR 298.

prove that I have taken all reasonable care to prevent it'.[10] On the other hand, it would be wrong to assume that the reasonableness of the defendant's conduct is an irrelevant consideration (especially where what is in question is whether the defendant has adopted or continued a nuisance[11]), for there exists an immutable inter-relationship between the unreasonableness of what the defendant does and the unreasonableness of the interference thereby caused to the claimant. Disturbances caused by malice[12] or reckless disregard for one's neighbour – such as persistently playing a musical instrument in the small hours of the morning – as opposed to those caused innocently and unavoidably,[13] are clearly unjustifiable.

As originally conceived, the law of nuisance was not designed to cover personal injuries. It was exclusively concerned with acts or omissions[14] causing violations of land or interests in or over land.[15] For a time it was thought that such injuries were actionable in nuisance. In *Hunter v Canary Wharf Ltd*, however, the House of Lords stated (*obiter*) that such injuries are not recoverable in private nuisance but rather, if at all, in negligence.[16] The fact that the law has fluctuated on this point, serves to demonstrate that the boundaries of the law of nuisance are by no means fixed or easy to identify.[17] This is in large part because the tort of negligence has, to a considerable extent, eclipsed (or, at least, subsumed) important elements of nuisance law.

(B) NUISANCE AND ENVIRONMENTAL LAW

Nuisance law – whether private or public – plays only a limited role in the protection of the environment.[18] The fact that there has been a steady growth in popular concern for the protection of the environment has resulted in the implementation of a number of

---

[10] [1893] 2 Ch 588, at 600. Similarly, in *Halsey v Esso Petroleum Co Ltd* [1961] 2 All ER 145, Veale J held D liable in nuisance for the noise generated by lorries driving in and out of D's depot at night, causing disturbance to C who lived opposite. And this was despite D's endeavours to do everything feasible to keep the noise to a minimum. See also *Read v J Lyons & Co Ltd* [1947] AC 156, at 183, *per* Lord Simmonds (*obiter*) and *Cambridge Water Co Ltd v Eastern Counties Leather plc* [1994] 2 AC 264, at 298, *per* Lord Goff (*obiter*).

[11] See, eg, *Leakey v National Trust* [1980] QB 485; *Transco plc v Stockport MBC* [2004] 2 AC 1, at [96], *per* Lord Walker (suggesting that such cases bring about an overlap between negligence and nuisance law).

[12] Eg, *Hollywood Silver Fox Farm Ltd v Emmett* [1936] 2 KB 468. In *Hunter v Canary Wharf Ltd* [1997] 2 All ER 426, at 465, Lord Cooke expressed the view (*obiter*) that the 'malicious erection of a structure for the purpose of interfering with television reception should be actionable in nuisance'.

[13] Eg, *Moy v Stoop* (1909) 25 TLR 262.

[14] Nuisance is actionable not just on the basis of misfeasance, but also nonfeasance: see, eg, *Goldman v Hargrave* [1967] 1 AC 645. Note also that the *positive* duty to prevent harm to others is more pronounced in nuisance than it is in negligence: see Markesinis, 'Negligence, Nuisance and Affirmative Duties of Action' (1989) 105 LQR 104.

[15] For an account of the genesis of private nuisance, see Murphy, 'The Merits of *Rylands v Fletcher*' (2004) 24 OJLS 643. See also *Hunter* [1997] 2 All ER 426, at 435ff, *per* Lord Goff; Gearty, 'The Place of Nuisance in the Modern Law of Torts' [1989] CLJ 214; Newark, 'The Boundaries of Nuisance' (1949) 65 LQR 480.

[16] [1997] 2 All ER 426, 438 and 442, *per* Lords Goff and Lloyd, respectively.

[17] In *Sedleigh-Denfield v O'Callaghan* [1940] AC 880, at 903, Lord Wright commented that 'The forms which nuisance may take are protean . . . many reported cases are no more than illustrations of particular matters of fact which have been held to be nuisances'.

[18] See Murphy, 'Noxious Emissions and Common Law Liability – Tort in the Shadow of Regulation' in Lowry and Edmunds (eds), *Environmental Protection and the Common Law* (1999); Steele, 'Private Law and the

statutes imposing a system of regulation that renders the common law very much a secondary means of protection. As Lord Goff put it:

[S]o much well-informed and carefully structured legislation is now being put in place to effect environmental protection . . . [that] there is less need for the courts to develop a common law principle to achieve the same end, and indeed it may be undesirable that they should do so.[19]

The point is this. Many of the sorts of conduct that would formerly have sounded in nuisance (and nuisance alone) are now also covered by statutes such as the Clean Air Act 1993 and the Environmental Protection Act 1990.[20] The implementation of such legislation has meant that it is easier and more effective to pursue a grievance via the local environmental health officers (who can prosecute such 'statutory nuisances') than through the courts where the costs of funding, especially in the light of recent restrictions on the availability of legal aid, may be prohibitively high.

A further, related cause of the diminution in the number of nuisance actions has been the effect of planning legislation. Essentially, the requirement that planning permission must be obtained prior to a change in use of existing premises, or the construction of new ones, has meant that some potential nuisances can be avoided prospectively. Thus, where a person is denied the planning permission to turn his house into a small printing works, the obvious potential for disturbance to a neighbour caused by vibrations is avoided in advance. In such cases, nuisance law, which operates retrospectively – that is, in response to an *extant* interference, or potentially injurious state of affairs – is clearly denied any role. It would be wrong, however, to assume that nuisance is now a redundant tort in the environmental context.[21] On the contrary, it retains the potential to perform at least three useful functions. First, it can operate as an enforcement procedure supplemental to those contained in the relevant statutes (yet where a particular activity has been authorized by planning permission, the courts will naturally be hesitant in finding that it has caused an actionable nuisance to the claimant[22]). Secondly, whenever such a case is decided in favour of the claimant, the effect of the judgment may be to establish standards in relation to, say, pollution control which are additional to those contained in the relevant statute.[23] Thirdly, some statutory nuisances are defined in terms that hinge on the common law concept of nuisance, so the common law elucidates the statutory meaning of nuisance.

Environment: Nuisance in Context' (1995) 15 *Legal Studies* 236; Ogus and Richardson 'Economics and the Environment: A Study in Private Nuisance' [1977] CLJ 284.

[19] *Cambridge Water Co Ltd v Eastern Counties Leather plc* [1994] 2 AC 264, at 305.

[20] For a good account of these and other acts creating statutory nuisances see Buckley, *The Law of Nuisance* (1996) chs 10–12.

[21] See Murphy, 'Noxious Emissions and Common Law Liability – Tort in the Shadow of Regulation' in Lowry and Edmunds (eds), *Environmental Protection and the Common Law* (1999).

[22] *Gillingham Borough Council v Medway (Chatham) Dock Co Ltd* [1993] QB 343. See also the supportive comment in *Hunter v Canary Wharf Ltd* [1997] 2 All ER 426, at 433, *per* Lord Goff that 'it will usually be open to local people to raise the possibility of [nuisance] . . . at the stage of the application for planning permission'.

[23] The extent to which nuisance can presently achieve this function is discussed, at length in Steele, 'Private Law and the Environment: Nuisance in Context' (1995) 15 *Legal Studies* 236.

(C) NUISANCE AND OTHER TORTS

As Erle CJ once remarked, the law of nuisance is 'immersed in undefined uncertainty'.[24] This uncertainty, Professor Newark forcefully argued, is mainly attributable to the fact that 'the boundaries of the tort of nuisance are blurred'.[25] To begin with, there is a considerable overlap and inter-relationship between nuisance and negligence. As Lord Wilberforce remarked in *Goldman v Hargrave*, a nuisance 'may comprise a wide variety of situations, in some of which negligence plays no part, in others of which it is decisive'.[26] Not only does this *dictum* reveal that the overlap is ill-defined and partial, it also forces us to ask one of the most vexed questions in the whole law of nuisance: namely, whether nuisance liability is strict or fault-based. Consideration of this matter is deferred until later in the chapter. For now, we are concerned only to note that concurrent liability in nuisance and negligence can arise out of a single set of facts. For example, if I were to light a fire next to my neighbour's fence and then leave it unattended, I might be held liable in either negligence or nuisance if the fire were to spread to his fence or shrubs. Indeed, in one case where the action was framed both in negligence and nuisance, the judge, in dismissing the negligence claim, stated that he 'need not discuss the alternative claim based on nuisance .. [since the latter] cannot be established unless negligence is proved'.[27] On a practical level, therefore, there is often a choice in terms of the way in which a claimant may frame his action. But on a jurisprudential level, one question that remains is why, when nuisance protects interests in the enjoyment of land, it is necessary to extend the boundaries of negligence to cover similar situations – especially at a time when the judicial trend is to restrain carefully the growth of negligence. Another question is whether nuisance law ought to be reined in and restored to its origins as a strict liability tort protecting only the amenities associated with land ownership.[28]

If the interface between negligence and nuisance leads to some difficult questions about the nature of nuisance liability, these have been compounded by similar questions concerning the inter-relationship between nuisance and the rule in *Rylands v Fletcher*[29] (discussed in the next chapter). In juridical terms, the two torts can be distinguished.[30] Yet they share a number of common features which have been taken by the courts and early commentators to form the basis for the mistaken idea that the rule in *Rylands v Fletcher* was derived from the law of nuisance.[31]

---

[24] *Brand v Hammersmith and City Rly Co* (1867) LR 2 QB 223.

[25] Newark, 'The Boundaries of Nuisance' (1949) 65 LQR 480.   [26] [1967] 1 AC 645, at 657.

[27] *Bolton v Stone* [1951] AC 850, at 860, *per* Lord Porter. This point was later endorsed by Lord Reid in *The Wagon Mound (No 2)* [1967] 1 AC 617, at 640: 'the similarities between nuisance and [negligence] . . . far outweigh any differences'.

[28] See Gearty, 'The Place of Nuisance in the Modern Law of Torts' [1989] CLJ 214; Murphy, 'The Merits of *Rylands v Fletcher*' (2004) 24 OJLS 643.   [29] (1866) LR 1 Exch 265.

[30] See *Leakey v National Trust* [1980] QB 485. See also Nolan, 'The Distinctiveness of *Rylands v Fletcher*' (2005) 121 LQR 421; Murphy, 'The Merits of *Rylands v Fletcher*' (2004) 24 OJLS 643.

[31] See, eg, *Cambridge Water Co Ltd v Eastern Counties Leather plc* [1994] 2 AC 264, at 298, *per* Lord Goff and Newark, 'The Boundaries of Nuisance' (1949) 65 LQR 480.

Trespass to land concerns direct rather than consequential harm and may therefore be distinguished easily from nuisance in both juristic and factual terms. For example, in being actionable *per se*, trespass does not require the claimant to prove damage.[32] Thus, in *Kelsen v Imperial Tobacco Co (of Great Britain and Ireland) Ltd*, where a sign erected by the defendants projected into the air space above the claimant's shop, it was held that the erection of the sign constituted a trespass but not a nuisance since 'the presence of this sign . . . caused no inconvenience and no interference with the [claimant's] use of his air'.[33] On the other hand, where damage does occur as a result of a trespass, 'it makes no difference to the result' whether the action is framed in trespass or in nuisance.[34]

The fact that there exists some degree of overlap between nuisance and the other torts mentioned in the preceding paragraph makes it difficult to classify any of them purely on the basis of the interest protected. If, for example, a neighbour's land is damaged because of an overflow of water, much will depend upon the directness of the invasion (central to trespass[35]); the role of fault (crucial in 'state of affairs' nuisance cases[36]), and whether the invasion was attributable to a foreseeably injurious escape (which lies at the heart of *Rylands v Fletcher* liability[37]).

A final characteristic of the tort of nuisance that should be noted is that the normal remedy sought by the claimant is an injunction rather than damages. His main concern, when subjected to the persistent late-night trumpet playing of his neighbour, for example, is that his neighbour should desist. But, as we shall see, injunctions are granted on a flexible basis reflecting the fact that they form a species of equitable remedy. They may therefore be refused even though an actionable nuisance can be proven. The courts' right to refuse an injunction despite the commission of an actionable nuisance enables them to pursue economic or social objectives.[38] For example, in one case concerning cricket balls being struck from a village green onto the claimants' land, it was stated that:

it does not seem just that a long-established activity, in itself innocuous, should be brought to an end because someone else chooses to build a house nearby and so turn an innocent pastime into an actionable nuisance.[39]

The extent to which the courts refuse injunctions where nuisance has been established should not, however, be exaggerated. In the vast preponderance of cases where the claimant can prove the commission of a nuisance, he will also succeed in obtaining an

---

[32] *Stoke-on-Trent Council v W & J Wass Ltd* [1988] 3 All ER 394.

[33] [1957] 2 QB 334, at 343, *per* McNair J. Cf *Smith v Giddy* [1904] 2 KB 448 where it was held to be a nuisance when D allowed his trees to overhang C's land and thus stymie the growth of C's fruit trees.

[34] *Home Brewery Co v William Davies & Co (Loughborough) Ltd* [1987] QB 339, at 354, *per* Piers Ashworth QC. See also Hudson, 'Trespass or Nuisance' (1960) 19 MLR 188.

[35] *Preston v Mercer* (1656) Hard 60.

[36] *Sedleigh-Denfield v O'Callaghan* [1940] AC 880. Cf Murphy, 'Rethinking Injunctions in Tort Law' (forthcoming). [37] (1868) LR 3 HL 330.

[38] Ogus and Richardson, 'Economics and the Environment: A Study in Private Nuisance' (1977) 36 CLJ 284; Campbell, 'Of Coase and Corn: a (sort of) Defence of Private Nuisance' (2000) 63 MLR 197.

[39] *Miller v Jackson* [1977] QB 966, at 986, *per* Geoffrey-Lane LJ. Cf *Kennaway v Thompson* [1981] QB 88.

injunction. Later in this chapter we shall see that the courts have developed a series of factors to which they will have regard before denying injunctive relief to those who can prove the commission of a nuisance.

SECTION 2 THE BASIS OF NUISANCE LIABILITY

According to the definition of nuisance offered earlier, the successful claimant must show a substantial interference either with his land, or with the use or the enjoyment of his land; and he must also demonstrate that the interference was an unreasonable one. As we shall see, the factors taken into account by the courts in assessing both the magnitude and reasonableness of an interference are both manifold and intricately inter-connected.

(A) SUBSTANTIAL INTERFERENCE

Before a claimant can succeed in a nuisance action, he must first be able to prove that he has suffered damage, for as we noted when distinguishing nuisance from trespass, nuisance is not a tort which is actionable *per se*.[40] Since the law of nuisance protects not just against physical damage to land, but also against interferences with the use or enjoyment of it, it is apparent that we require a definition of damage that embraces both tangible and intangible interferences. Thus, in addition to physical harm to land, our concept of damage must also embrace those cases in which the claimant's complaint related to, say, the emission of unpleasant smells, or the generation of loud noise; in short, with things that represented 'sensible discomfort',[41] being interferences with the amenities associated with land ownership.

Although, for the purposes of nuisance, both physical damage and disturbances to the enjoyment of land are actionable, it does not follow that we need not distinguish between the various kinds of interference. Indeed, as we shall see, the case law requires us to treat material harm quite differently from interferences with amenities.

(1) INTERFERENCE WITH THE USE OR ENJOYMENT OF LAND

Where interference with the use or enjoyment of land (amenity nuisance) is concerned, the law requires give and take on the part of neighbouring land owners. This principle is neatly encapsulated in the words of Lord Wright in *Sedleigh-Denfield v O'Callaghan* where he said that '[a] balance has to be maintained between the right of the occupier to do what he likes with his own [land], and the right of his neighbour not to be

---

[40] For a very few limited exceptions to this rule, see the 9th edition of this work.
[41] *Hunter v Canary Wharf Ltd* [1997] 2 All ER 426, at 452, *per* Lord Hoffmann.

interfered with'.[42] It is implicit in this that, as between neighbours, some measure of interference with the use and enjoyment of each other's land is permissible. In other words, only a *substantial* interference with a claimant's amenities constitute a nuisance. As Lord Selbourne said in *Gaunt v Fynney*: '[a] nuisance by noise . . . is emphatically a question of degree . . . Such things to offend against the law, must be done in a manner which, beyond fair controversy, are to be regarded as excessive'.[43] The same rule, that the nuisance must be substantial, applies equally in respect of other amenities. So, for example, an interference with the right to the free passage of light – acquired by grant or prescription,[44] and sometimes referred to as the right to 'ancient lights' – only amounts to a nuisance where it deprives the claimant of 'sufficient light, according to the ordinary notions of mankind, for the comfortable use and enjoyment of his house'.[45]

One key issue, then, turns on determining when an interference with amenities amounts to a substantial infringement of the claimant's interests. It is certainly the case that the claimant's health need not be shown to have suffered.[46] Indeed, the loss of a single night's sleep has been held to be sufficiently substantial to constitute a nuisance.[47] So, too, has using adjoining premises for the purposes of prostitution (despite the fact that this fails to impinge directly upon the senses of the claimant in the way that, for example, noxious fumes do[48]). The question of whether an interference is sufficiently substantial to amount to an actionable nuisance is one of fact and is to be determined on a case-by-case basis. Not every interference will constitute a nuisance, and an interference that comprises a nuisance in one context may not do so in another.[49] The most commonly cited formulation of the rule by which the interference is to be adjudged substantial is that supplied by Knight Bruce VC in *Walter v Selfe*:[50]

ought this inconvenience to be considered in fact as more than fanciful, more than one of mere delicacy or fastidiousness, as an inconvenience materially interfering with the ordinary comfort physically of human existence, not merely according to elegant or dainty modes and habits of living, but according to plain and simple notions among the English people?

Over the years, the courts have tended to gauge the seriousness of an interference by reference to two main considerations: the sensitivity of the claimant and the locality in which the alleged nuisance occurs. Neither of these factors is conclusive of whether an interference is sufficiently substantial to constitute a nuisance; they are merely *relevant* considerations which ought to be taken into account in all amenity nuisance cases.

---

[42] [1940] AC 880, at 903. The give and take principle also figured prominently in *Delaware Mansions Ltd v Westminster City Council* [2002] 1 AC 321.

[43] (1872) 8 Ch App 8, at 11–12.

[44] The acquisition of this right is a technical matter of land law. English common law recognises no automatic right to light, and such a right can only be acquired in connection with a building: *Harris v de Pinna* (1886) 33 Ch D 238. [45] *Colls v Home and Colonial Stores* [1904] AC 179, at 208, *per* Lord Lindley.

[46] *Crump v Lambert* (1867) LR 3 Eq 409, at 412, *per* Lord Romily MR.

[47] *Andreae v Selfridge & Co Ltd* [1938] Ch 1.

[48] *Thompson-Schwab v Costaki* [1956] 1 All ER 652. See also *Laws v Florinplace Ltd* [1981] 1 All ER 659 (sex shop established in a residential area). [49] *Sturges v Bridgman* (1879) 11 Ch D 852.

[50] (1851) 4 De G & Sm 315, at 322.

(a) The sensitivity of the claimant[51]

If the activity of which the claimant complains only disturbs the use or enjoyment of his land because he carries on there a 'delicate trade', heightening his sensitivity to interference, then the interference complained of will not amount to an actionable nuisance. The disturbance must be such that it would substantially inconvenience a claimant of ordinary sensitivities. The courts will not allow a claimant to turn an ordinarily innocuous activity into a nuisance. Take for example *Robinson v Kilvert*.[52]

A landlord who remained in occupation of the cellar let the superjacent floor to C. Because of the landlord's business it was necessary for the cellar to be dry and hot. The heat of the cellar passed through the ceiling to the floor above (which was used by C as a paper warehouse) and caused damage to a stock of brown paper kept there. The court rejected C's application for an injunction to restrain the landlord from keeping his cellar so hot since the heat transfer would not have caused a problem for anyone other than C.

It was only the fact that he was engaged in an 'exceptionally delicate trade' that caused the claimant in that case to suffer loss. Similarly, in *Bridlington Relay Ltd v Yorkshire Electricity Board* the defendants' power line was interfering with the claimant's business of providing a radio and television relay service to subscribers. It was said, *obiter*, that because interference with the recreational amenity of television viewing was not a substantial interference, the claimants could not sue for the business interference complained of: 'the claimants could not succeed in a claim for damages for nuisance if . . . an ordinary receiver of television by means of an aerial mounted on his house could not do so'.[53] It seems important that this case was decided in 1965 when television ownership was rare, rendering viewers unusually sensitive claimants. In the new Millennium, television viewing is far more common and less easily classified as a hypersensitive activity. Indeed, if the same facts were to arise today, it is possible that the court would hold there to be a nuisance.[54]

Such a possibility was certainly not ruled out in *Hunter v Canary Wharf Ltd* where two members of the House of Lords (Lords Goff and Cooke) suggested that, in certain circumstances, an action for this kind of interference might lie. However, in refusing to award damages to the claimants in that case, Lord Goff stated that while interferences with television reception 'might in appropriate circumstances be protected', it was also the case that 'more is required than the mere presence of a neighbouring building to give rise to an actionable private nuisance'.[55] In the wake of *Hunter*, then, it is unclear exactly if and when interferences with television viewing (and, by analogy, other such 'luxury'

---

[51] Though the hyper-sensitivity rule is well established, the point has been made that the reasonable user principle coupled with the requirement that C must suffer a foreseeable kind of harm may have rendered it more or less redundant: *Network Rail Infrastructure Ltd v CJ Morris* [2004] Env LR 41, at [35], *per* Buxton LJ.

[52] (1889) 41 Ch D 88.   [53] [1965] Ch 436, at 446, *per* Buckley J.

[54] Such is the case in Canada: see *Nor-Video Services Ltd v Ontario Hydro* (1978) 84 DLR (3d) 221, at 231 where Robins J, in the Ontario High Court, stated that: 'an inability to receive [a television broadcast] . . . would undoubtedly to my mind detract from the beneficial use and ownership of property'.

[55] [1997] 2 All ER 426, at 432. Much was made in the case of the fact that D had obtained planning permission to build the tower and the fact that the construction of buildings with such permission was a normal use of land. Qualifying this, however, Lord Cooke observed (at 465), that he could 'see no reason why neighbours

amenities) might form the basis of a nuisance action. Would there, for example, be an actionable nuisance where the interference is caused by the operation of an existing power station rather than by the construction of a tall building?[56] And bear in mind, too, that the decision in *Hunter* was grounded in part on a long-standing concern to allow landowners the freedom to build on their land (subject, of course, to planning restrictions).[57]

Leaving TV reception to one side, it is well established that '[a] man cannot increase the liabilities of his neighbour by applying his own property to special uses'.[58] On the other hand, he will be compensated in full for all the damage he suffers where a claimant of ordinary sensitivity would also have been able to found a nuisance action in respect of the interference complained of. So, in *McKinnon Industries Ltd v Walker*,[59] damage to the claimant's commercially grown orchids caused by the emission of sulphur dioxide gas from the defendant's factory was held to be actionable since it amounted to a non-remote consequence of what had already been proved to be a nuisance. That said, the fact that the claimant has suffered appreciable financial loss should not be taken, of itself, to amount to a substantial interference[60] (although the infliction of such business losses may be taken into account in deciding whether the interference *as a whole* was substantial[61]).

(b) Location of the claimant's premises

The locality in which the claimant's premises are situated is a second factor which assists the courts in determining whether the interference complained of is sufficiently substantial to amount to a nuisance. The expectations of the claimant, in terms of comfort, peace and quiet, will naturally vary according to the location of his house or business. The point was succinctly made in *Sturges v Bridgman*,[62] in which case a physician complained about the noise generated by a neighbouring confectioner who was operating a pestle and mortar. There, Thesiger LJ held that the court should take account of the fact that the area consisted largely of medical specialists' consulting rooms since:

[w]hether anything is a nuisance or not is a question to be determined, not merely by an abstract consideration of the thing itself, but in reference to its circumstances; what would be a nuisance in Belgrave Square would not necessarily be so in Bermondsey; and where a locality is devoted to a particular trade ... [the courts] would be justified in finding, and may be trusted to find, that the trade ... is not an actionable wrong.[63]

---

prejudicially affected should not be able to sue in nuisance if a building does exceed height, bulk or location restrictions. For then the developer is not making either a lawful or a reasonable use of his landowning rights.'

[56] See, on this question, the view of the Court of Appeal in *Hunter v Canary Wharf Ltd* [1996] 1 All ER 482.

[57] See *A-G (Ex rel Gray's Inn Society) v Doughty* (1752) 2 Ves Sen 453. One answer might be to allow the construction of tall buildings, allow a nuisance action, but restrict the remedy to one of damages: see O'Sullivan, 'A Poor Reception for Television Nuisance' [1996] CLJ 184.

[58] *Eastern and South African Telegraph Co Ltd v Cape Town Tramways Companies Ltd* [1902] AC 381, at 393, *per* Lord Robertson.   [59] [1951] 3 DLR 577.

[60] See, eg, the High Court of Australia's decision in *Victoria Park Racing and Recreation Grounds Ltd v Taylor* (1937) 58 CLR 479.   [61] *Thompson-Schwab v Costaki* [1956] 1 All ER 652.

[62] (1879) 11 Ch D 852. See also *Murdoch v Glacier Metal Co Ltd* [1998] LS Gaz R 31 (loud, night-time factory noise held not to be actionable in all the circumstances of the case (including C's proximity to a busy bypass).

[63] (1879) 11 Ch D 852, at 865.

Though locality is relevant in deciding amenity nuisance cases, it is not necessarily a conclusive consideration. Thus, although locality provides a compelling reason for the decision in *Adams v Ursell*[64] – where a fish and chip shop established in a fashionable street was held to be a nuisance – it was not determinative in *Rushmer v Polsue and Alfieri Ltd*[65] where printing presses were used at night in a printing district. Equally, it should be noted that the character of a locality is susceptible to change over time. Thus, the fact that an area was at one time wholly residential does not mean that the residents will always be entitled to a very high standard of peace and quiet. In *Gillingham Borough Council v Medway (Chatham) Dock Co Ltd*,[66] for example, it was held that planning permission which had been granted to change the use of an old naval dockyard into a commercial port (which turned out to be very noisy at night) should be taken to have effected a change in the character of the neighbourhood. As Buckley J put it: 'where planning permission is given . . . the question of nuisance will thereafter fall to be decided by reference to a neighbourhood with . . . [the new] development or use and not as it was previously'.[67]

On the other hand, *obiter dicta* in a decision of the Court of Appeal appears to constrain the effect of Buckley J's judgment to cases in which the interference complained of occurs *after* the character of the neighbourhood has already changed. The Court of Appeal took the view, in *Wheeler v JJ Saunders Ltd*,[68] that the simple grant of planning permission cannot be taken, *ipso facto*, to license what would otherwise be a nuisance. In other words, the court was chary of allowing administrative decisions (not susceptible to appeal) to be taken simply to extinguish existing private rights. But where planning permission has been obtained, it plays a part in the court's decision-making.[69]

(2) MATERIAL DAMAGE TO LAND

So far we have only been concerned with what amounts to a substantial interference with the use or enjoyment of land (otherwise known as 'amenity nuisance'). In this section we consider cases in which the activity complained of causes actual physical damage to the claimant's land. The kinds of nuisance that concern us here include collapses of the defendant's property onto the claimant's land,[70] drenching or flooding,[71] vegetation damage caused by the emission of noxious fumes,[72] the encroachment of roots[73] and vibration damage.[74] In such instances, the courts will approach the

---

[64] [1913] 1 Ch 269. See also *Thompson-Schwab v Costaki* [1956] 1 All ER 652, in which a brothel was set up in a high class street.

[65] [1906] 1 Ch 234; affd [1907] AC 121. Equally, the smell of oil on the border of an industrial area can constitute a nuisance: *Halsey v Esso Petroleum Co Ltd* [1961] 2 All ER 145. [66] [1993] QB 343.

[67] [1993] QB 343, at 361. [68] [1995] 2 All ER 697.

[69] The rationale here was explained by Lord Goff in *Hunter* when he observed (at 433) that: 'it will usually be open to local people to [complain] . . . at the stage of the application for planning permission'.

[70] *Wringe v Cohen* [1940] 1 KB 229. Cf *Sack v Jones* [1925] Ch 235 (not a nuisance where C's house caused D's house to collapse).

[71] *Sedleigh-Denfield v O'Callaghan* [1940] AC 880; *Hurdman v North Eastern Rly Co* (1878) 3 CPD 168; *Broder v Saillard* (1876) 2 Ch D 692.

[72] *St Helen's Smelting Co v Tipping* (1865) 11 HL Cas 642; *Manchester Corpn v Farnworth* [1930] AC 171.

[73] *Masters v Brent London Borough Council* [1978] QB 841.

[74] *Grosvenor Hotel Co v Hamilton* [1894] 2 QB 836.

question of substantial interference rather differently than where the claimant complains of amenity nuisance.

To begin with, where physical damage to property is concerned, the character of the district in which the claimant's land lies is *not* a material factor in assessing the gravity of the interference. In *St Helen's Smelting Co v Tipping*[75] – a case in which the claimant's shrubs had been damaged by fumes emitted from the defendants' copper-smelting plant – Lord Westbury held that:

It is a very desirable thing to mark the difference between an action brought for a nuisance upon the ground that the alleged nuisance produces material injury to the property, and an action . . . on the ground that the thing alleged . . . is productive of personal discomfort. With regard to the latter . . . a nuisance must undoubtedly depend greatly on the circumstances of the place where the thing complained of actually occurs. But where [physical damage is caused] . . . there unquestionably arises a very different consideration.[76]

One difficulty that arises from the fact that the claimant's location is irrelevant in physical damage cases is that physical damage and interference with amenities can often arise simultaneously, without there being any clear distinction between the two. If, for example, vibrations cause plaster to break off my walls, those same vibrations will probably also adversely affect the comfort and enjoyment of my home. Furthermore, the fact that the defendant engages in such a disturbing enterprise is likely to cause a diminution in the value of my house which is not easy to classify as either an amenity nuisance or an instance of physical damage.[77] Notwithstanding these problems, some attempts have been made by the courts to clarify the meaning of 'material damage'. A *dictum* of Lord Selbourne suggests that it is enough if science can trace a deleterious physical change in the property.[78] However, in the light of the fact that it can be difficult to distinguish between amenity nuisances and those involving physical damage,[79] it is best not to ignore the locality issue in all but the most clear-cut cases.

Just as in the case of amenity nuisance, it is also important to establish in physical damage cases that the nuisance complained of is substantial in nature. Hence, in *Darley Main Colliery Co v Mitchell*[80] it was held that minor subsidence (though identifiable and tangible) which caused the claimant no appreciable harm was not an actionable nuisance.

---

[75] (1865) 11 HL Cas 642.   [76] (1865) 11 HL Cas 642, at 650.

[77] Although the drop in value of the property is a form of economic loss, it is arguably implicit from *Bone v Seale* [1975] 1 All ER 787, that such loss should be treated as property damage insofar as, in that case, the court treated it separately from the award for the amenity nuisance. Does this mean that diminution in value is to be regarded, in nuisance, as physical damage? If so, since in *Halsey v Esso Petroleum Co Ltd* [1961] 2 All ER 145 it was presumed that the value of property will be affected wherever a substantial interference with enjoyment occurs, it could be argued that *all* amenity cases involve, at least some element of physical damage according to this conception. Problematic though this conception is, it is the one favoured in *Hunter v Canary Wharf Ltd* [1997] 2 All ER 426. Cf *Mayo v Seaton UDC* (1903) 68 JP 7 (the erection of public lavatories which depreciated the value of C's premises was held not to amount to a private nuisance).

[78] *Gaunt v Fynney* (1872) 8 Ch App 8, at 11–12.

[79] See Oliphant, 'Unblurring the Boundaries of Nuisance' (1998) 6 *Tort Law Review* 21.

[80] (1886) 11 App Cas 127.

(3) INTERFERENCE WITH SERVITUDES

For the sake of completeness we ought to note (but no more than that) a final category of damage that can, technically, form the basis of a nuisance action. It involves interferences with servitudes such as the right to light and air, and the right to support of land and buildings. The rules in relation to these rights are complex and more suitably the subject-matter of a textbook on property law than one on tort.

(B) UNREASONABLENESS

There is perhaps no more confusing matter in the whole of the law of private nuisance than the role played by unreasonableness in the ascription of liability. Conceivably, unreasonableness could relate to one or both of two inter-related issues: the conduct of the defendant and the nature of the interference with the claimant's land. Properly understood, it is the interference, rather than the defendant's conduct, which must be unreasonable.[81] This does not mean, however, that the nature of the defendant's conduct is irrelevant, since the unreasonableness of the defendant's user will impact upon the court's characterization of the nature of the interference. Imagine, for example, that I regularly fire a gun on my land in order to control vermin posing a threat to my crops. The noise made by the gun is precisely the same as if I were firing it out of wantonness. In both cases, the sound level remains constant and so, therefore, does the degree of disturbance that I cause my neighbour. In only the latter case, however, might a judge declare there to be a nuisance on the basis that the shooting in that instance was completely unwarranted. In the former case, by contrast, where the shooting was reasonable in order to effect pest control, the judge might easily reach the opposite conclusion.

The difference between the two cases lies in the way in which we characterize the nature of the interference (albeit by reference to the nature of the defendant's conduct). Yet not in every case in which the defendant acts unreasonably will he be liable in nuisance; for the disturbance must still be substantial. So, for example, if I play my CDs late at night and at full volume, I will not be liable in nuisance to my neighbour if she is almost entirely deaf and hears virtually nothing. The interference in such a case will be regarded as *de minimis*. As McNeill J insisted in *Tetley v Chitty*, the claimant must be able to demonstrate '*a real* interference with *his* use and enjoyment of his premises'.[82] The italicized words make it clear that there needs to be a subjective disturbance. So, it will not matter in such cases that every unreasonable user that gives rise to an

---

[81] See, eg, *Sampson v Hodson-Pressinger* [1981] 3 All ER 710 where the ordinary use of premises which, as a result of their being poorly constructed, caused intolerable noise to be perceived in adjoining premises, was held to be a nuisance. See also *Toff v McDowell* (1993) 25 HLR 650.

[82] [1986] 1 All ER 663, at 665. In *Bradford Corpn v Pickles* [1895] AC 587, at 601, Lord Macnaghten stated that no action would lie '[i]f the act . . . gives rise merely to damage without legal injury'. See also *Crown River Cruises Ltd v Kimbolton Fireworks Ltd* [1996] 2 Lloyd's Rep 533.

interference will *necessarily* give rise to an unreasonable interference. The fact that the interference is not *subjectively substantial* will defeat the claim.

There are several factors that the courts will typically take into account in deciding whether the interference is unreasonable.

(1) THE SERIOUSNESS OF THE INTERFERENCE

Generally, the more serious an interference with the claimant's interests, the more likely it is that the interference will be regarded by the court as unreasonable. In turn, the seriousness of the interference is influenced by four factors: the duration of the harm, the extent (or degree) of the harm, the character of the harm and the social value of the use interfered with.

(a) The duration of the harm

The persistence of an interference has a direct bearing on its reasonableness. In general terms, the more persistent an interference, the more likely it is that the courts will deem it to be unreasonable. Self-evidently, it is much less reasonable to expect one's neighbours to tolerate a nauseating smell that is more or less permanent than one that lasts for just a few moments. It follows from this that nuisances normally involve ongoing interferences as opposed to those which are merely transitory or isolated.[83] In some circumstances, however, even isolated or transitory interferences are actionable. For example, if the interference complained of is an isolated event but it causes physical damage, the courts appear willing to tolerate claims in nuisance so long as the damage arose out of a dangerous 'state of affairs'.[84] In *Spicer v Smee* – a case in which defective electrical wiring in the defendant's premises resulted in the claimant's bungalow being destroyed by fire – Atkinson J put the matter thus: '[a] private nuisance arises out of a state of things on one man's property whereby his neighbour's property is exposed to danger'.[85] Similarly, in *Midwood & Co Ltd v Manchester Corpn*,[86] where an accumulation of inflammable gas caused an explosion to occur which set fire to the claimant's

---

[83] Thus, in *Cunard v Antifyre Ltd* [1933] 1 KB 551 (where some of D's roofing fell into C's premises) Talbot J stated (at 557) that: 'nuisances, at least in the vast majority of cases, are interferences for a substantial length of time'.

[84] *Midwood & Co Ltd v Manchester Corpn* [1905] 2 KB 597; *Spicer v Smee* [1946] 1 All ER 489. For the suggestion that such cases ought better to be seen in terms of negligence (not nuisance) law, see Gearty, 'The Place of Nuisance in the Modern Law of Torts' [1989] CLJ 214 and Murphy, 'Rethinking Injunctions in Tort Law' (forthcoming). But while they remain part of the law of nuisance, note, also, that where there is a short-term interference the courts will allow claims for amenity nuisance: *Matania v National Provincial Bank Ltd and Elevenist Syndicate Ltd* [1936] 2 All ER 633 (C successfully sued on the basis of the excessive dust and noise generated by D's building work); *Crown River Cruises Ltd v Kimbolton Fireworks Ltd* [1996] 2 Lloyd's Rep 533 (C bothered by a 20-minute firework display). One possible explanation of why isolated events causing interferences with the enjoyment of land are not actionable is that there is no quantifiable loss to compensate.

[85] [1946] 1 All ER 489, at 493.

[86] [1905] 2 KB 597. See also *Stone v Bolton* [1949] 2 All ER 851 (person struck by a cricket ball hit out of the cricket ground); *British Celanese Ltd v A H Hunt (Capacitors) Ltd* [1969] 2 All ER 1252 (isolated escape of metal foil causing a short-circuit at a nearby electricity sub-station).

premises, the court again held there to be a nuisance by focusing upon the prevailing state of affairs.

Though it is a precondition of liability in respect of an isolated event that it arose from a dangerous state of affairs on the defendant's land, it is important to be clear that damages are only awarded for the harm caused. Nothing can be recovered in connection with the menacing state of affairs, *per se*, for this is merely a prerequisite for, and not the basis of, the defendant's liability. Nuisance law insists that the claimant must demonstrate that he has suffered actual damage.

(b) The extent of the harm

Whether an interference is serious (and hence unreasonable) must be assessed in the light of its impact on the defendant. Whenever I play my piano, I generate a level of noise that may be moderately irksome to my neighbour; but he may easily drown it out by turning on his television or radio. On the other hand, if I were to play my trombone, it would generate much more noise and be likely to remain heard and cause disturbance no matter what normal steps my neighbour might take. The relationship between the degree of interference and its unreasonableness is therefore clear: the louder I play an instrument, or the more odious the smell that my business generates, the more likely it is that the court will find the interference thereby caused to be not only substantial, but also unreasonable.

On the other hand, the gravity of the harm caused must not be gauged on a purely objective basis (for example, by reference only to the loudness of my trumpet playing). There is also an important role for a subjective element in the assessment of whether the interference was unreasonable. Although there is usually a correlation between the magnitude of an interference and its unreasonableness, this is not always the case. Where, for example, I play my trombone late at night generating, say, 20 decibels of noise, this would, nine times out of ten, be considered a very substantial (and hence unreasonable) disturbance to my next-door neighbour. Where, however, my neighbour is practically deaf, she may only faintly hear the trombone. Accordingly, despite the *objective* loudness of my playing, it will not *subjectively* be perceived to be an unreasonable interference. And, as we have already seen, the claimant must show that *she* has suffered a substantial interference, for 'the law does not regard trifling and small inconveniences, but only regards sensible inconveniences which sensibly diminish the comfort . . . *of the property which is affected*'.[87] It is also discernible from this that nuisance liability is not fault-based. I may wholly unreasonably play my CDs very loudly every night, but the fact that it does not diminish my deaf neighbour's enjoyment of her land negates any prospect of my being successfully sued by her in nuisance.

(c) The character of the harm

Harm, for the purposes of nuisance law, as we have already seen, may take the form either of physical damage to land or an interference with the use or enjoyment of it.

---

[87] *St Helen's Smelting Co v Tipping* (1865) 11 HL Cas 642, at 654, *per* Lord Wensleydale (emphasis added). See also *Sturges v Bridgman* (1879) 11 Ch D 852, at 863, *per* Thesiger LJ: '[where the interference is of] so trifling a character, that, upon the maxim *de minimis non curat lex*, we arrive at the conclusion that the defendant's acts would not have given rise to [liability]'.

Although all three forms are actionable, physical injury is generally regarded as being inherently of a more serious kind than interferences with a claimant's amenities. Indeed, the distinction drawn in *St Helen's Smelting Co v Tipping* between physical damage and amenity nuisance[88] has been taken by some commentators to support the proposition that physical injury is actionable regardless of whether the defendant's user of his land was objectively reasonable.[89] This proposition probably goes too far – especially in the light of what was said *(obiter) in Ellison v Ministry of Defence*[90] – but it does draw attention to the fact that, even in the context of nuisance, the English courts remain chary of protecting trifling personal discomforts falling short of physical injury.[91] The central issue is whether the interference is unreasonable.[92] So, in clear cases of physical injury – which can easily be proven and quantified in terms of damages, and which sit uppermost in the hierarchy of protected interests in tort law – it is simpler for the courts to find that the interference complained of was unreasonable than in cases of personal discomfort or annoyance.[93] Consequently, physical violations of the claimant's land are tolerated far less readily than disruptions to the peaceful enjoyment of it.

(d) Social value of the use interfered with

The final factor that can affect the seriousness of the harm is the nature of the use to which the claimant puts his land. Where the claimant uses his land in such a way that it can be classified as socially useful, it is more likely that the disruptive interference about which a complaint has been made will be regarded by the court as serious. In *Smith v Giddy*, for example, branches on the defendant's trees which overhung the claimant's land and prevented his commercially cultivated fruit trees from growing properly were held to be a nuisance whereas it was stated *obiter* that, had the claimant not been growing such trees, the mere blockage of light would not have been actionable.[94]

---

[88] (1865) 11 HL Cas 642, at 650, *per* Lord Westbury.

[89] See, eg, Ogus and Richardson, 'Economics and the Environment: A Study in Private Nuisance' [1977] CLJ 284, 297.

[90] (1996) 81 BLR 101. (D constructed large fuel containers on D's land. These trapped a large amount of rain-water which eventually flooded C's land. It was said that there was a reasonable use of land for the purposes of nuisance law and that the damage was not actionable in nuisance.) See also Steele, 'Private Law and the Environment: Nuisance in Context' (1995) 15 *Legal Studies* 236, 252.

[91] See the observations of Lord Hoffmann in *Hunter* (noted, at the beginning of this chapter).

[92] See, eg, *Watt v Jamieson* 1954 SC 56, at 58 where Lord President Cooper held that though D's vent pipe had caused plaster damage and dry-rot to occur in a neighbouring flat, the key question was 'whether what he was exposed to was *plus quam tolerabile*'. In short, his concern was with the unreasonableness of the harm rather than with its form.

[93] As Lord Selborne put it in *Gaunt v Fynney* (1872) 8 Ch App 8, at 1–12: '[amenity nuisance] is much more difficult to prove than when the injury complained of is the demonstrable effect of a visible or tangible cause'. See also *Hunter v Canary Wharf Ltd* [1997] 2 All ER 426, at 442, *per* Lord Lloyd: 'Damages for loss of amenity value cannot be assessed mathematically. But this does not mean that such damages cannot be awarded'. Note, too, *Ruxley Electronics and Construction Ltd v Forsyth* [1995] 3 All ER 268.

[94] [1904] 2 KB 448.

(2) REASONABLE USER OF THE DEFENDANT'S LAND

Strictly, as we have noted at several points, nuisance liability depends upon there being an unreasonable interference with the claimant's interests rather than there being unreasonable conduct *per se* on the part of the defendant. However, there is an immutable and fundamental inter-relationship between the reasonableness of the interference and the reasonableness of the user or activity. The fact that one is engaged in an unreasonable user will, *ipso facto*, render any interference thereby caused equally unreasonable: an interference that is caused by an unjustifiable activity cannot itself be justified.[95] The converse, as Lord Goff noted in *Cambridge Water Co Ltd v Eastern Counties Leather plc*, is also true: 'if the user is reasonable the defendant will not be liable for consequent harm to his neighbour's enjoyment of his -land'.[96] It thus follows that the question of negligent conduct is a highly relevant consideration, not in itself, but because of its impact on the characterization of the interference caused. Much may turn on the burden of proof, for, as the Court of Appeal explained in *Marcic v Thames Water Utilities Ltd*:

Once a claimant has proved that a nuisance has emanated from land in the possession or control of the defendant, the onus shifts to the defendant to show that he has a defence to the claim, whether this be absence of 'negligence' in a statutory authority case or that he took all reasonable steps to prevent the nuisance, [in other cases].[97]

In assessing the reasonableness of the defendant's user the courts have resort to a further wide range of factors. The following comprise the more important of these.

(a) The defendant's motive

In judging what constitutes an unreasonable user, the courts will take into account the main object of the defendant's activity. Thus, for example, in *Harrison v Southwark and Vauxhall Motor Co*[98] the useful nature of the defendants' construction work was part of the reason why the claimant's action was dismissed. Where, however, the defendant's primary aim is to injure his neighbour, there is considerable authority that his malicious motives may render the interference unreasonable. In *Christie v Davey*,[99] the claimants' action lay in respect of noises being made by their defendant neighbours. Central to North J's judgment that the noises were a nuisance was the fact that they were made 'deliberately and maliciously for the purpose of annoying the claimants'.[100] Similarly, in *Hollywood Silver Fox Farm Ltd v Emmett*[101] the court held the firing of guns

---

[95] Though the unreasonableness of the user will confirm the unreasonableness of the interference, it does not follow that all unreasonable users will result in liability. For example, an unreasonable user that causes minimal interference will not be actionable: the interference needs to be substantial as well as unreasonable. Cf Cross, 'Does only the Careless Polluter Pay? A Fresh Examination of the Nature of Private Nuisance' (1995) 111 LQR 445, fn 32.

[96] [1994] 2 AC 264, at 299. See also *Sanders-Clark v Grosvenor Mansions Co Ltd* [1900] 2 Ch 373, at 375–6, *per* Buckley J; *Bamford v Turnley* (1862) 3 B & S 66, at 83, *per* Bramwell B. On the other hand, reasonable user causing physical damage rather than amenity nuisance will almost certainly be actionable: *Halsey v Esso Petroleum Co Ltd* [1961] 2 All ER 145.

[97] [2002] QB 929, at [85] (revsd on appeal on different points of law: [2004] 2 AC 42).

[98] *Harrison v Southwark and Vauxhall Water Co* [1891] 2 Ch 409, at 414, *per* Vaughan Williams LJ.

[99] [1893] 1 Ch 316.   [100] [1893] 1 Ch 316, at 326.   [101] [1936] 2 KB 468.

to be actionable where they were fired out of spite, with the object of interfering with the breeding of silver foxes by the claimant. The defendant's malicious purpose was again emphasized. What stands reiteration is that, if nuisance is a strict liability tort, as Lord Goff proclaimed it to be in the *Cambridge Water* case, it is not the unreasonableness of the defendant's conduct, *per se*, that is of concern. Rather, it is the fact that this has a direct impact on the reasonableness of the interference. This is consistent with the definition of nuisance offered at the beginning of this chapter which does not stipulate unreasonable conduct – for this would blur the distinction between negligence and nuisance liability – but instead, an unreasonable interference.

An important, and arguably anomalous, case in this context is that of *Bradford Corpn v Pickles*.[102] There, the defendant was exercising his legal right to abstract water percolating beneath his land thereby preventing it from reaching the claimant's adjoining reservoir. In dismissing the claimant's nuisance action, Lord Macnaghten held that:

it is the act, not the motive for the act, that must be regarded. If the act, apart from motive, gives rise merely to damages without legal injury, the motive, however reprehensible it may be, will not supply that element.[103]

At first sight, this short passage from his Lordship's *dictum* would appear difficult to square with *Christie v Davey* and the *Hollywood Silver Fox Farm* case. Indeed, a number of commentators have been at pains to reconcile the cases on the basis that *Bradford Corpn v Pickles* is a *sui generis* type of case concerning, as it does, rights in respect of servitudes.[104] But this argument, turning on the claimant's *absolute* right to extract water, is unconvincing, for there is a no less absolute right to use one's land for lawful purposes that have been specifically sanctioned even where a substantial interference is caused to one's neighbour.[105] What the argument fails to recognize is that Lord Macnaghten's focus is not so much on the *reasonableness* of the interference, but rather upon its *gravity*. His concern, it is submitted, is primarily with whether the act complained of has occasioned a substantial interference, since the notions of *factual* and *legal* interference are by no means coextensive. His point, then, is that, in the absence of substantial harm, any action in nuisance based on the malicious conduct of the defendant must fail.[106] This accords with the principle *de minimis non curat lex*, long since deemed to be applicable to nuisance cases.[107] In any event, in *Hunter v Canary Wharf Ltd*, Lord Cooke reasserted the principle that the defendant actuated by malice may incur liability where the same interference, innocently caused, would not lead to this result.[108]

---

[102] [1895] AC 587.   [103] [1895] AC 587, at 601.   [104] For examples, see the 9th edition of this work.
[105] See, eg, *Hunter v Canary Wharf Ltd* [1997] 2 All ER 426, where Lord Goff refused to accept that the lawful construction of a tall building constituted nuisance when its construction caused interference to Cs' television reception. For an interesting account of various (unnecessary) attempts, at reconciling these cases see Cross, 'Does only the Careless Polluter Pay? A Fresh Examination of the Nature of Private Nuisance' (1995) 111 LQR 445, 453–5.
[106] His *dictum* is nonetheless misleading in so far as it appears to suggest that D's motive may *always* be disregarded. This is manifestly not the case as the *Christie* and *Silver Fox* cases amply demonstrate.
[107] *Sturges v Bridgman* (1879) 11 Ch D 852.   [108] [1997] 2 All ER 426, at 465ff.

Wanton ill-conduct serves no socially useful function. It necessarily amounts to an unreasonable user, and has the inevitable effect of rendering unreasonable any interference thereby caused to the claimant. Where, however, the defendant's activity does possess some social utility, and it is this social utility that motivates the defendant, the court will naturally be less inclined to declare any resulting interference to be unreasonable. The country must have power stations, factories and smelting works. By contrast, the need for motorcycle speedway tracks or racecourses is much less pressing and, consequently, such activities much more readily form the basis of successful nuisance actions.[109]

(b) Location of the defendant's enterprise

Just as the location of the *claimant's* premises is important in determining what constitutes a 'substantial interference' in cases of amenity nuisance, so too is the location of the *defendant's* premises important in assessing the reasonableness of the defendant's conduct. Put simply, we are concerned with the question 'what is it reasonable to do?' and not with the question (relevant when considering the location of the claimant's premises), 'what is it reasonable to put up with?'. Thus, in addition to considering the usefulness of the defendant's activity, we must also consider whether it is being carried on in a suitable locality. In this connection, the courts have recognized the national policy of segregating different uses of land and have furthered this policy by taking into account whether the defendant is putting his land to a use which is compatible with the main use to which land in that area is usually put. To take an example, the operation of a chemicals works would not, in every conceivable instance, be considered to be an unreasonable use of land. If it was operated in a residential area, it could be so regarded; but if the factory was located in an industrial area, the activity would probably be considered reasonable.[110]

(c) Fault

The undoubted role that fault can play in determining nuisance liability raises one of the most difficult questions in tort: is nuisance liability strict or fault-based? To answer this question, we must first identify the function served by identifying fault on the part of the defendant and, secondly, the limits to the role it plays in the ascription of nuisance liability. Much of the confusion that surrounds these issues stems from one famous passage in Lord Reid's Privy Council speech in *The Wagon Mound (No 2)* where he said:

Nuisance is a term used to cover a wide variety of tortious acts or omissions and in many negligence in the narrow sense is not essential. An occupier may incur liability for the emission of noxious fumes or noise although he has used the utmost care in building and

---

[109] See, eg, *A-G v Hastings Corpn* (1950) 94 Sol Jo 225 and *Dewar v City and Suburban Racecourse Co* [1899] 1 IR 345.

[110] It was decided in *Ball v Ray* (1873) 8 Ch App 467 that converting part of a house in a residential street into stables caused an unreasonable interference. But a similar degree of interference caused by a piano being played, or crying children, would not be a nuisance: see *Moy v Stoop* (1909) 25 TLR 262.

using his premises . . . [And yet] although negligence may not be necessary, *fault of some kind is almost always necessary* and fault generally involves foreseeability.[111]

At first sight, this passage may appear either intractable or inherently self-contradictory. Negligence is the archetypal fault-based tort. How then can it be asserted that while negligence is not required, fault is almost invariably a precondition of liability? The answer lies in Lord Reid's qualification that it is only *negligence in the narrow sense* that need not be shown. The first point to note is that 'negligence in the narrow sense' refers to no more than a failure to meet the standard of conduct of the reasonable man. The second point is that, though one undertakes an enterprise with all possible caution, one can seldom guarantee that certain, *foreseeable*, adverse consequences will not arise. I may, for example, drive my car in the winter with all due care but be unable to prevent a collision with another car caused by my skidding on a patch of 'black ice'. In such a case, though it could not be said that my driving was below the standard of the reasonable driver and thus negligent, it might still be said that I was at fault in the rather different sense that I knowingly took the risk of such an occurrence by deciding to drive in the first place. The element of fault in this second sense derives from the foreseeability of an accident even though I drive to an exemplary standard. It is submitted that it is this notion of fault that Lord Reid considered to be crucial to nuisance liability.

The question of whether nuisance involves strict or fault-based liability was revisited by the House of Lords in *Cambridge Water Co Ltd v Eastern Counties Leather plc.*[112] There, Lord Goff, with whom the other four Law Lords agreed, offered a similar interpretation of the role of fault to the one suggested here. He said:

[T]he fact that the defendant has taken all reasonable care will not of itself exonerate him . . . But it by no means follows that the defendant should be held liable for damage of a type which he could not reasonably foresee; and the development of the law of negligence in the past 60 years points strongly towards a requirement that such foreseeability be a prerequisite of liability in damages for nuisance, as it is of liability in negligence.[113]

This passage makes it clear that liability in nuisance is strict in the sense that a defendant may be found liable regardless of the care he took in doing what he did to avoid causing harm. But this does not exclude a residual role for fault in the second sense: that is, that liability will only attach to those users of land that involve a foreseeable risk of harm.[114]

(d) The kind of user

A penultimate factor that can influence the court's view of the reasonableness of the defendant's user is the kind of activity in which he is engaged. Here, the concern is simply with the actual use to which the defendant puts his land. If my neighbour

---

[111] [1967] 1 AC 617, at 639 (emphasis added).   [112] [1994] 2 AC 264.

[113] [1994] 2 AC 264, at 300.

[114] This is borne out by the case law. See, eg, *Leakey v National Trust* [1980] QB 485, at 526 (D had knowledge of the danger of a landslip, D was therefore liable); *Savage v Fairclough* [2000] Env LR 183 (farmer causing nitrate pollution had conformed with good farming practice and taken expert advice: there was no liability); *Delaware Mansions Ltd v Westminster City Council* [2002] 1 AC 321 (foreseeable root

disturbs me by operating a noisy printing press in order to produce illegal, pornographic literature, his activity can never be justified, for the activity is illegal and thus unreasonable. It follows that any substantial disturbance thereby caused can also never be justified. Illegal and extremely dangerous enterprises[115] are, by definition, unreasonable users of land and, apart from the criminal aspects of such activities, any disturbances they cause will, *ipso facto*, be regarded as unreasonable, *regardless* of motive.[116] By contrast, if the defendant is responsible for doing something that is socially useful, it may temper the willingness of the court to find his user to be unreasonable and help persuade the court not to grant injunctive relief even if it finds the activity in question to be a nuisance.[117]

The kinds of activity likely to be deemed unreasonable *per se* will commonly overlap with those which, for the purposes of liability under the rule in *Rylands v Fletcher*,[118] constitute 'non-natural' users of land. Yet, however clearly related the two notions are, it is nonetheless clear that they are not co-extensive. In *Fay v Prentice*,[119] for example, the defendant was found liable in nuisance in respect of water dripping from the eaves of his building although such a user would not be termed non-natural for the purposes of *Rylands v Fletcher* liability. On the other hand, the fact that a given user could be regarded as 'non-natural' for *Rylands* purposes might well be material in deciding whether it was also an 'unreasonable user' for the purposes of nuisance.[120] We return to the question of what constitutes a non-natural user in the next chapter.

(e) Practicability of preventing or avoiding the interference

It will always be material whether the defendant, by taking reasonable, practicable steps to prevent the interference, could still have achieved his purpose without interfering with the claimant's use of his land. If, without excessive expenditure, a factory owner could install equipment that would prevent him causing a disturbance to his neighbours, the courts might treat this as conclusive that the defendant's user was unreasonable. In *Andreae v Selfridge & Co Ltd*, for example, where building operations that were generating noise and dust interfered with the comfortable enjoyment of a

---

encroachment: D liable). For a fuller account of the role of foreseeability in nuisance and the rule in *Rylands and Fletcher* see Wilkinson, '*Cambridge Water Co Ltd v Eastern Counties Leather plc*: Diluting Liability for Continuing Escapes' (1994) 57 MLR 799.

[115] Eg, the storing of large quantities of high explosives in a private, terraced house.

[116] In *Cambridge Water Co Ltd v Eastern Counties Leather plc* [1994] 2 AC 264, at 298, Lord Goff identified that unreasonable land use is not necessarily to be equated with negligent land use, though wherever there is evidence of a negligently conducted activity, the courts may conclude that it amounts to an unreasonable user.

[117] *Dennis v Ministry of Defence* [2003] Env LR 34 (the noise from RAF training aircraft was held to be a nuisance, but damages only were awarded, and continuance of the nuisance permitted).

[118] (1868) LR 3 HL 330; see also ch 18.   [119] (1845) 1 CB 828.

[120] On the relationship between the two notions, see Murphy, 'Noxious Emissions and Common Law Liability – Tort in the Shadow of Regulation' in Lowry and Edmunds (eds), *Environmental Protection and the Common Law* (1999).

neighbour's hotel, it was held that the defendants who had undertaken an ostensibly reasonable user of the land were nonetheless under a duty:

to take proper precautions, and to see that the nuisance is reduced to a minimum. It is no answer for them to say: 'But this would mean that we should have to do the work more slowly than we would like to do it, or it would involve putting us to some extra expense'.[121]

Similarly, in *Leeman v Montagu*[122] a poultry farmer who made no attempt to rearrange his farm was held liable in nuisance in respect of 750 cockerels that crowed between the hours of 2.00am and 7.00am. On the other hand, in one case involving young children whose crying often caused a disturbance to the claimant, it was held that there was no liability as there was no evidence that the children had been neglected or suffered from a want of care.[123] What was crucial to this finding was the actual ability of the defendant to eradicate or minimize the interference. This principle was endorsed in *Leakey v National Trust* where, despite ultimately being found liable in respect of an earth-slide from their land, the Court of Appeal expressly declared that '[t]he extent of the defendant's duty [to minimize any interference], and the question of whether he has or has not fulfilled that duty, may . . . depend on the defendant's financial resources'.[124] Similarly, in *Holbeck Hall Hotel Ltd v Scarborough Borough Council*,[125] the Court of Appeal stated that in cases involving naturally occurring nuisances – in this case landslips – the defendants' duty would be in part restricted by their ability to avert the nuisance. On the other hand, the Court of Appeal has since held that where the defendant and claimant would both benefit from works done to avoid a nuisance, they should contribute to the cost of those works in proportion to their respective benefit.[126]

SECTION 3 WHO CAN SUE?

(A) OWNERS AND RESIDENT OCCUPIERS

Reflecting the fact that nuisance law has traditionally protected interests in land, the conventional approach adopted by the English courts was to allow only those who owned the land to bring an action in nuisance. As Lord Simmonds put it in *Read v J*

---

[121] [1938] Ch 1, at 9–10. See also the *obiter* endorsement of this approach by the House of Lords in *Southwark London Borough Council v Tanner* [2001] 1 AC 1.   [122] [1936] 2 All ER 1677.

[123] *Moy v Stoop* (1909) 25 TLR 262.

[124] [1980] QB 485, at 526, *per* Megaw LJ. Cf the wholly objective standard that applies in cases of public nuisance: *Wandsworth London Borough Council v Railtrack plc* [2002] QB 756 (council expected to take (objectively) reasonable steps to avoid pigeon infestation).

[125] [2000] 2 All ER 705. The court emphasized that liability in cases of this type involved nonfeasance and that, therefore, the duty to minimise or avoid an interference to C could be restricted for this reason. Their Lordships even considered, *obiter*, that issuing a warning to C of a known natural danger may suffice in some circumstances.

[126] *Abbahall v Smee* [2003] 1 All ER 465, at [41], *per* Munby J. In this case D and C both lived beneath a common roof which needed repairs. D was seeking to argue that her relative impecuniosity meant that she did not need to contribute to the cost of repairs.

Lyons & Co Ltd: 'he alone has a lawful claim who has suffered an invasion of some proprietary or other interest in land'.[127] It was this insistence on the existence of a proprietary interest that underpinned the decision of the Court of Appeal in *Malone v Laskey*.[128] In that case, a wife was injured when vibrations created by the defendant caused a lavatory cistern to fall off the wall and onto her head. Her claim failed because she had no legal or equitable interest in the property.[129] The same reasoning has been employed by the courts in a string of subsequent cases,[130] including, most notably, the decision of the House of Lords in *Hunter v Canary Wharf Ltd*.[131] There, Lord Goff said:

an action in private nuisance will only lie at the suit of a person who has a right to the land affected. Ordinarily such a person can only sue if he has the right to exclusive possession of the land, such as a freeholder or tenant in possession, or even a licensee with exclusive possession . . . But a mere licensee on the land has no right to sue.[132]

Notwithstanding the fact that *Hunter* is a decision of the highest court in the land, it is now nonetheless highly questionable in the light of the Human Rights Act 1998 whether this rule will survive for very long. The English courts are now required to develop the common law in a manner that is consistent with the rights embodied in the European Human Rights Convention;[133] and Article 8(1) of that Convention affords *all citizens* an equal respect for their private lives. Since this right is not contingent upon a proprietary interest in the land affected by the disturbance complained of it is arguable that the common law's insistence on such an interest is now inconsistent with the right to respect for privacy afforded by Article 8.[134]

Recognition of the potential significance of Article 8 in the present context (as well as of right to the peaceful enjoyment of his possessions under Art 1 of the First Protocol) occurred in *Marcic v Thames Water Utilities Ltd*.[135]

D was a sewerage undertaker appealing against a decision that it was liable for failing to prevent the regular flooding of C's property caused by the back-flow of waste-water from its sewerage system which in turn was attributable to a large increase in the volume of sewage entering the system. D had no control over the volume of sewage, and had not been negligent. Apart from arguing nuisance, C had alleged (1) that the flooding amounted to unjustified interference with the right to respect for private and family life under Article 8 and (2) that it was also an abrogation of C's right to the peaceful enjoyment of his possessions under the First Protocol.

---

[127] [1946]2 All ER 471, at 482(*obiter*).   [128] [1907]2 KB141.

[129] This reasoning *may not* apply today in respect of *a spouse* with no proprietary interest on the basis that, under the Family Law Act 1996, s 30, a spouse with no such interest is afforded a statutory right to occupy the matrimonial home (so long as the other spouse has a proprietary right to it). Such 'matrimonial home rights', as they are known, were somewhat glossed over in *Hunter v Canary Wharf Ltd* [1997] 2 All ER 426 and *Hunter* does not, therefore, conclusively settle the matter.

[130] See, eg, *Tate & Lyle Industries Ltd v Greater London Council* [1983] 2 AC 509; *Cunard v Antifyre Ltd* [1933] 1 KB 551 and *Metropolitan Properties Ltd v Jones* [1939] 2 All ER 202.   [131] [1997] 2 All ER 426.

[132] [1997] 2 All ER 426, at 438.   [133] Human Rights Act 1998, s 6.

[134] See, eg, *Hatton v United Kingdom* [2002] 1 FCR 732 and Wright, *Tort Law & Human Rights* (2001) ch 8.

[135] [2004] 2 AC 42.

It was held that the nuisance action failed for reasons associated with its incompatibility with the statutory scheme governing sewerage operations.[136] More importantly, it was also held that the claim under the Human Rights Act would also fail because the Water Industry Act 1991 required a statutory regulator (policing the Act's implementation) to balance the interests of the defendant's customers, whose properties were susceptible to flooding, with those of all its other customers. As such, the statutory scheme and the task of the regulator (albeit subject to judicial review) were compliant with the 1998 Act in achieving a proper balance of interests for the purposes of Article 8(2).[137]

Nonetheless, the case is important because it involves recognition in the House of Lords of the *possibility* of an action under the Human Rights Act 1998 in this context.[138] That being the case, it is entirely possible that the House of Lords, on some future occasion, may extrapolate from the approach adopted in *D v East Berkshire Community NHS Trust*[139] and hold that the existing law on *locus standi* has been superseded by the Human Rights Act so that it is no longer necessary to have a proprietary interest in the property affected. In short, they may invoke the broad principle enunciated in the *East Berkshire* case: namely, that it is pointless to continue to offer common law immunity in circumstances where an alternative action for damages would exist under Human Rights legislation. In the meantime, it may well be that, through a combination of sections 2 and 6 of the 1998 Act (which combination will require the courts to develop the common law consistently with the rights embodied in the Convention), there will be a much firmer line taken with respect to city and county councils that are alleged to have authorized, continued or adopted nuisances committed by others.

Leaving speculation to one side, it should be noted that Lord Goff recognized one exception to the general rule on *locus standi* in nuisance. Considering the decision in *Foster v Warblington UDC*[140] to be good law, he said that a person in actual possession (with no right to be there) is also allowed a right of action against a third party (that is, someone other than the true owner).[141] Apart from this instance, however, and subject to the courts adopting a new approach based on the right of all citizens to respect for their private lives, it is at present unlikely that anyone else – such as a squatter – would be entitled to bring a nuisance action.[142]

---

[136] [2004] 2 AC 42, at [34] and [70], *per* Lords Nicholls and Hoffmann respectively. The remaining Law Lords all signalled their agreement with Lord Nicholls.

[137] Article 8(2) permits derogation from the presumptive right to respect for privacy if some countervailing, legitimate and proportionate interest on behalf of the community generally can be raised: see *Hatton v UK* [2002] 1 FCR 732.

[138] Firm recognition of the availability of damages in connection with an abrogation Art 8 and/or the First Protocol exists in *Dennis v Ministry of Defence* [2003] Env LR 34.

[139] [2005] 2 AC 373. For details, see Ch 2.   [140] [1906] 1 KB 648.

[141] [1906] 1 KB 648, at 659–60, *per* Vaughan-Williams LJ.

[142] Cf the speech of Lord Hoffmann in *Hunter v Canary Wharf Ltd* [1997] 2 All ER 426 where he suggested (at 449) that it is sufficient if C 'was *de facto* in exclusive possession'.

(B) REVERSIONERS

Where a landowner is not in occupation at the time of the interference complained of, but where he retains a reversionary interest in the land, he may sue in respect of the nuisance so long as he can prove that *his* (the reversionary) interest in the land has been affected. If the damage is of a temporary nature, then he has no basis upon which to sue, and this is so even if the reversioner can show that it is likely that a similar, temporary interference will take place in the future.[143] In this context, the related concept of a 'permanent interference' has been described as one that:

> will continue indefinitely unless something is done to remove it. Thus a building which infringes ancient lights is permanent within the rule . . . On the other hand, a noisy trade and the exercise of an alleged right of way, are not in their nature permanent within the rule, for they cease of themselves, unless there be someone to continue them.[144]

In accordance with this principle, a reversioner may sue where an adjoining landowner constructs a house, the eaves of which project over his land and discharge rainwater onto it.[145] Similarly, physical damage caused to the reversioner's buildings will afford the reversioner a cause of action.[146] Conversely, no such action will lie where the nuisance complained of comprises merely temporary annoyance caused by the emission of smoke.[147]

(C) CLAIMANTS SUFFERING PERSONAL INJURIES, DAMAGE TO CHATTELS OR ECONOMIC LOSS

It was held in *Hunter v Canary Wharf Ltd*[148] that personal injuries are not, *per se*, recoverable in an action for private nuisance. Nonetheless, an action will lie where 'the injury to the amenity of the land consists in the fact that persons on it are liable to suffer inconvenience, annoyance or illness'.[149] The point is one of emphasis. The personal injury, to be recoverable, must be seen in terms of a diminution in the capacity of the land to be enjoyed. As such, where defective wiring in a neighbouring house causes a fire that spreads to the claimant's house, the claimant should be allowed to recover not only for the damage caused to his house but also for any burns he sustains because it is not only the land, but also the amenity of the land (characterized in terms of the ability to live there free from burns) that has been affected. The matter has resonance at the stage of quantifying damages: 'the reduction in amenity value is the same whether the land is occupied by the family man or the bachelor . . . the quantum of damages in

---

[143] *Simpson v Savage* (1856) 1 CBNS 347 (smoke discharged from a fire).
[144] *Jones v Llanrwst UDC* [1911] 1 Ch 393, at 404, *per* Parker J.
[145] *Tucker v Newman* (1839) 11 Ad & El 40.
[146] *Meux's Brewery Co v City of London Electric Lighting Co* [1895] 1 Ch 287.
[147] *Simpson v Savage* (1856) 1 CBNS 347.   [148] [1997] 2 All ER 426, at 442, *per* Lord Lloyd.
[149] *Hunter v Canary Wharf Ltd* [1997] 2 All ER 426, at 452, *per* Lord Hoffmann.

private nuisance does not depend on the number of those enjoying the land in question'.[150] In other words, there will be no multiplication of damages just because more than one person is affected.[151]

So far as damage to chattels is concerned, it is also reasonably well established that, again, private nuisance will afford a remedy. In *Midwood & Co Ltd v Manchester Corpn*,[152] for example, damages were awarded by the Court of Appeal for loss of stock in trade; while in *Halsey v Esso Petroleum Co Ltd*[153] they were awarded for damage to washing on a clothes line. Notwithstanding the fact that in *Hunter* their Lordships staunchly reasserted the principle that nuisance was a tort to *land*, it was also explicitly stated that an action in respect of *consequential* damage to chattels was recoverable.[154]

Finally, let us consider economic loss. In this context, it is clear, as Lord Hoffmann recognized in *Hunter*, that consequential economic loss in the form of the claimant's inability to use the land for the purposes of his business is recoverable.[155] Beyond this, matters are less clear. In two cases[156] decided according to the rule in *Rylands v Fletcher*[157] it has been suggested that, in principle, the recoverability of pure economic loss is possible. Since Lord Goff's view in the *Cambridge Water* case was that the rule in *Rylands v Fletcher* was a tort derived from nuisance, it could be argued that there should be no objection to pure economic losses being recovered in nuisance *so long as* they arise out of an interference with the amenity value of the land.[158]

SECTION 4 WHO CAN BE SUED?

A person is liable in nuisance only if he bears 'some degree of personal responsibility'.[159] Such persons can conveniently be identified under three main heads.

(A) CREATORS

If the actual wrongdoer is invested with the management and control of the premises from which the nuisance emanates, then he is liable irrespective of whether he is an occupier of those premises in the normal sense of the word.[160] Even though the person

---

[150] [1997] 2 All ER 426, at 442, *per* Lord Lloyd.

[151] But note that personal injuries are recoverable in the tort of public nuisance.   [152] [1905] 2 KB 597.

[153] [1961] 2 All ER 145. Though an award in respect of damaged furniture was denied in *Cunard v Antifyre Ltd* [1933] 1 KB 551, it should be noted that the case was ultimately decided in negligence.

[154] [1997] 2 All ER 426, at 452, *per* Lord Hoffmann. For critique, see Oliphant, 'Unblurring the Boundaries of Nuisance' (1998) 6 *Tort Law Review* 21.   [155] [1997] 2 All ER 426.

[156] *British Celanese Ltd v A H Hunt (Capacitors) Ltd* [1969] 2 All ER 1252; *Ryeford Homes Ltd v Sevenoaks District Council* [1989] 2 EGLR 281.   [157] (1868) LR 3 HL 330.

[158] But compare the (*obiter*) view that the cost of replacement cooking facilities necessitated by a disturbed gas supply is irrecoverable: *Anglian Water Services Ltd v Crawshaw Robbins & Co Ltd* 2002 WL 31523191, at [124], *per* Stanley Burnton J.   [159] *Sedleigh-Denfield v O'Callaghan* [1940] AC 880, at 897, *per* Lord Atkin.

[160] *Hall v Beckenham Corpn* [1949] 1 KB 716.

who created the interference was neither at the time of the proceedings, nor at the time when he created the interference, in occupation or control of the premises from which it emanated, but merely created it with the authority of the occupier of the premises, he may still be liable.[161] Nor will he be excused simply because he lacks the right to enter onto the premises in order to abate it.[162] In accordance with ordinary principles of tortious liability, anyone who authorizes another to commit a nuisance is himself also liable. So, for example, a local authority is liable where it authorizes the use of its land as a go-kart circuit, where a nuisance is the known and inevitable consequence of go-kart racing taking place there.[163] If, however, land is let by a local authority to persons who may or may not cause a nuisance, no such liability will attach as the eventuality of a nuisance is not inevitable.[164] Nor will a local authority be liable if it lets premises to tenants who, in poorly soundproofed buildings, cause annoyance to others simply by using their premises in the normal way.[165] It is only the authorization of conduct that will *definitely* cause a nuisance that enables the courts to treat the landowner as if he had caused the interference himself. Thus, it was held in *Hussain v Lancaster City Council*[166] that since the acts complained of – racial harassment committed by the defendant council's tenants against local shopkeepers – had no direct connection with the tenants' use of the premises they rented from the defendants, nuisance liability could not be imposed on the defendants. The council could only be held liable in respect of uses of the tenant's council houses that they had authorized and that had caused a nuisance. In this case, there was no such land use by the council tenants.[167]

Where the interference complained of arises from a 'state of affairs' that was created by the defendant,[168] he will again be held liable (even though his initial conduct does not, of itself, amount to a nuisance) *so long as* harm to the claimant is a foreseeable consequence of that initial conduct. Thus, he who plants poplar trees – itself an innocuous act – is liable in nuisance in respect of the indirect harm caused by their

---

[161] *Southwark London Borough Council v Tanner* [2001] 1 AC 1.

[162] *Thompson v Gibson* (1841) 7 M & W 456. In *Southport Corpn v Esso Petroleum Co Ltd* [1953] 2 All ER 1204, at 1207, Devlin J said *obiter*: 'I can see no reason why . . . if the defendant as a licensee or trespasser misuses someone else's land, he should not be liable for a nuisance in the same way as an adjoining occupier would be'. Despite this *dictum*, there has been no English case in which liability was imposed upon a person who had never been in occupation or control of the relevant premises in respect of conduct which was not authorized by someone who was in occupation. In Australia, there is direct authority that a trespasser is not liable in nuisance: *Beaudesert Shire Council v Smith* (1966) 40 ALJR 211.   [163] *Tetley v Chitty* [1986] 1 All ER 663.

[164] *Smith v Scott* [1973] Ch 314. In this case, undesirable tenants were always likely to annoy their neighbours by noise and vandalism; but that they would do so was not guaranteed. See also *Rich v Basterfield* (1847) 4 CB 783. Cf *Lippiatt v South Gloucestershire Council* [1999] 4 All ER 149 (travellers on D's land, and using D's land as a base for forays onto C's land, were known to D to interfere repeatedly with Cs' enjoyment of their land) and *Winch v Mid Bedfordshire District Council* 2002 WL 1876048.

[165] *Southwark London Borough Council v Tanner* [2001] 1 AC 1.

[166] [1999] 4 All ER 125. Cf *Lippiatt v South Gloucestershire Council* [1999] 4 All ER 149.

[167] But this decision skates rather too close for comfort to supporting the untenable proposition that a nuisance requires an improper use of D's land. For a rejection of this proposition, see *L E Jones (Insurance Brokers) Ltd v Portsmouth City Council* [2003] 1 WLR 427.

[168] Contrast those circumstances in which D only inherits or continues a state of affairs produced by a third party. In such cases, considered in the next section, D's liability attaches because of his failure to remedy the potentially injurious state of affairs: see *Delaware Mansions Ltd v Westminster City Council* [2002] 1 AC 321.

roots spreading under neighbouring land.[169] Equally, maintaining defective electric mains gives rise to liability for foreseeable damage that in fact ensues.[170] Where, on the other hand, the defendant creates a state of affairs that will not foreseeably result in a nuisance, the courts will refuse to attach liability.

In *Ilford UDC v Beal*,[171] D erected a retaining wall along the bank of a river. Because the wall was not constructed in accordance with the best engineering practice it was later completely undermined by the river. This undermining caused the wall to move forward a foot or two where it came to press against, and cause damage to, C's sewer. C neither knew, nor ought to have known, about the presence of the sewer. The damage to the sewer was therefore unforeseeable and D was held not liable in nuisance.

Although the key to liability in such cases is undoubtedly the remoteness of the injurious consequences of the defendant's initial conduct, it is not always easy to distinguish those cases in which the defendant genuinely created the dangerous state of affairs from those in which he merely failed to remedy it. The point can be illustrated by reference to *Goldman v Hargrave*.[172]

A redgum tree that was growing on D's land caught fire when it was struck by lightning. D took measures to fell the tree but because of changes in the weather conditions (including a strengthening in the wind) the embers which had not been completely extinguished, rekindled. The fire then spread to C's land. One of the Privy Council's findings of fact was that D's method of dealing with the fire gave rise to a foreseeable risk of the fire reviving and spreading.

It is not wholly clear whether the defendant's wrongdoing amounted to misfeasance (in that he dealt inappropriately with a burning tree thereby creating a risk to his neighbour) or nonfeasance (in that he failed to avert an extant risk of fire spreading). Had the tree not been felled in the manner adopted by the defendant, the fire may never have rekindled and spread to the defendant's land. On the other hand, had the tree not been struck by lightning in the first place, a hazardous state of affairs would never have arisen on the defendant's land. Whether cases such as this are better seen as involving misfeasance or nonfeasance is by no means easy to decide.[173]

(B) OCCUPIERS

As we noted in the previous section, the occupier of premises will be liable in respect of nuisances that he has himself created. But he may also be liable in other circumstances, too. In the main, these cases turn on the occupier having 'adopted' or 'continued' the nuisance by failing to take reasonable steps to remedy a potential hazard on land that he occupies. Broadly, an occupier adopts a nuisance if he makes

---

[169] *Butler v Standard Telephones and Cables Ltd* [1940] 1 KB 399; followed in *McCombe v Read* [1955] 2 QB 429.   [170] *Midwood & Co Ltd v Manchester Corpn* [1905] 2 KB 597.

[171] [1925] 1 KB 671.

[172] [1967] 1 AC 645. See also *Radstock Co-operative and Industrial Society Ltd v Norton-Radstock UDC* [1968] Ch 605.   [173] In the eventuality, the Privy Council treated *Goldman* as a nonfeasance case.

use of an 'erection, building, bank or artificial contrivance which constitutes the nuisance', whereas he continues the nuisance if he, with '[actual] knowledge or presumed knowledge of its existence, fails to take any reasonable means to bring it to an end'.[174] In determining what amounts to the reasonable means he might be expected to take, the court, for reasons of justice, *may* have regard to his limited financial and other resources;[175] especially if the claimant has had the state of affairs involuntarily thrust upon him.

So far as the liability of occupiers for nuisance is concerned, there are four main categories of case to consider. But before examining them, it is worth noting that the first three categories would also apparently apply in respect, not just of someone in control of the land (the test for occupation), but also someone in control of the hazard *but not in control of the land*.[176]

(1) ACTS OF A TRESPASSER

If the dangerous state of affairs on the defendant's land is created by a trespasser, so long as the occupier knows or ought to know about it, he is liable in nuisance in respect of damage thereby caused to his neighbour. The leading case is *Sedleigh-Denfield v O'Callaghan*.[177] There, the drainage system on the defendant's land became blocked because of the negligent acts of a trespasser. The defendant's servant who had been responsible for periodically cleansing the drainage system over a period of three years ought to have noticed the risk of flooding and for this reason the defendant was held liable for the flood damage that the blockage had caused to the claimant. In finding the defendant liable, the House of Lords stressed the importance of his (presumed) knowledge of the risk:

An occupier is not *prima facie* responsible for a nuisance created without his knowledge and consent. If he is to be liable a further condition is necessary, namely, that he had knowledge or means of knowledge, that he knew or should have known, of the nuisance in time to correct it.[178]

It is important to distinguish cases such as *Sedleigh-Denfield*, from two further kinds of case. First, from those such as *Smith v Littlewoods Organisation Ltd*[179] where the House of Lords held that there was no liability where the trespassers had, *in the absence of actual or presumed knowledge* on the part of the defendants, caused a fire in the defendants' disused cinema which spread to the claimant's property. Secondly, from those where the third party merely uses the defendant's land as a means of gaining access to the claimant's land rather than, as in *Sedleigh-Denfield*, where the third party's mischievous act or omission actually occurs on the defendant's land. In such cases the Court of Appeal has held that the defendant will be free of any general liability in

---

[174] *Sedleigh-Denfield v O'Callaghan* [1940] AC 880, at 894, *per* Viscount Maugham.
[175] But not always, see *Abbahall v Smee* [2003] 1 All ER 465 (discussed below).
[176] *Jones Ltd v Portsmouth City Council* [2003] 1 WLR 427.   [177] [1940] AC 880.
[178] [1940] AC 880, at 904, *per* Lord Wright. See also *Lippiatt v South Gloucestershire Council* [1999] 4 All ER 149.
[179] [1987] AC 241.

respect of the acts of such third parties.[180] A final point that ought to be noted is that, where the defendant's failure to abate a nuisance can be attributed to a pre-existing duty on his part to consult the interested parties before any remedial steps can permissibly be taken, the defendant's inaction will not be taken by the courts to be an unreasonable failure to erase the menacing state of affairs.[181]

(2) ACTS OF NATURE

If a dangerous state of affairs arises on the defendant's land due to an act of nature of which the occupier knows or ought to know, he is liable in nuisance if damage occurs to a neighbouring landowner. In *Goldman v Hargrave*, the facts of which we noted when considering the liability of the creator of a nuisance, the Privy Council extended the rule in *Sedleigh-Denfield v O'Callaghan* – that an occupier must take reasonable steps to remedy a potentially hazardous state of affairs – to cases in which the danger arises by an act of God. However, Lord Wilberforce added the important qualification that the unreasonableness of the defendant's attempts to avert such a danger must be judged in the light of his financial and other resources. He said:

[T]he law must take account of the fact that the occupier on whom the duty is cast has, *ex hypothesi*, had this hazard thrust upon him through no seeking or fault of his own. His interest and his resources, whether physical or material, may be of very modest character . . . A rule which required of him in such unsought circumstances in his neighbour's interest a physical effort of which he is not capable, or an excessive expenditure of money, would be unenforceable or unjust.[182]

Although *Goldman* is, strictly, an Australian decision, its underlying rationale was adopted in the English case of *Leakey v National Trust for Places of Historic Interest or Natural Beauty*.[183] There, the defendants owned land on which there stood a large mound of earth which the defendants knew to be prone to subsidence. When, following a particularly dry summer which caused cracks in the earth to appear, the mound finally gave way causing damage to the claimant's houses, it was held by the Court of Appeal that the defendants were liable in respect of the land-slip.[184] Although the defendants had given permission to the claimant to abate the cause of the nuisance, they had themselves done nothing to remove the danger.[185]

---

[180] *P Perl Exporters Ltd v Camden London Borough Council* [1984] QB 342.

[181] *Page Motors Ltd v Epsom and Ewell Borough Council* (1981) 80 LGR 337.

[182] [1967] 1 AC 645, at 663. This might be seen as undermining the supposed strictness of nuisance liability. On the other hand, it might be seen as being a not unreasonable user of the land (and, therefore, a not unreasonable interference).

[183] [1980] QB 485. See also *Davey v Harrow Corpn* [1958] 1 QB 60 (a landowner who allows the branches or roots of trees to encroach on a neighbour's land will be liable in nuisance).

[184] But note that where D's *nonfeasance* is in issue, the court's expectations of him will diminish, especially where preventative action would require great expense on D's part: see *Holbeck Hall Hotel Ltd v Scarborough Borough Council* [2000] 2 All ER 705.

[185] But note that it is doubtful whether liability arises for the presence of animals *ferae naturae* or failure to remove them: *Farrer v Nelson* (1885) 15 QBD 258; *Seligman v Docker* [1949] Ch 53.

(3) NUISANCES CREATED BY INDEPENDENT CONTRACTORS

An employer, naturally enough, is vicariously liable for nuisances created by an employee in the course of his employment.[186] But as regards independent contractors, the defendant is only liable in respect of their failure to take precautions if, as Slesser LJ held in *Matania v National Provincial Bank Ltd and Elevenist Syndicate Ltd*,[187] 'the act done is one which in its very nature involves a special danger of nuisance being complained of'. In that case, the occupier of the first floor of a building was held liable to the superjacent occupiers in respect of the dust and noise generated by the alteration works carried out by the independent contractors he had employed.

The nature of an occupier's liability for independent contractors was more widely stated by Cockburn CJ in *Bower v Peate*, when holding a principal liable for his independent contractor's withdrawing support from the buildings of the claimant:

a man who orders a work to be executed, from which, in the natural course of things, injurious consequences to his neighbour must be expected to arise . . . is bound to see to the doing of that which is necessary to prevent the mischief, and cannot relieve himself of his responsibility by employing someone else.[188]

(4) ACTS OF A PREVIOUS OCCUPIER

If the predecessor of the defendant occupier created a hazardous state of affairs and the defendant knows or ought to know of its existence then, according to Scrutton LJ in *St Anne's Well Brewery Co v Roberts*,[189] he is liable in respect of any damage to which it gives rise. Even if the construction created by the occupier's predecessor in title did not pose a threat at the time of its creation, that person may nonetheless be held liable in respect of any hazards it subsequently gives rise to so long as he knew, or ought to have known, that such a threat was posed.[190]

(c) LANDLORDS

We have already seen that a landlord who authorizes his tenant to commit a nuisance is treated, in law, as the creator of the nuisance, and will himself be liable for that nuisance.[191] But there are three further situations that call for discussion in which the landlord *may* be held liable *qua* landlord (as opposed to *qua* creator).

---

[186] *Spicer v Smee* [1946] 1 All ER 489, at 493, *per* Atkinson J (*obiter*).   [187] [1936] 2 All ER 633, at 646.

[188] (1876) 1 QBD 321, at 326. Cf Atkinson J, following *Bower v Peate* in *Spicer v Smee* [1946] 1 All ER 489, at 495: 'where danger is likely to arise unless work is properly done, there is a duty to see that it is properly done'. For a fuller discussion of liability for the acts of independent contractors, see Murphy, 'Juridical Foundations of Common Law Non-delegable Duties' in Neyers (ed), *Emerging Issues in Tort Law* (2007).

[189] (1928) 140 LT 1 (part of an ancient wall collapsed damaging C's inn but, on the facts, D was found not liable because of the lack of (constructive) knowledge that the wall was likely to collapse). Followed in *Wilkins v Leighton* [1932] 2 Ch 106.

[190] *Bybrook Barn Garden Centre Ltd v Kent County Council* [2001] Env LR 30.

[191] See, eg, *Lippiatt v South Gloucestershire Council* [1999] 4 All ER 149.

First, if at the date of letting the landlord knows or ought to know of the condition giving rise to the actionable nuisance, he will be liable despite the tenancy if he has not taken a covenant to repair the premises from the tenant.[192] According to Goddard J in *Wilchick v Marks and Silverstone*, a landlord ought to know not only of those defects that are patently obvious but also of those that are capable of being discovered by use of reasonable care.[193] Secondly, a landlord will also be liable for dangerous conditions that arise from want of repair during the currency of the tenancy if he has covenanted to perform such repairs,[194] reserves the right to enter and repair,[195] or has an implied right to enter and repair.[196] Furthermore, where the landlord's premises are situated on a highway, he will be liable to passers-by or neighbouring landowners regardless of whether the want of repair is attributable to his (that is, the landlord's) want of care.[197] Finally, where a landlord does something to the premises that leads inevitably to a nuisance if the premises are occupied, then he, rather than the tenants, will be liable. In *Toff v McDowell*,[198] for example, the tenants had used the premises in a perfectly normal fashion but, because the landlord had taken up the floor covering, anyone occupying the premises subsequently would sound unbearably loud to the subjacent claimant. The landlord was held liable and directed to replace the flooring.[199]

As regards the liability of a tenant, it is well established that, if he has covenanted to repair the premises, he is liable in nuisance for damage arising from a failure to effect those repairs.[200] On the other hand, the mere fact that the landlord has covenanted to repair the premises, will not, *ipso facto*, exonerate the tenant from nuisance liability.[201] As Lawrence LJ explained in *St Anne's Well Brewery Co v Roberts*:[202]

Any bargain made by the person responsible [ie, the occupier] to his neighbour or to the public that another person should perform that obligation may give rise to rights as between the two contracting parties, but does not, in my judgment, in any way affect any right of third parties, who are not parties or privy to such contract.

---

[192] *Todd v Flight* (1860) 9 CBNS 377; *Gandy v Jubber* (1864) 5 B & S 78; revsd (1865) 9 B & S 15; *Bowen v Anderson* [1894] 1 QB 164.   [193] [1934] 2 KB 56, at 67–8.

[194] *Payne v Rogers* (1794) 2 Hy Bl 350.

[195] *Wilchick v Marks and Silverstone* [1934] 2 KB 56; *Heap v Ind Coope and Allsopp Ltd* [1940] 2 KB 476; *Spicer v Smee* [1946] 1 All ER 489.   [196] *Mint v Good* [1951] 1 KB 517.

[197] *Wringe v Cohen* [1940] 1 KB 229 (followed in *Mint v Good* [1951] 1 KB 517). The importance of the rule in *Wringe v Cohen* has since been amplified by the imposition on landlords of onerous obligations to maintain houses, let for fewer than seven years, in a state of good repair (see the Landlord and Tenant Act 1985, ss 11–16). On the other hand, the rule in *Wringe v Cohen* does not apply to premises that do not lie on a highway, nor does it apply to nuisances arising from acts of trespassers or processes of nature: *Cushing v Peter Walker & Son (Warrington and Burton) Ltd* [1941] 2 All ER 693.

[198] (1993) 25 HLR 650. To similar effect, see *Stannard v Charles Pitcher Ltd* [2002] BLR 441.

[199] Cf *Southwark London Borough Council v Tanner* [2001] 1 AC 1 (D had not done anything to the rented premises so as to render a disturbance to C inevitable: D was not liable).

[200] *Brew Bros Ltd v Snax (Ross) Ltd* [1970] 1 QB 612. But note that the tenant's covenant to repair does not exonerate the landlord from liability for, as Sachs LJ observed (at 638): 'the test of an owner's duty to his neighbour depends on the degree of control exercised by the owner in law or in fact for the purpose of repairs'. And in this context it should be noted that the repair obligations placed upon landlords under the Landlord and Tenant Act 1985, ss 11–16 are made immutable.

[201] *Wilchick v Marks and Silverstone* [1934] 2 KB 56. Cf the *obiter* view of Heath J in *Payne v Rogers* (1794) 2 Hy Bl 350 that to hold the tenant liable would encourage circuity of action.   [202] (1928) 140 LT 1, at 8.

SECTION 5 MUST THE INTERFERENCE EMANATE FROM THE DEFENDANT'S LAND?

The land from which the interference has its source will normally be in the ownership or control of the defendant. Indeed, in so far as nuisance law is designed to provide a means of regulating competing land uses, it might even be argued that land ownership on the part of the defendant is as important as the classic requirement that the claimant must have a proprietary interest.[203] Nonetheless, *dicta* abounds to the effect that the defendant need not be the owner of the land from which the nuisance emanates. Thus, in *Sedleigh-Denfield v O'Callaghan* Lord Wright declared 'the ground of responsibility' to be merely 'the possession and control of the land from which the nuisance proceeds'.[204] And in *Halsey v Esso Petroleum Co Ltd*[205] the defendants were even held liable in respect of the noise generated by their lorries driving along a public street late at night.

SECTION 6 DEFENCES

(A) STATUTORY AUTHORITY

The fact that the activity giving rise to the interference complained of is authorized by statute is the single most important defence in the law of private nuisance. Many activities which interfere with the enjoyment of land are carried out by public or private enterprises in pursuance of an Act of Parliament. But if the statute merely confers a permissive power, then it has been held that the power must be exercised so as not to interfere with private rights.[206] Whether the activity complained of is explicitly authorized by statute, and whether any potential nuisance action is thereby defeated, is a matter of statutory interpretation.

In *Allen v Gulf Oil Refining Ltd*[207] D was authorized by statute compulsorily to acquire land near Milford Haven for the purpose of constructing and operating an oil refinery. C complained that the smell, noise and vibrations made by the refinery constituted a nuisance. D pleaded the defence of statutory authority.

The House of Lords held that the claimants would first have to establish a nuisance, and that the change in the local environment caused by authorizing the operation of the

---

[203] In *Miller v Jackson* [1977] QB 966, at 980, Lord Denning MR proclaimed that, '[i]t is the very essence of a private nuisance that it is the unreasonable use by a man of *his land* to the detriment of his neighbour' (emphasis added).

[204] [1940] AC 880, at 903. See also *J Lyons & Sons v Wilkins* [1899] 1 Ch 255; *Hubbard v Pitt* [1976] QB 142; *Ward Lock & Co Ltd v Operative Printers' Assistants' Society* (1906) 22 TLR 327; *Thomas v National Union of Mineworkers (South Wales Area)* [1986] Ch 20.   [205] [1961] 2 All ER 145.

[206] *Metropolitan Asylum District Managers v Hill* (1881) 6 App Cas 193.   [207] [1981] AC 1001.

refinery was relevant to that issue.[208] If a nuisance could be established, then the company had to prove that it was an inevitable result of carrying on a refinery there.[209]

It follows from this that the defendant must use all due diligence in performing the activity authorized by statute.[210] If he fails so to do, he will be held to have exceeded the level of damage for which he was granted immunity by the statute. So, in *Tate & Lyle Industries Ltd v Greater London Council*,[211] the defendants were held liable in public nuisance where reasonable care in the design and erection of new ferry terminals, which they had been authorized to build by statute, would have at least partially avoided the siltation of the River Thames which damaged the claimants' business.

One further matter that bedevils the law on the defence of statutory authority occurs where the defendant is a public authority. More particularly, the problem surfaces where the public body is invested with a *discretionary* statutory power and it is argued that it ought to have used that power in order to prevent a nuisance. In *Marcic v Thames Water Utilities Ltd*,[212] the Court of Appeal suggested that such powers may well need to be used in this way; but, on appeal, the matter was not considered by the House of Lords.[213] It remains to be seen how influential the approach of the Court of Appeal will be in future cases where the relevant legislation does not, as in *Marcic*, provide an exclusive statutory mechanism for dealing with complaints.

(B) PRESCRIPTION

The right to do something that would otherwise constitute private nuisance may be acquired as an easement by prescription. In order to decide whether this defence avails, one must look to the law of real property to identify whether the right claimed is capable of constituting an easement. The most common way of acquiring an easement is by 20 years' overt and undisturbed user. One may, for example, acquire the right to pour effluent into a stream, although not if it is done secretly.[214] Equally, one may acquire the right do such things as discharge surface water,[215] or rainwater from the eaves of one's house,[216] onto a neighbour's land. It is also well established that the user must be continuous. So, where there is a perpetual change in the amount of inconvenience caused – as in the case of fumes or noise – it is doubtful whether an easement can be obtained.[217]

---

[208] This point was endorsed by Buckley J in *Gillingham Borough Council v Medway (Chatham) Dock Co Ltd* [1993] QB 343, at 360 in relation to the (broadly) analogous defence of authorization by planning permission: 'Prior to 1984 [these] roads had been relatively quiet roads . . . [but] I must judge the present claim in nuisance pursuant to the planning permission for use of the dockyard as a commercial port'. But note that an injunction can exceptionally be obtained to restrain D from engaging in a land use authorized by planning permission: *Wheeler v JJ Saunders Ltd* [1995] 2 All ER 697. Cf the general position set out in *Hunter* and discussed above.

[209] In this respect, the House of Lords followed its earlier decision in *Manchester Corpn v Farnworth* [1930] AC 171, where a power station established under statute emitted poisonous fumes that damaged C's fields.

[210] *Marcic v Thames Water Utilities Ltd* [2004] 2 AC 42.

[211] [1983] 2 AC 509. See also *Department of Transport v North West Water Authority* [1984] AC 336.

[212] [2002] QB 929.   [213] [2004] 2 AC 42.   [214] *Liverpool Corpn v H Coghill & Son* [1918] 1 Ch 307.

[215] *A-G v Copeland* [1902] 1 KB 690.   [216] *Thomas v Thomas* (1835) 2 Cr M & R 34.

[217] *Hulley v Silversprings Bleaching and Dyeing Co Ltd* [1922] 2 Ch 268.

One matter that is beyond doubt is that if the user is prohibited by statute, it cannot be claimed as a prescriptive right.[218] Furthermore, 'acts which are *neither preventable nor actionable* cannot be relied upon to found an easement'.[219] Thus, where a defendant confectioner had for more than 20 years made certain noises on his land through the operation of his equipment, which then, for the first time, interfered with the claimant doctor's user of his land, the defendant could not plead a prescriptive right.[220] It was held that, as there had been no invasion of a legal right before the consulting room was built, there were no steps that the claimant could have taken to prevent the interference.

(c) THE CLAIMANT'S CONDUCT[221]

It is no defence that the claimant came to the nuisance by occupying the land adjoining it.[222] Nor is it a defence that the nuisance has only arisen because the claimant has chosen to use a particular part of his land in a way that heightens his sensitivity.[223] In any case, it may be assumed that the claimant has the normal duty in tort to take reasonable steps to mitigate his loss. He should, for instance, take reasonable steps to minimize the damage when his land is flooded in consequence of his neighbour's tortious conduct. The ordinary principles of causation apply in nuisance law and, if the nuisance is caused by the claimant's own acts, he cannot recover.[224] The defences of consent and assumption of risk are also available. *Pwllbach Colliery Co Ltd v Woodman*[225] illustrates the operation of the consent defence.

A lessor allowed his lessee to carry on the business of coal mining. The issue was whether he could complain when the lessee's non-negligent operations caused coal dust to be deposited on other land owned by the lessor. The House of Lords held that only if the terms of the lease could be construed as authorizing a nuisance was there any defence. Their Lordships held that, first, the nuisance was not a necessary consequence of carrying on that trade and, secondly, that there had been no express authorization of the nuisance in the lease. The defence of consent therefore failed.

As regards the assumption of risk defence, *Kiddle v City Business Properties Ltd*[226] is a case in point. There, the claimant complained of the damage caused to his shop when flooding from the gutter carrying water from a part of the premises retained by the defendant landlord occurred without negligence on the defendant's part. It was held that the tenant took the premises as he found them and must be deemed to have run this risk. Accordingly, his action in nuisance failed.

---

[218] *Liverpool Corpn v H Coghill & Son Ltd* [1918] 1 Ch 307.

[219] *Sturges v Bridgman* (1879) 11 Ch D 852, at 863, *per* Thesiger LJ (emphasis added).

[220] (1879) 11 Ch D 852.

[221] See also above for the inability of C to heighten his sensitivities in order to sue in nuisance.

[222] *Bliss v Hall* (1838) 4 Bing NC 183; *Miller v Jackson* [1977] QB 966 (no defence to a cricket club that the ground first became a nuisance when C built premises close to it).

[223] *Sturges v Bridgman* (1879) 11 Ch D 852; *Elliotson v Feetham* (1835) 2 Bing NC 134.

[224] Cf the case in public nuisance: *Almeroth v Chivers & Sons Ltd* [1948] 1 All ER 53.

[225] [1915] AC 634.   [226] [1942] 1 KB 269.

Contributory negligence on the part of the claimant might also, in principle, be raised as a defence to an action in nuisance; at least where the nuisance arises out of negligent conduct.[227] There is certainly an *obiter dictum* to this effect in the public nuisance case of *Trevett v Lee*.[228]

(D) OTHER DEFENCES

The Fires Prevention (Metropolis) Act 1774 provides that, in an action brought in respect of a fire, it is a defence to prove that the fire began accidentally.[229] But, as Atkinson J held in *Spicer v Smee*,[230] the defence has no application where the fire was caused by the negligence of the defendant, or was intentionally created by him or by those for whom he was responsible. Even when a fire starts accidentally, if the defendant negligently allows it to grow into a raging fire, the Act will not afford him a defence for the damage it later causes.[231] Accordingly, the defence has no application in nuisance law except, perhaps, where a person would be liable in nuisance even though his conduct was neither intentional nor negligent.

As we saw earlier, an occupier who unreasonably fails to avert a danger to his neighbour arising out of an act of God will be liable in nuisance. Where, however, there is an occurrence alleged by the claimant to be a nuisance, which in truth is an inevitable accident, it is well established that no liability will attach.[232] But it is no defence that the act of the defendant would not have been a nuisance but for the acts of others, provided that the defendant knew what the others were doing.[233]

SECTION 7 REMEDIES

(A) DAMAGES

The measure of damages in nuisance is similar to that awarded for trespass to land.[234] The claimant is entitled to full reparation for his loss. Where, for instance, a house (or a crop, or something analogous[235]) is destroyed or damaged, then the claimant will recover the difference between the monetary value to him of his interest (whether he is

---

[227] Query whether the courts would accept this defence where the nuisance was caused by D's deliberate and malicious conduct?   [228] [1955] 1 All ER 406, at 412, *per* Evershed MR.

[229] Note that the Act applies generally, not merely to London: *Filliter v Phippard* (1847) 11 QB 347.

[230] [1946] 1 All ER 489.   [231] *Goldman v Hargrave* [1967] 1 AC 645.

[232] *Tennent v Earl of Glasgow* (1864) 2 M 22.   [233] *Thorpe v Brumfitt* (1873) 8 Ch App 650.

[234] See ch 10. For an argument in favour of exemplary damages in private nuisance see Murphy, 'Noxious Emissions and Common Law Liability – Tort in the Shadow of Regulation' in Lowry and Edmunds (eds), *Environmental Protection and the Common Law* (1999).

[235] See *Marquis of Granby v Bakewell UDC* (1923) 87 JP 105 for a detailed calculation on this basis of the value of fish destroyed by pollution of a stream.

the landlord, tenant or otherwise) before and after the event.[236] Where business loss is suffered in consequence of the interference, whether by loss of custom[237] or the cost of moving elsewhere,[238] this is also recoverable in nuisance. Where, however, a hotel owner complained of loss of custom caused by nearby building operations, the Court of Appeal reversed an award of damages to the full extent of loss of custom, holding that a certain amount of the interference was reasonable in the circumstances, although likely to lead to some loss of custom. The court therefore assessed what proportion of the business loss was attributable to that excess of noise and dust which alone was actionable.[239] In 1966, in *The Wagon Mound (No 2)*,[240] the Privy Council held that, in public nuisance, it is not enough that the damage is a direct consequence of the wrongful act; it must also be a foreseeable consequence. *Obiter dicta* in the case stated this rule to be applicable also to private nuisance.

The amount to be awarded by way of damages increases the longer the nuisance continues. But, curiously, the law does not treat this as the continuance of the original nuisance complained of, but rather as a new and distinct nuisance. Thus, in one case where a defendant imposed a strain on the claimant's wall by piling earth against it and was sued in nuisance, it was stated that 'a fresh cause of action arises as each brick topples down, and that there is a continuing cause of action until the root of the trouble is eradicated'.[241] Whether the continuance of the interference is characterized as a fresh nuisance or as a prolongation of the original one is largely immaterial so far as the claimant is concerned.[242] He is much more interested in having the nuisance abated and will, in most cases, seek an injunction. However, as we shall see in the next section, the injunction is a flexible remedy and the court has a statutory power[243] to grant damages *in lieu* of an injunction (thus enabling it to make an award that takes account of future as well as past harm). The principles governing the exercise of the court's discretion in the exercise of this power were set out by Smith LJ in the leading case of *Shelfer v City of London Electric Lighting Co*.[244] There it was stated that the court has jurisdiction to

---

[236] *Moss v Christchurch RDC* [1925] 2 KB 750. The law does not grant damages based on the cost of restoring the damaged property to its prior state *if* C has no genuine interest in such restoration: *C R Taylor (Wholesale) Ltd v Hepworths Ltd* [1977] 2 All ER 784 (C not entitled to recover the cost of reinstating his destroyed billiard hall which he did not intend to use for that purpose again – the basis of assessment was simply the reduced value of the premises). See also *Lodge Holes Colliery Co Ltd v Wednesbury Corpn* [1908] AC 323;

[237] *Fritz v Hobson* (1880) 14 Ch D 542.

[238] *Grosvenor Hotel Co v Hamilton* [1894] 2 QB 836, at 840, *per* Lindley LJ.

[239] *Andrae v Selfridge & Co Ltd* [1938] Ch 1.   [240] [1967] 1 AC 617.

[241] *Maberley v Henry W Peabody & Co of London Ltd* [1946] 2 All ER 192, at 194, *per* Stable J. See also the acceptance of this approach by the House of Lords in *Delaware Mansions Ltd v Westminster City Council* [2002] 1 AC 321, *per* Lord Cooke.

[242] It can, however, be a concern to D who merely continues a nuisance begun by his predecessor. Yet where the nuisance has caused harm of a kind that now requires remedial work, the courts will award damages that reflect the cost of that remedial work regardless of whether some of the harm was occasioned prior to D 'inheriting' the nuisance: *Delaware Mansions Ltd v Westminster City Council* [2002] 1 AC 321, at [38], *per* Lord Cooke.

[243] Supreme Court Act 1981, s 50.

[244] [1895] 1 Ch 287, at 322–323. In this case the court was dealing with the equivalent provision to s 50 of the Supreme Court Act 1981 (Lord Cairns' Act, s 2). The principles enunciated have since been reiterated, however, in relation to the 1981 Act by Bingham MR in *Jaggard v Sawyer* [1995] 2 All ER 189, at 203.

grant damages *in lieu* where (i) the injury to the claimant is small, (ii) it is quantifiable in money, (iii) it is capable of being adequately compensated in money, and (iv) it would be oppressive to the defendant to grant an injunction.[245] The insistence that the harm complained of must be small places an important restriction on the court's ability to grant damages instead of an injunction.[246] In addition, it seems from *Elliott v London Borough of Islington*[247] that a restrictive definition of what amounts to a small degree of harm should be applied. In that case, the pressing of the defendant's tree against the claimant's wall – causing it to move only a very few inches – was regarded as 'very considerable harm'. Furthermore, in relation to the fourth limb of the *Shelfer* test, as Bingham MR observed in *Jaggard v Sawyer*, '[i]t is important to bear in mind that the test is one of *oppression*, and the court should not slide into application of a general balance of convenience test'.[248]

(B) INJUNCTION

An injunction is an order from the court directing the defendant to desist from the future commission of any tortious act. It is the remedy most often sought in nuisance cases and is granted on what is often (but inaccurately) described as being a discretionary basis.[249] Thus, even where the claimant can establish an actionable claim, he may nonetheless be refused an injunction. Broadly, there are two factors which influence the courts in deciding whether or not to grant an injunction: the gravity of the interference and the public interest.[250] As regards the first of these, the courts tend to view occasional interferences as insufficiently substantial to warrant the grant of an injunction. Take, for example, *Cooke v Forbes*.[251]

C used a certain bleaching chemical in making cocoa-nut matting. Occasionally, emission of a noxious chemical from D's plant damaged C's manufactures. Without prejudice to a claim in damages, the court refused an injunction because the interference was only occasional.

An example of the role that can be played by the public interest is evident in the judgment of Peter Gibson LJ in *Wheeler v JJ Saunders Ltd*. In that case, the nuisance was caused by the defendant running a pig farm. In relation to the application for an

---

[245] This means, in effect, that D buys the right to commit the nuisance: see Tromans, 'Nuisance – Prevention or Payment?' [1982] CLJ 87 and O'Sullivan, 'A Poor Reception for Television Nuisance' [1996] CLJ 184.

[246] *Wood v Conway Corpn* [1914] 2 Ch 47.   [247] [1991] 1 EGLR 167.

[248] [1995] 2 All ER 189, at 203.

[249] It is in fact misleading to describe it in such expansive terms. First, this is because 'appellate courts have quite readily undertaken the review of final equitable orders notwithstanding that they are called "discretionary" '; and secondly because, in any event, 'a judge exercising discretionary powers is not thereby authorized to act on "caprice", or in a manner that is "arbitrary or unregulated" ': Waddams, *Dimensions of Private Law: Categories and Concepts in Anglo-American Legal Reasoning* (2003) p 180 (footnotes omitted).

[250] For a full account of the principles governing the exercise of this discretion see Buckley, *The Law of Nuisance* (1996) ch 8.

[251] (1867) LR 5 Eq 166. Once C has established that a substantial interference has occurred, and is likely to recur, the burden is on D to adduce evidence of special circumstances why an injunction should not be granted: *McKinnon Industries Ltd v Walker* (1951) 3 DLR 577, at 581, *per* Lord Simonds.

injunction, his Lordship said: 'I can well see that in such a case the public interest must be allowed to prevail and that it would be inappropriate to grant an injunction.'[252]

The fact that the claimant's chief concern is with the future abatement of the nuisance does not mean that he will not also seek damages (as we have seen) in respect of the past harm that he has suffered. In consequence, the law of nuisance is complicated by the fact that the claimant may often seek two remedies at once. Of particular note in this context is the Canadian decision that, where both remedies are granted, any damages must not include an element in respect of permanent depreciation in the claimant's land: it is to be presumed that the injunction will be obeyed and that the value of the land will not further depreciate.[253]

SECTION 8 PUBLIC NUISANCE

(A) NATURE OF PUBLIC NUISANCE

Public nuisance is not susceptible to any precise definition. The term covers a miscellany of acts and omissions which 'endanger the life, health, property, morals or comfort of the public' or, alternatively, 'obstruct the public in the exercise or enjoyment of rights common to all Her Majesty's subjects'.[254] Despite this definitional obscurity, two general observations about the nature of public nuisance can be made. To begin with, it is clear that, at least in principle, a public nuisance is first and foremost a criminal offence at common law.[255] Secondly, it is equally clear that a public nuisance may form the basis of a civil action in three ways: by a relator action for an injunction (brought in the name of the Attorney-General on behalf of a private citizen to suppress the criminal activity of the defendant), by a local authority under section 222 of the Local Government Act 1972, or by an action in tort brought by a private citizen who can show that he has suffered 'special damage' beyond that suffered by the others of Her Majesty's subjects affected by the defendant's interference.

The criminal law aspects of public nuisance are not relevant in a book on torts. The focus here, therefore, is purely upon the civil law actions which may be brought in this context.

---

[252] [1995] 2 All ER 697, at 711. See also the similar view expressed by Buckley J in *Gillingham Borough Council v Medway (Chatham) Docks Co Ltd* [1993] QB 343, at 364. Cf the earlier Court of Appeal decision in *Kennaway v Thompson* [1981] QB 88.

[253] *Macievich v Anderson* [1952] 4 DLR 507 (Manitoba Court of Appeal).

[254] *Archbold's Criminal Practice* (1985) paras 27–44.

[255] Most established public nuisances are now prohibited by statutes such as the various Public Health Acts, the Food Act 1984 and the Highways Act 1980. See further Spencer, 'Public Nuisance – A Critical Examination' [1989] CLJ 55, 76–80.

(1) THE RELATOR ACTION

If the defendant is responsible for a nuisance that affects a large number of citizens but fails to occasion any of them special damage, then an individual citizen may seek to persuade the Attorney-General to suppress the defendant's activity on his behalf by way of a relator action for an injunction. To do so, the elements of the crime of public nuisance must be established. In practice, this method of obtaining injunctive relief is very seldom used. This is in large part explained by the fact that the Attorney-General is unlikely to entertain an application for a relator action where the victim has not experienced special harm; and where special harm has been suffered, the victim is entitled to bring a civil action in his own name.

(2) LOCAL AUTHORITY APPLICATIONS

Under section 222 of the Local Government Act 1972 a local authority is empowered to bring proceedings in its own name for injunctive relief where it considers it 'expedient to do so for the promotion and protection of the interests of the inhabitants'. This provision extends to injunctive relief to prevent a public nuisance. Thus, in *Nottingham City Council v Zain (a minor)*,[256] it was held that an injunction could be sought to exclude a known drug-dealer from one of the city council's housing estates.

(3) CIVIL ACTIONS FOR 'SPECIAL DAMAGE'

There are two situations in which a private citizen may mount a civil action for public nuisance. The first arises where the defendant is responsible for an interference which bears the characteristics of a private nuisance *except* that it affects a much greater number of people.[257] And here, just as in private nuisance, it is not a prerequisite that the act itself be unlawful: the nuisance derives from the detrimental effect of the act complained of. The second concerns cases where the interference would not bear the key characteristics of a private nuisance in that it does not affect the claimant's land, or his use or enjoyment of that land. Instead, the nuisance in such cases amounts to an inconvenience occasioned to the public generally, but causes special damage to the claimant (that is, damage beyond that suffered by other members of the public). Such nuisances typically involve obstructing, or creating a danger on, the highway.

Crucial to both kinds of public nuisance is the requirement that the claimant must suffer, or be at risk of, 'special damage'. Special damage – sometimes referred to as 'particular damage' – is a term almost as obscure in its meaning as public nuisance

---

[256] [2002] 1 WLR 607.

[257] The required number of people will vary from case to case; but it is at least clear that if it affects a public right – such as a public navigation right – it is immaterial if the number of persons suffering is quite small: *Jan de Nul (UK) Ltd v NV Royal Belge* [2000] 2 Lloyd's Rep 700, affd [2002] 1 Lloyd's Rep 583. Examples of such nuisances include driving heavy lorries through residential streets: *Gillingham Borough Council v Medway (Chatham) Dock Co Ltd* [1993] QB 343; blasting from a quarry causing vibrations, dust and noise: *A-G (on the relation of Glamorgan County Council and Pontardawe RDC) v PYA Quarries Ltd* [1957] 2 QB 169; holding 'acid-house parties': *R v Shorrock* [1994] QB 279.

itself.[258] Nonetheless, what is at least clear is that special damage must not be confused with 'special damages', which latter term is used in personal injury actions in negligence to describe pecuniary losses incurred up to the date of the trial which must be specifically pleaded and proved.

While it is difficult to supply a precise definition of special damage, it is possible to advert to a number of established categories of such loss. Pecuniary loss stemming from loss of business or custom, where the injury was of a 'substantial character, not fleeting or evanescent' has long been recognized as such a category.[259] But where other members of the public have also suffered economic loss, it is more difficult for the claimant to establish special damage, for he is able only to show the same kind of damage as that suffered by the others.[260] The claimant's problem in such a case is that the difference between his loss and that suffered by other citizens is merely one of degree and not one of kind. Since the claimant's loss, albeit greater in degree than that suffered by the generality of the public, is of the same kind, his action for public nuisance will fail.[261] In addition to pecuniary loss, personal injury[262] and property damage[263] have also been held to constitute special damage. So, too, have causing inconvenience or delay, provided that the harm thereby caused to the claimant is substantial and appreciably greater in degree than any suffered by the general public.[264] Thus, in one case, a claimant could recover in public nuisance both for damage to his vehicle on the highway and for interference with peaceful sleep in his adjoining house.[265]

The majority of public nuisance cases arise where the defendant either creates a danger on, or obstructs,[266] the highway.[267] As far as rendering the highway unsafe is concerned, there is a long line of cases that establishes liability in public nuisance in respect of walls,[268] fences,[269] windows[270] etc. that fall onto the highway from adjoining

---

[258] See Kodilinye, 'Public Nuisance and Particular Damage in the Modern Law' [1986] *Legal Studies* 182. See also Scholl J's earlier review of the authorities in *Walsh v Ervin* [1952] VLR 361; *Jan de Nul (UK) Ltd v Axa Royale Belge SA (formerly NV Royale Belge)* [2002] 1 Lloyd's Rep 583; *Harper v G N Haden & Sons* [1933] Ch 298; *Benjamin v Storr* (1874) LR 9 CP 400; *Wilkes v Hungerford Market Co* (1835) 2 Bing NC 281 and *Ricket v Directors etc of the Metropolitan Rly Co* (1867) LR 2 HL 175.

[259] *Benjamin v Storr* (1874) LR 9 CP 400, at 407, *per* Brett J (C's coffee shop lost custom when D parked horse-drawn vans outside his premises); *Lyons, Sons & Co v Gulliver* [1914] 1 Ch 631; *Blundy Clark & Co Ltd v London and North Eastern Rly Co* [1931] 2 KB 334. See also *Caledonian Rly Co v Walker's Trustees* (1882) 7 App Cas 259 (depreciation in the value of land) and *Tate and Lyle Industries Ltd v Greater London Council* [1983] 2 AC 509 (cost of dredging silted-up river in order to continue use of a ferry). In relation to economic loss, a curious anomaly exists where the loss is caused by negligence on the part of D. Take, eg, a defendant whose lorry breaks down and blocks the highway because he has failed properly to maintain it. If the action is framed in public nuisance it is likely to succeed, but if it is framed in negligence, it will almost certainly fail for want of sufficient proximity to establish a duty of care. For criticism of this anomaly, see the comments of Ambrose J in *Ball v Consolidated Rutile* [1991] Qd 524, at 546.   [260] *Martin v LCC* (1899) 80 LT 866.

[261] *Ricket v Directors etc of the Metropolitan Rly Co* (1867) LR 2 HL 175, at 190 and 199, *per* Lords Chelmsford and Cranworth, respectively.   [262] *Castle v St Augustine's Links Ltd* (1922) 38 TLR 615.

[263] *Halsey v Esso Petroleum Co Ltd* [1961] 2 All ER 145.

[264] *Walsh v Ervin* [1952] VLR 361; *Boyd v Great Northern Rly Co* [1895] 2 IR 555.

[265] *Halsey v Esso Petroleum Co Ltd* [1961] 2 All ER 145. But was Veale J correct in holding that C should recover even though he was unlawfully using the road to park his car when it was damaged?

[266] Whether there is an obstruction is a question of fact: *Harper v G N Haden & Sons* [1933] Ch 298.

[267] The same principles apply to navigable waterways: *Tate & Lyle Industries Ltd v Greater London Council* [1983] 2 AC 509; *Rose v Miles* (1815) 4 M & S 101.   [268] *Mint v Good* [1951] 1 KB 517.

[269] *Harrold v Watney* [1898] 2 QB 320.   [270] *Leanse v Lord Egerton* [1943] KB 323.

premises. But other examples include leaving dangerous articles such as defective cellar flaps or unlighted scaffolding there,[271] or conducting operations off the highway which menace the safety of those upon it.[272]

Cases involving a creation of danger on the highway help illustrate the rigid categorization of the law of torts. If someone falls over a projection on the forecourt (not forming part of the public footpath) leading to a shop, then his rights are merely those owed as an occupier to visitors to premises – he has no action in public nuisance.[273] Should this happen on the footpath, however, it becomes a case of public nuisance. Equally, if one deviates only slightly from the footpath in order to pass an obstruction, and is injured while thus off the highway, this might be within the area of public nuisance.[274]

As regards obstructing the highway, it is well established that temporary and reasonable obstructions of the highway will not attract liability. Consider *Trevett v Lee*.[275]

Ds, who had no mains connection, laid a hosepipe across the highway in a time of drought in order to obtain a water supply from the other side of the road. C, who tripped over it and suffered injury, failed in an action for public nuisance since Ds' user of the highway was reasonable 'judged both from their own point of view and from the point of view of the other members of the public'.[276]

Although an obstruction of the highway is only partial, it may nonetheless give rise to liability in public nuisance. As Lord Evershed MR explained in *Trevett v Lee*: '[a]n obstruction is something which permanently or temporarily removes the whole *or part of the highway* from public use'.[277] Accordingly, where a vehicle is parked in such a way as to narrow significantly the width of the road, its owner may be held liable in public nuisance.[278] The obstruction need not, of course, be caused by vehicles. A crowd – such as men picketing an employer's premises – may just as easily obstruct the highway and form the basis of an action in public nuisance.[279] But where a demonstration or picket takes place peacefully, the obstruction will *prima facie* be considered a reasonable (and thus non-actionable) use of the highway.[280]

---

[271] *Penny v Wimbledon UDC and Iles* [1899] 2 QB 72.

[272] *Castle v St Augustine's Links* (1922) 38 TLR 615 (C lost an eye when a golf ball smashed the window of his car). Cf *Stone v Bolton* [1950] 1 KB 201 (a cricket ball escaping the cricket ground was not a public nuisance as it was an isolated event).

[273] *Jacobs v LCC* [1950] AC 361; *Bromley v Mercer* [1922] 2 KB 126 (an unsafe wall adjoining a highway which amounted to a public nuisance, collapsed, not onto the highway, but onto a child playing on private land – the child was held to have no cause of action derived from public nuisance); *Creed v John McGeoch & Sons Ltd* [1955] 3 All ER 123 (road merely under construction, neither dedicated nor taken over by local authority; therefore not highway nuisance).   [274] *Barnes v Ward* (1850) 9 CB 392; *Barker v Herbert* [1911] 2 KB 633.

[275] [1955] 1 All ER 406 (applying the *dictum* of Romer LJ in *Harper v G N Haden & Sons* [1933] Ch 298, at 320). Whether it is a defence to say that the obstruction is reasonable because it is for the public benefit is unsettled. In *R v Russell* (1827) 6 B & C 566 it was held to be a defence, but the decision in this case was later doubted in *R v Ward* (1836) 4 Ad & El 384.   [276] [1955] 1 All ER 406, at 412, *per* Lord Evershed MR.

[277] [1955] 1 All ER 406, at 409 (emphasis added).

[278] *A-G v Gastonia Coaches Ltd* [1977] RTR 219; *Dymond v Pearce* [1972] 1 QB 496.

[279] *News Group Newspapers Ltd v SOGAT '82 (No 2)* [1987] ICR 181.   [280] *DPP v Jones* [1999] 2 AC 240.

(B) THE RELATIONSHIP BETWEEN PUBLIC NUISANCE AND PRIVATE NUISANCE

Though many of the decided cases on public nuisance – especially those involving obstructions to, and dangers on, the highway – are clearly incapable of founding an action in private nuisance, there are nonetheless, in certain respects, several important points of connection between the two torts. First, where an interference is of a kind capable of constituting a private nuisance – such as a disturbance caused by vibrations or noise – and it affects a sufficiently large class of Her Majesty's subjects, the action becomes curiously metamorphosed from being one in private nuisance, to one in public nuisance. The difference, as Denning LJ explained in *A-G (on the relation of Glamorgan County Council and Pontardawe RDC) v PYA Quarries Ltd*, lies in the fact that:

a public nuisance is a nuisance which is so widespread in its range or so indiscriminate in its effect that it would not be reasonable to expect one person to take proceedings on his own responsibility to put a stop to it, but that it should be taken on the responsibility of the community at large.[281]

Unfortunately, *dicta* in the case were unhelpful in identifying what amounts to a sufficiently large class of Her Majesty's subjects: it was merely stated that it was a question of fact whether the number of persons affected was sufficiently large.[282] This class need not, however, be very large as much depends on the nature of the public right interfered with. If there is only a relatively small section of the public that take advantage of such a right, the class affected need only be correspondingly small.[283]

A second connection between private and public nuisance occurs where the invasion of the claimant's interest arises from the defendant adopting or continuing a nuisance that was begun by a third party: the rules on who is deemed to be responsible for such an interference are the same.[284] Thirdly, as we have seen, the courts will consider the reasonableness of the defendant's conduct in determining whether an action for public nuisance may lie. Thus, whether one who has collided with a vehicle left standing without lights at night and obstructing a highway can sue will depend in part on whether the vehicle has been there for a long time, and whether there was a good excuse for its being there.[285]

Despite these affinities,[286] public and private nuisance are quite separate torts. The former is concerned with the protection of those who have a proprietary interest in the

---

[281] [1957] 2 QB 169, at 190–191.   [282] [1957] 2 QB 169, at 184, *per* Romer LJ.

[283] *Jan de Nul (UK) Ltd v NV Royal Belge* [2000] 2 Lloyd's Rep 700; affd [2002] 1 Lloyd's Rep 583.

[284] *Sedleigh-Denfield v O'Callaghan* [1940] AC 880, at 893 and 899, *per* Lord Atkin (and see also at 907, *per* Lord Wright). Similarly, constructive (as opposed to actual) knowledge is sufficient to secure a criminal conviction for public nuisance: *R v Shorrock* [1994] QB 279 (applying *Sedleigh-Denfield* to convict a landowner who, before he went away for the weekend, let his field to three people to hold a 15-hour 'acid-house party').

[285] *Trevett v Lee* [1955] 1 All ER 406; *Ware v Garston Haulage Co Ltd* [1944] 1 KB 30; *Maitland v Raisbeck and R T and J Hewitt Ltd* [1944] KB 689. Similarly, in *Stone v Bolton* [1950] 1 KB 201, the isolated escape of a cricket ball was not sufficient to amount to a public nuisance.

[286] Interestingly, the Privy Council drew no distinction between public and private nuisance in *The Wagon Mound (No 2)* [1967] 1 AC 617.

land affected while the latter only exists where an inconvenience is caused to the public generally. Equally, the distinction between the two torts is marked by the unavailability of the defence of prescription in public nuisance,[287] and by the fact that victims of private nuisances able to demonstrate a substantial interference need not prove more loss than their fellows. Finally, though it is well established that pure economic loss is recoverable in public nuisance, there is, to date, no authoritative statement on its recoverability in private nuisance.[288]

One particular case in which it is necessary to distinguish private and public nuisance concerns interferences with access to a highway or waterway. If the case is framed in terms of the landowner's inability to access the highway, the relevant tort will be private nuisance. Where, however, the action is framed in terms of the loss of custom – because access to the claimant's premises has been obstructed – the action will lie in public nuisance. The distinction is important because, in the former case, the private nuisance preventing the claimant's access is treated as analogous to trespass and is actionable *per se*.[289]

(c) REMEDIES IN PUBLIC NUISANCE

(1) INJUNCTION

As we have already seen, where the victim of a public nuisance cannot establish special damage, a relator action for an injunction may be brought by the Attorney-General on his behalf. Alternatively, as we have also seen, an injunction may be sought by a local authority under section 222 of the Local Government Act 1972 to secure 'the promotion and protection of the interests of the inhabitants'. Finally, individual applicants relying on their special damage are similarly able to obtain injunctions in public nuisance.[290]

(2) DAMAGES

Most commonly, a claim in public nuisance will be for damages in respect of personal injuries or pecuniary losses sustained by people using a public highway.[291] In addition,

---

[287] *Mott v Shoolbred* (1875) LR 20 Eq 22.

[288] But in relation to pure economic loss there are only *obiter* statements to the effect that such loss *may* be recovered in private nuisance: see *British Celanese Ltd v A H Hunt (Capacitors) Ltd* [1969] 2 All ER 1252; *Ryeford Homes Ltd v Sevenoaks District Council* [1989] 2 EGLR 281. See also *Dunton v Dover District Council* (1977) 76 LGR 87 where Griffiths J opined that consequential economic loss contingent upon an extant nuisance action would be recoverable (hotel bookings were lost because of the nuisance that had caused the proprietor to move out of the hotel).

[289] *Nicholls v Ely Beet Sugar Factory Ltd* [1936] Ch 343 (exclusive fishery rights alleged, but not proven, to be interfered with by C depositing refuse in the river in which those fishery rights existed).

[290] *Spencer v London and Birmingham Rly Co* (1836) 8 Sim 193.

[291] Note, however, that the creation of a mere hazard on the highway will suffice: *Wandsworth LBC v Railtrack plc* [2002] QB 756 (excessive pigeon droppings held to be a hazard to pedestrians).

however, occupiers of premises adjoining the highway may also recover in public nuisance when they suffer special damage as a result of a nuisance on a highway. And this is the case even though the damage complained of is not suffered by them *qua* users of the highway. For example, shopkeepers have succeeded in this tort where access to their premises has been interfered with,[292] or where their customers have been subjected to noxious smells and darkened rooms as a result of the parking of horses and carts outside their premises.[293]

It is clear from the decision of the Privy Council in *The Wagon Mound (No 2)*[294] that damages are available subject to the familiar remoteness of damage principle. That is, the claimant will only recover so far as the defendant ought to have foreseen the type of loss suffered by the claimant. In that case, the claimant's ship was damaged in a fire caused by the defendant carelessly allowing oil to overflow from the defendant's ship into the waters of Sydney Harbour. The defendant was held liable in public nuisance, but only because the fire on the claimant's ship was held to be a foreseeable consequence of the defendant's wrongful act. By contrast, in *Savage v Fairclough*,[295] a pig farmer who had relied on the advice of an expert agronomist was held not liable in respect of the ensuing pollution of the claimant's water since such pollution had not in fact been foreseen, nor had it been reasonably foreseeable.

Two further limitations exist with respect to the quantum of damages. First, as decided in *Gibbons v South West Water Services Ltd* – a case in which the public water supply in Cornwall was seriously polluted – that no matter how reprehensible the public nuisance, exemplary damages will never be available. An important element in the court's decision was the following question (which it was unable to answer):

[I]n the case of a public nuisance affecting hundreds or even thousands of [claimants] how can the court assess the sum of exemplary damages to be awarded to any one of them to punish or deter the defendant without knowing at the outset the number of successful [claimants] and the approximate size of the total bill for exemplary damages?[296]

Finally, an award of damages can be reduced or excluded altogether by operation of the defences of contributory negligence or *volenti non fit injuria* respectively.[297]

FURTHER READING

Cross, 'Does Only the Careless Polluter Pay? A Fresh Examination of the Nature of Private Nuisance' (1995) 111 LQR 445

Gearty, 'The Place of Nuisance in the Modern Law of Torts' [1989] CLJ 214

---

[292] *Fritz v Hobson* (1880) 14 Ch D 542.   [293] *Benjamin v Storr* (1874) LR 9 CP 400.

[294] [1967] 1 AC 617.   [295] [2000] Env LR 183.

[296] [1993] QB 507, at 531, *per* Sir Thomas Bingham MR. See also Law Commission, *Exemplary, Aggravated and Restitutionary Damages* (1997).

[297] *Dymond v Pearce* [1972] 1 QB 496 (motorcyclist collided with a lighted lorry parked on a straight, wide section of highway but he was held to be the sole author of his injuries).

Kodilinye, 'Public Nuisance and Particular Damage in the Modern Law' [1986] *Legal Studies* 182

Lee, 'What is Private Nuisance?' (2003) 119 LQR 298

Murphy, 'Noxious Emissions and Common Law Liability – Tort in the Shadow of Regulation' in Lowry and Edmunds (eds), *Environmental Protection and the Common Law* (1999)

Ogus and Richardson, 'Economics and the Environment: A Study in Private Nuisance' [1977] CLJ 284

O'Sullivan, 'A Poor Reception for Television Nuisance' [1996] CLJ 184

Spencer, 'Public Nuisance – A Critical Examination' [1989] CLJ 55

Steele, 'Private Law and the Environment: Nuisance in Context' (1995) 15 *Legal Studies* 236

Tromans, 'Nuisance – Prevention or Payment?' [1982] CLJ 87

18

THE RULE IN *RYLANDS V FLETCHER*

SECTION 1 INTRODUCTION

The rule in *Rylands v Fletcher*[1] is probably the best known example of a strict liability tort in English law and it derives from the nineteenth-century case of that name.

Ds employed independent contractors to build a reservoir on his land. Through the negligence of the independent contractors, disused shafts upon the site which communicated with C's mine beneath the reservoir were not blocked up. On the filling of the reservoir, the water escaped down the shafts and flooded C's mine.

Although the defendants were neither themselves negligent nor vicariously liable for the negligence of their independent contractors,[2] they were nonetheless held liable both by the Court of Exchequer Chamber and the House of Lords. Blackburn J, delivering the judgment of the Court of Exchequer Chamber, said:[3]

We think that the true rule of law is that the person who for his own purposes brings on his lands and collects and keeps there anything likely to do mischief if it escapes, must keep it in at his peril, and if he does not do so, is *prima facie* answerable for all the damage which is the natural consequence of its escape.

Lord Cairns in the House of Lords broadly agreed with this judgment, but he restricted the scope of the rule to instances where the defendant had engaged in 'a non-natural use' of the land.[4] Though seemingly innocuous at the time, this addition to Blackburn J's formulation of the rule gave rise to one of the most vexed questions in relation to *Rylands v Fletcher* liability: what is the essence of 'a non-natural use' of land? As we shall see in section 4 of this chapter, there is still no clear answer to this question.

One instructive point, however, is that Blackburn J did not consider himself to be making new law. The following quotation encapsulates his thinking.

The general rule, as above stated, seems on general principle just. The person whose grass or corn is eaten down by the escaping cattle of his neighbour, or whose mine is flooded by the

---

[1] (1866) LR 1 Exch 265; affd (1868) LR 3 HL 330.
[2] For discussion of vicarious liability and liability in relation to independent contractors, see ch 24.
[3] (1866) LR 1 Exch 265, at 279–80.   [4] (1866) LR 1 Exch 265, at 338–40.

water from his neighbour's reservoir, or whose cellar is invaded by the filth of his neighbour's privy, or whose habitation is made unhealthy by the fumes and noisome vapours of his neighbour's alkali works, is damnified without any fault of his own; and it seems but reasonable and just that the neighbour, who has brought something on his own property which was not naturally there, harmless to others so long as it is confined to his own property, but which he knows to be mischievous if it gets on his neighbour's, should be obliged to make good the damage which ensues if he does not succeed in confining it to his own property.[5]

Yet, close though the analogy with nuisance may ostensibly appear,[6] the fact remains that *Rylands v Fletcher* was the starting point for a form of liability which, as developed by the courts in subsequent decisions, was wider and quite different in kind to any that preceded it.[7] Indeed, this extension of liability gave rise to speculation about whether or not some comprehensive theory of strict liability for harm caused to persons by ultra-hazardous things was being formulated. Such a theory, whatever attraction it may once have had, is certainly no longer tenable after the interpretation put upon *Rylands v Fletcher* by the House of Lords in *Read v J Lyons & Co Ltd*.[8] There, the facts were as follows.

The appellant, while working in the respondent's factory, was injured by an explosion there. No allegation of negligence was made by her against the respondents, whom she sued in respect of her injuries. The basis of her claim was that the respondents carried on the manufacture of high-explosive shells, knowing that they were dangerous things.

The ground for the decision of the House of Lords in favour of the respondents was that the rule in *Rylands v Fletcher* does not apply unless there has been an escape from a place where the defendant has occupation or control over land to a place outside his control.[9] But the importance of the case does not end there. The decision in *Read v J Lyons & Co Ltd* constituted a denial of a general theory of strict liability for ultra-hazardous activities: there is only liability for non-negligent escapes where the several preconditions for *Rylands v Fletcher* liability (considered in the following sections) are satisfied. Where these preconditions are not met, the claimant's case can only be formulated in terms of the intentional or negligent conduct of the defendant.

---

[5] (1866) LR 1 Exch 265, at 280.

[6] For an early account of the relationship between liability in nuisance and liability under the rule in *Rylands v Fletcher* see Newark, 'The Boundaries of Nuisance' (1945) 65 LQR 480. See also *Cambridge Water Co Ltd v Eastern Counties Leather plc* [1994] 2 AC 264, at 298, *per* Lord Goff; *Transco v Stockport MBC* [2004] 2 AC 1, at [9], *per* Lord Bingham. For trenchant criticism of these understandings, see Murphy, 'The Merits of *Rylands v Fletcher*' (2004) 24 OJLS 643.

[7] See, eg, Nolan, 'The Distinctiveness of *Rylands v Fletcher*' (2005) 121 LQR 421.

[8] [1945] KB 216; affd, [1947] AC 156. In *Transco v Stockport MBC* [2004] 2 AC 1, there was a good deal of emphasis placed on extraordinary uses of land. Yet such uses do not (despite what some of their Lordships seemed to think in this case) require an ultra-hazardous agent to have been accumulated. It was really only Lord Bingham (at [11]) who took the view that the operation of the rule hinged on an especially dangerous agent. Those agreeing with Lord Bingham also signalled their agreement with Lord Hoffmann's approach to the case, which was markedly different. As such, it is impossible to identify any unequivocal support for Lord Bingham's view.

[9] There are *obiter dicta* to the effect that the escape of a dangerous thing from D's chattel, located on a highway (*Rigby v Chief Constable of Northamptonshire* [1985] 1 WLR 1242, at 1255) or from his vessel, situated on a navigable waterway (*Crown River Cruises Ltd v Kimbolton Fireworks Ltd* [1996] 2 Lloyd's Rep 533) is

Perhaps the most remarkable characteristic of this rule has been its fluidity. Stated in very broad terms by Blackburn J, it was at once modified in the case itself by the House of Lords, who confined it to instances involving a 'non-natural use' of land. But there nonetheless followed its widespread application: *often* cases properly sounding in nuisance alone were brought within the fold of *Rylands v Fletcher* . Then, the rule was given even greater elasticity by the interpretation of 'non-natural use' by the Privy Council in 1913. They considered it to mean 'some special use bringing with it increased danger to others, and [which] must not merely be the ordinary use of the land or such a use as is proper for the general benefit of the community'.[10] Even after 1913, the rule in *Rylands v Fletcher* continued to be invoked freely; and often it was not sufficiently sharply distinguished from nuisance.[11] Then, in 1947, came something of a *volte face* in the shape of *Read v J Lyons & Co Ltd* .[12] There, it was made clear that the earlier decisions of the lower courts which had appeared to extend the original rule must henceforth be closely scrutinized before they could be accepted as good authorities.

SECTION 2 'THINGS' WITHIN THE RULE

Blackburn J spoke of 'anything likely to do mischief if it escapes'. These things must not summarily be described as 'dangerous' and then equated (and, in turn, confused) with those things which have been considered 'dangerous' in the context of negligence. Indeed, it would be wise to eschew the word 'dangerous' altogether since it is an inherently protean concept. A simple example of the need for caution in this context can be supplied by reference to the mischievous 'thing' in *Rylands v Fletcher* itself – namely, water. Water is, of course, not 'dangerous' *per se*. Yet, as Du Parcq LJ observed in the Court of Appeal in *Read v J Lyons & Co Ltd*,[13] what matters is whether the thing is likely to do damage on escaping to other land.[14] Whether or not this involves personal danger is quite irrelevant. Thus, filth and water are both 'things' caught by the rule even though they are not inherently dangerous.

It is equally true that the ultra-hazardous quality of the thing (in the sense that it is intrinsically dangerous) is of no moment. In *Cambridge Water Co Ltd v Eastern*

---

sufficient to give rise to *Rylands* liability. These *dicta* are, however, difficult to sustain both in principle, and in the light of existing authority: see *Jones v Festiniog Rly Co* (1868) LR 3 QB 733; *Powell v Fall* (1880) 5 QBD 597; *West v Bristol Tramways Co* [1908] 2 KB 14. Such actions, it is submitted, should sound in negligence, not *Rylands v Fletcher* – which has always been a land-based tort – unless, as in the three cases cited, D has a statutory right to occupation of the public thoroughfare.

[10] *Rickards v Lothian* [1913] AC 263, at 280, *per* Lord Moulton.

[11] The most authoritative statement of the continuing affinity between the two torts is set out by Lord Goff in *Cambridge Water Co Ltd v Eastern Counties Leather plc* [1994] 2 AC 264, at 298–9. The remaining four Law Lords in that case concurred in his speech.   [12] [1945] KB 216, at 247.

[13] [1945] KB 216, at 247.   [14] Cf *Read v J Lyons & Co* [1947] AC 156, at 176, *per* Lord Porter.

Counties Leather plc[15] – a leading modern *Rylands v Fletcher* authority – it was held by Lord Goff that:

[T]here is much to be said for the view that the courts should not be proceeding down the path of developing such a theory [of liability for ultra-hazardous activities] . . . I incline to the view that, as a general rule, it is more appropriate for strict liability in respect of operations of high risk to be imposed by Parliament, than by the courts.[16]

In *Read v J Lyons & Co Ltd*, counsel argued that the thing must have the 'capacity for independent movement'[17] as well as being a potential cause of harm – so, for example, glass would be outside the rule. Provided that an extension is made to include a thing likely to give off something such as a gas, which itself has capacity for independent movement, this contention has much to commend it, and there is some (albeit limited) support for it in the cases.[18]

Things which have been held to be capable of giving rise to *Rylands v Fletcher* liability include electricity,[19] gas likely to pollute water supplies,[20] explosives,[21] fire and things likely to cause fires[22] (including a motor vehicle whether the tank contains,[23] or is empty of,[24] petrol), things likely to give off noxious gases or fumes,[25] water,[26] sewage,[27] and slag heaps.[28] Cases holding planted yew trees[29] and chair-o-planes[30] to be within the rule are also probably sound so long as there is movement of the mischievous thing beyond the boundary of the land under the defendant's control. Whether a decayed and rusty wire fence[31] and a flag-pole[32] have been rightly regarded as being within the rule is, however, doubtful.

A final, and interesting illustration of the kind of 'things' that may fall within the rule is supplied by the case of *A-G v Corke*.[33] There it was held that the owner of land who

---

[15] [1994] 2 AC 264.

[16] [1994] 1 All ER 53, at 76, *per* Lord Goff. In support of this approach see Stanton, 'The Legacy of *Rylands v Fletcher'* in Mullany and Linden (eds), *Torts Tomorrow: A Tribute to John Fleming* (1998).

[17] [1947] AC 156, at 158.

[18] Eg, *Wilson v Newberry* (1871) LR 7 QB 31, at 33, *per* Mellor J: 'things which have a tendency to escape and to do mischief'. [19] *National Telephone Co v Baker* [1893] 2 Ch 186.

[20] *Batchellor v Tunbridge Wells Gas Co* (1901) 84 LT 765.

[21] *Rainham Chemical Works Ltd v Belvedere Fish Guano Co* [1921] 2 AC 465; and CS gas canisters: *Rigby v Chief Constable of Northamptonshire* [1985] 1 WLR 1242.

[22] *Jones v Festiniog Rly Co* (1868) LR 3 QB 733 (sparks from railway engine); *Balfour v Barty-King* [1956] 2 All ER 555 (blowlamp), affd on other grounds [1957] 1 QB 496. [23] *Musgrove v Pandelis* [1919] 2 KB 43.

[24] *Perry v Kendricks Transport Ltd* [1956] 1 All ER 154.

[25] *West v Bristol Tramways Co* [1908] 2 KB 14; *Halsey v Esso Petroleum Co Ltd* [1961] 2 All ER 145 (acid smuts).

[26] *Rylands v Fletcher* (1868) LR 3 HL 330; *Western Engraving Co v Film Laboratories Ltd* [1936] 1 All ER 106.

[27] *Humphries v Cousins* (1877) 2 CPD 239. [28] *Kennard v Cory Bros & Co Ltd* [1921] AC 521.

[29] *Crowhurst v Amersham Burial Board* (1878) 4 Ex D 5. [30] *Hale v Jennings Bros* [1938] 1 All ER 579.

[31] *Firth v Bowling Iron Co* (1878) 3 CPD 254.

[32] *Shiffman v Grand Priory in British Realm of Venerable Order of the Hospital of St John of Jerusalem* [1936] 1 All ER 557.

[33] [1933] Ch 89. In *Smith v Scott* [1973] Ch 314 undesirable tenants were held to be outside the rule, because a landlord has no 'control' over the tenants.

allowed caravan dwellers to live on that land was answerable under the rule for the interferences which they perpetrated on adjoining land.[34]

The last characteristic of those 'things' whose escape may give rise to liability under the rule is that they must have been brought onto the land by the defendant. This final characteristic applies only to 'things artificially brought or kept upon the defendant's land'.[35]

SECTION 3 PARTIES

(A) WHO MAY BE SUED?

Blackburn J said that the rule applies to a 'person who for his own purposes brings on his lands and collects and keeps there' the thing in question. The thing may or may not be something which in its nature is capable of being naturally there: what matters is whether the particular thing has in fact been accumulated there. If, therefore, water flows from A's underground tunnels into B's mines, whether by force of gravitation or by percolation, A is not liable under the rule in *Rylands v Fletcher* for that escape if the water was naturally on A's land and he did nothing to accumulate it there.[36] On the other hand, there was liability in *Rylands v Fletcher* itself because steps had been taken by the defendants to accumulate the water on their land by constructing the reservoir.[37] The cases where flooding of neighbouring land results from pumping or diverting water from the land of the defendant to that of the claimant may be nuisance, or even perhaps trespass. But they cannot be within *Rylands v Fletcher* if the defendant has not artificially accumulated the water.[38] Similarly, the escape of rocks is outside the rule since there has been no accumulation.[39] If, however, rocks are blasted in quarrying, there may then be liability for accumulating the explosives.[40]

In the case of vegetation, assuming the other elements of the rule to be satisfied, it will be important to consider whether that vegetation was planted there deliberately, for the planting of it will constitute an accumulation.[41] *Giles v Walker*[42] (assuming the case

[34] On similar facts, liability has also been imposed under the principles of private nuisance: see *Lippiatt v South Gloucestershire Council* [1999] 4 All ER 149 (travellers on D's land were using D's land as a base for forays onto C's land).   [35] *Bartlett v Tottenham* [1932] 1 Ch 114, at 131, *per* Lawrence LJ.

[36] *Wilson v Waddell* (1876) 2 App Cas 95.

[37] And in *Broder v Saillard* (1876) 2 Ch D 692, where the water was brought onto the land in connection with the stabling of D's horses.

[38] Eg, *Palmer v Bowman* [2000] 1 All ER 22; *Baird v Williamson* (1863) 15 CBNS 376; *Whalley v Lancashire and Yorkshire Rly Co* (1884) 13 QBD 131. Cf *Hurdman v North Eastern Rly Co* (1878) 3 CPD 168.

[39] *Pontardawe RDC v Moore-Gwyn* [1929] 1 Ch 656.

[40] *Miles v Forest Rock Granite Co (Leicestershire) Ltd* (1918) 34 TLR 500. If it is not the explosives, but the rocks which have escaped, then presumably there needs to be an analogy drawn with those cases in which D accumulates agent X but X gives off a gas which escapes, in which case there can be liability: see, eg, *Wilson v Newberry* (1871) LR 7 QB 31.   [41] *Crowhurst v Amersham Burial Board* (1878) 4 Ex D 5.

[42] (1890) 62 LT 933. Cf *Seligman v Docker* [1949] Ch 53.

was decided on the basis of *Rylands v Fletcher*; and this is not clear), may be a relevant authority in this context.

In order to redeem some of his forest land, D ploughed it up. Thereafter, thistles grew all over the ploughed land. Thistle-down escaped from D's land to C's land, where it seeded itself.

Finding that the thistles were 'the natural growth of the soil', the court held that this was no tort.[43] Yet it seems, from an interjection of Lord Esher MR, during the argument, that the result would have been different had the court found that the defendant had been responsible for the thistles having come onto his land. In other words, had there been a finding of fact that the ploughing up of the land had caused the thistles to come onto, and grow upon the defendant's land when they otherwise would not have done, the requirement of artificial accumulation would have been satisfied.[44]

Problems of responsibility for accumulation were also considered by the House of Lords in *Rainham Chemical Works Ltd v Belvedere Fish Guano Co Ltd*.[45]

A and B contracted with the Ministry of Munitions to manufacture explosives on their land. They formed a limited company, C Ltd, and arranged for C Ltd to perform this contract on the land of A and B. C Ltd were thus the licensees of A and B. Neighbouring land-owners suffered damage to their land caused by an explosion on the land of A and B while C Ltd were using it, and they sued C Ltd as well as A and B.

It was decided that a licensee who himself accumulates something on the land of another is liable for the consequences of that accumulation.[46] Further, the House of Lords held that those who remain in occupation of land are also liable to land-owners injured by the escape of that which their licensee accumulates in discharge of a contractual duty owed by the occupiers to a third party.

Lord Sumner further stated (*obiter*) that if 'they [A and B] . . . simply suffered others to manufacture upon the site which they nevertheless continued to occupy' they would be liable for the consequences of an escape.[47] On the other hand, Eve J in *Whitmores (Edenbridge) Ltd v Stanford*[48] held that a land-owner, upon whose land some other person had a prescriptive right to accumulate water for his own purposes, would not be liable under the rule. The extent to which an occupier is liable in respect of the accumulations of his licensees cannot be regarded as entirely settled, but it is relevant to observe that in *Rylands v Fletcher* Blackburn J spoke only of a person who 'for his own purposes' brings things on his land.[49] Thus, a local authority which is required by

[43] But note the limited liability imposed in nuisance for damage resulting from the naturally occurring dangerous condition of land: *Leakey v National Trust* [1980] QB 485.

[44] (1890) 62 LT 933, at 934. Observations by the Court of Appeal in *Davey v Harrow Corpn* [1958] 1 QB 60 support the view taken in the text.   [45] [1921] 2 AC 465.

[46] Where, however, over 20 years had elapsed since the licensee had had the right to enter and accumulate water there, he was held not to be accountable for the escape of water, if he no longer had control of the land: *Westhoughton Coal and Cannel Co Ltd v Wigan Coal Corpn Ltd* [1939] Ch 800.

[47] [1921] 2 AC 465, at 480.   [48] [1909] 1 Ch 427.

[49] (1866) LR 1 Exch 265, at 279. But see *Humphries v Cousins* (1877) 2 CPD 239 where an occupier who was bound to receive sewage into drains on his land in circumstances where it was presumably not collected for his own purposes was nonetheless held liable for an escape. On the other hand, in *Read v Lyons*, Viscount Simon doubted whether D making munitions in his factory, at the Government's request in wartime brought things

statute to permit the discharge of sewage into its sewers is treated as responsible for the accumulation of that sewage.[50]

A person who authorizes another to commit a tort is normally also himself liable for that tort. Thus, a lessor is liable in nuisance if he lets land for a particular purpose in such circumstances that he is necessarily taken to have authorized the interference which the lessee in consequence causes.[51] There were *obiter dicta* in *Rainham Chemical Works Ltd v Belvedere Fish Guano Co Ltd* to the effect that the same rule applies in *Rylands v Fletcher* cases – in short, that a defendant may be liable although he does not occupy the land, if he has authorized another to accumulate something on it, when the thing so accumulated later escapes.[52]

What happens where the accumulation is not on the land owned or occupied by the defendant? In *Rigby v Chief Constable of Northamptonshire*, Taylor J relying on a passage in the then current edition of *Clerk and Lindsell on Torts* , suggested (*obiter*) that there was, so far as he could see, 'no difference in principle between allowing a man-eating tiger to escape from your land onto that of another and allowing it to escape from the back of your wagon parked on the highway'.[53] It is submitted that this view is wrong. How can the requirements that there be an artificial accumulation on, and a non-natural use of, the defendant's land be satisfied if both the accumulation and escape take place elsewhere? The preferable view, it is submitted, is that such cases should be actionable, if at all, as negligent omissions.[54] The rule in *Rylands v Fletcher* is a well-established land-based tort, yet the focus is on land owned by, or under the control of, the defendant.[55]

(B) WHO MAY SUE?

It is clear that this rule permits a land-owning claimant, as in *Rylands v Fletcher* itself, to sue in respect of damage to land. Similarly, in relation to damage to chattels, Blackburn

---

onto his land 'for his own purposes': [1947] AC 156, at 170. Gas, water and electricity boards, and inland waterways authorities carrying out statutory duties, do not accumulate for their own purposes. Accordingly, *Rylands v Fletcher* does not apply: *Dunne v North Western Gas Board* [1964] 2 QB 806; *Boxes Ltd v British Waterways Board* [1971] 2 Lloyd's Rep 183.

[50] *Smeaton v Ilford Corpn* [1954] Ch 450.   [51] See ch 17.

[52] [1921] 2 AC 465, at 476 and 489, *per* Lords Buckmaster and Parmoor, respectively. Cf *A-G v Cory Bros & Co* (1918) 34 TLR 621, but not considered, at [1921] 1 AC 521. Cf the *obiter dicta* of Scrutton and Greer LJJ in *St Anne's Well Brewery Co v Roberts* (1928) 140 LT 1, at 5 and 7.

[53] [1985] 1 WLR 1242, at 1255. There is a further *obiter dictum* to similar effect in *Crown River Cruises Ltd v Kimbolton Fireworks Ltd* [1996] 2 Lloyd's Rep 533, *per* Potter J.

[54] Negligent omissions, however, are only infrequently actionable: see Markesinis, 'Negligence, Nuisance and Affirmative Duties of Action' (1989) 105 LQR 104. On the other hand, creating an obvious source of danger, that is liable to be 'sparked off' by a third party may give rise to negligence liability: *Haynes v Harwood* [1935] 1 KB 146; *Smith v Littlewoods Organisation Ltd* [1987] AC 241, at 272, *per* Lord Goff (*obiter*); *Topp v London Country Bus (South West) Ltd* [1993] 1 WLR 976 (noted in Murphy, 'An Accident Waiting to Happen?' [1994] *Tort Law Review* 77).

[55] See Murphy, 'The Merits of *Rylands v Fletcher*' (2004) 24 OJLS 643. Cf *Read v Lyons* [1947] AC 156, at 173, *per* Lord Macmillan.

J later allowed a claim where sparks from a railway engine set fire to a haystack;[56] and several other cases support the proposition that liability for damage to chattels is recoverable.[57] But what of those who suffer no such property damage, but merely personal injuries? Arguably, the question needs to be addressed in two stages.[58]

First, where the claimant is an occupier of land, *Hale v Jennings Bros* is a binding Court of Appeal authority enabling occupiers to recover in respect of personal injuries.[59]

A tenant of a stall at a fair suffered personal injuries as the result of an escape of D's chair-o-plane. She was held to have a good cause of action based on the rule in *Rylands v Fletcher*.

But, secondly, what of the claimant who suffers personal injury but has no such proprietary interest? Here, the law is less clear; both in relation to the general question of whether such persons have a right to sue at all,[60] and in relation to the narrower question of whether they may sue in respect of personal injuries. In both *Perry v Kendricks Transport Ltd*[61] and *British Celanese Ltd v AH Hunt (Capacitors) Ltd*[62] it was suggested, *obiter*, that even those with no proprietary interests are able to bring an action for personal injuries on the basis of the rule in *Rylands v Fletcher*. Certainly, there was nothing in Blackburn J's judgment in *Rylands* to prohibit such a possibility. Indeed, to the contrary, his Lordship envisaged liability in respect of '*all the damage* which is the natural consequence of the escape'.[63] On this basis, it might by argued that a proprietary interest in land is not (and never has been) a prerequisite to recovery under this tort.[64] On the other hand, the House of Lords have twice stressed (wrongly, it is submitted) the fact that the rule in *Rylands v Fletcher* derives from, and is a sub-species of, private nuisance.[65] As such, on the present standing of English law, the rule in *Rylands*

---

[56] *Jones v Festiniog Rly Co* (1868) LR 3 QB 733. Cf *Cattle v Stockton Waterworks Co* (1875) LR 10 QB 453, at 457, *per* Blackburn J.

[57] Eg, *Midwood & Co Ltd v Manchester Corpn* [1905] 2 KB 597; *Musgrove v Pandelis* [1919] 2 KB 43; *Collingwood v Home and Colonial Stores Ltd* [1936] 3 All ER 200. Cf *Read v J Lyons & Co* [1947] AC 156, at 169, *per* Viscount Simon and *Transco v Stockport MBC* [2004] 2 AC 1 (*obiter*).

[58] The most recent pronouncement on the question exists in the speeches of Lords Bingham and Hoffmann in the *Transco* case. They both stated, *obiter*, that the rule does not permit claims for personal injuries or death. But as the following discussion reveals, this approach is highly suspect.

[59] [1938] 1 All ER 579. No doubt, in the wake of the modern tendency to assimilate *Rylands* and nuisance liability, such a case would no longer be explained along the lines proffered in *Hunter v Canary Wharf* [1997] 2 All ER 426: namely, that a land-owner who suffers personal injuries is entitled to point to those personal injuries as an indication of loss of amenity value in his land rather than as a recoverable head of loss *per se*. See further ch 17.

[60] See *McKenna v British Aluminium Ltd* [2002] Env LR 30, at [20]-[28], where Neuberger J questioned, in the context of a striking out action, (a) whether the increasingly close relationship between nuisance and the rule in *Rylands v Fletcher* meant that the proprietary entitlement rule in nuisance applied also to *Rylands v Fletcher* and (b), assuming it did, whether it was a sustainable rule in the wake of the passage of the Human Rights Act 1998. [61] [1956] 1 All ER 154.

[62] [1969] 2 All ER 1252. [63] (1866) LR 1 Exch 265, at 279.

[64] See Murphy, 'The Merits of *Rylands v Fletcher*' (2004) 24 OJLS 643. Cf *Hunter v Canary Wharf Ltd* [1997] 2 All ER 426.

[65] First, in *Cambridge Water Co Ltd v Eastern Counties Leather plc* [1994] 2 AC 264 and, secondly, in *Transco v Stockport MBC* [2004] 2 AC 1, at [9], [52] and [92], *per* Lords Bingham, Hobhouse and Walker, respectively.

v Fletcher, like the law of private nuisance, would seem to be available only those who possess a proprietary interest in the land affected by the escape.[66]

Recognizing the uncertainty surrounding this issue, and recognizing, too, that he was likely to fuel further academic debate on the matter, Ward LJ, in *Ribee v Norrie*,[67] steadfastly refused to draw any firm conclusion on the recoverability of personal injuries under the rule in *Rylands v Fletcher*. He contented himself by deciding the case before him on the basis of negligence. More recently, however, three members of the House of Lords have since re-asserted, but only *obiter*, the proposition that the rule in *Rylands v Fletcher* only protects interests in land.[68] The truth, then, is that the recovery of personal injuries under the rule is technically an open question.

In the absence of clear authority, it is submitted that the view that anyone suffering personal injury may recover is to be preferred since the similarities between nuisance and *Rylands v Fletcher* are, as we shall see later in this chapter, apt to be overstated. Even so, it should be pointed out that several of their Lordships in *Read v J Lyons & Co Ltd* specifically expressed the view (albeit *obiter*) that personal injuries were irrecoverable under the rule.[69] To some extent, however, the distinction between personal injuries and property damage is not always easy to sustain since, in the case of personal injury to the occupier or holder of a proprietary interest, injury to the person might be seen to merge into a general injury to the proprietary interest as a whole by way of a diminution in the amenity value of the land.[70]

A final question in this context is whether the claimant who suffers pure economic loss is able to claim for his losses under the rule in *Rylands v Fletcher*. Here, too, the law is somewhat uncertain. It was held in *Weller & Co v Foot and Mouth Disease Research Institute*[71] that the escape of a virus was not actionable by the claimant, a cattle auctioneer, when it caused a loss of profit to his business after making a third party's cattle unsaleable. But in the case of *Ryeford Homes v Sevenoaks District Council*,[72] the possibility of recovery for pure economic loss was again mooted, as a preliminary issue,

---

[66] See *Hunter v Canary Wharf Ltd* [1997] AC 655 (on nuisance) and *Transco v Stockport MBC* [2004] 2 AC 1, at [11], [47] and [68], *per* Lords Bingham, Hoffmann and Hobhouse respectively (on the rule in *Rylands v Fletcher*). In both cases, however, this approach is difficult to reconcile with Art 8 of the European Convention on Human Rights, which affords all citizens an equal right to respect for their private lives. This point was recognized in *McKenna v British Aluminium Ltd* [2002] Env LR 30, *per* Neuberger J. In addition, a further weakness in this approach is that it conflates nuisance law with the rule in *Rylands v Fletcher* without any heed to the historical fact that, in nuisance, the emphasis is placed on C having a proprietary interest, whereas under the rule in *Rylands v Fletcher* the emphasis rests upon D's property (or, at least, property under D's control): it is on *D's land* that an accumulation must occur, and from *D's land* that there must be an escape. See further, Murphy, 'The Merits of *Rylands v Fletcher*' (2004) 24 OJLS 643.   [67] [2001] PIQR P8, at [30].

[68] *Transco v Stockport MBC* [2004] 2 AC 1, at [9], [35] and [52], *per* Lords Bingham, Hoffmann and Hobhouse respectively. The first two named even stated in explicit terms their view that claims for personal injury and death were excluded under the rule.

[69] [1947] AC 156, at 173, 178 and 180–1, *per* Lords Macmillan, Porter and Simonds, respectively.

[70] See the analysis of *Hunter v Canary Wharf* in ch 17.

[71] [1966] 1 QB 569. See also, in similar vein, *Cattle v Stockton Waterworks Co* (1875) LR 10 QB 453 (escape of water which made it more expensive for C to carry out his contract to construct a tunnel; not actionable).

[72] [1989] 2 EGLR 281.

and not ruled out. There, Judge Newey QC expressed the view that pure economic loss was, *in principle*, recoverable under the rule in *Rylands v Fletcher* so long as it was 'a sufficiently direct result of an escape of water from sewers'.[73] This view is thought to be correct, and it is entirely consistent both with Blackburn J's judgment in *Rylands v Fletcher* and the decision in the *Weller* case.[74]

SECTION 4 THE NON-NATURAL USE OF LAND

Blackburn J said that the rule applied only to a thing 'which was not naturally there'.[75] In the House of Lords, Lord Cairns used more ambiguous words[76] which have since been construed as meaning that the defendant is only answerable if, in bringing the thing onto his land,[77] he is making 'a non-natural use' of the land. The expression 'non-natural use' is very flexible and the courts are afforded a great deal of latitude in construing whether the defendant has engaged in a 'non-natural use'. The form in which Lord Moulton, on behalf of the Privy Council, expressed this rule in *Rickards v Lothian* emphasized this flexibility.[78] He said: '[i]t must be some special use bringing with it increased danger to others, and must not merely be the ordinary use of the land or such a use as is proper for the general benefit of the community'.[79] Viscount Simon in *Read v J Lyons & Co Ltd* thought this statement to be 'of the first importance'[80] and Lord Porter said:

each seems to be a question of fact subject to a ruling of the judge as to whether . . . the particular use can be non-natural, and in deciding this question I think that all the circumstances of the time and place and practice of mankind must be taken into consideration so that what might be regarded as . . . non-natural may vary according to those circumstances. [81]

The current tendency is to interpret 'non-natural use' narrowly, and many earlier cases may no longer be followed. For instance, in *Read v J Lyons & Co Ltd*, despite the contrary previous decision of the House of Lords in *Rainham Chemical Works Ltd*

---

[73] On the facts, however, D was able to invoke the defence of statutory authority (see Section 7, below). For a contrary, *obiter*, suggestion: see the unconvincing, and slightly muddled, account provided at first instance in *Anglian Water Services Ltd v Crawshaw Robbins & Co Ltd* 2002 WL 31523191, at [149], *per* Stanley Burnton J.

[74] The fact that the auctioneer's loss in *Weller* was contingent upon the cattle owners' loss rendered the loss of profit from the would-be auctions an *indirect*, and hence (it was held) irrecoverable, economic loss.

[75] Viscount Simon in *Read v Lyons* [1947] AC 156, at 166, described this as 'a parenthetic reference to' the test of Lord Cairns.

[76] (1868) LR 3 HL 330, at 337–40. See Williams, 'Non-natural Use of Land' [1973] CLJ 310.

[77] What matters is whether the accumulation (as distinct from the escape) is a non-natural use: *Read v Lyons* [1947] AC 156, at 186, *per* Lord Uthwatt.   [78] [1913] AC 263, at 280.

[79] [1913] AC 263, at 280. It has since been qualified that this means the 'national community as a whole': *Ellison v Ministry of Defence* (1996) 81 BLR 101, at 119, *per* Judge Bowsher QC.

[80] [1947] AC 156, at 169.   [81] [1947] AC 156, at 176.

v Belvedere Fish Guano Co,[82] it was doubted whether building and running a munitions factory on land in wartime was a non-natural use.[83] Similarly, despite the words of Lord Moulton in *Rickards v Lothian* concerning uses that bring a 'general benefit to the community', Lord Goff emphatically denied the fact that the generation of employment for a local community was sufficient to transform the storage of chemicals used in the tanning industry into a natural use of the land. He said:

I myself, however, do not feel able to accept that the creation of employment as such, even in a small industrial complex, is sufficient of itself to establish a particular use as constituting a natural or ordinary use of land.[84]

Beyond this, his Lordship offered little to clarify the meaning of the term 'non-natural use'. Instead of taking the opportunity to do so in *Cambridge Water*, he declined to say more than that he did not consider it necessary to redefine the phrase in that context since 'the storage of chemicals on industrial premises should be regarded as *an almost classic case* of non-natural use'.[85] It thus fell to the House of Lords in the subsequent case of *Transco v Stockport MBC* to clarify this troublesome phrase. There – in holding that the supply of pressurised water to 66 flats constituted a natural use of land so that there could be no liability for the effects of a burst pipe – Lord Bingham offered the following thoughts.

I think it is clear that ordinary user is a preferable test to natural user, making it clear that the rule in *Rylands v Fletcher* is engaged only where the defendant's use is shown to be extraordinary and unusual. This is not a test to be inflexibly applied: a use may be extraordinary and unusual at one time or in one place but not so at another time or in another place . . . [T]he question is whether the defendant has done something out of the ordinary in the place and at the time when he does it. In answering that question, I respectfully think that little help is gained (and unnecessary confusion perhaps caused) by considering whether the use is proper for the general benefit of the community.[86]

By contrast, in the very same case, Lord Hoffmann was of the view that a test based on ordinary user was rather vague and preferred a test based on increased risk.[87] And confusingly, various other members of the House of Lords agreed with both analyses of the problem without indicating a preference for either one. As such, despite the effort to clear up the meaning of this troublesome phrase, a crepuscular haze continues to overhang its definition. On the other hand, however, the following instances can confidently be stated to be natural uses of land: water-pipe installations in buildings;[88] growing trees, even though planted by the defendant, so long as they are not poisonous;[89] working mines and minerals on land;[90] building or pulling down walls;[91] lighting a fire

---

[82] [1921] 2 AC 465.   [83] [1947] AC 156, at 169–70 and 173, *per* Viscount Simon and Lord Macmillan.
[84] [1994] 1 All ER 53, at 79.   [85] [1994] 1 All ER 53, at 79 (emphasis added).
[86] [2004] 2 AC 1, at [11].   [87] *Transco v Stockport MBC* [2004] 2 AC 1, at [37].
[88] *Rickards v Lothian* [1913] AC 263; *Tilley v Stevenson* [1939] 4 All ER 207.
[89] *Noble v Harrison* [1926] 2 KB 332.   [90] *Rouse v Gravelworks Ltd* [1940] 1 KB 489.
[91] *Thomas and Evans Ltd v Mid-Rhondda Co-operative Society Ltd* [1941] 1 KB 381; *St Anne's Well Brewery Co v Roberts* (1928) 140 LT 1.

in the fireplace of a house;[92] using a hot wire-cutter in proximity to flammable material;[93] installing necessary wiring for electric lighting;[94] storing metal foil in a factory;[95] supplying gas to flats in a tower block.[96] The provision for sewage disposal by a local authority,[97] and the escape from a ship of generated steam are probably also natural uses.[98] By contrast, it has been held that storing water, gas, electricity and the like in abnormal or excessive quantities,[99] as well as the use of a blowlamp to thaw pipes in a loft[100] and the storage of ignitable material in a barn[101] constitute non-natural uses of the land. Ultimately, it is difficult to resist the conclusion that the notion of 'non-natural use' is presently a narrow one, and that the current interpretation of the term is likely to restrict the scope of application of the rule in *Rylands v Fletcher*.

SECTION 5 ESCAPE

According to the orthodox view, an explosion which injures a claimant within the factory where the explosion occurs is outside the rule since there must be an 'escape from a place where the defendant has occupation of, or control over, land to a place which is outside his occupation or control'.[102] Accordingly, a yew tree that poisoned a horse which ate its leaves by reaching its head over onto the land of the defendant was outside the rule since the 'dangerous' leaves never went beyond the boundary of the defendant's land.[103] By contrast, where something escapes from one place of entertainment in a fairground to a stall tenanted by another fairground operative (but still within the fairground), there *is*, apparently, a sufficient escape.[104]

---

[92] *Sochaski v Sas* [1947] 1 All ER 344. *Ditto* holding a torch, at the top of the opening of a grate in order to test chimney draught: *J Doltis Ltd v Isaac Braithwaite & Sons (Engineers) Ltd* [1957] 1 Lloyd's Rep 522.

[93] *LMS International Ltd v Styrene Packaging & Insulation Ltd* [2005] EWHC 2065.

[94] *Collingwood v Home and Colonial Stores Ltd* [1936] 3 All ER 200.

[95] *British Celanese Ltd v A H Hunt (Capacitors) Ltd* [1969] 2 All ER 1252; *Mason v Levy Auto Parts of England Ltd* [1967] 2 QB 530 (storage of spare motor parts and engines; having regard to quantities of combustible material, manner of storage and character of neighbourhood).

[96] *British Gas plc v Stockport MBC* [2001] Env LR 44.

[97] *Pride of Derby and Derbyshire Angling Association v British Celanese Ltd* [1953] Ch 149, at 189, *per* Denning LJ. Cf *Smeaton v Ilford Corpn* [1954] Ch 450, at 470, *per* Upjohn J and *Ryeford Homes Ltd v Sevenoaks District Council* [1989] 2 EGLR 281.

[98] *Howard v Furness Houlder Argentine Lines Ltd and A and R Brown Ltd* [1936] 2 All ER 781.

[99] *Northwestern Utilities Ltd v London Guarantee and Accident Co Ltd* [1936] AC 108; *Western Engraving Co v Film Laboratories Ltd* [1936] 1 All ER 106 (water in unusual quantities brought onto land for manufacturing purposes of D). In *Transco*, the House of Lords expressly distinguished the substantially greater amount of water stored in *Rylands v Fletcher*.

[100] *Balfour v Barty-King* [1956] 2 All ER 555; affd on other grounds [1957] 1 QB 496.

[101] *E Hobbs (Farms) Ltd v Baxenden Chemical Co Ltd* [1992] 1 Lloyd's Rep 54.

[102] *Read v J Lyons & Co* [1947] AC 156, at 168, *per* Viscount Simon.

[103] *Ponting v Noakes* [1894] 2 QB 281.

[104] This point was essential to the decision in *Hale v Jennings Bros* [1938] 1 All ER 579. Similarly, an escape to the lower part of the same building is sufficient: *J Doltis v Isaac Braithwaite & Sons (Engineers) Ltd* [1957] 1

In *Midwood & Co Ltd v Manchester Corpn*[105] one of the two grounds of liability was the rule in *Rylands v Fletcher*.

After an explosion in a cable belonging to, and laid by, D in the highway, inflammable gas escaped into C's nearby house and set fire to its contents.

In *Charing Cross Electric Supply Co v Hydraulic Power Co*,[106] the Court of Appeal, relying on this case, held that there was a sufficient escape when water from a main, laid by the defendants under the highway, escaped and damaged the claimant's electric cable which was near to it and under the same highway. The House of Lords in *Read v J Lyons & Co Ltd* did not overrule these cases, and pointed out that there was in each of them an escape onto property over which the defendant had no control, from a container which the defendant had a licence to put in the highway.[107] On the other hand, the proposition that the rule also extends to cases where the defendant has no such licence in respect of a public thoroughfare is thought to be wrong.[108]

The actual harm wrought by the escape need not be immediately caused by the thing accumulated. So, for example, it was held in *Kennard v Cory Bros & Co* that where parts of a coal slag heap escaped and their pressure on a third party's quarry spoil caused that spoil to damage the claimant's land, the escape requirement of *Rylands v Fletcher* was satisfied.[109]

SECTION 6 FORESEEABILITY OF HARM

Since the important decision in the *Cambridge Water* case, it is clear that foreseeability of harm is required if a claimant is to succeed in an action based on the rule in *Rylands v Fletcher*. The facts in that case were as follows:

Solvents which had been used by Ds in their tannery for many years had a history of being spilt onto the floor of Ds' factory. From there, they seeped into a natural groundwater source drawn upon by C in order to fulfil its statutory duty to supply drinking water to the inhabitants of Cambridge. The seepage caused the water to become contaminated to the extent that it was unwholesome according to European Community standards. No-one had supposed that this contamination would take place, mainly because of the volatility of the solvents which it had been thought had simply evaporated from Ds' factory floor.

Lloyd's Rep 522. The key to these cases appears to be an escape onto land under another's control, regardless of property ownership on D's part.

[105] [1905] 2 KB 597.   [106] [1914] 3 KB 772.

[107] [1947] AC 156, at 177, *per* Lord Porter. Cf Viscount Simon (at 168) and Lord Simonds (at 183). See also *Hillier v Air Ministry* (1962) *Times*, 8 December (cows electrocuted by underground electric cable; liable within rule).

[108] See the *obiter* suggestion of Taylor J in *Rigby v Chief Constable of Northamptonshire* [1985] 1 WLR 1242, at 1255 to this effect. See also *Crown River Cruises Ltd v Kimbolton Fireworks Ltd* [1996] 2 Lloyd's Rep 533 (escape from a vessel on a navigable waterway).   [109] [1921] AC 521, at 538, *per* Viscount Finlay.

A unanimous House of Lords held the defendants not liable on the basis of the unforeseeability of the harm caused to the claimant's water supply. Lord Goff, who delivered the only full speech in the case, stated that: 'foreseeability of damage of the relevant type should be regarded as a prerequisite of liability in damages under the rule'.[110] What his Lordship failed to make clear, however, is whether damage had to be foreseeable (a) in terms of the *kind* of harm alone or (b) in terms of *both* an escape occurring *and* harm being thereby caused. In relation to the former notion of foreseeability of harm, the test would be akin to the one used to determine the remoteness of damage in negligence and nuisance.[111] If the second test were used – that is, if the foreseeability of harm were not simply gauged by reference to the potentially injurious nature of the accumulated substance, but also by reference to the likelihood of its escape – then foreseeability in this sense would undermine the strictness of *Rylands* liability by introducing a fault requirement. To insist on the foreseeability of *the escape* is to hinge liability upon the defendant's failure to confine something the escape of which he ought to have anticipated and exercised due diligence to contain.[112] Thus, even though his Lordship failed to make absolutely clear which model of foreseeability he favoured, it has since been held that it is the former that is required. As Lord Bingham put it in the *Transco* case:

It must be shown that the defendant has done something which he recognized, or judged by the standards appropriate at the relevant place and time, he ought reasonably to have recognized, as giving rise to an exceptionally high risk of danger or mischief if there should be an escape, however unlikely an escape may have been thought to be.[113]

SECTION 7 DEFENCES

(A) STATUTORY AUTHORITY

Sometimes, public bodies storing water, gas, electricity and the like, are by statute exempted from liability so long as they have taken reasonable care. It is a question of statutory interpretation whether (and, if so, to what extent) liability under the rule in *Rylands v Fletcher* has been excluded. Only if there is a statutory *duty* (as opposed to a

---

[110] [1994] 1 All ER 53, at 75.

[111] *Overseas Tankship (UK) Ltd v Morts Dock & Engineering Co Ltd, The Wagon Mound* [1961] AC 388. For an argument that it may be a broader test in *Rylands*, see McIntyre, 'Liability for Asbestos Related Injury' (1997) 4 *Irish Planning and Environmental Law Journal* 83.

[112] See, eg, *Bolton v Stone* [1951] AC 850.

[113] [2004] 2 AC 1, at [10]. This echoes the words of Lord Goff in the *Cambridge Water* Case (see [1994] 1 All ER 53, at 71) and the approach taken in *Hamilton v Papakura District Council* [2002] UKPC 9, where the Privy Council also emphasized the need to establish the foreseeability of the relevant damage.

mere *permission*) to perform the hazardous activity will there be a defence. *Smeaton v Ilford Corpn*[114] is illustrative:

Sewage accumulated by Ds in their sewers overflowed onto the land of C in circumstances which were held to constitute neither nuisance nor negligence. According to section 31 of the Public Health Act 1936, under which Ds had acted in receiving the sewage: 'A local authority shall so discharge their functions . . . as not to create a nuisance'. In interpreting this to mean that Ds were absolved from liability because they were *obliged* to fulfil the duty without creating a nuisance, the court held that Ds had a defence under the statute to an action based on *Rylands v Fletcher*.

Green v Chelsea Waterworks Co,[115] provides a further example of the statutory authority defence in operation. In that case, there was no liability when a water main burst because the Waterworks Company was under *a statutory obligation* to keep the mains charged at high pressure making a damaging escape an inevitable consequence of any non-negligent burst. By contrast, in *Charing Cross Electricity Co v Hydraulic Power Co*,[116] the defendant, upon the true construction of the legislation had a statutory permission (but no obligation) to keep their water mains charged at high pressure. On this basis, no immunity from liability could be claimed.

A final point in this context is that the defence only operates in respect of *Rylands v Fletcher* liability. So, if the reason for the escape is the defendant's negligence, the presence of a statutory duty to perform the hazardous activity will not afford a defence. This begs a further question: namely, 'Who is to bear the burden of proof, the claimant or the defendant?'. There is no English authority on the point but a majority decision of the High Court of Australia once held the onus to lie with the claimant to show negligence.[117] It is submitted that this decision has little to commend it, for '*prima facie*', according to Blackburn J in *Rylands v Fletcher*, a defendant is 'answerable for all the damage which is the natural consequence of [the thing's] . . . escape'.[118]

(B) CONSENT OF THE CLAIMANT

If the claimant has permitted the defendant to accumulate the thing the escape of which is complained of, then he cannot sue if it escapes.[119] For the purposes of this defence, implied consent will clearly suffice. Thus, a person becoming the tenant of business premises at a time when the condition or construction of adjoining premises is such that an escape is likely to ensue is deemed to have consented to the risk of such an event actually happening. This defence was the crux of *Kiddle v City Business Properties Ltd*[120]

---

[114] [1954] Ch 450.   [115] Eg, *Green v Chelsea Waterworks Co* (1894) 70 LT 547.

[116] [1914] 3 KB 772.

[117] *Benning v Wong* (1969) 43 ALJR 467. Since then, Australian law has ceased to recognize liability under the rule in *Rylands v Fletcher*: see *Burnie Port Authority v General Jones Pty Ltd* (1994) 179 CLR 520.

[118] (1866) LR 1 Exch 265, at 280.   [119] *Kennard v Cory Bros & Co Ltd* [1921] AC 521.

[120] [1942] 1 KB 269.

where an overflow of rainwater from a blocked gutter at the bottom of a sloping roof in the possession of the landlord, and above the tenant's premises, damaged the stock in the tenant's premises.[121]

If the accumulation benefits both claimant and defendant, this is an important element in deciding whether the claimant is deemed to have consented.[122] Where, therefore, for the benefit of the several occupants of a building, rainwater is collected on the roof,[123] or a water-closet is installed,[124] or water pipes are fitted,[125] the several occupants are presumed to have consented. On the other hand, the defence does not seem to be available as between a commercial supplier of gas (in respect of gas mains under the highway) and a consumer in premises adjoining the highway.[126] In any event, an occupier will not be presumed to have consented to installations being left in a dangerously unsafe state.[127]

(c) CONTRIBUTORY NEGLIGENCE AND RELATED MATTERS

Where the claimants worked a mine under the canal of the defendant, and had good reason to know that they would thereby cause the water from the canal to escape into this mine, it was held that the claimants could not invoke the rule in *Rylands v Fletcher* when the water actually escaped and damaged their mine. Cockburn CJ described the matter thus: 'the plaintiffs saw the danger and may be said to have courted it'.[128] Where the claimant is contributorily negligent, the apportionment provisions of the Law Reform (Contributory Negligence) Act 1945 will now apply. In addition, as was said in *Eastern and Southern African Telegraph Co Ltd v Cape Town Tramways Co Ltd*, 'a man cannot increase the liabilities of his neighbour by applying his own property to special uses, whether for business or pleasure'.[129] In that case, the claimant, who complained that the tramways of the defendant caused electrical interference with the receipt of messages through his submarine cable, failed in his action because no damage to the

---

[121] The principle of implied consent does not apply, however, where C and D are not in a tenant-landlord relationship: *Humphries v Cousins* (1877) 2 CPD 239.

[122] *Peters v Prince of Wales Theatre (Birmingham) Ltd* [1943] KB 73. Where C has, by inference, consented to receiving the benefit of D's watercourse, but contends he has not consented to a negligent accumulation of water, C must prove negligence: *Gilson v Kerrier RDC* [1976] 3 All ER 343.

[123] *Carstairs v Taylor* (1871) LR 6 Exch 217.　　[124] *Ross v Fedden* (1872) LR 7 QB 661.

[125] *Anderson v Oppenheimer* (1880) 5 QBD 602 (the reasoning is muddled, but this is the most likely basis of the decision).

[126] *Northwestern Utilities Ltd v London Guarantee and Accident Co Ltd* [1936] AC 108, at 120.

[127] *A Prosser & Sons Ltd v Levy* [1955] 3 All ER 577.

[128] *Dunn v Birmingham Canal Navigation Co* (1872) LR 7 QB 244, at 260; affd LR 8 QB 42. (Note that at the time of this decision contributory negligence was a *complete* defence.)

[129] [1902] AC 381, at 393. Cf *Hoare & Co v McAlpine* [1923] 1 Ch 167 which left open the question of whether C, who complains that his buildings have been damaged, could be met by the plea that they were damaged only because they were dilapidated buildings having insecure foundations.

cable itself was caused. The claimant suffered loss only because he relied on the cable for the transmission of messages.[130]

(D) ACT OF A THIRD PARTY: THE RULE IN *RYLANDS V FLETCHER* OR NEGLIGENCE?

What must next be considered is whether it is a defence that, although the defendant brought the thing onto his land, it has only escaped through the act of a third party. It is evident from *Rylands v Fletcher* itself that the defendant is liable for an escape attributable to his independent contractors.[131] Further, there is weighty support for the proposition that the defendant is liable for escapes caused by any other third party where the defendant ought reasonably to have foreseen the act of that third party and had enough control of the premises to be able to prevent it. The proprietor of a chair-o-plane was accordingly held liable for the escape of a chair caused by a passenger tampering with it;[132] the owner of a flag-pole was also liable when small children caused the pole to fall and injure the claimant.[133] Similarly, a gas company laying a main in a highway were liable for damage caused by an explosion of gas when the surrounding earth subsided due to a third party's subjacent mines.[134]

On the other hand, in *Rickards v Lothian*, the defendant was not liable where flooding of the claimant's premises was caused by an unknown third party who had maliciously turned on a water tap in the defendant's premises and blocked the waste pipe of the lavatory basin.[135] Nor was there liability in *Box v Jubb* where the defendant's reservoir overflowed when a third party, conducting operations higher up the stream supplying it, discharged downstream an unusually large volume of water without any warning.[136]

There has been a tendency – an example of which is *Perry v Kendricks*[137] – for these two cases to be taken to support the view that once the defendants have proved that the escape was the act of a stranger 'they avoid liability, unless the claimant can go on to show that the act which caused the escape was an act of the kind which the owner could reasonably have contemplated and guarded against'.[138] It is the present submission,

---

[130] This decision may, however, be better understood in terms of C's loss not being a sufficiently direct consequence of the escape.

[131] For analysis of the law's treatment of independent contractors see Murphy, 'The Juridical Foundations of Non-Delegable Duties' in Neyers (ed), *Emerging Issues in Tort Law* (2006).

[132] *Hale v Jennings Bros* [1938] 1 All ER 579.

[133] *Shiffman v Grand Priory in British Realm of Venerable Order of the Hospital of St John of Jerusalem* [1936] 1 All ER 557, at 561, *per* Atkinson J (*obiter* regarding *Rylands v Fletcher*).

[134] *Hanson v Wearmouth Coal Co Ltd and Sunderland Gas Co* [1939] 3 All ER 47.

[135] *Rickards v Lothian* [1913] AC 263.

[136] (1879) 4 Ex D 76. Cf *Black v Christchurch Finance Co Ltd* [1894] AC 48. Analogous cases to those last cited are those suggesting that there is no liability where an unobservable defect of nature causes the escape, or where there is flooding because a rat gnaws through a water cistern: *Carstairs v Taylor* (1871) LR 6 Exch 217.

[137] [1956] 1 All ER 154.

[138] *Perry v Kendricks Transport Ltd* [1956] 1 All ER 154, at 161, *per* Parker LJ. Likewise, Jenkins LJ held (at 160) that once the act of a stranger is made out, 'one reaches the point where the claim based on *Rylands v Fletcher* merges into the claim in negligence'.

however, that although the case law itself clearly supports such a proposition, it has nonetheless been somewhat misguided in its approach. Thus, while it is not suggested that the actual decisions in the two cases are wrong, it is nonetheless contended that the legal doctrine according which they ought to have been decided is mistaken: they are, by nature, more in line with negligence, not *Rylands*, principles. The reasoning for this assertion is as follows.

Since the rule in *Rylands v Fletcher* is a strict liability tort, it follows that negligence in the narrow sense (that is, the breach of a duty to take reasonable care) should play no part in determining liability. This much was made abundantly clear by Lord Goff in *Cambridge Water v Eastern Counties Leather plc* when he said: 'the defendant will be liable for harm caused to the claimant by the escape, notwithstanding that he has exercised all reasonable care and skill to prevent the escape from occurring'.[139] Similarly, in *Transco v Stockport MBC*, Lord Hoffmann stressed the immateriality of the fact that the defendant could not reasonably have foreseen an escape.[140] In other words, and contrary to the view in *Perry v Kendricks* just quoted, it should not matter whether the defendant 'could reasonably have contemplated and guarded against' the intervention of a third party. The better approach is to say that such reasoning has nothing to do with the rule in *Rylands v Fletcher*. In essence, they do not involve a failure to control (that is, keep in) a dangerous thing (*Rylands*); they centre, instead, upon the question of whether there was a failure to control the unforeseeable harmful acts of third parties (negligence). The distinction between these two classes of negligent omission was staunchly made by the House of Lords in *Smith v Littlewoods Organisation Ltd*.[141]

It is also quite clear that the rule in *Rylands v Fletcher* (which is concerned with escapes) is to be contrasted with deliberate discharges of the dangerous thing onto another's land. Those cases – at least where the discharge is by the person who accumulated the thing – should sound in trespass.[142]

(E) ACT OF GOD

This defence has received a prominence out of all proportion to its practical importance. It arises only where an escape is caused through natural causes and without human intervention, in 'circumstances which no human foresight can provide against, and of which human prudence is not bound to recognise the possibility'.[143]

---

[139] [1994] 1 All ER 53, at 71. In Australia, this tort has been abandoned and replaced by a 'non-delegable duty' in negligence: *Burnie Port Authority v General Jones Pty Ltd* (1994) 120 ALR 42. By contrast, European jurisdictions provide considerably greater scope for strict liability in this context: see Reid, 'Liability for Dangerous Activities: A Comparative Analysis' (1999) 48 ICLQ 731.   [140] [2004] 2 AC 1, at [27].

[141] [1987] 1 All ER 710. See also *Topp v London Country Bus (South West) Ltd* [1993] 1 WLR 976.

[142] *Rigby v Chief Constable of Northamptonshire* [1985] 1 WLR 1242, at 1255, *per* Taylor J.

[143] A definition of Lord Westbury in *Tennent v Earl of Glasgow* (1864) 2 M 22, at 26–7 (followed by the House of Lords in *Greenock Corpn v Caledonian Rly Co* [1917] AC 556). For Academic discussion, see Hall, 'An Unsearchable Providence: The Lawyer's Concept of Act of God' (1993) 12 OJLS 227.

Thus, the defence succeeded in *Nichols v Marsland*[144] where a most violent thunderstorm caused flooding. Yet the defence was put in its proper perspective by the House of Lords in *Greenock Corpn v Caledonian Rly Co*[145] where an extraordinary and unprecedented rainfall was held in similar circumstances not to be an act of God. The explanation of *Nichols v Marsland* in this case, was that, in *Nichols v Marsland*, the jury found that no reasonable person could have anticipated the storm and the court would not disturb this finding of fact.

The problem with the way in which the defence has been construed by the courts is that they make its incidence referable to reasonable foresight of the cause of an escape. This, on one construction, tends to undermine the strictness of *Rylands* liability because it makes the defendant's liability depend, just like the unforeseeable acts of a third party, just considered, upon the existence of fault.[146] However, a second (and preferable) construction of the defence is possible. This involves requiring that an act of God be beyond *all*, not just reasonable, human foresight. According to this construction, we are not excusing the defendant because the natural event causing the escape was beyond what could reasonably have been foreseen; instead, we are concerned with identifying the truly unique and freak occurrence (which should be distinguished from the highly unusual – but not unknown – event[147]). On this basis, it might be argued that few phenomena beyond earthquakes and tornadoes are likely to constitute an act of God for the purposes of this defence. Certainly, the paucity of occasions on which the defence has succeeded would tend to vindicate this view.

(F) NECESSITY

If an intentional release of a substance could ground liability under the rule in *Rylands v Fletcher*, then the defence of necessity ought, on principle, to be available in this tort.[148] However, it is probably better to treat such cases as trespass cases in which raising the defence of necessity is well established.[149] Certainly, in one first instance case in which police officers had fired CS gas canisters into the claimant's shop in order to flush out a psychopath, it was suggested that trespass would be the appropriate cause of action.[150]

---

[144] (1876) 2 Ex D 1.   [145] [1917] AC 556.

[146] If this construction is accepted, the failure to prevent the escape ought, instead, to sound in negligence.

[147] To allow reasonable foreseeability of the abnormal event to play a part in defining the defence is also, and inescapably, to suggest that foresight of such events is a factor which determines *prima facie* liability. And while, in the wake of the *Cambridge Water* case, it is clear that foreseeability is a relevant factor in a *Rylands* action, it is important to appreciate that it only operates to characterize a kind of harm, for which D would otherwise be *prima facie* liable, as too remote. If foreseeability of the 'freak' event were to play a part in defining this defence, however, it would operate at the level of the *definition* (as opposed to *limitation*) of *prima facie* liability. (For *obiter* judicial support for this view see *Ellison v Ministry of Defence* (1996) 81 BLR 101.)

[148] On the basis of the assumption that the rule in *Rylands v Fletcher* could apply to deliberate releases, this point was conceded in *Rigby v Chief Constable of Northamptonshire* [1985] 1 WLR 1242, at 1255, *per* Taylor J. However, the judge was of the view that the rule should not be applied to deliberate releases.

[149] On the defence of necessity, see ch 11.

[150] *Rigby v Chief Constable of Northamptonshire* [1985] 1 WLR 1242, at 1255, *per* Taylor J.

SECTION 8 NUISANCE AND THE RULE IN *RYLANDS V FLETCHER*

Apart from the fact that the *Cambridge Water* case continues the trend towards bringing *Rylands v Fletcher* closer to nuisance, there still remain important differences between the two torts.[151] To begin with, the category of things coming under the rule in *Rylands v Fletcher* is narrower than the category of occurrences that ground an action in nuisance. Under the rule, a tangible thing must be accumulated which, in its nature, is likely to cause mischief, either upon its own escape or upon its giving off fumes, gas, electricity, or possibly odours, which themselves escape. In nuisance, on the other hand, no physical object having that quality need be on the defendant's land.[152] Thus, in *Christie v Davey*,[153] a defendant who beat a tray against the wall of his house was held liable in nuisance to his neighbour for the interference caused by the noise; but because a tray is, in itself, likely neither to escape nor to give off fumes, smells, or noise, the defendant in that case could not have been liable in *Rylands v Fletcher*. More doubtfully, the list of mischief-making things giving rise to *Rylands* liability may be shorter than that for which liability in nuisance may be imposed. Whereas trees likely to fall may give rise to actions in nuisance, it was held in *Noble v Harrison*[154] that tree branches, which actually broke off causing damage, were not sufficiently likely to cause damage upon their 'escape' to fall within *Rylands v Fletcher*.

The justification for such a distinction may well be that since the scope of liability under the rule in *Rylands v Fletcher* is wider, the propensity of the thing to cause harm on escaping must be the more obvious. Likewise, although it is not in itself a defence to this tort that the defendant was unaware that the thing was likely to do harm, proof that it was not, according to the common experience of humanity, likely to cause harm *on escaping* will absolve the defendant.[155]

In addition, the rule in *Rylands v Fletcher* must still be examined separately because it will afford a remedy where nuisance will not in the following circumstances.

(1) If the defendant has accumulated 'a thing' which escapes, then, regardless of whether he was negligent in allowing it to escape or whether it was foreseeable that it would in the particular circumstances escape, he will be liable: 'the principle

---

[151] The rule in *Rylands v Fletcher*, therefore, continues to be considered separately from nuisance: see, eg, *British Gas plc v Stockport Metropolitan Borough Council* [2001] Env LR 44.

[152] The only case apparently inconsistent with this is *Hoare & Co v McAlpine* [1923] 1 Ch 167, a decision at first instance treating vibrations caused by a pile-driver as being within the rule. But note that the case might more appropriately have been decided in nuisance. It was disapproved of in *Barrette v Franki Compressed Pile Co of Canada Ltd* [1955] 2 DLR 665 (pile-driving vibrations not within *Rylands v Fletcher*, but held to be nuisance). [153] [1893] 1 Ch 316.

[154] [1926] 2 KB 332, at 342, *per* Wright J; there were other reasons why an action based on the rule in *Rylands v Fletcher* failed. [155] *West v Bristol Tramways Co* [1908] 2 KB 14, at 20–1, *per* Lord Alverstone.

is one of strict liability in the sense that the defendant may be held liable notwith-standing that he has exercised all due care to prevent the escape from occurring'.[156] In nuisance, the defendant is liable for damage resulting from a state of affairs on his land where the negligent management of that state of affairs makes it foresee-able that a substantial interference with C's use of his land will result.[157] Foresight of the escape, however, is not necessary in *Rylands v Fletcher*. Indeed, as we have seen, to insist on foresight of the escape is to introduce the requirement of fault into something that is a strict liability tort.[158]

(2) The occupier is liable in *Rylands v Fletcher* for the accumulation of, and the escape caused by, independent contractors. In nuisance, the liability for inde-pendent contractors is less extensive.[159]

(3) In nuisance the claimant must possess a proprietary interest in the land affected;[160] the same is apparently not true in *Rylands v Fletcher*.[161] On the other hand, while the escape must be from the defendant's land in *Rylands v Fletcher*, there is no requirement in nuisance that the defendant be an occupier of land.[162]

(4) Damage by fire may well be the subject of a claim in trespass or negligence, or the separate action on the case for fire.[163] It may also give rise to a claim in nuisance or under the rule in *Rylands v Fletcher*. It will be noted that the Fires Prevention (Metropolis) Act 1774 provides that the person on whose land a fire 'shall acci-dentally begin' has a defence. This defence is not available to suits based on *Rylands v Fletcher*,[164] although it is sometimes a defence in nuisance.

(5) Although the *Rylands v Fletcher* concept of 'non-natural use' is closely related to the nuisance concept of 'unreasonable user', the two are not (yet) co-extensive.[165] Indeed, it has long been recognized that a use may be natural and yet give rise to

---

[156] *Cambridge Water Co Ltd v Eastern Counties Leather plc* [1994] 2 AC 264, at 306, *per* Lord Goff.

[157] This explains why *quia timet* injunctions lie for a 'state of affairs' in nuisance but not necessarily for an 'accumulation' in *Rylands v Fletcher*. But for criticism, see Nolan, 'The Distinctiveness of *Rylands v Fletcher*' (2005) 121 LQR 421.

[158] See further Wilkinson, '*Cambridge Water Company v Eastern Counties Leather plc*: Diluting Liability for Continuing Escapes' (1994) 57 MLR 799, 803–7. Cf *Bolton v Stone* [1951] AC 850, on the role of foreseeability of an escape in determining the existence of *negligence* (in the narrow sense). [159] See ch 17.

[160] *Hunter v Canary Wharf Ltd* [1997] AC 655.

[161] *Hale v Jennings Bros* [1938] 1 All ER 579. But if – as is often dubiously suggested – the rule in *Rylands v Fletcher* derives from nuisance, why not?

[162] *L E Jones (Insurance Brokers) v Portsmouth City Council* [2003] 1 WLR 427.

[163] *Balfour v Barty-King* [1956] 2 All ER 555; *Mason v Levy Auto Parts of England Ltd* [1967] 2 QB 530. In *H & N Emanuel Ltd v Greater London Council* [1971] 2 All ER 835, it was held that an occupier is liable for an escape of fire caused by the negligence of anyone other than a stranger.

[164] *Musgrove v Pandelis* [1919] 2 KB 43; *Mulholland and Tedd Ltd v Baker* [1939] 3 All ER 253; *Perry v Kendricks Transport Ltd* [1956] 1 All ER 154; *Balfour v Barty-King* [1956] 2 All ER 555.

[165] See *Cambridge Water Co Ltd v Eastern Counties Leather plc* [1994] 1 All ER 53, at 71, where Lord Goff indi-cated that they were different but closely related concepts with similar functions. See also *Ellison v Ministry of Defence* (1996) 81 BLR 101 and *Graham and Graham v Rechem International Ltd* [1996] Env LR 158 (suggesting that they are virtually interchangeable concepts). Cf Cross, 'Does Only the Careless Polluter Pay? A Fresh Exam-ination of the Nature of Private Nuisance' (1995) 111 LQR 445 and Murphy, 'Noxious Emissions and Common

liability in nuisance.[166] Equally, the reasonableness of the defendant's user is merely one factor that may be taken into account in assessing nuisance liability; but it is not, *per se*, a precondition of liability since it is only the unreasonableness of the interference that counts.[167] By contrast, non-natural use is absolutely central to *Rylands* liability.

Beyond these five instances it is difficult to state with certainty further circumstances where the distinction between nuisance and the rule in *Rylands v Fletcher* exists. But this does not mean that such distinctions cannot be identified or that they ought not to exist in order to achieve harmony with juridical orthodoxy. For example, it is generally accepted that *Rylands v Fletcher* cases turn on an isolated escape, whereas in nuisance cases the interference is normally supposed to be ongoing one.[168] As such, it becomes difficult to square the 'state of affairs' nuisance cases with nuisance law orthodoxy. (Recall that in such cases it is said to suffice if there was a threatening state of affairs on the defendant's land from which an isolated interference emanated.[169])

FURTHER READING

Hall, 'An Unsearchable Providence: the Lawyer's Concept of Act of God' (1993) 12 OJLS 227

Murphy, 'Noxious Emissions and Common Law Liability: Tort in the Shadow of Regulation' in Lowry and Edmunds (eds), *Environmental Protection and the Common Law* (1999)

Murphy, 'The Merits of *Rylands v Fletcher*' (2004) 24 OJLS 643

Nolan, 'The Distinctiveness of *Rylands v Fletcher*' (2005) 121 LQR 421

Oliphant, '*Rylands v Fletcher* and the Emergence of Enterprise Liability in the Common Law' [2004] *European Tort Law* 81

Stanton, 'The Legacy of *Rylands v Fletcher*' in Mullany and Linden (eds), *Torts Tomorrow: A Tribute to John Fleming* (1998)

Reid, 'Liability for Dangerous Activities: A Comparative Analysis' (1999) 48 ICLQ 731

Wilkinson, '*Cambridge Water Company v Eastern Counties Leather plc*: Diluting Liability for Continuing Escapes' (1994) 57 MLR 799

Williams, 'Non-Natural Use of Land' [1973] CLJ 310

Law Liability: Tort in the Shadow of Regulation' in Lowry and Edmunds (eds), *Environmental Protection and the Common Law* (1999). See also Layard, 'Balancing Environmental Considerations' (1997) 113 LQR 254.

[166] Eg, *Leakey v National Trust* [1980] QB 485; *Sedleigh-Denfield v O'Callaghan* [1940] AC 880, at 888, *per* Viscount Maugham; *British Celanese Ltd v A H Hunt (Capacitors) Ltd* [1969] 2 All ER 1252.

[167] See, eg, *Sampson v Hodson-Pressinger* [1981] 3 All ER 710, where the ordinary use of premises which, as a result of their being poorly constructed, caused intolerable noise to be perceived in adjoining premises was held to be a nuisance. See also *Toff v McDowell* (1993) 25 HLR 650.

[168] Cf Newark, 'The Boundaries of Nuisance' (1949) 65 LQR 480, 488.

[169] *Midwood & Co Ltd v Manchester Corpn* [1905] 2 KB 597. But for compelling criticism of these cases, see Nolan, 'The Distinctiveness of *Rylands v Fletcher*' (2005) 121 LQR 421.

19

ANIMALS

SECTION 1 NEGLIGENCE AND STRICT LIABILITY

Persons who own or control animals are subject to the same duty of care in respect of the care and control of those animals as those responsible for any other chattels.[1] Thus, in *Aldham v United Dairies (London) Ltd*[2] the defendant was held liable when his unattended pony became restive and jabbed at a passing pedestrian, knocking her down. And in *Draper v Hodder*[3] the owner of a pack of terriers was found liable when the dogs bit a neighbour's child. He was negligent in failing to control and/or train the pack adequately. An occupier of premises may be liable under the Occupiers' Liability Acts in respect of injuries inflicted by dogs on his premises.[4] But liability for damage inflicted by animals extends beyond mere failure to control them properly.[5] The Animals Act 1971 provides a strict liability regime that covers a range of circumstances in which damage might be caused by both dangerous and non-dangerous animals.

SECTION 2 DAMAGE DONE BY DANGEROUS ANIMALS

(A) DANGEROUS SPECIES

Section 2(1) of the Animals Act 1971 imposes strict liability where any damage is caused by an animal that belongs to a dangerous species. A dangerous species, for these purposes, is one that is not commonly domesticated in the British Isles, and

---

[1] *Fardon v Harcourt-Rivington* [1932] All ER Rep 81; *Birch v Mills* [1995] 9 CL 354.

[2] [1940] 1 KB 507. And see *Brock v Richards* [1951] 1 KB 529.

[3] [1972] 2 QB 556 (the court rejected D's contention that while bowling over or scratching by the excited dogs was foreseeable, biting was harm of a distinct and unforeseeable type).

[4] *Hill v Lovett (OH)* 1992 SLT 994. But should an action for breach of statutory duty lie for failing to muzzle a pit bull terrier as *per* the Dangerous Dogs Act 1991 (which is silent on civil actions)?

[5] Eg, liability may sound in nuisance for the smell emanating from animals kept by D (*Wheeler v JJ Saunders Ltd* [1995] 2 All ER 697), or under the rule in *Rylands v Fletcher* for an animal that escapes (*Behrens v Bertram Mills Circus Ltd* [1957] 2 QB 1).

whose fully grown animals have such characteristics that (1) they are likely, unless restrained, to cause severe damage, or (2) they are of a kind that any damage they do cause is likely to be severe.[6] 'Damage' for the purposes of the Act embraces harm to either persons or property. The list is thus not confined to animals likely to attack man, such as bears, tigers, etc. An action also lies under the Act even though the damage caused is not of the kind in respect of which the species is known to be dangerous. And, similarly, liability arises even though the animal has not escaped from control: so a keeper would be liable if his elephant slips or stumbles and thereby causes damage. 'Damage' also includes the impairment of any mental condition.[7] So if someone suffered nervous shock with resulting psychiatric illness at the sudden appearance of a cobra, there would be liability.

(B) NON-DANGEROUS SPECIES

Section 2(2) of the Animals Act 1971 imposes liability in certain (convoluted) circumstances for an animal that does not belong to a dangerous species. It provides:

Where damage is caused by an animal which does not belong to a dangerous species, a keeper of the animal is liable for the damage if:

    (a) the damage is of a kind which the animal, unless restrained, was likely to cause or which, if caused by the animal, was likely to be severe; and

    (b) the likelihood of the damage or of its being severe was due to characteristics of the animal which are not normally found in animals of the same species or are not normally so found except at particular times or in particular circumstances; and

    (c) those characteristics were known to that keeper or were at any time known to a person who at that time had charge of the animal as that keeper's servant or, where that keeper is the head of a household, were known to another keeper of the animal who is a member of that household and under the age of sixteen.

According to the subsection, three conditions must be met before the keeper may be held liable.[8] First, the damage must be of a kind which the animal, unless restrained, was likely to cause[9] or which, if caused by the animal, was likely to be severe. (There is no need to show that the severity of the potential damage ensues from any abnormal characteristics in the animal.[10]) This formulation covers not only, say, a dog that attacks a man, but also an animal with a dangerous disease, such as foot and mouth, that spreads the infection to other animals.

---

    [6] Animals Act 1971, s 6(2).   [7] Animals Act 1971, s 11.

    [8] Note that one keeper may be liable to another keeper: *Flack v Hudson* [2001] QB 698 (C and D were joint keepers of D's horse).

    [9] In *Smith v Ainger* [1990] CLY 3297 it was held that it is enough to prove merely that the injurious occurrence was one 'such as might happen'. In *Mirvahedy v Henly* [2003] 2 AC 491, however, Lord Scott (at [97]-[98]) disagreed with this test. Instead, he opined (in his dissenting speech) that damage would be 'likely' if it was 'reasonably to be expected'.   [10] *Curtis v Betts* [1990] 1 All ER 769.

The second subparagraph focuses on unusual characteristics in the animal or those that are not normally found in animals of the same species[11] except at particular times or in particular circumstances. This requirement embraces behaviour that is normal for a particular species *but only* in special circumstances, such as where the animal is frightened. Thus, in *Mirvahedy v Henly*,[12] a cause of action lay where the claimant was injured by a horse that had been panicked and escaped from its field. A majority of their Lordships took the view that bolting was a normal characteristic of horses in certain circumstances and therefore within section 2(2)(b). The same applies to a bull mastiff dog defending his 'territory'.[13]

The third requirement of this subsection requires that the animal's unusual characteristics must have been known to the keeper, or to his servant, or to a member of his household under the age of 16. It further requires that a causal link between the 'abnormal' characteristic and the injury must be established.[14]

(C) LIABILITY FOR EITHER KIND OF DANGEROUS ANIMAL

Liability under the Animals Act 1971 is imposed on the keeper regardless of whether the animal in question belongs to a dangerous or a non-dangerous species. And a keeper for the purposes of the Act is defined in terms of the person who owns the animal or has it in his possession, or who is head of the household of which a member under the age of 16 owns the animal or has it in his possession.[15] This last provision prevents evasion of liability by making a child in the family the nominal owner. If a person ceases to keep, own or possess it, he continues to be liable until another person owns or possesses it.[16] While liability is imposed regardless of fault, the defendant is not liable for any damage which is due wholly to the fault of the person suffering it[17] and damages will be reduced under the Law Reform (Contributory Negligence) Act 1945 where the claimant's fault merely contributes to his damage.[18]

It is also a defence under the Act that the damage was suffered by a person who has voluntarily accepted the risk.[19] However, an employee who accepts a risk that is

[11] Section 11 of the Animals Act 1971 defines 'species' to include sub-species. It seems that different breeds of dogs are treated as sub-species: *Curtis v Betts* [1990] 1 All ER 769.

[12] [2003] 2 AC 491. See also *Cummings v Granger* [1977] QB 397 (C bitten by D's Alsatian dog which was used as a guard dog in his scrapyard. The dog barked and ran around when non-white people, like C, approached. This is not a usual characteristic in Alsatian dogs, except when used as guard dogs. Accordingly, this was held to be a particular circumstance within the Animals Act 1971 s 2(2)(b)).

[13] *Curtis v Betts* [1990] 1 All ER 769. A bitch protecting her pups would also be covered.

[14] *Jaundrill v Gillett* (1996) *Times*, 30 January.   [15] Animals Act 1971, s 6(3).

[16] Animals Act 1971, s 6(3). But a person who takes possession only for the purpose of preventing damage or restoring it to its owner is not thereby made liable: s 6(4).

[17] Animals Act 1971, s 5(1). It has been applied where C ignored police warnings to come out and subsequently was bitten by a police dog: *Dhesi v Chief Constable of West Midlands* 2000 WL 491455.

[18] Animals Act 1971, s 10.

[19] Animals Act 1971, s 5(2). In *Cummings v Granger* [1977] QB 397, the court found that when C knew of the dog she must be taken to have voluntarily accepted the risk. The court, especially Ormrod LJ (at 408), treated this defence as being wider than the common law defence of *volenti*.

necessarily incidental to his employment shall not be treated as accepting it voluntarily.[20] It is also a defence that the damage occurred on property where the claimant was a trespasser[21] if it is proved either that the animal was not kept there for the protection of persons or property or, if kept for those purposes, that thus keeping it there was not unreasonable.[22] Presumably it would be difficult to maintain this defence in respect of a dangerous species being kept for protection only, because that might well be unreasonable. Trespassers will never have a remedy when attacked by an animal of a dangerous species not kept for protection.

SECTION 3 LIABILITY FOR STRAYING LIVESTOCK

Section 4 of the Animals Act 1971 imposes liability on a person in possession of livestock which strays onto another's land.[23] Under the Act, 'livestock' means cattle, horses, asses, mules, hinnies, sheep, pigs, goats, poultry and deer not in the wild state.[24] Liability is for damage done by the livestock to the land or to any property on it.[25] Presumably, 'property' includes other animals as well as goods, but the claimant cannot recover under section 4 for his personal injuries. Either the person in possession or the owner (even though not in possession) can recover for damage to his land or property.

A claimant may incur expense in keeping livestock while it cannot be restored to its owner, or while it is detained in pursuance of the power conferred by the Animals Act 1971 to detain it.[26] He can recover any such expenses reasonably incurred.[27] Liability is strict under this section, but the defendant is not liable for any damage due wholly to the fault of the claimant.[28] Thus, if the claimant could have prevented the damage by

---

[20] Animals Act 1971, s 6(5); *Canterbury City Council v Howletts & Port Lympne Estates Ltd* [1997] ICR 925 (a tiger keeper was killed by one of the zoo's tigers; the zoo especially encouraged 'bonding' between the tigers and their keeper which necessitated entering the cage regularly: the keeper's dependants could recover damages).

[21] Since the creation in the Countryside and Rights of Way Act 2000 of certain rights to roam, there will now be a smaller number of potential trespassers in relation to whom this defence can be raised on the occasion of injury inflicted by livestock.

[22] Animals Act 1971, s 5(3); *Cummings v Granger* [1977] QB 397 (it was reasonable to keep an Alsatian dog, known to be ferocious, to protect old cars in a locked yard). Had the Guard Dogs Act 1975 been in force, Lord Denning MR would have held that failure to comply with the requirement of that Act that the dog had to be in the control of the handler would have made the keeping of the dog unreasonable.

[23] Where an animal strays onto the highway, the ordinary rules of negligence apply: see, eg, *Hole v Ross Skinner* [2003] EWCA Civ 774; *Wilson v Donaldson* [2004] EWCA Civ 972.   [24] Animals Act 1971, s 11.

[25] Cases involving loss (but no damage) would not be covered (eg, the Ministry of Agriculture makes a foot-and-mouth order restricting movement of cattle, but none of C's cattle are destroyed).

[26] Animals Act 1971, s 7. See *Matthews v Wicks* (1987) *Times*, 25 May; *Morris v Blaenau Gwent District Council* (1982) 80 LGR 793.   [27] Animals Act 1971, s 4(1)(b).

[28] Animals Act 1971, s 5(1); *Nelmes v Chief Constable of Avon and Somerset Constabulary* (9 February 1993, unreported) (C kicked a police dog, before his arrest, provoking it into biting him).

fencing,[29] and the claimant was under a duty (owed to a person having an interest in the land from which the livestock strayed) to fence, the defendant is not liable so long as the straying would not have occurred but for that breach on the part of the claimant.[30]

The Law Reform (Contributory Negligence) Act 1945 again applies in respect of damage in part caused by the claimant's own fault.[31] It is also a defence that the livestock strayed from a highway and its presence there was a lawful use of the highway. This is because the owner of property adjoining a highway is presumed to have accepted risks incidental to such ownership.[32]

SECTION 4 LIABILITY FOR INJURY DONE BY DOGS TO LIVESTOCK

Section 3 of the Animals Act 1971 provides that where a dog kills or injures livestock[33] its keeper is liable for the damage, even though he was not negligent. But a person is not liable if the livestock was killed or injured on land onto which it had strayed and either the dog belonged to the occupier or its presence on the land was authorized by the occupier.[34] It is a defence that the damage was due wholly to the fault of the person suffering it.[35]

FURTHER READING

Law Commission, *Civil Liability for Animals* (1967)

North, *The Modern Law of Animals* (1972)

---

[29] Fencing includes the construction of any obstacle designed to prevent animals from straying.

[30] Animals Act 1971, s 5(6). In the absence of any such duty to fence, there is no defence under the Act.

[31] Animals Act 1971, ss 10 and 11.   [32] Animals Act 1971, s 5(4), (5).

[33] Livestock for this purpose is a slightly wider category than the one under s 4 in that it includes pheasant, partridges and grouse while in captivity: Animals Act 1971, s 11.   [34] Animals Act 1971, s 5(4).

[35] Animals Act 1971, s 5(1). If C, by his own fault, has contributed to the damage, the Law Reform (Contributory Negligence) Act 1945 applies to permit a reduction of the damages awarded.

20

BREACH OF STATUTORY DUTY

SECTION 1 INTRODUCTION[1]

Exceptionally, a person suffering damage as a result of a violation of a statute may have an action in tort in respect of that damage, commonly called an action for breach of statutory duty. For the claimant, the great advantage of such an action is the fact that, in many cases, all he needs to prove is that the defendant failed to fulfil his statutory obligation. There is no requirement to establish that the breach was either intentional or negligent. The early cases on the tort rested on the broad principle that whenever a violation of a statute caused damage to an individual's interests, a right of action in tort arose.[2] Leading nineteenth-century decisions[3] markedly restricted the scope of the tort, however, and required that anyone claiming for breach of statutory duty must first establish that the legislature intended that a violation of his right or interest should be tortious.

Lord Denning MR attempted (ultimately unsuccessfully) to resurrect the broader principle in *Ex p Island Records Ltd*[4] arguing '[if] a private right is being interfered with by a criminal act, thus causing or threatening to cause him special damage over and above the generality of the public, then he can come to the court as a private individual and ask that his private right be protected'.[5] Had this 'Denning principle' taken root, it would have transformed the action for breach of statutory duty and opened up the way for greater protection of individual interests by the law of torts in two crucial respects. First, in respect of damage to economic and business interests, claimants could have taken advantage of the extensive provision made by statute to regulate the economy in order to obtain compensation for losses falling outside the compass of the economic torts.[6] Secondly, citizens aggrieved by the failure of public authorities to fulfil

---

[1] See generally Stanton, *Breach of Statutory Duty in Tort* (1986), Buckley, 'Liability in Tort for Breach of Statutory Duty' (1984) 100 LQR 204; Stanton, 'New Forms of the Tort of Breach of Statutory Duty' (2004) 120 LQR 324.

[2] *Couch v Steel* (1854) 3 E & B 402 was the last important case resting on the old broad principle.

[3] *Atkinson v Newcastle and Gateshead Waterworks Co* (1877) 2 Ex D 441; *Groves v Lord Wimborne* [1898] 2 QB 402.   [4] [1978] Ch 122.

[5] [1978] Ch 122, at 139.

[6] But see Part IV of this book and *Douglas v Hello! Ltd (No 6)* [2006] QB 125, at [174] in relation to what looks like the emergence of a general principle within the economic torts of liability for using unlawful means in order to inflict harm.

obligations designed to protect their welfare could have sought extensive redress from central and local government. The decisions of the House of Lords in *Lonrho Ltd v Shell Petroleum Co Ltd (No 2)*[7] and *X v Bedfordshire County Council*[8] appear, however, to have stifled the further development of the action for breach of statutory duty.

The claimant in *Lonrho* was an oil company which had suffered heavy losses because it had complied with government sanctions orders prohibiting trade with the illegal regime in Rhodesia while its competitors had flagrantly violated those orders. Relying on *Ex p Island Records*, the claimants sought to sue their competitors for breach of the orders. The House of Lords firmly rejected the 'Denning principle',[9] reasserting that the general rule in a claim for breach of statutory duty is that 'where an Act creates an obligation and enforces performance in a specified manner ... that performance cannot be enforced in any other manner'.[10] Where the only manner of enforcing performance for which the Act provides is the criminal process, there are only two classes of exception to this general rule. The first is where 'on the true construction of the Act it is apparent that the obligation or prohibition was imposed for the benefit of a particular class of individuals'.[11] The second arises where the statute creates a public right and an individual member of the public suffers damage which is 'particular, direct and substantial damage other and different from that which is common to the rest of the public'.[12] Lonrho's claim fell outside both exceptions. Sanctions orders prohibiting trade with Rhodesia were intended to end all trade and bring down the illegal regime. They were not imposed for the benefit of any class to which Lonrho belonged; nor did they confer a benefit on the public generally.

In *X v Bedfordshire County Council* the House of Lords held that no action for breach of statutory duty arose out of *either* legislation imposing duties on local authorities to safeguard the welfare of children in their area and protect them from child abuse, *or* legislation requiring local authorities to meet the educational needs of children in their district. Lord Browne-Wilkinson acknowledged that legislation to protect children at risk and to provide for education was undoubtedly designed to benefit those children, but found that it was not Parliament's intention to allow individual children harmed by a local authority's failure to meet its statutory obligations to recover compensation for that harm from the public purse. His Lordship noted that no case had been cited before the court where statutory provisions creating a general regulatory scheme to promote social welfare had been held to give rise to a private law claim for damages. He went on to say:

[a]lthough regulatory or welfare legislation affecting a particular area of activity does in fact provide protection to those individuals particularly affected by that activity, the legislation is

---

[7] [1982] AC 173.   [8] [1995] 2 AC 633.

[9] Technically, the *Lonrho* case involved a claim for damages whereas in *ex p Island Records* it was injunctive relief that had been sought. But even so, the *Lonrho* approach was subsequently stated by the Court of Appeal to be applicable regardless of whether it was an injunction or damages that was sought: *RCA Corp v Pollard* [1983] Ch 135.   [10] *Doe d Bishop of Rochester v Bridges* (1831) 1 B & Ad 847, at 859.

[11] [1982] AC 173, at 186, *per* Lord Diplock.

[12] [1982] AC 173, at 186, *per* Lord Diplock (citing a test formulated by Brett J in *Benjamin v Storr* (1874) LR 9 CP 400, at 407).

not to be treated as being passed for the benefit of those individuals *but for the benefit of society in general.*[13]

Subsequent to the House of Lords reaching its decision in the *Bedfordshire* case, the claimants pursued their case to the European Court of Human Rights where it was held that there had been a breach of both Articles 3 and 13 of the European Convention on Human Rights.[14] Respectively, these Articles provide for protection from inhuman or degrading treatment and the right to an adequate remedy under domestic law. However, the Strasbourg court's finding does not affect the action for breach of statutory duty. Instead, its repercussions have been felt in the context of common law negligence actions[15] and, of course, in relation to actions under section 7 of the Human Rights Act 1998 which provides a cause of action where 'a public authority has acted (or proposes to act) in a way which is made unlawful by section 6(1)' (that is, where the public authority fails to act consistently with a citizen's Convention rights).[16]

To succeed, then, in a claim for breach of statutory duty after the decisions in *Lonrho* and *X v Bedfordshire County Council*, the claimant must now satisfy a two-part test. He must establish that when Parliament enacted the relevant statute[17] (1) it was intended to protect a class of persons to which he belongs[18] and (2) Parliament envisaged that, in providing that protection of his interests, he should be able to claim compensation for any failure to protect those interests. The matter is in theory entirely one of construction of the statute in question. But as Lord Browne-Wilkinson has observed, while the principles of breach of statutory duty may be clear in theory, 'the application of those principles in any particular case remains difficult'.[19]

SECTION 2 ELUSIVE PARLIAMENTARY INTENT

The success or failure of any attempt to frame an action for breach of statutory duty will turn on Parliamentary intention. And as Lord Steyn observed in *Gorringe v Calderdale MBC*, 'the central question is whether from the provisions and structure of the statute an intention can be gathered to create a private law remedy'.[20] Yet in many instances it is probable that the legislature never even considered the issue of whether individuals

---

[13] [1995] 2 AC 633, at 731–732 (emphasis added). See also confirmation of this approach in *Phelps v Hillingdon LBC* [2001 2 AC 619.   [14] *Z v UK* (2001) 34 EHRR 97. See also ch 1.

[15] See, principally, *D v East Berkshire Community NHS Trust* [2005] 2 AC 373. And see also *Barrett v Enfield London Borough Council* [1999] 3 All ER 193 and *Phelps v Hillingdon London Borough Council* [2001] 2 AC 619.

[16] For detailed analysis, see Murphy, 'Children in Need – The Limits of Local Authority Accountability' [2003] *Legal Studies* 103.

[17] On the importance of timing, see *Issa v Hackney Borough Council* [1997] 1 All ER 999.

[18] It does not matter that the class may be very wide and for that reason hard to distinguish from the public in general: *Roe v Sheffield CC* [2004] QB 653 (the class 'road users' was regarded as being sufficiently specific).

[19] *X v Bedfordshire County Council* [1995] 2 AC 633, at 730.   [20] [2004] 1 WLR 1057.

should be able to claim damages for breach of the obligations embodied in the relevant statute. Only rarely does Parliament expressly declare that any breach of the statute should,[21] or should not,[22] be actionable in tort. On the other hand, since the courts may now refer to *Hansard* in interpreting statutes, Parliamentary intent may sometimes be gleaned from a study of the Parliamentary debates.[23] Nonetheless, in the majority of instances, the judges will continue to struggle with principles and policy developed over the years.

It cannot be stressed too forcefully, therefore, that an action for breach of statutory duty will only lie if the court finds that Parliament intended to confer a right to compensation on an individual injured by breach of that duty.[24] It is not enough simply to show that a statute was designed to protect the claimant in some general sense. Loss or injury of a recognized type must be shown, as must the intention of Parliament, that victims should be entitled to monetary compensation. Thus, in one case, unauthorized publication of information about the claimant in breach of the Mental Health Tribunal Rules was held to be insufficient since privacy was not a recognized head of damage.[25] And equally, in *Hague v Deputy Governor of Parkhurst Prison*,[26] where prisoners alleged that they had suffered injury as a result of being held in solitary confinement in breach of Prison Rules, it was held that mere evidence that the Rules were in part designed to protect prisoners was insufficient to show the required Parliamentary intention that they should be able to sue. Lord Jauncey put it this way:

The Prison Act 1952 is designed to deal with the administration of prisons and the management and control of prisoners. It covers such wide-ranging matters as central administration, prison officers, confinement and treatment of prisoners, release of prisoners on licence. Its objects are far removed from those of legislation such as the Factories and Coal Miners Acts whose prime concern is to protect the health and safety of persons[27] who work therein.[28]

The priority afforded to interests in bodily security by the law of torts (particularly within an employment context) is reflected in the willingness of the courts to interpret industrial safety legislation so as to confer a right of action on injured workmen. As Lord Jauncey intimated, breaches of statutory rules to fence machinery in the Factories Act[29] and regulations made for miners safety by the Mines and Quarries Acts[30]

---

[21] For two examples where Parliament expressly created a civil remedy for breach of statutory duty see the Protection from Harassment Act 1997, s 3 and the Consumer Protection Act 1987, s 41.

[22] See the Health and Safety at Work Act 1974, s 47(2).

[23] See *Richardson v Pitt-Stanley* [1995] QB 123.

[24] *Hague v Deputy Governor of Parkhurst Prison* [1991] 3 All ER 733, at 750, *per* Lord Jauncey.

[25] *Pickering v Liverpool Daily Post and Echo Newspapers plc* [1991] 1 All ER 622. But given the courts' obligation (*per* the Human Rights Act 1998) to develop the common law in line with the European Convention on Human Rights, would the same decision be reached today bearing in mind the Art 8 right to respect for private and family life? [26] [1991] 3 All ER 733.

[27] Note that Lord Bridge suggested ([1991] 3 All ER 733, at 741) that an action might lie for breach of those of the Prison Rules concerned with industrial safety in prison workshops.

[28] [1991] 3 All ER 733, at 750–1. [29] *Groves v Lord Wimborne* [1898] 2 QB 402.

[30] *Black v Fife Coal Co Ltd* [1912] AC 149; *National Coal Board v England* [1954] AC 403.

represent classic examples of the statutory provisions traditionally supporting tort actions. In such cases, the courts readily find that Parliament envisaged that an injured employee should be able to claim compensation from any employer who failed to provide his workforce with the protection Parliament demanded. Strict liability for injury to employees both offered an overwhelming incentive to employers to ensure that safety rules were complied with, and meant that the cost of any injury which befell a worker fell on the employer, not the luckless individual. Piecemeal legislation on industrial safety was originally intended to be replaced by a new all-embracing statutory regime introduced by the Health and Safety at Work Act 1974. Sections 2–9 of that Act imposed general safety duties on all employers. Breach of those general duties are expressly stated not to be actionable in tort.[31] But section 15 empowered the Secretary of State to make specific health and safety regulations for particular industries.[32] These abound and breaches are actionable unless the regulation in question provides otherwise.[33]

The duties imposed by such regulations vary in form. Some are absolute, thus requiring that employees' safety be guaranteed. Others demand only that the employer do what is reasonably practicable. In the interpretation of these and modern EU Regulations, case law on their predecessors (such as the Factories Acts) may remain relevant. More importantly, the general principle that employees injured at work should have generous access to compensation for industrial injury remains intact.

There are also precedents for the protection of interests in land and goods against violation of a statute.[34] Economic losses, too, have exceptionally been found recoverable where protection from that kind of loss is within the ambit of the statute. In *Monk v Warbey*,[35] for example, the claimant suffered bodily injuries in a road accident. Alas, the driver of the car was uninsured and impecunious. The claimant recovered his consequential financial loss by suing the owner of the car who, in breach of his statutory duty, had allowed his friend to drive uninsured against third party risks. Equally, in *Rickless v United Artists Corpn*,[36] the claimants won a massive award of damages for the defendants' unauthorized use of clips from old Peter Sellers films. The Court of Appeal found that violation of section 2 of the Dramatic and Musical Performers' Protection Act 1958, prohibiting use of such material without the performer's consent, did create a civil right of action. The purpose of the Act was protection of performers' rights and correlative financial interests.

On the other hand, in *Richardson v Pitt-Stanley*[37] a claim against the claimant's employer-company and its directors for failure to comply with provisions of the Employers' Liability (Compulsory Insurance) Act 1969 requiring employers to insure against liability for accidents at work failed. The Court of Appeal held that in respect of the company, the employee already enjoyed a range of remedies at common law

---

[31] Health and Safety at Work Act 1974, s 47(1)(a).
[32] Replacing earlier legislation such as the Factories Acts.
[33] Health and Safety at Work Act 1974, s 47(2). For examples of such regulations, see the 10th edition of this work.   [34] *Ross v Rugge-Price* (1876) 1 Ex D 269.
[35] [1935] 1 KB 75.   [36] [1988] QB 40.   [37] [1995] QB 123.

enforceable against company assets. If there were no such assets (and there were not because the company had gone into liquidation), and no insurance policy, no additional claim for breach of statutory duty under the 1969 Act would avail the claimant. The substantial criminal penalties under the Act militated against the existence of a civil claim and some slight indication that Parliament did not intend to create such a private right was to be found in Hansard. If no civil action for breach of statutory duty was intended against the company, their Lordships thought it unlikely that Parliament intended a claim to lie against individual directors.

In the light of the current judicial trend towards restricting liability for economic loss, very clear evidence that this type of loss was intended to be protected by the statute will be required. In *Richardson v Pitt-Stanley*, Stuart-Smith LJ signalled in the following words that only exceptionally would such losses be recoverable in an action for breach of statutory duty.

In my opinion, the court will more readily construe a statutory provision so as to provide a civil cause of action where the provision relates to the safety and health of a class of persons rather than where they have thereby suffered economic loss.[38]

So, in *Wentworth v Wiltshire County Council*,[39] a claimant seeking to recover for damage to his business caused by disrepair of the adjacent highway failed in his claim. The duty to maintain the highway existed to protect users against personal injury not to safeguard the profits of traders. Furthermore, a number of other factors will impact on the courts' readiness to find that Parliament intended that one of the class of persons for whose benefit an Act was passed should have an action for compensation for its breach.

(1) There is a great reluctance to allow a claim for breach of statutory duty against a public authority for failure to provide adequate public services. Claims have failed against health[40] and education ministers[41] for failure to meet their statutory obligations to ensure adequate health care to patients and education for the nation's children respectively. For example, in *X v Bedfordshire County Council*[42] Lord Browne-Wilkinson, addressing claims in respect of the child care protection system, had no doubt that the relevant statutes were intended to protect children from abuse, but that the language and framework of the legislation was not designed to allow individual children or families to sue.[43] Lord Bridge summed up the heart of the case against imposing liability for breach of statutory duty on public bodies when he issued this ringing warning against too great a readiness to do so:

... the shoulders of a public authority are only broad enough to bear the loss because they are financed by the public at large. It is pre-eminently for the legislature to decide whether these policy reasons should be accepted as sufficient for imposing on the

---

[38] [1995] QB 123, at 132.   [39] [1993] QB 654.

[40] *R v Secretary of State for Social Services, ex p Hincks* (1979) 123 Sol Jo 436.

[41] *Watt v Kesteven County Council* [1955] 1 QB 408.   [42] [1995] 2 AC 633.

[43] For a full review of the area, see further Murphy, 'Children in Need – The Limits of Local Authority Accountability' [1993] *Legal Studies* 103.

public the burden of providing compensation for financial losses. If they do so decide, it is not difficult for them to say so.[44]

Continuing in this vein, a seven-judge House of Lords ruled out an action based on breaches of the Education Acts 1944 and 1981 in *Phelps v Hillingdon London Borough Council*.[45] Their Lordships have also rejected a claim premised on a local authority's breach of a statutory duty to house homeless persons.[46]

(2) If the alleged breach of duty derives not from a breach of a statute itself, but a breach of a regulation made under a statute, the following tricky question arises. Did the enabling Act, as it must, empower the minister to make regulations conferring private rights of action on individuals?[47] In answering this question, all that is clear is that where a statute (a) permits a minister to establish rules concerned with the safety of a particular class of persons, and (b) the Act also empowers the minister to exempt certain potential defendants from the rules, the inference will be that there was no legislative intention that those rules would support an action for breach of statutory duty.[48]

(3) The statutory duty itself must be precise in its terms so as to make enforcing it by way of an action in tort fair to the defendant.[49]

(4) Finally it must be shown that, to intend that a private right of action should lie for violation of a statute, Parliament could have envisaged the circumstances in which the claimant came to suffer harm. In *Olotu v Home Office*[50] the claimant was remanded in custody for a period exceeding the 112-day limit set by Regulations. The court found that the Regulations were designed to achieve expedition in the prosecution of crime and to ensure that accused persons did 'not languish in prison for excessive periods awaiting trial'. Protecting accused persons – the class to which the claimant belonged – was clearly an object of the Regulations. However, no claim for breach of statutory duty lay because neither Parliament nor the secretary of state laying down the Regulations would have foreseen a scenario where not only would the Crown Prosecution Service fail to comply with its duty under the Regulations, but also the accused person would fail to apply for immediate bail.

SECTION 3 THE NATURE OF THE ACTION

Care must be taken to avoid confusion between this tort and negligence, albeit that in practice claimants will often make concurrent claims for breach of statutory duty and negligence. Lord Browne-Wilkinson offered an instructive analysis in *X v Bedfordshire*

---

[44] *Murphy v Brentwood District Council* [1990] 2 All ER 908, at 931.   [45] [2001] 2 AC 619.

[46] *O'Rourke v Camden London Borough Council* [1998] AC 188.

[47] *Hague v Deputy Governor of Parkhurst Prison* [1991] 3 All ER 733. Note the rather different answers to the question from Lords Bridge and Jauncey. See also *Olotu v Home Office* [1997] 1 WLR 328, at 339 and *Todd v Adams* [2002] 2 Lloyd's Rep 293.   [48] *Todd v Adams* [2002] 2 Lloyd's Rep 293, at [25], *per* Neuberger J.

[49] *Cutler v Wandsworth Stadium Ltd* [1949] AC 398; *X v Bedfordshire County Council* [1995] 2 AC 633.

[50] [1997] 1 WLR 328. See also *Issa v Hackney London Borough Council* [1997] 1 All ER 999.

County Council.[51] Addressing the extent of the defendant local authority's liabilities in tort generally for failure in child care and educational provision, he distinguished between three possible causes of action in tort.

(A) BREACH OF STATUTORY DUTY *SIMPLICITER*

Such a claim, in the tort which this chapter centrally addresses, 'depends neither on any breach of the [claimant's] common law rights nor on any allegation of negligence by the defendants'. If a private right of action lies for violation of a statute, the claimant has no need to prove negligence.

(B) THE COMMON LAW DUTY OF CARE

It may be that the performance of a statutory duty gives rise to a common law duty of care. The ordinary rules governing the existence of a duty of care in negligence will then apply subject to the caveat that the statutory duty cannot be taken to form the basis for establishing that duty of care. There must be other features of the case that, independently of the existence of the statutory duty, would ground a common law duty.[52]

(C) THE CARELESS PERFORMANCE OF A STATUTORY DUTY

If it is not established that Parliament intended to create an action for breach of statutory duty in respect of a particular obligation, and if it cannot be established, either, that the circumstances of the claimant's relationship with the defendant gave rise to a common law duty of care, no claim in tort lies simply for the careless performance of a statutory duty. On the other hand, if the claim is founded on another tort – say, for example, private nuisance – the fact that the statutory duty has been performed negligently will defeat an otherwise extant defence of statutory authority.[53]

A classic claim for breach of statutory duty, then – once a private right of action has been found to lie – requires only that the claimant should prove that the statutory obligation was not fulfilled. In many cases, liability is truly strict. In others, the statute may prescribe that some degree of negligence be proven. In still others, yet to like effect, the statute may even (on occasion) allow a defence if the defendant shows that avoiding

---

[51] [1995] 2 AC 633, at 731–736. See also *London Passenger Transport Board v Upson* [1949] AC 155, at 168, *per* Lord Wright.

[52] In *Gorringe v Calderdale MBC* [2004] 1 WLR 1057, Lord Scott said (at [71]): 'the [statutory] duty cannot create a duty of care that would not have been owed at common law'. Lords Steyn and Hoffmann expressed similar views at [23] and [38], respectively.

[53] *X v Bedfordshire County Council* [1995] 2 AC 633, at 728–729, *per* Lord Jauncey.

injury to the claimant was not 'reasonably practicable'.[54] In all cases, the nature of the conduct constituting violation of the Act is prescribed by the statute itself.

SECTION 4 WHAT THE CLAIMANT MUST PROVE

(A) AN OBLIGATION ON THE DEFENDANT

A mandatory duty must be imposed on the defendant if the action is to lie. The creation of a criminal offence prohibiting members of the public from engaging in certain conduct is insufficient.[55] Similarly, the conferral of a mere power to act is not enough to justify a civil action in respect of a failure to act in that way.

(B) THE STATUTE MUST IMPOSE THE BURDEN ON THE DEFENDANT

This issue has been raised most frequently in actions by workers against their employers where they have been injured by some act or omission of fellow workers. It is not always easy to decide whether the duty is imposed on the employer or on the worker. Just such a problem arose in *Harrison v National Coal Board*[56] where various duties relating to the running of mines were imposed by statute. In that case, the House of Lords held that, when expressed impersonally, the duties were to be understood as binding the mine owner. But where the duties were personal – such as duties relating to shot firing – those duties, expressly imposed on the shot firers were to be treated as binding the shot-firers alone.

Once the statute has been interpreted to impose a duty on the employer, the general principle is clear: the duty will be non-delegable. Thus:

the owner cannot relieve himself of his obligation by saying that he has appointed reasonably competent persons and that the breach is due to negligence on their part.[57]

It would therefore be no defence to an employer of a workman injured by an unfenced machine that the foreman has failed to carry out the instructions to fence which the employer issued to him. The rule is the same where the duty of the employer has been neglected by the independent contractor of the employer.[58] Other problems, however

---

[54] See, eg, the Highways Act 1980, s 41(1A) which provides that a highway authority is only required to keep a highway free from snow or ice so 'so far as is reasonably practicable'.

[55] *Lonrho Ltd v Shell Petroleum Co Ltd (No 2)* [1981] 2 All ER 456.   [56] [1951] AC 639.

[57] *Lochgelly Iron and Coal Co v M'Mullan* [1934] AC 1, at 13, *per* Lord Warrington.

[58] *Hosking v De Havilland Aircraft Co Ltd* [1949] 1 All ER 540; *Braham v J Lyons & Co Ltd* [1962] 3 All ER 281. Cf *Hole v Sittingbourne and Sheerness Rly Co* (1861) 6 H & N 488.

(which will be discussed later), are raised when the defendant has delegated the duty to the claimant himself, and the claimant is injured as a result of his own failure to perform the delegated duty.

(c) STATUTE PROTECTS THE CLAIMANT'S INTEREST BY WAY OF A CAUSE OF ACTION IN TORT

The fundamental issue is simply whether the Act was intended to create a right of action in tort.[59] Everything else is subordinate to that. The following considerations are no more than guides to the principles which the courts utilize in identifying (usually unexpressed) legislative intention. They must not be elevated to the status of inflexible rules of law overriding the root question of the purpose of the statute. As Lord Simonds said:

The only rule which in all circumstances is valid is that the answer must depend on a consideration of the whole Act and the circumstances, including the pre-existing law, in which it was enacted.[60]

(1) THE STATE OF THE PRE-EXISTING COMMON LAW

Sometimes, the law of torts in force before the passing of the Act[61] is considered to afford adequate compensation to victims in circumstances also covered by the statute,[62] and the object of the statute is merely to regulate certain activities in order to help prevent the occurrence of that loss which the existing law of tort would redress.[63] In such circumstances, the statute will not usually confer an additional cause of action for damages. For instance, the ordinary law of negligence affords adequate protection for the victims of road accidents: yet the need to reduce these accidents is so urgent that there is much legislation regulating road traffic (for example, on the use of headlights during hours of darkness). But the courts do not generally allow persons injured by motorists in breach of such statutory duties to sue in reliance on the relevant statute: they leave them to pursue their remedy in negligence, and regard the sanctions of the statute as limited to the imposition of the penalty prescribed.[64]

---

[59] Eg, *Hague v Deputy Governor of Parkhurst Prison* [1991] 3 All ER 733, at 705, *per* Lord Jauncey; *Atkinson v Newcastle and Gateshead Waterworks Co* (1877) 2 Ex D 441, at 448, *per* Lord Cairns LC; *Pasmore v Oswaldtwistle UDC* [1898] AC 387, at 397, *per* Lord Halsbury LC.

[60] *Cutler v Wandsworth Stadium Ltd* [1949] AC 398, at 407.

[61] So in *Issa v Hackney London Borough Council* [1997] 1 WLR 956, no claim lay in respect of a statutory nuisance because in 1936, when the relevant Act was passed, virtually all victims of such a nuisance would have been able to recover compensation from their landlords.

[62] See *Richardson v Pitt-Stanley* [1995] QB 123. If it is argued that there should be a claim for breach of statutory duty additional to common law remedies, it must be shown that the private action for breach of the statute will actually be independently effective.

[63] Sometimes, as in *Square v Model Farm Dairies (Bournemouth) Ltd* [1939] 2 KB 365 (sale of infected milk), the court might decide that no tort was intended to be created because existing contractual remedies were adequate.

[64] *Phillips v Britannia Hygienic Laundry Co* [1923] 2 KB 832 (a defective axle on lorry, in breach of the Motor Cars (Use and Construction) Order 1904 gave no cause of action to the owner of another vehicle damaged in

If, however, the statute merely affirms an interest of the claimant which the common law already recognizes, and does not purport to be giving that interest statutory protection for some quite different purpose, then the claimant may be free to sue for breach of the statute.[65] Thus, in *Ashby v White*, where the right to vote – a common law right – had been confirmed by statute, Holt CJ said:

And this statute . . . is only an enforcement of the common law; and if the Parliament thought the freedom of elections to be a matter of that consequence, as to give their sanction to it, and to enact that they should be free; it is a violation of that statute, to disturb the [claimant] in this case in giving his vote at an election, and consequently actionable.[66]

(2) ALTERNATIVE REMEDIES PROVIDED BY STATUTE

It has been suggested that where a statute fails to provide any alternative means of enforcement in the event of breach of the relevant duty, the claimant's task to establish that an action in tort was intended by the statute may be eased.[67] But the absence of an alternative remedy is not by any means irrefutable evidence that Parliament intended to grant the claimant redress via an action for breach of statutory duty. Counsel for prisoners claiming damages for breaches of the Prison Rules in *Hague v Deputy Governor of Parkhurst Prison* sought to argue that the absence of any other remedy available to them necessarily meant that an action lay. The House of Lords forcefully rejected that contention.[68] It is even doubtful whether the case stands as authority for the proposition that the absence of a statutory remedy can be taken as grounding a weak presumption that an action for breach of statutory duty will lie. In *every case*, according to their Lordships, evidence must be presented on the central question of parliamentary intent.

Accordingly, even in cases where an alternative remedy is available under the Act, the mere availability of that remedy is not *per se* determinative of the issue. As Lord Browne-Wilkinson forcefully put it in the *Hague* case, 'the mere existence of some other statutory remedy is not necessarily decisive'.[69] This is an important statement given that provision is often made for cases in which public authorities fail to carry out

---

consequence of the breach); *Clarke and Wife v Brims* [1947] KB 497 (failure to carry a red rear light on a car gave no right of action under this head to C who collided with the car); *Balmer v Hayes* 1950 SC 477 (the failure of a driver to disclose in an application for a driving licence that he was epileptic gave no cause of action to a passenger injured when an attack of epilepsy caused the driver to collide with another vehicle); *Verney v Wilkins* [1962] 106 Sol Jo 879 (a learner-driver was not liable for a passenger's injuries merely because there was a breach of the Act in that he was unaccompanied by a qualified driver); *Coote v Stone* [1971] 1 All ER 657 (parking on clearway not actionable in itself).

[65] *Wolverhampton New Waterworks Co v Hawkesford* (1859) 6 CBNS 336, at 356, *per* Willes J. He may then have the choice of the action for breach of statutory duty or the existing common-law remedy: see, eg, *Simon v Islington Borough Council* [1943] 1 KB 188, at 193, *per* Scott LJ (neglect of abandoned tramway).

[66] (1703) 2 Ld Raym 938, at 954. Cf the contrary approach in the analogous cases of *Watkins v Secretary of State for the Home Department* [2006] 2 WLR 807 concerning misfeasance in public office.

[67] *Thornton v Kirklees Metropolitan Borough Council* [1979] QB 626; but overruled on its facts in *O'Rourke v Camden London Borough Council* [1998] AC 188. And see *Booth & Co (International) Ltd v National Enterprise Board* [1978] 3 All ER 624.   [68] [1991] 3 All ER 733.

[69] *X v Bedfordshire County Council* [1995] 2 AC 633, at 731.

their duties for an administrative machinery according to which compliance with those duties may be secured.[70] For example, it may be provided that representations can be made to the relevant secretary of state (who can then order a recalcitrant public body to fulfil its responsibilities). But, importantly, the courts will need to be mindful of the extent to which the relevant administrative 'remedy' will provide the claimant with a means of obtaining financial redress.[71]

Where the 'alternative remedy' is the imposition of a criminal penalty, the onus will be on the claimant to establish that his claim falls within one of the two exceptions to the general rule of non-actionability set out by Lord Diplock in *Lonrho*.[72] Normally, then, this will mean that he must show that the purpose of the statute was not just to regulate a particular activity in the general public interest, but also to benefit a class of persons to which he belongs.[73] So, for example, the existence of criminal penalties in the Factories Acts did not bar concurrent remedies in tort since the duties imposed by those Acts were specifically designed to protect workmen.[74] By contrast, however, breach of statutory rules regulating the operation of greyhound tracks (and betting at those tracks), did not enable an aggrieved bookmaker to sue because the statute was not passed to safeguard or enhance the business of bookmakers.[75]

Special mention should finally be made of cases in which the alternative remedy available to the claimant would be judicial review. This is because the matter received detailed (but ultimately unsatisfactory) consideration by a divided House of Lords in *Cullen v Chief Constable of the Royal Ulster Constabulary*.[76]

C was detained in custody under terrorism legislation. Contrary to section 15 of the Northern Ireland (Temporary Provisions) Act 1987, C was denied the right to a private consultation with a solicitor. The fact that he was denied this right resulted in no measurable harm to C.

By a bare majority, their Lordships held that C did not have a civil claim for nominal damages based on breach of statutory duty. Material to the decisions of those in the majority was the fact that 'the speedy hearing of an application for judicial review . . . is a much more effective remedy for a claimant to seek than an action for nominal damages'.[77] Beyond the fact that this proposition is itself questionable,[78] however, the case leaves us

---

[70] See Murphy, 'Children in Need – The Limits of Local Authority Accountability' [2003] *Legal Studies* 103.

[71] See, eg, *Phelps v Hillingdon London Borough Council* [2001] 2 AC 619.

[72] *Atkinson v Newcastle and Gateshead Waterworks Co* (1877) 2 Ex D 441.

[73] See, eg, *Todd v Adams* [2002] 2 Lloyd's Rep 293.

[74] *Groves v Lord Wimborne* [1898] 2 QB 402. Breach of the duty to stop at a pedestrian crossing is a rare example of a road safety regulation being interpreted so as to create a right of action in tort: *London Passenger Transport Board v Upson* [1949] AC 155. Is this perhaps because pedestrians at zebra crossings constitute a defined class of persons?   [75] *Cutler v Wandsworth Stadium Ltd* [1949] AC 398.

[76] [2003] 1 WLR 1763.

[77] [2003] 1 WLR 1763, at [39], *per* Lord Hutton (with whom Lords Millett and Rodger agreed).

[78] These, as was pointed out in the joint dissenting speech of Lords Bingham and Steyn in the *Cullen* case, centre on the formidable obstacles that can sometimes stand in the way of demonstrating *locus standi* for the purposes of seeking judicial review: see [2003] 1 WLR 1763, at [20].

unclear on whether an action based on breach of statutory duty would have been available if the denial of access to a solicitor had resulted in measurable harm.[79]

(3) PUBLIC AND PRIVATE RIGHTS

Although the case-law is not entirely clear on this, one possible view seems to be that the claimant, in order to sue, must establish that a right or interest of his, *as a member of an ascertainable class of persons*, has been violated by the breach of duty. At one time, it was suggested that a duty owed to the public generally would suffice.[80] But some judicial fears about opening the floodgates, coupled with a wealth of contrary *dicta*, suggest that this view is no longer tenable. Lord Browne-Wilkinson, in *X v Bedfordshire County Council*, for example, saw actions for breach of statutory duty *simpliciter* arising only in favour of 'a limited class of the public'.[81]

Note, too, Lord Diplock's second exception[82] to the general rule of non-actionability where alternative criminal remedies are provided by the statute which refers to special damage resulting to the claimant in his enjoyment of a public right (a right available to all Her Majesty's subjects). It is somewhat difficult to discern whether Lord Diplock was simply endorsing the earlier approach according to which certain duties might be designed to benefit every member of the public individually, or whether he was initiating a new category of breach of statutory duty. Such a new category might ostensibly enable a person suffering special damage to sue without establishing a specific intention to protect his individual interest. The wording used by his Lordship is obscure and one of the authorities relied on is a leading judgment on public nuisance.[83] Accordingly, the better view is probably that any extension of the tort seems unlikely.

(D) THE HARM SUFFERED BY HIM IS WITHIN THE SCOPE OF THE GENERAL CLASS OF RISKS AT WHICH THE STATUTE IS DIRECTED

The leading case is *Gorris v Scott*.[84]

A statutory order required that those parts of a ship which were to be occupied by animals should be divided into pens of a specified size. D violated this order on a ship on which he was transporting sheep belonging to C. This violation caused C's sheep to be washed overboard.

---

[79] As regards those in the majority, Lord Hutton thought that it would be available (at [41]) while Lord Millett (despite elsewhere signalling his agreement with Lord Hutton) thought it would not (at [69]). Lord Rodger muddied the waters still further by agreeing with both of them, while Lords Bingham and Steyn, dissenting, were of the opinion that such an action would lie (although it is not clear what weight should be given to their dissenting view in the future).

[80] *Phillips v Britannia Hygenic Laundry Co* [1923] 2 KB 832, at 841, *per* Atkin LJ.

[81] [1995] 2 AC 633, at 731. See also, *O'Rourke v Camden London Borough Council* [1998] AC 188, at 194; *Mid Kent Holdings plc v General Utilities plc* [1997] 1 WLR 14.

[82] *Lonrho Ltd v Shell Petroleum Co Ltd (No 2)* [1982] AC 173.   [83] *Benjamin v Storr* (1874) LR 9 CP 400.

[84] (1874) LR 9 Exch 125. But see also *Tasci v Pekalp of London Ltd* [2001] ICR 633.

However, the statute was designed to prevent the spread of disease, not to prevent animals from being drowned. As such, an action for breach of statutory duty failed.

In similar vein, the duty imposed on highway authorities to repair the roads in order to protect users from injury was held not to embrace loss of profit to a local trader.[85] And, equally, breach of the requirement that employees be kitted out with steel toe-capped boots to prevent injury from falling objects does not ground an action based on frostbite.[86]

In the industrial context, too, the House of Lords has held that the statutory duty on an employer to fence every dangerous part of a machine was confined to the prevention of a workman coming into contact with moving parts of the machine and did not envisage protecting him from injury caused by ejected or flying pieces of the machine itself, or injury caused by the material on which the machine was working.[87] On the other hand, when a bogie was derailed by a stone that had been allowed to fall from the roof of a mine in breach of the defendants' statutory duty, and the claimant was consequently injured, the House of Lords held that 'where the object of the enactment is to promote safety there can be no implication that liability for a breach is limited to one which causes injury in a particular way'.[88] And in *Gerrard v Stafford-shire Potteries*[89] the defendant was found liable in respect of a breach of regulations requiring eye protection against any 'reasonably foreseeable risk engaged in the work from particles or fragments thrown off' where a foreign body flew out of a jar the claimant was glazing. The statute was designed to safeguard the worker from any object dangerous to the eye in the course of her work.

(E) THE CLAIMANT WAS ONE OF THE PERSONS PROTECTED BY THE STATUTE

Breach of a statute may give rise to an action in tort, but not necessarily in the hands of the particular claimant, as *Knapp v Railway Executive* shows.[90]

The Brighton & Chichester Railway Act 1844 provided for the erection of gates at level crossings, and the general supervision and maintenance of these gates. Knapp had stopped his car slightly short of a level crossing governed by this Act because it was closed against road traffic. Somehow, the brake of the car was released; the car moved forward and struck the gate. The gate had not been maintained in accordance with the Act, so that it swung back and

---

[85] *Wentworth v Wiltshire County Council* [1993] 2 All ER 256; and see *Merlin v British Nuclear Fuels plc* [1990] 2 QB 557 (damage to property means actual damage not diminished value through risk of contamination). Contrast the finding in *Merlin* with *Blue Circle Industries plc v Ministry of Defence* [1996] EGCS 190 (contamination requiring an intensive cleansing operation does constitute damage to land).

[86] *Fytche v Wincanton Logistics plc* [2004] 4 All ER 221.

[87] *Close v Steel Co of Wales Ltd* [1962] AC 367. Cf *Wearing v Pirelli Ltd* [1977] 1 All ER 339 (D, an employer, was liable when the unfenced dangerous part of the machine jerked his employee's hand against the materials being worked upon).

[88] *Grant v National Coal Board* [1956] AC 649, at 664, *per* Lord Tucker; *Donaghey v Boulton and Paul Ltd* [1968] AC 1; *Millard v Serck Tubes Ltd* [1969] 1 All ER 598.   [89] [1995] ICR 502.

[90] [1949] 2 All ER 508. Cf *Lavender v Diamints Ltd* [1949] 1 KB 585.

injured the driver of an oncoming train. It was held that the purpose of these provisions was to protect road users against danger from the railway only, and that an engine driver on the railway was thus not within the scope of the Act.

(F) WHEN DAMAGE MUST BE PROVED

In general the claimant must prove the relevant damage ensuing from the alleged breach of duty. The question is: what is the nature of the right or interest protected by the statute? If, for example, it is an interest in personal safety, then the courts will grant a remedy only if the claimant shows that he has sustained personal injury in consequence of a breach of the statutory duty.[91]

There are judgments in which it has been held that where, from its context, it is clear that the statute created a right in the claimant so absolute in its content that the claimant was to be protected against a violation, even though it caused no damage, then the tort is actionable *per se*. Thus, in *Ashby v White*,[92] interference with the statutory right to vote was held actionable *per se*, and in *Ferguson v Earl Kinnoull*[93] the refusal on the part of the defendant, in the face of a statute, to determine the suitability of the claimant for a living to which he had been presented, was held actionable *per se*. Yet in *Pickering v Liverpool Daily Post and Echo Newspapers plc*, Lord Bridge declared that an action could lie only on proof of 'loss or injury of a kind for which the law awards damages'.[94] Neither *Ashby* nor *Ferguson* were cited in that judgment.

(G) THE CONDUCT OF THE DEFENDANT WAS OF SUCH A CHARACTER AS TO VIOLATE THE STATUTE

Whether a defendant is liable for a breach, even though his act is neither intentional nor negligent, depends on the statute. Liability is strict in very many cases. For instance, non-negligent failure properly to maintain a lift in efficient working order was held by the House of Lords to be an actionable breach of the Factories Act 1937.[95] On the other hand, some statutes require the defendant only to do what is 'reasonably practicable'. So, regulation 11(2)(a) of the Provision and Use of Work Equipment Regulations 1998[96] requires the use of fixed guards for dangerous parts of machinery *if practicable* and, if not, sets in place a graded hierarchy of safety measures employers must take. There is a mass of case law on the interpretation of statutory provisions laying down such standards of conduct. The point to note here is that one must always turn to the statute imposing the duty to discover against

---

[91] Eg, *Watts v Enfield Rolling Mills (Aluminium) Ltd* [1952] 1 All ER 1013.
[92] (1703) 2 Ld Raym 938. Cf *Simmonds v Newport Abercarn Black Vein Steam Coal Co* [1921] 1 KB 616.
[93] (1842) 9 Cl & Fin 251.   [94] [1991] 1 All ER 622, at 632.
[95] *Galashiels Gas Co Ltd v Millar* [1949] AC 275.   [96] SI 1998 No 2306.

what particular types of conduct on the part of the defendant the claimant will be protected by an action in tort.

(H) CAUSATION

As with other torts, heads of damage are recoverable only when the breach of duty by the defendant 'caused' them. Moreover, as we have seen in many actions – especially those by workers for breach of safety regulations – success often depends on proof that injury to the claimant has been so 'caused'. In this tort 'the employee must in all cases prove his case by the ordinary standard of proof in civil actions: he must make it appear at least that on a balance of probabilities the breach of duty caused or materially contributed to his injury'.[97] Thus, where it was shown that a steel erector would not have worn a safety belt had it been provided, the House of Lords held that his employers were not liable to him for breach of their statutory duty to provide one.[98] Similarly, where a carpenter fell from a scaffold because the scaffold had been deliberately pushed over by a workmate, it was not the employer's breach of duty that had caused his injury. The employer was required to provide safe equipment and a safe place of work, but the duty incumbent upon him was to ensure that employees would be safe from foreseeable risks. The deliberate, wanton act of the workmate did not constitute such a risk:[99] it was a *novus actus interveniens* that broke the chain of causation.

SECTION 5 EUROPEAN LEGISLATION: THE ANALOGOUS ACTION

On the matter of European Community Law Rights, the English courts have for some time accepted that directly applicable European Community law can create obligations the breach of which entitles affected persons to sue for the harm thereby caused.[100] In *Francovich v Italy*,[101] however, the European Court broadened the bases of liability by holding that a failure by a member state to implement a Directive from the Community designed to create rights on the part of particular individuals would also give rise to a claim in damages on the part of those individuals. Strikingly, in *Francovich*, the Community legislation in question was not

---

[97] *Bonnington Castings Ltd v Wardlaw* [1956] AC 613, at 620, *per* Lord Reid. Cf *McGhee v National Coal Board* [1972] 3 All ER 1008 (a common law action in negligence). Even though C has proved the employer's breach of statutory duty with regard to a machine, and even though he has sustained injury from the machine, the onus of proving causation remains with C: *Lineker v Raleigh Industries Ltd* [1980] ICR 83.

[98] *Cummings (or McWilliams) v Sir William Arrol & Co Ltd* [1962] 1 All ER 623.

[99] *Horton v Taplin Contracts Ltd* [2003] ICR 179.

[100] *Garden Cottage Foods Ltd v Milk Marketing Board* [1984] AC 130.   [101] [1993] 2 CMLR 66.

directly effective which meant that, in the absence of an action against the state, there would have been no-one against whom an action could have been brought. Yet it has since been established by the European court that the *Francovich* principle applies in even more circumstances: where the legislation *is* of direct effect,[102] where the breach of Community law entails a legislative act (not merely an omission),[103] and in respect of administrative decisions.[104]

The conditions that must be satisfied in order to sue according to this 'eurotort' principle were set out by Lord Slynn in *R v Secretary of State for Transport, ex p Factortame Ltd*. He said:

Before a member state can be held liable, a national court must find that:

(i) the relevant rule of Community law is one which is intended to confer rights on individuals;

(ii) the breach must be sufficiently serious;

(iii) there must be a direct causal link between the breach and the loss complained of.[105]

The similarity between the first requirement and the test adopted in relation to an action for breach of statutory duty is immediately apparent; yet this connection between the two forms of action was arguably furthered in *Three Rivers District Council v Bank of England (No 3)*[106] where the House of Lords held that a failure to comply with a banking directive concerning the regulation of credit institutions was fundamentally concerned with harmonizing banking practice, rather than protecting depositors. In this way, their Lordships were not simply looking at whether the Community legislation in question was intended to confer rights on individuals, but whether it was intended to be for the benefit of the defined class of depositors. Since their Lordships answered this question in the negative, the action failed.

It has since been explained further, in relation to the second limb, that the pivotal phrase 'sufficiently serious' does not necessarily require negligence or fault (although fault may be a material consideration), and that the seriousness of the breach must be judged in the context of the clarity of the community rule breached and, where appropriate, the legislative discretion afforded to the member state.[107] Here, too, the similarities with ordinary breach of statutory duty principles are striking.

---

[102] *Brasserie du Pêcheur SA v Federal Republic of Germany* (Case C–46/93) [1996].

[103] *R v Secretary of State for Transport, ex p Factortame Ltd* (Case C–48/93).

[104] *R v Ministry of Agriculture, Fisheries and Food, ex p Hedley Lomas (Ireland)* (Case C5/94) [1996].

[105] [1999] 4 All ER 906, at 916. These conditions derive directly from the decision of the European Court of Justice in *Brasserie du Pêcheur SA v Federal Republic of Germany* (Case C–46/93) [1996], at [74].

[106] [2000] 2 WLR 1220.

[107] *R v Secretary of State for Transport, ex p Factortame Ltd (No 5)* [1999] 4 All ER 906.

SECTION 6 DEFENCES

(A) THE RELATION BETWEEN CRIMINAL AND TORTIOUS LIABILITY

Breaches of particular statutory duties may give rise both to criminal and tortious proceedings. It must not, however, be assumed that the defences in each case are identical. For example, the defences open to mine owners under the Coal Mines Act 1911 were held to be wider in criminal law than in actions for breach of statutory duty.[108]

(B) ASSUMPTION OF RISK

Wheeler v New Merton Board Mills Ltd[109] decided that *volenti non fit injuria* is not a defence to an action brought by a workman for breach by an employer of his statutory duty – at least where the statute makes the employer liable whether or not his conduct was intentional or negligent. In *ICI Ltd v Shatwell*,[110] the House of Lords approved the *Wheeler* case so far as employers' statutory duties are concerned; but it added that the defence of *volenti* 'should be available where the employer was not himself in breach of statutory duty and was not vicariously in breach of any statutory duty through the neglect of some person who was of superior rank to the [claimant] and whose commands the [claimant] was bound to obey'.[111] The grounds for the *Wheeler* decision are not obvious. This makes it all the harder, in the absence of any decision outside the sphere of such duties of employers to workers, to know whether the defence is generally inapplicable to actions for breach of statutory duty.[112] It may well be contrary to public policy for anybody (not merely employers) to contract out of a duty imposed by an Act of Parliament. If this is so, assumption of risk may never be a defence to this action.

(C) CONTRIBUTORY NEGLIGENCE

At common law, contributory negligence on the part of the claimant was once a complete defence.[113] Nowadays, apportionment of damages is possible under the Law Reform (Contributory Negligence) Act 1945.[114] The principles of the defence are the same as those already discussed, subject to the following points.[115] Legislation and

---

[108] [1933] 2 KB 669.   [109] [1965] AC 656.   [110] [1965] AC 656.   [111] [1965] AC 656, at 687.

[112] See *Alford v National Coal Board* [1952] 1 All ER 754, at 757, *per* Lord Normand (*obiter*).

[113] *Caswell v Powell Duffryn Associated Collieries Ltd* [1940] AC 152 (unanimous, but *obiter*).

[114] *Cakebread v Hopping Bros (Whetstone) Ltd* [1947] KB 641; *Tasci v Pekalp of London Ltd* [2001] ICR 633.

[115] It is difficult to accept the view of Denning J, in *Lavender v Diamints Ltd* [1948] 2 All ER 249 (not considered on appeal, [1949] 1 KB 585), that C, if contributorily negligent in an action for non-negligent violation of statutory duty, must be awarded no damages.

regulations designed to protect health and safety are often expressly designed to protect workers against acts or inattention. Accordingly, a 'risky act due to familiarity with the work or some inattention resulting from noise or strain' will not be contributory negligence,[116] although it might be sufficient negligence to make the employer vicariously liable to a negligently injured third party.[117] Frequently, the employer will have delegated to his employee responsibility for the performance of the statutory duty and that employee will then have been negligent. The House of Lords held in *Boyle v Kodak Ltd*[118] that 'once the [claimant] has established that there was a breach of enactment which made the employer absolutely liable, and that that breach caused the accident, he need do no more.'[119] But, 'if the employer can prove that the only act or default of anyone which caused or contributed to the non-compliance was the act or default of the [claimant] himself, he establishes a good defence'.[120]

In *Boyle v Kodak Ltd* the statutory duty to fix a ladder securely while a storage tank was painted was imposed on both the employers and the employee who was injured through its breach. The Court of Appeal dismissed the action on the ground that the claimant was the sole cause of the accident, but the House of Lords allowed his appeal. The employers had not proved that they had instructed the claimant on how to comply with the regulations. As such, their breach of statutory duty was a cause of the damage. The significance of the claimant also being in breach of his statutory duty was that it constituted a ground for apportionment of the damages: he was awarded one half. Had the statute imposed the duty on the employers alone, the claimant's damages would not have been reduced (even though performance of the duty was delegated to him by his employers), unless the employers proved that the claimant failed to take care for his own safety and was thus contributorily negligent.

(D) ACT OF A THIRD PARTY

This is no defence where the statute is deemed to impose liability so strict that the defendant is responsible for such acts. In other cases it may, but everything depends on the particular wording and interpretation of the Act.[121]

---

[116] Where, however, the risk has been consciously accepted by the employee, it will, apparently, be contributory negligence: see, eg, *Sherlock v Chester CC* [2004] EWCA Civ 201, at [32], *per* Latham LJ.

[117] *Staveley Iron and Chemical Co Ltd v Jones* [1956] AC 627, at 648, *per* Lord Tucker (explaining the similar decision of the House of Lords in *Caswell v Powell Duffryn Associated Collieries Ltd* [1939] 3 All ER 722). In *Mullard v Ben Line Steamers Ltd* [1971] 2 All ER 424, the deduction for contributory negligence was reduced because C's conduct 'was a monetary error, not to be judged too harshly when balanced against the defendants' flagrant and continuous breach of statutory duty', *per* Sachs LJ, at 428. On the difficulty of proving contributory negligence in this tort (as distinct from that of negligence) see *Westwood v Post Office* [1974] AC 1, and especially the statement by Lord Kilbrandon (at 17), that a workman's disobedience is not the same as contributory negligence.

[118] [1969] 2 All ER 439. This decision applied *Ross v Associated Portland Cement Manufacturers Ltd* [1964] 2 All ER 452 and *Ginty v Belmont Building Supplies Ltd* [1959] 1 All ER 414.

[119] [1969] 2 All ER 439, at 441, *per* Lord Reid.   [120] [1969] 2 All ER 439, at 446, *per* Lord Diplock.

[121] *Cooper v Railway Executive (Southern Region)* [1953] 1 All ER 477.

(E) *EX TURPI CAUSA*

The Court of Appeal has held that the defence of *ex turpi causa non oritur actio* may be invoked in cases where the claimant is relying on a breach of statutory duty.[122]

FURTHER READING

Buckley, 'Liability in Tort for Breach of Statutory Duty' (1984) 100 LQR 204

Stanton, 'New Forms of the Tort of Breach of Statutory Duty' (2004) 120 LQR 324

---

[122] *Hewison v Meridian Shipping Services Pte Ltd* (2003) 147 SJLB 24 (C's fraudulent concealment of his epilepsy led to the defeat of his claim).

PART VI

INTERESTS IN REPUTATION – DEFAMATION

21

DEFAMATION: FOUNDATIONAL PRINCIPLES

SECTION 1 INTRODUCTION

There are two types of defamation: libel which, in general, is written; and slander which, in general, is oral.[1] In some respects, different rules are applicable to each. Both, however, protect the interest in the reputation of the claimant. There is, therefore, no tort in either case unless there has been a communication of the defamatory matter to a third party, for it is the opinion held of the person defamed by others that matters.[2] Insults directed to the claimant himself do not in themselves constitute defamation, since the tort is not primarily concerned with the claimant's wounded feelings. Instead, the gist is that the defendant either lowers the claimant in the estimation of reasonable, right-thinking members of society, or causes such citizens to shun or avoid the claimant.

In many ways defamation is unique among torts, and it is best understood in the context of its historical development. Until the sixteenth century, the ecclesiastical courts exercised general jurisdiction over defamation. Thereafter, the common law courts developed an action on the case for slander where 'temporal' (as distinct from 'spiritual') damage could be established. Much later, the common law courts acquired jurisdiction over libels, too, and they then forged a distinction between libel and slander on the basis that damage would be presumed in libel, but that the claimant would have to prove 'special damage'[3] for slander.

In the late nineteenth and early twentieth centuries, liability in defamation was extended because of the menace to reputations occasioned by the mass circulation of the new, popular press. The recent history of defamation is marked by continuing conflict between the need to protect the character and privacy of individuals, on the one hand, and the right to freedom of speech, on the other.[4] The intensity of this conflict has

---

[1] It is inaccurate, however, to say that slander is always oral and that libel is always visual. The use of sign language as between two deaf persons, for example, is probably capable of constituting slander. Equally, television broadcasts and public theatre performances of a defamatory nature are, by statute, libellous rather than slanderous: see Section 3 below.

[2] For a powerful argument that it is not reputation, *per se*, that matters, but rather the concern that persons ought not wrongly to be judged by false information see Gibbons, 'Defamation Reconsidered' (1996) 16 OJLS 587.

[3] The phrase 'special damage' is to some extent misleading; 'actual damage' is a more accurate term to capture the sense of what must be proved: see Jolowicz, 'The Changing Use of "Special Damage" and its Effects on the Law' [1960] CLJ 214.

[4] See, eg, Barendt, 'Libel and Freedom of Speech in English Law' [1993] PL 449.

naturally been heightened with the enactment of the Human Rights Act 1998, bringing with it formal rights to both privacy (Article 8) and freedom of speech (Article 10). Of course, the press maintains that the latter is often disregarded at the expense of open and honest criticism of those in authority. And in *Derbyshire County Council v Times Newspapers Ltd*[5] the press scored a notable victory. The House of Lords ruled that public authorities and governmental bodies were not entitled to sue in defamation. As Lord Keith put it:

It is of the highest public importance that a democratically elected governmental body, or indeed any governmental body, should be open to uninhibited public criticism. The threat of a civil action for defamation must inevitably have an inhibiting effect on freedom of speech.[6]

Since that case was decided, the fundamentality of the right to freedom of speech conferred by Article 10 of the European Convention on Human Rights has been raised on a number of occasions. In *Tolstoy Miloslavsky v United Kingdom*,[7] for example, the European Court of Human Rights issued a declaration that a libel damages award of £1.5 m granted by an English jury had been excessive and thus a violation of the defendant's freedom of speech in that case. But apart from these decisions of rather limited scope, the English courts have consistently held defamation law to be broadly compatible with Article 10 of the European Convention.[8] Furthermore, in *Campbell v MGN*,[9] the House of Lords held that there was no presumption that the Article 10 right to freedom of speech should trump any competing interests, such as the Article 8 right to respect for privacy. It would simply need to be balanced against those interests (in respect of which there was, equally, no presumptive pre-eminence).

On the other hand, a move towards a freestanding right to privacy founded on Article 8 of the Human Rights Convention is becoming increasingly evident. In *Douglas v Hello! Ltd* Sedley LJ took a bold step towards the general protection of privacy: the thrust of his argument being that, since the courts are public authorities for the purposes of section 6 of the Human Rights Act 1998, they are now bound to develop the common law – including the law of defamation – in accordance with the Article 8 right to respect for privacy.[10] That said, it remains the case that English law has not yet reached the stage of recognizing a distinct cause of action based on the wrongful invasion of privacy.[11] But that it will in due course seems probable. Thus, while there are senior judicial figures who believe that it would be inappropriate for the courts (rather than Parliament) to introduce such an innovation,[12] the stated reluctance of Parliament to do so has since

---

[5] [1993] AC 534. Note, too, their Lordship's references to (but not reliance on) Art 10 of the European Convention on Human Rights.

[6] [1993] AC 534, at 547. The principle was extended to political parties in the course of an election campaign in *Goldsmith v Bhoyrul* [1997] 4 All ER 268. But what if an individual party member sues *qua* individual?

[7] (1995) 20 EHRR 442.

[8] See *Reynolds v Times Newspapers Ltd* [2001] 2 AC 127; *McCartan Turkington Breen v Times Newspapers Ltd* [2001] 2 AC 277; *Loutchansky v Times Newspapers Ltd (No 2)* [2002] 2 WLR 640.   [9] [2004] 2 AC 457.

[10] [2001] QB 967, at [129].   [11] See *Campbell v MGN Ltd* [2004] 2 AC 457, *per* Lord Nicholls at [11].

[12] See *Wainwright v Home Office* [2004] 2 AC 406, at [31]–[33], *per* Lord Hoffmann.

prompted the Master of the Rolls to comment that he cannot 'pretend to find it satisfactory to be required to shoehorn within the cause of action of breach of confidence' claims that are fundamentally about privacy.[13]

On the other hand, defamation law is already partly governed by statute; and some of this is ill-considered and badly drafted. The result of this admixture of legislation and common law is a tort characterized by many detailed and complex rules – some substantive, others procedural. Even so, defamation actions remain a popular recourse for wealthy public figures seeking, with the aid of expensive lawyers, to vindicate their reputations publicly in the law courts.[14] Indeed, the tort is to some extent a wealthy person's tort since legal aid is not *currently* available either to pursue, or to defend, a defamation action.[15]

Another notable feature of defamation law is the potentially very high level of damages that can be awarded by a jury.[16] To some extent this potential is mitigated by Rules of Court made under section 8 of the Courts and Legal Services Act 1990 which empower the Court of Appeal to substitute for an excessive award 'such sum as appears to the court to be proper'. Just such a substitution occurred in *John v MGN Ltd*.[17] There, a famous pop singer's libel action initially won him £350,000, but the damages were subsequently reduced to £50,000. In the course of his judgment, Sir Thomas Bingham MR suggested that in future the courts could provide guidance to juries on the level of awards either substituted or approved by the Court of Appeal in previous cases, that awards in personal injury cases might be looked at by jurors by way of comparison, and that the judge and the parties' respective counsel could indicate to the jury the award they consider to be appropriate.[18]

---

[13] *Douglas v Hello! (No 3)* [2005] 3 WLR 881, at [53]. See also ch 15.

[14] But note that the scope to litigate was partly curtailed by s 5 of the Defamation Act 1996 which reduced the normal limitation period from three years to one (extendable at the court's discretion – on which, see *Steedman v BBC* [2002] EMLR 17). Equally, the summary procedure under ss 8 – 10 of the 1996 Act confers considerable powers of disposal on the courts and helps avert protracted litigation, so long as adequate compensation can be achieved by an award not exceeding £10,000 (see, eg, *Burnstein v Times Newspapers Ltd* [2001] 1 WLR 579; *Loutchansky v Times Newspapers Ltd* [2001] 3 WLR 404).

[15] This absence of legal aid for Ds facing defamation charges from a powerful corporate entity amounts to a violation of the right to a fair trial under Art 6 of the European Convention on Human Rights: *Steel & Morris v United Kingdom* [2005] EMLR 15. It would seem, therefore, that it now falls to the UK government to make changes in the legal aid entitlements in defamation cases, and in principle not just for Ds.

[16] There is s strong *prima facie* right to a jury trial in defamation under the Supreme Court Act 1981, s 69(1). Thus, if D seeks to insist upon such a trial, the court will normally treat this *prima facie* right as being of fundamental importance: see *Safeway Stores v Tate* [2001] QB 1120. Exceptionally, under the Defamation Act 1996, s 8, a judge may determine the level of damages that C is to receive.

[17] [1996] 2 All ER 35. See also *Rantzen v Mirror Group Newspapers (1986) Ltd* [1994] QB 670 and *Jones v Pollard* [1997] EMLR 233 (award of £100,000 reduced to one of £40,000). On the other hand, the Court of Appeal will not reduce high (but not excessive) levels of damages: see *Kiam v MGN Ltd* [2002] 2 All ER 219.

[18] *John v MGN Ltd* [1996] 2 All ER 35, at 51–2. As a limit to such guidance, on the other hand, D is not permitted to mention to the jury any of the amounts he may have offered to C in their pre-trial correspondence: *Kiam v Neil* [1995] EMLR 1.

'Reputation' is treated as only a transitory interest since no cause of action will survive the defamed person's death.[19] Furthermore, the nature of the available defences in defamation serve to make it also a contingent interest that must sometimes give way to a more pressing public interest. For example, if one informs the police of one's suspicion that a neighbour is abusing a child, one may raise the defence of qualified privilege so long as the (ultimately unfounded) suspicion was honestly held. Similarly, as long as the basic facts are true, the defence of fair comment will protect the press when expressing views on the actions of politicians, public servants and others in the public eye.

The debate on how to achieve the correct balance between an individual's interest in his good name and freedom of speech is a vital attribute of a democratic society.[20] And with this in mind, there is an ancient rule that protects would-be defamers from court actions in respect of their criticism of the parliamentary conduct of MPs.[21] But there is also a sense in which defamation law has become a side issue. For protection of privacy and prevention of press harassment often enjoy a significantly higher profile.[22] But even bearing these developments in mind, it should not be forgotten that the tort of defamation has an ancient history and a remarkable capacity for survival.[23]

SECTION 2 ELEMENTS OF DEFAMATION

Whether a defamation action is framed in libel or slander, the claimant must always prove that the words, pictures, gestures etc are defamatory. Secondly, the claimant must show that they refer to him and, finally, that they were maliciously published.

(A) THE MEANING OF 'DEFAMATORY'

(1) INJURY TO REPUTATION

The classic definition of a defamatory statement is one 'which is calculated to injure the reputation of another, by exposing him to hatred, contempt or ridicule'.[24] It is clear that being made a laughing stock is not sufficient. *Blennerhasset v Novelty Sales Services Ltd*[25] provides an example. In that case, a newspaper advertisement was headed 'Beware of Yo Yo' and went on to imply that Mr Blennerhassett, a worthy man, had now been placed under supervision in a quiet place in the country by reason of his fascination with the

---

[19] See Law Reform (Miscellaneous Provisions) Act 1934, s 1(1). However, defaming a dead person may still constitute a criminal libel.

[20] See Loveland, 'A New Legal Landscape? Libel Law and Freedom of Political Expression in the UK' [2000] EHRLR 476.   [21] Bill of Rights 1689, Art 9.

[22] See, eg, *Douglas v Hello! Ltd* [2001] QB 967; *Douglas v Hello! Ltd (No3)* [2005] 3 WLR 881.

[23] See Barendt, 'What is the Point of Libel Law?' [1999] *CLP* 110.

[24] *Parmiter v Coupland* (1840) 6 M & W 105, at 108, *per* Parke B; *Emerson v Grimsby Times and Telegraph Co Ltd* (1926) 42 TLR 238.   [25] (1933) 175 LT Jo 393.

defendant's toy, the Yo Yo. Although the claimant, a stockbroker, showed that his arrival at the Stock Exchange on the day after the publication was greeted with 'jeers, ribaldry and laughter', the statement was held not to be defamatory.[26]

The inadequacy of the classic definition is now generally recognized, especially in that it does not embrace injury to trading reputation.[27] Lord Atkin once proposed the alternative test of whether: 'the words tend to lower the claimant in the estimation of right-thinking members of society generally?'[28] But, while this test cures some of the defects of the earlier one, the expression 'right-thinking members of society' is deeply problematic. For example, although it is established that it is defamatory to say that a person is insane,[29] or that she has been raped,[30] do right-thinking people think less well of those unfortunates? On the other hand, that one's associates (being themselves an ordinary cross-section of a respectable part of the community) think less well of one in consequence of a statement does not necessarily make that statement defamatory. Thus, in *Byrne v Deane*[31] it was held that to impute that a member of a golf club had informed the police about an illegal fruit-machine kept in the club was not defamatory even though it lowered him in the esteem of his fellow members. A certain class of society may think badly of police informers, but simply to impute this conduct to someone is nonetheless not defamatory.[32] Similarly, ought it to be regarded as defamatory to say of a worker who stayed at work during a strike that he was a 'scab' or a 'blackleg'?[33] And, do allegations that X is homosexual lower X in the estimation of anyone other than homophobes?[34]

The truth is that English law has not defined 'defamatory' with satisfactory precision.[35] With diffidence it is suggested that the 'right-thinking' person test (which has yet to be subject to an appellate court's close scrutiny) must be understood in one of two ways.

---

[26] On the other hand, so long as it inspires contempt or ridicule, even a caricature has been held to constitute defamation: *Dunlop Rubber Co Ltd v Dunlop* [1921] 1 AC 367. Cf *Dolby v Newnes* (1887) 3 TLR 393.

[27] Eg, *Capital and Counties Bank v George Henty & Sons* (1882) 7 App Cas 741, at 771, per Lord Blackburn; *Tournier v National Provincial and Union Bank of England* [1924] 1 KB 461, at 477 and 486–7, per Scrutton and Atkin LJJ respectively.

[28] *Sim v Stretch* [1936] 2 All ER 1237, at 1240. In *Rubber Improvement Ltd v Daily Telegraph Ltd* [1964] AC 234, at 285, Lord Devlin said that the test was the effect on the 'ordinary' man, not the 'logical' man. See also *Skuse v Granada Television Ltd* [1996] EMLR 278 and *Berkoff v Burchill* [1996] 4 All ER 1008 (to describe someone as 'hideously ugly' was held by a majority of their Lordships to be capable of lowering C's public standing). Cf *Norman v Future Publishing Ltd* [1999] EMLR 325 (gentle humour short of ridicule is not actionable).

[29] *Morgan v Lingen* (1863) 8 LT 800.

[30] *Youssoupoff v Metro-Goldwyn-Mayer Pictures Ltd* (1934) 50 TLR 581.   [31] [1937] 1 KB 818.

[32] *Sim v Stretch* [1936] 2 All ER 1237. On the other hand, not merely the golfing fraternity, but right-thinking persons will (it has been held) think worse of an amateur golfer who allows his name to be used in the advertising of chocolates: *Tolley v JS Fry & Sons Ltd* [1931] AC 333. Yet, in *Gibbings v O'Dea & Co Ltd* (1948–9) Macgillivray & Le Quesne Copyright Cases 31 it was held not to be libel for D to use the name of C, who was an author, on an advertisement for mattresses in the *Irish Times*.

[33] McCardie J thought not in *Myroft v Sleight* (1921) 90 LJKB 883.

[34] Probably not: see *Quilty v Windsor* 1999 SLT 346. See also *Arab News Network v Al Khazen* [2001] EWCA Civ 118 (a lowering of reputation within a particular racial group is insufficient).

[35] Gibbons' answer would be to change the basis of the action from damage to reputation to awarding a remedy for unsubstantiated allegations that cause C to be falsely judged: 'Defamation Reconsidered' (1996) 16 OJLS 587.

First, if most citizens would shun or avoid a person in consequence of the statement, then it will be classed as defamatory. Secondly, and alternatively, if a substantial and respectable proportion of society would think less well of a person then, again, the statement will be construed as defamatory provided that their reaction is not plainly anti-social or irrational.[36] Both these interpretations accord with *Byrne v Deane* and also support the view that it is defamatory to say that someone is a 'scab' or a member of the National Front.

(a) Words of abuse

To say that abuse is not defamatory is misleading. The cases relied on for this erroneous statement are cases of slander deciding that special damage must ordinarily be proved.[37] The test to be applied to words of abuse is exactly the same as for other allegedly defamatory statements. Thus, it may be defamatory to call a man a villain,[38] a black-sheep,[39] an habitual drunkard[40] or a pansy.[41] What matters is the context and manner in which the words are uttered. Thus, even a word like 'Mafia' can be understood to describe a close-knit group in a metaphorical, but not defamatory, sense.[42]

(b) Words of opinion

A statement may be defamatory, even though the maker states it, not as fact, but as mere opinion.[43] One must take into account circumstances of time and place.[44] Thus, in *Slazengers Ltd v C Gibbs & Co*,[45] it was defamatory to state during the war with Germany that the claimants were a German firm that were likely to be closed down.

(c) Other examples of injured reputation

Several further examples may help to illustrate what is, and what is not, defamatory. To say that a motorist drove negligently is defamatory.[46] But it is not *per se* defamatory to say that a trader has been put on a stop-list.[47] Nor is it defamatory to announce in a newspaper that the claimant was married on the day before the date fixed for the wedding.[48] On the other hand, it is defamatory to impute to a trader, businessman or

---

[36] If the words would not in themselves convey to the ordinary person the meaning which a special group of experts would give to them, then this interpretation would not apply (unless an innuendo were pleaded: see below) because the basic rule that words must be defamatory in their ordinary meaning would not be satisfied: *Mollo v BBC* (1963) *Times*, 2 February. Nor is it defamatory, without more, for D to say that C is Mr X, even though others have published defamatory articles about Mr X. The libel complained of must be in the statement published by D: *Astaire v Campling* [1965] 3 All ER 666.

[37] Eg, *Thorley v Lord Kerry* (1812) 4 Taunt 355. But in that case, it was explicitly stated (at 365) that, 'for mere general abuse spoken, no action lies'.   [38] *Bell v Stone* (1798) 1 Bos & P 331.

[39] *M'Gregor v Gregory* (1843) 11 M & W 287.   [40] *Alexander v Jenkins* [1892] 1 QB 797, at 804, *per* Kay LJ.

[41] *Thaarup v Hulton Press Ltd* (1943) 169 LT 309. For an example of a particularly abusive alleged libel see *Cornwell v Myskow* [1987] 2 All ER 504.

[42] *Brooks v Lind* 1997 Rep LR 83 (not defamation to suggest C was associated with a 'Council Mafia').

[43] *Braddock v Bevins* [1948] 1 KB 580.

[44] *Dolby v Newnes* (1887) 3 TLR 393 (a statement at a private dinner party, although not defamatory, may become so if repeated in a magazine).   [45] (1916) 33 TLR 35.

[46] *Groom v Crocker* [1939] 1 KB 194.

[47] *Ware and De Freville Ltd v Motor Trade Association* [1921] 3 KB 40.

[48] *Emerson v Grimsby Times and Telegraph Co Ltd* (1926) 42 TLR 238.

professional man a lack of qualification, knowledge, skill, capacity, judgment or efficiency in the conduct of his trade or business or professional activity (such as a severe attack on the special anaesthetising technique of a practising dental surgeon[49]). By contrast, it is not *per se* defamatory merely to criticise a trader's goods: the trader himself must be attacked for a defamation action to lie. If, however, one can read into a criticism of the product a criticism of its manufacturer, then the criticism may be defamatory.[50] Thus, to say that a baker's bread is *always unwholesome* is, for instance, defamatory.[51] But to say that a product does not answer its purpose is not.[52] To say that a trader is bankrupt or insolvent is defamatory;[53] but to say that he has ceased to be in business is not, for it does not reflect on his reputation.[54]

(2) WHO MAY BE DEFAMED?

Either a living person or the commercial reputation of a trading corporation may be defamed under English law,[55] so long as their reputation exists at least partly in this country.[56] Accordingly, it is defamation to claim that X Ltd indulges in black-market activities.[57] Importantly, the fact that commercial enterprises can sue for defamation is seen by the press as a powerful inhibition of vigorous criticism of such entities. The threat to sue for libel has a 'chilling effect' on investigations by the media and may allow corrupt practices to remain hidden from the public. By contrast, according to *Derbyshire County Council v Times Newspapers Ltd*,[58] public authorities cannot invoke defamation law to protect their 'governing reputation'.

Ds had published articles questioning the propriety of C's management of pension funds. The House of Lords struck out the claim holding that democratically elected government bodies and public authorities should be open to uninhibited public criticism. The 'chilling effect' of libel might prevent publication of matters about which the public ought to be informed.

---

[49] *Drummond-Jackson v British Medical Association* [1970] 1 All ER 1094.

[50] *Evans v Harlow* (1844) 5 QB 624.

[51] *Linotype Co Ltd v British Empire Type-Setting Machine Co Ltd* (1899) 81 LT 331.

[52] *Evans v Harlow* (1844) 5 QB 624.   [53] *Shepheard v Whitaker* (1875) LR 10 CP 502.

[54] *Ratcliffe v Evans* [1892] 2 QB 524. Nor is it defamatory to say that his business is suffering as a result of competition: *Stephenson v Donaldson & Sons* (1981) 262 *Estates Gazette* 148. In some circumstances it may constitute the separate tort of injurious falsehood.

[55] In relation to companies, the statement 'must attack the corporation or company in the method of conducting its affairs, must accuse it of fraud or mismanagement, or must attack its financial position': *South Hetton Coal Co v North-Eastern News Association* [1894] 1 QB 133, at 141, *per* Lopes LJ.

[56] In *King v Lewis* [2005] EMLR 4, a boxing promoter who was defamed in an American magazine was able to sue in the English courts on the twin bases that (a) he had a professional reputation in the UK and (b) the article, which had appeared over the net, had been downloaded in this country.

[57] *D & L Caterers Ltd and Jackson v D'Ajou* [1945] KB 364. Cf *Holdsworth Ltd v Associated Newspapers Ltd* [1937] 3 All ER 872 (actionable to say that a limited company refused to accept an interim wages award of the joint conciliation board for the industry). A company may recover substantial damages even though it suffers no financial loss: *Selby Bridge (Proprietors) v Sunday Telegraph Ltd* (1966) 197 EG 1077.

[58] [1993] 1 All ER 1011 (overruling *Bognor Regis UDC v Campion* [1972] 2 QB 169).

In effect, then, the right of free speech and freedom of the press (enshrined in Article 10 of the European Convention on Human Rights) outweighed the Council's claim to protection of its reputation.[59] On the other hand, the limitation on the authority suing in libel – be it a local council or government ministry – does not apply to any individual working there who can show that he personally has been defamed. So, for example, the Prime Minister is just as much entitled to sue for defamation as anyone else, regardless of whether the alleged defamatory statement concerns his personal or professional conduct. To some extent, then, what their Lordships had to say about libel and public authorities in the *Derbyshire* case may be viewed as somewhat specious given that uninhibited criticism may well be appropriate and healthy in respect of many individuals holding important public offices.

(3) THE INTERPRETATION OF DEFAMATORY STATEMENTS

It has so far been assumed that the meaning of the statement complained of is readily ascertainable. But this is not always so; and there are detailed rules of interpretation that must now be considered.

(a) Innuendo

The initial question in any defamation action is whether the words complained of are capable of bearing a defamatory meaning. In the absence of an allegation that those words possess an extended meaning, words must be construed (by a judge[60]) in their ordinary and natural sense.[61] The whole of the statement must be looked at, not merely that part which the claimant alleges to be defamatory (although, of course, it may be relevant to take account of the greater importance of some part of a statement – for example, the headlines of an article in a newspaper[62]). In *Charleston v News Group Newspapers Ltd*,[63] for instance, two soap opera stars sued in respect of material published in the defendants' newspaper which depicted the claimants' faces superimposed upon two near-naked torsos. The article printed beneath the picture castigated the makers of a pornographic computer game which had generated the images in question. It was held that, taken as a whole, the picture and the article were not capable of being defamatory.[64] On the other hand, where an article contains both a

---

[59] For critique see Loveland, 'Defamation and "Government": Taking Lessons from America' [1994] *Legal Studies* 206. Recall, also, that the Convention has all but been incorporated into English law by virtue of the Human Rights Act 1998.

[60] *Turner v Metro-Goldwyn-Mayer Pictures Ltd* [1950] 1 All ER 449, at 465, *per* Lord Greene.

[61] *Capital and Counties Bank Ltd v George Henty & Sons* (1882) 7 App Cas 741, at 772, *per* Lord Blackburn; *Skuse v Granada Television Ltd* [1996] EMLR 278: *Gillick v BBC* [1996] EMLR 267. In *Mitchell v Faber and Faber Ltd* [1998] EMLR 807, Hirst LJ stated (at 811) that, '[i]n deciding whether words are capable of conveying a defamatory meaning the court will reject those meanings which can only emerge as the product of some strained or forced or utterly unreasonable interpretation'. Similarly, in *Edwards v Times Newspapers Ltd* (1997) (unreported) it was held that the ordinary meaning of the words used must be construed in the light of the meaning that would be attached to them by 'the ordinary reader'.

[62] *Shipley v Todhunter* (1836) 7 C & P 680.   [63] [1995] 2 AC 65.

[64] For criticism see *Chakravarti v Advertisers Newspapers* [1998] HCA 37, at [134], *per* Kirby J.

defamatory statement *and* a denial of that statement, the court is unlikely to find that the denial necessarily neutralizes the defamatory comment. As Simon Brown LJ put it: 'I find it very difficult to conceive of circumstances in which the mere printing of a denial could of itself be said to constitute an antidote sufficient to neutralise the bane'.[65]

There may be circumstances, too, where the context in which the words were uttered must be taken into account. In *Bookbinder v Tebbit*,[66] for example, the alleged slander was made at a political meeting. The court said that the meaning to be attached to the defendant's words could be affected, among other things, by the form of the question to which the words were an answer or the general course of the speech in issue. Similarly, there may be circumstances where the claimant alleges that the statement is defamatory because specific facts known to the reader give to the statement a meaning other than, or additional to, its ordinary meaning. This is known as a 'true' or 'legal' innuendo, and here the claimant must plead and prove such facts[67] because the defendant is entitled to know the meaning of the statement on which the claimant seeks to rely so that he is able to argue either that, even thus construed, the statement is not defamatory or that it is true of the claimant.

There is also a third possibility: that the words may have a meaning beyond their literal meaning which is inherent in them and arises by inference or implication. This is sometimes known as a 'false innuendo' and it is something that the claimant must plead separately. Of course, if there is no obvious, ordinary or natural meaning to be ascribed to the words complained of, then this obscures the sense in which the words bear a 'false innuendo'. It was for this reason that the court in *Allsop v Church of England Newspaper Ltd*[68] held that the claimant must plead the particular meaning upon which he relies in such cases. A 'false innuendo' differs from a 'true innuendo' in that the pleader of a 'false innuendo' does not generally need to set out any extrinsic facts in support of his plea.

(i) True innuendoes

Here are some typical examples of 'true', or 'legal', innuendoes. In one case, the defendant, having engaged the claimant, a well-known singer, to perform at a concert, printed her name third in the order on the programme. The court accepted evidence that in the world of musical performances the best singer is always placed at the head of the programme with those holding only a lesser reputation in the middle. As such, the programme constituted a defamatory innuendo of the claimant.[69] In another case, a caption under a newspaper photograph of a man and a woman to the effect that it was a picture of Mr C and his fiancée conveyed to those who knew that the claimant lived with Mr C as his wife the defamatory meaning that she had done so without being

---

[65] *Mark v Associated Newspapers (No 1)* [2002] EMLR 38.   [66] [1989] 1 WLR 640.

[67] Case law insists that C must prove that those facts were actually known to some people (*Fullam v Newcastle Chronicle and Journal Ltd* [1977] 1 WLR 651) and that those facts were in existence and known to those people at the time of the publication (*Grapelli v Derek Block (Holdings) Ltd* [1981] 2 All ER 272).

[68] [1972] 2 QB 161.   [69] *Russell v Notcutt* (1896) 12 TLR 195.

married to him.[70] It has also been held that to include a cartoon of a well-known, amateur golfer in an advertisement for chocolate implied he was being paid for the advert and thus prostituting his amateur status.[71]

In *Hough v London Express Newspaper Ltd*,[72] the question that arose was whether a claimant relying on an innuendo has to prove that there was publication to somebody who interpreted the matter in the defamatory sense alleged.

D published an account and photograph of the 'curly-headed wife' of a named boxer. C, the boxer's real wife, produced witnesses who gave evidence that they had read the statement to mean that C was not the wife of the boxer. In the event, they were not misled into thinking that she was not his wife, nor was any person that was produced as a witness so misled. Nonetheless, it was held that the appropriate test was an objective one. The court found in C's favour: it was enough to prove that there are people who *might* understand the words in a defamatory sense, but no need for 'evidence that some person did so understand them'.[73]

(ii) False innuendoes

Problems also arise with regard to false innuendoes. In *Rubber Improvement Ltd v Daily Telegraph Ltd*,[74] the defendants published an article which stated that the Fraud Squad of the City of London Police were investigating the affairs of the claimants' company. The article was found to be defamatory in its ordinary meaning because the simple statement that the Fraud Squad was inquiring into his affairs may have damaged his reputation even though such investigation did not, *per se*, impugn his innocence. However, since what was said was true – the Fraud Squad were conducting the investigations mentioned – no action lay.[75] The claimants also alleged that the words were defamatory in a second way: that is, they carried with them the imputation that there was at least a basis for suspicion about the way in which the business was conducted. The thrust of the plea was that the imputation of reasonable suspicion (while still consistent with the claimants' innocence) was nonetheless capable of diminishing their trading reputation.

On the facts, their Lordships held that the words were not defamatory in this second sense; since there was a distinction between, on the one hand, imputing reasonable grounds for suspicion and, on the other (as here), simply reporting the fact of suspicion. This crucial distinction between a statement and imputation of suspicion has since been reasserted by the Court of Appeal in *Mapp v News Group Newspapers Ltd*.[76]

---

[70] *Cassidy v Daily Mirror Newspapers Ltd* [1929] 2 KB 331.

[71] *Tolley v JS Fry & Sons Ltd* [1931] AC 333.   [72] [1940] 2 KB 507.

[73] [1940] 2 KB 507, at 515, *per* Goddard LJ. See also *Theaker v Richardson* [1962] 1 All ER 229 (D liable for publishing a libel to C's husband although there was no evidence that the husband believed the accusation made against his wife).

[74] [1964] AC 234. But see *Hyams v Peterson* [1991] 1 NZLR 711 where the New Zealand Court of Appeal found a statement containing words of suspicion could impute guilt.

[75] There is an important difference between something being defamatory *simpliciter* and something being defamatory and *actionable*. To be defamatory, the statement must merely diminish C's reputation; but to be actionable, the statement must also be untrue. In short, both true and false statements may be defamatory, but only the latter may be actionable   [76] [1998] QB 520.

Nonetheless, the main point here is that the second plea in *Rubber Improvement Ltd* constituted the allegation of a false innuendo and therefore did not require the claimants to adduce evidence of any extrinsic facts which had to be set out in the pleading (such as details of individual readers who would interpret the words in a particular way). Furthermore, the presumption of falsity – which in fact is irrebuttable in English law (though this does not mean that substantial damage to reputation is also presumed[77]) – has since been confirmed by the European Court of Human Rights not to be incompatible with the Art 10 right to freedom of expression.[78]

When a defendant newspaper described a well-known broadcaster as 'bent', the claimant had to set out the meaning of the word on which he relied.[79] If a statement is capable of many different meanings and the claimant does not specify those on which he relies, the defendant is entitled to justify the statement according to any meaning which it reasonably bears.[80] If, in a long article which contains many different meanings in relation to him, the claimant fails to plead the meaning(s) on which he relies, the defendant is entitled to have the claimant's statement of claim struck out on the ground that it discloses no reasonable cause of action.[81]

(b) The roles of judge and jury in construing what is defamatory

The judge decides whether a statement is *capable* of bearing a defamatory meaning, whether in its normal meaning or by innuendo.[82] Once that is resolved in the affirmative, the jury then decides whether it *did* bear a defamatory meaning on the occasion complained of.[83] In order to fulfil his task, the judge must construe the particular words used to determine whether they are capable of bearing a defamatory meaning; only once he decides that they may bear such a meaning does the jury then decide whether in fact they were defamatory.[84] The claimant may contend that the statement has different defamatory meanings. In such instances, the judge decides which of those the statement is capable of conveying, and the jury then decides which particular meaning within that category the words in fact bear.[85] Take, for example, *Aspro Travel Ltd v Owners Abroad Group plc*.[86]

The allegations here were that Cs' family company was 'going bust' and the question was whether this was potentially defamatory. Among other things, the court had to consider the alleged false innuendo that it was defamatory in the sense that such allegations would lower

---

[77] *Jameel v Dow Jones* [2005] QB 946, at [30]–[32]. The Court of Appeal also added in this case that, although falsity is presumed, a claim may be struck out as an abuse of process where virtually no damage to reputation has occurred.　　　　[78] *Steel & Morris v United Kingdom* [2005] EMLR 15, at [93]–[94].

[79] *Allsop v Church of England Newspaper Ltd* [1972] 2 QB 161.

[80] *London Computer Operators Training Ltd v BBC* [1973] 2 All ER 170.

[81] *DDSA Pharmaceuticals Ltd v Times Newspapers Ltd* [1973] QB 21.

[82] *Adam v Ward* [1917] AC 309, at 329, *per* Lord Dunedin; *Lloyd v David Syme & Co Ltd* [1986] AC 350; *Mapp v News Group Newspapers Ltd* [1998] QB 520. By virtue of s 7 of the Defamation Act 1996, the judge must consider whether the statement is capable (as opposed to being merely 'arguably capable') of bearing a particular meaning.　　　　[83] *Cassidy v Daily Mirror Newspapers Ltd* [1929] 2 KB 331, at 340, *per* Scrutton LJ.

[84] *Jones v Skelton* [1963] 3 All ER 952.

[85] *Slim v Daily Telegraph Ltd* [1968] 2 QB 157.　　　　[86] [1995] 4 All ER 728.

the directors of such a company in the estimation of the public by implicitly suggesting that, notwithstanding the company's insolvency, the directors were nonetheless allowing it to continue trading.

Although jury trials are viewed as extremely important in libel cases,[87] it is nonetheless the case that an appellate court may set aside a jury's verdict and enter judgment for the defendant where the jury in the court of first instance found for the claimant after the first instance judge had entrusted the decision to them. Conversely, on the very rare occasions when an appellate court holds that a jury could not reasonably have found that the words were not defamatory, it will set aside the verdict and order a new trial.[88] Where the judge has misdirected the jury on the law, its verdict will also be set aside.[89] The courts seek to ensure that the issues which come to trial are clear cut in order to eschew the advantage that one party might obtain by clever tactics. It is a fundamental principle in defamation that:

the trial of the action should concern itself with the essential issues and the evidence relevant thereto and that public policy and the interests of the parties require that the trial should be kept strictly to the issues necessary for a fair determination of the dispute between the parties.[90]

Moreover, what holds for the claimant also holds for the defendant. Thus, defendants pleading the defence of justification must do so in a manner which makes it quite clear what meaning or meanings they seek to justify.[91] Time and again the Court of Appeal has deplored attempts to take advantage of the rules of pleading in order to acquire an unfair advantage at the actual trial.[92]

(4) IMMATERIALITY OF THE DEFENDANT'S KNOWLEDGE

The general common law position is that '[a] person charged with libel cannot defend himself by showing that he intended in his breast not to defame'.[93] Nor is it a defence that a person has no actual knowledge that his statement is defamatory. It is usually stated that liability at common law is strict: it matters not whether the defendant could have taken steps to discover that the statement was defamatory. The leading case is *Cassidy v Daily Mirror Newspapers Ltd.*[94]

With the authority of Mr C, Ds published a photograph, taken at a race meeting, with the following words underneath: 'Mr C, the racehorse owner, and Miss X, whose engagement has

---

[87] See, eg, *Safeway Stores plc v Tate* [2001] 2 WLR 1377. Cf *Alexander v Arts Council of Wales* [2001] 1 WLR 1840 (a finding of no possible malice justified the judge in withholding the case from a jury).

[88] The jurisdiction to do this exists under the Supreme Court Act 1981, s 69. However a decision to overturn the verdict of a jury can only be taken in exceptional circumstances where the jury's decision cannot be explained on any ground not indicative of perversity: see *Grobbelaar v News Group Newspapers* [2003] EMLR 1.

[89] *Tournier v National Provincial and Union Bank of England* [1924] 1 KB 461. Cf *Dakhyl v Labouchere* [1908] 2 KB 325.   [90] *Polly Peck (Holdings) plc v Trelford* [1986] 2 All ER 84, at 94, *per* O'Connor LJ.

[91] *Lucas-Box v News Group Newspapers Ltd* [1986] 1 All ER 177: *Morrell v International Thomson Publishing Ltd* [1989] 3 All ER 733.   [92] *Morrell v International Thomson Publishing Ltd* [1989] 3 All ER 733, at 733–5.

[93] *E Hulton & Co v Jones* [1910] AC 20, at 23, *per* Lord Loreburn LC.   [94] [1929] 2 KB 331.

been announced'. Ds published the photograph, not knowing that C was already married to the man in question, and having taken no steps whatever to find out whether he was already married. Ds were held liable to C for implying she had been living with him without being married to him.

The case provides clear authority for the proposition that, at common law, one may be liable for a statement which one does not actually know to be defamatory. To this strict general rule, however, there are two exceptions – one statutory; one rooted in the common law. These exceptions can be viewed in two ways: either as 'chinks' in the general rule or as defences to the application of the rule. The second approach is favoured here, and the exceptions are discussed in depth in the next chapter.

(B) REFERENCE TO THE CLAIMANT

'In order to be actionable the defamatory words must be understood to be published of and concerning the [claimant].'[95] The claimant need not be mentioned in the statement, nor need everyone reading it know that he was referred to; it suffices if ordinary sensible people, proved to have special knowledge of the facts, might reasonably believe that the statement referred to the claimant.[96] Thus, where the defendant publishes a biography about X, and the biography contains a picture of X together with the claimant *and* a known prostitute, it is defamatory of the claimant to publish that photograph where the claimant's friends would see the picture and identify him even though he is not actually named in the book.[97] On the other hand, in cases such as this, the damages will be lower where only a small proportion of those who read the book would know that it was defamatory of the claimant.

(1) CLASS LIBELS

Where a statement defamatory of a class of persons is made, the same test is applied to determine whether individuals within the class may sue. If the class is so small that persons would reasonably believe that every member of it is targeted, then each individual member may sue. Thus, where proceedings were pending against 17 persons, it was held that one of them could sue a third party who said of them all that 'these defendants helped to murder HF'.[98] A similar rule applies to directors of a small company,[99] and presumably also to trustees of an institution. But a statement that 'all estate agents are rogues' would not enable any one member of such a large class to sue.

---

[95] *Knupffer v London Express Newspaper Ltd* [1944] AC 116, at 121, *per* Lord Atkin. Cf *Farrington v Leigh* (1987) *Times*, 10 December.

[96] *Morgan v Odhams Press Ltd* [1971] 2 All ER 1156. If D publishes a statement defamatory on its face about someone described but not named, and a later publication by D names C so as to identify the subject to readers of the first article, for the first time, the second publication may be relied on to support the allegation that the first one referred to C: *Hayward v Thompson* [1982] QB 47.

[97] *Dwek v Macmillan Publishers Ltd* [2000] EMLR 284.

[98] *Foxcroft v Lacy* (1613) Hob 89. See also *Browne v Thomson & Co* 1912 SC 359.

[99] *Aspro Travel Ltd v Owners Abroad Group plc* [1995] 4 All ER 728 (defamation of company was also defamation of the directors of a family company). The same may be true in reverse: see *Elite Model Management Corp*

Even where the class is too large to permit every member to sue, an individual within the class may still be able to sue. So, for example, even if the claimant has a very common surname, other facts contained in the statement in question may narrow the class sufficiently for him to be defamed;[100] and, of course, if the claimant can show that the statement was especially referable to him, he may sue. Often this will rest on an innuendo which must be specifically pleaded; and the court will order the claimant to give full particulars of the facts on which the claim rests.[101]

Two cases illustrate the position. First, *Le Fanu v Malcomson*.[102]

D published an article suggesting that in some of the Irish factories cruelties were practised upon employees. There were circumstances in the article as a whole, including a reference to Waterford, which enabled the jury to identify C's Waterford factory as the one at which the article was aimed. C's action succeeded.

Secondly, *Knupffer v London Express Newspaper Ltd*:[103]

During the war, D's newspaper referred to the Quisling activities of the Young Russian Party. Although the party was international, and had a British branch of 24 members headed by C, the article referred only to the Party's activities in France and the US. But since the total membership was several thousand, each member could not be said to be identified. No facts were proved in evidence that could identify C as being singled out in the article, and therefore his action failed.

(2) UNINTENTIONAL REFERENCES TO THE CLAIMANT

The claimant may be defamed although the defendant did not intend it. Where the defamation is intentional, however, a greater level of damages may be awarded.[104] In several cases, newspaper proprietors who did not intend to defame the claimant have been held liable. In *Hulton v Jones*,[105] for example, the defendants published a fictional article about 'Artemus Jones'. The writer of the article did not know of the claimant, of that name, who was a former contributor to the newspaper. But the managing editor, on reading the article in proof, had thought at first that the claimant was intended. The defendants were held liable. Similarly, in *Newstead v London Express Newspaper Ltd*,[106] the defendant published an account of the trial for bigamy of 'Harold Newstead, thirty-year-old Camberwell man'. The reporter had included the address and occupation of the Harold Newstead of whom this was a correct report, but the sub-editor deleted it. This want of particularity caused readers to think that the claimant – another Harold

---

v BBC [2001] All ER (D) 334 (ie, defamation of company executives may also be defamatory of the company). Cf *Chomley v Watson* [1907] VLR 502 where the true statement 'Either you or Jones stole the money' was held not to be actionable by the innocent party, Jones.

[100] *Jameel v Dow Jones & Co Inc* [2005] QB 946.
[101] *Bruce v Odhams Press Ltd* [1936] 1 KB 697.   [102] (1848) 1 HL Cas 637.
[103] [1944] AC 116.   [104] *Bridgmont v Associated Newspapers Ltd* [1951] 2 KB 578.
[105] [1910] AC 20.
[106] [1940] 1 KB 377. And see *Grappelli v Derek Block (Holdings) Ltd* [1981] 2 All ER 272 and *Hayward v Thompson* [1982] QB 47 (effect of later publications identifying the person defamed).

Newstead of Camberwell, of about the same age – was meant. It was held to be no defence that the words were true of, and intended to refer to, another.[107]

Whether cases like these can now withstand the passage of the Human Rights Act 1998, with its requirement that the courts must develop the common law in accordance with the rights enshrined in the European Convention,[108] is now highly questionable. There is arguably an infringement of the Article 10 right to freedom of expression in such cases because, for example, the press would effectively be forced to check whether a genuine photograph of person X resembles closely enough any other person so as to amount to a defamation of that other person when a particular story accompanies the photograph. Certainly, the view was taken in *O'Shea v MGN Ltd* that such a requirement would place too onerous a burden on a publisher. As Morland J put it:

[T]he strict liability principle should not cover the 'look-alike' situation. To allow it to do so would be an unjustifiable interference with the vital right of freedom of expression disproportionate to the legitimate aim of protecting the reputations of 'look-alikes' and contrary to Article 10.[109]

But whether this first instance decision can be confined to cases involving 'look-alike' photographs, or whether it ought (logically) to be extended to cases where articles alone are printed in newspapers with no accompanying photograph, will be for future courts to decide. Perhaps Morland J simply felt obliged to confine his judgment to cases involving photographs because *Hulton v Jones* and *Newstead v London Express Newspaper Ltd* were decisions of the House of Lords and Court of Appeal respectively. At the very least, it is clear that the courts are increasingly concerned, in general terms, about infringements of Article 10.[110]

(C) 'MALICIOUS' PUBLICATION

Though always referred to as the need for 'malicious publication', the true requirement is for there to have been *mere* publication. The adjective 'malicious' is in practice otiose, save that the presence of malice serves to defeat the defences of fair comment and qualified privilege (both discussed in the next chapter). Publication is 'making known the defamatory matter after it has been written to some person other than the person of whom it is written'.[111] This requirement of publication to a third party merely underlines that the tort protects not an individual's opinion of himself but the estimation in which others hold him. Because of this rule, it is often important to

---

[107] By contrast, where D publishes details of a person whom he does not actually know (and it is clear that D does not know him), and C shares the same name as the person named by D, and that name is a common name, C seemingly will have to show that a reasonable person known to C would interpret it as a reference to C: *Jameel v Dow Jones* [2005] QB 946, at [45].   [108] See *Douglas v Hello! Ltd* [2001] QB 967, at [129], *per* Sedley LJ.

[109] [2001] EMLR 40, at [47].

[110] See, eg, *Jameel v Dow Jones* [2005] QB 946; *Steel & Morris v United Kingdom* [2005] EMLR 15.

[111] *Pullman v Walter Hill & Co* [1891] 1 QB 524, at 527, *per* Lord Esher MR.

know when the defendant, who perhaps addressed his remarks to the claimant alone, can be held responsible for the fact that third parties have learnt of the defamatory statement. The rule is that if he intended that it should be published to them, or ought to have foreseen such publication, he is liable, but not otherwise.[112] A defendant is not liable for an 'unsuspected overhearing of the words' spoken by him to the claimant.[113] He is not liable where a father opens his son's letter,[114] or the butler opens even the unsealed letter of his employer.[115] A correspondent should expect that clerks of a businessman-claimant might, in the ordinary course of business, open letters addressed to him at his place of business but not when they are marked 'personal', 'private', etc. He is therefore responsible for the publication to them where the correspondence is not so marked.[116] It has also been held that a husband can be expected to open an unstamped manila envelope lying on the door-mat which looks like a circular, even though it is sealed and addressed to his wife.[117] But whether this decision would be upheld today is questionable.

In general, the original maker of a statement is not liable for its republication by another; yet that other will be responsible even though he expressly states that he is merely reproducing what he has been told from a specified source.[118] So, the writer, newspaper proprietor and printer of a defamatory article in a newspaper are each liable for its publication.[119] This repetition rule has specifically been held to be compatible with Article 10 of the European Convention on Human Rights[120] even though it may be seen as forcing journalists to check scrupulously (or distance themselves from) comments made by others. Importantly, however:

where a man who makes a request to another to publish defamatory matter, of which, for the purpose, he gives him a statement, whether in full or in outline, and the agent publishes the matter, adhering to the sense and substance of it, although the language be to some extent his own, the man making the request is liable to an action as the publisher.[121]

---

[112] *Huth v Huth* [1915] 3 KB 32, at 38, *per* Lord Reading CJ; *Slipper v BBC* [1991] 1 All ER 165.

[113] *White v J and F Stone (Lighting and Radio) Ltd* [1939] 2 KB 827.

[114] *Powell v Gelston* [1916] 2 KB 615.

[115] *Huth v Huth* [1915] 3 KB 32. Cf the case if the sender knew that C was blind, and that the butler often opened letters for her.

[116] *Pullman v Walter Hill & Co* [1891] 1 QB 524. But what if one sent a letter marked 'private' to, say, the Prime Minister, or even to any other busy public figure? Might there not be publication to the secretary who opened it? [117] *Theaker v Richardson* [1962] 1 All ER 229.

[118] *M'Pherson v Daniels* (1829) 10 B & C 263. The republication principle extends to multiple publications by D: see *Loutchansky v Times Newspapers Ltd (No 2)* [2002] QB 783 (publications both in a printed newspaper and on the newspaper website).

[119] And distributors. In *Goldsmith v Sperrings Ltd* [1977] 2 All ER 566, it was held not to be an abuse of process for Goldsmith to pursue a claim arising from an article in *Private Eye* against 37 different distributors with a view to making them settle his claim on the basis of their undertaking to cease distributing the magazine. Note, too, that distributors may require the original publisher to indemnify them against liability. Thus, the original defamer may have to pay out damages several times over.

[120] *Chase v News Group Newspapers Ltd* [2003] EMLR 11. Cf the finding of the European Court of Human Rights in *Thoma v Luxembourg* (2003) 36 EHRR 21 that 'a general requirement for journalists to distance themselves from the content of a quotation' would be irreconcilable with the role of the press and thus an infringement of Art 10.

[121] *Parkes v Prescott* (1869) LR 4 Exch 169, at 179, *per* Montague Smith J.

A man who knows that reporters are present when he is making a speech is not thereby responsible for its publication in the press, but he is answerable if he gives the information to them with a view to publication.[122] On the other hand, when a television broadcast foreseeably invites comment in the next day's newspapers, the maker of the original defamatory statement will be liable for its repetition by the press.[123]

The requirement of publication to a third party is satisfied by dictating a letter to one's typist,[124] and probably also when office staff press-copy it.[125] A judge at first instance in Northern Ireland has held that a printer does not, by the very act of handing back in a parcel the printed handbills to the customer-author, publish those handbills.[126] The defendant's publication to his own wife is not enough[127] but publication to the wife of the claimant suffices.[128] Against these instances of minimal publication must be weighed a more recent authority, *Jameel v Dow Jones*,[129] in which it was held that a potentially widespread publication that was in fact confined to a very small number of persons should be struck out as an abuse of process. On the facts, only five people saw the libellous material; and of these, three were the claimants' agents while the remaining two had no connection whatsoever with the claimant. As such, there was no 'real and substantial tort' and the proceedings were an abuse of process in that there was hardly a genuine attempt to protect the claimant's reputation by way of injunction (since the source of the complaint had been removed from the website by the time of the claim) and any proceedings, if permitted, would have involved needless, substantial costs for all parties concerned. Furthermore, it has since been made clear that a claimant must bear the burden of proving a widespread publication in the case of internet defamation; for there is no legal presumption of substantial publication.[130]

Difficulties of proving publication are eased by certain rebuttable presumptions. If one can prove, for example, that a letter bore the correct address and that it was properly posted, there is a presumption of publication to the addressee.[131] Similarly, postcards and telegrams[132] (though not unsealed letters[133]) are presumed to have been

---

[122] *Adams v Kelly* (1824) Ry & M 157; *McWhirter v Manning* (1954) *Times*, 30 October.

[123] *Slipper v BBC* [1991] 1 All ER 165. In effect, this decision is no more than an application of the general law of causation; the foreseeable repetition of the statement by the press is too probable to be regarded as a *novus actus interveniens*.

[124] *Pullman v Walter Hill & Co* [1891] 1 QB 524. The circulation of inter-departmental memoranda within a company is also sufficient publication: *Riddick v Thames Board Mills Ltd* [1977] QB 881.

[125] The official report of *Pullman v Walter Hill & Co* [1891] 1 QB 524 does not expressly state that the press-copying in that case was held to be a publication, but Lord Esher MR said in *Boxsius v Goblet Frères* [1894] 1 QB 842, at 849 that the case had so decided, and he was a judge in both cases.

[126] *Eglantine Inn Ltd v Isaiah Smith* [1948] NI 29 (the printer was nevertheless held jointly liable for the subsequent distribution of the handbills by the author's agents).

[127] *Wennhak v Morgan* (1888) 20 QBD 635.   [128] *Wenman v Ash* (1853) 13 CB 836.

[129] [2005] QB 946.   [130] *Al Amoudi v Brisard* [2006] 3 All ER 294.

[131] *Warren v Warren* (1834) 1 Cr M & R 250.   [132] *Sadgrove v Hole* [1901] 2 KB 1.

[133] *Huth v Huth* [1915] 3 KB 32. It was stated, *obiter*, that had Post Office officials in fact read the letter to check whether it was properly stamped, that would have been publication. Cf *Clutterbuck v Chaffers* (1816) 1 Stark 471 (it was held to be no publication where D handed to X a folded, unsealed letter which X, without reading or showing to others, handed to C).

published to Post Office officials. On the other hand, there is no publication for the purposes of defamation law unless the defamatory meaning of the communication would be understood by the third party. Thus, a postcard defamatory of (but not known to be referable to the claimant by persons unaware of the special facts), was held not to be published to Post Office staff.[134]

On occasion, there may be publication by omission. Failure by a defendant who is authorized and able to remove or amend defamatory matter which is the work of another amounts to publication by him. Thus, those in charge of a club will be accountable for defamatory matter placed by another on the notice board of the club if they do not remove it within a reasonable time.[135]

SECTION 3 DISTINGUISHING LIBEL FROM SLANDER

(A) CRITERIA FOR DISTINGUISHING LIBEL FROM SLANDER

Any medium whereby thought and ideas can be expressed or conveyed may constitute the publication of defamation – words, pictures, gestures,[136] music and statues are all examples.[137] It is, however, the choice of medium which determines whether the defamation is libel or slander; and it is because the rules relating to the two torts differ in some important respects that it is necessary to distinguish between them.

There can be no doubt that anything communicated in the form of a permanent character and visible to the eye is libel, and that anything temporary and merely audible is slander. Thus, defamatory books, newspapers, letters and even effigies[138] are all libels, while spoken words are slander. What is more difficult, however, is how to characterize things which are in permanent form but only audible, and things which are visible but not in permanent form, such as material posted on the internet.[139] In *Youssoupoff v*

---

[134] *Sadgrove v Hole* [1901] 2 KB 1. The same applies to cipher messages and messages in foreign languages.

[135] *Byrne v Deane* [1937] 1 KB 818. Compare those cases where the matter is carved in stone, or D is not in control of the place where the libel is exhibited. Here the impracticability/impossibility of avoiding the publication negates any prospect of liability.

[136] See *Cook v Cox* (1814) 3 M & S 110, at 114, *per* Lord Ellenborough.

[137] Even the lighting of a lamp in the day-time in C's garden, thereby inferring that he keeps a brothel, is caught: *Jefferies v Duncombe* (1809) 2 Camp 3; and perhaps so is police shadowing of C's house.

[138] *Monson v Tussauds Ltd* [1894] 1 QB 671 (placing of a waxwork effigy of C holding a gun in a room next to another room in which there was a representation of a murder scene for which C was tried but acquitted).

[139] Defamatory material posted onto an internet website has been held to be a libel once downloaded in this country: *King v Lewis* [2005] EMLR 4. Merely being an internet service provider is enough to make that provider a publisher at common law; but liability for publication will not automatically follow for there may be a defence depending on whether the provider could and should have prevented further dissemination: *Godfrey*

Metro-Goldwyn-Mayer Pictures Ltd,[140] the scenes depicted on the screen in a talking film were held to constitute libel. Yet, at most, the case really only supports the view that permanency is an important element in the test for libel. It does not establish that permanency is the sole criterion. Slesser LJ put the *ratio* of the case thus:

There can be no doubt that, so far as the photographic part of the exhibition is concerned, that is a *permanent matter to be seen by the eye*, and is the proper subject of an action for libel, if defamatory. I regard the speech which is synchronized with the photographic reproduction and forms part of one complex, common exhibition as an ancillary circumstance, part of the surroundings explaining that which is to be seen.[141]

The case, therefore, does not settle authoritatively whether a defamatory anecdote in a film is libel. Nor does it tell us whether defamatory remarks on a CD are slander. Although there are *obiter dicta* in other cases suggesting that permanency alone is a sufficient criterion,[142] the point remains technically undecided. Accordingly, it follows that it is not possible to say into which category the following fall: tape recordings, talking parrots that have learnt certain phrases from their owners and sky-writing. On the other hand, dictation of a letter to a typist is only slander,[143] while forwarding of the typed letter is undoubtedly libel, and, moreover, a libel for which the dictator is accountable on the basis that he authorized his agent to forward it. The reading aloud of a letter written by another, where those to whom it was read were aware that the speaker was reading from the document, was held to be libel in *Forrester v Tyrrell*.[144] The short report of this case does not, however, mention whether the point that it may have been slander was argued.[145] In *Osborn v Boulter*,[146] Scrutton and Slesser LJJ thought that the reading aloud of a document was slander, while Greer LJ was inclined to think it libel. It is submitted that the approach in *Forrester v Tyrrell* is preferable since the defamatory material was both visible and in permanent form. The reading of it simply constituted the means of publication.[147]

The uncertainty at common law has prompted statutory intervention to cover mass media communications. Section 166 of the Broadcasting Act 1990 now provides that the publication of any words in the course of any broadcast programme on television or radio, shall be treated as publication in a permanent form. It no longer matters

---

v Demon Internet Ltd [2001] QB 201. See also, to similar effect, the Electronic Commerce (EC Directive) Regulations 2002.

[140] (1934) 50 TLR 581.   [141] (1934) 50 TLR 581, at 587 (emphasis added).

[142] Eg, in *Monson v Tussauds Ltd* [1894] 1 QB 671, at 692, Lopes LJ stated that: 'Libels are generally in writing or printing, but this is not necessary; the defamatory matter may be conveyed in some other permanent form. For instance, a statue, a caricature, an effigy, chalk marks on a wall, signs, or pictures may constitute a libel'.

[143] But when the typist listens to a dictaphone, a libel is probably being published.

[144] (1893) 57 JP 532. MacDermott J followed this decision with obvious reluctance in *Robinson v Chambers (No 2)* [1946] NI 148 where the audience was aware that D was reading out a letter.

[145] If the secretary simply hands or reads the letter back to the person who dictated it, then there can be no defamation, for there has been no publication.

[146] [1930] 2 KB 226. Slesser LJ left open (at 236) whether 'the circumstance of dictation, and the dictated matter being brought back and considered by the dictator, may constitute in certain cases a libel'.

[147] For additional judicial support for this view, see *Robinson v Chambers (No 2)* [1946] NI 148.

whether the broadcast is for general public reception or otherwise. Similarly, the Theatres Act 1968 provides that the publication of words in the course of a perform-ance of a play shall also be treated as publication in a permanent form.[148]

(B) JURIDICAL DIFFERENCES BETWEEN LIBEL AND SLANDER

There are two major juridical differences between libel and slander. First, a libel of sufficient seriousness may be punished as a crime whereas slander is always only tortious.[149] Secondly, libel is actionable *per se* whereas slander, subject to the exceptions discussed in the next section, is actionable only upon proof of actual damage.[150]

(C) EXCEPTIONAL CASES WHERE SLANDER IS ACTIONABLE *PER SE*

(1) IMPUTATION OF CRIME

The limits of this exception cannot precisely be defined because it is not settled whether the reason for it is the social ostracism resulting from such a slander, or the putting of the claimant in jeopardy, or even some other matter. At the very least, the following points are incontrovertible. The crime must be one for which the claimant could be imprisoned forthwith. The statement 'I know enough to put you in gaol' is therefore actionable *per se*.[151] If the perpetrator, having been arrested, can only be punished by a fine for the offence in question (and not by imprisonment) the imputation of the commission of the crime remains outside the exception.[152] And this is the case even though there is a power to commit for non-payment of the fine.[153]

The words used must also be clear and unambiguous. If they convey a mere suspicion – for example, of murder – they do not fall within the exception and the slander is not actionable *per se*.[154] In addition, in construing the meaning of the words, it is firmly established that they must be looked at in context in order to discover what was imputed. This rule is made clear by *Thompson v Bernard*.[155] The case also illustrates the obvious

---

[148] Section 4. But note that performances given 'on a domestic occasion in a private dwelling' are exempted by s 7 of the Act.

[149] Of course, spoken words may constitute a crime where the other elements of that crime are present: eg, blasphemy or sedition. Earlier views that to constitute a crime a libel must be calculated to provoke a breach of the peace were rejected in *Gleaves v Deakin* [1980] AC 477.

[150] Although the term 'special damage' is used frequently, this is misleading, as noted earlier, since the phrase has other meanings in other contexts. In fact, the use of the term 'special damage' in this context is to be attributed to the *dictum* of Lord Wensleydale in *Lynch v Knight* (1861) 9 HL Cas 577.

[151] *Webb v Beavan* (1883) 11 QBD 609. This illustration also shows that a general imputation of criminality without reference to a specific offence is sufficient.

[152] *Hellwig v Mitchell* [1910] 1 KB 609; *Ormiston v Great Western Rly Co* [1917] 1 KB 598.

[153] *Michael v Spiers and Pond Ltd* (1909) 101 LT 352.   [154] *Simmons v Mitchell* (1880) 6 App Cas 156.

[155] (1807) 1 Camp 48. (C was alleged to be 'a damned thief' because he had refused pay the wages of various mariners. In truth, therefore, this implied only a breach of contract.)

point that difficult problems of criminal law may need to be resolved in order to determine whether the facts imputed constituted a crime punishable by imprisonment.

If the claimant has to rely on some secondary meaning of the words spoken, he must, according to *Gray v Jones*,[156] prove that they were reasonably capable of being so interpreted. *Gray v Jones* also lends support to the view that the risk of social ostracism is at least one of the reasons for this exception. Having found that the words 'You are a convicted person' might reasonably mean that a crime punishable by imprisonment was imputed, Atkinson J held them to be within the exception because, although they would not place the claimant in jeopardy,[157] they would tend to cause him to be ostracized socially. On the other hand, there have been several cases where something criminal in character, but for technical reasons not punishable in the requisite way, has been held to be outside the rule – presumably because the claimant was not in jeopardy. In *Lemon v Simmons*,[158] for instance, saying that a husband stole from his wife while the couple lived together was held not to impute a crime since husbands were not at the time punishable for such thefts.

(2) IMPUTATION OF CERTAIN TYPES OF DISEASE

To impute that a person has a contagious venereal disease is also to commit a slander actionable *per se*.[159] Whether the exception has any greater scope is doubtful. There is weak authority that leprosy is within the exception.[160] Yet, even if it *is* defamatory to impute other communicable diseases, such as scarlet fever or tuberculosis, it is submitted that, unless suffering from the particular disease induces moral condemnation or loathing, it is probably not nowadays actionable *per se*. Even in the case of venereal disease, it is not actionable *per se* to say that the claimant has suffered from it in the past.[161] This makes good sense, since the rationale for making the imputation of contagious venereal diseases actionable *per se* was, historically, that it might dissuade people from associating with the victim. Today, with cures easily available for many, if not most, infectious or contagious diseases, it might be questioned whether this exception ought to survive. Indeed, the last reported case was *Bloodworth v Gray* in 1844.[162]

(3) SLANDER IN RESPECT OF OFFICE, PROFESSION, CALLING, TRADE OR BUSINESS

At common law, a slander in respect of an office, profession, trade or business was actionable *per se* if, first, it was calculated to disparage the claimant in his office, and, secondly,

---

[156] [1939] 1 All ER 798.   [157] On which see *Jackson v Adams* (1835) 2 Bing NC 402.

[158] (1888) 57 LJQB 260. *D & L Caterers Ltd and Jackson v D'Ajou* [1945] KB 364, raised, but did not decide, the point whether trading, as well as social ostracism, will be deemed sufficient. There, a crime punishable by imprisonment was imputed to a limited company engaged in trade.

[159] *Bloodworth v Gray* (1844) 7 Man & G 334. Even if AIDS is not strictly speaking a venereal disease, an imputation that a person is infected with the HIV virus may conceivably be actionable *per se*.

[160] *Taylor v Perkins* (1607) Cro Jac 144: the words 'Thou art a leprous knave' were held to be actionable *per se*.

[161] *Taylor v Hall* (1742) 2 Stra 1189.   [162] (1844) 7 Man & G 334.

it was spoken in relation to his office. Section 2 of the Defamation Act 1952 now recasts this most important of circumstances in which slander is actionable *per se*. It provides:

In an action for slander in respect of words calculated to disparage the [claimant] in any office, profession, calling, trade or business held or carried on by him at the time of the publication, it shall not be necessary to allege or prove special damage, whether or not the words are spoken of the [claimant] in the way of his office, profession, calling, trade or business.

The provision thus removes the second common law requirement: the words are actionable even though they are not said of the claimant in the actual conduct of his profession so long as the imputation they carry is designed to disparage him in his particular calling. Section 2 also nullifies decisions such as *Jones v Jones*[163] where it was held that an allegation that a headmaster had committed adultery with a school cleaner did not relate to his conduct in his profession. Today, such an allegation would certainly be actionable simply because it had prejudicial effects on his employment.

Words are also actionable *perse* if they impute some want of integrity or some corrupt or dishonest conduct in the office, whether an office of profit or of honour.[164] But as regards an office of honour, the slander is only actionable *per se* if it imputes such dishonesty, want of integrity or incompetence as to justify removal from office.[165]

(4) IMPUTATION OF THE UNCHASTITY OF A WOMAN

The loosely worded Slander of Women Act 1891 provides that 'words spoken and published . . . which impute unchastity or adultery to any woman or girl, shall not require special damage to render them actionable'. Imputation of 'unchastity' has also been held to include the imputation of lesbianism.[166] It is assumed, though the Act does not say so expressly, that it confers upon the woman alone the right to sue (but not her alleged male partner). Slang expressions of unchastity are probably enough, but gestures and other media of communication, not being 'words', fall outside the Act.[167]

(D) SPECIAL DAMAGE AND REMOTENESS OF DAMAGE

The question of what 'special damage' must be proved in respect of those forms of slander which are not actionable *per se* is closely bound up with the problem of remoteness of damage in defamation. Nonetheless, it is at least clear in principle that material loss is required if an allegation of special damage is to be substantiated. Examples include loss of employment,[168] the refusal of persons to enter into contracts

---

[163] [1916] 2 AC 481.

[164] The distinction between offices of honour and offices of profit are now immaterial. Section 2 applies equally to both: *Maccaba v Lichtenstein* [2004] EWHC 1578.

[165] *Robinson v Ward* (1958) 108 L Jo 491.   [166] *Kerr v Kennedy* [1942] 1 KB 409.

[167] Sign language is a probable exception.   [168] *Coward v Wellington* (1836) 7 C & P 531.

with the claimant,[169] the loss of hospitality from friends proved to have provided food or drink on former occasions.[170] A mere threat of material loss is insufficient,[171] but it is uncertain whether loss of spousal support, by either a husband or wife, is special damage. Consider *Lynch v Knight*.[172] There, the defendant told the claimant's husband that the claimant had almost been seduced before their marriage. The husband made her leave their home, and here her slander action (based on loss of consortium) failed. The ground of the decision, however, was not that loss of consortium is not special damage, but rather that the damage was too remote. It is submitted that Lord Campbell was correct in his assertion that loss of spousal support may constitute special damage.[173]

In *Allsop v Allsop*,[174] the claimant suffered physical illness as a result of the mental suffering she sustained following the slander. This was held not to be special damage. Noting that mental distress and bodily harm may be taken into account by way of aggravation in assessing damages in defamation,[175] *Allsop* must be taken as deciding that special damage in slander must be damage in respect of a primary interest – that is, loss of esteem or association – and that the primary purpose of the law of defamation is not to protect against psychiatric harm resulting from the apprehension of the effects of defamatory matter being published to third persons.

Despite the fact that historically the test for remoteness in defamation was one based on 'the natural and necessary consequences' of the defamation,[176] it now seems that the test is the same as in most other areas of tort law. Thus, the key question is now whether the kind of damage suffered by the claimant was a reasonably foreseeable consequence of the defendant's act? Accordingly, if a tabloid newspaper charges a distinguished law professor with sexual harassment and the university suspends him, he may claim compensation for the whole of that loss.

Particular problems arise in defamation where additional loss results from a repetition of the libel. In *Slipper v BBC*,[177] for example, allegations in an original broadcast were given even wider publicity in newspaper reviews of the programme. The Court of Appeal refused to strike out the part of the claim dealing with that damage. While unauthorized repetition might, on occasion, constitute a *novus actus interveniens*, there has never been an absolute rule that the original defamer cannot be held liable for the consequences of such a repetition. Thus, if I write to the Students' Union claiming a colleague is embezzling the Student Law Society's funds, it is very much foreseeable that this allegation will be repeated. If the letter had not been sent, but

---

[169] *Storey v Challands* (1837) 8 C & P 234.

[170] *Davies v Solomon* (1871) LR 7 QB 112. The rationale is that the loss of food and drink represents a loss of material value.   [171] *Michael v Spiers and Pond Ltd* (1909) 101 LT 352.

[172] (1861) 9 HL Cas 577.

[173] (1861) 9 HL Cas 577, at 589–9. His *dictum* was approved by Lord Goddard CJ in *Best v Samuel Fox & Co Ltd* [1952] AC 716, at 732. See also *Wright v Cedzich* (1930) 43 CLR 493, at 530, *per* Rich J, and *Lampert v Eastern National Omnibus Co Ltd* [1954] 2 All ER 719.   [174] (1860) 5 H & N 534.

[175] (1860) 5 H & N 534, at 539, *per* Bramwell B.   [176] *Ward v Weeks* (1830) 7 Bing 211.

[177] [1991] 1 QB 283. See also *Sutcliffe v Pressdram Ltd* [1991] 1 QB 153.

another colleague took it from my desk and sent it to the *Sun* newspaper, there would be a break in the chain of causation, in just the same way as in any other tort.[178]

FURTHER READING

Barendt, 'Libel and Freedom of Speech in English Law' [1993] *Public Law* 449

Barendt, 'What is the Point of Libel Law?' [1999] *CLP* 110

Gibbons, 'Defamation Reconsidered' (1996) 16 OJLS 587

Kaye, 'Libel and Slander – Two Torts or One?' (1975) 91 LQR 524

---

[178] See *Weld-Blundell v Stephens* [1920] AC 956.

22

DEFENCES AND REMEDIES
IN DEFAMATION

Most of the defences already discussed in relation to other torts are also available in defamation.[1] But several other defences, peculiar to defamation, warrant separate consideration in this chapter. To a large extent, these defences reflect the fact that defamation law recognises the vital interest in freedom of speech. The defence of absolute privilege, for example, allows comments to be made regardless of whether they are true, and regardless of the defendant's malicious motive.

SECTION 1 CONSENT AND
ASSUMPTION OF RISK

Although opinions vary, the better opinion is that consent is an independent defence in defamation.[2] Someone who telephones a newspaper with false information about himself will not be able to sue in defamation when the newspaper publishes it; but he does not consent to the publication in a newspaper of a story about himself that he told at a parish vestry meeting.[3] Importantly, consent may be implied or express, so consent explicitly supplied on a contractual basis will certainly defeat a defamation action.[4] On the other hand, implied consent can sometimes involve a difficult question of fact about whether a claimant has genuinely consented to the repetition of a defamatory statement. If, for instance, the claimant asked the defendant to repeat it, because he did not properly understand on the first occasion, he would not be consenting. Whether express or implied, consent will always be narrowly construed in defamation cases.[5]

The related defence of assumption of risk was applied in *Chapman v Lord Ellesmere*.[6] There the claimant maintained that even if he had consented to the publication of a report of an inquiry by the Jockey Club, he had not consented to its publication in such

---

[1] The exceptions are consent and assumption of risk, dealt with in Section 1 below.

[2] But see *Russell v Duke of Norfolk* [1949] 1 All ER 109, at 120, *per* Denning LJ. This issue may be crucial if, eg, A asks B for a reference and B is actuated by malice in providing one, unless the consent is deemed to be to a non-malicious reference only.   [3] *Cook v Ward* (1830) 6 Bing 409.

[4] *Cookson v Harewood* [1932] 2 KB 478n.   [5] *Howe v Burden* [2004] EWHC 196.

[6] [1932] 2 KB 431.

a form as to contain an innuendo against him. The Court of Appeal found for the defendant on the ground that the claimant had agreed to run the risk of the particular form that the statement might take.[7]

SECTION 2 JUSTIFICATION

It is no part of the claimant's case to establish that the defendant's statement was untrue: the claimant has merely to prove the publication of a statement defamatory of him. If, however, the defendant can prove that his statement was true, he has a complete defence even if he made the statement maliciously. The rationale is that 'the law will not permit a man to recover damages in respect of an injury to a character which he does not . . . possess'.[8] The defendant does not discharge this burden by proving that he honestly believed it to be true. He must prove that it was true.[9] Nor will it help simply to show that he repeated accurately to a third party what he had heard from another, even though he told the third party it was a mere repetition.[10] If the words impute the commission of a specific offence, it is not enough to prove that the claimant was suspected of that offence.[11] In order to invoke the defence of justification in these circumstances, the defendant must be able to identify specific conduct on the part of the claimant which justifies such a suspicion.[12] These restrictions on the defence are clearly necessary to prevent its abuse.

Before deciding whether the defendant can successfully plead justification, one must first discover what the statement complained of has been interpreted to mean.[13] If the statement contains an innuendo, that too must be justified.[14] And even if the defendant justifies the innuendo, he will still fail unless he also justifies the primary meaning of the words used; for they form a separate head of claim.[15] And just as the claimant must specifically plead the meanings he relies on as defamatory, so must the defendant pleading justification 'make it clear to the [claimant] what is the case he is seeking to set up'.[16]

---

[7] [1932] 2 KB 431, at 464, *per* Slesser LJ.   [8] *M'Pherson v Daniels* (1829) 10 B & C 263.

[9] *Peters v Bradlaugh* (1888) 4 TLR 414. In this context it is arguable that, the importation of the European Convention on Human Rights into English law might require a relaxation of this rule where the publication relates to matters of public importance: see Art 8(2).

[10] *M'Pherson v Daniels* (1829) 10 B & C 263. On the other hand, repetition of a prevalent rumour may be justified following *Aspro Travel v Owners Abroad Group plc* [1995] 4 All ER 728 where the Court of Appeal refused to strike out Ds' plea of justification on this basis.

[11] *Rubber Improvement Ltd v Daily Telegraph Ltd* [1964] AC 234, at 274–5, *per* Lord Hodson.

[12] *Shah v Standard Chartered Bank* [1999] QB 241, at 269–70, *per* May LJ (it is not enough merely to show that the suspicion emanates from a reliable source). The suggestion that this 'conduct rule' places an unjustifiable restriction on the Art 10 right to freedom of expression has been rejected: *Chase v Newsgroup Newspapers Ltd* [2002] EWCA Civ 1772.   [13] See ch 21.

[14] *Prior v Wilson* (1856) 1 CBNS 95.

[15] *Watkin v Hall* (1868) LR 3 QB 396, at 402, *per* Blackburn J; *Rubber Improvement Ltd v Daily Telegraph Ltd* [1964] AC 234.

[16] *Lucas-Box v Associated Newspapers Group* [1986] 1 All ER 177. See also *Morrell v International Thomson Publishing Ltd* [1989] 3 All ER 733.

Obviously, then, many problems with justification are merely points of interpretation where the material question is: 'Does that which is proved to be true tally with that which the defendant's statement is interpreted to mean?' In *Jameel v Wall Street Journal Europe (No 3)*,[17] the defendant made reference to 'those with potential terrorist ties'. The claimants argued that the words used meant, at the very least, that they were reasonably suspected of having terrorist links. The defendant counter-argued that the words implied no more than that there were reasonable grounds to undertake an enquiry or investigation of whether there were in fact terrorist links (this meaning being one stage removed from what the claimants alleged). The Court of Appeal accepted that both meanings were feasible and agreed with the claimants, holding that the issue should be left for a jury to decide. *Wakley v Cooke* is another case that turned, ultimately, on a point of interpretation.[18] There, the defendant called the claimant a 'libellous journalist'. He proved that a judgment against the claimant for libel had once been obtained; but because the defamatory statement complained of implied that the journalist habitually libelled people, the defendant ultimately failed to justify his remark.

The opposite result prevailed in *Bookbinder v Tebbit*.[19] The defendant had alleged at an electoral meeting that the claimant had squandered public money on a campaign to print 'support Nuclear Free Zones' on council stationery. He sought to justify his claim by advancing evidence of general financial mismanagement on the part of the claimant who was the leader of the local council. The Court of Appeal struck out those particulars of justification. They did not pertain to the very specific 'sting' of the libel. One cannot justify an express claim of misconduct by generalized evidence of the claimant's behaviour.

The defence will not fail if the statement is substantially true: inaccuracy on minor points of detail are disregarded.[20] Similarly, 'it is unnecessary to repeat every word which might have been the subject of the original comment. As much must be justified as meets the sting of the charge, and if anything be contained in a charge which does not add to the sting of it, that need not be justified'.[21] Consider *Clarke v Taylor*.[22]

D accused C of taking part in a 'grand swindling concern' at Manchester, and added that '[C] had been at Leeds for one or two days before his arrival in [Manchester] . . . and is supposed to have made considerable purchases there. It is hoped, however, that the detection of his plans in Manchester will be learnt in time to prevent any serious losses from taking place'. D justified the statement that C had swindled at Manchester, but not the remainder of the statement. It was held that this was a sufficient plea of justification because the remaining words did not allege any further act of criminality.

---

[17] [2005] QB 904. Revised on other grounds at [2006] UKHL 44.

[18] (1849) 4 Exch 511. On the question of whether it is more defamatory of a woman to allege that she has had an extra-marital affair with one man rather than another see *Khashoggi v IPC Magazines Ltd* [1986] 3 All ER 577.

[19] [1989] 1 All ER 1169.

[20] *Alexander v North Eastern Rly Co* (1865) 6 B & S 340 (Ds published notice that Cs had been sentenced to a fine of £1 with the alternative of three weeks' imprisonment: in fact, the alternative was only two weeks' imprisonment). See also *Henry v BBC* [2006] EWHC 386.

[21] *Edwards v Bell* (1824) 1 Bing 403, at 409, *per* Burrough J.   [22] (1836) 2 Bing NC 654.

Many statements contain both statements of fact and opinion: for example, 'X was drunk again last night; his behaviour was disgusting'. If the defendant relies on a plea of justification in respect of this, he must prove not only that X was drunk but also the accuracy of his claim that X's behaviour was disgusting (in so far as that comment adds to the sting of the libel). If the further statement introduces new matter, or implies the existence of further facts, he must prove those further facts which justify the terms in which he has described the claimant.[23]

At common law, every material statement had to be justified. Thus, if the defendant could prove the truth of three charges but not a fourth charge, the defence would fail (although proof of three would be relevant in assessing damages). This rule was modified by section 5 of the Defamation Act 1952 which stipulates:

In an action for libel or slander in respect of words containing two or more distinct charges against the [claimant], a defence of justification shall not fail by reason only that the truth of every charge is not proved if the words not proved to be true do not materially injure the [claimant's] reputation having regard to the truth of the remaining charges.[24]

It is now therefore important to know when there are several charges. The section can only apply when the defendant has proved first, that at least one charge is substantially true, after having been separated from the remaining charges and secondly, that this charge is itself incapable of further severance. At common law, the courts had also to consider when charges were severable, because any severable charge could be separately justified with a view to reducing damages or, perhaps, establishing some other defence in respect of that charge. Presumably, the common law rules on what is a severable charge also apply under the Act.[25]

The effect of the Act is illustrated by considering its application to the facts of the pre-Act decision in *Goodburne v Bowman*.[26]

C was alleged by D to have made, in each of his two periods of office as mayor, a small secret profit from the corporation on selling coals to the poor. D justified the statement by pleading that C did this in one of those terms of office only. The plea failed because it did not establish the truth of all the material statements in the libel.

Under the 1952 Act, it is open to the jury, on similar facts, to find that, in view of the truth of one of the two charges, the other did not separately, materially injure his reputation. The claimant cannot evade the section by basing his cause of action solely on those residual parts of the defendant's statement which are not true if the different parts of an article are not plainly severable. This is so because a defendant may well be able to base a defence of justification on the whole of the article.[27] Accordingly, where several defamatory allegations have a common 'sting' they are not to be regarded as

---

[23] *Cooper v Lawson* (1838) 8 Ad & El 746. There is sometimes another possible defence: fair comment.

[24] If D relies on s 5 he must plead it as a defence: *Moore v News of the World Ltd* [1972] 1 QB 441.

[25] See *Clarkson v Lawson* (1830) 6 Bing 587; *Davis v Billing* (1891) 8 TLR 58; *Fleming v Dollar* (1889) 23 QBD 388.

[26] (1833) 9 Bing 667.

[27] *S and K Holdings v Throgmorton Publications Ltd* [1972] 3 All ER 497 (distinguishing *Plato Films Ltd v Speidel* [1961] AC 1090).

separate and distinct: the defendant must justify the 'sting' and 'it is fortuitous that what is in fact similar fact evidence is found in the publication'.[28] Where separate allegations are made, however, and the claimant relies only on the allegation that cannot be justified (with no mention of the statement that can be justified) the defendant cannot invoke section 5.[29]

If a defendant persists in a plea of justification and thereby prolongs the period in which the damage from the publication continues to spread, a greater sum by way of aggravated damages may be awarded against him.[30]

Before the enactment of the Human Rights Act 1998, the completeness of the defence of justification required great emphasis. Even if the defendant was inspired by malice, or even if, when he made the statements, he did not believe them to be true, his defence was sound so long as they were true. As we saw in the previous chapter, defamation law offers no protection, *per se*, against even the grossest invasion of privacy.[31]

A further curb on the freedom of the press to dig up aspects of a person's past is contained in the Rehabilitation of Offenders Act 1974. In relation to 'spent' convictions of 'rehabilitated persons', the Act specifies that after the expiry of certain defined periods – the duration of which differs according to the length of sentence – most convictions become spent, and the convicted person becomes rehabilitated. Section 8(3) of the 1974 Act provides an exception to the general tenor of the legislation according to which convictions become totally spent. It entitles a defendant in a defamation action to adduce evidence of the claimant's conviction; but only so long as the defendant mentions this conviction without malice.[32] The onus of establishing the presence of malice – defined as some spiteful, irrelevant or improper motive – lies with the claimant.[33]

SECTION 3 INNOCENT DISSEMINATORS

There is, technically, still a common-law defence based on innocent dissemination. But this has been largely subsumed within section 1 of the 1996 Act. Furthermore, because the statutory defence is broader in scope, and (normally) no less onerous to invoke, it seems that the common-law defence is all but otiose nowadays. Accordingly, discussion of it is omitted from this book.

---

[28] *Polly Peck (Holdings) plc v Trelford* [1986] 2 All ER 84, at 102; *Khashoggi v IPC Magazines Ltd* [1986] 3 All ER 577.

[29] In *Cruise v Express Newspapers plc* [1999] QB 931, at 954, Brooke LJ said: 'It is no defence to a charge that "You called me A" to say "Yes, but I also called you B on the same occasion and that was true" '.

[30] *Cassell & Co Ltd v Broome* [1972] AC 1027, at 1125, *per* Lord Diplock.

[31] For the extent to which English tort law protects privacy as such, see ch 15.

[32] It is arguable that this qualification of the right to adduce evidence of a spent conviction is antithetical to the right to freedom of speech enshrined in Art 10 of the European Convention on Human Rights. It is therefore possible that an appellate court may, in the future, feel the need to issue a declaration of incompatibility between the 1974 Act and the Convention under s 4 of the Human Rights Act 1998.

[33] *Herbage v Pressdram Ltd* [1984] 2 All ER 769.

Under section 1(1), a person has a defence if he shows that he was not the 'author, editor or publisher'[34] of the matter complained of; that he took reasonable care in relation to its publication, and that he did not know (or have reason to believe) that what he did caused or contributed to the publication of defamatory matter. As such, the defence is not available where the defendant is an internet service provider through whose service an unknown third party posts defamatory material if, after notification of the defamatory nature of the material, the defendant fails to verify its defamatory content and remove it from the Web.[35] At this point, it does not lie in the mouth of the service provider to say that he or she is not contributing to the publication of the defamatory statement.

The defence is wider than the common-law defence of innocent dissemination in that a much wider class of persons may avail themselves of it.[36] But, again, the defendant has a burden and standard of proof that require him to show his innocence as regards knowledge of the defamatory nature of the statement,[37] and that he took reasonable care in relation to his part in its publication. So far as the reasonable care test is concerned, under section 1(5) of the Act, the court is directed to have regard to three specific factors: (1) the degree of the defendant's responsibility for the content of the statement complained of, or for the decision to publish it; (2) the nature or circumstances of the publication;[38] (3) the previous conduct or character of the author, editor or publisher.[39]

SECTION 4 OFFER OF AMENDS

Section 4 of the Defamation Act 1952 formerly provided a little used and widely criticized, technical defence in cases of innocent publication.[40] This section has now been repealed by Schedule 2 to the 1996 Act. In its stead a more modern, revamped

---

[34] The notion of publisher, for the purposes of the Act, is confined to that of 'commercial publisher'; ie, 'a person whose business is issuing material to the public': s 1(2).

[35] *Godfrey v Demon Internet Ltd* [2001] QB 201.

[36] Under s 1(3)(a) of the Act, those involved in the production process or printing of books, newspapers and magazines are also covered. So, too, are those who distribute information by way of electronic media such as internet users (s 1(3)(c)), those, such as chat-show and phone-in hosts, who broadcast information in live programmes (s 1(3)(d)) and those, such as internet service providers, who operate communications systems that are used to transmit defamatory statements (s 1(3)(e)).

[37] Strictly, *Vizetelly* required ignorance of *a libel* (a narrower concept than that of a defamatory remark). To this extent, the defence is more restrictive than its common law counterpart in that knowledge of a defamatory statement (eg, one known to be defamatory, but believed to be true) will defeat the defence.

[38] The Act is unclear on what is meant by 'the circumstances of the publication'. Presumably, however, remarks made about infamous or notorious persons would require greater concern than remarks about less well known people.

[39] Presumably, here, the standard of care demanded is greater in relation to publishers with a history of producing defamatory material.

[40] The principal problem with s 4 of the 1952 Act was that it placed the onus on D to demonstrate his innocence by proving the absence of negligence.

defence of 'offer to make amends' has been introduced.[41] The offer of amends defence is available only to those defendants who did not know, or had no reason to believe, that the statement in question referred to the claimant and was untrue and defamatory of him.[42] It has since been clarified that 'having a reason to believe' in this context requires that the defendant must have been reckless as to the matter and not merely that a reasonable person in his position would have realized that the statement was untrue or defamatory. In other words, the test is a subjective, not objective, one.[43]

The new defence may only be invoked where the offer to make amends is in writing and states that it is such an offer under the 1996 Act.[44] In addition, the offer must satisfy three further prerequisites: it must contain a correction to, and apology for, the original statement; it must state a willingness to publish that correction and apology; it must make clear that the publisher consents to pay to the aggrieved party such sum as may be agreed between them, or, as may be determined judicially.[45] Where an offer of amends has been made, it will probably serve as significant mitigation.[46]

If the offer of amends is accepted, section 3(2) prohibits the aggrieved party from subsequently bringing or continuing defamation proceedings. If, on the other hand, the offer is not accepted, the offer may nonetheless be invoked as a defence in any subsequent defamation proceedings brought by the claimant.[47] For this reason, it is suggested that it would normally be unwise for a claimant to reject an offer of amends. Should he instead pursue an action in the courts, in order for the offer not to constitute a defence, the claimant would have to show, first, that the defendant knew or had reason to believe that the statement referred to the claimant and, secondly, that it was both false and defamatory.[48]

The offer of amends defence does not require the alleged defamer to prove his innocence.[49] Accordingly, it effects a significant change in the location of the burden of proof. On the other hand, any defendant wishing to use this defence is debarred from resorting to any other defence (such as justification).[50] This means that he is forced to choose between (1) definitely paying moderate damages (either agreed with the claimant, or judicially determined) and (2) risking paying damages in full if another defence – such as justification – should be held not to be available.

---

[41] Defamation Act 1996, ss 2–4.   [42] Defamation Act 1996, s 4(3).

[43] *Milne v Express Newspapers (No 1)* [2005] 1 WLR 772.   [44] Defamation Act 1996, s 2(3).

[45] Defamation Act 1996, s 2(3), (4).

[46] *Nail v NGN Ltd* [2005] EMLR 12 (the damages in such cases serve no deterrent purpose, and need not be so high as in other cases where, eg, exemplary damages may be needed).

[47] Defamation Act 1996, s 4(2).

[48] C bears the burden of proof by virtue of the Defamation Act 1996, s 4(3) which introduced a statutory presumption of the publisher's innocence, thus giving him the right to invoke his offer of amends as a defence.

[49] This is now presumed under s 4(3). Cf s 4 of the 1952 Act, which it replaces. Another difference between the current provision and s 4 of the 1952 Act is as follows. If the offer is refused, the case will proceed but D may still use the making of the offer as a mitigatory defence (reducing the amount of damages payable) where he knew (1) that the publication was defamatory of C but (2) reasonably believed that what was said was true: s 4(5).

[50] Defamation Act 1996, s 4(4).

SECTION 5 ABSOLUTE PRIVILEGE

Certain occasions are deemed to be so important that those making statements upon them are not liable in defamation despite their statements being untrue and even malicious. These occasions – where the public interest in freedom of communication is paramount – are called cases of absolute privilege.

(A) PARLIAMENTARY PROCEEDINGS

By the law of Parliament, the courts for centuries had no jurisdiction to hear evidence of proceedings in Parliament.[51] This immunity extended beyond all statements made in the course of parliamentary proceedings to all reports, papers, votes, and proceedings published by, or under the authority of, either House.[52] This assertion of 'parliamentary privilege' meant not only that parliamentary proceedings could not found an action in defamation but also that such proceedings could not be relied on in relation to a claim arising out of a non-parliamentary publication. Thus, in one case, the court would not admit evidence of statements contained in *Hansard* that the claimant sought to introduce in order to demonstrate malice.[53]

Section 13 of the Defamation Act 1996 introduced a significant change in the law.[54] It permitted an MP to waive the prohibition on adducing evidence of parliamentary proceedings enshrined in Article 9 of the Bill of Rights 1688.[55] But where an MP waives that privilege in order to enter evidence of the proceedings of a parliamentary committee (or its findings), the waiver will override the privilege of the House as a whole, and thus entitle the defendant to challenge the parliamentary proceedings in question, and even the findings of a prior parliamentary inquiry into the conduct of the MP in question.[56] Section 13 is thus an extremely important (and not uncontroversial) provision. Furthermore, it is clear from section 13(5) that it extends not just to parliamentary proceedings *per se*, but also to evidence contained in such documents as reports produced by parliamentary committees.[57]

---

[51] Bill of Rights 1688, Art 9; *Ex p Wason* (1869) LR 4 QB 573, at 576, *per* Cockburn CJ. Hence, the frequent challenge by the victim to the MP to repeat outside the House his attacks on the victim's reputation. Comments outside Parliament, even if they refer to earlier privileged statements, do not attract absolute privilege: *Jennings v Buchanan* [2005] 1 AC 115.   [52] Parliamentary Papers Act 1840, s 1.

[53] *Church of Scientology of California v Johnson-Smith* [1972] 1 QB 522. See also *Hamilton v Al Fayed* [2001] 1 AC 395. Cf *Rost v Edwards* [1990] 2 QB 460 where Popplewell J did allow evidence drawn from the *Register of Members' Interests* on the basis that this was a public document.

[54] Cf the common law: *Prebble v Television New Zealand* [1995] 1 AC 321.

[55] Section 13 operates in favour of MPs only. The waiver enables an MP to vindicate his character in a defamation action by adducing evidence of parliamentary proceedings. It does not, by contrast, allow the MP to adduce evidence from a similar source in order to substantiate the main argument.

[56] *Hamilton v Al-Fayed* [2001] 1 AC 395. Note, however, that *the actual words used* by the MP remain privileged: Defamation Act 1996, s 13(4).

[57] See Sharland and Loveland, 'The Defamation Act 1996 and Political Libels' [1997] PL 113.

(B) EXECUTIVE MATTERS

In the leading case of *Chatterton v Secretary of State for India*,[58] it was held that a letter from the Secretary of State for India to his Parliamentary Under-Secretary providing the material for the answer to a parliamentary question was absolutely privileged. It is impossible to say how high in the hierarchy of civil servants a defendant must be before he enjoys this privilege, but a message from the High Commissioner for Australia to his Prime Minister about a matter of commerce which concerned the Government of Australia was certainly held to be privileged.[59] And complaints made to the European Commission relating to the enforcement of competition proceedings are similarly protected.[60]

It has been doubted whether those below the status of minister may claim the privilege;[61] and if it were not for the cases below relating to military communications, one might confidently suggest that routine communications between persons not in charge of government departments are outside the privilege. Indeed, one might even doubt whether the courts would extend it anywhere beyond the examples contained in the above cases.

In *Dawkins v Lord Paulet*[62] it was held that a report on the claimant from his superior officer to his commander-in-chief could not form the basis of an action for libel. The rationale of the case is not clear, however. Cockburn CJ dissented; Lush J based his judgment on the principle that the army was outside the jurisdiction of the courts,[63] yet one of the three grounds of Mellor J's judgment was that such letters were absolutely privileged.[64] It is submitted that this is not strong enough authority for the proposition that communications within the civil service generally, and relating to the character and ability of personnel, are absolutely privileged. Nor does the case decide that civil servants below ministerial rank enjoy this absolute privilege; but their communications, as we shall see, would be adequately protected by the qualified privilege which doubtless attaches to them.

A final point in this context is that absolute privilege must not be confused with the procedural rule that the Crown, whether or not it is a party, cannot be compelled in any litigation, to produce or disclose the existence of any documents the production or

---

[58] [1895] 2 QB 189. The Parliamentary Commissioner Act 1967, s 10(5) also gives an absolute privilege to the Parliamentary Commissioner for his reports to Parliament and for certain of his communications to MPs; the Local Commissioners have a similar absolute privilege under the Local Government Act 1974, s 32; so, too, does the Legal Services Ombudsman under s 23 of the Courts and Legal Services Act 1990.

[59] *M Isaacs & Sons Ltd v Cook* [1925] 2 KB 391.

[60] *Hasselblad (GB) Ltd v Orbinson* [1985] QB 475. But should this more properly be regarded as judicial privilege, or even witness immunity: see *Mahon v Rahn* [1998] QB 424.

[61] *Szalatnay-Stacho v Fink* [1946] 1 All ER 303, at 305, *per* Henn Collins J (not considered on appeal: [1947] KB 1).

[62] (1868) LR 5 QB 94.

[63] But see *Dawkins v Lord Rokeby* (1873) LR 8 QB 255 (affd (1875) LR 7 HL 744).

[64] In *Merricks v Nott-Bower* [1965] 1 QB 57, the report by one high ranking police officer to another about a third police officer was held not to be so clearly the subject of absolute privilege that a claim in libel should be struck out.

disclosure of which would be contrary to the public interest.[65] In practice, because the Crown can decide at its discretion whether to produce such documents, this rule has prevented claimants from maintaining libel suits, even for communications within the civil service, which were not absolutely privileged.[66]

(c) JUDICIAL PROCEEDINGS

Statements made in proceedings before superior and inferior courts of record and magistrates' courts are privileged. The privilege extends to other tribunals recognized by law,[67] provided they are 'exercising functions equivalent to those of an established court of justice'.[68] In cases of doubt, 'the overriding factor is whether there will emerge from the proceedings a determination the truth and justice of which is a matter of public concern'.[69] Thus, an enquiry before an Inn of Court into the conduct of a barrister was absolutely privileged,[70] even though the body had no power to issue a subpoena, or to take evidence on oath, and sat in private. The disciplinary committee of the Law Society,[71] courts-martial,[72] and select committees of the House of Commons[73] are also within the privilege. If the function of the body in question is merely administrative, and it does not determine the rights, guilt or innocence of anyone, there is no absolute privilege, even though procedures akin to judicial procedures – such as hearing evidence or summoning witnesses – are used.[74] Thus, justices dealing with applications for liquor licensing,[75] official industrial conciliation processes[76] and complaints to social security adjudication officers,[77] have all been held to be outside the scope of the privilege. Competition proceedings before the European Commission, by contrast, have been held to attract absolute privilege despite the essentially administrative nature of their procedures: the public interest in the Commission's duty to enforce European competition law was held to outweigh the private interests of litigants seeking to vindicate their reputations.[78]

The privilege is enjoyed by judges (even if their statements are malicious or irrelevant[79]), parties, witnesses questioned in relation to a crime,[80] counsel[81] and

---

[65] Crown Proceedings Act 1947, s 28. See also *Schneider v Leigh* [1955] 2 QB 195.

[66] *Home v Bentinck* (1820) 2 Brod & Bing 130, *Beatson v Skene* (1860) 5 H & N 838 and *West v West* (1911) 27 TLR 476, are examples of cases where the rule was successfully used for that purpose.

[67] Either under statute or royal prerogative of justice: *Lincoln v Daniels* [1962] 1 QB 237.

[68] *O'Connor v Waldron* [1935] AC 76, at 81.

[69] *Lincoln v Daniels* [1962] 1 QB 237, at 255–6, per Devlin LJ.   [70] *Lincoln v Daniels* [1962] 1 QB 237.

[71] *Addis v Crocker* [1961] 1 QB 11.   [72] *Wilson v Westney* [2001] EWCA Civ 839.

[73] On principle, these would seem to have been more properly within the 'legislative privilege', but this is not the basis of *Goffin v Donnelly* (1881) 6 QBD 307. But see now *Rost v Edwards* [1990] 2 QB 460.

[74] See, eg, *W v Westminster City Council and others* [2005] 1 FLR 816 (a communication made in a child protection case conference was not privileged); *O'Connor v Waldron* [1935] AC 76.

[75] *Attwood v Chapman* [1914] 3 KB 275.   [76] *Tadd v Eastwood* [1985] ICR 132.

[77] *Purdew and Purdew v Seress Smith* [1993] IRLR 77.

[78] *Hasselblad (GB) Ltd v Orbinson* [1985] QB 475.   [79] *Scott v Stansfield* (1868) LR 3 Exch 220.

[80] *Seaman v Netherclift* (1876) 2 CPD 53. See also *Mahon v Rahn (No 2)* [2000] 4 All ER 41 where a bankers' report sent in response to inquiries to both the Trading Standards Authority and the Serious Fraud Office was covered by absolute privilege.   [81] *Munster v Lamb* (1883) 11 QBD 588.

solicitors,[82] and presumably also jurors. Whether others engaged in the proceedings are privileged is doubtful.[83] They are certainly not protected where the statement is so irrelevant that it is no longer made by a person *qua* participant in the proceedings.[84] The privilege is probably lost when the court has no jurisdiction.

Finally, it should be noted that the privilege extends to documents initiating,[85] or made in the course of the proceedings (for example, pleadings and affidavits).[86] However, documents prepared prior to proceedings that do not have any *necessary* link with those proceedings are not privileged in this way. Accordingly, in one case where a defamatory letter was written by the defendant council to the claimant's solicitor in the course of pre-hearing negotiations, it was held that, since the letter's contents did not have any necessary import for any future legal proceedings, it was inappropriate to allow the defendant to claim a privilege.[87]

(D) SOLICITOR-CLIENT COMMUNICATIONS

Closely related to the privilege just discussed is the question of how far statements to solicitors by either clients or witnesses before trial, are protected. If the purpose of not restricting the prosecution of judicial proceedings is to be attained, it would be unrealistic to deny to a witness privilege in respect of a proof of his evidence made immediately before trial. The House of Lords has therefore held in *Watson v M'Ewan* that a witness making a proof after the issue of a writ, but before trial, is absolutely privileged.[88] This extension by the House of Lords of the privilege surrounding judicial proceedings is restricted to matters outside the proceedings which are necessary for the administration of justice. It does not extend to a complaint to the Bar Council, even though that is a recognised channel for complaints by the public about members of the Bar.[89]

---

[82] *Mackay v Ford* (1860) 5 H & N 792. But in non-contentious matters, a qualified privilege may be sufficient: see *Waple v Surrey County Council* [1998] 1 WLR 860.

[83] Doubt arises since judicial immunity may derive from the separate defence of judicial act, not that of privilege: *Hamilton v Anderson* (1858) 3 Macq 363. Cf *Law v Llewellyn* [1906] 1 KB 487.

[84] In answer to the question: 'Were you at York on a certain day?' a statement by a witness: 'Yes, and AB picked my pocket there', would not be made *qua* witness if the proceedings were entirely unconnected with AB: *Seaman v Netherclift* (1876) 2 CPD 53, at 57, *per* Cockburn CJ.

[85] But not, if the initiating document is wrongly sent to the Bar Council, instead of to an Inn of Court: *Lincoln v Daniels* [1962] 1 QB 237.

[86] See *Lilley v Roney* (1892) 61 LJQB 727; *Revis v Smith* (1856) 18 CB 126; *Taylor v Director of the Serious Fraud Office* [1999] 2 AC 177. The privilege confers a general defence to all torts, and not merely to defamation: *Marrinan v Vibart* [1963] 1 QB 528.

[87] *Waple v Surrey County Council* [1998] 1 All ER 624. See also *Daniels v Griffith* [1998] EMLR 489 (no privilege in respect of a defamatory statement (relating to C) given by D to the police which was later used by a parole board considering C's parole because the parole board was not a court of law). Cf *Mond v Hyde* [1998] 3 All ER 833 (official receiver covered by privilege in respect of statements made in bankruptcy proceedings in so far as those statements were made for the purpose of court proceedings). [88] [1905] AC 480.

[89] *Lincoln v Daniels* [1962] 1 QB 237.

Whether all communications between solicitor and client should be privileged is clearly a different matter. Yet consider *More v Weaver*:[90]

In a discussion between solicitor and client on whether a loan should be called in, C was defamed. Importantly, the discussion bore no relation to any actual or prospective litigation. The statement was held to be absolutely privileged.

By contrast, in *Minter v Priest*[91] the House of Lords expressly left open the question of whether *More v Weaver* had been rightly decided. It is submitted that *More v Weaver* was wrongly decided. In the cases which it purported to follow,[92] solicitor-client communications were only held to be absolutely privileged because they referred to judicial proceedings actually pending.

(E) REPORTS OF JUDICIAL PROCEEDINGS

A fair and accurate report of judicial proceedings heard in public and published contemporaneously with those proceedings, is absolutely privileged under section 14 of the Defamation Act 1996. For the purposes of this section, 'contemporaneous' publications include those that appear 'as soon as practicable after publication is permitted'.[93] And the 'judicial proceedings' to which the Act refers are specified to mean any proceedings in a UK court, the European Court of Justice or the European Court of Human Rights.[94] Unlike the corresponding provision in the previous legislation – which confined privilege to newspaper, television and radio reports – section 14 confers absolute privilege on *all* contemporaneous reports regardless of the medium of publication. However, nothing in the new legislation changes the common-law rule that the jury should decide if the report is a fair and accurate one.[95] And once any absolute privilege is established, it extends to consequential communications in the ordinary course of things to clerks, typists and the like.[96]

SECTION 6 QUALIFIED PRIVILEGE

In certain circumstances, it is thought desirable that reflections on the reputation of another, although untrue, should not give rise to tortious liability, provided those reflections were not published with 'malice'. These are occasions of qualified privilege. They are characterized by the fact that, in such circumstances, the interest in freedom of

---

[90] [1928] 2 KB 520.   [91] [1930] AC 558, at 579, *per* Lord Atkin.
[92] Eg, *Browne v Dunn* (1893) 6 R 67.   [93] Defamation Act 1996, s 14(2).
[94] Defamation Act 1996, s 14(3).
[95] Although legal precision is not required, a report of a conviction for stealing a car was held not to be a fair report of a conviction for taking it without the owner's consent: *Mitchell v Hirst, Kidd and Rennie Ltd* [1936] 3 All ER 872.   [96] *M Isaacs & Sons Ltd v Cook* [1925] 2 KB 391.

speech is more important than the claimant's interest in the protection of her reputation. In practical terms, this is the most widely used defence. It is generally underpinned by the notion that the defendant was under a duty – whether legal, social or moral – to make the communication complained of.[97] However, since malice – which will defeat this defence – may be evidenced in number of ways, that concept needs to be considered as a preliminary matter.

(A) MALICE

(1) ESTABLISHING MALICE

'Malice', for the purposes of defeating a claim to qualified privilege, means making use of the privileged occasion dishonestly or for some evil or improper purpose, and it may be established in any of the following ways.

(a) The defendant does not believe in the truth of his statement

By far the most important way of establishing malice (and thereby rebutting the privilege) is to show that the defendant did not believe in the truth of his statement or that he was reckless as to whether the statement was true or false. Thus, '[i]f a man is proved to have stated that which he knew to be false, no one need inquire further'.[98] As such, a solicitor who writes that his client has admitted his negligence when he knows that he has not admitted it has abused the privilege.[99] Equally, in *Fraser v Mirza*,[100] proof that the defendant had quite blatantly and deliberately lied in parts of the statement complained of was sufficient to establish malice and defeat his claim of privilege. On the other hand, mere proof that the defendant had no reasonable grounds for believing his statement to be true is not enough to rebut the qualified privilege.[101] In *Horrocks v Lowe*[102] it was held that if the defendant honestly believed his statement to be true, his privilege would not be lost merely because his conclusion that his statement was true resulted from unreasoning prejudice, or was irrational with regard to the subject matter. Equally, mere carelessness in the choice of one's words is insufficient to establish malice.[103]

There is probably one exception to the rule that a person who does not believe in the truth of a statement forfeits the privilege. Lord Bramwell established this exception thus:

A person may honestly make on a particular occasion a defamatory statement without believing it to be true; because the statement may be of such a character that on that occasion it may be proper to communicate it to a particular person who ought to be informed of it.[104]

---

[97] See *Adam v Ward* [1917] AC 309, at 334, *per* Lord Atkinson.
[98] *Clark v Molyneux* (1877) 3 QBD 237, at 247, *per* Brett LJ.   [99] *Groom v Crocker* [1939] 1 KB 194.
[100] 1993 SLT 527.
[101] *Clark v Molyneux* (1877) 3 QBD 237. Cf *Pitt v Donovan* (1813) 1 M & S 639. C may, however, be able to circumvent a plea of qualified privilege by suing in negligence: *Spring v Guardian Assurance plc* [1995] 2 AC 296.
[102] [1975] AC 135.   [103] *Oliver v Chief Constable of Northumbria Police* [2004] EWHC 790.
[104] *Clark v Molyneux* (1877) 3 QBD 237, at 244. Cf *Botterill v Whytehead* (1879) 41 LT 588, at 590, *per* Kelly CB.

Although authority is lacking, this exception seems sound in principle. There may well be circumstances where the obligation to communicate the defamatory matter is so pressing that the defendant should be free to do so: this is particularly true where such information as the defendant has, is properly requested by another, or where an important interest is subjected to a serious risk of harm if the defendant does not publish the information. A good example might be informing a school that the caretaker is a paedophile. Even if the maker of the statement does not believe it of the caretaker, although she heard it from another, she might nonetheless be excused from liability for erring on the side of caution and informing the school authorities.

(b) Abuse of the purpose of the privilege

If the defendant does not act for the purpose of protecting that interest for which the privilege is given, he loses it.[105] Thus, even if the defendant believes his statement to be true, if the court is satisfied that his dominant motive was an improper purpose, the privilege will be lost.[106] He must use the occasion in accordance with the purpose for which the occasion arose.[107] Thus, it was held that a letter sent to the BBC by a film company about a film critic would be 'malicious' if its purpose was to stifle criticism.[108]

With reference to this class of malice, the courts normally use such expressions as 'wrong motive', 'personal spite' or 'ill-will'.[109] If the defendant is actuated by any such motive, he abuses the privilege. But where he honestly believes in the truth of his statement, the court should be very slow to draw the inference that he is activated by improper motives.[110] The language occasionally used by the courts, and more often by writers, might seem to suggest that whenever, on a privileged occasion, the defendant has exhibited an improper motive, the privilege is rebutted. This is not quite correct: not only must there be an improper motive, that motive must have been a causative factor in the publishing of the defamation. Thus, in *Winstanley v Bampton*, a creditor who wrote a defamatory letter to the commanding officer of the claimant debtor, and believed what he wrote, forfeited his privilege because his indignation and anger had led him to defame the claimant.[111] If, however, the defendant was using the occasion for its proper purpose, but incidentally happened to have feelings of resentment towards the claimant, this would not deprive him of the privilege, which is not lost if the ill-will is not the defendant's primary purpose, but merely one purpose.[112]

In deciding whether there is the requisite ill-will, it is relevant to consider the violence of the language of the communication. That said, the courts will be very reluctant to infer malice from such evidence alone. In *Adam v Ward*, Lord Atkinson said:

a person making a communication on a privileged occasion is not restricted to the use of such language merely as is reasonably necessary to protect the interest or discharge the duty which

---

[105] (1877) 3 QBD 237, at 246, *per* Brett LJ.
[106] *Horrocks v Lowe* [1975] AC 135, at 149, *per* Lord Diplock.
[107] *Royal Aquarium and Summer and Winter Garden Society v Parkinson* [1892] 1 QB 431, *per* Lopes LJ.
[108] *Turner v Metro-Goldwyn-Mayer Pictures Ltd* [1950] 1 All ER 449, at 457–8, *per* Lord Porter.
[109] *Wright v Woodgate* (1835) 2 Cr M & R 573, approved in *Adam v Ward* [1917] AC 309, at 349, *per* Lord Shaw.   [110] *Horrocks v Lowe* [1975] AC 135, at 149–50, *per* Lord Diplock.
[111] [1943] KB 319.   [112] *Horrocks v Lowe* [1975] AC 135.

is the foundation of his privilege; but that, on the contrary, he will be protected, even though his language should be violent or excessively strong, if, having regard to all the circumstances of the case, he might have honestly and on reasonable grounds believed that what he wrote or said was true.[113]

(c) The inclusion of extraneous matter

The introduction of irrelevant matter in a communication may afford evidence of malice which will defeat the privilege that would otherwise attach to the communication.[114] On the other hand, in circumstances where the material is wholly extraneous to the main statement being made, there will be no privilege in the first place, and the question of whether a qualified privilege is defeated by malice will not arise.[115]

(d) Unreasonable publication to persons outside the scope of the privilege

Malice is present (and rebuts the privilege) if a defendant deliberately slanders another in the presence of persons to whom he has no privilege to communicate the matter (even if he has privilege to inform some of those present), or if he publishes in the press, when he could have protected his interest by a private communication.[116]

(2) JUDGE AND JURY AND THE BURDEN OF PROOF IN RESPECT OF MALICE

Lord Finlay summarised the functions of judge and jury in this context thus:

It is for the judge, and the judge alone, to determine as a matter of law whether the occasion is privileged, unless the circumstances attending it are in dispute, in which case the facts necessary to raise the question of law should be found by the jury. It is further for the judge to decide whether there is any evidence of express malice fit to be left to the jury – that is, whether there is any evidence on which a reasonable man could find malice.[117]

The burden of proving to the jury that the defendant was 'malicious' rests with the claimant. He discharges this burden if he proves the defendant malicious in any of the senses discussed above. In pleas of express malice, as in every other aspect of defamation law, questions may arise of exactly what meaning or meanings the defamatory statement properly bore. In *Fraser v Mirza*,[118] for example, the respondent alleged, in a complaint to the Chief Constable, that the appellant police officer had acted against him on racist motives. He expressly claimed that when questioned about two television sets he gave them up without hesitation and that a friend of his in the Pakistani community had been threatened by the officer. The House of Lords held that the whole substance of the complaint was intended to convey that the respondent had been

---

[113] [1917] AC 309, at 339. Cf *Spill v Maule* (1869) LR 4 Exch 232 for a good illustration of judicial refusal to deprive D of his privilege on the ground that he used extravagant language.

[114] *Adam v Ward* [1917] AC 309.

[115] *Adam v Ward* [1917] AC 309; *Watts v Times Newspapers Ltd* [1997] QB 650.

[116] *Oddy v Lord Paulet* (1865) 4 F & F 1009.   [117] *Adam v Ward* [1917] AC 309, at 318.

[118] 1993 SLT 527.

charged with offences relating to the television sets without any evidence. His allegations were shown to be deliberate untruths and constituted sufficient evidence of absence of belief in the overall sting of the libel: namely, that he had been charged on solely racist grounds.

(3) EXCESS OF PRIVILEGE AND MALICE

In *Adam v Ward*, the House of Lords held that there are two separate questions to be answered. The first is whether the privilege has been exceeded. The second is whether there is evidence of malice.[119] The primary importance of the distinction lies in the fact that the judge decides whether the privilege has been exceeded (and therefore lost), but the jury decides whether there is 'malice'. And observations made by judges in directing juries on what is evidence of malice are not necessarily applicable when they have to rule on excess of privilege.[120] There may be such an excess where statements quite unconnected with the main statement are introduced.[121]

An example of excess of privilege is where statements quite unconnected with the main statement are introduced. Take, for example, *Tuson v Evans*.[122]

In a letter to C's agent setting out the basis of his claim against C for arrears of rent, D added: 'This attempt to defraud me of the produce of land is as mean as it is dishonest'. This 'wholly unnecessary' addition deprived him of his qualified privilege.

The privilege will also be lost by publishing to more persons than is necessary. It was exceeded, for example, when the minutes of a *preliminary* inquiry by a committee of a local authority into alleged petrol thefts by employees were placed in the public library. At that stage, the body of ratepayers did not possess the necessary interest to receive that information.[123] On the other hand, an occasion does not cease to be privileged simply because the defendant publishes to clerks or others in the reasonable and ordinary course of business practice.[124] The fact that persons are present other than those to whom there is a duty to make the statement will not end the privilege if the ordinary 'business of life could not well be carried on' were such restrictions to be imposed.[125] So, for example, a company does not forfeit its protection if, in order to have circulated a copy of the auditor's report, it sends it to printers, for that is reasonable and necessary.[126]

---

[119] [1917] AC 309, at 318, 320–1 and 327 *per* Lord Finlay, Earl Loreburn and Lord Dunedin, respectively.

[120] [1917] AC 309, at 321, *per* Earl Loreburn.

[121] If the statement, though not in strict logic relevant to the privileged occasion, is reasonably germane to the subject matter, then it is material only as evidence of malice to take the case out of the privilege: *Horrocks v Lowe* [1975] AC 135, at 151, *per* Lord Diplock.   [122] (1840) 12 Ad & El 733.

[123] *De Buse v McCarthy* [1942] 1 KB 156.

[124] *Boxsius v Goblet Frères* [1894] 1 QB 842; *Edmondson v Birch & Co Ltd and Horner* [1907] 1 KB 371; *Bryanston Finance Co Ltd v De Vries* [1975] QB 703. The last cited case, following *Toogood v Spyring* (1834) 1 Cr M & R 181, established that where the publication is made only to C, and not to third parties, there is then a qualified privilege for the publication to clerks if it is fairly warranted by any reasonable occasion (but not, as in that case, for a threatening improper letter).   [125] *Toogood v Spyring* (1834) 1 Cr M & R 181, at 194, *per* Parke B.

[126] *Lawless v Anglo-Egyptian Cotton and Oil Co* (1869) LR 4 QB 262.

(4) JOINT PUBLISHERS AND MALICE

Some difficult problems relating to the abuse of privilege are raised when there is a publication by joint tortfeasors or the employees of the defendant. An agent through whom a person publishes a privileged communication enjoys the same privilege as his principal. Thus, a solicitor has the defence of qualified privilege when he publishes on behalf of his client some matter which his client had a privilege to publish.[127] Correspondingly, if a servant in the course of his employment publishes with malice, the fact that his master was not personally malicious will not exempt the master from vicarious liability since the servant who forfeits the privilege does so in the course of his employment.[128] Where each party responsible for a joint publication has an individual right to publish the statement – for example, trustees or members of a committee – each has an independent privilege which is not affected by the malice of one or more of the other joint publishers.[129] Sometimes, however, one of the persons sued for the publication is a mere ancillary (for example, a printer or typist). Such an ancillary publisher may probably still plead qualified privilege even if all his principals published maliciously. The key question would be whether the ancillary was himself actuated by malice.[130]

(B) INSTANCES OF QUALIFIED PRIVILEGE

(1) GENERAL PRINCIPLE

All the following instances of qualified privilege can be captured within the general principle of common interest: that is, they exist where the defendant has an interest or duty (whether legal, social or moral) to communicate intelligence about the claimant to a third party who has a corresponding interest or duty to receive such information.[131] The underlying rationale has also been summarized thus: it exists for 'the common convenience and welfare of society'.[132] Thus, 'originally and in principle there are not many different kinds of privilege, but rather for all privilege there is the same foundation of the public interest'.[133] The classic statement on the matter is that of Parke B:[134]

[The defendant is liable for a defamatory statement] unless it is fairly made by a person in the discharge of some public or private duty, whether legal or moral, or in the conduct of his own

---

[127] *Baker v Carrick* [1894] 1 QB 838.

[128] *Citizens' Life Assurance Co v Brown* [1904] AC 423; *Riddick v Thames Board Mills Ltd* [1977] QB 881.

[129] *Egger v Viscount Chelmsford* [1965] 1 QB 248.

[130] This was the view of the majority in *Egger v Viscount Chelmsford* [1965] 1 QB 248, who took the bold step of disregarding statements to the contrary in *Adam v Ward* [1917] AC 309 because their Lordships had not heard argument on the point.

[131] *Adam v Ward* [1917] AC 309. This even covers broad-based internet communications to all the members of a particular religious community if they have sufficient interest in receiving the information: *Hewitt v Grunwald* [2004] EWCA Civ 2959.　　　　　　　　　　[132] *Perera v Peiris* [1949] AC 1, at 20, *per* Lord Uthwatt.

[133] *Webb v Times Publishing Co Ltd* [1960] 2 QB 535, at 563, *per* Pearson J.

[134] *Toogood v Spyring* (1834) 1 Cr M & R 181, at 193, approved by Lord Shaw in *Adam v Ward* [1917] AC 309, at 349.

affairs, in matters where his interest is concerned. If fairly warranted by any reasonable occasion or exigency, and honestly made, such communications are protected for the common convenience and welfare of society; and the law has not restricted the right to make them within any narrow limits.

It is convenient to group the examples of statements afforded qualified privilege – and they are only examples – as follows: privileged reports, statements which protect an interest and those made in the public interest.

(2) PRIVILEGED REPORTS

Fair and accurate reports of proceedings in Parliament or in committees thereof, or a fair summary or sketch of that part of those proceedings which is of special interest,[135] are privileged at common law.[136] These, and other such common-law privileges, are expressly preserved by the Defamation Act 1996,[137] even though section 15 of that Act – read in conjunction with Schedule 1 – endeavours to establish a comprehensive range of reports that attract a statutory qualified privilege. The printing or broadcasting[138] of copies of, or extracts from, reports,[139] papers, votes or proceedings published by authority of either House of Parliament are also privileged independently of the 1996 Act.[140]

Judicial reports, too, remain privileged at common law, so long as they are both fair and accurate.[141] The question of whether such reports meet the criteria of fairness and accuracy falls to the jury. In view of the different rationale for this privilege, these 'judicial proceedings' (a report of which acquires a qualified privilege) are not the same as those 'judicial proceedings', a report of which attracts an absolute privilege.[142] The former is a much broader class of reports. Yet in *Stern v Piper*[143] it was held that qualified privilege does not stretch to a report of proceedings that are merely 'pending'. On the other hand, although a tribunal for the purposes of qualified privilege need not perform 'judicial functions' (in the narrow sense of the term), reports of its proceedings may be privileged, provided the public are admitted and the tribunal is not a mere domestic one, such as the Jockey Club.[144] The privilege still applies where the tribunal

---

[135] *Cook v Alexander* [1974] QB 279.   [136] *Wason v Walter* (1868) LR 4 QB 73.

[137] Defamation Act 1996, s 15(4)(b).

[138] Defamation Act 1952, s 9(1) extends this privilege to those forms of broadcasting to which the Act applies.

[139] Parliamentary Papers Act 1840, s 2.

[140] Including blue books and reports of Royal Commissions presented to Parliament: *Mangena v Edward Lloyd Ltd* (1908) 98 LT 640; on appeal (1909) 99 LT 824.

[141] *Furniss v Cambridge Daily News Ltd* (1907) 23 TLR 705, at 706, *per* Sir Gorell Barnes P. In *Stern v Piper* [1997] QB 123 it was said that blasphemous or obscene material would not be privileged; nor would pre-trial reporting of allegations in court documents not yet in the public domain.

[142] For the judicial proceedings covered by absolute privilege see s 14(3) of the Defamation Act 1996.

[143] [1997] QB 123.

[144] *Chapman v Lord Ellesmere* [1932] 2 KB 431. Cf *Allbutt v General Council of Medical Education and Registration* (1889) 23 QBD 400, at 410, *per* Lopes LJ. The privilege applied to foreign courts where the subject-matter was of legitimate interest to the English newspaper-reading public (eg, where it was closely connected with the administration of justice in England – as in *Webb v Times Publishing Co Ltd* [1960] 2 QB 535 – but not otherwise).

is simply considering the case in order to discover whether it has jurisdiction, even though in fact it has no such jurisdiction.[145]

By far the most comprehensive list of those reports and statements that are afforded a qualified privilege is contained in Schedule 1 to the Defamation Act 1996.[146] Importantly, however, there are limits to this statutory privilege. The Act offers no protection in the instance of a 'publication to the public, of matter which is not of public concern and the publication of which is not for the public benefit'.[147] Nor does it confer a qualified privilege in respect of anything published with malice,[148] or illegally.[149]

So far as it relates to qualified privilege, the protection provided by section 15 of the 1996 Act is broadly similar to its now repealed predecessor, section 7 of the Defamation Act 1952. That, in turn, was little more than a reiteration of section 3 of the Law of Libel Amendment Act 1888 and, importantly, there is authority under that nineteenth century statute that what has become section 15 requires *both* public concern *and* public benefit to be shown. Furthermore, the burden of proving these things lies with the defendant.[150] Both the questions of what constitutes a matter of public concern, and what constitutes a matter of public benefit, are for the jury to decide.[151]

Reports protected by the Act fall into two distinct groups: (1) those privileged without any explanation or contradiction[152] and (2) those privileged subject to explanation or contradiction.[153] In relation to the former category, protection is conferred, broadly, on a world-wide basis. It lies in respect of reports of judicial, legislative and international organization proceedings conducted in public, and reports on official publications. Unlike the absolute privilege that is conferred in relation to reports of judicial proceedings, the protection conferred under section 15 of the 1996 Act applies without requiring the report to be contemporaneous with the judicial proceedings.[154]

In relation to the second class of reports covered by section 15 – those which are privileged subject to explanation or contradiction – no protection will be afforded if the claimant proves that the defendant, despite a request to publish a letter or statement of explanation or contradiction in a suitable manner,[155] has refused or neglected so to

[145] *Usill v Hales* (1878) 3 CPD 319. This case is not an authority on absolute privilege for judicial acts done without jurisdiction.　　　　[146] The statutory list is too long to be reproduced here.

[147] Defamation Act 1996, s 15(3). In, eg, *Kelly v O'Malley* (1889) 6 TLR 62, for example, irrelevant, defamatory comments made at a public meeting were afforded no privilege.　　　[148] Defamation Act 1996, s 15(1).

[149] Defamation Act 1996, s 15(4)(a).　　　[150] *Kelly v O'Malley* (1889) 6 TLR 62, at 64, *per* Huddleston B.

[151] *Kingshott v Associated Kent Newspapers Ltd* [1991] 1 QB 88. But note that sufficient sections of society may well constitute 'the public' for these purposes: see *GKR Karate (UK) Ltd v Yorkshire Post Newspapers Ltd (No 2)* [2000] EMLR 410 (regional publication) and *Al-Fagih v HH Saudi Research and Marketing (UK) Ltd* [2002] EMLR 215 (publication aimed at Saudis only).　　　[152] Defamation Act 1996, Sch 1, Part I.

[153] Defamation Act 1996, Sch 1, Part II. Note that 'Reports' for these purposes will include the summary of a press release that is issued to accompany a press conference: *McCartan Turkington Breen v Times Newspapers Ltd* [2001] 2 AC 277.

[154] *Tsikata v Newspaper Publishing plc* [1997] 1 All ER 655 (case report appeared ten years after the case had been heard, but it was held to be privileged). 'Reports' privileged in this way under s 7 of the 1952 Act continue to be covered under the 1996 Act so the authority of the case remains intact.

[155] That is, in the same manner as the publication complained of or, alternatively, in a manner that is both reasonable and adequate in the circumstances: Defamation Act 1996, s 15(2).

do.[156] The kinds of reports and statements that fall into this second class include those concerning official parliamentary or judicial notices to the public, meetings of public or quasi-public bodies in this country and general meetings of UK public companies.

The essential difference between the first and second class of reports is that those in the latter category tend to be based on notices issued, and meetings held, in the UK or European Union. For this reason it is much more reasonable to expect, say, a newspaper to print a correction or explanation relating to the initial report. By contrast, it is seen as too much of an imposition to expect the newspaper to publish such explanations or corrections when the initial report was on an item of world news.

(3) STATEMENTS TO PROTECT AN INTEREST

(a) The public interest

(i) Statements by way of help in discovering criminals

Information given to the police[157] in order to detect crime is privileged.[158] Statements made by policemen in the course of their inquiries into suspected crimes are presumably also privileged; and statements made in the course of complaints about police conduct have also been held to be privileged.[159]

(ii) Statements about the misconduct of public officers

When a member of the public brings to the notice of the proper authority any misconduct or neglect of duty on the part of public officers, his doing so is afforded qualified privilege.[160] However, when the defendant, acting in good faith, complains to the wrong official, he is not privileged.[161] Yet a defendant who first addresses his complaint about misconduct to his MP will almost certainly be privileged.[162] One unanswered question, however, is whether the privilege in relation to the misconduct of public officers includes those employed in one of the now privatized public services? By reason of logic, it ought so to apply.

(iii) Statements more generally in the public interest

There is no general common-law defence of publication of 'fair information on a matter of public interest'. *General* interest in the subject-matter of a report made to the public as a whole is, by itself, an insufficient basis upon which to grant the report

---

[156] Defamation Act 1996, s 15(2).

[157] But not to the wife of the accused: *Wenman v Ash* (1853) 13 CB 836.

[158] *Padmore v Lawrence* (1840) 11 Ad & El 380.   [159] *Fraser v Mirza* 1993 SLT 527.

[160] Eg, *Harrison v Bush* (1855) 5 E & B 344 (statement to Home Secretary about county magistrate). But see *Blackshaw v Lord* [1984] QB 1: suspicions must be aired to the proper authority and not the public at large unless public safety is at risk.

[161] *Hebditch v MacIlwaine* [1894] 2 QB 54; *Beach v Freeson* [1972] 1 QB 14. Cf the *dictum* of Lord Atkinson in *London Association for Protection of Trade v Greenlands Ltd* [1916] 2 AC 15, at 34 (answers to an inquiry in the genuine mistaken belief that the inquirer had a legitimate interest were held to be privileged).

[162] *R v Rule* [1937] 2 KB 375.

a qualified privilege.[163] The correlative 'duty and interest' aspects that normally characterize instances of qualified privilege are absent in such cases; for the public at large can but rarely claim a *genuine* interest in the disclosure of information concerning a given individual. However, occasionally, an item of information will be of genuine public interest; and where this is so and a newspaper acts responsibly in publishing the item in the form that it does, it may claim a qualified privilege. A somewhat lengthy test for establishing whether a newspaper has acted in this fashion was set out by Lord Nicholls in the House of Lords in *Reynolds v Times Newspapers Ltd*. He said:

Depending on the circumstances, the matters to be taken into account include the following.

1 The seriousness of the allegation. The more serious the charge, the more the public is misinformed and the individual harmed, if the allegation is not true.

2 The nature of the information, and the extent to which the subject matter is a matter of public concern.

3 The source of the information. Some informants have no direct knowledge of the events. Some have their own axes to grind, or are being paid for their stories.

4 The steps taken to verify the information.

5 The status of the information. The allegation may have already been the subject of an investigation which commands respect.

6 The urgency of the matter. News is often a perishable commodity.

7 Whether comment was sought from the [claimant]. He may have information others do not possess or have not disclosed. An approach to the [claimant] will not always be necessary.

8 Whether the article contained the gist of the claimant's side of the story.

9 The tone of the article. A newspaper can raise queries or call for an investigation. It need not adopt allegations as statements of fact.

10 The circumstances of the publication, including the timing.

This list is not exhaustive. The weight to be given to these and any other relevant factors will vary from case to case.[164]

Notwithstanding a general caution regarding the free and easy application of the principle enunciated in *Reynolds*,[165] – after all, matters that are of interest to the public clearly extend beyond those which are strictly speaking in the public interest[166] – Lord Nicholls

---

[163] The 'public interest' of qualified privilege is narrower and broad in scope than the 'public interest' of fair comment (see below). *Chapman v Lord Ellesmere* [1932] 2 KB 431 illustrates its strictness, in qualified privilege, unlike fair comment, the defence will succeed although the facts are untrue. However, anything submitted to the public for its appraisal can be treated as a matter of 'public interest' in the fair comment defence.

[164] At [2001] 2 AC 127, at 205. For detailed analysis, see Williams, 'Defaming Politicians: the not so Common Law' (2000) 63 MLR 748.

[165] See, eg, *Al-Fagih v HH Saudi Research & Marketing (UK) Ltd* [2002] EMLR 215.

[166] For instance, a justification to publish to the public at large matters of speculation and suspicion will arise only in exceptional cases, such as those where public safety is endangered: see, eg, *Camporese v Parton* (1983) 150 DLR (3d) 208. See also *Henry v BBC* [2005] EWHC 2787 (no need for a certain party to be named in a regional television report).

did envisage that a more liberal approach should be taken in relation to defending comments made about political figures. He insisted that any 'court should be slow to conclude that a publication was not in the public interest and, therefore, the public had no right to know, especially when the information is in the field of political discussion'.[167] It has certainly been held that there is a public interest in learning, via a newspaper account, the details of a political dispute that is taking place in the public arena.[168] Since then, the point has been made that a better benchmark for claiming the privilege may well be 'responsible journalism'.[169] That said, a test of responsible journalism alone may be seen as too imprecise to constitute the sole test for *Reynolds* privilege because, by itself, it tends to conflate the questions of the existence of a privilege and the presence of malice. As such, the argument goes, while 'responsible journalism' might attract a privilege, it ought not to be seen as synonymous with a duty to publish,[170] for there must also be a public interest in publication. The argument, however, did not find favour with the House of Lords in its most recent consideration of this issue.[171]

It has never been directly decided whether the moral duty to publish an apology after having published a defamatory statement attracts a qualified privilege. In *Watts v Times Newspapers Ltd*,[172] the Court of Appeal failed to supply an authoritative answer to this question. In that case the defendant published a defamatory account of the claimant and then subsequently apologized in terms that reiterated the initial libel. Instead of stating generally that such apologies attract qualified privilege, it was merely held that no such claim to privilege could be sustained in the instant case for want of a reciprocal interest in publishing the apology on the part of the defendant.

As regards the social duty on Employer A to provide a reference on behalf of one of his (former) employees to Employer B, it is clear that such a reference would be afforded qualified privilege. On the other hand, in the light of the House of Lords' decision in *Spring v Guardian Assurance plc*,[173] this immunity may be of little use, since it was held in *Spring* that, subject to the usual requirements, the employee would be entitled to sue in negligence rather than defamation for the loss attributable to a carelessly written reference.[174]

---

[167] [2001] 2 AC 127, at 205. See, eg *Tsikata v Newspaper Publishing plc* [1997] 1 All ER 655. Cf the USA where all 'political speech' attracts a qualified privilege (*New York Times Co v Sullivan* (1964) 376 US 254) and in New Zealand where political speech concerning existing, former or prospective MPs is thus protected (*Lange v Atkinson* [1998] 3 NZLR 424; *Lange v Atkinson (No 2)* [2000] 3 NZLR 385).

[168] *Al-Fagih v HH Saudi Research and Marketing* [2002] EMLR 215.

[169] See, eg, *Bonnick v Morris* [2003] 1 AC 300; *Kearns v General Council of the Bar* [2003] 1 WLR 1357. The test of what is responsible journalism is to be judged by reference to whether the steps taken to gather and publish the information were responsible and fair: *Jameel v Wall Street Journal Europe (No 3)* [2006] UKHL 44, at [32], [53], [144] and [149], *per* Lords Bingham, Hoffman, Scott, and Baroness Hale respectively. But the test seems circular!

[170] *Loutchansky v Times Newspapers Ltd (No 2)* [2002] 1 All ER 652. See also *Al-Fagih v HH Saudi Research and Marketing (UK) Ltd* [2002] EMLR 215 (failure to verify allegations appearing in a newspaper does not necessarily amount to malice).

[171] The interest in publication can now be taken for granted in respect of matters of Public Interest: *Jameel v Wall Street Journal Europe (No 3)* [2006] UKHL 44.   [172] [1997] QB 650.

[173] [1995] 2 AC 296.

[174] But note that the remedy in negligence would be assessed by a judge and may well be lower than that awarded by a jury in a defamation action.

The defendant's duty to make a statement about the claimant is sometimes only a moral or social one – for example, to supply a third party with a warning about the claimant.[175] This, however, does not prohibit his statement attracting a qualified privilege. That said, in the absence of a legal or contractual duty to make such a statement, the court may well be wary of granting a privilege unless the defendant can show a strong relationship – for example, one of friendship – between himself and the third party to whom he feels obliged to make the statement.[176] Furthermore, in establishing the existence of such a duty, the defendant is entitled only to rely on matters that were known to him at the time of publication.[177]

If the duty is imposed by statute, the general defence of statutory authority will apply.[178] Otherwise, the list of moral and social duties is virtually endless. The following is by no means an exhaustive list of the situations under this head. It is merely illustrative, and includes the following: answers to confidential inquiries about servants;[179] supplying information about credit;[180] protection by a solicitor of his client's interests;[181] a host informing his guest of suspicions about the latter's servant;[182] a member of a woman's family warning her about her fiancé's character (or *vice versa*).[183] By contrast, the privilege does not cover idle gossip or officious intermeddling by strangers.[184] Consider *Watt v Longsdon*.[185]

A company director was held to be privileged in passing on to the chairman a report that an employee was associating with another woman and otherwise misconducting himself during his employment overseas, but he was not protected in informing the wife of the employee, although she had an interest in receiving that information.

(b) The self-interest of the publisher

Just as self-defence and protection of property are defences in torts against the person and property, so also is a statement made to protect or advance the defendant's interests a matter of qualified privilege in defamation.[186] Thus, a creditor may write to an auctioneer to protect his security.[187] Equally, a man who replied to a letter demanding payment of fees for medical services to his wife (who died from scarlet fever) saying, 'I shall never pay him unless the law compels me, and that I do not fancy it can, as I could more easily indict Dr S for manslaughter', was held to be privileged.[188] Privilege will also

---

[175] See, eg, *Amann v Damm* (1860) 8 CBNS 597; *S v Newham London Borough Council* (1998) 96 LGR 651 (Ds warned the DoH of the potential danger its employee, C, represented to young children).

[176] *Todd v Hawkins* (1837) 8 C & P 88.

[177] *Loutchansky v Times Newspapers Ltd* [2002] QB 321; *GKR Karate (UK) Ltd v Yorkshire Post Newspapers Ltd (No 2)* [2000] EMLR 410.

[178] Eg, *Moore v Canadian Pacific Steamship Co* [1945] 1 All ER 128 (there was a duty on a captain under the Merchant Shipping Act 1894 to record in the ship's log details of all desertions).

[179] *Kelly v Partington* (1833) 4 B & Ad 700.

[180] *London Association for Protection of Trade v Greenlands Ltd* [1916] 2 AC 15.

[181] Cf *Baker v Carrick* [1894] 1 QB 838, at 841, *per* Lopes LJ.   [182] *Stuart v Bell* [1891] 2 QB 341.

[183] *Todd v Hawkins* (1837) 8 C & P 88.   [184] *Coxhead v Richards* (1846) 2 CB 569.

[185] [1930] 1 KB 130.

[186] *Toogood v Spyring* (1834) 1 Cr M & R 181, at 193, *per* Parke B; *Aspro Travel Ltd v Owners Abroad Group plc* [1995] 4 All ER 728.   [187] *Blackman v Pugh* (1846) 2 CB 611.

[188] *Stevens v Kitchener* (1887) 4 TLR 159.

extend to reasonable steps taken by the publisher to collect money owing to him,[189] warnings issued to servants about the bad character of their associates,[190] and replies to attacks on the publisher's reputation.[191]

(c) Common interest

There are cases of privilege based on interest where neither the public nor the publisher *alone* has a sufficiently defensible interest for the case to be brought within either of the preceding headings. These cases attract a privilege on the basis that the publisher and the recipient of the communication have a 'common interest' in the subject-matter of the communication. A common interest of this kind exists between an employer and his employees. Thus, in one case, the defendants had posted up a circular in such of their premises as would be frequented by their employees, stating (among other things) that the claimant, another former employee, had been dismissed for neglect of duty. The privilege of common interest was held to extend to the defendants.[192]

The range of matters privileged because they are of common interest are manifold and include a bishop replying to an attack on him in the legislature before an assembly of his clergy,[193] communications within a family on matters affecting the welfare of a member of that family,[194] speeches by a company shareholder at a shareholders' meeting[195] or by a trustee at a friendly society meeting,[196] a statement made by a creditor to another creditor about their debtor,[197] and communications by the head of the Bar Council to members of the Bar.[198]

In one respect the scope of this privilege has been curtailed by section 10 of the Defamation Act 1952 which provides that publications, even to a qualified voter, by or on behalf of a candidate at a parliamentary or local government election, are not privileged on the ground that they are material to a question in issue in the election.[199]

SECTION 7 FAIR COMMENT

This defence covers comments about the claimant or the claimant's conduct[200] in connection with matters of public interest. Such comments must be in the form of reasonable remarks[201] upon true or privileged statements of fact. They must constitute an honestly

[189] *Winstanley v Bampton* [1943] KB 319.   [190] *Somerville v Hawkins* (1851) 10 CB 583.
[191] *Laughton v Bishop of Sodor and Man* (1872) LR 4 PC 495. But may a representative of the press, theatre, or other section of the community create a privilege by replying to an attack on that section as a whole by C? 'No', held Dixon J in *Penton v Caldwell* (1945) 70 CLR 219 (whose decision was reversed by the High Court of Australia on the ground that D, a newspaper, had itself been attacked by C.
[192] *Hunt v Great Northern Rly Co* [1891] 2 QB 189. See also *Bryanston Finance Ltd v De Vries* [1975] QB 703.
[193] *Laughton v Bishop of Sodor and Man* (1872) LR 4 PC 495.   [194] *Todd v Hawkins* (1837) 8 C & P 88.
[195] *Parsons v Surgey* (1864) 4 F & F 247.   [196] *Longdon-Griffiths v Smith* [1951] 1 KB 295.
[197] *Spill v Maule* (1869) LR 4 Exch 232.   [198] *Kearns v General Council of the Bar* [2003] 1 WLR 1357.
[199] *Braddock v Bevins* [1948] 1 KB 580 must now be read in the light of this section. See also *Plummer v Charman* [1962] 3 All ER 823.
[200] The comment may not be directed towards another matter but incidentally contain an unsubstantiated, defamatory allegation about C: *Baldwin v Rusbridger* [2001] EMLR 1062.
[201] The comment must pass an objective test (see below), but beyond this it is difficult to justify the use of the adjective 'fair' in this defence. It has even been said that the 'epithet "fair" is now meaningless and misleading': *Reynolds v Times Newspapers Ltd* [2001] 2 AC 127, at 193, *per* Lord Nicholls.

held opinion made by a person who did not believe the statements to be untrue and who was not therefore actuated by malice.[202]

(A) MATTERS OF PUBLIC INTEREST

The first requirement of this defence is that the statement in question must be made upon a matter of public interest. Here, the defence has been held to cover the public conduct of people in public offices,[203] but not their private conduct (except in so far as it throws light upon whether they possess qualities such as integrity and honesty which are thought to be essential to people in public life).[204] Matters of government and public administration,[205] including local government,[206] are also within its scope. The management of institutions of substantial public concern, such as the media itself,[207] or religious institutions, is also a matter for fair comment.[208]

Anything submitted to the public for its appraisal is of public interest. Books,[209] articles in periodicals and newspapers,[210] plays[211] and radio broadcasts (themselves being film criticisms),[212] are examples. The work of an architect[213] and the performance of actors in public entertainments[214] are also within the defence. Indeed, any circumstances that may fairly be said to invite comment are within its scope. Traders publishing handbills,[215] or those who issue public advertisements, invite comment on them. On the other hand – and notwithstanding the importance of the question – it remains undecided how far the quality of goods offered for sale to the public is, *ipso facto*, the object of fair comment. Even so, it is submitted that it would be artificially restrictive if the answer were to depend on the extent of the manufacturer's advertising campaign.

(B) COMMENT ON TRUE FACTS

A second part of the defence is that the comment, with one exception,[216] must be made upon true facts (and the rules relating to this part of the defence are unnecessarily complicated by many technical rules). At this point it is important to distinguish this defence from that of justification. Fair comment is available only in respect of expressions of opinion; justification is available in respect of both statements of fact and opinion. In fair comment, it is not necessary to prove the truth of the comment,

---

[202] *Reynolds v Times Newspapers Ltd* [2001] 2 AC 127, at 193, *per* Lord Nicholls.

[203] *Seymour v Butterworth* (1862) 3 F & F 372 (Recorder and MP).

[204] (1862) 3 F & F 372, at 382, *per* Cockburn CJ.

[205] Eg, *Henwood v Harrison* (1872) LR 7 CP 606 (the method by which D converted a naval vessel).

[206] *Purcell v Sowler* (1877) 2 CPD 215.

[207] *Telnikoff v Matusevitch* [1992] 2 AC 343 (recruiting policy for the BBC Russian service).

[208] *Kelly v Tinling* (1865) LR 1 QB 699.   [209] *Thomas v Bradbury, Agnew & Co Ltd* [1906] 2 KB 627.

[210] *Kemsley v Foot* [1952] AC 345.   [211] *Merivale v Carson* (1887) 20 QBD 275.

[212] *Turner v Metro-Goldwyn-Mayer Pictures Ltd* [1950] 1 All ER 449.

[213] *Soane v Knight* (1827) Mood & M 74.

[214] *Dibdin v Swan* (1793) 1 Esp 27; *Cooney v Edeveain* (1897) 14 TLR 34; *London Artists Ltd v Littler* [1969] 2 QB 375; *Cornwell v Myskow* [1987] 2 All ER 504.   [215] *Paris v Levy* (1860) 9 CBNS 342.

[216] Comments on statements of fact, not proved to be true, but themselves privileged, also attract the defence.

merely that the opinion was honestly held.[217] If justification is pleaded in respect of matters of opinion, the defendant must prove not merely that he honestly held the views expressed, but that they were correct views. Thus, if the statement complained of was: 'X's speech last night was inconsistent with his professions of Socialism', then, on a plea of justification, the defendant would have to prove that it was inconsistent. In fair comment, he would only need to show that he honestly held this opinion on X's speech.

Naturally, in many statements it will be very difficult to unravel fact from comment. Yet the two must be separated in due course by the court as the defence of fair comment only lies in relation to comments upon facts that are proved to be true or, exceptionally, statements that are untrue, but made on a privileged occasion (for example, a witness statement in court).[218] If the statement is not privileged, and the statement is untrue, the defendant will not be able to invoke the fair comment defence simply by proving that his comment is honestly made. Thus, in one case, a defendant who implied that a play was adulterous could not rely on fair comment where the court found as a fact that adultery was not dealt with in the play.[219] The words 'X is a disgrace' led the hearer to believe that they were based on unstated facts. Accordingly, the defendant could not plead fair comment in respect of those words alone. If, however, he had added 'he has deserted his wife and family', the original words might well be regarded as a comment on the stated facts.[220]

The full details of the procedural complexities associated with a plea of fair comment fall beyond the scope of this book. It suffices to say that defendants will attempt, whenever they can, to cloud the distinction between fact, which they must prove, and comment, which may be permissible if fair. Accordingly, the Court of Appeal has insisted that a plea of fair comment must be made 'with sufficient precision to enable the claimant to know what case he has to meet'.[221] Claimants can require details of the facts that are said to constitute the fair comment,[222] for not always will such facts be apparent. On the other hand, the absence of such facts in the defamatory statement will not necessarily be fatal to an attempt to invoke the defence. Consider *Kemsley v Foot*.[223]

D attacked a newspaper by publishing an article headed 'Lower than Kemsley'. Kemsley, a newspaper proprietor in no way connected to the newspaper that had been attacked, sued D arguing that the words amounted to a statement that that Kemsley's papers were worthy of contempt in their own right. D's counter argument was that this was indeed implied in what he had written, but that it was (1) a mere statement of opinion and (2) one that could be

---

[217] *Reynolds v Times Newspapers Ltd* [2001] 2 AC 127, at 193, *per* Lord Nicholls. But for criticism, see Young, 'Fact, Opinion and the Human Rights Act 1998' (2000) 20 OJLS 89.

[218] *Mangena v Wright* [1909] 2 KB 958; *Grech v Odhams Press Ltd* [1958] 1 QB 310; on appeal, [1958] 2 QB 275. It is not necessary for D to justify the facts contained in a privileged statement or report but he must establish that he has given a fair and accurate report of the proceedings in question: *Brent Walker Group plc v Time Out Ltd* [1991] 2 QB 33. The facts must exist at the time of the comment: *Cohen v Daily Telegraph Ltd* [1968] 2 All ER 407.　　　　　　　　　　　　　　　　　　　[219] *Merivale v Carson* (1887) 20 QBD 275.

[220] See *Cooper v Lawson* (1838) 8 Ad & El 746. For a more modern reassertion of the importance of taking the offending words in context, see *Branson v Bower* [2001] EMLR 800, at [12]–[13], *per* Latham LJ.

[221] See *Control Risks Ltd v New English Library Ltd* [1989] 3 All ER 577.

[222] *Cunningham-Howie v F W Dimbleby & Sons Ltd* [1951] 1 KB 360.

[223] [1952] AC 345; followed in *Lowe v Associated Newspapers* [2006] EWHC 320.

justified on the basis of fair comment. Kemsley contended that what D had said was a statement of fact, that no defence of fair comment could be invoked and that D's defence should be struck out. Their Lordships held that the words in question were, on their face, a mere statement of opinion even though no supporting factual evidence was provided to justify that opinion.

The case also established that 'where the facts relied on to justify the comment are contained only in the particulars, it is not incumbent on the defendant to prove the truth of every fact so stated in order to establish his plea of fair comment, but . . . he must establish sufficient facts to support the comment to the satisfaction of the jury'.[224]

A rather different question arose in *Telnikoff v Matusevitch*.[225] There, the defendant had written an angry and critical letter to the *Daily Telegraph* in response to an article written by the claimant. The key issue was whether, in determining which parts of the letter constituted allegations of fact and which were merely comment, the letter could be read alongside the offending article. The House of Lords held that only the contents of the letter itself could be considered as there were likely to be several readers who saw only the letter and not the article. Lord Keith advised both those writing to newspapers and the editors thereof to take care to use language distinguishing sufficiently clearly between fact and comment.[226]

Difficulties may arise where a defendant can prove some but not all of his factual allegations. It is thus provided in section 6 of the Defamation Act 1952 that:

a defence of fair comment shall not fail by reason only that the truth of every allegation of fact is not proved if the expression of opinion is fair comment having regard to such of the facts alleged or referred to in the words complained of as are proved.[227]

This provision has been held not to afford a defence where the facts on which the comment is based materially add to the harm to reputation. In such cases, the defendant must also prove those facts since their existence will not be assumed.[228] That said, even if the defence ultimately fails, where some of what the defendant said in relation to the claimant's bad character can be shown to be true, this can be invoked to mitigate the amount of damages payable.[229]

An imputation of corrupt or dishonourable motives will render a comment unfair unless, first, such an imputation is an inference that a fair-minded person might reasonably draw from such facts *and*, secondly, it also represents the honest opinion of the writer.[230]

---

[224] [1952] AC 345, at 362, *per* Lord Tucker.   [225] [1991] 4 All ER 817.

[226] [1991] 4 All ER 817, at 823. Note, however, the spirited dissent of Lord Ackner at 826–832.

[227] Where separate allegations have a common 'sting', O'Connor LJ has suggested that it is permissible in fair comment, as it is in justification, to rely on other uncomplained of parts of the relevant statement: *Polly Peck (Holding) plc v Trelford* [1986] 2 All ER 84, at 102.

[228] *Truth (NZ) Ltd v Avery* [1959] NZLR 274 (in this case there was an identically worded New Zealand statute); approved (*obiter*) in *Broadway Approvals Ltd v Odhams Press Ltd* [1965] 2 All ER 523.

[229] *Turner v News Group Newspapers Ltd* [2006] EWCA Civ 540.

[230] *Campbell v Spottiswoode* (1863) 3 B & S 769 (where Cockburn CJ variously uses the expressions 'well-founded', 'not without cause', and 'not without foundation'); *Peter Walker & Sons Ltd v Hodgson* [1909] 1 KB 239, at 253, *per* Buckley LJ; approved in *Harris v Lubbock* (1971) *Times*, 21 October.

(c) COMMENT MUST BE HONESTLY MADE AND NOT ACTUATED BY MALICE

There is only a *prima facie* case of fair comment if the comment in question is shown to be one that the defendant made honestly.[231] Lord Esher summarized the matter thus:

Every latitude must be given to opinion and to prejudice, and then an ordinary set of men with ordinary judgement must say whether any fair man[232] would have made such a comment on the work . . . Mere exaggeration, or even gross exaggeration, would not make the comment unfair. However wrong the opinion expressed may be in point of truth, or however prejudiced the writer, it may still be within the prescribed limit. The question which the jury must consider is this – would any fair man, however prejudiced he may be, however exaggerated or obstinate his views, have said that which this criticism has said of the work which is criticized?[233]

What is clear from this passage – and, in particular, those references to what 'ordinary men' and 'any fair man' might say – is that an objective test is to be applied in order to determine whether the comment in question is fair.[234] The court's task is to assess whether the comment in question fell within reasonable bounds.

When assessing whether the comment could honestly have been made by a fair-minded man, evidence of the claimant's standing and reputation among his fellows at the time of publication is relevant but evidence of enhanced reputation by the time of the trial is not. The vital issue is whether at the time of publication the comment could be thought fair.[235]

Surprisingly, perhaps, if the comment is objectively fair the defendant does not have to prove that he actually believes it to be fair.[236] It is for the claimant to establish that the relevant criticism was not an opinion honestly held by the defendant; that, in other words, the defendant was actuated by malice. If, for example, a newspaper publishes a defamatory letter from a reader expressing opinions which could reasonably be justified, the publishers and editor are not required to prove they concurred in the comment.[237]

It is a lack of belief in what was published that goes to the question of malice in connection with this defence.[238] It is therefore not malicious in this context to make a comment one believes to be true, even if one's reason for making that comment is associated with the pursuit of one's own private ends.[239] Conversely, even if the defendant

---

[231] *Plymouth Mutual Co-operative and Industrial Society Ltd v Traders' Publishing Association Ltd* [1906] 1 KB 403, at 418, *per* Fletcher Moulton LJ.

[232] This *dictum* was approved by Lord Porter in *Turner v Metro-Goldwyn-Mayer Pictures Ltd* [1950] 1 All ER 449 (except for the substitution of 'honest' for 'fair').

[233] *Merivale v Carson* (1887) 20 QBD 275, at 280–1. Note also that a comment may be unfair because a medical fact was omitted from the defamatory statement: *Dowling v Time Inc* (1954) *Times*, 25 June.

[234] For modern support of this objective test, see *Branson v Bower (No 2)* [2001] EMLR 809, *per* Eady J.

[235] *Cornwell v Myskow* [1987] 2 All ER 504.

[236] *Telnikoff v Matusevitch* [1991] 1 QB 102; affd on this point [1992] 2 AC 343.

[237] For a contrary judgment from Canada see *Cherneskey v Armadale Publishers Ltd* [1979] 1 SCR 1067.

[238] *Branson v Bower (No 2)* [2001] EMLR 809.

[239] Eg, *Grobbelaar v News Group Newspapers Ltd* [2001] 2 All ER 437 (reversed on other grounds [2003] EMLR 1). On the other hand, if the statement is made as part of a conspiracy, an action may lie in that tort, so long as a damage *beyond* mere damage to reputation can be shown.

survives this objective test of 'fair comment', his defence will still fail if he can be shown by the claimant to have been actuated by malice in making the comment.[240] If the purpose of the maker of the fair comment is not to give the public the benefit of his comment but instead to injure the claimant, then the defence does not lie.[241] The defendant 'is the person in whose motives the [claimant] in the libel action is concerned, and if he, the person sued, is proved to have allowed his view to be distorted by malice, it is quite immaterial that somebody else might without malice have written an equally damnatory criticism'.[242] Yet '[i]t is of course, possible for a person to have a spite against another and yet to bring a perfectly dispassionate judgment to bear upon his literary merits, but, given the existence of malice, it must be for the jury to say whether it has warped his judgement'.[243]

If an employee is malicious so as to lose his defence of fair comment, then in accordance with the ordinary principles of vicarious liability, his employer will also be deprived of the defence. Vicarious liability in defamation may also extend to a principal-agent relationship. Thus, the publisher of a periodical could not establish fair comment when the writer of a book review was malicious: the writer was an agent.[244] On the other hand, the publisher's defence of fair comment is not affected when the writer of a letter in the correspondence column of his newspaper is malicious.[245] A joint publisher probably does not lose his defence of fair comment because of the malice of another joint publisher unless he is vicariously liable for that other.[246]

(D) BURDEN OF PROOF AND THE FUNCTIONS OF JUDGE AND JURY

The defendant has the onus of proving that the matter is of public concern, that the facts on which the comment is based are true, and that the comment is such as an honest man might make. The claimant must then prove the defendant was actuated by malice. It is for the judge to decide whether the matter is one of public interest.[247] Lord Porter said:

It is for the jury in a proper case to determine what is comment and what is fact; but a prerequisite to their right is that the words are capable of being a statement of a fact or facts. It is for the judge alone to decide whether they are so capable, and whether his ruling is right or wrong is a matter of law for the decision of an appellate tribunal.[248]

---

[240] The separateness of these two matters was emphasized in *McQuire v Western Morning News Co* [1903] 2 KB 100.   [241] *Merivale v Carson* (1887) 20 QBD 275, at 281–2, *per* Lord Esher MR.

[242] *Thomas v Bradbury, Agnew & Co Ltd* [1906] 2 KB 627, at 638, *per* Collins MR.

[243] [1906] 2 KB 627, at 642.   [244] *Gros v Crook* (1969) 113 Sol Jo 408.

[245] *Lyon and Lyon v Daily Telegraph Ltd* [1943] KB 746.

[246] In *Gros v Crook* (1969) 113 Sol Jo 408 the court held that it would not have found D liable for the writer's malice had he not been vicariously liable. To the same effect, see *Egger v Viscount Chelmsford* [1965] 1 QB 248, at 265, *per* Lord Denning. Cf the judgment of Davies LJ (at 269).

[247] *South Hetton Coal Co v North-Eastern News Association* [1894] 1 QB 133, at 141, *per* Lopes LJ.

[248] *Turner v Metro-Goldwyn-Mayer Pictures Ltd* [1950] 1 All ER 449, at 461.

(E) SIMILARITY BETWEEN FAIR COMMENT AND QUALIFIED PRIVILEGE

The fair comment defence resembles that of qualified privilege in that the defendant, in order to raise a *prima facie* defence, must establish certain facts. Furthermore, both defences fail if the defendant was 'actuated by malice' in publishing the statement.

SECTION 8 APOLOGY

The offer or the making of an apology is not a defence at common law, although it may be given in evidence in mitigation of damages. Under statute, however, it is a defence.

In an action for a libel contained in any public newspaper or other periodical publication, it shall be competent to the defendant to plead that such libel was inserted in such newspaper or other periodical publication without actual malice, and without gross negligence, and that before the commencement of the action, or at the earliest opportunity afterwards, he inserted in such newspaper or other periodical publication a full apology for the said libel, or, if the newspaper or periodical publication . . . should be ordinarily published at intervals exceeding one week, had offered to publish the said apology in any newspaper or periodical publication to be selected by the [claimant] in such action.[249]

This defence is hardly ever used[250] and we need only note two further things in relation to it. First, every such defence must be accompanied by a payment of money into court by way of amends.[251] Secondly, the issues of malice, gross negligence, and the adequacy of the apology are to be decided separately by the jury.

SECTION 9 REMEDIES

(A) DAMAGES

The main function of the tort of defamation is to compensate the claimant for his loss of reputation: that is, the extent to which he is held in less esteem and respect, and suffers loss of goodwill and association.[252] Damages for this loss of reputation are at large in respect both of libel and slander actionable *per se*. The principles ordinarily applicable to damages at large[253] apply here equally. Accordingly, by way of parasitic damages,

---

[249] Libel Act 1843, s 2.   [250] For the reasons as to why this is so, see the 11th edition of this work.
[251] Libel Act 1845, s 2.
[252] The best judicial survey is in the judgment of Devlin LJ in Dingle v Associated Newspapers Ltd [1961] 2 QB 162.   [253] See ch 26.

compensation may be given for insult or injury to feelings.[254] In addition, circumstances of aggravation and mitigation are important. And damages may be aggravated by such matters as the mode, circumstances and extent of publication as well as the conduct of the defendant from publication to verdict.[255] By contrast, the defendant's belief in the truth of his statements,[256] the fairness of his reports[257] and his being provoked by the claimant[258] may all serve to mitigate the damages awarded.

Where partial justification is proved, even though the defendant may be unable to prove sufficient facts to establish justification at common law (or bring himself within section 5 of the Defamation Act 1952), he may nonetheless be able to rely on the facts proved to reduce the damages.[259] Indeed, in an exceptional case, he may do so to reduce the damages almost to vanishing point.[260] Persistence in an unsubstantiated plea of justification, however, will lead to a higher award of damages.

Exemplary damages may also be awarded where the defendant calculated that the money to be made out of his wrongdoing would probably exceed the compensation payable for the defamation, and where he defamed the claimant either knowing his conduct to be illegal, or where he was reckless as to its illegality.[261] Where several claimants are libelled, the amount of exemplary damages may properly take into account the fact that the defendant has libelled more than one person; but the total should not exceed the total representing a proper sum by way of punishment for the defendant.[262]

At one time, it was feared that damages awards were becoming excessive. The turning point came in *Sutcliffe v Pressdram Ltd*[263] when the Court of Appeal set aside a £600,000 award warning that in assessing any element of aggravated damages, misconduct by the defendant is relevant only in so far as it increases the injury to the claimant. The jury's own indignation at that conduct was irrelevant in assessing a proper quantum of compensatory damages. Importantly, section 8 of the Courts and Legal Services Act 1990 empowers the Court of Appeal to substitute 'such sum as appears to be proper' for the award of a jury where that award is quashed as excessive.[264] In relation to the meaning of 'excessive', the Court of Appeal has held the test to be whether a reasonable jury would have thought the award proposed was necessary to compensate the claimant and

---

[254] *Goslin v Corry* (1844) 7 Man & G 342; *Ley v Hamilton* (1935) 153 LT 384, at 386, *per* Lord Atkin. *Query*: are damages recoverable for injuries to C's feelings caused by publishing the libel to him? See *Hayward v Thompson* [1982] QB 47. [255] *Praed v Graham* (1889) 24 QBD 53.

[256] *Bryce v Rusden* (1886) 2 TLR 435; *Forsdike v Stone* (1868) LR 3 CP 607 (*bona fide* mistake of identity).

[257] *Smith v Scott* (1847) 2 Car & Kir 580; *East v Chapman* (1827) Mood & M 46.

[258] *Moore v Oastler* (1836) 1 Mood & R 451n.

[259] See, eg, *Burstein v Times Newspapers Ltd* [2001] 1 WLR 579. Note, however, that to introduce such evidence, it must be so clearly relevant to the subject matter of the libel or C's character as to produce an obvious risk of the jury assessing damages on a false basis: *Turner v News Group Newspapers* [2006] EWCA Civ 540.

[260] *Pamplin v Express Newspapers Ltd (No 2)* [1988] 1 All ER 282.

[261] *Cassell & Co Ltd v Broome* [1972] AC 1027.

[262] *Riches v News Group Newspapers Ltd* [1986] QB 256. [263] [1991] 1 QB 153.

[264] In *Rantzen v Mirror Group Newspapers (1986) Ltd* [1993] 4 All ER 975, the Court of Appeal made use of this section and reduced a jury award of £250,000 to one of £110,000. Cf *Kiam v Mirror Group Newspapers*

re-establish his reputation.[265] Finally, even beyond section 8 of the 1990 Act, it was held in *John v MGN Ltd*[266] that damages might permissibly be controlled in two further ways. First, by the court drawing the jury's attention to the levels of awards made in personal injuries cases (while recognizing that no direct analogy can be drawn because of the different nature of the 'injury' involved) and, secondly, by allowing the court and counsel to mention to the jury what they consider to be an appropriate award and its appropriate bracket. This last development helps particularly to curtail the huge awards made by juries in the past.

Occasionally the claimant's loss of reputation will cause him a knock-on pecuniary loss – for example, loss of business. That loss is recoverable as special damage and is awarded in addition to general damages so long as the loss can be shown with sufficient precision.[267] On the other hand, evidence of the bad reputation of the claimant will be a ground for mitigating the level of damages, since a reputation already largely lost is necessarily of less value. The rules governing evidence of reputation are complex and, in practice, a trial often becomes little more than a tactical battle over this issue. The governing principle is that general evidence alone is permitted (and then, only after prior notice and particulars have been given). Evidence of specific facts in order to demonstrate the disposition of the claimant is not currently admissible.[268] The court is concerned with the esteem in which the claimant is in fact held – with his established reputation, in other words.[269] It is not concerned with his actual character, or with the reputation that he may deserve. Thus, where, on a privileged occasion, a newspaper published extracts from a parliamentary report, and then embellished this report with details not found in the report, it could not mitigate its damage by asserting that the claimant's reputation was already tarnished by the privileged publication of the parliamentary report.[270] Where the defendant has persisted in a plea of justification, it is the claimant's reputation at the time of the trial which counts in assessing damage to reputation.[271] The ordinary rules of evidence apply. Thus, if the claimant gives evidence, he may be cross-examined as to credit, although evidence to rebut his answers is forbidden. The jury should be directed to disregard this cross-examination when fixing damages.[272]

In the case of slanders not actionable *per se*, actual damage must be proved. It is doubtful, therefore, whether any other damages than those for actual damage are

---

[2002] 2 All ER 219 (the jury awarded damages of £105,000 despite the trial judge's direction that an award up to £80,000 would be acceptable; yet the Court of Appeal refused to overrule the award under s 8 of the 1990 Act).

[265]   *Rantzen v Mirror Group Newspapers Ltd* [1993] 4 All ER 975.   [266]   [1997] QB 586.

[267]   See, eg, *Collins Stewart Ltd v Financial Times Ltd* [2005] EMLR 5 (claim for special damage struck out for lack of certainty and precision).

[268]   *Scott v Sampson* (1882) 8 QBD 491; *Turner v News Group Newspapers Ltd* [2006] EWCA Civ 540.

[269]   *Plato Films Ltd v Speidel* [1961] AC 1090 (approving *Scott v Sampson* (1882) 8 QBD 491 and *Hobbs v C T Tinling & Co Ltd* [1929] 2 KB 1).

[270]   *Associated Newspapers Ltd v Dingle* [1964] AC 371.   [271]   *Cornwell v Myskow* [1987] 2 All ER 504.

[272]   *Hobbs v C T Tinling & Co Ltd* [1929] 2 KB 1.

recoverable for such slanders.[273] If this is correct, the rules in relation to aggravated and exemplary damages, do not apply.

(B) INJUNCTIONS

Claimants in defamation actions often seek interlocutory injunctions as soon as they have served the writ so as to prevent further publication. The courts, concerned not to interfere unduly with press freedom, normally do not grant such injunctions when the case is contested and the claimant is unable to show that a defence of justification, fair comment or privilege is likely to fail at the eventual trial.[274] Section 12(3) of the Human Rights Act is also relevant in this context, for it provides that no injunctive relief may be granted to restrain a publication 'unless the court is satisfied that the applicant is likely to establish [at trial] that publication should not be allowed'. In *Cream Holdings v Banerjee*,[275] the House of Lords arguably watered down a prior Court of Appeal decision in which it had been stressed that section 12(3) had been specifically inserted into the 1998 Act in order to protect freedom of expression.[276] Their Lordships stated that for the purposes of section 12(3), 'likely', meant merely 'more probably than not'.

A somewhat specious case that is worth noting in this context involved the Attorney-General seeking an injunction to prevent further publication of an alleged contempt; it was said that the interest in the protection of justice (as perceived by the Attorney-General) prevailed over the interest in free speech.[277]

Finally, according to the Court of Appeal in *British Data Management plc v Boxer Commercial Removals plc*,[278] if publication of a libel is threatened but has not yet occurred, a *quia timet* injunction may be awarded if the claimant is able to set out with reasonable certainty the gist of the libel.[279] And the courts will also readily grant injunctions to successful claimants if further publication of the offending statement is likely.[280]

---

[273] There is an *obiter dictum* of Williams J in *Brown v Smith* (1853) 13 CB 596 to the effect that no other damages are available. In *Dixon v Smith* (1860) 5 H & N 450, C, a doctor, claimed a guinea, being the loss of a particular patient in consequence of the slander, together with damages for general decline in business, and deterioration of goodwill. After denying, on the grounds of remoteness, such general damages resulting from repetition of the slander, the court held the damages not to be limited to the guinea. Whether the further damages were at large, or for some non-remote business loss besides loss of the patient, is not clear, but an observation by Martin B (at 452), supports the latter interpretation.

[274] *Bonnard v Perryman* [1891] 2 Ch 269. For recent illustrations see *Crest Homes Ltd v Ascott* [1980] FSR 396; *Harakas v Baltic Mercantile and Shipping Exchange Ltd* [1982] 2 All ER 701.

[275] [2004] 3 WLR 918.   [276] *Greene v Associated Newspapers Ltd* [2005] 3 WLR 281.

[277] *A-G v News Group Newspapers Ltd* [1986] 2 All ER 833 (the rule in *Bonnard v Perryman* [1891] 2 Ch 269 does not apply to an action for conspiracy).

[278] [1996] 3 All ER 707.   [279] Note that C need not prove *verbatim* the wording of the threatened libel.

[280] *Monson v Tussauds Ltd* [1894] 1 QB 671.

FURTHER READING

Loveland, 'Defamation and "Government": Taking Lessons from America' [1994] *Legal Studies* 206

Loveland, 'A New Legal Landscape? Libel Law and Freedom of Political Expression in the UK' [2000] EHRLR 476

Sharland and Loveland, 'The Defamation Act 1996 and Political Libels' [1997] *Public Law* 113

Williams, 'Defaming Politicians: The Not So Common Law' (2000) 63 MLR 748

Young, 'Fact, Opinion and the Human Rights Act 1998' (2000) 20 OJLS 89

PART VII

MISUSE OF PROCESS

23

MISUSE OF PROCESS

The nature of the motive with which an act is done does not in general make that act tortious. As we shall see in this chapter there are certain limited exceptions to that general rule. The essence of the wrongful conduct in these torts is the misuse of rights conferred on individuals for the public good. It is the abuse of those rights for private benefit or other improper ends that gives rise to tortious liability. The tort of malicious prosecution is long established and in recent years seems to have revived from the degree of torpor which affected its development in the middle of the last century. At the same time, the evolution of the tort of misfeasance in public office continues to expand the role of tort law in controlling the conduct of public officials.

SECTION 1 MALICIOUS PROSECUTION AND RELATED CLAIMS

The torts considered in this section are concerned with protecting the interest in freedom from unjustifiable litigation. Their function comes very close to that of defamation: namely, the protection of reputation. The difference, however, is that the wrongful institution of proceedings will sometimes cause pecuniary loss or loss of personal liberty without damaging reputation.

It is also necessary to distinguish this tort from false imprisonment. In false imprisonment the initial act is wrongful in itself: for example, where an arrest is made without proper adherence to the procedural requirements. Malicious prosecution, by contrast, presupposes that the proper procedural formalities have been carried out, and is concerned with the purposes for which they were used. However, a point of connection between the two torts is that, in both instances, the claimant has a *prima facie* right to trial by jury.[1]

The delicate balance of public interests involved in malicious prosecution must not be underestimated. On the one hand, there is the freedom that everyone should enjoy to engage the legal process in order to prosecute crime, while on the other there is the need to discourage untruthful accusations made about innocent individuals.[2]

---

[1] *Cropper v Chief Constable of South Yorkshire Police* [1990] 2 All ER 1005.
[2] Noted in *Martin v Watson* [1994] 2 All ER 606, at 614 and 616 and *Gregory v Portsmouth City Council* [2000] 1 AC 419, at 426.

(A) INSTITUTION OF PROCEEDINGS

The rule is that the defendant must have been 'actively instrumental' in instigating the proceedings.[3] In *Martin v Watson*,[4] the House of Lords addressed just what that requirement involved. Their Lordships confirmed the ancient rule that if X merely gives information to a police officer[5] or a magistrate,[6] upon which the police officer or magistrate then *independently* decides to launch a prosecution, that does not render X a prosecutor for the purposes of this tort. The decision to prosecute rests with the public officials who determine that legal proceedings against the claimant should go ahead.[7] However, the deliberate provision of false information *may* need to be treated differently. The starting point on this issue is *Martin v Watson*[8] where the defendant had a history of ill-feeling towards the claimant. She deliberately set out to deceive police officers by making an entirely false allegation that the claimant had exposed himself to her. The House of Lords held her liable for malicious prosecution because the facts relating to the alleged offence were known only to her and therefore the police had virtually no discretion in the matter. It was thus appropriate to treat the defendant as having procured the subsequent prosecution.

As such, a defendant who complains to the police or magistrates will be regarded as the 'prosecutor' if:

(1) he falsely and maliciously gave information to the police, making it clear that he is prepared to be a witness for the prosecution in circumstances where it can be inferred that he desires and intends that the claimant should be prosecuted; and

(2) the facts of the alleged offence are such that they are exclusively within the defendant's knowledge, so that it is practically impossible for police officers to make any independent judgement about whether or not to proceed with the prosecution.[9]

But what happens if the authorities act upon, and are influenced by, information stemming from a variety of sources, only one of which is the false information knowingly

---

[3] *Danby v Beardsley* (1880) 43 LT 603, at 604, *per* Lopes J. In *Evans v London Hospital Medical College* [1981] 1 All ER 715, it was held that a hospital which provided pathology reports for the police did not institute proceedings. [4] [1996] AC 74.

[5] *Danby v Beardsley* (1880) 43 LT 603. Nor will supplying information to police, on the basis of which officers decide to make an arrest, engage liability for false imprisonment: *Davidson v Chief Constable of North Wales* [1994] 2 All ER 597. [6] *Cohen v Morgan* (1825) 6 Dow & Ry KB 8.

[7] This is in direct contrast to circumstances where D initiates a private prosecution. However, note that there may be cases where a public prosecution is brought, but on the facts of the case, D has effectively required that the prosecution go ahead, formally accepting responsibility for the initiation of the relevant proceedings: see, eg, *Mohamed Amin v Jogendra Kumar Bannerjee* [1947] AC 322; *Malz v Rosen* [1966] 2 All ER 10.

[8] [1996] AC 74.

[9] *Martin v Watson* [1995] 3 All ER 559, at 568, *per* Lord Keith. As to liability where D continues proceedings after learning of facts which negate the basis of the prosecution, see *Tims v John Lewis & Co Ltd* [1951] 2 KB 459 (revsd on another point [1952] AC 676). A lawyer who does more than advise his client in good faith may be deemed responsible for the prosecution: *Johnson v Emerson and Sparrow* (1871) LR 6 Exch 329.

supplied by the defendant? In such a case, it has been held, it will be much more difficult to sustain the argument that the malicious defendant was a 'prosecutor' in the sense that he or she procured the prosecution.[10] That said, actions against the authorities founded on either negligence or misfeasance in public office cannot necessarily be ruled out in such circumstances.[11]

(B) NATURE OF THE RELEVANT PROCEEDINGS

Where the claimant has been subjected to a criminal prosecution[12] as a consequence of which he lost, or risked losing,[13] his liberty and/or his reputation, a remedy in the tort of malicious prosecution will lie. What is less clear is whether maliciously instituting civil proceedings may incur liability. In 1698 Holt CJ delivered a judgment in *Savile v Roberts* which required that the proceedings must be such as to inflict one of the following:

1.... [D]amage to a man's fame, as if the matter whereof he is accused be scandalous ... 2.... such [damages] as are done to the person; as where a man is put in danger to lose his life, or limb, or liberty ... 3. Damage to a man's property, as where he is forced to expend his money in necessary charges, to acquit himself of the crime of which he is accused.[14]

Since then the courts have (at least *obiter*) resiled somewhat from this judgment.[15] Logically, the institution of a civil action should only exceptionally result in liability under this tort; for when the claimant loses that suit, the defendant's reputation is restored and he recovers his costs in defending the action.[16] However, malicious proceedings in bankruptcy and winding up can – so long as the defendant was the petitioning creditor[17] – ground liability in this tort.[18] The very institution of such proceedings may wreck the claimant's business, destroying confidence in his competence and integrity, and in his company's goodwill.

By contrast, in *Gregory v Portsmouth City Council*[19] the claimant sued the defendant for maliciously instituting disciplinary proceedings against him. He argued that

---

[10] *Mahon v Rahn (No 2)* [2000] 4 All ER 41 (D a banker, supplied information about C, but there had also been an investigation by the Serious Fraud Office therefore D was not liable).

[11] See *L v Reading Borough Council* [2001] 1 WLR 1575.

[12] It has never been decided formally whether maliciously instituting *civil* proceedings can incur liability; though the suggestions in the cases are against such a step: see *Quartz Hill Consolidated Gold Mining Co v Eyre* (1883) 11 QBD 674; *Gregory v Portsmouth City Council* [2000] 1 AC 419.

[13] *Berry v British Transport Commission* [1962] 1 QB 306. [14] (1698) 1 Ld Raym 374.

[15] See, eg, *Quartz Hill Consolidated Gold Mining Co v Eyre* (1883) 11 QBD 674; *Gregory v Portsmouth City Council* [2000] 1 AC 419.

[16] *Quartz Hill Consolidated Gold Mining Co v Eyre* (1883) 11 QBD 674, at 689–690, *per* Bowen LJ.

[17] *Tibbs v Islington London Borough Council* [2003] BPIR 743.

[18] *Chapman v Pickersgill* (1762) 2 Wils 145; *Gregory v Portsmouth City Council* [2000] AC 419.

[19] [2000] 1 AC 419.

the disciplinary process was analogous to the criminal process. The charges against him hurt his reputation and put him to expense in defending himself. Yet, the House of Lords stated that there were no grounds to extend the scope of a tort of maliciously instituting proceedings beyond criminal prosecutions and exceptional cases such as bankruptcy and winding up.[20] And in *Gizzonio v Chief Constable of Derbyshire*[21] the Court of Appeal also rejected an attempt to construct a tort of malicious refusal of bail.

Notwithstanding the position with respect to maliciously instituting civil proceedings, an action will lie for maliciously procuring a warrant of arrest.[22] And, similarly, maliciously procuring a search warrant is an actionable wrong, although actions typically fail[23] because the damage to the claimant ensues not from the warrant being granted, but from its execution in the form of entry into his premises, or the seizure of property. But exceptionally the issue of a warrant may constitute actionable harm.[24]

(C) TERMINATION IN FAVOUR OF THE CLAIMANT

In order to sue, the proceedings upon which the claim is based must have terminated in the claimant's favour.[25] Even though the claimant has been convicted of a lesser offence,[26] or has had his conviction quashed on appeal,[27] or has been acquitted on a technicality (for example, a defect in the indictment)[28] this requirement is satisfied. The same *may* be true where the claimant has escaped prosecution for offence X but the facts alleged in seeking to secure prosecution for offence X are later passed on by the police to a local authority in order that it may obtain an anti-social behaviour order against the claimant.[29] If, however, the conviction of the claimant stands, there is no cause of action in this tort.[30]

As regards demonstrating a favourable termination of proceedings, the claimant seems to satisfy the test if he proves that the defendant has discontinued the proceedings;[31] (but he cannot sue while the proceedings are still pending[32]).

---

[20] This is highly questionable, because even civil proceedings may damage one's reputation, and the immunity granted to those supplying evidence would defeat any action founded on defamation, conspiracy or malicious falsehood. As such, C stands to suffer damage in respect of which no cause of action currently lies.

[21] (1998) *Times*, 29 April.   [22] *Roy v Prior* [1971] AC 470.

[23] See *Gibbs v Rea* [1998] AC 786, at 797, *per* Gault J; *Reynolds v Metropolitan Police Comr* [1985] QB 881.

[24] *Gibbs v Rea* [1998] AC 786.

[25] This requirement is not imposed where, eg, an arrest or search warrant is procured. But it was considered applicable in an action based on an attempt to construct a tort of malicious refusal of bail: *Gizzonio v Chief Constable of Derbyshire* (1998) *Times*, 29 April.   [26] *Boaler v Holder* (1887) 51 JP 277, DC.

[27] *Reynolds v Kennedy* (1748) 1 Wils 232.   [28] *Wicks v Fentham* (1791) 4 Term Rep 247.

[29] *Daar v Chief Constable of Merseyside* [2005] EWCA Civ 1774.

[30] *Basébé v Matthews* (1867) LR 2 CP 684. Nor can C sue if he is merely bound over to keep the peace: *Everett v Ribbands* [1952] 2 QB 198.   [31] *Watkins v Lee* (1839) 5 M & W 270.

[32] *Gilding v Eyre* (1861) 10 CBNS 592, at 604, *per* Willes J (*obiter*).

(D) ABSENCE OF REASONABLE AND PROBABLE CAUSE

Malicious prosecution is treated with some caution by the courts, fearful of discouraging the enforcement of the law against suspected offenders and anxious to protect the interest in bringing litigation to a close.[33] This judicial attitude is reflected in the development of the requirement that there must be an absence of reasonable and probable cause on the part of the prosecutor. Thus, the claimant has the difficult task of proving a negative – a burden which he does not discharge merely by proving malice on the part of the defendant.[34] Furthermore, the court will not order the defendant to give particulars of the grounds on which he prosecuted.[35]

The House of Lords approved the following definition of reasonable and probable cause:

an honest belief in the guilt of the accused based upon a full conviction, founded upon reasonable grounds, of the existence of a state of circumstances, which, assuming them to be true, would reasonably lead any ordinary prudent and cautious man, placed in the position of the accuser, to the conclusion that the person charged was probably guilty of the crime imputed.[36]

Since then it has further been held that, in order for the claimant to succeed on the issue of reasonable and probable cause, he must prove one or other of the following.[37]

(1) That the defendant did not believe that the claimant was probably guilty of the offence. Evidence should be given by the claimant of some fact or facts which, either inherently or coupled with other matters proved in evidence, would permit the inference that the defendant did not believe in the claimant's guilt. Where there is powerful circumstantial evidence, the defendant's silence in the face of allegations made against him might afford some evidence of absence of reasonable and probable cause.[38] If such evidence is given, the question must be left to the jury, whether it has been proved to their satisfaction that the defendant did not believe in the claimant's guilt. But unless such evidence is given it is not proper to put a question to the jury as to the defendant's belief.[39] The question put to the jury must be formulated precisely and should not refer to reasonable cause. It should be either: 'Did the defendant honestly believe in the claimant's guilt?' or 'Did the defendant honestly believe in the charges he was preferring?'. It must not be: 'Did he honestly believe that there were reasonable grounds for the prosecution?', for that would cause the jury to reflect upon the whole issue of

---

[33] See, eg, *Martin v Watson* [1994] 2 All ER 606 (revsd [1996] AC 74).

[34] *Johnstone v Sutton* (1786) 1 Term Rep 510. [35] *Stapley v Annetts* [1969] 3 All ER 1541.

[36] *Hicks v Faulkner* (1881) 8 QBD 167, at 171, *per* Hawkins J (affd (1882) 46 LT 130); *Herniman v Smith* [1938] AC 305).

[37] *Glinski v McIver* [1962] AC 726; *Reynolds v Metropolitan Police Comr* [1985] QB 881.

[38] *Gibbs v Rea* [1998] AC 786.

[39] *Herniman v Smith* [1938] AC 305, at 317, *per* Lord Atkin; *Ward v Chief Constable of West Midlands Police* (1997) *Times*, 13 December.

reasonable and probable cause.[40] Merely to prove that the defendant had before him information which might or might not have led a reasonable man to form an opinion that the claimant was guilty is not evidence that the defendant did not believe him to be guilty. If this ground is relied on, the older cases suggest that the claimant must give some evidence from which an inference may be drawn as to what the defendant's belief actually was: it is not sufficient to give evidence from which a guess may be made as to what it was. Nor is it sufficient merely to supply evidence of reasons for non-belief. If such evidence is relied on, there must also be evidence that those reasons were in fact operative; but if silence affords some inference of absence of belief in cause, the heavy burden of proof on the claimant may now be somewhat eased.[41]

Or

(2) That a person of ordinary prudence and caution would not conclude, in the light of the facts in which he honestly believed, that the claimant was probably guilty. It is for the judge and not the jury to determine whether a man of ordinary prudence would have so concluded. It is for the judge alone to determine whether there is reasonable and probable cause.[42] The trouble experienced in splitting the functions of judge and jury in consequence of this rule accounts for most of the complexities of this tort. There is the ever-present danger that the questions addressed to the jury will be so general that the ultimate question left to the judge of reasonable cause is instead improperly decided by the jury. In conducting the trial the judge has two alternatives: he may direct the jury that, if they find certain facts, or arrive at certain answers to specific questions which he puts to them, there is reasonable and probable cause, leaving it to the jury to find a general verdict on this hypothetical direction; his alternative – and this is the better course – is to direct the jury to settle the facts in dispute, whereupon he decides, upon the whole case, whether there is reasonable and probable cause.[43]

It is impossible to enumerate all the factors which may be relevant in deciding whether there was reasonable and probable cause. Particularly important points would be that the defendant acted in good faith on the advice of counsel[44] (although this would not be conclusive[45]), or on the advice of the police,[46] where the defendant, however honest his act, had taken reasonable care to inform himself of the facts,[47] and regardless of whether the defendant's mistake was one of fact or law.[48]

---

[40] *Tempest v Snowden* [1952] 1 KB 130.   [41] *Gibbs v Rea* [1998] AC 786.

[42] *Lister v Perryman* (1870) LR 4 521.

[43] *Abrath v North Eastern Rly Co* (1883) 11 QBD 440, at 458, *per* Bowden LJ (affd (1886) 11 App Cas 247). See also *Green v De Havilland* (1968) 112 Sol Jo 766.

[44] *Ravenga v Mackintosh* (1824) 2 B & C 693. Cf *Bradshaw v Waterlow & Sons Ltd* [1915] 3 KB 527.

[45] *Abbott v Refuge Assurance Co Ltd* [1962] 1 QB 432.   [46] *Malz v Rosen* [1966] 2 All ER 10.

[47] *Abrath v North Eastern Rly Co* (1833) 11 QBD 440, at 451, *per* Brett MR.

[48] *Philips v Naylor* (1859) 4 H & N 565. In *Riches v DPP* [1973] 2 All ER 935, it was held that allegations of malice and want of reasonable cause in an action against the DPP stood no chance of success when the committing magistrate, the trial judge and the jury all shared the same view of the evidence held by the DPP.

(E) MALICE: IMPROPER PURPOSE

The claimant must also prove malice on the part of the defendant.[49] In this context, that means that he must show 'any motive other than that of simply instituting a prosecution for the purpose of bringing a person to justice'.[50] The judge decides whether there is any *prima facie* evidence of malice, but it falls to the jury to decide whether there is in fact any malice in the case.[51] There was, for instance, evidence of malice where a defendant landlord made a charge in order to evict the claimant tenant from his house,[52] and where a defendant accused the claimant of exposing himself to her as part of a long-running vendetta between neighbours.[53] The question is not whether the defendant is angry or inspired by hatred,[54] but whether the defendant has a purpose other than bringing an offender to justice. There is malice, for instance, if the defendant uses the prosecution as a means of blackmail or any other form of coercion. Where the motives of the defendant are mixed, the claimant will fail unless he establishes that the dominant purpose is something other than the vindication of the law.[55] However, it is crucial to note that a claimant who proves malice but who fails to prove want of reasonable and probable cause still fails.[56] Should a tenant, therefore, establish that his landlord has instituted proceedings against him for stealing the landlord's fixtures, with the object of determining his tenancy, the tenant's action in this tort will not succeed if he fails to prove absence of reasonable cause.[57]

(F) THE CROWN PROSECUTION SERVICE

As will be obvious, the vast majority of precedents establishing this tort predate the Prosecution of Offences Act 1985, albeit that many cases have been decided since its enactment. Under the 1985 Act, the Crown Prosecution Service, headed by the Director of Public Prosecutions, took over responsibility for prosecutions initiated by the police. Yet several questions relating to the potential liability of the CPS and the police remain unanswered. Assume the claimant is originally charged and remanded in custody at the instigation of the police. Imagine further that the CPS reviews the evidence and decides to discontinue proceedings. The claimant cannot sue for false imprisonment in respect of the period when he was detained by judicial order. But he

---

[49] *Brown v Hawkes* [1891] 2 QB 725. In *Wershof v Metropolitan Police Comr* [1978] 3 All ER 540, C proved absence of reasonable cause, but failed because he could not prove malice.

[50] *Stevens v Midland Counties Rly Co* (1854) 10 Exch 352, *per* Alderson B.

[51] *Brown v Hawkes* [1891] 2 QB 718.   [52] *Turner v Ambler* (1847) 10 QB 252.

[53] *Martin v Watson* [1995] 3 All ER 559.   [54] *Brown v Hawkes* [1891] 2 QB 718, at 722, *per* Cave J.

[55] Not malice when Ds' motive was to recoup themselves in a civil action, so that they first prosecuted in order to conform to the rule that prosecution for felony must precede civil actions relating thereto: *Abbott v Refuge Assurance Co Ltd* [1962] 1 QB 432.

[56] *Silcott v Metropolitan Police Comr* (1996) 8 Admin LR 633; *Gizzonio v Chief Constable of Derbyshire* (1998) Times, 29 April.   [57] *Turner v Ambler* (1847) 10 QB 252.

may sue under the present tort since discontinuance of the proceedings amounts to a termination of proceedings in his favour.[58] If the CPS continues proceedings, thus endorsing the judgement of police officers, proving absence of reasonable and proba-ble cause will be a mammoth task.

The CPS and its officers enjoy no general immunity in tort, in particular against claims for malicious prosecution or misfeasance in public office.[59] However, the CPS owes no *general* [60] duty of care in relation to the conduct of prosecutions. The Court of Appeal has held that such liability in negligence might have an 'inhibiting effect on the discharge by the CPS of its central function of prosecuting crime'.[61] Furthermore, the courts will be vigilant to ensure that any action in malicious prosecution brought against the CPS is not in reality a disguised claim for negligence. Incompetence is not evidence of malice.[62]

(G) DEFENCES

No questions on defences call for special comment other than that of whether it is a defence to establish that the claimant was guilty of the offence for which he was prose-cuted. Obviously, in the rare case where a defendant had no reasonable cause and was malicious, and the proceedings terminated in the claimant's favour, and yet, at the trial for malicious prosecution the defendant is able to establish the guilt of the claimant, the claimant would recover at best a very small sum of damages. There is, indeed, some authority for the view that in such a case the action fails altogether.[63]

SECTION 2 ABUSE OF PROCESS

For the purposes of this tort, the leading case is *Grainger v Hill*.[64]

D was liable when he had C arrested, ostensibly for non-payment of a debt, but in fact in order illegally to compel him to surrender the register of a vessel, without which C could not put to sea.

The case established that in this tort the claimant need not prove want of reasonable and probable cause; nor need the proceedings have terminated in his favour.[65] The

---

[58] *Watkins v Lee* (1839) 5 M & W 270.   [59] *Elguzouli-Daf v Metropolitan Police Comr* [1995] QB 335.
[60] But where prosecutors undertook to provide information to magistrates, a duty of care was owed to C: *Welsh v Chief Constable of Merseyside Police* [1993] 1 All ER 692.
[61] *Elguzouli-Daf v Metropolitan Police Comr* [1995] QB 335.
[62] *Thacker v Crown Prosecution Service* (1997) *Times*, 29 December.
[63] *Heslop v Chapman* (1853) 23 LJQB 49, at 52, *per* Jervis CJ and Pollock CB. Cf *Shrosbery v Osmaston* (1877) 37 LT 792, at 794, *per* Lindley J. Cf *Williams v Banks* (1859) 1 F & F 557, at 559, *per* Wightman J.
[64] (1838) 4 Bing NC 212; *Gibbs v Pike and Wells* (1842) 9 M & W 351 (maliciously registering a court order); *Speed Seal Products Ltd v Paddington* [1986] 1 All ER 91. See also Wells, 'The Abuse of Process' (1985) 102 LQR 9.
[65] *Speed Seal Products Ltd v Paddington* [1986] 1 All ER 91.

claimant must show simply that the predominant purpose of the other party in using the legal process has been other than that for which it was designed.[66] Thus, a defendant who issued by mistake a plaint note for a debt which had already been paid was held not liable.[67] By contrast with malicious prosecution, however, damage to fame, person or property need not be proved. *Any* special damage suffices.[68]

On the other hand, in *Metall und Rohstoff AG v Donaldson Lufkin & Jenrette Inc,*[69] the Court of Appeal somewhat grudgingly recognized the existence of a tort of abuse of process in *Grainger v Hill*. But it did doubt the existence of a more general tort of maliciously instituting civil proceedings.

SECTION 3 WITNESS IMMUNITY

It is a fundamental principle of the common law that no-one can be civilly liable for evidence given in court;[70] thus no action lies in defamation for words spoken as a witness in court,[71] nor will conspiracy lie against policemen who conspire to defame the claimant at a criminal trial.[72] A claimant who is imprisoned in consequence of the defendant giving false evidence on oath at the claimant's trial has no cause of action:[73] perjury is a crime, not a tort. Furthermore, witness immunity extends beyond the actual presentation of evidence to cover also the preparation of evidence that will (or would) be given in court.

On the other hand, a distinction must be drawn between evidence that a witness gives (or has stated he would give) in court, and evidence that has been fabricated (such as a fabricated interview). The House of Lords has made clear that immunity does not extend to the latter.[74] It has also been held that in proceedings for malicious arrest, the claimant can rely on statements made by the defendant in court when seeking the warrant: the wrong is the arrest with malice, of which the statement in court provides evidential support.[75]

---

[66] *Metall und Rohstoff AG v Donaldson Lufkin & Jenrette Inc* [1989] 3 All ER 14, at 50; *Clissold v Cratchley* [1910] 2 KB 244.

[67] *Corbett v Burge, Warren and Ridgley Ltd* (1932) 48 TLR 626. It was also said in this case that loss of business profits is not a recoverable head of damage. But why?

[68] Eg, if a suit in deceit was instituted for the purpose of damaging C's credit. In *Smith v East Elloe RDC* [1956] AC 736, their Lordships held there to be jurisdiction to hear a claim that a clerk to a council knowingly and in bad faith wrongfully procured a compulsory purchase order to be made and confirmed by a minister, even though a statute precluded the courts from challenging the validity of the order itself on the grounds of bad faith.   [69] [1989] 3 All ER 14.

[70] *Roy v Prior* [1971] AC 470.   [71] Ch 22.   [72] *Marrinan v Vibart* [1963] 1 QB 528.

[73] *Hargreaves v Bretherton* [1959] 1 QB 45, approved *obiter* in *Roy v Prior* [1971] AC 470, at 477, *per* Lord Morris of Borth-y-Gest. In *Evans v London Hospital Medical College* [1981] 1 All ER 715, it was held that this immunity extends to statements made before the issue of a writ or the institution of a prosecution, distinguishing *Saif Ali v Sydney Mitchell & Co* [1980] AC 198. But note *Palmer v Durnford Ford (a firm)* [1992] QB 483 (restricting immunities of expert witnesses).

[74] *Darker v Chief Constable of West Midlands Police* [2001] 1 AC 435. See also *L (A Child) v Reading Borough Council* [2001] 1 WLR 1575.   [75] *Roy v Prior* [1971] AC 470.

SECTION 4 MISFEASANCE IN PUBLIC OFFICE

A successful application for judicial review of administrative action which results in an administrative process being quashed as invalid or unlawful does not, of itself, create any liability in tort for loss or damage suffered by the applicant.[76] The tort of misfeasance in public office may, however, offer a remedy for misuse of administrative process.[77] Where an individual suffers loss or damage consequent upon improper administrative action which the relevant officer knows to be unlawful, that loss or damage is recoverable in tort.[78] The underlying rationale is that public power is conferred to be exercised only for the public good, and not for improper purposes.[79] Notwithstanding the fact that the tort allows the courts the opportunity to signal their disapproval of such abuses of public power, the tort is not actionable *per se* and no damages will be available unless special damage is proved. In one case, then, the action failed because the claimant-prisoner failed to show consequential loss resulting from the non-privileged opening of his letters by prison officers.[80] On the other hand, where material damage is proved and the courts are minded to signal their disapproval in strident terms, exemplary damages will be available.[81]

In *Three Rivers District Council v Bank of England (No 3)*,[82] the House of Lords laid down the test for liability in the tort of misfeasance in public office. According to their Lordships, liability arises where the wrongful actions of a public officer are carried out *either* in the knowledge of, *or* with reckless indifference to, the probability of injury being caused to the claimant as an individual, or the claimant as a member of a class of persons. The reckless indifference part of this proposition was later considered in more detail in *Akenzua v Secretary of State for the Home Department*.[83] There, the Court of Appeal had to consider whether the class of individuals to which the claimant belonged must be a particular, identifiable class of persons. In that case, X had been released from custody by the defendant in order to serve as a police informant. X later murdered a woman whose PRs subsequently brought an action for misfeasance in public office based on the fact that a man who had a history of violence and had violent proclivities had been recklessly released from custody. The Court of Appeal – notwithstanding the way in which the test for the tort had been expressed in the *Three Rivers* case – held that

---

[76] *Dunlop v Woollahra Municipal Council* [1982] AC 158.

[77] *Jones v Swansea City Council* [1990] 3 All ER 737.

[78] *David v Abdul Cader* [1963] 3 All ER 579; *Davis v Bromley Corpn* [1908] 1 KB 170.

[79] *Three Rivers District Council v Bank of England (No 3)* [2000] 2 WLR 1220; *Jones v Swansea City Council* [1990] 1 WLR 54.

[80] *Watkins v Secretary of State for the Home Department* [2006] 2 WLR 807 (misfeasance established; and the case remitted to the county court for a determination of what amount, if any, should be paid by way of exemplary damages). Cf *Ashby v White* (1703) 2 Ld Raym 938 where there was an analogous wrong without harm – the denial of a right to vote – which was held to be actionable.

[81] *Watkins v Secretary of State for the Home Department* [2006] 2 WLR 807; *Kuddus v Chief Constable of Leicestershire Constabulary* [2002] 2 AC 122;

[82] *Three Rivers District Council v Bank of England (No 3)* [2000] 2 WLR 1220.   [83] [2003] 1 WLR 741.

there was no need to identify a particular class of persons. As Sedley LJ explained, the reference in *Three Rivers* to knowledge of a class of persons to which the claimant belonged was 'not a freestanding requirement of [this] tort'; instead, it was a requirement 'derived from the antecedent proposition that the intent or recklessness must relate . . . to the kind of harm suffered'.[84] In other words, demonstrating knowledge of a class was not an end in itself, it was simply *a* means of showing the more fundamental factor: namely, that that the manner in which harm occurred was of kind foreseen by the defendant at the time of his act or omission.[85]

In the *Three Rivers* case, their Lordships further explained that the tort could be committed in two ways: either (1) by the exercise of public power for an improper or ulterior motive or (2) by the *ultra vires* conduct of a public officer in the knowledge that his or her actions would probably result in injury to the claimant. In relation to the second of these, it was made clear that reckless indifference was a sufficient way of acting in a manner that would probably result in damage to the claimant. In so saying, their Lordships embraced the possibility of the tort being caused by an omission, by the turning of a blind eye. Nonetheless, they emphasized that a conscious decision not to act would be required to meet the recklessness requirement.[86] In either form, it is clear that the tort may be invoked to provide a remedy where ordinary negligence principles would be of no avail for want of foreseeability and/or proximity for the purposes of establishing a duty of care.[87]

By definition, the tort can only be committed by those in public office. But this, of course, begs the question of how widely the term 'public office' is to be interpreted. *Roncarelli v Duplessis*[88] provides a good example of the tort being applied to a politician. The *Three Rivers* case clearly shows its applicability to an institution such as the Bank of England. (The case turned upon allegations that the Bank of England should never have granted a banking licence to the Bank of Credit and Commerce International *or* that it should have revoked the licence that was granted when it later became obvious that such action was necessary.) An action for misfeasance in public office may also lie against a local authority,[89] or a government department.[90]

It must be noted that unauthorized, unlawful conduct by an employee does not necessarily take him outside the scope of his employment. In order to do so, and thus to

---

[84] [2003] 1 WLR 741, at [19].

[85] On the facts, what was in the contemplation of D was not before the Court of Appeal. Their Lordships had simply been invited to strike out the action because of its failure to meet the preconditions in the *Three Rivers* case. They refused so to do.

[86] *Three Rivers District Council v Bank of England (No 3)* [2000] 2 WLR 1220, at 1267 and 1269, *per* Lords Hutton and Hobhouse, respectively.

[87] See further Chamberlain, 'Misfeasance in a Public Office: In Defence of the Power/Duty Distinction' in Neyers (ed), *Emerging Issues in Tort Law* (2007).

[88] (1959) 16 DLR (2d) 689: C lost his liquor licence after D, the then Prime Minister of Quebec, ordered the Quebec Licensing Commission to revoke the licence. D acted against C as part of his campaign against Jehovah's Witnesses. C recovered damages for this malicious abuse of the licensing process.

[89] *Jones v Swansea City Council* [1990] 3 All ER 737 (where the action lies against a local council, C must show that the majority of those supporting the relevant resolution did so with intent to harm him).

[90] *Racz v Home Office* [1994] 2 WLR 23.

relieve the employer of his vicarious liability for the employee's tortious conduct, the unlawful conduct must be so far beyond the authorized duties of the employee as to amount to a 'frolic of his own'. Thus, it was necessary in one case to have a full trial to identify the precise nature of the actions of prison officers towards a prisoner.[91] What was crucial was whether the action complained of fell within the scope of the officers' employment. What remains to be seen is whether such authorities will survive the broader-based, 'close connection' test for vicarious liability promulgated in *Lister v Hesley Hall Ltd*.[92] But it is submitted that that test should apply to this tort just as it applies to other intentional torts, such as battery.

Fabrication of evidence by police officers and malicious refusal of bail are further examples of possible misfeasance in office. However, the usual rules on witness immunity apply to this tort;[93] and misfeasance in public office cannot be used to circumvent the requirements in malicious prosecution of proof of absence of reasonable and probable cause.

FURTHER READING

Chamberlain, 'Misfeasance in a Public Office: In Defence of the Power/Duty Distinction' in Neyers (ed), *Emerging Issues in Tort Law* (2007)

Wells, 'The Abuse of Process' (1985) 102 LQR 9

---

[91] *Racz v Home Office* [1994] 2 WLR 23.   [92] [2002] 1 AC 215.
[93] *Silcott v Metropolitan Police Comr* (1996) 8 Admin LR 633; *Gizzonio v Chief Constable of Derbyshire* (1998) *Times*, 29 April.

PART VIII

PARTIES AND REMEDIES

24

VICARIOUS LIABILITY

SECTION 1 IMPORTANCE OF DISTINGUISHING EMPLOYEES FROM INDEPENDENT CONTRACTORS

For present purposes, the law divides employed persons into two groups:

(1) Those employed to perform services in connection with the affairs of the employer and over whom the employer has control in the performance of those services. In tort, these persons have traditionally been termed 'servants'. That word, in modern parlance, tends to be taken to refer to domestic help alone. As such, the term 'employee' will be used as the term of choice in this chapter.

(2) Those who do work for another, but who are not controlled by that other in the performance of that work. Normally, such work will be carried out in pursuance of a contract for services, and the persons doing it are therefore called 'independent contractors'.

The distinction is primarily important for the following reason. If an employee commits a tort in the course of his employment, then the employer is liable regardless of whether he himself has committed a tort: 'every act which is done by a servant in the course of his duty is regarded as done by his master's orders, and consequently is the same as if it were the master's own act.'[1] This is the clearest case of strict tortious liability, yet it should not be forgotten that the employee, too, may be sued for his torts. It is simply that the employer will normally have the deeper pockets and thus make the more attractive defendant (though this will not always be the case[2]). Partly, this will be because he is generally better able to insure against the loss and partly because he may well be in a position to pass on the cost to the public in the form of increased prices. In addition, the prospect of vicarious liability may encourage employers to maintain high standards of conduct in the running of their businesses. There is also the argument that because the employer stands to make a profit from his employee working for him, it is

---

[1] *Bartonshill Coal Co v McGuire* (1858) 3 Macq 300, at 306, *per* Lord Chelmsford LC.

[2] See, eg, *Merrett v Babb* [2001] 3 WLR 1 (the action was brought against an individual negligent surveyor after the firm for which he had worked had ceased to trade); *Shapland v Palmer* [1999] 1 WLR 2068 (employee and employer sued as co-defendants). Where just the employer is sued, he may later seek an indemnity from the employee under the Civil Liability (Contribution) Act 1978.

only right that he should also bear the risk of potential liability arising from the work done.[3]

If the act complained of is not that of an employee, then the employer is not, without more, liable. He can be sued only if he himself has acted in a way so as to be treated as a joint tortfeasor[4] (or if he was in breach of a non-delegable duty).[5] An employer may be vicariously liable for the torts of his employees, but he is not liable for the torts of those who are his independent contractors. For this reason, it is vital to distinguish the two classes of person.

SECTION 2 DISTINGUISHING EMPLOYEES FROM INDEPENDENT CONTRACTORS[6]

(A) CONTROL

The formula most often used by the courts to mark the distinction between an employee and an independent contractor is that of 'control'.[7] According to this test, a person is an employee where the employer 'retains the control of the actual perform-ance' of the work.[8] This was a more meaningful test in bygone years when this country was predominantly an agricultural and industrial nation in which work was largely done by labourers or craftsmen under the directions of employers who had the same or even greater technical skill than their workmen. It would ordinarily be enough to say that the employer could tell the worker not merely what task was to be performed, but also how it should be performed. If the employer could do both these things, the man was a servant. However, nowadays, working patterns have changed so much that it is difficult to slot employment relationships into the traditional analytical framework.[9] For example, many more employees work at home these days, or possess some techni-cal skill which is often not possessed by their employers. In consequence, the control test does not by itself prove adequate on every occasion.[10] In addition, for policy reasons

---

[3] For other putative justifications for vicarious liability see Feldthusen, 'Vicarious Liability for Sexual Torts' in Mullany & Linden (eds), *Torts Tomorrow: A Tribute to John Fleming* (1998) but for critical analysis of all of these justifications see Neyers, 'A Theory of Vicarious Liability' (2005) *Alberta L Rev* 1.   [4] See ch 25.

[5] *Bull v Devon Area Health Authority* [1993] 4 Med LR 117.

[6] See Kidner, 'Vicarious Liability: For Whom Should the Employers be Liable?' [1995] *Legal Studies* 47.

[7] 'The final test . . . lies in the nature and degree of detailed control over the person alleged to be a servant': *Performing Right Society Ltd v Mitchell and Booker (Palais de Danse) Ltd* [1924] 1 KB 762, at 767, *per* McCardie J.

[8] *Honeywill and Stein Ltd v Larkin Bros (London's Commercial Photographers) Ltd* [1934] 1 KB 191, at 196, *per* Slesser LJ.

[9] See McKendrick, 'Vicarious Liability and Independent Contractors – A Re-examination' (1990) 53 MLR 770.

[10] *Short v J & W Henderson Ltd* (1946) 62 TLR 427, at 429, *per* Lord Thankerton. The inadequacy of this test was expressly stated in *Cassidy v Ministry of Health* [1951] 2 KB 343, at 352, *per* Somerville LJ.

the courts may hold someone to be an employee even though aspects of his work suggest more that he is an independent contractor. In *Lane v Shire Roofing Co (Oxford) Ltd*,[11] for example, the Court of Appeal drew attention to the policy reasons that exist within the field of health and safety at work to decide a borderline case in favour of classifying the worker as an employee.

Notwithstanding its limitations and other inadequacies,[12] the control test does remain helpful in some instances, and in deciding whether enough 'control' is exercised over another to make him an employee one must take into account several factors, no single one of which is conclusive. The criteria include the extent to which the employer can control the details of the work, whether the method of payment is on a time or a job basis,[13] whose tools, equipment and premises are to be used,[14] the skill called for in the work, the freedom of selection of labour by the employer,[15] and the power to dismiss. All these matters, and possibly more besides, but especially and increasingly the one mentioned in the quotation below from Denning LJ, must be considered in order to decide whether a power to control can be inferred. His Lordship said:

It is often easy to recognise a contract of service when you see it, but difficult to say wherein the difference [between a contract of service and a contract for services] lies.[16] A ship's master, a chauffeur, and a reporter on the staff of a newspaper are all employed under a contract of service; but a ship's pilot, a taxi-man, and a newspaper contributor are employed under a contract for services. *One feature which seems to run through the instances is that, under a contract of service, a man is employed as part of the business, and his work is done as an integral part of the business; whereas, under a contract for services, his work, although done for the business, is not integrated into it but is only accessory to it.*[17]

Of particular note in relation to the ongoing relevance of the control test is the decision in *Viasystems (Tyneside) Ltd v Thermal Transfer (Northern) Ltd*.[18] In this case, the question facing the Court of Appeal was whether a fitter's mate supplied on a labour-only basis by A to B could trigger the vicarious liability of A or B. It was found that both A and B (through their respective fitters) had sufficient control of the mate to prevent his negligence. As such, it was held by May LJ that both A and B could be held vicariously liable for the flooding he caused through his negligence.[19] The route to the same conclusion adopted by Rix LJ, however, was rather different. In his view, the critical test to

---

[11] [1995] IRLR 493.   [12] See Stevens, 'A Servant of Two Masters' (2006) 122 LQR 201.

[13] Employees are generally paid by the hour whereas independent contractors are normally paid for the complete job.   [14] *Quarman v Burnett* (1840) 6 M & W 499.

[15] At common law the owner of a ship was not liable for the negligence of a compulsory pilot: *The Halley* (1868) LR 2 PC 193 (see now Pilotage Act 1987; *Oceangas (Gibraltar) Ltd v Port of London Authority* [1993] 2 Lloyd's Rep 292).

[16] Terms 'contract of service' and 'contract for services' correspond to 'employee' and 'independent contractor' respectively.

[17] *Stevenson, Jordan & Harrison Ltd v MacDonald and Evans* [1952] 1 TLR 101, at 111 (emphasis added). Cf somewhat similar observations by Lord Wright in *Montreal v Montreal Locomotive Works Ltd* [1947] 1 DLR 161, at 169; *Bank Voor Handel en Scheepvaart NV v Slatford* [1953] 1 QB 248, at 295, *per* Denning LJ: 'It depends on whether the person is part and parcel of the organization' (revsd on other grounds [1954] AC 584).

[18] [2006] 2 WLR 428.   [19] [2006] 2 WLR 428, at [16].

apply is whether the employee 'is so much a part of the work, business or organization of both employers that is it just to make both employers answer for his negligence'.[20] Importantly, both members of this two-man Court of Appeal recognized that there was never a formal contract of employment between B and the careless mate! They were content to deem him to be the employee of B and impose liability equally on A and B.[21] This is a radical step, and, in the wrong hands, it potentially threatens to undermine the principle that one cannot be liable for the torts of an independent contractor, for all one would need to do would be to look to the control or degree of integration into the temporary employer's workforce in order to deem that contractor to be an employee of the temporary employer.

It was almost inevitable that *Viasystems* would not supply the final word on dual vicarious liability. And, indeed, the ink was barely dry on the judgments in that case when another case, *Hawley v Luminar Leisure*,[22] came before the Court of Appeal. Disappointingly, that case failed to clarify whose was the preferable test: there were echoes in the court's decision of both May LJ's control test and Rix LJ's integration test.[23] What the case does seem to entrench is the appropriateness of dual vicarious liability (even though in *Hawley*, the court held that the imposition of dual vicarious liability was inappropriate on the facts of that case[24]).

(B) PERSONAL INVESTMENT IN THE ENTERPRISE

Another approach to the central issue of who is an employee is to ask: 'Is the worker in business on his own account?'.[25] In answering this question the courts will look at who owns the tools used, who paid for the materials and whether the worker stands to make anything from a profit to a loss on completion of the enterprise. Thus, where a building worker is simply paid, and neither hires his own help nor provides his own equipment and has no say in the control of the site, his position will be that of an employee rather than an independent contractor.[26]

There is, however, another sense in which the phrase 'personal investment in the enterprise' may be used and may also be pertinent to the question in hand. If the person engaged need not personally invest his own endeavour into the enterprise, but has the option of delegating the task to some other person, this is likely to be indicative of a contract for services rather than a contract of service.[27]

---

[20] [2006] 2 WLR 428, at [79].

[21] Since vicarious liability does not require fault to be shown on the part of the employer, it naturally followed that liability would ordinarily be split evenly between the two employers (assuming equal control): [2006] 2 WLR 428, at [52] and [85], *per* May and Rix LJJ, respectively.   [22] [2006] EWCA Civ 30.

[23] [2006] EWCA Civ 30, at [83] and [85].

[24] For a theoretical justification of dual vicarious liability, see Stevens, 'A Servant of Two Masters' (2006) 122 LQR 201.

[25] *Lee Tin Sang v Chung Chi-Keung* [1990] 2 AC 374. See also *Lane v Shire Roofing Co (Oxford) Ltd* [1995] IRLR 493.   [26] *Montreal v Montreal Locomotive Works* [1947] 1 DLR 161.

[27] *MacFarlane v Glasgow City Council* [2001] IRLR 7.

(C) INTENTION OF THE PARTIES

The intention of the parties, recorded in the terms of their agreement, can also provide a useful guide as to whether there is a contract of service or a contract for services.[28] On the other hand, their express intentions will not necessarily be conclusive of the matter. Thus, in one case where the parties agreed that the worker should be treated as self-employed for reasons of tax and national insurance payments, the court nonetheless held there to be a contract of employment.[29] The intention of the parties was simply one factor to which the court had regard.

Interestingly, it has been said that the question of the interpretation of documents governing the nature of the parties' relationship is one of law;[30] yet the appellate courts will be loath to reverse the findings of lower courts or tribunals unless there has been a clear misdirection or a conclusion reached that is wholly unsupportable.[31]

(D) SOME PARTICULAR CASES EXAMINED

In the majority of cases, there is no difficulty in determining the status of the worker.[32] Factory hands, office clerical staff, agricultural workers and the like are clearly employees; whereas garage proprietors, house builders, and dry-cleaners are the independent contractors of the members of the public who employ them. Similarly, a chauffeur is an employee, but a taxi driver is not. There will, however, arise borderline or hybrid cases from time to time. Sales representatives, for example, might conceivably fall into either category, depending on the circumstances.[33]

(1) AGENCY WORKERS

Those who work *ad hoc* on temporary contracts acquired through an employment agency, may, on occasion, be treated as employees of the agency for the purposes of each separate engagement.[34] Whether the general arrangement – that is, the worker being registered on the agency's books – could amount to a contract of employment would appear to turn on the question whether there is a mutuality of obligation between the

[28] *Johnson v Coventry Churchill International Ltd* [1992] 3 All ER 14.
[29] *Young & Woods Ltd v West* [1980] IRLR 201. See also *Ferguson v Dawson Partners (Contractors) Ltd* [1976] 1 WLR 1213.   [30] *Davies v Presbyterian Church of Wales* [1986] 1 WLR 323.
[31] See, eg, *Lee Ting Sang v Cheung Chi-Keung* [1990] 2 AC 374; *Kapfunde v Abbey National plc* [1999] ICR 1.
[32] For the special statutory provisions defining when a trade union is vicariously liable for various torts involving industrial action, see the Trade Union and Labour Relations (Consolidation) Act 1992, s 15.
[33] Or the holder of a university research fellowship who is required also to act as a part-time demonstrator.
[34] *McMeechan v Secretary of State for Employment* [1997] IRLR 353. Cf *Montgomery v Johnson Underwood Ltd* [2001] IRLR 269 (the worker here was not an employee because, unlike in *McMeechan*, there was no review or grievance procedure between the agency and the worker that could be taken to be indicative of the formality of their relationship).

worker and agency (that is, a duty to provide work on the part of the agency and a duty to accept it on the part of the worker).[35] In turn, this question can be answered not merely by reference to the documentary evidence associated with the engagement[36] but also by reference to what was actually said and done at the time of the engagement.[37] If the agency has no day-to-day control over the tasks performed by the worker, this will tend to indicate that he or she is not an employee of the agency.[38]

(2) HOSPITAL STAFF

The courts were once much concerned to decide which members of hospital staff are employees. This issue exposed the problems of the 'control' test. How could lay members of a hospital board be said to 'control' a highly skilled neurosurgeon? After much uncertainty, it is now settled that nurses, radiographers,[39] house surgeons,[40] and assistant medical officers[41] in the full-time service of hospitals are employees.[42] Part-time anaesthetists have also been held to be employees on the basis that they are members of the organization of the hospital.[43] Surgeons and consultants working under the National Health Service, even though only engaged part-time, will for the same reason be employees. They are all operating as part and parcel of the NHS enterprise. It is only when the surgeon or consultant treats the patient under a private contract between himself and the patient that the hospital is not answerable for his torts.

(3) BORROWED EMPLOYEES

It is often difficult to decide whose employee a person is when he is lent by his employer to another. The leading decision here is *Mersey Docks and Harbour Board v Coggins and Griffiths (Liverpool) Ltd.*[44]

The Board owned many mobile cranes, each operated by skilled drivers who were engaged and paid by the Board. In the ordinary course of its business, the Board hired out a crane to the respondents, a stevedoring company, for use in unloading a ship. The power to dismiss the

---

[35] In *Carmichael v National Power plc* [1999] 1 WLR 2042 Lord Irvine said (at 2047) that a contract of employment required an 'irreducible minimum of mutual obligations'. See also *Clark v Oxfordshire Health Authority* [1998] IRLR 125; *Dacas v Brook Street Bureau (UK) Ltd* [2004] IRLR 358; *Stevedoring and Haulage Services Ltd v Fuller* [2001] IRLR 627.

[36] Eg, the fact that the agency only pays the worker according to time sheets supplied by the employer (suggesting that the worker is not an employee of the agency): *Montgomery v Johnson Underwood* [2001] IRLR 269.

[37] *Franks v Reuters Ltd* [2003] EWCA 417.   [38] *Dacas v Brook Street Bureau (UK) Ltd* [2004] IRLR 358.

[39] *Gold v Essex County Council* [1942] 2 KB 293.

[40] *Collins v Hertfordshire County Council* [1947] KB 598; *Cassidy v Ministry of Health* [1951] 2 KB 343.

[41] *Cassidy v Ministry of Health* [1951] 2 KB 343.

[42] Soo, too, are educational psychologists and teachers engaged by a local education authority (*Phelps v Hillingdon London Borough Council* [2001] 2 AC 619), as are education officers performing the statutory functions of such authorities (*Carty v London Borough of Croydon* [2005] EWCA Civ 19).

[43] *Roe v Minister of Health* [1954] 2 QB 66.

[44] [1947] AC 1; *Karuppan Bhoomidas v Port of Singapore Authority* [1978] 1 All ER 956 (even though a byelaw provided that those loading and discharging vessels shall be under the superintendence of the ship's officers, stevedores were held to remain employees of the port authority, which was vicariously liable for their torts).

driver remained with the board even though the contract provided that he was to be the servant of the hirers. While loading the cargo, the driver was under the immediate control of the hirers in the sense that the hirers could tell him which boxes to load and where to place them, but they could not tell him how to manipulate the controls of the crane. A third party was injured by virtue of negligent handling of the crane by the driver. The House of Lords was called upon to decide whose servant he was at the time of the accident.

It was held that the Board was solely liable. There is a very strong presumption[45] that someone remains the employee of the general or permanent employer although another employer borrows his services. Where cranes or vehicles are let out on hire with a driver, the owner is responsible for his employee's negligence unless he specifically divested himself of all possession and control.[46] But if the system of work that is used is unsafe, then, according to *Morris v Breaveglen Ltd*,[47] the general employer is liable, for he has a non-delegable duty to ensure the provision and operation of a safe system of work. (On the other hand, it should not be forgotten that, as we have already seen, where both the general employer and the employer to whom the employee has been loaned have control over the employee, both employers can be held vicariously liable in respect of the employee's torts.[48])

(4) POLICE OFFICERS

Under section 88 of the Police Act 1996 the chief officer of police for any police area is vicariously liable for those torts committed by constables exercising or purporting to exercise their functions. Thus, vicarious liability may be imposed even if the tort in question is committed by an off-duty officer who makes it clear that he is by profession a police officer.[49]

SECTION 3 IS THERE A SEPARATE CATEGORY OF AGENTS?

We have seen that a person who does work for another may be either an employee or an independent contractor. But such a person *may* simultaneously be an agent. This is because the category of 'agent' partially overlaps with the categories of both 'employee' and 'independent contractor'. And while agency is primarily of importance within the law of contract, it is not without some significance in this context, too.

---

[45] For an example where the company 'borrowing' employees did become vicariously liable, even though there was no formal contract of employment between the temporary employer and the employee, see *Hawley v Luminar Leisure* [2006] EWCA Civ 30.

[46] And the original employer will of course be primarily liable if he hires out an incompetent driver: *McConkey v Amec plc* (1990) 27 Con LR 88.   [47] [1993] PIQR P294.

[48] *Viasystems (Tyneside) Ltd v Thermal Transfer (Northern) Ltd* [2006] 2 WLR 428.

[49] *Weir v Bettison* [2003] EWCA Civ 111.

An agent may or may not be an employee. A person employed on a weekly wage to sell vacuum cleaners and under orders as to his times and place of employment will be both an agent (in contracting to sell cleaners) and an employee.[50] By contrast, no-one would suggest that, if the defendant employed a chartered accountant to settle his liability for income tax on his behalf, the defendant would be liable if the accountant negligently knocked down a pedestrian while driving to the tax office in order to discuss the matter. The accountant would be both an agent and an independent contractor of the defendant.

The tort of deceit provides an important example of where tort law *is* concerned with the existence of an agency arrangement. Where a principal delegates authority to another person to negotiate a contract on his behalf, he may be liable for the fraud of his 'agent'. So, for example, if an estate agent, in the course of negotiating the sale of a house of his principal, knowingly makes untrue statements about that house to a third party who acts on them to his detriment, the principal will be liable in deceit. And yet the estate agent is not the principal's employee. This liability exists only where the principal can be said to have held out the estate agent as someone authorized to make such representations in the course of making the contract.[51] This provides a valuable clue to the key issue here – such misrepresentations, though capable of giving rise to tortious liability, are so intimately associated with, and inseparable from, the contractual relation to which end the agency is directed that they assume the quality of contract, where agency, of course, is important *per se*.[52]

The concept of agency is also applicable to merely negligent statements made by an estate agent.[53] But it is an essential prerequisite of liability of the principal that the agent acted within the scope of the authority which the principal's acts led the claimant to believe the agent enjoyed. Where the agent is an employee of the principal, the agent cannot act beyond the scope of his authority yet still remain within the general course of his employment.[54]

---

[50] Cf a schoolboy distributing milk in his school who will not be the servant of a local education authority, although he may well be an agent: *Watkins v Birmingham CC* (1975) 126 NLJ 442.

[51] Cf *Uxbridge Permanent Benefit Building Society v Pickard* [1939] 2 KB 248, at 254–5, *per* Lord Greene MR. For further endorsement of the 'holding out' principle, see *Lloyd v Grace, Smith & Co* [1912] AC 716; but for criticism of the way in which this case has subsequently been interpreted by the House of Lords, see Murphy, 'Juridical Foundations of Common Law Non-Delegable Duties' in Neyers (ed), *Emerging Issues in Tort Law* (2007).

[52] Whether this exception will be restricted to deceit because of the need for a contractual element, or whether the parallel concept of 'holding out' will permit its extension to any tort where D has held out a person to represent him in performing a transaction with others, is uncertain. The High Court of Australia has held an insurance company liable when its agent (not an employee) defamed a rival company while soliciting business: *Colonial Mutual Life Assurance Society Ltd v Producers and Citizens Assurance Co of Australia Ltd* (1931) 46 CLR 41. *Dicta* in *Houldsworth v City of Glasgow Bank* (1880) 5 App Cas 317, at 326, *per* Lord Selbourne and *Lloyd v Grace, Smith & Co* [1912] AC 716, at 734–5, *per* Lord Macnaghten lean towards the Australian position.

[53] *Kooragang Investments Pty Ltd v Richardson & Wrench Ltd* [1982] AC 462. In that case, therefore, the principal was held not liable for the agent's negligent statement because the agent was not authorized to make the valuations, the subject of the negligent statements.

[54] *Armagas Ltd v Mundogas SA, The Ocean Frost* [1986] AC 717. But acting in manner closely connected to his contractual obligations will probably suffice in the wake of *Lister v Hesley Hall Ltd* [2002] 1 AC 215.

The other area which demands special attention is the liability of the owner of a vehicle when it is driven by someone else. Of course, the owner is liable if his employee drives it negligently in the course of his employment. The courts have not stopped there, however, and the House of Lords in *Morgans v Launchbury*[55] affirmed that if the vehicle is driven by the owner's agent, and the user is driving as the owner's agent for the owner's purposes, the owner is again liable. The facts in *Morgans v Launchbury* were as follows.

D owned the car. With her permission, her husband took it on a pub-crawl. When he was too drunk to drive, he asked his drinking companion to drive. D was held not liable for the damage caused by the companion's negligent driving.

The House of Lords held that the driver was not the agent of the owner, and that a car owner is liable only if the driver is his employee acting in the course of his employment or is his authorized agent driving for, and on behalf of, the owner. Lord Wilberforce added that 'agency' in such a context was merely a concept the meaning and purpose of which is that the owner ought to pay.[56] The House rejected the argument that it was so desirable to find someone liable who was covered by compulsory third-party insurance, that it should hold the owner liable for anyone who drove with his permission: only Parliament, not the courts, could make that extension of liability.[57] *Morgans v Launchbury* does not, therefore, upset the general rule in vicarious liability that a principal is not liable merely because his agent commits a tort while acting as agent.[58]

SECTION 4 LIABILITY IN RESPECT OF AN INDEPENDENT CONTRACTOR

The employer is not normally liable merely because an independent contractor commits a tort in the course of his employment. He is liable only if he himself is deemed to have committed a tort. This may happen in one of three ways.

(A) AUTHORIZING HIM TO COMMIT A TORT

In many circumstances the law will attribute to a man the conduct of another being, whether human or animal, if he has instigated that conduct. If X sets his dog upon Y it is as much a battery as if X had struck Y with his fist. He who instigates or procures

---

[55] [1973] AC 127.   [56] [1973] AC 127, at 135.

[57] In *Norwood v Navan* [1981] RTR 457, a husband was held not liable for the negligence of his wife when driving his car for family shopping. In *Nelson v Raphael* [1979] RTR 437, the seller of a car asked a friend to hand over the car to the buyer and collect his cheque. When the friend demonstrated the controls to the buyer, the seller was held vicariously liable for the friend's negligence while doing so.

[58] *Nottingham v Aldridge* [1971] 2 QB 739.

another to commit a tort is deemed to have committed the tort himself.[59] It matters not whether that other was an employee, an independent contractor or an agent (human or otherwise). In *Ellis v Sheffield Gas Consumers Co* the facts were as follows.[60]

Having no legal power to do so, Ds' gas undertaking employed an independent contractor to dig up a part of a street. C fell over a heap of earth and stones made by the contractor in the course of digging, and Ds were held liable on the ground that they had authorized this nuisance.

It is not always easy, however, to decide whether the defendant can be said to have authorized the tortious act. Where a lessee was empowered to erect certain structures, but the lease reserved to the lessor the right to approve the plans for such structures (which right the lessor is not reported to have exercised), this was not enough to make the lessor answerable for the lessee's negligence in the course of building the structure.[61] On the other hand, although a taxi driver is certainly not an employee, if his fare orders him to drive fast or to take other risks, he is jointly responsible for any ensuing tort.[62]

If a person commits a tort while purporting to act on behalf of another, but in fact does so without his authority, and that other later ratifies the act which amounted to a tort, he thereby becomes answerable for the tort in the same way as if he had given authority prior to its commission. However, to be liable on this basis, the principal must know at the time of ratification[63] of the commission of the act which constitutes a tort. On the other hand, the principal is not excused simply because he was unaware that the ratified act was a tort for which he would have been liable had he performed the act himself. As such, if he ratifies the purchase of goods which the vendor had no right to sell, he is liable in conversion, even though he is unaware that the sale was unlawful.[64]

(B) TORTS WHERE INTENTIONAL OR NEGLIGENT CONDUCT NEED NOT ALWAYS BE PROVED

The torts of 'strict liability' discussed in previous chapters revealed that, in some instances, liability may be imposed even in the absence of an intentional or negligent act by the defendant's independent contractors. In nuisance,[65] the rule in *Rylands v Fletcher*[66] and breach of statutory duty,[67] for example, we saw that a defendant may in some circumstances be liable for the conduct of his independent contractor.

---

[59] And even if that other has a defence, the principal may still be liable: *Bsarker v Braham* (1773) 3 Wils 368 (D authorized a sheriff to arrest C on an illegal warrant; although the sheriff was protected from liability by reason of acting under the warrant, D was still liable in false imprisonment).   [60] (1853) 2 E & B 767.

[61] *Hurlstone v London Electric Rly Co* (1914) 30 TLR 398.

[62] Cf *M'Laughlin v Pryor* (1842) 4 Man & G 48. Mere failure to object or other acquiescence would not be enough.   [63] *Freeman v Rosher* (1849) 13 QB 780.

[64] *Hilbery v Hatton* (1864) 2 H & C 822.

[65] Eg, *Matania v National Provincial Bank Ltd* [1936] 2 All ER 633. Cf *Hole v Sittingbourne and Sheerness Rly Co* (1861) 6 H & N 488; *Dalton v Angus & Co* (1881) 6 App Cas 740 (the right of support); *Bower v Peate* (1876) 1 QBD 321; *Alcock v Wraith* (1991) 58 BLR 20.   [66] (1868) LR 3 HL 330.

[67] *Hosking v De Havilland Aircraft Co Ltd* [1949] 1 All ER 540.

(c) NEGLIGENCE

An employer may be liable in negligence for damage caused by the acts of his independent contractors in the following circumstances.[68]

(1) PERSONAL NEGLIGENCE ON THE PART OF THE EMPLOYER

First, there may be such an element of personal negligence on the part of the employer as to make him liable for the acts of his independent contractor, and this may be so even though the duty of care owed by the employer in a particular case is not so extensive as to make the employer liable merely because his independent contractor has been negligent. For example, the employer is liable where he carelessly appoints an incompetent contractor. Equally, where the risk of harm is foreseeable in the absence of precautions, a failure by the employer to provide in the contract for those precautions, is actionable negligence.[69] *Robinson v Beaconsfield RDC*[70] furnishes another example of personal negligence on the part of the employer.

Ds employed contractors to clean out cesspools in their district. No arrangements were made for the removal of the deposits of sewage upon their being taken from the cesspools by the contractors. The contractors deposited sewage on C's land. Ds were held liable for their failure to take proper precautions to dispose of the sewage.

It probably follows from the decision in *Robinson* that it would also be negligence to fail to make a proper inspection after a job has been completed. Certainly, in the context of the operation of the Occupiers' Liability Act 1957, proper discharge of the common duty of care where contractors have been engaged involves making such inspections after the work has been completed.[71]

(2) NON-DELEGABLE DUTIES

In some categories of negligence, the duty to take care has been so widely drawn that it is not discharged by properly instructing and supervising a competent contractor: there is a positive duty to see that care is taken. Such duties are often termed non-delegable duties and they involve such high standards of care that they often appear to (and sometimes do) impose strict liability.[72] It must be emphasized that not all duties of care in

---

[68] But for these purposes, a sub-contractor who himself engages a sub-sub-contractor will not be treated in law as an employer: *MTM Construction Ltd v William Reid Engineering Ltd* 1998 SLT 211.

[69] Cf *Hughes v Percival* (1883) 8 App Cas 443.   [70] [1911] 2 Ch 188.

[71] Occupiers' Liability Act 1957, s 2(4)(b).

[72] The standard of care involved where the non-delegable duty exists as a sub-species of the law of negligence is often pitched at a very high level because of the degree of risk typically present in such cases. Where, however, the non-delegable duty exists as a sub-species of nuisance, the duty is necessarily strict. But for the novel view that the non-delegable duty is an independent tort involving strict liability in every case, see Witting, 'Breach of Non-delegable Duty: Defending Limited Strict Liability in Tort' (forthcoming). Cf Murphy, 'Common Law Non-Delegable Duties – Theorizing the Basis of Liability' (forthcoming).

negligence are treated as non-delegable. It is a question of law whether such a duty is owed.[73]

Where the activity is particularly hazardous – for example, where open fires on bush land are lit,[74] where re-roofing takes place on a row of terraced houses where difficulties with the 'joins' between the properties is well known,[75] or where flash-light photographs in a cinema are taken[76] – the duty of care has been held to be non-delegable. Where employers are carrying out inherently dangerous operations on or near a highway, and those operations may foreseeably harm highway users, and the negligence of their independent contractors does cause such harm, the employers are again liable on this basis. Consider *Holliday v National Telephone Co*.[77]

Ds, in laying telephone wires along a street, employed an independent contractor to solder the tubes in which these wires were carried. In negligently using a benzolene lamp, the contractor injured a passer-by. Ds were held liable.

Where one carries out structural operations that threaten damage to neighbouring premises, these too may ground a non-delegable duty;[78] while a railway company owes a duty to passengers to see that bridges along its lines are carefully built by independent contractors engaged for this purpose.[79] By contrast, removing a hawthorn tree from a garden adjoining a highway is not an inherently dangerous activity. Accordingly, its owner is not liable for harm caused to the claimant by his contractor removing it negligently.[80]

The categories of non-delegable duties are not closed; and danger is not the only criterion according to which they may be ascribed. It seems equally plausible that an assumption of responsibility on the part of the employer will suffice.[81] Thus, a patient who is accepted for treatment in an NHS hospital will be able to invoke a non-delegable

---

[73] For an attempt to theorize the little understood prerequisites for such duties, see Murphy, 'Juridical Foundations of Common Law Non-Delegable Duties' in Neyers (ed), *Emerging Issues in Tort Law* (2007).

[74] *Black v Christchurch Finance Co* [1894] AC 48. And see *Balfour v Barty-King* [1957] 1 QB 496 (owner liable for a fire when an independent contractor plumber used a blowlamp in a loft to thaw D's frozen pipes).

[75] *Alcock v Wraith* (1991) 58 BLR 20.

[76] *Honeywill and Stein Ltd v Larkin Bros (London's Commercial Photographer) Ltd* [1934] 1 KB 191.

[77] [1899] 2 QB 392. Cf *Hardaker v Idle District Council* [1896] 1 QB 335 (damaging a gas pipe while laying a sewer under the highway); *Penny v Wimbledon UDC and Iles* [1899] 2 QB 72 (a heap of soil was left unlighted on a highway); *Walsh v Holst & Co Ltd* [1958] 3 All ER 33. In *Pickard v Smith* (1861) 10 CBNS 470, the same principle was applied to hold a railway refreshment room proprietor liable to a passenger who fell down a hole which the employee of D's independent contractor negligently left on the platform.

[78] *Hughes v Percival* (1883) 8 App Cas 443 (party wall negligently cut into while contractor was rebuilding part of adjoining premises); *Alcock v Wraith* (1991) 58 BLR 20.

[79] *Grote v Chester and Holyhead Rly Co* (1848) 2 Exch 251.   [80] *Salsbury v Woodland* [1970] 1 QB 324.

[81] Indeed, in some instances it has been said that undertaking an enterprise that carries with it certain severe risks will form the basis for the imputation of such an 'assumption of responsibility' (even though this involves a measure of linguistic inelegance): see Murphy, 'Juridical Foundations of Common Law Non-Delegable Duties' in Neyers (ed), *Emerging Issues in Tort Law* (2007). As such, an assumption of responsibility may, more so than the creation of an especial danger, lie at the heart of such non-delegable duties.

duty in order to sue the NHS authorities that stand behind those engaged to provide the patient's actual specialist treatment. The rationale here is that hospital authorities have a duty to provide proper treatment at all stages, and this involves a duty that they cannot cast off by simply entrusting it to competent staff. *Lindsey County Council v Marshall*,[82] *Gold v Essex County Council*[83] and *Collins v Hertfordshire County Council*[84] all suggest that such a non-delegable duty formed the basis of Denning LJ's judgment in *Cassidy v Ministry of Health*[85] where it was held that a hospital authority that ran a casualty department had a duty to provide proper medical and nursing care for all those who presented themselves complaining of illness or injury.[86]

A direct, non-delegable duty to patients may have several consequences in today's health service. Perhaps until about 1980 it did not matter very much whether Denning LJ was right in *Cassidy*.[87] If all the professionals caring for a patient were employees, and it could be proved that someone was negligent, the hospital authority was necessarily vicariously liable for the tort of one of their employees. However, with the increasing use of agency staff, the hospital may be able to escape liability by arguing that the patient is unable to prove that a person for whom the hospital is vicariously responsible was at fault. The fact that there may be a personal, non-delegable duty owed by the hospital authorities means that such an escape-route is readily blocked. It could be invoked, for example, where a child falls ill in the night and a doctor from the deputizing service engaged by the family GP fails to diagnose meningitis. Equally, it could be invoked where, say, an elderly lady finally gets a date for a hip replacement and the health authority contracts her operation out to a private clinic. In these examples, if the GP and health authority are subject to *Cassidy*-type, non-delegable duties, they will be placed in breach of this duty by virtue of the negligent treatment performed by their independent contractors, the deputizing services and the private clinic.[88]

The Employer's Liability (Defective Equipment) Act 1969 must also be noted at this juncture. It applies when, for the purposes of his business, an employer provides equipment (which includes any plant and machinery, vehicle, aircraft and clothing) for his employee and the employee suffers personal injury in the course of his employment in consequence of a defect in that equipment. The injury is then deemed also to be attributable to the negligence of the employer if the defect is attributable wholly or partly to the negligence, or other tort, of an independent contractor or other third party. This Act therefore imposes an extensive statutory duty on employers. But it leaves unchanged the common-law duty of the employer to provide and ensure the operation of a safe system of work in respects other than the provision of equipment.[89] And this duty is

---

[82] [1937] AC 97.   [83] [1942] 2 KB 293, at 301, *per* Lord Greene MR.   [84] [1947] KB 598.

[85] [1951] 2 KB 343, at 362–3.

[86] *Barnett v Chelsea and Kensington Hospital Management Committee* [1969] 1 QB 428.

[87] For a view that he was wrong see *Yepremian v Scarborough General Hospital* (1980) 110 DLR (3d) 513.

[88] See *M v Calderdale and Kirklees Health Authority* [1998] Lloyd's Rep Med 157.

[89] Note the obligation to insure under the Employers' Liability (Compulsory Insurance) Act 1969.

an especially onerous one as *McDermid v Nash Dredging and Reclamation Co Ltd*[90] illustrates.

C was employed as a deck hand by Ds. He was instructed to go and work on another tug owned by a different company within the same group as Ds. As a result of the negligence of that tug master, who was not an employee of Ds, C suffered severe injuries. Ds were held liable for failing to provide and ensure the operation of a safe system of work.

It was no excuse that they did not in fact have any control over the operation of the system in question. The breach of the non-delegable duty in respect of the safety of their employee was not discharged by delegating that duty to the master of the tug. The duty was one not just to devise, but also to *ensure the operation of* a safe system of work.[91] Even so, it must be stressed that that duty remains a duty to take reasonable care, not an absolute duty to guarantee the employee's safety.[92] In *Cook v Square D Ltd*,[93] for example, an employee working in Saudi Arabia was injured falling over an unguarded raised tile. The Court of Appeal held that the employers, who were 8,000 miles away, could not be responsible for every day-to-day event in the workplace.[94] The real question was whether they had done what a reasonable employer should do in order to set up, operate and monitor a safe system of work.

In one or two instances, the courts have been prepared to extend the categories of non-delegable duty. In *Rogers v Night Riders*,[95] for example, the claimant's mother telephoned the defendants for a taxi to take her daughter to the station and the mother paid for the cab. During the journey, a door flew open and the claimant was injured. The taxi driver was not an employee but an independent contractor for the defendants. Nevertheless the defendants were held to be in breach of their primary duty to the claimant. As far as she knew, it was the defendants who undertook to convey her safely and carefully to her destination.

What is really required in this area is that the courts set out clearly the bases for such duties. This need arises not simply because such analysis is conspicuous by its absence in the English case law, but also because there has been a tendency for the boundaries between non-delegable duties and vicarious liability to become remarkably confused in recent years, especially in the House of Lords decision in *Lister v Hesley Hall Ltd*[96] which case is explored in more detail below.[97]

---

[90] [1987] AC 906. See also *Davie v New Merton Board Mills Ltd* [1959] AC 604, at 646, *per* Lord Reid.

[91] For the argument that this case more closely resembles vicarious liability than non-delegable duty, see McKendrick, 'Vicarious Liability and Independent Contractors – A Re-examination' (1990) 53 MLR 770.

[92] As such, it is possible for the partial defence of contributory negligence to be raised in relation to the employer's non-delegable duty towards his employees: see, eg, *McGarvey v Eve NCI Ltd* [2002] EWCA Civ 374.

[93] [1992] ICR 262.

[94] But note that the incident in *McDermid* also took place abroad. Are the distinctions made between the two cases convincing: see [1992] ICR 262 at 270–1, *per* Farquharson LJ.

[95] [1983] RTR 324. See also *Cynat Products Ltd v Landbuild (Investment and Property) Ltd* [1984] 3 All ER 513.   [96] [2002] 1 AC 215.

[97] For more detail than is offered here, see Murphy, 'Juridical Foundations of Common Law Non-Delegable Duties' in Neyers (ed), *Emerging Issues in Tort Law* (2007).

SECTION 5 WHERE THE EMPLOYER IS NOT LIABLE FOR THE ACTS OF AN INDEPENDENT CONTRACTOR

(A) NO BREACH BY EMPLOYER OF ANY DUTY IMPOSED ON HIM BY THE LAW OF TORTS

An employer is liable for damage caused by tortious acts of his independent contractor only where he himself is in breach of a duty of care. In the case of non-delegable duties, the standard of care will typically be so high that any tort committed by an independent contractor is likely to place the employer in breach of his own personal duty. But in other cases, where the duty is not a non-delegable one – and there are many such instances – the key question will concern the extent of the risk against which the employer has the duty to guard.[98] And here a less stringent standard of care would seem to obtain. *Phillips v Britannia Hygienic Laundry Co*[99] provides a useful example. In that case, the owner of a lorry was held not liable when a third party's vehicle was damaged in consequence of the negligent repair of his lorry by a garage proprietor.

(B) COLLATERAL NEGLIGENCE

Employers of independent contractors are never liable for, as it is commonly termed, the 'collateral negligence' of their contractors. *Padbury v Holiday and Greenwood Ltd*[100] both furnishes facts which illustrate the principle and contains what seems to be the soundest statement of it.

A employed B to fit casement windows into certain premises. B's employee negligently put a tool on the sill of the window on which he was working at the time. The wind blew the casement open and the tool was knocked off the sill onto a passer-by.

Holding the employer not liable, Fletcher Moulton LJ said:

[B]efore a superior employer could be held liable for the negligent act of a servant of a sub-contractor it must be shown that the work which the sub-contractor was employed to do was work the nature of which, and not merely the performance of which, cast on the superior employer the duty of taking precautions.[101]

---

[98] *Dalton v Angus & Co* (1881) 6 App Cas 740, at 831, *per* Lord Watson.

[99] [1923] 1 KB 539 (affd [1923] 2 KB 832); followed in *Stennett v Hancock and Peters* [1939] 2 All ER 578. But would the garage be liable for the negligent repair by its independent contractor? See *Taylor v Rover Co Ltd* [1966] 2 All ER 181; *Rivers v Cutting* [1982] 3 All ER 69 (a policeman arranged, under powers given by the Removal and Disposal of Vehicles Regulations 1968, for a garage to tow away a car broken down on the M1 motorway; he was not liable for the garage's negligent towing). [100] (1912) 28 TLR 494.

[101] (1912) 28 TLR 494, at 495. Cf *Hardaker v Idle District Council* [1896] 1 QB 335, at 342, *per* Lindley LJ; *Thompson v Anglo-Saxon Petroleum Co Ltd* [1955] 2 Lloyd's Rep 363.

In short, the employer is liable for those risks of harm created by the work itself which the employer is having done. 'Collateral' means collateral to the risk which marks the limit of the duty of the employer. If the employer is to be liable, the danger must be inherent in the work; it is not enough that the contractor chooses a negligent way of performing it where the normal manner of performance would create no reasonably foreseeable peril to the claimant.

The negligence must be 'in the employer's department of duty'.[102] A householder who employs a contractor to repair his lamp over the highway is liable if the contractor repairs it in such a way that it falls onto a passer-by, for that is the very risk in respect of which the duty of the householder is imposed on him, but he is not liable if the contractor, while repairing it, allows a hammer to drop onto the passer-by, for that act would be outside the employer's range of duty. If a hospital owes a non-delegable duty to patients in respect of their treatment, it does not follow that the hospital is liable when an agency doctor negligently backs his car into yours when driving from one part of the hospital to another. That act is not within the non-delegable duty to patients. *Wilson v Hodgson's Kingston Brewery Co*[103] also demonstrates how liability for the acts of independent contractors falls short of vicarious liability for the torts of an employee.

Ds employed X, an independent contractor, to deliver beer at a public house. X delivered it through a cellar flap on the highway, and he negligently left the flap open, causing C, who was passing along the pavement, to be injured. Pointing out that X could have delivered it through the front door, the court held that the incident was not within the scope of any duty on the part of Ds to take care.

SECTION 6 LIABILITY IN RESPECT OF EMPLOYEES

(A) INTRODUCTION

An employer is liable whenever his employee commits a tort in the course of his employment or in circumstances sufficiently closely connected to his employment. All the elements of the particular tort[104] must generally occur within, or in close connection with, the employer-employee relationship. However, the employer will still be answerable if the tort was committed before, but the harm occurred after, the employment relationship ceased to exist.[105]

---

[102] *Cassidy v Ministry of Health* [1951] 2 KB 343, at 365, *per* Denning LJ. This judgment contains a lucid statement of the nature of collateral negligence. For the difficulty in ascertaining exactly D's duty for the purpose of this rule, see *Salsbury v Woodland* [1970] 1 QB 324, at 349, *per* Sachs LJ.   [103] (1915) 85 LJKB 270.

[104] A procedural bar against suing the servant will not prevent the master from being vicariously liable: *Staveley Iron and Chemicals Co Ltd v Jones* [1956] 1 All ER 403; *Broom v Morgan* [1953] 1 QB 597.

[105] *Briess v Woolley* [1954] AC 333.

Where a duty of care imposed on the employer has been broken, but the claimant cannot prove which employee of the employer is responsible for the breach, the employer is nonetheless liable as one might expect.[106] Thus in *Roe v Minister of Health* all three judges in the Court of Appeal stated (*obiter*) that where a claimant established negligence on the part of one or more of several employees of the defendant hospital authority, the defendant authority was vicariously liable although the claimant could not prove which of those employees committed the negligent act.[107] Further, the *ratio decidendi* of *Cassidy v Ministry of Health* is that where the claimant has been injured as a result of some operation in the control of one or more employees of a hospital authority (and he cannot identify the particular employee who was in control), and in all other respects the requirements of the *res ipsa loquitur* rule in respect of the act are satisfied, the hospital authority is vicariously liable unless it ousts the operation of that rule.[108] These two decisions were arrived at on the basis of vicarious liability,[109] *not* on the basis of a breach of non-delegable duty by the employer.

(B) IN THE COURSE OF THE EMPLOYEE'S EMPLOYMENT

At one time, vicarious liability could only be imposed when the employee did the act complained of 'in the course of his employment'.[110] While a rival test has since emerged, based on acts closely connected to the employee's contract of employment, it is nonetheless still true that any tortious act committed within the course of an employee's employment will suffice to invoke vicarious liability. To hold otherwise would be to negate the rationale behind a vast body of case law that is still regarded as sound. As such, the *legal* question of when an act falls within a 'course of employment' is by no means redundant (even though it is admittedly of far less significance than it was formerly).

(1) THE COURSE OF EMPLOYMENT: GENERAL PRINCIPLES

At one time, it was generally accepted that the crucial distinction to be made lay between an employee's wrongful mode of doing authorized work (for which the

---

[106] *Grant v Australian Knitting Mills Ltd* [1936] AC 85; *Olley v Marlborough Court Ltd* [1949] 1 KB 532 (a guest left the bedroom key at the hotel office; upon the key being taken and the bedroom being burgled, the onus was cast on the hotel to prove that they and their staff had taken reasonable care of the key).

[107] [1954] 2 QB 66. [108] [1951] 2 KB 343.

[109] Although Denning LJ would have preferably founded liability in Cassidy's case on breach of a non-delegable duty (as we saw in Section 3), he also agreed with Somervell and Singleton LJJ, in respect of the statement in the text.

[110] Even though the act is outside the scope of employment the employer may still be liable for breach of his own duty to provide a safe system of work. Eg, in *Hudson v Ridge Manufacturing Co Ltd* [1957] 2 QB 348, an employer was held liable to an employee for failure to prevent horseplay by one workman known to be likely to harm other workmen. It seems that a claim based on vicarious liability would have failed.

employer would be liable), and his performance of some unauthorized act (for which the employer would not be liable).[111] Such a simplistic distinction was never entirely satisfactory,[112] especially from a compensation point of view, for some cases involving deliberate misconduct could best be viewed as having been 'massaged' in order to fit the somewhat rigid 'unauthorized mode' (as opposed to 'unauthorized act') category.[113] Of course, it is quite properly uncontentious to regard negligence in the performance of a job as a wrongful mode of doing an authorized act; but deliberate, heinous acts by an employee are far more difficult to classify in such terms. That said, the decided cases have on occasion regarded such egregious (even criminal) conduct in terms of wrongful modes of performing authorised acts. Examples will be considered below. But it is useful to begin this section by making the general observation that the possible variations of fact in this context bedevil the exposition of any clear, uncontroversial and universally applicable formula. Here, as in many areas of tort law, some of the decisions are based more on policy than principle. That said, a few examples do help to illustrate the breadth of the factual variations that may occur. Take first, *Century Insurance Co Ltd v Northern Ireland Road Transport Board*.[114]

The driver of a petrol lorry, while transferring petrol from the lorry to an underground tank at a petrol station, struck a match in order to light a cigarette and then threw it, still alight, on the floor. An explosion and a fire ensued.

His employers were held liable for the damage caused: he did the act in the course of carrying out his task of delivering petrol. It was an unauthorized way of doing what he was actually employed to do. Similarly, in *Bayley v Manchester, Sheffield and Lincolnshire Rly Co*,[115] erroneously thinking that the claimant was on the wrong train, a porter of the defendants forcibly removed him. The defendants were held liable. Consider, too, *Harrison v Michelin Tyre Co Ltd*.[116]

C was injured when an employee of Ds deliberately steered the truck which he was driving a few inches off the designated passageway and knocked C over as he stood at his machine. Ds were held liable. The momentary horseplay engaged in by Ds' servant did not take him outside the course of his employment.

In recent years, however, there has been a rash of cases the Commonwealth over in which the employee committed various crimes of violence and sexual abuse which have forced the courts to abandon their somewhat artificial endeavours to squeeze these cases of deliberate wrongdoing into the traditional 'unauthorized mode' framework.[117] The same could be said of another case in which an employer was held liable for the

---

[111] *Goh Choon Seng v Lee Kim Soo* [1925] AC 550.

[112] See Weekes, 'Vicarious liability for Violent Employees' [2004] CLJ 53; Cane, 'Vicarious Liability for Sexual Abuse' (2000) 116 LQR 21.   [113] For details, see the 10th edition of this book.

[114] [1942] AC 509.   [115] (1873) LR 8 CP 148.

[116] [1985] 1 All ER 918. See also *Duffy v Thanet District Council* (1984) 134 NLJ 680.

[117] See, eg, *Mattis v Pollock* [2003] 1 WLR 2158, *New South Wales v Lepore* [2003] HCA 4, *Bazley v Curry* [1999] 2 SCR 534 and *Jacobi v Griffiths* (1999) 174 DLR (4th) 71; *Lister v Hesley Hall Ltd* [2002] 1 AC 215.

racist taunts of, and assaults upon, employee A by employees B, C and D.[118] Here, it was arguably nonsensical to describe such conduct as being within the course of employment. Another example is *Aldred v Nacanco*[119] where an employee knew that a basin in a washroom was unsteady and she deliberately shoved it against a colleague causing her injury. In that case, the Court of Appeal held her act to be quite unrelated to her work and so outside her course of employment. Similarly, a transport company was not liable when the conductor turned a bus round on his own initiative at the terminus and injured a third party.[120] So far as any firm guiding principles can be evinced from the older cases, they might well be the following.

(2) AUTHORIZED CONDUCT WITHIN LIMITS OF TIME AND SPACE

The conduct of an employee is normally only within the scope of his employment during his authorized period of work. However, he will still be treated as being within the scope of his employment during a period which is not unreasonably disconnected from the authorized period. Thus, someone paid for working until 6 pm who stays on for a few minutes in order to finish a job will still be within the scope of his employment.[121] But an employee who comes into his employer's premises without permission during his holiday is not within the scope of his job.[122]

By extension from the foregoing, employees travelling to and from their place of work are not ordinarily regarded as being within the course of their employment. However, there are instances where travel is so closely connected with a person's work that the ordinary principle cannot apply. In *Smith v Stages*,[123] for example, an employee had been working away from his home and his usual workplace. He was involved in a road accident driving home in his own car so that he could resume work at his usual place of employment the next day. He was paid for the day he needed to drive back as a normal working day. The House of Lords held that he remained within the course of his employment. His journey from A to B was part and parcel of his job in those circumstances, and his employers, in effect, directed that he make the journey.

There are of course many jobs where travel is itself the essence of the employment. The work of sales representatives is an obvious example. But what if such employees make a detour from their set pattern of work for their own purposes, say, to visit a friend or to do some shopping? The courts have sometimes been called upon to decide

---

[118] *Tower Boot Co Ltd v Jones* [1997] 2 All ER 406 (the importance of the Race Relations Act 1976 demanded that the provisions governing vicarious liability be given a broad interpretation).

[119] [1987] IRLR 292. Their Lordships expressed some disapproval of *Harrison v Michelin Tyre Co Ltd*. Yet perhaps the decisions can be reconciled. The driver in *Harrison* was still doing what he was employed to do, driving. In *Aldred*, nothing relating to the employee's act was concerned with the job she was engaged to do.

[120] *Beard v London General Omnibus Co* [1900] 2 QB 530. Cf *Kay v ITW Ltd* [1968] 1 QB 140; *Iqbal v London Transport Executive* (1973) 16 KIR 329.   [121] See, eg, *Ruddiman & Co v Smith* (1889) 60 LT 708.

[122] *Compton v McClure* [1975] ICR 378.

[123] [1989] AC 928. See also *Vandyke v Fender* [1970] 2 QB 292; *Elleanor v Cavendish Woodhouse Ltd and Comerford* [1973] 1 Lloyd's Rep 313.

whether such detours fall within the scope of employment. The classic ruling is that of Parke B in *Joel v Morison*.

If he was going out of his way, against his master's implied commands when driving on his master's business, he will make his master liable; but if he was going on a frolic of his own, without being at all on his master's business, the master will not be liable.[124]

Whether the detour by the employee is a 'frolic of his own' is clearly a matter of degree. Here are two cases, one on each side of the line.

A carter was in charge of a horse and cart during the day. Without permission he drove them home, a ¼-mile out of his way, for his midday meal, and left the horse unattended outside his home. His employer was held liable for damage done by the horse when it ran away.[125]

A carman, having delivered wine, was to bring back some empties directly to the shop of his employers. On the return journey, before reaching the shop, he deviated from his route in order to pick up a cask at the home of the clerk accompanying him and take it elsewhere for that clerk's private purposes. While on the way to the clerk's home he drove the cart negligently and injured C. His employers were held not liable.[126]

Consider carefully, in each case, exactly what job the employee was engaged to do. If an employee is found to have gone on a 'frolic of his own', can he be deemed to have re-entered his employer's service? An attempt to establish such a resumption failed in *Rayner v Mitchell*.[127]

X was employed to deliver beer and pick up empties. He took out the cart on an unauthorized trip and on his return picked up some empties. This was held not enough to constitute a resumption of his employment, and his employer was held not liable for his negligent driving while returning to the employer's premises with the empties on board.

(3) EXPRESS PROHIBITIONS

Often, of course, an employer expressly forbids certain acts. But it does not follow from this that an act done in defiance of the prohibition is thereby placed outside the scope of employment. If it were so, the employer would only have to issue specific orders not to be negligent in order to escape liability for his employee's negligence. The House of Lords has laid down the rule as follows:

[T]here are prohibitions which limit the sphere of employment, and prohibitions which only deal with conduct within the sphere of employment. A transgression of a prohibition of the latter class leaves the sphere of employment where it was, and consequently will not prevent recovery of compensation. A transgression of the former class carries with it the result that the man has gone outside the sphere.[128]

---

[124] (1834) 6 C & P 501, at 503.   [125] *Whatman v Pearson* (1868) LR 3 CP 422.
[126] *Storey v Ashton* (1869) LR 4 QB 476.   [127] (1877) 2 CPD 357.
[128] *Plumb v Cobden Flour Mills Co Ltd* [1914] AC 62, at 67, *per* Lord Dunedin (a workmen's compensation case, but the principles are the same).

Again, a few illustrative examples are helpful. First, consider *Canadian Pacific Rly Co v Lockhart*.[129]

Ds prohibited their staff from driving uninsured cars on the company's business. In breach of this instruction, S drove an uninsured car negligently, while engaged on the company's business, and injured C.

Holding the defendants liable, the Judicial Committee stated:

[I]t was not the acting as driver that was prohibited, but that non-insurance of the motor car, if used as a means incidental to the execution of the work which he was employed to do. It follows that the prohibition merely limited the way in which, or by means of which, the servant was to execute the work which he was employed to do, and that breach of the prohibition did not exclude the liability of the master to third parties.[130]

Likewise, a garage hand employed to move vehicles in a garage, but forbidden to drive them, was acting in the course of his employment when he drove a van out of the garage onto the highway (in order to make room in the garage for another vehicle), and collided on the highway with the claimant's van.[131] These cases may be contrasted with *Rand v Craig*.[132] There, the defendant employed his servants to carry rubbish from X to Y. Instead they deposited some of this rubbish on the claimant's land. The defendant was held not liable for this trespass because the employees were employed, not to carry rubbish generally, but only to carry it from X to Y. The act was therefore of a kind that the defendant was impliedly forbidden to do.

If a driver gives a lift to a third party in breach of his employer's instructions and tortiously injures that passenger through careless driving, the courts approach the question of the employer's liability as follows. The issue does not turn on the fact that the passenger is a trespasser.[133] Instead, the employer will be held not liable if his prohibition has marked the limits of the scope of employment, so that giving the lift was outside that scope. On the other hand, if the prohibition affects only the mode in which the employee is to perform his duties, the employer may be vicariously liable. Two cases show the distinction.

In *Twine v Bean's Express Ltd*,[134] the facts were as follows.

The employer had a contract to employ his vans on Post Office business. Contrary to his express instruction his driver gave a lift to a third party.

It was held that giving the lift was outside the scope of employment. Operating what was in effect a 'free taxi service' was not the job the driver was employed to do. But contrast this case with that of *Rose v Plenty*.[135]

---

[129] [1942] AC 591.   [130] [1942] AC 591, at 601.

[131] *LCC v Cattermoles (Garages) Ltd* [1953] 2 All ER 582. Cf *Limpus v London General Omnibus Co Ltd* (1862) 1 H & C 526 (a bus driver, contrary to instructions, raced a rival bus in order to get custom – a direction to the jury that these instructions defined the scope of employment was held wrong in law). Cf *Iqbal v London Transport Executive* (1973) 16 KIR 329.   [132] [1919] 1 Ch 1.

[133] *Young v Box & Co* [1951] 1 TLR 798; *Rose v Plenty* [1976] 1 All ER 97.   [134] (1946) 175 LT 131.

[135] [1976] 1 All ER 97. As to the principles applicable when a prohibition is statutory, see *Alford v National Coal Board* [1952] 1 All ER 754.

A milkman employed a 13-year-old boy to deliver and collect milk bottles on his milk round contrary to his employer's order that children were not to be employed by roundsmen in the performance of their duties. The driver negligently injured the boy.

The employer was held vicariously liable because the prohibition affected only the manner in which the roundsman was to perform his duties of delivering milk and did not limit the scope of those duties. He was still delivering milk, and the boy he had wrongly recruited to assist him was part of that enterprise.

(c) CLOSE CONNECTION BETWEEN THE WRONGFUL ACT AND THE EMPLOYEE'S WORK

Frequently, employees do acts which they have no express authority to do, but which are nevertheless calculated to further some proper objective of their employer. Unless the method of accomplishing this objective is so outrageous that no employer could reasonably be taken to have contemplated such an act as being within the scope of employment, the employer will be liable for torts thus committed, as the following cases show.

Poland v John Parr & Sons is the leading case.[136]

H, an employee of Ds, while going home to dinner, reasonably believed that a boy was stealing sugar from a bag on a passing lorry of his employers. He struck the boy, who fell and, in consequence, had to have a leg amputated. Although his act in defence of his employer's property was unreasonable enough to be tortious, it was not sufficiently excessive to be outside the scope of his employment.

Holding that 'a servant has an implied authority upon an emergency to endeavour to protect his employer's property if he sees it in danger or has reasonable ground for thinking that he sees it in danger',[137] the Court of Appeal found the defendants liable. Atkin LJ did, however, point out that:

where the servant does more than the emergency requires, the excess may be so great as to take the act out of the class. For example, if H had fired a shot at the boy, the act might have been in the interest of his employers, but that is not the test.[138]

Now consider *Warren v Henlys Ltd.*[139]

A garage attendant employed by Ds accused C, in violent language, of leaving the garage without paying for his petrol. After paying, C called the police and said that he would report the attendant to his employers. The attendant on hearing this assaulted C.

It was held that there was no evidence that 'this assault . . . was so connected with the acts which the servant was expressly or impliedly authorized to do as to be a mode of

---

[136] [1927] 1 KB 236.   [137] [1927] 1 KB 236, at 240, *per* Bankes LJ.   [138] [1927] 1 KB 236, at 245.
[139] [1948] 2 All ER 935. In *Keppel Bus Co Ltd v Sa'ad bin Ahmad* [1974] 2 All ER 700, a bus conductor struck a passenger after a quarrel. Although the conductor's duties extended to keeping order, his employer was not vicariously liable because there was no evidence of disorder.

doing those acts'.[140] A very obvious example of conduct unconnected with the employer's work is seen in *Makanjuola v Metropolitan Police Comr*.[141] There, a police officer extracted sexual favours from the claimant in return for a promise not to report her to the immigration authorities. It was held that his act was entirely for his own purposes and not an act his employer in any sense authorized. Of course, were the officer's proclivities known to senior officers, it might have been possible to argue that there was a breach of a primary duty of care to the public; but those proclivities were not known. Finally, where the acts of prison officers are broadly in furtherance of the interests of the Home Office, the Home Office remains liable even though the officers' acts amount to misfeasance in a public office.[142]

(1) CRIMINAL ASSAULTS ETC.

Evidence that the employee's conduct was a criminal or otherwise wilful wrongdoing will not necessarily negate the possibility of imposing vicarious liability.[143] For example, an employer may be liable where an over-enthusiastic defence of his interests results in an assault which is in the circumstances a crime as well as a tort.[144] Similarly, in *Vasey v Surrey Free Inns*,[145] an employer was held liable in respect of an assault upon the claimant committed by two doormen in his employ. The doormen's acts were, crucially, in response to the claimant having caused damage to the employer's premises by kicking them. Accordingly, the doormen's actions were construed as being in furtherance of the employer's interests.[146]

There may be cases, however, where the wrongful conduct is in no sense in the employers' interests, but it is so bound up with the employee's job that the employers may be held vicariously liable for that conduct. To put it more bluntly, dishonest or criminal acts are no bar, *per se*, to the imposition vicarious liability.[147] The crucial question is whether the act in question was committed either directly in the course of the employee's employment,[148] or whether it was sufficiently connected to it to warrant the imposition of vicarious liability. Thus, the theft of the mink stole in *Morris v C W Martin & Sons Ltd*[149] by the man entrusted with the job of cleaning it has been viewed by the House of Lords in *Lister v Hesley Hall Ltd* as being a case in which the employee used an unlawful mode of doing his job.[150] The theft of the stole by a cook in the canteen

---

[140] [1948] 2 All ER 935, at 938, *per* Hilbery J.   [141] [1992] 3 All ER 617.

[142] *Racz v Home Office* [1994] 2 AC 45.

[143] *Barwick v English Joint Stock Bank* (1867) LR 2 Exch 259; *Lloyd v Grace, Smith & Co* [1912] AC 716.

[144] *Poland v Parr* [1927] 1 KB 236.   [145] [1996] PIQR P373.

[146] See also *Mattis v Pollock* [2003] 1 WLR 2158 (where a doorman committed an assault some hundreds of metres from the nightclub at which the trouble had started and vicarious liability was still imposed); *Weir v Bettison* [2003] EWCA Civ 111 (a chief constable was held vicariously liable for an assault committed by off-duty police officer who assaulted a would-be thief after indicating that he was a police officer and that he proposed to take the culprit to a police station).   [147] *Port Swettenham Authority v TW Wu & Co* [1979] AC 580.

[148] *T v North Yorkshire County Council* (1998) *Times*, 10 September.   [149] [1966] 1 QB 716.

[150] [2002] 1 AC 215. This interpretation is highly questionable since two members of the Court of Appeal seem to have viewed the case as turning primarily upon the non-delegable duty arising out of the bailment of the fur: see Murphy, 'Juridical Foundations of Common Law Non-Delegable Duties' in Neyers (ed), *Emerging Issues in Tort Law* (2007). It is particularly notable that Lord Nicholls deliberately left this case to one side when

at the firm's factory would, however, be an act totally unrelated to his employment. Accordingly, the employer would not in such circumstances be held vicariously liable (which is not to say that he would escape personal liability in negligence – for example, in employing persons known to be dishonest, or for breach of a non-delegable duty to care properly for the fur). The short point is that the employer cannot be held *vicariously liable* simply for supplying an opportunity for the employee to commit the crime. Instead, the criminal act must be much more closely connected with the contract of employment. The leading case is *Lister v Hesley Hall Ltd.*[151]

A warden living in a boarding house attached to a school owned and managed by Ds had systematically sexually abused for about three years Cs, who were boys at the school with emotional and behavioural difficulties. Ds had no knowledge of these facts. Cs claimed damages against Ds for the personal injuries they suffered, arguing, *inter alia*, that Ds were vicariously liable for the torts committed by the warden. The House of Lords held Ds vicariously liable emphasizing the close contact he had had with the pupils by virtue of his job and the inherent risks his job carried with it.

At the heart of their Lordships' decision was the fact that there was a sufficiently close connection between the work that the warden had been employed to do and the acts of abuse that he had committed for those acts to justify the defendants' vicarious liability. As Lord Steyn put it, in terms reflecting the role of policy in this context:

The question is whether the warden's torts were so closely connected with his employment that it would be fair and just to hold the employers vicariously liable. On the facts of the case the answer is yes. After all, the sexual abuse was inextricably interwoven with the carrying out by the warden of his duties in [the children's] House.[152]

And for Lord Clyde:

The opportunity to be at the premises would not in itself constitute a sufficient connection between his wrongful actings and his employment. In addition to the opportunity which access gave him, his position as warden and the close contact with the boys which that work involved created a sufficient connection between the acts of abuse which he committed and the work which he had been employed to do.[153]

What seems to lie at the heart of *Lister*, then, is not that the job provided the mere circumstances in which the tort took place, but rather that the tort in question constituted a particular risk which was inextricably linked to the employer's type of business. As Lord Clyde further explained: '[t]he fact that his employment gave the employee

---

considering the new test for vicarious liability in *Dubai Aluminium Co Ltd v Salaam* [2003] 2 AC 366, at [27]–[28]. Note also, in bailment, however, that a gratuitous bailee has the burden of proving that he was not negligent if the bailed goods are lost: *Port Swettenham Authority v T W Wu & Co Sdn Bhd* [1979] AC 580. A bailee is also liable for the negligence of the servants of his independent contractor: *British Road Service Ltd v Arthur V Crutchley & Co Ltd* [1967] 2 All ER 785. In *Fairline Shipping Corpn v Adamson* [1975] QB 180, a director who was not himself a bailee, assumed responsibility for refrigerated goods and was held liable for carelessly allowing them to defrost.

[151] [2002] 1 AC 215.   [152] [2002] 1 AC 215, at [28].   [153] [2002] 1 AC 215, at [50].

the opportunity to commit the wrong is not enough to make the employer liable. He is liable only if the risk is one which experience shows is inherent in the nature of the business'.[154]

In the wake of *Lister*, then, it is unwise to regard earlier decisions treating wanton, egregious conduct as falling beyond the bounds of a course of employment as cast-iron precedents on vicarious liability. A moment's reflection reveals that child abuse, by whatever means, could never plausibly be viewed as a mere unauthorized mode of performing an authorized act. Instead, it is better simply to recognize that the decision in *Lister* establishes a new test for vicarious liability based upon language that stresses the intimate connection between the employee's tort and the nature of his employment.[155] Of course, while this approach goes a long way towards providing compensation to those who might otherwise go without (if forced to sue, for example, a relatively impecunious warden), it nonetheless gives rise to more problems than it solves. In particular, the language used in *Lister* is more in tune with non-delegable duty than vicarious liability.[156] Equally, as Lord Nicholls subsequently pointed out in *Dubai Aluminium Co Ltd v Salaam*, the close connection test 'affords no guidance on the type or degree of connection . . . [that will be] sufficiently close to prompt the legal conclusion that the risk of the wrongful act occurring, and any loss resulting . . . should fall on the firm or employer'.[157] In other words, in ensuring the claimants with a remedy in *Lister*, the House of Lords adopted a very vague test the application of which will prove remarkably popular,[158] but no doubt problematic in the future.

(2) FRAUD

Leaving cases involving violence of one form or another to one side, it is clear that an employee's fraud may also form the basis of vicarious liability. *Barwick v English Joint Stock Bank*,[159] made this clear where a bank manager caused his employers to be held vicariously liable for his fraudulent misrepresentations. Before 1912 it had been thought that the employer would only be liable for wilful wrongdoing where, as in *Barwick's* case, the act was done for his benefit. In that year, however, *Lloyd v Grace, Smith & Co*[160] was decided by the House of Lords.

In an action to recover title deeds by C (who was a client of D, a firm of solicitors), the material point was whether the firm were liable for the act of their managing clerk, who, when C

---

[154] [2002] 1 AC 215, at [65]. It might be argued that the focus on the nature of the employer's business tends to blur the distinction between the employer's primary and vicarious liability (see *Balfon Trustees Ltd v Peterson* [2001] IRLR 758, at [28], *per* Laddie J). But the decision in *Lister* is assuredly based on the latter.

[155] In similar vein, see *Bazley v Curry* (1999) 174 DLR (4th) 45; *Jacobi v Griffiths* (1999) 174 DLR (4th) 71.

[156] *Lister v Hesley Hall Ltd* [2002] 1 AC 215, at [55] and [82]-[83], *per* Lords Hobhouse and Millett respectively.

[157] [2003] 2 AC 366.

[158] The test has already been adopted on many occasions: see *Dubai Aluminium v Salaam* [2003] 2 AC 366; *JJ Coughlan Ltd v Ruparelia* [2003] EWCA Civ 1057; *Marsh v Chief Constable of Lancashire* [2003] EWCA Civ 284; *Mattis v. Pollock* [2003] 1 WLR 2158; *Att-Gen v Hartwell* [2004] UKPC 12; *Bernard v Att-Gen of Jamaica* [2004] UKPC 47; *Brown v Robinson* [2004] UKPC 56; *Godden v Kent and Medway Strategic Health Authority* [2004] UKHC 1629; *Frans Maas (UK) Ltd v Samsung Electronics* [2004] 2 Lloyd's Rep 251; *Majrowski v Guy's and St Thomas' NHS Trust* [2006] UKHL 34. [159] (1867) LR 2 Exch 259.

[160] [1912] AC 716.

consulted him about selling her property and realizing a mortgage, fraudulently induced her to sign documents transferring those properties to him. The managing clerk was employed, among other things, to carry out conveyancing transactions. Although the firm derived no benefit from these frauds, perpetrated by their employee for his own purposes, they were held liable for his acts.

But the issue of vicarious liability in that case must be approached cautiously. The liability of an employer for a fraud perpetrated by an employee is not to be treated identically with liability for other forms of wrongdoing. Lord Keith put it this way:

[D]ishonest conduct is of a different character from blundering attempts to promote the employer's business interests involving negligent ways of carrying out the employer's work or excessive zeal and errors of judgment in the performance of it. Dishonest conduct perpetrated with no intention of benefiting the employer but solely with that of procuring a personal gain or advantage to the servant is governed, in the field of vicarious liability, by a set of principles and a line of authority of particular application.[161]

The key question where it is sought to make an employer vicariously liable for a fraud committed by the employee, ought on principle to be whether the fraud was intended to benefit the employer or the employee alone. If it is only intended to benefit the latter (as in *Lloyd*) and the fraud is not intimately bound up with the employee's employment,[162] it may well be preferable to view the employer's liability as turning on a non-delegable duty.[163] Certainly, in *Dubai Aluminium Co Ltd v Salaam*,[164] all the acts necessary to make the employee personally liable took place within the course of his employment and vicarious liability was accordingly imposed. By contrast, however, in *Crédit Lyonnais Bank Nederland NV v Export Credits Guarantee Department*,[165] part of the fraud was committed by the employee (by his non-tortious conduct) and part of it by a third party. The House of Lords therefore refused to combine the two sets of acts so as to make the employer vicariously liable for the combined acts of the two fraudsters.

SECTION 7 STATUTORY DUTY AND VICARIOUS LIABILITY

For a time it was unclear whether an employer could be held vicariously liable for an employee's breach of a statutory duty imposed directly on the employee but not the employer. Happily, the matter has now been resolved authoritatively in *Majrowski v*

---

[161] *Armagas Ltd v Mundogas SA, The Ocean Frost* [1986] AC 717.

[162] In *JJ Coughlan v Ruparelia* [2003] EWCA Civ 1057 the Court of Appeal stressed the importance of considering whether the transaction in question 'viewed fairly and properly' was the kind of transaction that forms part of the ordinary business of a solicitor.

[163] Certainly, relying on the emphasis placed on the delegation of the task of conveyancing in that case, there were those in the Australian Supreme Court who preferred to see *Lloyd* as a case of non-delegable duty: see *New South Wales v Lepore* [2003] HCA 4, at [110], *per* Gaudron J; at [235], *per* Gummow and Hayne JJ. Furthermore, it also worth noting that Lord Nicholls deliberately left this case to one side when considering the new test for vicarious liability in *Dubai Aluminium Co Ltd v Salaam* [2003] 2 AC 366, at [27]–[28].

[164] [2003] 1 Lloyd's Rep 65.   [165] [2000] 1 AC 486.

Guy's and St Thomas' NHS Trust where it was held that an employer can be so liable. In that case, Lord Nicholls said: 'Unless the statute expressly or impliedly indicates otherwise, the principle of vicarious liability is applicable where an employee commits a breach of a statutory obligation sounding in damages while acting in the course of his employment'.[166] So far as the Crown is concerned there is specific statutory provision. The rather obscurely worded s 2(3) of the Crown Proceedings Act 1947 has the effect of making the Crown liable for breaches of statutory duty by its employees.

FURTHER READING

Cane, 'Vicarious Liability for Sexual Abuse' (2000) 116 LQR 21

Feldthusen, 'Vicarious Liability for Sexual Torts' in Mullany and Linden (eds), *Torts Tomorrow: A Tribute to John Fleming* (1998)

McKendrick, 'Vicarious Liability and Independent Contractors – A Re-Examination' (1990) 53 MLR 770

Murphy, 'Juridical Foundations of Common Law Non-Delegable Duties' in Neyers (ed), *Emerging Issues in Tort Law* (2007)

Stevens, 'Non-Delegable Duties and Vicarious Liability' in Neyers (ed), *Emerging Issues in Tort Law* (2007)

Weekes, 'Vicarious Liability for Violent Employees' [2004] CLJ 53; Cane, 'Vicarious Liability for Sexual Abuse' (2000) 116 LQR 21

---

[166] [2006] UKHL 34, at [17].

25

CAPACITY AND PARTIES

SECTION 1 THE CROWN

(A) VICARIOUS LIABILITY

According to section 2(1) of the Crown Proceedings Act 1947, 'the Crown shall be subject to all those liabilities in tort to which, if it were a private person of full age and capacity, it would be subject in respect of torts committed by its servants or agents'. However, notwithstanding this general statement of the Crown's vicarious liability, it is also clear that an employee must *normally* be directly or indirectly appointed by the Crown and paid wholly out of the Consolidated Fund or other specified national funds for this vicarious liability to be triggered.[1] The Crown is not, therefore, vicariously liable for the torts of police officers,[2] or for the torts of borrowed employees.

The Act does not define the term 'Crown', yet it is clear that the Crown Proceedings Act 1947 does not apply to the employees of those bodies that are not deemed to be agents of the Crown. In such cases, the ordinary law affecting public bodies and public officers will apply, and it is clear that many public bodies fall outside the Act.[3] It is thus important to be able to determine which public bodies constitute agents of the Crown. Yet resolving this matter is often difficult. That said, it is certainly the case that the nature of the functions of the body in question and the extent to which it is under ministerial control, are especially relevant considerations.[4]

(B) NON-VICARIOUS LIABILITY

Section 2(1)(b) and (c) of the Crown Proceedings Act 1947 make the Crown liable for any breach of those duties owed at common law to employees, agents or independent contractors by an employer, and for any breach of the duties attaching at common law to the ownership, occupation, possession or control of property.

---

[1] Crown Proceedings Act 1947, s 2(6). The exception, under s 3, is that no such liability can be imposed in respect of the infringement of intellectual property rights except in accordance with s 3.

[2] For the liability of a chief constable to pay damages out of public funds to those harmed by a policeman's torts, see the Police Act 1996, s 88 and *Weir v Bettison* [2003] EWCA Civ 111.

[3] *Tamlin v Hannaford* [1950] 1 KB 18.

[4] *Bank voor Handel en Scheepvaart NV v Administrator of Hungarian Property* [1954] AC 584.

Section 2(1) does not seem sufficiently wide to take account of all the cases where an employer is liable otherwise than vicariously. While employers are frequently answerable for the acts of independent contractors – not because the independent contractor has committed a tort in the course of his work, but because the duty is a personal one imposed on the employer – section 2 would not seem wide enough to cover non-delegable duties of this sort.[5] The Crown is liable in tort to the same extent as private persons for breaches of statutory duty that have been imposed on it, provided the duty is also imposed on persons other than the Crown and its officers.[6] If the duty is imposed, not on the Crown, but directly on its employees, and an employee commits a tort while performing or purporting to perform those statutory functions, 'the liabilities of the Crown in respect of the tort shall be such as they would have been if those functions had been conferred or imposed solely by virtue of instructions lawfully given by the Crown'.[7] The Crown also has the same liability as other employers under the Employers' Liability (Defective Equipment) Act 1969.

(c) EXCEPTIONS

(1) JUDICIAL ERRORS

Section 2(5) of the Crown Proceedings Act 1947 provides that the Crown shall not be liable 'in respect of anything done or omitted to be done by any person while discharging or purporting to discharge any responsibilities of a judicial nature vested in him, or any responsibilities which he has in connection with the execution of the judicial process'. The first part of the subsection would be otiose if it merely provided that the Crown shall not be liable wherever the judge has the defence of 'judicial act'. It seems, therefore, that whatever doubts there may be about the liability of inferior courts for acts done in excess of jurisdiction which purport to be in discharge of the judicial function, the Crown is exempted from liability.[8] Presumably, also, the first part of the subsection extends not only to that limited class of bodies not being courts, *stricto sensu*, to which the defence of 'judicial acts' applies, but also to other administrative tribunals.

(2) ARMED FORCES

The Crown Proceedings (Armed Forces) Act 1987 repealed section 10 of the 1947 Act which prevented members of the armed forces suing the Crown in respect of injuries

---

[5] Cf *Egerton v Home Office* [1978] Crim LR 494 (a duty was owed to a sexual offender in prison to keep a protective watch to guard against his being attacked by fellow prisoners).

[6] Crown Proceedings Act 1947, s 2(2). The Occupiers' Liability Act 1957, s 6 provides that that Act shall bind the Crown and that the common duty of care imposed by it shall apply as a statutory duty for the purpose of the Crown Proceedings Act 1947.

[7] Crown Proceedings Act 1947, s 2(3). Presumably, this rule also applies where the duty in question is not also imposed on persons other than employees of the Crown.

[8] *Welsh v Chief Constable of the Merseyside Police* [1993] 1 All ER 692. Under s 31(1) of the Courts Act 2003, immunity is granted to a justice of the peace only in respect of acts or omissions 'in the execution of his duty as a justice of the peace', and then only so far as those acts or omissions fall 'within his jurisdiction'.

suffered in the course of their duties, caused by another member of the armed forces who was on duty. Beyond the statute, it was also established in *Mulcahy v Ministry of Defence*[9] that no alternative liability at common law exists. In that case, the Court of Appeal held that a serviceman did not owe his fellow servicemen a duty of care in war-like conditions for it would not be fair, just and reasonable to impose such a duty.[10]

(3) CERTAIN STATUTES IMPOSING LIABILITY IN TORT

It is doubtful whether the Crown is bound by statutes imposing tortious liability unless the particular statute has clearly made the Crown liable. However, most modern Acts making substantial changes in the law of torts have been made expressly applicable to the Crown.[11]

SECTION 2 CORPORATIONS

(A) LIABILITY

Where the liability of an ordinary employer for the acts of his employees is in issue, there are normally four possible situations.

(1) The act may be treated as the act of the employer himself so that no issue of vicarious liability arises.

(2) The employer has specifically directed the employee to commit the tort.[12]

(3) The employer is vicariously liable for the employee's acts in accordance with the principles discussed in the previous chapter.

(4) The employer is not vicariously liable for the employee because the act or omission in question falls outside the principles discussed in the previous chapter.[13]

The same four possibilities presumably also apply where the employer is a corporation. However, in addition, we must bear in mind a fifth possibility specific to corporations as set out in *Lennard's Carrying Co Ltd v Asiatic Petroleum Co Ltd*[14] by Viscount Haldane:

[it] has no mind of its own any more than it has a body of its own; its active and directing will must consequently be sought in the person of somebody who for some purposes may be called an agent, but who is really the directing mind and will of the corporation . . . That

---

[9] [1996] QB 732.

[10] Note that this decision must now be read in the light of *Barrett v Enfield London Borough Council* [2001] 2 AC 550 and *Phelps v Hillingdon London Borough Council* [2000] 3 WLR 776.

[11] Eg, Law Reform (Contributory Negligence) Act 1945, the Congenital Disabilities (Civil Liability) Act 1976, the Civil Liability (Contribution) Act 1978 and the Limitation Act 1980. Statutes about which the doubt persists include the Defamation Acts of 1952 and 1996.

[12] See, eg, *Campbell v Paddington Corpn* [1911] 1 KB 869.

[13] See, eg, *Poulton v London and South Western Rly Co* (1867) LR 2 QB 534.   [14] [1915] AC 705.

person may be under the direction of the shareholders in general meeting; that person may be the board of directors itself.[15]

In order, then, to be the act of the company in this sense, the act must be of 'somebody who is not merely a servant or agent for whom the company is liable on the footing *respondeat superior*, but somebody for whom the company is liable because his action is the very action of the company itself'.[16] If somebody of such authority in the company acts tortiously on behalf of the company, the company is liable, not by way of vicarious liability, but because the tortious act is that of the company itself.[17] On this reasoning, a corporation may even be liable for torts that require a particular state of mind, such as harassment.[18]

(B) POWER TO SUE

Corporations (but not their members[19]) can sue for any tort other than those of which, in the nature of things, they could not be victims – for example, assault. That said, in the context of defamation – for which a corporation may in principle sue – it is important to identify whether the words in question refer to the corporation or an individual. Thus, to say of the sole owner of a company that he is a 'bloody crook' is a slur on the individual rather than his company.[20]

SECTION 3 PARTNERSHIPS AND LIMITED LIABILITY PARTNERSHIPS

Partners may be jointly and severally liable to any persons not themselves partners[21] for torts committed by any one of them either while acting in the ordinary course of the business of the firm, or with the authority of his fellow partners.[22] The claimant must

---

[15] [1915] AC 705, at 713.

[16] [1915] AC 705. In *The Lady Gwendolen* [1965] P 294, the Guinness company were liable for their managerial failure to detect and stop the habitual practice of their ship's captain in going full steam ahead in fog, relying on the fact that his ship was fitted with radar.

[17] The director may be personally liable as bailee when goods are stored with his company and he assumes personal responsibility for their storage: *Fairline Shipping Corpn v Adamson* [1975] QB 180. For other circumstances in which a company director may be personally liable see *C Evans & Sons Ltd v Spritebrand Ltd* [1985] 2 All ER 415. Cf *Williams v Natural Life Health Foods Ltd* [1998] 1 WLR 830 (no personal assumption of responsibility by a director); *Standard Chartered Bank v Pakistan National Shipping Corp (No 2)* [2000] 1 Lloyd's Rep 218 (no liability where a director was merely carrying out his constitutional role in the company's governance). See also Watts, 'The Company's *Alter Ego* – An Impostor in Private Law' (2000) 116 LQR 525.

[18] See, eg, *Mainstream Properties v Young* [2005] EWCA Civ 861.

[19] Thus if a shareholder suffers a loss in the value of his shareholding due to a tort committed against the company, it is the company, not the shareholder who can recover: see *Johnson v Gore Wood & Co* [2002] 2 AC 1.

[20] *Shendish Manor Ltd v Coleman* [2001] EWCA Civ 913.

[21] *Mair v Wood* 1948 SC 83 (M was one of five partners of a trawler injured through negligence of another partner. Under neither the Partnership Act 1890 nor under any common-law rule unaffected by the Act could the other three partners be vicariously liable for the negligence of one partner to a fellow partner).

[22] Partnership Act 1890, ss 10 and 12; *Dubai Aluminium Co Ltd v Salaam* [2003] 1 All ER 97.

show that he relied on the individual partner's status *as a partner*.[23] In addition to this vicarious liability, each partner may have a primary duty in tort: for example, the occupier's duty of care to visitors is owed by each partner in a partnership that occupies those premises.[24]

Where the partnership has been established as a limited liability partnership,[25] the commission of a tort by any one partner will render liable both that partner personally, and the limited liability partnership (as principal). The other partners will not be liable personally on the face of the legislation. But one important issue that is unclear from the Limited Liability Partnerships Act 2000 is whether the personal involvement of one partner in linking a client to a second partner can invoke that partner's personal liability. Suppose senior partner X recommends to a client, C, that junior partner Y should do C's conveyance. Suppose further that X misrepresents that Y is competent. In such a case, it is clear that Y could be held liable for a negligently performed conveyance, as could the limited liability partnership. But would X remain immune, or would the personal assumption of responsibility principle that causes a director to be personally liable in the case of a limited company[26] be applied in this context, too?

SECTION 4 HUSBAND AND WIFE

The liability of one spouse for the torts of the other is to be decided on the same principles as those applying where the parties are not married. Put simply, there is no presumption that one is responsible for the other.[27] As regards liability, *inter se*, section 1(1) of the Law Reform (Husband and Wife) Act 1962 provides that 'each of the parties to a marriage shall have the like right of action in tort against the other as if they were not married'. This provision is not so peculiar as it may first seem because, of course, the first spouse may well be a mere nominal defendant, the real defendant being an insurance company (for example, where spouse A is injured by spouse B's negligent driving[28]). Notwithstanding section 1(1), Parliament was also anxious to discourage actions founded on petty grievances between spouses. As such, section 1(2) allows the court to stay the action 'if it appears . . . that no substantial benefit would accrue to either party from the continuation of the proceedings'.[29]

---

[23] *Nationwide Building Society v Lewis* [1998] Ch 482. Note that the existence of a partnership may be implied from an agreement to carry on a business in common even where the term 'partnership' is not expressly used: *Grant v Langley* [2001] WL 513090.   [24] See *Meekins v Henson* [1964] 1 QB 472.

[25] This legal entity was created by the Limited Liability Partnerships Act 2000.

[26] *Williams v Natural Life Health Foods Ltd* [1998] 1 WLR 830.

[27] Law Reform (Married Women and Tortfeasors) Act 1935, s 3. Husband and wife can be jointly liable in conspiracy: *Midland Bank Trust Co Ltd v Green (No 3)* [1982] Ch 529.

[28] Where another negligent driver is involved, his or her insurers may claim a contribution from the insurers of the negligent spouse in accordance with the principles discussed in Section 7 of this chapter.

[29] Note, too, the provision in s 1(2)(b) to allow property disputes to be dealt with under the Married Women's Property Act 1882, s 17.

SECTION 5 MENTALLY DISORDERED PERSONS

The problems here arise mainly from the incomplete analyses often made by the judges of the states of mind required in particular torts. The case most directly in point is *Morriss v Marsden*.[30]

D violently attacked C, a complete stranger, while he was standing in the entrance hall of a hotel, and D was sued for battery. The defence raised was insanity. The judge found that D was not in a condition of automatism or trance at the time of the attack on C, but that his mind directed the blows which he struck. He also found that at the material time D was a certifiable lunatic who knew the nature and quality of his act but, because of his lunacy, did not know that what he was doing was wrong. He nevertheless held the defence of insanity to be inapplicable.

The case is therefore authority for the proposition that if a mentally disordered person has that state of mind which is required for liability in battery, then his insanity is no defence.[31] All that is required in battery is that the defendant must intend to strike the blow at the claimant. The judge in *Morriss* found that the defendant did so intend, and that it therefore followed that he was liable. At a more general level, the case also supports the proposition that, in tort (as distinct from criminal law), a defendant who intentionally invades the claimant's protected interest will not be excused simply because he was unaware that the invasion was a wrongful act. Thus, as Stable J observed in *Morriss v Marsden*:

if a person in a condition of complete automatism inflicted grievous injury, that would not be actionable. In the same way, if a sleepwalker inadvertently, without intention or without carelessness, broke a valuable vase, that would not be actionable.[32]

The logic of this *dictum* means that a defence will lie in respect of all torts – including those of 'strict' liability – in which the defendant's conduct was, because of his mental disorder, involuntary. But there will also be a defence even if the conduct was intended, but the tort in question – for example, simple conspiracy – requires an improper purpose or malice.

---

[30] [1952] 1 All ER 925.

[31] This is so even if the defendant's insanity causes him to be under a delusion about the surrounding circumstances. The critical thing is simply that he possessed the state of mind required by the tort in relation to the act done: *Buckley and Toronto Transportation Commission v Smith Transport Ltd* [1946] 4 DLR 721.

[32] [1952] 1 All ER 925, at 927.

SECTION 6 CHILDREN

(A) LIABILITY

A person is a child until he attains the age of 18 years.[33] Childhood as such is not a defence: but like all other defendants, a child is not liable for a specific tort if it is shown that he lacked the required state of mind. Should a one-year-old child pick up a letter defamatory of X, written by his father, and throw it through the window, whereupon Y picks it up and reads it, X will have no cause of action for libel against the baby. On the other hand, a 15-year-old youth who pushes a man into a swimming pool, can be held liable in negligence and trespass.[34]

(1) WHERE THE ACT OF THE CHILD IS ALSO A BREACH OF CONTRACT

With certain exceptions, a child is not liable for breach of contract.[35] Therefore, where the act of the child is merely an improper performance of one of the acts contemplated by such a contract, it will not be open to the person aggrieved to sue him in tort so as to evade the contractual immunity. On the other hand, if the act complained of, though performed upon the occasion of a contract, is independent of it, the claimant may then sue in tort. Of course, this rule is difficult to apply in marginal cases, but its judicial recognition is clear. Thus, a child who had possession of goods under a hire-purchase agreement, and who wrongfully disposed of them to a third party was liable to the true owner for the independent tort of detinue which he committed by wrongfully disposing of them.[36] The hirer of a mare, hired for riding only, is liable in tort for doing an act of a nature not contemplated by the contract (namely jumping the mare); but if he were merely to ride her too far, this would not be an act of a different nature and no action in tort would lie.[37] The fact that the contract was in both cases void against the child would not, *per se*, prevent him from being liable in tort.

In this context, the question of suing a child in tort arises most often where he has obtained goods or a loan of money under contract by misrepresenting his real age. In such cases, the courts have held that no action in deceit will lie because that would be tantamount to allowing the enforcement of a void contract.[38]

---

[33] Family Law Reform Act 1969, s 1(1).

[34] *Williams v Humphrey* (1975) *Times*, 20 February. Cf *Wilson v Pringle* [1987] QB 237 (13-year-old schoolboy pulling bag off another).   [35] See Minors' Contracts Act 1987.

[36] *Ballett v Mingay* [1943] KB 281.

[37] *Burnard v Haggis* (1863) 14 CBNS 45; *Jennings v Rundall* (1799) 8 Term Rep 335. See also *Walley v Holt* (1876) 35 LT 631 and *Fawcett v Smethurst* (1914) 84 LJKB 473.

[38] *R Leslie Ltd v Sheill* [1914] 3 KB 607, at 612, *per* Lord Sumner MR.

(2) LIABILITY OF THE PARENT

Although a claimant may have no cause of action against the child, he may sometimes be able to recover from the child's parent. The parent is liable only where he is accountable according to some other general principle of tort law. He may be vicariously liable – for example, if the child is acting as her father's chauffeur and drives the car negligently. Similarly, the father will be liable if he instigates the son's commission of a tort, and he will be liable if he himself has been personally negligent.[39] In other words, a father is not necessarily liable merely because his son has thrown a stone through his neighbour's window. Unless the father ordered him to do so, or unless his negligent supervision is proved to have caused the act complained of, he will not be liable.

(B) CAPACITY TO SUE

Except that he must normally sue by his next friend, a child is in the same position as any other claimant when suing in tort. A child may sue either parent, and may wish to do so where the parent has an insurance policy (usually comprehensive household insurance) which covers the particular liability.[40] The Court of Appeal has warned against the danger of too readily imposing liability for the 'rough and tumble of family life'.[41] And it is certainly well established that a parent (or someone with quasi-parental responsibility) may lawfully exercise reasonable chastisement in respect of the child.[42] But is there not a danger here that children's rights would be circumscribed?

One case of particular importance in this context is *Stubbings v Webb*.[43] By imposing an absolute six-year-limitation period for actions in trespass to the person, victims of child abuse are effectively denied a remedy for their suffering. Another matter to bear in mind is the capacity of children to sue their parents for injuries sustained before birth; but this was dealt with in Chapter 3.

SECTION 7 JOINT TORTS

(A) CATEGORIES

There are three broad categories of circumstances where one person may suffer damage as the result of torts committed by two or more defendants: joint tortfeasors, several

---

[39] *Donaldson v McNiven* [1952] 2 All ER 691; *Newton v Edgerley* [1959] 3 All ER 337. The duty of school authorities is also to take the care which a reasonable parent would take: see, eg, *Ricketts v Erith Borough Council* [1943] 2 All ER 629 and *Rich v LCC* [1953] 2 All ER 376.

[40] See, eg, *Ash v Lady Ash* (1696) Comb 357 (a daughter sued her mother in false imprisonment and battery and succeeded, subject to a new trial, to fix damages). See also *Young v Rankin* 1934 SC 499 (a child, who was injured by the negligent driving of his father, could sue his father).

[41] *Surtees v Kingston-upon-Thames Borough Council* [1991] 2 FLR 559.

[42] See, eg, *R v H* [2001] 2 FLR 431 (allegation of assault by father of his son).   [43] [1993] AC 498.

concurrent tortfeasors causing the same damage and several tortfeasors causing different damage.[44]

(1) JOINT TORTFEASORS[45]

In this category there are the following:[46]

(a) An employer and employee in those cases where the employer is vicariously liable for the tort of the employee.[47]

(b) One person together with another whom he prompts to commit a tort. Thus, for example, a landlord who invited his lodger to help him detect an escape of gas on the premises by striking a match was a joint tortfeasor along with the lodger in respect of the damage caused by the ensuing explosion.[48] But a person who merely facilitated (rather than procured) a tort would not be a joint tortfeasor.[49]

(c) Two or more persons who are in breach of a duty imposed on them jointly. Thus, two occupiers of the same premises are joint tortfeasors if they are sued by a visitor for failure to take reasonable care in respect of those premises.

(d) All those persons who take 'concerted action to a common end'[50] where, in the course of executing that joint purpose, any one of them commits a tort. The liability of partners for a tort committed by one of them in connection with the firm's business, the director 'sufficiently bound up in the company's acts',[51] and the liability of joint employers of an employee who commits a tort in the course of his employment, are three examples. *Brooke v Bool*[52] furnishes another. The landlord and his lodger were looking for an escape of gas, and an explosion occurred as a result of the careless exposure of a naked light to the escaping gas by the lodger. Besides holding that they were joint tortfeasors because the landlord had 'permitted and invited'[53] the lodger to do the act, the court held that they were joint tortfeasors for the further reasons that 'the enterprise in which . . . [they] were engaged was the joint enterprise of both, and that the act which was the immediate cause of the explosion was their joint act done in pursuance of a concerted purpose'.[54] Similarly, where the first

---

[44] For full discussion, see *Clerk and Lindsell on Torts* (2006), ch 4.

[45] Carty, 'Joint Tortfeasance and Assistance Liability' [1999] *Legal Studies* 489.

[46] Cf Scrutton LJ in *The Koursk* [1924] P 140, at 155.   [47] See ch 24.

[48] *Brooke v Bool* [1928] 2 KB 578.   [49] *PLG Research Ltd v Ardon International Ltd* [1993] FSR 197.

[50] *The Koursk* [1924] P 140, at 152, *per* Bankes LJ. Directors may be joint tortfeasors with a limited company where they directed or procured the tortious act, or informed the company for the express purpose of doing a wrongful act: *Rainham Chemical Works Ltd v Belvedere Fish Guano Co* [1921] 2 AC 465, at 476, *per* Lord Buckmaster; or if, after formation, the company adopted a deliberate policy of wrongdoing: *Oertli (T) A-G v E J Bowman (London) Ltd* [1956] RPC 282, at 292.

[51] *Koninklijke Philips Electronics NV v Princo Digital Disc GmbH* [2003] EWHC 2588.

[52] [1928] 2 KB 578. Perhaps *Scarsbrook v Mason* [1961] 3 All ER 767 furnishes the most remarkable example. There it was held that where passengers and the driver of a car combine on equal terms for the enterprise of a specific journey by the car of another, each is jointly liable for the driver's negligence.

[53] [1928] 2 KB 578, at 585, *per* Salter J.   [54] [1928] 2 KB 578, at 585, *per* Salter J.

defendant imprisoned the claimant, and the second defendant threatened to strike the claimant if he resisted, they were joint tortfeasors in respect of the claimant's false imprisonment even though the second defendant's act was also an assault.[55]

The Porter Committee summarized the position in defamation as follows:[56]

Where defamatory matter is contained in a book, periodical or newspaper, there is normally a series of publications each of which constitutes a separate tort. First, there is a publication by the author to the publisher for which the author is solely liable. Secondly, there is the publication by the author and publisher jointly to the printer, for which the author and publisher are jointly liable. Thirdly, there is the publication of the printed work to the trade and the public, for which the author, publisher and printer are jointly liable.

(2) SEVERAL CONCURRENT TORTFEASORS CAUSING THE SAME DAMAGE

Several, or separate, or independent tortfeasors are of two kinds: either those whose tortious acts combine to produce the same damage, or those whose acts cause different damage, to the same claimant. It is convenient to call the first group *several concurrent tortfeasors*, and they alone are illustrated in this section, which is concerned with acts that do not fit into any of the four sub-categories of joint tortfeasors just listed, but which result in the infliction of the same damage to the claimant. In *Drinkwater v Kimber*,[57] a passenger in a motor car was injured in a collision between that car and another. Morris LJ said that the two drivers, both of whom were negligent, 'were separate tortfeasors whose concurrent acts caused injury to the female claimant'. *Thompson v LCC*[58] provides a further example.

C's house was damaged when its foundations subsided due to a combination of two things: first, negligent excavation by D1 and, secondly, a water company, D2, negligently allowing water to escape from their main.

Finally, the facts in *The Koursk* also illustrate a case in which there was only one unit of damage that was impossible to divide between the various tortfeasors.[59]

The Koursk, while sailing in convoy, negligently changed course so that it bore down on the *Clan Chisholm*, which was careless in failing to reverse its engines in order to avoid a collision. Immediately after the impact, the *Clan Chisholm* collided with the *Itria*. Having recovered damages against the *Clan Chisholm* for an amount less than the loss suffered (because of a special statutory provision), the *Itria* sued *The Koursk*. *The Koursk* and *Clan Chisholm* were held not to be joint tortfeasors, but only several tortfeasors causing the same damage.

---

[55] *Boyce v Douglas* (1807) 1 Camp 60. See also the view of Bankes LJ (at 149) in *The Koursk* [1924] P 140, that if X, Y and Z conspired to attack C, and X and Y carried out the attack, the fact that X and Y were sued in battery, and Z was sued in conspiracy, would not prevent them from being joint tortfeasors.

[56] Cmd 7536, at p 29. If C must prove malice in order to defeat a plea of qualified privilege, only Ds who are malicious are joint tortfeasors: *Gardiner v Moore* [1969] 1 QB 55.

[57] [1952] 2 QB 281, at 292. See also *Fitzgerald v Lane* [1989] AC 328.

[58] [1899] 1 QB 840. Cf *Sadler v Great Western Rly Co* [1896] AC 450.   [59] [1924] P 140.

(3) SEVERAL TORTFEASORS CAUSING DIFFERENT DAMAGE

Where two or more persons not acting in concert cause different damage to the same claimant, they are treated differently in law from either joint or several concurrent tortfeasors. In the straightforward kind of case, the two defendants inflict quite separate harm on the claimant. For example, the first defendant gouges out the claimant's eye, and the second defendant fractures his skull, whereupon the first defendant is answerable only for the damage resulting from the loss of the eye and the second defendant solely for the damage attributable to the fracture of the skull. Similarly, suppose that a motorist carelessly knocked down a pedestrian who sustained multiple injuries to his leg, and a surgeon later amputated the wrong leg. Since the motorist would not be answerable for the further damage caused to the pedestrian by the surgeon's negligence, the motorist and the surgeon would be several tortfeasors causing different damage to the same claimant.

While the notional distinction between this category and several concurrent tortfeasors is clear in theory, there are some cases in which it is very difficult to decide whether there was an indivisible unit of damage, or whether the harm was capable of apportionment among the several defendants. The courts appear to have taken a sensible attitude in such cases, avoiding, if possible, saddling any one defendant with responsibility for more harm than he has caused. Accordingly, they display a marked a preparedness to declare harm to be divisible.[60] Thus, in the common kinds of case of harm caused by the independent acts of various defendants – for example, pollution of rivers, or nuisance by smell or noise – the courts will not hold each defendant liable for the entire damage. They will endeavour to ascertain the respective contributions to the harm made by each defendant, and, failing that, they will generally apportion the loss equally between them.[61]

Flooding cases, however, can present difficulties. If C's land is flooded for 30 days by the combined flood water of the first defendant and the second defendant, and would have been flooded for 15 days by the flood water of either of them, each is liable for 15-days' loss of farming activity. If, on the other hand, the flooding does not hinder the claimant's work, but actually destroys his crops in circumstances where the flood water of either the first defendant or the second defendant alone would not have destroyed the crops, the first and second defendants will both be liable for the entire loss – the harm being indivisible. When the act of the defendant impinges on existing circumstances – for example, where the first and second defendants are already discharging water into a stream and not causing a flood – and the third defendant, knowing of the

---

[60] See, eg, *Royal Brompton Hospital NHS Trust v Hammond (No 3)* [2002] 1 WLR 1397; *Niru Battery Manufacturing Co v Milestone Trading Ltd (No 2)* [2003] 2 All ER (Comm) 365.

[61] *Bank View Mills Ltd v Nelson Corpn* [1942] 2 All ER 477, especially *per* Stable J at 483 (revsd [1943] KB 337); *Pride of Derby and Derbyshire Angling Association Ltd v British Celanese Ltd* [1953] 1 All ER 179. See also *Dingle v Associated Newspapers Ltd* [1961] 1 All ER 897, at 916, *per* Devlin LJ. The point was not discussed in the House of Lords: [1964] AC 371. Sometimes the cumulative effect of D1 and D2's actions is greater than the sum of their respective contributions – this does not deter the courts from making them liable proportionately to the amount of harm which each would have caused in any event.

first and second defendants acts, discharges such a further amount as causes the claimant's lands to be flooded, then the third defendant is answerable for the entire flood damage.

Another difficult case concerns a claimant who has contracted mesothelioma in consequence of wrongful exposure to asbestos dust on the part of a number of former employers. In *Barker v Corus UK Ltd*,[62] it was held that where more than one employer had been in breach of a duty (and may therefore have been responsible for the claimant's mesothelioma), liability should be distributed among the various former employers according to their respective contributions to the risk of contracting the disease (gauged according to the length and intensity of exposure to asbestos dust[63]). While this indicates a clear desire to treat each employer as a several tortfeasor,[64] it is not at all clear why the different periods of risk were viewed as different damage, or even damage at all (given that risk is not generally treated as actionable loss in negligence law[65]). This difficulty, and others besides,[66] prompted the government to introduce legislation designed to reverse the decision in *Barker*, and to put in its place some form of statutory basis for claims by mesothelioma victims. This has now occurred in the shape of the Compensation Act 2006 (discussed fully in Chapter 5). But the Act only applies to cases of mesothelioma, leaving in doubt what would happen in the case of other forms of industrial diseases.

(B) DISTINGUISHING BETWEEN JOINT TORTFEASORS, SEVERAL CONCURRENT TORTFEASORS AND OTHER TORTFEASORS

There are four points of note that can be made in relation to the distinctions that exist between the various categories of multiple tortfeasors.

(1) Concurrent tortfeasors, whether joint or several, are each answerable in full for the whole damage caused to the claimant. Several non-concurrent tortfeasors are merely answerable for that damage which each has caused. It is therefore often of prime importance to decide whether the defendants were acting in concert. Suppose that A and B are engaged on a hunting expedition and both of them simultaneously fire across a highway at game beyond the highway. If a shot injures a highway user, but it is not known which of A or B fired it, they are joint tortfeasors acting in concert, enabling the claimant to recover full damages from either.[67] If, however, they are several tortfeasors, they have not

---

[62] [2006] 2 WLR 1027.

[63] [2006] 2 WLR 1027, at [48] and [109], *per* Lords Hoffmann and Rodger respectively.

[64] [2006] 2 WLR 1027, at [62], *per* Lord Scott.

[65] This point was made in the speeches of both Lord Rodger and Baroness Hale.

[66] The most prominent other problem was identified by Lord Rodger: namely, that he could see no 'logical or otherwise compelling connection between the *Fairchild* exception and the introduction of several liability': [2006] 2 WLR 1027, at [87].　　　　　　　　　　　　　　[67] *Arneil v Paterson* [1931] AC 560.

committed the same damage (for only one has caused damage), and the success of the action depends on proof of the commission of a tort by the one who is sued.[68] Questions of divisible harm do not arise where the defendants are joint tortfeasors because each joint tortfeasor is liable in full for all the harm sustained by the claimant.

(2) Satisfaction[69] by any concurrent tortfeasor discharges the liability of all the others, whereas satisfaction by a several non-concurrent one does not.[70]

(3) The courts are less willing to exercise their discretion under the Civil Procedure Rules to allow joinder of the defendants where the defendants concerned are not concurrent tortfeasors.

(4) There is in general a right to contribution in the case of concurrent tortfeasors, but not in respect of other tortfeasors.

(c) JOINT TORTFEASORS AND SEVERAL CONCURRENT TORTFEASORS

The distinction between joint and several concurrent tortfeasors is of much less importance since the enactment of the Law Reform (Married Woman and Tortfeasors) Act 1935. Section 6(1) of that Act[71] abolished the rule in *Brinsmead v Harrison*[72] according to which a judgment against one joint tortfeasor barred a separate action, or the continuance of the first action, against the others.[73]

The following two rules apply to both joint and several concurrent tortfeasors.

(1) A claimant who has obtained judgment against one wrongdoer for any damage is free to obtain judgment later against anyone else jointly liable for that damage.[74]

(2) The damages in the later actions can exceed the award in the first action. However, the claimant is not entitled to costs in any such later action unless the court is of the opinion that there were reasonable grounds for bringing that action at this later stage.[75]

---

[68] Cf *Cook v Lewis* [1952] 1 DLR 1.

[69] But note that a mere accord – ie, an agreement by C to accept some consideration in substitution for his strict legal remedy – with a several concurrent tortfeasor does not necessarily have this effect: everything turns on the interpretation of the accord: *Jameson v Central Electricity Generating Board* [2000] 1 AC 455; *Heaton v AXA Equity & Law Life Assurance Society plc* [2002] UKHL 15.

[70] And see *Bryanston Finance Ltd v de Vries* [1975] QB 703. For the effect of C's accepting payment into court by D1 on his right to sue those others jointly liable, see *Townsend v Stone Toms & Partners* [1981] 2 All ER 690.

[71] Section 6(1) has been repealed but substantially re-enacted in the Civil Liability (Contribution) Act 1978, s 1.

[72] (1872) LR 7 CP 547.

[73] If C had an unsatisfied judgment against D1 and a retrial is ordered of his action against D2 the judgment against D1 does not prevent C from recovering judgment against D2: *Wah Tat Bank Ltd v Chan Cheng Kum* [1975] AC 507.   [74] Civil Liability (Contribution) Act 1978, s 3.

[75] Civil Liability (Contribution) Act 1978, s 4.

(D) CONTRIBUTION

(1) SCOPE

Section 1(1) of the Civil Liability (Contribution) Act 1978 provides that 'any person liable in respect of any damage suffered by another person may recover contribution from any other person liable in respect of the same damage (whether jointly with him or otherwise)'. At one time, the courts gave a wide interpretation to the meaning of the phrase 'same damage'.[76] However, the House of Lords overruled this broad approach in *Royal Brompton Hospital NHS Trust v Hammond (No 3)*.[77]

A firm of architects had negligently issued extension certificates to contractors in respect of certain construction work commissioned by a developer. The building work was delayed and the developer sued the architects in respect of their negligence. The architects were unable to claim a contribution from the contractors who actually carried out the delayed construction. The contractors were responsible for delayed construction *per se*, whereas the architects (by issuing the extension certificates) had caused the developer to lose the opportunity to sue the contractors for liquidated damages in respect of that delay. The question was whether the loss of opportunity to sue for liquidated damages was to be regarded as the same damage as the delay, *per se*.

Their Lordships insisted that the words 'liable in respect of the same damage' were to receive their ordinary and natural meaning and held that the loss of opportunity to sue for liquidated damage was not the same damage as the delayed construction.

(2) WHO MAY CLAIM A CONTRIBUTION?

The Civil Liability (Contribution) Act 1978 reaffirms the general principle that a person who is liable is entitled to claim contribution from anyone else who is also liable.[78] This applies even if an out-of-court settlement is reached. Thus, if a defendant can show that, assuming that the factual basis of the claim against him could be established, he would have been liable, he may claim a contribution from anyone else who would have been liable with him.[79] If the defendant has settled because he was doubtful about his liability in law (even though the facts were established), he can obtain a contribution only if he can prove that he was legally answerable, however *bona fide* and reasonable his decision to settle the claim. Furthermore, if he were liable at the time he made, was ordered to make, or agreed to make the payment, he is still entitled to recover a contribution, even though he has since ceased to be liable either because of the expiry of a limitation period, or otherwise.[80] And the right to claim a contribution passes on the

---

[76] For details, see *Friends' Provident Life Office v Hillier Parker May and Rowden* [1997] QB 85.

[77] [2002] UKHL 14.

[78] Civil Liability (Contribution) Act 1978, s 1(1). A contribution may still be claimed from D2 where D1 made a payment in kind (ie, free remedial work): *Baker & Davies plc v Leslie Wilks* [2005] 3 All ER 603.

[79] Civil Liability (Contribution) Act 1978, s 1(4); *Arab Monetary Fund v Hashim (No 8)* (1993) *Times*, 17 June.   [80] Civil Liability (Contribution) Act 1978, s 1(2).

defendant's death to his personal representatives, whether or not his liability had, before his death, been established or admitted.[81]

(3) THOSE FROM WHOM A CONTRIBUTION MAY BE CLAIMED

Contribution is recoverable from anyone who is liable for the same damage,[82] and on the authority of *K v P*[83] it is clear that the defence of *ex turpi causa* may not be raised in order to defeat a claim for contribution.[84] If one party was originally liable, but then ceased to be liable since the time the damage occurred – perhaps because the claimant waived his claim against that person – he would nonetheless remain liable to make a contribution to the other tortfeasor, if that second tortfeasor were to be sued.[85] By contrast, where a settlement is reached with tortfeasor X, but a later action is pursued against tortfeasor Y, the question of whether X (who settled) may later be required to contribute to the damages later paid by Y will turn on the construction of the settlement agreement. *Jameson v Central Electricity Generating Board*[86] is the leading case.

Jameson was exposed to asbestos at work due to the fault both of his employer, X, and the CEGB where the exposure occurred. Jameson agreed a 'full and final settlement' with X. When Jameson died, his executors made an additional claim for loss of dependency under the Fatal Accidents Act 1976 from CEGB. It was held that this action could not be brought because of the finality of the wording of the settlement between X and Jameson. As such, there was no prospect of CEGB paying the additional sum, and then seeking a contribution to this sum from X.

If, on its proper construction, the settlement between X and Jameson had not ruled out a subsequent action brought by his executors against CEGB, then, in principle, X could have been required to contribute.[87] More commonly, the period of limitation for the claimant suing that defendant may have expired (the limitation period being two years after the right to contribution arose).[88] So long as contribution is sought before the expiry of the limitation period, however, the contribution will be payable.[89]

---

[81] *Ronex Properties Ltd v John Laing Construction Ltd* [1983] QB 398.

[82] Civil Liability (Contribution) Act 1978, s 1(1).   [83] [1993] Ch 140.

[84] On the other hand, those factors relevant to raising the defence are also factors of which the court may take note in fixing the level of contribution (which may be 0%).

[85] Civil Liability (Contribution) Act 1978, s 1(3).

[86] [2000] 1 AC 455. For a similar 'constructionist' approach, see *Co-operative Retail Services Ltd v Taylor Young Partnership Ltd* [2002] UKHL 17. But note that a properly interested third party may later invite the court to re-examine the meaning of any such agreement: *AB v British Coal Corp* [2004] EWHC 1372.

[87] See, eg, *Logan v Uttlesford District Council and Hammond* [1986] NLJ Rep 541.

[88] The relevant date is the date of judgment or, where the case has been settled out of court, the date of the agreement to pay: Limitation Act 1980, s 10(3), (4). The period may be extended where the person seeking contribution is under a disability or is the victim of fraud, concealment or mistake Limitation Act 1980, s 10(5).

[89] Civil Liability (Contribution) Act 1978, s 1(3). The subsection has a proviso that he is not liable if, on the expiry of the period of limitation or prescription, the right on which the claim against him was based, was extinguished. But because most tort actions are not extinguished by limitation – conversion is the important exception – this proviso is of very limited importance in tort.

(4) AMOUNT OF CONTRIBUTION RECOVERABLE

By section 2(1) of the Civil Liability (Contribution) Act 1978:

in any proceedings for contribution under section 1 above the amount of the contribution recoverable from any person shall be such as may be found by the court to be just and equitable having regard to the extent of that person's responsibility for the damage in question.

Section 2(2) of the same Act provides that:

The court shall have power in any such proceedings to exempt any person from liability to make contribution, or to direct that the contribution to be recovered from any person shall amount to a complete indemnity.

Neither causation nor culpability is the sole test to be applied in making the apportionment.[90] Both the moral blameworthiness and the extent to which the act is directly connected to the damage caused are material in making this apportionment.[91] This view that moral blame is not the only criterion is supported by the cases which have authorized apportionment between a defendant liable for negligence at common law and one who was not negligent but who was nonetheless in breach of a strict statutory duty.[92] On the other hand, it has been held that moral blame alone will suffice where there is no causative potency on the part of one of the defendants.[93] This seems odd because it means that one can be liable to pay a contribution even though, if sued directly, one would incur no liability. Less controversially, where two employers are both vicariously liable for the tort of a shared employee, it has been held to follow from the fact that there is no requirement of fault on the part of the employers held vicariously liable, that their liability should be shared equally.[94]

If there is a limit on the amount for which a defendant could be liable to the claimant, by reason of an agreement between the claimant and the defendant, or if the amount would have been reduced by reason of the Law Reform (Contributory Negligence) Act 1945,[95] then the maximum amount of contribution is that amount so limited or reduced.[96]

It will be noted that the statute contemplates tortfeasors being entitled to a complete indemnity in some circumstances. Where, for example, a person who knows that he is

---

[90] *Weaver v Commercial Process Co Ltd* (1947) 63 TLR 466.

[91] *Miraflores (Owners) v George Livanos (Owners)* [1967] 1 AC 826, at 845, *per* Lord Pearce; *Brown v Thompson* [1968] 2 All ER 708, at 709, *per* Winn LJ; *Cavanagh v London Passenger Transport Executive* (1956) *Times*, 23 October, *per* Devlin J.

[92] *Eg, Jerred v Roddam Dent & Son Ltd* [1948] 2 All ER 104; *Dooley v Cammell Laird & Co Ltd* [1951] 1 Lloyd's Rep 271.   [93] *Brian Warwicker Partnership plc v HOK International Ltd* [2005] EWCA Civ 962.

[94] *Viasystems (Tyneside) Ltd v Thermal Transfer (Northern) Ltd* [2006] 2 WLR 428.

[95] Suppose that C was injured by defective goods which he bought, but that C was also contributorily negligent. As contributory negligence is not a defence to actions for breach of strict contractual duties (*Barclays Bank plc v Fairclough Building Ltd* [1995] QB 214), the retailer will be liable in full to C, but his claim for contribution against the negligent manufacturer will be reduced to the extent to which a claim by C against the manufacturer would have been scaled down on account of C's contributory negligence.

[96] Civil Liability (Contribution) Act 1978, s 2(3). The reduction to represent the degree of C's contributory negligence must be made before assessing the respective contributions of the tortfeasors: *Fitzgerald v Lane* [1989] AC 328.

not entitled to sell goods authorizes an auctioneer to sell them, and he immediately does, the auctioneer, having been held liable in conversion, is entitled to an indemnity from his principal.[97]

Most important is the relationship between employer and employee. In *Lister v Romford Ice and Cold Storage Co Ltd* the facts were as follows.[98]

D, employed by C, took his father with him as mate. In reversing his lorry, D injured his father who, in an action against C, recovered damages in respect of D's negligent act. C brought an action against D claiming an indemnity in respect of the amount of the judgment and costs awarded against it.

The House of Lords held that the claimant was entitled to recover from the defendant for breach of the defendant's contractual obligation of care to his employer.[99] It follows that an employer who has been made vicariously liable for the tort of his employee can claim an indemnity from the employee. It was clearly recognized before this decision that when the employer himself was also at fault he would not obtain a complete indemnity but must suffer a reduction in respect of his own fault.[100] But these cases were based on section 6 of the Law Reform (Married Women and Tortfeasors) Act 1935.[101] What remains to be decided is whether, and if so on what principles, a reduction can be made in a claim by the employer based on a breach by the employee of his contract of employment.[102]

FURTHER READING

Carty, 'Joint Tortfeasance and Assistance Liability' [1999] *Legal Studies* 489

Watts, 'The Company's *Alter Ego* – An Impostor in Private Law' (2000) 116 LQR 525

---

[97] *Adamson v Jarvis* (1827) 4 Bing 66. For an illustration of a statutory right of indemnity, see the Civil Aviation Act 1982, s 76(3).

[98] [1957] AC 555; distinguished in *Harvey v R G O'Dell Ltd* [1958] 2 QB 78, at 106, *per* McNair J. And see *Vandyke v Fender* [1970] 2 QB 292, at 303, *per* Lord Denning MR.

[99] The Report of the Inter-Departmental Committee (1959) set up by the Ministry of Labour and National Service concluded that the decision raised no practical problem and that no legislative change was called for at that time. Moreover, in *Morris v Ford Motor Co Ltd* [1973] QB 792, it was held that the agreement in that case, being in an industrial setting so that subrogation against employees was unrealistic, contained an implied term excluding subrogation against them.

[100] Eg, *Jones v Manchester Corpn* [1952] 2 QB 852. Where the master's liability is purely vicarious, involving no personal fault, the master will obtain a 100% contribution from the negligent servant under the Civil Liability (Contribution) Act 1978, as in *Harvey v R G O'Dell Ltd* [1958] 2 QB 78.

[101] *Lister v Romford Ice and Cold Storage Co Ltd* [1957] AC 555 left open the question of whether an indemnity under the Act could also have been given.

[102] How far the Law Reform (Contributory Negligence) Act 1945 applies to a suit in contract is obviously pertinent. But see *Barclays Bank plc v Fairclough Building Ltd* [1995] QB 214 ruling out its applicability in relation to strict contractual duties.

26

REMEDIES IN TORT: BASIC PRINCIPLES

SECTION 1 SELF-HELP

The availability of a limited number of extra-judicial self-help remedies has been touched on earlier.[1] In general, however, the person invoking self-help should remember that he acts at his peril.

SECTION 2 JUDICIAL

(A) DAMAGES[2]

(1) NOMINAL

Some interests, for example, freedom of movement, the exercise of a vote at an election and the possession of one's property are considered to be so important that any violation of them is a tort.[3] The damages are said to be at large in all these torts. This means that although the interest protected may not have a precise cash value, the court is free, on proof of the commission of the tort, to award substantial damages.[4] By contrast, nominal damages (of typically £5) will be awarded where the court decides in the light of all the facts that no damage has been sustained.[5] The function of nominal damages is simply to mark the vindication of a right which is held to be so important that any infringement of it is actionable *per se*: that is, even where no tangible damage has been

---

[1] See ch 11 in the contexts of self-defence, abatement etc.

[2] Burrows, *Remedies for Torts and Breach of Contract* (2004); Harris, Campbell and Halson, *Remedies in Contract & Tort* (2002).

[3] For the difficulties involved in deciding whether an action on the case is actionable *per se*, see the opinion of Viscount Haldane in *Hammerton v Earl of Dysart* [1916] 1 AC 57.

[4] Eg, £5 damages was awarded to C in *Ashby v White* (1703) 2 Ld Raym 938 (right to vote); £50 damages was treated as appropriate in *Nicholls v Ely Beet Sugar Factory Ltd* [1936] Ch 343 (interference with fishery).

[5] *The Mediana* [1900] AC 113, at 116, *per* Earl of Halsbury LC; *Neville v London Express Newspaper Ltd* [1919] AC 368, at 392, *per* Viscount Haldane.

suffered. *Grobbelaar v News Group Newspapers Ltd*[6] provides a good example. There, a professional footballer had been libelled in so far as he had been accused of actually fixing football matches. He had not technically fixed the result of the matches, thus the statement was untrue and libellous. He had, however, accepted money in exchange for his attempts to throw the games, and was awarded £1 in nominal damages by the House of Lords.

Nominal damages are nowadays given *only* in respect of torts actionable *per se*[7] and must not be confused with a small sum intended to compensate only limited actual damage. On the other hand, one case runs counter to these principles: *Constantine v Imperial Hotels Ltd.*[8]

C, a famous black cricketer, was improperly refused accommodation at Ds' hotel. This was a tort derived from the former action on the case, and actionable *per se*. Birkett J held that he could not grant substantial damages.

The decision seems wrong because damages were at large in accordance with the above principles and he found that the claimant suffered unjustifiable humiliation and distress. He should, therefore, have awarded damages that reflected the injury to feelings.[9]

(2) CONTEMPTUOUS DAMAGES

These are derisory damages marking the court's low opinion of the claimant's claim, or its disapproval of his conduct. They differ from nominal damages in that they may be awarded in respect of any tort, not merely those actionable *per se*. Moreover, the award of only contemptuous damages may be material in deciding whether to allow costs to the claimant.

(3) DISTINGUISHING BETWEEN GENERAL AND SPECIAL DAMAGES

These expressions have various meanings but the basic principle is this. General damages are those damages that the law presumes to have resulted from the defendant's tort; special damages are awarded for a loss that will not be presumed. Thus, to avoid injustice to the defendant, the claimant must give notice in his pleadings of, and substantiate any claim for, 'special damages'.[10] The expenses incurred by the claimant prior to the date of the hearing – for example, costs of medical treatment in a personal injury case – constitute special damages. In short, the substantial damage capable of pecuniary assessment that must be proved in the case of all torts not actionable *per se* is called 'special damage'. All other heads of damage constitute general damage.[11]

---

[6] [2002] 1 WLR 3024.   [7] Cf *Embrey v Owen* (1851) 6 Exch 353, at 368, *per* Parke B.

[8] [1944] KB 693.

[9] And see below for general confirmation of this approach in *Cassell & Co Ltd v Broome* [1972] AC 1027.

[10] See, eg, *Domsalla v Barr* [1969] 1 WLR 630.

[11] In *R v Secretary of State for the Home Department, ex p Greenfield* [2005] 1 WLR 673, at [11]–[12], Lord Bingham put it even more tersely equating special damages with pecuniary loss, and general damages with non-pecuniary loss.

(4) DAMAGES FOR PERSONAL INJURIES

Detailed discussion of the principles governing compensation for personal injuries and the relationship of those principles to other compensation systems is located in the next chapter.

(5) DAMAGES AND TAX

If the award of damages is not subject to income tax and damages are calculated by reference to income that would be taxable, then tax must be deducted in calculating the damages. An allowance for tax must therefore be made in calculating loss of earnings,[12] or, in awarding damages in trespass, for loss of rent.[13]

(6) 'PARASITIC' DAMAGES

There is no general rule that simply because a particular head of damage is recoverable in one tort, the same head of damage is recoverable in any other tort. In that sense, English law does not recognize any principle of 'parasitic' damages.[14] Thus, while personal injuries are recoverable in, say, negligence, they are not *per se* recoverable in private nuisance.[15]

(7) AGGRAVATED DAMAGES

The object of an award of damages in tort is normally to compensate the claimant for what he has lost or suffered as a consequence of the tort. Nonetheless, in certain torts, an award of damages may sometimes take into account the motives and conduct of the defendant where they cause anger and annoyance in the claimant. There may be malevolence or spite on the part of the defendant, or it may be that the manner in which he commits the wrong is such as to injure the claimant's proper feelings of dignity and pride. Such damages are traditionally called 'aggravated damages' and are they intimately linked to arrogant conduct that inspires outrage or anger in the claimant.[16] So much is clear.

What is far from certain, however, is whether aggravated damages constitute a special form of compensation or whether they are non-compensatory in nature. There are arguments both ways, and both arguments enjoy some measure of support from the decided cases. The traditional view is that such damages represent a special form of

---

[12] *British Transport Commission v Gourley* [1956] AC 185. For an assessment of the *Gourley* principle see *Burrows, Remedies for Torts and Breach of Contract* (2004) pp 132–5.

[13] *Hall & Co Ltd v Pearlberg* [1956] 1 All ER 297. *Gourley* has also been applied to awards for libel: *Rubber Improvement Ltd v Daily Telegraph* [1964] AC 234.

[14] *Spartan Steel and Alloys Ltd v Martin & Co (Contractors) Ltd* [1973] QB 27, at 35, *per* Lord Denning MR.

[15] *Hunter v Canary Wharf Ltd* [1997] 2 All ER 426.

[16] In *Horsford v Bird* [2006] UKPC 3, at [14], *per* Lord Scott, the Privy Council spoke of 'high-handed, insulting or oppressive conduct'.

compensation for the distress associated with the commission of a tort, or for the defendant's behaviour (perhaps, in his conduct at trial) subsequent to the commission of a tort. Sir Thomas Bingham MR, for example, once said that the aggravated damages in defamation cases are not a true exception 'since injury to the [claimant's] feelings and self-esteem is an important part of the damage for which compensation is awarded'.[17] But there is, it is submitted, a more compelling, second view; and this is that aggravated damages are non-compensatory in nature – that is, that they are intimately bound up with *conduct* causing anger and outrage that goes beyond the damage usually caused by any given tort. Consider *KD v Chief Constable of Hampshire*.[18]

C sought damages in respect of repeated acts of harassment committed by a police constable. The constable had sexually harassed C over the phone and in person by interviewing her several times in such a way as to extract sexually explicit information about her that was irrelevant for the purposes of the investigation, and in truth gained purely for the satisfaction of the constable's prurient interest. C was awarded £10,000 general damages in respect of the anxiety and injury to her feelings by virtue of the constable's harassing visits and telephone calls. She was also awarded £10,000 by way of aggravated damages in respect of the additional anger and annoyance caused by the constable persistently denying the allegations when it was clear that they had been established from the five typed and signed statements that had been taken.

On the basis of this case, it could be said that aggravated damages were awarded simply to appease or pacify the claimant. Harassment, by its very nature, causes distress. And the award of general damages was granted with a view to effecting compensation for the distress and anxiety caused (especial note being taken of the fact that this fell short of PTSD). This award was entirely claimant-centred. By contrast, the award of aggravated damages in the case focused *both* upon the arrogant conduct of the constable after the tort had been committed *as well as* the annoyance and additional distress caused to the claimant. This award was neither wholly defendant-centred nor wholly claimant-centred.[19] As Tugendhat J made clear, his concern in awarding aggravated damages was not merely with the fact that the constable had 'caused the claimant to undergo a prolonged cross-examination' but also with the fact that 'she had to listen to [him] continue to deny everything, including the correctness of the findings of the disciplinary tribunal'.[20] In concentrating on both facets of the case – the defendant's arrogant and groundless defence together with the additional distress caused to the claimant by defending the case in the way she had to – these damages were not concerned simply with compensating measurable harm suffered by the claimant.

---

[17] *AB v South West Water Services Ltd* [1993] QB 507, at 532. In similar vein, see *Rookes v Barnard* [1964] AC 1129, at 1221, *per* Lord Devlin; *Cassell & Co Ltd v Broome* [1972] AC 1027, at 1124, *per* Lord Diplock. Cf *Richardson v Howie* [2004] EWCA Civ 1127 where it was said that aggravated damages should not be thought of – except in an exceptional case (whatever that may be) – as being granted in relation to feelings of indignity and anger inspired in C. Compare this, however, with Beever's view that aggravated damages are precisely about compensation for an affront to moral dignity: 'The Structure of Aggravated and Exemplary Damages' (2003) 23 OJLS 87.   [18] [2005] EWHC 2550.

[19] In similar vein see the Privy Council decision in *Horsford v Bird* [2006] UKPC 3; and for an Australian judicial objection to the traditional, compensatory understanding of aggravated damages see *Uren v John Fairfax & Sons Pty Ltd* (1965–66) 117 CLR 118, at 151, *per* Windeyer J.   [20] [2005] EWHC 2550, at [192].

The range of torts in relation to which aggravated damages may be awarded is broad. It includes the following: trespass to the person[21] and to land,[22] defamation[23] and other torts based on deliberate falsehoods,[24] and private nuisance.[25] The question of whether such damages should be available in negligence was considered by the Court of Appeal in *AB v South West Water Services Ltd*.[26] The view taken in that case – just as in an earlier case[27] – was that they should not be available in negligence. What seemingly underlies this approach, however, is the assumption that negligence can only be committed through inadvertent or otherwise non-intentional conduct. A common thread linking those torts in which such damages are available is the capacity of those torts to be committed by wanton, arrogant conduct likely to inflame the claimant in the requisite way.[28] If, however, one accepts that negligence liability can be imposed in respect of deliberate acts of wrongdoing – as logically it must[29] – then there is ample scope for the defendant to behave in such a way as to justify aggravated damages in a case of negligence. Certainly it is hard to see any plausible reason of principle why negligence should not support such damages.

(8) EXEMPLARY DAMAGES

Exemplary damages (which in theory turn upon conduct which outrages the court) may be seen as an anomaly in the law of torts.[30] Their object is to punish and deter. The preponderance of opinion until relatively recently was that exemplary damages should be abolished.[31] Their continued existence, it has been objected, confuses the functions of the civil and criminal law.[32] Furthermore, since the standard of proof is lower in a tort case than in a criminal law case, it might be argued that a defendant can end up being 'punished' in tort without being afforded the same kinds of safeguards (including the higher standard of proof) provided for accused persons in criminal proceedings. Finally, such damages have also been opposed on the basis that they bestow upon a claimant an unwarranted windfall. On the other hand, this argument only holds good so long as one accepts that the law of tort is exclusively concerned with securing compensation for harm caused, which (it would be widely accepted) it is not.[33] Tort, for

---

[21] See, eg, *Thompson v Metropolitan Police Comr* [1998] QB 498.

[22] *Drane v Evangelou* [1978] 1 WLR 455.   [23] *Sutcliffe v Pressdram Ltd* [1991] 1 QB 153.

[24] *Khodaparast v Shad* [2000] 1 All ER 545; (malicious falsehood); *Archer v Brown* [1985] QB 401 (deceit).

[25] *Thompson v Hill* (1870) LR 5 CP 564.   [26] [1993] 1 All ER 609, at 629, *per* Sir Thomas Bingham MR.

[27] *Kralj v McGrath* [1986] 1 All ER 54.   [28] For a full list, see *Clerk and Lindsell on Torts* (2006) p 1882.

[29] See Murphy, 'Rethinking Injunctions in Tort Law' (forthcoming).

[30] Despite the endorsement of exemplary damages in *Kuddus v Chief Constable of Leicestershire* [2002] 2 AC 122, their Lordships nonetheless expressly recognized their anomalous nature in tort.

[31] See, *inter alia*, the proposals for abolition of exemplary damages in defamation in the Faulks Report, *Report of the Committee in Defamation* Cmnd 5609 (1975). See also Law Commission Consultation Paper No 132, *Aggravated, Exemplary and Restitutionary Damages* (1993) and Law Commission Report, *Exemplary, Aggravated and Restitutionary Damages* (1997).

[32] See, eg, *Cassell & Co Ltd v Broome* [1972] AC 1027, at 1088, *per* Lord Reid. But note that this makes an assumption about a *necessary separation* of crime from tort that is difficult to ground when the truth is that virtually all crimes are also torts. See further, Reiff, *Punishment, Compensation and the Law* (2005).

[33] This point was made forcefully by Lord Wilberforce in *Cassell & Co Ltd v Broome* [1972] AC 1027. See also the way in which the Compensation Act 2006 affetcs the way in which a breach of duty is to be assessed in negligence cases in ch 4.

example, can clearly be shown to possess a deterrent function in reinforcing the civil liberties of the individual.[34] As such, conferring such a benefit on the 'undeserving' claimant may well secure other objectives that are equally the concern of tort law as compensation.[35]

But leaving such arguments to one side, it is now clear from the decision of the House of Lords in *Kuddus v Chief Constable of Leicestershire*[36] that exemplary damages may nowadays be obtained in connection with virtually any tort.[37] In sweeping away the previous approach – which limited their availability to specific torts that need no longer concern us – the House of Lords rendered the argument about the rights and wrongs of exemplary damages within tort a largely academic one. All that really concerns us in the remainder of this section – in the present edition, at least[38] – is an examination of the bases upon which such damages will be awarded.[39] (That said, this section will conclude with a brief consideration of what the future *may* hold for exemplary damages.)

The starting point is *Rookes v Barnard*.[40] In that case, Lord Devlin limited exemplary damages awards to three categories of case.

(a) Where the claimant has been the victim of oppressive, arbitrary or unconstitutional action by servants of government.

It has been established that the phrase 'oppressive, arbitrary or unconstitutional' is to be understood *disjunctively*, so that it is enough if the action was merely oppressive, or arbitrary or unconstitutional. As such, if unlawful conduct by a police officer can be proved, it is not necessary to show that it was also arbitrary or oppressive.[41] As regards those who constitute 'servants of government', it has been held that the notion embraces central and local government officers and includes, also, police officers[42] and prison officers guilty of misfeasance in public office.[43] Public utilities, such as the electricity and water companies, fall outside the category, as do other privatized monopoly

---

[34] This has been supplied by the decision in *Lancashire County Council v Municipal Mutual Insurance Ltd* [1997] QB 897 (even exemplary damages may be claimed from the tortfeasor's insurers).

[35] For a powerful justification of exemplary damages in cases where either (a) the protected interest can be protected by an injunction, or (b) the tort in question (whether intentional or not) causes a fatality or (c) the tort in question is morally repugnant in that it generates a benefit that, on moral grounds, ought to be disgorged, see Ogus, 'Exemplary Damages and Economic Analysis' in Hawkins (ed), *The Human Face of Law: Essays in Honour of Donald Harris* (1997).   [36] [2002] 2 AC 122.

[37] The only doubt that exists relates to the availability of exemplary damages for breach of statutory duty where the statute in question *does not* specifically authorize such an award: see *Kuddus v Chief Constable of Leicestershire* [2002] 2 AC 122, at [45]. But see *Design Progression Ltd v Thurloe Properties Ltd* for use (at first instance) of exemplary damages in connection with a breach of s 1(3) of the Landlord and Tenant Act 1998.

[38] It is likely, given the tenor of the decision in the *Kuddus* case (in which rather a narrow question was put to their Lordships) that the broader question about what to do *generally* about exemplary damages in tort will have to be revisited sooner rather than later, and if not by the House of Lords, then by Parliament.

[39] For more detailed academic discussion, see Beever, 'The Structure of Aggravated and Exemplary Damages' (2003) 23 OJLS 87; Burrows, 'Reforming Exemplary Damages' and McBride, 'Punitive Damages' both in Birks (ed), *Wrongs and Remedies in the 21st Century* (1996).   [40] [1964] AC 1129.

[41] *Holden v Chief Constable of Lancashire* [1987] QB 380.

[42] *Casssell & Co Ltd v Broome* [1972] AC 1027; *Thompson v Metropolitan Police Comr* [1998] QB 498.

[43] *Racz v Home Office* [1994] 2 WLR 23.

suppliers; for even though they are endowed with statutory powers and obligations, they are not exercising executive functions.[44]

(b) Where the defendant's conduct has been calculated by him to make a profit for himself which may well exceed the compensation payable to the claimant.

Within this category fall those such as publishers who, as in *Cassell & Co Ltd v Broome*,[45] calculate that a libel may well sell so many copies of a publication that they will still profit despite having to pay compensatory damages to the victim.[46] The idea is that they should learn that 'tort does not pay'.[47] In this context, it is important to stress that 'carelessness alone, however extreme, is not enough' unless the inference may be drawn 'that the publisher had no honest belief in the truth of what he published'.[48] But the category is not limited to cases of defamation; it can equally well be invoked where landlords commit torts against tenants by driving them out of their property in order to profit from selling the property or letting it to someone else at a higher rent.[49]

(c) Where authorized by statute

There are very few examples of this final, and least important, category in which the statute expressly permits the claimant to sue for exemplary damages.[50]

(d) Three further considerations

Beyond establishing that the tort in question falls into one of the three categories outlined in *Rookes v Barnard*, it also seems that three further requirements must obtain. First, the claimant must able to show that he himself was the victim of the tort.[51] (This requirement is certain, and also means that relatives invested with a cause of action upon the victim's death do not possess the right to sue for exemplary damages.[52]) Secondly, it must also be shown that exemplary damages are necessary to effect proper punishment of the defendant. (This requirement is also certain,[53] and means that if, for

---

[44] *AB v South West Water Services Ltd* [1993] 1 All ER 609, at 622 and 628, *per* Stuart-Smith LJ and Sir Thomas Bingham MR, respectively. [45] [1972] AC 1027.

[46] Judging whether there is a likely profit is to be construed widely so that not just potential damages awards are assessed, but also benefits in kind that may be recovered by C: *Borders (UK) Ltd v Commissioner of the Police of the Metropolis* [2005] EWCA Civ 197, at [23], *per* Sedley LJ.

[47] But could an action for unjust enrichment achieve the same laudable aim? Note also the limits of this argument exposed in *AB v South West Water Services Ltd* [1993] 1 All ER 609.

[48] *John v MGN Ltd* [1996] 2 All ER 35, at 57, *per* Sir Thomas Bingham MR.

[49] *Drane v Evangelou* [1978] 2 All ER 437 (simply acquiring vacant possession of the property so that they could be let to relatives was sufficient).

[50] See, eg, the Reserve and Auxiliary Forces (Protection of Civil Interests) Act 1951, s 3(2).

[51] *Rookes v Barnard* [1964] AC 1129, at 1227–1228, *per* Lord Devlin.

[52] There is, indeed, specific provision to this effect in s 1(2)(a)(i) of the Law Reform (Miscellaneous Provisions) Act 1934.

[53] *Watkins v Secretary of State for the Home Dept* [2006] 2 WLR 807. However, the point was also made in that case that their Lordships would not extend the law of exemplary damages so as to enable a claimant to receive exemplary damages simply because (at least in the context of misfeasance in public office) he or she has suffered no material loss and therefore cannot sue for compensatory damages.

example, the defendant has been prosecuted for the equivalent crime, no such award should be made[54]). Finally, but slightly less certainly, it was established by a bare majority in *A v Bottrill*[55] that when considering an award of exemplary damages, a third fundamental consideration is whether the defendant's conduct met the criterion of outrageous conduct warranting condemnation. Since *Bottrill* is strictly an authority on New Zealand law, it remains to be confirmed by the English courts. However, it seems overwhelmingly likely that it will be so confirmed given that *Bottrill* was a decision of the Privy Council.

(e) The future

If the English courts were to adopt the general approach laid down in *Bottrill*, then it might be used to expand both the first and second *Rookes v Barnard* categories. For sure, there is no good reason in principle why outrageous conduct on the part of servants of the Crown should be frowned upon more than outrageous conduct on the part of any other citizen. Nor is it logical to confine the availability of exemplary damages to instances of intentional wrongdoing or subjective recklessness where the defendant's conduct is motivated by the prospect of making a profit. Intentional wrongdoing motivated purely by simple spite or malevolence would seem to be perfectly suitable, too. Thus, if the English courts were to adopt and run with the *Bottrill* criterion of outrageous conduct that calls for condemnation, they might well pave the way for a more logical, coherent and principled law on exemplary damages even if, as their Lordships' most recent statement on the matter makes clear, such damages are not to be encouraged.[56]

A second point that requires final determination is whether a person held vicariously liable for the tort of another can be required to pay exemplary damages. There is Court of Appeal authority suggesting that such a person can be required to pay such damages;[57] but this has since been doubted in the House of Lords by one Law Lord, while his brethren declined to reach a settled view on the matter.[58] On principle, since vicarious liability is a form of liability without fault, it seems inappropriate to impose exemplary damages on someone held vicariously liable.

(9) MITIGATION OF DAMAGE AND RELATED PRINCIPLES

This expression covers two separate rules in the law of torts.

(1) There is the situation which is the converse of the circumstances in which aggravated damages may be awarded. That is, evidence may be given of

---

[54] See, eg, *Archer v Brown* [1985] QB 401 (no exemplary damages where D had been imprisoned for the offence). [55] [2002] 3 WLR 1406.

[56] *Watkins v Secretary of State for the Home Dept* [2006] 2 WLR 807.

[57] *Thompson v Metropolitan Police Comr* [1998] QB 498.

[58] *Kuddus v Chief Constable of Leicestershire* [2002] 2 AC 122.

circumstances which justify a lesser award of damages at large.[59] For example, damages in defamation may be reduced where the claimant has provoked the defendant.[60]

(2) The discussion of causation showed that it is the policy of the law not to allow a claimant to recover to the extent to which he has brought the loss upon himself by his own act.[61] Similarly, where a claimant is negligent after the commission of the tort against him, he cannot recover further damages caused by that carelessness. *The Flying Fish*[62] illustrates the point.

C's ship was damaged by the negligence of those in charge of D's vessel. C's captain showed want of nautical skill in that he refused aid after the collision. In consequence of this negligent refusal, the ship was destroyed. C was able to recover the damage caused by the collision but not that additional damage accruing when the ship was destroyed by the negligence of the captain.

In short, contributory negligence is concerned with negligence of the claimant before the cause of action has matured by the occurrence of some damage. After damage has occurred and an action in tort is vested in the claimant, he has a duty to take care to mitigate his loss. The burden of showing an unreasonable failure to mitigate lies with the defendant. Thus, where a claimant refuses treatment or surgery that could have lessened the consequences of her injury, the onus is on the defendant to show that the refusal was unreasonable.[63] Even if the claimant shows that the refusal of treatment is presently reasonable, there may still be a discount if it can be shown that there is a chance both (a) that the claimant will accept the treatment in the longer term *and* (b) that the treatment might succeed.[64]

Where the claimant does take reasonable steps to minimize the consequences of the defendant's tort, he can recover for the harm sustained by him in consequence of his action[65] or expenses thereby incurred,[66] regardless of whether his total loss would have been less had he not acted at all. Thus, in *Rogers v Austin*[67] it was held to be reasonable to hire a replacement car at above the market rate for such a vehicle where the basis of

---

[59] *Peruvian Guano Co Ltd v Dreyfus Bros & Co* [1892] AC 166, at 174, *per* Lord Macnaghten; *Drane v Evangelou* [1978] 2 All ER 437.   [60] *Moore v Oastler* (1836) 1 Mood & R 451n.

[61] See ch 5. In *Dodd Properties Ltd v Canterbury City Council* [1980] 1 All ER 928 C's premises were damaged in 1970, but when he repaired them in 1978 the cost of repairs was much greater. He was allowed the 1978 repair costs on the ground that, in deciding what it was reasonable for C to do in mitigation, it was relevant to ask whether C could afford to repair sooner. See also *Perry v Sidney Phillips & Son* [1982] 3 All ER 705.

[62] (1865) 2 Moo PCCNS 77.

[63] *Geest plc v Lansiquot* [2002] UKPC 48, at [14], *per* Lord Bingham. Note that a woman's refusal of an abortion after Ds' negligence resulted in an unplanned pregnancy did not constitute an unreasonable failure to mitigate damages: *Emeh v Kensington and Chelsea and Westminster Area Health Authority* [1985] QB 1012.

[64] *Thomas v Bath District Health Authority* [1995] PIQR Q19.   [65] *The Oropesa* [1943] P 32.

[66] *Kirkham v Boughey* [1958] 2 QB 338. Note also that in *Lagden v O'Connor* [2004] 1 AC 1067 the House of Lords held generally that losses flowing from the higher-than-usual expenses incurred by C because of C's impecuniosity are recoverable.   [67] [1997] CLY 1791.

the hire agreement was that no hire payment would be required of the claimant until completion of her legal proceedings against the defendant. Equally, if a claimant takes a new job because, by virtue of his injury he can no longer do the old one, and the new job proves to be beyond him, there can be no reduction in the tortfeasor's liability based on the loss of that second job.[68]

Although not strictly mitigation issues, the courts have been required to decide what to do in relation to a claimant whose loss is either covered by an insurance policy held by the claimant, or in relation to a claimant who, consequent upon the defendant's tort, happens to benefit from some future windfall. As regards insurance cover, it was held in *Bradburn v Great Western Railway Co*[69] that the amount received under the insurance policy is *not* to be deducted from the claimant's damages. A claimant pays the insurance premiums; and these would be totally wasted if the claimant's tort damages were to be reduced by the amount payable under the policy.

The second issue – namely, that of a windfall payment – arose for consideration in *Needler Financial Services Ltd v Taber*.[70] In that case, the claimant changed to a new pension scheme in line with the defendant's negligent advice. The scheme, taken out with Norwich Union, was less favourable than the claimant's initial scheme, but it did entitle the claimant to a windfall payment when the Norwich Union de-mutalised. It was held, rather curiously, that this windfall was *not* to be deducted from the loss attributable to the defendant's negligent advice.

(10) SUCCESSIVE ACTIONS ON THE SAME FACTS

The difficulties presented by this topic are of the same character as those arising from the undefined stand of English law with regard to parasitic damages. The following principles may be gleaned from the decided cases.

The guiding rule can be stated shortly. The difficulty lies in defining its terms. If one and the same act produces two different heads of damage, but it does not give rise to two separate causes of action, the claimant cannot bring successive actions but must recover in respect of all his damage in the first proceedings. The policy is to avoid excessive litigation. The leading case is *Fitter v Veal*.[71]

C recovered £11 damages from D for assault and battery. Some years later, C discovered that his injuries were much more serious than he had at first thought, and he underwent a surgical operation for removal of part of his skull. He was held unable to recover any damages in a second action for his additional injuries.

(a) Violation of two rights separately protected

If a single act violates two rights which are accorded separate protection by the law of torts, then there are two separate causes of action, the pursuit of one of which will

---

[68] *Morris v Richards* [2003] EWCA Civ 232.   [69] (1874) LR 10 Ex 1.   [70] [2002] 3 All ER 501.
[71] (1701) 12 Mod Rep 542.

not necessarily bar proceedings in respect of the other.[72] *Brunsden v Humphrey*[73] is illustrative.

A cab driven by C collided with D's van through the negligent driving of D's servant. In county court proceedings, C recovered compensation for the damage to his cab. He then brought a second action in the High Court for personal injuries sustained by him in the same collision, and the Court of Appeal held that this action was not barred by the earlier one.

The interest in bodily security is separate from that in one's goods – hence there were two separate causes of action.[74] Where a single act caused a shortened expectation of life and damaged goods, two actions lay.[75] On the other hand, the interest in length of life and in freedom from pain are deemed to be subsumed under the one interest, namely that in bodily security. Accordingly, only one action may be brought.[76] The following interests are distinct for present purposes: interests in land, in reputation, in freedom of the person and freedom from excessive litigation (that is, malicious prosecution).[77]

(b) Consequential damage where two torts protect the same interest

If the primary purpose of two different torts is to protect the same interest, then merely consequential damage that could have been recovered in proceedings for the first tort cannot be claimed in an action on the second tort. *Gibbs v Cruikshank*[78] makes this clear:

D executed an illegal distress on C's land. In an action of replevin, C recovered the goods and the replevin expenses. This action did not preclude a subsequent suit in trespass to land, but it did preclude a later action in trespass to goods for consequential business loss, since both replevin and trespass to goods primarily protect one's interest in goods and, parasitically, one's business interests.

---

[72] But note that it may be regarded as an abuse of process to return to court raising issues that might have been raised against the same wrongdoer in earlier proceedings: see, eg, *Talbot v Berkshire County Council* [1994] QB 290 and *Bradford and Bingley Building Society v Seddon* [1999] 4 All ER 217. If it is such an abuse, the second claim will be struck out. In some circumstances, this approach may be thought extremely harsh. Thus, in *Wain v F Sherwood & Sons Transport Ltd* [1999] PIQR P159 the rule operated to prevent a second action worth £100,000 being brought in respect of a back injury that had not been sued for in the first action due to the negligence of C's (then immune) counsel. Happily, the House of Lords has adopted a more relaxed approach to this rule in more recent times: *Johnson v Gore Wood & Co* [2001] 2 WLR 72. See also *Toth v Ledger* [2002] PIQR P1.

[73] (1884) 14 QBD 141. *Brunsden v Humphrey* was accepted as correct in *O'Sullivan v Williams* [1992] 3 All ER 385 and *Barrow v Bankside Members Agency Ltd* [1995] 2 Lloyd's Rep 472.

[74] But does a man have distinct interests in, say, a leg, and an arm? Coleridge CJ, dissenting in *Brunsden v Humphrey*, said that was the logical consequence of the decision in the case, but one of the judges in the majority subsequently said that the case 'is no authority for holding that if there be an actionable injury to the person one action may be brought for injury to one part of the body and another action for injury to another part': *MacDougall v Knight* (1890) 25 QBD 1, at 8, *per* Lord Esher MR. Note also the power to strike out an unreasonable claim as an abuse of process: *The Indian Grace* [1992] 1 Lloyd's Rep 124.

[75] *The Oropesa* [1943] P 32.

[76] *Derrick v Williams* [1939] 2 All ER 559. Cf *Chant v Read* [1939] 2 KB 346.

[77] *Guest v Warren* (1854) 9 Exch 379. And see *Ash v Hutchinson & Co (Publishers) Ltd* [1936] Ch 489, for a further addition to the list.   [78] (1873) LR 8 CP 454.

It would seem that if the chief purpose of the second tort is to protect an interest different from that primarily protected by the first, then damages for the violation of the main interest protected by the second tort can be recovered in proceedings for the second tort even though those damages could have been recovered consequentially in the first action.[79] If, as is supposed, damages for interference with land are recoverable in replevin, *Gibbs v Cruikshank* would be authority for this.[80]

Imagine, also, that X took letters from Z which were in Z's possession and which were defamatory of Z; and then suppose that X gave them to Y. Suppose further that in proceedings in conversion against X, Z recovered damages for his loss of the letters *qua* goods, but did not claim or recover (as he could by way of consequential damages[81]) damages for loss of reputation. It is submitted that, in such circumstances, he would be able to bring a further action for defamation against X (because defamation primarily protects the interest in one's reputation, quite different in kind from the primary interest covered by conversion).

(c) Successive acts

Successive actions are barred only in respect of one and the same act. If, then, A assaults B today and again tomorrow, two actions lie. Should A, however, in one and the same fight break B's nose and knock out some of his teeth, then B has only one cause of action. In less straightforward cases, one must look to the pleadings of the first action to discover whether the facts there relied on do or do not include those later complained of.

(d) One tortious act causing damage on different occasions

Sometimes, a single act may cause the same damage over and over again. If X digs a hole in Y's land, Y's cattle may fall into it and suffer injury both before and after Y has sued X for trespass to land. There is, however, only one act of a tortious nature – digging the hole. It follows, therefore, that only one suit in trespass to land can be brought. If, on the other hand, A throws an object on B's land and B recovers in trespass to land, and thereafter B's cattle stumble over it and are injured, B can bring a second action; for leaving an object on the land of another is an act of trespass in itself, separate from the earlier trespass constituted by throwing the object onto the land.[82]

(B) ACCOUNT OF PROFITS

Sometimes it is more advantageous for the claimant to seek an account of the defendant's profits resulting from the tort rather than to claim damages. Frequently, the

---

[79] So if D causes subsidence on C's land, C may not claim for later depreciation in the value of the land *although* he can claim for the cost of remedial work that will help to prevent further loss: *Delaware Mansions Ltd v Westminster City Council* [2002] 1 AC 321.   [80] See also *Guest v Warren* (1854) 9 Exch 379.

[81] *Thurston v Charles* (1905) 21 TLR 659.

[82] In principle, the same rules should apply to torts not actionable *per se*. In *Maberley v Henry W Peabody & Co London Ltd* [1946] 2 All ER 192 it was held that where two separate torts are committed, two successive actions may be brought.

victim of passing off will obtain an injunction *and* an account of the defendant's profits, but the remedy is not confined to that tort.

(c) INJUNCTIONS

(1) AS A REMEDY *PER SE*, OR AS AN ADDITION TO DAMAGES

A remedy in damages alone may sometimes be inappropriate or insufficient to vindicate the claimant's rights. Where there is a risk a tort may be repeated, what the claimant wants is an order to prohibit that repetition: an injunction. Injunctions are a critical remedy in many tort claims, but they will be dealt with only briefly here.[83]

There are two broad kinds of injunctions: *viz*, prohibitory injunctions and mandatory injunctions. A prohibitory injunction may, for example, be issued against someone who has committed a trespass or a nuisance so that he will be restrained from repeating the tort in the future. A mandatory injunction, by contrast, requires the defendant to undertake a positive act to put an end to a state of affairs amounting to an actionable interference with some proprietary interest on the part of the claimant, whether or not that interference is causing actual damage.[84] For example, a mandatory injunction may require him to pull down a wall which interferes with the claimant's right to light.

Where an injunction is granted before the trial of an action, pending fuller investigation into the case that will take place at the trial, and in order to prevent the commission or continuance of an act alleged to be tortious, it is called an interim injunction.[85] Such an injunction is commonly applied for in respect of alleged economic torts where the claimant contends that the state of affairs resulting from the defendant's act is so serious that the defendant ought not to be allowed to continue to create that state of affairs pending the hearing. At one level, the granting of an interim injunction might seem to be a prejudgment of the case because it is, of course, a remedy granted to a claimant who has yet to prove that he has had his legal right infringed by the defendant. This begs the question of whether such injunctions should, in justice, ever be granted.[86] So far as the courts are concerned, the matter is clear: there is no offence caused in considering the respective strength of both parties cases and, if the claimant has a strong *prima facie* case, in granting such an order.[87] Where, however, an interim injunction would effectively ruin the defendant's livelihood, the courts will be very slow to grant one without a hearing having taken place.[88]

A further restriction on the availability of interim injunctions operates in relation to breach of confidence and is to be found in s 12(3) of the Human Rights Act 1998. There

---

[83] For fuller treatment see Burrows, *Remedies for Torts and Breach of Contract* (2004). And for an argument in favour of a wider use of injunctions *before* any measurable harm has occurred, see Murphy, 'Rethinking Injunctions in Tort Law' (forthcoming). [84] See, eg, *Jones v Llanrwst UDC* [1911] 1 Ch 393.

[85] See Gray, 'Interlocutory Injunctions since *Cyanamid*' [1981] CLJ 307.

[86] For the general argument that injunctions should be available even before any form of measurable harm – and outside an interference with a proprietary interest – has occurred, see Murphy, 'Rethinking Injunctions in Tort Law' (forthcoming). [87] *Series 5 Software Ltd v Clarke* [1996] 1 All ER 853.

[88] *Series 5 Software Ltd v Clarke* [1996] 1 All ER 853.

it is provided that no such injunction should be granted if it is likely to restrict freedom of expression *unless* the court is satisfied that the applicant is likely to establish that the publication in question should not be permitted.[89] Of course, everything here turns on what is meant by 'likely'. And the House of Lords, in *Cream Holdings Ltd v Banerjee*,[90] held that the term is susceptible to more or less restrictive interpretations depending on the circumstances of the case, including the severity of the consequences associated with publication. By itself, this is a fairly unhelpful thing to say. But three observations can be made that help to clarify matters.

First, it was held by the Court of Appeal in *Greene v Associated Newspapers Ltd*[91] that the common law on defamation has not been changed by section 12(3). Secondly, and by contrast, it was held in the *Cream Holdings* case that section 12(3) may be especially relevant in cases of breach of confidence; for while one's reputation can be restored for the purposes of defamation law, confidentiality once breached is lost for good. Thirdly, Lord Nicholls did suggest in the *Cream Holdings* case that in a non-exceptional case, the crucial word, 'likely', should be understood to mean 'more likely than not'.

Two highly important forms of interim injunction are the search order and the freezing injunction. A search order is a mandatory injunction (formerly known as an *Anton Piller* order) that requires the defendant to allow the claimant entry to premises to search for property infringing the claimant's rights, or documents relevant to his claim. In actions for breach of intellectual property rights, such orders are crucial to ensure the defendant cannot destroy incriminating documents prior to the trial of the action. By contrast, a freezing injunction prohibits the defendant from moving his assets abroad or from disposing of assets within the jurisdiction.[92] In this way, the claimant ensures that if he obtains judgment against the defendant, there will be property in England against which to enforce that judgment. Both search orders and freezing injunctions are draconian measures[93] and claimants will always be required not only to justify their claim for such orders, but also to give undertakings to return property seized and compensate the defendants should their suit ultimately fail.

A perpetual injunction is a final order issued after the hearing of the action. A *quia timet* injunction may be issued to restrain a tort which has not yet been committed, but commission of which is threatened, so long as substantial damage appears imminent.[94]

The jurisdiction of the High Court[95] to grant injunctions is often said to be discretionary; but this is not strictly a fair description.[96] An interim injunction may be granted even though the claimant has not made out a *prima facie* case provided there is a 'serious question' to address and the court decides on the balance of convenience that such an

---

[89] See *Douglas v Hello! Ltd* [2001] QB 967.   [90] [2005] 1 AC 253.   [91] [2005] 1 All ER 30.

[92] *Mareva Cia Naviera SA v International Bulkcarriers SA* [1975] 2 Lloyd's Rep 509. See also *Practice Direction* [1997] 1 All ER 288.   [93] See *Columbia Pictures Industries Inc v Robinson* [1987] Ch 38.

[94] *Lemos v Kennedy Leigh Development Co Ltd* (1961) 105 Sol Jo 178.

[95] Supreme Court Act 1981, s 37(1).

[96] As Waddams has pointed out, this is a somewhat misleading description since 'appellate courts have quite readily undertaken the review of final equitable orders notwithstanding that they are called "discretionary"': *Dimensions of Private Law – Categories and Concepts in Anglo-American Legal Reasoning* (2003) p 180 (footnotes omitted). If they were *truly* granted at the court's discretion, no such appellate reviews would be possible.

order is warranted.[97] The courts exercise sparingly their discretion to grant mandatory injunctions, and will refuse unless very serious damage would otherwise occur.[98] A prohibitory injunction will be granted to a claimant on proof that his proprietary rights are wrongfully being interfered with unless special circumstances exist.[99]

The public interest in not restraining the activity in question will sometimes be a relevant consideration.[100] But even so, it should be noted that the courts will be most reluctant to leave the victim of a serious interference with merely a remedy in damages.[101] The most that the courts seem willing to do as almost a matter of course in order to mitigate the consequences of their granting injunctions is suspend the coming into force of the injunction for a short period,[102] or impose time restrictions on it.[103]

(2) INJUNCTIONS WHERE AN ACTION IN TORT DOES NOT LIE

The courts have occasionally granted injunctions to protect title to property, even where no tort is established.[104] But this is an exceptional use. The normal rule is that a final injunction will not be granted unless the relevant elements of an extant tort have been shown to be present. The rationale underpinning this general approach, of course, is that it is wrong to restrain another from engaging in some form of lawful conduct in this way, and that it is similarly wrong to compel another to act in particular way when that other has not transgressed any law. But as regards the title to property exception, *Gee v Pritchard*[105] is instructive. In that case, the claimant obtained an injunction to prevent

---

[97] *American Cyanamid Co v Ethicon Ltd* [1975] AC 396. Lord Diplock enumerated at length the factors to be weighed in deciding where the balance of convenience lay. See also *Garden Cottage Foods Ltd v Milk Marketing Board* [1982] QB 1114 where Sir John Donaldson MR preferred the phrase 'balance of justice'. It is clear that public policy considerations enter the equation and not simply factors relating to the convenience of the parties: *Department of Social Security v Butler* [1995] 1 WLR 1528.

[98] *Redland Bricks Ltd v Morris* [1970] AC 652 sets out detailed rules governing the exercise of this 'discretion'.

[99] *Pride of Derby and Derbyshire Angling Association Ltd v British Celanese Ltd* [1953] Ch 149.

[100] See, eg, *Miller v Jackson* [1977] QB 966, at 981 and 988, *per* Lord Denning MR and Cumming-Bruce LJ, respectively; *Dennis v Ministry of Defence* [2003] EWHC 793.

[101] *Shelfer v City of London Electric Lighting Co* [1895] 1 Ch 287. See also *Kennaway v Thompson* [1981] QB 88 which probably went too far in refusing to consider the public interest and held *Miller v Jackson* not to be binding.

[102] In *Woollerton & Wilson Ltd v Richard Costain Ltd* [1970] 1 All ER 483, Ds (building contractors) operated a crane in Cs' air space. The court suspended the injunction until Ds completed the building because Cs had refused reasonable compensation and the air space had become valuable only because of Ds' activities. In *Charrington v Simons & Co Ltd* [1971] 2 All ER 588, the soundness of that decision concerning the injunction was left open by the court and in *John Trenberth Ltd v National Westminster Bank Ltd* (1979) 253 *Estates Gazette* 151, the court held that the *Woollerton* case was wrongly decided and refused to follow it.

[103] Eg, *Dunton v Dover District Council* (1977) 76 LGR 87 (the use of a playground was confined to children under 12, and between 10am and 6.30pm).

[104] See *Loudon v Ryder (No 2)* [1953] Ch 423; *Springhead Spinning Co v Riley* (1868) LR 6 Eq 551. The possibility of an injunction, even though no tort has been committed, is doubly important when it is noted that s 50 of the Supreme Court Act 1981 enables the court to grant damages in addition to, or in substitution for, an injunction. For judicial discussion of the provision, see *Marcic v Thames Water Utilities Ltd (No 2)* [2001] 4 All ER 326.

[105] (1818) 2 Swan 402. In *Savoy Hotel plc v BBC* (1982) *Times*, 28 December the BBC filmed a barman in the Savoy bar allegedly giving short measure. Because this was without permission, the court granted an interim injunction forbidding the televising of the film.

the defendant from disclosing confidential and private material contained in letters (which had already been returned to the claimant, but of which the defendant had kept copies) written by the claimant to the defendant. Crucially, according to the court, an injunction would serve to protect the claimant's right of property in the letters. English tort law does not protect privacy as such,[106] but it is interesting that this English case has been the cornerstone of the development in the US of the tort of infringement of privacy.

Until 1982 it seemed that an injunction could be available to protect victims of criminal violations of statutes even though no action for breach of statutory duty lay. However, we saw earlier how *RCA Corpn v Pollard*[107] has ruled against the availability of injunctions in such cases.[108]

SECTION 3 LIMITATION OF ACTIONS[109]

(A) INTRODUCTION

At common law there was no time limit restricting the right to sue. Successive statutes from 1623 onwards introduced limitation periods after the expiry of which an action in tort is time-barred. The victim of an alleged tort must serve his writ within a specified number of years or forfeit his remedy.

The need for limitation periods is self-evident. Potential defendants would otherwise face years of uncertainty not knowing whether or not they will be sued. A fair trial becomes increasingly difficult as witnesses' memories fade and in some cases witnesses even die or leave the country. Accordingly, even if the claimant begins his cause of action within the statutory limitation period, his claim may still be struck out if he pursues it in a dilatory manner on the basis that this will amount to an abuse of process of the court.[110]

Very short and rigid time limits, however, also result in injustice to the claimant. He may not discover for some years that he has been the victim of a tort. Common examples include persons contracting industrial diseases, and the losses suffered by the owners of negligently constructed buildings. Taking first damage to the body from working conditions: this is likely to be stealthy and progressive with definitive symptoms of disease not manifesting themselves until years after the disease was in fact well established.[111] Similarly, when a building is erected on defective foundations, cracks

---

[106] But it is moving in this direction, see ch 15.

[107] [1983] Ch 135 and holding that *Ex p Island Records Ltd* [1978] Ch 122 was overruled by *Lonrho Ltd v Shell Petroleum Co Ltd* (No 2) [1982] AC 173.   [108] See Ch 20.

[109] See generally, McGee, *Limitation of Actions* (2002); Law Commission, *Limitation of Actions* (2001).

[110] *Grovit v Doctor* [1997] 1 WLR 640, at 647, *per* Lord Woolf; *Arbuthnot Latham Bank Ltd v Trafalgar Holdings Ltd* [1998] 2 All ER 181.

[111] See, eg, *Cartledge v E Jopling & Sons Ltd* [1963] AC 758 (pneumoconiosis from inhaling dust); *Thompson v Smiths Shiprepairers (North Shields) Ltd* [1984] QB 405 (industrial deafness); *Fairchild v Glenhaven Funeral Services Ltd* [2002] 3 All ER 305 (mesothelioma from inhaling asbestos dust).

may begin to ruin the fabric of the building years before they become apparent to even the most observant homeowner.[112] It would scarcely be fair to deny the worker suffering from disease or the unfortunate homeowner any remedy at all simply because a rigid limitation period had expired before they could have realized that they might have a right to compensation.

The relevant and complex law on limitation is now mainly contained in the Limitation Act 1980 (as amended by the Latent Damage Act 1986).[113] In the case of actions for injury caused by negligence, nuisance or breach of duty – whether the duty exists by virtue of a contract, a statute[114] or independently of either a contract or a statute – when the damages claimed by the claimant consist of, or include, damages in respect of personal injuries to the claimant or any other person, the period of limitation is three years.[115] In cases of actions for negligence, other than for personal injuries or death, the Latent Damage Act 1986[116] introduced a primary limitation period of six years (with provision in special circumstances for a further period of three years to run from the 'starting date' set by that Act). In either case, there is a final 'long-stop' of 15 years from the date of the act or omission constituting the negligence.[117]

An action for libel and slander must ordinarily be brought within one year, but there is a discretion to allow the action to proceed even after the expiry of the one-year period.[118] Where the claimant sues in respect of a defective product under the Consumer Protection Act 1987, he or she must normally bring the action within three years of suffering the relevant damage, or within three years of acquiring the necessary knowledge of the facts to sue if that date be later.[119] No action may be brought under the Consumer Protection Act 1987 more than 10 years after the product was first put into circulation.[120] The claimant may still have an action in negligence after that date where, even by then, he has not discovered his injury or damage or other relevant facts pertaining to his right of action in negligence. The limitation period for other tort actions remains six years.[121]

The three-year period of limitation for personal injuries applies only to 'any action for negligence, nuisance or breach of duty (whether the duty exists by virtue of a contract . . . a statute or independently of any contract or any such provision)'.[122]

The term 'personal injuries' includes any disease and any impairment of a person's physical or mental condition.[123] But what exactly is meant by the broad phrase 'breach

---

[112] See, eg, *Murphy v Brentwood District Council* [1991] 1 AC 398.

[113] For recommendations in favour of a streamlined, unitary approach to the limitation of actions in this context, see Law Com 270, *Limitation of Actions* (2001).

[114] A breach of a duty embodied in Community law that causes C to suffer the infringement of a right created by Community law will be treated in the same way as the breach of a domestic statutory duty: *R v Secretary of State for Transport, ex p Factortame Ltd (No 7)* [2001] 1 WLR 942. [115] Limitation Act 1980, s 11(1).

[116] By inserting a new s 14A into the Limitation Act 1980. [117] Limitation Act 1980, s 14B.

[118] Limitation Act 1980, s 4A. [119] Consumer Protection Act 1987, s 5(5) and Sch I.

[120] Consumer Protection Act 1987, s 5(5) and Sch I. [121] Limitation Act 1980, s 2.

[122] Limitation Act 1980, s 11(1).

[123] Limitation Act 1980, s 38(1). It also seems capable of embracing the failure to make proper provision for someone suffering from a congenital learning difficulty: *Phelps v Hillingdon London Borough Council* [2000] 3 WLR 776.

of duty'? In *Letang v Cooper*,[124] Lord Denning MR held those words to include *any* breach of *any* duty imposed by the law of tort. Thus where a claimant sought to sue for trespass to the person more than three years after the commission of the alleged trespass,[125] her action was barred. However, the House of Lords has now ruled in *Stubbings v Webb*[126] that Lord Denning was wrong. Availing themselves of their new freedom to consult *Hansard*,[127] their Lordships held that Parliament never intended the three-year limitation period to apply to deliberate torts such as trespass to the person.[128] Such torts were governed by the standard six-year period of limitation.

Any apparent advantage to the victim of a trespass action is, however, misleading. For although trespass does not fall within the three-year personal injuries rule, the claimant cannot take advantage of the special provisions permitting a claim exceptionally to be brought well after the original limitation period has expired.[129] *Stubbings v Webb* itself illustrates the claimant's dilemma. The claimant claimed that her adoptive father and stepbrother had sexually abused her in childhood. She sought to sue them in battery when she was 35 years old and came to appreciate the link between her ongoing psychiatric problems and that childhood abuse. The House of Lords ruled that her suit was subject to an absolute six-year limitation period. But had she, for example, been able to sue social workers whom she might have contended had negligently ignored her plight, the personal injuries rules in negligence would have come into play giving the court the discretion to allow her to proceed even after such a long period of time.[130]

(B) WHEN DOES A CAUSE OF ACTION ACCRUE?

A cause of action accrues, and hence the limitation period begins to run, at that moment in time when a potential claimant is entitled to succeed in an action against a potential defendant.[131] There must then be in existence such a claimant and defendant. If, for example, a tort is committed against the estate of a deceased person, and if his goods are taken away, the cause of action does not accrue until an executor or administrator

---

[124] [1965] 1 QB 232.

[125] Even where the trespass was intentional: *Long v Hepworth* [1968] 3 All ER 248.   [126] [1993] AC 498.

[127] See *Pepper (Inspector of Taxes) v Hart* [1993] AC 593.

[128] But note that positively giving permission for an uninsured third party to drive one's car is not treated as an intentional tort: *Norman v Ali* [2000] PIQR P72.

[129] If, however, the gist of C's action is that D was under a duty to prevent a third party from committing trespass against C, then the case does not fall to be dealt with as a (six-year) trespass case: *S v W* [1995] 3 FCR 649.

[130] For confirmation of this anomaly (whereby a claimant may be worse off relying on intentional wrongdoing rather than negligence) see *S v W* [1995] 1 FLR 862; *KR v Bryn Alyn Community Holdings Ltd* [2003] QB 1441; *A v Hoare* [2006] EWCA Civ 395. Note also that the failure of the argument (for reasons of being bound by the House of Lords) that the *Stubbings v Webb* approach should now be abandoned in the light of s 3 of the Human Rights Act 1998 requiring the courts to interpret legislation so far as possible in line with Convention Rights: *A v Hoare* [2006] EWCA Civ 395.

[131] More than one cause of action may arise from a single set of circumstances. In *Duke of Brunswick and Luneberg v Harmer* (1849) 14 QB 185, D's newspaper had published a statement defamatory of C. C's agent purchased a copy at D's office. 17 years later C's cause of action accrued upon the sale of this copy, not when the newspaper was first published.

is appointed.[132] A cause of action against an ambassador does not accrue until his diplomatic immunity ends.[133] On the other hand, a claimant whose car has been stolen by a thief whom he does not know and cannot trace has a cause of action against that thief from the time of the theft.[134] When a cause of action lies without proof of damage, time clearly always runs from the date of the wrongful act.

By contrast, in negligence, the cause of action accrues only when damage is suffered. In fact, this is the case in all torts where damage is essential to the cause of action. But ascertaining when damage occurs may be difficult. The crucial date is the date of the damage not its discoverability.[135] So when a negligently constructed security gate is the reason for a burglary's commission, the time runs from the date of the burglary, not the time of the negligent construction of the gate.[136] Where the relevant negligence consists of negligent advice, the question arises whether the damage founding the cause of action is suffered when the claimant relies on that advice,[137] or when the subsequent financial loss is suffered. The leading case of *Nykredit Mortgage Bank plc v Edwards Erdman Group Ltd (No 2)*[138] supports the latter approach. There, it was held that a purchaser's cause of action accrues at the time of the purchase. For, as Lord Nicholls explained, '[h]e suffers damage by parting with his money and receiving in exchange property worth less than the price he paid'.[139] This, of course, makes sense in that reliance is only relevant to the question of causation; and it is not *per se* a measurable head of loss.

The injustice to a claimant who would otherwise lose his right to a remedy before he could know of its existence explains why in the tort of negligence special provision is now made for all forms of latent damage with separate rules for personal injuries and other forms of damage.

(c) SPECIAL RULES FOR PERSONAL INJURIES[140]

The impetus for reform of the limitation rules concerning personal injuries came from cases relating to industrial disease. Where, for example, the claimant contracts pneumoconiosis from inhaling dust, his cause of action in negligence arises even though he is unaware of the onset of the disease. In *Cartledge v E Jopling & Sons Ltd*[141] the House of Lords held that, at common law, time started to run as soon as the damage was suffered. In this case, therefore, time ran once material scarring of the lung tissue had occurred, even though an X-ray examination would *not* have revealed it.

---

[132] *Murray v East India Co* (1821) 5 B & Ald 204; *Pratt v Swaine* (1828) 8 B & C 285.

[133] *Musurus Bey v Gadban* [1894] 2 QB 352.   [134] *R B Policies at Lloyd's v Butler* [1950] 1 KB 76.

[135] *Pirelli General Cable Works Ltd v Oscar Faber & Partners* [1983] 2 AC 1. Cf the position in New Zealand, established by the Privy Council, which renders uncertain the authority of *Pirelli*: *Invercargill City Council v Hamlin* [1996] 1 All ER 756.   [136] *Dove v Banhams Patent Locks Ltd* [1983] 2 All ER 833.

[137] *Forster v Outred & Co* [1982] 2 All ER 753; *Secretary of State for the Environment v Essex Goodman & Suggitt* [1986] 2 All ER 69.   [138] [1997] 1 WLR 1627.

[139] [1997] 1 WLR 1627.   [140] See Jones, *Limitation Periods in Personal Injury Actions* (1995).

[141] [1963] AC 758.

The Limitation Act 1980[142] seeks to avoid the injustice that would otherwise arise in such circumstances where a cause of action for personal injuries would become time-barred before the claimant knew of it. Thus, under the Act, the three-year limitation period begins to run either from the date of the accrual of the cause of action (that is, the date of the damage) or from the date of the claimant's knowledge of that damage, whichever is the later. The limitation period ends only three years after the date of the claimant's knowledge of the cause of action if that date is after three years from the accrual of the cause of action. If the claimant dies before the expiration of the period, the period as regards the cause of action surviving for the benefit of the estate of the deceased by virtue of section 1 of the Law Reform (Miscellaneous Provisions) Act 1934, is three years from the date of death or the date of knowledge of the personal representative.[143]

Section 14 of the Law Reform (Miscellaneous Provisions) Act 1934 provides a detailed definition of 'knowledge', the interpretation of which has given rise to complicated case law. When, in a personal injuries case, time runs from the date of a person's knowledge, the date is the date on which he first had knowledge of the following facts:[144]

(1) that the injury in question was significant;[145]

(2) that the injury was attributable in whole or in part to the alleged wrongful act or omission;[146]

(3) the identity of the defendant;[147]

(4) the identity of a third person (and any additional facts supporting the bringing of an action against the defendant) where that third person was guilty of the act or omission on which the claimant's case hangs.

The case law surrounding these factors has been summarized by the Court of Appeal and reduced to the following four rules:

1 The knowledge required to satisfy section 14(1)(b) of the Law Reform (Miscellaneous Provisions) Act 1934 is a broad knowledge of the essence of the causally relevant act or omission to which the injury is attributable.

---

[142] Limitation Act 1980, s 11.

[143] Limitation Act 1980, s 11(5), (6). For the corresponding application of these provisions to claims under the Fatal Accidents Act 1976 see ss 12(1) and 33.

[144] Law Reform (Miscellaneous Provisions) Act 1934, s 14(1). Note that there is an important distinction between 'knowledge' and 'belief': see *Nash v Eli Lilly & Co* [1993] 4 All ER 383. C's intelligence is relevant here (*McCafferty v Metropolitan Police District Receiver* [1977] 2 All ER 756), though his reasons for not suing are not (*Miller v London Electrical Manufacturing Co Ltd* [1976] 2 Lloyd's Rep 284).

[145] Under the Law Reform (Miscellaneous Provisions) Act 1934, s14(2), an injury is deemed significant if the person whose date of knowledge is in question would reasonably have considered it sufficiently serious to justify his instituting proceedings for damages against D who does not dispute liability and is able to satisfy a judgment.

[146] See *Wilkinson v Ancliff (BLT) Ltd* [1986] 3 All ER 427. C need not know the precise details of D's acts or omissions to set time running, only the essence of the act or omission: *Nash v Eli Lilly & Co* [1993] 1 WLR 782. He need not know that the act constitutes an actionable tort: *Brooks v J & P Coates (UK) Ltd* [1984] 1 All ER 702; *Broadley v Guy Clapham Co* [1994] 4 All ER 439; *Dobbie v Medway Health Authority* [1994] 4 All ER 450.

[147] C may have been knocked down by a hit-and-run driver, or D's firm may be a member of a group of interlocking companies – see *Simpson v Norwest Holst Southern Ltd* [1980] 2 All ER 471.

2 'Attributable' in this context means 'capable of being attributed to', in the sense of being a real possibility.

3 A [claimant] has the requisite knowledge when she knows enough to make it reasonable for her to begin to investigate whether or not she has a case against the defendant. Another way of putting this is to say that she will have such knowledge if she so firmly believes that her condition is capable of being attributed to an act or omission which she can identify (in broad terms) that she goes to a solicitor to seek advice about making a claim for compensation.[148]

4 On the other hand she will not have the requisite knowledge if she thinks she knows the acts or omissions she should investigate but in fact is barking up the wrong tree; or if her knowledge of what the defendant did or did not do is so vague or general that she cannot fairly be expected to know what she should investigate; or if her state of mind is such that she thinks her condition is capable of being attributed to the act or omission alleged to constitute negligence, but she is not sure about this, and would need to check with an expert before she could properly be said to know that it was.[149]

Section 14(1) expressly states that knowledge that any acts or omissions did, or did not, as a matter of law, involve negligence, nuisance or breach of duty is irrelevant.[150] In effect the claimant is deemed to know the legal significance of facts.[151] Furthermore, as regards knowledge of facts, it is clear that it is not just the claimant's *actual* knowledge that is relevant. Section 14(3) makes the following provision for constructive knowledge of the facts:

For the purposes of this section, a person's knowledge includes knowledge which he might reasonably have been expected to acquire:

(a) from facts observable or ascertainable by him; or

(b) from facts ascertainable by him with the help of medical or other appropriate expert advice which it is reasonable for him to seek; but a person shall not be fixed under this subsection with knowledge of a fact ascertainable only with the help of expert advice so long as he has taken all reasonable steps to obtain (and, where appropriate, act on) that advice.

The point of section 14(3) is to encourage a claimant to seek expert advice expeditiously. If he fails to do so, and remains ignorant in consequence, the burden lies with the defendant to show that it was unreasonable for the claimant not to seek advice taking account of purely objective criteria, but excluding subjective factors such as the intellect and character of the particular claimant.[152] If the claimant does consult an

---

[148] Cf someone who merely suspects that they may have suffered and whose investigation takes the form of seeking medical (as opposed to legal) advice in order to clarify matters: *Sniezek v Bundy (Letchworth) Ltd* [2000] PIQR P213.

[149] *Spargo v North Essex District Health Authority* [1997] PIQR P235, at P242, *per* Brooke LJ. See also *Griffin, Lawson and Williams v Clwyd Health Authority* [2001] EWCA Civ 818.

[150] That said, where C's action relies on D's omission, 'knowledge' cannot exist until C knows that something else could and should have been done: *Forbes v Wandsworth Health Authority* [1997] QB 402.

[151] See *Brooks v J & P Coates (UK) Ltd* [1984] 1 All ER 702.

[152] *Adams v Bracknell Forest BC* [2005] 1 AC 76.

expert, he is not prejudiced if the expert fails to find, or inform him of, the ascertainable facts.[153] Furthermore, since the subsection only applies to knowledge of a 'fact', it follows that a claimant who delays suing because he has received erroneous legal advice, will find that time runs against him if he has not issued a writ.[154] Similarly, since the subsection is confined to knowledge and what ought to be known, it does not extend to reasonable belief or reasonable suspicion.[155]

Nevertheless, in exceptional cases, the victim of personal injuries who fails to start his action in due time may, with permission of the court, still be able to proceed. Thus, the claimant who had knowledge of all the relevant facts but was unaware of his legal rights, or the claimant who has received hopeless legal advice, has one last chance to seek a remedy. By section 33(1) of the 1980 Act, the court may still allow an action to proceed notwithstanding the expiry of the limitation periods.[156] The court has a discretion to extend the statutory time limits if it considers it equitable to do so having regard to the degree to which the ordinary limitation rules prejudice the claimant, and the degree to which any exercise of the power would prejudice the defendant. The court must have regard to all the circumstances,[157] including:

(a) the length of, and the reasons for, the delay on the part of the claimant;[158]

(b) the effect of the delay on the cogency of the evidence in the case;

(c) the conduct of the defendant after the cause of action arose, including his response to the claimant's request for information;

(d) the duration of any disability of the claimant arising after the cause of action;[159]

(e) the extent to which the claimant acted promptly and reasonably once he knew of the facts which afforded him a cause of action; and

(f) the steps taken by the claimant to obtain medical, legal, or other expert advice and the nature of any such advice received.[160]

A very wide discretion, and one not limited to the six named factors, is given to the court.[161] So, for example, the fact that the defendant is insured is a relevant

---

[153] *Marston v British Railways Board* [1976] ICR 124.

[154] *Leadbitter v Hodge Finance Ltd* [1982] 2 All ER 167.   [155] *Nash v Eli Lilly & Co* [1993] 4 All ER 383.

[156] For detailed discussion, see *Clerk and Lindsell on Torts* (2006) pp 2009–2015.

[157] A balancing exercise is central to the deployment of this discretion and it is unacceptable simply to consider the effects of not exercising the discretion on either C or D: *KR v Bryn Alyn Community (Holdings) Ltd* [2003] 1 FCR 385. Furthermore, it has also been held that the courts should be slow to find the balance of prejudice in favour of C in the absence of cogent medical evidence showing a serious effect on C's health: *Robinson v St Helen's Metropolitan Borough Council* [2002] EWCA Civ 1099.

[158] *Thompson v Brown Construction (Ebbw Vale) Ltd* [1981] 2 All ER 296; *Long v Tolchard & Sons Ltd* [2001] PIQR P18.   [159] See, eg, *Barrow v Consignia plc* [2003] EWCA Civ 249.

[160] But note that C is not necessarily to be associated with his dilatory (or otherwise negligent) legal advisers *Das v Ganju* [1999] Lloyd's Rep Med 198.

[161] See, eg, *Firman v Ellis* [1978] QB 886. See also *Birkett v James* [1978] AC 297; *Liff v Peasley* [1980] 1 All ER 623; *Hartley v Birmingham City District Council* [1992] 2 All ER 213; *Shapland v Palmer* [1999] 3 All ER 50; *Steeds v Peverel Management Services Ltd* [2001] EWCA Civ 419.

consideration[162] as, too, is the fact that the case may involve putting the defendant to greater expense in defending the action than the action is actually worth.[163] There is, however, one restriction. Where the claimant has commenced proceedings and then discontinued them, only in the most exceptional case will the discretion be exercised in his favour.[164] Recall also that the decision of the House of Lords in *Stubbings v Webb*[165] denied the benefit of any such discretion to the victim of a deliberate tort.

(D) LATENT DAMAGE IN NON-PERSONAL INJURIES CASES

The special provision made by section 11 of the Limitation Act 1980 to assist claimants who lacked the necessary knowledge to start an action was restricted to actions for personal injuries. Yet the problems limitation periods pose for the victim of a latent defect can be just as acute in relation to damage to property. A series of Court of Appeal decisions sought to establish that the cause of action in such cases accrued only when the defect was discoverable.[166] But in *Pirelli General Cable Works Ltd v Oscar Faber & Partners*[167] the House of Lords overruled those decisions as inconsistent with *Cartledge v E Jopling & Sons Ltd*.[168] The facts in *Pirelli* highlight the problems of latent damage.

In 1969, Cs engaged Ds to advise them in relation to building a new chimney. Ds' design was negligently produced. Cracks occurred in the chimney and it had to be replaced. Cs first discovered the cracks in 1977 but they in fact first occurred in 1970. Cs served their writ in 1978 contending that the (six-year) limitation period did not begin to run until 1977 when they could first reasonably have discovered the defect.

The House of Lords held that the cause of action accrued in 1970 when the damage first occurred so the claim was time-barred. Two further acute difficulties for claimants emerged from the decision in *Pirelli*. Lord Fraser, in an *obiter dictum*,[169] suggested that where a defect was so gross that the building was 'doomed from the start',[170] time would begin to run even earlier: from the completion of the building. The result of such a doctrine – that is, that the worse the negligence, the more favourable the limitation period would be to the defendant – did not find favour in later decisions.[171]

---

[162] *Kelly v Bastible* (1996) 36 BMLR 51.   [163] *Nash v Eli Lilly & Co* [1993] 4 All ER 383.

[164] *Walkley v Precision Forgings Ltd* [1979] 2 All ER 548; *Deerness v John R Keeble & Son (Brantham) Ltd* [1983] 2 Lloyd's Rep 260.

[165] [1993] AC 498, at 552. See also *Halford v Brookes* [1992] PIQR P175 though in substance the judgment must now be considered incorrect.

[166] See *Sparham-Souter v Town and Country Developments (Essex) Ltd* [1976] QB 858; *Dennis v Charnwood Borough Council* [1983] QB 409.   [167] [1983] 2 AC 1.

[168] [1963] AC 758.   [169] [1983] 2 AC 1, at 16.

[170] See *Dove v Banhams Patent Locks Ltd* [1983] 2 All ER 833; *Jones v Stroud District Council* [1988] 1 All ER 5.

[171] See, eg, *Ketteman v Hansel Properties Ltd* [1987] AC 189 where the House of Lords adopted a severely restrictive view of 'doomed from the start'. The doctrine, if it existed, did not embrace any latent defect bound at some stage to result in damage to the property: [1987] AC 189.

The second difficulty arising from the case in relation to latent defects affected 'subsequent owners' of buildings. In *Pirelli* it was said that time did not start to run again in favour of the subsequent owner once he acquired the property.[172] But subsequent owners' problems were in fact more acute than simply being entitled only to the tag end of their predecessors' limitation period. Had they any claim at all in respect of damage to property to which, at the time damage occurred, they had no title? The essence of the claim in such a case is a claim for economic loss associated with the diminished value of the property that the subsequent owner has acquired. According to the House of Lords' decision in *Murphy v Brentwood District Council*,[173] such claims will now generally be inadmissible; yet their Lordships also managed to approve *Pirelli* on the basis that it was said to fall within the principle enunciated in *Hedley Byrne v Heller*.[174] As a consequence, there has been continuing confusion.[175]

The Law Reform Committee reported on these several problems concerning latent damage to property in 1984.[176] Their proposals were largely incorporated into the Latent Damage Act 1986 which applies not solely to latent damage to property, but also to all negligence actions other than claims in respect of personal injury or death. The Act took effect by inserting two new sections – sections 14A and 14B – into the Limitation Act 1980. The limitation period in actions to which sections 14A and 14B apply are now either six years from the date on which the cause of action accrued, or three years from the 'starting date' when the claimant had the necessary knowledge of the facts to bring an action.

'Knowledge' in this context is defined in section 14A(6)-(8) in terms virtually identical to those used to define 'knowledge' in the original section 14 for the purpose of extending the three-year period to bring an action in respect of personal injuries.[177] Section 14B of the 1980 Act imposes a 'long-stop' of 15 years from the date of the act or omission constituting the alleged negligence. Once 15 years have elapsed, no action at all may be brought, even though the claimant may not have discovered the relevant damage. This is because section 14B contains no provision similar to section 33 of the 1980 Act, which, as we have already seen, gives a judge the discretion to override this final limitation period.[178]

The Latent Damage Act 1986 represents a worthy attempt at compromise between the rights of claimants and defendants, but it still leaves some key questions unanswered. First, sections 14A and 14B apply to actions for negligence. But are they also applicable to actions for nuisance or breach of statutory duty where the essence of the wrong complained of is also often the absence of reasonable care?[179] Secondly, no clear definition of damage is provided.

---

[172] [1983] 2 AC 1, at 18.   [173] [1990] 2 All ER 908.
[174] [1990] 2 All ER 908, at 919, *per* Lord Keith.
[175] See McKendrick, '*Pirelli* Re-examined' [1991] *Legal Studies* 326.
[176] Twenty-fourth Report; *Latent Damage* (Cmnd 9390).
[177] See, eg, *Spencer-Ward v Humberts* [1995] 06 EG 148. In assessing C's knowledge, account will be taken of misleading advice that has been provided by 'experts' in the past that now prevents C from knowing that an actionable case exists: *Oakes v Hopcroft* [2000] Lloyd's Rep Med 294.
[178] But see the Latent Damage Act 1986, s 2 regarding fraud, concealment or mistake.
[179] For a 'yes' answer, see James, 'Statutory Liability for Negligence and the Latent Damage Act 1986' [1994] *Northern Ireland Legal Quarterly* 301.

One matter – concerning overlapping duties in contract and tort – that was once unclear has now been clarified. The Latent Damage Act 1986 is applicable only to actions in tort.[180] But, notwithstanding its inapplicability to contractual duties of care, some contractual relationships may still be governed by this limitation period where concurrent duties in contract and tort are owed.[181] According to *Henderson v Merrett Syndicates Ltd*,[182] the claimant is entitled to rely on that limitation period which is most advantageous to him; so in such circumstances, a claimant may well have recourse to the extendable limitation periods in tort.

Section 3 of the Latent Damage Act 1986 addresses the rights of successive owners of property. It provides that where a cause of action has accrued to A while he has an interest in that property, 'then providing B acquires the property', after the date on which the original cause of action accrued,

but before the material facts about the damage have become known to any person who, at the time when he first had knowledge of the facts, has any interest in the property; a fresh cause of action in respect of that negligence shall accrue to that other person on the date on which he acquires his interest in the property.

The limitation period as against the new owner is once again either six years from when his cause of action accrued (that is, his acquisition of the property) or three years from when he acquired knowledge of the relevant facts (subject once again to the 15-year 'long stop' in section 14B of the Limitation Act 1980).

Three further points must be noted about section 3 of the Latent Damage Act 1986. First, and most importantly, how can section 3 be reconciled with *Murphy v Brentwood District Council* which generally denies the existence of any duty of care in such cases?[183] Note that in *Murphy*, section 3 did not even get a passing mention from their Lordships! Secondly, although drafted with defective buildings in mind, the section applies to all property including goods. Finally, the new cause of action for the subsequent property owner arises only where his predecessor did not have any actual or constructive knowledge of the relevant defect.[184]

(E) CONTINUING WRONGS

Where the act of the defendant is a continuing wrong – for example, if he erects a building on the claimant's land and there is a continuing trespass – then, so long as it endures, a cause of action will lie providing it is based on the continuance of that

---

[180] *Iron Trades Mutual Insurance Co Ltd v JK Buckenham Ltd* [1990] 1 All ER 808; *Société Commerciale de Réassurance v ERAS (International) Ltd* [1992] 2 All ER 82.

[181] Note that many professional-client relationships would fall into this bracket.   [182] [1995] 2 AC 145.

[183] *Murphy* does not deny a duty of care where the defective property poses a threat of damage to other property, nor does it do so where the property damage is of the kind often referred to as 'complex structure' damage. These would appear to be the only two exceptions to the seeming redundancy of s 3 in this context.

[184] In what circumstances (if any) could the subsequent owner sue the vendor who failed to disclose his knowledge of the relevant defects?

wrong during the six years (or three years in the case of personal injuries) immediately preceding the action.[185] To put it another way, once the wrong ceases, the claimant can claim for all the harm that occurred by virtue of the continuance within the previous six or three years, depending on the kind of harm. An example of a continuing wrong is an ongoing failure to implement an EC Directive as required by statute. The loss associated with failure so to implement is of an ongoing nature and therefore not time barred.[186]

(F) EFFECT OF DISABILITY OF THE CLAIMANT

If, on the date when any right of action accrued, the person to whom it accrued was a minor or a person of unsound mind,[187] the action may be brought at any time before the expiration of six years (or three years in the case of personal injuries) from the date when the person ceased to be under that disability, or died, whichever event first occurred.[188]

Where the cause of action has once vested in a person who is free from disability, and the period has therefore began to run, should that person (or some other person to whom the cause of action has passed subsequently) become disabled, the period will not on that account be further extended.[189] When a right of action which has accrued to a person under disability vests, on the death of that person while still under a disability, in another person also under a disability, there, too, there is no further extension of time permitted by reason of the disability of the second person.[190] Where a person, in whom a cause of action has vested, was, at the moment of vesting, under one disability – for example, minority – and, at or before the cessation of that disability, the person becomes insane, time does not begin to run until he has 'ceased to be under a disability',[191] that is until the last of his disabilities has ended.

The fact that disability may persist for a very long time obviously works to the disadvantage of the defendant. But according to *Headford v Bristol and District Health Authority*[192] it was not an abuse of process to institute proceedings after a 28-year delay, even though the delay was apparently unjustified other than in terms of the Act's provision for an extension of the limitation period.

---

[185] *Hardy v Ryle* (1829) 9 B & C 603; *Earl of Harrington v Derby Corpn* [1905] 1 Ch 205.

[186] *Phonographic Performance Ltd v DTI* [2004] 1 WLR 2893.

[187] By the Limitation Act 1980, s 38(3) 'a person is of unsound mind if he is a person who, by reason of mental disorder within the meaning of the Mental Health Act 1983 is incapable of managing and administering his property and affairs'. The court will not strike out an action by an infant claimant for negligence for mere inactivity on his part before his twenty-first birthday: *Tolley v Morris* [1979] 2 All ER 561.

[188] Limitation Act 1980, ss 28(1) and 28A. For an illustration of the operation of these provisions see again *Stubbings v Webb* [1993] AC 498; *Tolley v Morris* [1979] 2 All ER 561.

[189] Limitation Act 1980, s 28(2). But in personal injury actions, the court may take account of this factor in deciding whether to exercise its s 33 discretion to extend the limitation period.

[190] Limitation Act 1980, s 28(3).   [191] Limitation Act 1980, s 28(1).   [192] [1995] 6 Med LR 1.

(G) POSTPONEMENT OF LIMITATION PERIODS IN CASES OF FRAUD OR CONCEALMENT

Where the action is based on the fraud of the defendant or his agent, or of any person through whom he claims (or that person's agent),[193] or where any fact relevant to the right of action is deliberately concealed by any such person, the period shall not begin to run until the claimant has, or with reasonable diligence could have, discovered the fraud or concealment.[194] It is not sufficient if the defendant has merely concealed facts that would strengthen the claimant's claim; they must be central to him framing such a claim in the first place.[195] On the other hand, once a cause of action has arisen, subsequent concealment of facts relevant to the claimant's action will postpone the running of the limitation period.[196]

A tort is 'based upon fraud' only where fraud is a necessary allegation in order to constitute the cause of action.[197] (Presumably, deceit is the only tort based upon fraud in this sense.) Deliberate commission of a breach of duty in circumstances in which it is unlikely to be discovered for some time amounts to deliberate concealment of the facts involved in that breach of duty.[198] The House of Lords – despite the ambiguity of the language used in the provision ('deliberate conduct' does not necessarily imply deliberate harm) – has made it clear that moral wrongdoing on the part of the defendant is an essential ingredient.[199] 'Fraud' in the Act is to be interpreted very widely.[200] It appears, rather than to bear any technical meaning, to signify simply 'conscious wrongdoing'.[201]

SECTION 4 TORT AND CONTRACT

For a time, the Court of Appeal, in a series of decisions,[202] gave support to *dicta* by Lord Scarman in *Tai Hing Cotton Mills Ltd v Liu Chong Hing Bank Ltd*[203] to the effect that where the relationship between two parties is contractual, no concurrent duty should lie in tort. Yet it has since been authoritatively determined that concurrent duties in contract and tort may in fact lie.[204] Furthermore, the claimant is at complete liberty to

---

[193] In *Eddis v Chichester Constable* [1969] 2 Ch 345, these words included the tenant for life where Cs were the trustees and owners of an heirloom fraudulently sold by the tenant for life.

[194] Limitation Act 1980, s 32(1). [195] *C v Mirror Group Newspapers Ltd* [1996] 4 All ER 511.

[196] *Sheldon v RHM Outhwaite (Underwriting Agencies) Ltd* [1996] AC 102.

[197] *Beaman v ARTS Ltd* [1949] 1 KB 550 (conversion was held not to be an action based on fraud).

[198] Section 32(2). See also *Beaman v ARTS* [1949] 1 KB 550.

[199] *Cave v Robinson Jarvis & Rolf* [2003] 1 AC 384: the moral wrongdoing on the part of D must exist *either* in respect of the act that constitutes the breach of a duty *or* in connection with the concealment of a duty that was breached without any malice.

[200] *Beaman v ARTS* [1949] 1 KB 550; *Kitchen v Royal Air Force Association* [1958] 2 All ER 241.

[201] *Beaman v ARTS* [1949] 1 KB 550, at 572, *per* Singleton LJ.

[202] *National Bank of Greece SA v Pinios Shipping Co* [1990] 1 AC 637; *Lee v Thompson* (1989) 2 PN 91; *Johnstone v Bloomsbury Area Health Authority* [1992] QB 333. [203] [1985] 2 All ER 947, at 957.

[204] *Henderson v Merrett Syndicates Ltd* [1995] 2 AC 145.

choose whichever cause of action he thinks will be most advantageous to him.[205] That choice may be crucial for the following reasons:

(1) Causes of action for liquidated damages may perhaps be assignable if they lie in contract,[206] but not if they lie in tort.

(2) Although the claimant may not freely evade the contractual immunities of minors and mentally disordered persons by suing in tort, in some circumstances he can sue them for torts committed in the course of a contractual relationship.

(3) There are circumstances in which an action in contract will give greater damages than one under the Fatal Accidents Acts.[207] Although the Fatal Accidents Acts may perhaps bind the Crown in tort proceedings, they do not bind the Crown in contract actions (to which they also extend).

(4) The Crown is answerable in tort for the acts of a restricted class of 'servants'.[208] That restricted definition does not apply to actions against the Crown for breaches of contracts made by servants of the Crown.

(5) Trade unions are partially immune from tortious liability but are fully liable for breaches of contract.[209]

(6) Most importantly, the rules relating to limitation of actions differ depending on whether the claimant sues in contract or tort. In contract, time starts to run from the date of the breach of contract; in negligence it runs only from the date damage was suffered, or the date when the claimant had the necessary knowledge of the facts to sue, if that is later. The claimant-friendly provisions of the Latent Damage Act 1986 do not apply to an action for breach of a contractual duty of care.[210] But note that the availability of the defence of contributory negligence no longer depends on which remedy the claimant seeks where the essence of the claim is breach of a duty of care rather than of a strict contractual obligation.[211]

SECTION 5 TORT AND UNJUST ENRICHMENT[212]

(A) ELECTION OF REMEDIES

It has been held that, in appropriate circumstances, a claimant has the choice of suing either in tort or in the law of unjust enrichment.[213] For example, if the defendant wrongfully takes the claimant's goods and sells them, the claimant is said to have the choice of

---

[205] [1995] 2 AC 145, at 194, per Lord Goff.

[206] County Hotel and Wine Co Ltd v London and North Western Rly Co [1918] 2 KB 251, at 258, per McCardie J (not considered on appeal when affirmed on other grounds: [1919] 2 KB 29, [1921] 1 AC 85).

[207] Sellars v Best [1954] 2 All ER 389.   [208] Crown Proceedings Act 1947, s 2.   [209] See below.

[210] Iron Trades Mutual Insurance Co Ltd v J K Buckenham Ltd [1990] 1 All ER 808.

[211] Forsikringsaktieselskapet Vesta v Butcher [1989] AC 852.

[212] See Edelman, Gain-Based Damages: Contract, Tort, Equity and Intellectual Property (2002) ch 4; Cane, The Anatomy of Tort Law (1997) ch 5.   [213] A-G v Blake [2001] 1 AC 268, at 280, per Lord Nicholls.

suing in conversion or bringing an action for restitution of an unjust enrichment for the price received by the defendant. It is not proposed to examine here the intricacies of the law of unjust enrichment (which would be necessary if every possible circumstance giving rise to both tortious and restitutionary remedies were to be considered).[214] It suffices to note two things: first, that the torts in which such an election is likely to arise are conversion,[215] trespass to goods,[216] trespass to land by removing minerals,[217] and deceit;[218] and secondly, that it is questionable whether in juridical terms there is a straightforward election between a compensatory remedy (in tort) and a restitutionary remedy (based on the defendant's unjust enrichment).[219] In conversion cases, the loss suffered by the defendant will frequently coincide exactly with the gain made by the defendant. Imagine A steals B's watch and sells it for the market value of £60. If B sues on the basis of A's gain he will receive just the same amount as if he sues on the basis of his own loss. But if B sues on the former basis, this does not *ipso facto* render the damages received restitutionary in nature. In as much as B suffered a loss, and in so far as the damages he receives perform corrective justice, they may perfectly well be viewed as compensatory in nature.[220]

This election by the claimant to sue for 'restitution' has sometimes been erroneously described as a 'waiver' of the tort. The claimant does not 'waive' the tort if he elects to sue for restitution.[221] He is free at any time before he has signed judgment to abandon his restitutionary claim and pursue, instead, a remedy in tort. Equally, his suit in unjust enrichment will not bar proceedings in tort on the same facts against another wrongdoer unless the claimant has not merely obtained judgment, but has also had satisfaction of it. It is true that if he signs judgment in unjust enrichment, his claim in tort against that defendant is barred,[222] but that is merely an illustration of the rule that where the claimant has succeeded in one cause of action he has no further cause of action, howsoever framed, in respect of that very same interest for which the first cause of action lay.

These rules are clearly illustrated by the leading case of *United Australia Ltd v Barclays Bank Ltd.*[223]

A cheque payable to Cs was wrongfully endorsed by M & Co, presented by M & Co for payment to, and collected for it by, Ds (its bankers). Cs discontinued an unjust enrichment action against M & Co for money had and received without obtaining final judgment. Cs then sued Ds for

---

[214] On this, see Edelman, *Gain-Based Damages: Contract, Tort, Equity and Intellectual Property* (2002).

[215] *Lamine v Dorrell* (1705) 2 Ld Raym 1216; *Thomas v Whip* (1715) cited in 1 Burr 458.

[216] *Oughton v Seppings* (1830) 1 B & Ad 241; *Rodgers v Maw* (1846) 15 M & W 444; *Neate v Harding* (1851) 6 Exch 349. [217] *Powell v Rees* (1837) 7 Ad & El 426.

[218] *Hill v Perrott* (1810) 3 Taunt 274; *Mahesan S/O Thambiah v Malaysian Government Officers' Co-operative Housing Society* [1979] AC 374.

[219] The true nature of damages for unjust enrichment is a matter of great disagreement. Compare the account in Edelman, *Gain-Based Damages: Contract, Tort, Equity and Intellectual Property* (2002) with Giglio, 'Restitution for Wrongs: A Structural Analysis' (2007) XX *Canadian Journal of Law and Jurisprudence* (forthcoming)

[220] For a good analysis of the nature of the remedies supported by an action in conversion see Tettenborn, 'Conversion, Tort and Restitution' in Palmer and McKendrick (eds), *Interests in Goods* (1998) p 825.

[221] Hedley, 'The Myth of Waiver of Tort' (1984) 100 LQR 653; Edelman, *Gain-Based Damages: Contract, Tort, Equity and Intellectual Property* (2002) p 124. And see *Maheson S/O Thambiah v Malaysian Government Officers' Co-operative Housing Society* [1979] AC 374, where the court also held that a principal whose agent had received a bribe could either sue for deceit or recover the bribe in unjust enrichment, but that he could not be compensated twice over. [222] *United Australia Ltd v Barclays Bank Ltd* [1941] AC 1, at 30, *per* Lord Atkin.

[223] [1941] AC 1.

conversion of the cheque. The House of Lords held that Cs could not be said to have 'waived' their right to sue Ds by having instituted proceedings against M & Co – nothing less than satisfaction of a judgment in the first proceedings would have barred this action in tort for the same damage. Cs, therefore, were not precluded from bringing the present action in tort.

(B) ADVANTAGES OF PROCEEDINGS IN TORT OR UNJUST ENRICHMENT

The crucial difference between proceeding on the basis of normal tort principles and suing for the restitutionary remedy lies in the different measure of damages.[224] For example, if A converts B's watch valued at £10, a suit in conversion will allow B to recover £10. But if A sells it to C for £15, B can recover £15 in unjust enrichment as money had and received by A!

Some of the differences between contract and tort mentioned in the previous section are also relevant here: for example, the disabling effect in contract of infancy or insanity[225] and the operation of the Crown Proceedings Act 1947 in relation to tort actions. Finally, if X makes use of Y's land without causing any tangible harm to that land, a restitutionary remedy based on a fair rental value, will be available.[226]

FURTHER READING

Beever, 'The Structure of Aggravated and Exemplary Damages' (2003) 23 OJLS 87

Burrows, 'Reforming Exemplary Damages' in Birks (ed), *Wrongs and Remedies in the 21st Century* (1996)

Burrows, *Remedies for Torts and Breach of Contract* (2004)

Gray, 'Interlocutory Injunctions since *Cyanamid*' [1981] CLJ 307

Hedley, 'The Myth of Waiver of Tort' (1984) 100 LQR 653

James, 'Statutory Liability for Negligence and the Latent Damage Act 1986' [1994] *Northern Ireland Legal Quarterly* 301

Law Commission, *Limitation of Actions* (2001)

McBride, 'Punitive Damages' in Birks (ed), *Wrongs and Remedies in the 21st Century* (1996)

McKendrick, '*Pirelli* Re-examined' [1991] *Legal Studies* 326

Ogus, 'Exemplary Damages and Economic Analysis' in Hawkins (ed), *The Human Face of Law: Essays in Honour of Donald Harris* (1997)

Tettenborn, 'Conversion, Tort and Restitution' in Palmer and McKendrick (eds), *Interests in Goods* (1998)

---

[224] In *Universe Tankships Inc of Monrovia v International Transport Workers' Federation* [1983] 1 AC 366, the House of Lords held that by bringing an action in unjust enrichment (instead of inducing breach of contract) against a trade union, the immunity of trade unions under s 13 of the Trade Union and Labour Relations Act 1974 was evaded by C.   [225] See *Morriss v Marsden* [1952] 1 All ER 925, at 927, *per* Stable J.
[226] *A–G v Blake* [2001] 1 AC 268, at 279, *per* Lord Nicholls. For the analytically compelling, but judicially unsupported, argument that this is *not* a restitutionary award, see Giglio, 'Restitution for Wrongs: A Structural Analysis' (2007) XX *Canadian Journal of Law and Jurisprudence* (forthcoming).

27

PRINCIPLES OF COMPENSATION FOR PERSONAL INJURIES AND ASSOCIATED LOSSES

SECTION 1 INTRODUCTION

The function and the anomalies of tort law as a system of loss distribution in society are well illustrated when we consider the overall provision made for compensation of personal injuries today. The victim's financial future may well turn on whether he is successful in establishing that his injuries are someone else's 'fault'; essentially, that a tort was committed. Should he succeed, he and his family will receive a level of compensation, which, while its method of assessment may be criticized, will help to meet his material needs and will far exceed the total of social welfare benefits available to an equally severely injured person unable to prove 'fault'[1] on the part of another.

Consider this rough example. X, Y and Z, all aged 25, suffer severe brain damage rendering them incapable of continuing paid employment. X's accident happens while he is swimming in a cold lake. He gets into difficulties and by the time he is rescued from drowning and resuscitated, the brain damage inflicted by lack of oxygen is irreversible. Y suffers brain damage in the course of surgery to remove his appendix. Proceedings are started on his behalf but allegations of negligence against the hospital are not substantiated. Z's injuries are inflicted in a road accident for which the driver of the other car accepts liability. All three accident victims, before their misfortunes, were earning £25,000 a year.

Providing X and Y are successful in obtaining the maximum available social security benefits they will still receive far less than Z, the only victim to benefit from the torts system.[2] This then begs the question of how this discrepancy can be explained or justified. In the case of X, is it that his accident was his own 'fault' and that he took the risk upon himself?[3] What about Y? Anaesthesia is inherently risky. Does Y have to accept the risk

---

[1] For a thoroughgoing critique and indictment of the 'fault' principle, see Cane (ed), *Atiyah's Accidents Compensation and the Law* (2006).

[2] For an illustration of the degree of discrepancy, see the 11th edition of this work (with figures current as of tax year 2003–2004).   [3] See *Tomlinson v Congleton Borough Council* [2004] 1 AC 46.

to attain the benefit of the surgery? It could even be argued that X and Y should have insured themselves against their respective injuries. But then so could Z. Yet, even if Z had insured himself, he would still receive his insurance monies *in addition to* his award of damages, as we shall see later.

Considerations such as these lead inevitably to a fundamental questioning about the operation of the 'fault' system upon which tort law is widely thought to be premised.[4] This is a huge question involving considerations of corrective justice (upon which there is no settled notion) and economic analysis of tort law (a subject in itself[5]) as well as a careful study of the inter-relationship between tort law and insurance.[6] The pros and cons of various no-fault compensation schemes – such as the one implemented in New Zealand, and others partially implemented elsewhere in the common-law world – have been discussed elsewhere (including previous editions of this book) both ably and amply.[7] Yet, while the debate on compensating personal injuries via tort law has raged for over three decades, there seems little to no present prospect of the tort system being overhauled in this country. Even so, for the sake of completeness, a short section appears at the end of the this chapter which describes briefly various alternative compensation schemes.

SECTION 2 AWARDS OF DAMAGES TO LIVING CLAIMANTS

It must not be forgotten that the overwhelming majority of claims for damages for personal injuries never come to court.[8] Furthermore, damages have historically been granted on a once-and-for-all basis,[9] which inevitably – because of the role played by speculation – leads to imperfections in the compensatory awards made. Indeed, the process of assessing lump sum damages in this way often consists, in truth, of little more than judicial guesstimates: 'How long will the claimant actually live?', 'Will she develop epilepsy in five years' time?'. Such awards, by their very nature, cannot provide comprehensively and accurately for all such contingencies *except* as a matter of luck. A claimant whose medical prognosis is judged overly pessimistically will gain a bonus, while the converse is also true. In short, individual corrective justice gets sacrificed in the interests

---

[4] See especially *Report of the Royal Commission on Civil Liability and Compensation for Personal Injury* (1978) (Cmnd 7054–1) (hereafter *Pearson Report*) paras 1716–7.

[5] See, eg, Calabresi, *The Cost of Accidents* (1970). Cf Schwartz, 'Reality in the Economic Analysis of Tort Law: Does Tort Law Really Deter?' (1994) UCLA Law Rev 377.

[6] See, eg, Atiyah, *The Damages Lottery* (1997); Stapleton, 'Tort, Insurance and Ideology' (1995) 58 MLR 820.

[7] See, eg, Sugarman, *Doing Away with Personal Injury Law* (1989); Atiyah, *The Damages Lottery* (1997); Palmer, *Compensation for Incapacity* (1979); Harris, 'Accident Compensation in New Zealand: A Comprehensive Insurance System' (1974) 37 MLR 361.

[8] See Genn, *Hard Bargaining* (1987) and *id*, *Compensation and Support for Illness and Injury* (1984).

[9] One exception is where a provisional award is made enabling C to re-apply for further damages if a risk of further damage (eg, epilepsy) does in fact materialize: see the Supreme Court Act 1981, s32A.

of finality and predictability. Unsurprisingly, such imperfections have attracted much criticism; even from leading members of the judiciary.[10] In particular, a system of periodic payments that can be adjusted over time to meet the claimant's needs are generally regarded as a more effective and just compensation mechanism in cases of severe injury.[11] Thus, while lump sum awards can and will still be made in respect of run-of-the-mill injuries, it is also now possible to obtain a periodic payment order in respect of severely injured claimants (and these may even be made on a reviewable basis in certain circumstances[12]). Such periodical payments were first made available on a statutory footing in 2005.[13] Unlike the voluntary structured settlements that they replaced, these orders can be imposed on the parties even if they are individually or jointly opposed to such an arrangement. Drawing up the necessary initial schedule can be a complex matter, and it is for this reason that periodical payments orders were made reviewable in certain circumstances so that modifications to the order can be effected in the future in the light of, typically, a serious deterioration in the claimant's condition.[14] On the other hand, it is important to stress that the order needs to be made reviewable at the outset, and that reviewability is by no means the norm.

Whether paid in the form of a lump sum or in the form of periodic payments, compensatory damages in tort can be broken down into three main components:

(1) pecuniary losses – primarily but not exclusively those resulting from loss of earnings or earning capacity;

(2) cost of further care such as medical and hospital expenses. (The aim of compensation under both these preliminary heads will be to restore the claimant, so far as money alone ever can, to the position which he would have enjoyed had the tort never been committed[15]);

(3) non-pecuniary loss – that is, pain and suffering and loss of amenity.[16]

---

[10] See, eg, *Wright v British Railways Board* [1983] 2 AC 773, at 776–8, *per* Lord Diplock.

[11] But for criticism and doubt, see Lewis, 'Appearance and Reality in Reforming Periodical Payments of Tort Damages in the UK' in Neyers (ed), *Emerging Issues in Tort Law* (2007).

[12] See the Damages Act 1996, ss 2–2B (as substituted by the Courts Act 2003 and the Damages (Variation of Periodical Payments) Order 2005). Part of what now falls under the rubric of periodical payments was formerly known as 'structured settlements'. Some of the relevant literature therefore refers to structured settlements.

[13] Damages Act 1996 (as amended by the Courts Act 2003 and the Damages (Variation of Periodical Payments) Order 2005). The impetus for this statute was provided largely by the Law Commission in its review of such settlements: Consultation Paper No 125, *Structured Settlements and Interim and Provisional Damages* (1992). See also Law Com No 224, *Structured Settlements and Interim Provisional Damages* (1994).

[14] But note that, controversially, no facility for review is made in respect of the escalating costs of health care provision that may well rise at a rate in excess of inflation. See further Lewis, 'Appearance and Reality in Reforming Periodical Payments of Tort Damages in the UK' in Neyers (ed), *Emerging Issues in Tort Law* (2007) and *Clerk and Lindsell on Torts* (2006) pp 1844–1845.

[15] For recognition of the artificiality of this exercise, see *Heil v Rankin* [2000] PIQR Q187, at Q193, *per* Lord Woolf MR. See also Stapleton, 'The Normal Expectancies Measure in Tort Damages' (1997) 113 LQR 257.

[16] For a detailed account of the composition of non-pecuniary loss see Law Com No 257, *Damages for Personal Injury: Non-Pecuniary Loss* (1999). See also Ogus, 'Damages for Lost Amenities: For a Foot, a Feeling or a Function?' (1972) 35 MLR 1 and Rogers (ed), *Damages for Non-Pecuniary Loss in a Comparative Perspective* (2001).

The Court of Appeal exercises overall supervision over the level of awards and sets the 'tariff' for non-pecuniary losses. Itemisation of awards is now encouraged to enable awards from individual High Court judges to be scrutinized properly.[17]

(A) PECUNIARY LOSSES

(1) LOSS OF EARNINGS

A number of years is likely to elapse between the infliction of the relevant injuries and the trial.[18] Loss of earnings up to the date of trial are part of the claimant's 'special damages' and must be specifically pleaded.[19] In making such pleas it is important to realise that all claims for loss of earnings (including business profits[20]) are computed in a way that is consistent with deductions that would have been made by way of tax.[21] Loss of perquisites, will also be taken into account.[22]

One's prospective loss of earnings is, of course, recoverable.[23] And in this context the court is forced to estimate the claimant's future employment prospects,[24] his future incapacity[25] and the number of working years of which he has been deprived.[26] The traditional judicial method is to arrive at a multiplicand (which represents an estimate of the claimant's net annual loss); and then to multiply this by a multiplier (which represents the number of working years lost by the claimant). The starting point for arriving at the multiplier is the number of remaining years in the claimant's working life.[27] This figure is then reduced to take account of contingencies such as future unemployment and sickness and, above all (in the case of a lump sum), the fact that the claimant may

---

[17] *George v Pinnock* [1973] 1 WLR 118. For an example see *Housecroft v Burnett* [1986] 1 All ER 332. And see also *Practice Direction (personal injuries actions: particulars of claim)* [1984] 3 All ER 165.

[18] Matters have improved to some extent in the wake of the changes made to the availability of legal aid and the introduction of tracking of claims within the Civil Justice System.

[19] *Ilkiw v Samuels* [1963] 2 All ER 879.　　　[20] *Kent v British Railways Board* [1995] PIQR Q42.

[21] *British Transport Commission v Gourley* [1956] AC 185. The case sets out in detail how the notional tax liability is to be calculated.

[22] *Clay v Pooler* [1982] 3 All ER 570. Where a director is able to show that his company suffered a loss of profits through his incapacity, so that his earnings fell, damages for this loss were awarded: *Lee v Sheard* [1956] 1 QB 192.

[23] But not if the claim is barred by illegality. So, if C lied to his employer in order to get the job, he may not sue for the lost earnings he would otherwise have received: *Hewison v Meridian Shipping PTE* [2002] EWCA Civ 1822.

[24] Or, in the case of a professional sportsperson, his or her likely winnings by comparison with the previous year: *Raitt v Lunn* 2002 WL 31599780.

[25] But note that this estimate is now subject to variation if the award takes the form of a reviewable periodic payment: Damages Act 1996, s 2B.

[26] This paragraph is based mainly on the speeches of the House of Lords in *Taylor v O'Connor* [1971] AC 115 and *Cookson v Knowles* [1979] AC 556. For the most modern statement on the correct approach to the computation of loss of earnings in cases of long-term disability, see *Herring v Ministry of Defence* [2003] EWCA Civ 528. See also *Clenshaw v Tanner* [2002] EWCA Civ 1848 on the deductions that can be made in order to take account of the likely effects of C's alcohol abuse on his future earning potential.

[27] If there is great uncertainty associated with the calculation, the courts will, instead, grant a lump-sum based on the best estimate the court can make as to C's loss: *Chase International Express Ltd v McRae* [2003] EWCA Civ 505.

receive a capital sum which he is expected to invest in interest-bearing securities. In the important House of Lords decision in *Wells v Wells*,[28] it was held that there is an expectation that the prudent claimant will take advantage of index-linked government securities which yield a low but safe average net return. The relatively low return associated with such securities has to be reflected in a higher initial lump sum than would formerly have been made.[29] The award is calculated on the basis that the claimant will spend the income and part of the capital annually so that the capital will be exhausted at the age the court has assessed to be the appropriate age having regard to all the contingencies. Currently, the courts assume a 2.5% rate of interest which is net after tax.[30] In practice, the experience of the court has resulted in a multiplier which, for example, in the case of a 30-year-old, would ordinarily be about 17, reducing to about 14 in the case of a man of about 40.[31] Practitioners are familiar with current judicial trends and out of court settlements are negotiated on the basis of these current 'going rates'.[32]

Until *Wells v Wells*, actuarial evidence was discouraged by the courts despite the fact that actuaries are accustomed to using statistical tables to work out expectancies and to 'discount' capital awards so as to reflect contingencies and the immediate receipt of the capital sum.[33] The main criticism made against actuarial tables was that, being produced for insurers, they were designed to deal with average expectancies within *groups* rather than with the actual expectancies of particular individuals (with whom the courts had to deal). Put thus, this criticism is somewhat misleading, for it takes no account of the fact that actuarial tables can be drawn up more specifically – for example, on an occupation-specific basis – than the criticism suggests. Furthermore, it fails to indicate why a judicial guesstimate would be any more accurate than such tables. In recognition of this fact, there was support in *Wells v Wells* for counsel generally endeavouring to calculate their clients' claims in accordance with the most well-known set of such tables – the *Ogden Tables*.[34] If it ever comes into force, section 10 of the Civil Evidence Act 1995 will afford statutory recognition to the use of these *Ogden Tables*.

---

[28] [1998] 3 All ER 481.

[29] In terms of presumed rates of return, *Wells* was decided on the basis of a 3% return (compared with something in the region of 4.5% which had previously been the expectation). Since June 1998, however, the Lord Chancellor (exercising his powers under the Damages Act 1996, s 1 to prescribe 'from time to time' a rate of return which serves as an official guide to the courts) has set a discount rate of 2.5%: see Damages (Personal Injury) Order 2001.

[30] This was set by the Damages (Personal Injury) Order 2001. However, if any party to the proceedings can show that a different rate is more appropriate in the particular case, the court may use that rate: Damages Act 1996, s 1(2). For details of s 1(2) in operation, see *Clerk and Lindsell on Torts* (2006) p 1821.

[31] See *Pritchard v JH Cobden Ltd* [1988] Fam 22.

[32] Relying heavily on publications such as the looseleaf Kemp and Kemp, *The Quantum of Damages* (1975).

[33] *Mitchell v Mulholland (No 2)* [1972] 1 QB 65. In *Auty v National Coal Board* [1985] 1 All ER 930, at 939, Oliver LJ commented: 'the predictions of an actuary can only be a little more likely to be accurate (and will almost certainly be less entertaining) than those of an astrologer'. The courts seem to take a very different attitude to actuarial evidence when approving those periodical payments formerly known as structured settlements: see Law Com 125, *Structured Settlements and Interim and Provisional Damages* (1992) pp 53–4. See also, Kemp, 'Discounting Damages for Future Loss' (1997) 113 LQR 195.

[34] *Actuarial Tables for use in Personal Injury and Fatal Accident Cases* (2004).

The courts will not hear evidence from economists on future inflationary trends.[35] The House of Lords has stated that such evidence is too speculative[36] and has taken the view that, by prudent investment, the claimant can offset the effects of inflation.[37] Only in very exceptional cases will any allowance be made for inflation to offset the effect of higher-rate tax on very large awards.[38]

Although there is no shortage of examples of the courts showing faith in the efficacy of fine tuning the multiplicand and multiplier in order to provide an award which is both just and meets the claimant's needs,[39] considerable problems have from time to time been encountered. One of these problems centres on the time that may elapse between the date of the accident and the date of the trial. In such a case, the claimant will of course receive his actual loss of earnings up to the trial. Yet the defendants in *Pritchard v J H Cobden Ltd*[40] sought to argue that the multiplier – fixed by reference to the period likely to elapse between the date of the trial and the end of the claimant's working life – should be reduced to allow for the actual loss recovered as special damages and to discourage delay in bringing personal injuries actions to trial. Their contentions were ultimately rejected. The Court of Appeal stressed the need that the claimants had for a certain and predictable sum in lost earnings to defray their immediate post-injury expenses.

A second difficulty that has been encountered concerns fixing a suitable multiplier where the medical evidence suggests that the claimant will die early as a result of his injuries. Should he be able to recover compensation for his 'lost years' when, but for the fatal injury, he would have lived longer? Loss of income in the 'lost years' is now recoverable[41] subject to a deduction for the claimant's living expenses during those 'lost years'.[42] For claimants injured in the middle of their working life when they have families and dependants, such income should clearly be recoverable. It is needed to ensure that even after the claimant's premature death his family does not suffer and that the claimant himself can enjoy some relative peace of mind in what remains of his life. Section 3 of the Damages Act 1996 now provides for this eventuality, allowing dependants to claim for those losses not compensated by the original award of damages.

It is now clear that the courts will compensate loss of earning capacity[43] as readily as loss of earnings. So a married woman who at the time of her injuries is engrossed in child rearing will be compensated for any loss of earning capacity running from the

---

[35] *Mitchell v Mulholland (No 2)* [1972] 1 QB 65. But see again Law Com 125, pp 12–14 deploring this stance.

[36] See *Lim Poh Choo v Camden and Islington Area Health Authority* [1980] AC 174, at 193, *per* Lord Scarman.

[37] *Cookson v Knowles* [1979] AC 556; *Wells v Wells* [1998] 3 All ER 481.

[38] *Hodgson v Trapp* [1989] AC 807, at 835, *per* Lord Oliver.

[39] For an exception see *Read v Harries* [1995] PIQR Q 25.   [40] [1988] Fam 22.

[41] *Pickett v British Rail Engineering Ltd* [1980] AC 136.

[42] Including a *pro rata* sum for his consumption of housing, electricity costs etc: *Harris v Empress Motors Ltd* [1983] 3 All ER 561.

[43] *Smith v Manchester Corpn* (1974) 17 KIR 1; *Dhaliwal v Personal Representatives of Hunt* [1995] PIQR Q56. But what of C who elects to paint unprofitably rather than do well-paid commercial work? See *Keating v Elvan Reinforced Concrete Co Ltd* [1967] 3 All ER 611.

time when she would have been likely to return to remunerated work outside the home.[44] Children and young people who have not started earning will receive compensation for the damage to, or destruction of, their employment prospects. The older the child and the more evidence there is of her prospects of remunerated work, the larger the award will be.[45] With a very young child, the highly speculative nature of assessing her loss of earning capacity will not disentitle her from such an award, but it may mean a relatively small amount is received under this head. In *Croke v Wiseman*,[46] for example, a 21-month old boy was permanently incapacitated in a medical accident. He was seven at the date of the trial and likely to survive until he was 40. To compensate him for his loss of earnings, a multiplicand of £5,000, and a multiplier of five years, were set by the Court of Appeal. No award was made in respect of loss of earnings in the 'lost years'. This now seems standard for children and young people.[47]

(2) MEDICAL, NURSING AND HOSPITAL EXPENSES[48]

A claimant is entitled to recover as special damages those medical, nursing and hospital expenses which he has reasonably incurred up to the date of trial. His predicted future expenses will then be estimated and awarded as general damages. Where the claimant has received private health care or plans to arrange future treatment privately, the possibility that the claimant could have avoided these expenses by using the facilities of the NHS is to be disregarded.[49] Yet, if it is clear that private medical care will not be used, the courts will refuse to entertain any claim that the claimant makes in respect of any such care he *might have elected* to use.[50] In other respects, the expenditure must be reasonable both in relation to the claimant's condition and the amount paid. If he has to live in a special institution or in special accommodation, the additional expense is recoverable.[51] He cannot claim the capital cost of acquiring special accommodation since he continues to own that accommodation.[52] But he can claim the additional annual cost over his lifetime of providing special accommodation and the capital cost of any alterations or conversions needed to meet his disability that do not enhance the value of the property.[53] Any saving to the claimant which is attributable to his maintenance at public expense in a hospital, nursing home or other institution is set off against any loss of earnings.[54]

---

[44] *Daly v General Steam Navigation Co Ltd, The Dragon* [1980] 3 All ER 696.

[45] See *Housecroft v Burnett* [1986] 1 All ER 332 (£56,000 for loss of earning capacity awarded to an intelligent 16-year-old girl).   [46] [1981] 3 All ER 852.

[47] See *Housecroft v Burnett* [1986] 1 All ER 332. Cf *Harvey v Northumberland County Council* [2003] EWCA Civ 338 (C, a young adult, got £9,000 for his thwarted ambition to become a police officer).

[48] See Law Com No 262, *Damages for Personal Injury: Medical, Nursing and Other Expenses: Collateral Benefits* (1999).

[49] Law Reform (Personal Injuries) Act 1948, s 2(4). If C does make use of the NHS he cannot recover what he would have had to pay if he had had private treatment: *Lim Poh Choo v Camden and Islington Area Health Authority* [1980] AC 174.   [50] *Woodrup v Nicol* [1993] PIQR Q 14.

[51] *Shearman v Folland* [1950] 2 KB 43; *George v Pinnock* [1973] 1 All ER 926.

[52] *Cunningham v Harrison* [1973] QB 942.   [53] *Roberts v Johnstone* [1989] QB 878.

[54] Administration of Justice Act 1982, s 5.

The claimant is able to claim his nursing expenses. If the court finds, however, that at some future time he will be unable to obtain all the private nursing services required, and will have to enter an NHS hospital, an appropriate deduction from future nursing expenses will be made.[55] On the other hand, where the burden of caring for the claimant is largely shouldered by relatives or friends, the claimant's right to compensation to pay for such services is normally unaffected.[56] He is entitled to receive a sum to recompense, for example, his wife, mother or friend.[57] That the carer has given up gainful employment must be taken into account and generally his or her loss should be made good, although the total cost of care should not exceed current commercial rates for professional nursing care.[58] Recompense is also available even though the relative is simply caring for the claimant voluntarily, out of love.[59] On the other hand, if a spouse provides gratuitous assistance in running her injured husband's business, no award will be made in relation to the value of these essentially commercial services.[60]

There is no need for the injured party to enter into any contractual agreement with his relative or friend. Indeed, any such agreement made for the purpose of increasing the award for care will be treated as a sham.[61] The need for additional help for the family by way of night sleepers to help a paralysed claimant, and substitute help to give family members a holiday, must not be overlooked, however. Nor must the monetary value of gratuitous care formerly provided by the claimant for another member of the family. So, for example, if X is injured by virtue of Y's tort, X may claim the value of the care he used to provide gratuitously for his disabled brother Z.[62]

Exceptionally, nursing care cannot be recouped in the case where the carer was also the tortfeasor who inflicted the injury. In *Hunt v Severs*,[63] for example, a wife had run over her husband in a car but no award was made in relation to the nursing care she later provided, since the House of Lords stated that this head of damage was only to be awarded in circumstances where the claimant had a moral duty to account for those damages to the carer. In other words, the objection was that such damages would have been a perverse award 'compensating the [tortfeasor] carer'.[64]

---

[55] *Cunningham v Harrison* [1973] QB 942.

[56] *Hunt v Severs* [1994] 2 AC 350; *Donnelly v Joyce* [1974] QB 454 (mother gave up job to care for six-year-old C); *Cunningham v Harrison* [1973] QB 942 (a wife gave up her job to nurse her husband); *Roberts v Johnstone* [1989] QB 878 (care provided by adoptive mother). But note the important distinction between caring services and business services: *Hardwick v Hudson* [1999] 1 WLR 1770.

[57] In *Croke v Wiseman* [1981] 3 All ER 852, C had a life expectancy of 33 years, throughout which he would need continuous nursing by professional nurses and his parents. In awarding £119,000 for the future cost of nursing care the court took account of the mother losing her teacher's pension rights, valued at £7,000, on giving up her post.

[58] *Housecroft v Burnett* [1986] 1 All ER 332. Where, however, the carer's net loss of earnings is a lesser amount than the commercial rate for caring, the amount will nonetheless be confined to the carer's net loss: *Fitzgerald v Ford* [1996] PIQR Q72.

[59] But here, it has been suggested that the amount should be equal to 75% of the commercial rate for help: *Fairhurst v St Helens and Knowsley Health Authority* [1995] PIQR Q1.

[60] *Hardwick v Hudson* [1999] PIQR Q202.

[61] *Fairhurst v St Helens and Knowsley Health Authority* [1995] PIQR Q 1.

[62] *Lowe v Guise* [2002] QB 1369.   [63] [1994] 2 AC 350.

[64] [1994] 2 AC 350, at 394, *per* Lord Bridge. But why should the loss be so seen? Why is it not to be regarded in terms of C's need for such care? For criticism see Matthews and Lunney, 'A Tortfeasor's Lot is not a Happy

(3) ADDITIONAL PECUNIARY LOSSES AND EXPENSES

Loss of earnings or earning capacity, and medical and nursing expenses commonly form the bulk of the pecuniary loss resulting from personal injuries. But other losses and expenses which can be shown to flow from the claimant's injuries will also generally be recoverable. These include obvious additional costs of coping with a life of disability,[65] expenses of removal to a specially adapted dwelling,[66] a specially built invalid car or some other means of giving the claimant mobility,[67] a telephone for emergencies[68] etc. Similarly, losses resulting from no longer being able to pursue a profitable hobby will also be recoverable. And a married woman whose injuries impaired her capability to do housework received an award for that impairment based on the cost of obtaining household help.[69]

But certain 'losses' resulting from injury are more problematic. Historically, young unmarried women received an award for loss of marriage prospects where they suffered disabling or disfiguring injuries. That award was generally regarded as part of the claimant's recompense for loss of amenity. But young female claimants paid for it in that, in assessing the multiplier for loss of future earnings, account was taken of the likelihood of marriage and motherhood reducing the number of years in which the claimant was likely to be earning.[70] In a break with the past, the judge in *Hughes v McKeown*[71] made no award for loss of marriage prospects and consequently declined to reduce the multiplier used to calculate the award for loss of earnings from that appropriate to a young man of similar age. The Court of Appeal later suggested that either approach is acceptable.[72] But in the modern era, loss of a young woman's marriage prospects coupled with a presumed dependency upon a husband would seem to be sexist. If anything, the loss of marriage and parenthood prospects should be reflected in the award for loss of amenity and be available equally to young men.

A second problematic 'loss' occurs where injuries lead to the breakdown of the claimant's marriage. Can he or she recover the additional expenditure involved in running two homes and maintaining a former spouse? The Court of Appeal has held such expenses to be irrecoverable.[73] They are not 'losses' resulting from the injuries but merely a redistribution of assets. In any case, such 'losses' should be excluded as a matter of policy, since the spectre of sham 'divorces' clearly cannot be ignored.

One' (1995) 58 MLR 395. Note also the fact that the Australian Courts have refused to follow the *Hunt v Severs* approach: *Kars v Kars* (1996) 141 ALR 37.

[65] In *Kroeker v Jansen* (1995) 123 DLR (4th) 652 an award was made to a woman 'disabled from some of her housework beyond the level that her husband ought reasonably to do for her'.

[66] *Moriarty v McCarthy* [1978] 2 All ER 213 (paraplegic moving to a bungalow).

[67] *Housecroft v Burnett* [1986] 1 All ER 332.   [68] *Moriarty v McCarthy* [1978] 2 All ER 213.

[69] The award was made regardless of whether it was actually used to obtain domestic help: *Daly v General Steam Navigation Co Ltd, The Dragon* [1980] 3 All ER 696.   [70] *Moriarty v McCarthy* [1978] 2 All ER 213.

[71] [1985] 3 All ER 284.

[72] *Housecroft v Burnett* [1986] 1 All ER 332; but what of the 20-year-old law student who has a training contract at a London firm? Her prospective earnings may be higher than her speculative 'husband's' and she may well never give up paid work. And what about the financial loss to a young man deprived of the chance of marrying a high-earning wife?   [73] *Pritchard v J H Cobden Ltd* [1988] Fam 22.

The exclusion of damages on policy grounds has also surfaced in other contexts. In one case, a rapist who had earlier recovered damages for the change of personality he suffered after a traumatic injury, attempted to obtain an indemnity for the damages he was ordered to pay his victims. His attempt failed.[74] In cases in which mothers have attempted to obtain damages for wrongful birth, it is now clear that no award will lie in respect of the ordinary costs associated with raising a healthy child;[75] but damages will be available in respect of the special costs associated with raising a disabled child.[76]

Where a claimant was permanently incapacitated and, in addition to loss of earnings, there was a 'cost of care' claim, the House of Lords sought to avoid any duplication of damages as follows.[77] A full award for loss of earnings was made in the usual way with no deduction for living expenses except in respect of the 'lost years'. In calculating the award for cost of care, however, a deduction was made for the living expenses the claimant would have incurred in any event had she not been injured.

Other miscellaneous losses that would fall into this category include the loss of the opportunity of obtaining affordable health or life insurance,[78] the loss of lodgings which have to be surrendered when the claimant is unable to work any longer because those lodgings had been provided by the employer,[79] and the loss of a company car.[80]

(4) DEDUCTION FOR BENEFITS RECEIVED[81]

The pecuniary losses and expenses resulting from injury may on occasion be offset by benefits received whether from social security, insurance provision or charity. But on what bases should such benefits be set off against the award to be made to the claimant? Social security benefits are now dealt with in the Social Security (Recovery of Benefits) Act 1997. That Act provides protection for damages awards made in respect of pain, suffering and loss of amenity against the recoupment of social security benefits. Taken together, section 8 and Schedule 2 of the Act permit recoupment only as against compensation for loss of earnings, the cost of care and loss of mobility. The scheme affects the defendant in the following way. As regards those damages that represent the amount payable in respect of pain, suffering and loss of amenity, the defendant is directly liable to the claimant. As regards the amount now paid to the claimant by way of state benefits in respect of loss of earnings etc, the defendant is, instead, liable to the Secretary of State. The principle is simple: the state shall not bear the pecuniary cost of the defendant's tort, while the claimant at the same time should not be compensated twice over.

---

[74] *Meah v McCreamer (No 2)* [1986] 1 All ER 943. See also *Clunis v Camden and Islington Health Authority* [1998] 3 All ER 180.

[75] *McFarlane v Tayside Health Board* [1999] 3 WLR 1301; *AD v East Kent Community NHS Trust* [2002] EWCA Civ 1872.

[76] *Parkinson v St James and Seacroft University Hospital NHS Trust* [2002] QB 266; *Groom v Selby* [2002] PIQR P201.   [77] *Lim Poh Choo v Camden and Islington Area Health Authority* [1980] AC 174.

[78] *A v National Blood Authority* [2001] 3 All ER 289.   [79] *Liffen v Watson* [1940] 1 KB 556.

[80] *Clay v Pooler* [1982] 3 All ER 570.

[81] For comprehensive coverage, see Lewis, *Deducting Benefits from Damages for Personal Injury* (2000).

But one possible exception to this principle is contained in Part II of Sch 1 to the Social Security (Recovery of Benefits) Act 1997 which allows for regulations to be made for disregarding small payments.[82]

Social security benefits are not the only collateral benefits which may result from the claimant's injury and consequent disability. Few general principles can be deduced from the authorities about when such benefits should be deducted from the award of damages for loss of earnings and additional expenditure. As such, any attempt to present a rational picture of the rules is likely to fail. Nonetheless, it does seem clear that the courts will generally make every effort to encourage benevolence so that charitable payments made to the claimant – for example, from a disaster fund – will not be deducted;[83] nor generally will *ex gratia* payments made by employers be deducted.[84] In addition, proceeds of personal insurance policies provided for by the claimant or his family will not be deducted.[85] But where, even despite his sickness or disability, the claimant receives sick pay as part of his contract of employment, he must account for those monies[86] (unless the contract provides that sick pay must be refunded in the event of a successful tort claim[87]).

In *Parry v Cleaver*[88] the House of Lords held that an occupational disability pension was not deductible regardless of whether it was contributory or discretionary. The test, their Lordships held, was twofold: was the money received of the same nature as what was lost; and, if not, was it a benefit still intended to be paid even if the claimant were to be reimbursed from another source? In the light of this test, statutory sick pay payable by the employer under the Social Security and Housing Benefits Act 1982 was held to be deductible.[89] It was seen as essentially the same as a contractual entitlement to sick pay.

In *Hussain v New Taplow Paper Mills Ltd*[90] the injured claimant received long-term sickness benefit provided for by a permanent health insurance scheme arranged by his employers and taken out for their (that is, the employers') benefit. The monies received were held to be indistinguishable from contractual sick pay and were not seen as analogous to a disability pension or private insurance monies. The Court of Appeal suggested that, as between claimant employees and their employers, *ex gratia* benefits ought to be accounted for and that the claimant should generally only recover his net loss. But difficulties arise because two basic principles of compensatory damages conflict. First, as *Hussain* affirmed, the claimant should receive only his actual estimated loss, and should not gain a net benefit from his injuries. Yet, on the other hand, the tortfeasor should not benefit either from the claimant's own prudence in insuring himself, or from the benevolence of others.

---

[82] 'Small payments' are those of £2,500 or less. There is no sign of any such regulations at present.

[83] *Redpath v Belfast and County Down Rly* [1947] NI 167; approved in *Parry v Cleaver* [1970] AC 1.

[84] *Cunningham v Harrison* [1973] QB 942. Cf *Hussain v New Taplow Paper Mills Ltd* [1987] 1 All ER 417 (where D was the employer).

[85] *Bradburn v Great Western Rly Co* (1874) LR 10 Exch 1; approved in *Parry v Cleaver* [1970] AC 1.

[86] *Turner v Ministry of Defence* (1969) 113 Sol Jo 585.   [87] *Browning v War Office* [1963] 1 QB 750.

[88] [1970] AC 1; followed in *Longden v British Coal Corpn* [1998] AC 653.

[89] *Palfrey v Greater London Council* [1985] ICR 437.

[90] [1988] AC 514. See also *College v Bass Mitchells & Butlers Ltd* [1988] 1 All ER 536 (redundancy payments).

'Victory' for the net loss principle in *Hussain* was short-lived. In *Smoker v London Fire and Civil Defence Authority*,[91] the House of Lords affirmed *Parry v Cleaver*. Thus, a contributory disability pension remains non-deductible even if provided and partly paid for by the employer. Similarly, in *McCamley v Cammell Laird Shipbuilders Ltd*[92] the defendant employers took out and paid for personal accident policies on behalf of all their employees. The proceeds of such policies were held to be non-deductible as these were payable whenever an employee suffered a qualifying injury regardless of fault. It was a product of the employers' benevolence not a consequence of the tort which later materialized. *Hussain*, then, is probably best seen as confined it to its own particular facts.[93] As such, only if part of the claimant's claim is that he has lost the opportunity to accumulate greater pension rights will the pension payable after the normal date of retirement be taken into account.[94]

(B) NON-PECUNIARY LOSSES[95]

(1) PAIN AND SUFFERING

The claimant is entitled to compensation for the pain and suffering, both actual and prospective, which is caused by the initial injury or subsequent surgical operations.[96] If his expectation of life has been reduced by his injuries, an award of damages for pain and suffering shall take account of any suffering caused or likely to be caused to him by awareness that his expectation of life has been shortened.[97] A permanently unconscious claimant has no claim for pain and suffering.[98] Nor, according to *Kerby v Redbridge Health Authority*,[99] is mere sorrow or upset at the loss of a child actionable.

(2) LOSS OF AMENITIES

Compensation is also recoverable for loss of faculty. Even though the accident has rendered the claimant a 'human vegetable' so that he is unaware of his injuries, he is still

---

[91] [1991] 2 AC 502.   [92] [1990] 1 All ER 854.

[93] Tentatively suggested in *McCamley v Cammell Laird Shipbuilders Ltd*, [1990] 1 All ER 854, at 860.

[94] *Longden v British Coal Corpn* [1998] AC 653.

[95] For a full review of the current law and potential reforms in respect of amenity loss, quantum of damage and interest on awards see Law Com No 257, *Damages for Personal Injury: Non-Pecuniary Loss* (1999). For the role of the Court of Appeal in setting levels of damages see *Heil v Rankin* [2000] PIQR Q187.

[96] *H West & Son Ltd v Shephard* [1964] AC 326; *Cutler v Vauxhall Motors Ltd* [1971] 1 QB 418. In *Sutton v Population Services Family Planning Programme Ltd* (1981) *Times*, 7 November, damages were awarded for the premature onset of the menopause. And in *Kralj v McGrath* [1986] 1 All ER 54, C received damages for her trepidation concerning a further wanted pregnancy after an obstetric 'nightmare', while in *Barber v Somerset County Council* [2004] 1 WLR 1089 a nervous breakdown caused by work-related stress was treated as falling under this head.

[97] Administration of Justice Act 1982, s 1(1)(b). Damages for loss of expectation of life as such, and as a separate head of damage, were abolished by this Act.   [98] *Wise v Kaye* [1962] 1 QB 638.

[99] [1994] PIQR Q 1.

entitled to claim for any loss of bodily function.[100] Damages cannot be refused simply because the claimant will be unable to enjoy the damages in view of the severity of his injuries.[101] This is because the award for loss of amenities must be made on the basis of amenities lost; awareness of deprivation being irrelevant. The court will take into account deprivation of sexual pleasures,[102] loss of a holiday,[103] inability to fish,[104] disfigurement,[105] as well as more obvious losses, such as inability to play games or to walk. In short, damages under this head may take account of a wide range of subjective factors.

(3) ASSESSING THE QUANTUM

Non-pecuniary damages differ from pecuniary damages in that there is no scientific method of deciding what sum should be awarded. Damages for loss of amenity and pain and suffering have traditionally been awarded as an aggregate lump sum. This sum represents an amount that society deems fair (fairness being interpreted by the courts in the light of previous decisions); and in this regard there has evolved a set of conventional principles which provide a provisional guide to the comparative severity of different forms of injury. This guide uses a system of brackets of damages into which particular types of injury fall. In other words, loss is generally[106] compensated according to a tariff – for example, a sum between £A and £B for the loss of an arm, and between £X and £Y for the loss of an eye. However, the particular circumstances of the claimant, including his age and any unusual deprivation which he suffers are also taken into account. So, too, is the fact that the injuries were inflicted in the context of a rape.[107]

One particular problem for these guidelines is the continual fall in the value of money. This, of course, necessitates an ongoing reassessment of these awards.[108] What happens in practice, then, is that practitioners' books and periodicals[109] regularly publish judicial awards under all the relevant heads – for example, blindness, loss of a leg, etc – with brief details of the claimant's circumstances. This enables the claimant's lawyers and the defendant's insurers to agree likely awards, and it also assists the judges in conforming to the (real value) levels of awards made by their brethren. Nonetheless,

---

[100] *H West & Son Ltd v Shephard* [1964] AC 326; *Lim Poh Choo v Camden and Islington Area Health Authority* [1980] AC 174. [101] *H West & Son Ltd v Shephard* [1964] AC 326.

[102] *Cook v JL Kier & Co Ltd* [1970] 2 All ER 513. [103] *Ichard v Frangoulis* [1977] 2 All ER 461.

[104] *Moeliker v A Reyrolle & Co Ltd* [1977] 1 All ER 9.

[105] Where a husband's disfigurement caused his wife to leave him and his children, £7,000 was awarded to him under that head in *Oakley v Walker* (1977) 121 Sol Jo 619. Financial losses resulting from divorce are generally irrecoverable: *Pritchard v JH Cobden Ltd* [1988] Fam 22.

[106] The courts may depart from the standard tariff where the circumstances of a particular case require it. See, eg, *Griffiths v Williams* (1995) *Times*, 24 November (the court took account of the fact that C was a rape victim).

[107] In *Griffiths v Williams* (1995) *Times*, 24 November, the Court of Appeal stated that the consequences of injuries incurred in such cases placed them in a distinct category from the generality of personal injuries cases.

[108] *Birkett v Hayes* [1982] 2 All ER 710.

[109] Especially Kemp and Kemp, *The Quantum of Damages* (1975) and the monthly publication, *Current Law*, under the heading of 'Damages'.

the difficulty of awarding a sum given the constant fall in the value of money is well illustrated in *Housecroft v Burnett*.[110]

The injuries sustained by the 16-year-old claimant resulted in tetraplegia. The life which she could have expected with its pleasures, career prospects and the hope of a family was replaced by complete dependence on her mother for every aspect of her care. The court recognised the imprecise nature of the task but stressed the need for uniformity where possible. As such, it was held that the bracket of acceptable awards should be set by reference to recent decisions.

However, when considering the exact amount to award within the appropriate bracket, extreme physical pain, or the impairment of speech or hearing ought to justify an award above the average; whereas as a lack of awareness of one's disability might be taken to justify an award at the lower end of the range. But the difficulty of comparing levels of injury is well illustrated in *McCamley v Cammell Laird Shipbuilders Ltd*.[111] There, the claimant lost most of an arm and a leg on one side. He continued to suffer great pain and regained very little mobility. The trial judge awarded him £85,000, equivalent to the then going rate for tetraplegia. The Court of Appeal considered the award to be very generous, yet refused to overturn it. This decision points to the fact that the superior courts are generally reluctant to overturn damages awards unless they are *drastically* out of line with common practice (making the amount awarded, at least in part, a matter of luck). Furthermore, the reluctance of the superior courts to exercise their supervisory function in this context can be quite remarkable on occasion. In *Kiam v MGN Ltd*[112] – admittedly a defamation case – the Court of Appeal refused to disturb an award of £105,000 made by the jury even though the trial judge had suggested a bracket of between £40,000 and £80,000. The amount was not, according to the court, out of all proportion to what might sensibly have been thought appropriate.

(4) PROVISIONAL AWARDS

Sometimes, the courts are called upon to award prospective damages where the claimant's medical prognosis is imprecise. For example, the injury may have created a risk of, say, epilepsy developing later in life. The courts used to estimate the percentage chance of such a condition developing and award an equivalent proportion of damages for the results of that condition. Claimants were consequently over-compensated if the risk did not materialize and under-compensated if it did. The Administration of Justice Act 1982 accordingly provided an alternative. Where there is a chance that the claimant at some time in the future will, as a result of the tort, develop some serious disease or suffer some serious deterioration in his physical or mental condition, the court will assess damages on the assumption that the development or deterioration will not occur, but award further damages at a future date if it does so occur, upon an application made by the claimant.[113]

---

[110] [1986] 1 All ER 332.   [111] [1990] 1 All ER 854.   [112] [2002] 2 All ER 219.

[113] The 1982 Act merely provided for rules to be made under it that grant this jurisdiction. They have now been made. See Supreme Court Act 1981, s 32A(1) and (2). See also RSC Ord 37, rr 8–10.

The rules on provisional damages have in the past given rise to problems of application,[114] and it is submitted that the courts will now, where the facility exists, much prefer to make use of the facility for reviewable periodical payments (considered above) that have been able to be ordered since 2005.

(5) INTEREST

The courts have the power to award interest on all or any part of an award of damages and should do so on awards for personal injuries or death unless there are 'special reasons' not to do so.[115] Detailed exposition of the rules on interest is beyond the scope of this work.[116] It suffices to note simply the general rule that interest on pre-trial pecuniary loss will be payable at half the average rate on short-term investment accounts for that period.[117] No deduction of interest is normally made to take account of social security benefits received by the claimant.[118] Interest payable on non-pecuniary loss will be low – not more than 2% at present.[119]

(C) DAMAGE OR DESTRUCTION OF GOODS

Claimants in personal injury actions often also have a claim for damage to goods such as their cars. Where the car or other goods are destroyed, damages are made up of the cost of buying a replacement, together with compensation for loss of use pending replacement, with a deduction for the salvage value of the destroyed goods.[120] Where there is damage to goods, the measure is the diminution in value, normally based on the cost of repair.[121] Damages are also given for loss of use, even though the goods were non-profit earning and not replaced during repair.[122] If a substitute has been hired, then the cost can be claimed provided the goods hired and the price paid are reasonable.[123]

SECTION 3 DEATH

Two issues arise when death ensues from a tort. First, the deceased's estate may wish to proceed with the cause of action which the deceased himself would have had if he had

---

[114] For examples, see the 11th edition of this work.   [115] Supreme Court Act, s 34A.

[116] See Burrows, *Remedies for Torts and Breach of Contract* (2004) pp 256–62.

[117] *Jefford v Gee* [1970] 2 QB 130.

[118] *Wisely v John Fulton (Plumbers) Ltd* [2000] 2 All ER 545. But where the benefits exceed the damages due to be paid, such a deduction may be made: *Griffiths v British Coal Corpn* [2001] 1 WLR 1493.

[119] *Lawrence v Chief Constable of Staffordshire* [2000] PIQR Q349; *Wright v British Railways Board* [1983] 2 AC 773. The reasons are (1) damages should take into account inflation up to the time of judgment and (2) damages for non-pecuniary loss are often difficult to quantify until C's condition has stabilized.

[120] *Moore v DER Ltd* [1971] 3 All ER 517; *Thatcher v Littlejohn* [1978] RTR 369. See also *Liesbosch Dredger v SS Edison* [1933] AC 449.   [121] *Dodd Properties (Kent) Ltd v Canterbury City Council* [1980] 1 All ER 928.

[122] *The Mediana* [1900] AC 113; *HL Motor Works (Willesden) Ltd v Alwahbi* [1977] RTR 276.

[123] *HL Motor Works (Willesden) Ltd v Alwahbi* [1977] RTR 276 (reasonable to hire a Rolls Royce until C's Rolls Royce was repaired).

not died. Secondly, others – but especially relatives – may claim that they have suffered a loss in consequence of the death. Two statutes need therefore to be examined: the Law Reform (Miscellaneous Provisions) Act 1934 (dealing with the survival of actions), and the Fatal Accidents Act 1976 (dealing with death itself giving rise to a cause of action).

(A) SURVIVAL OF ACTIONS

The Law Reform (Miscellaneous Provisions) Act 1934 provides that, subject to three significant exceptions, on the death of any person, all causes of action vested in him survive for the benefit of his estate.[124] The first exception is that actions for defamation do not survive. Secondly, the right of a person to claim under section 1A of the Fatal Accidents Act 1976 for bereavement does not survive for the benefit of his estate.[125] Thirdly, exemplary damages do not survive in the hands of the deceased's estate.[126] The reason why these actions die with the initial victim is that they are all regarded as claims personal to the deceased; although why this should be true of exemplary (as opposed to aggravated) damages is hard to fathom.

Where the death of the deceased has been caused by an act or omission giving rise to a cause of action, the 1934 Act enables his estate to bring proceedings in tort against the defendant.[127] His estate may claim damages according to the usual principles for the period between when the cause of action arose and the death. Thus, damages may be awarded for the pain, suffering[128] and loss of amenity[129] for that period during which the deceased actually suffered such deprivations. Damages may also be awarded for lost earnings[130] and medical expenses incurred up to the time of death.[131]

The damages awarded to his estate 'shall be calculated without reference to any loss or gain to his estate consequent on his death'.[132] Thus, if the deceased loses an annuity to which he was entitled, or if insurance monies become payable upon his death, these losses and gains are disregarded in computing damages under the 1934 Act. The rights conferred by the Act are in addition to any rights conferred by the Fatal Accidents Act 1976.[133] The award of damages under the earlier legislation is the same whether or not an award is also made under the 1976 Act.

---

[124] Section 1(1).

[125] Administration of Justice Act 1982, s 4(1). It does, however, extend to a registered same-sex civil partner.

[126] Administration of Justice Act 1982, s 4(2).

[127] For the limitation periods within which these proceedings must be brought, see the Limitation Act 1980, s 11(5)–(7).

[128] *Andrews v Freeborough* [1967] 1 QB 1 (£2,000 awarded to the estate of a child aged 8 who remained unconscious for a year between the accident and death); *Murray v Shuter* [1976] QB 972 (£11,000 awarded to the estate of a man aged 36 in respect of loss of amenity during the four years he survived the accident in a coma).

[129] *Rose v Ford* [1937] AC 826 (£2 awarded for loss of leg amputated two days before death).

[130] *Murray v Shuter* [1976] QB 927.   [131] *Rose v Ford* [1937] AC 826.

[132] Law Reform (Miscellaneous Provisions) Act 1934, s 1(2). For application see *Harland and Wolff plc v McIntyre* [2006] EWCA Civ 287.

[133] Law Reform (Miscellaneous Provisions) Act 1934, s 1(5); *Yelland v Powell Duffryn Associated Collieries Ltd (No 2)* [1941] 1 KB 519.

No damages may now be awarded to the estate in respect of loss of income in the deceased's 'lost years'.[134] The potential overlap between claims by dependants under the Fatal Accidents Act for loss of dependency and an estate's claims for lost income from the 'lost years' is thus avoided.[135]

Technically, the 1934 Act applies even though death occurs instantaneously upon the commission of the tort (thus removing the possibility that the victim experiences any pain and suffering).[136] But since the Administration of Justice Act 1982 came into force, there is only one circumstance in which a claim may, in reality, be made under the 1934 Act where death is immediate;[137] and even that is of restricted application. However, whether or not the deceased died immediately, a claim for funeral expenses may be made.[138]

Finally, we must consider the situation where a claimant has been awarded provisional damages under section 32A of the Supreme Court Act 1981. If he subsequently dies due to deterioration in his condition, his dependants may now claim those losses that were not compensated by the initial award of damages.[139]

(B) DEATH AS A CAUSE OF ACTION[140]

(1) INTRODUCTION

Historically, at common law, no action in tort could be brought by third parties who suffered loss through the killing of another.[141] But fatal accidents became so frequent with the development of railways that in 1846 Parliament had to pass the Fatal Accidents Act of that year which made considerable inroads into the common-law rule. The modern principles are now embodied in the Fatal Accidents Act 1976.

The 1976 Act only benefits certain dependants; and even then the class of dependants entitled to sue varies according to whether the claim lies in respect of loss of support, bereavement or funeral expenses (the three heads of claim permitted under the Act). But for present purposes, the initial point to make is that the Act is rather exceptional in creating an interest for one person in the life of another. No such general principle exists in tort law. Thus, an employee cannot sue a tortfeasor for the resulting death of his employer so that the employee loses his job. Nor can an insurance company sue simply because it has to discharge its obligations under a life policy sooner than it otherwise

---

[134] Law Reform (Miscellaneous Provisions) Act 1934, s 1(2)(a).

[135] See *Gammell v Wilson* [1982] AC 27.

[136] In *Hicks v Chief Constable of the South Yorkshire Police* [1992] 2 All ER 65 it was held that momentary pain was merely part of the dying process and not an independent period of pain prior to death.

[137] The problem is that, with immediate death, there is no time for the victim to appreciate pain, suffering etc and for the cause of action to vest. The better view is probably that the cause of action is completed by the injuries, and vests in the deceased at the moment of death.

[138] Law Reform (Miscellaneous Provisions) Act 1934, ss 1(2)(c) and 3(5); *Stanton v Ewart F Youlden Ltd* [1960] 1 All ER 429   [139] Damages Act 1996, s 3.

[140] See generally Law Com No 263, *Claims for Wrongful Death* (1999).

[141] *Baker v Bolton* (1808) 1 Camp 493; *Admiralty Comrs v SS Amerika* [1917] AC 38.

would. In short, interests beyond those of the deceased's family have no recognition when death occurs.

Section 1(1) of the Fatal Accidents Act 1976 provides:

If death is caused by any wrongful act, neglect or default which is such as would (if death had not ensued) have entitled the person injured to maintain an action and recover damages in respect thereof, the person who would have been liable if death had not ensued shall be liable to an action for damages, notwithstanding the death of the person injured.[142]

(2) WHO MAY SUE?

The action is brought in the name of the executor or administrator[143] of the deceased, and lies in respect of loss of support for the benefit of the following relatives:[144] a wife, husband or former wife or husband;[145] registered same-sex civil partners and former registered same-sex civil partners;[146] children, grandchildren, fathers, mothers, step-parents, grandparents, brothers, sisters, uncles, aunts and their issue; adopted and illegitimate dependants; step children of the several categories.[147] If there is no executor or administrator, or if he fails to bring the action within six months after the death of the deceased, any dependant may bring the action.[148] The Administration of Justice Act 1982 responded to social changes by including for the first time any person who was living with the deceased in the same household[149] for at least two years before that date, and was living during the whole of that period as the husband or wife of the deceased.[150] The provision now made for same-sex (and former same-sex) partners to claim is a further example of this branch of law responding to social change.

(3) NATURE OF THE ACT COMPLAINED OF

It must first be proved that the act caused the death.[151] Thereafter, it must be shown that there was a 'wrongful act, neglect or default' by the defendant. These words presumably

---

[142] For transport accidents in the course of an international journey see the Carriage by Air Act 1961, Carriage of Passengers by Road Act 1974, Merchant Shipping Act 1995 and International Transport Conventions Act 1983.   [143] Fatal Accidents Act 1976, s 2(1).

[144] Fatal Accidents Act 1976, s 1(2)–(5).

[145] By the Fatal Accidents Act 1976, s 1(4), a former spouse includes a person whose marriage has been annulled or declared void as well as a divorced person. This provision still applies even if the surviving former spouse has remarried: *Shepherd v Post Office* (1995) *Times*, 15 June. An equivalent definition is made in respect of a 'former civil partner': Fatal Accidents Act, s 1(4A).

[146] Fatal Accidents Act 1976, ss 1(4)–(5) as amended by s 83 of the Civil Partnership Act 2004.

[147] Fatal Accidents Act 1976, s 1(5)(a): 'any relationship by affinity shall be treated as a relationship by consanguinity, any relationship of the half-blood as a relationship of the whole blood, and the stepchild of any person as his child'. D must be given particulars of the dependants for whom a claim is made and of the nature of this claim: Fatal Accidents Act 1976, s 2(4).   [148] Fatal Accidents Act 1976, s 2(2).

[149] Note that it is possible for a person to be living in more than one household at any one time: *Pounder v London Underground Ltd* [1995] PIQR P 217.

[150] Fatal Accidents Act 1976, s 1(3)(b). But note that the Act is not so progressive as to recognize same-sex cohabitational relationships unless a registered a civil partnership has been entered into. Cf Family Law Act 1996, s 62.

[151] In *Pigney v Pointer's Transport Services Ltd* [1957] 2 All ER 807, the deceased committed suicide while in a depressive state induced by D's negligent act; the death was held to have been caused by that act, so that an

embrace any tort.[152] Consequently, if the defendant's act was never actionable because he would have had a defence to any action brought by the deceased in his lifetime, no action will lie.[153] Where the deceased died partly as the result of his own fault and partly as the result of the fault of any other person, damages are reduced to a proportionate extent[154] in the same way that they are under the Law Reform (Contributory Negligence) Act 1945.[155] If a dependant's contributory negligence is a cause of the deceased's death, that dependant's damages are reduced but the awards to other dependants are unaffected.[156]

At the time of his death, the deceased must have been in a position to sue the defendant had he not died because of the wrongful act. If the limitation period expired between the injury and his death, the Limitation Act 1980 stipulates that no Fatal Accidents Act claim can come into existence.[157] This ordinarily[158] means that if more than three years have elapsed between the injury and death, the claim will be time-barred.[159] The Limitation Act 1980 also provides that if the deceased had settled his own claim,[160] no action lies under the Fatal Accidents Act,[161] but an action still lies (and without any limit on the damages) if the claimant had merely agreed beforehand that no more than, say, £1000 damages should be recoverable in the event of his being the victim of this tort.[162]

(4) SPECIFIC LIMITATIONS ON CLAIMS UNDER THE 1976 ACT

We have already noted the three kinds of action that can be brought under the Act. But there are certain important limitations on the ability to sue for these. Let us begin with the action for bereavement.[163] This claim – quite distinct from the action for loss of support already considered – may be brought only for the benefit of, (1) the surviving 'life partner' of he deceased (that is the deceased's wife, husband or civil partner[164]), or (2) the relevant parent or parents of any unmarried children.[165] The bereavement action does not extend to former spouses, former civil partners or a heterosexual cohabitant who had been living with the deceased as his or her wife or husband.

---

action under the Fatal Accidents Act 1976 was successful (as was a similar claim in *Watson v Willmott* [1991] 1 QB 140).

[152] And a negligent breach of contract: *Grein v Imperial Airways Ltd* [1937] 1 KB 50.

[153] *Murphy v Culhane* [1977] QB 94 (if the deceased had failed because of the defence of *ex turpi causa* – see ch 11 – no action would lie under the Act). [154] Fatal Accidents Act 1976, s 5.

[155] See ch 6.

[156] *Dodds v Dodds* [1978] QB 543. The negligent dependant may also be required to make a contribution (under the Civil Liability (Contribution) Act 1978) towards the damages which D has to pay for the benefit of the dependants. [157] Limitation Act 1980, s 12(1).

[158] The three-year period can be extended if the deceased did not have 'relevant knowledge' of his cause of action. [159] Limitation Act 1980, s 11(1).

[160] *Pickett v British Rail Engineering Ltd* [1980] AC 136, at 146–7 and 152, *per* Lords Wilberforce and Salmon respectively. [161] Limitation Act 1980, s 12(1).

[162] *Nunan v Southern Rly Co* [1924] 1 KB 223. [163] Fatal Accidents Act 1976, s 1A(1).

[164] Fatal Accidents Act 1976, s 1A(2)(a).

[165] Both parents may claim if he was legitimate; but only his mother if he was illegitimate: Fatal Accidents Act 1976, s 1A(2)(b).

There are limits, too, on the ability to sue for loss of support. In particular, any claim by a dependant lies only upon proof of pecuniary loss (that is, financial support that he or she would have received).[166] The language ordinarily used by the courts is that there must be a loss of 'prospective pecuniary advantage' and that a 'speculative possibility' of pecuniary gain is not enough.[167] A parent could recover, therefore, when his 16-year-old daughter died, having almost completed her unpaid dressmaking apprenticeship.[168] But the parent of a three-year-old child has been held to have no cause of action.[169] Although it is not essential that the dependant should have a legal right to that aid[170] – the loss of services gratuitously rendered is enough.[171] However, a distinction must be made between a pecuniary benefit to the dependant that would have accrued *qua* business relationship (as opposed to *qua* family relationship). If the loss is business loss, no action is permitted under the Act. Thus, a father could not sue in respect of the loss of business contracts occasioned by the death of his son, who worked for the father's firm.[172] On the other hand, in *Pym v Great Northern Rly Co*[173] it was held that younger children of the deceased had sustained loss of pecuniary advantage because most of the income from the settlement of which the deceased had been tenant for life passed on his death to his widow and eldest child.

For public policy reasons, where the pecuniary loss is attributable to an illegal enterprise in which the deceased was engaged, no action will lie under the 1976 Act. Thus, in *Hunter v Butler*[174] it was held that no claim lay where the deceased had been earning wages while fraudulently claiming social security benefits. The court was concerned not to allow monies illegally gained to form the basis of a claim for dependency.

(5) PERIOD OF LIMITATION

The action under the 1976 Act must be brought within three years from either the date of the death, or the date on which the claimant had (actual or constructive) knowledge of the death, whichever is the later.[175] Where there are several potential claimants, the limitation period runs separately against each. Where the dependant's limitation

---

[166] *Duckworth v Johnson* (1859) 4 H & N 653.

[167] *Davies v Taylor* [1974] AC 207: wife deserted husband five weeks before his death; shortly before his death he instructed a solicitor to begin divorce proceedings. The deserting wife had no claim, for she had to show a reasonable expectation of pecuniary benefit – ie, there had to be a significant prospect, not a mere speculative possibility, of reconciliation with the husband had he lived, and this she failed to prove. In *Kandalla v British Airways Board* [1981] QB 158, the elderly parents of two young women doctors were awarded damages on proof that the doctors intended to flee from Iraq (where they had been working) to England where they would have supported their parents.   [168] *Taff Vale Rly Co v Jenkins* [1913] AC 1.

[169] *Barnett v Cohen* [1921] 2 KB 461.

[170] *Stimpson v Wood & Son* (1888) 57 LJQB 484 (the mere fact that a wife by her adultery had lost her legal right to maintenance did not bar her claim).   [171] *Berry v Humm & Co* [1915] 1 KB 627.

[172] *Sykes v North Eastern Rly Co* (1875) 44 LJCP 191. The decision was followed in *Burgess v Florence Nightingale Hospital for Gentlewomen* [1955] 1 QB 349 (husband could not recover for loss of services of wife as dancing partner). See also *Behrens v Bertram Mills Circus Ltd* [1957] 2 QB 1 and *Malyon v Plummer* [1964] 1 QB 330.

[173] (1863) 4B & S 396.

[174] [1996] RTR 396. See also *Burns v Edman* [1970] 2 QB 541: no claim could be made by a widow who knew that her support came from the proceeds of her husband's crimes.   [175] Limitation Act 1980, s 12(2).

period has expired before an action was brought, the court has a further discretionary power to extend the period.[176]

(6) ASSESSMENT OF DAMAGES

The sum to be awarded as damages for bereavement is £10,000.[177] Where both parents claim this sum, it is divided equally between them.[178] Damages other than damages for bereavement are set proportionate to the injury[179] each dependant suffers.[180] Thus, the actual pecuniary loss resulting to each dependant from the death is ascertained separately[181] and the question of division is dealt with later.[182] So, for example, where an award is made to a widow and her children it has been suggested that the proportion awarded to the children should represent their genuine dependency,[183] and not simply to award the bulk of the money to the widow on the assumption that she will provide for her children.[184] Among other things, the children need protection against the risk of their mother dying and the money passing into the hands of a stepfather.

Lord Wright has explained the traditional method of measuring the damages.

The starting point is the amount of wages which the deceased was earning, the ascertainment of which to some extent may depend on the regularity of his employment. Then there is an estimate of how much was required or expended for his own personal and living expenses. The balance will give a datum or basic figure which will generally be turned into a lump sum . . . That sum, however, has to be taxed down by having due regard to uncertainties.[185]

The House of Lords elaborated upon this in *Taylor v O'Connor*.[186] The damages to a widow must make available to her, to spend each year, a sum free of tax equal to the amount of the dependency – an award sufficient to buy an annuity of that amount is not enough because part of the annuity will be taxable. The multiplier must be

---

[176] Limitation Act 1980, s 33.

[177] Damages for Bereavement (Variation of Sum) (England and Wales) Order 2002.

[178] Fatal Accidents Act 1976, s 1A(4). Would this be so where one parent was the tortfeasor who caused the death?

[179] 'Injury' includes any disease and any impairment of a person's physical or mental condition: Fatal Accidents Act 1976, s 1(6).

[180] Fatal Accidents Act 1976, s 3(1). This is an oddly worded provision. For elucidation of its meaning, see *Jameson v Central Electricity Generating Board* [2000] 1 AC 455.

[181] *Davies v Powell Duffryn Associated Collieries Ltd* [1942] AC 601, at 612, *per* Lord Wright. A dependant's damages are not reduced because his mother was contributorily negligent: *Dodds v Dodds* [1978] QB 543. Where a husband and wife with either separate incomes or a joint income share their living expenses, the amount by which their joint living expenses are less than twice the expenses of each one living separately is a benefit arising from the relationship, and may be the subject of a claim under the Fatal Accidents legislation by the husband in respect of the death of his wife: *Burgess v Florence Nightingale Hospital for Gentlewomen* [1955] 1 QB 349.

[182] *Dietz v Lennig Chemicals Ltd* [1969] 1 AC 170, at 183, *per* Lord Morris of Borth-y-Gest. The court is to direct how the award is to be divided: Fatal Accidents Act 1976, s 3(2).

[183] *Benson v Biggs Wall & Co Ltd* [1982] 3 All ER 300.

[184] *Clay v Pooler* [1982] 3 All ER 570 (the children merely received pocket money).

[185] *Davies v Powell Duffryn Associated Collieries Ltd* [1942] AC 601, at 617.   [186] [1971] AC 115.

calculated from the date of the victim's death[187] and should be such that the capital sum awarded, together with the income earned by its investment, will be exhausted by the end of the period intended to be covered. It is supposed that the dependants will spend annually a part of the capital as well as the whole of the income they receive from so much of the capital as remains.[188] The multiplier of the annual loss of dependency is seldom fixed at more than 16 times that annual figure; so if the dependants have lost £8,000 a year from the death, the award will rarely exceed £128,000.

In assessing future earnings, probable deductions for income tax are to be made.[189] No account may be taken of the fact that the dependant is of independent means, except in so far as it shows what pecuniary aid to that dependant was made by the deceased.[190] So, if a professional woman loses her husband who is also a professional, it is no answer to say that she could well support herself and her children. The question is simply how much of his income the deceased husband spent on his family rather than himself.

In *Cookson v Knowles*,[191] the House of Lords refined further the method of calculation. As a general rule, damages up to the date of trial are to be assessed separately from those after that date. For the first part, the loss of dependency will be multiplied by the actual period between the accident and the trial. Interest on that sum will then be awarded at half the short-term investment rate current during that period. For the second part, the court will arrive at the amount of dependency (the multiplicand) by estimating the probable rate of earnings of the deceased at the date of the trial. It will calculate the multiplier in the usual way. The multiplier will be fixed by reference to the date of the death, and the number of years actually elapsing between the death and the trial will then be deducted.[192] Interest is not awarded on the second sum.[193] Inflation is disregarded except in estimating earnings at the date of trial.

If the dependants have incurred funeral expenses in respect of the deceased, damages may be awarded in respect of those expenses.[194] But in assessing damages payable to a widow in respect of the death of her husband, the court must not take into account the widow's remarriage or her prospects of remarriage.[195]

It will be recalled that subject to certain conditions, persons living together as man and wife, though not married, are treated as 'dependants'.[196] In assessing their damages the court has to take into account the fact that the dependant had no enforceable right to financial support by the deceased as a result of their living together.[197]

---

[187] *Graham v Dodds* [1983] 2 All ER 953.

[188] *Young v Percival* [1974] 3 All ER 677. See also *Taylor v O'Connor* [1971] AC 115.

[189] *Bishop v Cunard White Star Co Ltd* [1950] P 240, at 250, *per* Hodson J.

[190] *Shiels v Cruikshank* [1953] 1 All ER 874, a Scottish case, but presumably also applicable to England.

[191] [1979] AC 556; *Corbett v Barking, Havering and Brentwood Health Authority* [1991] 2 QB 408 (but the multiplier should be adjusted to take account of known facts). [192] *Graham v Dodds* [1983] 2 All ER 953.

[193] The court's power to award interest in respect of personal injuries is strictly limited: Supreme Court Act 1981, s 35A. [194] Section 3(3) of the Fatal Accidents Act 1976, s 3(5).

[195] Fatal Accidents Act 1976, s 3(3). Her remarriage prospects might affect awards to her children: *Thompson v Price* [1973] QB 838.

[196] If an unmarried father is killed, even if the mother of his children has no claim, their children recover the loss of all the benefits which their father had provided for them, including such benefits given to the mother for the children's advantage – eg, the cost of her air fares for a family holiday: *K v JMP Co Ltd* [1976] QB 85.

[197] Fatal Accidents Act 1976, s 3(4).

To what extent can the courts take account of events occurring between the death and trial? If such an event enables the courts to fix more precisely that which they are otherwise called upon to estimate, they must have regard to that event.[198] Thus, they have taken into account that, before trial, the defendant died;[199] that war broke out (reducing the deceased's life expectancy);[200] that tax rates had been reduced.[201] Each of these events enables the courts to quantify more precisely a dependant's loss of contribution from the deceased. Hypothetical events which would, but for the deceased's death, have increased the dependant's dependency will not be taken into account. So the claimant widow's greater prospective loss had she, as she would have so desired, given up work to have a family, was rightly disregarded in *Malone v Rowan*.[202] Also to be disregarded under the 1976 Act are benefits which have accrued or will, or may, accrue to any person from his estate, or otherwise, as a result of the death.[203]

The assessment of damages in a Fatal Accidents Act claim can thus be seen to be relatively straightforward where what is in issue is the loss of a family breadwinner. The dependent family seeks to replace the lost income of the deceased parent. In recent years the courts have recognized that the death of a parent gives rise to other pecuniary losses over and above any loss of earned income. A series of cases have considered how damages should be assessed where a mother is tortiously killed. It may be that at the time of her death she was not working outside her home, or was only doing so on a part-time basis. The fundamental principle is that the widower and children are entitled to compensation based on the reasonable cost to them of replacing the mother's services in the home.[204] The starting point for that assessment where the children are under school age,[205] will be the national cost of hiring a child-minder/housekeeper.[206] Allowance will be made for the fact that mothers do not work fixed hours and do not limit themselves to cooking, cleaning and routine tasks. They provide more general care and moral guidance and those wider 'motherly services'[207] should be reflected in the award of damages. Where the father,[208] or other relative,[209] then gives up work to take over these duties, and in the light of the children's needs, that is a reasonable course of action, compensation may be based on his (or their) loss of earnings rather than the cost of a child-minder.

What is said above assumes the existence of a nuclear family where the mother stays at home providing 100% of the child care and the father earns 100% of the family income. That, of course, is seldom the case these days. If the mother, too, is in regular employment, the children will suffer a loss of family income which they can obviously

---

[198] *Corbett v Barking, Havering and Brentwood Health Authority* [1991] 2 QB 408.

[199] *Williamson v John I Thornycroft & Co Ltd* [1940] 4 All ER 61.   [200] *Hall v Wilson* [1939] 4 All ER 85.

[201] *Daniels v Jones* [1961] 3 All ER 24.   [202] [1984] 3 All ER 402.

[203] Fatal Accidents Act 1976, s 4.

[204] *Hay v Hughes* [1975] QB 790; *Corbett v Barking, Havering and Brentwood Health Authority* [1991] 2 QB 408.

[205] The court in *Spittle v Bunney* [1988] 3 All ER 1031 assumed a diminishing need for 'motherly services' once a child is settled at school.

[206] Based on the net rather than the gross wage payable: *Spittle v Bunney* [1988] 3 All ER 1031.

[207] *Regan v Williamson* [1976] 2 All ER 241.

[208] *Mehmet v Perry* [1977] 2 All ER 529 (note the special needs of these children who suffered from the hereditary disease thalassaemia).

[209] *Cresswell v Eaton* [1991] 1 All ER 484 (aunt gave up job as a traffic warden).

claim. They will also lose her 'motherly services' which can be compensated (subject to a 'modest' discount because the mother did not provide full-time care[210]). Interestingly, in *Hayden v Hayden*,[211] it was held that if the father in effect undertook most of the mother's responsibilities after her death, there was no loss to the child in this respect. Yet *Hayden v Hayden* must be contrasted with *Stanley v Saddique*[212] where the child's parents were not married. On the death of the mother, the father undertook full responsibility for his son and soon remarried. The evidence suggested that the stepmother was likely to make a much better parent than the deceased mother. The defendants argued that the benefit conferred by the acquisition of a stepmother more than cancelled out the loss of the original mother's services. But the court held that section 4 of the Fatal Accidents Act 1976 prevented any such 'benefit' being taken into account.[213] *Stanley v Saddique* was followed, but with a critical qualification added, in *H v S*.[214] There it was said that the principle enunciated in *Hunt v Severs*[215] should be applied to such cases so that the amount representing the value of the lost gratuitous services should be held on trust for the benefit of the new voluntary carer (in this case, the father who had not previously provided care for the claimant children whose mother had been killed).

SECTION 4 ALTERNATIVE COMPENSATION SYSTEMS[216]

(A) RESPONSIBILITY AND THE WELFARE STATE[217]

Public responsibility for personal injury victims is recognized in the existence of a safety net of a number of benefits and provisions made for such persons. The complexity of the social welfare system means that a detailed exposition of its workings fall beyond the scope of this book. However, a brief sketch of that system's mechanics can be offered to good effect for anyone trying to assess the comparative merits (or otherwise) of the tort system.

(1) The welfare state provides essential services for accident victims in two main respects. Medical advice and treatment are largely available free of charge within the National Health Service. Where long-term care is required, this may prove to be of significant benefit to the victim. Even beyond hospital care, there

---

[210] *Cresswell v Eaton* [1991] 1 All ER 484.   [211] [1992] 4 All ER 681.   [212] [1992] QB 1.

[213] On the broad meaning of 'benefit' in this context see also *O'Loughlin v Cape Distribution Ltd* [2001] EWCA Civ 178 (business flair of the deceased a benefit for the purposes of s 4).   [214] [2003] QB 965.

[215] But for criticism see Matthews and Lunney, 'A Tortfeasor's Lot is not a Happy One' (1995) 58 MLR 395. See *Dimond v Lovell* [2002] 1 AC 384.

[216] See especially Cane, *Atiyah's Accidents, Compensation and the Law* (1999); Stapleton, 'Tort, Insurance and Ideology' (1995) 58 MLR 820.

[217] See generally Oxford Socio-Legal Studies, *Compensation and Support for Illness and Injury* (1984) and McLean (ed), *Compensation for Damage: an International Perspective* (1993).

is the possibility of various forms of assistance being provided by local authorities to, for example, the aged and the disabled. In practice, however, pressure on local authority budgets often means that only minimal benefits and services are in fact supplied.

(2) A wide range of social security benefits is available to persons incapable of work by reason of accident or disease. The level of payments made is at a subsistence rate, and generally far lower than the loss of earnings suffered by the incapacitated victim. Certain of the non-means-tested benefits are also payable to tort victims but the social security legislation now provides that the state recovers these payments from the tortfeasor.[218]

One thing is clear in this context: the better off one is to start with, the more one stands to lose and is likely to suffer from an incapacity in respect of which one has no remedy in tort. Thus, the solicitor who succumbs to an inherent risk of surgery stands to lose a great deal more than the single mother already on social security benefits before she is incapacitated. However, if the state has only limited resources to compensate for disability, it can be argued that high earners should have no especial claim for preferential treatment. The solicitor could, after all, have taken out an insurance policy covering her against all forms of personal injury or disease.

(3) Certain groups of the disabled may, in addition, receive extra payments related to their disability. For example, the Vaccine Damage Payments Act 1979 provides for payments to persons suffering 80% disablement consequent on vaccination.

(B) OTHER COMPENSATION SYSTEMS

(1) CRIMINAL INJURIES COMPENSATION SCHEME

The Criminal Injuries Compensation Authority administers from government funds a statutory scheme[219] for compensating victims of crimes of violence. If they suffer personal injury as a result of violent crime or while apprehending (or seeking to apprehend) a suspect, the Authority may award compensation according to a statutory tariff.

(2) OCCUPATIONAL SICK PAY

Many members of the workforce are entitled to continued payments from their employer in replacement of loss of earnings (at least in part), for a limited absence from work through sickness or injury.[220] But the number so entitled is on the wane.

---

[218] Social Security (Recovery of Benefits) Act 1997, s 6. Note that this provision requires that the 'compensator' – usually D's insurer – must pay the *full amount* of recoverable benefits which may well exceed the sum that would have been payable as compensation. This means that the state never loses out although, plainly, D might (as might C, depending on future contingencies).

[219] The basis for this scheme is the Criminal Injuries Compensation Act 1995.

[220] *Pearson Report*, para 137.

(3) OCCUPATIONAL PENSIONS

Many millions of employees are members of pension schemes run by their employers. These entitle the relevant employees to compensation beyond that available under the social security system in the event of personal injury requiring their early retirement.[221]

(4) INDUSTRIAL INJURIES SCHEME

Where injury occurs at work as a result of an industrial accident, a much more generous scheme provides higher levels of disability benefit than that available within the basic social security system.

(5) INSURANCE

In many cases, the person killed or injured will have taken out an insurance policy providing for benefits in the event of his death or personal injury.[222] There are three main forms of this first-party insurance.[223] The most common is a life policy providing a guaranteed minimum sum on death. Personal accident policies cover death, loss or disability resulting from accidents for a prescribed period. Permanent health policies provide periodic payments if the insured person becomes unable to pursue his usual occupation because of sickness or accident. Sometimes these forms of insurance are provided by employers for their staff.

The *Pearson Report*[224] estimated that about half the total compensation paid in respect of personal injury and death comes from social security and about a quarter from the tort system. The remaining quarter comes from the other sources listed above. These figures show how limited a view of accident compensation is obtained if one examines only tort, and ignores these other sources of compensation.

(C) THE FUTURE

In 1974 the Royal Commission on Civil Liability and Compensation for Personal Injury was set up under the chairmanship of Lord Pearson. It reported in 1978. Its basic proposal was to retain the mixed system of tort law and social security, with a gradual swing towards social security. It made 188 detailed proposals of which one of the most interesting was a proposal to bring road traffic accidents within social security schemes on the model of industrial injuries.[225] Nearly 30 years later, it seems that a wholesale

---

[221] For details, see *Pearson Report*, para 145 *et seq*.

[222] Much more widespread is insurance against fire or damage to one's buildings, homes, furniture or car, where the insured has a right of subrogation against tortfeasors.

[223] For greater detail and for arguments in favour of augmenting first-party insurance, see Atiyah, *The Damages Lottery* (1997).   [224] *Pearson Report* (1978).

[225] For the problems of such a scheme actually implemented in France, see Redmond-Cooper, 'No Fault Liability on French Roads' in McLean (ed), *Compensation for Damage: an International Perspective* (1993) p 115.

change to a social welfare system that abandons 'fault' is highly improbable in this country, at least in the foreseeable future. In particular categories of accident, there has been some pressure for limited 'no-fault' compensation systems. But on what rational grounds should victims of particular types of mishaps – such as medical accidents – be singled out for special treatment? It is equally to be noted that a piecemeal implementation of 'no fault' schemes would be potentially problematic in that it would simply add to the highly complex interweaving of various compensation systems.

FURTHER READING

Atiyah, *The Damages Lottery* (1997)

Cane (ed), *Atiyah's Accidents Compensation and the Law* (2006)

Harris, 'Accident Compensation in New Zealand: A Comprehensive Insurance System' (1974) 37 MLR 361

Kemp, 'Discounting Damages for Future Loss' (1997) 113 LQR 195

Lewis, 'Appearance and Reality in Reforming Periodical Payments of Tort Damages in the UK' in Neyers (ed), *Emerging Issues in Tort Law* (2007)

Lewis, *Deducting Benefits from Damages for Personal Injury* (2000)

Matthews and Lunney, 'A Tortfeasor's Lot is Not a Happy One' (1995) 58 MLR 395

Ogus, 'Damages for Lost Amenities: For a Foot, a Feeling or a Function?' (1972) 35 MLR 1

Rogers (ed), *Damages for Non-Pecuniary Loss in a Comparative Perspective* (2001)

Stapleton, 'Tort, Insurance and Ideology' (1995) 58 MLR 820

INDEX